THE OXFORD
DICTIONARY OF
MODERN
QUOTATIONS

Tony Augarde has compiled and
edited a number of Oxford reference
books and is the author of *The Oxford
Guide to Word Games*.

THE OXFORD
DICTIONARY OF
MODERN
QUOTATIONS

Edited by

TONY AUGARDE

Oxford   New York

OXFORD UNIVERSITY PRESS

1992

Oxford University Press, Walton Street, Oxford OX2 6DP

Oxford New York Toronto
Delhi Bombay Calcutta Madras Karachi
Petaling Jaya Singapore Hong Kong Tokyo
Nairobi Dar es Salaam Cape Town
Melbourne Auckland

and associated companies in
Berlin Ibadan

Oxford is a trade mark of Oxford University Press

British Library Cataloguing in Publication Data
Data available

Library of Congress Cataloging in Publication Data
The Oxford dictionary of modern quotations / edited by Tony Augarde.
p. cm Includes Index.
I. Quotations. I. Augarde, Tony
PN6080.094 1991 080–dc20 90–26588
ISBN 0–19–283086–4

1 3 5 7 9 10 8 6 4 2

Typeset by Latimer Trend & Company Ltd.
Printed in Great Britain by
Clays Ltd.
Bungay, Suffolk

Preface

THIS is a completely new dictionary, containing about 5,000 quotations.

What is a 'quotation'? It is a saying or piece of writing that strikes people as so true or memorable that they quote it (or allude to it) in speech or writing. Often they will quote it directly, introducing it with a phrase like 'As —— says' but equally often they will assume that the reader or listener already knows the quotation, and they will simply allude to it without mentioning its source (as in the headline 'A rosé is a rosé is a rosé', referring obliquely to a line by Gertrude Stein).

This dictionary has been compiled from extensive evidence of the quotations that are actually used in this way. The dictionary includes the commonest quotations which were found in a collection of more than 200,000 citations assembled by combing books, magazines, and newspapers. For example, our collections contained more than thirty examples each for Edward Heath's 'unacceptable face of capitalism' and Marshall McLuhan's 'The medium is the message', so both these quotations had to be included.

As a result, this book is not—like many quotations dictionaries—a subjective anthology of the editor's favourite quotations, but an objective selection of the quotations which are most widely known and used. Popularity and familiarity are the main criteria for inclusion, although no reader is likely to be familiar with all the quotations in this dictionary.

The book can be used for reference or for browsing: to trace the source of a particular quotation or to find an appropriate saying for a special need.

The quotations are drawn from novels, plays, poems, essays, speeches, films, radio and television broadcasts, songs, advertisements, and even book titles. It is difficult to draw the line between quotations and similar sayings like proverbs, catch-phrases, and idioms. For example, some quotations (like 'The opera ain't over till the fat lady sings') become proverbial. These are usually included if

they can be traced to a particular originator. However, we have
generally omitted phrases like 'agonizing reappraisal' which are
covered adequately in the *Oxford English Dictionary*. Catch-phrases
are included if there is evidence that they are widely remembered or
used.

We have taken care to verify all the quotations in original or
authoritative sources—something which few other quotations dictionaries have tried to do. We have corrected many errors found in
other dictionaries, and we have traced the true origins of such
phrases as 'There ain't no such thing as a free lunch' and 'Shaken
and not stirred'.

The quotations are arranged in alphabetical order of authors, with
anonymous quotations in the middle of 'A'. Under each author, the
quotations are listed in alphabetical order of the titles of their
sources. The anonymous quotations are arranged in alphabetical
order of their first words. Foreign quotations are, wherever possible,
given in the original language as well as in translation.

Authors are cited under the names by which they are best known:
for example, Graham Greene (not Henry Graham Greene); F. Scott
Fitzgerald (not Francis Scott Key Fitzgerald); George Orwell (not Eric
Blair); W. C. Fields (not William Claude Dukenfield). Authors' dates
of birth and death are given when ascertainable. The actual writers
of the words are credited for quotations from songs, film-scripts, etc.

The references after each quotation are designed to be as helpful as
possible, enabling the reader to trace quotations in their original
sources if desired.

The index has been carefully prepared—with ingenious computer
assistance—to help the reader to trace quotations from their most
important keywords. Each reference includes not only the page and
the number of the quotation on the page but also the first few letters
of the author's name. The index includes references to book-titles
which have become well known as quotations in their own right.

One difficulty in a dictionary of modern quotations is to decide
what the word 'modern' means. In this dictionary it means 'twen-
tieth-century'. Quotations are eligible if they originated from
someone who was still alive after 1900. Where an author (like
George Bernard Shaw, who died in 1950) said memorable things
before and after 1900, these are all included.

This dictionary could not have been compiled without the work of many people, most notably Paula Clifford, Angela Partington, Fiona Mullan, Penelope Newsome, Julia Cresswell, Michael McKinley, Charles McCreery, Heidi Abbey, Jean Harker, Elizabeth Knowles, George Chowdharay-Best, Tracey Ward, and Ernest Trehern. I am also very grateful to the OUP Dictionary Department's team of checkers, who verified the quotations at libraries in Oxford, London, Washington, New York, and elsewhere. James Howes deserves credit for his work in computerizing the index.

The Editor is responsible for any errors, which he will be grateful to have drawn to his attention. As the quotation from Simeon Strunsky reminds us, 'Famous remarks are very seldom quoted correctly', but we have endeavoured to make this book more accurate, authoritative, and helpful than any other dictionary of modern quotations.

TONY AUGARDE

Contents

How to Use this Dictionary

GENERAL PRINCIPLES

The arrangement is alphabetical by the names of authors: usually the names by which each person is best known. So look under *Maya Angelou*, not *Maya Johnson*; *Princess Anne*, not *HRH The Princess Royal*; *Lord Beaverbrook*, not *William Maxwell Aitken*; *Irving Berlin*, not *Israel Balin*; *Greta Garbo*, not *Greta Lovisa Gustafsson*.

Anonymous quotations are all together, starting on page 5. They are arranged in alphabetical order of their first significant word.

Under each author, quotations are arranged by the alphabetical order of the titles of the works from which they come, even if those works were not written by the person who is being quoted. Poems are usually cited from the first book in which they appeared.

Quotations by foreign authors are, where possible, given in the original language and also in an English translation.

A reference is given after each quotation to its original source or to an authoritative record of its use. The reference usually consists of either (*a*) a book-title with its date of publication and a reference to where the quotation occurs in the book; or (*b*) the title of a newspaper or magazine with its date of publication. The reference is preceded by 'In' if the quotation comes from a secondary source: for example if a writer is quoted by another author in a newspaper article, or if a book refers to a saying but does not indicate where or when it was made.

EXAMPLES

Here are some typical entries, with notes to clarify the meaning of each part.

*Charlie Chaplin (Sir Charles
Spencer Chaplin)* 1889–1977

8 All I need to make a comedy is a park, a
policeman and a pretty girl.
My Autobiography (1964) ch. 10

Charlie Chaplin is the name by which this person is best known but
Sir Charles Spencer Chaplin is the name which would appear in
reference books such as *Who's Who*. Charlie Chaplin was born in
1889 and died in 1977. The number '8' indicates that this is the
eighth quotation on the page (page 49). The quotation comes from
the tenth chapter of Chaplin's autobiography, which was published
in 1964.

Martin Luther King 1929–1968

11 Injustice anywhere is a threat to justice
everywhere.
Letter from Birmingham Jail, Alabama, 16
Apr. 1963, in *Atlantic Monthly* Aug. 1963,
p. 78

Martin Luther King wrote these words in a letter that he sent from
Birmingham Jail on 16 April 1963. The letter was published later
that year on page 78 of the August issue of the *Atlantic Monthly*.

Dorothy Parker 1893–1967

14 One more drink and I'd have been under
the host.
In Howard Teichmann *George S. Kaufman*
(1972) p. 68

Dorothy Parker must have said this before she died in 1967 but the
earliest reliable source we can find is a 1972 book by Howard
Teichmann. 'In' signals the fact that the quotation is cited from a
secondary source.

INDEX

If you remember part of a quotation and want to know the rest of it,
or who said it, you can trace it by means of the index.

The index lists the most significant words from each quotation.
These keywords are listed alphabetically in the index, each with a
section of the text to show the context of every keyword. These
sections are listed in strict alphabetical order under each keyword.
Foreign keywords are included in their alphabetical place.

The references show the first few letters of the author's name, followed by the page and item numbers (e.g. 163:15 refers to the fifteenth quotation on page 163).

As an example, suppose that you want to verify a quotation which you remember contains the line 'to purify the dialect of the tribe'. If you decide that *tribe* is a significant word and refer to it in the index, you will find this entry:

tribe: To purify the dialect of the t.   ELIOT 74:19

This will lead you to the poem by T. S. Eliot which is the nineteenth quotation on page 74.

Quotations

Bud Abbott 1895–1974 and *Lou Costello (Louis Francis Cristillo)* 1906–1959

1 ABBOTT: Now, on the St Louis team we have Who's on first, What's on second, I Don't Know is on third.
COSTELLO: That's what I want to find out.
Naughty Nineties (1945 film), in R. J. Anobile *Who's On First?* (1973) p. 224

Dannie Abse 1923–

2 I know the colour rose, and it is lovely,
But not when it ripens in a tumour;
And healing greens, leaves and grass, so springlike,
In limbs that fester are not springlike.
A Small Desperation (1968) 'Pathology of Colours'

3 So in the simple blessing of a rainbow,
In the bevelled edge of a sunlit mirror,
I have seen visible, Death's artifact
Like a soldier's ribbon on a tunic tacked.
A Small Desperation (1968) 'Pathology of Colours'

4 That Greek one then is my hero, who watched the bath water rise above his navel and rushed out naked, 'I found it, I found it' into the street in all his shining, and forgot that others would only stare at his genitals.
Walking under Water (1952) 'Letter to Alex Comfort'

Goodman Ace 1899–1982

5 Jane and I got mixed up with a television show—or as we call it back east here, TV—a clever contraction derived from the words Terrible Vaudeville. However, it is our latest medium—we call it a medium because nothing's well done. It was discovered, I suppose you've heard, by a man named Fulton Berle, and it has already revolutionized social grace by cutting down parlour conversation to two sentences: 'What's on television?' and 'Good night'.
Letter to Groucho Marx, in The Groucho Letters (1967) p. 114

Dean Acheson 1893–1971

6 The first requirement of a statesman is that he be dull. This is not always easy to achieve.
In *Observer* 21 June 1970

7 I will undoubtedly have to seek what is happily known as gainful employment, which I am glad to say does not describe holding public office.
In *Time* 22 Dec. 1952

8 Great Britain has lost an empire and has not yet found a role.
Speech at the Military Academy, West Point, 5 Dec. 1962, in *Vital Speeches* 1 Jan. 1963, p. 163

9 A memorandum is written not to inform the reader but to protect the writer.
In *Wall Street Journal* 8 Sept. 1977

J. R. Ackerley 1896–1967

10 I was born in 1896 and my parents were married in 1919.
My Father and Myself (1968) ch. 1

Douglas Adams 1952–

11 Don't panic.
Hitch Hiker's Guide to the Galaxy (1979) preface

12 'Life,' said Marvin, 'don't talk to me about Life.'
Hitch Hiker's Guide to the Galaxy (1979) ch. 11

13 And of course I've got this terrible pain in all the diodes down my left hand side.
Hitch Hiker's Guide to the Galaxy (1979) ch. 13

14 The Answer to the Great Question Of. . . . Life, the Universe and Everything. . . . Is. . . . Forty-two.
Hitch Hiker's Guide to the Galaxy (1979) ch. 27

1 'The first ten million years were the worst,' said Marvin, 'and the second ten million years, they were the worst too. The third ten million I didn't enjoy at all. After that I went into a bit of a decline.'
   Restaurant at the End of the Universe (1980) ch. 18

Frank Adams and Will M. Hough

2 I wonder who's kissing her now.
   Title of song (1909)

Franklin P. Adams 1881–1960

3 When the political columnists say 'Every thinking man' they mean themselves, and when candidates appeal to 'Every intelligent voter' they mean everybody who is going to vote for them.
   Nods and Becks (1944) p. 3

4 Years ago we discovered the exact point, the dead centre of middle age. It occurs when you are too young to take up golf and too old to rush up to the net.
   Nods and Becks (1944) p. 53

5 The trouble with this country is that there are too many politicians who believe, with a conviction based on experience, that you can fool all of the people all of the time.
   Nods and Becks (1944) p. 74

6 Elections are won by men and women chiefly because most people vote against somebody rather than for somebody.
   Nods and Becks (1944) p. 206

Henry Brooks Adams 1838–1918

7 Politics, as a practice, whatever its professions, has always been the systematic organization of hatreds.
   Education of Henry Adams (1907) ch. 1

8 A friend in power is a friend lost.
   Education of Henry Adams (1907) ch. 7

9 Chaos often breeds life, when order breeds habit.
   Education of Henry Adams (1907) ch. 16

10 One friend in a lifetime is much; two are many; three are hardly possible. Friendship needs a certain parallelism of life, a community of thought, a rivalry of aim.
   Education of Henry Adams (1907) ch. 20

11 What one knows is, in youth, of little moment; they know enough who know how to learn.
   Education of Henry Adams (1907) ch. 21

12 Practical politics consists in ignoring facts.
   Education of Henry Adams (1907) ch. 22

13 Some day science may have the existence of mankind in its power, and the human race commit suicide, by blowing up the world.
   Letter 11 Apr. 1862, in *Letters of Henry Adams* (1982) vol. 1, p. 290

Harold Adamson 1906–1980

14 Comin' in on a wing and a pray'r.
   Title of song (1943)

George Ade 1866–1944

15 'Whom are you?' he asked, for he had attended business college.
   Chicago Record 16 Mar. 1898, 'The Steel Box'

16 Anybody can Win, unless there happens to be a Second Entry.
   Fables in Slang (1900) p. 133

17 After being Turned Down by numerous Publishers, he had decided to write for posterity.
   Fables in Slang (1900) p. 158

18 If it were not for the presents, an elopement would be preferable.
   Forty Modern Fables (1901) p. 218

19 R-E-M-O-R-S-E!
   Those dry Martinis did the work for me;
   Last night at twelve I felt immense,
   Today I feel like thirty cents.
   My eyes are bleared, my coppers hot,
   I'll try to eat, but I cannot.
   It is no time for mirth and laughter,
   The cold, gray dawn of the morning
       after.
   Sultan of Sulu (1903) act 2, p. 63

Konrad Adenauer 1876–1967

20 A thick skin is a gift from God.
   In *New York Times* 30 Dec. 1959, p. 5

Alfred Adler 1870–1937

21 It is always easier to fight for one's principles than to live up to them.
   In Phyllis Bottome *Alfred Adler* (1939) p. 76

1 The truth is often a terrible weapon of aggression. It is possible to lie, and even to murder, for the truth.
Problems of Neurosis (1929) ch. 2

Polly Adler 1900–1962

2 A house is not a home.
Title of book (1954)

AE (A.E., Æ) (George William Russell) 1867–1935

3 In ancient shadows and twilights
Where childhood had strayed,
The world's great sorrows were born
And its heroes were made.
In the lost boyhood of Judas
Christ was betrayed.
Vale and Other Poems (1931) 'Germinal'

Herbert Agar 1897–1980

4 The truth which makes men free is for the most part the truth which men prefer not to hear.
Time for Greatness (1942) ch. 7

James Agate 1877–1947

5 I don't know very much, but what I do know I know better than anybody, and I don't want to argue about it. I know what I think about an actor or an actress, and am not interested in what anybody else thinks. My mind is not a bed to be made and re-made.
Ego 6 (1944) 9 June 1943

Spiro T. Agnew 1918–

6 I didn't say I wouldn't go into ghetto areas. I've been in many of them and to some extent I would have to say this: If you've seen one city slum you've seen them all.
In *Detroit Free Press* 19 Oct. 1968

7 A spirit of national masochism prevails, encouraged by an effete corps of impudent snobs who characterize themselves as intellectuals.
Speech in New Orleans, 19 Oct. 1969, in *Frankly Speaking* (1970) ch. 3

Max Aitken

See LORD BEAVERBROOK

Zoë Akins 1886–1958

8 The Greeks had a word for it.
Title of play (1930)

Alain (Émile-Auguste Chartier) 1868–1951

9 *Rien n'est plus dangereux qu'une idée, quand on n'a qu'une idée.*

Nothing is more dangerous than an idea, when you have only one idea.
Propos sur la religion (Remarks on Religion, 1938) no. 74

Edward Albee 1928–

10 Who's afraid of Virginia Woolf?
Title of play (1962). Cf. Frank E. Churchill

11 I have a fine sense of the ridiculous, but no sense of humour.
Who's Afraid of Virginia Woolf? (1962) act 1

Richard Aldington 1892–1962

12 Patriotism is a lively sense of collective responsibility. Nationalism is a silly cock crowing on its own dunghill.
Colonel's Daughter (1931) pt. 1, ch. 6

Brian Aldiss 1925–

13 Keep violence in the mind
Where it belongs.
Barefoot in the Head (1969) (last lines of concluding poem 'Charteris')

Nelson Algren 1909–

14 Never play cards with a man called Doc. Never eat at a place called Mom's. Never sleep with a woman whose troubles are worse than your own.
In *Newsweek* 2 July 1956

15 A walk on the wild side.
Title of novel (1956)

16 I got a glimpse into the uses of a certain kind of criticism this past summer at a writers' conference into how the avocation of assessing the failures of better men can be turned into a comfortable livelihood, providing you back it up with a Ph.D. I saw how it was possible to gain a chair of literature on no qualification other than persistence in nipping the heels of Hemingway, Faulkner, and Steinbeck. I know, of

course, that there are true critics, one or
two. For the rest all I can say is, Deal
around me.

> In Malcolm Cowley (ed.) *Writers at Work*
> (1958) 1st Ser. p. 222

Muhammad Ali (*Cassius Clay*)
1942–

1 Float like a butterfly, sting like a bee.

> Catch-phrase used from *c*.1964, in G.
> Sullivan *Cassius Clay Story* (1964) ch. 8

2 I'm the greatest.

> Catch-phrase used from 1962, in *Louisville
> Times* 16 Nov. 1962

Fred Allen (*John Florence
Sullivan*) 1894–1956

3 California is a fine place to live—if you
happen to be an orange.

> *American Magazine* Dec. 1945, p. 120

4 Hollywood is a place where people from
Iowa mistake each other for stars.

> In Maurice Zolotow *No People like Show
> People* (1951) ch. 8

5 Committee—a group of men who
individually can do nothing but as
a group decide that nothing can be
done.

> In Laurence J. Peter *Quotations for our Time*
> (1978) p. 120

Woody Allen
(*Allen Stewart Konigsberg*) 1935–

6 It's not that I'm afraid to die. I just don't
want to be there when it happens.

> *Death* (1975) p. 63

7 Is sex dirty? Only if it's done right.

> *Everything You Always Wanted to Know about
> Sex* (1972 film)

8 If it turns out that there is a God, I don't
think that he's evil. But the worst that
you can say about him is that basically
he's an underachiever.

> *Love and Death* (1975 film)

9 The lion and the calf shall lie down
together but the calf won't get much
sleep.

> *New Republic* 31 Aug. 1974 'The Scrolls'

10 Not only is there no God, but try getting
a plumber on weekends.

> *New Yorker* 27 Dec. 1969 'My Philosophy'

11 If only God would give me some clear
sign! Like making a large deposit in my
name at a Swiss bank.

> *New Yorker* 5 Nov. 1973 'Selections from
> the Allen Notebooks'

12 On bisexuality: It immediately doubles
your chances for a date on Saturday
night.

> *New York Times* 1 Dec. 1975, p. 33

13 More than any other time in history,
mankind faces a crossroads. One path
leads to despair and utter hopelessness.
The other, to total extinction. Let us
pray we have the wisdom to choose
correctly.

> *Side Effects* (1980) 'My Speech to the
> Graduates'

14 Take the money and run.

> Title of film (1968)

15 On the plus side, death is one of the few
things that can be done as easily lying
down.

> *Without Feathers* (1976) 'Early Essays'

16 Money is better than poverty, if only for
financial reasons.

> *Without Feathers* (1976) 'Early Essays'

17 My one regret in life is that I am not
someone else.

> Epigraph to Eric Lax *Woody Allen and his
> Comedy* (1975)

18 And my parents finally realize that I'm
kidnapped and they snap into action
immediately: They rent out my room.

> In Eric Lax *Woody Allen and his Comedy*
> (1975) ch. 1

19 I don't want to achieve immortality
through my work. . . . I want to achieve
it through not dying.

> In Eric Lax *Woody Allen and his Comedy*
> (1975) ch. 12

20 It was partially my fault that we got
divorced. . . . I tended to place my wife
under a pedestal.

> At night-club in Chicago, Mar. 1964,
> recorded on *Woody Allen Volume Two* (Colpix
> CP 488) side 1, band 6

21 I must say . . . a fast word about oral
contraception. I asked a girl to go to bed
with me and she said 'no'.

> At night-club in Washington, Apr. 1965,
> recorded on *Woody Allen Volume Two* (Colpix
> CP 488) side 4, band 6

Woody Allen
(*Allen Stewart Konigsberg*) 1935–
and *Marshall Brickman* 1941–

1 That [sex] was the most fun I ever had
without laughing.
Annie Hall (1977 film)

2 Don't knock masturbation. It's sex with
someone I love.
Annie Hall (1977 film)

3 I feel that life is—is divided up into the
horrible and the miserable.
Annie Hall (1977 film)

4 My brain? It's my second favourite
organ.
Sleeper (1973 film)

5 I'm not the heroic type, really. I was
beaten up by Quakers.
Sleeper (1973 film)

Margery Allingham 1904–1966

6 Once sex rears its ugly 'ead it's time to
steer clear.
Flowers for the Judge (1936) ch. 4

Joseph Alsop

7 Gratitude, like love, is never
a dependable international emotion.
In *Observer* 30 Nov. 1952

Robert Altman 1922–

8 After all, what's a cult? It just means
not enough people to make a minority.
In *Guardian* 11 Apr. 1981

Leo Amery 1873–1955

9 I will quote certain other words. I do it
with great reluctance, because I am
speaking of those who are old friends
and associates of mine, but they are
words which, I think, are applicable to
the present situation. This is what
Cromwell said to the Long Parliament
when he thought it was no longer fit to
conduct the affairs of the nation: 'You
have sat too long here for any good you
have been doing. Depart, I say, and let

us have done with you. In the name of
God, go.'
Hansard 7 May 1940, col. 1150. Cf. *Oxford
Dictionary of Quotations* (1979) 169:26

10 Speak for England.
Said to Arthur Greenwood in House of
Commons, 2 Sept. 1939, in *My Political Life*
(1955) vol. 3, p. 324

11 For twenty years he [H. H. Asquith] has
held a season-ticket on the line of least
resistance and has gone wherever the
train of events has carried him, lucidly
justifying his position at whatever point
he has happened to find himself.
Quarterly Review July 1914, p. 276

Sir Kingsley Amis 1922–

12 The delusion that there are thousands of
young people about who are capable of
benefiting from university training, but
have somehow failed to find their way
there, is . . . a necessary component of
the expansionist case. . . . More will
mean worse.
Encounter July 1960

13 The point about white Burgundies is
that I hate them myself. I take whatever
my wine supplier will let me have at
a good price (which I would never dream
of doing with any other drinkable).
I enjoyed seeing those glasses of Chablis
or Pouilly Fuissé, so closely resembling
a blend of cold chalk soup and alum
cordial with an additive or two to bring
it to the colour of children's pee, being
peered and sniffed at, rolled round the
shrinking tongue and forced down
somehow by parties of young technology
dons from Cambridge or junior television
producers and their girls.
The Green Man (1969) ch. 1

14 Dixon . . . tried to flail his features into
some sort of response to humour.
Mentally, however, he was making
a different face and promising himself
he'd make it actually when next alone.
He'd draw his lower lip in under his top
teeth and by degrees retract his chin as
far as possible, all this while dilating his
eyes and nostrils. By these means he
would, he was confident, cause a deep
dangerous flush to suffuse his face.
Lucky Jim (1953) ch. 1

ANDERSON

6

ANONYMOUS

1 Alun's life was coming to consist more and more exclusively of being told at dictation speed what he knew.
The Old Devils (1986) ch. 7

2 Outside every fat man there was an even fatter man trying to close in.
One Fat Englishman (1963) ch. 3. See also Cyril Connolly 59:12 and George Orwell 164:11

3 He was of the faith chiefly in the sense that the church he currently did not attend was Catholic.
One Fat Englishman (1963) ch. 8

Maxwell Anderson 1888–1959

4 But it's a long, long while
From May to December;
And the days grow short
When you reach September.
September Song (1938 song; music by Kurt Weill)

Maxwell Anderson 1888–1959 and Lawrence Stallings 1894–1968

5 What price glory?
Title of play (1924)

Robert Anderson 1917–

6 All you're supposed to do is every once in a while give the boys a little tea and sympathy.
Tea and Sympathy (1957) act 1

James Anderton 1932–

7 God works in mysterious ways. Given my love of God and my belief in God and in Jesus Christ, I have to accept that I may well be used by God in this way [as a prophet].
In radio interview, 18 Jan. 1987, in *Daily Telegraph* 19 Jan. 1987

8 Everywhere I go I see increasing evidence of people swirling about in a human cesspit of their own making.
Speech at seminar on AIDS, 11 Dec. 1986, in *Guardian* 12 Dec. 1986

Sir Norman Angell 1872–1967

9 The great illusion.
Title of book (1910), first published as 'Europe's optical illusion' (1909), on the futility of war

Maya Angelou (Maya Johnson) 1928–

10 I know why the caged bird sings.
Title of book (1969), taken from the last line of 'Sympathy' by Paul Laurence Dunbar in *Lyrics of Hearthside* (1899). Cf. *Oxford Dictionary of Quotations* (1979) 567:10

Paul Anka 1941–

11 And now the end is near
And so I face the final curtain,
My friend, I'll say it clear,
I'll state my case of which I'm certain.
I've lived a life that's full, I've travelled each and ev'ry highway
And more, much more than this. I did it my way.
My Way (1969 song; music by Claude François and Jacques Revaux)

Princess Anne (HRH the Princess Royal) 1950–

12 It could be said that the Aids pandemic is a classic own-goal scored by the human race against itself.
In *Daily Telegraph* 27 Jan. 1988

Anonymous

13 Access—your flexible friend.
Advertising slogan for Access credit cards, 1981 onwards, in Nigel Rees *Slogans* (1982) p. 91

14 All the way with LBJ.
US Democratic Party campaign slogan, in *Washington Post* 4 June 1960

15 American Express? . . . That'll do nicely, sir.
Advertisement for American Express credit card, 1970s, in F. Jenkins *Advertising* (1985) ch. 1

16 *Arbeit macht frei.*
Work liberates.
Words inscribed on the gates of Dachau concentration camp, 1933

17 Australians wouldn't give a XXXX for anything else.
Advertisement for Castlemaine lager, 1986 onwards, in Philip Kleinman *The Saatchi and Saatchi Story* (1987) ch. 5

1 Ban the bomb.
US anti-nuclear slogan, 1953 onwards, adopted by the Campaign for Nuclear Disarmament

2 A bayonet is a weapon with a worker at each end.
British pacifist slogan (1940)

3 The best defence against the atom bomb is not to be there when it goes off.
Contributor to *British Army Journal*, in *Observer* 20 Feb. 1949

4 Better red than dead.
Slogan of nuclear disarmament campaigners, late 1950s

5 Bigamy is having one husband too many. Monogamy is the same.
In Erica Jong *Fear of Flying* (1973) ch. 1 (epigraph)

6 A bigger bang for a buck.
Description of Charles E. Wilson's defence policy, in *Newsweek* 22 Mar. 1954

7 Black is beautiful.
Slogan of American civil rights campaigners in the mid-1960s, cited in *Newsweek* 11 July 1966

8 Burn, baby, burn.
Black extremist slogan used in Los Angeles riots, August 1965, in *Los Angeles Times* 15 Aug 1965, p. 1

9 The butler did it!
In Nigel Rees *Sayings of the Century* (1984) p. 45 (as a solution for detective stories. Rees cannot trace the origin of the phrase, but he quotes a correspondent who recalls hearing it at a cinema *c.*1916)

10 A camel is a horse designed by a committee.
In *Financial Times* 31 Jan. 1976

11 Can't act. Slightly bald. Also dances.
Studio official's comment on Fred Astaire, in Bob Thomas *Astaire* (1985) ch. 3

12 Can you tell Stork from butter?
Advertisement for Stork margarine, from *c.*1956

13 Careless talk costs lives.
World War II security slogan, in J. Darracott and B. Loftus *Second World War Posters* (1972) p. 28

14 Coughs and sneezes spread diseases. Trap the germs in your handkerchief.
1942 health slogan, in J. Darracott and B. Loftus *Second World War Posters* (1972) p. 19

15 [Death is] nature's way of telling you to slow down.
Newsweek 25 Apr. 1960, p. 70

16 Do not fold, spindle or mutilate in any way.
1950s instruction on punched cards, found in various forms *c.*1935 onwards

17 Don't ask a man to drink and drive.
UK road safety slogan, from 1964

18 Don't die of ignorance.
Slogan used in AIDS publicity campaign, 1987: see *The Times* 9 and 13 Jan. 1987

19 *Ein Reich, ein Volk, ein Führer.*
One realm, one people, one leader.
Nazi Party slogan, early 1930s

20 Even your closest friends won't tell you.
US advertisement for Listerine mouthwash, in *Woman's Home Companion* Nov. 1923, p. 63

21 Every picture tells a story.
Advertisement for Doan's Backache Kidney Pills, in *Daily Mail* 26 Feb. 1904

22 Expletive deleted.
Submission of Recorded Presidential Conversations to the Committee on the Judiciary of the House of Representatives by President Richard M. Nixon 30 Apr. 1974, app. 1, p. 2

23 Faster than a speeding bullet! More powerful than a locomotive! Able to leap tall buildings at a single bound! Look! Up in the sky! It's a bird! It's a plane! It's Superman! Yes, it's Superman! Strange visitor from another planet, who came to earth with powers and abilities far beyond those of mortal men. Superman! Who can change the course of mighty rivers, bend steel with his bare hands, and who—disguised as Clark Kent, mild-mannered reporter for a great metropolitan newspaper—fights a never ending battle for truth, justice and the American way!
Preamble to *Superman*, US radio show, 1940 onwards

24 The following is a copy of Orders issued by the German Emperor on August 19th: 'It is my Royal and Imperial command that you concentrate your energies for the immediate present upon one single purpose, and that is that you address all your skill and all the valour of my soldiers to exterminate first, the treacherous English, walk over General French's contemptible little army. . . . '

Annexe to B.E.F. [British Expeditionary Force] Routine Orders of 24 September 1914, in Arthur Ponsonby *Falsehood in Wartime* (1928) ch. 10 (although this is often attributed to Kaiser Wilhelm II, it was most probably fabricated by the British)

1 Frankie and Albert were lovers, O Lordy, how they could love.
Swore to be true to each other, true as the stars above;
He was her man, but he done her wrong.

'Frankie and Albert' in John Huston *Frankie and Johnny* (1930) p. 95 (St Louis ballad later better known as 'Frankie and Johnny')

2 Full of Eastern promise.
Advertising slogan for Fry's Turkish Delight, 1950s onwards

3 God gave Noah the rainbow sign,
No more water, the fire next time.
Home in that Rock (Negro spiritual). Cf. James Baldwin 16:14

4 God is not dead but alive and well and working on a much less ambitious project.
Graffito quoted in *Guardian* 26 Nov. 1975

5 Gotcha!
Headline on the sinking of the *General Belgrano*, in *Sun* 4 May 1982

6 Go to work on an egg.
Advertising slogan for the British Egg Marketing Board, from 1957; perhaps written by Fay Weldon or Mary Gowing: see Nigel Rees *Slogans* (1982) p. 133

7 The Governments of the States parties to this Constitution on behalf of their peoples declare, that since wars begin in the minds of men, it is in the minds of men that the defences of peace must be constructed.
Constitution of the United Nations Educational, Scientific and Cultural Organisation (1945), in *UK Parliamentary Papers* 1945–6 vol. 26

8 The hands that do dishes can be soft as your face, with mild green Fairy Liquid.
Advertising slogan for Procter & Gamble's washing-up liquid

9 Hark the herald angels sing
Mrs Simpson's pinched our king.
1936 children's rhyme quoted in letter from Clement Attlee, 26 Dec. 1938, in Kenneth Harris *Attlee* (1982) ch. 11

10 Have you heard? The Prime Minister [Lloyd George] has resigned and Northcliffe has sent for the King.
1919 saying in Hamilton Fyfe *Northcliffe, an Intimate Biography* (1930) ch. 16

11 Here we go, here we go, here we go.
Song sung by football supporters etc., 1980s

12 His [W. S. Gilbert's] foe was folly and his weapon wit.
Inscription on memorial to Gilbert on the Victoria Embankment, London, 1915

13 I don't like the family Stein!
There is Gert, there is Ep, there is Ein.
Gert's writings are punk,
Ep's statues are junk,
Nor can anyone understand Ein.
In R. Graves and A. Hodge *The Long Weekend* (1940) ch. 12 (rhyme current in the USA in the 1920s)

14 If it moves, salute it; if it doesn't move, pick it up; and if you can't pick it up, paint it.
1940s saying, in Paul Dickson *The Official Rules* (1978) p. 21

15 If you want to get ahead, get a hat.
Advertising slogan for the Hat Council, UK, 1965

16 *Ils ne passeront pas.*

They shall not pass.
Slogan used by French army at defence of Verdun in 1916; variously attributed to Marshal Pétain and to General Robert Nivelle. Cf. Dolores Ibarruri 109:18

17 I'm backing Britain.
Slogan coined by workers at the Colt factory, Surbiton, Surrey and subsequently used in a national campaign, in *The Times* 1 Jan. 1968

18 I'm worried about Jim.
Frequent line in *Mrs Dale's Diary*, BBC radio series 1948–69: see Denis Gifford *The Golden Age of Radio* (1985) p. 179 (where the line is given as 'I'm a little worried about Jim')

19 The iron lady.
In *Sunday Times* 25 Jan. 1976 (name given to Margaret Thatcher, then Leader of the Opposition, by the Soviet defence ministry newspaper *Red Star*, which accused her of trying to revive the cold war)

20 Is your journey *really* necessary?
1939 slogan (coined to discourage Civil Servants from going home for Christmas), in Norman Longmate *How We Lived Then* (1971) ch. 25

1 It became necessary to destroy the town to save it.
> Comment by unidentified US Army Major in Associated Press Report, *New York Times* 8 Feb. 1968 [the town referred to is Ben Tre, Vietnam]

2 It's for you-hoo!
> Slogan for British Telecom television advertisements, 1985 onwards

3 It's that man again . . . ! At the head of a cavalcade of seven black motor cars Hitler swept out of his Berlin Chancellery last night on a mystery journey.
> Headline in *Daily Express* 2 May 1939 [the abbreviation ITMA was used as title of a BBC radio show from 19 Sept. 1939]

4 It will play in Peoria.
> In *New York Times* 9 June 1973 (catch-phrase of the Nixon administration)

5 *Je suis Marxiste—tendance Groucho.*

I am a Marxist—of the Groucho tendency.
> Slogan used at Nanterre in Paris, 1968

6 Just when you thought it was safe to go back in the water.
> Advertisement for *Jaws 2* (1978 film)

7 Kentucky Fried Chicken. . . . '*It's finger lickin' good.*'
> *American Restaurant Magazine* June 1958

8 King's Moll Reno'd in Wolsey's Home Town.
> In Frances Donaldson *Edward VIII* (1974) ch. 7 (American newspaper headline referring to Mrs Simpson's divorce proceedings in Ipswich)

9 Labour isn't working.
> In Philip Kleinman *The Saatchi and Saatchi Story* (1987) ch. 2 (British Conservative Party slogan, 1978–9, on poster showing a long queue outside an unemployment office)

10 LBJ, LBJ, how many kids have you killed today?
> In Jacquin Sanders *The Draft and the Vietnam War* (1966) ch. 3 (anti-Vietnam marching slogan)

11 Let's get out of these wet clothes and into a dry Martini.
> Line coined in 1920s by press agent for Robert Benchley (and often attributed to Benchley), in Howard Teichmann *Smart Alec* (1976) ch. 9. Cf. Mae West 225:10

12 Let the train take the strain.
> British Rail advertising slogan, 1970 onwards

13 Let your fingers do the walking.
> 1960s advertisement for Bell system Telephone Directory Yellow Pages, in Harold S. Sharp *Advertising Slogans of America* (1984) p. 44

14 Liberty is always unfinished business.
> Title of 36th Annual Report of the American Civil Liberties Union, 1 July 1955–30 June 1956

15 Life is a sexually transmitted disease.
> In D. J. Enright (ed.) *Faber Book of Fevers and Frets* (1989) (graffito in the London Underground)

16 Life's better with the Conservatives. Don't let Labour ruin it.
> In David Butler and Richard Rose *British General Election of 1959* (1960) ch. 3 (Conservative Party election slogan)

17 Lloyd George knows my father,
My father knows Lloyd George.
> Comic song consisting of these two lines sung over and over again to the tune of *Onward, Christian Soldiers*, perhaps originally by Tommy Rhys Roberts (1910–75); sometimes with 'knew' instead of 'knows'

18 Lousy but loyal.
> London East End slogan at George V's Jubilee (1935), in Nigel Rees *Slogans* (1982)

19 Mademoiselle from Armenteers,
Hasn't been kissed for forty years,
Hinky, dinky, parley-voo.
> Song of World War I, variously ascribed to Edward Rowland and Harry Carlton

20 Make do and mend.
> Wartime slogan, 1940s

21 Make love not war.
> Student slogan, 1960s

22 The man from Del Monte says 'Yes'.
> Advertising slogan for tinned fruit, 1985

23 The man you love to hate.
> Billing for Erich von Stroheim in the film *The Heart of Humanity* (1918), in Peter Noble *Hollywood Scapegoat* (1950) ch. 2

24 Mother may I go and bathe?
Yes, my darling daughter.
Hang your clothes on yonder tree,
But don't go near the water.
> In Iona and Peter Opie *Oxford Dictionary of Nursery Rhymes* (1951) p. 314. Cf. Walter de la Mare 66:20

1 The nearest thing to death in life
Is David Patrick Maxwell Fyfe,
Though underneath that gloomy shell
He does himself extremely well.

In E. Grierson *Confessions of a Country
Magistrate* (1972) p. 35 (rhyme about Sir
David Maxwell Fyfe, said to
have been current on the Northern circuit
in the late
1930s)

2 *Nil carborundum illegitimi.*

Mock-Latin proverb translated as 'Don't let
the bastards grind you down'; often simply
'nil carborundum' or 'illegitimi non
carborundum'

3 No manager ever got fired for buying
IBM.

IBM advertising slogan

4 Nice one, Cyril.

1972 television advertising campaign for
Wonderloaf; taken up by supporters of Cyril
Knowles, Tottenham Hotspur footballer; the
Spurs team later made a record featuring the
line

5 No more Latin, no more French,
No more sitting on a hard board bench.

Rhyme used by children at the end of school
term: see Iona and Peter Opie *Lore and
Language of Schoolchildren* (1959) ch. 13;
also found with variants such as: No more
Latin, no more Greek, No more cares to
make me squeak

6 Nostalgia isn't what it used to be.

Graffito, used as title of book by Simone
Signoret

7 Not so much a programme, more a way
of life!

Title of BBC television series, 1964

8 O Death, where is thy
sting-a-ling-a-ling,
O grave, thy victory?
The bells of Hell go ting-a-ling-a-ling
For you but not for me.

For You But Not For Me (song of World War
I) in S. Louis Guiraud (ed.) *Songs That Won
the War* (1930). Cf.
1 Corinthians 15:55

9 Once again we stop the mighty roar of
London's traffic and from the great
crowds we bring you some of the
interesting people who have come by
land, sea and air to be *in town tonight.*

In Town Tonight (BBC radio series, 1933–60)
introductory words

10 Power to the people.

Slogan of the Black Panther movement,
c.1968 onwards, in *Black Panther* 14 Sept.
1968

11 *Puella Rigensis ridebat
Quam tigris in tergo vehebat;
Externa profecta,
Interna revecta,
Risusque cum tigre manebat.*

There was a young lady of Riga
Who went for a ride on a tiger;
They returned from the ride
With the lady inside,
And a smile on the face of the tiger.

In R. L. Green (ed.) *A Century of Humorous
Verse* (1959) p. 285

12 The [*or* A] quick brown fox jumps over
the lazy dog.

Sentence used by typists etc. to ensure that
all letters of the alphabet are printing
properly: see R. Hunter Middleton's
introduction to *The Quick Brown Fox* (1945)
by Richard H. Templeton Jr.

13 The rabbit has a charming face:
Its private life is a disgrace.
I really dare not name to you
The awful things that rabbits do.

The Rabbit, in *The Week-End Book* (1925)
p. 171

14 See the happy moron,
He doesn't give a damn,
I wish I were a moron,
My God! perhaps I am!

Eugenics Review July 1929

15 She was poor but she was honest
Victim of a rich man's game.
First he loved her, than he left her,
And she lost her maiden name.

See her on the bridge at midnight,
Saying 'Farewell, blighted love.'
Then a scream, a splash and goodness,
What is she a-doin' of?

It's the same the whole world over,
It's the poor wot gets the blame,
It's the rich wot gets the gravy.
Ain't it all a bleedin shame?

She was Poor but she was Honest (song sung
by British soldiers in World War I)

16 Shome mishtake, shurely?

Catch-phrase in *Private Eye* magazine,
1980s

17 Snap! Crackle! Pop!

Slogan for Kellogg's Rice Krispies, from
c.1928

1 So farewell then. . . .
> Frequent opening of poems by 'E. J. Thribb'
> in *Private Eye* magazine, 1970s onwards,
> usually as an obituary

2 Some television programmes are so
much chewing gum for the eyes.
> John Mason Brown, quoting a friend of his
> young son, in interview 28 July 1955, in
> James Beasley Simpson *Best Quotes of '50,
> '55, '56* (1957) p. 233

3 Sticks nix hick pix.
> *Variety* 17 July 1935 (headline on lack of
> interest for farm dramas in rural areas)

4 Stop-look-and-listen.
> Safety slogan current in the US from 1912

5 Take me to your leader.
> Catch-phrase from science-fiction stories

6 Tell Sid.
> Advertising slogan for the privatization of
> British Gas, 1986, in Philip Kleinman *The
> Saatchi and Saatchi Story* (1987) ch. 11

7 There is one thing stronger than all the
armies in the world; and that is an idea
whose time has come.
> *Nation* 15 Apr. 1943. Cf. *Oxford Dictionary of
> Quotations* (1979) 267:11

8 There is so much good in the worst of
us,
And so much bad in the best of us,
That it hardly becomes [*or* behooves]
  any of us
To talk about the rest of us.
> Attributed to many authors, especially
> Edward Wallis Hoch (1849–1945) because
> printed in the *Marion Record* (Kansas) which
> he owned, but disclaimed by him

9 There was a faith-healer of Deal
Who said, 'Although pain isn't real,
If I sit on a pin
And it punctures my skin,
I dislike what I fancy I feel.'
> *The Week-End Book* (1925) p. 158

10 They [Jacob Epstein's sculptures for the
former BMA building in the Strand] are
a form of statuary which no careful
father would wish his daughter, or no
discerning young man his fiancée, to
see.
> *Evening Standard* 19 June 1908

11 They come as a boon and a blessing to
men,

The Pickwick, the Owl, and the
  Waverley pen.
> Advertisement by MacNiven and H.
> Cameron Ltd., *c.*1920

12 [This film] is so cryptic as to be almost
meaningless. If there is a meaning, it is
doubtless objectionable.
> The British Board of Film Censors, banning
> Jean Cocteau's film *The Seashell and the
> Clergyman* (1929), in J. C. Robertson *Hidden
> Cinema* (1989) ch. 1

13 Though I yield to no one in my
admiration for Mr Coolidge, I do wish he
did not look as if he had been weaned
on a pickle.
> Anonymous remark reported in Alice
> Roosevelt Longworth *Crowded Hours* (1933)
> ch. 21

14 To err is human but to really foul things
up requires a computer.
> *Farmers' Almanac for 1978* (1977) 'Capsules
> of Wisdom'

15 Top people take The Times.
> Advertising slogan for *The Times* newspaper
> from Jan. 1959: see I. McDonald *History of
> The Times* (1984) vol. 5, ch. 16

16 *Tous les êtres humains naissent libres et
égaux en dignité et en droits.*

All human beings are born free and
equal in dignity and rights.
> *Universal Declaration of Human Rights* (1948)
> Article 1 (modified from a draft by René
> Cassin)

17 Ulster says no.
> Slogan coined in response to the Anglo-Irish
> Agreement of 15 Nov. 1985, in *Irish Times*
> 25 Nov. 1985

18 *Vorsprung durch Technik.*

Progress through technology.
> Advertising slogan for Audi cars, from 1986

19 Vote early. Vote often.
> Chicago (and Irish) election proverb, in
> David Frost and Michael Shea *Mid-Atlantic
> Companion* (1986) p. 95

20 Wall St. lays an egg.
> *Variety* 30 Oct. 1929 (headline on the Wall
> Street Crash)

21 War will cease when men refuse to
fight.
> Pacifist slogan, from *c.*1936 (often 'Wars
> will cease . . . '): see *Birmingham Gazette*
> 21 Nov. 1936, p. 3, and *Peace News* 15 Oct.
> 1938, p. 12

22 We are the Ovaltineys,

Little [*or* Happy] girls and boys.
We are the Ovaltineys (song promoting the drink Ovaltine, from *c*.1935)

1 The weekend starts here.
Catch-phrase of *Ready, Steady, Go*, British television series, *c*.1963

2 We're number two. We try harder.
Advertising slogan for Avis car rentals

3 We're here
Because
We're here
Because
We're here
Because we're here.
In John Brophy and Eric Partridge *Songs and Slang of the British Soldier 1914–18* (1930) p. 33 (sung to the tune of *Auld Lang Syne*)

4 We shall not be moved.
Title of (1931) song

5 We shall not pretend that there is nothing in his long career which those who respect and admire him would wish otherwise.
The Times 23 Jan. 1901 (leading article on the accession of Edward VII)

6 We shall overcome,
We shall overcome,
We shall overcome some day.
Oh, deep in my heart
I do believe
We shall overcome some day.
We Shall Overcome (song derived from several sources, notably the singers Zilphia Horton and Pete Seeger)

7 Who dares wins.
Motto on badge of British Special Air Service regiment, from 1942 (see J. L. Collins *Elite Forces: the SAS* (1986) introduction)

8 Whose finger do you want on the trigger?
Daily Mirror 21 Sept. 1951

9 Winston is back.
Board of Admiralty signal to the Fleet on Winston Churchill's reappointment as First Sea Lord, 3 Sept. 1939, in Martin Gilbert *Winston S. Churchill* (1976) vol. 5, ch. 53

10 Would you like to sin
With Elinor Glyn
On a tiger-skin?
Or would you prefer
To err
With her

On some other fur?
In A. Glyn *Elinor Glyn* (1955) bk. 2

Jean Anouilh 1910–1987

11 *Dieu est avec tout le monde. . . . Et, en fin de compte, il est toujours avec ceux qui ont beaucoup d'argent et de grosses armées.*

God is on everyone's side. . . . And, in the last analysis, he is on the side with plenty of money and large armies.
L'Alouette (The Lark, 1953) p. 120

12 *Il y a l'amour bien sûr. Et puis il y a la vie, son ennemie.*

There is love of course. And then there's life, its enemy.
Ardèle (1949) p. 8

13 *Vous savez bien que l'amour, c'est avant tout le don de soi!*

You know very well that love is, above all, the gift of oneself!
Ardèle (1949) p. 79

14 *C'est très jolie la vie, mais cela n'a pas de forme. L'art a pour objet de lui en donner une précisément et de faire par tous les artifices possibles—plus vrai que le vrai.*

Life is very nice, but it has no shape. The object of art is actually to give it some and to do it by every artifice possible—truer than the truth.
La Répétition (The Rehearsal, 1950) act 2

Guillaume Apollinaire 1880–1918

15 *Sous le pont Mirabeau coule la Seine.
Et nos amours, faut-il qu'il m'en souvienne?
La joie venait toujours après la peine.
Vienne la nuit, sonne l'heure,
Les jours s'en vont, je demeure.*

Under Mirabeau Bridge flows the Seine.
And our loves, must I remember them?
Joy always came after pain.
Let night come, ring out the hour,
The days go by, I remain.
Les Soirées de Paris Feb. 1912 'Le Pont Mirabeau'

16 *Les souvenirs sont cors de chasse
Dont meurt le bruit parmi le vent.*

Memories are hunting horns
Whose sound dies on the wind.
Les Soirées de Paris Sept. 1912 'Cors de Chasse'

Sir Edward Appleton 1892–1965

1 I do not mind what language an opera is sung in so long as it is a language I don't understand.
In *Observer* 28 Aug. 1955

Louis Aragon 1897–1982

2 *Ô mois des floraisons mois des métamorphoses*
Mai qui fut sans nuage et Juin poignardé
Je n'oublierai jamais les lilas ni les roses
Ni ceux que le printemps dans ses plis
a gardé.

O month of flowerings, month of metamorphoses,
May without cloud and June that was stabbed,
I shall never forget the lilac and the roses
Nor those whom spring has kept in its folds.
Le Crève-Cœur (Heartbreak, 1940) 'Les lilas et les roses'

Hannah Arendt 1906–1975

3 Under conditions of tyranny it is far easier to act than to think.
In W. H. Auden *A Certain World* (1970) p. 369

4 It was as though in those last minutes he [Eichmann] was summing up the lessons that this long course in human wickedness had taught us—the lesson of the fearsome, word-and-thought-defying banality of evil.
Eichmann in Jerusalem: a Report on the Banality of Evil (1963) ch. 15

5 It is well known that the most radical revolutionary will become a conservative on the day after the revolution.
New Yorker 12 Sept. 1970, p. 88

G. D. Armour 1864–1949

6 Look here, Steward, if this is coffee, I want tea; but if this is tea, then I wish for coffee.
Punch 23 July 1902 (cartoon caption)

Harry Armstrong 1879–1951

7 There's an old mill by the stream, Nellie Dean,

Where we used to sit and dream, Nellie Dean.
And the waters as they flow
Seem to murmur sweet and low,
'You're my heart's desire; I love you, Nellie Dean.'
Nellie Dean (1905 song)

Louis Armstrong 1901–1971

8 All music is folk music, I ain't never heard no horse sing a song.
In *New York Times* 7 July 1971, p. 41

9 If you still have to ask ... shame on you.
Habitual reply when asked what jazz is, in Max Jones et al. *Salute to Satchmo* (1970) p. 25

Neil Armstrong 1930–

10 That's one small step for a man, one giant leap for mankind.
In *New York Times* 31 July 1969, p. 20

Lord Robert Armstrong 1927–

11 It [a letter] contains a misleading impression, not a lie. It was being economical with the truth.
In Supreme Court, New South Wales, 18 Nov. 1986, in *Daily Telegraph* 19 Nov. 1986. Cf. Edmund Burke's *Two letters on Proposals for Peace* (1796) pt. 1, p. 137: Falsehood and delusion are allowed in no case whatsoever: But, as in the exercise of all the virtues, there is an economy of truth.

Raymond Aron 1905–

12 *La pensée politique, en France, est rétrospective ou utopique.*

Political thought, in France, is retrospective or utopian.
L'opium des intellectuels (The opium of the intellectuals, 1955) ch. 1

George Asaf 1880–1951

13 What's the use of worrying?
It never was worth while,
So, pack up your troubles in your old kit-bag,
And smile, smile, smile.
Pack up your Troubles (1915 song; music by Felix Powell)

Dame Peggy Ashcroft 1907–1991

1 It seems silly that more people should
see me in 'Jewel in the Crown' than in
all my years in the theatre.
   In *Observer* 18 Mar. 1984

Daisy Ashford 1881–1972

2 Mr Salteena was an elderly man of 42
and was fond of asking peaple to stay
with him.
   Young Visiters (1919) ch. 1

3 I do hope I shall enjoy myself with you.
I am fond of digging in the garden and
I am parshial to ladies if they are nice
I suppose it is my nature. I am not quite
a gentleman but you would hardly
notice it but can't be helped anyhow.
   Young Visiters (1919) ch. 1

4 You look rather rash my dear your
colors dont quite match your face.
   Young Visiters (1919) ch. 2

5 My own room is next the bath room
said Bernard it is decerated dark red as I
have somber tastes. The bath room has
got a tip up bason and a hose thing for
washing your head.
   Young Visiters (1919) ch. 2

6 Bernard always had a few prayers in the
hall and some whiskey afterwards as he
was rarther pious but Mr Salteena was
not very addicted to prayers so he
marched up to bed.
   Young Visiters (1919) ch. 3

7 It was a sumpshous spot all done up in
gold with plenty of looking glasses.
   Young Visiters (1919) ch. 5

8 Oh I see said the Earl but my own idear
is that these things are as piffle before
the wind.
   Young Visiters (1919) ch. 5

9 The bearer of this letter is an old friend
of mine not quite the right side of the
blanket as they say in fact he is the son
of a first rate butcher but his mother was
a decent family called Hyssopps of the
Glen so you see he is not so bad and is
desireus of being the correct article.
   Young Visiters (1919) ch. 5

10 Ethel patted her hair and looked very
sneery.
   Young Visiters (1919) ch. 8

11 My life will be sour grapes and ashes
without you.
   Young Visiters (1919) ch. 8

12 Oh Bernard muttered Ethel this is so
sudden. No no cried Bernard and taking
the bull by both horns he kissed her
violently on her dainty face. My bride to
be he murmered several times.
   Young Visiters (1919) ch. 9

Isaac Asimov 1920–1992

13 The three fundamental Rules of
Robotics. . . . One, a robot may not
injure a human being, or, through
inaction, allow a human being to come
to harm. . . . Two . . . a robot must obey
the orders given it by human beings
except where such orders would conflict
with the First Law . . . three, a robot
must protect its own existence as long as
such protection does not conflict with
the First or Second Laws.
   I, Robot (1950) 'Runaround'

Elizabeth Asquith (Princess Antoine Bibesco) 1897–1945

14 Kitchener is a great poster.
   In Margot Asquith *More Memories* (1933)
   ch. 6

Herbert Henry Asquith (Earl of Oxford and Asquith) 1852–1928

15 We had better wait and see.
   Hansard 3 Mar. 1910, col. 972 (expression
   used in various forms when answering
   questions on the Finance Bill)

16 Happily there seems to be no reason
why we should be anything more than
spectators [of the approaching war].
   Letters to Venetia Stanley (1982) 24 July
   1914

17 Youth would be an ideal state if it came
a little later in life.
   In *Observer* 15 Apr. 1923

18 [The War Office kept three sets of
figures:] one to mislead the public,
another to mislead the Cabinet, and the
third to mislead itself.
   In Alistair Horne *Price of Glory* (1962) ch. 2

19 We shall never sheath the sword which
we have not lightly drawn until Belgium

recovers in full measure all and more than all that she has sacrificed, until France is adequately secured against the menace of aggression, until the rights of the smaller nationalities of Europe are placed upon an unassailable foundation, and until the military domination of Prussia is wholly and finally destroyed.

Speech at the Guildhall, 9 Nov. 1914, in *The Times* 10 Nov. 1914

1 It is fitting that we should have buried the Unknown Prime Minister [Bonar Law] by the side of the Unknown Soldier.

In Robert Blake *The Unknown Prime Minister* (1955) p. 531

Margot Asquith (Countess of Oxford and Asquith) 1864–1945

2 It [10 Downing Street] is an inconvenient house with three poor staircases, and after living there a few weeks I made up my mind that owing to the impossibility of circulation I could only entertain my Liberal friends at dinner or at garden parties.

Autobiography (1922) vol. 2, ch. 5

3 Ettie [Lady Desborough] is an ox: she will be made into Bovril when she dies.

In Jeanne Mackenzie *Children of the Souls* (1986) ch. 4

4 Jean Harlow kept calling Margot Asquith by her first name, or kept trying to: she pronounced it Mar*got*. Finally Margot set her right. 'No, no, Jean. The *t* is silent, as in *Harlow*.'

T. S. Matthews *Great Tom* (1973) ch. 7

5 The King [George V] told me he would never have died if it had not been for that fool Dawson of Penn.

In letter from Mark Bonham Carter to Kenneth Rose 23 Oct. 1978, quoted in Kenneth Rose *King George V* (1983) ch. 9

6 Lord Birkenhead is very clever but sometimes his brains go to his head.

In *Listener* 11 June 1953 'Margot Oxford: a Personal Impression' by Lady Violet Bonham Carter

7 She [Lady Desborough] tells enough white lies to ice a wedding cake.

In *Listener* 11 June 1953 'Margot Oxford: a Personal Impression' by Lady Violet Bonham Carter

8 He [Lloyd George?] can't see a belt without hitting below it.

In *Listener* 11 June 1953 'Margot Oxford: a Personal Impression' by Lady Violet Bonham Carter

Raymond Asquith 1878–1916

9 The sun like a Bishop's bottom
Rosy and round and hot
Looked down upon us who shot 'em
And down on the devils we shot.
And the stink of the damned dead niggers
Went up to the Lord high God
But we stuck to our starboard triggers
Though we yawned like dying cod.

Letter, 4 Mar. 1900, in J. Jolliffe *Raymond Asquith Life and Letters* (1980) p. 64

Nancy Astor (Viscountess Astor) 1879–1964

10 One reason why I don't drink is because I wish to know when I am having a good time.

In *Christian Herald* June 1960, p. 31

11 I married beneath me, all women do.

In *Dictionary of National Biography 1961–1970* (1981) p. 43

12 After a heated argument on some trivial matter Nancy ... shouted, 'If I were your wife I would put poison in your coffee!' Whereupon Winston [Churchill] with equal heat and sincerity answered, 'And if I were your husband I would drink it.'

Consuelo Vanderbilt Balsan *Glitter and Gold* (1952) ch. 7

13 Jakie, is it my birthday or am I dying?

In J. Grigg *Nancy Astor* (1980) p. 184

Brooks Atkinson 1894–1984

14 After each war there is a little less democracy to save.

Once Around the Sun (1951) 7 Jan.

15 In every age 'the good old days' were a myth. No one ever thought they were good at the time. For every age has consisted of crises that seemed intolerable to the people who lived through them.

Once Around the Sun (1951) 8 Feb.

16 There is a good deal of solemn cant about the common interests of capital

and labour. As matters stand, their only common interest is that of cutting each other's throat.
Once Around the Sun (1951) 7 Sept.

E. L. Atkinson 1882–1929 and Apsley Cherry-Garrard 1882–1959

1 Hereabouts died a very gallant gentleman, Captain L. E. G. Oates of the Inniskilling Dragoons. In March 1912, returning from the Pole, he walked willingly to his death in a blizzard to try and save his comrades, beset by hardships.
Epitaph on cairn erected in the Antarctic, 15 Nov. 1912, in Apsley Cherry-Garrard *Worst Journey in the World* (1922) p. 487

Clement Attlee 1883–1967

2 Few thought he was even a starter
There were many who thought themselves smarter
But he ended PM
CH and OM
An earl and a knight of the garter.
Letter to Tom Attlee, 8 Apr.1956, in Kenneth Harris *Attlee* (1982) p. 545 (describing himself)

3 I should be a sad subject for any publicity expert. I have none of the qualities which create publicity.
In Harold Nicolson *Diary* (1968) 14 Jan. 1949

4 I think the British have the distinction above all other nations of being able to put new wine into old bottles without bursting them.
Hansard 24 Oct. 1950, col. 2705

5 The voice we heard was that of Mr Churchill but the mind was that of Lord Beaverbrook.
Speech on radio, 5 June 1945, in Francis Williams *Prime Minister Remembers* (1961) ch. 6

6 I remember he [Winston Churchill] complained once in Opposition that a matter had been brought up several times in Cabinet and I had to say, 'I must remind the Right Honourable Gentleman that a monologue is not a decision.'
In Francis Williams *Prime Minister Remembers* (1961) ch. 7

7 You have no right whatever to speak on behalf of the Government. Foreign Affairs are in the capable hands of Ernest Bevin. . . . I can assure you there is widespread resentment in the Party at your activities and a period of silence on your part would be welcome.
Letter to Harold Laski, 20 Aug. 1945, in Francis Williams *Prime Minister Remembers* (1961) ch. 11

8 [Russian Communism is] the illegitimate child of Karl Marx and Catherine the Great.
Speech at Aarhus University, 11 Apr. 1956, in *The Times* 12 Apr. 1956

9 Democracy means government by discussion, but it is only effective if you can stop people talking.
Speech at Oxford, 14 June 1957, in *The Times* 15 June 1957

W. H. Auden 1907–1973

10 Some thirty inches from my nose
The frontier of my Person goes,
And all the untilled air between
Is private *pagus* or demesne.
Stranger, unless with bedroom eyes
I beckon you to fraternize,
Beware of rudely crossing it:
I have no gun, but I can spit.
About the House (1966) 'Prologue: the Birth of Architecture'

11 Sob, heavy world,
Sob as you spin
Mantled in mist, remote from the happy.
Age of Anxiety (1947) p. 104

12 I'll love you, dear, I'll love you
Till China and Africa meet
And the river jumps over the mountain
And the salmon sing in the street.

I'll love you till the ocean
Is folded and hung up to dry
And the seven stars go squawking
Like geese about the sky.
Another Time (1940) 'As I Walked Out One Evening'

13 O plunge your hands in water,
Plunge them in up to the wrist;
Stare, stare in the basin
And wonder what you've missed.

The glacier knocks in the cupboard,
The desert sighs in the bed,
And the crack in the tea-cup opens

A lane to the land of the dead.
Another Time (1940) 'As I Walked Out One
Evening'

1 Perfection, of a kind, was what he was
after,
And the poetry he invented was easy to
understand;
He knew human folly like the back of
his hand,
And was greatly interested in armies
and fleets;
When he laughed, respectable senators
burst with laughter,
And when he cried the little children
died in the streets.
Another Time (1940) 'Epitaph on a Tyrant'

2 To us he is no more a person
Now but a whole climate of opinion.
Another Time (1940) 'In Memory of Sigmund
Freud'

3 He disappeared in the dead of winter:
The brooks were frozen, the airports
almost deserted,
And snow disfigured the public statues;
The mercury sank in the mouth of the
dying day.
What instruments we have agree
The day of his death was a dark cold
day.
Another Time (1940) 'In Memory of W. B.
Yeats'

4 You were silly like us: your gift survived
it all;
The parish of rich women, physical
decay,
Yourself; mad Ireland hurt you into
poetry.
Now Ireland has her madness and her
weather still,
For poetry makes nothing happen: it
survives
In the valley of its saying where
executives
Would never want to tamper; it flows
south
From ranches of isolation and the busy
griefs,
Raw towns that we believe and die in; it
survives,
A way of happening, a mouth.
Another Time (1940) 'In Memory of W. B.
Yeats'

5 Earth, receive an honoured guest;
William Yeats is laid to rest:
Let the Irish vessel lie

Emptied of its poetry.
Another Time (1940) 'In Memory of W. B.
Yeats'

6 In the nightmare of the dark
All the dogs of Europe bark,
And the living nations wait,
Each sequestered in its hate;

Intellectual disgrace
Stares from every human face,
And the seas of pity lie
Locked and frozen in each eye.
Another Time (1940) 'In Memory of W. B.
Yeats'

7 In the deserts of the heart
Let the healing fountain start,
In the prison of his days
Teach the free man how to praise.
Another Time (1940) 'In Memory of W. B.
Yeats'

8 About suffering they were never wrong,
The Old Masters: how well they
understood
Its human position; how it takes place
While someone else is eating or opening
a window or just walking dully along.
Another Time (1940) 'Musée des Beaux Arts'

9 They never forgot
That even the dreadful martyrdom must
run its course
Anyhow in a corner, some untidy spot
Where the dogs go on with their doggy
life and the torturer's horse
Scratches its innocent behind on a tree.
Another Time (1940) 'Musée des Beaux Arts'

10 Lay your sleeping head, my love,
Human on my faithless arm;
Time and fevers burn away
Individual beauty from
Thoughtful children, and the grave
Proves the child ephemeral:
But in my arms till break of day
Let the living creature lie,
Mortal, guilty, but to me
The entirely beautiful.
Another Time (1940) no. 18, p. 43

11 I and the public know
What all schoolchildren learn,
Those to whom evil is done
Do evil in return.
Another Time (1940) 'September 1, 1939'

12 All I have is a voice
To undo the folded lie,
The romantic lie in the brain
Of the sensual man-in-the-street

And the lie of Authority
Whose buildings grope the sky:
There is no such thing as the State
And no one exists alone;
Hunger allows no choice
To the citizen or the police;
We must love one another or die.
   Another Time (1940) 'September 1, 1939'

1 Our researchers into Public Opinion are
      content
   That he held the proper opinions for the
      time of year;
   When there was peace, he was for ·
      peace; when there was war, he went.
   Another Time (1940) 'The Unknown Citizen'

2 Was he free? Was he happy? The
      question is absurd:
   Had anything been wrong, we should
      certainly have heard.
   Another Time (1940) 'The Unknown Citizen'

3 All sin tends to be addictive, and the
   terminal point of addiction is what is
   called damnation.
   A Certain World (1970) 'Hell'

4 Of course, Behaviourism 'works'. So
   does torture. Give me a no-nonsense,
   down-to-earth behaviourist, a few
   drugs, and simple electrical appliances,
   and in six months I will have him
   reciting the Athanasian Creed in public.
   A Certain World (1970) 'Behaviourism'

5 A poet's hope: to be,
   like some valley cheese,
   local, but prized elsewhere.
   Collected Poems (1976) p. 639

6 It is a sad fact about our culture that
   a poet can earn much more money
   writing or talking about his art than he
   can by practising it.
   Dyer's Hand (1963) foreword

7 Between the ages of twenty and forty we
   are engaged in the process of discovering
   who we are, which involves learning the
   difference between accidental limitations
   which it is our duty to outgrow and the
   necessary limitations of our nature
   beyond which we cannot trespass with
   impunity.
   Dyer's Hand (1963) 'Reading'

8 Some books are undeservedly forgotten;
   none are undeservedly remembered.
   Dyer's Hand (1963) 'Reading'

9 One cannot review a bad book without
   showing off.
   Dyer's Hand (1963) 'Reading'

10 No poet or novelist wishes he were the
   only one who ever lived, but most of
   them wish they were the only one alive,
   and quite a number fondly believe their
   wish has been granted.
   Dyer's Hand (1963) 'Writing'

11 It takes little talent to see clearly what
   lies under one's nose, a good deal of it to
   know in which direction to point that
   organ.
   Dyer's Hand (1963) 'Writing'

12 The true men of action in our time,
   those who transform the world, are not
   the politicians and statesmen, but the
   scientists. Unfortunately poetry cannot
   celebrate them, because their deeds are
   concerned with things, not persons, and
   are, therefore, speechless. When I find
   myself in the company of scientists, I feel
   like a shabby curate who has strayed by
   mistake into a drawing room full of
   dukes.
   Dyer's Hand (1963) 'The Poet and the City'

13 The image of myself which I try to
   create in my own mind in order that
   I may love myself is very different from
   the image which I try to create in the
   minds of others in order that they may
   love me.
   Dyer's Hand (1963) 'Hic et Ille'

14 Almost all of our relationships begin and
   most of them continue as forms of
   mutual exploitation, a mental or
   physical barter, to be terminated when
   one or both parties run out of goods.
   Dyer's Hand (1963) 'Hic et Ille'

15 Man is a history-making creature who
   can neither repeat his past nor leave it
   behind.
   Dyer's Hand (1963) 'D. H. Lawrence'

16 Among those whom I like or admire,
   I can find no common denominator, but
   among those whom I love, I can: all of
   them make me laugh.
   Dyer's Hand (1963) 'Notes on the Comic'

17 At Dirty Dick's and Sloppy Joe's
   We drank our liquor straight,
   Some went upstairs with Margery,
   And some, alas, with Kate.
   For the Time Being (1944) 'The Sea and the
   Mirror'—'Master and Boatswain'

1 My Dear One is mine as mirrors are
   lonely.
   For the Time Being (1944) 'The Sea and the
   Mirror'—'Miranda'

2 The desires of the heart are as crooked
   as corkscrews
   Not to be born is the best for man
   The second best is a formal order
   The dance's pattern, dance while you
   can.
   Dance, dance, for the figure is easy
   The tune is catching and will not stop
   Dance till the stars come down with the
   rafters
   Dance, dance, dance till you drop.
   Letter from Iceland (1937, by Auden and
   MacNeice) 'Letter to William Coldstream,
   Esq.'

3 And make us as Newton was, who in
   his garden watching
   The apple falling towards England,
   became aware
   Between himself and her of an eternal
   tie.
   Look, Stranger! (1936) no. 1

4 Out on the lawn I lie in bed,
   Vega conspicuous overhead.
   Look, Stranger! (1936) no. 2

5 Let the florid music praise,
   The flute and the trumpet,
   Beauty's conquest of your face:
   In that land of flesh and bone,
   Where from citadels on high
   Her imperial standards fly,
   Let the hot sun
   Shine on, shine on.
   Look, Stranger! (1936) no. 4

6 Look, stranger, at this island now
   The leaping light for your delight
   discovers,
   Stand stable here
   And silent be,
   That through the channels of the ear
   May wander like a river
   The swaying sound of the sea.
   Look, Stranger! (1936) no. 5

7 O what is that sound which so thrills
   the ear
   Down in the valley drumming,
   drumming?
   Only the scarlet soldiers, dear,
   The soldiers coming.
   Look, Stranger! (1936) no. 6

8 O it's broken the lock and splintered the
   door,
   O it's the gate where they're turning,
   turning;
   Their boots are heavy on the floor
   And their eyes are burning.
   Look, Stranger! (1936) no. 6

9 A shilling life will give you all the facts.
   Look, Stranger! (1936) no. 13

10 August for the people and their favourite
    islands.
    Daily the steamers sidle up to meet
    The effusive welcome of the pier.
    Look, Stranger! (1936) no. 30

11 Geniuses are the luckiest of mortals
    because what they must do is the same
    as what they most want to do.
    In Dag Hammarskjöld *Markings* (1964)
    foreword

12 I see it often since you've been away:
    The island, the veranda, and the fruit;
    The tiny steamer breaking from the bay;
    The literary mornings with its hoot;
    Our ugly comic servant; and then you,
    Lovely and willing every afternoon.
    New Verse Oct. 1933, p. 15

13 At the far end of the enormous room
    An orchestra is playing to the rich.
    New Verse Oct. 1933, p. 15

14 To the man-in-the-street, who, I'm
    sorry to say,
    Is a keen observer of life,
    The word 'Intellectual' suggests straight
    away
    A man who's untrue to his wife.
    New Year Letter (1961) note to l. 1277

15 This is the Night Mail crossing the
    Border,
    Bringing the cheque and the postal
    order,
    Letters for the rich, letters for the poor,
    The shop at the corner, the girl next
    door.
    Pulling up Beattock, a steady climb:
    The gradient's against her, but she's on
    time.
    Past cotton-grass and moorland border,
    Shovelling white steam over her
    shoulder.
    Night Mail (1936) in *Collected Shorter Poems*
    (1966)

16 Letters of thanks, letters from banks,
    Letters of joy from girl and boy,

Receipted bills and invitations
To inspect new stock or to visit
    relations,
And applications for situations,
And timid lovers' declarations,
And gossip, gossip from all the nations.
  Night Mail (1936) in *Collected Shorter Poems*
  (1966)

1 Altogether elsewhere, vast
Herds of reindeer move across
Miles and miles of golden moss,
Silently and very fast.
  Nones (1951) 'The Fall of Rome'

2 Private faces in public places
Are wiser and nicer
Than public faces in private places.
  Orators (1932) dedication

3 Sir, no man's enemy, forgiving all
But will his negative inversion, be
    prodigal:
Send to us power and light, a sovereign
    touch
Curing the intolerable neutral itch,
The exhaustion of weaning, the liar's
    quinsy,
And the distortions of ingrown virginity.
  Poems (1930) 'Sir, No Man's Enemy'

4 Harrow the house of the dead; look
    shining at
New styles of architecture, a change of
    heart.
  Poems (1930) 'Sir, No Man's Enemy'

5 Let us honour if we can
The vertical man
Though we value none
But the horizontal one.
  Poems (1930) 'To Christopher Isherwood'

6 To ask the hard question is simple.
  Poems (1933) no. 27

7 This great society is going smash;
They cannot fool us with how fast they
    go,
How much they cost each other and the
    gods!
A culture is no better than its woods.
  Shield of Achilles (1955) 'Bucolics'

8 To save your world you asked this man
    to die:
Would this man, could he see you now,
    ask why?
  Shield of Achilles (1955) 'Epitaph for the
  Unknown Soldier'

9 Out of the air a voice without a face
Proved by statistics that some cause was
    just
In tones as dry and level as the place.
  Shield of Achilles (1955) 'The Shield of
  Achilles'

10 Tomorrow for the young the poets
    exploding like bombs,
The walks by the lake, the weeks of
    perfect communion;
Tomorrow the bicycle races
Through the suburbs on summer
    evenings. But today the struggle.
  Spain (1937) p. 11

11 The stars are dead. The animals will not
    look:
We are left alone with our day, and the
    time is short, and
History to the defeated
May say Alas but cannot help nor
    pardon.
  Spain (1937) p. 12

12 In a garden shady this holy lady
With reverent cadence and subtle psalm,
Like a black swan as death came on
Poured forth her song in perfect calm:
And by ocean's margin this innocent
    virgin
Constructed an organ to enlarge her
    prayer,
And notes tremendous from her great
    engine
Thundered out on the Roman air.

Blonde Aphrodite rose up excited,
Moved to delight by the melody,
White as an orchid she rode quite naked
In an oyster shell on top of the sea.
  Three Songs for St Cecilia's Day (1941).
  Dedicated to Benjamin Britten, and set to
  music by Britten as *Hymn to St Cecilia* op. 27
  (1942)

13 Blessed Cecilia, appear in visions
To all musicians, appear and inspire:
Translated Daughter, come down and
    startle
Composing mortals with immortal fire.
  Three Songs for St Cecilia's Day (1941)

14 No opera plot can be sensible, for in
sensible situations people do not sing.
An opera plot must be, in both senses of
the word, a melodrama.
  Times Literary Supplement 2 Nov. 1967,
  p. 1038

1 Your cameraman might enjoy himself
because my face looks like
a wedding-cake left out in the rain.
In Humphrey Carpenter *W. H. Auden* (1981)
pt. 2, ch. 6

2 You [Stephen Spender] are so infinitely
capable of being humiliated. Art is born
of humiliation.
In Stephen Spender *World Within World*
(1951) ch. 2

W. H. Auden 1907–1973 and
Christopher Isherwood 1904–1986

3 Happy the hare at morning, for she
cannot read
The Hunter's waking thoughts.
Dog beneath the Skin (1935) chorus following
act 2, sc. 2

Tex Avery (Fred Avery)
1907–1980

4 What's up, Doc?
Catch-phrase in Bugs Bunny cartoons, from
*c.*1940

Earl of Avon
See SIR ANTHONY EDEN

Revd W. Awdry 1911–

5 You've a lot to learn about trucks, little
Thomas. They are silly things and must
be kept in their place. After pushing
them about here for a few weeks you'll
know almost as much about them as
Edward. Then you'll be a Really Useful
Engine.
Thomas the Tank Engine (1946) p. 46

Alan Ayckbourn 1939–

6 My mother used to say, Delia, if S-E-X
ever rears its ugly head, close your eyes
before you see the rest of it.
Bedroom Farce (1978) act 2

7 This place, you tell them you're
interested in the arts, you get messages
of sympathy.
Chorus of Disapproval (1986) act 2

8 Do you realize, Mrs Foster, the hours
I've put into that woman? When I met
her, you know, she was nothing.
Nothing at all. With my own hands
I have built her up. Encouraging her to

join the public library and make use of
her non-fiction tickets.
How the Other Half Loves (1972) act 2, sc. 1

9 I only wanted to make you happy.
Round and Round the Garden (1975) act 2,
sc. 2

10 If you gave Ruth a rose, she'd peel all
the petals off to make sure there weren't
any greenfly. And when she'd done
that, she'd turn round and say, do you
call that a rose? Look at it, it's all in
bits.
Table Manners (1975) act 1, sc. 2

11 I always feel with Norman that I have
him on loan from somewhere. Like one
of his library books.
Table Manners (1975) act 2, sc. 1

Sir A. J. Ayer 1910–1989

12 No moral system can rest solely on
authority.
Humanist Outlook (1968) introduction

13 It seems that I have spent my entire time
trying to make life more rational and
that it was all wasted effort.
In *Observer* 17 Aug. 1986

Pam Ayres 1947–

14 I am a bunny rabbit,
Sitting in me hutch,
I like to sit up this end,
I don't care for that end, much,
I'm glad tomorrow's Thursday,
'Cause with a bit of luck,
As far as I remember,
That's the day they pass the buck.
Some of Me Poetry (1976) 'The Bunny
Poem'

15 Oh, I wish I'd looked after me teeth,
And spotted the perils beneath,
All the toffees I chewed,
And the sweet sticky food,
Oh, I wish I'd looked after me teeth.
Some of Me Poetry (1976) 'Oh, I wish I'd
looked after me teeth'

16 I might have been a farmyard hen,
Scratchin' in the sun,
There might have been a crowd of
chicks,
After me to run,
There might have been a cockerel fine,
To pay us his respects,
Instead of sittin' here,

Till someone comes and wrings our
   necks.

I see the Time and Motion clock,
Is sayin' nearly noon,
I 'spec me squirt of water,
Will come flyin' at me soon,
And then me spray of pellets,
Will nearly break me leg,
And I'll bite the wire nettin'
And lay one more bloody egg.
   Some of Me Poetry (1976) 'The Battery Hen'

1 Medicinal discovery,
It moves in mighty leaps,
It leapt straight past the common cold
And gave it us for keeps.
Now I'm not a fussy woman,
There's no malice in me eye
But I wish that they could cure
the common cold. That's all. Goodbye.
   Some of Me Poetry (1976) 'Oh no, I got
   a cold'

Robert Baden-Powell (Baron Baden-Powell) 1857–1941

2 The scouts' motto is founded on my
initials, it is: BE PREPARED, which means,
you are always to be in a state of
readiness in mind and body to do your
DUTY.
   Scouting for Boys (1908) pt. 1

Joan Baez 1941–

3 The only thing that's been a worse flop
than the organization of non-violence
has been the organization of violence.
   Daybreak (1970) 'What Would You Do If?'

Sydney D. Bailey 1916–

4 It has been said that this Minister [the
Lord Privy Seal] is neither a Lord, nor
a privy, nor a seal.
   British Parliamentary Democracy (ed. 3,
   1971) ch. 8

Bruce Bairnsfather 1888–1959

5 Well, if you knows of a better 'ole, go to
it.
   Fragments from France (1915) p. 1

Hylda Baker 1908–1986

6 She knows, you know!
   Catch-phrase used in comedy act, about her
   friend Cynthia

James Baldwin 1924–1987

7 Money, it turned out, was exactly like
sex, you thought of nothing else if you
didn't have it and thought of other
things if you did.
   Esquire May 1961 'Black Boy looks at the
   White Boy'

8 The fire next time.
   Title of book (1963). Cf. Anonymous 6:12

9 At the root of the American Negro
problem is the necessity of the American
white man to find a way of living with
the Negro in order to be able to live with
himself.
   Harper's Magazine Oct. 1953 'Stranger in
   a Village'

10 If the concept of God has any validity or
any use, it can only be to make us
larger, freer, and more loving. If God
cannot do this, then it is time we got rid
of Him.
   New Yorker 17 Nov. 1962 'Down at the
   Cross'

11 If they take you in the morning, they
will be coming for us that night.
   New York Review of Books 7 Jan. 1971 'Open
   Letter to my Sister, Angela Davis'

12 It comes as a great shock around the age
of 5, 6 or 7 to discover that the flag to
which you have pledged allegiance,
along with everybody else, has not
pledged allegiance to you. It comes as
a great shock to see Gary Cooper killing
off the Indians and, although you are
rooting for Gary Cooper, that the
Indians are you.
   Speech at Cambridge University, 17 Feb.
   1965, in *New York Times Magazine* 7 March
   1965, p. 32

13 The situation of our youth is not
mysterious. Children have never been
very good at listening to their elders,
but they have never failed to imitate
them. They must, they have no other
models.
   Nobody Knows My Name (1961) 'Fifth
   Avenue, Uptown: a letter from Harlem'

14 Anyone who has ever struggled with
poverty knows how extremely expensive
it is to be poor.
   Nobody Knows My Name (1961) 'Fifth
   Avenue, Uptown: a letter from Harlem'

15 Freedom is not something that anybody
can be given; freedom is something

people take and people are as free as
they want to be.
Nobody Knows My Name (1961) 'Notes for
a Hypothetical Novel'

Stanley Baldwin (*Earl Baldwin of Bewdley*) 1867–1947

1 Do not run up your nose dead against
the Pope or the NUM!
In Lord Butler *Art of Memory* (1982) p. 110

2 They [parliament] are a lot of hard-faced
men who look as if they had done very
well out of the war.
In J. M. Keynes *Economic Consequences of the
Peace* (1919) ch. 5

3 A platitude is simply a truth repeated
until people get tired of hearing it.
Hansard 29 May 1924, col. 727

4 I think it is well also for the man in the
street to realize that there is no power
on earth that can protect him from
being bombed. Whatever people may tell
him, the bomber will always get
through. The only defence is in offence,
which means that you have to kill more
women and children more quickly than
the enemy if you want to save
yourselves.
Hansard 10 Nov. 1932, col. 632

5 Let us never forget this; since the day of
the air, the old frontiers are gone. When
you think of the defence of England you
no longer think of the chalk cliffs of
Dover; you think of the Rhine. That is
where our frontier lies.
Hansard 30 July 1934, col. 2339

6 I shall be but a short time tonight. I have
seldom spoken with greater regret, for
my lips are not yet unsealed. Were these
troubles over I would make a case, and
I guarantee that not a man would go
into the lobby against us.
Hansard 10 Dec. 1935, col. 856

7 I put before the whole House my own
views with an appalling frankness. . . .
Supposing I had gone to the country and
said that Germany was rearming and
that we must rearm, does anybody think
that this pacific democracy would have
rallied to that cry at that moment?
I cannot think of anything that would
have made the loss of the election from
my point of view more certain.
Hansard 12 Nov. 1936, col. 1144

8 There are three classes which need
sanctuary more than others—birds, wild
flowers, and Prime Ministers.
In *Observer* 24 May 1925

9 Then comes Winston with his
hundred-horse-power mind and what
can I do?
In G. M. Young *Stanley Baldwin* (1952)
ch. 11

10 The intelligent are to the intelligentsia
what a gentleman is to a gent.
In G. M. Young *Stanley Baldwin* (1952)
ch. 13

11 'Safety first' does not mean a smug
self-satisfaction with everything as it is.
It is a warning to all persons who are
going to cross a road in dangerous
circumstances.
The Times 21 May 1929

12 Had the employers of past generations
all of them dealt fairly with their men
there would have been no unions.
Speech in Birmingham, 14 Jan. 1931, in *The
Times* 15 Jan. 1931

Arthur James Balfour (*Earl of Balfour*) 1848–1930

13 His Majesty's Government view with
favour the establishment in Palestine of
a national home for the Jewish people,
and will use their best endeavours to
facilitate the achievement of this object,
it being clearly understood that nothing
shall be done which may prejudice the
civil and religious rights of existing
non-Jewish communities in Palestine, or
the rights and political status enjoyed by
Jews in any other country.
Letter to Lord Rothschild 2 Nov. 1917, in K.
Young *A. J. Balfour* (1963) p. 478

14 Frank Harris . . . said . . . 'The fact is, Mr
Balfour, all the faults of the age come
from Christianity and journalism.' To
which Arthur replied . . . 'Christianity, of
course . . . but why journalism?'
Margot Asquith *Autobiography* (1920) vol. 1,
ch. 10

15 I never forgive but I always forget.
In R. Blake *Conservative Party* (1970) ch. 7

1 I thought he [Churchill] was a young man of promise, but it appears he is a young man of promises.
  In Winston Churchill *My Early Life* (1930) ch. 17

2 Biography should be written by an acute enemy.
  In *Observer* 30 Jan. 1927

3 It is unfortunate, considering that enthusiasm moves the world, that so few enthusiasts can be trusted to speak the truth.
  Letter to Mrs Drew, 19 May 1891, in *Some Hawarden Letters* (1917) ch. 7

Whitney Balliett 1926–

4 Critics are biased, and so are readers. (Indeed, a critic is a bundle of biases held loosely together by a sense of taste.) But intelligent readers soon discover how to allow for the windage of their own and a critic's prejudices.
  Dinosaurs in the Morning (1962) introductory note

5 The sound of surprise.
  Title of book on jazz (1959)

Pierre Balmain 1914–1982

6 The trick of wearing mink is to look as though you were wearing a cloth coat. The trick of wearing a cloth coat is to look as though you are wearing mink.
  In *Observer* 25 Dec. 1955

Tallulah Bankhead 1903–1968

7 I'm as pure as the driven slush.
  Quoted by Maurice Zolotow in *Saturday Evening Post* 12 Apr. 1947

8 There is less in this than meets the eye.
  In Alexander Woollcott *Shouts and Murmurs* (1922) ch. 4 describing a revival of Maeterlinck's play 'Aglavaine and Selysette')

9 Cocaine habit-forming? Of course not. I ought to know. I've been using it for years.
  Tallulah (1952) ch. 4

Nancy Banks-Smith

10 In my experience, if you have to keep the lavatory door shut by extending your left leg, it's modern architecture.
  Guardian 20 Feb. 1979

11 I'm still suffering from the big dénouement in [Jeffrey Archer's book] Not A Penny More when 'the three stood motionless like sheep in the stare of a python.' The whole thing keeps me awake at night. Here are these sheep, gambolling about in the Welsh jungle, when up pops a python. A python, what's more, who thinks he's a cobra.
  Guardian 26 Mar. 1990

Imamu Amiri Baraka (Everett LeRoi Jones) 1934–

12 A rich man told me recently that a liberal is a man who tells other people what to do with their money.
  Kulchur Spring 1962 'Tokenism'

13 A man is either free or he is not. There cannot be any apprenticeship for freedom.
  Kulchur Spring 1962 'Tokenism'

14 God has been replaced, as he has all over the West, with respectability and airconditioning.
  Midstream (1963) p. 39

W. N. P. Barbellion (Bruce Frederick Cummings) 1889–1919

15 Give me the man who will surrender the whole world for a moss or a caterpillar, and impracticable visions for a simple human delight. Yes, that shall be my practice. I prefer Richard Jefferies to Swedenborg and Oscar Wilde to Thomas à Kempis.
  Enjoying Life and Other Literary Remains (1919) 'Crying for the Moon'

16 Am writing an essay on the life-history of insects and have abandoned the idea of writing on 'How Cats Spend their Time'.
  Journal of a Disappointed Man (1919) 3 Jan. 1903

17 I can remember wondering as a child if I were a young Macaulay or Ruskin and secretly deciding that I was. My infant mind even was bitter with those who insisted on regarding me as a normal child and not as a prodigy.
  Journal of a Disappointed Man (1919) 23 Oct. 1910

Maurice Baring 1874–1945

1 In Mozart and Salieri we see the contrast
between the genius which does what it
must and the talent which does what it
can.
  Outline of Russian Literature (1914) ch. 3

Ronnie Barker 1929–

2 The marvellous thing about a joke with
a double meaning is that it can only
mean one thing.
  Sauce (1977) 'Daddie's Sauce'

Frederick R. Barnard

3 One picture is worth ten thousand
words.
  Printers' Ink 10 Mar. 1927

Clive Barnes 1927–

4 This [*Oh, Calcutta!*] is the kind of show
to give pornography a dirty name.
  New York Times 18 June 1969, p. 33

Julian Barnes 1946–

5 What does this journey seem like to
those who aren't British—as they head
towards the land of embarrassment and
breakfast?
  Flaubert's Parrot (1984) ch. 7

6 The writer must be universal in
sympathy and an outcast by nature:
only then can he see clearly.
  Flaubert's Parrot (1984) ch. 10

7 Do not imagine that Art is something
which is designed to give gentle uplift
and self-confidence. Art is not
a *brassière*. At least, not in the English
sense. But do not forget that *brassière* is
the French for life-jacket.
  Flaubert's Parrot (1984) ch. 10

8 Books say: she did this because. Life
says: she did this. Books are where
things are explained to you; life is where
things aren't. I'm not surprised some
people prefer books. Books make sense of
life. The only problem is that the lives
they make sense of are other people's
lives, never your own.
  Flaubert's Parrot (1984) ch. 13

Peter Barnes 1931–

9 CLAIRE: How do you know you're . . .
  God?

EARL OF GURNEY: Simple. When I pray
to Him I find I'm talking to myself.
  The Ruling Class (1969) act 1, sc. 4

Sir J. M. Barrie 1860–1937

10 I'm not young enough to know
everything.
  The Admirable Crichton (performed 1902,
  pubd. 1914) act 1

11 His lordship may compel us to be equal
upstairs, but there will never be equality
in the servants' hall.
  The Admirable Crichton (performed 1902,
  pubd. 1914) act 1

12 It's my deserts; I'm a second eleven sort
of chap.
  The Admirable Crichton (performed 1902,
  pubd. 1914) act 3

13 Times have changed since a certain
author was executed for murdering his
publisher. They say that when the
author was on the scaffold he said
goodbye to the minister and to the
reporters, and then he saw some
publishers sitting in the front row below,
and to them he did not say goodbye. He
said instead, 'I'll see you later.'
  Speech at Aldine Club, New York, 5 Nov.
  1896, in *Critic* 14 Nov. 1896

14 The life of every man is a diary in which
he means to write one story, and writes
another; and his humblest hour is when
he compares the volume as it is with
what he vowed to make it.
  The Little Minister (1891) vol. 1, ch. 1

15 It's grand, and you canna expect to be
baith grand and comfortable.
  The Little Minister (1891) vol. 1, ch. 10

16 I loathe entering upon explanations to
anybody about anything.
  My Lady Nicotine (1890) ch. 14

17 When the first baby laughed for the first
time, the laugh broke into a thousand
pieces and they all went skipping about,
and that was the beginning of fairies.
  Peter Pan (1928) act 1

18 Every time a child says 'I don't believe in
fairies' there is a little fairy somewhere
that falls down dead.
  Peter Pan (1928) act 1

19 To die will be an awfully big adventure.
  Peter Pan (1928) act 3. Cf. Charles Frohman

1 Do you believe in fairies? Say quick that you believe! If you believe, clap your hands!

   Peter Pan (1928) act 4

2 That is ever the way. 'Tis all jealousy to the bride and good wishes to the corpse.

   Quality Street (performed 1901, pubd. 1913) act 1

3 The printing press is either the greatest blessing or the greatest curse of modern times, one sometimes forgets which.

   Sentimental Tommy (1896) ch. 5

4 Someone said that God gave us memory so that we might have roses in December.

   Rectorial Address at St Andrew's, 3 May 1922, in *The Times* 4 May 1922

5 Never ascribe to an opponent motives meaner than your own.

   Rectorial Address at St Andrew's, 3 May 1922, in *The Times* 4 May 1922

6 Courage is the thing. All goes if courage goes!

   Rectorial Address at St Andrews, 3 May 1922, in *The Times* 4 May 1922

7 For several days after my first book was published I carried it about in my pocket, and took surreptitious peeps at it to make sure that the ink had not faded.

   Speech at the Critics' Circle in London, 26 May 1922, in *The Times* 27 May 1922

8 Have you ever noticed, Harry, that many jewels make women either incredibly fat or incredibly thin?

   The Twelve-Pound Look and Other Plays (1921) p. 27

9 One's religion is whatever he is most interested in, and yours is Success.

   The Twelve-Pound Look and Other Plays (1921) p. 28

10 Oh the gladness of her gladness when she's glad,
   And the sadness of her sadness when she's sad,
   But the gladness of her gladness
   And the sadness of her sadness
   Are as nothing, Charles,
   To the badness of her badness when she's bad.

   Rosalind in *Half Hours* (1914) p. 113

11 Charm ... it's a sort of bloom on a woman. If you have it, you don't need to have anything else; and if you don't have it, it doesn't much matter what else you have. Some women, the few, have charm for all; and most have charm for one. But some have charm for none.

   What Every Woman Knows (1918) act 1

12 A young Scotsman of your ability let loose upon the world with £300, what could he not do? It's almost appalling to think of; especially if he went among the English.

   What Every Woman Knows (1918) act 1

13 My lady, there are few more impressive sights in the world than a Scotsman on the make.

   What Every Woman Knows (1918) act 2

14 You've forgotten the grandest moral attribute of a Scotsman, Maggie, that he'll do nothing which might damage his career.

   What Every Woman Knows (1918) act 2

15 The tragedy of a man who has found himself out.

   What Every Woman Knows (1918) act 4

16 Every man who is high up loves to think that he has done it all himself; and the wife smiles, and lets it go at that. It's our only joke. Every woman knows that.

   What Every Woman Knows (1918) act 4

Ethel Barrymore 1879–1959

17 For an actress to be a success, she must have the face of a Venus, the brains of a Minerva, the grace of Terpsichore, the memory of a Macaulay, the figure of Juno, and the hide of a rhinoceros.

   In George Jean Nathan *The Theatre in the Fifties* (1953) p. 30

John Barrymore 1882–1942

18 He [Barrymore] would quote from Genesis the text which says, 'It is not good for man to be alone,' and then add, 'But O my God, what a relief.'

   Alma Power-Waters *John Barrymore* (1941) ch. 13

19 My only regret in the theatre is that I could never sit out front and watch me.

   In Eddie Cantor *The Way I See It* (1959) ch. 2

1 Die? I should say not, old fellow. No
Barrymore would allow such
a conventional thing to happen to him.
In Lionel Barrymore *We Barrymores* (1951)
ch. 26

Lionel Bart 1930–

See FRANK NORMAN

Karl Barth 1886–1968

2 *Die Menschen aber waren nie gut, sind es
nicht und werden es auch nie sein.*

Men have never been good, they are not
good and they never will be good.
Christliche Gemeinde (Christian Community,
1948) p. 36

3 Whether the angels play only Bach in
praising God I am not quite sure; I am
sure, however, that en famille they play
Mozart.
In *New York Times* 11 Dec. 1968, p. 42

Roland Barthes 1915–1980

4 *Ce que le public réclame, c'est l'image de la
passion, non la passion elle-même.*

What the public wants is the image of
passion, not passion itself.
Esprit (1952) vol. 20, pt. 10, p. 412 'Le
monde où l'on catche' (The world of
wrestling)

5 *Je crois que l'automobile est aujourd'hui
l'équivalent assez exact des grandes
cathédrales gothiques: je veux dire une
grande création d'époque, conçue
passionnément par des artistes inconnus,
consommée dans son image, sinon dans son
usage, par un peuple entier qui s'approprie
en elle un objet parfaitement magique.*

I think that cars today are almost the
exact equivalent of the great Gothic
cathedrals: I mean the supreme creation
of an era, conceived with passion by
unknown artists, and consumed in
image if not in usage by a whole
population which appropriates them as
a purely magical object.
Mythologies (1957) 'La nouvelle Citroën'
(The new Citroën)

Bernard Baruch 1870–1965

6 To me old age is always fifteen years
older than I am.
In *Newsweek* 29 Aug. 1955

7 Vote for the man who promises least;
he'll be the least disappointing.
In Meyer Berger *New York* (1960)

8 Let us not be deceived—we are today in
the midst of a cold war.
Speech to South Carolina Legislature
16 Apr. 1947, in *New York Times* 17 Apr.
1947, p. 21 (the expression 'cold war' was
suggested to him by H. B. Swope, former
editor of the *New York World*)

9 A political leader must keep looking over
his shoulder all the time to see if the
boys are still there. If they aren't still
there, he's no longer a political leader.
In *New York Times* 21 June 1965, p. 16

10 You can talk about capitalism and
communism and all that sort of thing,
but the important thing is the struggle
everybody is engaged in to get better
living conditions, and they are not
interested too much in forms of
government.
In *The Times* 20 Aug. 1964

Jacques Barzun 1907–

11 If it were possible to talk to the unborn,
one could never explain to them how it
feels to be alive, for life is washed in the
speechless real.
The House of Intellect (1959) ch. 6

12 Art distils sensation and embodies it
with enhanced meaning in memorable
form—or else it is not art.
The House of Intellect (1959) ch. 6

L. Frank Baum 1856–1919

13 The road to the City of Emeralds is
paved with yellow brick.
Wonderful Wizard of Oz (1900) ch. 2

Vicki Baum 1888–1960

14 *Verheiratet sein verlangt immer und überall
die feinste Kunst der Unaufrichtigkeit
zwischen Mensch und Mensch.*

Marriage always demands the finest arts
of insincerity possible between two
human beings.
Zwischenfall in Lohwinckel (1930) p. 140,
translated by Margaret Goldsmith as *Results
of an Accident* (1931) p. 140

Sir Arnold Bax 1883–1953

15 A sympathetic Scot summed it all up
very neatly in the remark, 'You should

make a point of trying every experience once, excepting incest and folk-dancing.'
Farewell, My Youth (1943) p. 17

Sir Beverley Baxter 1891–1964

1 Beaverbrook is so pleased to be in the Government that he is like the town tart who has finally married the Mayor!
In Sir Henry Channon *Chips: the Diaries* (1967) 12 June 1940

Beachcomber

See J. B. MORTON

David, First Earl Beatty 1871–1936

2 There seems to be something wrong with our bloody ships today [at the Battle of Jutland].
In S. Roskill *Beatty* (1980) ch. 8

3 The German flag will be hauled down at sunset to-day (Thursday) and will not be hoisted again without permission.
Signal to the Fleet, 21 Nov. 1918, in *The Times* 22 Nov. 1918

Lord Beaverbrook (William Maxwell Aitken, first Baron Beaverbrook) 1879–1964

4 I ran the paper [*Daily Express*] purely for propaganda, and with no other purpose.
Evidence to Royal Commission on the Press, 18 Mar. 1948, in A. J. P. Taylor *Beaverbrook* (1972) ch. 23

5 This is my final word. It is time for me to become an apprentice once more. I have not settled in which direction. But somewhere, sometime soon.
Speech at Dorchester Hotel, 25 May 1964, in A. J. P. Taylor *Beaverbrook* (1972) ch. 25

6 The Flying Scotsman is no less splendid a sight when it travels north to Edinburgh than when it travels south to London. Mr Baldwin denouncing sanctions was as dignified as Mr Baldwin imposing them. At times it seemed that there were two Mr Baldwins on the stage, a prudent Mr Baldwin, who scented the danger in foolish projects, and a reckless Mr Baldwin, who plunged into them head down, eyes shut. But there was, in fact, only one Mr Baldwin,

a well-meaning man of indifferent judgement, who, whether he did right or wrong, was always sustained by a belief that he was acting for the best.
Daily Express 29 May 1937

7 The Daily Express declares that Great Britain will not be involved in a European war this year or next year either.
Daily Express 19 Sept. 1938

8 He [Lloyd George] did not seem to care which way he travelled providing he was in the driver's seat.
Decline and Fall of Lloyd George (1963) ch. 7

9 Now who is responsible for this work of development on which so much depends? To whom must the praise be given? To the boys in the back rooms. They do not sit in the limelight. But they are the men who do the work.
Listener 27 Mar. 1941. Cf. Frank Loesser

10 With the publication of his [Earl Haig's] Private Papers in 1952, he committed suicide 25 years after his death.
Men and Power (1956) p. xviii

11 Churchill on top of the wave has in him the stuff of which tyrants are made.
Politicians and the War (1932) vol. 2, ch. 6

Carl Becker 1873–1945

12 The significance of man is that he is that part of the universe that asks the question, What is the significance of Man? He alone can stand apart imaginatively and, regarding himself and the universe in their eternal aspects, pronounce a judgment: The significance of man is that he is insignificant and is aware of it.
Progress and Power (1936) ch. 3

Samuel Beckett 1906–1989

13 It is suicide to be abroad. But what is it to be at home, Mr Tyler, what is it to be at home? A lingering dissolution.
All That Fall (1957) p. 10

14 We could have saved sixpence. We have saved fivepence. (*Pause*) But at what cost?
All That Fall (1957) p. 25

15 CLOV: Do you believe in the life to come?

HAMM: Mine was always that.
Endgame (1958) p. 35

1 Personally I have no bone to pick with graveyards, I take the air there willingly, perhaps more willingly than elsewhere, when take the air I must.
First Love (1973) p. 8

2 If I had the use of my body I would throw it out of the window.
Malone Dies (1958) p. 44

3 Where I am, I don't know, I'll never know, in the silence you don't know, you must go on, I can't go on, I'll go on.
The Unnamable (1959) p. 418

4 Nothing to be done.
Waiting for Godot (1955) act 1

5 One of the thieves was saved. (*Pause*) It's a reasonable percentage.
Waiting for Godot (1955) act 1

6 ESTRAGON: Charming spot. Inspiring prospects. Let's go.
VLADIMIR: We can't.
ESTRAGON: Why not?
VLADIMIR: We're waiting for Godot.
Waiting for Godot (1955) act 1

7 Nothing happens, nobody comes, nobody goes, it's awful!
Waiting for Godot (1955) act 1

8 He can't think without his hat.
Waiting for Godot (1955) act 1

9 VLADIMIR: That passed the time.
ESTRAGON: It would have passed in any case.
VLADIMIR: Yes, but not so rapidly.
Waiting for Godot (1955) act 1

10 We always find something, eh, Didi, to give us the impression that we exist?
Waiting for Godot (1955) act 2

11 We are not saints, but we have kept our appointment. How many people can boast as much?
Waiting for Godot (1955) act 2

12 We all are born mad. Some remain so.
Waiting for Godot (1955) act 2

13 They give birth astride of a grave, the light gleams an instant, then it's night once more.
Waiting for Godot (1955) act 2

14 The air is full of our cries. (*He listens.*) But habit is a great deadener.
Waiting for Godot (1955) act 2

Harry Bedford and *Terry Sullivan*

15 I'm a bit of a ruin that Cromwell knock'd about a bit.
It's a Bit of a Ruin that Cromwell Knocked about a Bit (1920 song; written for Marie Lloyd)

Sir Thomas Beecham 1879–1961

16 A musicologist is a man who can read music but can't hear it.
In H. Proctor-Gregg *Beecham Remembered* (1976) pt. 2, p. 154

17 There are two golden rules for an orchestra: start together and finish together. The public doesn't give a damn what goes on in between.
In Harold Atkins and Archie Newman *Beecham Stories* (1978) p. 27

18 [The harpsichord] sounds like two skeletons copulating on a corrugated tin roof.
In Harold Atkins and Archie Newman *Beecham Stories* (1978) p. 34

19 In the first movement alone, of the Seventh Symphony [by Bruckner], I took note of six pregnancies and at least four miscarriages.
In Harold Atkins and Archie Newman *Beecham Stories* (1978) p. 50

20 [Herbert von Karajan is] a kind of musical Malcolm Sargent.
In Harold Atkins and Archie Newman *Beecham Stories* (1978) p. 61

21 I am not the greatest conductor in this country. On the other hand I'm better than any damned foreigner.
In *Daily Express* 9 Mar. 1961

22 Musicians did not like the piece [Strauss's *Elektra*] at all. One eminent British composer on leaving the theatre was asked what he thought of it. 'Words fail me,' he replied, 'and I'm going home at once to play the chord of C major twenty times over to satisfy myself that it still exists.'
Mingled Chime (1944) ch. 18

23 The plain fact is that music *per se* means nothing; it is sheer sound, and the interpreter can do no more with it than his own capacities, mental and spiritual, will allow, and the same applies to the listener.
Mingled Chime (1944) ch. 33

1 The English may not like music, but they absolutely love the noise it makes.
   In *New York Herald Tribune* 9 Mar. 1961

2 Good music is that which penetrates the ear with facility and quits the memory with difficulty.
   Speech, *c*.1950, in *New York Times* 9 Mar. 1961

3 All the arts in America are a gigantic racket run by unscrupulous men for unhealthy women.
   In *Observer* 5 May 1946

4 Hark! the herald angels sing!
   Beecham's Pills are just the thing,
   Two for a woman, one for a child . . .
   Peace on earth and mercy mild!
   In Neville Cardus *Sir Thomas Beecham* (1961) p. 23

5 At a rehearsal I let the orchestra play as they like. At the concert I make them play as *I* like.
   In Neville Cardus *Sir Thomas Beecham* (1961) p. 111

6 Dear old Elgar—he is furious with me for drastically cutting his A flat symphony—it's a very long work, the musical equivalent of the Towers of St Pancras Station—neo-Gothic, you know.
   In Neville Cardus *Sir Thomas Beecham* (1961) p. 113

7 I am entirely with you in your obvious reluctance to rehearse on a morning as chilly and dismal as this—but please do try to keep in touch with us from time to time.
   In Neville Cardus *Sir Thomas Beecham* (1961) p. 113

8 Why do we have to have all these third-rate foreign conductors around—when we have so many second-rate ones of our own?
   In L. Ayre *Wit of Music* (1966) p. 70

Sir Max Beerbohm 1872–1956

9 I have known no man of genius who had not to pay, in some affliction or defect either physical or spiritual, for what the gods had given him.
   And Even Now (1920) 'No. 2, The Pines'

10 One might well say that mankind is divisible into two great classes: hosts and guests.
   And Even Now (1920) 'Hosts and Guests'

11 I maintain that though you would often in the fifteenth century have heard the snobbish Roman say, in a would-be off-hand tone, 'I am dining with the Borgias tonight,' no Roman ever was able to say, 'I dined last night with the Borgias.'
   And Even Now (1920) 'Hosts and Guests'

12 They so very indubitably *are*, you know!
   Christmas Garland (1912) 'Mote in the Middle Distance'

13 Of course he [William Morris] was a wonderful all-round man, but the act of walking round him has always tired me.
   Letter to S. N. Behrman *c*.1953, in *Conversations with Max* (1960) ch. 2

14 A swear-word in a rustic slum
   A simple swear-word is to some,
   To Masefield something more.
   Fifty Caricatures (1912) no. 12

15 Not that I had any special reason for hating school! Strange as it may seem to my readers, I was not unpopular there. I was a modest, good-humoured boy. It is Oxford that has made me insufferable.
   More (1899) 'Going Back to School'

16 Undergraduates owe their happiness chiefly to the consciousness that they are no longer at school. The nonsense which was knocked out of them at school is all put gently back at Oxford or Cambridge.
   More (1899) 'Going Back to School'

17 I have the satiric temperament: when I am laughing at anyone I am generally rather amusing, but when I am praising anyone, I am always deadly dull.
   Saturday Review 28 May 1898

18 The only tribute a French translator can pay Shakespeare is not to translate him—even to please Sarah [Bernhardt].
   Saturday Review 17 June 1899

19 'I'm afraid I found [the British Museum] rather a depressing place. It—it seemed to sap one's vitality.' 'It does. That's why I go there. The lower one's vitality, the more sensitive one is to great art.'
   Seven Men (1919) 'Enoch Soames'

20 Enter Michael Angelo. Andrea del Sarto appears for a moment at a window. Pippa passes.
   Seven Men (1919) ' Savonarola Brown' act 3

1 Most women are not so young as they
are painted.
  Yellow Book (1894) vol. 1, p. 67

2 'After all,' as a pretty girl once said to
me, 'women are a sex by themselves, so
to speak.'
  Yellow Book (1894) vol. 1, p. 70

3 Fate wrote her [Queen Caroline of
Brunswick] a most tremendous tragedy,
and she played it in tights.
  Yellow Book (1894) vol. 3, p. 260

4 There is always something rather absurd
about the past.
  Yellow Book (1895) vol. 4, p. 282

5 To give an accurate and exhaustive
account of the period would need a far
less brilliant pen than mine.
  Yellow Book (1895) vol. 4, p. 283

6 None, it is said, of all who revelled with
the Regent, was half so wicked as Lord
George Hell.
  Yellow Book (1896) vol. 11, p. 11 ' Happy
  Hypocrite' ch. 1

7 The fading signals and grey eternal walls
of that antique station, which, familiar
to them and insignificant, does yet
whisper to the tourist the last
enchantments of the Middle Age.
  Zuleika Dobson (1911) ch. 1

8 Zuleika, on a desert island, would have
spent most of her time in looking for
a man's footprint.
  Zuleika Dobson (1911) ch. 2

9 The dullard's envy of brilliant men is
always assuaged by the suspicion that
they will come to a bad end.
  Zuleika Dobson (1911) ch. 4

10 Women who love the same man have
a kind of bitter freemasonry.
  Zuleika Dobson (1911) ch. 4

11 You will find that the woman who is
really kind to dogs is always one who
has failed to inspire sympathy in men.
  Zuleika Dobson (1911) ch. 6

12 Beauty and the lust for learning have
yet to be allied.
  Zuleika Dobson (1911) ch. 7

13 You will think me lamentably crude: my
experience of life has been drawn from
life itself.
  Zuleika Dobson (1911) ch. 7

14 He held, too, in his enlightened way,
that Americans have a perfect right to
exist. But he did often find himself
wishing Mr Rhodes had not enabled
them to exercise that right in Oxford.
  Zuleika Dobson (1911) ch. 8

15 She was one of the people who say 'I
don't know anything about music
really, but I know what I like.'
  Zuleika Dobson (1911) ch. 9. Cf. Henry James
  112:3

16 You cannot make a man by standing
a sheep on its hind-legs. But by standing
a flock of sheep in that position you can
make a crowd of men.
  Zuleika Dobson (1911) ch. 9

17 Deeply regret inform your grace last
night two black owls came and perched
on battlements remained there through
night hooting at dawn flew away none
knows whither awaiting instructions
Jellings.
  Zuleika Dobson (1911) ch. 14

18 Prepare vault for funeral Monday
Dorset.
  Zuleika Dobson (1911) ch. 14

19 The Socratic manner is not a game at
which two can play. Please answer my
question, to the best of your ability.
  Zuleika Dobson (1911) ch. 15

20 Byron!—he would be all forgotten today
if he had lived to be a florid old
gentleman with iron-grey whiskers,
writing very long, very able letters to
The Times about the Repeal of the Corn
Laws.
  Zuleika Dobson (1911) ch. 18

Brendan Behan 1923–1964

21 He was born an Englishman and
remained one for years.
  Hostage (1958) act 1

22 PAT: He was an Anglo-Irishman.
  MEG: In the blessed name of God what's
  that?
  PAT: A Protestant with a horse.
  Hostage (1958) act 1

23 Meanwhile I'll sing that famous old
song, 'The Hound that Caught the Pubic
Hare'.
  Hostage (1958) act 1

24 When I came back to Dublin, I was
courtmartialled in my absence and

sentenced to death in my absence, so
I said they could shoot me in my
absence.
Hostage (1958) act 1

1 SOLDIER: What's a mixed infant?
TERESA: A little boy or girl under five
years old. They were called mixed
infants because until that time the
boys and girls were mixed together.
SOLDIER: I wish I'd been a mixed infant.
Hostage (1958) act 2

2 I am a sociable worker. Have you your
testament?
Hostage (1958) act 2

3 Go on, abuse me—your own husband
that took you off the streets on a Sunday
morning, when there wasn't a pub open
in the city.
Hostage (1958) act 2

4 We're here because we're queer
Because we're queer because we're here.
Hostage (1958) act 3

5 There's no such thing as bad publicity
except your own obituary.
In Dominic Behan *My Brother Brendan*
(1965) p. 158

John Hay Beith

See IAN HAY

Clive Bell 1881–1964

6 One account . . . given me by a very
good artist, is that what he tries to
express in a picture is 'a passionate
apprehension of form'.
Art (1914) pt. 1, ch. 3

7 It would follow that 'significant form'
was form behind which we catch a sense
of ultimate reality.
Art (1914) pt. 1, ch. 3

8 Art and Religion are, then, two roads by
which men escape from circumstance to
ecstasy. Between aesthetic and religious
rapture there is a family alliance. Art
and Religion are means to similar states
of mind.
Art (1914) pt. 2, ch. 1

9 I will try to account for the degree of my
aesthetic emotion. That, I conceive, is
the function of the critic.
Art (1914) pt. 3 ch. 3

10 Only reason can convince us of those
three fundamental truths without

a recogniton of which there can be no
effective liberty: that what we believe is
not necessarily true; that what we like
is not necessarily good; and that all
questions are open.
Civilization (1928) ch. 5

Henr; Bellamann

11 'Randy—where—where's the rest of
me?' His voice rose to a sharp wail.
King's Row (1940) pt. 5, ch. 1 (also used in
the 1941 film of the book, where the line
was spoken by Ronald Reagan)

Hilaire Belloc 1870–1953

12 Child! do not throw this book about;
Refrain from the unholy pleasure
Of cutting all the pictures out!
Preserve it as your chiefest treasure.
Bad Child's Book of Beasts (1896) dedication

13 I call you bad, my little child,
Upon the title page,
Because a manner rude and wild
Is common at your age.
Bad Child's Book of Beasts (1896)
introduction

14 Who take their manners from the Ape,
Their habits from the Bear,
Indulge in loud unseemly jape,
And never brush their hair.
Bad Child's Book of Beasts (1896)
introduction

15 Mothers of large families (who claim to
common sense)
Will find a Tiger well repay the trouble
and expense.
Bad Child's Book of Beasts (1896) 'The Tiger'

16 I shoot the Hippopotamus
With bullets made of platinum,
Because if I use leaden ones
His hide is sure to flatten 'em.
Bad Child's Book of Beasts (1896) 'The
Hippopotamus'

17 When people call this beast to mind,
They marvel more and more
At such a little tail behind,
So large a trunk before.
Bad Child's Book of Beasts (1896) 'The
Elephant'

18 And always keep a-hold of Nurse
For fear of finding something worse.
Cautionary Tales (1907) 'Jim'

19 The Chief Defect of Henry King

Was chewing little bits of String.
Cautionary Tales (1907) 'Henry King'

1 Physicians of the Utmost Fame
Were called at once; but when they
    came
They answered, as they took their Fees,
'There is no Cure for this Disease.'
Cautionary Tales (1907) 'Henry King'

2 'Oh, my Friends, be warned by me,
That Breakfast, Dinner, Lunch, and Tea
Are all the Human Frame requires . . .
With that, the Wretched Child expires.
Cautionary Tales (1907) 'Henry King'

3 Matilda told such Dreadful Lies,
It made one Gasp and Stretch one's
    Eyes;
Her Aunt, who, from her Earliest Youth,
Had kept a Strict Regard for Truth,
Attempted to Believe Matilda:
The effort very nearly killed her.
Cautionary Tales (1907) 'Matilda'

4 It happened that a few Weeks later
Her Aunt was off to the Theatre
To see that Interesting Play
The Second Mrs Tanqueray.
Cautionary Tales (1907) 'Matilda'

5 For every time She shouted 'Fire!'
They only answered 'Little Liar!'
And therefore when her Aunt returned,
Matilda, and the House, were Burned.
Cautionary Tales (1907) 'Matilda'

6 In my opinion, Butlers ought
To know their place, and not to play
The Old Retainer night and day.
Cautionary Tales (1907) 'Lord Lundy'

7 Sir! you have disappointed us!
We had intended you to be
The next Prime Minister but three:
The stocks were sold; the Press was
    squared;
The Middle Class was quite prepared.
But as it is! . . . My language fails!
Go out and govern New South Wales!
Cautionary Tales (1907) 'Lord Lundy'

8 A Trick that everyone abhors
In Little Girls is slamming Doors.
Cautionary Tales (1907) 'Rebecca'

9 She was not really bad at heart,
But only rather rude and wild:
She was an aggravating child.
Cautionary Tales (1907) 'Rebecca'

10 The nicest child I ever knew

Was Charles Augustus Fortescue.
He never lost his cap, or tore
His stockings or his pinafore:
In eating Bread he made no Crumbs,
He was extremely fond of sums.
Cautionary Tales (1907) 'Charles Augustus
Fortescue'

11 The pleasure politicians take in their
limelight pleases me with a sort of
pleasure I get when I see a child's eyes
gleam over a new toy.
Conversation with a Cat (1931) ch. 17

12 Gentlemen, I am a Catholic. As far as
possible, I go to Mass every day. This is
a rosary. As far as possible, I kneel down
and tell these beads every day. If you
reject me on account of my religion,
I shall thank God that He has spared me
the indignity of being your
representative.
Speech to voters of South Salford, 1906, in
R. Speaight *Life of Hilaire Belloc* (1957)
ch. 10

13 I always like to associate with a lot of
priests because it makes me understand
anti-clerical things so well.
Letter to E. S. P. Haynes, 9 Nov. 1909, in R.
Speaight *Life of Hilaire Belloc* (1957) ch. 17

14 Whatever happens we have got
The Maxim Gun, and they have not.
Modern Traveller (1898) pt. 6

15 I had an Aunt in Yucatan
Who bought a Python from a man
And kept it for a pet.
She died, because she never knew
These simple little rules and few;—
The Snake is living yet.
More Beasts for Worse Children (1897) 'The
Python'

16 The Llama is a woolly sort of fleecy hairy
    goat,
With an indolent expression and an
    undulating throat
Like an unsuccessful literary man.
More Beasts for Worse Children (1897) 'The
Llama'

17 The Microbe is so very small
You cannot make him out at all.
More Beasts for Worse Children (1897) 'The
Microbe'

18 Oh! let us never, never doubt
What nobody is sure about!
More Beasts for Worse Children (1897) 'The
Microbe'

1 Lord Finchley tried to mend the Electric
   Light
   Himself. It struck him dead: And serve
   him right!
   It is the business of the wealthy man
   To give employment to the artisan.
   More Peers (1911) 'Lord Finchley'

2 Lord Hippo suffered fearful loss
   By putting money on a horse
   Which he believed, if it were pressed,
   Would run far faster than the rest.
   More Peers (1911) 'Lord Hippo'

3 Like many of the Upper Class
   He liked the Sound of Broken Glass.
   New Cautionary Tales (1930) 'About John'.
   Cf. Evelyn Waugh 222:19

4 Birds in their little nests agree
   With Chinamen, but not with me.
   New Cautionary Tales (1930) 'On Food'

5 It is the best of all trades, to make songs,
   and the second best to sing them.
   On Everything (1909) 'On Song'

6 Is there no Latin word for Tea? Upon
   my soul, if I had known that I would
   have let the vulgar stuff alone.
   On Nothing (1908) 'On Tea'

7 Strong brother in God and last
   companion, Wine.
   Short Talks with the Dead (1926) 'Heroic
   Poem upon Wine'

8 Sally is gone that was so kindly
   Sally is gone from Ha'nacker Hill.
   Sonnets and Verse (1923) 'Ha'nacker Mill'

9 Do you remember an Inn,
   Miranda?
   Do you remember an Inn?
   And the tedding and the spreading
   Of the straw for a bedding,
   And the fleas that tease in the High
   Pyrenees
   And the wine that tasted of the tar?
   Sonnets and Verse (1923) 'Tarantella'

10 When I am dead, I hope it may be said:
   'His sins were scarlet, but his books
   were read.'
   Sonnets and Verse (1923) 'On His Books'

11 The Devil, having nothing else to do,
   Went off to tempt My Lady Poltagrue.
   My Lady, tempted by a private whim,
   To his extreme annoyance, tempted him.
   Sonnets and Verse (1923) 'On Lady
   Poltagrue'

12 Of this bad world the loveliest and the
   best
   Has smiled and said 'Good Night', and
   gone to rest.
   Sonnets and Verse (1923) 'On a Dead
   Hostess'

13 The accursed power which stands on
   Privilege
   (And goes with Women, and
   Champagne, and Bridge)
   Broke—and Democracy resumed her
   reign:
   (Which goes with Bridge, and Women
   and Champagne).
   Sonnets and Verse (1923) 'On a Great
   Election'

14 Lady, when your lovely head
   Droops to sink among the Dead,
   And the quiet places keep
   You that so divinely sleep;
   Then the dead shall blessèd be
   With a new solemnity,
   For such Beauty, so descending,
   Pledges them that Death is ending,
   Sleep your fill—but when you wake
   Dawn shall over Lethe break.
   Sonnets and Verse (1923) 'On a Sleeping
   Friend'

15 I'm tired of Love: I'm still more tired of
   Rhyme.
   But Money gives me pleasure all the
   time.
   Sonnets and Verse (1923) 'Fatigued'

16 Pale Ebenezer thought it wrong to fight,
   But Roaring Bill (who killed him)
   thought it right.
   Sonnets and Verse (ed. 2, 1938) 'The Pacifist'

17 I am a sundial, and I make a botch
   Of what is done much better by a watch.
   Sonnets and Verse (ed. 2, 1938) 'On
   a Sundial'

18 From the towns all Inns have been
   driven: from the villages most. . . .
   Change your hearts or you will lose
   your Inns and you will deserve to have
   lost them. But when you have lost your
   Inns drown your empty selves, for you
   will have lost the last of England.
   This and That (1912) 'On Inns'

19 When I am living in the Midlands
   That are sodden and unkind,
   I light my lamp in the evening:
   My work is left behind;
   And the great hills of the South Country

Come back into my mind.
Verses (1910) 'The South Country'

1 If I ever become a rich man,
Or if ever I grow to be old,
I will build a house with deep thatch
To shelter me from the cold,
And there shall the Sussex songs be
     sung
And the story of Sussex told.

I will hold my house in the high wood
Within a walk of the sea,
And the men that were boys when I was
     a boy
Shall sit and drink with me.
Verses (1910) 'The South Country'

2 Of Courtesy, it is much less
Than Courage of Heart or Holiness,
Yet in my Walks it seems to me
That the Grace of God is in Courtesy.
Verses (1910) 'Courtesy'

3 Balliol made me, Balliol fed me,
Whatever I had she gave me again:
And the best of Balliol loved and led me.
God be with you, Balliol men.
Verses (1910) 'To the Balliol Men Still in
Africa'

4 From quiet homes and first beginning,
Out to the undiscovered ends,
There's nothing worth the wear of
     winning,
But laughter and the love of friends.
Verses (1910) 'Dedicatory Ode'

5 Remote and ineffectual Don
That dared attack my Chesterton.
Verses (1910) 'Lines to a Don'

6 Don different from those regal Dons!
With hearts of gold and lungs of bronze,
Who shout and bang and roar and bawl
The Absolute across the hall,
Or sail in amply billowing gown
Enormous through the Sacred Town,
Bearing from College to their homes
Deep cargoes of gigantic tomes;
Dons admirable! Dons of Might!
Uprising on my inward sight
Compact of ancient tales, and port
And sleep—and learning of a sort.
Verses (1910) 'Lines to a Don'

7 A smell of burning fills the startled Air—
The Electrician is no longer there!
Verses (1910) 'Newdigate Poem'

8 I said to Heart, 'How goes it?' Heart
replied:

'Right as a Ribstone Pippin!' But it lied.
Verses (1910) 'The False Heart'

9 The Moon on the one hand, the Dawn
     on the other;
The Moon is my sister, the Dawn is my
     brother.
The Moon on my Left and the Dawn on
     my right.
My Brother, good morning: my Sister
     good night.
Verses and Sonnets (1896) 'The Early
Morning'

Saul Bellow 1915–

10 If I am out of my mind, it's all right with
me, thought Moses Herzog.
Herzog (1961) p. 1 (opening sentence)

11 The idea, anyway, was to ward off
trouble. But now the moronic inferno
had caught up with me. My elegant car
... was mutilated.
Humboldt's Gift (1975) p. 35

12 The only real distinction at this
dangerous moment in human history
and cosmic development has nothing to
do with medals and ribbons. Not to fall
asleep is distinguished. Everything else is
mere popcorn.
Humboldt's Gift (1975) p. 283

13 I feel that art has something to do with
the achievement of stillness in the midst
of chaos. A stillness which characterizes
prayer, too, and the eye of the storm.
I think that art has something to do
with an arrest of attention in the midst
of distraction.
In George Plimpton *Writers at Work* (1967)
3rd series, p. 190

Robert Benchley 1889–1945

14 I haven't been abroad in so long that
I almost speak English without an accent
now.
After 1903—What? (1938) p. 241

15 On a summer vacation trip Benchley
arrived in Venice and immediately wired
a friend: 'STREETS FLOODED. PLEASE
ADVISE.'
In R. E. Drennan *Algonquin Wits* (1968)
p. 45

16 I do most of my work sitting down;
that's where I shine.
In R. E. Drennan *Algonquin Wits* (1968)
p. 55

1 My only solution for the problem of habitual accidents and, so far, nobody has asked me for my solution, is to stay in bed all day. Even then, there is always the chance that you will fall out.
Chips off the old Benchley (1949) 'Safety Second'

2 I had just dozed off into a stupor when I heard what I thought was myself talking to myself. I didn't pay much attention to it, as I knew practically everything I would have to say to myself, and wasn't particularly interested.
Chips off the old Benchley (1949) 'First Pigeon of Spring '

3 A great many people have come up to me and asked how I manage to get so much work done and still keep looking so dissipated.
Chips off the old Benchley (1949) 'How to get things Done'

4 The biggest obstacle to professional writing is the necessity for changing a typewriter ribbon.
Chips off the old Benchley (1949) 'Learn to Write'

5 Bob Benchley was one of the few writers I knew who always laughed at other writers' lines. I always laughed at one of his. When he returned for his twenty-fifth homecoming at Harvard [in 1937], he stated to underclassmen, 'I feel as I always have, except for an occasional heart attack.'
Groucho Marx Grouchophile (1976) p. 204

6 The surest way to make a monkey of a man is to quote him.
My Ten Years in a Quandary (1936) p. 204

7 Tell us your phobias and we will tell you what you are afraid of.
My Ten Years in a Quandary (1936) p. 295

8 He [Benchley] came out of a night club one evening and, tapping a uniformed figure on the shoulder, said, 'Get me a cab.' The uniformed figure turned around furiously and informed him that he was not a doorman but a rear admiral. 'O.K.,' said Benchley, 'Get me a battleship.'
New Yorker 5 Jan. 1946

9 The famous office that Benchley and Dorothy Parker shared in the Metropolitan Opera House . . . was a cramped triangle stolen from a hallway. 'One square foot less and it would be adulterous,' said Benchley.
New Yorker 5 Jan. 1946

10 In America there are two classes of travel—first class, and with children.
Pluck and Luck (1925) p. 6

11 Often Daddy sat up very late working on a case of Scotch.
Pluck and Luck (1925) p. 198

12 A friend told him that the particular drink he was drinking was slow poison, and he replied, 'So who's in a hurry?'
Nathaniel Benchley Robert Benchley (1955) ch. 1

13 It took me fifteen years to discover that I had no talent for writing, but I couldn't give it up because by that time I was too famous.
In Nathaniel Benchley Robert Benchley (1955) ch. 1
See also: MAE WEST

Julien Benda 1867–1956

14 La trahison des clercs.

The treachery of the intellectuals.
Title of book (1927)

Stephen Vincent Benét 1898–1943

15 We thought we were done with these things but we were wrong.
We thought, because we had power, we had wisdom.
Atlantic Monthly Sept. 1935 'Litany for Dictatorships'

16 I have fallen in love with American names,
The sharp, gaunt names that never get fat,
The snakeskin-titles of mining-claims,
The plumed war-bonnet of Medicine Hat,
Tucson and Deadwood and Lost Mule Flat.
Yale Review (1927) vol. 17, p. 63 'American Names'

17 I shall not rest quiet in Montparnasse.
I shall not lie easy at Winchelsea.

You may bury my body in Sussex grass,
You may bury my tongue at
  Champmédy.
I shall not be there, I shall rise and pass.
Bury my heart at Wounded Knee.

  Yale Review (1927) vol. 17, p. 64 'American
  Names'

William Rose Benét 1886–1950

1 Blake saw a treefull of angels at
    Peckham Rye,
  And his hands could lay hold on the
    tiger's terrible heart.
  Blake knew how deep is Hell, and
    Heaven how high,
  And could build the universe from one
    tiny part.

  Burglar of Zodiac (1918) 'Mad Blake'

Tony Benn 1925–

2 A holy war with atom bombs could end
  the human family for ever. I say this as
  a socialist whose political commitment
  owes much more to the teachings of
  Jesus—without the mysteries within
  which they are presented—than to the
  writings of Marx whose analysis seems
  to lack an understanding of the deeper
  needs of humanity.

  Arguments for Democracy (1981) ch. 7

3 The distortion of the Marxist idea that
  developed in Russia was as great, and of
  the same character, as the
  distortion of the Christian teaching at
  the time of the Inquisition. But it is as
  wholly wrong to blame Marx for what
  was done in his name, as it is to blame
  Jesus for what was done in his.

  In Alan Freeman *The Benn Heresy* (1982)
  p. 172

4 In developing our industrial strategy for
  the period ahead, we have the benefit of
  much experience. Almost everything has
  been tried at least once.

  Hansard 13 Mar. 1974, col. 197

5 Broadcasting is really too important to
  be left to the broadcasters.

  In Anthony Sampson *The New Anatomy of
  Britain* (1971) ch. 24

6 It is arguable that what has really
  happened has amounted to such a

breakdown in the social contract, upon
which parliamentary democracy by
universal suffrage was based, that that
contract now needs to be re-negotiated
on a basis that shares power much more
widely, before it can win general assent
again.

  The New Politics (1970) ch. 4

7 The British House of Lords is the British
  Outer Mongolia for retired politicians.

  In *Observer* 4 Feb. 1962

8 We thought we could put the economy
  right in five years. We were wrong. It
  will probably take ten.

  Speech at Bristol, 18 Apr. 1968 , in *The
  Times* 19 Apr. 1968

George Bennard 1873–1958

9 I will cling to the old rugged cross,
  And exchange it some day for a crown.

  The Old Rugged Cross (1913 hymn)

Alan Bennett 1934–

10 Life, you know, is rather like opening
   a tin of sardines. We are all of us looking
   for the key. And, I wonder, how many
   of you here tonight have wasted years of
   your lives looking behind the kitchen
   dressers of this life for that key. I know
   I have. Others think they've found the
   key, don't they? They roll back the lid of
   the sardine tin of life, they reveal the
   sardines, the riches of life, therein, and
   they get them out, they enjoy them.
   But, you know, there's always a little bit
   in the corner you can't get out.
   I wonder—I wonder, is there a little bit
   in the corner of your life? I know there
   is in mine.

   Beyond the Fringe (1961 revue) 'Take
   a Pew', in Roger Wilmut *Complete Beyond
   the Fringe* (1987) p. 104

11 I have never understood this liking for
   war. It panders to instincts already
   catered for within the scope of any
   respectable domestic establishment.

   Forty Years On (1969) act 1

12 We started off trying to set up a small
   anarchist community, but people
   wouldn't obey the rules.

   Getting On (1972) act 1

1 One of the few lessons I have learned in life is that there is invariably something odd about women who wear ankle socks.
Old Country (1978) act 1

2 We were put to Dickens as children but it never quite took. That unremitting humanity soon had me cheesed off.
Old Country (1978) act 2

Arnold Bennett 1867–1931

3 I place it upon record frankly—the Clayhanger trilogy is good . . . .The scene, for instance, where Darius Clayhanger dies that lingering death could scarcely be bettered . . . .And why? . . . Because I took infinite pains over it. All the time my father was dying, I was at the bedside making copious notes. You can't just slap these things down. You have to take trouble.
Overheard conversation with Hugh Walpole c.1926, in P. G. Wodehouse and Guy Bolton *Bring on the Girls* (1954) ch. 15

4 His opinion of himself, having once risen, remained at 'set fair'.
The Card (1911) ch. 1

5 'Ye can call it influenza if ye like,' said Mrs Machin. 'There was no influenza in my young days. We called a cold a cold.'
The Card (1911) ch. 8

6 'And yet,' demanded Councillor Barlow, 'what's he done? Has he ever done a day's work in his life? What great cause is he identified with?' 'He's identified,' said the first speaker, 'with the great cause of cheering us all up.'
The Card (1911) ch. 12

7 My general impression is that Englishmen act better than Frenchmen, and Frenchwomen better than Englishwomen.
Cupid and Commonsense (1909) preface

8 Good taste is better than bad taste, but bad taste is better than no taste, and men without individuality have no taste—at any rate no taste that they can impose on their publics.
Evening Standard 21 Aug. 1930

9 'Bah!' she said. 'With people like you, love only means one thing.' 'No,' he

replied. 'It means twenty things, but it doesn't mean nineteen.'
Journal (1932) 20 Nov. 1904

10 A test of a first-rate work, and a test of your sincerity in calling it a first-rate work, is that you finish it.
Things that have Interested Me (1921) 'Finishing Books'

11 In the meantime alcohol produces a delightful social atmosphere that nothing else can produce.
Things that have Interested Me (1921) 'For and Against Prohibition'

12 Seventy minutes had passed before Mr Lloyd George arrived at his proper theme. He spoke for a hundred and seventeen minutes, in which period he was detected only once in the use of an argument.
Things that have Interested Me (1921) 'After the March Offensive.'

13 Pessimism, when you get used to it, is just as agreeable as optimism. Indeed, I think it must be more agreeable, must have a more real savour, than optimism—from the way in which pessimists abandon themselves to it.
Things that have Interested Me (1921) 'Slump in Pessimism'

14 The price of justice is eternal publicity.
Things that have Interested Me (2nd series, 1923) 'Secret Trials'

15 A cause may be inconvenient, but it's magnificent. It's like champagne or high heels, and one must be prepared to suffer for it.
The Title (1918) act 1

16 Examine the Honours List and you can instantly tell how the Government feels in its inside. When the Honours List is full of rascals, millionaires, and—er—chumps, you may be quite sure that the Government is dangerously ill.
The Title (1918) act 1

17 Being a husband is a whole-time job. That is why so many husbands fail. They cannot give their entire attention to it.
The Title (1918) act 1

18 Journalists say a thing that they know isn't true, in the hope that if they keep on saying it long enough it will be true.
The Title (1918) act 2

1 Literature's always a good card to play
for Honours. It makes people think that
Cabinet ministers are educated.
The Title (1918) act 3

Ada Benson and *Fred Fisher*
1875–1942

2 Your feet's too big,
Don't want you 'cause your feet's too
big,
Mad at you 'cause your feet's too big,
Hates you 'cause your feet's too big.
Your Feet's Too Big (1936 song)

A. C. Benson 1862–1925

3 I don't like authority, at least I don't like
other people's authority.
Excerpts from Letters to M. E. A. (1926)
p. 41

4 Land of Hope and Glory, Mother of the
Free,
How shall we extol thee who are born of
thee?
Wider still and wider shall thy bounds
be set;
God who made thee mighty, make thee
mightier yet.
Land of Hope and Glory (1902 song; music
by Sir Edward Elgar)

Stella Benson 1892–1933

5 Call no man foe, but never love
a stranger.
This is the End (1917) p. 63

Edmund Clerihew Bentley
1875–1956

6 When their lordships asked Bacon
How many bribes he had taken
He had at least the grace
To get very red in the face.
Baseless Biography (1939) 'Bacon'

7 The Art of Biography
Is different from Geography.
Geography is about Maps,
But Biography is about Chaps.
Biography for Beginners (1905) introd.

8 Sir Christopher Wren
Said, 'I am going to dine with some
men.
If anybody calls

Say I am designing St Paul's.'
Biography for Beginners (1905) 'Sir
Christopher Wren'

9 Sir Humphrey Davy
Abominated gravy.
He lived in the odium
Of having discovered Sodium.
Biography for Beginners (1905) 'Sir
Humphrey Davy'

10 John Stuart Mill,
By a mighty effort of will,
Overcame his natural bonhomie
And wrote 'Principles of Political
Economy'.
Biography for Beginners (1905) 'John Stuart
Mill'

11 What I like about Clive
Is that he is no longer alive.
There is a great deal to be said
For being dead.
Biography for Beginners (1905) 'Clive'

12 Edward the Confessor
Slept under the dresser.
When that began to pall,
He slept in the hall.
Biography for Beginners (1905) 'Edward the
Confessor'

13 Chapman & Hall
Swore not at all.
Mr Chapman's yea was yea,
And Mr Hall's nay was nay.
Biography for Beginners (1905) 'Chapman &
Hall'

14 George the Third
Ought never to have occurred.
One can only wonder
At so grotesque a blunder.
More Biography (1929) 'George the Third'

Eric Bentley 1916–

15 The theatre of farce is the theatre of the
human body but of that body in a state
as far from the natural as the voice of
Chaliapin is from my voice or yours. It is
a theatre in which, though the
marionettes are men, the men are
supermarionettes. It is the theatre of the
surrealist body.
Life of Drama (1964) ch. 7

16 Ours is the age of substitutes: instead of
language, we have jargon; instead of
principles, slogans; and, instead of
genuine ideas, Bright Ideas.
New Republic 29 Dec. 1952

Nikolai Berdyaev 1874–1948

1 Утопии осуществимы, они осуществимее того, цто представлялось «реальной политикой» и что было лишь рационалистическим расчетом кабинетных людей. Жизнь движется к утопиям. И открывается, быть может, новое столетие мечтаний интеллигенции и культурнаго слоя о том, как избежать утопий, как вернуться к не утопическому обществу, к менее «соьершенному» и более свободному обществу.

Utopias are realizable, they are more realizable than what has been presented as 'realist politics' and what has simply been the calculated rationalism of armchair politicians. Life is moving towards utopias. But perhaps a new age is opening up before us, in which the intelligentsia and the cultured classes will dream of ways to avoid utopias and to return to a non-utopian society, to a less 'perfect' a freer society.
Novoe srednevekov'e (New Middle Ages, 1924) p. 122

Lord Charles Beresford 1846–1919

2 On one occasion, when at the eleventh hour he [Beresford] had been summoned to dine with the then Prince of Wales, he is said to have telegraphed back: 'Very sorry can't come. Lie follows by post.' This story has been told of several other people, but Lord Charles was the real originator.
Ralph Nevill *World of Fashion 1837–1922* (1923) ch. 5. Cf. Marcel Proust 176:5

Henri Bergson 1859–1941

3 *La fonction essentielle de l'univers, qui est une machine à faire des dieux.*

The essential function of the universe, which is a machine for making gods.
Les Deux sources de la morale et de la religion (The Two Sources of Morality and Religion, 1932) ch. 4

Irving Berlin (Israel Baline) 1888–1989

4 Come on and hear,
Come on and hear,
Alexander's ragtime band,
Come on and hear,
Come on and hear,
It's the best band in the land.
Alexander's Ragtime Band (1911 song)

5 Anything you can do, I can do better,
I can do anything better than you.
Anything You Can Do (1946 song)

6 God bless America,
Land that I love,
Stand beside her and guide her
Thru the night with a light from above.
From the mountains to the prairies,
To the oceans white with foam,
God bless America,
My home sweet home.
God Bless America (1939 song)

7 Oh! how I hate to get up in the morning,
Oh! how I'd love to remain in bed;
For the hardest blow of all,
Is to hear the bugler call,
You've got to get up, you've got to get up,
You've got to get up this morning!
Oh! How I Hate to Get Up in the Morning (1918 song)

8 A pretty girl is like a melody
That haunts you night and day.
A Pretty Girl is like a Melody (1919 song)

9 The song is ended (but the melody lingers on).
Title of song (1927)

10 There's no business like show business.
Title of song (1946)

11 I'm puttin' on my top hat,
Tyin' up my white tie,
Brushin' off my tails.
Top Hat, White Tie and Tails (1935 song)

12 I'm dreaming of a white Christmas,
Just like the ones I used to know,
Where the tree-tops glisten
And children listen
To hear sleigh bells in the snow.
White Christmas (1942 song)

Sir Isaiah Berlin 1909–

13 There exists a great chasm between those, on one side, who relate everything to a single central vision ... and, on the other side, those who pursue many ends, often unrelated and

even contradictory. .... The first kind of intellectual and artistic personality belongs to the hedgehogs, the second to the foxes.
Hedgehog and Fox (1953) ch. 1

1 Rousseau was the first militant lowbrow.
Observer 9 Nov. 1952

2 Liberty is liberty, not equality or fairness or justice or human happiness or a quiet conscience.
Two Concepts of Liberty (1958) p. 10

Georges Bernanos 1888–1948

3 *Le désir de la prière est déjà une prière.*

The wish for prayer is a prayer in itself.
Journal d'un curé de campagne (Diary of a Country Priest, 1936) ch. 2

4 *L'enfer, madame, c'est de ne plus aimer.*

Hell, madam, is to love no more.
Journal d'un curé de campagne (Diary of a Country Priest, 1936) ch. 2

Jeffrey Bernard

5 When people say, 'You're breaking my heart,' they do in fact usually mean that you're breaking their genitals.
Spectator 31 May 1986

Eric Berne 1910–1970

6 The sombre picture presented in Parts I and II of this book, in which human life is mainly a process of filling in time until the arrival of death, or Santa Claus, with very little choice, if any, of what kind of business one is going to transact during the long wait, is a commonplace but not the final answer.
Games People Play (1964) ch. 18

7 Games people play: the psychology of human relationships.
Title of book (1964)

Carl Bernstein 1944–
and Bob Woodward 1943–

8 All the President's men.
Title of book (1974)

Chuck Berry 1931–

9 Roll over, Beethoven, and tell Tchaikovsky the news.
Roll Over, Beethoven (1956 song)

John Berryman 1914–1972

10 Blossomed Sarah, and I blossom. Is that thing alive? I hear a famisht howl.
Partisan Review (1953) vol. 20, p. 494 'Homage to Mistress Bradstreet'

11 We must travel in the direction of our fear.
Poems (1942) 'A Point of Age'

12 Life, friends, is boring. We must not say so.
77 Dream Songs (1964) no. 14

13 And moreover my mother taught me as a boy
(repeatedly) 'Ever to confess you're bored
means you have no
Inner Resources.' I conclude now I have no
inner resources, because I am heavy bored.
77 Dream Songs (1964) no. 14

14 I seldom go to films. They are too exciting,
said the Honourable Possum.
77 Dream Songs (1964) no. 53

Pierre Berton 1920–

15 [Definition of a Canadian:] Somebody who knows how to make love in a canoe.
Toronto Star, Canadian Mag. 22 Dec. 1973

Theobald von Bethmann Hollweg 1856–1921

16 He [Bethmann Hollweg] said that the step taken by His Majesty's Government was terrible to a degree, just for a word 'neutrality'—a word which in wartime had so often been disregarded—just for a scrap of paper, Great Britain was going to make war on a kindred nation who desired nothing better than to be friends with her.
Report by Sir E. Goschen to Sir Edward Grey, in *British Documents on Origins of the War 1898–1914* (1926) vol. 11, p. 351

Sir John Betjeman 1906–1984

17 He sipped at a weak hock and seltzer

As he gazed at the London skies
Through the Nottingham lace of the
    curtains
Or was it his bees-winged eyes?
    Continual Dew (1937) 'Arrest of Oscar Wilde
    at the Cadogan Hotel'

1 He rose, and he put down The Yellow
    Book.
He staggered—and, terrible-eyed,
He brushed past the palms on the
    staircase
And was helped to a hansom outside.
    Continual Dew (1937) 'Arrest of Oscar
    Wilde at the Cadogan Hotel'

2 Come, friendly bombs, and fall on Slough!
It isn't fit for humans now,
There isn't grass to graze a cow.
Swarm over, Death!
    Continual Dew (1937) 'Slough'

3 Rime Intrinsica, Fontmell Magna,
    Sturminster Newton and Melbury
    Bubb,
Whist upon whist upon whist upon
    whist drive, in Institute, Legion and
    Social Club.
Horny hands that hold the aces which
    this morning held the plough—
While Tranter Reuben, T. S. Eliot, H. G.
    Wells and Edith Sitwell lie in Mellstock
    churchyard now.
    Continual Dew (1937) 'Dorset'

4 Spirits of well-shot woodcock, partridge,
    snipe
Flutter and bear him up the Norfolk sky:
In that red house in a red mahogany
    book-case
The stamp collection waits with mounts
    long dry.
    Continual Dew (1937) 'Death of King George
    V'

5 And girls in slacks remember Dad,
And oafish louts remember Mum,
And sleepless children's hearts are glad,
And Christmas-morning bells say 'Come!'
Even to shining ones who dwell
Safe in the Dorchester Hotel.

And is it true? And is it true,
This most tremendous tale of all,
Seen in a stained-glass window's hue,
A Baby in an ox's stall?
The Maker of the stars and sea
Become a Child on earth for me?
    Few Late Chrysanthemums (1954)
    'Christmas'

6 In the licorice fields at Pontefract
My love and I did meet
And many a burdened licorice bush
Was blooming round our feet;
Red hair she had and golden skin,
Her sulky lips were shaped for sin,
Her sturdy legs were flannel-slack'd,
The strongest legs in Pontefract.
    Few Late Chrysanthemums (1954) 'The
    Licorice Fields at Pontefract'

7 In the Garden City Café with its murals
    on the wall
Before a talk on 'Sex and Civics'
I meditated on the Fall.
    Few Late Chrysanthemums (1954) 'Huxley
    Hall'

8 Gaily into Ruislip Gardens
Runs the red electric train,
With a thousand Ta's and Pardon's
Daintily alights Elaine;
Hurries down the concrete station
With a frown of concentration,
Out into the outskirt's edges
Where a few surviving hedges
Keep alive our lost Elysium—rural
    Middlesex again.
    Few Late Chrysanthemums (1954)
    'Middlesex'

9 There was sun enough for lazing upon
    beaches,
There was fun enough for far into the
    night.
But I'm dying now and done for,
What on earth was all the fun for?
For God's sake keep that sunlight out of
    sight.
    Few Late Chrysanthemums (1954) 'Sun and
    Fun'

10 It's awf'lly bad luck on Diana,
Her ponies have swallowed their bits;
She fished down their throats with
    a spanner
And frightened them all into fits.
    Few Late Chrysanthemums (1954) 'Hunter
    Trials'

11 Oh wasn't it naughty of Smudges?
Oh, Mummy, I'm sick with disgust.
She threw me in front of the Judges
And my silly old collarbone's bust.
    Few Late Chrysanthemums (1954) 'Hunter
    Trials'

12 Phone for the fish-knives, Norman
As Cook is a little unnerved;
You kiddies have crumpled the serviettes

And I must have things daintily served.
Few Late Chrysanthemums (1954) 'How to get on in Society'

1 Milk and then just as it comes dear?
I'm afraid the preserve's full of stones;
Beg pardon, I'm soiling the doileys
With afternoon tea-cakes and scones.
Few Late Chrysanthemums (1954) 'How to get on in Society'

2 Ghastly good taste, or a depressing story of the rise and fall of English architecture.
Title of book (1933)

3 Oh! Chintzy, Chintzy cheeriness,
Half dead and half alive!
Mount Zion (1931) 'Death in Leamington'

4 The Church's Restoration
In eighteen-eighty-three
Has left for contemplation
Not what there used to be.
Mount Zion (1931) 'Hymn'

5 Sing on, with hymns uproarious,
Ye humble and aloof,
Look up! and oh how glorious
He has restored the roof!
Mount Zion (1931) 'Hymn'

6 Broad of Church and 'broad of Mind',
Broad before and broad behind,
A keen ecclesiologist,
A rather dirty Wykehamist.
Mount Zion (1931) 'The Wykehamist'

7 Oh shall I see the Thames again?
The prow-promoted gems again,
As beefy ATS
Without their hats
Come shooting through the bridge?
And 'cheerioh' or 'cheeri-bye'
Across the waste of waters die
And low the mists of evening lie
And lightly skims the midge.
New Bats in Old Belfries (1945) 'Henley-on-Thames'

8 Rumbling under blackened girders,
  Midland, bound for Cricklewood,
Puffed its sulphur to the sunset where
  that Land of Laundries stood.
Rumble under, thunder over, train and
  tram alternate go.
Shake the floor and smudge the ledger,
  Charrington, Sells, Dale and Co.,
Nuts and nuggets in the window, trucks
  along the lines below.
New Bats in Old Belfries (1945) 'Parliament Hill Fields'

9 Miss J. Hunter Dunn, Miss J. Hunter Dunn,
Furnish'd and burnish'd by Aldershot sun,
What strenuous singles we played after tea,
We in the tournament—you against me.

Love-thirty, love-forty, oh! weakness of joy,
The speed of a swallow, the grace of a boy,
With carefullest carelessness, gaily you won,
I am weak from your loveliness, Joan Hunter Dunn.

Miss Joan Hunter Dunn, Miss Joan Hunter Dunn,
How mad I am, sad I am, glad that you won.
The warm-handled racket is back in its press,
But my shock-headed victor, she loves me no less.
New Bats in Old Belfries (1945) 'Subaltern's Love-Song'

10 The scent of the conifers, sound of the bath,
The view from my bedroom of moss-dappled path,
As I struggle with double-end evening tie,
For we dance at the Golf Club, my victor and I.
New Bats in Old Belfries (1945) 'Subaltern's Love-Song'

11 By roads 'not adopted', by woodlanded ways,
She drove to the club in the late summer haze,
Into nine-o'clock Camberley, heavy with bells
And mushroomy, pine-woody, evergreen smells.

Miss Joan Hunter Dunn, Miss Joan Hunter Dunn,
I can hear from the car park the dance has begun.
Oh! full Surrey twilight! importunate band!
Oh! strongly adorable tennis-girl's hand!
New Bats in Old Belfries (1945) 'Subaltern's Love-Song'

12 We sat in the car park till twenty to one

And now I'm engaged to Miss Joan
  Hunter Dunn.
  New Bats in Old Belfries (1945) 'Subaltern's
  Love-Song'

1 Belbroughton Road is bonny, and pinkly
  bursts the spray
  Of prunus and forsythia across the
  public way,
  For a full spring-tide of blossom seethed
  and departed hence,
  Leaving land-locked pools of jonquils by
  sunny garden fence.

  And a constant sound of flushing
  runneth from windows where
  The toothbrush too is airing in this new
  North Oxford air.
  New Bats in Old Belfries (1945) 'May-Day
  Song for North Oxford'

2 Bells are booming down the bohreens,
  White the mist along the grass.
  Now the Julias, Maeves and Maureens
  Move between the fields to Mass.
  New Bats in Old Belfries (1945) 'Ireland with
  Emily'

3 The gas was on in the Institute,
  The flare was up in the gymn,
  A man was running a mineral line,
  A lass was singing a hymn,
  When Captain Webb the Dawley man,
  Captain Webb from Dawley,
  Came swimming along in the old canal
  That carries the bricks to Lewley.
  Old Lights for New Chancels (1940) 'A
  Shropshire Lad'

4 Pam, I adore you, Pam, you great big
  mountainous sports girl,
  Whizzing them over the net, full of the
  strength of five:
  That old Malvernian brother, you zephyr
  and khaki shorts girl,
  Although he's playing for Woking,
  Can't stand up to your wonderful
  backhand drive.
  Old Lights for New Chancels (1940) 'Pot
  Pourri from a Surrey Garden'

5 Think of what our Nation stands for,
  Books from Boots' and country lanes,
  Free speech, free passes, class
  distinction,
  Democracy and proper drains.
  Lord, put beneath Thy special care
  One-eighty-nine Cadogan Square.
  Old Lights for New Chancels (1940) 'In
  Westminster Abbey'

6 The dread of beatings! Dread of being
  late!
  And, greatest dread of all, the dread of
  games!
  Summoned by Bells (1960) ch. 7

7 Balkan Sobranies in a wooden box,
  The college arms upon the lid; Tokay
  And sherry in the cupboard; on the
  shelves
  The University Statutes bound in blue,
  Crome Yellow, Prancing Nigger, Blunden,
  Keats.
  Summoned by Bells (1960) ch. 9

8 As one more solemn of our number
  said:
  'Spiritually I was at Eton, John.'
  Summoned by Bells (1960) ch. 9

Aneurin Bevan 1897–1960

9 He [Winston Churchill] is a man
  suffering from petrified adolescence.
  In Vincent Brome *Aneurin Bevan* (1953)
  ch. 11

10 Listening to a speech by Chamberlain is
  like paying a visit to Woolworth's:
  everything in its place and nothing
  above sixpence.
  In Michael Foot *Aneurin Bevan* (1962) vol. 1,
  ch. 8

11 I know that the right kind of leader for
  the Labour Party is a desiccated
  calculating machine who must not in
  any way permit himself to be swayed by
  indignation. If he sees suffering,
  privation or injustice he must not allow
  it to move him, for that would be
  evidence of the lack of proper education
  or of absence of self-control. He must
  speak in calm and objective accents and
  talk about a dying child in the same way
  as he would about the pieces inside an
  internal combustion engine.
  In Michael Foot *Aneurin Bevan* (1973) vol. 2,
  ch. 11

12 Damn it all, you can't have the crown of
  thorns and the thirty pieces of silver.
  In Michael Foot *Aneurin Bevan* (1973) vol. 2,
  ch. 13

13 This island is made mainly of coal and
  surrounded by fish. Only an organizing
  genius could produce a shortage of coal
  and fish at the same time.
  Speech at Blackpool 24 May 1945, in *Daily
  Herald* 25 May 1945

1 I do not think Winston Churchill wants war, but the trouble with him is that he doesn't even know how to avoid it. He does not talk the language of the 20th century but that of the 18th. He is still fighting Blenheim all over again. His only answer to a difficult situation is send a gun-boat.

> Speech at Scarborough 2 Oct. 1951, in *Daily Herald* 3 Oct. 1951

2 If you carry this resolution you will send Britain's Foreign Secretary naked into the conference chamber.

> Speech at Brighton, in *Daily Herald* 4 Oct. 1957

3 The worst thing I can say about democracy is that it has tolerated the Right Honourable Gentleman [Neville Chamberlain] for four and a half years.

> *Hansard* 23 July 1929, col. 1191

4 Why read the crystal when he can read the book?

> *Hansard* 29 Sept. 1949, col. 319

5 I am not going to spend any time whatsoever in attacking the Foreign Secretary. Quite honestly, I am beginning to feel extremely sorry for him. If we complain about the tune, there is no reason to attack the monkey when the organ grinder is present.

> *Hansard* 16 May 1957, col. 680

6 We know what happens to people who stay in the middle of the road. They get run down.

> In *Observer* 6 Dec. 1953

7 The language of priorities is the religion of Socialism.

> Speech at Labour Party Conference in Blackpool, 8 June 1949, in *Report of 48th Annual Conference* (1949) p. 172

8 No amount of cajolery, and no attempts at ethical or social seduction, can eradicate from my heart a deep burning hatred for the Tory Party that inflicted those bitter experiences on me. So far as I am concerned they are lower than vermin. They condemned millions of first-class people to semi-starvation.

> Speech at Manchester, 4 July 1948, in *The Times* 5 July 1948

9 I read the newspapers avidly. It is my one form of continuous fiction.

> *The Times* 29 Mar. 1960

William Henry Beveridge (First Baron Beveridge) 1879–1963

10 Ignorance is an evil weed, which dictators may cultivate among their dupes, but which no democracy can afford among its citizens.

> *Full Employment in a Free Society* (1944) pt. 7

11 The object of government in peace and in war is not the glory of rulers or of races, but the happiness of the common man.

> *Social Insurance and Allied Services* (1942) pt. 7

12 The state is or can be master of money, but in a free society it is master of very little else.

> *Voluntary Action* (1948) ch. 12

Ernest Bevin 1881–1951

13 If you open that Pandora's Box [the Council of Europe], you never know what Trojan 'orses will jump out.

> In Sir Roderick Barclay *Ernest Bevin and Foreign Office* (1975) ch. 3

14 A Ministerial colleague with whom Ernie [Bevin] was almost always on bad terms was Nye Bevan. There was a well-known occasion when the latter had incurred Ernie's displeasure, and one of those present, seeking to excuse Nye, observed that he was sometimes his own worst enemy. 'Not while I'm alive 'e aint!' retorted Ernie.

> Sir Roderick Barclay *Ernest Bevin and Foreign Office* (1975) ch. 4

15 There never has been a war yet which, if the facts had been put calmly before the ordinary folk, could not have been prevented. . . . The common man, I think, is the great protection against war.

> *Hansard* 23 Nov. 1945, col. 786

16 The most conservative man in this world is the British Trade Unionist when you want to change him.

> Speech, 8 Sept. 1927, in *Report of Proceedings of the Trades Union Congress* (1927) p. 298

1 I didn't ought never to have done it. It was you, Willie, what put me up to it.
   To Lord Strang, after officially recognizing Communist China, in C. Parrott *Serpent and Nightingale* (1977) ch. 3

2 My policy is to be able to take a ticket at Victoria Station and go anywhere I damn well please.
   In *Spectator* 20 Apr. 1951, p. 514

Georges Bidault 1899–1983

3 The weak have one weapon: the errors of those who think they are strong.
   In *Observer* 15 July 1962

Ambrose Bierce 1842–?1914

4 Acquaintance, n. A person whom we know well enough to borrow from, but not well enough to lend to. A degree of friendship called slight when its object is poor or obscure, and intimate when he is rich or famous.
   Cynic's Word Book (1906) p. 12

5 Admiration, n. Our polite recognition of another's resemblance to ourselves.
   Cynic's Word Book (1906) p. 13

6 Advice, n. The smallest current coin.
   Cynic's Word Book (1906) p. 14

7 Alliance, n. In international politics, the union of two thieves who have their hands so deeply inserted in each other's pocket that they cannot separately plunder a third.
   Cynic's Word Book (1906) p. 16

8 Ambition, n. An overmastering desire to be vilified by enemies while living and made ridiculous by friends when dead.
   Cynic's Word Book (1906) p. 17

9 Applause, n. The echo of a platitude.
   Cynic's Word Book (1906) p. 19

10 Auctioneer, n. The man who proclaims with a hammer that he has picked a pocket with his tongue.
   Cynic's Word Book (1906) p. 24

11 Battle, n. A method of untying with the teeth a political knot that would not yield to the tongue.
   Cynic's Word Book (1906) p. 30

12 Bore, n. A person who talks when you wish him to listen.
   Cynic's Word Book (1906) p. 37

13 Brain, n. An apparatus with which we think that we think.
   Cynic's Word Book (1906) p. 39

14 Calamity, n. . . . Calamities are of two kinds: misfortune to ourselves, and good fortune to others.
   Cynic's Word Book (1906) p. 41

15 Conservative, n. A statesman who is enamoured of existing evils, as distinguished from the Liberal, who wishes to replace them with others.
   Cynic's Word Book (1906) p. 56

16 Cynic, n. A blackguard whose faulty vision sees things as they are, not as they ought to be.
   Cynic's Word Book (1906) p. 63

17 Education, n. That which discloses to the wise and disguises from the foolish their lack of understanding.
   Cynic's Word Book (1906) p. 86

18 Egotist, n. A person of low taste, more interested in himself than in me.
   Cynic's Word Book (1906) p. 86

19 Future, n. That period of time in which our affairs prosper, our friends are true, and our happiness is assured.
   Cynic's Word Book (1906) p. 129

20 History, n. An account, mostly false, of events, mostly unimportant, which are brought about by rulers, mostly knaves, and soldiers, mostly fools.
   Cynic's Word Book (1906) p. 161

21 Marriage, n. The state or condition of a community consisting of a master, a mistress and two slaves, making in all, two.
   Devil's Dictionary (1911) p. 213

22 Noise, n. A stench in the ear. . . . The chief product and authenticating sign of civilization.
   Devil's Dictionary (1911) p. 228

23 Patience, n. A minor form of despair, disguised as a virtue.
   Devil's Dictionary (1911) p. 248

24 Peace, n. In international affairs, a period of cheating between two periods of fighting.
   Devil's Dictionary (1911) p. 248

25 Prejudice, n. A vagrant opinion without visible means of support.
   Devil's Dictionary (1911) p. 264

1 Saint, n. A dead sinner revised and
edited.
  Devil's Dictionary (1911) p. 306

2 Destiny, n. A tyrant's authority for
crime and a fool's excuse for failure.
  Enlarged Devil's Dictionary (1967) p. 64

Laurence Binyon 1869–1943

3 Now is the time for the burning of the
leaves.
  Horizon Oct. 1942, 'The Ruins'

4 With proud thanksgiving, a mother for
  her children,
England mourns for her dead across the
  sea.
Flesh of her flesh they were, spirit of her
  spirit,
Fallen in the cause of the free.
  The Times 21 Sept. 1914, 'For the Fallen'

5 They shall grow not old, as we that are
  left grow old.
Age shall not weary them, nor the years
  condemn.
At the going down of the sun and in the
  morning
We will remember them.
  The Times 21 Sept. 1914, 'For the Fallen'

Nigel Birch (Baron Rhyl)
1906–1981

6 My God! They've shot our fox! [said
13 Nov. 1947, when hearing of the
resignation of Hugh Dalton, Chancellor
of the Exchequer in the Labour
Government].
  In Harold Macmillan *Tides of Fortune* (1969)
  ch. 3

John Bird

7 That was the week that was.
  Title of BBC television series, 1962–3: see
  Ned Sherrin *A Small Thing—Like an
  Earthquake* (1983) p. 62

Earl of Birkenhead
See F. E. Smith

Lord Birkett (William Norman
Birkett, Baron Birkett) 1883–1962

8 I do not object to people looking at their
watches when I am speaking. But

I strongly object when they start shaking
them to make certain they are still
going.
  In *Observer* 30 Oct. 1960

Eric Blair
See George Orwell

Eubie Blake (James Hubert Blake)
1883–1983

9 If I'd known I was gonna live this long
[100 years], I'd have taken better care
of myself.
  In *Observer* 13 Feb. 1983

Lesley Blanch 1907–

10 She was an Amazon. Her whole life was
spent riding at breakneck speed towards
the wilder shores of love.
  The Wilder Shores of Love (1954) pt. 2, ch. 1

Alan Bleasdale 1946–

11 YOSSER HUGHES: Gizza job. . . . I can do
  that.
  Boys from the Blackstuff (1985) p. 7 (often
  quoted as 'Gissa job')

Karen Blixen
See Isak Dinesen

Edmund Blunden 1896–1974

12 Dance on this ball-floor thin and wan,
Use him as though you love him;
Court him, elude him, reel and pass,
And let him hate you through the glass.
  Masks of Time (1925) 'Midnight Skaters'

13 I have been young, and now am not too
  old;
And I have seen the righteous forsaken,
His health, his honour and his quality
  taken.
This is not what we were formerly told.
  Near and Far (1929) 'Report on Experience'

14 This was my country and it may be yet,
But something flew between me and the
  sun.
  Retreat (1928) 'The Resignation'

15 I am for the woods against the world,
But are the woods for me?
  To Themis (1931) 'The Kiss'

Alfred Blunt (Bishop of Bradford) 1879–1957

1 The benefit of the King's Coronation depends, under God, upon two elements: First, on the faith, prayer, and self-dedication of the King himself, and on that it would be improper for me to say anything except to commend him, and ask you to commend him, to God's grace, which he will so abundantly need ... if he is to do his duty faithfully. We hope that he is aware of his need. Some of us wish that he gave more positive signs of his awareness.
Speech to Bradford Diocesan Conference, 1 Dec. 1936, in *The Times* 2 Dec. 1936

Wilfrid Scawen Blunt 1840–1922

2 To the Grafton Gallery to look at ... the Post-Impressionist pictures sent over from Paris. ... The drawing is on the level of that of an untaught child of seven or eight years old, the sense of colour that of a tea-tray painter, the method that of a schoolboy who wipes his fingers on a slate after spitting on them. ... These are not works of art at all, unless throwing a handful of mud against a wall may be called one. They are the works of idleness and impotent stupidity, a pornographic show.
My Diaries (1920) 15 Nov. 1910

3 I like the hunting of the hare
Better than that of the fox.
New Pilgrimage (1889) 'The Old Squire'

Ronald Blythe 1922–

4 As for the British churchman, he goes to church as he goes to the bathroom, with the minimum of fuss and with no explanation if he can help it.
Age of Illusion (1963) ch. 12

5 An industrial worker would sooner have a £5 note but a countryman must have praise.
Akenfield (1969) ch. 5

Enid Blyton 1897–1968

6 Five go off in a caravan.
Title of children's story (1946)

7 The naughtiest girl in the school.
Title of children's story (1940)

Louise Bogan 1897–1970

8 Women have no wilderness in them,
They are provident instead,
Content in the tight hot cell of their hearts
To eat dusty bread.
Body of this Death (1923) 'Women'

Humphrey Bogart 1899–1957

9 Contrary to legend, as a juvenile I never said 'Tennis, anyone?' just as I never said 'Drop the gun, Louie' as a heavy.
In Ezra Goodman *Bogey: the Good-Bad Guy* (1965) ch. 4. Cf. George Bernard Shaw 199:4

See also Julius J. Epstein *et al.*

John B. Bogart 1848–1921

10 When a dog bites a man, that is not news, because it happens so often. But if a man bites a dog, that is news.
In F. M. O'Brien *Story of the Sun* (1918) ch. 10 (the quotation is often attributed to Charles A. Dana)

Niels Bohr 1885–1962

11 One of the favourite maxims of my father was the distinction between the two sorts of truths, profound truths recognized by the fact that the opposite is also a profound truth, in contrast to trivialities where opposites are obviously absurd.
In S. Rozental *Niels Bohr* (1967) p. 328

Alan Bold 1943–

12 They mattered more than they should have. It is so
In Scotland, land of the omnipotent No.
Perpetual Motion Machine (1969) 'A Memory of Death'

Robert Bolt 1924–

13 Morality's *not* practical. Morality's a gesture. A complicated gesture learned from books.
A Man for All Seasons (1960) act 2

Andrew Bonar Law 1858–1923

14 If, therefore, war should ever come between these two countries [Great Britain and Germany], which Heaven

forbid! it will not, I think, be due to
irresistible natural laws; it will be due to
the want of human wisdom.
Hansard 27 Nov. 1911, col. 167

1 If I am a great man, then all great men
are frauds.
In Lord Beaverbrook *Politicians and the War*
(1932) vol. 2, ch. 4

Carrie Jacobs Bond 1862–1946

2 When you come to the end of a perfect
day,
And you sit alone with your thought,
While the chimes ring out with a carol
gay
For the joy that the day has brought,
Do you think what the end of a perfect
day
Can mean to a tired heart,
When the sun goes down with a flaming
ray,
And the dear friends have to part?

Well, this is the end of a perfect day,
Near the end of a journey, too;
But it leaves a thought that is big and
strong,
With a wish that is kind and true.
For mem'ry has painted this perfect day
With colours that never fade,
And we find, at the end of a perfect day,
The soul of a friend we've made.
A Perfect Day (1910 song)

Sir David Bone 1874–1959

3 It's 'Damn you, Jack—I'm all right!'
with you chaps.
Brassbounder (1910) ch. 3

Dietrich Bonhoeffer 1906–1945

4 *Es ist der Vorzug und das Wesen der
Starken, dass sie die grossen
Entscheidungsfragen stellen und zu ihnen
klar Stellung nehmen können. Die
Schwachen müssen sich immer zwischen
Alternativen entscheiden, die nicht die ihren
sind.*

It is the nature, and the advantage, of
strong people that they can bring out
the crucial questions and form a clear
opinion about them. The weak always
have to decide between alternatives that
are not their own.
Widerstand und Ergebung (Resistance and
Submission, 1951)

5 *Jesus ist nur 'für andere da'. . . . Gott in
Menschengestalt! . . . nicht die griechische
Gott-Menschgestalt des 'Menschen an sich',
sondern 'der Mensch für andere', darum der
Gekreuzigte.*

Jesus is there only for others. . . . God in
human form! not . . . in the Greek
divine-human form of 'man in himself',
but 'the man for others', and therefore
the crucified.
Widerstand und Ergebung (Resistance and
Submission, 1951)

Sonny Bono (Salvatore Bono) 1953–

6 The beat goes on.
Title of song (1966)

Daniel J. Boorstin 1914–

7 The celebrity is a person who is known
for his well-knownness.
The Image (1961) ch. 2

8 A bestseller was a book which somehow
sold well simply because it was selling
well.
The Image (1961) ch. 4

James H. Boren 1925–

9 Guidelines for bureaucrats: (1) When in
charge, ponder. (2) When in trouble,
delegate. (3) When in doubt, mumble.
In *New York Times* 8 Nov. 1970, p. 45

Jorge Luis Borges 1899–1986

10 *El original es infiel a la traducción.*

The original is unfaithful to the
translation [Henley's translation of
Beckford's *Vathek*].
Sobre el 'Vathek' de William Beckford (1943)
in *Obras Completas* (1974) p. 730

11 *Para uno de esos gnósticos, el visible
universo era una ilusión ó (mas
precisamente) un sofisma. Los espejos y la
paternidad son abominables porque lo
multiplican y lo divulgan.*

For one of those gnostics, the visible
universe was an illusion or, more
precisely, a sophism. Mirrors and
fatherhood are abominable because they
multiply it and extend it.
Tlön, Uqbar, Orbis, Tertius (1941) in *Obras
Completas* (1974) p. 431

1 The Falklands thing [the Falklands War of 1982] was a fight between two bald men over a comb.
In *Time* 14 Feb. 1983

Max Born 1882–1970

2 The human race has today the means for annihilating itself—either in a fit of complete lunacy, i.e., in a big war, by a brief fit of destruction, or by careless handling of atomic technology, through a slow process of poisoning and of deterioration in its genetic structure.
Bulletin of Atomic Scientists (1957) vol. 13, p. 186

John Collins Bossidy 1860–1928

3 And this is good old Boston,
The home of the bean and the cod,
Where the Lowells talk to the Cabots
And the Cabots talk only to God.
Verse spoken at Holy Cross College alumni dinner in Boston, Mass., 1910, in *Springfield Sunday Republican* 14 Dec. 1924

Gordon Bottomley 1874–1948

4 When you destroy a blade of grass
You poison England at her roots:
Remember no man's foot can pass
Where evermore no green life shoots.
Chambers of Imagery (1912) 'To Ironfounders and Others'

5 Your worship is your furnaces,
Which, like old idols, lost obscenes,
Have molten bowels; your vision is
Machines for making more machines.
Chambers of Imagery (1912) 'To Ironfounders and Others'

Horatio Bottomley 1860–1933

6 During his incarceration at the Scrubbs [1922–3], Bottomley was largely employed in the making of mail-bags. It was while he was so engaged one afternoon that a prison visitor . . . saw him busily stitching away. 'Ah, Bottomley,' he remarked brightly, 'sewing?' 'No,' grunted the old man without looking up, 'reaping.'
In S.T. Felstead *Horatio Bottomley* (1936) ch. 16

7 Gentlemen: I have not had your advantages. What poor education I have received has been gained in the University of Life.
Speech at Oxford Union, 2 Dec. 1920, in Beverley Nichols 25 (1926) ch. 7

Sir Harold Edwin Boulton 1859–1935

8 When Adam and Eve were dispossessed
Of the garden hard by Heaven,
They planted another one down in the west,
'Twas Devon, glorious Devon!
Lyrics and other Poems (1902) 'Glorious Devon'

9 Speed, bonnie boat, like a bird on the wing,
'Onward,' the sailors cry;
Carry the lad that's born to be king,
Over the sea to Skye.
National Songs and Some Ballads (1908) 'Skye Boat Song'

Elizabeth Bowen 1899–1973

10 Experience isn't interesting till it begins to repeat itself—in fact, till it does that, it hardly *is* experience.
Death of the Heart (1938) pt. 1, ch. 1

11 In fact, it is about five o'clock in an evening that the first hour of spring strikes—autumn arrives in the early morning, but spring at the close of a winter day.
Death of the Heart (1938) pt. 2, ch. 1

12 Some people are moulded by their admirations, others by their hostilities.
Death of the Heart (1938) pt. 2, ch. 2

13 The heart may think it knows better: the senses know that absence blots people out. We have really no absent friends.
Death of the Heart (1938) pt. 2, ch. 2

14 Elizabeth Bowen said that she [Edith Sitwell] looked like 'a high altar on the move'.
V. Glendinning *Edith Sitwell* (1981) ch. 25

15 I suppose art is the only thing that can go on mattering once it has stopped hurting.
Heat of the Day (1949) ch. 16

16 There is no end to the violations committed by children on children, quietly talking alone.
House in Paris (1935) pt. 1, ch. 2

1 Nobody speaks the truth when there's
something they must have.
House in Paris (1935) pt. 1, ch. 5

2 Meetings that do not come off keep
a character of their own. They stay as
they were projected.
House in Paris (1935) pt. 2, ch. 1

3 Fate is not an eagle, it creeps like a rat.
House in Paris (1935) pt. 2, ch. 2

4 Jealousy is no more than feeling alone
against smiling enemies.
House in Paris (1935) pt. 2, ch. 8

5 My failing to have a nice ear for vowel
sounds, and the Anglo-Irish slurred,
hurried way of speaking made me take
the words 'Ireland' and 'island' to be
synonymous. Thus, all other countries
quite surrounded by water took (it
appeared) their generic name from ours.
Seven Winters (1942) p. 12

David Bowie (David Jones) 1947–

6 Ground control to Major Tom.
Space Oddity (1969 song)

Sir Maurice Bowra 1898–1971

7 There is also that story, perhaps
apocryphal, of Maurice [Bowra]'s
decision to get married. When he
announced that he had at last chosen
a girl, a friend remonstrated: 'But you
can't marry anyone as plain as that.'
Maurice answered: 'My dear fellow,
buggers can't be choosers.'
Francis King in Hugh Lloyd-Jones *Maurice
Bowra: a Celebration* (1974) p. 150

8 I'm a man more dined against than
dining.
In John Betjeman *Summoned by Bells* (1960)
ch. 9

Charles Boyer 1898–1978

9 Come with me to the Casbah.
Catch-phrase often attributed to Boyer, but
L. Swindell *Charles Boyer* (1983) ch. 7 says:
Algiers ... is the picture in which Charles
Boyer did *not* say 'Come wiz me to zee
Casbah' to Hedy Lamarr.... Boyer and
Lamarr were *in* the Casbah in most of their
Algiers scenes, and they *did* have an
important scene in which they were not in
the Casbah, but the dialogue was nowhere
close.

Lord Brabazon (Baron Brabazon of Tara) 1884–1964

10 I take the view, and always have, that if
you cannot say what you are going to
say in twenty minutes you ought to go
away and write a book about it.
Hansard (Lords) 21 June 1955, col. 207

Charles Brackett 1892–1969, Billy Wilder 1906– , and D. M. Marshman Jr.

11 JOE GILLIS: You used to be in pictures.
You used to be big.
NORMA DESMOND: I am big. It's the
pictures that got small.
Sunset Boulevard (1950 film)

12 All right, Mr de Mille, I'm ready for my
close-up now.
Sunset Boulevard (1950 film)

Charles Brackett 1892–1969, Billy Wilder 1906– , and Walter Reisch 1903–1983

13 IRANOFF: What a charming idea for
Moscow to surprise us with a lady
Comrade.
KOPALSKI: If we had known we would
have greeted you with flowers.
IRANOFF: Ahh—yes.
NINOTCHKA: Don't make an issue of my
womanhood.
Ninotchka (1939 film)

14 NINOTCHKA: Why should you carry
other people's bags?
PORTER: Well, that's my business,
Madame.
NINOTCHKA: That's no business. That's
social injustice.
PORTER: That depends on the tip.
Ninotchka (1939 film)

F. H. Bradley 1846–1924

15 The propriety of some persons seems to
consist in having improper thoughts
about their neighbours.
Aphorisms (1930) no. 9

16 True penitence condemns to silence.
What a man is ready to recall he would
be willing to repeat.
Aphorisms (1930) no. 10

1 The secret of happiness is to admire without desiring. And that is not happiness.
   Aphorisms (1930) no. 33

2 Metaphysics is the finding of bad reasons for what we believe upon instinct; but to find these reasons is no less an instinct.
   Appearance and Reality (1893) preface

3 Of Optimism I have said that 'The world is the best of all possible worlds, and everything in it is a necessary evil.'
   Appearance and Reality (1893) preface

4 That the glory of this world . . . is appearance leaves the world more glorious, if we feel it is a show of some fuller splendour; but the sensuous curtain is a deception . . . if it hides some colourless movement of atoms, some . . . unearthly ballet of bloodless categories.
   Principles of Logic (1883) bk. 3, pt. 2, ch. 4

Omar Bradley 1893–1981

5 The way to win an atomic war is to make certain it never starts.
   Speech to Boston Chamber of Commerce, 10 Nov. 1948, in *Collected Writings* (1967) vol. 1, p. 588

6 We have grasped the mystery of the atom and rejected the Sermon on the Mount.
   Speech to Boston Chamber of Commerce, 10 Nov. 1948, in *Collected Writings* (1967) vol. 1, p. 588

7 Red China is not the powerful nation seeking to dominate the world. Frankly, in the opinion of the Joint Chiefs of Staff, this strategy would involve us in the wrong war, at the wrong place, at the wrong time, and with the wrong enemy.
   US Cong. Senate Comm. on Armed Services (1951) vol. 2, p. 732

Caryl Brahms (Doris Caroline Abrahams) 1901–1982 and S. J. Simon (Simon Jasha Skidelsky)

8 The suffragettes were triumphant. Woman's place was in the gaol.
   No Nightingales (1944) pt. 6, ch. 37

John Braine 1922–

9 Room at the top.
   Title of novel (1957). Cf. *Oxford Dictionary of Quotations* (1979) 566:9

Ernest Bramah (Ernest Bramah Smith) 1868–1942

10 It is a mark of insincerity of purpose to spend one's time in looking for the sacred Emperor in the low-class tea-shops.
   Wallet of Kai Lung (1900) p. 6

11 In his countenance this person read an expression of no-encouragement towards his venture.
   Wallet of Kai Lung (1900) p. 224

12 The whole narrative is permeated with the odour of joss-sticks and honourable high-mindedness.
   Wallet of Kai Lung (1900) p. 330

Georges Braque 1882–1963

13 L'Art est fait pour troubler, la Science rassure.
   Art is meant to disturb, science reassures.
   Le Jour et la Nuit: Cahiers 1917–52 (Day and Night, Notebooks, 1952) p. 11

14 La vérité existe; on n'invente que le mensonge.
   Truth exists; only lies are invented.
   Le Jour et la Nuit: Cahiers 1917–52 (Day and Night, Notebooks, 1952) p. 20

John Bratby 1928–

15 A real art student wears coloured socks, has a fringe and a beard, wears dirty jeans and an equally dirty seaman's pullover, carries a sketch-book, is despised by the rest of society, and loafs in a coffee bar.
   Breakdown (1960) ch. 8

Irving Brecher 1914–

16 I'll bet your father spent the first year of your life throwing rocks at the stork.
   (*Marx Brothers*) *At the Circus* (1939 film)

17 Time wounds all heals.
   Marx Brothers Go West (1940 film)

Bertolt Brecht 1898–1956

18 Und der Haifisch, der hat Zähne

Und die trägt er im Gesicht
Und Macheath, der hat ein Messer
Doch das Messer sieht man nicht.

Oh, the shark has pretty teeth, dear,
And he shows them pearly white.
Just a jack-knife has Macheath, dear
And he keeps it out of sight.
  Dreigroschenoper (Threepenny Opera, 1928)
  prologue

1 *Erst kommt das Fressen, dann kommt die*
  Moral.

  Food comes first, then morals.
  Dreigroschenoper (Threepenny Opera, 1928)
  act 2, sc. 3

2 *Was ist ein Einbruch in eine Bank gegen*
  die Gründung einer Bank?

  What is robbing a bank compared with
  founding a bank?
  Dreigroschenoper (Threepenny Opera, 1928)
  act 3, sc. 3

3 ANDREA: *Unglücklich das Land, das keine*
  Helden
  hat! . . .
  GALILEI: *Nein. Unglücklich das Land, das*
  Helden nötig hat.

  ANDREA: Unhappy the land that has no
  heroes! . . .
  GALILEO: No. Unhappy the land that
  needs heroes.
  Leben des Galilei (Life of Galileo, 1939) sc. 13

4 *Man merkts, hier ist zu lang kein Krieg*
  gewesen. Wo soll da Moral herkommen,
  frag ich? Frieden, das ist nur Schlamperei,
  erst der Krieg schafft Ordnung.

  One observes, they have gone too long
  without a war here. What is the moral,
  I ask? Peace is nothing but slovenliness,
  only war creates order.
  Mutter Courage (Mother Courage, 1939)
  sc. 1

5 *Weil ich ihm nicht trau, sind wir*
  befreundet.

  Because I don't trust him, we are
  friends.
  Mutter Courage (Mother Courage, 1939)
  sc. 3

6 *Die schönsten Plän sind schon zuschanden*
  geworden durch die Kleinlichkeit von denen,
  wo sie ausführen sollten, denn die Kaiser
  selber können ja nix machen.

  The finest plans are always ruined by
  the littleness of those who ought to

carry them out, for the Emperor himself
can actually do nothing.
  Mutter Courage (Mother Courage, 1939)
  sc. 6

7 *Der Krieg findet immer einen Ausweg.*

  War always finds a way.
  Mutter Courage (Mother Courage, 1939)
  sc. 6

8 *Sagen Sie mir nicht, dass Friede*
  ausgebrochen ist, wo ich eben neue Vorräte
  eingekauft hab.

  Don't tell me peace has broken out,
  when I've just bought some new
  supplies.
  Mutter Courage (Mother Courage, 1939)
  sc. 8

Gerald Brenan 1894–1987

9 Those who have some means think that
  the most important thing in the world is
  love. The poor know that it is money.
  Thoughts in a Dry Season (1978) p. 22

10 Religions are kept alive by heresies,
  which are really sudden explosions of
  faith. Dead religions do not produce
  them.
  Thoughts in a Dry Season (1978) p. 45

Aristide Briand 1862–1932

11 *Les hautes parties contractantes déclarent*
  solennellement . . . qu'elles condamnent le
  recours à la guerre . . . et y renoncent en tant
  qu'instrument de politique nationale dans
  leurs relations mutuelles . . . le règlement ou
  la solution de tous les différends ou
  conflits—de quelque nature ou de quelque
  origine qu'ils puissent être—qui pourront
  surgir entre elles ne devra jamais être cherché
  que par des moyens pacifiques.

  The high contracting powers solemnly
  declare . . . that they condemn recourse
  to war and renounce it . . . as an
  instrument of their national policy
  towards each other. . . . The settlement
  or the solution of all disputes or conflicts
  of whatever nature or of whatever origin
  they may be which may arise . . . shall
  never be sought by either side except by
  pacific means.
  Draft, 20 June 1927, which became part of
  the Kellogg Pact, 1928, in *Le Temps* 13 Apr.
  1928

Vera Brittain 1893–1970

1 Politics are usually the executive
expression of human immaturity.
Rebel Passion (1964) ch. 1

David Broder 1929–

2 Anybody that wants the presidency so
much that he'll spend two years
organizing and campaigning for it is not
to be trusted with the office.
Washington Post 18 July 1973, p. A 25

Jacob Bronowski 1908–1974

3 We have to understand that the world
can only be grasped by action, not by
contemplation. The hand is more
important than the eye.... The hand is
the cutting edge of the mind.
Ascent of Man (1973) ch. 3

4 That is the essence of science: ask an
impertinent question, and you are on
the way to a pertinent answer.
Ascent of Man (1973) ch. 4

5 The wish to hurt, the momentary
intoxication with pain, is the loophole
through which the pervert climbs into
the minds of ordinary men.
Face of Violence (1954) ch. 5

6 The world is made of people who never
quite get into the first team and who
just miss the prizes at the flower show.
Face of Violence (1954) ch. 6

7 Man masters nature not by force but by
understanding. This is why science has
succeeded where magic failed: because it
has looked for no spell to cast on nature.
Universities Quarterly (1956) vol. 10, no. 3,
p. 252

Rupert Brooke 1887–1915

8 Breathless, we flung us on the windy
hill,
Laughed in the sun, and kissed the
lovely grass.
Cambridge Review 8 Dec. 1910, 'Sonnet'

9 Then, the cool kindliness of sheets, that
soon
Smooth away trouble; and the rough
male kiss
Of blankets; grainy wood; live hair that
is
Shining and free; blue-massing clouds;
the keen

Unpassioned beauty of a great machine;
The benison of hot water; furs to touch;
The good smell of old clothes.
New Numbers no. 3 (1914) 'The Great
Lover'

10 Now, God be thanked Who has matched
us with His hour,
And caught our youth, and wakened us
from sleeping,
With hand made sure, clear eye, and
sharpened power,
To turn, as swimmers into cleanness
leaping,
Glad from a world grown old and cold
and weary,
Leave the sick hearts that honour could
not move,
And half-men, and their dirty songs and
dreary,
And all the little emptiness of love!
Oh! we, who have known shame, we
have found release there,
Where there's no ill, no grief, but sleep
has mending,
Naught broken save this body, lost but
breath;
Nothing to shake the laughing heart's
long peace there
But only agony, and that has ending;
And the worst friend and enemy is but
Death.
New Numbers no. 4 (1914) 'Peace'

11 War knows no power. Safe shall be my
going,
Secretly armed against all death's
endeavour;
Safe though all safety's lost; safe where
men fall;
And if these poor limbs die, safest of all.
New Numbers no. 4 (1914) 'Safety'

12 Blow out, you bugles, over the rich
Dead!
There's none of these so lonely and poor
of old,
But, dying, has made us rarer gifts than
gold.
These laid the world away; poured out
the red
Sweet wine of youth; gave up the years
to be
Of work and joy, and that unhoped
serene,
That men call age; and those that would
have been,

Their sons, they gave, their immortality.
New Numbers no. 4 (1914) 'The Dead'

1 Honour has come back, as a king, to earth,
And paid his subjects with a royal wage;
And Nobleness walks in our ways again;
And we have come into our heritage.
New Numbers no. 4 (1914) 'The Dead'

2 If I should die, think only this of me:
That there's some corner of a foreign field
That is for ever England. There shall be
In that rich earth a richer dust concealed;
A dust whom England bore, shaped, made aware,
Gave, once, her flowers to love, her ways to roam,
A body of England's, breathing English air,
Washed by the rivers, blest by suns of home.
And think, this heart, all evil shed away,
A pulse in the eternal mind, no less
Gives somewhere back the thoughts by England given;
Her sights and sounds; dreams happy as her day;
And laughter, learnt of friends; and gentleness,
In hearts at peace, under an English heaven.
New Numbers no. 4 (1914) 'The Soldier'

3 Fish say, they have their Stream and Pond;
But is there anything Beyond?
1914 and Other Poems (1915) 'Heaven'

4 But somewhere, beyond Space and Time
Is wetter water, slimier slime!
1914 and Other Poems (1915) 'Heaven'

5 Oh! never fly conceals a hook,
Fish say, in the Eternal Brook,
But more than mundane weeds are there,
And mud, celestially fair;
Fat caterpillars drift around,
And Paradisal grubs are found;
Unfading moths, immortal flies,
And the worm that never dies.
And in that Heaven of all their wish,
There shall be no more land, say fish.
1914 and Other Poems (1915) 'Heaven'

6 But there's wisdom in women, of more than they have known,
And thoughts go blowing through them, are wiser than their own.
1914 and Other Poems (1915) 'There's Wisdom in Women'

7 Just now the lilac is in bloom,
All before my little room.
1914 and Other Poems (1915) 'The Old Vicarage, Grantchester'

8 Here tulips bloom as they are told;
Unkempt about those hedges blows
An English unofficial rose;
And there the unregulated sun
Slopes down to rest when day is done,
And wakes a vague unpunctual star,
A slippered Hesper; and there are
Meads towards Haslingfield and Coton
Where *das Betreten*'s not *verboten*.
εἴθε γενοίμην. ... would I were
In Grantchester, in Grantchester!
1914 and Other Poems (1915) 'The Old Vicarage, Grantchester'

9 And in that garden, black and white,
Creep whispers through the grass all night;
And spectral dance, before the dawn,
A hundred Vicars down the lawn;
Curates, long dust, will come and go
On lissom, clerical, printless toe;
And oft between the boughs is seen
The sly shade of a Rural Dean.
1914 and Other Poems (1915) 'The Old Vicarage, Grantchester'

10 God! I will pack, and take a train,
And get me to England once again!
For England's the one land, I know,
Where men with Splendid Hearts may go;
And Cambridgeshire, of all England,
The shire for Men who Understand;
And of *that* district I prefer
The lovely hamlet Grantchester.
For Cambridge people rarely smile,
Being urban, squat, and packed with guile.
1914 and Other Poems (1915) 'The Old Vicarage, Grantchester'

11 They love the Good; they worship Truth;
They laugh uproariously in youth;
(And when they get to feeling old,
They up and shoot themselves, I'm told).
1914 and Other Poems (1915) 'The Old Vicarage, Grantchester'

1 Oh, is the water sweet and cool,
Gentle and brown, above the pool?
And laughs the immortal river still
Under the mill, under the mill?
Say, is there Beauty yet to find?
And Certainty? and Quiet kind?
Deep meadows yet, for to forget
The lies, and truths, and pain? . . . oh!
    yet
Stands the Church clock at ten to three?
And is there honey still for tea?
> *1914 and Other Poems* (1915) 'The Old
> Vicarage, Grantchester'

Anita Brookner 1938–

2 Good women always think it is their
fault when someone else is being
offensive. Bad women never take the
blame for anything.
> *Hotel du Lac* (1984) ch. 7

3 Blanche Vernon occupied her time most
usefully in keeping feelings at bay.
> *Misalliance* (1986) ch. 1

Mel Brooks 1926–

4 That's it baby, when you got it, flaunt
it.
> *The Producers* (1968 film)

Heywood Broun 1888–1939

5 Free speech is about as good a cause as
the world has ever known. But, like the
poor, it is always with us and gets
shoved aside in favour of things which
seem at some given moment more
vital. . . . Everybody favours free speech
in the slack moments when no axes are
being ground.
> *New York World* 23 Oct. 1926, p. 13

6 Just as every conviction begins as
a whim so does every emancipator serve
his apprenticeship as a crank. A fanatic
is a great leader who is just entering the
room.
> *New York World* 6 Feb. 1928, p. 11

7 Men build bridges and throw railroads
across deserts, and yet they contend
successfully that the job of sewing on
a button is beyond them. Accordingly,
they don't have to sew buttons.
> *Seeing Things at Night* (1921) 'Holding
> a Baby'

8 Posterity is as likely to be wrong as
anybody else.
> *Sitting on the World* (1924) 'The Last
> Review'

H. Rap Brown 1943–

9 I say violence is necessary. It is as
American as cherry pie.
> Speech at Washington, 27 July 1967, in
> *Washington Post* 28 July 1967, p. A7

Helen Gurley Brown 1922–

10 Sex and the single girl.
> Title of book (1962)

Ivor Brown 1891–1974

11 For nearly a century after his death,
Shakespeare remained more a theme for
criticism by the few than a subject of
adulation by the many.
> *Shakespeare* (1949) ch. 1

John Mason Brown 1900–1969

12 Tallulah Bankhead barged down the
Nile last night as Cleopatra—and sank.
> *New York Post* 11 Nov. 1937, p. 18

Lew Brown (Louis Brownstein) 1893–1958

13 Life is just a bowl of cherries.
> Title of song (1931; music by Ray
> Henderson)

Nacio Herb Brown 1896–1964

See ARTHUR FREED

Cecil Browne

14 But not so odd
As those who choose
A Jewish God,
But spurn the Jews.
> Reply to verse by William Norman Ewer: see
> 78:4

Sir Frederick Browning 1896–1965

15 I think we might be going a bridge too
far.
> Expressing reservations about the Arnhem
> 'Market Garden' operation to Field Marshal
> Montgomery on 10 Sept. 1944, in R. E.
> Urquhart *Arnhem* (1958) p. 4

Lenny Bruce (Leonard Alfred Schneider) 1925–1966

1 The liberals can understand everything but people who don't understand them.
In John Cohen *Essential Lenny Bruce* (1970) p. 59

Anita Bryant 1940–

2 If homosexuality were the normal way, God would have made Adam and Bruce.
In *New York Times* 5 June 1977, p. 22

Martin Buber 1878–1965

3 *Der Mensch wird am Du zum Ich.*

Through the Thou a person becomes I.
Ich und Du (I and Thou, 1923) in *Werke* (1962) vol. 1, p. 97

John Buchan (Baron Tweedsmuir) 1875–1940

4 To live for a time close to great minds is the best kind of education.
Memory Hold-the-Door (1940) ch. 2

5 'Back to Glasgow to do some work for the cause,' I said lightly. 'Just so,' he said, with a grin. 'It's a great life if you don't weaken.'
Mr Standfast (1919) ch. 5

6 An atheist is man who has no invisible means of support.
In H. E. Fosdick *On Being a Real Person* (1943) ch. 10

Frank Buchman 1878–1961

7 I thank heaven for a man like Adolf Hitler, who built a front line of defence against the anti-Christ of Communism.
New York World-Telegram 26 Aug. 1936

8 Suppose everybody cared enough, everybody shared enough, wouldn't everybody have enough? There is enough in the world for everyone's need, but not enough for everyone's greed.
Remaking the World (1947) p. 56

Gene Buck (Edward Eugene Buck) 1885–1957 and Herman Ruby 1891–1959

9 That Shakespearian rag,—

Most intelligent, very elegant.
That Shakespearian Rag (1912 song; music by David Stamper). Cf. T. S. Eliot 76:21

Richard Buckle 1916–

10 John Lennon, Paul McCartney and George Harrison are the greatest composers since Beethoven, with Paul McCartney way out in front.
Sunday Times 29 Dec. 1963

Arthur Buller 1874–1944

11 There was a young lady named Bright, Whose speed was far faster than light; She set out one day In a relative way And returned on the previous night.
Punch 19 Dec. 1923, 'Relativity'

Ivor Bulmer-Thomas 1905–

12 If he [Harold Wilson] ever went to school without any boots it was because he was too big for them.
Speech at Conservative Party Conference, in *Manchester Guardian* 13 Oct. 1949

Luis Buñuel 1900–1983

13 *Le charme discret de la bourgeoisie.*

The discreet charm of the bourgeoisie.
Title of film (1972)

14 *Grâce à Dieu, je suis toujours athée.*

Thanks to God, I am still an atheist.
In *Le Monde* 16 Dec. 1959

Anthony Burgess 1917–

15 Who ever heard of a clockwork orange? Then I read a malenky bit out loud in a sort of very high type preaching goloss: 'The attempt to impose upon man, a creature of growth and capable of sweetness, to ooze juicily at the last round the bearded lips of God, to attempt to impose, I say, laws and conditions appropriate to a mechanical creation, against this I raise my sword-pen.'
A Clockwork Orange (1962) p. 21

16 It was the afternoon of my eighty-first birthday, and I was in bed with my catamite when Ali announced that the archbishop had come to see me.
Earthly Powers (1980) p. 7

1 He said it was artificial respiration, but now I find I am to have his child.
   Inside Mr Enderby (1963) pt. 1, ch. 4

2 The possession of a book becomes a substitute for reading it.
   New York Times Book Review 4 Dec. 1966, p. 74

Johnny Burke 1908–1964

3 Every time it rains, it rains
   Pennies from heaven.
   Don't you know each cloud contains
   Pennies from heaven?
   You'll find your fortune falling
   All over town
   Be sure that your umbrella
   Is upside down.
   Pennies from Heaven (1936 song; music by Arthur Johnston)

4 Like Webster's Dictionary, we're Morocco bound.
   The Road to Morocco (1942 song from film *The Road to Morocco*; music by James van Heusen)

John Burns 1858–1943

5 'What have you in the Mississippi?' he [John Burns] asked an American who had spoken disparagingly of the Thames. The American replied that there was water—miles and miles of it. 'Ah, but you see, the Thames is liquid history,' said Burns.
   Daily Mail 25 Jan. 1943

William S. Burroughs 1914–

6 I think there are innumerable gods. What we on earth call God is a little tribal God who has made an awful mess. Certainly forces operating through human consciousness control events.
   Paris Review Fall 1965

Benjamin Hapgood Burt 1880–1950

7 One evening in October, when I was one-third sober,
   An' taking home a 'load' with manly pride;
   My poor feet began to stutter, so I lay down in the gutter,
   And a pig came up an' lay down by my side;

Then we sang 'It's all fair weather when good fellows get together,'
Till a lady passing by was heard to say:
'You can tell a man who "boozes" by the company he chooses'
And the pig got up and slowly walked away.
   The Pig Got Up and Slowly Walked Away (1933 song)

Nat Burton

8 There'll be bluebirds over the white cliffs of Dover,
   Tomorrow, just you wait and see.
   White Cliffs of Dover (1941 song; music by Walter Kent)

R. A. Butler (Baron Butler of Saffron Walden) 1902–1982

9 Politics is the Art of the Possible. That is what these pages show I have tried to achieve—not more—and that is what I have called my book.
   The Art of the Possible (1971) p. xi. Cf. Bismarck's 'Die Politik ist die Lehre vom Möglichen', *Oxford Dictionary of Quotations* (1979) 84:20

10 REPORTER: Mr Butler, would you say that this [Anthony Eden] is the best Prime Minister we have?
   R. A. BUTLER: Yes.
   Interview at London Airport, 8 Jan. 1956, in R. A. Butler *The Art of the Possible* (1971) ch. 9

Ralph Butler and Noel Gay (Richard Moxon Armitage) 1898–1954

11 The sun has got his hat on
   Hip hip hip hooray!
   The sun has got his hat on
   And he's coming out today.
   The Sun Has Got His Hat On (1932 song)

Samuel Butler 1835–1902

12 Yet meet we shall, and part, and meet again

Where dead men meet, on lips of living
men.
Athenaeum 4 Jan. 1902, 'Μέλλοντα ταῦτα'

1 It has been said that the love of money
is the root of all evil. The want of money
is so quite as truly.
Erewhon (1872) ch. 20

2 It has been said that though God cannot
alter the past, historians can; it is
perhaps because they can be useful to
Him in this respect that He tolerates
their existence.
Erewhon Revisited (1901) ch. 14

3 Life is like playing a violin solo in public
and learning the instrument as one goes
on.
Speech at the Somerville Club, 27 Feb.
1895, in R. A. Streatfield *Essays on Life, Art
and Science* (1904) p. 69

4 An honest God's the noblest work of
man.
Further Extracts from Notebooks (1934)
p. 26. Cf. *Oxford Dictionary of Quotations*
(1979) 270:17 and 379:24

5 A lawyer's dream of heaven: every man
reclaimed his own property at the
resurrection, and each tried to recover it
from all his forefathers.
Further Extracts from Notebooks (1934) p. 27

6 The three most important things a man
has are, briefly, his private parts, his
money, and his religious opinions.
Further Extracts from Notebooks (1934) p. 93

7 The course of true anything never does
run smooth.
Further Extracts from Notebooks (1934)
p. 260

8 Conscience is thoroughly well-bred and
soon leaves off talking to those who do
not wish to hear it.
Further Extracts from Notebooks (1934)
p. 279

9 I heard a man say that brigands demand
your money *or* your life, whereas
women require both.
Further Extracts from Notebooks (1934)
p. 315

10 It was very good of God to let Carlyle
and Mrs Carlyle marry one another and
so make only two people miserable
instead of four, besides being very
amusing.
*Letters between Samuel Butler and Miss E. M.
A. Savage 1871–1885* (1935) 21 Nov. 1884

11 The most perfect humour and irony is
generally quite unconscious.
Life and Habit (1877) ch. 2

12 It has, I believe, been often remarked
that a hen is only an egg's way of
making another egg.
Life and Habit (1877) ch. 8

13 Life is one long process of getting tired.
Notebooks (1912) ch. 1

14 Life is the art of drawing sufficient
conclusions from insufficient premises.
Notebooks (1912) ch. 1

15 All progress is based upon a universal
innate desire on the part of every
organism to live beyond its income.
Notebooks (1912) ch. 1

16 The healthy stomach is nothing if not
conservative. Few radicals have good
digestions.
Notebooks (1912) ch. 6

17 Always eat grapes downwards—that is,
always eat the best grape first; in this
way there will be none better left on the
bunch, and each grape will seem good
down to the last. If you eat the other
way, you will not have a good grape in
the lot. Besides you will be tempting
providence to kill you before you come
to the best.
Notebooks (1912) ch. 7

18 How thankful we ought to be that
Wordsworth was only a poet and not
a musician. Fancy a symphony by
Wordsworth! Fancy having to sit it out!
And fancy what it would have been if he
had written fugues!
Notebooks (1912) ch. 8

19 The history of art is the history of
revivals.
Notebooks (1912) ch. 8

20 Genius . . . has been defined as
a supreme capacity for taking trouble.
. . . It might be more fitly described as
a supreme capacity for getting its
possessors into trouble of all kinds and
keeping them therein so long as the
genius remains.
Notebooks (1912) ch. 11

21 An apology for the Devil: It must be
remembered that we have only heard
one side of the case. God has written all
the books.
Notebooks (1912) ch. 14

1 The great pleasure of a dog is that you may make a fool of yourself with him and not only will he not scold you, but he will make a fool of himself too.
Notebooks (1912) ch. 14

2 A definition is the enclosing a wilderness of idea within a wall of words.
Notebooks (1912) ch. 14

3 To live is like to love—all reason is against it, and all healthy instinct for it.
Notebooks (1912) ch. 14

4 The public buys its opinions as it buys its meat, or takes in its milk, on the principle that it is cheaper to do this than to keep a cow. So it is, but the milk is more likely to be watered.
Notebooks (1912) ch. 17

5 I do not mind lying, but I hate inaccuracy.
Notebooks (1912) ch. 19

6 Stowed away in a Montreal lumber room
The Discobolus standeth and turneth his face to the wall;
Dusty, cobweb-covered, maimed, and set at naught,
Beauty crieth in an attic, and no man regardeth.
O God! O Montreal!
Spectator 18 May 1878, 'Psalm of Montreal'

7 I do not like books. I believe I have the smallest library of any literary man in London, and I have no wish to increase it. I keep my books at the British Museum and at Mudie's, and it makes me very angry if any one gives me one for my private library.
Universal Review Dec. 1890, 'Ramblings in Cheapside'

8 Adversity, if a man is set down to it by degrees, is more supportable with equanimity by most people than any great prosperity arrived at in a single lifetime.
Way of All Flesh (1903) ch. 5

9 They would have been equally horrified at hearing the Christian religion doubted, and at seeing it practised.
Way of All Flesh (1903) ch. 15

10 All animals, except man, know that the principal business of life is to enjoy it—and they do enjoy it as much as man and other circumstances will allow.
Way of All Flesh (1903) ch. 19

11 The advantage of doing one's praising for oneself is that one can lay it on so thick and exactly in the right places.
Way of All Flesh (1903) ch. 34

12 Young as he was, his instinct told him that the best liar is he who makes the smallest amount of lying go the longest way.
Way of All Flesh (1903) ch. 39

13 Beyond a haricot vein in one of my legs, I'm as young as ever I was. Old indeed! There's many a good tune played on an old fiddle!
Way of All Flesh (1903) ch. 61

14 'Tis better to have loved and lost than never to have lost at all.
Way of All Flesh (1903) ch. 67. Cf. Tennyson in *Oxford Dictionary of Quotations* (1979) 536:16

Max Bygraves 1922–

See ERIC SYKES and MAX BYGRAVES

James Branch Cabell 1879–1958

15 The optimist proclaims that we live in the best of all possible worlds; and the pessimist fears this is true.
Silver Stallion (1926) bk. 4, ch. 26

Irving Caesar 1895–

16 Picture you upon my knee,
Just tea for two and two for tea.
Tea for Two (1925 song; music by Vincent Youmans)

John Cage 1912–

17 I have nothing to say and I am saying it and that is poetry.
Silence (1961) 'Lecture on nothing'

James Cagney 1899–1986

18 Frank Gorshin—oh, Frankie, just in passing: I never said [in any film] 'Mmm, you dirty rat!' What I actually did say was 'Judy! Judy! Judy!'
Speech at American Film Institute banquet, 13 Mar. 1974, in *Cagney by Cagney* (1976) ch. 14

Sammy Cahn (Samuel Cohen) 1913–

19 Love and marriage, love and marriage,

Go together like a horse and carriage,
This I tell ya, brother,
Ya can't have one without the other.
Love and Marriage (1955 song; music by
James Van Heusen)

1 It's that second time you hear your love
song sung,
Makes you think perhaps, that
Love like youth is wasted on the young.
The Second Time Around (1960 song; music
by James Van Heusen)

James M. Cain 1892–1977

2 The postman always rings twice.
Title of novel (1934) and play (1936)

Michael Caine (*Maurice Joseph Micklewhite*) 1933–

3 Not many people know that.
Title of book (1984)

Sir Joseph Cairns 1920–

4 The betrayal of Ulster, the cynical and
entirely undemocratic banishment of its
properly elected Parliament and
a relegation to the status of a fuzzy
wuzzy colony is, I hope, a last betrayal
contemplated by Downing Street because
it is the last that Ulster will
countenance.
Speech on retiring as Lord Mayor of Belfast,
31 May 1972, in *Daily Telegraph* 1 June
1972

Charles Calhoun 1897–1972

5 Shake, rattle and roll.
Title of song (1954)

James Callaghan (*Leonard James Callaghan, Baron Callaghan of Cardiff*) 1912–

6 We say that what Britain needs is a new
social contract. That is what this
document [*Labour's Programme for
Britain*] is about.
Speech at Labour Party Annual Conference,
2 Oct. 1972, in *Conference Report* (1972)
p. 115

7 I don't think other people in the world
would share the view there is mounting
chaos.
In interview at London Airport, 10 Jan.
1979, in the *Sun* 11 Jan. 1979; the *Sun*
headlined its report: 'Crisis? What Crisis?'

Joseph Campbell (*Seosamh MacCathmhaoil*) 1879–1944

8 As a white candle
In a holy place,
So is the beauty
Of an agéd face.
Irishry (1913) 'Old Woman'

Mrs Patrick Campbell (*Beatrice Stella Campbell*) 1865–1940

9 Oh dear me—its too late to do anything
but *accept* you and *love* you—but when
you were quite a little boy somebody
ought to have said 'hush' just once!
Letter to G. B. Shaw, 1 Nov. 1912, cited in
Alan Dent *Bernard Shaw and Mrs Patrick
Campbell* (1952) p. 52

10 A popular anecdote describes a well
known actor-manager [Sir Herbert
Beerbohm Tree] as saying one day at
rehearsal to an actress of distinguished
beauty [Mrs Patrick Campbell], 'Let us
give Shaw a beefsteak and put some red
blood into him.' 'For heaven's sake,
don't,' she exclaimed: 'he is bad enough
as it is; but if you give him meat no
woman in London will be safe.'
G. B. Shaw in Frank Harris *Contemporary
Portraits* (1919) p. 331

11 It doesn't matter what you do in the
bedroom as long as you don't do it in
the street and frighten the horses.
In Daphne Fielding *Duchess of Jermyn Street*
(1964) ch. 2

12 Tallulah [Bankhead] is always skating
on thin ice. Everyone wants to be there
when it breaks.
In *The Times* 13 Dec. 1968

13 It was Mrs Campbell, for instance, who,
on a celebrated occasion, threw her
companion into a flurry by describing her recent marriage as 'the deep,
deep peace of the
double-bed after the hurly-burly of the
chaise-longue.'
Alexander Woollcott *While Rome Burns*
(1934) 'The First Mrs Tanqueray'

Roy Campbell 1901–1957

1 Of all the clever people round me here
I most delight in Me—
Mine is the only voice I care to hear,
And mine the only face I like to see.
   Adamastor (1930) 'Home Thoughts in
   Bloomsbury'

2 You praise the firm restraint with which
   they write—
I'm with you there, of course:
They use the snaffle and the curb all
   right,
But where's the bloody horse?
   Adamastor (1930) 'On Some South African
   Novelists'

3 I hate 'Humanity' and all such
abstracts: but I love *people*. Lovers of
'Humanity' generally hate *people and
children,* and keep parrots or puppy dogs.
   Light on a Dark Horse (1951) ch. 13

4 Translations (like wives) are seldom
strictly faithful if they are in the least
attractive.
   Poetry Review June–July 1949

5 Giraffes!—a People
Who live between the earth and skies,
Each in his lone religious steeple,
Keeping a light-house with his eyes.
   Talking Bronco (1946) 'Dreaming Spires'

6 South Africa, renowned both far and
   wide
For politics and little else beside.
   The Wayzgoose (1928) p. 7

Sir Henry Campbell-Bannerman
1836–1908

7 There is a phrase which seems in itself
somewhat self-evident, which is often
used to account for a good deal—that
'war is war'. But when you come to ask
about it, then you are told that the war
now going on is not war. [Laughter]
When is a war not a war? When it is
carried on by methods of barbarism in
South Africa.
   Speech to National Reform Union, 14 June
   1901, in *Daily News* 15 June 1901

8 Good government could never be
a substitute for government by the
people themselves.
   Speech at Stirling, 23 Nov. 1905, in *Daily
   News* 24 Nov. 1905

Albert Camus 1913–1960

9 *Intellectuel = celui qui se dédouble.*

An intellectual is someone whose mind
watches itself.
   Carnets, 1935–42 (Notebooks, 1962) p. 41

10 *La politique et le sort des hommes sont
formés par des hommes sans idéal et sans
grandeur. Ceux qui ont une grandeur en
eux ne font pas de politique.*

Politics and the fate of mankind are
formed by men without ideals and
without greatness. Those who have
greatness within them do not go in for
politics.
   Carnets, 1935–42 (Notebooks, 1962) p. 99

11 *Vous savez ce qu'est le charme: une
manière de s'entendre répondre oui sans
avoir posé aucune question claire.*

You know what charm is: a way of
getting the answer yes without having
asked any clear question.
   La Chute (The Fall, 1956) p. 62

12 *Nous sommes tous des cas exceptionnels.
Nous voulons tous faire appel de quelque
chose! Chacun exige d'être innocent, à tout
prix, même si, pour cela, il faut accuser le
genre humain et le ciel.*

We are all special cases. We all want to
appeal against something! Everyone
insists on his innocence, at all costs,
even if it means accusing the rest of the
human race and heaven.
   La Chute (The Fall, 1956) p. 95

13 *C'est si vrai que nous nous confions
rarement à ceux qui sont meilleurs que
nous.*

It is very true that we seldom confide in
those who are better than ourselves.
   La Chute (The Fall, 1956) p. 97

14 *Je vais vous dire un grand secret, mon cher.
N'attendez pas le jugement dernier. Il a lieu
tous les jours.*

I'll tell you a great secret, my friend.
Don't wait for the last judgement. It
happens every day.
   La Chute (The Fall, 1956) p. 129

15 *Aujourd'hui, maman est morte. Ou
peut-être hier, je ne sais pas.*

Mother died today. Or perhaps it was yesterday, I don't know.
L'Étranger (The Outsider, 1944) p. 9

1 *Qu'est-ce qu'un homme révolté ? Un homme qui dit non.*

What is a rebel? A man who says no.
L'Homme révolté (The Rebel, 1951) p. 25

2 *Toutes les révolutions modernes ont abouti à un renforcement de l'État.*

All modern revolutions have ended in a reinforcement of the State.
L'Homme révolté (The Rebel, 1951) p. 221

3 *Tout révolutionnaire finit en oppresseur ou en hérétique.*

Every revolutionary ends as an oppressor or a heretic.
L'Homme révolté (The Rebel, 1951) p. 306

4 *La lutte elle-même vers les sommets suffit à remplir un cœur d'homme. Il faut imaginer Sisyphe heureux.*

The struggle itself towards the heights is enough to fill a human heart. One must imagine that Sisyphus is happy.
Le Mythe de Sisyphe (The Myth of Sisyphus, 1942) p. 168

Elias Canetti 1905–

5 *Alles was man vergessen hat, schreit im Traum um Hilfe.*

All the things one has forgotten scream for help in dreams.
Die Provinz der Menschen (The Human Province, 1973) p. 269

Hughie Cannon 1877–1912

6 Won't you come home Bill Bailey, won't you come home?
Bill Bailey, Won't You Please Come Home (1902 song)

John R. Caples 1900–

7 They laughed when I sat down at the piano. But when I started to play!
Advertisement for US School of Music, in *Physical Culture* Dec. 1925, p. 95

Al Capone 1899–1947

8 Don't you get the idea I'm one of these goddam radicals. Don't get the idea I'm knocking the American system.
Interview, c.1929, in Claud Cockburn *In Time of Trouble* (1956) ch. 16

9 Once in the racket you're always in it.
Philadelphia Public Ledger 18 May 1929

Truman Capote 1924–1984

10 Mr Capote . . . commented on the difficulty he had reading the Beat novels. He had tried but he had been unable to finish any one of them. . . . 'None of these people have anything interesting to say,' he observed, 'and none of them can write, not even Mr Kerouac.' What they do, he added, 'isn't writing at all—it's typing.'
Report of television discussion, in *New Republic* 9 Feb. 1959

11 Venice is like eating an entire box of chocolate liqueurs in one go.
In *Observer* 26 Nov. 1961

12 Other voices, other rooms.
Title of novel (1948)

Al Capp 1909–1979

13 [Abstract art is] a product of the untalented, sold by the unprincipled to the utterly bewildered.
In *National Observer* 1 July 1963

Ethna Carbery (Anna MacManus) 1866–1902

14 Oh, Kathaleen Ní Houlihan, your road's a thorny way,
And 'tis a faithful soul would walk the flints with you for aye,
Would walk the sharp and cruel flints until his locks grew grey.
Four Winds Of Eirinn (1902) 'Passing of the Gael'

Hoagy Carmichael (Hoagland Howard Carmichael) 1899–1981

See STUART GORRELL

Stokely Carmichael 1941– and Charles Vernon Hamilton 1929–

15 The adoption of the concept of Black Power is one of the most legitimate and healthy developments in American politics and race relations in our time. . . . It is a call for black people in this country to unite, to recognize their heritage, to build a sense of

community. It is a call for black people
to begin to define their own goals, to
lead their own organizations and to
support those organizations. It is a call
to reject the racist institutions and
values of this society.

Black Power (1967) ch. 2

Dale Carnegie 1888–1955

1 How to win friends and influence people.
Title of book (1936)

J. L. Carr

2 'I've never been spoken to like this
before in all my thirty years'
experience,' she wails. '*You* have not
had thirty years' experience, Mrs
Grindle-Jones,' he says witheringly. '*You*
have had one year's experience 30
times.'

Harpole Report (1972) p. 128

Edward Carson (Baron Carson)
1854–1935

3 My only great qualification for being put
at the head of the Navy is that I am very
much at sea.
In Ian Colvin *Life of Lord Carson* (1936)
vol. 3, ch. 23

Jimmy Carter 1924–

4 We should live our lives as though
Christ were coming this afternoon.
Speech to Bible class at Plains, Georgia,
March 1976, in *Boston Sunday Herald
Advertiser* 11 Apr. 1976

5 I'm Jimmy Carter, and I'm going to be
your next president.
Said to the son of a campaign supporter,
Nov. 1975, in *I'll Never Lie to You* (1976)
ch. 1

6 I've looked on a lot of women with lust.
I've committed adultery in my heart
many times. This is something that God
recognizes I will do—and I have done
it—and God forgives me for it.
Playboy Nov. 1976

Sydney Carter 1915–

7 I danced in the morning
When the world was begun
And I danced in the moon
And the stars and the sun
And I came down from heaven

And I danced on the earth—
At Bethlehem I had my birth.
Dance then wherever you may be,
I am the Lord of the Dance, said he,
And I'll lead you all, wherever you may
be
And I'll lead you all in the dance, said
he.
Nine Carols or Ballads (1967) 'Lord of the
Dance'

8 It's God they ought to crucify
Instead of you and me,
I said to the carpenter
A-hanging on the tree.
Nine Carols or Ballads (1967) 'Friday
Morning'

Pablo Casals 1876–1973

9 It [the cello] is like a beautiful woman
who has not grown older, but younger
with time, more slender, more supple,
more graceful.
In *Time* 29 Apr. 1957

Ted Castle (Baron Castle of Islington) 1907–1979

10 In place of strife.
Title of Labour Government's White Paper,
17 Jan. 1969, suggested by Castle to his
wife, Barbara Castle (Secretary of State for
Employment): see Barbara Castle *Diaries*
(1984) 15 Jan. 1969

Harry Castling and C. W. Murphy

11 Let's all go down the Strand!
Let's all go down the Strand!
I'll be leader, you can march behind
Come with me, and see what we can
find
Let's all go down the Strand!
Let's All Go Down the Strand! (1909 song)

Fidel Castro 1926–

12 *La historia me absolverá.*
History will absolve me.
Title of pamphlet (1953)

Willa Cather 1873–1947

13 Religion and art spring from the same
root and are close kin. Economics and
art are strangers.
Commonweal 17 Apr. 1936

1 The history of every country begins in the heart of a man or a woman.
   O Pioneers! (1913) pt. 1, ch. 5

2 I like trees because they seem more resigned to the way they have to live than other things do.
   O Pioneers! (1913) pt. 2, ch. 8

Mr Justice Caulfield (Sir Bernard Caulfield) 1914–

3 Remember Mary Archer in the witness box. Your vision of her will probably never disappear. Has she elegance? Has she fragrance? Would she have— without the strain of this trial— a radiance?
   Summing up of court case between Jeffrey Archer and the *News of the World,* July 1987, in *The Times* 24 July 1987

Charles Causley 1917–

4 O are you the boy
   Who would wait on the quay
   With the silver penny
   And the apricot tree?
   Farewell, Aggie Weston (1951) 'Nursery Rhyme of Innocence and Experience'

5 Timothy Winters comes to school
   With eyes as wide as a football-pool,
   Ears like bombs and teeth like splinters:
   A blitz of a boy is Timothy Winters.
   Union Street (1957) 'Timothy Winters'

Constantine Cavafy 1863–1933

6 Τί περιμένουμε στῆν ἀγορά συναθροισμένοι;
   Εἶναι οἱ βάρβαροι νά φθάσουν σήμερα.

   What are we all waiting for, gathered together like this on the public square?
   The Barbarians are coming today.
   Περιμενοντας τους βαρβαρους (Waiting for the Barbarians, 1904) in *Poems* (1963)

7 Καινούριους τόπους δὲν θὰ βρεῖς, δὲν θάβρεις ἄλλες θάλασσες,
   Ἡ πόλις θὰ σὲ ἀκολουθεῖ.

   You will find no new places, no other seas,
   The town will follow you.
   Ποημata (Poems, 1911) 'Ἡ Πόλις ('The Town')

Edith Cavell 1865–1915

8 They have all been very kind to me here. But this I would say, standing, as I do, in view of God and eternity, I realize that patriotism is not enough. I must have no hatred or bitterness towards anyone.
   Words spoken in prison the night before her execution, in *The Times* 23 Oct. 1915

Lord David Cecil 1902–1986

9 The primary object of a student of literature is to be delighted. His duty is to enjoy himself: his efforts should be directed to developing his faculty of appreciation.
   Reading as one of the Fine Arts (1949) p. 4

Patrick Reginald Chalmers 1872–1942

10 What's lost upon the roundabouts we pulls up on the swings!
   Green Days and Blue Days (1912) 'Roundabouts and Swings'

Joseph Chamberlain 1836–1914

11 In politics, there is no use looking beyond the next fortnight.
   In letter from A. J. Balfour to 3rd Marquess of Salisbury, 24 Mar. 1886, in A. J. Balfour *Chapters of Autobiography* (1930) ch. 16

12 It is said that the City is the centre of the world's finance, that the fate of our manufactures therefore is a secondary consideration; that, provided that the City of London remains, as it is at present, the clearing-house of the world, any other nation may be its workshop. Now I ask you, gentlemen, whether ... that is not a very short-sighted view.
   Speech at the Guildhall, 19 Jan. 1904, in *The Times* 20 Jan. 1904

13 In the great revolution which separated the United States from Great Britain the greatest man that that revolution produced ... was Alexander Hamilton ... he left a precious legacy to his countrymen when he disclosed to them the secrets of union and when he said to them, 'Learn to think continentally.' And, my fellow-citizens, if I may venture

to give you a message, now I would say to you, 'Learn to think Imperially.'

Speech at the Guildhall, 19 Jan. 1904, in *The Times* 20 Jan. 1904

1 The day of small nations has long passed away. The day of Empires has come.

Speech at Birmingham, 12 May 1904, in *The Times* 13 May 1904

2 We are not downhearted. The only trouble is we cannot understand what is happening to our neighbours.

Speech at Smethwick, 18 Jan. 1906, in *The Times* 19 Jan. 1906

Neville Chamberlain 1869–1940

3 In war, whichever side may call itself the victor, there are no winners, but all are losers.

Speech at Kettering, 3 July 1938, in *The Times* 4 July 1938

4 How horrible, fantastic, incredible it is that we should be digging trenches and trying on gas-masks here because of a quarrel in a far away country [Czechoslovakia] between people of whom we know nothing.

Broadcast speech, 27 Sept. 1938, in *The Times* 28 Sept. 1938

5 This morning I had another talk with the German Chancellor, Herr Hitler, and here is the paper which bears his name upon it as well as mine. . . . 'We regard the agreement signed last night and the Anglo-German Naval Agreement, as symbolic of the desire of our two peoples never to go to war with one another again.'

Speech at Heston Airport, 30 Sept. 1938, in *The Times* 1 Oct. 1938

6 My good friends, this is the second time in our history that there has come back from Germany to Downing Street peace with honour. I believe it is peace for our time. We thank you from the bottom of our hearts. And now I recommend you to go home and sleep quietly in your beds.

Speech from window of 10 Downing Street, 30 Sept. 1938, in *The Times* 1 Oct. 1938

7 This morning, the British Ambassador in Berlin handed the German government a final Note stating that, unless we heard from them by eleven o'clock that they were prepared at once to withdraw their troops from Poland, a state of war would exist between us. I have to tell you now that no such undertaking has been received, and that consequently this country is at war with Germany.

Radio broadcast, 3 Sept. 1939, in *The Times* 4 Sept. 1939

8 Whatever may be the reason—whether it was that Hitler thought he might get away with what he had got without fighting for it, or whether it was that after all the preparations were not sufficiently complete—however, one thing is certain—he missed the bus.

Speech at Central Hall, Westminster, 4 Apr. 1940, in *The Times* 5 Apr. 1940

Harry Champion 1866–1942

See CHARLES COLLINS, E. A. SHEPPARD, and FRED TERRY

Raymond Chandler 1888–1959

9 Down these mean streets a man must go who is not himself mean, who is neither tarnished nor afraid.

Atlantic Monthly Dec. 1944 'The Simple Art of Murder'

10 It was about eleven o'clock in the morning, mid October, with the sun not shining and a look of hard wet rain in the clearness of the foothills. I was wearing my powder-blue suit, with dark blue shirt, tie and display handkerchief, black brogues, black wool socks with dark blue clocks on them. I was neat, clean, shaved and sober, and I didn't care who knew it.

The Big Sleep (1939) ch. 1

11 It was a blonde. A blonde to make a bishop kick a hole in a stained glass window.

Farewell, My Lovely (1940) ch. 13

12 Would you convey my compliments to the purist who reads your proofs and tell him or her that I write in a sort of broken-down patois which is something like the way a Swiss waiter talks, and that when I split an infinitive, God damn it, I split it so it will stay split.

Letter to Edward Weeks, 18 Jan. 1947, in F. MacShane *Life of Raymond Chandler* (1976) ch. 7

1 A big hard-boiled city with no more
personality than a paper cup.
  The Little Sister (1949) ch. 26 (of Los
  Angeles)

2 If my books had been any worse,
I should not have been invited to
Hollywood, and if they had been any
better, I should not have come.
  Letter to Charles W. Morton, 12 Dec. 1945,
  in Dorothy Gardiner and Katherine S.
  Walker *Raymond Chandler Speaking* (1962)
  p. 126

Coco Chanel 1883–1971

3 Youth is something very new: twenty
years ago no one mentioned it.
  In Marcel Haedrich *Coco Chanel, Her Life,
  Her Secrets* (1971) ch. 1

Charlie Chaplin (Sir Charles Spencer Chaplin) 1889–1977

4 All I need to make a comedy is a park,
a policeman and a pretty girl.
  My Autobiography (1964) ch. 10

Arthur Chapman 1873–1935

5 Out where the handclasp's a little
    stronger,
Out where the smile dwells a little
    longer,
That's where the West begins.
  Out Where the West Begins (1916) p. 1

Graham Chapman 1941–89, John Cleese 1939– , Terry Gilliam 1940– , Eric Idle 1943– , Terry Jones 1942– , and Michael Palin 1943–

6 I'm a lumberjack
And I'm OK
I sleep all night
And I work all day.
  Monty Python's Big Red Book (1971)

7 And now for something completely
different.
  Catch-phrase popularized in *Monty Python's
  Flying Circus* (BBC TV programme,
  1969–74)

8 Your wife interested in . . . *photographs*?
Eh? Know what I mean—*photographs*?

He asked him knowingly . . . nudge
nudge, snap snap, grin grin, wink wink,
say no more.
  Monty Python's Flying Circus (BBC TV
  programme, 1969), in Roger Wilmut *From
  Fringe to Flying Circus* (1980) ch. 11

9 CUSTOMER: I wish to complain about
this parrot what I purchased not half
an hour ago from this very boutique.
SHOPKEEPER: Oh yes, the Norwegian
Blue—what's wrong with it?
CUSTOMER: I'll tell you what's wrong
with it—it's dead that's what's wrong
with it.
SHOPKEEPER: No, no—it's resting. . . .
It's probably pining for the fiords. . . .
CUSTOMER: It's not pining—it's passed
on! This parrot is no more! It has
ceased to be! It's expired and gone to
meet its maker! This is a late parrot!
It's a stiff! Bereft of life it rests in
peace—if you hadn't nailed it to the
perch it would be pushing up the
daisies! It's rung down the curtain
and joined the choir invisible! THIS IS
AN EX–PARROT!
  Monty Python's Flying Circus (BBC TV
  programme, 1969), in Roger Wilmut *From
  Fringe to Flying Circus* (1980) ch. 11

10 Nobody expects the Spanish Inquisition!
Our chief weapon is surprise—surprise
and fear . . . fear and surprise . . . our
two weapons are fear and surprise—and
ruthless efficiency . . . our *three* weapons
are fear and surprise and ruthless
efficiency and an almost fanatical
devotion to the Pope . . . our *four* . . . no.
. . . *Amongst* our weapons—amongst our
weaponry—are such elements as fear,
surprise. . . . I'll come in again.
  Monty Python's Flying Circus (BBC TV
  programme, 1970), in Roger Wilmut *From
  Fringe to Flying Circus* (1980) ch. 11

Prince Charles (Charles Philip Arthur George, Prince of Wales) 1948–

11 I have not the slightest hesitation in
making the observation that much of
British management doesn't seem to
understand the importance of the
human factor.
  Speech to Parliamentary and Scientific
  Committee, 21 Feb. 1979, in *Daily Telegraph*
  22 Feb. 1979

1 I just come and talk to the plants, really—very important to talk to them, they respond I find.
  Television interview, 21 Sept. 1986, in *Daily Telegraph* 22 Sept. 1986

2 We do need a sense of urgency in our outlook in the regeneration of industry and enterprise, because otherwise what really worries me is that we are going to end up as a fourth-rate country and I don't want to see that.
  Speech at Edinburgh, 26 Nov. 1985, in *Scotsman* 27 Nov. 1985

3 Instead of designing an extension to the elegant façade of the National Gallery which complements it . . . it looks as if we may be presented with a kind of vast municipal fire station. . . . I would understand better this type of high-tech approach if you demolished the whole of Trafalgar Square and started again . . . but what is proposed is like a monstrous carbuncle on the face of a much-loved and elegant friend.
  Speech to Royal Institute of British Architects, 30 May 1984, in *The Times* 31 May 1984. Cf. Countess Spencer

Apsley Cherry-Garrard 1882–1959
See E. L. ATKINSON

G. K. Chesterton 1874–1936

4 An adventure is only an inconvenience rightly considered. An inconvenience is only an adventure wrongly considered.
  All Things Considered (1908) 'On Running after one's Hat'

5 No animal ever invented anything so bad as drunkenness—or so good as drink.
  All Things Considered (1908) 'Wine When it is Red'

6 Of those days the tale is told that I once sent a telegram to my wife in London, which ran: 'Am in Market Harborough. Where ought I to be?' I cannot remember whether this story is true; but it is not unlikely, or, I think, unreasonable.
  Autobiography (1936) ch. 16

7 They died to save their country and they only saved the world.
  Ballad of St Barbara and Other Verses (1922) 'English Graves'

8 Before the gods that made the gods
  Had seen their sunrise pass,
  The White Horse of the White Horse Vale
  Was cut out of the grass.
  Ballad of the White Horse (1911) bk. 1, p. 1

9 I tell you naught for your comfort,
  Yea, naught for your desire,
  Save that the sky grows darker yet
  And the sea rises higher.
  Ballad of the White Horse (1911) bk. 1, p. 18

10 For the great Gaels of Ireland
  Are the men that God made mad,
  For all their wars are merry,
  And all their songs are sad.
  Ballad of the White Horse (1911) bk. 2, p. 35

11 The thing on the blind side of the heart,
  On the wrong side of the door,
  The green plant groweth, menacing
  Almighty lovers in the Spring;
  There is always a forgotten thing,
  And love is not secure.
  Ballad of the White Horse (1911) bk. 3, p. 52

12 Literature is a luxury; fiction is a necessity.
  Defendant (1901) 'Defence of Penny Dreadfuls'

13 All slang is metaphor, and all metaphor is poetry.
  Defendant (1901) 'Defence of Slang'

14 'My country, right or wrong', is a thing that no patriot would think of saying except in a desperate case. It is like saying, 'My mother, drunk or sober'.
  Defendant (1901) 'Defence of Patriotism'

15 And Noah he often said to his wife when he sat down to dine,
  'I don't care where the water goes if it doesn't get into the wine.'
  Flying Inn (1914) ch. 5 'Wine and Water'

16 God made the wicked Grocer
  For a mystery and a sign,
  That men might shun the awful shops
  And go to inns to dine.
  Flying Inn (1914) ch. 6 'Song against Grocers'

17 He keeps a lady in a cage
  Most cruelly all day,
  And makes her count and calls her 'Miss'
  Until she fades away.
  Flying Inn (1914) ch. 6 'Song against Grocers'

18 The folk that live in Liverpool, their heart is in their boots;
  They go to hell like lambs, they do, because the hooter hoots.
  Flying Inn (1914) ch. 7 'Me Heart'

1 They haven't got no noses,
  The fallen sons of Eve.
  Flying Inn (1914) ch. 15 'Song of Quoodle'

2 And goodness only knowses
  The Noselessness of Man.
  Flying Inn (1914) ch. 15 'Song of Quoodle'

3 The rich are the scum of the earth in
  every country.
  Flying Inn (1914) ch. 15

4 Tea, although an Oriental,
  Is a gentleman at least;
  Cocoa is a cad and coward,
  Cocoa is a vulgar beast.
  Flying Inn (1914) ch. 18 'Song of Right and
  Wrong'

5 Before the Roman came to Rye or out to
  Severn strode,
  The rolling English drunkard made the
  rolling English road.
  A reeling road, a rolling road, that
  rambles round the shire,
  And after him the parson ran, the sexton
  and the squire;
  A merry road, a mazy road, and such as
  we did tread
  The night we went to Birmingham by
  way of Beachy Head.
  Flying Inn (1914) ch. 21 'Rolling English
  Road'

6 For there is good news yet to hear and
  fine things to be seen,
  Before we go to Paradise by way of Kensal
  Green.
  Flying Inn (1914) ch. 21 'Rolling English
  Road'

7 Ten thousand women marched through
  the streets of London [in support of
  women's suffrage] saying: 'We
  will not be dictated to,' and then went off
  to become stenographers.
  In M. Ffinch *G. K. Chesterton* (1986) ch. 11

8 The word 'orthodoxy' not only no longer
  means being right; it practically means
  being wrong.
  Heretics (1905) ch. 1

9 There is no such thing on earth as an
  uninteresting subject; the only thing that
  can exist is an uninterested person.
  Heretics (1905) ch. 3

10 The artistic temperament is a disease that
   afflicts amateurs. It is a disease which
   arises from men not having sufficient

power of expression to utter and get rid of
the element of art in their being.
Heretics (1905) ch. 17

11 Bigotry may be roughly defined as the
   anger of men who have no opinions.
   Heretics (1905) ch. 20

12 After the first silence the small man said
   to the other: 'Where does a wise man hide
   a pebble?'
   And the tall man answered in a low
   voice: 'On the beach.'
   The small man nodded, and after a short
   silence said: 'Where does a wise man hide
   a leaf?'
   And the other answered: 'In the forest.'
   Innocence of Father Brown (1911) 'The Sign of
   the Broken Sword'

13 Thieves respect property. They merely
   wish the property to become their
   property that they may more perfectly
   respect it.
   Man who was Thursday (1908) ch. 4

14 The human race, to which so many of my
   readers belong, has been playing at
   children's games from the beginning, and
   will probably do it till the end, which is
   a nuisance for the few people who grow
   up.
   Napoleon of Notting Hill (1904) bk. 1, ch. 1

15 Why do you rush through the fields in
   trains,
   Guessing so much and so much.
   Why do you flash through the flowery
   meads,
   Fat-head poet that nobody reads;
   And why do you know such a frightful lot
   About people in gloves and such?
   New Poems (1933) 'The Fat White Woman
   Speaks' (an answer to Frances Cornford, see
   61:8)

16 Democracy means government by the
   uneducated, while aristocracy means
   government by the badly educated.
   New York Times 1 Feb. 1931, pt. 5, p. 1

17 The men who really believe in themselves
   are all in lunatic asylums.
   Orthodoxy (1908) ch. 2

18 Poets do not go mad; but chess-players
   do. Mathematicians go mad, and cashiers;
   but creative artists very seldom. I am not,
   as will be seen, in any sense attacking
   logic: I only say that this danger does lie
   in logic, not in imagination.
   Orthodoxy (1908) ch. 2

1 Mr Shaw is (I suspect) the only man on
earth who has never written any poetry.
  Orthodoxy (1908) ch. 3

2 Tradition may be defined as an extension
of the franchise. Tradition means giving
votes to the most obscure of all classes,
our ancestors. It is the democracy
of the dead. Tradition refuses to submit to
the small and arrogant oligarchy of those
who merely happen to be walking about.
All democrats object to men being
disqualified by the accident of birth;
tradition objects to their being disqualified
by the accident of death. Democracy tells
us not to neglect a good man's opinion,
even if he is our groom; tradition asks us
not to neglect a good man's opinion, even
if he is our father.
  Orthodoxy (1908) ch. 4

3 All conservatism is based upon the idea
that if you leave things alone you leave
them as they are. But you do not. If you
leave a thing alone you leave it to
a torrent of change.
  Orthodoxy (1908) ch. 7

4 Angels can fly because they take
themselves lightly.
  Orthodoxy (1908) ch. 7

5 White founts falling in the Courts of the
  sun,
And the Soldan of Byzantium is smiling as
  they run.
  Poems (1915) 'Lepanto'

6 Strong gongs groaning as the guns boom
  far,
Don John of Austria is going to the war,
Stiff flags straining in the night-blasts cold
In the gloom black-purple, in the glint
  old-gold,
Torchlight crimson on the copper
  kettle-drums,
Then the tuckets, then the trumpets, then
  the cannon, and he comes.
  Poems (1915) 'Lepanto'

7 From all that terror teaches,
From lies of tongue and pen,
From all the easy speeches
That comfort cruel men,
From sale and profanation
Of honour and the sword,
From sleep and from damnation,
Deliver us, good Lord!
  Poems (1915) 'A Hymn'

8 Are they clinging to their crosses, F. E.
  Smith?
  Poems (1915) 'Antichrist'

9 Talk about the pews and steeples
And the Cash that goes therewith!
But the souls of Christian peoples . . .
Chuck it, Smith!
  Poems (1915) 'Antichrist'

10 The souls most fed with Shakespeare's
  flame
Still sat unconquered in a ring,
Remembering him like anything.
  Poems (1915) 'Shakespeare Memorial'

11 John Grubby, who was short and stout
And troubled with religious doubt,
Refused about the age of three
To sit upon the curate's knee.
  Poems (1915) 'New Freethinker'

12 And I dream of the days when work was
  scrappy,
And rare in our pockets the mark of the
  mint,
When we were angry and poor and
  happy,
And proud of seeing our names in print.
  Poems (1915) 'Song of Defeat'

13 Smile at us, pay us, pass us; but do not
  quite forget.
For we are the people of England, that
  never have spoken yet.
  Poems (1915) 'The Secret People'

14 We only know the last sad squires ride
  slowly towards the sea,
And a new people takes the land: and still
  it is not we.
  Poems (1915) 'The Secret People'

15 They spoke of Progress spiring round,
Of Light and Mrs Humphry Ward—
It is not true to say I frowned,
Or ran about the room and roared;
I might have simply sat and snored—
I rose politely in the club
And said,'I feel a little bored.
Will someone take me to a pub?'
  Poems (1915) 'Ballade of an Anti-Puritan'

16 The gallows in my garden, people say,
Is new and neat and adequately tall.
I tie the noose on in a knowing way
As one that knots his necktie for a ball;
But just as all the neighbours—on the
  wall—
Are drawing a long breath to shout
  'Hurray!'

The strangest whim has seized me. . . .
  After all
I think I will not hang myself today.
  Poems (1915) 'Ballade of Suicide'

1 It isn't that they can't see the solution. It
is that they can't see the problem.
  Scandal of Father Brown (1935) 'Point of a Pin'

2 Lying in bed would be an altogether
perfect and supreme experience if only one
had a coloured pencil long enough to
draw on the ceiling.
  Tremendous Trifles (1909) 'On Lying in Bed'

3 Hardy went down to botanize in the
swamp, while Meredith climbed towards
the sun. Meredith became, at his best,
a sort of daintily dressed Walt Whitman:
Hardy became a sort of village atheist
brooding and blaspheming over the village
idiot.
  Victorian Age in Literature (1912) ch. 2

4 He [Tennyson] could not think up to the
height of his own towering style.
  Victorian Age in Literature (1912) ch. 3

5 The Christian ideal has not been tried and
found wanting. It has been found difficult;
and left untried.
  What's Wrong with the World (1910) pt. 1,
  ch. 5

6 She was maintaining the prime truth of
woman, the universal mother: that if
a thing is worth doing, it is worth doing
badly.
  What's Wrong with the World (1910) pt. 4,
  ch. 14

7 When fishes flew and forests walked
And figs grew upon thorn,
Some moment when the moon was blood
Then surely I was born.

With monstrous head and sickening cry
And ears like errant wings,
The devil's walking parody
On all four-footed things.
  Wild Knight and Other Poems (1900) 'The
  Donkey'

8 Fools! For I also had my hour;
One far fierce hour and sweet:
There was a shout about my ears,
And palms before my feet.
  Wild Knight and Other Poems (1900) 'The
  Donkey'

9 But Higgins is a Heathen,
And to lecture rooms is forced,

Where his aunts, who are not married,
Demand to be divorced.
  Wine, Water and Song (1915) 'Song of the
  Strange Ascetic'

10 To be clever enough to get all that
money, one must be stupid enough to
want it.
  Wisdom of Father Brown (1914) 'Paradise of
  Thieves'

11 Journalism largely consists in saying 'Lord
Jones Dead' to people who never knew
that Lord Jones was alive.
  Wisdom of Father Brown (1914) 'The Purple
  Wig'

Maurice Chevalier 1888–1972

12 On his seventy-second birthday in 1960,
he [Chevalier] was asked what he felt
about the advancing years. 'Considering
the alternative,' he said, 'it's not too bad
at all.'
  Michael Freedland *Maurice Chevalier* (1981)
  ch. 20

Erskine Childers 1870–1922

13 The riddle of the sands.
  Title of novel (1903)

14 The [firing] squad took up their positions
across the prison yard. 'Come closer,
boys,' Childers called out to them. 'It will
be easier for you.'
  Burke Wilkinson *Zeal of Convert* (1976) ch. 26

Charles Chilton 1914–

See JOAN LITTLEWOOD

Noam Chomsky 1928–

15 As soon as questions of will or decision or
reason or choice of action arise, human
science is at a loss.
  Television interview, 30 Mar. 1978, in *Listener*
  6 Apr. 1978

16 The notion 'grammatical' cannot be
identified with 'meaningful' or 'significant'
in any semantic sense. Sentences (1) and
(2) are equally nonsensical, but . . . only
the former is grammatical.
  (1) Colourless green ideas sleep
    furiously.
  (2) Furiously sleep ideas green
    colourless.
  Syntactic Structures (1957) ch. 2

Dame Agatha Christie 1890–1976

1 One is left with the horrible feeling now that war settles *nothing*; that to *win* a war is as disastrous as to lose one!
  Autobiography (1977) pt. 10

2 'This affair must all be unravelled from within.' He [Hercule Poirot] tapped his forehead. 'These little grey cells. It is "up to them"—as you say over here.'
  The Mysterious Affair at Styles (1920) ch. 10

3 Trust the train, Mademoiselle, for it is *le bon Dieu* who drives it.
  The Mystery of the Blue Train (1928) ch. 36

Frank E. Churchill 1901–1942

4 Who's afraid of the big bad wolf?
  Title of song (1933; probably written in collaboration with Ann Ronell)

Sir Winston Churchill 1874–1965

5 In defeat unbeatable: in victory unbearable.
  In Edward Marsh *Ambrosia and Small Beer* (1964) ch. 5 (describing Viscount Montgomery)

6 After the war one quip which went the rounds of Westminster was attributed to Churchill himself. 'An empty taxi arrived at 10 Downing Street, and when the door was opened [Clement] Attlee got out.' When [John] Colville repeated this, and its attribution, to Churchill he obviously did not like it. His face set hard, and 'after an awful pause' he said: 'Mr Attlee is an honourable and gallant gentleman, and a faithful colleague who served his country well at the time of her greatest need. I should be obliged if you would make it clear whenever an occasion arises that I would never make such a remark about him, and that I strongly disapprove of anybody who does.'
  Kenneth Harris *Attlee* (1982) ch. 16

7 Always remember, Clemmie, that I have taken more out of alcohol than alcohol has taken out of me.
  In Quentin Reynolds *By Quentin Reynolds* (1964) ch. 11

8 [Clement Attlee is] a modest man who has a good deal to be modest about.
  In *Chicago Sunday Tribune Magazine of Books* 27 June 1954

9 QUESTION: What are the desirable qualifications for any young man who wishes to become a politician?
  MR CHURCHILL: It is the ability to foretell what is going to happen tomorrow, next week, next month, and next year. And to have the ability afterwards to explain why it didn't happen.
  In B. Adler *Churchill Wit* (1965) p. 4

10 The British people have taken for themselves this motto—'Business carried on as usual during alterations on the map of Europe'. They expect the navy, on which they have lavished so much care and expense, to make that good, and that is what, upon the whole, we are actually achieving at the present time.
  Speech at the Guildhall, 9 Nov. 1914, in *Complete Speeches* (1974) vol. 3, p. 2341

11 Here is the answer which I will give to President Roosevelt. . . . We shall not fail or falter; we shall not weaken or tire. Neither the sudden shock of battle nor the long-drawn trials of vigilance and exertion will wear us down. Give us the tools and we will finish the job.
  Speech on radio, 9 Feb. 1941, in *Complete Speeches* (1974) vol. 6, p. 6350

12 The people of London with one voice would say to Hitler: 'You have committed every crime under the sun. . . . We will have no truce or parley with you, or the grisly gang who work your wicked will. You do your worst—and we will do our best.'
  Speech at County Hall, London, 14 July 1941, in *Complete Speeches* (1974) vol. 6, p. 6451

13 Do not let us speak of darker days; let us rather speak of sterner days. These are not dark days: these are great days—the greatest days our country has ever lived; and we must all thank God that we have been allowed, each of us according to our stations, to play a part in making these days memorable in the history of our race.
  Speech at Harrow School, 29 Oct. 1941, in *Complete Speeches* (1974) vol. 6, p. 6500

14 It becomes still more difficult to reconcile Japanese action with prudence or even

with sanity. What kind of a people do they think we are?

Speech to US Congress, 26 Dec. 1941, in *Complete Speeches* (1974) vol. 6, p. 6540

1 When I warned them [the French Government] that Britain would fight on alone whatever they did, their generals told their Prime Minister and his divided Cabinet, 'In three weeks England will have her neck wrung like a chicken.' Some chicken! Some neck!

Speech to Canadian Parliament, 30 Dec. 1941, in *Complete Speeches* (1974) vol. 6, p. 6544

2 There is no finer investment for any community than putting milk into babies. Healthy citizens are the greatest asset any country can have.

Speech on radio, 21 Mar. 1943, in *Complete Speeches* (1974) vol. 7, p. 6761

3 From Stettin in the Baltic to Trieste in the Adriatic an iron curtain has descended across the Continent.

Speech at Westminster College, Fulton, Missouri, 5 Mar. 1946, in *Complete Speeches* (1974) vol. 7, p. 7290

4 Somebody said, 'One never hears of Baldwin nowadays—he might as well be dead.' 'No,' said Winston, 'not dead. But the candle in that great turnip has gone out.'

Harold Nicolson *Diary* 17 Aug. 1950, in *Diaries and Letters* (1968) p. 193

5 Now this is not the end. It is not even the beginning of the end. But it is, perhaps, the end of the beginning.

Speech at the Mansion House, London, 10 Nov. 1942, in *End of the Beginning* (1943) p. 214

6 We mean to hold our own. I have not become the King's First Minister in order to preside over the liquidation of the British Empire.

Speech in London, 10 Nov. 1942, in *End of the Beginning* (1943) p. 215

7 Once he [Churchill] said to me, 'Alfred, if you met Picasso coming down the street, would you join with me in kicking his something something something?' I said, 'Yes, sir, I would.'

Sir Alfred Munnings in speech at Royal Academy, 28 Apr. 1949, in *The Finish* (1952) ch. 22

8 Don't talk to me about naval tradition. It's nothing but rum, sodomy and the lash.

In Sir Peter Gretton *Former Naval Person* (1968) ch. 1

9 A labour contract into which men enter voluntarily for a limited and for a brief period, under which they are paid wages which they consider adequate, under which they are not bought or sold and from which they can obtain relief ... on payment of £17.10s, the cost of their passage, may not be a healthy or proper contract, but it cannot in the opinion of His Majesty's Government be classified as slavery in the extreme acceptance of the word without some risk of terminological inexactitude.

Hansard 22 Feb. 1906, col. 555

10 He [Lord Charles Beresford] is one of those orators of whom it was well said, 'Before they get up, they do not know what they are going to say; when they are speaking, they do not know what they are saying; and when they have sat down, they do not know what they have said.'

Hansard 20 Dec. 1912, col. 1893

11 The whole map of Europe has been changed. The position of countries has been violently altered. The modes of thought of men, the whole outlook on affairs, the grouping of parties, all have encountered violent and tremendous changes in the deluge of the world, but as the deluge subsides and the waters fall short we see the dreary steeples of Fermanagh and Tyrone emerging once again. The integrity of their quarrel is one of the few institutions that has been unaltered in the cataclysm which has swept the world.

Hansard 16 Feb. 1922, col. 1270

12 I decline utterly to be impartial as between the fire brigade and the fire.

Hansard 7 July 1926, col. 2216 (replying to complaints of his bias in editing the *British Gazette* during the General Strike)

13 I remember, when I was a child, being taken to the celebrated Barnum's circus, which contained an exhibition of freaks and monstrosities, but the exhibit on the programme which I most desired to see was the one described as 'The Boneless

Wonder'. My parents judged that that spectacle would be too revolting and demoralizing for my youthful eyes, and I have waited 50 years to see the boneless wonder [Ramsay Macdonald] sitting on the Treasury Bench.

Hansard 28 Jan. 1931, col. 1021

1 So they [the Government] go on in strange paradox, decided only to be undecided, resolved to be irresolute, adamant for drift, solid for fluidity, all-powerful to be impotent.

Hansard 12 Nov. 1936, col. 1107

2 The utmost he [Neville Chamberlain] has been able to gain for Czechoslovakia and in the matters which were in dispute has been that the German dictator, instead of snatching his victuals from the table, has been content to have them served to him course by course.

Hansard 5 Oct. 1938, col. 361

3 I would say to the House, as I said to those who have joined this Government: 'I have nothing to offer but blood, toil, tears and sweat.'

Hansard 13 May 1940, col. 1502

4 You ask, what is our policy? I will say: It is to wage war, by sea, land and air, with all our might and with all the strength that God can give us; to wage war against a monstrous tyranny, never surpassed in the dark, lamentable catalogue of human crime. That is our policy. You ask, what is our aim? I can answer in one word: Victory, victory at all costs, victory in spite of all terror; victory, however long and hard the road may be; for without victory, there is no survival.

Hansard 13 May 1940, col. 1502

5 At this time I feel entitled to claim the aid of all, and I say, 'Come then, let us go forward together with our united strength.'

Hansard 13 May 1940, col. 1502

6 Even though large tracts of Europe and many old and famous States have fallen or may fall into the grip of the Gestapo and all the odious apparatus of Nazi rule, we shall not flag or fail. We shall go on to the end. We shall fight in France, we shall fight on the seas and oceans, we shall fight with growing confidence and growing strength in the air, we shall defend our island, whatever the cost may be. We shall fight on the beaches, we shall fight on the landing grounds, we shall fight in the fields and in the streets, we shall fight in the hills; we shall never surrender, and even if, which I do not for a moment believe, this island or a large part of it were subjugated and starving, then our Empire beyond the seas, armed and guarded by the British Fleet, would carry on the struggle, until, in God's good time, the new world, with all its power and might, steps forth to the rescue and the liberation of the old.

Hansard 4 June 1940, col. 796

7 What General Weygand called the 'Battle of France' is over. I expect that the Battle of Britain is about to begin. Upon this battle depends the survival of Christian civilization. Upon it depends our own British life and the long continuity of our institutions and our Empire. The whole fury and might of the enemy must very soon be turned on us. Hitler knows that he will have to break us in this island or lose the war. If we can stand up to him all Europe may be free and the life of the world may move forward into broad, sunlit uplands; but if we fail then the whole world, including the United States, and all that we have known and cared for, will sink into the abyss of a new dark age made more sinister, and perhaps more prolonged, by the lights of a perverted science. Let us therefore brace ourselves to our duty, and so bear ourselves that, if the British Commonwealth and its Empire lasts for a thousand years, men will still say, 'This was their finest hour.'

Hansard 18 June 1940, col. 60

8 The gratitude of every home in our Island, in our Empire, and indeed throughout the world, except in the abodes of the guilty, goes out to the British airmen who, undaunted by odds, unwearied in their constant challenge and mortal danger, are turning the tide of world war by their prowess and by their devotion. Never in the field of human conflict was so much owed by so many to so few.

Hansard 20 Aug. 1940, col. 1166

1 The British nation is unique in this respect. They are the only people who like to be told how bad things are, who like to be told the worst.
Hansard 10 June 1941, col. 152

2 We make this wide encircling movement in the Mediterranean, having for its primary object the recovery of the command of that vital sea, but also having for its object the exposure of the under-belly of the Axis, especially Italy, to heavy attack.
Hansard 11 Nov. 1942, col. 28 (often misquoted as 'the soft under-belly of the Axis')

3 He [President Roosevelt] devised the extraordinary measure of assistance called Lend-Lease, which will stand forth as the most unselfish and unsordid financial act of any country in all history.
Hansard 17 Apr. 1945, col. 76

4 Unless the right hon. Gentleman [Mr Bevan] changes his policy and methods and moves without the slightest delay, he will be as great a curse to this country in time of peace, as he was a squalid nuisance in time of war.
Hansard 6 Dec. 1945, col. 2544

5 Many forms of Government have been tried, and will be tried in this world of sin and woe. No one pretends that democracy is perfect or all-wise. Indeed, it has been said that democracy is the worst form of Government except all those other forms that have been tried from time to time.
Hansard 11 Nov. 1947, col. 206

6 I cannot forecast to you the action of Russia. It is a riddle wrapped in a mystery inside an enigma: but perhaps there is a key. That key is Russian national interest.
Radio talk, 1 Oct. 1939, in *Into Battle* (1941) p. 131

7 *Nous attendons l'invasion promise de longue date. Les poissons aussi.*

We are waiting for the long-promised invasion. So are the fishes.
Radio broadcast to the French people, 21 Oct. 1940, in *Into Battle* (1941) p. 298

8 Shortly after returning from his tour of the Near East, Anthony Eden submitted a long-winded report to the Prime Minister on his experiences and impressions. Churchill, it is told, returned it to his War Minister with a note saying: 'As far as I can see you have used every cliché except "God is Love" and "Please adjust your dress before leaving".'
Life 9 Dec. 1940 (when this story was repeated in the Daily Mirror, Churchill denied that it was true)

9 I wrote my name at the top of the page. I wrote down the number of the question '1'. After much reflection I put a bracket round it thus '(1)'. But thereafter I could not think of anything connected with it that was either relevant or true. . . . It was from these slender indications of scholarship that Mr Welldon drew the conclusion that I was worthy to pass into Harrow. It is very much to his credit.
My Early Life (1930) ch. 2

10 By being so long in the lowest form [at Harrow] I gained an immense advantage over the cleverer boys. They all went on to learn Latin and Greek. . . . But I was taught English. . . . Thus I got into my bones the essential structure of the ordinary British sentence—which is a noble thing. . . . Naturally I am biased in favour of boys learning English. I would make them all learn English: and then I would let the clever ones learn Latin as an honour, and Greek as a treat.
My Early Life (1930) ch. 2

11 Headmasters have powers at their disposal with which Prime Ministers have never yet been invested.
My Early Life (1930) ch. 2

12 So they told me how Mr Gladstone read Homer for fun, which I thought served him right.
My Early Life (1930) ch. 2

13 It is a good thing for an uneducated man to read books of quotations.
My Early Life (1930) ch. 9

14 To jaw-jaw is always better than to war-war.
Speech at White House, 26 June 1954, in *New York Times* 27 June 1954, p. 1

15 I am prepared to meet my Maker. Whether my Maker is prepared for the

great ordeal of meeting me is another matter.

At news conference in Washington, 1954, in *New York Times* 25 Jan. 1965 (Suppl.) p. 7

1 The empires of the future are the empires of the mind.

Speech at Harvard, 6 Sept. 1943, in *Onwards to Victory* (1944) p. 238

2 It is said that Mr Winston Churchill once made this marginal comment against a sentence that clumsily avoided a prepositional ending: 'This is the sort of English up with which I will not put.'

Ernest Gowers *Plain Words* (1948) ch. 9

3 Moral of the Work. In war: resolution. In defeat: defiance. In victory: magnanimity. In peace: goodwill.

Second World War (1948) vol. 1, epigraph (Sir Edward Marsh in *A Number of People* (1939) p. 152, says that this motto occurred to Churchill shortly after the First World War)

4 One day President Roosevelt told me that he was asking publicly for suggestions about what the war should be called. I said at once 'The Unnecessary War'.

Second World War (1948) vol. 1, p. viii

5 I felt as if I were walking with destiny, and that all my past life had been but a preparation for this hour and this trial. Eleven years in the political wilderness had freed me from ordinary Party antagonisms. My warnings over the last six years had been so numerous, so detailed, and were now so terribly vindicated, that no one could gainsay me. I could not be reproached either for making the war or with want of preparation for it. I thought I knew a good deal about it all, and I was sure I should not fail. Therefore, although impatient for the morning, I slept soundly and had no need for cheering dreams. Facts are better than dreams.

Second World War (1948) vol. 1, p. 526

6 No one can guarantee success in war, but only deserve it.

Letter to Lord Wavell, 26 Nov. 1940, in *Second World War* (1949) vol. 2, ch. 27

7 It may almost be said, 'Before Alamein we never had a victory. After Alamein we never had a defeat.'

Second World War (1951) vol. 4, ch. 33

8 Dictators ride to and fro upon tigers which they dare not dismount. And the tigers are getting hungry.

Letter, 11 Nov. 1937, in *Step by Step* (1939) p. 186. Cf. the proverb 'He who rides a tiger is afraid to dismount' (see *Concise Oxford Dictionary of Proverbs* under *rides*)

9 You must rank me and my colleagues as strong partisans of national compulsory insurance for all classes for all purposes from the cradle to the grave.

Radio broadcast, 21 Mar. 1943, in *The Times* 22 Mar. 1943

10 I have never accepted what many people have kindly said—namely, that I inspired the nation. . . . It was the nation and the race dwelling all round the globe that had the lion's heart. I had the luck to be called upon to give the roar. I also hope that I sometimes suggested to the lion the right place to use his claws.

Speech at Westminster Hall, 30 Nov. 1954, in *The Times* 1 Dec. 1954

11 Mr Attlee, whom Churchill once playfully described as a 'sheep in sheep's clothing'.

Lord Home *Way the Wind Blows* (1976) ch. 6. Cf. Sir Edmund Gosse

12 Take away that pudding—it has no theme.

In Lord Home *Way the Wind Blows* (1976) ch. 16

13 We are all worms. But I do believe that I am a glow-worm.

In Violet Bonham-Carter *Winston Churchill as I Knew Him* (1965) ch. 1

14 Jellicoe was the only man on either side who could lose the war in an afternoon.

World Crisis (1927) pt. 1, ch. 5

Count Galeazzo Ciano 1903–1944

15 *La vittoria trova cento padri, e nessuno vuole riconoscere l'insuccesso.*

Victory has a hundred fathers, but defeat is an orphan.

Diary 9 Sept. 1942 (1946) vol. 2, p. 196

Brian Clark 1932–

16 Whose life is it anyway?

Title of play (1977)

Kenneth Clark (Baron Clark)
1903–1983

1 Perrault's façade [of the Louvre] reflects the triumph of an authoritarian state, and of those logical solutions that Colbert, the great administrator of the seventeenth century, was imposing on politics, economics and every department of contemporary life, including, above all, the arts. This gives French Classical architecture a certain inhumanity. It was the work not of craftsmen, but of wonderfully gifted civil servants.

> *Civilization* (1969) ch. 9

Arthur C. Clarke 1917–

2 If an elderly but distinguished scientist says that something is possible he is almost certainly right, but if he says that it is impossible he is very probably wrong.

> In *New Yorker* 9 Aug. 1969

Grant Clarke 1891–1931 and Edgar Leslie 1885–1976

3 He'd have to get under, get out and get under
And fix up his automobile.

> *He'd Have to Get Under—Get Out and Get Under* (1913 song; music by Maurice Abrahams)

Eldridge Cleaver 1935–

4 What we're saying today is that you're either part of the solution or you're part of the problem.

> Speech in San Francisco, 1968, in R. Scheer *Eldridge Cleaver, Post Prison Writings and Speeches* (1969) p. xxxii

John Cleese 1939–

> See GRAHAM CHAPMAN et al.

John Cleese 1939– and Connie Booth

5 They're Germans. Don't mention the war.

> *Fawlty Towers* 'The Germans' (BBC TV programme, 1975), in *Complete Fawlty Towers* (1988) p. 153

6 So Harry says, 'You don't like me any more. Why not?' And he says, 'Because you've got so terribly pretentious.' And Harry says, 'Pretentious? *Moi?*'

> *Fawlty Towers* 'The Psychiatrist' (BBC TV programme, 1979), in *Complete Fawlty Towers* (1988) p. 190

Sarah Norcliffe Cleghorn
1876–1959

7 The golf-links lie so near the mill
That almost every day
The labouring children can look out
And watch the men at play.

> *New York Tribune* 23 Jan. 1914 'For Some Must Watch, While—'

Georges Clemenceau 1841–1929

8 *La guerre, c'est une chose trop grave pour la confier à des militaires.*

War is too serious a matter to entrust to military men.

> Attributed to Clemenceau e.g. in Hampden Jackson *Clemenceau and the Third Republic* (1946) p. 228, but also attributed to Briand and Talleyrand

9 *Politique intérieure, je fais la guerre; politique extérieure, je fais toujours la guerre. Je fais toujours la guerre.*

My home policy: I wage war; my foreign policy: still I wage war. All the time I wage war.

> Speech to French Chamber of Deputies, 8 Mar. 1918, in *Discours de Guerre* (War Speeches, 1968) p. 172

10 *Il est plus facile de faire la guerre que la paix.*

It is easier to make war than to make peace.

> Speech at Verdun, 20 July 1919, in *Discours de Paix* (Peace Speeches, 1938) p. 122

Harlan Cleveland 1918–

11 In 1950 he [Harlan Cleveland] invented the phrase, so thrashed to death in later years, 'the revolution of rising expectations'.

> Arthur Schlesinger *Thousand Days* (1965) ch. 16

Richard Cobb 1917–

1 In an operation of this kind one would
not go for a Proust or a Joyce—not that
I would know about that, never having
read either.
  Speech at Booker Prize awards in London,
  18 Oct. 1984, in *The Times* 19 Oct. 1984

Claud Cockburn 1904–1981

2 Small earthquake in Chile. Not many
dead.
  In Time of Trouble (1956) ch. 10 (the words
  with which Cockburn claims to have won
  a competition at *The Times* for the dullest
  headline)

Jean Cocteau 1889–1963

3 *Le tact dans l'audace c'est de savoir
jusqu'où on peut aller trop loin.*

  Being tactful in audacity is knowing
  how far one can go too far.
  Le Coq et l'Arlequin (1918) in *Le Rappel à
  l'ordre* (Recall to Order, 1926) p. 2

4 *Le pire drame pour un poète, c'est d'être
admiré par malentendu.*

  The worst tragedy for a poet is to be
  admired through being misunderstood.
  Le Coq et l'Arlequin (1918) in *Le Rappel à
  l'ordre* (Recall to Order, 1926) p. 20

5 *S'il faut choisir un crucifié, la foule sauve
toujours Barabbas.*

  If it has to choose who is to be crucified,
  the crowd will always save Barabbas.
  Le Coq et l'Arlequin (1918) in *Le Rappel à
  l'ordre* (Recall to Order, 1926) p. 39

6 *L'Histoire est un alliage de réel et de
mensonge. Le réel de l'Histoire devient un
mensonge. L'irréel de la fable devient vérité.*

  History is a combination of reality and
  lies. The reality of History becomes a lie.
  The unreality of the fable becomes the
  truth.
  Journal d'un inconnu (Diary of an Unknown
  Man, 1953) p. 143

7 *Vivre est une chute horizontale.*

  Life is a horizontal fall.
  Opium (1930) p. 37

8 *Quand j'ai écrit que Victor Hugo était un
fou qui se croyait Victor Hugo, je ne
plaisantais pas.*

  When I wrote that Victor Hugo was
  a madman who thought he was Victor
  Hugo, I was not joking.
  Opium (1930) p. 77

Lenore Coffee ?1897–1984

9 What a dump!
  Beyond the Forest (1949 film; line spoken by
  Bette Davis, entering a room)

George M. Cohan 1878–1942

10 It was Cohan who first said to
a newspaperman (who wanted some
information about *Broadway Jones* in
1912), 'I don't care what you say about
me, as long as you say *something* about
me, and as long as you spell my name
right.'
  John McCabe *George M. Cohan* (1973) ch. 13

11 Give my regards to Broadway,
Remember me to Herald Square,
Tell all the gang at Forty-Second Street
That I will soon be there.
  Give My Regards to Broadway (1904 song)

12 Over there, over there,
Send the word, send the word over there
That the Yanks are coming, the Yanks
    are coming,
The drums rum-tumming everywhere.
So prepare, say a prayer,
Send the word, send the word to
    beware.
We'll be over, we're coming over
And we won't come back till it's over,
    over there.
  Over There (1917 song)

13 I'm a Yankee Doodle Dandy,
A Yankee Doodle, do or die;
A real live nephew of my Uncle Sam's,
Born on the fourth of July.
I've got a Yankee Doodle sweetheart,
She's my Yankee Doodle joy.
Yankee Doodle came to London,
Just to ride the ponies;
I am the Yankee Doodle Boy.
  Yankee Doodle Boy (1904 song)

Desmond Coke 1879–1931

14 His blade struck the water a full second
before any other: the lad had started
well. Nor did he flag as the race wore
on: as the others tired, he seemed to
grow more fresh, until at length, as the

boats began to near the winning-post,
his oar was dipping into the water
nearly twice as often as any other.
> *Sandford of Merton* (1903) ch. 12 (often
> misquoted as 'All rowed fast, but none so
> fast as stroke')

Colette (Sidonie-Gabrielle Colette) 1873–1954

1 *Il découvrait . . . le monde des émotions
qu'on nomme, à la légère, physiques.*

He was discovering . . . the world of the
emotions that are so lightly called
physical.
> *Le Blé en herbe* (Ripening Seed, 1923) p. 161

2 *Quand elle lève ses paupières, on dirait
qu'elle se déshabille.*

When she raises her eyelids, it is as if
she is undressing.
> *Claudine s'en va* (Claudine Goes Away, 1931)
> p. 59

3 *Ne porte jamais de bijoux artistiques, ça
déconsidère complètement une femme.*

Don't ever wear artistic jewellery; it
wrecks a woman's reputation.
> *Gigi* (1944) p. 40

R. G. Collingwood 1889–1943

4 Perfect freedom is reserved for the man
who lives by his own work and in that
work does what he wants to do.
> *Speculum Mentis* (1924) p. 25

Charles Collins and Fred W. Leigh

5 My old man said, 'Follow the van,
Don't dilly-dally on the way!'
Off went the cart with the home packed
   in it,
I walked behind with my old cock
   linnet.
But I dillied and dallied, dallied and
   dillied,
Lost the van and don't know where to
   roam.
You can't trust the 'specials' like the old
   time 'coppers'
When you can't find your way home.
> *Don't Dilly-Dally on the Way* (1919 song;
> made famous by Marie Lloyd)

Charles Collins and Fred Murray

6 Boiled beef and carrots.
> Title of song (1910; made famous by Harry
> Champion)

Charles Collins, E. A. Sheppard, and Fred Terry

7 Any old iron, any old iron,
Any any old old iron?
You look neat
Talk about a treat,
You look dapper from your napper to
   your feet.
Dressed in style, brand new tile,
And your father's old green tie on,
But I wouldn't give you tuppence for
   your old watch chain;
Old iron, old iron?
> *Any Old Iron* (1911 song; made famous by
> Harry Champion; the second line is often
> sung as 'Any any any old iron?')

John Churton Collins 1848–1908

8 To ask advice is in nine cases out of ten
to tout for flattery.
> In L. C. Collins *Life of John Churton Collins*
> (1912) p. 316

Michael Collins 1890–1922

9 Think—what I have got for Ireland?
Something which she has wanted these
past seven hundred years. Will anyone
be satisfied at the bargain? Will anyone?
I tell you this—early this morning
I signed my death warrant. I thought at
the time how odd, how ridiculous—
a bullet may just as well have done the
job five years ago.
> Letter, 6 Dec. 1921, in T. R. Dwyer *Michael
> Collins and the Treaty* (1981) ch. 4

Betty Comden 1919– and Adolph Green 1915–

10 New York, New York,—a helluva town,
The Bronx is up but the Battery's down,
And people ride in a hole in the ground:
New York, New York,—It's a helluva
   town.
> *New York, New York* (1945 song; music by
> Leonard Bernstein)

11 The party's over.
> Title of song (1956; music by Jule Styne)

Dame Ivy Compton-Burnett
1884–1969

1 'Well, of course, people are only human,' said Dudley to his brother, as they walked to the house behind the women. 'But it really does not seem much for them to be.'
A Family and a Fortune (1939) ch. 2

2 There are different kinds of wrong. The people sinned against are not always the best.
The Mighty and their Fall (1961) ch. 7

3 There is more difference within the sexes than between them.
Mother and Son (1955) ch. 10

4 As regards plots I find real life no help at all. Real life seems to have no plots.
In R. Lehmann et al. *Orion I* (1945) p. 25

Billy Connolly 1942–

5 Marriage is a wonderful invention; but, then again, so is a bicycle repair kit.
In Duncan Campbell *Billy Connolly* (1976) p. 92

Cyril Connolly 1903–1974

6 Literature is the art of writing something that will be read twice; journalism what will be read once.
Enemies of Promise (1938) ch. 3

7 As repressed sadists are supposed to become policemen or butchers, so those with an irrational fear of life become publishers.
Enemies of Promise (1938) ch. 10

8 Whom the gods wish to destroy they first call promising.
Enemies of Promise (1938) ch. 13

9 There is no more sombre enemy of good art than the pram in the hall.
Enemies of Promise (1938) ch. 14

10 All charming people have something to conceal, usually their total dependence on the appreciation of others.
Enemies of Promise (1938) ch. 16

11 I have called this style the Mandarin style, since it is beloved by literary pundits, by those who would make the written word as unlike as possible to the spoken one. It is the style of those writers whose tendency is to make their language convey more than they mean or more than they feel, it is the style of most artists and all humbugs.
Enemies of Promise (1938) ch. 20

12 In the eighteenth century he [Alec Douglas-Home] would have become Prime Minister before he was thirty; as it was he appeared honourably ineligible for the struggle of life.
Enemies of Promise (1938) ch. 23

13 Were I to deduce any system from my feelings on leaving Eton, it might be called *The Theory of Permanent Adolescence.*
Enemies of Promise (1938) ch. 24

14 It is closing time in the gardens of the West and from now on an artist will be judged only by the resonance of his solitude or the quality of his despair.
Horizon Dec. 1949—Jan. 1950, p. 362

15 Better to write for yourself and have no public, than to write for the public and have no self.
New Statesman 25 Feb. 1933

16 Destroy him as you will, the bourgeois always bounces up—execute him, expropriate him, starve him out *en masse*, and he reappears in your children.
In *Observer* 7 Mar. 1937

17 He [George Orwell] could not blow his nose without moralising on the state of the handkerchief industry.
Sunday Times 29 Sept. 1968

18 The more books we read, the sooner we perceive that the only function of a writer is to produce a masterpiece. No other task is of any consequence.
Unquiet Grave (1944) pt. 1

19 There is no fury like a woman looking for a new lover.
Unquiet Grave (1944) pt. 1. Cf. *Oxford Dictionary of Quotations* (1979) 160:15

20 In the sex-war thoughtlessness is the weapon of the male, vindictiveness of the female.
Unquiet Grave (1944) pt. 1

21 Life is a maze in which we take the wrong turning before we have learnt to walk.
Unquiet Grave (1944) pt. 1

1 The civilization of one epoch becomes the manure of the next. Everything over-ripens in the same way. The disasters of the world are due to its inhabitants not being able to grow old simultaneously.
Unquiet Grave (1944) pt. 2

2 Imprisoned in every fat man a thin one is wildly signalling to be let out.
Unquiet Grave (1944) pt. 2. See also George Orwell 164:11

3 The true index of a man's character is the health of his wife.
Unquiet Grave (1944) pt. 2

4 We are all serving a life-sentence in the dungeon of self.
Unquiet Grave (1944) pt. 2

5 Peeling off the kilometres to the tune of 'Blue Skies', sizzling down the long black liquid reaches of Nationale Sept, the plane trees going sha-sha-sha through the open window, the windscreen yellowing with crushed midges, she with the Michelin beside me, a handkerchief binding her hair.
Unquiet Grave (1944) pt. 3

6 Our memories are card-indexes consulted, and then put back in disorder by authorities whom we do not control.
Unquiet Grave (1944) pt. 3

James Connolly 1868–1916

7 The worker is the slave of capitalist society, the female worker is the slave of that slave.
Re-conquest of Ireland (1915) p. 38

Joseph Conrad (Teodor Josef Konrad Korzeniowski) 1857–1924

8 In plucking the fruit of memory one runs the risk of spoiling its bloom.
Arrow of Gold (author's note, 1920, to 1924 Uniform Edition) p. viii

9 The conquest of the earth, which mostly means the taking it away from those who have a different complexion or slightly flatter noses than ourselves, is not a pretty thing when you look into it.
Heart of Darkness ch. 1, in *Youth* (1902)

10 We live, as we dream—alone.
Heart of Darkness ch. 1, in *Youth* (1902)

11 Exterminate all the brutes!
Heart of Darkness ch. 2, in *Youth* (1902)

12 He [Kurtz] cried in a whisper at some image, at some vision,—he cried out twice, a cry that was no more than a breath—'The horror! The horror!'
Heart of Darkness ch. 3, in *Youth* (1902)

13 Mistah Kurtz—he dead.
Heart of Darkness ch. 3, in *Youth* (1902)

14 A man that is born falls into a dream like a man who falls into the sea. If he tries to climb out into the air as inexperienced people endeavour to do, he drowns—*nicht wahr*? . . . No! I tell you! The way is to the destructive element submit yourself, and with the exertions of your hands and feet in the water make the deep, deep sea keep you up. . . . In the destructive element immerse. . . . That was the way. To follow the dream, and again to follow the dream—and so—*ewig*—*usque ad finem*.
Lord Jim (1900) ch. 20

15 You shall judge of a man by his foes as well as by his friends.
Lord Jim (1900) ch. 34

16 Any work that aspires, however humbly, to the condition of art should carry its justification in every line.
The Nigger of the Narcissus, author's note, in *New Review* Dec. 1897

17 Action is consolatory. It is the enemy of thought and the friend of flattering illusions.
Nostromo (1904) pt. 1, ch. 6

18 It's only those who do nothing that make no mistakes, I suppose.
Outcast of the Islands (1896) pt. 3, ch. 2

19 The terrorist and the policeman both come from the same basket.
Secret Agent (1907) ch. 4

20 All ambitions are lawful except those which climb upwards on the miseries or credulities of mankind.
Some Reminiscences (1912; in USA entitled 'A Personal Record') p. 19

21 The scrupulous and the just, the noble, humane, and devoted natures; the unselfish and the intelligent may begin

a movement—but it passes away from them. They are not the leaders of a revolution. They are its victims.
> *Under Western Eyes* (1911) pt. 2, ch. 3

1 A belief in a supernatural source of evil is not necessary; men alone are quite capable of every wickedness.
> *Under Western Eyes* (1911) pt. 2, ch. 4

2 I remember my youth and the feeling that will never come back any more—the feeling that I could last for ever, outlast the sea, the earth, and all men; the deceitful feeling that lures us on to joys, to perils, to love, to vain effort—to death; the triumphant conviction of strength, the heat of life in the handful of dust, the glow in the heart that with every year grows dim, grows cold, grows small, and expires—and expires, too soon, too soon—before life itself.
> *Youth* (1902) p. 41

Shirley Conran 1932–

3 OUR MOTTO: *Life is too short to stuff a mushroom.*
> *Superwoman* (1975) p. 15

4 First things first, second things never.
> *Superwoman* (1975) p. 157

A. J. Cook 1885–1931

5 Not a penny off the pay, not a second on the day.
> Speech at York, 3 Apr. 1926, in *The Times* 5 Apr. 1926 (referring to miners' slogan)

Dan Cook

6 The opera ain't over 'til the fat lady sings.
> In *Washington Post* 3 June 1978

Peter Cook 1937–

7 I have recently been travelling round the world—on your behalf, and at your expense—visiting some of the chaps with whom I hope to be shaping your future. I went first to Germany, and there I spoke with the German Foreign Minister, Herr ... Herr and there, and

we exchanged many frank words in our respective languages.
> *Beyond the Fringe* (1961 revue) 'TVPM', in Roger Wilmut *Complete Beyond the Fringe* (1987) p. 54

8 Yes, I could have been a judge but I never had the Latin, never had the Latin for the judging, I just never had sufficient of it to get through the rigorous judging exams. They're noted for their rigour. People come staggering out saying, 'My God, what a rigorous exam'—and so I became a miner instead.
> *Beyond the Fringe* (1961 revue) 'Sitting on the Bench', in Roger Wilmut *Complete Beyond the Fringe* (1987) p. 97

Calvin Coolidge 1872–1933

9 Shortly after Mr Coolidge had gone to the White House, Mrs Coolidge was unable to go to church with him one Sunday. At lunch she asked what the sermon was about. 'Sins,' he said. 'Well, what did he say about sin?' 'He was against it.'
> John H. McKee *Coolidge: Wit and Wisdom* (1933) p. 4 (but Edward C. Lathem's *Meet Calvin Coolidge* (1960) p. 151 quotes Mrs Coolidge as saying that this was one of 'the stories which might reasonably be attributed to him [Coolidge] but which did not originate with him')

10 Mr Coolidge ... interrupted a discussion of cancellation of the war debts with: 'Well, they hired the money, didn't they?'
> John H. McKee *Coolidge: Wit and Wisdom* (1933) p. 118

11 There is no right to strike against the public safety by anybody, anywhere, any time.
> Telegram to Samuel Gompers, 14 Sept. 1919, in *Have Faith in Massachusetts* (1919) p. 223

12 Civilization and profits go hand in hand.
> Speech in New York, 27 Nov. 1920, in *New York Times* 28 Nov. 1920, p. 20

13 The chief business of the American people is business.
> Speech in Washington, 17 Jan. 1925, in *New York Times* 18 Jan. 1925, p. 19

14 I do not choose to run for President in nineteen twenty-eight.
> Statement issued at Rapid City, South Dakota, 2 Aug. 1927, in *New York Times* 3 Aug. 1927, p. 1

Ananda Coomaraswamy
1877–1947

1 The artist is not a special kind of man,
but every man is a special kind of artist.
Transformation of Nature in Art (1934) ch. 2

Alfred Duff Cooper (Viscount Norwich) 1890–1954

2 I really did enjoy Belvoir you know. . . .
You must I think have enjoyed it too,
with your two stout lovers frowning at
one another across the hearth rug,
while your small, but perfectly formed
one kept the party in a roar.
*Letter to Lady Diana Manners, Oct. 1914, in
Artemis Cooper* Durable Fire *(1983) p. 17*

Tommy Cooper 1921–1984

3 Just like that!
*Title of autobiography (1975), from his
catch-phrase.*

Wendy Cope 1945–

4 I used to think all poets were Byronic—
Mad, bad and dangerous to know.
And then I met a few. Yes it's ironic—
I used to think all poets were Byronic.
They're mostly wicked as a ginless tonic
And wild as pension plans.
Making Cocoa for Kingsley Amis (1986)
'Triolet'. Cf. *Oxford Dictonary of Quotations*
(1979) 306:25

5 It's nice to meet serious people
And hear them explain their views:
Your concern for the rights of women
Is especially welcome news.

I'm sure you'd never exploit one;
I expect you'd rather be dead;
I'm thoroughly convinced of it—
Now can we go to bed?
Making Cocoa for Kingsley Amis (1986) 'From
June to December'

6 There are so many kinds of awful men—
One can't avoid them all. She often said
She'd never make the same mistake
again:
She always made a new mistake instead.
Making Cocoa for Kingsley Amis (1986)
'Rondeau Redoublé'

7 It was a dream I had last week
And some kind of record seemed vital.
I knew it wouldn't be much of a poem

But I love the title.
Making Cocoa for Kingsley Amis (1986)
title-poem

Aaron Copland 1900–1990

8 The whole problem can be stated quite
simply by asking, 'Is there a meaning to
music?' My answer to that would be,
'Yes.' And 'Can you state in so many
words what the meaning is?' My answer
to that would be, 'No.'
What to Listen for in Music (1939) ch. 2

Bernard Cornfeld 1927–

9 Do you sincerely want to be rich?
*Question often asked by Cornfeld of
salesmen in the 1960s, in Charles Raw et
al.* Do You Sincerely Want to be Rich? *(1971)
p. 67*

Frances Cornford 1886–1960

10 Whoso maintains that I am humbled now
(Who wait the Awful Day) is still a liar;
I hope to meet my Maker brow to brow
And find my own the higher.
Collected Poems (1954) 'Epitaph for
a Reviewer'

11 A young Apollo, golden-haired,
Stands dreaming on the verge of strife,
Magnificently unprepared
For the long littleness of life.
Poems (1910) 'Youth'

12 O why do you walk through the fields in
gloves,
Missing so much and so much?
O fat white woman whom nobody loves,
Why do you walk through the fields in
gloves,
When the grass is soft as the breast of
doves
And shivering-sweet to the touch?
O why do you walk through the fields in
gloves,
Missing so much and so much?
Poems (1910) 'To a Fat Lady seen from the
Train'. Cf. G. K. Chesterton 51:8

13 How long ago Hector took off his plume,
Not wanting that his little son should
cry,
Then kissed his sad Andromache
goodbye—

And now we three in Euston
  waiting-room.
    Travelling Home (1948) 'Parting in Wartime'

Francis Macdonald Cornford
1874–1943

1 If you persist to the threshold of old
age—your fiftieth year, let us say—you
will be a powerful person yourself, with
an accretion of peculiarities which other
people will have to study in order to
square you. The toes you will have
trodden on by this time will be as sands
on the sea-shore; and from far below
you will mount the roar of a ruthless
multitude of young men in a hurry. You
may perhaps grow to be aware what
they are in a hurry to do. They are in
a hurry to get you out of the way.
  Microcosmographia Academica (1908) p. 2

2 Every public action, which is not
customary, either is wrong, or, if it is
right, is a dangerous precedent. It
follows that nothing should ever be done
for the first time.
  Microcosmographia Academica (1908) p. 28

Baron Pierre de Coubertin
1863–1937

3 *L'important dans la vie ce n'est point le
triomphe mais le combat; l'essentiel ce
n'est pas d'avoir vaincu mais de s'être bien
battu.*

The important thing in life is not the
victory but the contest; the essential
thing is not to have won but to have
run the race.
  Speech at government banquet in London,
  24 July 1908, in T. A. Cook *Fourth Olympiad*
  (1909) p. 793

Émile Coué 1857–1926

4 *Tous les jours, à tous points de vue, je vais
de mieux en mieux.*

Every day, in every way, I am getting
better and better.
  De la suggestion et de ses applications (On
  Suggestion and its Applications, 1915) p. 17
  (Coué advised his patients to repeat this
  phrase 15 to 20 times, morning and
  evening)

Noël Coward 1899–1973

5 Let's drink to the spirit of gallantry and
courage that made a strange Heaven out
of unbelievable Hell, and let's drink to
the hope that one day this country of
ours, which we love so much, will find
dignity and greatness and peace again.
  Cavalcade (1932) act 3

6 Dance, dance, dance, little lady!
Dance, dance, dance, little lady!
Leave tomorrow behind.
  Dance, Little Lady (1928 song)

7 Don't let's be beastly to the Germans
When our Victory is ultimately won.
  Don't Let's Be Beastly to the Germans (1943
  song)

8 I believe that since my life began
The most I've had is just
A talent to amuse.
Heigho, if love were all!
  If Love Were All (1929 song)

9 I'll see you again,
Whenever Spring breaks through again.
  I'll See You Again (1929 song)

10 Dear 338171 (May I call you 338?)
  Letter to T. E. Lawrence, 25 Aug. 1930, in
  D. Garnett (ed.) *Letters of T. E. Lawrence*
  (1938) p. 696

11 London Pride has been handed down to
us.
London Pride is a flower that's free.
London Pride means our own dear town
to us,
And our pride it for ever will be.
  London Pride (1941 song)

12 Mad about the boy,
It's pretty funny but I'm mad about the
boy.
He has a gay appeal
That makes me feel
There may be something sad about the
boy.
  Mad about the Boy (1932 song)

13 Mad dogs and Englishmen
Go out in the midday sun.
The Japanese don't care to,
The Chinese wouldn't dare to,
The Hindus and Argentines sleep firmly
from twelve to one,
But Englishmen detest a siesta.
In the Philippines, there are lovely
screens

To protect you from the glare;
In the Malay states, they have hats like
    plates
Which the Britishers won't wear.
At twelve noon, the natives swoon,
And no further work is done;
But mad dogs and Englishmen go out in
    the midday sun.
Mad Dogs and Englishmen (1931 song)

1 Don't put your daughter on the stage,
    Mrs Worthington,
Don't put your daughter on the stage.
Mrs Worthington (1935 song)

2 Poor little rich girl
You're a bewitched girl,
Better beware!
Poor Little Rich Girl (1925 song)

3 Extraordinary how potent cheap music is.
Private Lives (1930) act 1 (in a gramophone
recording also made in 1930, Gertrude
Lawrence spoke the line as 'Strange how
potent cheap music is')

4 AMANDA: I've been brought up to
    believe that it's beyond the pale, for
    a man to strike a woman.
ELYOT: A very poor tradition. Certain
    women should be struck regularly,
    like gongs.
Private Lives (1930) act 3

5 Someday I'll find you,
Moonlight behind you,
True to the dream I am dreaming.
Someday I'll Find You (1930 song)

6 Dear Mrs A.,
Hooray, hooray,
At last you are deflowered.
On this as every other day
I love you—Noel Coward.
Telegram to Gertrude Lawrence, 5 July
1940 (the day after her wedding), in
Gertrude Lawrence *A Star Danced* (1945)
p. 201

7 The Stately Homes of England,
How beautiful they stand,
To prove the upper classes
Have still the upper hand;
Though the fact that they have to be
    rebuilt
And frequently mortgaged to the hilt
Is inclined to take the gilt
Off the gingerbread,
And certainly damps the fun

Of the eldest son.
The Stately Homes of England (1938 song).
Cf. *Oxford Dictionary of Quotations* (1979)
244:21

8 Tho' the pipes that supply the bathroom
    burst
And the lavatory makes you fear the
    worst,
It was used by Charles the First
Quite informally,
And later by George the Fourth
On a journey North.
The Stately Homes of England (1938 song)

9 The Stately Homes of England,
Tho' rather in the lurch,
Provide a lot of chances
For Psychical Research—
There's the ghost of a crazy younger son
Who murdered, in thirteen fifty-one,
An extremely rowdy Nun
Who resented it,
And people who come to call
Meet her in the hall.
The Stately Homes of England (1938 song)

Hart Crane 1899–1932

10 Cowslip and shad-blow, flaked like
    tethered foam
Around bared teeth of stallions, bloomed
    that spring
When first I read thy lines, rife as the
    loam
Of prairies, yet like breakers cliffward
    leaping!
. . . My hand
in yours,
Walt Whitman—
so—
The Bridge (1930) pt. 4

11 O Sleepless as the river under thee,
Vaulting the sea, the prairies' dreaming
    sod,
Unto us lowliest sometime sweep,
    descend
And of the curveship lend a myth to
    God.
Dial June 1927, p. 490 'To Brooklyn Bridge'

12 You who desired so much—in vain to
    ask—
Yet fed your hunger like an endless task,
Dared dignify the labor, bless the
    quest—
Achieved that stillness ultimately best,

Being, of all, least sought for: Emily,
  hear!
Nation 29 June 1927, p. 718 'To Emily
Dickinson'

James Creelman 1901–1941 and Ruth Rose

1 Oh no, it wasn't the aeroplanes. It was
Beauty killed the Beast.
King Kong (1933 film; final words)

Bishop Mandell Creighton 1843–1901

2 No people do so much harm as those
who go about doing good.
In Louise Creighton *Life* (1904) vol. 2,
p. 503

Quentin Crisp 1908–

3 There was no need to do any housework
at all. After the first four years the dirt
doesn't get any worse.
Naked Civil Servant (1968) ch. 15

4 I became one of the stately homos of
England.
Naked Civil Servant (1968) ch. 24

5 An autobiography is an obituary in
serial form with the last instalment
missing.
Naked Civil Servant (1968) ch. 29

Julian Critchley 1930–

6 The only safe pleasure for
a parliamentarian is a bag of boiled
sweets.
Listener 10 June 1982

7 She [Margaret Thatcher] has been
beastly to the Bank of England, has
demanded that the BBC 'set its house in
order' and tends to believe the worst of
the Foreign and Commonwealth Office.
She cannot see an institution without
hitting it with her handbag.
The Times 21 June 1982

Richmal Crompton (Richmal Crompton Lamburn) 1890–1969

8 'If anyone trith to hang me,' said Violet
Elizabeth complacently, 'I'll thcream and

thcream and thcream till I'm thick.
I can.'
Still—William (1925) ch. 8

Bing Crosby (Harry Lillis Crosby) 1903–1977

9 Half joking, he [Crosby] asked that his
epitaph read, 'He was an average guy
who could carry a tune.'
Newsweek 24 Oct. 1977, p. 102

Bing Crosby 1903–1977, Roy Turk 1892–1934, and Fred Ahlert 1892–1933

10 Where the blue of the night
Meets the gold of the day,
Someone waits for me.
Where the Blue of the Night (1931 song)

Richard Crossman 1907–1974

11 The Civil Service is profoundly
deferential—'Yes, Minister! No,
Minister! If you wish it, Minister!'
Diary, 22 Oct. 1964, in *Diaries of a Cabinet
Minister* (1975) vol. 1, p. 21

Aleister Crowley 1875–1947

12 Do what thou wilt shall be the whole of
the Law.
Book of the Law (1909) l. 40. Cf. *Oxford
Dictionary of Quotations* (1979) 403:28

Leslie Crowther 1933–

13 Come on down!
Catch-phrase in 'The Price is Right', ITV
programme, 1984 onwards.

Robert Crumb 1943–

14 Keep on truckin'.
Catch-phrase used in cartoons from *c*.1972

Bruce Frederick Cummings

See W. N. P. BARBELLION

e. e. cummings 1894–1962

15 anyone lived in a pretty how town
(with up so floating many bells down)

spring summer autumn winter
he sang his didn't he danced his did.
  50 Poems (1949) no. 29

1 Humanity i love you because
when you're hard up you pawn your
intelligence to buy a drink.
  XLI Poems (1925) 'La Guerre', no. 2

2 'next to of course god america i
love you land of the pilgrims' and so
forth oh
say can you see by the dawn's early my
country 'tis of centuries come and go
and are no more what of it we should
worry
in every language even deafanddumb
thy sons acclaim your glorious name by
gorry
by jingo by gee by gosh by gum
why talk of beauty what could be more
beaut-
iful than these heroic happy dead
who rushed like lions to the roaring
slaughter
they did not stop to think they died
instead
then shall the voices of liberty be mute?

He spoke. And drank rapidly a glass of
water.
  is 5 (1926) p. 62

3 Buffalo Bill's
defunct
who used to
ride a watersmooth-silver
stallion
and break onetwothreefourfive pigeons-
justlikethat
Jesus
he was a handsome man
and what i want to know is
how do you like your blueeyed boy
Mister Death.
  Tulips and Chimneys (1923) 'Portraits' no. 8

4 the Cambridge ladies who live in
furnished souls
are unbeautiful and have comfortable
minds.
  Tulips and Chimneys (1923)
  'Sonnets-Realities' no. 1

5 (i do not know what it is about you that
closes
and opens; only something in me
understands
the voice of your eyes is deeper than all
noses)

nobody, not even the rain, has such
small hands.
  W (1931) 'somewhere I have never
  travelled'

6 a politician is an arse upon
which everyone has sat except a man.
  1 × 1 (1944) no. 10

7 pity this busy monster, manunkind,
not. Progress is a comfortable disease.
  1 × 1 (1944) no. 14

8 We doctors know
a hopeless case if—listen: there's a hell
of a good universe next door; let's go.
  1 × 1 (1944) no. 14

William Thomas Cummings
1903–1945

9 There are no atheists in the foxholes.
  In Carlos P. Romulo *I Saw the Fall of the
  Philippines* (1943) ch. 15

Will Cuppy 1884–1949

10 The Dodo never had a chance. He seems
to have been invented for the sole
purpose of becoming extinct and that
was all he was good for.
  How to Become Extinct (1941) p. 163

Edwina Currie 1946–

11 Good Christian people who wouldn't
dream of misbehaving will not catch
Aids. My message to the businessmen of
this country when they go abroad on
business is that there is one thing above
all they can take with them to stop them
catching Aids—and that is the wife.
  Speech at Runcorn, 12 Feb. 1987, in
  Guardian 13 Feb. 1987

12 We have problems here of high smoking
and alcoholism. Some of these problems
are things we can tackle by impressing
on people the need to look after
themselves better. That is something
which is taken more seriously down
South. . . . I honestly don't think the
problem has anything to do with
poverty. . . . The problem very often for
people is, I think, just ignorance and
failing to realise that they do have some
control over their lives.
  Speech at Newcastle upon Tyne, 23 Sept.
  1986, in *Guardian* 24 Sept. 1986

Michael Curtiz 1888–1962

1 Bring on the empty horses!

In David Niven *Bring on the Empty Horses*
(1975) ch. 6 (said while Curtiz was directing
the 1936 film, *The Charge of the Light
Brigade*)

Lord Curzon (George Nathaniel Curzon, Marquess Curzon of Kedleston) 1859–1925

2 Not even a public figure. A man of no
experience. And of the utmost
insignificance.

In Harold Nicolson *Curzon: the Last Phase*
(1934) ch. 12 (said by Stanley Baldwin on
his being appointed Prime Minister in 1923)

3 The Domestic Bursar of Balliol
(according to his own story) sent Curzon
a specimen menu [for a luncheon for
Queen Mary in 1921], beginning with
soup. The menu came back with one
sentence written across the corner in
Curzon's large and old-fashioned hand:
'Gentlemen do not take soup at
luncheon.'

E. L. Woodward *Short Journey* (1942) ch. 7

4 Dear me, I never knew that the lower
classes had such white skins.

In K. Rose *Superior Person* (1969) ch. 12
(words supposedly said by Curzon when
watching troops bathing during the First
World War)

Paul Daniels 1938–

5 You're going to like this . . . not a lot . . .
but you'll like it!

Catch-phrase used in his conjuring act,
especially on television from 1981 onwards

Charles Brace Darrow 1889–1967

6 Go to jail. Go directly to jail. Do not pass
go. Do not collect £200.

Instructions on 'Community Chest' card in
the game 'Monopoly', invented by Darrow
in 1931

Clarence Darrow 1857–1938

7 When I was a boy I was told that
anybody could become President. I'm
beginning to believe it.

In Irving Stone *Clarence Darrow for the
Defence* (1941) ch. 6

8 I do not consider it an insult, but rather
a compliment to be called an agnostic.
I do not pretend to know where many
ignorant men are sure—that is all that
agnosticism means.

Speech at trial of John Thomas Scopes,
15 July 1925, in *The World's Most Famous
Court Trial* (1925) ch. 4

Sir Francis Darwin 1848–1925

9 In science the credit goes to the man
who convinces the world, not to the
man to whom the idea first occurs.

Eugenics Review Apr. 1914, 'Francis Galton'

Jules Dassin 1911–

10 Ποτέ τήν Κυριακή.

Never on Sunday.
Title of film (1959)

Worton David and Lawrence Wright

11 Not tonight, Josephine.

Title of song (1915; popularized by Florrie
Forde)

Jack Davies and Ken Annakin

12 Those magnificent men in their flying
machines, or How I flew from London to
Paris in 25 hours and 11 minutes.
Title of film (1965)

W. H. Davies 1871–1940

13 A rainbow and a cuckoo's song
May never come together again;
May never come
This side the tomb.

Bird of Paradise (1914) 'A Great Time'

14 And hear the pleasant cuckoo, loud and
long—
The simple bird that thinks two notes
a song.

Child Lovers (1916) 'April's Charms'

15 Girls scream,
Boys shout;
Dogs bark,
School's out.

Complete Poems (1963) 'School's Out'

16 It was the Rainbow gave thee birth,
And left thee all her lovely hues.

Farewell to Poesy (1910) 'Kingfisher'

1 Sweet Stay-at-Home, sweet
    Well-content,
  Thou knowest of no strange continent:
  Thou hast not felt thy bosom keep
  A gentle motion with the deep;
  Thou hast not sailed in Indian Seas,
  Where scent comes forth in every
    breeze.
      Foliage (1913) 'Sweet Stay-At-Home'

2 What is this life if, full of care,
  We have no time to stand and stare.
      Songs of Joy (1911) 'Leisure'

Bette Davis (*Ruth Elizabeth Davis*)
1908–1989

See LENORE COFFEE, JOSEPH L.
MANKIEWICZ, and
OLIVE HIGGINS PROUTY

Lord Dawson of Penn (*Bertrand Edward Dawson, Viscount Dawson of Penn*) 1864–1945

3 The King's life is moving peacefully
  towards its close.
      Bulletin on George V, 20 Jan. 1936, in
      History Today Dec. 1986, p. 28

C. Day-Lewis 1904–1972

4 Do not expect again a phoenix hour,
  The triple-towered sky, the dove
    complaining,
  Sudden the rain of gold and heart's first
    ease
  Traced under trees by the eldritch light
    of sundown.
      Collected Poems, 1929–33 (1935) 'From
      Feathers to Iron'

5 Hurry! We burn
  For Rome so near us, for the phoenix
    moment
  When we have thrown off this
    traveller's trance,
  And mother-naked and ageless-ancient
  Wake in her warm nest of renaissance.
      Italian Visit (1953) 'Flight to Italy'

6 Tempt me no more; for I
  Have known the lightning's hour,
  The poet's inward pride,
  The certainty of power.
      Magnetic Mountain (1933) pt. 3, no. 24

7 You that love England, who have an ear
  for her music,

The slow movement of clouds in
    benediction,
  Clear arias of light thrilling over her
    uplands,
  Over the chords of summer sustained
    peacefully.
      Magnetic Mountain (1933) pt. 4, no. 32

8 It is the logic of our times,
  No subject for immortal verse—
  That we who lived by honest dreams
  Defend the bad against the worse.
      Word over All (1943) 'Where are the War
      Poets?'

Simone de Beauvoir 1908–1986

9 *On ne naît pas femme: on le devient.
  Aucun destin biologique, psychique,
  économique ne définit la figure que revêt au
  sein de la société la femelle humaine.*

  One is not born a woman: one becomes
  a woman. No biological, psychological or
  economic destiny can determine how the
  human female will appear in society.
      Le deuxième sexe (The Second Sex, 1949)
      vol. 2, pt. 1, ch. 1

Edward de Bono 1933–

10 Unhappiness is best defined as the
  difference between our talents and our
  expectations.
      In *Observer* 12 June 1977

Eugene Victor Debs 1855–1926

11 I said then, I say now, that while there
  is a lower class, I am in it; while there is
  a criminal element, I am of it; while
  there is a soul in prison, I am not free.
      Speech at trial in Cleveland, Ohio, 14 Sept.
      1918, in *Liberator* Nov. 1918, p. 12

12 When great changes occur in history,
  when great principles are involved, as
  a rule the majority are wrong. The
  minority are right.
      Speech at Federal Court, Cleveland, Ohio,
      11 Sept. 1918, in *Speeches* (1928) p. 66

Edgar Degas 1834–1917

13 *L'art, c'est le vice. On ne l'épouse pas
  légitimement, on le viole.*

  Art is vice. You don't marry it
  legitimately, you rape it.
      In Paul Lafond *Degas* (1918) p. 140

Charles de Gaulle 1890–1970

1 *Les traités, voyez-vous, sont comme les jeunes filles et comme les roses : ça dure ce que ça dure.*

Treaties, you see, are like girls and roses: they last while they last.

> Speech at Elysée Palace, 2 July 1963, in André Passeron *De Gaulle parle 1962–6* (1966) p. 340

2 *Vive Le Québec Libre.*

Long Live Free Quebec.

> Speech in Montreal, 24 July 1967, in *Discours et messages* (1970) p. 192

3 *La France a perdu une bataille! Mais la France n'a pas perdu la guerre!*

France has lost a battle. But France has not lost the war!

> Proclamation, 18 June 1940, in *Discours, messages et déclarations du Général de Gaulle* (1941)

4 *Comment voulez-vous gouverner un pays qui a deux cent quarante-six variétés de fromage?*

How can you govern a country which has 246 varieties of cheese?

> In Ernest Mignon *Les Mots du Général* (1962) p. 57

5 *Comme un homme politique ne croit jamais ce qu'il dit, il est tout étonné quand il est cru sur parole.*

Since a politician never believes what he says, he is quite surprised to be taken at his word.

> In Ernest Mignon *Les Mots du Général* (1962) p. 67

6 I reviewed a book of his after the war. I said, 'General de Gaulle is a very good soldier and a very bad politician.' So he wrote back to me and said, 'I have come to the conclusion that politics are too serious a matter to be left to the politicians.'

> Clement Attlee *Prime Minister Remembers* (1961) ch. 4

J. de Knight (*James E. Myers*) 1919–   and M. Freedman 1893–1962

7 (We're gonna) rock around the clock.

> Title of song (1953)

Walter de la Mare 1873–1956

8 Oh, no man knows
Through what wild centuries
Roves back the rose.

> *The Listeners and Other Poems* (1912) 'All That's Past'

9 Softly along the road of evening,
In a twilight dim with rose,
Wrinkled with age, and drenched with dew,
Old Nod, the shepherd, goes.

> *The Listeners and Other Poems* (1912) 'Nod'

10 He is crazed with the spell of far Arabia,
They have stolen his wits away.

> *The Listeners and Other Poems* (1912) 'Arabia'

11 'Is there anybody there?' said the Traveller,
Knocking on the moonlit door;
And his horse in the silence champed the grasses
Of the forest's ferny floor.

> *The Listeners and Other Poems* (1912) 'The Listeners'

12 'Tell them I came, and no one answered,
That I kept my word,' he said.

> *The Listeners and Other Poems* (1912) 'The Listeners'

13 Here lies a most beautiful lady,
Light of step and heart was she;
I think she was the most beautiful lady
That ever was in the West Country.
But beauty vanishes; beauty passes;
However rare—rare it be;
And when I crumble, who will remember
This lady of the West Country?

> *The Listeners and Other Poems* (1912) 'Epitaph'

14 A face peered. All the grey night
In chaos of vacancy shone;
Nought but vast Sorrow was there—
The sweet cheat gone.

> *Motley and Other Poems* (1918) 'The Ghost'

15 Look thy last on all things lovely,
Every hour. Let no night
Seal thy sense in deathly slumber
Till to delight
Thou have paid thy utmost blessing;
Since that all things thou wouldst praise
Beauty took from those who loved them
In other days.

> *Motley and Other Poems* (1918) 'Fare Well'

1 Ann, Ann!
Come! quick as you can!
There's a fish that *talks*
In the frying-pan.
    Peacock Pie (1913) 'Alas, Alack'

2 Three jolly gentlemen,
In coats of red,
Rode their horses
Up to bed.
    Peacock Pie (1913) 'The Huntsmen'

3 It's a very odd thing—
As odd as can be—
That whatever Miss T eats
Turns into Miss T.
    Peacock Pie (1913) 'Miss T'

4 Three jolly Farmers
Once bet a pound
Each dance the others would
Off the ground.
    Peacock Pie (1913) 'Off the Ground'

5 Slowly, silently, now the moon
Walks the night in her silver shoon.
    Peacock Pie (1913) 'Silver'

6 What is the world, O soldiers?
It is I:
I, this incessant snow,
This northern sky;
Soldiers, this solitude
Through which we go
Is I.
    Poems (1906) 'Napoleon'

7 Hi! handsome hunting man
Fire your little gun.
Bang! Now the animal
Is dead and dumb and done.
Nevermore to peep again, creep again,
    leap again,
Eat or sleep or drink again, Oh, what
fun!
    Poems for Children (1930) 'Hi!'

8 'Holiday tasks always remind me, my
dear, of the young lady who wanted to
go out to swim:
Mother may I go out to swim?
Yes, my darling daughter.
Fold your clothes up neat and trim,
And don't go near the water.'
'The rhyme I know,' said Laetitia, 'is,
Hang your clothes on a hickory limb.'
'That's all very well,' said her uncle,
'but just you show me one!'
    The Scarecrow (1945) p. 11. Cf. Anonymous
    7:25

Shelagh Delaney 1939–

9 Women never have young minds. They
are born three thousand years old.
    A Taste of Honey (1959) act 1, sc. 2

Jack Dempsey 1895–1983

10 Honey, I just forgot to duck.
    Comment to his wife Estelle after losing his
    World Heavyweight title, 23 Sept. 1926, in
    J. and B. P. Dempsey *Dempsey* (1977) p. 202
    (after someone tried to assassinate Ronald
    Reagan in 1981, Reagan told his wife:
    'Honey, I forgot to duck')

Nigel Dennis 1912–

11 I am a well-to-do, revered and powerful
figure. That Establishment which we call
England has taken me in: I am become
her Fortieth Article. I sit upon her
Boards, I dominate her stage, her
museums, her dances and her costumes;
I have an honoured voice in her elected
House. To her—and her alone—I bend
the knee, and in return for my homage
she is gently blind to my small failings,
asking only that I indulge them
privately.
    Cards of Identity (1955) pt. 2, p. 230

Buddy De Sylva (George Gard De Sylva) 1895–1950 and Lew Brown 1893–1958

12 The moon belongs to everyone,
The best things in life are free,
The stars belong to everyone,
They gleam there for you and me.
    The Best Things in Life are Free (1927 song;
    music by Ray Henderson)

Peter De Vries 1910–

13 You can make a sordid thing sound like
a brilliant drawing-room comedy.
Probably a fear we have of facing up to
the real issues. Could you say we were
guilty of Noel Cowardice?
    Comfort me with Apples (1956) ch. 15

14 It is the final proof of God's omnipotence
that he need not exist in order to save
us.
    Mackerel Plaza (1958) ch. 1

15 Who of us is mature enough for
offspring before the offspring themselves

arrive? The value of marriage is not that
adults produce children but that
children produce adults.

Tunnel of Love (1954) ch. 8

Lord Dewar 1864–1930

1 Lord Dewar ... made the famous
epigram about there being only two
classes of pedestrians in these days of
reckless motor traffic—the quick, and
the dead.

George Robey *Looking Back on Life* (1933)
ch. 28

Sergei Diaghilev 1872–1929

2 *Étonne-moi.*

Astonish me.

In *Journals of Jean Cocteau* (1957) ch. 1

Paul Dickson 1939–

3 Rowe's Rule: the odds are five to six
that the light at the end of the tunnel is
the headlight of an oncoming train.

Washingtonian Nov. 1978. Cf. Robert Lowell
139:21

Joan Didion 1934–

4 That is one last thing to remember:
writers are always selling somebody out.
Slouching towards Bethlehem (1968) p. xvi

Howard Dietz

5 *Ars gratia artis.*

Art for art's sake.

Motto of Metro-Goldwyn-Mayer film studios:
see Bosley Crowthier *The Lion's Share* (1957)
p. 64

William Dillon

6 I want a girl (just like the girl that
married dear old dad).

Title of song (1911; music by Harry von
Tilzer)

Ernest Dimnet

7 Architecture, of all the arts, is the one
which acts the most slowly, but the
most surely, on the soul.

What We Live By (1932) pt. 2, ch. 12

Isak Dinesen (Karen Blixen)
1885–1962

8 Out of Africa.

English title of her novel *Den Afrikanske
Farm* (1937. Cf. Pliny the Elder's *Historia
Naturalis* bk. 8, sec. 6: *Ex Africa semper
aliquid novi.* Always something new out of
Africa.

9 What is man, when you come to think
upon him, but a minutely set, ingenious
machine for turning, with infinite
artfulness, the red wine of Shiraz into
urine?

Seven Gothic Tales (1934) p. 275

Mort Dixon 1892–1956

10 Bye bye blackbird.

Title of song (1926; music by Ray
Henderson)

11 I'm looking over a four leaf clover
That I overlooked before.

I'm Looking Over a Four Leaf Clover (1927
song; music by Harry Woods)

Milovan Djilas 1911–

12 The Party line is that there is no Party
line.

Comment on reforms of Yugoslavian
Communist Party, Nov. 1952, in Fitzroy
Maclean *Disputed Barricade* (1957)
caption facing p. 416

Austin Dobson (Henry Austin
Dobson) 1840–1921

13 Fame is a food that dead men eat,—
I have no stomach for such meat.

Century Nov. 1906, 'Fame is a Food'

14 I intended an Ode,
And it turned to a Sonnet.
It began *à la mode*,
I intended an Ode;
But Rose crossed the road
In her latest new bonnet;
I intended an Ode;
And it turned to a Sonnet.

Graphic 23 May 1874, 'Rose-Leaves'

15 The ladies of St James's!
They're painted to the eyes;
Their white it stays for ever,
Their red it never dies:
But Phyllida, my Phyllida!
Her colour comes and goes;

It trembles to a lily,—
It wavers to a rose.
Harper's Jan. 1883, 'Ladies of St James's'

1 Time goes, you say? Ah no!
Alas, Time stays, we go.
Proverbs in Porcelain (1877) 'Paradox of Time'

Ken Dodd 1931–

2 The trouble with [Sigmund] Freud is
that he never played the Glasgow
Empire Saturday night.
In *The Times* 7 Aug. 1965

J. P. Donleavy 1926–

3 But Jesus, when you don't have any
money, the problem is food. When you
have money, it's sex. When you have
both it's health, you worry about getting
rupture or something. If everything is
simply jake then you're frightened of
death.
Ginger Man (1955) ch. 5

4 When I die I want to decompose in
a barrel of porter and have it served in
all the pubs in Dublin. I wonder would
they know it was me?
Ginger Man (1955) ch. 31

Sir Reginald Dorman-Smith 1899–1977

5 Half a million more allotments properly
worked will provide potatoes and
vegetables that will feed another million
adults and 1½ million children for eight
months out of 12. The matter is not one
that can wait. So—let's get going. Let
'Dig for Victory' be the motto of every
one with a garden and of every
able-bodied man and woman capable of
digging an allotment in their spare time.
Radio broadcast, 3 Oct. 1939, in *The Times*
4 Oct. 1939

Keith Douglas 1920–1944

6 And all my endeavours are unlucky
explorers
come back, abandoning the expedition;
the specimens, the lilies of ambition
still spring in their climate, still
unpicked:
but time, time is all I lacked

to find them, as the great collectors
before me.
Alamein to Zem Zem (1946) 'On Return from
Egypt, 1943–4'

7 Remember me when I am dead
And simplify me when I'm dead.
Collected Poems (1966) 'Simplify me when
I'm Dead' (1941)

8 But she would weep to see today
how on his skin the swart flies move;
the dust upon the paper eye
and the burst stomach like a cave.

For here the lover and killer are mingled
who had one body and one heart.
And death, who had the soldier singled
has done the lover mortal hurt.
Collected Poems (1966) 'Vergissmeinnicht,
1943'

9 If at times my eyes are lenses
through which the brain explores
constellations of feeling
my ears yielding like swinging doors
admit princes to the corridors
into the mind, do not envy me.
I have a beast on my back.
Collected Poems (1966) 'Bête Noire' (1944)

Norman Douglas 1868–1952

10 To find a friend one must close one eye.
To keep him—two.
Almanac (1941) p. 77

11 The bishop was feeling rather sea-sick.
Confoundedly sea-sick, in fact.
South Wind (1917) ch. 1

12 You can tell the ideals of a nation by its
advertisements.
South Wind (1917) ch. 6

13 Many a man who thinks to found
a home discovers that he has merely
opened a tavern for his friends.
South Wind (1917) ch. 20

Sir Alec Douglas-Home
See LORD HOME

Caroline Douglas-Home 1937–

14 He [Lord Home] is used to dealing with
estate workers. I cannot see how anyone
can say he is out of touch.
Comment on her father becoming Prime
Minister, in *Daily Herald* 21 Oct. 1963

Sir Arthur Conan Doyle
1859–1930

1 To Sherlock Holmes she [Irene Adler] is always *the* woman. I have seldom heard him mention her under any other name. In his eyes she eclipses and predominates the whole of her sex.
Adventures of Sherlock Holmes (1892) 'Scandal in Bohemia'

2 You see, but you do not observe.
Adventures of Sherlock Holmes (1892) 'Scandal in Bohemia'

3 It is quite a three-pipe problem, and I beg that you won't speak to me for fifty minutes.
Adventures of Sherlock Holmes (1892) 'Red-Headed League'

4 It has long been an axiom of mine that the little things are infinitely the most important.
Adventures of Sherlock Holmes (1892) 'Case of Identity'

5 The case has, in some respects, been not entirely devoid of interest.
Adventures of Sherlock Holmes (1892) 'Case of Identity'

6 Singularity is almost invariably a clue. The more featureless and commonplace a crime is, the more difficult is it to bring it home.
Adventures of Sherlock Holmes (1892) 'Boscombe Valley Mystery'

7 A man should keep his little brain attic stocked with all the furniture that he is likely to use, and the rest he can put away in the lumber room of his library, where he can get it if he wants it.
Adventures of Sherlock Holmes (1892) 'Five Orange Pips'

8 It is my belief, Watson, founded upon my experience, that the lowest and vilest alleys in London do not present a more dreadful record of sin than does the smiling and beautiful countryside.
Adventures of Sherlock Holmes (1892) 'Copper Beeches'

9 Matilda Briggs ... was a ship which is associated with the giant rat of Sumatra, a story for which the world is not yet prepared.
Case-Book of Sherlock Holmes (1927) 'Sussex Vampire'

10 But here, unless I am mistaken, is our client.
His Last Bow (1917) 'Wisteria Lodge'

11 All other men are specialists, but his specialism is omniscience.
His Last Bow (1917) 'Bruce-Partington Plans'

12 'I [Sherlock Holmes] followed you.' 'I saw no one.' 'That is what you may expect to see when I follow you.'
His Last Bow (1917) 'Devil's Foot'

13 Good old Watson! You are the one fixed point in a changing age.
His Last Bow (1917) title story

14 They were the footprints of a gigantic hound!
Hound of the Baskervilles (1902) ch. 2

15 A long shot, Watson; a very long shot!
Memoirs of Sherlock Holmes (1894) 'Silver Blaze'

16 'Is there any other point to which you would wish to draw my attention?' 'To the curious incident of the dog in the night-time.' 'The dog did nothing in the night-time.' 'That was the curious incident,' remarked Sherlock Holmes.
Memoirs of Sherlock Holmes (1894) 'Silver Blaze'

17 'Excellent,' I [Dr Watson] cried. 'Elementary,' said he [Sherlock Holmes].
Memoirs of Sherlock Holmes (1894) 'The Crooked Man' ('Elementary' is often expanded into 'Elementary, my dear Watson' but the longer phrase is not found in any book by Conan Doyle, although a review of the film *The Return of Sherlock Holmes* in New York Times 19 Oct. 1929, p. 22, says: In the final scene Dr Watson is there with his 'Amazing Holmes', and Holmes comes forth with his 'Elementary, my dear Watson, elementary'.)

18 Ex-Professor Moriarty of mathematical celebrity ... is the Napoleon of crime, Watson.
Memoirs of Sherlock Holmes (1894) 'The Final Problem'

19 You mentioned your name as if I should recognise it, but I assure you that, beyond the obvious facts that you are a bachelor, a solicitor, a Freemason, and an asthmatic, I know nothing whatever about you.
Return of Sherlock Holmes (1905) 'The Norwood Builder'

1 Now, Watson, the fair sex is your
department.
Return of Sherlock Holmes (1905) 'The
Second Stain'

2 Detection is, or ought to be, an exact
science, and should be treated in the
same cold and unemotional manner.
You have attempted to tinge it with
romanticism, which produces much the
same effect as if you worked a love-story
or an elopement into the fifth
proposition of Euclid.
Sign of Four (1890) ch. 1

3 Yes, I have been guilty of several
monographs.... Here ... is one 'Upon
the Distinction between the Ashes of the
Various Tobaccos'. In it I enumerate
a hundred and forty forms of cigar,
cigarette and pipe tobacco.
Sign of Four (1890) ch. 1

4 In an experience of women that extends
over many nations and three separate
continents, I have never looked upon
a face which gave a clearer promise of
a refined and sensitive nature.
Sign of Four (1890) ch. 2

5 How often have I said to you that when
you have eliminated the impossible,
whatever remains, *however improbable*,
must be the truth?
Sign of Four (1890) ch. 6

6 You know my methods. Apply them.
Sign of Four (1890) ch. 6

7 'It is the unofficial force—the Baker
Street irregulars.' As he spoke, there
came a swift pattering of naked feet
upon the stairs, a clatter of high voices,
and in rushed a dozen dirty and ragged
little street Arabs.
Sign of Four (1890) ch. 8

8 London, that great cesspool into which
all the loungers and idlers of the Empire
are irresistibly drained.
Study in Scarlet (1888) ch. 1

9 It is a capital mistake to theorize before
you have all the evidence. It biases the
judgement.
Study in Scarlet (1888) ch. 3

10 Where there is no imagination there is
no horror.
Study in Scarlet (1888) ch. 5

11 It is a mistake to confound strangeness
with mystery. The most commonplace

crime is often the most mysterious,
because it presents no new or special
features from which deductions may be
drawn.
Study in Scarlet (1888) ch. 7

12 'I am inclined to think—' said I [Dr
Watson]. 'I should do so,' Sherlock
Holmes remarked, impatiently.
Valley of Fear (1915) ch. 1

13 The vocabulary of 'Bradshaw' is nervous
and terse, but limited. The selection of
words would hardly lend itself to the
sending of general messages.
Valley of Fear (1915) ch. 1

14 Mediocrity knows nothing higher than
itself, but talent instantly recognizes
genius.
Valley of Fear (1915) ch. 1

15 What of the bow?
The bow was made in England,
Of true wood, of yew wood,
The wood of English bows.
White Company (1891) 'Song of the Bow'

Maurice Drake

16 Beanz meanz Heinz.
Advertising slogan for Heinz baked beans
c.1967, in Nigel Rees *Slogans* (1982) p. 131

William A. Drake 1899–

See GRETA GARBO

John Drinkwater 1882–1937

17 In the corridors under there is nothing
but sleep.
And stiller than ever on orchard boughs
they keep
Tryst with the moon, and deep is the
silence, deep
On moon-washed apples of wonder.
Tides (1917) 'Moonlit Apples'

Alexander Dubček 1921–

18 *Proto vedení strany klade takový důraz na
to, aby ... naše země hospodářsky a
kulturně nezaostávala a hlavně abychom ve
službách lidu dělali takovou politiku, aby
socialismus neztrácel svou lidskou tvář.*

That is why the leadership of the
country has put such emphasis on
ensuring that ... our land did not lag
behind economically or culturally, and,

most important, why in the service of the people we followed a policy so that socialism would not lose its human face.
In *Rudé Právo* 19 July 1968

Al Dubin 1891–1945

1 Tiptoe through the tulips.
Title of song (1929; music by Joseph Burke)

W. E. B. DuBois 1868–1963

2 One thing alone I charge you. As you live, believe in life! Always human beings will live and progress to greater, broader and fuller life.
    The only possible death is to lose belief in this truth simply because the great end comes slowly, because time is long.
Last message (written 26 June, 1957) read at his funeral, 1963, in *Journal of Negro History* Apr. 1964

3 The problem of the twentieth century is the problem of the colour line—the relation of the darker to the lighter races of men in Asia and Africa, in America and the islands of the sea.
Souls of Black Folk (1903) ch. 2

Georges Duhamel 1884–1966

4 *Je respecte trop l'idée de Dieu pour la rendre responsable d'un monde aussi absurde.*

I have too much respect for the idea of God to make it responsible for such an absurd world.
Le désert de Bièvres (1937) in *Chronique des Pasquier* (1948) vol. 5, p. 249

Raoul Duke

See HUNTER S. THOMPSON

John Foster Dulles 1888–1959

5 You have to take chances for peace, just as you must take chances in war. Some say that we were brought to the verge of war. Of course we were brought to the verge of war. The ability to get to the verge without getting into the war is the necessary art. If you cannot master it, you inevitably get into war. If you try to run away from it, if you are scared to go to the brink, you are lost. We've had to look it square in the face—on the question of enlarging the Korean war, on the question of getting into the

Indochina war, on the question of Formosa. We walked to the brink and we looked it in the face.
In *Life* 16 Jan. 1956

6 If . . . the European Defence Community should not become effective; if France and Germany remain apart. . . . That would compel an agonizing reappraisal of basic United States policy.
Speech to NATO Council in Paris, 14 Dec. 1953, in *New York Times* 15 Dec. 1953, p. 14

Dame Daphne du Maurier 1907–1989

7 Last night I dreamt I went to Manderley again.
Rebecca (1938) ch. 1 (opening sentence)

Isadora Duncan 1878–1927

8 *Adieu, mes amis. Je vais à la gloire.*

Farewell, my friends. I am going to glory.
Last words before her scarf caught in a car wheel and broke her neck, in Mary Desti *Isadora Duncan's End* (1929) ch. 25

Ian Dunlop

9 The shock of the new: seven historic exhibitions of modern art.
Title of book (1972)

Jimmy Durante 1893–1980

10 Everybody wants to get inta the act!
Catch-phrase, in W. Cahn *Good Night, Mrs Calabash* (1963) p. 95

Leo Durocher 1906–1991

11 I called off his players' names as they came marching up the steps behind him, 'Walker, Cooper, Mize, Marshall, Kerr, Gordon, Thomson. Take a look at them. All nice guys. They'll finish last. Nice guys. Finish last.'
Said on 6 July 1946, in *Nice Guys Finish Last* (1975) pt. 1, p. 14 (generally quoted as 'Nice guys finish last')

Ian Dury

12 Sex and drugs and rock and roll.
Title of song (1977; music by Chaz Jankel)

1 I could be the catalyst that sparks the
    revolution.
  I could be an inmate in a long term
    institution
  I could lean to wild extremes I could do
    or die,
  I could yawn and be withdrawn and
    watch them gallop by,
  What a waste, what a waste, what
    a waste, what a waste.
    What a Waste (1978 song; music by Chaz
    Jankel)

Lillian K. Dykstra

2 He [Thomas Dewey] is just about the
  nastiest little man I've ever known. He
  struts sitting down.
    Letter to Franz Dykstra, 8 July 1952, in
    James T. Patterson *Mr Republican* (1972)
    ch. 35

Bob Dylan (Robert Zimmerman)
1941–

3 How many roads must a man walk
    down
  Before you can call him a man? . . .
  The answer, my friend, is blowin' in the
    wind,
  The answer is blowin' in the wind.
    Blowin' in the Wind (1962 song)

4 Don't think twice, it's all right.
    Title of song (1963)

5 I saw ten thousand talkers whose
    tongues were all broken,
  I saw guns and sharp swords, in the
    hands of young children,
  And it's a hard, and it's a hard, it's
    a hard, it's a hard,
  And it's a hard rain's a gonna fall.
    A Hard Rain's A Gonna Fall (1963 song)

6 Money doesn't talk, it swears.
    It's Alright, Ma (1965 song)

7 How does it feel
  To be on your own
  With no direction home
  Like a complete unknown
  Like a rolling stone?
    Like a Rolling Stone (1965 song)

8 She knows there's no success like failure
  And that failure's no success at all.
    Love Minus Zero/No Limit (1965 song)

9 I ain't gonna work on Maggie's Farm no
    more.
    Maggie's Farm (1965 song)

10 Hey! Mr Tambourine Man, play a song
    for me.
  I'm not sleepy and there is no place I'm
    going to.
    Mr Tambourine Man (1965 song)

11 'Equality,' I spoke the word
  As if a wedding vow
  Ah, but I was so much older then,
  I'm younger than that now.
    My Back Pages (1964 song)

12 Don't follow leaders
  Watch the parkin' meters.
    Subterranean Homesick Blues (1965 song)

13 Come mothers and fathers,
  Throughout the land
  And don't criticize
  What you can't understand.
  Your sons and your daughters
  Are beyond your command
  Your old road is
  Rapidly agin'
  Please get out of the new one
  If you can't lend your hand
  For the times they are a-changin'!
    The Times They Are A-Changing (1964 song)

14 But I can't think for you
  You'll have to decide,
  Whether Judas Iscariot
  Had God on his side.
    With God on our Side (1963 song)

Stephen T. Early 1889–1951

15 I received a card the other day from
  Steve Early which said, 'Don't Worry
  Me—I am an 8 Ulcer Man on 4 Ulcer
  Pay.'
    William Hillman *Mr President; the First
    Publication from the Personal Diaries, Private
    Letters, Papers and Revealing Interviews of
    Harry S. Truman* (1952) pt. 5, p. 222

Clint Eastwood 1930–

See HARRY JULIAN FINK, RITA M. FINK,
and DEAN RIESNER

Abba Eban 1915–

16 History teaches us that men and nations
  behave wisely once they have exhausted
  all other alternatives.
    Speech in London, 16 Dec. 1970, in *The
    Times* 17 Dec. 1970

Sir Anthony Eden (Earl of Avon) 1897–1977

1 We are in an armed conflict; that is the phrase I have used. There has been no declaration of war.

   Hansard 1 Nov. 1956, col. 1641

Clarissa Eden (Countess of Avon) 1920–

2 For the past few weeks I have really felt as if the Suez Canal was flowing through my drawing room.

   Speech at Gateshead, 20 Nov. 1956, in *Gateshead Post* 23 Nov. 1956

Marriott Edgar 1880–1951

3 There's a famous seaside place called Blackpool,
That's noted for fresh air and fun,
And Mr and Mrs Ramsbottom
Went there with young Albert, their son.
A grand little lad was young Albert,
All dressed in his best; quite a swell
With a stick with an 'orse's 'ead 'andle,
The finest that Woolworth's could sell.

They didn't think much to the Ocean:
The waves, they were fiddlin' and small,
There was no wrecks and nobody drownded,
Fact, nothing to laugh at at all.

   The Lion and Albert (1932) in *Albert, 'Arold and Others* (1937)—monologue recorded by Stanley Holloway in 1932

4 The Magistrate gave his opinion
That no one was really to blame
And he said that he hoped the Ramsbottoms
Would have further sons to their name.

At that Mother got proper blazing,
'And thank you, sir, kindly,' said she.
'What, waste all our lives raising children
To feed ruddy Lions? Not me!'

   The Lion and Albert (1932) in *Albert, 'Arold and Others* (1937)

Duke of Edinburgh 1921–

See Prince Philip, Duke of Edinburgh

Thomas Alva Edison 1847–1931

5 Genius is one per cent inspiration, ninety-nine per cent perspiration.

   Harper's Monthly Magazine Sept. 1932 (quoted by M. A. Rosanoff as having been said by Edison *c*.1903)

John Maxwell Edmonds 1875–1958

6 When you go home, tell them of us and say,
'For your tomorrows these gave their today.'

   Inscriptions Suggested for War Memorials (1919)

King Edward VII 1841–1910

7 That's the fourth time that infernal noise has roused me.

   Said to his secretary 'Fritz' Ponsonby at the first performance of 'The Wreckers', an opera by Dame Ethel Smyth, quoted in H. Atkins and A. Newman *Beecham Stories* (1978) p. 43

8 I thought everyone must know that a *short* jacket is always worn with a silk hat at a private view in the morning.

   In Sir P. Magnus *Edward VII* (1964) ch. 19 (said to Sir Frederick Ponsonby, who had proposed to accompany him in a tail-coat)

9 Because a man has a black face and a different religion from our own, there is no reason why he should be treated as a brute.

   Letter to Lord Granville, 30 Nov. 1875, in Sir Sydney Lee *King Edward VII* (1925) vol. 1, ch. 21

King Edward VIII (Duke of Windsor) 1894–1972

10 The thing that impresses me most about America is the way parents obey their children.

   Look 5 Mar. 1957

11 At long last I am able to say a few words of my own. I have never wanted to withhold anything, but until now it has not been constitutionally possible for me to speak. A few hours ago I discharged my last duty as King and Emperor, and now that I have been succeeded by my brother, the Duke of York, my first words must be to declare

allegiance to him. This I do with all my
heart.You all know the reasons which
have impelled me to renounce the
throne. But I want you to understand
that in making up my mind I did not
forget the country or the Empire which
as Prince of Wales, and lately as King,
I have for twenty-five years tried to
serve. But you must believe me when
I tell you that I have found it impossible
to carry the heavy burden of
responsibility and to discharge my duties
as King as I would wish to do without
the help and support of the woman I
love. . . .

   This decision has been made less
difficult to me by the sure knowledge
that my brother, with his long training
in the public affairs of this country and
with his fine qualities, will be able
to take my place forthwith, without
interruption or injury to the life and
progress of the Empire. And he has
one matchless blessing, enjoyed by so
many of you and not bestowed on
me—a happy home with his wife and
children. . . .

   I now quit altogether public affairs,
and I lay down my burden. . . . God bless
you all. God save the King.

> Broadcast, 11 Dec. 1936, in *The Times*
> 12 Dec. 1936

1 These works [the derelict Dowlais Iron
and Steel Works] brought all these
people here. Something should be done
to get them at work again.

> Spoken to Charles Keen, 18 Nov. 1936, in
> *Western Mail* 19 Nov. 1936

John Ehrlichman 1925–

2 I think we ought to let him [Patrick
Gray] hang there. Let him twist slowly,
slowly in the wind.

> Telephone conversation with John Dean, 7
> or 8 Mar. 1973, in *Washington Post* 27 July
> 1973, p. A27 (regarding Patrick Gray's
> nomination as Director of the FBI)

Albert Einstein 1879–1955

3 Nationalism is an infantile sickness. It is
the measles of the human race.

> In Helen Dukas and Banesh Hoffman *Albert
> Einstein, the Human Side* (1979) p. 38

4 I am an absolute pacifist. . . . It is an
instinctive feeling. It is a feeling that

possesses me, because the murder of
men is disgusting.

> Interview with Paul Hutchinson, in *Christian
> Century* 28 Aug. 1929

5 *Raffiniert ist der Herrgott, aber boshaft ist
er nicht.*

   God is subtle but he is not malicious.

> Remark made during a week at Princeton
> beginning 9 May 1921, later carved above
> the fireplace of the Common Room of Fine
> Hall (the Mathematical Institute), Princeton
> University – in R. W. Clark *Einstein* (1973)
> ch. 14

6 *Jedenfalls bin ich überzeugt, dass der nicht
würfelt.*

   At any rate, I am convinced that *He*
[God] does not play dice.

> Letter to Max Born, 4 Dec. 1926, in *Einstein
> und Born Briefwechsel* (1969) p. 130 (often
> quoted as *Gott würfelt nicht* God does not
> play dice, e.g. in B. Hoffmann *Albert Einstein*
> (1973) ch. 10)

7 If my theory of relativity is proven
correct, Germany will claim me as
a German and France will declare that
I am a citizen of the world. Should my
theory prove untrue, France will say
that I am a German and Germany will
declare that I am a Jew.

> Address at the Sorbonne, Paris, ?early Dec.
> 1929, in *New York Times* 16 Feb. 1930

8 The unleashed power of the atom has
changed everything save our modes of
thinking and we thus drift toward
unparalleled catastrophe.

> Telegram sent to prominent Americans,
> 24 May 1946, in *New York Times* 25 May
> 1946

9 If *A* is a success in life, then *A* equals *x*
plus *y* plus *z*. Work is *x*; *y* is play; and *z*
is keeping your mouth shut.

> In *Observer* 15 Jan. 1950

10 If I would be a young man again and
had to decide how to make my living,
I would not try to become a scientist or
scholar or teacher. I would rather
choose to be a plumber or a peddler in
the hope to find that modest degree of
independence still available under
present circumstances.

> *Reporter* 18 Nov. 1954

11 Science without religion is lame, religion
without science is blind.

> *Science, Philosophy and Religion: a Symposium*
> (1941) ch. 13

Dwight D. Eisenhower 1890–1969

1 This conjunction of an immense military establishment and a large arms industry is new in the American experience. . . . We recognize the imperative need for this development. Yet we must not fail to comprehend its grave implications. . . . In the councils of government, we must guard against the acquisition of unwarranted influence, whether sought or unsought, by the military-industrial complex. The potential for the disastrous rise of misplaced power exists and will persist.

Farewell broadcast, 17 Jan. 1961, in *New York Times* 18 Jan. 1961

2 Every gun that is made, every warship launched, every rocket fired signifies, in the final sense, a theft from those who hunger and are not fed, those who are cold and are not clothed. This world in arms is not spending money alone. It is spending the sweat of its laborers, the genius of its scientists, the hopes of its children.

Speech in Washington, 16 Apr. 1953, in *Public Papers of Presidents 1953* (1960) p. 182

3 You have broader considerations that might follow what you might call the 'falling domino' principle. You have a row of dominoes set up. You knock over the first one, and what will happen to the last one is that it will go over very quickly. So you have the beginning of a disintegration that would have the most profound influences.

Speech at press conference, 7 Apr. 1954, in *Public Papers of Presidents 1954* (1960) p. 383

4 I think that people want peace so much that one of these days governments had better get out of the way and let them have it.

Broadcast discussion, 31 Aug. 1959, in *Public Papers of Presidents 1959* (1960) p. 625

T. S. Eliot 1888–1965

5 Where are the eagles and the trumpets?

Buried beneath some snow-deep Alps.
Over buttered scones and crumpets
Weeping, weeping multitudes

Droop in a hundred A.B.C.'s.
Ara Vus Prec (1920) 'Cooking Egg'

6 Here I am, an old man in a dry month
Being read to by a boy, waiting for rain.
Ara Vus Prec (1920) 'Gerontion'

7 After such knowledge, what forgiveness?
Think now
History has many cunning passages, contrived corridors
And issues, deceives with whispering ambitions,
Guides us by vanities.
Ara Vus Prec (1920) 'Gerontion'

8 Tenants of the house,
Thoughts of a dry brain in a dry season.
Ara Vus Prec (1920) 'Gerontion'

9 A cold coming we had of it,
Just the worst time of the year
For a journey, and such a long journey:
The ways deep and the weather sharp,
The very dead of winter.
Ariel Poems (1927) 'Journey of the Magi'

10 But set down
This set down
This: were we led all that way for
Birth or Death? There was a Birth, certainly,
We had evidence and no doubt. I had seen birth and death
But had thought they were different; this Birth was
Hard and bitter agony for us, like Death, our death.
We returned to our places, these Kingdoms,
But no longer at ease here, in the old dispensation,
With an alien people clutching their gods.
I should be glad of another death.
Ariel Poems (1927) 'Journey of the Magi'

11 Because I do not hope to turn again
Because I do not hope
Because I do not hope to turn.
Ash-Wednesday (1930) pt. 1

12 Because these wings are no longer wings to fly
But merely vans to beat the air
The air which is now thoroughly small and dry
Smaller and dryer than the will
Teach us to care and not to care
Teach us to sit still.
Ash-Wednesday (1930) pt. 1

1 Lady, three white leopards sat under
  a juniper-tree
  In the cool of the day.
  Ash-Wednesday (1930) pt. 2

2 You've missed the point completely,
  Julia:
  There *were* no tigers. *That* was the point.
  Cocktail Party (1950) act 1, sc. 1

3 What is hell?
  Hell is oneself,
  Hell is alone, the other figures in it
  Merely projections. There is nothing to
  escape from
  And nothing to escape to. One is always
  alone.
  Cocktail Party (1950) act 1, sc. 3

4 How unpleasant to meet Mr Eliot!
  With his features of clerical cut,
  And his brow so grim
  And his mouth so prim
  And his conversation, so nicely
  Restricted to What Precisely
  And If and Perhaps and But.
  Collected Poems (1936) 'Five-Finger
  Exercises'

5 Time present and time past
  Are both perhaps present in time future,
  And time future contained in time past.
  Collected Poems (1936) 'Burnt Norton' pt. 1

6 Footfalls echo in the memory
  Down the passage which we did not
  take
  Towards the door we never opened
  Into the rose-garden. My words echo
  Thus, in your mind.
  Collected Poems (1936) 'Burnt Norton' pt. 1

7 Human kind
  Cannot bear very much reality.
  Collected Poems (1936) 'Burnt Norton' pt. 1.

8 At the still point of the turning world.
  Neither flesh nor fleshless;
  Neither from nor towards; at the still
  point, there the dance is,
  But neither arrest nor movement.
  Collected Poems (1936) 'Burnt Norton' pt. 2

9 Words strain,
  Crack and sometimes break, under the
  burden,
  Under the tension, slip, slide, perish,
  Decay with imprecision, will not stay in
  place,
  Will not stay still.
  Collected Poems (1936) 'Burnt Norton' pt. 5

10 I do not know much about gods; but
   I think that the river
   Is a strong brown god—sullen, untamed
   and intractable.
   Dry Salvages (1941) pt. 1

11 In my beginning is my end.
   East Coker (1940) pt. 1

12 That was a way of putting it—not very
   satisfactory:
   A periphrastic study in a worn-out
   poetical fashion,
   Leaving one still with the intolerable
   wrestle
   With words and meanings. The poetry
   does not matter.
   East Coker (1940) pt. 2

13 The houses are all gone under the sea.
   The dancers are all gone under the hill.
   East Coker (1940) pt. 2

14 O dark dark dark. They all go into the
   dark,
   The vacant interstellar spaces, the
   vacant into the vacant.
   East Coker (1940) pt. 3

15 The wounded surgeon plies the steel
   That questions the distempered part;
   Beneath the bleeding hands we feel
   The sharp compassion of the healer's art
   Resolving the enigma of the fever chart.
   East Coker (1940) pt. 4

16 Each venture
   Is a new beginning, a raid on the
   inarticulate
   With shabby equipment always
   deteriorating
   In the general mess of imprecision of
   feeling.
   East Coker (1940) pt. 5

17 Success is relative:
   It is what we can make of the mess we
   have made of things.
   Family Reunion (1939) pt. 2, sc. 3

18 Agatha! Mary! come!
   The clock has stopped in the dark!
   Family Reunion (1939) pt. 2, sc. 3

19 Round and round the circle
   Completing the charm
   So the knot be unknotted
   The cross be uncrossed
   The crooked be made straight
   And the curse be ended.
   Family Reunion (1939) pt. 2, sc. 3

1 And what the dead had no speech for,
     when living,
  They can tell you, being dead: the
     communication
  Of the dead is tongued with fire beyond
     the language of the living.
     Little Gidding (1942) pt. 1

2 Ash on an old man's sleeve
  Is all the ash the burnt roses leave.
  Dust in the air suspended
  Marks the place where a story ended.
  Dust inbreathed was a house—
  The wall, the wainscot and the mouse.
  The death of hope and despair,
  This is the death of air.
     Little Gidding (1942) pt. 2

3 Since our concern was speech, and
     speech impelled us
  To purify the dialect of the tribe
  And urge the mind to aftersight and
     foresight.
     Little Gidding (1942) pt. 2

4 We shall not cease from exploration
  And the end of all our exploring
  Will be to arrive where we started
  And know the place for the first time.
     Little Gidding (1942) pt. 5

5 What we call the beginning is often the
     end
  And to make an end is to make
     a beginning.
  The end is where we start from.
     Little Gidding (1942) pt. 5

6 A people without history
  Is not redeemed from time, for history is
     a pattern
  Of timeless moments. So, while the light
     fails
  On a winter's afternoon, in a secluded
     chapel
  History is now and England.
     Little Gidding (1942) pt. 5

7 A condition of complete simplicity
  (Costing not less than everything)
  And all shall be well and
  All manner of thing shall be well
  When the tongues of flame are in-folded
  Into the crowned knot of fire
  And the fire and the rose are one.
     Little Gidding (1942) pt. 5

8 Yet we have gone on living,
  Living and partly living.
     Murder in the Cathedral (1935) pt. 1

9 The last temptation is the greatest
     treason:
  To do the right deed for the wrong
     reason.
     Murder in the Cathedral (1935) pt. 1

10 Clear the air! clean the sky! wash the
     wind! take the stone from stone, take
     the skin from the arm, take the muscle
     from bone, and wash them.
     Murder in the Cathedral (1935) pt. 2

11 Culture may even be described simply as
     that which makes life worth living.
     Notes Towards a Definition of Culture (1948)
     ch. 1

12 Macavity, Macavity, there's no one like
     Macavity,
  There never was a Cat of such
     deceitfulness and suavity.
  He always has an alibi, and one or two
     to spare:
  At whatever time the deed took
     place—MACAVITY WASN'T THERE!
  And they say that all the Cats whose
     wicked deeds are widely known
  (I might mention Mungojerrie, I might
     mention Griddlebone)
  Are nothing more than agents for the
     Cat who all the time
  Just controls their operations: the
     Napoleon of Crime!
     Old Possum's Book of Practical Cats (1939)
     'Macavity: the Mystery Cat'. Cf. Conan
     Doyle 69:16

13 The host with someone indistinct
  Converses at the door apart,
  The nightingales are singing near
  The Convent of the Sacred Heart,

  And sang within the bloody wood
  When Agamemnon cried aloud
  And let their liquid siftings fall
  To stain the stiff dishonoured shroud.
     Poems (1919) 'Sweeney among the
     Nightingales'

14 The hippopotamus's day
  Is passed in sleep; at night he hunts;
  God works in a mysterious way—
  The Church can feed and sleep at once.
     Poems (1919) 'The Hippopotamus'

15 Polyphiloprogenitive
  The sapient sutlers of the Lord
  Drift across window-panes
  In the beginning was the Word.
     Poems (1919) 'Mr Eliot's Sunday Morning
     Service'

1 Webster was much possessed by death
And saw the skull beneath the skin;
And breastless creatures underground
Leaned backward with a lipless grin.
Poems (1919) 'Whispers of Immortality'

2 Grishkin is nice: her Russian eye
Is underlined for emphasis;
Uncorseted, her friendly bust
Gives promise of pneumatic bliss.
Poems (1919) 'Whispers of Immortality'

3 We are the hollow men
We are the stuffed men
Leaning together
Headpiece filled with straw. Alas!
Poems 1909–1925 (1925) 'The Hollow
Men'

4 *Here we go round the prickly pear*
Prickly pear prickly pear
Here we go round the prickly pear
At five o'clock in the morning.

Between the idea
And the reality
Between the motion
And the act
Falls the Shadow.
Poems 1909–1925 (1925) 'The Hollow
Men'

5 This is the way the world ends
Not with a bang but a whimper.
Poems 1909–1925 (1925) 'The Hollow
Men'

6 Let us go then, you and I,
When the evening is spread out against
the sky
Like a patient etherized upon a table.
Prufrock (1917) 'Love Song of J. Alfred
Prufrock'

7 In the room the women come and go
Talking of Michelangelo.

The yellow fog that rubs its back upon
the window-panes.
The yellow smoke that rubs its muzzle
on the window-panes.
Licked its tongue into the corners of the
evening.
Prufrock (1917) 'Love Song of J. Alfred
Prufrock'

8 I have measured out my life with coffee
spoons.
Prufrock (1917) 'Love Song of J. Alfred
Prufrock'

9 I should have been a pair of ragged claws
Scuttling across the floors of silent seas.
Prufrock (1917) 'Love Song of J. Alfred
Prufrock'

10 I have seen the moment of my greatness
flicker,
And I have seen the eternal Footman
hold my coat, and snicker,
And in short, I was afraid.
Prufrock (1917) 'Love Song of J. Alfred
Prufrock'

11 No! I am not Prince Hamlet, nor was
meant to be;
Am an attendant lord, one that will do
To swell a progress, start a scene or two,
Advise the prince.
Prufrock (1917) 'Love Song of J. Alfred
Prufrock'

12 I grow old ... I grow old ...
I shall wear the bottoms of my trousers
rolled.

Shall I part my hair behind? Do I dare to
eat a peach?
I shall wear white flannel trousers, and
walk upon the beach.
I have heard the mermaids singing, each
to each.

I do not think that they will sing to me.
Prufrock (1917) 'Love Song of J. Alfred
Prufrock'

13 The winter evening settles down
With smell of steaks in passageways.
Six o'clock.
The burnt-out ends of smoky days.
Prufrock (1917) 'Preludes'

14 Every street lamp that I pass
Beats like a fatalistic drum,
And through the spaces of the dark
Midnight shakes the memory
As a madman shakes a dead geranium.
Prufrock (1917) 'Rhapsody on a Windy
Night'

15 I am aware of the damp souls of
housemaids
Sprouting despondently at area gates.
Prufrock (1917) 'Morning at the Window'

16 Stand on the highest pavement of the
stair—
Lean on a garden urn—
Weave, weave the sunlight in your hair.
Prufrock (1917) 'La Figlia Che Piange'

17 Sometimes these cogitations still amaze

The troubled midnight and the noon's
repose.
Prufrock (1917) 'La Figlia Che Piange'

1 Where is the Life we have lost in living?
Where is the wisdom we have lost in
knowledge?
Where is the knowledge we have lost in
information?
The Rock (1934) pt. 1

2 And the wind shall say: 'Here were
decent godless people:
Their only monument the asphalt road
And a thousand lost golf balls.'
The Rock (1934) pt. 1

3 Poetry is not a turning loose of emotion,
but an escape from emotion; it is not the
expression of personality but an escape
from personality. But, of course, only
those who have personality and
emotions know what it means to want
to escape from these things.
Sacred Wood (1920) 'Tradition and
Individual Talent'

4 The only way of expressing emotion in
the form of art is by finding an 'objective
correlative'; in other words, a set of
objects, a situation, a chain of events
which shall be the formula of that
particular emotion; such that when the
external facts, which must terminate in
sensory experience, are given, the
emotion is immediately evoked.
Sacred Wood (1920) 'Hamlet and his
Problems'

5 Immature poets imitate; mature poets
steal.
Sacred Wood (1920) 'Philip Massinger'

6 Birth, and copulation, and death.
That's all the facts when you come to
brass tacks:
Birth, and copulation, and death.
I've been born, and once is enough.
Sweeney Agonistes (1932) p. 24

7 In the seventeenth century a dissociation
of sensibility set in, from which we have
never recovered; and this dissociation,
as is natural, was due to the influence of
the two most powerful poets of the
century, Milton and Dryden.
Times Literary Supplement 20 Oct. 1921

8 We can only say that it appears likely
that poets in our civilization, as it exists
at present, must be *difficult*.
Times Literary Supplement 20 Oct. 1921

9 Stone, bronze, stone, steel, stone,
oakleaves, horses' heels
Over the paving.
Triumphal March (1931)

10 April is the cruellest month, breeding
Lilacs out of the dead land, mixing
Memory and desire, stirring
Dull roots with spring rain.
Winter kept us warm, covering
Earth in forgetful snow, feeding
A little life with dried tubers.
Waste Land (1922) pt. 1

11 I read, much of the night, and go south
in the winter.
Waste Land (1922) pt. 1

12 And I will show you something different
from either
Your shadow at morning striding behind
you
Or your shadow at evening rising to
meet you;
I will show you fear in a handful of dust.
Waste Land (1922) pt. 1. Cf. Joseph Conrad
60:4

13 Madame Sosostris, famous clairvoyante,
Had a bad cold, nevertheless
Is known to be the wisest woman in
Europe,
With a wicked pack of cards.
Waste Land (1922) pt. 1

14 Unreal City,
Under the brown fog of a winter dawn,
A crowd flowed over London Bridge, so
many,
I had not thought death had undone so
many.
Sighs, short and infrequent, were
exhaled,
And each man fixed his eyes before his
feet
Flowed up the hill and down King
William Street,
To where Saint Mary Woolnoth kept the
hours
With a dead sound on the final stroke of
nine.
Waste Land (1922) pt. 1

15 The Chair she sat in, like a burnished
throne,
Glowed on the marble.
Waste Land (1922) pt. 2 (cf. Shakespeare's
Antony and Cleopatra act 2, sc. 2, l. 199)

16 And still she cried, and still the world
pursues,

'Jug Jug' to dirty ears.

Waste Land (1922) pt. 2

1 I think we are in rats' alley
Where the dead men lost their bones.

Waste Land (1922) pt. 2

2 O O O O that Shakespeherian Rag—
It's so elegant
So intelligent.

Waste Land (1922) pt. 2. Cf. Gene Buck and
Herman Ruby

3 Hurry up please it's time.

Waste Land (1922) pt. 2

4 But at my back from time to time I hear
The sound of horns and motors, which
shall bring
Sweeney to Mrs Porter in the spring.
O the moon shone bright on Mrs Porter
And on her daughter
They wash their feet in soda water.

Waste Land (1922) pt. 3. Cf. *Oxford
Dictionary of Quotations* (1979) 332:19

5 At the violet hour, when the eyes and
back
Turn upward from the desk, when the
human engine waits
Like a taxi throbbing waiting,
I, Tiresias, though blind, throbbing
between two lives,
Old man with wrinkled female breasts,
can see
At the violet hour, the evening hour
that strives
Homeward, and brings the sailor home
from sea,
The typist home at teatime, clears her
breakfast, lights
Her stove, and lays out food in tins.

Waste Land (1922) pt. 3

6 I Tiresias, old man with wrinkled dugs
Perceived the scene, and foretold the
rest—
I too awaited the expected guest.
He, the young man carbuncular,
arrives,
A small house agent's clerk, with one
bold stare,
One of the low on whom assurance sits
As a silk hat on a Bradford millionaire.

Waste Land (1922) pt. 3

7 When lovely woman stoops to folly and
Paces about her room again, alone,
She smoothes her hair with automatic
hand,
And puts a record on the gramophone.

Waste Land (1922) pt. 3

8 Phlebas the Phoenician, a fortnight
dead,
Forgot the cry of gulls, and the deep sea
swell
And the profit and loss.

Waste Land (1922) pt. 4

9 Who is the third who walks always
beside you?
When I count, there are only you and
I together
But when I look ahead up the white
road
There is always another one walking
beside you.

Waste Land (1922) pt. 5

10 A woman drew her long black hair out
tight
And fiddled whisper music on those
strings
And bats with baby faces in the violet
light
Whistled.

Waste Land (1922) pt. 5

11 These fragments I have shored against
my ruins.

Waste Land (1922) pt. 5

Queen Elizabeth II 1926–

12 I declare before you all that my whole
life, whether it be long or short, shall be
devoted to your service and the service
of our great Imperial family to which we
all belong.

Broadcast speech (as Princess Elizabeth) to
the Commonwealth from Cape Town,
21 Apr. 1947, in *The Times* 22 Apr. 1947

13 I think everybody really will concede
that on this, of all days, I should begin
my speech with the words 'My husband
and I'.

Speech at Guildhall on her 25th wedding
anniversary, 20 Nov. 1972, in *The Times*
21 Nov. 1972

Queen Elizabeth, the Queen Mother 1900–

1 I'm glad we've been bombed. It makes me feel I can look the East End in the face.

> Said to a policeman, 13 Sept. 1940, in John Wheeler-Bennett *King George VI* (1958) pt. 3, ch. 6

Alf Ellerton

2 Belgium put the kibosh on the Kaiser.

> Title of song (1914)

Havelock Ellis (Henry Havelock Ellis) 1859–1939

3 It is certainly strange to observe ... how many people seem to feel vain of their own unqualified optimism when the place where optimism most flourishes is the lunatic asylum.

> *Dance of Life* (1923) ch. 3

4 The sanitary and mechanical age we are now entering makes up for the mercy it grants to our sense of smell by the ferocity with which it assails our sense of hearing. As usual, what we call 'Progress' is the exchange of one Nuisance for another Nuisance.

> *Impressions and Comments* (1914) 31 July 1912

5 Every artist writes his own autobiography.

> *New Spirit* (1890) 'Tolstoi'

Paul Éluard 1895–1952

6 *Adieu tristesse*
Bonjour tristesse
Tu es inscrite dans les lignes du plafond.
Farewell sadness
Good-day sadness
You are inscribed in the lines of the ceiling.

> *La vie immédiate* (1930) 'À peine défigurée', in *Œuvres complètes* (1968) vol. 1, p. 365

Sir William Empson 1906–1984

7 Slowly the poison the whole blood stream fills.
It is not the effort nor the failure tires.
The waste remains, the waste remains and kills.

> *Poems* (1935) 'Missing Dates'

8 Seven types of ambiguity.

> Title of book (1930)

Julius J. Epstein 1909– , Philip G. Epstein 1909–1952, and Howard Koch 1902–

9 Of all the gin joints in all the towns in all the world, she walks into mine.

> *Casablanca* (1942 film), words spoken by Humphrey Bogart

10 If she can stand it, I can. Play it!

> *Casablanca* (1942 film), words spoken by Humphrey Bogart, often misquoted as 'Play it again, Sam' (earlier in the film, Ingrid Bergman says: 'Play it, Sam. Play *As Time Goes By*.')

11 Here's looking at you, kid.

> *Casablanca* (1942 film), words spoken by Humphrey Bogart

12 Major Strasser has been shot. Round up the usual suspects.

> *Casablanca* (1942 film), words spoken by Claude Rains

Susan Ertz 1894–1985

13 Someone has somewhere commented on the fact that millions long for immortality who don't know what to do with themselves on a rainy Sunday afternoon.

> *Anger in the Sky* (1943) p. 137

Dudley Erwin 1917–1984

14 Mr Dudley Erwin, former Air Minister [in Australia], claimed last night that the secretary of Mr John Gorton, the Prime Minister, had cost him his job in the reshuffled Government announced earlier this week. At first Mr Erwin said he was dropped because of a 'political manoeuvre'. Later, when asked to explain what this meant, he said: 'It wiggles, it's shapely and its name is Ainsley Gotto.'

> *The Times* 14 Nov. 1969

Howard Estabrook and Harry Behn

15 Excuse me while I slip into something more comfortable.

> *Hell's Angels* (1930 film), words spoken by Jean Harlow

Gavin Ewart 1916–

1 Miss Twye was soaping her breasts in
   the bath
 When she heard behind her a meaning
   laugh
 And to her amazement she discovered
 A wicked man in the bathroom
   cupboard.
   Poems and Songs (1939) 'Miss Twye'

William Norman Ewer 1885–1976

2 I gave my life for freedom—This I know:
 For those who bade me fight had told
   me so.
   Five Souls and Other Verses (1917) 'Five
   Souls'

3 How odd
 Of God
 To choose
 The Jews.
   In *Week-End Book* (1924) p. 117 (for the
   reply, see Cecil Browne)

Clifton Fadiman 1904–

4 Provided it be well and truly made there
 is really for the confirmed turophile no
 such thing as a *bad* cheese. A cheese
 may disappoint. It may be dull, it may
 be naive, it may be oversophisticated.
 Yet it remains cheese, milk's leap toward
 immortality.
   Any Number Can Play (1957) p. 105

5 On November 17 . . . I encountered the
 mama of dada [Gertrude Stein] again
 (something called *Portraits and Prayers*)
 and as usual withdrew worsted.
   Party of One (1955) p. 90

Eleanor Farjeon 1881–1965

6 Morning has broken
 Like the first morning,
 Blackbird has spoken
 Like the first bird.
 Praise for the singing!
 Praise for the morning!
 Praise for them, springing
 Fresh from the Lord!
   Children's Bells (1957) 'A Morning Song (for
   the First Day of Spring)'

7 King's Cross!
 What shall we do?
 His Purple Robe
 Is rent in two!

Out of his Crown
He's torn the gems!
He's thrown his Sceptre
Into the Thames!
The Court is shaking
In its shoe—
King's Cross!
What shall we do?
*Leave him alone
For a minute or two.*
   Nursery Rhymes of London Town (1916)
   'King's Cross'

King Farouk of Egypt 1920–1965

8 The whole world is in revolt. Soon there
 will be only five Kings left—the King of
 England, the King of Spades, the King of
 Clubs, the King of Hearts and the King
 of Diamonds.
   Said to Lord Boyd-Orr at a conference in
   Cairo, 1948, in Lord Boyd-Orr *As I Recall*
   (1966) ch. 21

William Faulkner 1897–1962

9 The long summer.
   The Hamlet (1940), title of bk. 3. Cf. Irving
   Ravetch and Harriet Frank

10 The writer's only responsibility is to his
 art. He will be completely ruthless if he
 is a good one. He has a dream. It
 anguishes him so much he must get rid
 of it. He has no peace until then.
 Everything goes by the board: honor,
 pride, decency, security, happiness, all,
 to get the book written. If a writer has to
 rob his mother, he will not hesitate; the
 Ode on a Grecian Urn is worth any
 number of old ladies.
   In *Paris Review* Spring 1956, p. 30

11 He [the writer] must teach himself that
 the basest of all things is to be afraid
 and, teaching himself that, forget it
 forever, leaving no room in his
 workshop for anything but the old
 verities and truths of the heart, the old
 universal truths lacking which any story
 is ephemeral and doomed—love and
 honor and pity and pride and
 compassion and sacrifice.
   Nobel Prize speech, 1950, in *Les Prix Nobel
   en 1950* (1951) p. 71

12 I believe man will not merely endure, he
 will prevail. He is immortal, not because
 he, alone among creatures, has an
 inexhaustible voice but because he has

a soul, a spirit capable of compassion and sacrifice and endurance.

Nobel Prize speech, 1950, in *Les Prix Nobel en 1950* (1951) p. 71

1 There is no such thing ... as bad whiskey. Some whiskeys just happen to be better than others. But a man shouldn't fool with booze until he's fifty; then he's a damn fool if he doesn't.

In James M. Webb and A. Wigfall Green *William Faulkner of Oxford* (1965) p. 110

George Fearon 1901–1972

2 In my capacity as Press Representative for the English Stage Company I had read John Osborne's play [*Look Back in Anger*]. When I met the author I ventured to prophesy that his generation would praise his play while mine would, in general, dislike it. I then told him jokingly that Sloane Square might well become a bloody battleground. 'If this happens,' I told him, 'you would become known as the Angry Young Man.' In fact, we decided then and there that henceforth he was to be known as that.

Daily Telegraph 2 Oct. 1957

James Fenton 1949–

3 It is not what they built. It is what they knocked down.
It is not the houses. It is the spaces between the houses.
It is not the streets that exist. It is the streets that no longer exist.
German Requiem (1981) p. 1

Edna Ferber 1887–1968

4 Mother knows best.
Title of story (1927)

5 Being an old maid is like death by drowning, a really delightful sensation after you cease to struggle.

In R. E. Drennan *Wit's End* (1973)

Kathleen Ferrier 1912–1953

6 Enid and I visited her just before the end to be greeted by her with smiling affection. She tired quickly and gently

sent us away by murmuring, 'Now I'll have eine kleine Pause.' Those were the last words we heard her utter.

Gerald Moore *Am I Too Loud?* (1962) ch. 19

Eric Field

7 Towards the end of July 1914, I ... received a surprise call from Colonel Strachey, the A.A.G. (Recruiting). He swore me to secrecy, told me that war was imminent and that the moment it broke out we should have to start advertising at once. ... That night I worked out a draft schedule and wrote an advertisement headed 'Your King and Country need you' with the inevitable Coat of Arms at the top.

Advertising (1959) ch. 2

Dorothy Fields 1905–1974

8 The minute you walked in the joint,
I could see you were a man of distinction,
A real big spender.
Good looking, so refined,
Say, wouldn't you like to know what's going on in my mind?
So let me get right to the point.
I don't pop my cork for every guy I see.
Hey! big spender, spend a little time with me.
Big Spender (1966 song; music by Cy Coleman)

9 A fine romance with no kisses.
A fine romance, my friend, this is.
We should be like a couple of hot tomatoes,
But you're as cold as yesterday's mashed potatoes.
A Fine Romance (1936 song; music by Jerome Kern)

10 I can't give you anything but love (baby).
Title of song (1928; music by Jimmy McHugh)

11 Grab your coat, and get your hat,
Leave your worry on the doorstep,
Just direct your feet
To the sunny side of the street.
On the Sunny Side of the Street (1930 song; music by Jimmy McHugh)

Dame Gracie Fields (Grace Stansfield) 1898-1979

See JIMMY HARPER *et al.*

W. C. Fields (William Claude Dukenfield) 1880-1946

1 Some weasel took the cork out of my lunch.

> *You Can't Cheat an Honest Man* (1939 film), in William K. Everson *Art of W. C. Fields* (1968) p. 167

2 Never give a sucker an even break.

> In *Collier's* 28 Nov. 1925. It was W. C. Fields's catch-phrase, and he is said to have used it in the musical comedy *Poppy* (1923), although it does not occur in the libretto. It was used as the title of a W. C. Fields film in 1941.

3 Last week, I went to Philadelphia, but it was closed.

> In Richard J. Anobile *Godfrey Daniels* (1975) p. 6

4 I was in love with a beautiful blonde once, dear. She drove me to drink. That's the one thing I'm indebted to her for.

> *Never Give a Sucker an Even Break* (1941 film), in Richard J. Anobile *Flask of Fields* (1972) p. 219

5 I always keep a supply of stimulant handy in case I see a snake—which I also keep handy.

> In Corey Ford *Time of Laughter* (1970) p. 182

6 Here lies W. C. Fields. I would rather be living in Philadelphia.

> Suggested epitaph for himself, in *Vanity Fair* June 1925

7 Fifteen years ago, I made the line 'It ain't a fit night out for man or beast' a by-word by using it in my sketch in Earl Carroll's *Vanities*. Later on, I used it as a title for a moving picture I did for Mack Sennett. I do not claim to be the originator of this line as it was probably used long before I was born in some old melodrama.

> Letter, 8 Feb. 1944, in R. J. Fields (ed.) *W. C. Fields by Himself* (1974) pt. 2 (also used by Fields in his 1933 film *The Fatal Glass of Beer*)

8 Hell, I never vote *for* anybody. I always vote *against*.

> In Robert Lewis Taylor *W. C. Fields: His Follies and Fortunes* (1950) p. 228

Harry Julian Fink, Rita M. Fink, and Dean Riesner

9 Go ahead, make my day.

> *Dirty Harry* (1971 film; words spoken by Clint Eastwood)

Ronald Firbank 1886-1926

10 'O! help me, heaven,' she prayed, 'to be decorative and to do right!'

> *Flower Beneath the Foot* (1923) ch. 2

11 Looking back, I remember the average curate at home as something between a eunuch and a snigger.

> *Flower Beneath the Foot* (1923) ch. 4

12 There was a pause—just long enough for an angel to pass, flying slowly.

> *Vainglory* (1915) ch. 6

13 All millionaires love a baked apple.

> *Vainglory* (1915) ch. 13

14 'I know of no joy,' she airily began, 'greater than a cool white dress after the sweetness of confession.'

> *Valmouth* (1919) ch. 4

Fred Fisher 1875-1942

See ADA BENSON

H. A. L. Fisher 1856-1940

15 One intellectual excitement has, however, been denied me. Men wiser and more learned than I have discerned in history a plot, a rhythm, a predetermined pattern. These harmonies are concealed from me. I can see only one emergency following upon another as wave follows upon wave, only one great fact with respect to which, since it is unique, there can be no generalizations, only one safe rule for the historian: that he should recognize in the development of human destinies

the play of the contingent and the unforeseen.

History of Europe (1935) p. vii

John Arbuthnot Fisher (*Baron Fisher*) 1841–1920

1 The essence of war is violence. Moderation in war is imbecility.

Lecture notes 1899–1902, in R. H. Bacon *Life of Lord Fisher* (1929) vol. 1, ch. 7

2 Yours till Hell freezes.

Letter to George Lambert, 5 Apr. 1909, in A. J. Marder *Fear God and Dread Nought* (1956) vol. 2, pt. 1, ch. 2. Cf. F. Ponsonby *Reflections of Three Reigns* (1951) p. 131: Once an officer in India wrote to me and ended his letter 'Yours till Hell freezes'. I used this forcible expression in a letter to Fisher, and he adopted it instead of 'Yours sincerely' and used it a great deal.

3 You must be ruthless, relentless, and remorseless! Sack the lot!

Letter to *The Times* 2 Sept. 1919

4 This letter is not to argue with your leading article of September 2. (It's only d—d fools who argue!)
  Never contradict
  Never explain
  Never apologize
(Those are the secrets of a happy life!)

Letter to *The Times*, 5 Sept.1919

Marve Fisher

5 I want an old-fashioned house
With an old-fashioned fence
And an old-fashioned millionaire.

Old-Fashioned Girl (1954 song; popularized by Eartha Kitt)

Albert H. Fitz

6 You are my honey, honeysuckle, I am the bee.

The Honeysuckle and the Bee (1901 song; music by William H. Penn)

F. Scott Fitzgerald 1896–1940

7 Let me tell you about the very rich. They are different from you and me.

All Sad Young Men (1926) 'Rich Boy' (Ernest Hemingway's rejoinder in his story 'The Snows of Kilimanjaro'—in *Esquire* Aug. 1936—was: 'Yes, they have more money')

8 The beautiful and damned.

Title of novel (1922)

9 No grand idea was ever born in a conference, but a lot of foolish ideas have died there.

Note-Books E, in Edmund Wilson (ed.) *The Crack-Up* (1945)

10 Show me a hero and I will write you a tragedy.

Note-Books E, in Edmund Wilson (ed.) *The Crack-Up* (1945)

11 The test of a first-rate intelligence is the ability to hold two opposed ideas in the mind at the same time, and still retain the ability to function.

Esquire Feb. 1936, 'The Crack-Up'

12 In a real dark night of the soul it is always three o'clock in the morning, day after day.

Esquire Mar. 1936, 'Handle with Care'

13 In my younger and more vulnerable years my father gave me some advice I've been turning over in my mind ever since.

Great Gatsby (1925) ch. 1

14 In his blue gardens, men and girls came and went like moths among the whisperings and the champagne and the stars.

Great Gatsby (1925) ch. 3

15 Her voice is full of money.

Great Gatsby (1925) ch. 7

16 Gatsby believed in the green light, the orgastic future that year by year recedes before us. It eluded us then, but that's no matter—to-morrow we will run faster, stretch out our arms farther. . . . And one fine morning—
  So we beat on, boats against the current, borne back ceaselessly into the past.

Great Gatsby (1925) ch. 9

17 There are no second acts in American lives.

In Edmund Wilson (ed.) *The Last Tycoon* (1949) 'Hollywood, etc. Notes'

18 She had once been a Catholic, but discovering that priests were infinitely more attentive when she was in process of losing or regaining faith in Mother Church, she maintained an enchantingly wavering attitude.

This Side of Paradise (1921) bk. 1, ch. 1

Zelda Fitzgerald 1900–1948

1 Ernest, don't you think Al Jolson is
greater than Jesus?
  In Ernest Hemingway *Moveable Feast* (1964)
  ch. 18. Cf. John Lennon 135:2

Robert Fitzsimmons 1862–1917

2 You know the old saying, 'The bigger
they are, the further they have to fall.'
  In *Brooklyn Daily Eagle* 11 Aug. 1900

Bud Flanagan (Chaim Reeven Weintrop) 1896–1968

3 Underneath the Arches,
I dream my dreams away,
Underneath the Arches,
On cobble-stones I lay.
  Underneath the Arches (1932 song;
  additional words by Reg Connelly)

Michael Flanders 1922–1975 and Donald Swann 1923–

4 I'm a gnu
A gnother gnu.
  The Gnu (1956 song)

5 Mud! Mud! Glorious mud!
Nothing quite like it for cooling the
  blood.
So, follow me, follow,
Down to the hollow,
And there let us wallow
In glorious mud.
  Hippopotamus Song (1952)

6 I don't eat people,
I won't eat people,
I don't eat people,
Eating people is wrong!
  The Reluctant Cannibal (1956 song)

James Elroy Flecker 1884–1915

7 We who with songs beguile your
  pilgrimage
And swear that beauty lives though
  lilies die,
We Poets of the proud old lineage
Who sing to find your hearts, we know
  not why,—
What shall we tell you? Tales,
  marvellous tales
Of ships and stars and isles where good
  men rest.
  Golden Journey to Samarkand (1913)
  'Prologue'

8 When the great markets by the sea shut
  fast
All that calm Sunday that goes on and
  on:
When even lovers find their peace at
  last,
And earth is but a star, that once had
  shone.
  Golden Journey to Samarkand (1913)
  'Prologue'

9 Sweet to ride forth at evening from the
  wells,
When shadows pass gigantic on the
  sand,
And softly through the silence beat the
  bells
Along the Golden Road to Samarkand.
  Golden Journey to Samarkand (1913) p. 8

10 For lust of knowing what should not be
  known,
We take the Golden Road to Samarkand.
  Golden Journey to Samarkand (1913) p. 8

11 How splendid in the morning glows the
  lily; with what grace he throws
His supplication to the rose.
  Golden Journey to Samarkand (1913)
  'Yasmin'

12 And some to Meccah turn to pray, and
  I toward thy bed, Yasmin.
  Golden Journey to Samarkand (1913)
  'Yasmin'

13 For one night or the other night
Will come the Gardener in white, and
  gathered flowers are dead, Yasmin.
  Golden Journey to Samarkand (1913)
  'Yasmin'

14 The dragon-green, the luminous, the
  dark, the serpent-haunted sea.
  Golden Journey to Samarkand (1913) 'Gates of
  Damascus'

15 A ship, an isle, a sickle moon—
With few but with how splendid stars
The mirrors of the sea are strewn
Between their silver bars!
  Golden Journey to Samarkand (1913) 'A Ship,
  an Isle, and a Sickle Moon'

16 For pines are gossip pines the wide
  world through
And full of runic tales to sigh or sing.
  Golden Journey to Samarkand (1913)
  'Brumana'

17 Half to forget the wandering and pain,

Half to remember days that have gone
by,
And dream and dream that I am home
again!

Golden Journey to Samarkand (1913)
'Brumana'

1 Noon strikes on England, noon on
Oxford town,
Beauty she was statue cold—there's
blood upon her gown:
Noon of my dreams, O noon!
Proud and godly kings had built her,
long ago,
With her towers and tombs and statues
all arow,
With her fair and floral air and the love
that lingers there,
And the streets where the great men go.

Golden Journey to Samarkand (1913) 'Dying
Patriot'

2 West of these out to seas colder than the
Hebrides
I must go
Where the fleet of stars is anchored and
the young
Star captains glow.

Golden Journey to Samarkand (1913) 'Dying
Patriot'

3 I have seen old ships sail like swans
asleep
Beyond the village which men still call
Tyre,
With leaden age o'ercargoed, dipping
deep
For Famagusta and the hidden sun
That rings black Cyprus with a lake of
fire.

Old Ships (1915) title poem

4 And with great lies about his wooden
horse
Set the crew laughing, and forgot his
course.

Old Ships (1915) title poem

5 It was so old a ship—who knows, who
knows?
—And yet so beautiful, I watched in
vain
To see the mast burst open with a rose,
And the whole deck put on its leaves
again.

Old Ships (1915) title poem

6 How shall we conquer? Like a wind
That falls at eve our fancies blow,

And old Maeonides the blind
Said it three thousand years ago.

36 Poems (1910) 'To a Poet a Thousand
Years Hence'

7 O friend unseen, unborn, unknown,
Student of our sweet English tongue,
Read out my words at night, alone:
I was a poet, I was young.

36 Poems (1910) 'To a Poet a Thousand
Years Hence'

Ian Fleming 1908–1964

8 Bond said, 'And I would like a medium
Vodka dry Martini—with a slice of
lemon peel. Shaken and not stirred,
please. I would prefer Russian or Polish
vodka.'

Dr No (1958) ch. 14

9 From Russia with love.

Title of novel (1957)

10 Live and let die.

Title of novel (1954)

Robert, Marquis de Flers 1872–1927 and Arman de Caillavet 1869–1915

11 Démocratie est le nom que nous donnons au
peuple toutes les fois que nous avons besoin
de lui.

Democracy is the name we give the
people whenever we need them.

L'habit vert act 1, sc. 12, in La petite
illustration série théâtre 31 May 1913

Dario Fo 1926–

12 Non si paga, non si paga.

We won't pay, we won't pay.

Title of play (1975; translated by Lino
Pertile in 1978 as 'We Can't Pay? We
Won't Pay!' and performed in London in
1981 as 'Can't Pay? Won't Pay!')

Marshal Ferdinand Foch 1851–1929

13 Mon centre cède, ma droite recule, situation
excellente, j'attaque.

My centre is giving way, my right is
retreating, situation excellent, I am
attacking.
> Message sent during the first Battle of the
> Marne, Sept. 1914, in R. Recouly *Foch*
> (1919) ch. 6

1 *Ce n'est pas un traité de paix, c'est un
armistice de vingt ans.*

This [the treaty signed at Versailles in
1919] is not a peace treaty, it is an
armistice for twenty years.
> In Paul Reynaud *Mémoires* (1963) vol. 2,
> p. 457

J. Foley

2 Old soldiers never die,
They simply fade away.
> *Old Soldiers Never Die* (1920 song;
> copyrighted by J. Foley but perhaps
> a 'folk-song' from the First World War)

Michael Foot 1913–

3 A speech from Ernest Bevin on a major
occasion had all the horrific fascination
of a public execution. If the mind was
left immune, eyes and ears and emotions
were riveted.
> *Aneurin Bevan* (1962) vol. 1, ch. 13

4 Think of it! A second Chamber selected
by the Whips. A seraglio of eunuchs.
> *Hansard* 3 Feb. 1969, col. 88

5 It is not necessary that every time he
[Norman Tebbit] rises he should give his
famous imitation of a semi-house-
trained polecat.
> *Hansard* 2 Mar. 1978, col. 668

Anna Ford 1943–

6 Let's face it, there are no plain women
on television.
> In *Observer* 23 Sept. 1979

Gerald Ford 1909–

7 I believe that truth is the glue that holds
Government together, not only our
Government, but civilization itself.
> Speech, 9 Aug. 1974, in G. J. Lankevich
> *Gerald R. Ford* (1977)

8 My fellow Americans, our long national
nightmare is over. Our Constitution
works; our great Republic is

a Government of laws and not of men.
Here the people rule.
> Speech, 9 Aug. 1974, in G. J. Lankevich
> *Gerald R. Ford* (1977)

9 There is no Soviet domination of Eastern
Europe and there never will be under
a Ford administration.
> In television debate with Jimmy Carter,
> 6 Oct. 1976, in
> S. Kraus *Great Debates* (1979) p. 482

10 If the Government is big enough to give
you everything you want, it is big
enough to take away everything you
have.
> In John F. Parker *If Elected* (1960) p. 193

11 I am a Ford, not a Lincoln. My addresses
will never be as eloquent as Lincoln's.
But I will do my best to equal his brevity
and plain speaking.
> Speech on taking vice-presidential oath,
> 6 Dec. 1973, in *Washington Post* 7 Dec.
> 1973

Henry Ford 1863–1947

12 History is more or less bunk. It's
tradition. We don't want tradition. We
want to live in the present and the only
history that is worth a tinker's damn is
the history we make today.
> *Chicago Tribune* 25 May 1916 (interview
> with Charles N. Wheeler)

13 People can have the Model T in any
colour—so long as it's black.
> In Allan Nevins *Ford* (1957) vol. 2, ch. 15

Lena Guilbert Ford 1870–1916

14 Keep the Home-fires burning,
While your hearts are yearning,
Though your lads are far away
They dream of Home.
There's a silver lining
Through the dark cloud shining;
Turn the dark cloud inside out,
Till the boys come Home.
> *'Till the Boys Come Home!* (1914 song;
> music by Ivor Novello)

Howell Forgy 1908–1983

15 Lieutenant Forgy . . . said that on Dec. 7
he was at Pearl Harbor directing
preparations for church services aboard
his ship . . . when general quarters were

sounded as the Japanese attacked. He reported to his battle station. The power was off on a powder hoist, he said, and so Lieutenant Edwin Woodhead formed a line of sailors to pass the ammunition by hand to the deck. The chaplain moved along the line, encouraging the passers and repeating, 'Praise the Lord and pass the ammunition.'

New York Times 1 Nov. 1942. Cf. Frank Loesser's 1942 song Praise the Lord and Pass the Ammunition.

E. M. Forster 1879–1970

1 They [public schoolboys] go forth into a world that is not entirely composed of public-school men or even of Anglo-Saxons, but of men who are as various as the sands of the sea; into a world of whose richness and subtlety they have no conception. They go forth into it with well-developed bodies, fairly developed minds, and undeveloped hearts.

Abinger Harvest (1936) 'Notes on English Character'

2 It is not that the Englishman can't feel—it is that he is afraid to feel. He has been taught at his public school that feeling is bad form. He must not express great joy or sorrow, or even open his mouth too wide when he talks—his pipe might fall out if he did.

Abinger Harvest (1936) 'Notes on English Character'

3 Everything must be like something, so what is this like?

Abinger Harvest (1936) 'Doll Souse'

4 American women shoot the hippopotamus with eyebrows made of platinum.

Abinger Harvest (1936) 'Mickey and Minnie'. Cf. 24:8

5 It is frivolous stuff, and how rare, how precious is frivolity! How few writers can prostitute all their powers! They are always implying 'I am capable of higher things.'

Abinger Harvest (1936) 'Ronald Firbank'

6 The historian must have a third quality as well: some conception of how men who are not historians behave.

Otherwise he will move in a world of the dead.

Abinger Harvest (1936) 'Captain Edward Gibbon'

7 Yes—oh dear yes—the novel tells a story.

Aspects of the Novel (1927) ch. 2

8 That old lady in the anecdote . . . was not so much angry as contemptuous. . . . 'How can I tell what I think till I see what I say?'

Aspects of the Novel (1927) ch. 5. Cf. Graham Wallas 222:8

9 I am only touching on one aspect of Ulysses: it is of course far more than a fantasy—it is a dogged attempt to cover the universe with mud, an inverted Victorianism, an attempt to make crossness and dirt succeed where sweetness and light failed, a simplification of the human character in the interests of Hell.

Aspects of the Novel (1927) ch. 6

10 Long books, when read, are usually overpraised, because the reader wishes to convince others and himself that he has not wasted his time.

Note from commonplace book, in O. Stallybrass (ed.) Aspects of the Novel and Related Writings (1974) p. 129

11 Like many others who have lived long in a great capital, she had strong feelings about the various railway termini. They are our gates to the glorious and the unknown. Through them we pass out into adventure and sunshine, to them, alas! we return.

Howards End (1910) ch. 2

12 It will be generally admitted that Beethoven's Fifth Symphony is the most sublime noise that has ever penetrated into the ear of man.

Howards End (1910) ch. 5

13 The music [the scherzo of Beethoven's 5th Symphony] started with a goblin walking quietly over the universe, from end to end. Others followed him. They were not aggressive creatures; it was that that made them so terrible to Helen. They merely observed in passing that there was no such thing as splendour or heroism in the world. After the interlude of elephants dancing, they returned and made the observation for

a second time. Helen could not contradict them, for, once at all events, she had felt the same, and had seen the reliable walls of youth collapse. Panic and emptiness! The goblins were right.
Howards End (1910) ch. 5

1 All men are equal—all men, that is to say, who possess umbrellas.
Howards End (1910) ch. 6

2 Personal relations are the important thing for ever and ever, and not this outer life of telegrams and anger.
Howards End (1910) ch. 19

3 She would only point out the salvation that was latent in his own soul, and in the soul of every man. Only connect! That was the whole of her sermon. Only connect the prose and the passion, and both will be exalted, and human love will be seen at its height. Live in fragments no longer. Only connect, and the beast and the monk, robbed of the isolation that is life to either, will die.
Howards End (1910) ch. 22 (the title-page also has 'Only connect . . . ')

4 Death destroys a man: the idea of Death saves him.
Howards End (1910) ch. 27 (chapter 41 has 'Death destroys a man, but the idea of death saves him')

5 'I don't think I understand people very well. I only know whether I like or dislike them.'
'Then you are an Oriental.'
Passage to India (1924) ch. 2

6 The so-called white races are really pinko-grey.
Passage to India (1924) ch. 7

7 The echo in a Marabar cave is not like these, it is entirely devoid of distinction. Whatever is said, the same monotonous noise replies, and quivers up and down the walls until it is absorbed into the roof. 'Boum' is the sound as far as the human alphabet can express it, or 'bou-oum', or 'ou-boum',—utterly dull. Hope, politeness, the blowing of a nose, the squeak of a boot, all produce 'boum'.
Passage to India (1924) ch. 14

8 The echo began in some indescribable way to undermine her hold on life. Coming at a moment when she chanced to be fatigued, it had managed to murmur, 'Pathos, piety, courage—they

exist, but are identical, and so is filth. Everything exists, nothing has value.'
Passage to India (1924) ch. 14

9 The inscriptions which the poets of the State had composed were hung where they could not be read, or had twitched their drawing-pins out of the stucco, and one of them (composed in English to indicate His universality) consisted, by an unfortunate slip of the draughtsman, of the words, 'God si Love.'
God si Love. Is this the first message of India?
Passage to India (1924) ch. 33

10 A room with a view.
Title of novel (1908)

11 The traveller who has gone to Italy to study the tactile values of Giotto, or the corruption of the Papacy, may return remembering nothing but the blue sky and the men and women under it.
Room with a View (1908) ch. 2

12 I hate the idea of causes, and if I had to choose between betraying my country and betraying my friend, I hope I should have the guts to betray my country.
Two Cheers for Democracy (1951) 'What I Believe'

13 So Two cheers for Democracy: one because it admits variety and two because it permits criticism. Two cheers are quite enough: there is no occasion to give three. Only Love the Beloved Republic deserves that.
Two Cheers for Democracy (1951) 'What I Believe' ('Love, the Beloved Republic' is a phrase from Swinburne's poem *Hertha*)

14 Think before you speak is criticism's motto; speak before you think creation's.
Two Cheers for Democracy (1951) 'Raison d'être of Criticism'

15 I suggest that the only books that influence us are those for which we are ready, and which have gone a little farther down our particular path than we have yet got ourselves.
Two Cheers for Democracy (1951) 'Books That Influenced Me'

16 Creative writers are always greater than the causes that they represent.
Two Cheers for Democracy (1951) 'Gide and George'

Bruce Forsyth 1928–

1 Didn't she [or he or they] do well?
   Catch-phrase in 'The Generation Game' on
   BBC Television, 1973 onwards

2 Nice to see you—to see you, nice.
   Catch-phrase in 'The Generation Game' on
   BBC Television, 1973 onwards

3 I'm in charge.
   Catch-phrase in 'Sunday Night at the
   London Palladium' on ITV, 1958 onwards

Harry Emerson Fosdick
1878–1969

4 I renounce war for its consequences, for
   the lies it lives on and propagates, for
   the undying hatred it arouses, for the
   dictatorships it puts in the place of
   democracy, for the starvation that stalks
   after it. I renounce war and never again,
   directly or indirectly, will I sanction or
   support another.
   Sermon in New York on Armistice Day
   1933, in *Secret of Victorious Living* (1934)
   p. 97

Anatole France
(Jacques-Anatole-François
Thibault) 1844–1924

5 *Dans tout État policé, la richesse est chose
   sacrée; dans les démocraties elle est la seule
   chose sacrée.*

   In every well-governed state, wealth is
   a sacred thing; in democracies it is the
   only sacred thing.
   L'Ile des pingouins (Penguin Island, 1908)
   pt. 6, ch. 2

6 *Ils [les pauvres] y doivent travailler devant
   la majestueuse égalité des lois, qui interdit
   au riche comme au pauvre de coucher sous
   les ponts, de mendier dans les rues et de
   voler du pain.*

   They [the poor] have to labour in the
   face of the majestic equality of the law,
   which forbids the rich as well as the
   poor to sleep under bridges, to beg in the
   streets, and to steal bread.
   Le Lys rouge (The Red Lily, 1894) ch. 7

7 *Le bon critique est celui qui raconte les
   aventures de son âme au milieu des
   chefs-d'œuvre.*

The good critic is he who relates the
adventures of his soul among
masterpieces.
   La Vie littéraire (The Literary Life, 1888)
   dedicatory letter

Georges Franju 1912–

See JEAN-LUC GODARD

Sir James George Frazer
1854–1941

8 The awe and dread with which the
   untutored savage contemplates his
   mother-in-law are amongst the most
   familiar facts of anthropology.
   The Golden Bough (ed. 2, 1900) vol. 1,
   p. 288

Stan Freberg 1926–

9 It's too loud, man. . . . It's too shrill,
   man, it's too piercing.
   Banana Boat (Day-O) (1957 record; lines
   spoken by Peter Leeds)

10 Excuse me, you ain't any kin to the
   snare drummer, are you?
   Yellow Rose of Texas (1955 record; words
   spoken to a loud banjo-player)

Arthur Freed 1894–1973

11 Singin' in the rain.
   Title of song (1929; music by Nacio Herb
   Brown)

Ralph Freed

12 I like New York in June,
   How about you?
   How About You (1941 song; music by
   Burton Lane)

Cliff Freeman

13 Where's the beef?
   Advertising slogan for Wendy's Hamburgers
   in campaign launched 9 Jan. 1984 (taken
   up by Walter Mondale in a televised debate
   with Gary Hart from Atlanta, 11 March
   1984: 'When I hear your new ideas I'm
   reminded of that ad, "Where's the beef?"')

John Freeman 1880–1929

14 It was the lovely moon—she lifted
   Slowly her white brow among

Bronze cloud–waves that ebbed and
drifted
Faintly, faintlier afar.
Stone Trees (1916) 'It Was the Lovely Moon'

Marilyn French 1929–

1 Whatever they may be in public life,
whatever their relations with men, in
their relations with women, all men are
rapists, and that's all they are. They
rape us with their eyes, their laws, and
their codes.
The Women's Room (1977) bk. 5, ch. 19

Sigmund Freud 1856–1939

2 *Die Anatomie ist das Schicksal.*

Anatomy is destiny.
Gesammelte Schriften (Collected Writings,
1924) vol. 5, p. 210

3 *'Itzig, wohin reit'st Du?' 'Weiss ich, frag
das Pferd.'*

'Itzig, where are you riding to?' 'Don't
ask me, ask the horse.'
Letter to Wilhelm Fliess, 7 July 1898, in *Aus
den Anfängen der Psychoanalyse* (Origins of
Psychoanalysis, 1950) p. 275

4 *Wir sind so eingerichtet, dass wir nur den
Kontrast intensiv geniessen können, den
Zustand nur sehr wenig.*

We are so made, that we can only
derive intense enjoyment from
a contrast, and only very little from
a state of things.
Das Unbehagen in der Kultur (Civilization and
its Discontents, 1930) ch. 2

5 *Vergleiche entscheiden nichts, das ist wahr,
aber sie können machen, dass man sich
heimischer fühlt.*

Analogies decide nothing, that is true,
but they can make one feel more at
home.
*Neue Folge der Vorlesungen zur Einführung in
die Psychoanalyse* (New Introductory
Lectures on Psychoanalysis, 1933) ch. 31

6 The great question that has never been
answered and which I have not yet been
able to answer, despite my thirty years
of research into the feminine soul, is
'What does a woman want?'
Letter to Marie Bonaparte, in Ernest Jones
Sigmund Freud: Life and Work (1955) vol. 2,
pt. 3, ch. 16

Max Frisch 1911–

7 *Diskussion mit Hanna!—über Technik (laut
Hanna) als Kniff, die Welt so einzurichten,
dass wir sie nicht erleben müssen.*

Discussion with Hanna—about
technology (according to Hanna) as the
knack of so arranging the world that we
need not experience it.
Homo Faber (1957) pt. 2

Charles Frohman 1860–1915

8 Why fear death? It is the most beautiful
adventure in life.
Last words before drowning in the *Lusitania*,
7 May 1915, in I. F. Marcosson and D.
Frohman *Charles Frohman* (1916) ch. 19. Cf.
J. M. Barrie 19:9

Erich Fromm 1900–1980

9 Man's main task in life is to give birth to
himself, to become what he potentially
is. The most important product of his
effort is his own personality.
Man for Himself (1947) ch. 4

10 In the nineteenth century the problem
was that *God is dead*; in the twentieth
century the problem is that *man is dead*.
In the nineteenth century inhumanity
meant cruelty; in the twentieth century
it means schizoid self-alienation. The
danger of the past was that men became
slaves. The danger of the future is that
men may become robots.
The Sane Society (1955) ch. 9

David Frost 1939–

11 Hello, good evening, and welcome.
Catch-phrase in 'The Frost Programme' on
BBC Television, 1966 onwards

12 Seriously, though, he's doing a grand
job!
Catch-phrase in 'That Was The Week That
Was', on BBC Television, 1962–3

Robert Frost 1874–1963

13 It should be of the pleasure of a poem
itself to tell how it can. The figure
a poem makes. It begins in delight and
ends in wisdom. The figure is the same
as for love.
Collected Poems (1939) 'Figure a Poem
Makes'

1 No tears in the writer, no tears in the reader.
> Collected Poems (1939) 'Figure a Poem Makes'

2 Like a piece of ice on a hot stove the poem must ride on its own melting. A poem may be worked over once it is in being, but may not be worried into being.
> Collected Poems (1939) 'Figure a Poem Makes'

3 They cannot scare me with their empty spaces
Between stars—on stars where no human race is.
I have it in me so much nearer home
To scare myself with my own desert places.
> Further Range (1936) 'Desert Places'

4 I never dared be radical when young
For fear it would make me conservative when old.
> Further Range (1936) 'Precaution'

5 Never ask of money spent
Where the spender thinks it went.
Nobody was ever meant
To remember or invent
What he did with every cent.
> Further Range (1936) 'Hardship of Accounting'

6 I've given offence by saying that I'd as soon write free verse as play tennis with the net down.
> In Edward Lathem Interviews with Robert Frost (1966) p. 203

7 Forgive, O Lord, my little jokes on Thee
And I'll forgive Thy great big one on me.
> In the Clearing (1962) 'Cluster of Faith'

8 I shall be telling this with a sigh
Somewhere ages and ages hence:
Two roads diverged in a wood, and I—
I took the one less travelled by,
And that has made all the difference.
> Mountain Interval (1916) 'Road Not Taken'

9 I'd like to get away from earth awhile
And then come back to it and begin over.
May no fate wilfully misunderstand me
And half grant what I wish and snatch me away
Not to return. Earth's the right place for love:

I don't know where it's likely to go better.
I'd like to go by climbing a birch tree,
And climb black branches up a snow-white trunk
Toward heaven, till the tree could bear no more,
But dipped its top and set me down again.
That would be good both going and coming back.
One could do worse than be a swinger of birches.
> Mountain Interval (1916) 'Birches'

10 Some say the world will end in fire,
Some say in ice.
From what I've tasted of desire
I hold with those who favour fire.
But if it had to perish twice,
I think I know enough of hate
To say that for destruction ice
Is also great
And would suffice.
> New Hampshire (1923) 'Fire and Ice'

11 The woods are lovely, dark and deep.
But I have promises to keep,
And miles to go before I sleep,
And miles to go before I sleep.
> New Hampshire (1923) 'Stopping by Woods on a Snowy Evening'

12 I'm going out to clean the pasture spring;
I'll only stop to rake the leaves away
(And wait to watch the water clear, I may):
I shan't be gone long.—You come too.
> North of Boston (1914) 'The Pasture'

13 Something there is that doesn't love a wall,
That sends the frozen-ground-swell under it.
> North of Boston (1914) 'Mending Wall'

14 My apple trees will never get across
And eat the cones under his pines, I tell him.
He only says, 'Good fences make good neighbours.'
> North of Boston (1914) 'Mending Wall'

15 Before I built a wall I'd ask to know
What I was walling in or walling out,
And to whom I was like to give offence.
> North of Boston (1914) 'Mending Wall'

16 And nothing to look backward to with pride,

And nothing to look forward to with hope.
North of Boston (1914) 'Death of the Hired Man'

1 'Home is the place where, when you have to go there,
They have to take you in.'
'I should have called it
Something you somehow haven't to deserve.'
North of Boston (1914) 'Death of the Hired Man'

2 Most of the change we think we see in life
Is due to truths being in and out of favour.
North of Boston (1914) 'Black Cottage'

3 Len says one steady pull more ought to do it.
He says the best way out is always through.
North of Boston (1914) 'Servant to Servants'

4 I've broken Anne of gathering bouquets.
It's not fair to the child. It can't be helped though:
Pressed into service means pressed out of shape.
North of Boston (1914) 'Self-Seeker'

5 Poetry is what is lost in translation. It is also what is lost in interpretation.
In Louis Untermeyer *Robert Frost: a Backward Look* (1964) p. 18

6 Asked ... whether he would define poetry as 'escape' he answered hardily: 'No. Poetry is a way of taking life by the throat.'
Elizabeth S. Sergeant *Robert Frost: the Trial by Existence* (1960) ch. 18

7 I have been one acquainted with the night.
West-Running Brook (1928) 'Acquainted with the Night'

8 Happiness makes up in height for what it lacks in length.
Title of poem in *Witness Tree* (1942)

9 The land was ours before we were the land's.
She was our land more than a hundred years
Before we were her people.
Witness Tree (1942) 'Gift Outright'

10 And were an epitaph to be my story
I'd have a short one ready for my own.

I would have written of me on my stone:
I had a lover's quarrel with the world.
Witness Tree (1942) 'Lesson for Today'

11 We dance round in a ring and suppose,
But the Secret sits in the middle and knows.
Witness Tree (1942) 'The Secret Sits'

Christopher Fry 1907–

12 The dark is light enough.
Title of play (1954)

13 I travel light; as light,
That is, as a man can travel who will
Still carry his body around because
Of its sentimental value.
The Lady's not for Burning (1949) act 1

14 What after all
Is a halo? It's only one more thing to keep clean.
The Lady's not for Burning (1949) act 1

15 What is official
Is incontestable. It undercuts
The problematical world and sells us life
At a discount.
The Lady's not for Burning (1949) act 1

16 Where in this small-talking world can I find
A longitude with no platitude?
The Lady's not for Burning (1949) act 3

17 The moon is nothing
But a circumambulating aphrodisiac
Divinely subsidized to provoke the world
Into a rising birth-rate.
The Lady's not for Burning (1949) act 3

18 I hear
A gay modulating anguish, rather like music.
The Lady's not for Burning (1949) act 3

19 The Great Bear is looking so geometrical
One would think that something or other could be proved.
The Lady's not for Burning (1949) act 3

20 The best
Thing we can do is to make wherever we're lost in
Look as much like home as we can.
The Lady's not for Burning (1949) act 3

21 Try thinking of love, or something.
Amor vincit insomnia.
A Sleep of Prisoners (1951) p. 37

1 I hope
I've done nothing so monosyllabic as to
  cheat,
A spade is never so merely a spade as
  the word
Spade would imply.
Venus Observed (1950) act 2, sc. 1

2 I tell you,
Miss, I knows an undesirable character
When I see one; I've been one myself for
  years.
Venus Observed (1950) act 2, sc. 1

Roger Fry 1866–1934

3 Mr Fry . . . brought out a screen upon
which there was a picture of a circus.
The interviewer was puzzled by the long
waists, bulging necks and short legs of
the figures. 'But how much wit there is
in those figures,' said Mr Fry. 'Art is
significant deformity.'
Virginia Woolf *Roger Fry* (1940) ch. 8

4 Bach almost persuades me to be
a Christian.
In Virginia Woolf *Roger Fry* (1940) ch. 11

R. Buckminster Fuller 1895–1983

5 Right now I am a passenger on space
vehicle Earth zooming about the Sun at
60,000 miles per hour somewhere in
the solar system.
In Gene Youngblood *Expanded Cinema*
(1970) p. 24

6 Either war is obsolete or men are.
In *New Yorker* 8 Jan. 1966, p. 93

7 Here is God's purpose—
for God, to me, it seems,
is a verb
not a noun,
proper or improper.
No More Secondhand God (1963) p. 28 (poem
written in 1940)

8 Now there is one outstandingly
important fact regarding Spaceship
Earth, and that is that no instruction
book came with it.
Operating Manual for Spaceship Earth (1969)
ch. 4

Alfred Funke 1869–?

9 *Gott strafe England!*

God punish England!
Schwert und Myrte (Sword and Myrtle,
1914) p. 78

Sir David Maxwell Fyfe
1900–1967
See LORD KILMUIR

Will Fyffe 1885–1947

10 I belong to Glasgow
Dear Old Glasgow town!
But what's the matter wi' Glasgow?
For it's going round and round.
I'm only a common old working chap,
As anyone can see,
But when I get a couple of drinks on
  a Saturday,
Glasgow belongs to me.
I Belong to Glasgow (1920 song)

Rose Fyleman 1877–1957

11 There are fairies at the bottom of our
garden!
Punch 23 May 1917 'Fairies'

Zsa Zsa Gabor (Sari Gabor) 1919–

12 You mean apart from my own?
When asked how many husbands she had
had, in K. Edwards *I Wish I'd Said That*
(1976) p. 75

13 A man in love is incomplete until he has
married. Then he's finished.
In *Newsweek* 28 Mar. 1960, p. 89

14 I never hated a man enough to give him
diamonds back.
In *Observer* 25 Aug. 1957

Norman Gaff d. 1988

15 A Mars a day helps you work, rest and
play.
Advertising slogan for Mars bar, *c*.1960
onwards

Hugh Gaitskell 1906–1963

16 I say this to you: we may lose the vote
today [on retaining nuclear weapons]
and the result may deal this Party
a grave blow. It may not be possible to
prevent it, but I think there are many of
us who will not accept that this blow
need be mortal, who will not believe
that such an end is inevitable. There are
some of us, Mr Chairman, who will fight
and fight and fight again to save the
Party we love. We will fight and fight

and fight again to bring back sanity and honesty and dignity, so that our Party with its great past may retain its glory and its greatness.

Speech at Labour Party Conference, 5 Oct. 1960, in *Report of 59th Annual Conference* p. 201

1 It [a European federation] does mean, if this is the idea, the end of Britain as an independent European state. . . . It means the end of a thousand years of history.

Speech at Labour Party Conference, 3 Oct. 1962, in *Report of 61st Annual Conference* p. 159

J. K. Galbraith 1908–

2 These are the days when men of all social disciplines and all political faiths seek the comfortable and the accepted; when the man of controversy is looked upon as a disturbing influence; when originality is taken to be a mark of instability; and when, in minor modification of the scriptural parable, the bland lead the bland.

Affluent Society (1958) ch. 1

3 Perhaps the thing most evident of all is how new and varied become the problems we must ponder when we break the nexus with the work of Ricardo and face the economics of affluence of the world in which we live. It is easy to see why the conventional wisdom resists so stoutly such a change. It is a far, far better thing to have a firm anchor in nonsense than to put out on the troubled seas of thought.

Affluent Society (1958) ch. 11

4 In a community where public services have failed to keep abreast of private consumption things are very different. Here, in an atmosphere of private opulence and public squalor, the private goods have full sway.

Affluent Society (1958) ch. 18. Cf. Sallust's *Catiline* 1ii. 22: *Habemus publice egestatem, privatim opulentiam.* We have public poverty and private opulence.

5 Politics is not the art of the possible. It consists in choosing between the disastrous and the unpalatable.

Letter to President Kennedy, 2 Mar. 1962, in *Ambassador's Journal* (1969) p. 312. Cf. R. A. Butler 43:1

John Galsworthy 1867–1933

6 He [Jolyon] was afflicted by the thought that where Beauty was, nothing ever ran quite straight, which, no doubt, was why so many people looked on it as immoral.

In Chancery (1920) pt. 1, ch. 13

7 I s'pose Jolyon's told you something about the young man. From all *I* can learn, he's got no business, no income, and no connection worth speaking of; but then, I know nothing—nobody tells me anything.

Man of Property (1906) pt. 1, ch. 1

Ray Galton 1930– and Alan Simpson 1929–

8 I came in here in all good faith to help my country. I don't mind giving a reasonable amount [of blood], but a pint . . . why that's very nearly an armful. I'm sorry. I'm not walking around with an empty arm for anybody.

The Blood Donor (1961 television programme) in *Hancock's Half Hour* (1974) p. 113 (words spoken by Tony Hancock)

Mohandas Karamchand Gandhi 1869–1948

9 Recently I saw a film of Gandhi when he came to England in 1930. He disembarked in Southampton and on the gangway he was already overwhelmed by journalists asking questions. One of them asked, 'Mr Gandhi, what do you think of modern civilization?' And Mr Gandhi said, 'That would be a good idea.'

E. F. Schumacher *Good Work* (1979) ch. 2

10 What difference does it make to the dead, the orphans and the homeless, whether the mad destruction is wrought under the name of totalitarianism or the holy name of liberty or democracy?

Non-Violence in Peace and War (1942) vol. 1, ch. 142

11 The moment the slave resolves that he will no longer be a slave, his fetters fall. He frees himself and shows the way

to others. Freedom and slavery are
mental states.
> *Non-Violence in Peace and War* (1949) vol. 2,
> ch. 5

1 I wanted to avoid violence. Non-violence
is the first article of my faith. It is also
the last article of my creed.
> Speech at Shahi Bag, 18 Mar. 1922, in
> *Young India* 23 Mar. 1922

Greta Garbo (Greta Lovisa Gustafsson) 1905–1990

2 I want to be alone. . . . I just want to be
alone.
> *Grand Hotel* (1932 film; script by William A.
> Drake)

3 I tank I go home.
> On being refused a pay rise by Louis B.
> Mayer, in Norman Zierold *Moguls* (1969)
> ch. 9

Ed Gardner 1905–1963

4 Opera is when a guy gets stabbed in the
back and, instead of bleeding, he sings.
> In *Duffy's Tavern* (1940s American radio
> programme)

John Nance Garner 1868–1967

5 The vice-presidency isn't worth a pitcher
of warm piss.
> In O. C. Fisher *Cactus Jack* (1978) ch. 11

Bamber Gascoigne 1935–

6 Your starter for ten.
> Phrase often used in *University Challenge*
> (ITV quiz series, 1962–1987)

Noel Gay (Richard Moxon Armitage) 1898–1954

7 I'm leaning on a lamp-post at the corner
of the street,
In case a certain little lady comes by.
> *Leaning on a Lamp-Post* (1937 song; sung by
> George Formby in film *Father Knew Best*)

Noel Gay 1898–1954 and Ralph Butler

8 Run, rabbit, run, rabbit, run, run, run.
Run, rabbit, run, rabbit, run, run, run.
Bang, bang, bang, bang, goes the
farmer's gun,
Run, rabbit, run, rabbit, run, run, run.
> *Run Rabbit Run!* (1939 song)

Sir Eric Geddes 1875–1937

9 The Germans, if this Government is
returned, are going to pay every penny;
they are going to be squeezed as a lemon
is squeezed—until the pips squeak. My
only doubt is not whether we can
squeeze hard enough, but whether there
is enough juice.
> Speech at Cambridge, 10 Dec. 1918, in
> *Cambridge Daily News* 11 Dec. 1918

Bob Geldof 1954–

10 Most people get into bands for three very
simple rock and roll reasons: to get laid,
to get fame, and to get rich.
> *Melody Maker* 27 Aug. 1977

Bob Geldof 1954– and Midge Ure

11 Feed the world
Feed the world.
Feed the world
Let them know it's Christmas time
again.
> *Do They Know it's Christmas?* (1984 song)

King George V 1865–1936

12 After I am dead, the boy [Edward VIII]
will ruin himself in twelve months.
> In Keith Middlemas and John Barnes
> *Baldwin* (1969) ch. 34

13 I said to your predecessor: 'You know
what they're all saying, no more coals
to Newcastle, no more Hoares to Paris.'
The fellow didn't even laugh.
> Remark to Anthony Eden, 23 Dec. 1935,
> following Samuel Hoare's resignation as
> Foreign Secretary on 18 Dec. 1935, in Earl
> of Avon *Facing the Dictators* (1962) pt. 2,
> ch. 1

14 I venture to allude to the impression
which seemed generally to prevail
among their brethren across the seas,
that the Old Country must wake up if
she intends to maintain her old position
of pre-eminence in her Colonial trade
against foreign competitors.
> Speech at Guildhall, 5 Dec. 1901, in Harold
> Nicolson *King George V* (1952) p. 73 (the
> speech was reprinted in 1911 with the title
> 'Wake up, England')

1 Bugger Bognor.

> Remark said to have been made either in
> 1929 when the King was informed that
> a deputation of leading citizens was asking
> that the town should be named Bognor
> Regis because of his convalescence there
> after a serious illness, or on his death-bed in
> 1936 when one of his doctors sought to
> soothe him with the remark 'Cheer up, your
> Majesty, you will soon be at Bognor again.'
> See Kenneth Rose *King George V* (1983)
> ch. 9

2 The last time I talked to the King
[George V] on the morning of his death,
Monday 20th, he had *The Times* on his
table in front of him opened at the
'Imperial and Foreign' page and I think
his remark to me, 'How's the Empire?'
was prompted by some para. he had
read on this page.

> Letter from Lord Wigram, 31 Jan. 1936, in
> J. E. Wrench *Geoffrey Dawson and Our Times*
> (1955) ch. 28

3 Gentlemen, I am so sorry for keeping
you waiting like this. I am unable to
concentrate.

> Words spoken on his death-bed, reported in
> memorandum by Lord Wigram, 20 Jan.
> 1936, in *History Today* Dec. 1986

4 I have many times asked myself whether
there can be more potent advocates of
peace upon earth through the years to
come than this massed multitude of
silent witnesses to the desolation of war.

> Message read at Terlincthun Cemetery,
> Boulogne, 13 May 1922, in *The Times*
> 15 May 1922

Daniel George (Daniel George Bunting)

5 O Freedom, what liberties are taken in
thy name!

> In Sagittarius and D. George *Perpetual
> Pessimist* (1963) p. 58

George Gershwin 1898–1937

See IRA GERSHWIN

Ira Gershwin 1896–1983

6 A foggy day in London Town
Had me low and had me down.
I viewed the morning with alarm,
The British Museum had lost its charm.
How long, I wondered, could this thing
last?

But the age of miracles hadn't passed,
For, suddenly, I saw you there
And through foggy London town the
sun was shining everywhere.

> *A Foggy Day* (1937 song; music by George
> Gershwin)

7 I got rhythm,
I got music,
I got my man
Who could ask for anything more?

> *I Got Rhythm* (1930 song; music by George
> Gershwin)

8 Lady, be good!

> Title of musical (1924; music by George
> Gershwin)

9 You like potato and I like po-tah-to,
You like tomato and I like to-mah-to;
Potato, po-tah-to, tomato, to-mah-to—
Let's call the whole thing off!

> *Let's Call the Whole Thing Off* (1937 song;
> music by George Gershwin)

10 Holding hands at midnight
'Neath a starry sky,
Nice work if you can get it,
And you can get it if you try.

> *Nice Work If You Can Get It* (1937 song;
> music by George Gershwin)

Stella Gibbons 1902–1989

11 Every year, in the fulness o' summer,
when the sukebind hangs heavy from
the wains . . . 'tes the same. And when
the spring comes her hour is upon her
again. 'Tes the hand of Nature and we
women cannot escape it.

> *Cold Comfort Farm* (1932) ch. 5

12 When you were very small—so small
that the lightest puff of breeze blew your
little crinoline skirt over your head—you
had seen something nasty in the
woodshed.

> *Cold Comfort Farm* (1932) ch. 10

13 Mr Mybug, however, did ask Rennett to
marry him. He said that, by god, D. H.
Lawrence was right when he had said
there must be a dumb, dark, dull, bitter
belly-tension between a man and
a woman, and how else could this be
achieved save in the long monotony of
marriage?

> *Cold Comfort Farm* (1932) ch. 20

Wolcott Gibbs 1902–1958

1 Backward ran sentences until reeled the mind.
  New Yorker 28 Nov. 1936 'Time ... Fortune ... Life ... Luce' (satirizing the style of *Time* magazine)

2 Where it will all end, knows God!
  New Yorker 28 Nov. 1936 'Time ... Fortune ... Life ... Luce' (satirizing the style of *Time* magazine)

Kahlil Gibran 1883–1931

3 Your children are not your children.
  They are the sons and daughters of
    Life's longing for itself.
  They came through you but not from
    you
  And though they are with you yet they
    belong not to you.
  You may give them your love but not
    your thoughts,
  For they have their own thoughts.
  You may house their bodies but not
    their souls,
  For their souls dwell in the house of
    tomorrow, which you cannot visit,
    not even in your dreams.
  You may strive to be like them, but seek
    not to make them like you,
  For life goes not backward nor tarries
    with yesterday.
  You are the bows from which your
    children as living arrows are sent
    forth.
  Prophet (1923) 'On Children'

4 Work is love made visible. And if you
  cannot work with love but only with
  distaste, it is better that you should
  leave your work and sit at the gate of
  the temple and take alms of those who
  work with joy.
  Prophet (1923) 'On Work'

5 An exaggeration is a truth that has lost
  its temper.
  Sand and Foam (1926) p. 59

Wilfrid Wilson Gibson 1878–1962

6 But we, how shall we turn to little
    things
  And listen to the birds and winds and
    streams
  Made holy by their dreams,

Nor feel the heart-break in the heart of
    things?
  Whin (1918) 'Lament'

André Gide 1869–1951

7 *M'est avis ... que le profit n'est pas toujours
  ce qui mène l'homme; qu'il y a des actions
  désintéressées. ... Par désintéressé
  j'entends: gratuit. Et que le mal, ce que l'on
  appelle: le mal, peut être aussi gratuit que
  le bien.*

  I believe ... that profit is not always
  what motivates man; that there are
  disinterested actions. ... By *disinterested*
  I mean: gratuitous. And that evil acts,
  what people call evil, can be as
  gratuitous as good acts.
  Les Caves du Vatican (The Vatican Cellars, 1914) bk. 4, ch. 7

8 *Hugo—hélas!*

  Hugo—alas!
  Answer when he was asked who was the
  greatest 19th-century poet, in Claude
  Martin *La Maturité d'André Gide* (1977)
  p. 502

Eric Gill 1882–1940

9 That state is a state of Slavery in which
  a man does what he likes to do in his
  spare time and in his working time that
  which is required of him.
  Art-nonsense and Other Essays (1929)
  'Slavery and Freedom'

Terry Gilliam 1940–

See GRAHAM CHAPMAN *et al.*

Penelope Gilliatt 1933–

10 It would be unfair to suggest that one of
  the most characteristic sounds of the
  English Sunday is the sound of Harold
  Hobson barking up the wrong tree.
  Encore Nov.-Dec. 1959

11 Sunday, bloody Sunday.
  Title of film (1971)

Allen Ginsberg 1926–

12 What if someone gave a war & Nobody
    came?
  Life would ring the bells of Ecstasy and
    Forever be Itself again.
  Fall of America (1972) 'Graffiti'

1 I saw the best minds of my generation
   destroyed by madness, starving
   hysterical naked,
dragging themselves through the negro
   streets at dawn looking for an angry
   fix,
angelheaded hipsters burning for the
   ancient heavenly connection to the
   starry dynamo in the machinery of
   the night.
   Howl (1956) p. 9

George Gipp d. 1920

2 'Some time, Rock,' he said, 'when the
team's up against it, when things are
wrong and the breaks are beating the
boys—tell them to go in there with all
they've got and win just one for the
Gipper.'
   Knut Rockne 'Gipp the Great' in *Collier's*
   22 Nov. 1930

Jean Giraudoux 1882–1944

3 *Nous savons tous ici que le droit est la plus
puissante des écoles de l'imagination.
Jamais poète n'a interprété la nature aussi
librement qu'un juriste la réalité.*

We all know here that the law is the
most powerful of schools for the
imagination. No poet ever interpreted
nature as freely as a lawyer interprets
the truth.
   La Guerre de Troie n'aura pas lieu (The Trojan
   War Will Not Take Place, 1935) act. 2, sc.
   5

George Glass 1910–1984

4 An actor is a kind of a guy who if you
ain't talking about him ain't listening.
   In Bob Thomas *Brando* (1973) ch. 8 (said to
   be often quoted by Marlon Brando, who is
   cited as quoting it in *Observer* 1 Jan. 1956)

John A. Glover-Kind d. 1918

5 I do like to be beside the seaside.
   Title of song (1909)

Jean-Luc Godard 1930–

6 *La photographie, c'est la vérité. Le cinéma:
la vérité vingt-quatre fois par seconde.*

Photography is truth. The cinema is
truth twenty-four times per second.
   Le Petit Soldat (1960 film), in *Lettres
   Françaises* 31 Jan. 1963

7 'Movies should have a beginning,
a middle and an end,' harrumphed
French Film Maker Georges Franju at
a symposium some years back.
'Certainly,' replied Jean-Luc Godard.
'But not necessarily in that order.'
   Time 14 Sept. 1981

A. D. Godley 1856–1925

8 What is this that roareth thus?
Can it be a Motor Bus?
Yes, the smell and hideous hum
Indicat Motorem Bum! ...
How shall wretches live like us
Cincti Bis Motoribus?
Domine, defende nos
Contra hos Motores Bos!
   Letter to C. R. L. Fletcher, 10 Jan 1914, in
   Reliquiae (1926) vol. 1, p. 292

Joseph Goebbels 1897–1945

9 *Ohne Butter werden wir fertig, aber nicht
beispielsweise ohne Kanonen. Wenn wir
einmal überfallen werden, dann können wir
uns nicht mit Butter, sondern nur mit
Kanonen verteidigen.*

We can manage without butter but not,
for example, without guns. If we are
attacked we can only defend ourselves
with guns not with butter.
   Speech in Berlin, 17 Jan. 1936, in *Deutsche
   Allgemeine Zeitung* 18 Jan. 1936. Cf.
   Hermann Goering

Hermann Goering 1893–1946

10 We have no butter, *meine Volksgenossen*
[my countrymen], but I ask you—
would you rather have butter or guns?
Shall we import lard or metal ores?
Let me tell you—preparedness makes
us powerful. Butter merely makes us
fat.
   Speech at Hamburg, 1936, in W.
   Frischauer *Goering* (1951) ch. 10

Ivan Goff 1910– and Ben Roberts (Benjamin Eisenberg) 1916–1984

11 Anyway, Ma, I made it. .... Top of the
world!
   White Heat (1949 film; last lines—spoken
   by James Cagney)

Isaac Goldberg 1887–1938

1 Diplomacy is to do and say
The nastiest thing in the nicest way.
   Reflex Oct. 1927, p. 77

William Golding 1911–

2 Lord of the flies.
   Title of novel (1954)

Emma Goldman 1869–1940

3 Anarchism, then, really, stands for the
liberation of the human mind from the
dominion of religion; the liberation of
the human body from the dominion of
property; liberation from the shackles
and restraints of government.
   Anarchism and Other Essays (1910) p. 68

Barry Goldwater 1909–

4 I would remind you that extremism in
the defence of liberty is no vice! And let
me remind you also that moderation in
the pursuit of justice is no virtue!
   Speech accepting the presidential
   nomination, 16 July 1964, in *New York
   Times* 17 July 1964, p. 1

Sam Goldwyn (Samuel Goldfish) 1882–1974

5 Pictures are for entertainment, messages
should be delivered by Western Union.
   In Arthur Marx *Goldwyn* (1976) ch. 15

6 Gentlemen, include me out.
   Said on resigning from the Motion Picture
   Producers and Distributors of America, Oct.
   1933, in Michael Freedland
   The Goldwyn Touch (1986) ch. 10

7 A verbal contract isn't worth the paper
it is written on.
   In Alva Johnston *The Great Goldwyn* (1937)
   ch. 1

8 'I can answer you in two words,
"im-possible"' is almost the cornerstone
of the Goldwyn legend, but Sam did not
say it. It was printed late in 1925 in
a humorous magazine and credited to an
anonymous Potash or Perlmutter.
   Alva Johnston *The Great Goldwyn* (1937)
   ch. 1

9 That's the way with these directors,
they're always biting the hand that lays
the golden egg.
   In Alva Johnston *The Great Goldwyn* (1937)
   ch. 1

10 Any man who goes to a psychiatrist
should have his head examined.
   In Norman Zierold *Moguls* (1969) ch. 3

11 It is doubtful that Goldwyn made the
remark attributed to him by several
authors: 'The reason so many people
showed up at his [Louis B. Mayer's]
funeral was because they wanted to
make sure he was dead.' In Hollywood
one hears that sentiment attributed to
other moguls at other funerals. It's
a good story, and the temptation to use
it is almost irresistible. Goldwyn,
however, denies making the remark. He
did not go to the funeral, was in fact not
invited, but his son who was with him
on that day says he was deeply moved
despite the fact that he never liked
Mayer.
   Norman Zierold *Moguls* (1969) ch. 3

12 Why should people go out and pay to
see bad movies when they can stay at
home and see bad television for
nothing?
   In *Observer* 9 Sept. 1956

Paul Goodman 1911–1972

13 All men are creative but few are artists.
   Growing up Absurd (1961) ch. 9

Mack Gordon 1904–1959

14 Pardon me boy is that the Chattanooga
   Choo-choo,
Track twenty nine,
Boy you can gimme a shine.
I can afford to board a Chattanooga
   Choo-choo,
I've got my fare and just a trifle to spare.
You leave the Pennsylvania station
   'bout a quarter to four,
Read a magazine and then you're in
   Baltimore,
Dinner in the diner nothing could be
   finer
Than to have your ham'n eggs in
   Carolina.
   Chattanooga Choo-choo (1941 song; music by
   Harry Warren)

Stuart Gorrell 1902–1963

1 Georgia, Georgia, no peace I find,
Just an old sweet song keeps Georgia on
my mind.
  Georgia on my Mind (1930 song; music by
  Hoagy Carmichael)

Sir Edmund Gosse 1849–1928

2 At a lunch at the House of Lords
[c.1906] given by Edmund Gosse ... the
woolly-bearded poet, Sturge Moore ...
entered late. Gosse, a naughty host,
whispered in my ear, 'A sheep in sheep's
clothing.'
  F. Greenslet *Under the Bridge* (1943) ch. 10.
  Cf. Winston Churchill 56:3

Lord Gowrie (2nd Earl of Gowrie) 1939–

3 [£1,500 a month] is not what people
need for living in central London, and
which I am more or less obliged to do.
  In BBC radio interview, 4 Sept. 1985, in *The
  Times* 5 Sept. 1985 (giving reason for
  resigning as Minister for the Arts)

Lew Grade (Baron Grade) 1906–

4 All my shows are great. Some of them
are bad. But they are all great.
  In *Observer* 14 Sept. 1975

D. M. Graham 1911–

5 That this House will in no circumstances
fight for its King and Country.
  Motion worded by Graham (the
  then-Librarian) for debate at the Oxford
  Union, 9 Feb. 1933, and passed by 275
  votes to 153

Harry Graham 1874–1936

6 Weep not for little Léonie
Abducted by a French Marquis!
Though loss of honour was a wrench
Just think how it's improved her French.
  More Ruthless Rhymes for Heartless Homes
  (1930) 'Compensation'

7 Aunt Jane observed, the second time
She tumbled off a bus,
'The step is short from the Sublime
To the Ridiculous.'
  Ruthless Rhymes for Heartless Homes (1899)
  'Equanimity'

8 Billy, in one of his nice new sashes,
Fell in the fire and was burnt to ashes;
Now, although the room grows chilly,
I haven't the heart to poke poor Billy.
  Ruthless Rhymes for Heartless Homes (1899)
  'Tender-Heartedness'

9 O'er the rugged mountain's brow
Clara threw the twins she nursed,
And remarked, 'I wonder now
Which will reach the bottom first?'
  Ruthless Rhymes for Heartless Homes (1899)
  'Calculating Clara'

10 'There's been an accident,' they said,
'Your servant's cut in half; he's dead!'
'Indeed!' said Mr Jones, 'and please,
Send me the half that's got my keys.'
  Ruthless Rhymes for Heartless Homes (1899)
  'Mr Jones' (poem attributed to 'G.W.')

Kenneth Grahame 1859–1932

11 The curate faced the laurels—
hesitatingly. But Aunt Maria flung
herself on him. 'O Mr Hodgitts!' I heard
her cry, 'you are brave! for my sake do
not be rash!' He was not rash.
  The Golden Age (1895) 'The Burglars'

12 Monkeys, who very sensibly refrain from
speech, lest they should be set to earn
their livings.
  The Golden Age (1895) 'Lusisti Satis'

13 Believe me, my young friend, there is
nothing—absolutely nothing—half so
much worth doing as simply messing
about in boats.
  Wind in the Willows (1908) ch. 1

14 'There's cold chicken inside it,' replied
the Rat briefly; 'coldtonguecoldhamcold-
beefpickledgerkinssaladfrenchrollscress-
sandwidgespottedmeatgingerbeer-
lemonadesodawater—'
  Wind in the Willows (1908) ch. 1

15 'Glorious, stirring sight!' murmured
Toad, never offering to move. 'The
poetry of motion! The *real* way to travel!
The *only* way to travel! Here today—in
next week tomorrow! Villages skipped,
towns and cities jumped—always
somebody else's horizon! O bliss! O
poop-poop! O my! O my!'
  Wind in the Willows (1908) ch. 2

16 The clever men at Oxford
Know all that there is to be knowed.

But they none of them know one half as
much
As intelligent Mr Toad!
Wind in the Willows (1908) ch. 10

Bernie Grant 1944–

1 The police were to blame for what
happened on Sunday night and what
they got was a bloody good hiding.
Speech as leader of Haringey Council outside
Tottenham Town Hall, 8 Oct. 1985, in *The
Times* 9 Oct. 1985

Ethel Watts-Mumford Grant
1878–1940

See ETHEL WATTS MUMFORD

Robert Graves 1895–1985

2 'What did the mayor do?'
'I was coming to that.'
Collected Poems (1938) 'Welsh Incident'

3 Goodbye to all that.
Title of autobiography (1929)

4 If there's no money in poetry, neither is
there poetry in money.
Speech at London School of Economics,
6 Dec. 1963, in *Mammon and Black Goddess*
(1965) p. 3

5 His eyes are quickened so with grief,
He can watch a grass or leaf
Every instant grow; he can
Clearly through a flint wall see,
Or watch the startled spirit flee
From the throat of a dead man.
Pier-Glass (1921) 'Lost Love'

6 As you are woman, so be lovely:
As you are lovely, so be various,
Merciful as constant, constant as
various,
So be mine, as I yours for ever.
Poems (1927) 'Pygmalion to Galatea'

7 Children are dumb to say how hot the
day is,
How hot the scent is of the summer
rose.
Poems (1927) 'Cool Web'

8 Counting the beats,
Counting the slow heart beats,
The bleeding to death of time in slow
heart beats,
Wakeful they lie.
Poems and Satires (1951) 'Counting the
Beats'

9 Far away is close at hand
Close joined is far away,
Love shall come at your command
Yet will not stay.
Whipperginny (1923) 'Song of Contrariety'

Hannah Green (Joanne Greenberg)

10 I never promised you a rose garden.
Title of novel (1964)

Graham Greene 1904–1991

11 Catholics and Communists have
committed great crimes, but at least
they have not stood aside, like an
established society, and been indifferent.
I would rather have blood on my hands
than water like Pilate.
Comedians (1966) pt. 3, ch. 4

12 Against the beautiful and the clever and
the successful, one can wage a pitiless
war, but not against the unattractive.
Heart of the Matter (1948) bk. 1, pt. 1, ch. 2

13 Despair is the price one pays for setting
oneself an impossible aim.
Heart of the Matter (1948) bk. 1, pt. 1, ch. 2

14 He [Harris] felt the loyalty we all feel to
unhappiness—the sense that that is
where we really belong.
Heart of the Matter (1948) bk. 2, pt. 2, ch. 1

15 Any victim demands allegiance.
Heart of the Matter (1948) bk. 3, pt. 1, ch. 1

16 His hilarity was like a scream from
a crevasse.
Heart of the Matter (1948) bk. 3, pt. 1, ch. 1

17 Our man in Havana.
Title of novel (1958)

18 There is always one moment in
childhood when the door opens and lets
the future in.
The Power and the Glory (1940) pt. 1, ch. 1

Oswald Greene

19 Greene and Bevan's research largely
consisted of visiting pubs and asking
people why they drank Guinness. Again
and again they received the . . . reply—
they drank Guinness because it was
good for them. So universal was this
idea, Greene decided he need look no
further for a copyline. 'Guinness' the

advertisements would simply say 'is
good for you.'

> Brian Sibley *Book of Guinness Advertising*
> (1985) ch. 4

Germaine Greer 1939–

1 Human beings have an inalienable right
to invent themselves; when that right is
pre-empted it is called brain-washing.

> *The Times* 1 Feb. 1986

Hubert Gregg 1914–

2 Maybe it's because I'm a Londoner
That I love London so,
Maybe it's because I'm a Londoner—
That I think of her—Wherever I go.
I get a funny feeling inside of me—
Just walking up and down,—
Maybe it's because I'm a Londoner
That I love London Town.

> *Maybe It's Because I'm a Londoner* (1947
> song)

Joyce Grenfell 1910–1979

3 George—don't do that.

> Recurring line in monologues about
> a nursery school, from the 1950s, in
> *George—Don't Do That* (1977) p. 24

4 Stately as a galleon, I sail across the
floor,
Doing the Military Two-step, as in the
days of yore.

> *Stately as a Galleon* (1978) p. 31

Julian Grenfell 1888–1915

5 The naked earth is warm with Spring,
And with green grass and bursting trees
Leans to the sun's kiss glorying,
And quivers in the sunny breeze;

And Life is Colour and Warmth and
Light
And a striving evermore for these;
And he is dead, who will not fight;
And who dies fighting has increase.

The fighting man shall from the sun
Take warmth, and life from the glowing
earth.
Speed with the light-foot winds to run,
And with the trees to newer birth.

> *The Times* 28 May 1915 'Into Battle'

Clifford Grey 1887–1941

6 If you were the only girl in the world
And I were the only boy.

> *If You Were the only Girl in the World* (song
> from musical *The Bing Boys* (1916); music
> by Nat Ayer)

Sir Edward Grey (Viscount Grey of Fallodon) 1862–1933

7 A friend came to see me on one of the
evenings of the last week—he thinks it
was on Monday August 3 [1914]. We
were standing at a window of my room
in the Foreign Office. It was getting
dusk, and the lamps were being lit in
the space below on which we were
looking. My friend recalls that
I remarked on this with the words: 'The
lamps are going out all over Europe; we
shall not see them lit again in our
lifetime.'

> *25 Years* (1925) vol. 2, ch. 18

Mervyn Griffith-Jones 1909–1979

8 You may think that one of the ways in
which you can test this book [*Lady
Chatterley's Lover* by D. H. Lawrence],
and test it from the most liberal outlook,
is to ask yourselves the question when
you have read it through: 'Would you
approve of your young sons and
daughters—because girls can read as
well as boys—reading this book?' Is it
a book you would have lying around in
your own house? Is it a book you would
even wish your wife or your servants to
read?

> Speech for the prosecution at the Central
> Criminal Court, Old Bailey, 20 Oct. 1960, in
> *The Times* 21 Oct. 1960

Leon Griffiths

9 'Er indoors.

> Used in ITV television series *Minder* (1979
> onwards) by Arthur Daley (played by George
> Cole) to refer to his wife

Jo Grimond (Baron Grimond) 1913–

10 In bygone days, commanders were
taught that when in doubt, they should
march their troops towards the sound of

gunfire. I intend to march my troops towards the sound of gunfire.

Speech at Liberal Party Annual Assembly, 14 Sept. 1963, in *Guardian* 16 Sept. 1963

Philip Guedalla 1889–1944

1 Any stigma, as the old saying is, will serve to beat a dogma.

Masters and Men (1923) 'Ministers of State'

2 History repeats itself. Historians repeat each other.

Supers and Supermen (1920) 'Some Historians'

3 The cheerful clatter of Sir James Barrie's cans as he went round with the milk of human kindness.

Supers and Supermen (1920) 'Some Critics'

4 The work of Henry James has always seemed divisible by a simple dynastic arrangement into three reigns: James I, James II, and the Old Pretender.

Supers and Supermen (1920) 'Some Critics'

R. Guidry

5 See you later, alligator,
After 'while, crocodile;
Can't you see you're in my way, now,
Don't you know you cramp my style?

See You Later Alligator (1956 song)

Texas Guinan (Mary Louise Cecilia Guinan) 1884–1933

6 Fifty million Frenchmen can't be wrong.

In *New York World–Telegram* 21 Mar. 1931, p. 25, which asserts that Guinan used the phrase at her night club at least six or seven years previously. The saying is also attributed to Jack Osterman and Mae West; it was the title of a 1927 song (see Billy Rose and Willie Raskin) and a film of 1931. The latter was inspired by Cole Porter's 1929 musical *Fifty Million Frenchmen*. Cf. Billy Rose and Willie Raskin

Nubar Gulbenkian 1896–1972

7 The best number for a dinner party is two—myself and a dam' good head waiter.

In *Daily Telegraph* 14 Jan. 1965

Thom Gunn 1929–

8 You know I know you know I know you know.

Fighting Terms (1954) 'Carnal Knowledge'

Dorothy Frances Gurney 1858–1932

9 The kiss of the sun for pardon,
The song of the birds for mirth,
One is nearer God's Heart in a garden
Than anywhere else on earth.

Poems (1913) 'God's Garden'

Woody Guthrie (Woodrow Wilson Guthrie) 1912–1967

10 This land is your land, this land is my land,
From California to the New York Island.
From the redwood forest to the Gulf Stream waters
This land was made for you and me.

This Land is Your Land (1956 song)

Earl Haig 1861–1928

11 D. [the 17th Earl of Derby] is a very weak-minded fellow I am afraid, and, like the feather pillow, bears the marks of the last person who has sat on him! I hear he is called in London 'genial Judas'!

Letter to Lady Haig, 14 Jan. 1918, in R. Blake *Private Papers of Douglas Haig* (1952) ch. 16

12 Every position must be held to the last man: there must be no retirement. With our backs to the wall, and believing in the justice of our cause, each one of us must fight on to the end. The safety of our Homes and the Freedom of mankind alike depend upon the conduct of each one of us at this critical moment.

Order to British troops, 12 Apr. 1918, in A. Duff Cooper *Haig* (1936) vol. 2, ch. 23

Lord Hailsham (Baron Hailsham, Quintin Hogg) 1907–

13 A great party is not to be brought down because of a scandal by a woman of easy virtue and a proved liar.

In BBC television interview on the Profumo affair, 13 June 1963, in *The Times* 14 June 1963

14 If the British public falls for this [the programme of the Labour party], I think

it will be stark, raving bonkers.

> In press conference at Conservative Central Office, 12 Oct. 1964, in *The Times* 13 Oct. 1964

J. B. S. Haldane 1892–1964

1 Now, my own suspicion is that the universe is not only queerer than we suppose, but queerer than we *can* suppose. I have read and heard many attempts at a systematic account of it, from materialism and theosophy to the Christian system or that of Kant, and I have always felt that they were much too simple. I suspect that there are more things in heaven and earth than are dreamed of, or can be dreamed of, in any philosophy. That is the reason why I have no philosophy myself, and must be my excuse for dreaming.

> *Possible Worlds and Other Essays* (1927) 'Possible Worlds'

2 From the fact that there are 400,000 species of beetles on this planet, but only 8,000 species of mammals, he [Haldane] concluded that the Creator, if He exists, has a special preference for beetles, and so we might be more likely to meet them than any other type of animal on a planet which would support life.

> Report of lecture, 7 Apr. 1951, cited in *Journal of the British Interplanetary Society* (1951) vol. 10, p. 156

H. R. Haldeman 1929–

3 Once the toothpaste is out of the tube, it is awfully hard to get it back in.

> Comment to John Wesley Dean on Watergate affair, 8 Apr. 1973, in *Hearings Before the Select Committee on Presidential Campaign Activities of US Senate: Watergate and Related Activities* (1973) vol. 4, p. 1399

Sir William Haley 1901–

4 It *is* a moral issue.

> Heading of leading article on the Profumo affair, in *The Times* 11 June 1963

Henry Hall 1899–1989

5 This *is* Henry Hall speaking, and tonight is my guest night.

> Catch-phrase on BBC Radio's *Guest Night* from 1934 (see Henry Hall's *Here's to the Next Time* (1955) ch. 11)

Sir Peter Hall 1930–

6 Sir Peter [Hall] has always maintained that, although nobody appeared to want a National Theatre when it was first promulgated, the public has consistently supported it with cash at the box office—with 'bottoms on seats' to use his own earthy phrase.

> *Spectator* 10 May 1980 (the phrase is often 'bums on seats')

Margaret Halsey 1910–

7 Englishwomen's shoes look as if they had been made by someone who had often heard shoes described but had never seen any.

> *With Malice Toward Some* (1938) pt. 2, p. 107

8 Towards people with whom they disagree the English gentry, or at any rate that small cross section of them which I have seen, are tranquilly good-natured. It is not *comme il faut* to establish the supremacy of an idea by smashing in the faces of all the people who try to contradict it. The English never smash in a face. They merely refrain from asking it to dinner.

> *With Malice Toward Some* (1938) pt. 3, p. 208

Oscar Hammerstein II 1895–1960

9 Climb ev'ry mountain, ford ev'ry stream
Follow ev'ry rainbow, till you find your dream!

> *Climb Ev'ry Mountain* (1959 song; music by Richard Rodgers)

10 June is bustin' out all over.

> Title of song (1945; music by Richard Rodgers)

11 The last time I saw Paris
Her heart was warm and gay,
I heard the laughter of her heart in ev'ry street café.

> *The Last Time I saw Paris* (1940 song; music by Jerome Kern)

12 The corn is as high as an elephant's eye,
An' it looks like it's climbin' clear up to the sky.

> *Oh, What a Beautiful Mornin'* (1943 song; music by Richard Rodgers)

13 Oh, what a beautiful mornin',

Oh, what a beautiful day!
I got a beautiful feelin'
Ev'rything's goin' my way.
Oh, What a Beautiful Mornin' (1943 song;
music by Richard Rodgers)

1 Ol' man river, dat ol' man river,
He must know sumpin', but don't say
    nothin',
He just keeps rollin',
He keeps on rollin' along.
Ol' Man River (1927 song; music by Jerome
Kern)

2 Some enchanted evening,
You may see a stranger,
You may see a stranger,
Across a crowded room.
Some Enchanted Evening (1949 song; music
by Richard Rodgers)

3 The hills are alive with the sound of
    music,
With songs they have sung for
    a thousand years.
The hills fill my heart with the sound of
    music,
My heart wants to sing ev'ry song it
    hears.
The Sound of Music (1959 song; music by
Richard Rodgers)

4 There is nothin' like a dame.
Title of song (1949; music by Richard
Rodgers)

5 You'll never walk alone.
Title of song (1945; music by Richard
Rodgers)

Christopher Hampton 1946–

6 Masturbation is the thinking man's
television.
Philanthropist (1970) act. 1, sc. 3

7 If I had to give a definition of capitalism
I would say: the process whereby
American girls turn into American
women.
Savages (1974) sc. 16

Learned Hand 1872–1961

8 A self-made man may prefer a self-made
name.
In Bosley Crowther *Lion's Share* (1957) ch. 7
(referring to Samuel Goldfish changing his
name to Samuel Goldwyn)

Minnie Hanff 1880–1942

9 High o'er the fence leaps Sunny Jim
'Force' is the food that raises him.
Advertising slogan (1903)

Brian Hanrahan 1949–

10 I'm not allowed to say how many planes
joined the raid [on Port Stanley in the
Falkland Islands] but I counted them all
out and I counted them all back.
Report broadcast by BBC, 1 May 1982, in
Battle for the Falklands (1982) p. 21

Otto Harbach 1873–1963

11 When a lovely flame dies,
Smoke gets in your eyes.
Smoke Gets in your Eyes (1933 song; music
by Jerome Kern)

E. Y. 'Yip' Harburg 1898–1981

12 Once I built a railroad. Now it's done—
Brother can you spare a dime?
Brother Can You Spare a Dime? (1932 song;
music by Jay Gorney)

13 Somewhere over the rainbow
Way up high,
There's a land that I heard of
Once in a lullaby.
Over the Rainbow (1939 song; music by
Harold Arlen)

14 When I'm not near the girl I love,
I love the girl I'm near.
When I'm Not Near the Girl I Love (1947
song; music by Burton Lane)

Gilbert Harding 1907–1960

15 Before he [Gilbert Harding] could go to
New York he had to get a US visa at the
American consulate in Toronto. He was
called upon to fill in a long form with
many questions, including 'Is it your
intention to overthrow the Government
of the United States by force?' By the
time Harding got to that one he was so
irritated that he answered: 'Sole purpose
of visit.'
W. Reyburn *Gilbert Harding* (1978) ch. 2

16 If, sir, I possessed, as you suggest, the
power of conveying unlimited sexual
attraction through the potency of my
voice, I would not be reduced to
accepting a miserable pittance from the

BBC for interviewing a faded female in a damp basement.

In S. Grenfell *Gilbert Harding by his Friends* (1961) p. 118 (reply to Mae West's manager who asked 'Can't you sound a bit more sexy when you interview her?')

Warren G. Harding 1865–1923

1 America's present need is not heroics, but healing; not nostrums but normalcy; not revolution, but restoration.

Speech at Boston, 14 May 1920, in Frederick E. Schortemeier *Rededicating America* (1920) ch. 17

Godfrey Harold Hardy 1877–1947

2 Beauty is the first test: there is no permanent place in the world for ugly mathematics.

A Mathematician's Apology (1940) p. 25

Thomas Hardy 1840–1928

3 A local thing called Christianity.
Dynasts (1904) pt. 1, act 1, sc. 6

4 My argument is that War makes rattling good history; but Peace is poor reading.
Dynasts (1904) pt. 1, act 2, sc. 5

5 A lover without indiscretion is no lover at all.
Hand of Ethelberta (1876) ch. 20

6 A piece of paper was found upon the floor, on which was written, in the boy's hand, with the bit of lead pencil that he carried: 'Done because we are too menny.'
Jude the Obscure (1896) pt. 6, ch. 2

7 The bower we shrined to Tennyson,
Gentlemen,
Is roof-wrecked; damps there drip upon
Sagged seats, the creeper-nails are rust,
The spider is sole denizen;
Even she who voiced those rhymes is
dust,
Gentlemen!
Late Lyrics and Earlier (1922) 'An Ancient to Ancients'

8 This is the weather the cuckoo likes,
And so do I;
When showers betumble the chestnut
spikes,
And nestlings fly:
And the little brown nightingale bills his
best,

And they sit outside at 'The Travellers'
Rest',
And maids come forth sprig-muslin
drest,
And citizens dream of the south and
west,
And so do I.
Late Lyrics and Earlier (1922) 'Weathers'

9 And meadow rivulets overflow,
And drops on gate-bars hang in a row,
And rooks in families homeward go,
And so do I.
Late Lyrics and Earlier (1922) 'Weathers'

10 Life's little ironies.
Title of book (1894)

11 'Well, poor soul; she's helpless to hinder that or anything now,' answered Mother Cuxsom. 'And all her shining keys will be took from her, and her cupboards opened; and things a' didn't wish seen, anybody will see; and her little wishes and ways will all be as nothing!'
Mayor of Casterbridge (1886) ch. 18

12 One grievous failing of Elizabeth's was her occasional pretty and picturesque use of dialect words—those terrible marks of the beast to the truly genteel.
Mayor of Casterbridge (1886) ch. 20

13 I am the family face;
Flesh perishes, I live on,
Projecting trait and trace
Through time to times anon,
And leaping from place to place
Over oblivion.
Moments of Vision (1917) 'Heredity'

14 In the third-class seat sat the journeying
boy
And the roof-lamp's oily flame
Played down on his listless form and
face,
Bewrapt past knowing to what he was
going,
Or whence he came.
Moments of Vision (1917) 'Midnight on the Great Western'

15 Only a man harrowing clods
In a slow silent walk
With an old horse that stumbles and nods
Half asleep as they stalk.

Only thin smoke without flame
From the heaps of couch-grass;
Yet this will go onward the same
Though Dynasties pass.

Yonder a maid and her wight
Come whispering by:
War's annals will cloud into night
Ere their story die.
> Moments of Vision (1917) 'In Time of "The
> Breaking of Nations"'

1 When the Present has latched its
    postern behind my tremulous stay,
And the May month flaps its glad green
    leaves like wings,
Delicate-filmed as new-spun silk, will
    the neighbours say,
'He was a man who used to notice such
    things'?
> Moments of Vision (1917) 'Afterwards'

2 At once a voice outburst among
The bleak twigs overhead
In a full-hearted evensong
Of joy illimited;
An aged thrush, frail, gaunt, and small,
In blast-beruffled plume,
Had chosen thus to fling his soul
Upon the growing gloom.

So little cause for carollings
Of such ecstatic sound
Was written on terrestrial things
Afar or nigh around,
That I could think there trembled
    through
His happy good-night air
Some blessed Hope, whereof he knew
And I was unaware.
> Poems of Past and Present (1902) 'Darkling
> Thrush'

3 If way to the Better there be, it exacts
    a full look at the worst.
> Poems of Past and Present (1902) 'De
> Profundis'

4 In a solitude of the sea
Deep from human vanity,
And the Pride of Life that planned her,
    stilly couches she.

Steel chambers, late the pyres
Of her salamandrine fires,
Cold currents thrid, and turn to
    rhythmic tidal lyres.

Over the mirrors meant
To glass the opulent
The sea-worm crawls—grotesque,
    slimed, dumb, indifferent.
> Satires of Circumstance (1914) 'Convergence
> of the Twain'

5 The Immanent Will that stirs and urges
    everything.
> Satires of Circumstance (1914) 'Convergence
> of the Twain'

6 When I set out for Lyonnesse,
A hundred miles away,
The rime was on the spray,
And starlight lit my lonesomeness
When I set out for Lyonnesse
A hundred miles away.
> Satires of Circumstance (1914) p. 20

7 What of the faith and fire within us
Men who march away
Ere the barn-cocks say
Night is growing grey,
To hazards whence no tears can win us;
What of the faith and fire within us
Men who march away?
> Satires of Circumstance (1914) 'Men Who
> March Away'

8 'Justice' was done, and the President of
the Immortals (in Aeschylean phrase)
had ended his sport with Tess.
> Tess of the D'Urbervilles (1891) ch. 59

9 Let me enjoy the earth no less
Because the all-enacting Might
That fashioned forth its loveliness
Had other aims than my delight.
> Time's Laughing Stocks (1909) 'Let me Enjoy'

10 Yes; quaint and curious war is!
You shoot a fellow down
You'd treat if met where any bar is,
Or help to half-a-crown.
> Time's Laughing Stocks (1909) 'Man he
> Killed'

11 Good, but not religious-good.
> Under the Greenwood Tree (1872) ch. 2

12 Well, World, you have kept faith with me,
Kept faith with me;
Upon the whole you have proved to be
Much as you said you were.
> Winter Words (1928) 'He Never Expected
> Much'

13 'Peace upon earth!' was said. We sing it,
And pay a million priests to bring it.
After two thousand years of mass
We've got as far as poison-gas.
> Winter Words (1928) 'Christmas: 1924'

Maurice Evan Hare 1886–1967

14 There once was an old man who said,
    'Damn!
It is borne in upon me I am
An engine that moves

In determinate grooves,
I'm not even a bus, I'm a tram.'
Limerick (1905)

Robertson Hare 1891–1979

1 Oh, calamity!
Catch-phrase, in *Yours Indubitably* (1956)
p. 32

W. F. Hargreaves 1846–1919

2 I'm Burlington Bertie
I rise at ten thirty and saunter along like
a toff,
I walk down the Strand with my gloves
on my hand,
Then I walk down again with them off.
Burlington Bertie from Bow (1915 song)

3 I acted so tragic the house rose like magic,
The audience yelled 'You're sublime.'
They made me a present of Mornington
Crescent
They threw it a brick at a time.
The Night I Appeared as Macbeth (1922 song)

Lord Harlech (David Ormsby Gore) 1918–1985

4 In the end it may well be that Britain
will be honoured by historians more for
the way she disposed of an empire than
for the way in which she acquired it.
In *New York Times* 28 Oct. 1962, sec. 4, p. 11

Jimmy Harper, Will E. Haines, and Tommie Connor

5 The biggest aspidistra in the world.
Title of song (1938; popularized by Gracie
Fields)

Frank Harris (James Thomas Harris) 1856–1931

6 Christ went deeper than I have, but I've
had a wider range of experience.
In conversation with Hugh Kingsmill, in
Hesketh Pearson and Malcolm Muggeridge
About Kingsmill (1951) ch. 3

7 Sex is the gateway to life.
In Enid Bagnold *Autobiography* (1969) ch. 4

H. H. Harris

8 Bovril. . . . Prevents that sinking feeling.
Advertising slogan (1920)

Lorenz Hart 1895–1943

9 Bewitched, bothered and bewildered.
Title of song (1941; music by Richard
Rodgers)

10 When love congeals
It soon reveals
The faint aroma of performing seals,
The double crossing of a pair of heels.
I wish I were in love again!
I Wish I Were in Love Again (1937 song;
music by Richard Rodgers)

11 I get too hungry for dinner at eight.
I like the theatre, but never come late.
I never bother with people I hate.
That's why the lady is a tramp.
The Lady is a Tramp (1937 song; music by
Richard Rodgers)

12 On the first of May
It is moving day;
Spring is here, so blow your job—
Throw your job away;
Now's the time to trust
To your wanderlust.
In the city's dust you wait.
Must you wait?
Just you wait:

In a mountain greenery
Where God paints the scenery—
Just two crazy people together;
While you love your lover, let
Blue skies be your coverlet—
When it rains we'll laugh at the
weather.
Mountain Greenery (1926 song; music by
Richard Rodgers)

Moss Hart 1904–1961 and George Kaufman 1889–1961

13 You can't take it with you.
Title of play (1936)

L. P. Hartley 1895–1972

14 The past is a foreign country: they do
things differently there.
The Go-Between (1953) prologue

F. W. Harvey 1888–?

15 From troubles of the world
I turn to ducks
Beautiful comical things.
Ducks and Other Verses (1919) 'Ducks'

Minnie Louise Haskins 1875–1957

1 And I said to the man who stood at the gate of the year: 'Give me a light that I may tread safely into the unknown.'
And he replied:
'Go out into the darkness and put your hand into the Hand of God. That shall be to you better than light and safer than a known way.'
Desert (1908) 'God Knows'

Lord Haw-Haw

See WILLIAM JOYCE

Ian Hay (John Hay Beith) 1876–1952

2 What do you mean, funny? Funny-peculiar or funny ha-ha?
Housemaster (1938) act 3

J. Milton Hayes 1884–1940

3 There's a one-eyed yellow idol to the north of Khatmandu,
There's a little marble cross below the town,
There's a broken-hearted woman tends the grave of Mad Carew,
And the Yellow God forever gazes down.
The Green Eye of the Yellow God (1911)

Lee Hazlewood 1929–

4 These boots are made for walkin'.
Title of song (1966)

Denis Healey 1917–

5 That part of his [Sir Geoffrey Howe's] speech was rather like being savaged by a dead sheep.
Hansard 14 June 1978, col. 1027

6 I plan to be the Gromyko of the Labour Party.
In *Sunday Times* 5 Feb. 1984

7 I warn you there are going to be howls of anguish from the 80,000 people who are rich enough to pay over 75% [tax] on the last slice of their income.
Speech at Labour Party Conference, 1 Oct. 1973, in *The Times* 2 Oct. 1973

Seamus Heaney 1939–

8 Between my finger and my thumb
The squat pen rests.
I'll dig with it.
Death of a Naturalist (1966) 'Digging'

9 All agog at the plasterer on his ladder
Skimming our gable and writing our name there
With his trowel point, letter by strange letter.
The Haw Lantern (1987) 'Alphabets'

10 Who would connive
in civilised outrage
yet understand the exact
and tribal, intimate revenge.
North (1975) 'Punishment'

11 The famous
Northern reticence, the tight gag of place
And times: yes, yes. Of the 'wee six' I sing
Where to be saved you only must save face
And whatever you say, you say nothing.
North (1975) 'Whatever You Say Say Nothing'

12 Is there a life before death? That's chalked up
In Ballymurphy. Competence with pain,
Coherent miseries, a bite and sup,
We hug our little destiny again.
North (1975) 'Whatever You Say Say Nothing'

13 Don't be surprised
If I demur, for, be advised
My passport's green.
No glass of ours was ever raised
To toast *The Queen*.
Open Letter (Field Day pamphlet no. 2, 1983) p. 9 (rebuking the editors of *The Penguin Book of Contemporary British Poetry* for including his work)

Edward Heath 1916–

14 It is the unpleasant and unacceptable face of capitalism.
Hansard 15 May 1973, col. 1243 (on the Lonrho affair)

15 The alternative is to break into the wage/price spiral by acting directly to reduce prices. This can be done by reducing those taxes which bear directly on prices and costs, such as the selective employment tax, and by taking a firm

grip on public sector prices and charges such as coal, steel, gas, electricity, transport charges and postal charges. This would, at a stroke, reduce the rise in prices, increase production and reduce unemployment.

Press release, 16 June 1970, in *The Times* 17 June 1970

Fred Heatherton

1 I've got a loverly bunch of cocoanuts, There they are a-standing in a row, Big ones, small ones, some as big as your head, Give 'em a twist, a flick of the wrist, That's what the showman said.

I've Got a Lovely Bunch of Cocoanuts (1944 song; revised version 1948)

Robert A. Heinlein 1907–

2 'Oh, "tanstaafl". Means "There ain't no such thing as a free lunch." And isn't,' I added, pointing to a FREE LUNCH sign across room, 'or these drinks would cost half as much. Was reminding her that anything free costs twice as much in the long run or turns out worthless.'

Moon is Harsh Mistress (1966) ch. 11

Werner Heisenberg 1901–1976

3 *Ein Fachmann ist ein Mann, der einige der gröbsten Fehler kennt, die man in dem betreffenden Fach machen kann und der sie deshalb zu vermeiden versteht.*

An expert is someone who knows some of the worst mistakes that can be made in his subject and how to avoid them.

Der Teil und das Ganze ('The Part and the Whole', 1969) ch. 17 (translated by A. J. Pomerans in 1971 as *Physics and Beyond*)

Joseph Heller 1923–

4 There was only one catch and that was Catch-22, which specified that a concern for one's own safety in the face of dangers that were real and immediate was the process of a rational mind. Orr was crazy and could be grounded. All he had to do was ask; and as soon as he did, he would no longer be crazy and would have to fly more missions. Orr would be crazy to fly more missions and sane if he didn't, but if he was sane he had to fly them. If he flew them he was

crazy and didn't have to; but if he didn't want to he was sane and had to. Yossarian was moved very deeply by the absolute simplicity of this clause of Catch-22 and let out a respectful whistle.

'That's some catch, that Catch-22,' he observed.

'It's the best there is,' Doc Daneeka agreed.

Catch-22 (1961) ch. 5 (the first chapter of this novel was published as *Catch-18* in *New World Writing* (1955) No. 7—see Kiley and MacDonald '*Catch-22*' *Casebook* (1973) 294)

5 Some men are born mediocre, some men achieve mediocrity, and some men have mediocrity thrust upon them. With Major Major it had been all three.

Catch-22 (1961) ch. 9. Cf. *Oxford Dictionary of Quotations* (1979) 489:14

6 Good God, how much reverence can you have for a Supreme Being who finds it necessary to include such phenomena as phlegm and tooth-decay in His divine system of creation?

Catch-22 (1961) ch. 18

7 'You put so much stock in *winning* wars,' the grubby iniquitous old man scoffed. 'The real trick lies in *losing* wars, and in knowing which wars can be *lost*. Italy has been losing wars for centuries, and just see how splendidly we've done nonetheless. France wins wars and is in a continual state of crisis. Germany loses and prospers. Look at our own recent history. Italy won a war in Ethiopia and promptly stumbled into serious trouble. Victory gave us such insane delusions of grandeur that we helped start a world war we hadn't a chance of winning. But now that we are losing again, everything has taken a turn for the better, and we will certainly come out on top again if we succeed in being defeated.'

Catch-22 (1961) ch. 23

Lillian Hellman 1905–1984

8 Cynicism is an unpleasant way of saying the truth.

The Little Foxes (1939) act 1

9 I do not like subversion or disloyalty in any form and if I had ever seen any I would have considered it my duty to

have reported it to the proper authorities. But to hurt innocent people whom I knew many years ago in order to save myself is to me inhuman and indecent and dishonorable. I cannot and will not cut my conscience to fit this year's fashions, even though I long ago came to the conclusion that I was not a political person and could have no comfortable place in any political group.
Letter to John S. Wood, 19 May 1952, in *US Congress Committee Hearing on Un-American Activities* (1952) pt. 8, p. 3546

Sir Robert Helpmann 1909–1986

1 No. You see there are portions of the human anatomy which would keep swinging after the music had finished.
In Elizabeth Salter *Helpmann* (1978) ch. 21 [reply to question on whether the fashion for nudity would extend to dance]

Ernest Hemingway 1899–1961

2 All good books are alike in that they are truer than if they had really happened and after you are finished reading one you will feel that all that happened to you and afterwards it all belongs to you: the good and the bad, the ecstasy, the remorse and sorrow, the people and the places and how the weather was. If you can get so that you can give that to people, then you are a writer.
Esquire Dec. 1934 'Old Newsman Writes'

3 'Just kiss me.'
She kissed him on the cheek.
'No.'
'Where do the noses go? I always wondered where the noses would go.'
'Look, turn thy head' and then their mouths were tight together.
For Whom the Bell Tolls (1940) ch. 7

4 He said, 'Maria . . . I feel as though I wanted to die when I am loving thee.'
'Oh,' she said. 'I die each time. Do you not die?'
'No. Almost. But did thee feel the earth move?'
'Yes. As I died. Put thy arm around me, please.'
For Whom the Bell Tolls (1940) ch. 13

5 All modern American literature comes from one book by Mark Twain called *Huckleberry Finn*.
Green Hills of Africa (1935) ch. 1

6 Cowardice, as distinguished from panic, is almost always simply a lack of ability to suspend the functioning of the imagination.
Men at War (1942)

7 If you are lucky enough to have lived in Paris as a young man, then wherever you go for the rest of your life, it stays with you, for Paris is a movable feast.
Movable Feast (1964) epigraph

8 'Exactly what do you mean by "guts"?'
'I mean,' Ernest Hemingway said, 'grace under pressure.'
Interview with Dorothy Parker, in *New Yorker* 30 Nov. 1929

9 I started out very quiet and I beat Mr Turgenev. Then I trained hard and I beat Mr de Maupassant. I've fought two draws with Mr Stendhal, and I think I had an edge in the last one. But nobody's going to get me in any ring with Mr Tolstoy unless I'm crazy or I keep getting better.
New Yorker 13 May 1950

10 A man can be destroyed but not defeated.
The Old Man and the Sea (1952) p. 103

11 The most essential gift for a good writer is a built-in, shock-proof shit detector. This is the writer's radar and all great writers have had it.
Paris Review Spring 1958

12 The sun also rises.
Title of novel (1926)

13 Switzerland is a small, steep country, much more up and down than sideways, and is all stuck over with large brown hotels built on the cuckoo clock style of architecture.
Toronto Star Weekly 4 Mar. 1922, in William White *By-line: Ernest Hemingway* (1967) p. 18

See also F. SCOTT FITZGERALD

Arthur W. D. Henley

14 Nobody loves a fairy when she's forty
Title of song (1934)

O. Henry (William Sydney Porter) 1862–1910

15 Life is made up of sobs, sniffles, and smiles, with sniffles predominating.
Four Million (1906) 'Gift of the Magi'

1 If men knew how women pass the time
when they are alone, they'd never
marry.
> *Four Million* (1906) 'Memoirs of a Yellow
> Dog'

2 It was beautiful and simple as all truly
great swindles are.
> *Gentle Grafter* (1908) 'Octopus Marooned'

3 Turn up the lights; I don't want to go
home in the dark.
> Last words, quoting 1907 song by Harry
> Williams 'I'm afraid to come home in the
> dark', in Charles Alphonso Smith *O. Henry
> Biography* (1916) ch. 9

A. P. Herbert 1890–1971

4 Other people's babies—
That's my life!
Mother to dozens,
And nobody's wife.
> *Ballads for Broadbrows* (1930) 'Other
> People's Babies' (also a 1934 song, with
> music by Vivian Ellis)

5 Let's find out what everyone is doing,
And then stop everyone from doing it.
> *Ballads for Broadbrows* (1930) 'Let's Stop
> Somebody from Doing Something!'

6 As my poor father used to say
In 1863,
Once people start on all this Art
Goodbye, moralitee!
And what my father used to say
Is good enough for me.
> *Ballads for Broadbrows* (1930) 'Lines for
> a Worthy Person'

7 Holy deadlock.
> Title of novel (1934)

8 Don't tell my mother I'm living in sin,
Don't let the old folks know.
> *Laughing Ann* (1925) 'Don't Tell My Mother
> I'm Living in Sin'

9 Not huffy, or stuffy, not tiny or tall,
But fluffy, just fluffy, with no brains at
all.
> *Plain Jane* (1927) 'I Like them Fluffy'

10 Don't let's go to the dogs tonight,
For mother will be there.
> *She-Shanties* (1926) 'Don't Let's Go to the
> Dogs Tonight'

11 The Farmer will never be happy again;
He carries his heart in his boots;
For either the rain is destroying his
grain
Or the drought is destroying his roots.
> *Tinker Tailor* (1922) 'The Farmer'

12 This high official, all allow,
Is grossly overpaid;
There wasn't any Board, and now
There isn't any Trade.
> *Tinker Tailor* (1922) 'The President of the
> Board of Trade'

13 Nothing is wasted, nothing is in vain:
The seas roll over but the rocks remain.
> *Tough at the Top* (c.1949 operetta), in *A.P.H.*
> (1970) ch. 7

14 The Common Law of England has been
laboriously built about a mythical
figure—the figure of 'The Reasonable
Man'.
> *Uncommon Law* (1935) 'The Reasonable
> Man'

15 People must not do things for fun. We
are not here for fun. There is no
reference to fun in any Act of
Parliament.
> *Uncommon Law* (1935) 'Is it a Free
> Country?'

16 The critical period in matrimony is
breakfast-time.
> *Uncommon Law* (1935) 'Is Marriage
> Lawful?'

17 The Englishman never enjoys himself
except for a noble purpose.
> *Uncommon Law* (1935) 'Fox-Hunting Fun'

18 Milord, in that case an Act of God was
defined as 'something which no
reasonable man could have expected'.
> *Uncommon Law* (1935) 'Act of God'

Oliver Herford 1863–1935

19 'Perhaps it is only a whim,' said the
Queen. The King laughed mirthlessly.
'King Barumph has a whim of iron!'
> *Excuse it Please* (1929) 'Impossible Pudding'

See also ETHEL WATTS MUMFORD

Jerry Herman 1933–

20 Hello, Dolly, well, hello Dolly
It's so nice to have you back where you
belong.
> *Hello, Dolly* (1964 song from the musical
> *Hello, Dolly*)

June Hershey

1 Deep in the heart of Texas.
   Title of song (1941; music by Don Swander)

Hermann Hesse 1877–1962

2 *Wenn wir einen Menschen hassen, so
   hassen wir in seinem Bild etwas, was in
   uns selber sitzt. Was nicht in uns selber ist,
   das regt uns nicht auf.*

   If you hate a person, you hate
   something in him that is part of
   yourself. What isn't part of ourselves
   doesn't disturb us.
   Demian (1919) ch. 6

3 *Auf Kosten der Intensität also erreicht er
   [der Bürger] Erhaltung und Sicherheit,
   statt Gottbesessenheit erntet er
   Gewissensruhe, statt Lust Behagen, statt
   Freiheit Bequemlichkeit, statt tödlicher Glut
   eine angenehme Temperatur.*

   The bourgeois prefers comfort to
   pleasure, convenience to liberty, and
   a pleasant temperature to the deathly
   inner consuming fire.
   Der Steppenwolf (1927) 'Tractat vom
   Steppenwolf' (Treatise on the Steppenwolf)

Gordon Hewart (Viscount Hewart) 1870–1943

4 A long line of cases shows that it is not
   merely of some importance, but is of
   fundamental importance that justice
   should not only be done, but should
   manifestly and undoubtedly be seen to
   be done.
   Rex v Sussex Justices, 9 Nov. 1923, in *Law
   Reports King's Bench Division* (1924) vol. 1,
   p. 259

Patricia Hewitt 1948–

5 It is obvious from our polling, as well as
   from the doorstep, that the 'London
   Effect' is now really noticeable. The
   'loony Labour left' is taking its toll; the
   gays and lesbians issue is costing us dear
   among the pensioners, and fear of
   extremism and higher rates/taxes is
   particularly prominent in the Greater
   London Council area.
   Letter to Frank Dobson and other Labour
   leaders, in *The Times* 6 Mar. 1987

Du Bose Heyward 1885–1940 and Ira Gershwin 1896–1983

6 It ain't necessarily so.
   Title of song (1935; music by George
   Gershwin)

7 Summer time an' the livin' is easy.
   Summer Time (1935 song; music by George
   Gershwin)

Sir Seymour Hicks 1871–1949

8 You will recognize, my boy, the first sign
   of old age: it is when you go out into
   the streets of London and realize for the
   first time how young the policemen
   look.
   In C. R. D. Pulling *They Were Singing* (1952)
   ch. 7

Jack Higgins (Henry Patterson) 1929–

9 The eagle has landed.
   Title of novel (1975)

Joe Hill 1879–1915

10 I will die like a true-blue rebel. Don't
   waste any time in mourning—organize.
   Farewell telegram to Bill Haywood, 18 Nov.
   1915, before his death by firing squad, in
   Salt Lake (Utah) Tribune 19 Nov. 1915

11 You will eat, bye and bye,
   In that glorious land above the sky;
   Work and pray, live on hay,
   You'll get pie in the sky when you die.
   Songs of the Workers (Industrial Workers of
   the World, 1911) 'Preacher and the Slave'

Pattie S. Hill 1868–1946

12 Happy birthday to you.
   Title of song (1935; music by Mildred J.
   Hill)

Sir Edmund Hillary 1919–

13 [After the ascent of Everest] George
   [Lowe] met us with a mug of soup just
   above camp, and seeing his stalwart
   frame and cheerful face reminded me
   how fond of him I was. My comment
   was not specially prepared for public
   consumption but for George. . . . 'Well,
   we knocked the bastard off!' I told him

and he nodded with pleasure. . . .
'Thought you must have!'
Nothing Venture (1975) ch. 10

Fred Hillebrand 1893–

1 Home James, and don't spare the horses.
Title of song (1934)

Lady Hillingdon 1857–1940

2 I am happy now that Charles calls on
my bedchamber less frequently than of
old. As it is, I now endure but two calls
a week and when I hear his steps outside
my door I lie down on my bed, close my
eyes, open my legs and think of
England.
Journal 1912, in J. Gathorne-Hardy *Rise and
Fall of the British Nanny* (1972) ch. 3

James Hilton 1900–1954

3 Nothing really wrong with him—only
anno domini, but that's the most fatal
complaint of all, in the end.
Goodbye, Mr Chips (1934) ch. 1

Alfred Hitchcock 1899–1980

4 Television has brought back murder into
the home—where it belongs.
In *Observer* 19 Dec. 1965

5 Actors are cattle.
In *Saturday Evening Post* 22 May 1943, p. 56

Adolf Hitler 1889–1945

6 *Die neue and diesmal blutige Erhebung—die
Nacht der langen Messer, wie man sie
grauenvoll bezeichnete—entspräche meinem
eigenen Sinn.*

The new, and this time bloody,
rising—'The Night of the Long Knives'
was their ghastly name for it—was
exactly what I myself desired.
Speech to the Reichstag, 13 July 1934, in
Max Domarus (ed.) *Hitler: Reden und
Proklamationen 1932–1945* (1962) p. 418

7 *Ich gehe mit traumwandlerischer Sicherheit
den Weg, den mich die Vorsehung gehen
heisst.*

I go the way that Providence dictates
with the assurance of a sleepwalker.
Speech in Munich, 15 Mar. 1936, in Max
Domarus (ed.) *Hitler: Reden und
Proklamationen 1932–1945* (1962) p. 606

8 *Und nun steht vor uns das letzte Problem,
das gelöst werden muss und gelöst werden
wird! Es [das Sudetenland] ist die letzte
territoriale Forderung, die ich Europa zu
stellen habe, aber es ist die Forderung, von
der ich nicht abgehe, und die ich, so Gott
will, erfüllen werde.*

And now before us stands the last
problem that must be solved and will be
solved. It [the Sudetenland] is the last
territorial claim which I have to make in
Europe, but it is the claim from which
I will not recede and which, God-willing,
I will make good.
Speech at Berlin Sportpalast, 26 Sept. 1938,
in Max Domarus (ed.) *Hitler: Reden und
Proklamationen 1932–1945* (1962)
p. 927

9 *In bezug auf das sudetendeutsche Problem
ist meine Geduld jetzt zu Ende!*

With regard to the problem of the
Sudeten Germans, my patience is now at
an end!
Speech at Berlin Sportpalast, 26 Sept. 1938,
in Max Domarus (ed.) *Hitler: Reden und
Proklamationen 1932–1945* (1962) p. 932

10 *Brennt Paris?*

Is Paris burning?
Question, 25 Aug. 1944, in Larry Collins
and Dominique Lapierre *Is Paris Burning?*
(1965) ch. 5

11 *Die breite Masse eines Volkes . . . fällt einer
grossen Lüge leichter zum Opfer als einer
kleinen.*

The broad mass of a nation . . . will more
easily fall victim to a big lie than to
a small one.
Mein Kampf (My Struggle, 1925) vol. 1,
ch. 10

Ralph Hodgson 1871–1962

12 Time, you old gipsy man,
Will you not stay,
Put up your caravan
Just for one day?
Poems (1917) 'Time, You Old Gipsy Man'

13 I climbed a hill as light fell short,
And rooks came home in scramble sort,
And filled the trees and flapped and
    fought
And sang themselves to sleep.
Poems (1917) 'Song of Honour'

14 I stood and stared; the sky was lit,
The sky was stars all over it,

I stood, I knew not why,
Without a wish, without a will,
I stood upon that silent hill
And stared into the sky until
My eyes were blind with stars and still
I stared into the sky.
  Poems (1917) 'Song of Honour'

1 When stately ships are twirled and spun
Like whipping tops and help there's
   none
And mighty ships ten thousand ton
Go down like lumps of lead.
  Poems (1917) 'Song of Honour'

2 'Twould ring the bells of Heaven
The wildest peal for years,
If Parson lost his senses
And people came to theirs,
And he and they together
Knelt down with angry prayers
For tamed and shabby tigers
And dancing dogs and bears,
And wretched, blind, pit ponies,
And little hunted hares.
  Poems (1917) 'Bells of Heaven'

3 See an old unhappy bull,
Sick in soul and body both,
Slouching in the undergrowth
Of the forest beautiful,
Banished from the herd he led,
Bulls and cows a thousand head.
  Poems (1917) 'The Bull'

4 Reason has moons, but moons not hers,
Lie mirror'd on her sea,
Confounding her astronomers,
But, O! delighting me.
  Poems (1917) 'Reason Has Moons'

'Red' Hodgson

5 I blow through here;
The music goes 'round and around.
Whoa-ho-ho-ho-ho-ho, and it comes up
   here.
  Music Goes 'round and Around (1935 song;
  music by Edward Farley and Michael Riley)

Eric Hoffer 1902–1983

6 It is easier to love humanity as a whole
than to love one's neighbour.
  New York Times Magazine 15 Feb. 1959,
  p. 12

7 When people are free to do as they
please, they usually imitate each other.

Originality is deliberate and forced, and
partakes of the nature of a protest.
  Passionate State of Mind (1955) p. 21

Al Hoffman 1902–1960 and Dick Manning 1912–

8 Takes two to tango.
  Title of song (1952)

Gerard Hoffnung 1925–1959

9 Standing among savage scenery, the
hotel offers stupendous revelations.
There is a French widow in every
bedroom, affording delightful prospects.
  Speech at Oxford Union, 4 Dec. 1958
  (supposedly quoting a letter from a Tyrolean
  landlord)

Lancelot Hogben 1895–1975

10 This is not the age of pamphleteers. It is
the age of the engineers. The spark-gap
is mightier than the pen. Democracy will
not be salvaged by men who talk
fluently, debate forcefully and quote
aptly.
  Science for the Citizen (1938) epilogue

Billie Holiday (Eleanor Fagan) 1915–1959 and Arthur Herzog Jr. 1901–1983

11 Them that's got shall get,
Them that's not shall lose,
So the Bible said,
And it still is news;
Mama may have, papa may have,
But God bless the child that's got his
   own!
That's got his own.
  God Bless the Child (1941 song)

Stanley Holloway 1890–1982

12 Sam, Sam, pick up tha' musket.
  Pick Up Tha' Musket (1930 recorded
  monologue)

John H. Holmes 1879–1964

13 This, now, is the judgement of our
scientific age—the third reaction of man
upon the universe! This universe is not
hostile, nor yet is it friendly. It is simply
indifferent.
  The Sensible Man's View of Religion (1932)
  ch. 4

Lord Home (Baron Home of the Hirsel, formerly Sir Alec Douglas-Home) 1903–

1 As far as the fourteenth earl is concerned, I suppose Mr [Harold] Wilson, when you come to think of it, is the fourteenth Mr Wilson.

> Television interview, 21 Oct. 1963, in *Daily Telegraph* 22 Oct. 1963 (replying to question on how he was going to meet attacks by the Labour Party on his then position as a 'fourteenth Earl, a reactionary, and an out-of-date figure')

2 When I have to read economic documents I have to have a box of matches and start moving them into position to simplify and illustrate the points to myself.

> In *Observer* 16 Sept. 1962

Arthur Honegger 1892–1955

3 *Il est certain que la première qualité d'un compositeur, c'est d'être mort.*

There is no doubt that the first requirement for a composer is to be dead.

> *Je suis compositeur* (I am a Composer, 1951) p. 16

Herbert Hoover 1874–1964

4 Older men declare war. But it is youth who must fight and die. And it is youth who must inherit the tribulation, the sorrow, and the triumphs that are the aftermath of war.

> Speech at the Republican National Convention, Chicago, 27 June 1944, in *Addresses upon the American Road* (1946) p. 254.

5 Our country has deliberately undertaken a great social and economic experiment, noble in motive and far-reaching in purpose (i.e. 18th Amendment on Prohibition).

> Letter to Senator W. H. Borah, 23 Feb. 1928, in Claudius O. Johnson *Borah of Idaho* (1936) ch. 21

6 When the war closed ... we were challenged with a peace-time choice between the American system of rugged individualism and a European philosophy of diametrically opposed doctrines—doctrines of paternalism and state socialism.

> Speech in New York City, 22 Oct. 1928, in *New Day* (1928) p. 154

7 Another proposal of our opponents which would wholly alter our American system of life is to reduce the protective tariff to a competitive tariff for revenue. ... The grass will grow in the streets of a hundred cities, a thousand towns; the weeds will overrun the fields of millions of farms if that protection be taken away.

> Speech, 31 Oct. 1932, in *State Papers of Herbert Hoover* (1934) vol. 2, p. 418

Anthony Hope (Sir Anthony Hope Hawkins) 1863–1933

8 Economy is going without something you do want in case you should, some day, want something you probably won't want.

> *Dolly Dialogues* (1894) no. 12

9 'You oughtn't to yield to temptation.' 'Well, somebody must, or the thing becomes absurd,' said I.

> *Dolly Dialogues* (1894) no. 14

10 'Bourgeois,' I observed, 'is an epithet which the riff-raff apply to what is respectable, and the aristocracy to what is decent.' 'But it's not a nice thing to be, all the same,' said Dolly, who is impervious to the most penetrating remark.

> *Dolly Dialogues* (1894) no. 17

11 I wish you would read a little poetry sometimes. Your ignorance cramps my conversation.

> *Dolly Dialogues* (1894) no. 22

12 Anthony Hope—a friend, a true friend, yet pledged always to his own and far more Attic interpretation of life—sat there [at the first night of J. M. Barrie's *Peter Pan* in 1904] looking primmer and drier at every extravagance, and more and more as if, in his opinion, children should be kept in their right place. When he spoke, his comment was also far more succinct. 'Oh, for an hour of Herod!' he said.

> Denis Mackail *Story of JMB* (1941) ch. 17

Bob Hope 1903–

1 A bank is a place that will lend you
money if you can prove that you don't
need it.
> In Alan Harrington *Life in the Crystal Palace*
> (1959) 'The Tyranny of Farms'

Francis Hope 1938–1974

2 And scribbled lines like fallen hopes
On backs of tattered envelopes.
> *Instead of a Poet and Other Poems* (1965)
> 'Instead of a Poet'

Laurence Hope (*Adela Florence Nicolson*) 1865–1904

3 Less than the dust, beneath thy Chariot
wheel,
Less than the rust, that never stained
thy Sword,
Less than the trust thou hast in me, Oh,
Lord,
Even less than these!
Less than the weed, that grows beside
thy door,
Less than the speed, of hours, spent far
from thee,
Less than the need thou hast in life of
me.
Even less am I.
> *Garden of Kama* (1901) 'Less than the Dust'

4 Pale hands I loved beside the Shalimar,
Where are you now? Who lies beneath
your spell?
... Pale hands, pink tipped, like lotus
buds that float
On those cool waters where we used to
dwell,
I would have rather felt you round my
throat
Crushing out life; than waving me
farewell!
> *Garden of Kama* (1901) 'Kashmiri Song'

Zilphia Horton 1907–1957
See ANONYMOUS 9:13

A. E. Housman 1859–1936

5 Mud's sister, not himself, adorns my
legs.
> *Fragment of a Greek Tragedy* (*Bromsgrovian*
> vol. 2, no. 5, 1883) in *Alfred Edward
> Housman*, the Housman Memorial
> Supplement of the Bromsgrovian (1936)

6 This great College, of this ancient
University, has seen some strange sights.
It has seen Wordsworth drunk and
Porson sober. And here am I, a better
poet than Porson, and a better scholar
than Wordsworth, betwixt and between.
> Speech at Trinity College, Cambridge, in G.
> K. Chesterton *Autobiography* (1936) ch. 12

7 If I were the Prince of Peace, I would
choose a less provocative Ambassador.
> In Alan Wood *Bertrand Russell: Passionate
> Sceptic* (1957) p. 103

8 Oh who is that young sinner with the
handcuffs on his wrists?
And what has he been after that they
groan and shake their fists?
And wherefore is he wearing such
a conscience-stricken air?
Oh they're taking him to prison for the
colour of his hair.

'Tis a shame to human nature, such
a head of hair as his;
In the good old time 'twas hanging for
the colour that it is;
Though hanging isn't bad enough and
flaying would be fair
For the nameless and abominable colour
of his hair.
> *Collected Poems* (1939) 'Additional Poems'
> no. 18

9 That is indeed very good. I shall have to
repeat that on the Golden Floor!
> In *Daily Telegraph* 21 Feb. 1984 (said to his
> physician who told him a risqué story to
> cheer him up just before he died)

10 The Grizzly Bear is huge and wild;
He has devoured the infant child.
The infant child is not aware
He has been eaten by the bear.
> *Infant Innocence* in *Oxford Book of Light Verse*
> (1938) p. 489

11 Pass me the can, lad; there's an end of
May.
> *Last Poems* (1922) no. 9

12 May will be fine next year as like as not:
Oh, ay, but then we shall be
twenty-four.
> *Last Poems* (1922) no. 9

13 We for a certainty are not the first
Have sat in taverns while the tempest
hurled
Their hopeful plans to emptiness, and
cursed

Whatever brute and blackguard made
the world.
Last Poems (1922) no. 9

1 The troubles of our proud and angry
dust
Are from eternity, and shall not fail.
Bear them we can, and if we can we
must.
Shoulder the sky, my lad, and drink
your ale.
Last Poems (1922) no. 9

2 But men at whiles are sober
And think by fits and starts,
And if they think, they fasten
Their hands upon their hearts.
Last Poems (1922) no. 10

3 The laws of God, the laws of man,
He may keep that will and can;
Not I: let God and man decree
Laws for themselves and not for me;
And if my ways are not as theirs
Let them mind their own affairs.
Last Poems (1922) no. 12

4 And how am I to face the odds
Of man's bedevilment and God's?
I, a stranger and afraid
In a world I never made.
Last Poems (1922) no. 12

5 The candles burn their sockets,
The blinds let through the day,
The young man feels his pockets
And wonders what's to pay.
Last Poems (1922) no. 21

6 To think that two and two are four
And neither five nor three
The heart of man has long been sore
And long 'tis like to be.
Last Poems (1922) no. 35

7 These, in the day when heaven was
falling,
The hour when earth's foundations fled,
Followed their mercenary calling
And took their wages and are dead.

Their shoulders held the sky suspended;
They stood, and earth's foundations
stay;
What God abandoned, these defended,
And saved the sum of things for pay.
Last Poems (1922) no. 37

8 For nature, heartless, witless nature,
Will neither care nor know
What stranger's feet may find the
meadow

And trespass there and go,
Nor ask amid the dews of morning
If they are mine or no.
Last Poems (1922) no. 40

9 Experience has taught me, when I am
shaving of a morning, to keep watch
over my thoughts, because, if a line of
poetry strays into my memory, my skin
bristles so that the razor ceases to act. . . .
The seat of this sensation is the pit of the
stomach.
Lecture at Cambridge, 9 May 1933, *The
Name and Nature of Poetry* (1933) p. 47

10 The rainy Pleiads wester,
Orion plunges prone,
The stroke of midnight ceases,
And I lie down alone.
More Poems (1936) no. 11

11 Life, to be sure, is nothing much to lose;
But young men think it is, and we were
young.
More Poems (1936) no. 36

12 Good-night. Ensured release
Imperishable peace,
Have these for yours,
While earth's foundations stand
And sky and sea and land
And heaven endures.
More Poems (1936) no. 48 'Alta Quies'

13 Loveliest of trees, the cherry now
Is hung with bloom along the bough,
And stands about the woodland ride
Wearing white for Eastertide.

Now, of my threescore years and ten,
Twenty will not come again,
And take from seventy springs a score,
It only leaves me fifty more.

And since to look at things in bloom
Fifty springs are little room,
About the woodlands I will go
To see the cherry hung with snow.
Shropshire Lad (1896) no. 2

14 Clay lies still, but blood's a rover;
Breath's a ware that will not keep.
Up, lad: when the journey's over
There'll be time enough to sleep.
Shropshire Lad (1896) no. 4

15 And naked to the hangman's noose
The morning clocks will ring
A neck God made for other use
Than strangling in a string.
Shropshire Lad (1896) no. 9

1 When I was one-and-twenty
I heard a wise man say,
'Give crowns and pounds and guineas
But not your heart away;
Give pearls away and rubies,
But keep your fancy free.'
But I was one-and-twenty,
No use to talk to me.
Shropshire Lad (1896) no. 13

2 Oh, when I was in love with you,
Then I was clean and brave,
And miles around the wonder grew
How well I did behave.

And now the fancy passes by,
And nothing will remain,
And miles around they'll say that I
Am quite myself again.
Shropshire Lad (1896) no. 18

3 In summertime on Bredon
The bells they sound so clear;
Round both the shires they ring them
In steeples far and near,
A happy noise to hear.

Here of a Sunday morning
My love and I would lie,
And see the coloured counties,
And hear the larks so high
About us in the sky.
Shropshire Lad (1896) no. 21

4 'Come all to church, good people,'—
Oh, noisy bells, be dumb;
I hear you, I will come.
Shropshire Lad (1896) no. 21

5 The lads in their hundreds to Ludlow
come in for the fair,
There's men from the barn and the forge
and the mill and the fold,
The lads for the girls and the lads for the
liquor are there,
And there with the rest are the lads that
will never be old.
Shropshire Lad (1896) no. 23

6 Is my team ploughing,
That I was used to drive
And hear the harness jingle
When I was man alive?
Shropshire Lad (1896) no. 27

7 On Wenlock Edge the wood's in trouble;
His forest fleece the Wrekin heaves;
The wind it plies the saplings double,
And thick on Severn snow the leaves.
Shropshire Lad (1896) no. 31

8 The gale, it plies the saplings double,

It blows so hard, 'twill soon be gone:
To-day the Roman and his trouble
Are ashes under Uricon.
Shropshire Lad (1896) no. 31

9 From far, from eve and morning
And yon twelve-winded sky,
The stuff of life to knit me
Blew hither: here am I.
Shropshire Lad (1896) no. 32

10 Speak now, and I will answer;
How shall I help you, say;
Ere to the wind's twelve quarters
I take my endless way.
Shropshire Lad (1896) no. 32

11 Into my heart an air that kills
From yon far country blows:
What are those blue remembered hills,
What spires, what farms are those?

That is the land of lost content,
I see it shining plain,
The happy highways where I went
And cannot come again.
Shropshire Lad (1896) no. 40

12 And bound for the same bourn as I,
On every road I wandered by,
Trod beside me, close and dear,
The beautiful and death-struck year.
Shropshire Lad (1896) no. 41

13 Clunton and Clunbury,
Clungunford and Clun,
Are the quietest places
Under the sun.
Shropshire Lad (1896) no. 50, epigraph

14 With rue my heart is laden
For golden friends I had,
For many a rose-lipt maiden
And many a lightfoot lad.

By brooks too broad for leaping
The lightfoot boys are laid;
The rose-lipt girls are sleeping
In fields where roses fade.
Shropshire Lad (1896) no. 54

15 Say, for what were hop-yards meant,
Or why was Burton built on Trent?
Oh many a peer of England brews
Livelier liquor than the Muse,
And malt does more than Milton can
To justify God's ways to man.
Ale, man, ale's the stuff to drink
For fellows whom it hurts to think.
Shropshire Lad (1896) no. 62

16 Oh I have been to Ludlow fair
And left my necktie God knows where,

And carried half-way home, or near,
Pints and quarts of Ludlow beer:
Then the world seemed none so bad,
And I myself a sterling lad;
And down in lovely muck I've lain,
Happy till I woke again.
Shropshire Lad (1896) no. 62

1 I tell the tale that I heard told.
Mithridates, he died old.
Shropshire Lad (1896) no. 62

Sidney Howard

See MARGARET MITCHELL

Elbert Hubbard 1859–1915

2 Never explain—your friends do not need
it and your enemies will not believe you
anyway.
Motto Book (1907) p. 31

3 Life is just one damned thing after
another.
Philistine Dec. 1909, p. 32. The saying is
often attributed to Frank Ward O'Malley

4 Editor: a person employed by
a newspaper, whose business it is to
separate the wheat from the chaff, and
to see that the chaff is printed.
Roycroft Dictionary (1914) p. 46

5 Little minds are interested in the
extraordinary; great minds in the
commonplace.
Thousand and One Epigrams (1911) p. 133

6 One machine can do the work of fifty
ordinary men. No machine can do the
work of one extraordinary man.
Thousand and One Epigrams (1911) p. 151

Frank McKinney ('Kin') Hubbard 1868–1930

7 Classic music is th'kind that we keep
thinkin'll turn into a tune.
Comments of Abe Martin and His Neighbors
(1923)

8 It's no disgrace t'be poor, but it might as
well be.
Short Furrows (1911) p. 42

L. Ron Hubbard 1911–1986

9 Hubbard . . . told us that writing science
fiction for about a penny a word was no
way to make a living. If you really want

to make a million, he said, the quickest
way is to start your own religion.
Sam Moscowitz recalling Hubbard speaking
to the Eastern Science Fiction Association at
Newark, New Jersey, in 1947, in B.
Corydon and L. Ron Hubbard Jr. *L. Ron
Hubbard* (1987) ch. 3

Howard Hughes Jr. 1905–1976

10 That man's ears make him look like
a taxi-cab with both doors open.
In Charles Higham and Joel Greenberg
Celluloid Muse (1969) p. 156 (describing
Clark Gable)

Jimmy Hughes and Frank Lake

11 Bless 'em all! Bless 'em all!
The long and the short and the tall.
Bless 'Em All (1940 song)

Langston Hughes 1902–1967

12 'It's powerful,' he said.
'What?'
'That one drop of Negro
blood—because just *one* drop of black
blood makes a man coloured. *One*
drop—you are a Negro!'
Simple Takes a Wife (1953) p. 85

13 I, too, sing America.

I am the darker brother.
They send me to eat in the kitchen
When company comes.
But I laugh,
And eat well,
And grow strong.

Tomorrow
I'll sit at the table
When company comes
Nobody'll dare
Say to me,
'Eat in the kitchen'
Then.

Besides, they'll see how
beautiful I am
And be ashamed,—

I, too, am America.
Survey Graphic Mar. 1925, 'I, Too'

Ted Hughes 1930–

14 It took the whole of Creation
To produce my foot, my each feather:
Now I hold Creation in my foot.
Lupercal (1960) 'Hawk Roosting'

Josephine Hull ?1886–1957

1 [Josephine Hull's] stage reminiscences
are not the least of her charms.
'Shakespeare,' she recalls, 'is so tiring.
You never get a chance to sit down
unless you're a king.'
   Time 16 Nov. 1953, p. 90

Hubert Humphrey 1911–1978

2 There are not enough jails, not enough
policemen, not enough courts to enforce
a law not supported by the people.
   Speech at Williamsburg, 1 May 1965, in
   New York Times 2 May 1965, sec. 1, p. 34

3 The right to be heard does not
automatically include the right to be
taken seriously.
   Speech to National Student Association at
   Madison, 23 Aug. 1965, in *New York Times*
   24 Aug. 1965, p. 12

4 And here we are, just as we ought to be,
here we are, the people, here we are in
a spirit of dedication, here we are the
way politics ought to be in America, the
politics of happiness, the politics of
purpose and the politics of joy.
   Speech in Washington, 27 Apr. 1968, in
   New York Times 28 Apr. 1968, p. 66

Herman Hupfeld 1894–1951

5 You must remember this, a kiss is still
a kiss,
A sigh is just a sigh;
The fundamental things apply,
As time goes by.
   As Time Goes By (1931 song)

Aldous Huxley 1894–1963

6 Christlike in my behaviour,
Like every good believer,
I imitate the Saviour,
And cultivate a beaver.
   Antic Hay (1923) ch. 4

7 There are few who would not rather be
taken in adultery than in provincialism.
   Antic Hay (1923) ch. 10

8 Official dignity tends to increase in
inverse ratio to the importance of the
country in which the office is held.
   Beyond the Mexique Bay (1934) p. 34

9 The sexophones wailed like melodious
cats under the moon.
   Brave New World (1932) ch. 5

10 That men do not learn very much from
the lessons of history is the most
important of all the lessons that history
has to teach.
   Collected Essays (1959) 'Case of Voluntary
   Ignorance'

11 The proper study of mankind is books.
   Crome Yellow (1921) ch. 28

12 Too much consistency is as bad for the
mind as it is for the body. Consistency is
contrary to nature, contrary to life. The
only completely consistent people are the
dead.
   Do What You Will (1929) 'Wordsworth in
   the Tropics'

13 The end cannot justify the means, for
the simple and obvious reason that the
means employed determine the nature of
the ends produced.
   Ends and Means (1937) ch. 1

14 So long as men worship the Caesars and
Napoleons, Caesars and Napoleons will
duly arise and make them miserable.
   Ends and Means (1937) ch. 8

15 Chastity—the most unnatural of all the
sexual perversions, he added
parenthetically, out of Remy de
Gourmont.
   Eyeless in Gaza (1936) ch. 27

16 'Death,' said Mark Staithes. 'It's the
only thing we haven't succeeded in
completely vulgarizing.'
   Eyeless in Gaza (1936) ch. 31

17 'Bed,' as the Italian proverb succinctly
puts it, 'is the poor man's opera.'
   Heaven and Hell (1956) p. 41

18 A million million spermatozoa,
All of them alive:
Out of their cataclysm but one poor
   Noah
Dare hope to survive.

And among that billion minus one
Might have chanced to be
Shakespeare, another Newton, a new
   Donne—
But the One was Me.
   Leda (1920) 'Fifth Philosopher's Song'

19 Beauty for some provides escape,
Who gain a happiness in eyeing
The gorgeous buttocks of the ape
Or Autumn sunsets exquisitely dying.
   Leda (1920) 'Ninth Philosopher's Song'

1 Then brim the bowl with atrabilious
liquor!
We'll pledge our Empire vast across the
flood:
For Blood, as all men know, than
Water's thicker,
But Water's wider, thank the Lord, than
Blood.
Leda (1920) 'Ninth Philosopher's Song'

2 Ragtime . . . but when the wearied Band
Swoons to a waltz, I take her hand,
And there we sit in peaceful calm,
Quietly sweating palm to palm.
Leda (1920) 'Frascati's'

3 I can sympathize with people's pains,
but not with their pleasures. There is
something curiously boring about
somebody else's happiness.
Limbo (1920) 'Cynthia'

4 After silence, that which comes nearest
to expressing the inexpressible is music.
Music at Night (1931) p. 17

5 'And besides,' he added, forgetting that
several excuses are always less
convincing than one, 'Lady Edward's
inviting an American editor specially for
my sake.'
Point Counter Point (1928) ch. 1

6 A bad book is as much of a labour to
write as a good one; it comes as
sincerely from the author's soul.
Point Counter Point (1928) ch. 13

7 There is no substitute for talent.
Industry and all the virtues are of no
avail.
Point Counter Point (1928) ch. 13

8 Brought up in an epoch when ladies
apparently rolled along on wheels, Mr
Quarles was peculiarly susceptible to
calves.
Point Counter Point (1928) ch. 20

9 Parodies and caricatures are the most
penetrating of criticisms.
Point Counter Point (1928) ch. 28

10 That all men are equal is a proposition
to which, at ordinary times, no sane
human being has ever given his assent.
Proper Studies (1927) 'The Idea of Equality'

11 Those who believe that they are
exclusively in the right are generally
those who achieve something.
Proper Studies (1927) 'Note on Dogma'

12 Facts do not cease to exist because they
are ignored.
Proper Studies (1927) 'Note on Dogma'

13 Experience is not what happens to
a man; it is what a man does with what
happens to him.
Texts and Pretexts (1932) p. 5

14 Most human beings have an almost
infinite capacity for taking things for
granted.
Themes and Variations (1950) 'Variations on
a Philosopher'

15 'There's only one corner of the universe
you can be certain of improving, and
that's your own self. Your own self,' he
repeated. So you have to begin there,
not outside, not on other people. That
comes afterwards, when you've worked
on your own corner.
Time Must Have a Stop (1945) ch. 7

Sir Julian Huxley 1887–1975

16 Operationally, God is beginning to
resemble not a ruler but the last fading
smile of a cosmic Cheshire cat.
Religion without Revelation (1957 edn.) ch. 3

Dolores Ibarruri ('*La Pasionaria*') 1895–1989

17 *Il vaut mieux mourir debout que de vivre à
genoux!*

It is better to die on your feet than to
live on your knees.
Speech in Paris, 3 Sept. 1936, in *L'Humanité*
4 Sept. 1936 (also attributed to Emiliano
Zapata)

18 *No pasarán.*

They shall not pass.
Radio broadcast, Madrid, 19 July 1936, in
Speeches and Articles 1936–38 (1938) p. 7
(cf. Anonymous 6:25)

Henrik Ibsen 1828–1906

19 *Luftslotte,—de er så nemme at ty ind i, de.
Og nemme at bygge også.*

Castles in the air—they are so easy to
take refuge in. And so easy to build, too.
Bygmester Solness (The Master Builder,
1892) act 3

1 *Flertallet har aldrig retten på sin side.
Aldrig, siger jeg! Det er en af disse
samfundsløgne, som en fri, tænkende mand
må gøre oprør imod. Hvem er det, som
udgør flertallet af beboerne i et land? Er det
de kloge folk, eller er det dè dumme? Jeg
taenker, vi får være enige om, at dumme
mennesker er tilstede i en ganske forskraek
kelig overvældende majoritet rundt omkring
på den hele vide jord. Men det kan da vel,
for fanden, aldrig i evighed vaere ret, at de
dumme skal herske over de kloge!*

The majority never has right on its side.
Never I say! That is one of the social lies
that a free, thinking man is bound to
rebel against. Who makes up the
majority in any given country? Is it the
wise men or the fools? I think we must
agree that the fools are in a terrible
overwhelming majority, all the wide
world over.
  En Folkefiende (An Enemy of the People,
  1882) act 4

2 *En skulde aldrig ha' sine bedste buxer på,
når en er ude og strider for frihed og
sandhed.*

You should never have your best
trousers on when you go out to fight for
freedom and truth.
  En Folkefiende (An Enemy of the People,
  1882) act 5

3 *Sagen er den, ser I, at den stærkeste mand i
verden, det er han, som står mest alene.*

The thing is, you see, that the strongest
man in the world is the man who stands
most alone.
  En Folkefiende (An Enemy of the People,
  1882) act 5

4 *Mor, gi' mig solen.*

Mother, give me the sun.
  Gengangere (Ghosts, 1881) act 3

5 *Men, gud sig forbarme,—sligt noget gør
man da ikke!*

But good God, people don't do such
things!
  Hedda Gabler (1890) act 4

6 *Hvad skal manden være? Sig selv, det er
mit korte svar.*

What ought a man to be? Well, my
short answer is 'himself'.
  Peer Gynt (1867) act 4

7 *Tar de livsløgnen fra et
gennemsnitsmenneske, så tar De lykken fra
ham med det samme.*

Take the life-lie away from the average
man and straight away you take away
his happiness.
  Vildanden (The Wild Duck, 1884) act 5

Harold L. Ickes 1874–1952

8 The trouble with Senator Long ... is
that he is suffering from halitosis of the
intellect. That's presuming Emperor
Long has an intellect.
  Speech, 1935, in G. Wolfskill and J. A.
  Hudson *All But the People: Franklin D.
  Roosevelt and his Critics, 1933–39* (1969)
  ch. 11

9 Dewey threw his diaper into the ring.
  On the Republican candidate for the
  presidency, in *New York Times* 12 Dec.
  1939, p. 32

Eric Idle 1943–

See GRAHAM CHAPMAN *et al.*

Francis Iles (*Anthony Berkeley Cox*) 1893–1970

10 It was not until several weeks after he
had decided to murder his wife that Dr
Bickleigh took any active steps in the
matter. Murder is a serious business.
  Malice Aforethought (1931) p. 7

Ivan Illich 1926–

11 Man must choose whether to be rich in
things or in the freedom to use them.
  Deschooling Society (1971) ch. 4

12 In a consumer society there are
inevitably two kinds of slaves: the
prisoners of addiction and the prisoners
of envy.
  Tools for Conviviality (1973) ch. 3

Charles Inge 1868–1957

13 This very remarkable man
Commends a most practical plan:
You can do what you want

If you don't think you can't,
So don't think you can't think you can.
  Weekend Book (1928) 'On Monsieur Coué'

William Ralph Inge (Dean Inge)
1860–1954

1 The aim of education is the knowledge
not of facts but of values.
  'The Training of the Reason' in A. C.
  Benson (ed.) *Cambridge Essays on Education*
  (1917) ch. 2

2 The enemies of Freedom do not argue;
they shout and they shoot.
  End of an Age (1948) ch. 4

3 The effect of boredom on a large scale in
history is underestimated. It is a main
cause of revolutions, and would soon
bring to an end all the static Utopias and
the farmyard civilization of the Fabians.
  End of an Age (1948) ch. 6

4 To become a popular religion, it is only
necessary for a superstition to enslave
a philosophy.
  Idea of Progress (Romanes Lecture delivered
  at Oxford, 27 May 1920) p. 9

5 Many people believe that they are
attracted by God, or by Nature, when
they are only repelled by man.
  More Lay Thoughts of a Dean (1931) pt. 4,
  ch. 1

6 It takes in reality only one to make
a quarrel. It is useless for the sheep to
pass resolutions in favour of
vegetarianism, while the wolf remains of
a different opinion.
  Outspoken Essays: First Series (1919)
  'Patriotism'

7 The nations which have put mankind
and posterity most in their debt have
been small states—Israel, Athens,
Florence, Elizabethan England.
  Outspoken Essays: Second Series (1922)
  'State, visible and invisible'

8 A man may build himself a throne of
bayonets, but he cannot sit on it; and
he cannot avow that the bayonets are
meant to keep his own subjects quiet.
  Philosophy of Plotinus (1923) vol. 2, lecture
  22

9 Literature flourishes best when it is half
a trade and half an art.
  Victorian Age (Rede Lecture delivered at
  Cambridge, 1922) p. 49

Eugène Ionesco 1912–

10 *C'est une chose anormale de vivre.*

  Living is abnormal.
  Le Rhinocéros (1959) act 1

11 *Tu ne prévois les événements que lorsqu'ils
sont déjà arrivés.*

  You can only predict things after they
  have happened.
  Le Rhinocéros (1959) act 3

12 *Un fonctionnaire ne plaisante pas.*

  A civil servant doesn't make jokes.
  Tueur sans gages (The Killer, 1958) act 1

Weldon J. Irvine

13 Young, gifted and black.
  Title of song (1969; music by Nina Simone)

Christopher Isherwood 1904–1986

14 The common cormorant (or shag)
Lays eggs inside a paper bag,
You follow the idea, no doubt?
It's to keep the lightning out.

  But what these unobservant birds
  Have never thought of, is that herds
  Of wandering bears might come with
    buns
  And steal the bags to hold the crumbs.
    Exhumations (1966) 'Common Cormorant'

15 I am a camera with its shutter open,
quite passive, recording, not thinking.
Recording the man shaving at the
window opposite and the woman in the
kimono washing her hair. Some day, all
this will have to be developed, carefully
printed, fixed.
  Goodbye to Berlin (1939) 'Berlin Diary'
  Autumn 1930

16 Mr Norris changes trains.
  Title of novel (1935)

  See also W. H. AUDEN and CHRISTOPHER
  ISHERWOOD

Holbrook Jackson 1874–1948

17 A mother never realizes that her
children are no longer children.
  All Manner of Folk (1912) 'On a Certain
  Arrangement' p. 89

18 Pedantry is the dotage of knowledge.
  Anatomy of Bibliomania (1930) vol. 1, p. 150

1 As soon as an idea is accepted it is time to reject it.
   Platitudes in the Making (1911) p. 13

Joe Jacobs 1896–1940

2 We was robbed!
   Shouted into the microphone after Jack Sharkey beat Max Schmeling (of whom Jacobs was manager) in the heavyweight title fight, 21 June 1932, in Peter Heller *In This Corner* (1975) p. 44

3 I should of stood [i.e. have stayed] in bed.
   Said after he left his sick-bed in October 1935 to attend the World Baseball Series in Detroit and he bet on the losers, in John Lardner *Strong Cigars* (1951) p. 61

Mick Jagger 1943– and Keith Richard (*Keith Richards*) 1943–

4 It's only rock 'n' roll.
   Title of song (1974)

5 Ev'rywhere I hear the sound of
      marching, charging feet, oh, boy,
   'Cause summer's here and the time is
      oh, right for fighting in the street,
      boy.
   But what can a poor boy do
   Except to sing for a rock 'n' roll band,
   'Cause in sleepy London town
   There's just no place for street fighting
      man!
   Street Fighting Man (1968 song)

Henry James 1843–1916

6 The ever-importunate murmur, 'Dramatize it, dramatize it!'
   Altar of the Dead (1909 ed.) preface

7 The terrible *fluidity of self-revelation.*
   Ambassadors (1909 ed.) preface

8 Live all you can; it's a mistake not to. It doesn't so much matter what you do in particular, so long as you have your life. If you haven't had that, what *have* you had?
   Ambassadors (1903) bk. 5, ch. 11

9 The deep well of unconscious cerebration.
   The American (1909 ed.) preface

10 The historian, essentially, wants more documents than he can really use; the dramatist only wants more liberties than he can really take.
   Aspern Papers (1909 ed.) preface

11 Summer afternoon—summer afternoon; to me those have always been the two most beautiful words in the English language.
   In Edith Wharton *Backward Glance* (1934) ch. 10

12 He [Henry James] is said to have told his old friend Lady Prothero, when she saw him after the first stroke, that in the very act of falling (he was dressing at the time) he heard in the room a voice which was distinctly, it seemed, not his own saying: 'So here it is at last, the distinguished thing!'
   Edith Wharton *Backward Glance* (1934) ch. 14

13 To kill a human being is, after all, the least injury you can do him.
   Complete Tales (1962) vol. 1 'My Friend Bingham' (1867 short story)

14 We work in the dark—we do what we can—we give what we have. Our doubt is our passion and our passion is our task. The rest is the madness of art.
   Complete Tales (1964) vol. 9 'Middle Years' (1893 short story)

15 Vereker's secret, my dear man—the general intention of his books: the string the pearls were strung on, the buried treasure, the figure in the carpet.
   Figure in the Carpet (1896) ch. 11

16 It takes a great deal of history to produce a little literature.
   Hawthorne (1879) ch. 1

17 Whatever question there may be of his [Thoreau's] talent, there can be none, I think, of his genius. It was a slim and crooked one; but it was eminently personal. He was imperfect, unfinished, inartistic; he was worse than provincial—he was parochial.
   Hawthorne (1879) ch. 4

18 Cats and monkeys—monkeys and cats—all human life is there!
   Madonna of the Future (1879) vol. 1, p. 59 ('All human life is there' was used by Maurice Smelt as an advertising slogan for the *News of the World* in the late 1950s)

1 They have fairly faced the full, the monstrous demonstration that Tennyson was not Tennysonian.
Middle Years (1917 autobiography) ch. 6

2 The only reason for the existence of a novel is that it does attempt to represent life.
Partial Portraits (1888) 'Art of Fiction'

3 The only obligation to which in advance we may hold a novel, without incurring the accusation of being arbitrary, is that it be interesting.
Partial Portraits (1888) 'Art of Fiction'

4 Experience is never limited, and it is never complete; it is an immense sensibility, a kind of huge spider-web of the finest silken threads suspended in the chamber of consciousness, and catching every air-borne particle in its tissue.
Partial Portraits (1888) 'Art of Fiction'

5 What is character but the determination of incident? What is incident but the illustration of character? What is either a picture or a novel that is *not* character?
Partial Portraits (1888) 'Art of Fiction'

6 We must grant the artist his subject, his idea, his *donnée*: our criticism is applied only to what he makes of it.
Partial Portraits (1888) 'Art of Fiction'

7 I don't care anything about reasons, but I know what I like.
Portrait of a Lady (1881) vol. 2, ch. 5. Cf. Max Beerbohm 23:14

8 I didn't, of course, stay her hand—there never *is* in such cases 'time'; and I had once more the full demonstration of the fatal futility of Fact.
Spoils of Poynton (1909 ed.) preface

9 We were alone with the quiet day, and his little heart, dispossessed, had stopped.
Turn of the Screw (1898) p. 169

William James 1842–1910

10 Man, biologically considered, and whatever else he may be into the bargain, is simply the most formidable of all the beasts of prey, and, indeed, the only one that preys systematically on its own species.
Atlantic Monthly Dec. 1904, p. 845

11 I now perceive one immense omission in my Psychology,—the deepest principle of Human Nature is the *craving to be appreciated*, and I left it out altogether from the book, because I had never had it gratified till now.
Letter to his class at Radcliffe College, 6 Apr. 1896, in *Letters* (1920) vol. 2, p. 33

12 The moral flabbiness born of the exclusive worship of the bitch-goddess *success*. That—with the squalid cash interpretation put on the word success—is our national disease.
Letter to H. G. Wells, 11 Sept. 1906, in *Letters* (1920) vol. 2, p. 260

13 Real culture lives by sympathies and admirations, not by dislikes and disdains—under all misleading wrappings it pounces unerringly upon the human core.
McClure's Magazine Feb. 1908, p. 422

14 So long as antimilitarists propose no substitute for war's disciplinary function, no *moral equivalent* of war, analogous, as one might say, to the mechanical equivalent of heat, so long they fail to realize the full inwardness of the situation.
Memories and Studies (1911) 'The Moral Equivalent of War' p. 283

15 There is no more miserable human being than one in whom nothing is habitual but indecision.
Principles of Psychology (1890) vol. 1, ch. 4

16 The art of being wise is the art of knowing what to overlook.
Principles of Psychology (1890) vol. 2, ch. 22

17 The first thing to learn in intercourse with others is non-interference with their own peculiar ways of being happy, provided those ways do not assume to interfere by violence with ours.
Talks to Teachers (1899) 'What makes a Life Significant?'

18 If merely 'feeling good' could decide, drunkenness would be the supremely valid human experience.
Varieties of Religious Experience (1902) lecture 1, p. 16

19 An idea, to be suggestive, must come to the individual with the force of a revelation.
Varieties of Religious Experience (1902) lectures 4 and 5, p. 113

1 There is no worse lie than a truth
misunderstood by those who hear it.
Varieties of Religious Experience (1902)
lectures 14 and 15, p. 355

Randall Jarrell 1914–1965

2 One of the most obvious facts about
grown-ups, to a child, is that they have
forgotten what it is like to be a child.
Introduction to Christina Stead *The Man
Who Loved Children* (1965) p. xxvi

Douglas Jay 1907–

3 It was Bert Amey who asked me to send
him a brief rhyming North Battersea
slogan [for the 1946 by-election].
I suggested: 'Fair Shares for All, is
Labour's Call'; and from this by-election
'Fair Shares for All' spread in a few
years round the country.
Change and Fortune (1980) ch. 7

4 For in the case of nutrition and health,
just as in the case of education, the
gentleman in Whitehall really does
know better what is good for people
than the people know themselves.
Socialist Case (1939) ch. 30

Sir James Jeans 1877–1946

5 Taking a very gloomy view of the future
of the human race, let us suppose that it
can only expect to survive for two
thousand million years longer, a period
about equal to the past age of the earth.
Then, regarded as a being destined to
live for three-score years and ten,
humanity, although it has been born in
a house seventy years old, is itself only
three days old.
Eos (1928) p. 12

6 Life exists in the universe only because
the carbon atom possesses certain
exceptional properties.
Mysterious Universe (1930) ch. 1

7 From the intrinsic evidence of his
creation, the Great Architect of the
Universe now begins to appear as a pure
mathematician.
Mysterious Universe (1930) ch. 5

Patrick Jenkin 1926–

8 People can clean their teeth in the dark,
use the top of the stove instead of the
oven, all sorts of savings, but they must
use less electricity.
Radio broadcast, 15 Jan. 1974, in *The Times*
16 Jan. 1974

Rt. Revd David Jenkins (Bishop of Durham) 1925–

9 I wouldn't put it past God to arrange
a virgin birth if he wanted to, but I very
much doubt if he would—because it
seems to be contrary to the way in
which he deals with persons and brings
his wonders out of natural personal
relationships.
In *Church Times* 4 May 1984

10 The withdrawal of an imported, elderly
American [Ian MacGregor] to leave
a reconciling opportunity for some local
product is surely neither dishonourable
nor improper.
In *The Times* 22 Sept. 1984

Roy Jenkins (Baron Jenkins of Hillhead) 1920–

11 The politics of the left and centre of this
country are frozen in an out-of-date
mould which is bad for the political and
economic health of Britain and
increasingly inhibiting for those who live
within the mould. Can it be broken?
Speech to Parliamentary Press Gallery,
9 June 1980, in *The Times* 10 June 1980

Paul Jennings 1918–1989

12 I am prepared to testify on oath that on
the portico pillars of one building there
is a bronze office sign which simply says:
ACTIVATED SLUDGE.
Oddly Enough (1950) 'Activated Sludge'

13 Clark-Trimble arranged four hundred
pieces of carpet in ascending degrees of
quality, from coarse matting to priceless
Chinese silk. Pieces of toast and
marmalade, graded, weighed, and
measured, were then dropped on each
piece of carpet, and the marmalade-
downwards incidence was statistically
analysed. The toast fell right-side-up
every time on the cheap carpet . . . and it
fell marmalade-downwards every time on
the Chinese silk.
Town and Country Sept. 1949, 'Report on
Resistentialism'

Jerome K. Jerome 1859–1927

1 It is always the best policy to speak the truth—unless, of course, you are an exceptionally good liar.
The Idler Feb. 1892, p. 118

2 It is impossible to enjoy idling thoroughly unless one has plenty of work to do.
Idle Thoughts of an Idle Fellow (1886) 'On Being Idle'

3 Love is like the measles; we all have to go through it.
Idle Thoughts of an Idle Fellow (1886) 'On Being in Love'

4 We drink one another's healths, and spoil our own.
Idle Thoughts of an Idle Fellow (1886) 'On Eating and Drinking'

5 The world must be getting old, I think; it dresses so very soberly now.
Idle Thoughts of an Idle Fellow (1886) 'On Dress and Deportment'

6 I did not intend to write a funny book, at first. I did not know I was a humorist. I have never been sure about it. In the middle ages, I should probably have gone about preaching and got myself burnt or hanged.
My Life and Times (1926) ch. 6

7 The passing of the third floor back.
Title of story (1907) and play (1910)

8 I want a house that has got over all its troubles; I don't want to spend the rest of my life bringing up a young and inexperienced house.
They and I (1909) ch. 11

9 It is a most extraordinary thing, but I never read a patent medicine advertisement without being impelled to the conclusion that I am suffering from the particular disease therein dealt with in its most virulent form.
Three Men in a Boat (1889) ch. 1

10 But there, everything has its drawbacks, as the man said when his mother-in-law died, and they came down upon him for the funeral expenses.
Three Men in a Boat (1889) ch. 3

11 I like work: it fascinates me. I can sit and look at it for hours. I love to keep it by me: the idea of getting rid of it nearly breaks my heart.
Three Men in a Boat (1889) ch. 15

William Jerome 1865–1932

12 Any old place I can hang my hat is home sweet home to me.
Title of song (1901; music by Jean Schwartz)

13 You needn't try to reason,
Your excuse is out of season,
Just kiss yourself goodbye.
Just Kiss Yourself Goodbye (1902 song; music by Jean Schwartz)

C. E. M. Joad 1891–1953

14 It all depends what you mean by ...
Frequent opening to replies on the BBC radio series 'The Brains Trust' (originally 'Any Questions'), 1941–8

15 My life is spent in a perpetual alternation between two rhythms, the rhythm of attracting people for fear I may be lonely, and the rhythm of trying to get rid of them because I know that I am bored.
In *Observer* 12 Dec. 1948, p. 2

Pope John XXIII (Angelo Giuseppe Roncalli) 1881–1963

16 If civil authorities legislate for or allow anything that is contrary to that order and therefore contrary to the will of God, neither the laws made or the authorizations granted can be binding on the consciences of the citizens, since God has more right to be obeyed than man.
Pacem in Terris (1963) p. 142

17 The social progress, order, security and peace of each country are necessarily connected with the social progress, order, security and peace of all other countries.
Pacem in Terris (1963) p. 150

18 John XXIII said that during the first months of his pontificate he often woke during the night, thinking himself still a cardinal and worried over a difficult decision to be made, and he would say to himself: 'I'll talk it over with the

Pope!' Then he would remember where he was. 'But *I'm* the Pope!' he said to himself. After which he would conclude: 'Well I'll talk it over with Our Lord!'
Henri Fesquet *Wit and Wisdom of Good Pope John* (1964) p. 59

1 Anybody can be pope; the proof of this is that I have become one.
Henri Fesquet *Wit and Wisdom of Good Pope John* (1964) p. 112

Lyndon Baines Johnson
1908–1973

2 I don't want loyalty. I want *loyalty*. I want him to kiss my ass in Macy's window at high noon and tell me it smells like roses. I want his pecker in my pocket.
In David Halberstam *Best and Brightest* (1972) ch. 20

3 It's probably better to have him [J. Edgar Hoover] inside the tent pissing out, than outside pissing in.
In David Halberstam *Best and Brightest* (1972) ch. 20

4 Jerry Ford is so dumb he can't fart and chew gum at the same time.
In Richard Reeves *A Ford, not a Lincoln* (1975) ch. 2

5 For the first time in our history, it is possible to conquer poverty.
Speech to Congress, 16 Mar. 1964, in *New York Times* 17 Mar. 1964, p. 22

6 All I have I would have given gladly not to be standing here today.
Speech to Congress, 27 Nov. 1963, in *Public Papers of the Presidents of the United States: Lyndon B. Johnson 1963–64* vol. 1, p. 8 (after the previous president, J. F. Kennedy, was assassinated)

7 We have talked long enough in this country about equal rights. We have talked for a hundred years or more. It is time now to write the next chapter, and to write it in the books of law.
Speech to Congress, 27 Nov. 1963, in *Public Papers of the Presidents of the United States: Lyndon B. Johnson 1963–64* vol. 1, p. 9

8 We hope that the world will not narrow into a neighbourhood before it has broadened into a brotherhood.
Speech at lighting of the Nation's Christmas Tree, 22 Dec. 1963, in *Public Papers of the Presidents of the United States: Lyndon B. Johnson 1963–64*, vol. 1, item 65

9 This administration today, here and now declares unconditional war on poverty in America.
State of the Union address to Congress, 8 Jan. 1964, in *Public Papers of the Presidents of the United States: Lyndon B. Johnson 1963–64* vol. 1, p. 114

10 In your time we have the opportunity to move not only toward the rich society and the powerful society, but upward to the Great Society.
Speech at University of Michigan, 22 May 1964, in *Public Papers of the Presidents of the United States: Lyndon B. Johnson 1963–64* vol. 1, p. 704

11 We Americans know, although others appear to forget, the risks of spreading conflict. We still seek no wider war.
Speech on radio and television, 4 Aug. 1964, in *Public Papers of the Presidents of the United States: Lyndon B. Johnson 1963–64* vol. 2, p. 927

12 We are not about to send American boys 9 or 10,000 miles away from home to do what Asian boys ought to be doing for themselves.
Speech at Akron University, 21 Oct. 1964, in *Public Papers of the Presidents of the United States: Lyndon B. Johnson 1963–64* vol. 2, p. 1391

13 Extremism in the pursuit of the Presidency is an unpardonable vice. Moderation in the affairs of the nation is the highest virtue.
Speech in New York, 31 Oct. 1964, in *Public Papers of the Presidents of the United States: Lyndon B. Johnson 1963–64* vol. 2, p. 1559

14 A President's hardest task is not to *do* what is right, but to *know* what is right.
State of the Union address to Congress, 4 Jan. 1965, in *Public Papers of the Presidents of the United States: Lyndon B. Johnson 1965* vol. 1, p. 9

15 I am a free man, an American, a United States Senator, and a Democrat, in that order.
Texas Quarterly Winter 1958

Philander Chase Johnson
1866–1939

16 Cheer up! the worst is yet to come!
Everybody's Magazine May 1920

Philip Johnson 1906–

1 Architecture is the art of how to waste space.

New York Times 27 Dec. 1964, p. 9E)

Hanns Johst 1890–1978

2 *Wenn ich Kultur höre ... entsichere ich meinen Browning!*

Whenever I hear the word culture ... I release the safety-catch of my Browning [pistol]!

Schlageter (1933) act 1, sc. 1. Often attributed to Hermann Goering

Al Jolson 1886–1950

3 It can be revealed for the first time that it was in San Francisco [in 1906] that Al Jolson first uttered his immortal slogan, 'You ain't heard nuttin' yet!' One night at the cafe he had just finished a song when a deafening burst of noise from a building project across the street drowned out the applause. At the top of his lungs, Jolson screamed, 'You think that's noise—you ain't heard nuttin' yet!' And he proceeded to deliver an encore which for sheer blasting power put to everlasting shame all the decibels of noise the carpenters, the brick-layers and the drillers could scare up between them.

Martin Abramson *Real Story of Al Jolson* (1950) p. 12

James Jones 1921–

4 From here to eternity.

Title of novel (1951). Cf. Rudyard Kipling 123:16

LeRoi Jones

See IMAMU AMIRI BARAKA

Erica Jong 1942–

5 The zipless fuck is the purest thing there is. And it is rarer than the unicorn. And I have never had one.

Fear of Flying (1973) ch. 1

Janis Joplin 1943–1970

6 Oh, Lord, won't you buy me a Mercedes Benz
My friends all drive Porsches,
I must make amends.

Mercedes Benz (1970 song)

7 Fourteen heart attacks and he had to die in my week. In MY week.

Said when Eisenhower's death prevented her photograph from being on the front cover of *Newsweek*, in *New Musical Express* 12 Apr. 1969

Sir Keith Joseph 1918–

8 Perhaps there is at work here a process, apparent in many situations but imperfectly understood, by which problems reproduce themselves from generation to generation. If I refer to this as a 'cycle of deprivation' I do not want to be misunderstood.

Speech in London to Pre-School Playgroups Association, 29 June 1972

James Joyce 1882–1941

9 Yes, the newspapers were right: snow was general all over Ireland. It was falling on every part of the dark central plain, on the treeless hills, falling softly upon the Bog of Allen and, farther westward, softly falling into the dark mutinous Shannon waves. It was falling, too, upon every part of the lonely churchyard on the hill where Michael Furey lay buried. It lay thickly drifted on the crooked crosses and headstones, on the spears of the little gate, on the barren thorns. His soul swooned slowly as he heard the snow falling faintly through the universe and faintly falling, like the descent of their last end, upon all the living and the dead.

Dubliners (1914) 'The Dead'

10 riverrun, past Eve and Adam's, from swerve of shore to bend of bay, brings us by a commodious vicus of recirculation back to Howth Castle and Environs.

Finnegans Wake (1939) pt. 1, p. 3

11 That ideal reader suffering from an ideal insomnia.

Finnegans Wake (1939) pt. 1, p. 120

1 The flushpots of Euston and the hanging
garments of Marylebone.
  Finnegans Wake (1939) pt. 1, p. 192

2 O
  tell me all about
  Anna Livia! I want to hear all
  about Anna Livia. Well, you know
    Anna Livia?
  Yes, of course, we all know Anna Livia.
  Tell me all. Tell me now.
  Finnegans Wake (1939) pt. 1, p. 196

3 Tell me, tell me, tell me, elm! Night
night! Telmetale of stem or stone.
Beside the rivering waters of
hitherandthithering waters of. Night!
  Finnegans Wake (1939) pt. 1, p. 216

4 All moanday, tearsday, wailsday,
thumpsday, frightday, shatterday till the
fear of the Law.
  Finnegans Wake (1939) pt. 2, p. 301

5 Three quarks for Muster Mark!
  Finnegans Wake (1939) pt. 2, p. 383

6 The Gracehoper was always jigging
ajog, hoppy on akkant of his joyicity.
  Finnegans Wake (1939) pt. 3, p. 414

7 If I seen him bearing down on me now
under whitespread wings like he'd come
from Arkangels, I sink I'd die down over
his feet, humbly dumbly, only to
washup. Yes, tid. There's where. First.
We pass through grass behush the bush
to. Whish! A gull. Gulls. Far calls.
Coming, far! End here. Us then. Finn,
again! Take. Bussoftlhee, mememormee!
Till thousendsthee. Lps. The keys to.
Given! A way a lone a last a loved a long
the
  Finnegans Wake (1939) pt. 4, p. 627

8 Once upon a time and a very good time
it was there was a moocow coming
down along the road and this moocow
that was down along the road met
a nicens little boy named baby tuckoo.
  A Portrait of the Artist as a Young Man
  (1916) ch. 1

9 The artist, like the God of the creation,
remains within or behind or beyond or
above his handiwork, invisible, refined
out of existence, indifferent, paring his
fingernails.
  A Portrait of the Artist as a Young Man
  (1916) ch. 5

10 Ireland is the old sow that eats her
farrow.
  A Portrait of the Artist as a Young Man
  (1916) ch. 5

11 Pity is the feeling which arrests the
mind in the presence of whatsoever is
grave and constant in human sufferings
and unites it with the human sufferer.
Terror is the feeling which arrests the
mind in the presence of whatsoever is
grave and constant in human sufferings
and unites it with the secret cause.
  A Portrait of the Artist as a Young Man
  (1916) ch. 5

12 Welcome, O life! I go to encounter for
the millionth time the reality of
experience and to forge in the smithy of
my soul the uncreated conscience of my
race. . . . Old father, old artificer, stand
me now and ever in good stead.
  A Portrait of the Artist as a Young Man
  (1916) ch. 5

13 I will not serve that in which I no longer
believe whether it call itself my home,
my fatherland or my church: and I will
try to express myself in some mode of
life or art as freely as I can and as
wholly as I can, using for my defence
the only arms I allow myself to use,
silence, exile, and cunning.
  A Portrait of the Artist as a Young Man
  (1916) ch. 5

14 Stately, plump Buck Mulligan came from
the stairhead, bearing a bowl of lather
on which a mirror and a razor lay
crossed. A yellow dressinggown,
ungirdled, was sustained gently behind
him by the mild morning air. He held
the bowl aloft and intoned:
    —*Introibo ad altare Dei.*
  Ulysses (1922) p. 1

15 The snotgreen sea. The
scrotumtightening sea.
  Ulysses (1922) p. 5

16 It is a symbol of Irish art. The cracked
lookingglass of a servant.
  Ulysses (1922) p. 7

17 When I makes tea I makes tea, as old
mother Grogan said. And when I makes
water I makes water. . . . *Begob, ma'am,*
says Mrs. Cahill, *God send you don't make
them in the one pot.*
  Ulysses (1922) p. 12

1 I fear those big words, Stephen said,
which make us so unhappy.
Ulysses (1922) p. 31

2 History, Stephen said, is a nightmare
from which I am trying to awake.
Ulysses (1922) p. 34

3 Lawn Tennyson, gentleman poet.
Ulysses (1922) p. 50

4 Mr Leopold Bloom ate with relish the
inner organs of beasts and fowls. He
liked thick giblet soup, nutty gizzards,
a stuffed roast heart, liver slices fried
with crustcrumbs, fried hencod's roes.
Most of all he liked grilled mutton
kidneys which gave to his palate a fine
tang of faintly scented urine.
Ulysses (1922) p. 53

5 Come forth, Lazarus! And he came fifth
and lost the job.
Ulysses (1922) p. 102

6 She used to say Ben Dollard had a base
barreltone voice.
Ulysses (1922) p. 147

7 A man of genius makes no mistakes. His
errors are volitional and are the portals
of discovery.
Ulysses (1922) p. 182 ,

8 Greater love than this, he said, no man
hath that a man lay down his wife for
his friend. Go thou and do likewise.
Thus, or words to that effect, saith
Zarathustra, sometime regius professor
of French letters to the university of
Oxtail.
Ulysses (1922) p. 375

9 The heaventree of stars hung with
humid nightblue fruit.
Ulysses (1922) p. 651

10 He kissed me under the Moorish wall
and I thought well as well him as
another and then I asked him with my
eyes to ask again yes and then he asked
me would I yes to say yes my mountain
flower and first I put my arms around
him yes and drew him down to me so
he could feel my breasts all perfume yes
and his heart was going like mad and
yes I said yes I will Yes.
Ulysses (1922) p. 732

11 When a young man came up to him in
Zurich and said, 'May I kiss the hand
that wrote Ulysses?' Joyce replied,

somewhat like King Lear, 'No, it did lots
of other things too.'
Richard Ellmann *James Joyce* (1959) p. 114

William Joyce (Lord Haw-Haw)
1906–1946

12 Germany calling! Germany calling!
Habitual introduction to propaganda
broadcasts to Britain during the Second
World War

Jack Judge 1878–1938 and
Harry Williams 1874–1924

13 It's a long way to Tipperary,
It's a long way to go;
It's a long way to Tipperary,
To the sweetest girl I know!
Goodbye, Piccadilly,
Farewell, Leicester Square,
It's a long, long way to Tipperary,
But my heart's right there!
It's a Long Way to Tipperary (1912 song)

Carl Gustav Jung 1875–1961

14 *Ein Mensch, der nicht durch die Hölle
seiner Leidenschaften gegangen ist, hat sie
auch nie überwunden.*

A man who has not passed through the
inferno of his passions has never
overcome them.
Erinnerungen, Träume, Gedanken (Memories,
Dreams, Reflections, 1962) ch. 9

15 *Soweit wir zu erkennen vermögen, ist es der
einzige Sinn der menschlichen Existenz, ein
Licht anzuzünden in der Finsternis des
blossen Seins.*

As far as we can discern, the sole
purpose of human existence is to kindle
a light in the darkness of mere being.
Erinnerungen, Träume, Gedanken (Memories,
Dreams, Reflections, 1962) ch. 11

16 *Jede Form von Süchtigkeit ist von übel,
gleichgültig, ob es sich um Alkohol oder
Morphium oder Idealismus handelt.*

Every form of addiction is bad, no matter
whether the narcotic be alcohol or
morphine or idealism.
Erinnerungen, Träume, Gedanken (Memories,
Dreams, Reflections, 1962) ch. 12

17 I do not believe. . . . I know.
In L. van der Post *Jung and the Story of our
Time* (1976) p. 215

1 *Wo die Liebe herrscht, da gibt es keinen*
Machtwillen, und wo die Macht den
Vorrang hat, da fehlt die Liebe. Das eine ist
der Schatten des andern.

Where love rules, there is no will to
power, and where power predominates,
love is lacking. The one is the shadow of
the other.

   Über die Psychologie des Unbewussten (On the
   Psychology of the Unconscious, 1917) in
   Gesammelte Werke (1964) vol. 7, p. 58

2 *Alles, was wir an den Kindern ändern*
wollen, sollten wir zunächst wohl
aufmerksam prüfen, ob es nicht etwas sei,
was besser an uns zu ändern wäre.

If there is anything that we wish to
change in the child, we should first
examine it and see whether it is not
something that could better be changed
in ourselves.

   Vom Werden der Persönlichkeit (On the
   Development of Personality, 1932) in
   Gesammelte Werke (1972) vol. 17, p. 194

3 *Persönlichkeit ist höchste Verwirklichung*
der eingeborenen Eigenart des besonderen
lebenden Wesens. Persönlichkeit ist einer
Tat des höchsten Lebensmutes, der
absoluten Bejahung des individuell Seienden
und der erfolgreichsten Anpassung an das
universal Gegebene bei grösstmöglicher
Freiheit der eigenen Entscheidung.

Personality is the supreme realization of
the innate individuality of a particular
living being. Personality is an act of the
greatest courage in the face of life, the
absolute affirmation of all that
constitutes the individual, and the most
successful adaptation to the universal
conditions of existence coupled with the
greatest possible freedom of personal
decision.

   Vom Werden der Persönlichkeit (On the
   Development of Personality, 1932) in
   Gesammelte Werke (1972) vol. 17, p. 195

4 *Eine gewissermassen oberflächliche Schicht*
des Unbewussten ist zweifellos persönlich.
Wir nennen sie das persönliche
Unbewusste. Dieses ruht aber auf einer
tieferen Schicht, welche nicht mehr
persönlicher Erfahrung und Erwerbung
entstammt, sondern angeboren ist. Diese
tiefere Schicht ist das sogenannte kollektive
Unbewusste. . . . Die Inhalte des

persönlichen Unbewussten sind in der
Hauptsache die sogenannten
gefühlsbetonten Komplexe. . . . *Die*
Inhalte des kollektiven Unbewussten
dagegen sind die sogenannten Archetypen.

A more or less superficial layer of the
unconscious is undoubtedly personal.
I call it the *personal unconscious*. But this
personal unconscious rests upon
a deeper layer, which does not derive
from personal experience and is not
a personal acquisition but is inborn.
This deeper layer I call the *collective*
unconscious. . . . The contents of
the personal unconscious are chiefly
the *feeling-toned complexes*. . . . The
contents of the collective unconscious,
on the other hand, are known as
archetypes.

   Eranos Jahrbuch (Eranos Yearbook, 1934)
   p. 180

Pauline Kael 1919–

5 The words 'Kiss Kiss Bang Bang' which
I saw on an Italian movie poster, are
perhaps the briefest statement
imaginable of the basic appeal of movies.

   Kiss Kiss Bang Bang (1968) 'Note on the
   Title'

6 She [Barbra Streisand in *What's Up,*
Doc?] does her own shtick—the rapid,
tricky New Yorkese line readings . . . but
she doesn't do anything she hasn't
already done. She's playing herself—and
it's awfully soon for that.

   New Yorker 25 Mar. 1972, p. 122

Franz Kafka 1883–1924

7 *Jemand musste Josef K. verleumdet haben,*
denn ohne dass er etwas Böses getan hätte,
wurde er eines Morgens verhaftet.

Someone must have traduced Joseph K.,
for without having done anything
wrong he was arrested one fine
morning.

   Der Prozess (The Trial, 1925) opening
   sentence

8 *Sie können einwenden, dass es ja überhaupt*
kein Verfahren ist, Sie haben sehr recht,

denn es ist ja nur ein Verfahren, wenn ich es als solches anerkenne.

You may object that it is not a trial at all; you are quite right, for it is only a trial if I recognize it as such.
Der Prozess (The Trial, 1925) ch. 2

1 *Es ist oft besser, in Ketten als frei zu sein.*

It's often better to be in chains than to be free.
Der Prozess (The Trial, 1925) ch. 8

2 *Als Gregor Samsa eines Morgens aus unruhigen Träumen erwachte, fand er sich in seinem Bett zu einem ungeheueren Ungeziefer verwandelt.*

When Gregor Samsa awoke one morning from uneasy dreams he found himself transformed in his bed into a gigantic insect.
Die Verwandlung (The Metamorphosis, 1915) opening sentence

Gus Kahn 1886–1941 and Raymond B. Egan 1890–1952

3 There's nothing surer,
The rich get rich and the poor get children.
In the meantime, in between time,
Ain't we got fun.
Ain't We Got Fun (1921 song; music by Richard A. Whiting)

Bert Kalmar 1884–1947, Harry Ruby 1895–1974, Arthur Sheekman 1891–1978, and Nat Perrin

4 Remember, you're fighting for this woman's honour . . . which is probably more than she ever did.
Duck Soup (1933 film; said by Groucho Marx)

5 If you can't leave in a taxi you can leave in a huff. If that's too soon, you can leave in a minute and a huff.
Duck Soup (1933 film; said by Groucho Marx)

George S. Kaufman 1889–1961

6 Satire is what closes Saturday night.
In Scott Meredith *George S. Kaufman and his Friends* (1974) ch. 6

George S. Kaufman 1889–1961 and Moss Hart 1904–1961

7 The man who came to dinner.
Title of play (1939)

George S. Kaufman 1889–1961 and Morrie Ryskind 1895–1985

8 One morning I shot an elephant in my pajamas. How he got into my pajamas I'll never know.
Animal Crackers (1930 film; said by Groucho Marx) in Richard J. Anobile *Hooray for Captain Spaulding* (1974) p. 168

9 DRIFTWOOD (Groucho Marx): It's all right. That's—that's in every contract. That's—that's what they call a sanity clause.
FIORELLO (Chico Marx): You can't fool me. There ain't no Sanity Claus.
Night at the Opera (1935 film), in Richard J. Anobile *Why a Duck?* (1971) p. 206

Gerald Kaufman 1930–

10 Our second handicap was an election manifesto which Gerald Kaufman rightly described as 'the longest suicide note in history'.
Denis Healey *Time of My Life* (1989) ch. 23 (describing the Labour Party's *New Hope for Britain*, published in 1983)

Paul Kaufman and Mike Anthony

11 Poetry in motion.
Title of song (1960)

Patrick Kavanagh 1905–1967

12 I hate what every poet hates in spite
Of all the solemn talk of contemplation.
Oh, Alexander Selkirk knew the plight
Of being king and government and nation.
A road, a mile of kingdom, I am king
Of banks and stones and every blooming thing.
Ploughman and Other Poems (1936), 'Inniskeen Road: July Evening'

13 Cassiopeia was over
Cassidy's hanging hill,
I looked and three whin bushes rode across
The horizon—the Three Wise Kings.
Soul for Sale (1947) 'Christmas Childhood'

1 Clay is the word and clay is the flesh
Where the potato-gatherers like
    mechanized scarecrows move
Along the side-fall of the hill—Maguire
    and his men.
    Soul for Sale (1947) 'The Great Hunger'

2 That was how his life happened.
No mad hooves galloping in the sky,
But the weak, washy way of true
    tragedy—
A sick horse nosing around the meadow
    for a clean place to die.
    Soul for Sale (1947) 'The Great Hunger'

Ted Kavanagh 1892–1958

3 CECIL: After you, Claude.
    CLAUDE: No, after you, Cecil.
    Catch-phrase in *ITMA* (BBC radio
    programme, 1939–49)

4 Can I do you now, sir?
    Catch-phrase spoken by 'Mrs Mopp' in
    ITMA (BBC radio programme, 1939–49)

5 Don't forget the diver.
    Catch-phrase spoken by 'The Diver' in *ITMA*
    (BBC radio programme, 1939–49); in *ITMA*
    1939–1948 (1948) p. 19, Francis Worsley
    says: This character was a memory of the
    pier at New Brighton where Tommy
    [Handley] used to go as a child. . . . A man
    in a bathing suit . . . whined 'Don't forget
    the diver, sir.'

6 I don't mind if I do.
    Catch-phrase spoken by 'Colonel Chinstrap'
    in *ITMA* (BBC radio programme, 1939–49)

7 I go—I come back.
    Catch-phrase spoken by 'Ali Oop' in *ITMA*
    (BBC radio programme, 1939–49)

8 It's being so cheerful as keeps me going.
    Catch-phrase spoken by 'Mona Lott' in
    ITMA (BBC radio programme, 1939–49)

Helen Keller 1880–1968

9 Science may have found a cure for most
evils; but it has found no remedy for the
worst of them all—the apathy of human
beings.
    My Religion (1927) ch. 6

Jaan Kenbrovin and John William Kellette

10 I'm forever blowing bubbles.
    Title of song (1919)

Florynce Kennedy 1916–

11 If men could get pregnant, abortion
would be a sacrament.
    In *Ms.* Mar. 1973, p. 89

Jimmy Kennedy 1902–1984

12 If you go down in the woods today
You're sure of a big surprise
If you go down in the woods today
You'd better go in disguise
For every Bear that ever there was
Will gather there for certain because,
Today's the day the Teddy Bears have
    their Picnic.
    Teddy Bear's Picnic (1932 song; music by
    John W. Bratton)

Jimmy Kennedy 1902–1984 and Michael Carr 1904–1968

13 South of the Border—down Mexico way.
    South of the Border (1939 song)

14 We're gonna hang out the washing on
the Siegfried Line.
    Title of song (1939)

Jimmy Kennedy 1902–1984 and Hugh Williams (Will Grosz)

15 Red sails in the sunset.
    Title of song (1935)

John F. Kennedy 1917–1963

16 I just received the following wire from
my generous Daddy [Joseph P.
Kennedy]—'Dear Jack. Don't buy
a single vote more than necessary. I'll be
damned if I'm going to pay for
a landslide.'
    Speech in Washington, 1958, in J. F. Cutler
    Honey Fitz (1962) p. 306

17 When we got into office, the thing that
surprised me most was to find that
things were just as bad as we'd been
saying they were.
    Speech at White House, 27 May 1961, in
    New York Times 28 May 1961, p. 39

1 Mankind must put an end to war or war will put an end to mankind.

Speech to United Nations General Assembly, 25 Sept. 1961, in *New York Times* 26 Sept. 1961, p. 14

2 The President described the dinner [for Nobel Prizewinners] as 'probably the greatest concentration of talent and genius in this house except for perhaps those times when Thomas Jefferson ate alone.'

New York Times 30 Apr. 1962, p. 1

3 Two thousand years ago the proudest boast was '*civis Romanus sum*'. Today, in the world of freedom the proudest boast is '*Ich bin ein Berliner*'. . . . All free men, wherever they may live, are citizens of Berlin. And, therefore, as a free man, I take pride in the words, '*Ich bin ein Berliner*'.

Speech in West Berlin, 26 June 1963, in *New York Times* 27 June 1963, p. 12

4 When power leads man toward arrogance, poetry reminds him of his limitations. When power narrows the areas of man's concern, poetry reminds him of the richness and diversity of his existence. When power corrupts, poetry cleanses. For art establishes the basic human truths which must serve as the touchstone of our judgement.

Speech at Amherst College, Mass., 26 Oct. 1963, in *New York Times* 27 Oct. 1963, p. 87

5 In free society art is not a weapon. . . . Artists are not engineers of the soul.

Speech at Amherst College, Mass., 26 Oct. 1963, in *New York Times* 27 Oct. 1963, p. 87

6 It was involuntary. They sank my boat.

Reply when asked how he became a war hero, in Arthur M. Schlesinger Jr. *A Thousand Days* (1965) ch. 4

7 We stand today on the edge of a new frontier—the frontier of the 1960s—a frontier of unknown opportunities and perils—a frontier of unfulfilled hopes and threats. Woodrow Wilson's New Freedom promised our nation a new political and economic framework. Franklin Roosevelt's New Deal promised security and succor to those in need. But the New Frontier of which I speak is not a set of promises—it is a set of challenges. It sums up not what I intend to offer the American people, but what I intend to ask of them.

Speech accepting Democratic nomination in Los Angeles, 15 July 1960, in *Vital Speeches* 1 Aug. 1960, p. 611

8 Let the word go forth from this time and place, to friend and foe alike, that the torch has been passed to a new generation of Americans—born in this century, tempered by war, disciplined by a hard and bitter peace, proud of our ancient heritage—and unwilling to witness or permit the slow undoing of those human rights to which this nation has always been committed, and to which we are committed today at home and around the world.

Let every nation know, whether it wishes us well or ill, that we shall pay any price, bear any burden, meet any hardship, support any friend, oppose any foe to assure the survival and the success of liberty.

Inaugural address, 20 Jan. 1961, in *Vital Speeches* 1 Feb. 1961, p. 226

9 If a free society cannot help the many who are poor, it cannot save the few who are rich.

Inaugural address, 20 Jan. 1961, in *Vital Speeches* 1 Feb. 1961, p. 226

10 Let us never negotiate out of fear. But let us never fear to negotiate.

Inaugural address, 20 Jan. 1961, in *Vital Speeches* 1 Feb. 1961, p. 227

11 All this will not be finished in the first 100 days. Nor will it be finished in the first 1,000 days, nor in the life of this Administration, nor even perhaps in our lifetime on this planet. But let us begin.

Inaugural address, 20 Jan. 1961, in *Vital Speeches* 1 Feb. 1961, p. 227

12 Now the trumpet summons us again—not as a call to bear arms, though arms we need—not as a call to battle, though embattled we are—but a call to bear the burden of a long twilight struggle, year in and year out, 'rejoicing in hope, patient in tribulation'—a struggle against the common enemies of man: tyranny, poverty, disease and war itself.

Inaugural address, 20 Jan. 1961, in *Vital Speeches* 1 Feb. 1961, p. 227

1 And so, my fellow Americans: ask not what your country can do for you—ask what you can do for your country. My fellow citizens of the world: ask not what America will do for you, but what together we can do for the freedom of man.

> Inaugural address, 20 Jan. 1961, in *Vital Speeches* 1 Feb. 1961, p. 227. Cf. Oliver Wendell Holmes Jr., speech at Keene, New Hampshire, 30 May 1884: 'We pause to ... recall what our country has done for each of us and to ask ourselves what we can do for our country in return.'

2 I believe that this Nation should commit itself to achieving the goal, before this decade is out, of landing a man on the Moon and returning him safely to earth.

> Supplementary State of the Union message to Congress, 25 May 1961, in *Vital Speeches* 15 June 1961, p. 518

3 Those who make peaceful revolution impossible will make violent revolution inevitable.

> Speech at White House, 13 Mar. 1962, in *Vital Speeches* 1 Apr. 1962, p. 356

Joseph P. Kennedy 1888–1969

4 When the going gets tough, the tough get going.

> In J. H. Cutler *Honey Fitz* (1962) p. 291 (also attributed to Knute Rockne) *See also* JOHN F. KENNEDY

Robert F. Kennedy 1925–1968

5 About one-fifth of the people are against everything all the time.

> Speech at University of Pennsylvania, 6 May 1964, in *Philadelphia Inquirer* 7 May 1964

Jack Kerouac 1922–1969

6 John Clellon Holmes ... and I were sitting around trying to think up the meaning of the Lost Generation and the subsequent Existentialism and I said, 'You know, this is really a beat generation' and he leapt up and said 'That's it, that's right!'

> *Playboy* June 1959, p. 32

Jean Kerr 1923–

7 As someone pointed out recently, if you can keep your head when all about you are losing theirs, it's just possible you haven't grasped the situation.

> *Please Don't Eat the Daisies* (1957) introduction. Cf. Rudyard Kipling 126:13

8 I'm tired of all this nonsense about beauty being only skin-deep. That's deep enough. What do you want—an adorable pancreas?

> *The Snake has all the Lines* (1958) p. 142

Joseph Kesselring 1902–1967

9 Arsenic and old lace.

> Title of play (1941)

John Maynard Keynes (Baron Keynes) 1883–1946

10 I work for a Government I despise for ends I think criminal.

> Letter to Duncan Grant, 15 Dec. 1917, in *British Library Add. MSS 57931* fo. 119

11 He [Clemenceau] felt about France what Pericles felt of Athens—unique value in her, nothing else mattering; but his theory of politics was Bismarck's. He had one illusion—France; and one disillusion—mankind, including Frenchmen, and his colleagues not least.

> *Economic Consequences of the Peace* (1919) ch. 3

12 Like Odysseus, the President [Woodrow Wilson] looked wiser when he was seated.

> *Economic Consequences of the Peace* (1919) ch. 3

13 Lenin was right. There is no subtler, no surer means of overturning the existing basis of society than to debauch the currency. The process engages all the hidden forces of economic law on the side of destruction, and does it in a manner which not one man in a million is able to diagnose.

> *Economic Consequences of the Peace* (1919) ch. 6

14 A study of the history of opinion is a necessary preliminary to the emancipation of the mind. I do not know which makes a man more conservative—to know nothing but the present, or nothing but the past.

> *End of Laissez-Faire* (1926) pt. 1

15 Marxian Socialism must always remain a portent to the historians of Opinion—

how a doctrine so illogical and so dull can have exercised so powerful and enduring an influence over the minds of men, and, through them, the events of history.
End of Laissez-Faire (1926) pt. 3

1 The important thing for Government is not to do things which individuals are doing already, and to do them a little better or a little worse; but to do those things which at present are not done at all.
End of Laissez-Faire (1926) pt. 4

2 I think that Capitalism, wisely managed, can probably be made more efficient for attaining economic ends than any alternative system yet in sight, but that in itself it is in many ways extremely objectionable.
End of Laissez-Faire (1926) pt. 5

3 How can I convey to the reader, who does not know him, any just impression of this extraordinary figure of our time, this syren, this goat-footed bard, this half-human visitor to our age from the hag-ridden magic and enchanted woods of Celtic antiquity? One catches in his company that flavour of final purposelessness, inner irresponsibility, existence outside or away from our Saxon good and evil, mixed with cunning, remorselessness, love of power, that lend fascination, enthralment, and terror to the fair-seeming magicians of North European folklore.
Essays in Biography (1933) 'Mr Lloyd George'

4 It is better that a man should tyrannize over his bank balance than over his fellow-citizens.
General Theory of Employment (1936) ch. 24

5 The ideas of economists and political philosophers, both when they are right and when they are wrong, are more powerful than is commonly understood. Indeed the world is ruled by little else. Practical men, who believe themselves to be quite exempt from any intellectual influences, are usually the slaves of some defunct economist. Madmen in authority, who hear voices in the air, are distilling their frenzy from some academic scribbler of a few years back. I am sure that the power of vested

interests is vastly exaggerated compared with the gradual encroachment of ideas. Not, indeed, immediately, but after a certain interval; for in the field of economic and political philosophy there are not many who are influenced by new theories after they are twenty-five or thirty years of age, so that the ideas which civil servants and politicians and even agitators apply to current events are not likely to be the newest. But soon or late, it is ideas, not vested interests, which are dangerous for good or evil.
General Theory of Employment (1936; 1947 ed.) ch. 24

6 I remember in my youth asking Maynard Keynes, 'What do you think happens to Mr Lloyd George when he is alone in the room?' And Keynes replied, 'When he is alone in the room there is nobody there.'
Lady Violet Bonham-Carter *Impact of Personality in Politics* (Romanes Lecture, 1963) p. 6

7 But this *long run* is a misleading guide to current affairs. *In the long run* we are all dead.
Tract on Monetary Reform (1923) ch. 3

Nikita Khrushchev 1894–1971

8 Comrades! We must abolish the cult of the individual decisively, once and for all.
Speech to secret session of 20th Congress of the Communist Party, 25 Feb. 1956, in *Dethronement of Stalin* (Manchester Guardian) 11 June 1956, p. 27

9 If anyone believes that our smiles involve abandonment of the teaching of Marx, Engels and Lenin he deceives himself. Those who wait for that must wait until a shrimp learns to whistle.
Speech in Moscow, 17 Sept. 1955, in *New York Times* 18 Sept. 1955, p. 19

10 If you start throwing hedgehogs under me, I shall throw a couple of porcupines under you.
In *New York Times* 7 Nov. 1963

11 Кто считает, что можно убаюкать рабочего хорошей революционной фразой, тот ошибается. ... Если же не проявлять заботы о росте материалбных и духовных богатств, то люди сегодня послушают, завтра послушают, а потом могут сказать:

что вы нам все обещаете в будущем,
говорите, так сказать, о загробной
жизни. Нам уже поп говорил об
этом.

Anyone who believes that the worker
can be lulled by fine revolutionary
phrases is mistaken. . . . If no concern is
shown for the growth of material and
spiritual riches, the people will listen
today, they will listen tomorrow, and
then they may say: 'Why do you
promise us everything for the future?
You are talking, so to speak, about life
beyond the grave. The priest has already
told us about this.'

Speech at World Youth Forum, 19 Sept.
1964, in *Pravda* 22 Sept. 1964

1 If one cannot catch the bird of paradise,
better take a wet hen.

In *Time* 6 Jan. 1958·

2 We say this not only for the socialist
states, who are more akin to us. We
base ourselves on the idea that we must
peacefully co-exist. About the capitalist
States, it doesn't depend on you whether
or not we exist. If you don't like us,
don't accept our invitations and don't
invite us to come to see you. Whether
you like it or not, history is on our side.
We will bury you.

Speech to Western diplomats at reception in
Moscow for Polish leader Mr Gomulka,
18 Nov. 1956, in *The Times* 19 Nov. 1956

Joyce Kilmer 1886–1918

3 I think that I shall never see
A poem lovely as a tree.

Trees and Other Poems (1914) 'Trees'

4 Poems are made by fools like me,
But only God can make a tree.

Trees and Other Poems (1914) 'Trees'

Lord Kilmuir (Sir David Maxwell Fyfe) 1900–1967

5 Loyalty is the Tory's secret weapon.

In Anthony Sampson *Anatomy of Britain*
(1962) ch. 6

Martin Luther King 1929–1968

6 Injustice anywhere is a threat to justice
everywhere.

Letter from Birmingham Jail, Alabama,
16 Apr. 1963, in *Atlantic Monthly* Aug.
1963, p. 78

7 I have almost reached the regrettable
conclusion that the Negro's great
stumbling block in the stride toward
freedom is not the White Citizens
Councillor or the Ku Klux Klanner but
the white moderate who is more devoted
to order than to justice; who prefers
a negative peace which is the absence of
tension to a positive peace which is the
presence of justice.

Letter from Birmingham Jail, Alabama,
16 Apr. 1963, in *Atlantic Monthly* Aug.
1963, p. 81

8 I submit to you that if a man hasn't
discovered something he will die for, he
isn't fit to live.

Speech in Detroit, 23 June 1963, in J.
Bishop *Days of M. L. King Jr.* (1971) ch. 4

9 I want to be the white man's brother,
not his brother-in-law.

In *New York Journal-American* 10 Sept.
1962, p. 1

10 Now, I say to you today my friends,
even though we face the difficulties of
today and tomorrow, I still have
a dream. It is a dream deeply rooted in
the American dream. I have a dream
that one day this nation will rise up and
live out the true meaning of its
creed:—'We hold these truths to be
self-evident, that all men are created
equal.'

I have a dream that one day on the
red hills of Georgia the sons of former
slaves and the sons of former slave
owners will be able to sit down together
at the table of brotherhood.

I have a dream that one day even the
state of Mississippi, a state sweltering
with the people's injustice, sweltering
with the heat of oppression, will be
transformed into an oasis of freedom and
justice.

I have a dream that my four little
children will one day live in a nation
where they will not be judged by the
color of their skin but by the content of
their character.

Speech at Civil Rights March in
Washington, 28 Aug. 1963, in *New York
Times* 29 Aug. 1963, p. 21

11 Well, I don't know what will happen
now. We've been to the mountain top.
I won't mind. Like anybody, I would like
to have a long life. Longevity has its

place. But I'm not concerned about that now. I just want to do God's will. And he's allowed me to go up to the mountain. And I've looked over, and I've seen the promised land. I may not get there with you, but I want you to know tonight that we as a people will get to the promised land. So I'm happy tonight. I'm not worried about anything. I'm not fearing any man. Mine eyes have seen the glory of the coming of the Lord.

> Speech in Memphis, 3 Apr. 1968 (the day before King was assassinated), in *New York Times* 4 Apr. 1968, p. 24

1 The ultimate measure of a man is not where he stands in moments of comfort and convenience, but where he stands at times of challenge and controversy.
> *Strength to Love* (1963) ch. 3

2 Nothing in all the world is more dangerous than sincere ignorance and conscientious stupidity.
> *Strength to Love* (1963) ch. 4

3 Jesus eloquently affirmed from the cross a higher law. He knew that the old eye-for-an-eye philosophy would leave everyone blind. He did not seek to overcome evil with evil. He overcame evil with good.
> *Strength to Love* (1963) ch. 4

4 The means by which we live have outdistanced the ends for which we live. Our scientific power has outrun our spiritual power. We have guided missiles and misguided men.
> *Strength to Love* (1963) ch. 7

5 If we assume that mankind has a right to survive, then we must find an alternative to war and destruction. In our day of space vehicles and guided ballistic missiles, the choice is either nonviolence or nonexistence.
> *Strength to Love* (1963) ch. 17

6 We must learn to live together as brothers or perish together as fools.
> Speech at St. Louis, 22 Mar. 1964, in *St Louis Post-Dispatch* 23 Mar. 1964

7 A riot is at bottom the language of the unheard.
> *Where Do We Go From Here?* (1967) ch. 4

Stoddard King 1889–1933

8 There's a long, long trail awinding
Into the land of my dreams,
Where the nightingales are singing
And a white moon beams;
There's a long, long night of waiting
Until my dreams all come true,
Till the day when I'll be going down
That long, long trail with you.
> *There's a Long, Long Trail* (1913 song; music by Zo (Alonso) Elliott)

David Kingsley, Dennis Lyons, and Peter Lovell-Davis

9 Yesterday's men (they failed before!).
> Advertising slogan for the Labour Party (referring to the Conservatives), 1970, in David Butler and Michael Pinto-Duschinsky *British General Election of 1970* (1971) ch. 6

Hugh Kingsmill (Hugh Kingsmill Lunn) 1889–1949

10 Friends . . . are God's apology for relations.
> In Michael Holroyd *Best of Hugh Kingsmill* (1970) p. 12

11 What still alive at twenty-two,
A clean upstanding chap like you?
Sure, if your throat 'tis hard to slit,
Slit your girl's, and swing for it.
Like enough, you won't be glad,
When they come to hang you, lad:
But bacon's not the only thing
That's cured by hanging from a string.
> *Table of Truth* (1933) 'Two Poems, after A. E. Housman', no. 1

12 'Tis Summer Time on Bredon,
And now the farmers swear:
The cattle rise and listen
In valleys far and near,
And blush at what they hear.

But when the mists in autumn
On Bredon top are thick,
And happy hymns of farmers
Go up from fold and rick,
The cattle then are sick.
> *Table of Truth* (1933) 'Two Poems, after A. E. Housman', no. 2

Neil Kinnock 1942–

13 If Margaret Thatcher wins on Thursday, I warn you not to be ordinary, I warn

you not to be young, I warn you not to
fall ill, and I warn you not to grow old.
    Speech at Bridgend, 7 June 1983, in
    Guardian 8 June 1983

1 Mr Shultz went off his pram.
    Comment after a meeting with the US
    Secretary of State, in *Guardian* 15 Feb. 1984

2 I would die for my country but I could
never let my country die for me.
    Speech at Labour Party Conference, 30 Sept.
    1986, in *Guardian* 1 Oct. 1986

3 Why am I the first Kinnock in
a thousand generations to be able to get
to a university? Why is Glenys the first
woman in her family in a thousand
generations to be able to get to
a university? Was it because all our
predecessors were thick? Did they lack
talent? Those people who could sing and
play and write poetry? Those people
who could make wonderful beautiful
things with their hands? Those people
who could dream dreams, see visions?
Was it because they were weak, those
people who could work eight hours
underground and then come up and
play football, weak? Does anybody really
think that they didn't get what we had
because they didn't have the talent or
the strength or the endurance or the
commitment? Of course not. It's because
they didn't have a platform on which
they could stand.
    Speech in party political broadcast, 21 May
    1987, in *New York Times* 12 Sept. 1987,
    p. 1 (this speech was later plagiarized by the
    American politician Joe Biden)

Rudyard Kipling 1865–1936

4 But I consort with long-haired things
In velvet collar-rolls,
Who talk about the Aims of Art,
And 'theories' and 'goals',
And moo and coo with women-folk
About their blessed souls.
    Abaft the Funnel (1909) 'In Partibus'

5 When you've shouted 'Rule Britannia',
    when you've sung 'God save the
    Queen'—
When you've finished killing Kruger
    with your mouth—
Will you kindly drop a shilling in my
    little tambourine
For a gentleman in *Kharki* ordered
    South?

He's an absent-minded beggar and his
    weaknesses are great—
But we and Paul must take him as we
    find him—
He is out on active service, wiping
    something off a slate—
And he's left a lot o' little things behind
    him!
    Absent-Minded Beggar (1899) p. 1

6 There is sorrow enough in the natural
    way
From men and women to fill our day;
But when we are certain of sorrow in
    store,
Why do we always arrange for more?
*Brothers and Sisters, I bid you beware
Of giving your heart to a dog to tear.*
    Actions and Reactions (1909) 'The Power of
    the Dog'

7 There are nine and sixty ways of
    constructing tribal lays,
And—every—single—one—of—them—
    is—right!
    Ballads and Barrack-Room Ballads (1893) 'In
    the Neolithic Age'

8 'What are the bugles blowin' for?' said
    Files-on-Parade.
'To turn you out, to turn you out,' the
    Colour-Sergeant said.
    Barrack-Room Ballads (1892) 'Danny
    Deever'

9 For they're hangin' Danny Deever, you
    can hear the Dead March play,
The regiment's in 'ollow square—they're
    hangin' him to-day;
They've taken of his buttons off an' cut
    his stripes away,
An' they're hangin' Danny Deever in
    the mornin'.
    Barrack-Room Ballads (1892) 'Danny
    Deever'

10 O it's Tommy this, an' Tommy that, an'
    'Tommy, go away';
But it's 'Thank you, Mister Atkins,'
    when the band begins to play.
    Barrack-Room Ballads (1892) 'Tommy'

11 Then it's Tommy this, an' Tommy that,
    an 'Tommy 'ow's yer soul?'
But it's 'Thin red line of 'eroes' when
    the drums begin to roll.
    Barrack-Room Ballads (1892) 'Tommy'

12 For it's Tommy this, an' Tommy that,
    an' 'Chuck him out, the brute!'

But it's 'Saviour of 'is country' when the
    guns begin to shoot.
Barrack-Room Ballads (1892) 'Tommy'

1 So 'ere's *to* you, Fuzzy-Wuzzy, at your
    'ome in the Soudan;
You're a pore benighted 'eathen but
    a first-class fightin' man;
An' 'ere's *to* you, Fuzzy-Wuzzy, with
    your 'ayrick 'ead of 'air—
You big black boundin' beggar—for you
    broke a British square!
Barrack-Room Ballads (1892) 'Fuzzy-Wuzzy'

2 The uniform 'e wore
Was nothin' much before,
An' rather less than 'arf o' that be'ind.
    Barrack-Room Ballads (1892) 'Gunga Din'

3 Though I've belted you and flayed you,
By the livin' Gawd that made you,
You're a better man than I am, Gunga
    Din!
Barrack-Room Ballads (1892) 'Gunga Din'

4 'Ave you 'eard o' the Widow at Windsor
With a hairy gold crown on 'er 'ead?
She 'as ships on the foam—she 'as
    millions at 'ome,
An' she pays us poor beggars in red.
    Barrack-Room Ballads (1892) 'The Widow at
    Windsor'

5 When you're wounded and left on
    Afghanistan's plains
And the women come out to cut up
    what remains
Just roll to your rifle and blow out your
    brains
An' go to your Gawd like a soldier.
    Barrack-Room Ballads (1892) 'The Young
    British Soldier'

6 By the old Moulmein Pagoda, lookin'
    eastward to the sea,
There's a Burma girl a-settin', and
    I know she thinks o' me;
For the wind is in the palm-trees, an'
    the temple-bells they say:
'Come you back, you British soldier;
    come you back to Mandalay!'
Come you back to Mandalay,
Where the old Flotilla lay:
Can't you 'ear their paddles chunkin'
    from Rangoon to Mandalay?
On the road to Mandalay,
Where the flyin'-fishes play,
An' the dawn comes up like thunder
    outer China 'crost the Bay!
Barrack-Room Ballads (1892) 'Mandalay'

7 An' I seed her first a-smokin' of
    a whackin' white cheroot,
An' a-wastin' Christian kisses on an
    'eathen idol's foot.
Barrack-Room Ballads (1892) 'Mandalay'

8 Ship me somewheres east of Suez, where
    the best is like the worst,
Where there aren't no Ten
    Commandments an' a man can raise
    a thirst.
Barrack-Room Ballads (1892) 'Mandalay'

9 We're poor little lambs who've lost our
    way,
Baa! Baa! Baa!
We're little black sheep who've gone
    astray,
Baa-aa-aa!
Gentlemen-rankers out on the spree,
Damned from here to Eternity,
God ha' mercy on such as we,
Baa! Yah! Bah!
    Barrack-Room Ballads (1892)
    'Gentlemen-Rankers'

10 Oh, East is East, and West is West, and
    never the twain shall meet,
Till Earth and Sky stand presently at
    God's great Judgement Seat;
But there is neither East nor West,
    Border, nor Breed, nor Birth,
When two strong men stand face to
    face, tho' they come from the ends of
    earth!
    Barrack-Room Ballads (1892) 'The Ballad of
    East and West'

11 And the talk slid north, and the talk slid
    south,
With the sliding puffs from the
    hookah-mouth.
Four things greater than all things
    are,—
Women and Horses and Power and
    War.
    Barrack-Room Ballads (1892) 'The Ballad of
    the King's Jest'

12 When the flush of a new-born sun fell
    first on Eden's green and gold,
Our father Adam sat under the Tree and
    scratched with a stick in the mould;
And the first rude sketch that the world
    had seen was joy to his mighty heart,
Till the Devil whispered behind the
    leaves, 'It's pretty, but is it Art?'
    Barrack-Room Ballads (1892) 'The
    Conundrum of the Workshops'

1 We know that the tail must wag the
  dog, for the horse is drawn by the
  cart;
  But the Devil whoops, as he whooped of
  old: 'It's clever, but is it Art?'
  Barrack-Room Ballads (1892) 'The
  Conundrum of the Workshops'

2 Winds of the World, give answer! They
  are whimpering to and fro—
  And what should they know of England
  who only England know?—
  The poor little street-bred people that
  vapour and fume and brag.
  Barrack-Room Ballads (1892) 'The English
  Flag'

3 For the sin ye do by two and two ye
  must pay for one by one!
  Barrack-Room Ballads (1892) 'Tomlinson'

4 There be triple ways to take, of the eagle
  or the snake,
  Or the way of a man with a maid;
  But the sweetest way to me is a ship's
  upon the sea
  In the heel of the North-East Trade.
  Barrack-Room Ballads (1892) 'L'Envoi'

5 What the horses o' Kansas think to-day,
  the horses of America will think
  tomorrow; an' I tell *you* that when the
  horses of America rise in their might,
  the day o' the Oppressor is ended.
  The Day's Work (1898) 'A Walking Delegate'

6 The toad beneath the harrow knows
  Exactly where each tooth-point goes;
  The butterfly upon the road
  Preaches contentment to that toad.
  Departmental Ditties (1886) 'Pagett, MP'

7 A Nation spoke to a Nation,
  A Throne sent word to a Throne:
  'Daughter am I in my mother's house,
  But mistress in my own.
  The gates are mine to open,
  As the gates are mine to close,
  And I abide by my Mother's House.'
  Said our Lady of the Snows.
  Departmental Ditties (1898 US ed.) 'Our Lady
  of the Snows'

8 Who hath desired the Sea?—the sight of
  salt water unbounded—
  The heave and the halt and the hurl and
  the crash of the comber
  wind-hounded?
  The sleek-barrelled swell before storm,
  grey, foamless, enormous, and
  growing—

Stark calm on the lap of the Line or the
crazy-eyed hurricane blowing.
The Five Nations (1903) 'The Sea and the
Hills'

9 And here the sea-fogs lap and cling
  And here, each warning each,
  The sheep-bells and the ship-bells ring
  Along the hidden beach.
  The Five Nations (1903) 'Sussex'

10 God gives all men all earth to love,
   But since man's heart is small,
   Ordains for each one spot shall prove
   Belovèd over all.
   Each to his choice, and I rejoice
   The lot has fallen to me
   In a fair ground—in a fair ground—
   Yea, Sussex by the sea!
   The Five Nations (1903) 'Sussex'

11 Then ye returned to your trinkets; then
   ye contented your souls
   With the flannelled fools at the wicket or
   the muddied oafs at the goals.
   The Five Nations (1903) 'The Islanders'

12 We're foot—slog—slog—slog—sloggin'
   over Africa!—
   Foot—foot—foot—foot—sloggin' over
   Africa—
   (Boots—boots—boots—boots—movin'
   up and down again!)
   There's no discharge in the war!
   The Five Nations (1903) 'Boots' (for the last
   line, cf. *Oxford Dictionary of Quotations*
   (1979) 55:25)

13 An' it all goes into the laundry,
   But it never comes out in the wash,
   'Ow we're sugared about by the old men
   ('Eavy-sterned amateur old men!)
   That 'amper an' 'inder an' scold men
   For fear o' Stellenbosh!
   The Five Nations (1903) 'Stellenbosh'

14 For all we have and are,
   For all our children's fate,
   Stand up and take the war.
   The Hun is at the gate!
   For All We Have and Are (1914) p. 1

15 There is but one task for all—
   For each one life to give.
   What stands if freedom fall?
   Who dies if England live?
   For All We Have and Are (1914) p. 2

16 It is always a temptation to a rich and
   lazy nation,
   To puff and look important and to say:-

'Though we know we should defeat you,
  we have not the time to meet you,
We will therefore pay you cash to go
  away.'

And that is called paying the Dane-geld;
But we've proved it again and again,
That if once you have paid him the
  Dane-geld
You never get rid of the Dane.
  History of England (1911) 'Dane-Geld'

1 'Oh, where are you going to, all you Big
  Steamers,
With England's own coal, up and down
  the salt seas?'
'We are going to fetch you your bread
  and your butter,
Your beef, pork, and mutton, eggs,
  apples, and cheese.'
  History of England (1911) 'Big Steamers'

2 Our England is a garden that is full of
  stately views,
Of borders, beds and shrubberies and
  lawns and avenues,
With statues on the terraces and
  peacocks strutting by;
But the Glory of the Garden lies in more
  than meets the eye.
  History of England (1911) 'The Glory of the
  Garden'

3 Our England is a garden, and such
  gardens are not made
By singing:—'Oh, how beautiful!' and
  sitting in the shade,
While better men than we go out and
  start their working lives
At grubbing weeds from gravel paths
  with broken dinner-knives.
  History of England (1911) 'The Glory of the
  Garden'

4 Oh, Adam was a gardener, and God who
  made him sees
That half a proper gardener's work is
  done upon his knees,
So when your work is finished, you can
  wash your hands and pray
For the Glory of the Garden that it may
  not pass away!
*And the Glory of the Garden it shall never
  pass away!*
  History of England (1911) 'The Glory of the
  Garden'

5 Lalun is a member of the most ancient
  profession in the world.
  In Black and White (1888) 'On the City Wall'

6 'We be one blood, thou and I', Mowgli
  answered. 'I take my life from thee
  to-night. My kill shall be thy kill if ever
  thou art hungry, O Kaa.'
  Jungle Book (1894) 'Kaa's Hunting'

7 Brother, thy tail hangs down behind!
  The Jungle Book (1894) 'Road Song of the
  Bandar-Log'

8 You must *not* forget the suspenders, Best
  Beloved.
  Just So Stories (1902) 'How the Whale got
  his Throat'

9 Then the Whale stood up on his Tail
  and said, 'I'm hungry.' And the small
  'Stute Fish said in a small 'stute voice,
  'Noble and generous Cetacean, have you
  ever tasted Man?' 'No,' said the Whale.
  'What is it like?' 'Nice,' said the small
  'Stute Fish. 'Nice but nubbly.'
  Just So Stories (1902) 'How the Whale got
  his Throat'

10 He had his Mummy's leave to paddle, or
  else he would never have done it,
  because he was a man of infinite-
  resource-and-sagacity.
  Just So Stories (1902) 'How the Whale got
  his Throat'

11 The Camel's hump is an ugly lump
  Which well you may see at the Zoo;
  But uglier yet is the hump we get
  From having too little to do.
  Just So Stories (1902) 'How the Camel got
  his Hump'

12 We get the hump—
  Cameelious hump—
  The hump that is black and blue!
  Just So Stories (1902) 'How the Camel got
  his Hump'

13 The cure for this ill is not to sit still,
  Or frowst with a book by the fire;
  But to take a large hoe and a shovel
  also,
  And dig till you gently perspire.
  Just So Stories (1902) 'How the Camel got
  his Hump'

14 But there was one Elephant—a new
  Elephant—an Elephant's Child—who
  was full of 'satiable curtiosity, and that
  means he asked ever so many questions.
  Just So Stories (1902) 'The Elephant's Child'

15 Then Kolokolo Bird said, with
  a mournful cry, 'Go to the banks of the
  great grey-green, greasy Limpopo River,

all set about with fever-trees, and find out.'
Just So Stories (1902) 'The Elephant's Child'

1 Then the Elephant's Child put his head down close to the Crocodile's musky, tusky mouth, and the Crocodile caught him by his little nose. . . . At this, O Best Beloved, the Elephant's Child was much annoyed, and he said, speaking through his nose, like this, 'Led go! You are hurtig be!'
Just So Stories (1902) 'The Elephant's Child'

2 I keep six honest serving-men
(They taught me all I knew);
Their names are What and Why and When
And How and Where and Who.
Just So Stories (1902) 'The Elephant's Child'

3 Yes, weekly from Southampton,
Great steamers, white and gold,
Go rolling down to Rio
(Roll down—roll down to Rio!).
And I'd like to roll to Rio
Some day before I'm old!
Just So Stories (1902) 'Beginning of the Armadilloes'

4 But the wildest of all the wild animals was the Cat. He walked by himself, and all places were alike to him.
Just So Stories (1902) 'The Cat that Walked by Himself'

5 And he went back through the Wet Wild Woods, waving his wild tail and walking by his wild lone. But he never told anybody.
Just So Stories (1902) 'The Cat that Walked by Himself'

6 When [Max] Aitken acquired the *Daily Express* his political views seemed to Kipling to become more and more inconsistent, and one day Kipling asked him what he was really up to. Aitken is supposed to have replied: 'What I want is power. Kiss 'em one day and kick 'em the next'; and so on. 'I see,' said Kipling. 'Power without responsibility: the prerogative of the harlot throughout the ages.' So, many years later, when [Stanley] Baldwin deemed it necessary to deal sharply with such lords of the press, he obtained leave of his cousin [Kipling] to borrow that telling phrase, which he used to some effect on the 18th March,

1931, at . . . the old Queen's Hall in Langham Place.
Speech by Earl Baldwin to the Kipling Society, 5 Oct. 1971, in *Kipling Journal* Dec. 1971

7 If I were hanged on the highest hill,
Mother o' mine, O mother o' mine!
I know whose love would follow me still,
Mother o' mine, O mother o' mine!

If I were drowned in the deepest sea,
Mother o' mine, O mother o' mine!
I know whose tears would come down to me,
Mother o' mine, O mother o' mine.

If I were damned of body and soul,
I know whose prayers would make me whole,
Mother o' mine, O mother o' mine.
The Light That Failed (1891) dedication

8 The man who would be king.
Title of story (1888)

9 And the end of the fight is a tombstone white, with the name of the late deceased,
And the epitaph drear: 'A fool lies here who tried to hustle the East.'
The Naulahka (1892) ch. 5

10 Take my word for it, the silliest woman can manage a clever man; but it takes a very clever woman to manage a fool.
Plain Tales from the Hills (1888) 'Three and—an Extra'

11 Every one is more or less mad on one point.
Plain Tales from the Hills (1888) 'On the Strength of a Likeness'

12 Of all the trees that grow so fair,
Old England to adorn,
Greater are none beneath the Sun,
Than Oak, and Ash, and Thorn.
Puck of Pook's Hill (1906) 'Tree Song'

13 England shall bide till Judgement Tide
By Oak, and Ash, and Thorn!
Puck of Pook's Hill (1906) 'Tree Song'

14 What is a woman that you forsake her,
And the hearth-fire and the home-acre,
To go with the old grey Widow-maker?
Puck of Pook's Hill (1906) 'Harp Song of the Dane Women'

15 If you wake at midnight, and hear a horse's feet,
Don't go drawing back the blind, or looking in the street,

Them that asks no questions isn't told
  a lie.
Watch the wall, my darling, while the
  Gentlemen go by!
Five and twenty ponies,
Trotting through the dark—
Brandy for the Parson,
'Baccy for the Clerk;
Laces for a lady, letters for a spy,
Watch the wall, my darling, while the
  Gentlemen go by!
  Puck of Pook's Hill (1906) 'Smuggler's Song'

1 Land of our birth, we pledge to thee
Our love and toil in the years to be;
When we are grown and take our place,
As men and women with our race.
  Puck of Pook's Hill (1906) 'Children's Song'

2 Teach us Delight in simple things,
And Mirth that has no bitter springs;
Forgiveness free of evil done,
And Love to all men 'neath the sun!
  Puck of Pook's Hill (1906) 'Children's Song'

3 The tumult and the shouting dies—
The captains and the kings depart—
Still stands Thine ancient Sacrifice,
An humble and a contrite heart.
Lord God of Hosts, be with us yet,
Lest we forget—lest we forget!
  Recessional, in *The Times* 17 July 1897

4 Far-called our navies melt away—
On dune and headland sinks the fire—
Lo, all our pomp of yesterday
Is one with Nineveh, and Tyre!
  Recessional, in *The Times* 17 July 1897

5 If, drunk with sight of power, we loose
Wild tongues that have not Thee in
  awe—
Such boasting as the Gentiles use,
Or lesser breeds without the Law.
  Recessional, in *Times* 17 July 1897

6 They shut the road through the woods
Seventy years ago.
Weather and rain have undone it again,
And now you would never know
There was once a road through the
  woods.
  Rewards and Fairies (1910) 'Way through
  the Woods'

7 If you can keep your head when all
  about you
Are losing theirs and blaming it on you;
If you can trust yourself when all men
  doubt you,

But make allowance for their doubting
  too;
If you can wait and not be tired by
  waiting,
Or being lied about, don't deal in lies,
Or being hated, don't give way to
  hating,
And yet don't look too good, nor talk
  too wise;
If you can dream—and not make
  dreams your master;
If you can think—and not make
  thoughts your aim,
If you can meet with Triumph and
  Disaster
And treat those two imposters just the
  same . . .
  Rewards and Fairies (1910) 'If—'

8 If you can make one heap of all your
  winnings
And risk it on one turn of
  pitch-and-toss,
And lose, and start again at your
  beginnings
And never breathe a word about your
  loss . . .
  Rewards and Fairies (1910) 'If—'

9 If you can talk with crowds and keep
  your virtue,
Or walk with Kings—nor lose the
  common touch,
If neither foes nor loving friends can
  hurt you,
If all men count with you, but none too
  much;
If you can fill the unforgiving minute
With sixty seconds' worth of distance
  run,
Yours is the Earth and everything that's
  in it,
And—which is more—you'll be a Man,
  my son!
  Rewards and Fairies (1910) 'If—'

10 One man in a thousand, Solomon says,
Will stick more close than a brother.
  Rewards and Fairies (1910) 'The Thousandth
  Man'

11 The female of the species is more deadly
  than the male.
  Rudyard Kipling's Verse (1919) 'The Female
  of the Species'

12 As it will be in the future, it was at the
  birth of Man—

There are only four things certain since
Social Progress began:—
That the Dog returns to his Vomit and
the Sow returns to her Mire,
And the burnt Fool's bandaged finger
goes wabbling back to the Fire.
Rudyard Kipling's Verse (1927) 'The Gods of
the Copybook Headings'

1 England's on the anvil—hear the
hammers ring—
Clanging from the Severn to the Tyne!
Never was a blacksmith like our Norman
King—
England's being hammered, hammered,
hammered into line!
Rudyard Kipling's Verse (1927) 'The Anvil'

2 Now this is the Law of the Jungle—as
old and as true as the sky;
And the Wolf that shall keep it may
prosper, but the Wolf that shall break
it must die.
Second Jungle Book (1895) 'The Law of the
Jungle'

3 Keep ye the law—be swift in all
obedience—
Clear the land of evil, drive the road and
bridge the ford.
Make ye sure to each his own
That he reap where he hath sown;
By the peace among our peoples let men
know we serve the Lord!
The Seven Seas (1896) 'A Song of the
English'

4 We have fed our sea for a thousand
years
And she calls us, still unfed,
Though there's never a wave of all her
waves
But marks our English dead:
We have strawed our best to the weed's
unrest
To the shark and sheering gull.
If blood be the price of admiralty,
Lord God, we ha' paid in full!
The Seven Seas (1896) 'The Song of the
Dead'

5 And Ye take mine honour from me if Ye
take away the sea!
The Seven Seas (1896) 'Last Chantey'

6 The Liner she's a lady, an' she never
looks nor 'eeds—
The Man-o'-War's 'er 'usband, 'an 'e
gives 'er all she needs;

But, oh, the little cargo boats that sail
the wet seas roun',
They're just the same as you 'an me
a-plyin' up and down!
The Seven Seas (1896) 'The Liner She's
a Lady'

7 When 'Omer smote 'is bloomin' lyre,
He'd 'eard men sing by land an' sea;
An' what he thought 'e might require,
'E went an' took—the same as me!
The Seven Seas (1896) p. 162

8 I've taken my fun where I've found it,
An' now I must pay for my fun,
For the more you 'ave known o' the
others
The less will you settle to one;
An' the end of it's sittin' and thinkin',
An' dreamin' Hell-fires to see;
So be warned by my lot (which I know
you will not),
An' learn about women from me!
The Seven Seas (1896) 'The Ladies'

9 An' I learned about women from 'er!
The Seven Seas (1896) 'The Ladies'

10 When you get to a man in the case,
They're like as a row of pins—
For the Colonel's Lady an' Judy O'Grady
Are sisters under their skins!
The Seven Seas (1896) 'The Ladies'

11 The 'eathen in 'is blindness bows down
to wood an' stone;
'E don't obey no orders unless they is 'is
own;
'E keeps 'is side-arms awful: 'e leaves
'em all about,
An' then comes up the Regiment an'
pokes the 'eathen out.
The Seven Seas (1896) 'The 'Eathen'

12 The 'eathen in 'is blindness must end
where 'e began.
But the backbone of the Army is the
non-commissioned man!
The Seven Seas (1896) 'The 'Eathen'

13 And only the Master shall praise us, and
only the Master shall blame;
And no one shall work for money, and
no one shall work for fame,
But each for the joy of the working, and
each, in his separate star,
Shall draw the Thing as he sees It for
the God of Things as They are!
The Seven Seas (1896) 'When Earth's Last
Picture is Painted'

1 Words are, of course, the most powerful
drug used by mankind.
  Speech, 14 Feb. 1923, in *A Book of Words*
  (1928), p. 223

2 Mr Raymond Martin, beyond question,
was born in a gutter, and bred in
a Board-School, where they played
marbles. He was further (I give the
barest handful from great store)
a Flopshus Cad, an Outrageous Stinker,
a Jelly-bellied Flag-flapper (this was
Stalky's contribution), and several other
things which it is not seemly to put
down.
  Stalky & Co. (1899) p. 214

3 Being kissed by a man who didn't wax
his moustache was—like eating an egg
without salt.
  The Story of the Gadsbys (1889) 'Poor Dear
  Mamma'

4 Down to Gehenna or up to the Throne,
He travels the fastest who travels alone.
  The Story of the Gadsbys (1890) 'L'Envoi'

5 'Tisn't beauty, so to speak, nor good talk
necessarily. It's just It. Some women'll
stay in a man's memory if they once
walked down a street.
  Traffics and Discoveries (1904) 'Mrs Bathurst'

6 It's north you may run to the
    rime-ringed sun,
Or south to the blind Horn's hate;
Or east all the way into Mississippi Bay,
Or west to the Golden Gate.
  Twenty Poems (1918) 'The Long Trail'

7 A fool there was and he made his prayer
    (Even as you and I!)
To a rag and a bone and a hank of hair
(We called her the woman who did not
    care)
But the fool he called her his lady fair—
    (Even as you and I!)
  The Vampire (1897) p. 1

8 Take up the White Man's burden—
Send forth the best ye breed—
Go, bind your sons to exile
To serve your captives' need;
To wait, in heavy harness,
On fluttered folk and wild—
Your new-caught, sullen peoples,
Half devil and half child.
  The White Man's Burden (1899)

9 By all ye will or whisper,
By all ye leave or do,

The silent sullen peoples
Shall weigh your God and you.
  The White Man's Burden (1899)

10 If any question why we died,
Tell them, because our fathers lied.
  The Years Between (1919) 'Common Form'

Henry Kissinger 1923–

11 'We are the President's men,' he
[Kissinger] would exclaim, 'and we must
behave accordingly.'
  M. and B. Kalb *Kissinger* (1974) ch. 7

12 There cannot be a crisis next week. My
schedule is already full.
  In *New York Times Magazine* 1 June 1969,
  p. 11

13 Power, he [Kissinger] has observed, 'is
the great aphrodisiac.'
  New York Times 19 Jan. 1971, p. 12

Fred Kitchen 1872–1950

14 Meredith, we're in!
  Catch-phrase originating in *The Bailiff* (1907
  stage sketch) —see J. P. Gallagher *Fred
  Karno* (1971) ch. 9, p. 90

Lord Kitchener 1850–1916

15 You are ordered abroad as a soldier of
the King to help our French comrades
against the invasion of a common
enemy. You have to perform a task
which will need your courage, your
energy, your patience. Remember that
the honour of the British Army depends
on your individual conduct. It will be
your duty not only to set an example of
discipline and perfect steadiness under
fire, but also to maintain the most
friendly relations with those whom you
are helping in this struggle. The
operations in which you are engaged
will, for the most part, take place in
a friendly country, and you can do your
own country no better service than in
showing yourself in France and Belgium
in the true character of a British soldier.
  Be invariably courteous, considerate,
and kind. Never do anything likely to
injure or destroy property, and always
look upon looting as a disgraceful act.
You are sure to meet with a welcome
and to be trusted; your conduct must
justify that welcome and that trust.

Your duty cannot be done unless your health is sound. So keep constantly on your guard against any excesses. In this new experience you may find temptations both in wine and women. You must entirely resist both temptations, and, while treating all women with perfect courtesy, you should avoid any intimacy. Do your duty bravely. Fear God. Honour the King.

Message to soldiers of the British Expeditionary Force (1914), in *The Times* 19 Aug. 1914

Paul Klee 1879–1940

1 *Eine aktive Linie, die sich frei ergeht, ein Spaziergang um seiner selbst willen, ohne Ziel. Das agens ist ein Punkt, der sich verschiebt.*

An active line on a walk, moving freely without a goal. A walk for walk's sake. The agent is a point that shifts position.
Pädagogisches Skizzenbuch (Pedagogical Sketchbook, 1925) p. 6

2 *Kunst gibt nicht das Sichtbare wieder, sondern macht sichtbar.*

Art does not reproduce the visible; rather, it makes visible.
Schöpferische Konfession (Creative Credo, 1920) in *Im Zwischenreich* (1957) (Inward Vision, 1958) p. 5

Charles Knight and *Kenneth Lyle*

3 Here we are! here we are!! here we are again!!!
There's Pat and Mac and Tommy and Jack
and Joe.
When there's trouble brewing,
When there's something doing,
Are we downhearted?
No! Let 'em all come!
Here we are! Here we are again!! (1914 song)

Frederick Knott 1916–

4 Dial 'M' for murder.
Title of play (1952)

Monsignor Ronald Knox 1888–1957

5 There once was a man who said, 'God

Must think it exceedingly odd
If he finds that this tree
Continues to be
When there's no one about in the Quad.'
In Langford Reed *Complete Limerick Book* (1924) p. 44
(This reply was written by an unknown author:
Dear Sir,
Your astonishment's odd:
I am always about in the Quad.
And that's why the tree
Will continue to be,
Since observed by
Yours faithfully,
God.)

6 The tumult and the shouting dies,
The captains and the kings depart,
And we are left with large supplies
Of cold blancmange and rhubarb tart.
[sic] L. E. Eyres (ed.) *In Three Tongues* (1959) p. 130 'After the Party'—a parody of Kipling 126:9

7 It is stupid of modern civilization to have given up believing in the devil, when he is the only explanation of it.
Let Dons Delight (1939) ch. 8

Arthur Koestler 1905–1983

8 The most persistent sound which reverberates through man's history is the beating of war drums.
Janus (1978) prologue

9 Man can leave the earth and land on the moon, but cannot cross from East to West Berlin. Prometheus reaches for the stars with an insane grin on his face and a totem-symbol in his hand.
Janus (1978) prologue

Jiddu Krishnamurti d. 1986

10 I maintain that Truth is a pathless land, and you cannot approach it by any path whatsoever, by any religion, by any sect.
Speech in Holland, 3 Aug. 1929, in Lilly Heber *Krishnamurti* (1931) ch. 2

Kris Kristofferson 1936– and *Fred Foster*

11 Freedom's just another word for nothin' left to lose,
Nothin' ain't worth nothin', but it's free.
Me and Bobby McGee (1969 song)

Joseph Wood Krutch 1893–1970

1 The most serious charge which can be brought against New England is not Puritanism but February.
Twelve Seasons (1949) 'February'

2 Cats seem to go on the principle that it never does any harm to ask for what you want.
Twelve Seasons (1949) 'February'

Stanley Kubrick 1928–

3 The great nations have always acted like gangsters, and the small nations like prostitutes.
In Guardian 5 June 1963

Satish Kumar 1937–

4 Lead me from death to life, from falsehood to truth.
Lead me from despair to hope, from fear to trust.
Lead me from hate to love, from war to peace.
Let peace fill our heart, our world, our universe.
Prayer for Peace (1981; adapted from the Upanishads)

Henry Labouchere 1831–1912

5 Mr Labouchere's jest about Mr Gladstone laying upon Providence the responsibility of always placing the ace of trumps up his sleeve was a good one. In one of his private letters I find the quip worded a little more pungently. 'Who cannot refrain,' he says, referring to the then Prime Minister, 'from perpetually bringing an ace down his sleeve, even when he has only to play fair to win the trick.'
A. L. Thorold Life of Henry Labouchere (1913) ch. 15. Cf. Earl Curzon's Modern Parliamentary Eloquence (1913) p. 25 'I recall a phrase of that incorrigible cynic Labouchere, alluding to Mr Gladstone's frequent appeals to a higher power, that he did not object to the old man always having a card up his sleeve, but he did object to his insinuating that the Almighty had placed it there.'

Fiorello La Guardia 1882–1947

6 When I make a mistake, it's a beaut!
In William Manners Patience and Fortitude (1976) p. 219 (on the appointment of Herbert O'Brien as a judge in 1936)

R. D. Laing 1927–1989

7 Schizophrenia cannot be understood without understanding despair.
The Divided Self (1960) ch. 2

8 Few books today are forgivable.
Politics of Experience (1967) introduction

9 We are effectively destroying ourselves by violence masquerading as love.
Politics of Experience (1967) ch. 3

10 The brotherhood of man is evoked by particular men according to their circumstances. But it seldom extends to all men. In the name of our freedom and our brotherhood we are prepared to blow up the other half of mankind and to be blown up in turn.
Politics of Experience (1967) ch. 4

11 The experience and behaviour that gets labelled schizophrenic is a special strategy that a person invents in order to live in an unlivable situation.
Politics of Experience (1967) ch. 5

12 Madness need not be all breakdown. It may also be break-through. It is potential liberation and renewal as well as enslavement and existential death.
Politics of Experience (1967) ch. 6

Arthur J. Lamb 1870–1928

13 She's a bird in a gilded cage.
Title of song (1900; music by Harry von Tilzer)

Constant Lambert 1905–1951

14 To put it vulgarly, the whole trouble with a folk song is that once you have played it through there is nothing much you can do except play it over again and play it rather louder.
Music Ho! (1934) ch. 3

15 The average English critic is a don manqué, hopelessly parochial when not exaggeratedly teutonophile, over whose desk must surely hang the motto

(presumably in Gothic lettering) 'Above all no enthusiasm'.

Opera Dec. 1950

Giuseppe di Lampedusa 1896–1957

1 *Se vogliamo che tutto rimanga come è, bisogna che tutto cambi.*

If we want things to stay as they are, things will have to change.

Il Gattopardo (The Leopard, 1957) p. 33

Sir Osbert Lancaster 1908–1986

2 Today, when the passer-by is a little unnerved at being suddenly confronted with a hundred and fifty accurate reproductions of Anne Hathaway's cottage, each complete with central heating and garage, he should pause to reflect on the extraordinary fact that all over the country the latest and most scientific methods of mass-production are being utilized to turn out a stream of old oak beams, leaded window-panes and small discs of bottle-glass, all structural devices which our ancestors lost no time in abandoning as soon as an increase in wealth and knowledge enabled them to do so.

Pillar to Post (1938) 'Stockbroker's Tudor'

Bert Lance 1931–

3 Bert Lance believes he can save Uncle Sam billions if he can get the government to adopt a single motto: 'If it ain't broke, don't fix it.' He explains: 'That's the trouble with government: Fixing things that aren't broken and not fixing things that are broken.'

Nation's Business 27 May 1977, p.27

Andrew Lang 1844–1912

4 St Andrews by the Northern sea, A haunted town it is to me!

Ballades and Verses Vain (1884) p. 79

5 They hear like ocean on a western beach The surge and thunder of the Odyssey.

Poetical Works (1923) vol. 2, 'The Odyssey'

6 If the wild bowler thinks he bowls, Or if the batsman thinks he's bowled, They know not, poor misguided souls, They too shall perish unconsoled. I am the batsman and the bat, I am the bowler and the ball,

The umpire, the pavilion cat, The roller, pitch, and stumps, and all.

Poetical Works (1923) vol. 2, 'Brahma' (a parody of Emerson—see Oxford Dictionary of Quotations (1979) 206:17)

Julia Lang 1921–

7 Are you sitting comfortably? Then we'll begin.

Introduction to stories on Listen with Mother, BBC Radio programme, 1950–1982 (sometimes 'Then I'll begin')

Suzanne K. Langer 1895–1985

8 Art is the objectification of feeling, and the subjectification of nature.

Mind (1967) vol. 1, pt. 2, ch. 4

Ring Lardner 1885–1933

9 Are you lost daddy I arsked tenderly. Shut up he explained.

The Young Immigrunts (1920) ch. 10

Philip Larkin 1922–1985

10 Rather than words comes the thought of high windows: The sun-comprehending glass, And beyond it, the deep blue air, that shows Nothing, and is nowhere, and is endless.

High Windows (1974) 'High Windows'

11 Perhaps being old is having lighted rooms Inside your head, and people in them, acting. People you know, yet can't quite name.

High Windows (1974) 'The Old Fools'

12 Next year we are to bring the soldiers home For lack of money, and it is all right. Places they guarded, or kept orderly, Must guard themselves, and keep themselves orderly.

High Windows (1974) 'Homage to a Government'

13 Next year we shall be living in a country That brought its soldiers home for lack of money. The statues will be standing in the same Tree-muffled squares, and look nearly the same. Our children will not know it's a different country.

All we can hope to leave them now is
  money.
  High Windows (1974) 'Homage to
  a Government'

1 They fuck you up, your mum and dad.
  They may not mean to, but they do.
  They fill you with the faults they had
  And add some extra, just for you.
  High Windows (1974) 'This Be The Verse'

2 Man hands on misery to man.
  It deepens like a coastal shelf.
  Get out as early as you can,
  And don't have any kids yourself.
  High Windows (1974) 'This Be The Verse'

3 Sexual intercourse began
  In nineteen sixty-three
  (Which was rather late for me)—
  Between the end of the *Chatterley* ban
  And the Beatles' first LP.
  High Windows (1974) 'Annus Mirabilis'

4 Hatless, I take off
  My cycle-clips in awkward reverence.
  The Less Deceived (1955) 'Church Going'

5 A serious house on serious earth it is,
  In whose blent air all our compulsions
  meet,
  Are recognised, and robed as destinies.
  The Less Deceived (1955) 'Church Going'

6 Why should I let the toad *work*
  Squat on my life?
  Can't I use my wit as a pitchfork
  And drive the brute off?

  Six days of the week it soils
  With its sickening poison—
  Just for paying a few bills!
  That's out of proportion.
  The Less Deceived (1955) 'Toads'

7 Nothing, like something, happens
  anywhere.
  The Less Deceived (1955) 'I Remember,
  I Remember'

8 Far too many [of the books entered for
  the 1977 Booker Prize] relied on the
  classic formula of a beginning, a muddle,
  and an end.
  New Fiction no. 15, Jan. 1978

9 Deprivation is for me what daffodils were
  for Wordsworth.
  Reply to question 'Do you think people go
  around feeling they haven't got out of life
  what life has to offer?'–*Required Writing*
  (1983) p. 47

10 Give me your arm, old toad;
   Help me down Cemetery Road.
   The Whitsun Weddings (1964) 'Toads
   Revisited'

11 I thought of London spread out in the
   sun,
   Its postal districts packed like squares of
   wheat.
   The Whitsun Weddings (1964) 'The Whitsun
   Weddings'

12 What are days for?
   Days are where we live.
   They come, they wake us
   Time and time over.
   They are to be happy in:
   Where can we live but days?
   The Whitsun Weddings (1964) 'Days'

13 Never such innocence,
   Never before or since,
   As changed itself to past
   Without a word—the men
   Leaving the gardens tidy,
   The thousands of marriages
   Lasting a little while longer:
   Never such innocence again.
   The Whitsun Weddings (1964) 'MCMXIV'

14 Don't read too much now: the dude
   Who lets the girl down before
   The hero arrives, the chap
   Who's yellow and keeps the store,
   Seem far too familiar. Get stewed:
   Books are a load of crap.
   The Whitsun Weddings (1964) 'Study of
   Reading Habits'

15 Life is first boredom, then fear.
   Whether or not we use it, it goes,
   And leaves what something hidden from
   us chose,
   And age, and then the only end of age.
   The Whitsun Weddings (1964) 'Dockery &
   Son'

16 Time has transfigured them into
   Untruth. The stone fidelity
   They hardly meant has come to be
   Their final blazon, and to prove
   Our almost-instinct almost true:
   What will survive of us is love.
   The Whitsun Weddings (1964) 'An Arundel
   Tomb'

Sir Harry Lauder 1870–1950

17 Keep right on to the end of the road,
   Keep right on to the end.

Tho' the way be long, let your heart be
strong,
Keep right on round the bend.
Tho' you're tired and weary,
Still journey on
Till you come to your happy abode,
Where all you love you've been
dreaming of
Will be there at the end of the road.
The End of the Road (1924 song)

1 I love a lassie, a bonnie, bonnie lassie,
She's as pure as the lily in the dell.
She's as sweet as the heather, the
bonnie bloomin' heather—
Mary, ma Scotch Bluebell.
I Love a Lassie (1905 song)

2 It's nice to get up in the mornin' (but
it's nicer to lie in bed).
Title of song (1913)

3 Roamin' in the gloamin',
On the bonnie banks o' Clyde.
Roamin' in the gloamin'
Wae my lassie by my side.
Roamin' in the Gloamin' (1911 song)

Stan Laurel (*Arthur Stanley Jefferson*) 1890–1965

4 Well, here's another nice mess you've
gotten me into.
Another Fine Mess (1930 film; words spoken
by Oliver Hardy in many Laurel and Hardy
films: often 'another fine mess')

5 Why don't you do something to *help*
me?
Drivers' Licence Sketch (1947), in J. McCabe
Comedy World of Stan Laurel (1974) p. 107
(words spoken by Oliver Hardy)

James Laver 1899–1975

The same costume will be
Indecent ... 10 years before its time
Shameless ... 5 years before its time
Outré ... 1 year before its time
(daring)
Smart
Dowdy ... 1 year after its time
Hideous ... 10 years after its time
Ridiculous ... 20 years after its time
Amusing ... 30 years after its time
Quaint ... 50 years after its time
Charming ... 70 years after its time
Romantic ... 100 years after its time
Beautiful ... 150 years after its time
Taste and Fashion (1937) ch. 18

Andrew Bonar Law 1858–1923

See BONAR LAW

D. H. Lawrence 1885–1930

7 Is it the secret of the long-nosed
Etruscans?
The long-nosed, sensitive-footed,
subtly-smiling Etruscans
Who made so little noise outside the
cypress groves?
Birds, Beasts and Flowers (1923) 'Cypresses'

8 Men! The only animal in the world to
fear!
Birds, Beasts and Flowers (1923) 'Mountain
Lion'

9 A snake came to my water-trough
On a hot, hot day, and I in pyjamas for
the heat,
To drink there.
Birds, Beasts and Flowers (1923) 'Snake'

10 And I thought of the albatross,
And I wished he would come back, my
snake.
For he seemed to me again like a king,
Like a king in exile, uncrowned in the
underworld,
Now due to be crowned again.
And so, I missed my chance with one of
the lords
Of life.
And I have something to expiate:
A pettiness.
Birds, Beasts and Flowers (1923) 'Snake'

11 Curse the blasted, jelly-boned swines,
the slimy, the belly-wriggling
invertebrates, the miserable sodding
rotters, the flaming sods, the snivelling,
dribbling, dithering, palsied, pulse-less
lot that make up England today. They've
got white of egg in their veins, and their
spunk is that watery it's a marvel they
can breed. They *can* nothing but

frog-spawn—the gibberers! God, how
I hate them!

> Letter to Edward Garnett, 3 July 1912, in
> *Collected Letters* (1962) vol. 1, p. 134

1 I like to write when I feel spiteful; it's
like having a good sneeze.

> Letter to Lady Cynthia Asquith, ?25 Nov.
> 1913, in *Collected Letters* (1962) vol. 1,
> p. 246

2 The dead don't die. They look on and
help.

> Letter to J. Middleton Murry, 2 Feb. 1923,
> in *Collected Letters* (1962) vol. 2, p. 736

3 The autumn always gets me badly, as it
breaks into colours. I want to go south,
where there is no autumn, where the
cold doesn't crouch over one like
a snow-leopard waiting to pounce. The
heart of the North is dead, and the
fingers of cold are corpse fingers.

> Letter to J. Middleton Murry, 3 Oct. 1924, in
> *Collected Letters* (1962) vol. 2, p. 812

4 I'd like to write an essay on [Arnold]
Bennett—sort of pig in clover.

> Letter to Aldous Huxley, 27 Mar. 1928, in
> *Collected Letters* (1962) vol. 2, p. 1048

5 My God, what a clumsy *olla putrida*
James Joyce is! Nothing but old fags and
cabbage-stumps of quotations from the
Bible and the rest, stewed in the juice of
deliberate, journalistic dirty-mindedness.

> Letter to Aldous and Maria Huxley, 15 Aug.
> 1928, in *Collected Letters* (1962) vol. 2,
> p. 1074

6 To the Puritan all things are impure, as
somebody says.

> *Etruscan Places* (1932) 'Cerveteri'

7 Ours is essentially a tragic age, so we
refuse to take it tragically.

> *Lady Chatterley's Lover* (1928) ch. 1

8 Some things can't be ravished. You
can't ravish a tin of sardines.

> *Lady Chatterley's Lover* (1928) ch. 8

9 John Thomas says good-night to Lady
Jane, a little droopingly, but with
a hopeful heart.

> *Lady Chatterley's Lover* (1928) ch. 19

10 Now it is autumn and the falling fruit
And the long journey towards
oblivion . . .
Have you built your ship of death, O
have you?

O build your ship of death, for you will
need it.

> *Last Poems* (1932) 'Ship of Death'

11 Along the avenue of cypresses
All in their scarlet cloaks, and surplices
Of linen go the chanting choristers,
The priests in gold and black, the
villagers.

> *Look! We Have Come Through!* (1917)
> 'Giorno dei Morti'

12 Not I, not I, but the wind that blows
through me!
A fine wind is blowing the new direction
of Time.

> *Look! We Have Come Through!* (1917) 'Song
> of a Man who has Come Through'

13 So now it is vain for the singer to burst
into clamour
With the great black piano
appassionato. The glamour
Of childish days is upon me, my
manhood is cast
Down in the flood of remembrance,
I weep like a child for the past.

> *New Poems* (1918) 'Piano'

14 Don't be sucked in by the su-superior,
don't swallow the culture bait,
don't drink, don't drink and get beerier
and beerier,
do learn to discriminate.

> *Pansies* (1929) 'Don'ts'

15 How beastly the bourgeois is
Especially the male of the species.

> *Pansies* (1929) 'How Beastly the Bourgeois
> Is'

16 I never saw a wild thing
Sorry for itself.

> *Pansies* (1929) 'Self-Pity'

17 For while we have sex in the mind, we
truly have none in the body.

> *Pansies* (1929) 'Leave Sex Alone'

18 When I read Shakespeare I am struck
with wonder
That such trivial people should muse
and thunder
In such lovely language.

> *Pansies* (1929) 'When I Read Shakespeare'

19 Pornography is the attempt to insult sex,
to do dirt on it.

> *Phoenix* (1936) 'Pornography and
> Obscenity' ch. 3

1 The very first copy of The White Peacock that was ever sent out, I put into my mother's hands when she was dying. She looked at the outside, and then at the title-page, and then at me, with darkening eyes. And though she loved me so much, I think she doubted whether it could be much of a book, since no one more important than I had written it. Somewhere, in the helpless privacies of her being, she had wistful respect for me. But for me in the face of the world, not much. This David would never get a stone across at Goliath. And why try? Let Goliath alone! Anyway, she was beyond reading my first immortal work. It was put aside, and I never wanted to see it again. She never saw it again.

   After the funeral, my father struggled through half a page, and it might as well have been Hottentot.

   'And what dun they gi'e thee for that, lad?'

   'Fifty pounds, father.'

   'Fifty pounds!' He was dumbfounded, and looked at me with shrewd eyes, as if I were a swindler. 'Fifty pounds! An' tha's niver done a day's hard work in thy life.'

   Phoenix (1936) p. 232

2 Never trust the artist. Trust the tale. The proper function of a critic is to save the tale from the artist who created it.
   Studies in Classic American Literature (1923) ch. 1

3 'Be a good animal, true to your instincts,' was his motto.
   White Peacock (1911) pt. 2, ch. 2

4 Don't you find it a beautiful clean thought, a world empty of people, just uninterrupted grass, and a hare sitting up?
   Women in Love (1920) ch. 11

T. E. Lawrence 1888–1935

5 Many men would take the death-sentence without a whimper to escape the life-sentence which fate carries in her other hand.
   The Mint (1955) pt. 1, ch. 4

6 The seven pillars of wisdom.
   Title of book (1926). Cf. *Oxford Dictionary of Quotations* (1979) 53:27

7 I loved you, so I drew these tides of men into my hands and wrote my will across the sky in stars
   To earn you Freedom, the seven pillared worthy house, that your eyes might be shining for me
      When we came.
   The Seven Pillars of Wisdom (1926) dedication 'to S.A.'

Sir Edmund Leach 1910–

8 Far from being the basis of the good society, the family, with its narrow privacy and tawdry secrets, is the source of all our discontents.
   BBC Reith Lectures, 1967, in *Listener* 30 Nov. 1967

Stephen Leacock 1869–1944

9 The parent who could see his boy as he really is, would shake his head and say: 'Willie, is no good; I'll sell him.'
   Essays and Literary Studies (1916) 'Lot of a Schoolmaster'

10 Advertising may be described as the science of arresting human intelligence long enough to get money from it.
   Garden of Folly (1924) 'The Perfect Salesman'

11 I am what is called a *professor emeritus*—from the Latin *e*, 'out', and *meritus*, 'so he ought to be'.
   Here are my Lectures (1938) ch. 14

12 There are no handles to a horse, but the 1910 model has a string to each side of its face for turning its head when there is anything you want it to see.
   Literary Lapses (1910) 'Reflections on Riding'

13 I detest life-insurance agents; they always argue that I shall some day die, which is not so.
   Literary Lapses (1910) 'Insurance up to Date'

14 Get your room full of good air, then shut up the windows and keep it. It will keep for years. Anyway, don't keep using your lungs all the time. Let them rest.
   Literary Lapses (1910) 'How to Live to be 200'

15 A sportsman is a man who, every now and then, simply has to get out and kill

something. Not that he's cruel. He
wouldn't hurt a fly. It's not big enough.
My Remarkable Uncle (1942) p. 73

1 Lord Ronald said nothing; he flung
himself from the room, flung himself
upon his horse and rode madly off in all
directions.
Nonsense Novels (1911) 'Gertrude the
Governess'

2 A decision of the courts decided that the
game of golf may be played on Sunday,
not being a game within the view of the
law, but being a form of moral effort.
Over the Footlights (1923) 'Why I Refuse to
Play Golf'

3 The general idea, of course, in any
first-class laundry, is to see that no shirt
or collar ever comes back twice.
Winnowed Wisdom (1926) ch. 6

Timothy Leary 1920–

4 If you take the game of life seriously, if
you take your nervous system seriously,
if you take your sense organs seriously,
if you take the energy process seriously,
you must turn on, tune in and drop out.
Lecture, June 1966, in *Politics of Ecstasy*
(1968) ch. 21

F. R. Leavis 1895–1978

5 It is well to start by distinguishing the
few really great—the major novelists
who count in the same way as the
major poets, in the sense that they not
only change the possibilities of the art
for practitioners and readers, but that
they are significant in terms of the
human awareness they promote;
awareness of the possibilities of life.
The Great Tradition (1948) ch. 1

6 The Sitwells belong to the history of
publicity rather than of poetry.
New Bearings in English Poetry (1932) ch. 2

Fran Lebowitz

7 All God's children are not beautiful.
Most of God's children are, in fact,
barely presentable.
Metropolitan Life (1978) p. 6

8 There is no such thing as inner peace.
There is only nervousness or death. Any
attempt to prove otherwise constitutes
unacceptable behaviour.
Metropolitan Life (1978) p. 6

9 Life is something to do when you can't
get to sleep.
Metropolitan Life (1978) p. 101

10 Food is an important part of a balanced
diet.
Metropolitan Life (1978) p. 110

11 Being a woman is of special interest only
to aspiring male transsexuals. To actual
women, it is merely a good excuse not to
play football.
Metropolitan Life (1978) p. 144

Stanislaw Lec 1909–1966

12 Is it progress if a cannibal uses knife and
fork?
Myśli Nieuczesane (Unkempt Thoughts,
1962) p. 78

John le Carré (David John Moore Cornwell) 1931–

13 The spy who came in from the cold.
Title of novel (1963)

Le Corbusier (Charles Édouard Jeanneret) 1887–1965

14 *Une maison est une machine-à-habiter.*

A house is a machine for living in.
Vers une architecture (Towards an
Architecture, 1923) p. ix

Harper Lee 1926–

15 Shoot all the bluejays you want, if you
can hit 'em, but remember it's a sin to
kill a mockingbird.
To Kill a Mockingbird (1960) ch. 10

Laurie Lee 1914–

16 I was set down from the carrier's cart at
the age of three; and there with a sense
of bewilderment and terror my life in the
village began.
Cider with Rosie (1959) p. 9

17 Such a morning it is when love
leans through geranium windows
and calls with a cockerel's tongue.

When red-haired girls scamper like roses
over the rain-green grass,
and the sun drips honey.
Sun is my Monument (1947) 'Day of these
Days'

Ernest Lehman

1 Somebody up there likes me.
Title of film (1956)

2 Sweet smell of success.
Title of book and film (1957)

Tom Lehrer 1928–

3 Life is like a sewer. What you get out of it depends on what you put into it.
Preamble to song 'We Will All Go Together When We Go', in *An Evening Wasted with Tom Lehrer* (1953 record album)

4 Plagiarize! Let no one else's work evade your eyes,
Remember why the good Lord made your eyes,
So don't shade your eyes but plagiarize, plagiarize, plagiarize!
Lobachevski (1953 song)

5 And we will all go together when we go—
Every Hottentot and every Eskimo.
We Will All Go Together When We Go (1953 song)

Jerry Leiber 1933–
and Mike Stoller 1933–

6 You ain't nothin' but a hound dog,
Cryin' all the time.
Hound Dog (1956 song)

Fred W. Leigh d. 1924

7 There was I, waiting at the church,
Waiting at the church, waiting at the church,
When I found he'd left me in the lurch,
Lor, how it did upset me!
All at once he sent me round a note,
Here's the very note,
This is what he wrote—
'Can't get away to marry you today,
My wife won't let me!'
Waiting at the Church (My Wife Won't Let Me) (1906 song; music by Henry E. Pether)

Fred W. Leigh d. 1924, Charles Collins, and Lily Morris

8 Why am I always the bridesmaid,
Never the blushing bride?
Why Am I Always the Bridesmaid? (1917 song)

Fred W. Leigh d. 1924 and George Arthurs

9 A little of what you fancy does you good.
Title of song (1915)

Curtis E. LeMay 1906–1990

10 My solution to the problem would be to tell them [the North Vietnamese] frankly that they've got to draw in their horns and stop their aggression, or we're going to bomb them back into the Stone Age.
Mission with LeMay (1965) p. 565

Lenin (Vladimir Ilich Ulyanov) 1870–1924

11 We must now set about building a proletarian socialist state in Russia.
Speech in Petrograd, 7 Nov. 1917, in *Collected Works* (1964) vol. 26, p. 240

12 Коммунизм—это есть Советская власть плюс электрификация всей страны.

Communism is Soviet power plus the electrification of the whole country.
Report to 8th Congress, 1920, in *Collected Works* (ed. 5) vol. 42, p. 30

13 He [George Bernard Shaw] is a good man fallen among Fabians.
In Arthur Ransome *Six Weeks in Russia in 1919* (1919) 'Notes of Conversations with Lenin'

14 It is true that liberty is precious—so precious that it must be rationed.
In Sidney and Beatrice Webb *Soviet Communism* (1936) p. 1036

15 Нет. Демократия *не* тождественна с подчинением меньшинства большинству. Демократия есть признающее подчинение меньшинства большинству *государство*, т.е. организация для систематического *насилия* одного класса над другим, одной части населения над другою.

No, Democracy is *not* identical with majority rule. Democracy is a *State* which recognizes the subjection of the minority to the majority, that is, an organization for the systematic use of *force* by one class against the other, by

one part of the population against another.
State and Revolution (1919) ch. 4

1 Пока есть государство, нет свободы. Когда будет свобода не будет государства.

While the State exists, there can be no freedom. When there is freedom there will be no State.
State and Revolution (1919) ch. 5

John Lennon 1940–1980

2 Imagine there's no heaven,
It's easy if you try,
No hell below us,
Above us only sky,
Imagine all the people
Living for today.
Imagine (1971 song)

3 Will the people in the cheaper seats clap your hands? All the rest of you, if you'll just rattle your jewellery.
At Royal Variety Performance, 4 Nov. 1963, in R. Colman *John Winston Lennon* (1984) pt. 1, ch. 11

4 Christianity will go. It will vanish and shrink. I needn't argue about that; I'm right and I will be proved right. We're [the Beatles are] more popular than Jesus now; I don't know which will go first—rock 'n' roll or Christianity.
Interview with Maureen Cleave in *Evening Standard* 4 Mar. 1966. Cf. Zelda Fitzgerald

John Lennon 1940–1980 and Paul McCartney 1942–

5 All you need is love.
Title of song (1967)

6 Back in the USSR.
Title of song (1968)

7 For I don't care too much for money,
For money can't buy me love.
Can't Buy Me Love (1964 song)

8 I heard the news today, oh boy.
Four thousand holes in Blackburn Lancashire.
And though the holes were rather small,
They had to count them all.
Now they know how many holes it takes to fill the Albert Hall.
I'd love to turn you on.
A Day in the Life (1967 song)

9 Give peace a chance.
Title of song (1969)

10 It's been a hard day's night,
And I've been working like a dog.
A Hard Day's Night (1964 song)

11 Magical mystery tour.
Title of song and TV film (1967)

12 She loves you, yeh, yeh, yeh,
And with a love like that, you know you should be glad.
She Loves You (1963 song)

13 Strawberry fields forever.
Title of song (1967)

14 She's got a ticket to ride, but she don't care.
Ticket to Ride (1965 song)

15 Will you still need me, will you still feed me,
When I'm sixty four?
When I'm Sixty Four (1967 song)

16 Oh I get by with a little help from my friends.
With a Little Help From My Friends (1967 song)

17 We all live in a yellow submarine,
yellow submarine, yellow submarine.
Yellow Submarine (1966 song)

18 Yesterday, all my troubles seemed so far away,
Now it looks as though they're here to stay.
Oh I believe in yesterday.
Yesterday (1965 song)

Dan Leno (George Galvin) 1860–1904

19 Ah! what is man? Wherefore does he why? Whence did he whence? Whither is he withering?
Dan Leno Hys Booke (1901) ch. 1

Alan Jay Lerner 1918–1986

20 I'm getting married in the morning,
Ding! dong! the bells are gonna chime.
Pull out the stopper;
Let's have a whopper;
But get me to the church on time!
Get Me to the Church on Time (1956 song; music by Frederick Loewe)

21 Why can't a woman be more like a man?

Men are so honest, so thoroughly
    square;
Eternally noble, historically fair;
Who, when you win, will always give
    your back a pat.
Why can't a woman be like that?
A Hymn to Him (1956 song; music by
Frederick Loewe)

1 Ah yes! I remember it well.
I Remember it Well (1958 song; music by
Frederick Loewe)

2 I've grown accustomed to the trace
Of something in the air;
Accustomed to her face.
I've Grown Accustomed to her Face (1956
song; music by Frederick Loewe)

3 On a clear day (you can see forever).
Title of song from musical *On a Clear Day*
(1965; music by Burton Lane)

4 The rain in Spain stays mainly in the
plain.
The Rain in Spain (1956 song; music by
Frederick Loewe)

5 Thank heaven for little girls!
For little girls get bigger every day.
Thank Heaven for Little Girls (1958 song;
music by Frederick Loewe)

6 All I want is a room somewhere,
Far away from the cold night air,
With one enormous chair;
Oh, wouldn't it be loverly?
Wouldn't it be Loverly (1956 song; music by
Frederick Loewe)

Doris Lessing 1919–

7 There's only one real sin, and that is to
persuade oneself that the second-best is
anything but the second-best.
Golden Notebook (1962) p. 554

8 When a white man in Africa by accident
looks into the eyes of a native and sees
the human being (which it is his chief
preoccupation to avoid), his sense of
guilt, which he denies, fumes up in
resentment and he brings down the
whip.
The Grass is Singing (1950) ch. 8

Winifred Mary Letts 1882–1972

9 I saw the spires of Oxford
As I was passing by,
The grey spires of Oxford
Against a pearl-grey sky;

My heart was with the Oxford men
Who went abroad to die.
Hallow-e'en (1916) 'The Spires of Oxford'

Oscar Levant 1906–1972

10 Epigram: a wisecrack that played
Carnegie Hall.
Coronet Sept. 1958

11 Underneath this flabby exterior is an
enormous lack of character.
Memoirs of an Amnesiac (1965) ch. 11

12 I don't drink liquor. I don't like it. It
makes me feel good.
Time 5 May 1958

Ros Levenstein

13 I'm only here for the beer.
Slogan for Double Diamond beer, 1971
onwards, in Nigel Rees *Slogans* (1982) p. 11

Viscount Leverhulme (William Hesketh Lever) 1851–1925

14 Half the money I spend on advertising is
wasted, and the trouble is I don't know
which half.
In David Ogilvy *Confessions of an Advertising
Man* (1963) ch. 3

Ada Leverson 1865–1936

15 He [Oscar Wilde] seemed at ease and to
have the look of the last gentleman in
Europe.
Letters to the Sphinx (1930) p. 34

16 You don't know a woman until you
have had a letter from her.
Tenterhooks (1912) ch. 7

Bernard Levin 1928–

17 [Tony] Benn flung himself into the
Sixties technology with the enthusiasm
(not to say language) of a newly enrolled
Boy Scout demonstrating knot-tying to
his indulgent parents.
The Pendulum Years (1970) ch. 11

18 I have heard tell of a Professor of
Economics who has a sign on the wall of
his study, reading 'the future is not
what it was'. The sentiment was
admirable; unfortunately, the past is not
getting any better either.
Sunday Times 22 May 1977

Claude Lévi-Strauss 1908–

1 *La langue est une raison humaine qui a ses raisons, et que l'homme ne connaît pas.*

Language is a form of human reason and has its reasons which are unknown to man.
La Pensée sauvage (The Savage Mind, 1962) ch. 9. Cf. Pascal in *Oxford Dictionary of Quotations* (1979) 369:10

Cecil Day Lewis

See C. DAY-LEWIS

C. S. Lewis 1898–1963

2 There is wishful thinking in Hell as well as on Earth.
Screwtape Letters (1942) preface

3 We have trained them [men] to think of the Future as a promised land which favoured heroes attain—not as something which everyone reaches at the rate of sixty minutes an hour, whatever he does, whoever he is.
Screwtape Letters (1942) no. 25

4 She's the sort of woman who lives for others—you can always tell the others by their hunted expression.
Screwtape Letters (1942) no. 26

5 I remember summing up what I took to be our destiny, in conversation with my best friend at Chartres, by the formula, 'Term, holidays, term, holidays, till we leave school, and then work, work, work till we die.'
Suprised by Joy (1955) ch. 4

John Spedan Lewis 1885–1963

6 Service to customers: never knowingly undersold.
Slogan (c.1920) in *Partnership for All* (1948) ch. 29

Percy Wyndham Lewis 1882–1957

7 'The Art of Being Ruled' might be described from some points of view as an infernal Utopia. ... An account, comprising many chapters, of the decadence occupying the trough between the two world wars introduces us to a moronic inferno of insipidity and decay (which is likewise the inferno of 'The Apes of God').
Rude Assignment (1950) ch. 31

8 Gertrude Stein's prose-song is a cold, black suet-pudding. We can represent it as a cold suet-roll of fabulously-reptilian length. Cut it at any point, it is the same thing; the same heavy, sticky, opaque mass all through, and all along. It is weighted, projected, with a sibylline urge. It is mournful and monstrous, composed of dead and inanimate material. It is all fat, without nerve. Or the evident vitality that informs it is vegetable rather than animal. Its life is a low-grade, if tenacious one; of the sausage, by-the-yard, variety.
Time and Western Man (1927) pt. 1, ch. 13

Sam M. Lewis 1885–1959 and Joe Young 1889–1939

9 How 'ya gonna keep 'em down on the farm (after they've seen Paree)?
Title of song (1919; music by Walter Donaldson)

Sinclair Lewis 1885–1951

10 Our American professors like their literature clear and cold and pure and very dead.
The American Fear of Literature (Nobel Prize Address, 12 Dec. 1930), in H. Frenz *Literature 1901–1967* (1969) p. 285

11 His name was George F. Babbitt. He was forty-six years old now, in April, 1920, and he made nothing in particular, neither butter nor shoes nor poetry, but he was nimble in the calling of selling houses for more than people could afford to pay.
Babbitt (1922) ch. 1

12 To George F. Babbitt, as to most prosperous citizens of Zenith, his motor car was poetry and tragedy, love and heroism. The office was his pirate ship but the car his perilous excursion ashore.
Babbitt (1922) ch. 3

13 In other countries, art and literature are left to a lot of shabby bums living in attics and feeding on booze and spaghetti, but in America the successful writer or picture-painter is indistinguishable from any other decent business man.
Babbitt (1922) ch. 14

1 It can't happen here.
  Title of novel (1935)

Robert Ley 1890–1945

2 *Kraft durch Freude.*

  Strength through joy.
  German Labour Front slogan, in *The Times*
  30 Nov. 1933, p. 13

Liberace (Wladziu Valentino Liberace) 1919–1987

3 He [Liberace] begins to belabour the
  critics announcing that *he* doesn't mind
  what they say but that poor George [his
  brother] 'cried all the way to the bank'.
  Collier's 17 Sept. 1954 (Cf. Liberace's
  Autobiography (1973) ch. 2: 'When the
  reviews are bad I tell my staff that they can
  join me as I cry all the way to the bank')

Beatrice Lillie 1894–1989

4 At one early, glittering dinner party at
  Buckingham Palace, the trembling hand
  of a nervous waiter spilled a spoonful of
  decidedly hot soup down my neck. How
  could I manage to ease his mind and
  turn his embarrassed apologies into
  a smile, except to put on a pretended
  frown and say, without thinking: 'Never
  darken my Dior again!'
  Every Other Inch a Lady (1973) ch. 14

R. M. Lindner 1914–1956

5 Rebel without a cause . . . the
  hypnoanalysis of a criminal psychopath.
  Title of book (1944)

Audrey Erskine Lindop 1920–1986

6 The singer not the song.
  Title of book (1953)

Howard Lindsay 1888–1968 and Russel Crouse 1893–1966

7 Call me madam.
  Title of musical (1950; music by Irving
  Berlin)

Vachel Lindsay 1879–1931

8 Booth led boldly with his big brass
  drum—

  (Are you washed in the blood of the
  Lamb?)
  The Saints smiled gravely and they said:
  'He's come.'
  (Are you washed in the blood of the
  Lamb?)
  Walking Lepers followed, rank on rank,
  Lurching bravos from the ditches dank,
  Drabs from the alleyways and drug
  fiends pale—
  Minds still passion-ridden, soul-power
  frail:—
  Vermin-eaten saints with moldy breath,
  Unwashed legions with the ways of
  Death—
  (Are you washed in the blood of the
  Lamb?)
  Collected Poems (1934) 'General William
  Booth Enters into Heaven' (1913)

9 Booth died blind and still by faith he
  trod,
  Eyes still dazzled by the ways of God.
  Collected Poems (1934) 'General William
  Booth Enters into Heaven' (1913)

10 Then I saw the Congo, creeping through
  the black,
  Cutting through the forest with a golden
  track.
  The Congo and Other Poems (1922) 'The
  Congo' (1914) pt. 1

Eric Linklater 1899–1974

11 'There won't be any revolution in
  America,' said Isadore. Nikitin agreed.
  'The people are all too clean. They spend
  all their time changing their shirts and
  washing themselves. You can't feel
  fierce and revolutionary in a bathroom.'
  Juan in America (1931) bk. 5, pt. 3

Art Linkletter 1912–

12 The four stages of man are infancy,
  childhood, adolescence and
  obsolescence.
  A Child's Garden of Misinformation (1965)
  ch. 8

Walter Lippmann 1889–1974

13 Mr Coolidge's genius for inactivity is
  developed to a very high point. It is far
  from being an indolent activity. It is a
  grim, determined, alert inactivity which

keeps Mr Coolidge occupied constantly. Nobody has ever worked harder at inactivity, with such force of character, with such unremitting attention to detail, with such conscientious devotion to the task. Inactivity is a political philosophy and a party program with Mr Coolidge.
Men of Destiny (1927) p. 12

1 The final test of a leader is that he leaves behind him in other men the conviction and the will to carry on.
New York Herald Tribune 14 Apr. 1945

Joan Littlewood and Charles Chilton 1914–

2 Oh what a lovely war.
Title of stage show (1963)

Maxim Litvinov 1876–1951

3 Peace is indivisible.
Note to the Allies, 25 Feb. 1920, in A. U. Pope *Maxim Litvinoff* (1943) p. 234

Ken Livingstone 1945–

4 The problem is that many MPs never see the London that exists beyond the wine bars and brothels of Westminster.
The Times 19 Feb. 1987

Richard Llewellyn (Richard Dafydd Vivian Llewellyn Lloyd) 1907–1983

5 How green was my valley.
Title of book (1939)

Jack Llewelyn-Davies 1894–1959

6 *Little Mary* [by J.M. Barrie] opened at Wyndham's Theatre on September 24th, 1903, and . . . it contained a sprinkling of lines contributed by the boys, including a remark from Jack [Llewelyn-Davies]. When stuffing himself with cakes at tea, Sylvia had warned him, 'You'll be sick tomorrow.' 'I'll be sick tonight,' replied Jack cheerily.
Andrew Birkin *J. M. Barrie and the Lost Boys* (1979) p. 99

David Lloyd George (Earl Lloyd-George of Dwyfor) 1863–1945

7 Negotiating with de Valera . . . is like trying to pick up mercury with a fork.
In M. J. MacManus *Eamon de Valera* (1944) ch. 6 (to which de Valera replied, 'Why doesn't he use a spoon?')

8 This [The House of Lords] is the leal and trusty mastiff which is to watch over our interests, but which runs away at the first snarl of the trade unions. . . . A mastiff? It is the right hon. Gentleman's [Mr Balfour's] poodle.
Hansard 26 June 1907, col. 1429

9 Those are the conditions of the armistice. Thus at eleven o'clock this morning came to an end the cruellest and most terrible War that has ever scourged mankind. I hope we may say that thus, this fateful morning, came to an end all wars.
Hansard 11 Nov. 1918, col. 2463. Cf. H. G. Wells 225:4

10 Winston was nervous before a speech, but he was not shy. L.G. said he himself was both nervous and shy. Winston would go up to his Creator and say that he would very much like to meet His Son, about Whom he had heard a great deal and, if possible, would like to call on the Holy Ghost. Winston *loved* meeting people.
A. J. Sylvester *Diary* 2 Jan. 1937, in *Life with Lloyd George* (1975) p. 166

11 He [Ramsay MacDonald] had sufficient conscience to bother him, but not sufficient to keep him straight.
In A. J. Sylvester *Life with Lloyd George* (1975) p. 216

12 A fully-equipped duke costs as much to keep up as two Dreadnoughts; and dukes are just as great a terror and they last longer.
Speech at Newcastle, 9 Oct. 1909, in *The Times* 11 Oct. 1909

13 The great peaks of honour we had forgotten—Duty, Patriotism, and—clad in glittering white—the great pinnacle of Sacrifice, pointing like a rugged finger to Heaven.
Speech at Queen's Hall, London, 19 Sept. 1914, in *The Times* 20 Sept. 1914

1 What is our task? To make Britain a fit country for heroes to live in.
  Speech at Wolverhampton, 23 Nov. 1918, in *The Times* 25 Nov. 1918

2 M. Clemenceau ... is one of the greatest living orators, but he knows that the finest eloquence is that which gets things done and the worst is that which delays them.
  Speech at Paris Peace Conference, 18 Jan. 1919, in *The Times* 20 Jan. 1919

3 The world is becoming like a lunatic asylum run by lunatics.
  In *Observer* 8 Jan. 1933

4 What were politicians? A politician was a person with whose politics you did not agree. When you did agree, he was a statesman.
  Speech at Central Hall, Westminster, 2 July 1935, in *The Times* 3 July 1935

David Lodge 1935–

5 Literature is mostly about having sex and not much about having children. Life is the other way round.
  The British Museum is Falling Down (1965) ch. 4

Frank Loesser 1910–1969

6 See what the boys in the back room will have
  And tell them I'm having the same.
  Boys in the Back Room (1939 song; music by Frederick Hollander)

7 I'd love to get you
  On a slow boat to China,
  All to myself, alone.
  Slow Boat to China (1948 song)

8 Spring will be a little late this year.
  Title of song (1944)

Jack London (John Griffith London) 1876–1916

9 The call of the wild.
  Title of novel (1903)

Alice Roosevelt Longworth 1884–1980

10 [Warren] Harding was not a bad man. He was just a slob.
  Crowded Hours (1933) ch. 20

11 If you haven't got anything good to say about anyone come and sit by me.
  Maxim embroidered on a cushion, in Michael Teague *Mrs L: Conversations with Alice Roosevelt Longworth* (1981) p. xi

Frederick Lonsdale 1881–1954

12 'Don't keep finishing your sentences,' he said to me once when I was telling him something; 'I'm not a bloody fool.'
  Frances Donaldson *Child of the Twenties* (1959) p. 11

Anita Loos 1893–1981

13 So this gentleman said a girl with brains ought to do something with them besides think.
  Gentlemen Prefer Blondes (1925) ch. 1

14 Gentlemen always seem to remember blondes.
  Gentlemen Prefer Blondes (1925) ch. 1

15 She said she always believed in the old addage, 'Leave them while you're looking good.'
  Gentlemen Prefer Blondes (1925) ch. 1

16 So I really think that American gentlemen are the best after all, because kissing your hand may make you feel very very good but a diamond and safire bracelet lasts forever.
  Gentlemen Prefer Blondes (1925) ch. 4

17 You have got to be a Queen to get away with a hat like that.
  Gentlemen Prefer Blondes (1925) ch. 4

18 Fun is fun but no girl wants to laugh all of the time.
  Gentlemen Prefer Blondes (1925) ch. 4

19 So then Dr Froyd said that all I needed was to cultivate a few inhibitions and get some sleep.
  Gentlemen Prefer Blondes (1925) ch. 5

20 So then he said that he used to be a member of the choir himself, so who was he to cast the first rock at a girl like I.
  Gentlemen Prefer Blondes (1925) ch. 5

Frederico García Lorca 1899–1936

21 *A las cinco de la tarde.*
  Eran las cinco en punto de la tarde.
  Un niño trajo la blanca sábana
  a las cinco de la tarde.

At five in the afternoon.
It was exactly five in the afternoon.
A boy brought the white sheet
at five in the afternoon.

> *Llanto por Ignacio Sánchez Mejías* (Lament for Ignacio Sánchez Mejías, 1935) 'La Cogida y la muerte'

1 *Verde que te quiero verde.*
Verde viento.
Verde ramas.
El barco sobre la mar
y el caballo en la montaña.

Green how I love you green.
Green wind.
Green boughs.
The ship on the sea
and the horse on the mountain.

> *Romancero Gitano* (Gypsy Romances, 1924–1927) 'Romance Sonámbulo'

Konrad Lorenz 1903–1989

2 *Überhaupt ist es für den Forscher ein guter Morgensport, täglich vor dem Frühstück eine Lieblingshypothese einzustampfen—das erhält jung.*

It is a good morning exercise for a research scientist to discard a pet hypothesis every day before breakfast. It keeps him young.

> *Das sogenannte Böse* (The So-Called Evil, 1963; translated 1966 by Marjorie Latzke as *On Aggression*) ch. 2

Joe Louis 1914–1981

3 He [Billy Conn] can run, but he can't hide.

> In *New York Herald Tribune* 9 June 1946

Terry Lovelock

4 Heineken refreshes the parts other beers cannot reach.

> Slogan for Heineken lager, 1975 onwards, in Nigel Rees *Slogans* (1982) p. 16

Robert Loveman 1864–1923

5 It isn't raining rain to me,
It's raining violets.

> *Gates of Silence* (1903) 'Song' (words adapted by Buddy De Sylva in 1921 song *April Showers*; music by Louis Silver)

David Low 1891–1963

6 I have never met anyone who wasn't against war. Even Hitler and Mussolini were, according to themselves.

> *New York Times Magazine* 10 Feb. 1946

Amy Lowell 1874–1925

7 And the softness of my body will be guarded by embrace
By each button, hook, and lace.
For the man who should loose me is dead,
Fighting with the Duke in Flanders,
In a pattern called a war.
Christ! What are patterns for?

> *Men, Women and Ghosts* (1916) 'Patterns'

8 I [Death] was astonished to see him in Baghdad, for I had an appointment with him tonight in Samarra.

> *Sheppy* (1933) act 3

9 All books are either dreams or swords,
You can cut, or you can drug, with words.

> *Sword Blades and Poppy Seed* (1914) title poem

Robert Lowell 1917–1977

10 We feel the machine slipping from our hands
As if someone else were steering;
If we see light at the end of the tunnel,
It's the light of the oncoming train.

> *Day by Day* (1977) 'Since 1939'. Cf. Paul Dickson

11 My eyes have seen what my hand did.

> *The Dolphin* (1973) 'Dolphin'

12 The aquarium is gone.
Everywhere,
giant finned cars nose forward like fish;
a savage servility
slides by on grease.

> *For the Union Dead* (1964) title poem

13 These are the tranquillized *Fifties*,
and I am forty. Ought I to regret my seed-time?
I was a fire-breathing Catholic C.O.,
and made my manic statement,
telling off the state and president, and then

sat waiting sentence in the bull pen
beside a Negro boy with curlicues
of marijuana in his hair.

> *Life Studies* (1956) 'Memories of West Street and Lepke'

1 I saw the spiders marching through the
air,
Swimming from tree to tree that
mildewed day
In latter August when the hay
Came creaking to the barn.

> *Poems 1938–1949* (1950) 'Mr Edwards and the Spider'

2 This is death.
To die and know it. This is the Black
Widow, death.

> *Poems 1938–1949* (1950) 'Mr Edwards and the Spider'

3 The Lord survives the rainbow of His
will.

> *Poems 1938–1949* (1950) 'The Quaker Graveyard in Nantucket'

L. S. Lowry 1887–1976

4 I'm a simple man, and I use simple
materials.

> In Mervyn Levy *Paintings of L. S. Lowry* (1975) p. 11

Malcolm Lowry 1909–1957

5 How alike are the groans of love to
those of the dying.

> *Under the Volcano* (1947) ch. 12

E. V. Lucas 1868–1938

6 Poor G.K.C., his day is past—
Now God will know the truth at last.

> Mock epitaph for G. K. Chesterton, in Dudley Barker
> *G. K. Chesterton* (1973) ch. 16

7 There can be no defence like elaborate
courtesy.

> *Reading, Writing and Remembering* (1932) ch. 8

8 I have noticed that the people who are
late are often so much jollier than the
people who have to wait for them.

> *365 Days and One More* (1926) p. 277

George Lucas 1944–

9 The Empire strikes back.

> Title of film (1980)

10 Then man your ships, and may the force
be with you.

> *Star Wars: from the Adventures of Luke Skywalker* (1976) ch. 11

Clare Booth Luce 1903–

11 But if God had wanted us to think just
with our wombs, why did He give us
a brain?

> *Life* 16 Oct. 1970

Joanna Lumley

12 To be a judge you don't have to know
about books, you have to be skilled at
picking shrapnel out of your head.

> In *Observer* 17 Nov. 1985 (comment on the Booker Prize)

Sir Edwin Lutyens 1869–1944

13 I had proposed that we should lunch
together at the Garrick Club, because
I had obviously to ask father if he had
any serious objection to the writing or
the writer of this essay. But, when
I broached the matter, he merely
mumbled in obvious embarrassment:
'Oh, my!'—just as his father was used
to do. Then, as the fish was served, he
looked at me seriously over the rims of
his two pairs of spectacles and
remarked: ' The piece of cod passeth all
understanding'!

> Robert Lutyens *Sir Edwin Lutyens* (1942) p. 74

Rosa Luxemburg 1871–1919

14 *Freiheit ist immer nur Freiheit des anders
Denkenden.*

Freedom is always and exclusively
freedom for the one who thinks
differently.

> *Die Russische Revolution* (The Russian Revolution, 1918) sec. 4

Lady Lytton (Pamela Frances Audrey, Countess of Lytton) 1874–1971

1 The first time you meet Winston [Churchill] you see all his faults and the rest of your life you spend in discovering his virtues.

> Letter to Sir Edward Marsh, Dec. 1905, in Edward Marsh
> *A Number of People* (1939) ch. 8

Alexander McArthur and H. Kingsley Long

2 Battles and sex are the only free diversions in slum life. Couple them with drink, which costs money, and you have the three principal outlets for that escape complex which is for ever working in the tenement dweller's subconscious mind.

> *No Mean City* (1935) ch. 4

Charles MacArthur 1895–1956 and Ben Hecht 1894–1964

3 The son of a bitch stole my watch!

> *Front Page* (1928) last line

General Douglas MacArthur 1880–1964

4 In war, indeed, there can be no substitute for victory.

> *Congressional Record* 19 Apr. 1951, vol. 97, pt. 3, p. 4125

5 The President of the United States ordered me to break through the Japanese lines and proceed from Corregidor to Australia for the purpose, as I understand it, of organizing the American offensive against Japan. A primary purpose of this is relief of the Philippines. I came through and I shall return.

> Statement in Adelaide, 20 Mar. 1942, in *New York Times* 21 Mar. 1942, p. 1

Dame Rose Macaulay 1881–1958

6 'Take my camel, dear,' said my aunt Dot, as she climbed down from this animal on her return from High Mass.

> *Towers of Trebizond* (1956) p. 9

General Anthony McAuliffe 1898–1975

7 Nuts!

> Response to German demand to surrender at Bastogne, Belgium, 22 Dec. 1944, in *New York Times* 28 Dec. 1944, p. 4, and 30 Dec. 1944, p. 1

Sir Desmond MacCarthy 1877–1952

8 A biographer is an artist who is on oath, and anyone who knows anything about artists, knows that that is almost a contradiction in terms.

> *Memories* (1953) 'Lytton Strachey and the Art of Biography'

9 The whole of art is an appeal to a reality which is not without us but in our minds.

> *Theatre* (1954) 'Diction and Realism'

Joe McCarthy

10 You made me love you, I didn't want to do it.

> *You Made Me Love You* (1913 song; music by James V. Monaco)

Joseph McCarthy 1908–1957

11 McCarthyism is Americanism with its sleeves rolled.

> Speech in Wisconsin, 1952, in Richard Rovere *Senator Joe McCarthy* (1973) p. 8

Mary McCarthy 1912–1989

12 I once said in an interview that every word she [Lillian Hellman] writes is a lie, including 'and' and 'the'.

> *New York Times* 16 Feb. 1980, p. 12

13 When an American heiress wants to buy a man, she at once crosses the Atlantic. The only really materialistic people I have ever met have been Europeans.

> *On the Contrary* (1961) 'America the Beautiful'

14 The immense popularity of American movies abroad demonstrates that Europe is the unfinished negative of which America is the proof.

> *On the Contrary* (1961) 'America the Beautiful'

15 There are no new truths, but only truths that have not been recognized by those

who have perceived them without noticing. A truth is something that everyone can be shown to know and to have known, as people say, all along.

On the Contrary (1961) 'Vita Activa'

1 In violence, we forget who we are.
On the Contrary (1961) 'Characters in Fiction'

2 If someone tells you he is going to make a 'realistic decision', you immediately understand that he has resolved to do something bad.
On the Contrary (1961) 'American Realist Playwrights'

Paul McCartney 1942–

3 He [John Lennon] could be a manœuvring swine, which no one ever realized.
In Hunter Davies The Beatles (1985) p. 469

See also JOHN LENNON

David McCord 1897–

4 By and by
God caught his eye.
Bay Window Ballads (1935) 'Remainders' (epitaph for a waiter)

Horace McCoy 1897–1955

5 They shoot horses don't they.
Title of novel (1935)

John McCrae 1872–1918

6 In Flanders fields the poppies blow
Between the crosses, row on row,
That mark our place; and in the sky
The larks, still bravely singing, fly
Scarce heard amid the guns below.
Punch 8 Dec. 1915 'In Flanders Fields'

7 To you from failing hands we throw
The torch; be yours to hold it high.
If ye break faith with us who die
We shall not sleep, though poppies grow.
Punch 8 Dec. 1915, 'In Flanders Fields'

Carson McCullers 1917–1967

8 The heart is a lonely hunter.
Title of novel (1940; taken from The Lonely Hunter (1896), a poem by 'Fiona Macleod' (William Sharp): 'My heart is a lonely hunter that hunts on a lonely hill')

Derek McCulloch 1897–1967

9 Goodnight, children ... everywhere.
Children's Hour (BBC Radio programme; closing words normally spoken by 'Uncle Mac' in the 1930s and 1940s)

Hugh MacDiarmid (Christopher Murray Grieve) 1892–1978

10 I'll ha'e nae hauf-way hoose, but aye be whaur
Extremes meet—it's the only way I ken
To dodge the curst conceit o' bein' richt
That damns the vast majority o' men.
A Drunk Man Looks at the Thistle (1926) p. 6

11 He's no a man ava',
And lacks a proper pride,
Gin less than a' the world
Can ser' him for a bride!
A Drunk Man Looks at the Thistle (1926) p. 36

Ramsay MacDonald 1866–1937

12 Yes, tomorrow every Duchess in London will be wanting to kiss me!
Comment after forming the National Government, 25 Aug. 1931, in Philip Viscount Snowden Autobiography (1934) vol. 2, p. 957

13 If God were to come to me and say 'Ramsay, would you rather be a country gentleman than a prime minister?', I should reply, 'Please God, a country gentleman.'
In Harold Nicolson Diary 5 Oct. 1930, in Diaries and Letters (1966) p. 57

14 We hear war called murder. It is not: it is suicide.
In Observer 4 May 1930

A. G. Macdonell 1889–1941

15 England, their England.
Title of novel (1933)

John McEnroe 1959–

16 You cannot be serious!
Said to tennis umpire at Wimbledon, early 1980s

17 This must be the pits.
Comment after disagreement with Wimbledon umpire, in Sun 23 June 1981

Arthur McEwen d. 1907

1 'What we're after,' said Arthur McEwen, 'is the 'gee-whiz' emotion.' Pressed for further explanation, he said: 'We run our paper so that when the reader opens it he says: "Gee-whiz!" An issue is a failure which doesn't make him say that.'

Colliers 18 Feb. 1911

Roger McGough 1937–

2 Let me die a youngman's death
Not a clean & in-between-
The-sheets, holy-water death,
Not a famous-last-words
Peaceful out-of-breath death.

'Let Me Die a Youngman's Death' in Edward Lucie Smith (ed.) *The Liverpool Scene* (1967) p. 47

3 Girls are simply the prettiest things
My cat and i believe
And we're always saddened
When it's time for them to leave

We watch them titivating
(that often takes a while)
and though they keep us waiting
My cat and i just smile

We like to see them to the door
Say how sad it couldn't last
Then my cat and i go back inside
And talk about the past.

Watchwords (1969) 'My Cat and i'

Sir Ian MacGregor 1912–

4 People are now discovering the price of insubordination and insurrection. And boy, are we going to make it stick!

Comment during the coal-miners' strike, in *Sunday Telegraph* 10 Mar. 1985

Jimmy McGregor

5 Oh, he's football crazy, he's football mad
And the football it has robbed him o' the wee bit sense he had.
And it would take a dozen skivvies, his clothes to wash and scrub,
Since our Jock became a member of that terrible football club.

Football Crazy (1960 song)

Dennis McHarrie

6 'He died who loved to live,' they'll say,
'Unselfishly so we might have today!'

Like hell! He fought ...
fight;
He died that's all. It was ...
night.

In V. Selwyn et al *Return to Oasis* ... pt. 3, p. 172 'Luck'

Colin MacInnes 1914–1976

7 And I thought, 'My lord, one thing is certain, and that's that they'll make musicals one day about the glamour-studded 1950s.' And I thought, my heaven, one thing is certain too, I'm miserable.

Absolute Beginners (1959) p. 81

Claude McKay 1890–1948

8 If we must die, let it not be like hogs
Hunted and penned in an inglorious spot,
While round us bark the mad and hungry dogs,
Making their mock at our accursed lot.
If we must die, O let us nobly die,
So that our precious blood may not be shed
In vain; then even the monsters we defy
Shall be constrained to honor us though dead!
O, kinsmen! we must meet the common foe!
Though far outnumbered let us show us brave,
And for their thousand blows deal one deathblow!
What though before us lies the open grave?
Like men we'll face the murderous, cowardly pack,
Pressed to the wall, dying, but fighting back!

Selected Poems (1953) 'If We Must Die'

Sir Compton Mackenzie 1883–1972

9 Women do not find it difficult nowadays to behave like men, but they often find it extremely difficult to behave like gentlemen.

Literature in My Time (1933) ch. 22

10 You are offered a piece of bread and butter that feels like a damp

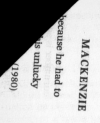

...hen
...wet one.

...because he had to
...is unlucky
... (1980)

MACKENZIE

...have skied
...de with

...rates' Court,
... 1977

Alexander Maclaren 1826–1910

2 'The Church is an anvil which has worn
out many hammers', and the story of
the first collision is, in essentials, the
story of all.
*Expositions of Holy Scripture: Acts of the
Apostles* (1907) ch. 4

Alistair Maclean 1923–1987

3 Where eagles dare.
Title of novel (1967)

Archibald MacLeish 1892–1982

4 A Poem should be palpable and mute
As a globed fruit

Dumb
As old medallions to the thumb

Silent as the sleeve-worn stone
Of casement ledges where the moss has
grown—

A poem should be wordless
As the flight of birds
Streets in the Moon (1926) 'Ars Poetica'

5 A poem should not mean
But be.
Streets in the Moon (1926) 'Ars Poetica'

Irene Rutherford McLeod
1891–1964

6 I'm a lean dog, a keen dog, a wild dog,
and lone;
I'm a rough dog, a tough dog, hunting
on my own;
I'm a bad dog, a mad dog, teasing silly
sheep;
I love to sit and bay at the moon, to
keep fat souls from sleep.
Songs to Save a Soul (1915) 'Lone Dog'

Marshall McLuhan 1911–1980

7 The new electronic interdependence
recreates the world in the image of
a global village.
Gutenberg Galaxy (1962) p. 31

8 One matter Englishmen don't think in
the least funny is their happy
consciousness of possessing a deep sense
of humour.
Mechanical Bride (1951) 'The Ballet Luce'

9 The medium is the message.
Understanding Media (1964) title of ch. 1

10 The name of a man is a numbing blow
from which he never recovers.
Understanding Media (1964) p. 32

11 The car has become an article of dress
without which we feel uncertain, unclad
and incomplete in the urban compound.
Understanding Media (1964) p. 217

12 The car has become the carapace, the
protective and aggressive shell, of urban
and suburban man.
Understanding Media (1964) p. 224

Ed McMahon 1923–

13 And now ... heeeeere's Johnny!
Introduction to Johnny Carson on NBC-TV's
Tonight show (from 1961; also used by Jack
Nicholson in the 1980 film *The Shining*)

Harold Macmillan (Lord Stockton)
1894–1986

14 He [Aneurin Bevan] enjoys prophesying
the imminent fall of the capitalist system
and is prepared to play a part, any part,
in its burial, except that of mute.
In Michael Foot *Aneurin Bevan* (1962) pt. 1,
ch. 5

15 After a long experience of politics I have
never found that there is any inhibition
caused by ignorance as regards
criticism.
Hansard 11 July 1963, col. 1411

16 I was determined that no British
government should be brought down by
the action of two tarts.
Comment on the Profumo affair, July 1963,
in Anthony Sampson *Macmillan* (1967)
p. 243

17 There ain't gonna be no war.
Said at London press conference, 24 July
1955, after Geneva summit, in *News
Chronicle* 25 July 1955

1 He [a Foreign Secretary] is forever poised between a cliché and an indiscretion.

In *Newsweek* 30 Apr. 1956

2 Even before Mr Heath's troubles of 1972 and 1974, Mr Harold Macmillan was fond of remarking that there were three bodies no sensible man directly challenged: the Roman Catholic Church, the Brigade of Guards and the National Union of Mineworkers.

Alan Watkins in *Observer* 22 Feb. 1981

3 The most striking of all the impressions I have formed since I left London a month ago is of the strength of this African national consciousness. In different places it takes different forms, but it is happening everywhere. The wind of change is blowing through this continent, and, whether we like it or not, this growth of national consciousness is a political fact. We must all accept it as a fact, and our national policies must take account of it.

Speech at Cape Town, 3 Feb. 1960, *Pointing the Way* (1972) p. 475

4 Indeed, let us be frank about it: most of our people have never had it so good. Go around the country, go to the industrial towns, go to the farms, and you will see a state of prosperity such as we have never had in my lifetime—nor indeed ever in the history of this country. What is beginning to worry some of us is, Is it too good to be true?—or perhaps I should say, Is it too good to last?

Speech at Bedford, 20 July 1957, in *The Times* 22 July 1957

5 I thought the best thing to do was to settle up these little local difficulties, and then turn to the wider vision of the Commonwealth.

Statement at London airport on leaving for Commonwealth tour, 7 Jan. 1958, following the resignation of the Chancellor of the Exchequer and others, in *The Times* 8 Jan. 1958

6 As usual the Liberals offer a mixture of sound and original ideas. Unfortunately none of the sound ideas is original and none of the original ideas is sound.

Speech to London Conservatives, 7 Mar. 1961, in *The Times* 8 Mar. 1961

7 First of all the Georgian silver goes, and then all that nice furniture that used to be in the saloon. Then the Canalettos go.

Speech on privatization to the Tory Reform Group, 8 Nov. 1985, in *The Times* 9 Nov. 1985

Louis MacNeice 1907–1963

8 Better authentic mammon than a bogus god.

Autumn Journal (1939) p. 49

9 The sunlight on the garden
Hardens and grows cold,
We cannot cage the minute
Within its net of gold,
When all is told
We cannot beg for pardon.

Earth Compels (1938) 'Sunlight on the Garden'

10 Our freedom as free lances
Advances towards its end;
The earth compels, upon it
Sonnets and birds descend;
And soon, my friend,
We shall have no time for dances.

Earth Compels (1938) 'Sunlight on the Garden'

11 It's no go the merrygoround, it's no go the rickshaw,
All we want is a limousine and a ticket for the peepshow.

Earth Compels (1938) 'Bagpipe Music'

12 It's no go the picture palace, it's no go the stadium,
It's no go the country cot with a pot of pink geraniums,
It's no go the Government grants, it's no go the elections,
Sit on your arse for fifty years and hang your hat on a pension.

Earth Compels (1938) 'Bagpipe Music'

13 It's no go my honey love, it's no go my poppet;
Work your hands from day to day, the winds will blow the profit.
The glass is falling hour by hour, the glass will fall for ever,
But if you break the bloody glass you won't hold up the weather.

Earth Compels (1938) 'Bagpipe Music'

14 I take a rather common-sense view of poetry. I think that the poet is a sensitive instrument designed to record anything

which interests his mind or affects his emotions.
Listener 27 July 1939

1 By a high star our course is set,
Our end is Life. Put out to sea.
London Magazine Feb. 1964 'Thalassa' (poem published posthumously)

2 And under the totem poles—the ancient terror—
Between the enormous fluted Ionic columns
There seeps from heavily jowled or hawk-like foreign faces
The guttural sorrow of the refugees.
Plant and Phantom (1941) 'The British Museum Reading Room'

3 Time was away and somewhere else,
There were two glasses and two chairs
And two people with the one pulse
(Somebody stopped the moving stairs):
Time was away and somewhere else.
Plant and Phantom (1941) 'Meeting Point'

4 So they were married—to be the more together—
And found they were never again so much together,
Divided by the morning tea,
By the evening paper,
By children and tradesmen's bills.
Plant and Phantom (1941) 'Les Sylphides'

5 Crumbling between the fingers, under the feet,
Crumbling behind the eyes,
Their world gives way and dies
And something twangs and breaks at the end of the street.
Plant and Phantom (1941) 'Débâcle'

6 Down the road someone is practising scales,
The notes like little fishes vanish with a wink of tails,
Man's heart expands to tinker with his car
For this is Sunday morning, Fate's great bazaar.
Poems (1935) 'Sunday Morning'

7 World is crazier and more of it than we think,
Incorrigibly plural. I peel and portion
A tangerine and spit the pips and feel
The drunkenness of things being various.
Poems (1935) 'Snow'

8 I am not yet born; O fill me

With strength against those who would freeze my
humanity, would dragoon me into a lethal automaton,
would make me a cog in a machine, a thing with
one face, a thing, and against all those
who would dissipate my entirety, would
blow me like thistledown hither and thither or hither and thither
like water held in the
hands would spill me.
Let them not make me a stone and let them not spill me,
Otherwise kill me.
Springboard (1944) 'Prayer Before Birth'

Salvador de Madariaga 1886–1978

9 Since, in the main, it is not armaments that cause wars but wars (or the fears thereof) that cause armaments, it follows that every nation will at every moment strive to keep its armament in an efficient state as required by its fear, otherwise styled security.
Morning Without Noon (1974) pt. 1, ch. 9

Maurice Maeterlinck 1862–1949

10 *Il n'y a pas de morts.*

There are no dead.
L'Oiseau bleu (The Blue Bird, 1909) act 4

John Gillespie Magee 1922–1941

11 Oh! I have slipped the surly bonds of earth
And danced the skies on laughter-silvered wings;
Sunward I've climbed, and joined the tumbling mirth
Of sun-split clouds—and done a hundred things
You have not dreamed of—wheeled and soared and swung
High in the sunlit silence. Hov'ring there
I've chased the shouting wind along, and flung
My eager craft through footless halls of air.

Up, up the long, delirious, burning blue
I've topped the wind-swept heights with easy grace,
Where never lark, nor even eagle flew—
And, while with silent lifting mind I've trod

The high, untrespassed sanctity of space,
Put out my hand and touched the face
    of God.

In K. Rhys *More Poems from the Forces*
(1943) 'High Flight'

Magnus Magnusson 1929–

1 I've started so I'll finish.

Said when a contestant's time runs out
while a question is being put in *Mastermind*,
BBC television (1972 onwards)

Sir John Pentland Mahaffy
1839–1919

2 In Ireland the inevitable never happens
and the unexpected constantly occurs.

In W. B. Stanford and R. B. McDowell
Mahaffy (1971) ch. 4

Gustav Mahler 1860–1911

3 On seeing Niagara Falls, Mahler
exclaimed: 'Fortissimo at last!'

K. Blaukopf *Gustav Mahler* (1973) ch. 8

Derek Mahon 1941–

4 'I am just going outside and may be
    some time.'
The others nod, pretending not to know.
At the heart of the ridiculous, the
    sublime.

Antarctica (1985) title poem (for the first
line, cf. Captain Lawrence Oates)

Norman Mailer 1923–

5 Sentimentality is the emotional
promiscuity of those who have no
sentiment.

Cannibals and Christians (1966) p. 51

6 Hip is the sophistication of the wise
primitive in a giant jungle.

Dissent Summer 1957, p. 281

7 Once a newspaper touches a story, the
facts are lost forever, even to the
protagonists.

Esquire June 1960

8 The horror of the Twentieth Century
was the size of each event, and the
paucity of its reverberation.

A Fire on the Moon (1970) pt. 1, ch. 2

9 So we think of Marilyn who was every
man's love affair with America, Marilyn
Monroe who was blonde and beautiful

and had a sweet little rinky-dink of
a voice and all the cleanliness of all the
clean American backyards.

Marilyn (1973) p. 15

10 Ultimately a hero is a man who would
argue with the Gods, and so awakens
devils to contest his vision.

The Presidential Papers (1976) Special Preface
to the 1st Berkeley Edition

Bernard Malamud 1914–1986

11 I think I said 'All men are Jews except
they don't know it.' I doubt I expected
anyone to take the statement literally.
But I think it's an understandable
statement and a metaphoric way of
indicating how history, sooner or later,
treats all men.

Leslie and Joyce Field (ed.) *Bernard Malamud*
(1975) 'An interview with Bernard
Malamud' p. 11

12 The past exudes legend: one can't make
pure clay of time's mud. There is no life
that can be recaptured wholly; as it
was. Which is to say that all biography
is ultimately fiction.

Dubin's Lives (1979) p. 20

George Leigh Mallory 1886–1924

13 Because it's there.

Response to question 'Why do you want to
climb Mount Everest?', in *New York Times*
18 Mar. 1923

André Malraux 1901–1976

14 *L'art est un anti-destin.*

Art is a revolt against fate.

Les Voix du silence (Voices of Silence, 1951)
pt. 4, ch. 7

Lord Mancroft (Baron Mancroft)
1914–

15 Our soft grass and mild climate has
enabled us to foster new sports. Racing,
golf, football and particularly cricket—a
game which the English, not being
a spiritual people, have invented in order
to give themselves some conception of
eternity—all owe their development to
our climate.

Bees in Some Bonnets (1979) p. 185

Winnie Mandela 1936–

1 We are going to dismantle apartheid ourselves. That programme will be brought to you by the ANC. Together, hand in hand, with that stick of matches, with our necklace, we shall liberate this country.
   Speech in black townships, 14 Apr. 1986, in *Guardian* 15 Apr. 1986

Osip Mandelstam 1891–1938

2 Perhaps my whisper was already born before my lips.
   Selected Poems (1973, trans. by D. McDuff) p. 129

Herman J. Mankiewicz 1897–1953 and Orson Welles 1915–1985

3 KATHERINE: What's Rosebud?
   RAYMOND: That's what he said when he died. . . .
   LOUISE: If you could have found out what Rosebud meant, I bet that would've explained everything.
   THOMPSON: No, I don't think so. No. Mr Kane was a man who got everything he wanted, and then lost it. Maybe Rosebud was something he couldn't get or something he lost. Anyway, it wouldn't have explained anything. I don't think any word can explain a man's life. No, I guess Rosebud is just a piece in a jigsaw puzzle, a missing piece.
   Citizen Kane (1941 film)

Joseph L. Mankiewicz 1909–

4 Fasten your seat-belts, it's going to be a bumpy night.
   All About Eve (1950 film; words spoken by Bette Davis)

Thomas Mann 1875–1955

5 *Der Tod in Venedig.*

   Death in Venice.
   Title of novella (1912)

6 *Tatsächlich ist unser Sterben mehr eine Angelegenheit der Weiterlebenden als unserer selbst.*

It is a fact that a man's dying is more the survivors' affair than his own.
   Der Zauberberg (The Magic Mountain, 1924) ch. 6, pt. 8

Katherine Mansfield (Kathleen Mansfield Beauchamp) 1888–1923

7 E. M. Forster never gets any further than warming the teapot. He's a rare fine hand at that. Feel this teapot. Is it not beautifully warm? Yes, but there ain't going to be no tea.
   Journal May 1917 (1927) p. 69

8 Whenever I prepare for a journey I prepare as though for death. Should I never return, all is in order. This is what life has taught me.
   Journal 29 Jan. 1922 (1927) p. 224

9 Looking back, I imagine I was always writing. Twaddle it was, too. But better far write twaddle or anything, anything, than nothing at all.
   Journal 1922 (1927) p. 243

Mao Tse-Tung 1893–1976

10 Letting a hundred flowers blossom and a hundred schools of thought contend is the policy for promoting progress in the arts and the sciences and a flourishing socialist culture in our land.
   Speech at Peking, 27 Feb. 1957, in *Quotations of Chairman Mao* (1966) p. 302

11 A revolution is not the same as inviting people to dinner, or writing an essay, or painting a picture. . . . A revolution is an insurrection, an act of violence by which one class overthrows another.
   Report, Mar. 1927, in *Selected Works* (1954) vol. 1, p. 27

12 The atom bomb is a paper tiger which the United States reactionaries use to scare people. It looks terrible, but in fact it isn't. Of course, the atom bomb is a weapon of mass slaughter, but the outcome of a war is decided by the people, not by one or two new types of weapon.
   Interview with Anne Louise Strong, Aug. 1946, in *Selected Works* (1961) vol. 4, p. 100

13 All reactionaries are paper tigers. In appearance, the reactionaries are terrifying, but in reality they are not so

powerful. From a long-term point of view, it is not the reactionaries but the people who are really powerful.

> Interview with Anne Louise Strong, Aug. 1946, in *Selected Works* (1961) vol. 4, p. 100

1 Politics is war without bloodshed while war is politics with bloodshed.

> Lecture, 1938, in *Selected Works* (1965) vol. 2, p. 153

2 Every Communist must grasp the truth, 'Political power grows out of the barrel of a gun'.

> Speech at 6th Plenary Session of 6th Central Committee, 6 Nov. 1938, in *Selected Works* (1965) vol. 2, p. 224

Edwin Markham 1852–1940

3 Bowed by the weight of centuries he leans
Upon his hoe and gazes on the ground,
The emptiness of ages in his face,
And on his back the burden of the world.
Who made him dead to rapture and despair,
A thing that grieves not and that never hopes,
Stolid and stunned, a brother to the ox?

> *Man with the Hoe and Other Poems* (1899) 'Man with the Hoe'

4 He drew a circle that shut me out—
Heretic, rebel, a thing to flout.
But Love and I had the wit to win:
We drew a circle that took him in!

> *Shoes of Happiness* (1915) 'Outwitted'

Dewey 'Pigmeat' Markham 1906–1981

5 Here comes the judge.

> Title of song (1968; written with Dick Alen, Bob Astor, and Sarah Harvey; subsequently a catch-phrase, often in the form 'Here come de judge')

Johnny Marks 1909–1985

6 Rudolph, the Red-Nosed Reindeer
Had a very shiny nose,
And if you ever saw it,
You would even say it glows.

> *Rudolph, the Red-Nosed Reindeer* (1949 song), based on a Robert L. May story (1939)

Don Marquis 1878–1937

7 but wotthehell wotthehell
oh i should worry and fret
death and I will coquette
there s a dance in the old dame yet
toujours gai toujours gai.

> *archy and mehitabel* (1927) 'the song of mehitabel'

8 procrastination is the
art of keeping
up with yesterday.

> *archy and mehitabel* (1927) 'certain maxims of archy'

9 an optimist is a guy
that has never had
much experience.

> *archy and mehitabel* (1927) 'certain maxims of archy'

10 I have got you out here
in the great open spaces
where cats are cats.

> *archy and mehitabel* (1927) 'mehitabel has an adventure'

11 but wotthehell
archy wotthehell
it s cheerio
my deario that
pulls a lady through.

> *archy and mehitabel* (1927) 'cheerio, my deario'

12 but wotthehell archy wotthehell
jamais triste archy jamais triste
that is my motto.

> *archy and mehitabel* (1927) 'mehitabel sees paris'

13 boss there is always
a comforting thought
in time of trouble when
it is not our trouble

> *archy does his part* (1935) 'comforting thoughts'

14 honesty is a good
thing but
it is not profitable to
its possessor
unless it is
kept under control.

> *archys life of mehitabel* (1933) 'archygrams'

15 did you ever
notice that when
a politician
does get an idea

he usually
gets it all wrong.
archys life of mehitabel (1933) no. 40
'archygrams'

1 now and then
there is a person born
who is so unlucky
that he runs into accidents
which started to happen
to somebody else.
archys life of mehitabel (1933) 'archy says'

2 Writing a book of poetry is like dropping
a rose petal down the Grand Canyon and
waiting for the echo.
In E. Anthony *O Rare Don Marquis* (1962)
p. 146

3 The art of newspaper paragraphing is to
stroke a platitude until it purrs like an
epigram.
In E. Anthony *O Rare Don Marquis* (1962)
p. 354

Anthony Marriott 1931–
and Alistair Foot

4 No sex please—we're British.
Title of play (1971)

Arthur Marshall 1910–1989

5 Oh My! Bertha's got a bang on the boko.
Keep a stiff upper lip, Bertha dear. What,
knocked a tooth out? Never mind, dear,
laugh it off, laugh it off; it's all part of
life's rich pageant.
The Games Mistress (recorded monologue,
1937)

Thomas R. Marshall 1854–1925

6 What this country needs is a really good
5-cent cigar.
In *New York Tribune* 4 Jan. 1920, pt. 7, p. 1

Dean Martin 1917–

7 You're not drunk if you can lie on the
floor without holding on.
In Paul Dickson *Official Rules* (1978) p. 112

Holt Marvell

8 A cigarette that bears a lipstick's traces,
An airline ticket to romantic places;
And still my heart has wings

These foolish things
Remind me of you.
These Foolish Things Remind Me of You (1935
song; music by Jack Strachey and Harry
Link)

Chico Marx 1891–1961

9 I wasn't kissing her, I was just
whispering in her mouth.
In Groucho Marx and Richard J. Anobile
Marx Brothers Scrapbook (1973) ch. 24

Groucho Marx 1895–1977

10 From the moment I picked up your book
until I laid it down, I was convulsed with
laughter. Some day I intend reading it.
In Hector Arce *Groucho* (1979) p. 188 (a
blurb written for S. J. Perelman's 1928 book
Dawn Ginsberg's Revenge)

11 I sent the club a wire stating, PLEASE
ACCEPT MY RESIGNATION. I DON'T WANT TO
BELONG TO ANY CLUB THAT WILL ACCEPT
ME AS A MEMBER.
Groucho and Me (1959) ch. 26

12 I never forget a face, but in your case I'll
be glad to make an exception.
In Leo Rosten *People I have Loved, Known or
Admired* (1970) 'Groucho'

Queen Mary 1867–1953

13 'Well, Mr Baldwin!' Queen Mary
exclaimed, stepping briskly into the
room, her hands held out before her in
a gesture of despair, '*this* is a pretty
kettle of fish!'
James Pope-Hennessy *Life of Queen Mary*
(1959) pt. 4, ch. 7 (said on 17 Nov. 1936,
after Edward VIII had told her he was
prepared to give up the throne to marry Mrs
Simpson)

14 So *that's* what hay looks like.
James Pope-Hennessy *Life of Queen Mary*
(1959) pt. 4, ch. 8 (said at Badminton
House, where she was evacuated during the
Second World War)

Eric Maschwitz 1901–1969

15 A nightingale sang in Berkeley Square.
Title of song (1940; music by Manning
Sherwin)

John Masefield 1878–1967

16 Quinquireme of Nineveh from distant
Ophir

Rowing home to haven in sunny
  Palestine,
With a cargo of ivory,
And apes and peacocks,
Sandalwood, cedarwood, and sweet
  white wine.
  Ballads (1903) 'Cargoes'

1 Dirty British coaster with a salt-caked
  smoke stack,
Butting through the Channel in the mad
  March days,
With a cargo of Tyne coal,
Road-rails, pig lead,
Firewood, ironware, and cheap tin trays.
  Ballads (1903) 'Cargoes'

2 Oh some are fond of Spanish wine, and
  some are fond of French,
And some'll swallow tay and stuff fit
  only for a wench.
  Ballads (1903) 'Captain Stratton's Fancy'

3 Oh some are fond of fiddles, and a song
  well sung,
And some are all for music for a lilt
  upon the tongue;
But mouths were made for tankards,
  and for sucking at the bung,
Says the old bold mate of Henry
  Morgan.
  Ballads (1903) 'Captain Stratton's Fancy'

4 I have seen dawn and sunset on moors
  and windy hills,
Coming in solemn beauty like slow old
  tunes of Spain.
  Ballads (1903) 'Beauty'

5 But the loveliest things of beauty God
  ever has showed to me,
Are her voice, and her hair, and eyes,
  and the dear red curve of her lips.
  Ballads (1903) 'Beauty'

6 One road leads to London,
One road runs to Wales,
My road leads me seawards
To the white dipping sails.
  Ballads (1903) 'Roadways'

7 In the dark womb where I began
My mother's life made me a man.
Through all the months of human birth
Her beauty fed my common earth.
I cannot see, nor breathe, nor stir,
But through the death of some of her.
  Ballads and Poems (1910) 'C.L.M.'

8 Jane brought the bowl of stewing gin
And poured the egg and lemon in,

And whisked it up and served it out
While bawdy questions went about.
Jack chucked her chin, and Jim accost
  her
With bits out of the 'Maid of Gloster'.
And fifteen arms went round her waist.
(And then men ask, Are Barmaids
  Chaste?)
  The Everlasting Mercy (1911) st. 26

9 And he who gives a child a treat
Makes joy-bells ring in Heaven's street.
And he who gives a child a home
Builds palaces in Kingdom come,
And she who gives a baby birth
Brings Saviour Christ again to Earth,
For life is joy, and mind is fruit,
And body's precious earth and root.
  The Everlasting Mercy (1911) st. 47

10 The corn that makes the holy bread
By which the soul of man is fed,
The holy bread, the food unpriced,
Thy everlasting mercy, Christ.
  The Everlasting Mercy (1911) st. 86

11 Death opens unknown doors. It is most
  grand to die.
  Pompey The Great (1910) act 2

12 And all the way, that wild high crying,
To cold his blood with the thought of
  dying.
  Reynard the Fox (1919) pt. 2, st. 49

13 The stars grew bright in the winter sky,
The wind came keen with a tang of
  frost,
The brook was troubled for new things
  lost,
The copse was happy for old things
  found,
The fox came home and he went to
  ground.
  Reynard the Fox (1919) pt. 2, st. 137

14 I must down to the seas again, to the
  lonely sea and the sky,
And all I ask is a tall ship and a star to
  steer her by,
And the wheel's kick and the wind's
  song and the white sail's shaking,
And a grey mist on the sea's face and
  a grey dawn breaking.
  Salt-Water Ballads (1902) 'Sea Fever'

15 I must down to the seas again, for the
  call of the running tide
Is a wild call and a clear call that may
  not be denied.
  Salt-Water Ballads (1902) 'Sea Fever'

1 I must down to the seas again, to the
  vagrant gypsy life,
To the gull's way and the whale's way
  where the wind's like a whetted knife;
And all I ask is a merry yarn from
  a laughing fellow-rover,
And quiet sleep and a sweet dream when
  the long trick's over.
  Salt-Water Ballads (1902) 'Sea Fever'

2 It's a warm wind, the west wind, full of
  birds' cries;
I never hear the west wind but tears are
  in my eyes.
For it comes from the west lands, the old
  brown hills,
And April's in the west wind, and
  daffodils.
  Salt-Water Ballads (1902) 'West Wind'

3 It is good to be out on the road, and
  going one knows not where,
Going through meadow and village, one
  knows not whither nor why.
  Salt-Water Ballads (1902) 'Tewkesbury
  Road'

4 In this life he laughs longest who laughs
  last.
  Widow in Bye Street (1912) ch. 4, p. 66

Donald Mason 1913–

5 Sighted sub, sank same.
  Radio message, 28 Jan. 1942, in *New York
  Times* 27 Feb. 1942 (on sinking Japanese
  submarine in the Atlantic region, the first
  US naval success in the war)

Sir James Mathew 1830–1908

6 In England, justice is open to all—like
  the Ritz Hotel.
  In R. E. Megarry *Miscellany-at-Law* (1955)
  p. 254

Melissa Mathison 1950–

7 E.T. phone home.
  E.T. (1982 film; directed by Steven
  Spielberg)

Henri Matisse 1869–1954

8 *Ce que je rêve, c'est un art d'équilibre, de
  pureté, de tranquillité, sans sujet inquiétant
  ou préoccupant, qui soit . . . un lénifiant, un
  calmant cérébral, quelque chose d'analogue*
  *à un bon fauteuil qui le délasse de ses
  fatigues physiques.*

What I dream of is an art of balance, of
  purity and serenity devoid of troubling
  or depressing subject matter . . . a
  soothing, calming influence on the
  mind, something like a good armchair
  which provides relaxation from physical
  fatigue.
  Notes d'un peintre (Notes of a Painter, 1908)
  in Dominique Fourcade *Écrits et propos sur
  l'art* (1972) p. 30

Reginald Maudling 1917–1979

9 There comes a time in every man's life
  when he must make way for an older
  man.
  Remark after he was dropped from the
  Shadow Cabinet and replaced by an older
  man, in *Guardian* 20 Nov. 1976

W. Somerset Maugham
1874–1965

10 Hypocrisy is the most difficult and
  nerve-racking vice that any man can
  pursue; it needs an unceasing vigilance
  and a rare detachment of spirit. It
  cannot, like adultery or gluttony, be
  practised at spare moments; it is
  a whole-time job.
  Cakes and Ale (1930) ch. 1

11 This is not so strange when you reflect
  that from the earliest times the old have
  rubbed it into the young that they are
  wiser than they, and before the young
  had discovered what nonsense this was
  they were old too, and it profited them
  to carry on the imposture.
  Cakes and Ale (1930) ch. 11

12 Poor Henry [James], he's spending
  eternity wandering round and round
  a stately park and the fence is just too
  high for him to peep over and they're
  having tea just too far away for him to
  hear what the countess is saying.
  Cakes and Ale (1930) ch. 11

13 You can't learn too soon that the most
  useful thing about a principle is that it
  can always be sacrificed to expediency.
  Circle (1921) act 3

14 A woman will always sacrifice herself if
  you give her the opportunity. It is her

favourite form of self-indulgence.
Circle (1921) act 3

1 'Dying' he [Maugham] said to me, 'is
a very dull, dreary affair.' Suddenly he
smiled. 'And my advice to you is to have
nothing whatever to do with it,' he
added.
Robin Maugham *Escape from the Shadows*
(1972) pt. 5, p. 233

2 There can be nothing so gratifying to an
author as to arouse the respect and
esteem of the reader. Make him laugh
and he will think you a trivial fellow,
but bore him in the right way and your
reputation is assured.
Gentleman in the Parlour (1930) ch. 11

3 God knows that I have never been that
[anti-Semitic]; some of my best friends
both in England and America are Jews.
Letter, May 1946, in Ted Morgan *Somerset
Maugham* (1980) ch. 6

4 I forget who it was that recommended
men for their soul's good to do each day
two things they disliked: it was a wise
man, and it is a precept that I have
followed scrupulously; for every day
I have got up and I have gone to bed.
Moon and Sixpence (1919) ch. 2

5 Impropriety is the soul of wit.
Moon and Sixpence (1919) ch. 4

6 She saw shrewdly that the world is
quickly bored by the recital of
misfortune, and willingly avoids the
sight of distress.
Moon and Sixpence (1919) ch. 16

7 It is not true that suffering ennobles the
character; happiness does that
sometimes, but suffering, for the most
part, makes men petty and vindictive.
Moon and Sixpence (1919) ch. 17

8 'A woman can forgive a man for the
harm he does her,' he said, 'but she can
never forgive him for the sacrifices he
makes on her account.'
Moon and Sixpence (1919) ch. 41

9 Like all weak men he laid an
exaggerated stress on not changing
one's mind.
Of Human Bondage (1915) ch. 39

10 People ask you for criticism, but they
only want praise.
Of Human Bondage (1915) ch. 50

11 Money is like a sixth sense without
which you cannot make a complete use
of the other five.
Of Human Bondage (1915) ch. 51

12 It was such a lovely day I thought it was
a pity to get up.
Our Betters (1923) act 3

13 I would sooner read a time-table or
a catalogue than nothing at all. . . . They
are much more entertaining than half
the novels that are written.
Summing Up (1938) p. 92

14 The common idea that success spoils
people by making them vain, egotistic
and self-complacent is erroneous; on the
contrary it makes them, for the most
part, humble, tolerant and kind. Failure
makes people bitter and cruel.
Summing Up (1938) p. 187

15 *Lucky Jim* [by Kingsley Amis] is
a remarkable novel. It has been greatly
praised and widely read, but I have not
noticed that any of the reviewers have
remarked on its ominous significance.
I am told that today rather more than
60 per cent of the men who go to the
universities go on a Government grant.
This is a new class that has entered
upon the scene. . . . They are scum.
Sunday Times 25 Dec. 1955

16 At a dinner party one should eat wisely
but not too well, and talk well but not
too wisely.
Writer's Notebook (1949) p. 17 (written in
1896)

17 Few misfortunes can befall a boy which
bring worse consequences than to have
a really affectionate mother.
Writer's Notebook (1949) p. 27 (written in
1896)

Bill Mauldin 1921–

18 I feel like a fugitive from th' law of
averages.
Up Front (1945) cartoon caption

James Maxton 1885–1946

19 All I say is, if you cannot ride two horses
you have no right in the circus.
Said at Scottish Independent Labour Party
Conference on being told that he could not
be in two parties, in *Daily Herald* 12 Jan.
1931

John May

1 You're never alone with a Strand.
Slogan for Strand cigarettes, 1960, in Nigel Rees *Slogans* (1982) p. 108

Percy Mayfield 1920–1984

2 Hit the road, Jack.
Title of song (1961)

Charles H. Mayo 1865–1939

3 The definition of a specialist as one who 'knows more and more about less and less' is good and true.
Modern Hospital Sept. 1938, p. 69

Margaret Mead 1901–1978

4 Women want mediocre men, and men are working hard to be as mediocre as possible.
In *Quote Magazine* 15 June 1958

Shepherd Mead 1914–

5 How to succeed in business without really trying.
Title of book (1952)

Hughes Mearns 1875–1965

6 As I was walking up the stair
I met a man who wasn't there.
He wasn't there again today.
I wish, I wish he'd stay away.
The Psycho-ed (1910 play), in *Newsweek* 15 Jan. 1940

Dame Nellie Melba (Helen Porter Mitchell) 1861–1931

7 So you're going to Australia! Well, *I* made twenty thousand pounds on my tour there, but of course *that* will never be done again. Still, it's a wonderful country, and you'll have a good time. What are you going to sing? All I can say is—sing 'em muck! It's all they can understand!
Advice to Dame Clara Butt, in W. H. Ponder *Clara Butt* (1928) ch. 12

H. L. Mencken 1880–1956

8 Here, indeed, was his [Calvin Coolidge's] one peculiar *Fach*, his one really notable talent. He slept more than any other

President, whether by day or by night. Nero fiddled, but Coolidge only snored.
American Mercury Apr. 1933

9 The saddest life is that of a political aspirant under democracy. His failure is ignominious and his success is disgraceful.
Baltimore Evening Sun 9 Dec. 1929

10 No one in this world, so far as I know— and I have searched the records for years, and employed agents to help me—has ever lost money by underestimating the intelligence of the great masses of the plain people.
Chicago Tribune 19 Sept. 1926

11 When women kiss it always reminds one of prize-fighters shaking hands.
Chrestomathy (1949) ch. 30

12 Love is the delusion that one woman differs from another.
Chrestomathy (1949) ch. 30

13 Men have a much better time of it than women. For one thing, they marry later. For another thing, they die earlier.
Chrestomathy (1949) ch. 30

14 Puritanism. The haunting fear that someone, somewhere, may be happy.
Chrestomathy (1949) ch. 30

15 Democracy is the theory that the common people know what they want, and deserve to get it good and hard.
Little Book in C major (1916) p. 19

16 Conscience: the inner voice which warns us that someone may be looking.
Little Book in C major (1916) p. 42

17 I've made it a rule never to drink by daylight and never to refuse a drink after dark.
New York Post 18 Sept. 1945

18 It is now quite lawful for a Catholic woman to avoid pregnancy by a resort to mathematics, though she is still forbidden to resort to physics and chemistry.
Notebooks (1956) 'Minority Report'

19 The capacity of human beings to bore one another seems to be vastly greater than that of any other animals. Some of their most esteemed inventions have no other apparent purpose, for example, the dinner party of more than two, the epic poem, and the science of metaphysics.
Notebooks (1956) 'Minority Report'

1 All successful newspapers are ceaselessly
querulous and bellicose. They never
defend any one or anything if they can
help it; if the job is forced upon them,
they tackle it by denouncing some one
or something else.
Prejudices (1919) 1st ser., ch. 13

2 Poetry is a comforting piece of fiction set
to more or less lascivious music.
Prejudices (1922) 3rd ser., ch. 7

3 Faith may be defined briefly as an
illogical belief in the occurrence of the
improbable.
Prejudices (1922) 3rd ser., ch. 14

4 If, after I depart this vale, you ever
remember me and have thought to
please my ghost, forgive some sinner
and wink your eye at some homely girl.
Smart Set Dec. 1921

David Mercer 1928–1980

5 A suitable case for treatment.
Title of play (1962) in *Three TV Comedies*
(1966)

Johnny Mercer 1909–1976

6 You've got to ac-cent-tchu-ate the
positive
Elim-my-nate the negative
Latch on to the affirmative
Don't mess with Mister In-between.
Ac-cent-tchu-ate the Positive (1944 song;
music by Harold Arlen)

7 We're drinking my friend,
To the end of a brief episode,
Make it one for my baby
And one more for the road.
One For My Baby (1943 song; music by
Harold Arlen)

8 That old black magic.
Title of song (1942; music by Harold Arlen)

Bob Merrill

9 How much is that doggie in the
window?
Title of song (1953)

Dixon Lanier Merritt 1879–1972

10 Oh, a wondrous bird is the pelican!
His beak holds more than his belican.
He takes in his beak
Food enough for a week.

But I'll be darned if I know how the
helican.
Nashville Banner 22 Apr. 1913

Viola Meynell 1886–1956

11 The dust comes secretly day after day,
Lies on my ledge and dulls my shining
things.
But O this dust that I shall drive away
Is flowers and Kings,
Is Solomon's temple, poets, Nineveh.
Verses (1919) 'Dusting'

Princess Michael of Kent 1945–

12 I don't enjoy my public obligations.
I was not made to cut ribbons and kiss
babies.
Life Nov. 1986

George Mikes 1912–

13 On the Continent people have good food;
in England people have good table
manners.
How to be an Alien (1946) p. 10

14 Continental people have sex life; the
English have hot-water bottles.
How to be an Alien (1946) p. 25

15 An Englishman, even if he is alone,
forms an orderly queue of one.
How to be an Alien (1946) p. 44

Edna St Vincent Millay
1892–1950

16 Down, down, down into the darkness of
the grave
Gently they go, the beautiful, the tender,
the kind;
Quietly they go, the intelligent, the
witty, the brave.
I know. But I do not approve. And I am
not resigned.
Buck in the Snow (1928) 'Dirge Without
Music'

17 My candle burns at both ends;
It will not last the night;
But ah, my foes, and oh, my friends—
It gives a lovely light.
A Few Figs From Thistles (1920) 'First Fig'

18 Safe upon solid rock the ugly houses
stand:
Come and see my shining palace built
upon the sand!
A Few Figs From Thistles (1920) 'Second Fig'

1 I only know that summer sang in me
 A little while, that in me sings no more.
   Harp-Weaver and Other Poems (1923) sonnet
   19

2 Euclid alone
 Has looked on Beauty bare. Fortunate
   they
 Who, though once only and then but far
   away,
 Have heard her massive sandal set on
   stone.
   Harp-Weaver and Other Poems (1923) sonnet
   22

3 It's not true that life is one damn thing
 after another—it's one damn thing over
 and over.
   Letter to Arthur Davison Ficke, 24 Oct.
   1930, in A. R. Macdougal *Letters of Edna St
   V. Millay* (1952) p. 240

4 Death devours all lovely things;
 Lesbia with her sparrow
 Shares the darkness—presently
 Every bed is narrow.
   Second April (1921) 'Passer Mortuus Est'

5 After all, my erstwhile dear,
 My no longer cherished,
 Need we say it was not love,
 Now that love is perished?
   Second April (1921) 'Passer Mortuus Est'

6 Childhood is not from birth to a certain
   age and at a certain age
 The child is grown, and puts away
   childish things.
 Childhood is the kingdom where nobody
   dies.
 Nobody that matters, that is.
   Wine from these Grapes (1934) 'Childhood is
   the Kingdom where Nobody dies'

Alice Duer Miller 1874–1942

7 I am American bred,
 I have seen much to hate here—much
   to forgive,
 But in a world where England is finished
   and dead,
 I do not wish to live.
   White Cliffs (1940) p. 70

Arthur Miller 1915–

8 I don't say he's a great man. Willy
 Loman never made a lot of money. His
 name was never in the paper. He's not
 the finest character that ever lived. But
 he's a human being, and a terrible thing

is happening to him. So attention must
be paid. He's not to be allowed to fall
into his grave like an old dog. Attention,
attention must be finally paid to such
a person.
   Death of a Salesman (1949) act 1

9 Willy was a salesman. And for
 a salesman, there is no rock bottom to
 the life. He don't put a bolt to a nut, he
 don't tell you the law or give you
 medicine. He's a man way out there in
 the blue, riding on a smile and
 a shoeshine. And when they start not
 smiling back—that's an earthquake.
 And then you get yourself a couple of
 spots on your hat, and you're finished.
 Nobody dast blame this man.
 A salesman is got to dream, boy. It
 comes with the territory.
   Death of a Salesman (1949) 'Requiem'

10 I used . . . to keep a book in which
 I would talk to myself. One of the
 aphorisms I wrote was, 'The structure of
 a play is always the story of how the
 birds came home to roost.'
   Harper's Magazine Aug. 1958

11 Roslyn: 'How do you find your way
 back in the dark?' Gay nods, indicating
 the sky before them: 'Just head for that
 big star straight on. The highway's
 under it; take us right home.'
   The Misfits (1961) ch. 12

12 A good newspaper, I suppose, is a nation
 talking to itself.
   In *Observer* 26 Nov. 1961

Henry Miller 1891–1980

13 Even before the music begins there is
 that bored look on people's faces.
 A polite form of self-imposed torture, the
 concert.
   Tropic of Cancer (1934) p. 84

14 Every man with a bellyful of the classics
 is an enemy to the human race.
   Tropic of Cancer (1934) p. 280

Jonathan Miller 1934–

15 In fact, I'm not really a *Jew*. Just Jew-*ish*.
 Not the whole hog, you know.
   Beyond the Fringe (1960) 'Real Class', in
   Alan Bennett et al. *Complete Beyond the
   Fringe* (1987) p. 84

Spike Milligan (Terence Alan Milligan) 1918–

1 GRYTPYPE-THYNNE: You silly twisted boy.

Dreaded Batter Pudding Hurler in The Goon Show (BBC radio series) 12 Oct. 1954, in Goon Show Scripts (1972) p. 26

2 SEAGOON: Ying tong iddle I po.

Dreaded Batter Pudding Hurler in The Goon Show (BBC radio series) 12 Oct. 1954, in Goon Show Scripts (1972) p. 27; catch-phrase also used in The Ying Tong Song (1956)

3 He's fallen in the water.

Catch-phrase used by 'Little Jim' (Spike Milligan) in The Goon Show (BBC radio series, used from 1956 onwards)

4 BLUEBOTTLE: You rotten swines. I told you I'd be deaded.

Hastings Flyer in The Goon Show (BBC radio series) 3 Jan. 1956, in Goon Show Scripts (1972) p. 170

5 I'm walking backwards for Christmas
Across the Irish Sea.

I'm Walking Backwards for Christmas (1956 song)

6 MORIARTY: Sapristi Nuckoes—do you always drink ink?
SEAGOON: Only in the mating season.
MORIARTY: Shall we dance?

Napoleon's Piano in The Goon Show (BBC radio series) 11 Oct. 1955, in Goon Show Scripts (1972) p. 100

7 BLUEBOTTLE: I don't like this game, let's play another game—let's play doctor and nurses.

The Phantom Head-Shaver in The Goon Show (BBC radio series) 15 Oct. 1954, in Goon Show Scripts (1972) p. 54 (the catch-phrase was often 'I do not like this game')

8 Money couldn't buy friends but you got a better class of enemy.

Puckoon (1963) ch. 6

A. J. Mills, Fred Godfrey, and Bennett Scott

9 Take me back to dear old Blighty,
Put me on the train for London town.

Take Me Back to Dear Old Blighty (1916 song)

Irving Mills 1894–1985

10 It don't mean a thing
If it ain't got that swing.

It Don't Mean a Thing (1932 song; music by Duke Ellington)

A. A. Milne 1882–1956

11 The more it snows
(Tiddely pom),
The more it goes
(Tiddely pom),
The more it goes
(Tiddely pom)
On snowing.
And nobody knows
(Tiddely pom),
How cold my toes
(Tiddely pom),
How cold my toes
(Tiddely pom),
Are growing.

House at Pooh Corner (1928) ch. 1

12 Tiggers don't like honey.

House at Pooh Corner (1928) ch. 2

13 King John was not a good man—
He had his little ways.
And sometimes no one spoke to him
For days and days and days.

Now We Are Six (1927) 'King John's Christmas'

14 When I was young, we *always* had mornings like this.

Toad of Toad Hall (1929) act 2, sc. 3 (Milne's dramatization of Kenneth Grahame's Wind in the Willows)

15 They're changing guard at Buckingham Palace—
Christopher Robin went down with Alice.
Alice is marrying one of the guard.
'A soldier's life is terrible hard,'
Says Alice.

When We Were Very Young (1924) 'Buckingham Palace'

16 John had
Great Big
Waterproof
Boots on;
John had a
Great Big
Waterproof
Hat;
John had a
Great Big

Waterproof
Mackintosh—
And that
(Said John)
Is
That.
> *When We Were Very Young* (1924)
> 'Happiness'

1 James James
Morrison Morrison
Weatherby George Dupree
Took great
Care of his Mother,
Though he was only three.
James James
Said to his Mother,
'Mother,' he said, said he;
'You must never go down to the end of
    the town, if you don't go down with
    me.'
> *When We Were Very Young* (1924)
> 'Disobedience'

2 *What* is the matter with Mary Jane?
She's perfectly well and she hasn't
    a pain,
*And it's lovely rice pudding for dinner
    again!*
What *is* the matter with Mary Jane?
> *When We Were Very Young* (1924) 'Rice
> Pudding'

3 The King asked
The Queen, and
The Queen asked
The Dairymaid:
'Could we have some butter for
The Royal slice of bread?'
> *When We Were Very Young* (1924) 'The
> King's Breakfast'

4 The King said
'Butter, eh?'
And bounced out of bed.
> *When We Were Very Young* (1924) 'The
> King's Breakfast'

5 Nobody,
My darling,
Could call me
A fussy man—
BUT
I do like a little bit of butter to my bread!
> *When We Were Very Young* (1924) 'The
> King's Breakfast'

6 Little Boy kneels at the foot of the bed,
Droops on the little hands little gold
    head.

Hush! Hush! Whisper who dares!
Christopher Robin is saying his prayers.
> *When We Were Very Young* (1924) 'Vespers'

7 Isn't it funny
How a bear likes honey?
Buzz! Buzz! Buzz!
I wonder why he does?
> *Winnie-the-Pooh* (1926) ch. 1

8 How sweet to be a Cloud
Floating in the Blue!
It makes him very proud
To be a little cloud.
> *Winnie-the-Pooh* (1926) ch. 1

9 Pooh always liked a little something at
eleven o'clock in the morning, and he
was very glad to see Rabbit getting out
the plates and mugs; and when Rabbit
said, 'Honey or condensed milk with
your bread?' he was so excited that he
said, 'Both,' and then, so as not to seem
greedy, he added, 'But don't bother
about the bread, please.' And for a long
time after that he said nothing ... until
at last, humming to himself in a rather
sticky voice, he got up, shook Rabbit
lovingly by the paw, and said that he
must be going on.
> *Winnie-the-Pooh* (1926) ch. 2

10 'Well,' said Owl, 'the customary
procedure in such cases is as follows.'
'What does Crustimoney Proseedcake
mean?' said Pooh. 'For I am a Bear of
Very Little Brain, and long words Bother
me.'
> *Winnie-the-Pooh* (1926) ch. 4

11 Eeyore, the old grey Donkey, stood by
the side of the stream, and looked at
himself in the water. 'Pathetic,' he said.
'That's what it is. Pathetic.'
> *Winnie-the-Pooh* (1926) ch. 6

12 Cottleston, Cottleston, Cottleston Pie.
A fly can't bird, but a bird can fly.
Ask me a riddle and I reply:
'Cottleston, Cottleston, Cottleston Pie.'
> *Winnie-the-Pooh* (1926) ch. 6

13 Time for a little something.
> *Winnie-the-Pooh* (1926) ch. 6

14 My spelling is Wobbly. It's good spelling
but it Wobbles, and the letters get in the
wrong places.
> *Winnie-the-Pooh* (1926) ch. 6

15 On Monday, when the sun is hot
I wonder to myself a lot:

'Now is it true, or is it not,
'That what is which and which is
    what?'
Winnie-the-Pooh (1926) ch. 7

1 3 Cheers for Pooh!
(*For Who?*)
For Pooh—
(*Why what did he do?*)
I thought you knew;
He saved his friend from a wetting!
Winnie-the-Pooh (1926) ch. 10

Lord Milner (*Alfred, Viscount Milner*) 1854–1925

2 If we believe a thing to be bad, and if we
have a right to prevent it, it is our duty
to try to prevent it and to damn the
consequences.
Speech at Glasgow, 26 Nov. 1909, in *The
Times* 27 Nov. 1909

Adrian Mitchell 1932–

3 Most people ignore most poetry
because
most poetry ignores most people.
Poems (1964) p. 8

Joni Mitchell 1945–

4 I've looked at life from both sides now,
From win and lose and still somehow
It's life's illusions I recall;
I really don't know life at all.
Both Sides Now (1967 song)

5 They paved paradise
And put up a parking lot,
With a pink hotel,
A boutique, and a swinging hot spot.
Big Yellow Taxi (1970 song)

6 We are stardust,
We are golden,
And we got to get ourselves
Back to the garden.
Woodstock (1969 song)

Margaret Mitchell 1900–1949

7 Death and taxes and childbirth! There's
never any convenient time for any of
them.
Gone with the Wind (1936) ch. 38

8 Scarlett . . . I wish I could care what you
do or where you go but I can't. . . . My
dear, I don't give a damn.
Gone with the Wind (1936) ch. 57 (in Sidney
Howard's script for the film version (1939)
this became 'Frankly, my dear, I don't give
a damn!')

9 Tomorrow, I'll think of some way to get
him back. After all, tomorrow is another
day.
Gone with the Wind (1936) ch. 57 (closing
words)

Jessica Mitford 1917–

10 According to one of my correspondents,
Jessica Mitford was overheard to remark,
'I have nothing against undertakers
personally. It's just that I wouldn't want
one to bury my sister.'
Saturday Review 1 Feb. 1964

Nancy Mitford 1904–1973

11 'Always be civil to the girls, you never
know who they may marry' is an
aphorism which has saved many an
English spinster from being treated like
an Indian widow.
Love in a Cold Climate (1949) pt. 1, ch. 2

12 'Twenty three and a quarter minutes
past,' Uncle Matthew was saying
furiously, 'in precisely six and
three-quarter minutes the damned fella
will be late.'
Love in a Cold Climate (1949) pt. 1, ch. 13

13 An aristocracy in a republic is like
a chicken whose head has been cut off:
it may run about in a lively way, but in
fact it is dead.
Noblesse Oblige (1956) p. 39

14 I have only ever read one book in my
life, and that is *White Fang*. It's so
frightfully good I've never bothered to
read another.
Pursuit of Love (1945) ch. 9

15 Uncle Matthew's four years in France
and Italy between 1914 and 1918 had
given him no great opinion of foreigners.
'Frogs,' he would say, 'are slightly better
than Huns or Wops, but abroad is
unutterably bloody and foreigners are
fiends.'
Pursuit of Love (1945) ch. 15

Addison Mizner 1892–1933

See ETHEL WATTS MUMFORD

Wilson Mizner 1876–1933

1 Among his [Mizner's] philosophical maxims were 'Be nice to people on your way up because you'll meet 'em on your way down', 'Treat a whore like a lady and a lady like a whore', and 'If you steal from one author, it's plagiarism; if you steal from many, it's research'.

Alva Johnston *The Legendary Mizners* (1953) ch. 4

2 Mizner's comment on Hollywood, 'It's a trip through a sewer in a glass-bottomed boat', was converted by Mayor Jimmy Walker into 'A reformer is a guy who rides through a sewer in a glass-bottomed boat'.

Alva Johnston *The Legendary Mizners* (1953) ch. 4

Walter Mondale 1928–

See CLIFF FREEMAN

William Cosmo Monkhouse 1840–1901

3 There once was an old man of Lyme
Who married three wives at a time,
When asked 'Why a third?'
He replied, 'One's absurd!
And bigamy, Sir, is a crime!'

Nonsense Rhymes (1902)

Harold Monro 1879–1932

4 When the tea is brought at five o'clock,
And all the neat curtains are drawn with care,
The little black cat with bright green eyes
Is suddenly purring there.

Children of Love (1914) 'Milk for the Cat'

Marilyn Monroe 1926–1962

5 Asked if she really had nothing on in the [calendar] photograph, Marilyn, her blue eyes wide, purred: 'I had the radio on.'

Time 11 Aug. 1952

C. E. Montague 1867–1928

6 War hath no fury like a non-combatant.

Disenchantment (1922) ch. 16

Field-Marshal Montgomery (Viscount Montgomery of Alamein) 1887–1976

7 Rule 1, on page 1 of the book of war, is: 'Do not march on Moscow'. Various people have tried it, Napoleon and Hitler, and it is no good. That is the first rule. I do not know whether your Lordships will know Rule 2 of war. It is: 'Do not go fighting with your land armies in China.' It is a vast country, with no clearly defined objectives, and an army fighting there would be engulfed by what is known as the Ming Bing, the people's insurgents.

Hansard (Lords) 30 May 1962, col. 227

8 Far from helping these unnatural practices along, surely our task is to build a bulwark which will defy evil influences which are seeking to undermine the very foundations of our national character—defy them; do not help them. I have heard some say—and, indeed, the noble Earl said so himself—that such practices are allowed in France and in other NATO countries. We are not French, and we are not other nationals. We are British, thank God!

Hansard (Lords) 24 May 1965, col. 648 (2nd reading of Sexual Offences Bill)

George Moore 1852–1933

9 All reformers are bachelors.

Bending of the Bough (1900) act 1

10 A man travels the world in search of what he needs and returns home to find it.

Brook Kerith (1916) ch. 11

11 Had I not myself written, only half conscious of the truth, that art must be parochial in the beginning to become cosmopolitan in the end?

Hail and Farewell: Ave (1911) p. 3

12 The lot of critics is to be remembered by what they failed to understand.

Impressions and Opinions (1891) 'Balzac'

13 Our contention is . . . that acting is therefore the lowest of the arts, if it be an art at all.

Impressions and Opinions (1891) 'Mummer-Worship'

Marianne Moore 1887–1972

1 O to be a dragon,
  a symbol of the power of Heaven—of silkworm
size or immense; at times invisible.
Felicitous phenomenon!
   O To Be a Dragon (1959) title poem

2 I, too, dislike it: there are things that are important beyond all this fiddle.
  Reading it, however, with a perfect contempt for it, one discovers in it, after all, a place for the genuine.
   Selected Poems (1935) 'Poetry'

3 Nor till the poets among us can be 'literalists of
the imagination'—above
insolence and triviality and can present
for inspection, imaginary gardens with
  real toads in them, shall we have it.
   Selected Poems (1935) 'Poetry'

4 My father used to say,
  'Superior people never make long visits,
have to be shown Longfellow's grave
or the glass flowers at Harvard.'
   Selected Poems (1935) 'Silence'

5 Nor was he insincere in saying, 'Make my house your inn.'
Inns are not residences.
   Selected Poems (1935) 'Silence'

Larry Morey 1905–1971

6 Heigh-ho, heigh-ho,
It's off to work we go.
   Heigh-Ho (1937 song; music by Frank Churchill)

7 Whistle while you work.
   Title of song (1937; music by Frank Churchill)

Robin Morgan 1941–

8 Sisterhood is powerful.
   Title of book (1970)

Christian Morgenstern 1871–1914

9 *Es war einmal ein Lattenzaun,*
mit Zwischenraum, hindurchzuschaun.
Ein Architekt, der dieses sah,
Stand eines Abends plötzlich da—
und nahm den Zwischenraum heraus
und baute draus ein grosses Haus.

One time there was a picket fence
With space to gaze from hence to thence.
An architect who saw this sight
Approached it suddenly one night,
Removed the spaces from the fence
And built of them a residence.
   Galgenlieder (Gallows Songs, 1905) 'Der Lattenzaun'; tr. Max Knight 1963

Christopher Morley 1890–1957

10 Life is a foreign language: all men mispronounce it.
   Thunder on the Left (1925) ch. 14

Lord Morley (John, Viscount Morley of Blackburn) 1838–1923

11 Simplicity of character is no hindrance to subtlety of intellect.
   Life of Gladstone (1903) vol. 1, p. 194

12 You have not converted a man, because you have silenced him.
   On Compromise (1874) ch. 5

Desmond Morris 1928–

13 Clearly, then, the city is not a concrete jungle, it is a human zoo.
   The Human Zoo (1969) p. 8

14 There are one hundred and ninety-three living species of monkeys and apes. One hundred and ninety-two of them are covered with hair. The exception is a naked ape self-named *Homo sapiens*.
   The Naked Ape (1967) p. 9

Herbert Morrison (Baron Morrison of Lambeth) 1888–1965

15 Work is the call. Work at war speed. Good-night—and go to it.
   Broadcast as Minister of Supply, 22 May 1940, in *Daily Herald* 23 May 1940

Jim Morrison 1943–1971, Ray Manzarek 1935– , Robby Krieger 1946– , and John Densmore 1945–

16 C'mon, baby, light my fire.
   Light My Fire (1967 song)

R. F. Morrison

1 Just a wee deoch-an-doris,
Just a wee yin, that's a'.
Just a wee deoch-an-doris,
Before we gang awa'.
There's a wee wifie waitin',
In a wee but-an-ben;
If you can say
'It's a braw bricht moonlicht nicht',
Ye're a' richt, ye ken.

  Just a Wee Deoch-an-Doris (1911 song;
  music by Whit Cunliffe; sung by Harry
  Lauder)

Dwight Morrow 1873–1931

2 The world is divided into people who do
things and people who get the credit.
Try, if you can, to belong to the first
class. There's far less competition.

  Letter to his son, in Harold Nicolson *Dwight
  Morrow* (1935) ch. 3

John Mortimer 1923–

3 No brilliance is needed in the law.
Nothing but common sense, and
relatively clean finger nails.

  Voyage Round My Father (1971) act 1

J. B. Morton ('Beachcomber')
1893–1975

4 One disadvantage of being a hog is that
at any moment some blundering fool
may try to make a silk purse out of your
wife's ear.

  By the Way (1931) p. 282

5 Hush, hush,
Nobody cares!
Christopher Robin
Has
  Fallen
    Down-
      Stairs.

  By the Way (1931) p. 367

6 Mr Justice Cocklecarrot began the
hearing of a very curious case yesterday.
A Mrs Tasker is accused of continually
ringing the doorbell of a Mrs Renton,
and then, when the door is opened,
pushing a dozen red-bearded dwarfs into
the hall and leaving them there.

  Diet of Thistles (1938) pt. 7

7 The Doctor is said also to have invented
an extraordinary weapon which will
make war less brutal. It is described as
a very powerful liquid which rots braces
at a distance of a mile.

  Gallimaufry (1936) 'Bracerot'

8 The man with the false nose had gone to
that bourne from which no
hollingsworth returns.

  Gallimaufry (1936) 'Another True Story'

9 Dr Strabismus (Whom God Preserve) of
Utrecht has patented a new invention. It
is an illuminated trouser-clip for
bicyclists who are using main roads at
night.

  Morton's Folly (1933) p. 99

Rogers Morton 1914–1979

10 After losing five of the last six primaries,
President Ford's campaign manager,
Rogers Morton, was asked if he plans
any change in strategy. Said Morton:
'I'm not going to rearrange the furniture
on the deck of the Titanic.'

  Washington Post 16 May 1976, p. C8

Sir Oswald Mosley 1896–1980

11 I am not, and never have been, a man of
the right. My position was on the left
and is now in the centre of politics.

  Letter in *The Times* 26 Apr. 1968

Lord Louis Mountbatten (Viscount
Mountbatten of Burma)
1900–1979

12 I can't think of a more wonderful
thanksgiving for the life I have had than
that everyone should be jolly at my
funeral.

  In Richard Hough *Mountbatten* (1980) p. 3

13 As a military man who has given half
a century of active service, I say in all
sincerity that the nuclear arms race has
no military purpose. Wars cannot be
fought with nuclear weapons. Their
existence only adds to our perils because
of the illusions which they have
generated.

  Speech at Strasbourg, 11 May 1979, in P.
  Ziegler *Mountbatten* (1985) ch. 52

Lord Moynihan (Berkeley Moynihan, Baron Moynihan) 1865–1936

1 Lord Dawson of Penn
Has killed lots of men.
So that's why we sing
God save the King.
   In Kenneth Rose *King George V* (1983) ch. 9

Robert Mugabe 1924–

2 Cricket civilizes people and creates good gentlemen. I want everyone to play cricket in Zimbabwe; I want ours to be a nation of gentlemen.
   In *Sunday Times* 26 Feb. 1984

Kitty Muggeridge

3 David Frost has risen without trace.
   Said *c*.1965 to Malcolm Muggeridge

Malcolm Muggeridge 1903–1990

4 An orgy looks particularly alluring seen through the mists of righteous indignation.
   The Most of Malcolm Muggeridge (1966)
   'Dolce Vita in a Cold Climate'

5 Once in the lobby of the Midland Hotel in Manchester when I happened to be in some public disfavour, a man came up to me, grasped my hand and observed: 'Never forget that only dead fish swim with the stream.'
   Radio Times 9 July 1964

6 Good taste and humour . . . are a contradiction in terms, like a chaste whore.
   Time 14 Sept. 1953

7 The orgasm has replaced the Cross as the focus of longing and the image of fulfilment.
   Tread Softly (1966) p. 46

8 As has truly been said in his days as an active politician, he [Sir Anthony Eden] was not only a bore; he bored for England.
   Tread Softly (1966) p. 147

Edwin Muir 1887–1959

9 And without fear the lawless roads
Ran wrong through all the land.
   Journeys and Places (1937) 'Hölderlin's Journey'

Herbert J. Muller 1905–

10 Few have heard of Fra Luca Pacioli, the inventor of double-entry book-keeping; but he has probably had much more influence on human life than has Dante or Michelangelo.
   Uses of the Past (1957) ch. 8

Ethel Watts Mumford 1878–1940, Oliver Herford 1863–1935, and Addison Mizner 1872–1933

11 In the midst of life we are in debt.
   Altogether New Cynic's Calendar (1907)—a parody of Book of Common Prayer: see *Oxford Dictionary of Quotations* (1979) 389:12

12 God gives us our relatives—thank God we can choose our friends.
   Cynic's Calendar (1903)

Lewis Mumford 1895–

13 Every generation revolts against its fathers and makes friends with its grandfathers.
   The Brown Decades (1931) p. 3

14 Our national flower is the concrete cloverleaf.
   Quote Magazine 8 Oct. 1961

Sir Alfred Munnings 1878–1959

15 I find myself a President of a body of men who are what I call shilly-shallying. They feel that there is something in this so-called modern art. . . . I myself would rather have—excuse me, my Lord Archbishop—a damned bad failure, a bad, dusty old picture where somebody has tried to do something, to set down something that they have seen and felt, than all this affected juggling, this following of well—shall we call it the school of Paris? . . . Anthony Blunt . . . once stood in this room with me when the King's pictures were here. And there was a Reynolds hanging there and he said, 'That Reynolds isn't as great as a Picasso.' Believe me, what an extraordinary thing for a man to say.
   Speech at Royal Academy, 28 Apr. 1949, in *The Finish* (1952) ch. 22

Richard Murdoch 1907–1990 and Kenneth Horne 1900–1969

1 Have you read any good books lately?
   Catch-phrase used by Richard Murdoch in
   radio comedy series
   Much-Binding-in-the-Marsh (started 2 Jan.
   1947)

2 Good morning, sir—was there
   something?
   Catch-phrase used by Sam Costa in radio
   comedy series *Much-Binding-in-the-Marsh*
   (started 2 Jan. 1947), in Norman Hackforth
   Solo for Horne (1976) p. 58

C. W. Murphy and Will Letters

3 Has anybody here seen Kelly?
   Kelly from the Isle of Man?
   Has Anybody Here Seen Kelly? (1909 song)

Ed Murphy

4 I was project manager at Edwards
   Airforce Base during Colonel J. P.
   Stapp's experimental crash research
   testing on the track at North Base. The
   law's namesake was Captain Ed
   Murphy—a development engineer from
   Wright aircraft lab. Frustration with
   a strap transducer which was
   malfunctioning due to an error by a lab
   technician in the wiring of the strain
   gauge bridges caused Murphy to
   remark: 'If there's *any* way to do it
   wrong, he will!' I assigned Murphy's
   Law to the statement and the associated
   variations.
   George E. Nichols in *Listener* 16 Feb. 1984

Fred Murray

5 Ginger, you're balmy!
   Title of song (1910)

6 I'm Henery the Eighth, I am!
   Henery the Eighth, I am, I am!
   I got married to the widow next door,
   She's been married seven times before.
   Every one was a Henery,
   She wouldn't have a Willie or a Sam.
   I'm her eighth old man named Henery
   I'm Henery the Eighth, I am!
   I'm Henery the Eighth, I Am! (1911 song)

Edward R. Murrow 1908–1965

7 As Ed Murrow once said about Vietnam,
   anyone who isn't confused doesn't really
   understand the situation.
   Walter Bryan *The Improbable Irish* (1969)
   ch. 1

8 This—is London.
   Words used to open his broadcasts from
   London, 1938–45: see E. R. Murrow *In
   Search of Light* (1967) p. 7

9 He [Winston Churchill] mobilized the
   English language and sent it into battle
   to steady his fellow countrymen and
   hearten those Europeans upon whom
   the long dark night of tyranny had
   descended.
   Broadcast, 30 Nov. 1954, in *In Search of
   Light* (1967) p. 276

Benito Mussolini 1883–1945

10 *Voglio partire in perfetto orario. . . . D'ora
   innanzi ogni cosa deve camminare alla
   perfezione.*

   We must leave exactly on time. . . .
   From now on everything must function
   to perfection.
   In Giorgio Pini *Mussolini* (1939) vol. 2,
   ch. 6, p. 251 (said to a station-master). Cf.
   HRH Infanta Eulalia of Spain *Courts and
   Countries after the War* (1925) ch. 13: 'The
   first benefit of Benito Mussolini's direction in
   Italy begins to be felt when one crosses the
   Italian Frontier and hears 'Il treno arriva
   all'orario' [i.e. 'the train is arriving on
   time']

A. J. Muste 1885–1967

11 There is no way to peace. Peace is the
   way.
   In *New York Times* 16 Nov. 1967, p. 46

Vladimir Nabokov 1899–1977

12 Her exotic daydreams do not prevent her
   from being small-town bourgeois at
   heart, clinging to conventional ideas or
   committing this or that conventional
   violation of the conventional, adultery
   being a most conventional way to rise
   above the conventional.
   Lectures on Literature (1980) 'Madame
   Bovary'

1 Lolita, light of my life, fire of my loins.
My sin, my soul. Lo-lee-ta: the tip of the
tongue taking a trip of three steps down
the palate to tap, at three, on the teeth.
Lo. Lee. Ta.
  Lolita (1955) ch. 1

2 Life is a great surprise. I do not see why
death should not be an even greater
one.
  Pale Fire (1962) p. 225

3 The cradle rocks above an abyss, and
common sense tells us that our existence
is but a brief crack of light between two
eternities of darkness.
  Speak, Memory (1951) ch. 1

4 I think like a genius, I write like
a distinguished author, and I speak like
a child.
  Strong Opinions (1973) foreword

5 A work of art has no importance
whatever to society. It is only important
to the individual, and only the
individual reader is important to me.
  Strong Opinions (1973) p. 33

Ralph Nader 1934–

6 Unsafe at any speed.
  Title of book (1965)

Sarojini Naidu 1879–1949

7 If only Bapu [Gandhi] knew the cost of
setting him up in poverty!
  In A. Campbell-Johnson *Mission with
  Mountbatten* (1951) ch. 12

Fridtjof Nansen 1861–1930

8 He [Nansen] once told me the rules by
which, in his explorations and at
Geneva, his work was done. There were
three of them, and they were very
simple: 'Never stop because you are
afraid—you are never so likely to be
wrong.' 'Never keep a line of retreat: it
is a wretched invention.' 'The difficult is
what takes a little time; the impossible is
what takes a little longer.'
  Philip Noel-Baker in *Listener* 14 Dec. 1939

Ogden Nash 1902–1971

9 The camel has a single hump;

The dromedary, two;
Or else the other way around,
I'm never sure. Are you?
  Bad Parents' Garden of Verse (1936) 'The
  Camel'

10 The trouble with a kitten is
THAT
Eventually it becomes a
CAT.
  The Face is Familiar (1940) 'The Kitten'

11 Oh, what a tangled web do parents
  weave
When they think that their children are
  naïve.
  The Face is Familiar (1940) 'Baby, What
  Makes the Sky Blue'

12 Sure, deck your lower limbs in pants;
Yours are the limbs, my sweeting.
You look divine as you advance—
Have you seen yourself retreating?
  The Face is Familiar (1940) 'What's the
  Use?'

13 The cow is of the bovine ilk;
One end is moo, the other, milk;
  Free Wheeling (1931) 'The Cow'

14 A bit of talcum
Is always walcum.
  Free Wheeling (1931) 'The Baby'

15 Life is not having been told that the man
has just waxed the floor.
  Good Intentions (1942) 'You and Me and P.
  B. Shelley'

16 Beneath this slab
John Brown is stowed.
He watched the ads,
And not the road.
  Good Intentions (1942) 'Lather as You Go'

17 I have a bone to pick with Fate.
Come here and tell me, girlie,
Do you think my mind is maturing late,
Or simply rotted early?
  Good Intentions (1942) 'Lines on Facing
  Forty'

18 I test my bath before I sit,
And I'm always moved to wonderment
That what chills the finger not a bit
Is so frigid upon the fundament.
  Good Intentions (1942) 'Samson Agonistes'

19 Women would rather be right than be
  reasonable.
  Good Intentions (1942) 'Frailty, Thy Name is
  a Misnomer'

1 Parsley
Is gharsley.
Good Intentions (1942) 'Further Reflections
on Parsley'

2 God in His wisdom made the fly
And then forgot to tell us why.
Good Intentions (1942) 'The Fly'

3 Any kiddie in school can love like a fool,
But hating, my boy, is an art.
Happy Days (1933) 'Plea for Less Malice
Toward None'

4 I think that I shall never see
A billboard lovely as a tree.
Perhaps, unless the billboards fall,
I'll never see a tree at all.
Happy Days (1933) 'Song of the Open Road'.
Cf. Joyce Kilmer 121:8

5 Children aren't happy with nothing to
ignore,
And that's what parents were created
for.
Happy Days (1933) 'The Parent'

6 One would be in less danger
From the wiles of the stranger
If one's own kin and kith
Were more fun to be with.
Hard Lines (1931) 'Family Court'

7 A girl whose cheeks are covered with
paint
Has an advantage with me over one
whose ain't.
Hard Lines (1931) 'Biological Reflection'

8 Candy
Is dandy
But liquor
Is quicker.
Hard Lines (1931) 'Reflections on
Ice-breaking'

9 The turtle lives 'twixt plated decks
Which practically conceal its sex.
I think it clever of the turtle
In such a fix to be so fertile.
Hard Lines (1931) 'Autres Bêtes, Autres
Moeurs'

10 Let us pause to consider the English,
Who when they pause to consider
themselves they get all reticently
thrilled and tinglish,
Because every Englishman is convinced
of one thing, viz.:
That to be an Englishman is to belong to
the most exclusive club there is.
I'm a Stranger Here Myself (1938) 'England
Expects'

11 There was a young belle of old Natchez
Whose garments were always in
patchez.
When comment arose
On the state of her clothes,
She drawled, When Ah itchez, Ah
scratchez.
I'm a Stranger Here Myself (1938) 'Requiem'

12 Home is heaven and orgies are vile,
But you *need* an orgy, once in a while.
Primrose Path (1935) 'Home, $99^{44}/_{100}$%
Sweet Home'

13 He tells you when you've got on too
much lipstick,
And helps you with your girdle when
your hips stick.
Versus (1949) 'The Perfect Husband'

George Jean Nathan 1882–1958

14 The test of a real comedian is whether
you laugh at him before he opens his
mouth.
American Mercury Sept. 1929

Terry Nation

15 Exterminate! Exterminate!
Said by the Daleks in BBC television series
Dr Who from Dec. 1963, in David Whitaker
and Terry Nation *Dr Who* (1964) ch. 9

James Ball Naylor 1860–1945

16 King David and King Solomon
Led merry, merry lives,
With many, many lady friends,
And many, many wives;
But when old age crept over them—
With many, many qualms!—
King Solomon wrote the Proverbs
And King David wrote the Psalms.
Vagrant Verse (1935) 'King David and King
Solomon'

Jawaharlal Nehru 1889–1964

17 Friends and comrades, the light has
gone out of our lives and there is
darkness everywhere. I do not know
what to tell you and how to say it. Our
beloved leader, Bapu as we called him,
the father of the nation, is no more.
Broadcast, 30 Jan. 1948 (after Gandhi's
assassination), in Richard J. Walsh *Nehru on
Gandhi* (1948) ch. 6

1 Democracy and socialism are means to an end, not the end itself.

'Basic Approach', repr. in Vincent Shean *Nehru: the Years of Power* (1960) p. 294

2 Normally speaking, it may be said that the forces of a capitalist society, if left unchecked, tend to make the rich richer and the poor poorer and thus increase the gap between them.

'Basic Approach', repr. in Vincent Shean *Nehru: the Years of Power* (1960) p. 295

Allan Nevins 1890–1971

3 The former Allies had blundered in the past by offering Germany too little, and offering even that too late, until finally Nazi Germany had become a menace to all mankind.

In *Current History* (New York) May 1935, p. 178

Anthony Newley 1931–
and Leslie Bricusse 1931–

4 Stop the world, I want to get off.

Title of musical (1961)

Huey Newton 1942–

5 I suggested [in 1966] that we use the panther as our symbol and call our political vehicle the Black Panther Party. The panther is a fierce animal, but he will not attack until he is backed into a corner; then he will strike out.

Revolutionary Suicide (1973) ch. 16

Vivian Nicholson 1936–

6 I want to spend, and spend, and spend.

Said to reporters on arriving to collect her husband's football pools winnings of £152,000, in *Daily Herald* 28 Sept. 1961

Sir Harold Nicolson 1886–1968

7 Chamberlain (who has the mind and manner of a clothes-brush) aims only at assuring temporary peace at the price of ultimate defeat.

Diary 6 June 1938, in *Diaries and Letters* (1966) p. 345

8 Attlee is a charming and intelligent man, but as a public speaker he is, compared to Winston [Churchill], like a village fiddler after Paganini.

Diary 10 Nov. 1947, in *Diaries and Letters* (1968) p. 113

Reinhold Niebuhr 1892–1971

9 Man's capacity for justice makes democracy possible, but man's inclination to injustice makes democracy necessary.

Children of Light and Children of Darkness (1944) foreword

10 God, give us the serenity to accept what cannot be changed;
Give us the courage to change what should be changed;
Give us the wisdom to distinguish one from the other.

In Richard Wightman Fox *Reinhold Niebuhr* (1985) ch. 12 (prayer said to have been first published in 1951)

Carl Nielsen 1865–1931

11 *Musik er liv, som dette uudslukkelig.*

Music *is* life, and like it is inextinguishable.

4th Symphony ('The Inextinguishable', 1916) preface

Martin Niemöller 1892–1984

12 When Hitler attacked the Jews I was not a Jew, therefore, I was not concerned. And when Hitler attacked the Catholics, I was not a Catholic, and therefore, I was not concerned. And when Hitler attacked the unions and the industrialists, I was not a member of the unions and I was not concerned. Then, Hitler attacked me and the Protestant church—and there was nobody left to be concerned.

In *Congressional Record* 14 Oct. 1968, p. 31636

Florence Nightingale 1820–1910

13 On December 5 [1907], Sir Douglas Dawson . . . brought the Order [of Merit]

... to South Street. Miss Nightingale understood that some kindness had been done to her, but hardly more. 'Too kind, too kind,' she said.

E. Cook *Life of Florence Nightingale* (1913) vol. 2, pt. 7, ch. 9

Richard Milhous Nixon 1913–

1 When the President does it, that means that it is not illegal.

In David Frost *I Gave Them a Sword* (1978) ch. 8

2 I brought myself down. I gave them a sword. And they stuck it in. And they twisted it with relish. And, I guess, if I'd been in their position, I'd have done the same thing.

Television interview with David Frost, 19 May 1977, in David Frost *I Gave Them a Sword* (1978) ch. 10

3 I leave you gentlemen now and you will now write it. You will interpret it. That's your right. But as I leave you I want you to know—just think how much you're going to be missing. You won't have Nixon to kick around any more because, gentlemen, this is my last press conference. . . . I hope that what I have said today will at least make television, radio, the press first recognize the great responsibility they have to report all the news and, second, recognize that they have a right and a responsibility, if they're against a candidate, to give him the shaft, but also recognize if they give him the shaft, put one lonely reporter on the campaign who will report what the candidate says now and then. Thank you gentlemen, and good day.

After losing the election for Governor of California, 5 Nov. 1962, in *New York Times* 8 Nov. 1962, p. 8

4 Let us begin by committing ourselves to the truth, to see it like it is and tell it like it is, to find the truth, to speak the truth and to live the truth. That's what we will do.

Nomination acceptance speech, Miami, 8 Aug. 1968, in *New York Times* 9 Aug. 1968, p. 20

5 Hello, Neil and Buzz. I'm talking to you by telephone from the Oval Room at the White House, and this certainly has to be the most historic telephone call ever made.

Speaking to the first men to land on the moon, 20 July 1969, in *New York Times* 21 July 1969, p. 2

6 This is the greatest week in the history of the world since the Creation.

Speech 24 July 1969, welcoming the return of the first men to land on the moon, in *New York Times* 25 July 1969, p. 29

7 There can be no whitewash at the White House.

Television speech on Watergate, 30 Apr. 1973, in *New York Times* 1 May 1973, p. 31

8 I made my mistakes, but in all my years of public life, I have never profited, never profited from public service. I've earned every cent. And in all of my years in public life I have never obstructed justice. And I think, too, that I can say that in my years of public life that I welcome this kind of examination because people have got to know whether or not their President is a crook. Well, I'm not a crook. I've earned everything I've got.

Speech at press conference, 17 Nov. 1973, in *New York Times* 18 Nov. 1973, p. 62

9 This country needs good farmers, good businessmen, good plumbers, good carpenters.

Farewell address at White House, 9 Aug. 1974, cited in *New York Times* 10 Aug. 1974, p. 4

10 Pat and I have the satisfaction that every dime that we've got is honestly ours. I should say this—that Pat doesn't have a mink coat. But she does have a respectable Republican cloth coat. And I always tell her that she'd look good in anything. One other thing I probably should tell you, because if I don't they'll probably be saying this about me too, we did get something—a gift—after the election. . . . It was a little cocker-spaniel dog. . . . And our little girl—Tricia, the 6-year-old—named it Checkers. And you know the kids love that dog and I just want to say this right now, that regardless of what they say about it, we're going to keep it.

Speech on television, 23 Sept. 1952, in P. Andrews *This Man Nixon* (1952) p. 60

David Nobbs

1 'This one's going to be a real winner,'
said C. J. 'I didn't get where I am today
without knowing a real winner when
I see one.'

> Death of Reginald Perrin (1975) p. 9
> (subsequently a catch-phrase in BBC
> television series The Fall and Rise of Reginald
> Perrin, 1976–80)

Milton Nobles 1847–1924

2 The villain still pursued her.
> Phoenix (1900) act 1, sc. 3

Albert J. Nock 1873–1945

3 It is an economic axiom as old as the
hills that goods and services can be paid
for only with goods and services.
> Memoirs of a Superfluous Man (1943) ch. 13

Frank Norman 1931–
and Lionel Bart 1930–

4 Fings ain't wot they used t'be.
> Title of musical (1959). Cf. Ted Persons
> 170:9

Lord Northcliffe (Alfred Charles William Harmsworth, Viscount Northcliffe) 1865–1922

5 Harmsworth had always said: 'When
I want a peerage, I shall buy it like an
honest man.'
> Tom Driberg Swaff: the Life and Times of
> Hannen Swaffer (1974) ch. 2

Jack Norworth 1879–1959

6 Oh, shine on, shine on, harvest moon
Up in the sky.
I ain't had no lovin'
Since April, January, June, or July.
> Shine On, Harvest Moon (1908 song; music
> by Nora Bayes-Norworth)

7 Take me out to the ball game.
> Title of song (1908; music by Albert Von
> Tilzer)

Alfred Noyes 1880–1958

8 Go down to Kew in lilac-time, in
lilac-time, in lilac-time,
Go down to Kew in lilac-time (it isn't far
from London!)

And you shall wander hand in hand
with love in summer's wonderland;
Go down to Kew in lilac-time (it isn't far
from London!)
> Poems (1904) 'The Barrel-Organ'

9 The wind was a torrent of darkness
among the gusty trees,
The moon was a ghostly galleon tossed
upon cloudy seas,
The road was a ribbon of moonlight over
the purple moor,
And the highwayman came riding—
Riding—riding—
The highwayman came riding, up to the
old inn-door.
> Forty Singing Seamen and Other Poems
> (1907) 'The Highwayman'

10 He whistled a tune to the window, and
who should be waiting there
The landlord's black-eyed daughter,
Bess, the landlord's daughter,
Plaiting a dark red love-knot into her
long black hair.
> Forty Singing Seamen and Other Poems
> (1907) 'The Highwayman'

11 Look for me by moonlight;
Watch for me by moonlight;
I'll come to thee by moonlight, though
hell should bar the way!
> Forty Singing Seamen and Other Poems
> (1907) 'The Highwayman'

Bill Nye (Edgar Wilson Nye)

12 The late Bill Nye once said, 'I have been
told that Wagner's music is better than
it sounds.'
> Mark Twain Autobiography (1924) vol. 1,
> p. 338

Captain Lawrence Oates 1880–1912

13 I am just going outside and may be
some time.
> Last words, quoted in R. F. Scott Diary
> 16–17 Mar. 1912, in Last Expedition (1913)
> p. 593

Edna O'Brien 1932–

14 August is a wicked month.
> Title of novel (1965)

15 The vote, I thought, means nothing to
women. We should be armed.
> In Erica Jong Fear of Flying (1973) ch. 16

1 Oh, God, who does not exist, you hate
women, otherwise you'd have made
them different.
 Girls in their Married Bliss (1964) ch. 10

Flann O'Brien (Brian O'Nolan or O Nuallain) 1911–1966

2 The Pooka MacPhellimey, a member of
the devil class, sat in his hut in the
middle of a firwood meditating on the
nature of the numerals and segregating
in his mind the odd ones from the even.
 At Swim-Two-Birds (1939) ch. 1

3 The conclusion of your syllogism, I said
lightly, is fallacious, being based upon
licensed premises.
 At Swim-Two-Birds (1939) ch. 1

4 A pint of plain is your only man.
 At Swim-Two-Birds (1939) 'The Workman's
Friend'

5 It is not that I half knew my mother.
I knew half of her: the lower half—her
lap, legs, feet, her hands and wrists as
she bent forward.
 The Hard Life (1961) p. 11

6 People who spend most of their natural
lives riding iron bicycles over the rocky
roadsteads of this parish get their
personalities mixed up with the
personalities of their bicycles as a result
of the interchanging of the atoms of
each of them and you would be
surprised at the number of people in
these parts who nearly are half people
and half bicycles.
 The Third Policeman (1967) p. 85

Sean O'Casey 1884–1964

7 He's an oul' butty o' mine—oh, he's
a darlin' man, a daarlin' man.
 Juno and the Paycock (1925) act 1

8 The whole worl's in a state o' chassis!
 Juno and the Paycock (1925) act 1

9 I often looked up at the sky an' assed
meself the question—what is the stars,
what is the stars?
 Juno and the Paycock (1925) act 1

10 Sacred Heart of the Crucified Jesus, take
our hearts o' stone ... an' give us
hearts o' flesh! ... Take away this
murdherin' hate ... an' give us Thine
own eternal love!
 Juno and the Paycock (1925) act 2

11 The Polis as Polis, in this city, is Null
an' Void!
 Juno and the Paycock (1925) act 3

12 When one has reached 81 ... one likes
to sit back and let the world turn by
itself, without trying to push it.
 New York Times 25 Sept. 1960, pt. 2, p. 3

13 There's no reason to bring religion into
it. I think we ought to have as great
a regard for religion as we can, so as to
keep it out of as many things as possible.
 The Plough and the Stars (1926) act 1

14 It's my rule never to lose me temper till
it would be dethrimental to keep it.
 The Plough and the Stars (1926) act 2

15 English literature's performing flea [P. G.
Wodehouse].
 In P. G. Wodehouse *Performing Flea* (1953)
p. 217

Edwin O'Connor 1918–1968

16 The last hurrah.
 Title of novel (1956)

Seán O'Faoláin 1900–

17 Stories, like whiskey, must be allowed to
mature in the cask.
 Atlantic Monthly Dec. 1956, p. 76

David Ogilvy 1911–

18 The consumer isn't a moron; she is your
wife. You insult her intelligence if you
assume that a mere slogan and a few
vapid adjectives will persuade her to buy
anything.
 Confessions of an Advertising Man (1963)
ch. 5

Geoffrey O'Hara 1882–1967

19 K-K-K-Katy, beautiful Katy,
You're the only g-g-g-girl that
 I adore;—
When the m-m-m-moon shines,
Over the cow shed,
I'll be waiting at the k-k-k-kitchen door.
 K-K-K-Katy (1918 song)

John O'Hara 1905–1970

20 George [Gershwin] died on July 11,
1937, but I don't have to believe that if
I don't want to.
 Newsweek 15 July 1940, p. 34

Patrick O'Keefe 1872–1934

1 Say it with flowers.
   Slogan for the Society of American Florists,
   in *Florists' Exchange* 15 Dec. 1917, p. 1268

Chauncey Olcott and George Graff Jr.

2 When Irish eyes are smiling.
   Title of song (1912; music by Ernest R. Ball)

Frederick Scott Oliver 1864–1934

3 A wise politician will never grudge
   a genuflexion or a rapture if it is
   expected of him by prevalent opinion.
   The Endless Adventure (1930) vol. 1, pt. 1,
   ch. 20

Laurence Olivier (Baron Olivier of Brighton) 1907–1989

4 Acting is a masochistic form of
   exhibitionism. It is not quite the
   occupation of an adult.
   In *Time* 3 July 1978, p. 33

Frank Ward O'Malley 1875–1932

See ELBERT HUBBARD

Mary O'Malley 1941–

5 Once a Catholic always a Catholic.
   That's the rule.
   Once a Catholic (1971) act 1, sc. 2. Cf.
   Angus Wilson

Eugene O'Neill 1888–1953

6 For de little stealin' dey gits you in jail
   soon or late. For de big stealin' dey
   makes you Emperor and puts you in de
   Hall o' Fame when you croaks.
   The Emperor Jones (1921) sc. 1

7 The iceman cometh.
   Title of play (1946)

8 Life is for each man a solitary cell whose
   walls are mirrors.
   Lazarus Laughed (1927) act 2, sc. 1

9 When men make gods, there is no God!
   Lazarus Laughed (1927) act 2, sc. 2

10 A long day's journey into night.
   Title of play (written 1940–1; published
   1956)

11 Life is perhaps most wisely regarded as
   a bad dream between two awakenings,
   and every day is a life in miniature.
   Marco Millions (1928) act 2, sc. 2

12 The sea hates a coward!
   Mourning becomes Electra (1931) pt. 2, act 4

13 What beastly incidents our memories
   insist on cherishing! . . . the ugly and
   disgusting . . . the beautiful things we
   have to keep diaries to remember!
   Strange Interlude (1928) pt. 1, act 2

14 The only living life is in the past and
   future . . . the present is an interlude . . .
   strange interlude in which we call on
   past and future to bear witness we are
   living.
   Strange Interlude (1928) pt. 2, act 8

15 Strange interlude! Yes, our lives are
   merely strange dark interludes in the
   electrical display of God the Father!
   Strange Interlude (1928) pt. 2, act 9

Brian O'Nolan 1911–1966

See FLANN O'BRIEN

J. Robert Oppenheimer 1904–1967

16 In some sort of crude sense which no
   vulgarity, no humour, no overstatement
   can quite extinguish, the physicists have
   known sin; and this is a knowledge
   which they cannot lose.
   Lecture at Massachusetts Institute of
   Technology, 25 Nov. 1947, in *Open Mind*
   (1955) ch. 5

Susie Orbach 1946–

17 Fat is a feminist issue.
   Title of book (1978)

Baroness Orczy 1865–1947

18 We seek him here, we seek him there,
   Those Frenchies seek him everywhere.
   Is he in heaven?—Is he in hell?
   That demmed, elusive Pimpernel?
   The Scarlet Pimpernel (1905) ch. 12

David Ormsby Gore 1918–1985

See LORD HARLECH

José Ortega y Gasset 1883–1955

1 *Yo soy yo y mi circunstancia, y si no la salvo a ella no me salvo yo.*

I am I plus my surroundings and if I do not preserve the latter, I do not preserve myself.
   Meditaciones del Quijote (Meditations of Quixote, 1914) in *Obras Completas* (1946) vol. 1, p. 322

2 *La civilización no es otra cosa que el ensayo de reducir la fuerza a ultima ratio.*

Civilization is nothing more than the effort to reduce the use of force to the last resort.
   La Rebelión de las Masas (The Revolt of the Masses, 1930) in *Obras Completas* (1947) vol. 4, p. 191

Joe Orton 1933–1967

3 I'd the upbringing a nun would envy and that's the truth. Until I was fifteen I was more familiar with Africa than my own body.
   Entertaining Mr Sloane (1964) act 1

4 KATH: Can he be present at the birth of his child? ...
   ED: It's all any reasonable child can expect if the dad is present at the conception.
   Entertaining Mr Sloane (1964) act 3

5 Every luxury was lavished on you— atheism, breast-feeding, circumcision. I had to make my own way.
   Loot (1967) act 1

6 Policemen, like red squirrels, must be protected.
   Loot (1967) act 1

7 Reading isn't an occupation we encourage among police officers. We try to keep the paper work down to a minimum.
   Loot (1967) act 2

8 The kind of people who always go on about whether a thing is in good taste invariably have very bad taste.
   Transatlantic Review Spring 1967, p. 95

9 You were born with your legs apart. They'll send you to the grave in a Y-shaped coffin.
   What the Butler Saw (1969) act 1

George Orwell (Eric Blair) 1903–1950

10 Man is the only creature that consumes without producing.
   Animal Farm (1945) ch. 1

11 Four legs good, two legs bad.
   Animal Farm (1945) ch. 3

12 All animals are equal but some animals are more equal than others.
   Animal Farm (1945) ch. 10

13 At 50, everyone has the face he deserves.
   Last words in his notebook, 17 April 1949, in *Collected Essays* (1968) vol. 4, p. 515

14 I'm fat, but I'm thin inside. Has it ever struck you that there's a thin man inside every fat man, just as they say there's a statue inside every block of stone?
   Coming up For Air (1939) pt. 1, ch. 3. See also 59:12

15 [Clement] Attlee reminds me of nothing so much as a recently dead fish, before it has had time to stiffen.
   Diary 19 May 1942, in *Essays* (1968) vol. 2, p. 426

16 He was an embittered atheist (the sort of atheist who does not so much disbelieve in God as personally dislike Him), and took a sort of pleasure in thinking that human affairs would never improve.
   Down and Out in Paris and London (1933) ch. 30

17 Whatever is funny is subversive, every joke is ultimately a custard pie. ... A dirty joke is a sort of mental rebellion.
   Horizon Sept. 1941 'The Art of Donald McGill'

18 Most revolutionaries are potential Tories, because they imagine that everything can be put right by altering the *shape* of society; once that change is effected, as it sometimes is, they see no need for any other.
   Inside the Whale (1940) 'Charles Dickens'

19 Keep the aspidistra flying.
   Title of novel (1936)

20 England is not the jewelled isle of Shakespeare's much-quoted passage, nor is it the inferno depicted by Dr Goebbels. More than either it resembles a family, a rather stuffy Victorian family, with not many black

sheep in it but with all its cupboards bursting with skeletons. . . . A family with the wrong members in control—that, perhaps, is as near as one can come to describing England in a phrase.

The Lion and the Unicorn (1941) pt. 1
'England Your England'

1 Probably the battle of Waterloo *was* won on the playing-fields of Eton, but the opening battles of all subsequent wars have been lost there.

The Lion and the Unicorn (1941) pt. 1
'England Your England'

2 It was a bright cold day in April, and the clocks were striking thirteen.

Nineteen Eighty-Four (1949) pt. 1, ch. 1

3 On each landing, opposite the lift shaft, the poster with the enormous face gazed from the wall. It was one of those pictures which are so contrived that the eyes follow you about when you move. BIG BROTHER IS WATCHING YOU, the caption beneath it ran.

Nineteen Eighty-Four (1949) pt. 1, ch. 1

4 War is peace. Freedom is slavery. Ignorance is strength.

Nineteen Eighty-Four (1949) pt. 1, ch. 1

5 'Who controls the past,' ran the Party slogan, 'controls the future: who controls the present controls the past.'

Nineteen Eighty-Four (1949) pt. 1, ch. 3

6 Freedom is the freedom to say that two plus two make four. If that is granted, all else follows.

Nineteen Eighty-Four (1949) pt. 1, ch. 7

7 *Doublethink* means the power of holding two contradictory beliefs in one's mind simultaneously, and accepting both of them.

Nineteen Eighty-Four (1949) pt. 2, ch. 9

8 Power is not a means, it is an end. One does not establish a dictatorship in order to safeguard a revolution; one makes the revolution in order to establish the dictatorship.

Nineteen Eighty-Four (1949) pt. 3, ch. 3

9 If you want a picture of the future, imagine a boot stamping on a human face—for ever.

Nineteen Eighty-Four (1949) pt. 3, ch. 3

10 The Catholic and the Communist are alike in assuming that an opponent cannot be both honest and intelligent.

Polemic Jan. 1946 'The Prevention of Literature'

11 The quickest way of ending a war is to lose it.

Polemic May 1946 'Second Thoughts on James Burnham'

12 It is only because miners sweat their guts out that superior persons can remain superior.

The Road to Wigan Pier (1937) ch. 2

13 A person of bourgeois origin goes through life with some expectation of getting what he wants, within reasonable limits. Hence the fact that in times of stress 'educated' people tend to come to the front.

The Road to Wigan Pier (1937) ch. 3

14 There can hardly be a town in the South of England where you could throw a brick without hitting the niece of a bishop.

The Road to Wigan Pier (1937) ch. 7

15 As with the Christian religion, the worst advertisement for Socialism is its adherents.

The Road to Wigan Pier (1937) ch. 11

16 The typical Socialist is . . . a prim little man with a white-collar job, usually a secret teetotaller and often with vegetarian leanings, with a history of Nonconformity behind him, and, above all, with a social position which he has no intention of forfeiting.

The Road to Wigan Pier (1937) ch. 11

17 To the ordinary working man, the sort you would meet in any pub on Saturday night, Socialism does not mean much more than better wages and shorter hours and nobody bossing you about.

The Road to Wigan Pier (1937) ch. 11

18 The high-water mark, so to speak, of Socialist literature is W. H. Auden, a sort of gutless Kipling.

The Road to Wigan Pier (1937) ch. 11

19 We of the sinking middle class . . . may sink without further struggles into the working class where we belong, and probably when we get there it will not

be so dreadful as we feared, for, after all, we have nothing to lose but our aitches.

The Road to Wigan Pier (1937) ch. 13

1 In our time, political speech and writing are largely the defence of the indefensible.

Shooting an Elephant (1950) 'Politics and the English Language'

2 The great enemy of clear language is insincerity. When there is a gap between one's real and one's declared aims, one turns as it were instinctively to long words and exhausted idioms, like a cuttlefish squirting out ink.

Shooting an Elephant (1950) 'Politics and the English Language'

3 Political language—and with variations this is true of all political parties, from Conservatives to Anarchists—is designed to make lies sound truthful and murder respectable, and to give an appearance of solidity to pure wind.

Shooting an Elephant (1950) 'Politics and the English Language'

4 Saints should always be judged guilty until they are proved innocent.

Shooting an Elephant (1950) 'Reflections on Gandhi'

5 To see what is in front of one's nose needs a constant struggle.

Tribune 22 Mar. 1946, 'In Front of your Nose'

John Osborne 1929–

6 Don't clap too hard—it's a very old building.

The Entertainer (1957) no. 7

7 Thank God we're normal, normal, normal,
Thank God we're normal,
Yes, this is our finest shower!

The Entertainer (1957) no. 7

8 But I have a go, lady, don't I? I 'ave a go. I do.

The Entertainer (1957) no. 7

9 Never believe in mirrors or newspapers.

The Hotel in Amsterdam (1968) act 1

10 Oh heavens, how I long for a little ordinary human enthusiasm. Just enthusiasm—that's all. I want to hear a warm, thrilling voice cry out Hallelujah! Hallelujah! I'm alive!

Look Back in Anger (1956) act 1

11 His knowledge of life and ordinary human beings is so hazy, he really deserves some sort of decoration for it—a medal inscribed 'For Vaguery in the Field'.

Look Back in Anger (1956) act 1

12 I don't think one 'comes down' from Jimmy's university. According to him, it's not even red brick, but white tile.

Look Back in Anger (1956) act 2, sc. 1

13 They spend their time mostly looking forward to the past.

Look Back in Anger (1956) act 2, sc. 1

14 There aren't any good, brave causes left. If the big bang does come, and we all get killed off, it won't be in aid of the old-fashioned, grand design. It'll just be for the Brave New-nothing-very-much-thank-you. About as pointless and inglorious as stepping in front of a bus.

Look Back in Anger (1956) act 3, sc. 1

15 This is a letter of hate. It is for you my countrymen, I mean those men of my country who have defiled it. The men with manic fingers leading the sightless, feeble, betrayed body of my country to its death. . . . I only hope it [my hate] will keep me going. I think it will. I think it may sustain me in the last few months. Till then, damn you England. You're rotting now, and quite soon you'll disappear. My hate will outrun you yet, if only for a few seconds. I wish it could be eternal.

Tribune 18 Aug. 1961

Sir William Osler 1849–1919

16 That man can interrogate as well as observe nature, was a lesson slowly learned in his evolution.

In *Aphorisms from his Bedside Teachings* (1961) p. 62

17 Failure to examine the throat is a glaring sin of omission, especially in children. One finger in the throat and one in the rectum makes a good diagnostician.

In *Aphorisms from his Bedside Teachings* (1961) p. 104

1 One of the first duties of the physician is to educate the masses not to take medicine.

In *Aphorisms from his Bedside Teachings* (1961) p. 105

2 It is strange how the memory of a man may float to posterity on what he would have himself regarded as the most trifling of his works.

In *Aphorisms from his Bedside Teachings* (1961) p. 112

3 The desire to take medicine is perhaps the greatest feature which distinguishes man from animals.

In H. Cushing *Life of Sir William Osler* (1925) vol. 1, ch. 14

4 My second fixed idea is the uselessness of men above sixty years of age, and the incalculable benefit it would be in commercial, political, and in professional life, if as a matter of course, men stopped work at this age.

Speech at Johns Hopkins University, 22 Feb. 1905, in H. Cushing *Life of Sir William Osler* (1925) vol. 1, ch. 24

5 To talk of diseases is a sort of *Arabian Nights* entertainment.

In Oliver Sacks *The Man Who Mistook his Wife for a Hat* (1985) epigraph

6 The greater the ignorance the greater the dogmatism.

Montreal Medical Journal Sept. 1902, p. 696

7 The natural man has only two primal passions, to get and beget.

Science and Immortality (1904) ch. 2

Peter Demianovich Ouspensky
1878–1947

8 Truths that become old become decrepit and unreliable; sometimes they may be kept going artificially for a certain time, but there is no life in them. This explains why reverting to old ideas, when people become disappointed in new ideas, does not help much. Ideas can be too old.

A New Model of the Universe (ed. 2, 1934) preface

David Owen 1938–

9 We are fed up with fudging and mudging, with mush and slush. We need courage, conviction, and hard work.

Speech to his supporters at Labour Party Conference in Blackpool, 2 Oct. 1980, in *Guardian* 3 Oct. 1980

10 The price of championing human rights is a little inconsistency at times.

Hansard 30 Mar. 1977, p. 397

11 I don't care if you criticize us, agree with us or disagree with us. Just mention us, that is all we ask.

Observer 28 Apr. 1985

Wilfred Owen 1893–1918

12 Above all I am not concerned with Poetry.
My subject is War, and the pity of War.
The Poetry is in the pity.
Yet these elegies are to this generation in no sense consolatory. They may be to the next. All a poet can do today is warn. That is why the true Poets must be truthful.

Poems (1963 ed.) preface

13 What passing-bells for these who die as cattle?
Only the monstrous anger of the guns.
Only the stuttering rifles' rapid rattle
Can patter out their hasty orisons.
No mockeries now for them; no prayers nor bells,
Nor any voice of mourning save the choirs,—
The shrill, demented choirs of wailing shells;
And bugles calling for them from sad shires.

What candles may be held to speed them all?
Not in the hands of boys, but in their eyes
Shall shine the holy glimmers of good-byes.
The pallor of girls' brows shall be their pall;
Their flowers the tenderness of patient minds,
And each slow dusk a drawing-down of blinds.

Poems (1963 ed.) 'Anthem for Doomed Youth'

14 If you could hear, at every jolt, the blood

Come gargling from the froth-corrupted
  lungs,
Obscene as cancer, bitter as the cud
Of vile, incurable sores on innocent
  tongues,—
My friend, you would not tell with such
  high zest
To children ardent for some desperate
  glory,
The old Lie: Dulce et decorum est
Pro patria mori.
  Poems (1963 ed.) 'Dulce et Decorum Est'

1 Move him into the sun—
Gently its touch awoke him once,
At home, whispering of fields unsown,
Always it woke him, even in France,
Until this morning and this snow.
If anything might rouse him now
The kind old sun will know.
  Poems (1963 ed.) 'Futility'

2 Was it for this the clay grew tall?
—O what made fatuous sunbeams toil
To break earth's sleep at all?
  Poems (1963 ed.) 'Futility'

3 Red lips are not so red
As the stained stones kissed by the
  English dead.
  Poems (1963 ed.) 'Greater Love'

4 So secretly, like wrongs hushed-up, they
  went.
They were not ours:
We never heard to which front these
  were sent.

Nor there if they yet mock what women
  meant
Who gave them flowers.
  Poems (1963 ed.) 'The Send-Off'

5 It seemed that out of battle I escaped
Down some profound dull tunnel, long
  since scooped
Through granites which titanic wars
  had groined.
  Poems (1963 ed.) 'Strange Meeting'

6 'Strange friend,' I said, 'here is no cause
  to mourn.'
'None,' said that other, 'save the
  undone years,
The hopelessness. Whatever hope is
  yours,
Was my life also; I went hunting wild
After the wildest beauty in the world.
  Poems (1963 ed.) 'Strange Meeting'

7 Courage was mine, and I had mystery,
Wisdom was mine, and I had mastery:
To miss the march of this retreating
  world
Into vain citadels that are not walled.
  Poems (1963 ed.) 'Strange Meeting'

8 I am the enemy you killed, my friend.
I knew you in this dark: for you so
  frowned
Yesterday through me as you jabbed
  and killed.
I parried; but my hands were loath and
  cold.
Let us sleep now . . .
  Poems (1963 ed.) 'Strange Meeting'

Oxford and Asquith, Countess of
1864–1945
See MARGOT ASQUITH

Oxford and Asquith, Earl of
1852–1928
See HERBERT HENRY ASQUITH

Vance Packard 1914–
9 The hidden persuaders.
  Title of book (1957)

William Tyler Page 1868–1942
10 I believe in the United States of America
as a government of the people, by the
people, for the people, whose just powers
are derived from the consent of the
governed; a democracy in a republic;
a sovereign Nation of many sovereign
States; a perfect Union, one and
inseparable, established upon those
principles of freedom, equality, justice,
and humanity for which American
patriots sacrificed their lives and
fortunes. I therefore believe it is my duty
to my country to love it, to support its
Constitution, to obey its laws, to respect
its flag, and to defend it against all
enemies.
  American's Creed (prize-winning competition
  entry, 3 Apr. 1918) in *Congressional Record*
  vol. 56, pt. 12 (appendix), p. 286

Reginald Paget 1908–
11 There is no disguise or camouflage about
the Prime Minister. He is the original

banana man, yellow outside and a softer yellow inside.

Of Sir Anthony Eden in a House of Commons debate, *Hansard* 14 Sept. 1956, col. 432

Gerald Page-Wood

1 It beats as it sweeps as it cleans.

Advertising slogan for Hoover vacuum cleaners, devised in 1919, in Nigel Rees *Slogans* (1982) p. 40

Revd Ian Paisley 1926–

2 I would rather be British than just.

Remark to Bernadette Devlin, Oct. 1969, reported by *Sunday Times* Insight Team in *Ulster* (1972) ch. 3

Michael Palin 1943–

See GRAHAM CHAPMAN *et al.*

Norman Panama 1914–
and Melvin Frank 1913–1988

3 The pellet with the poison's in the vessel with the pestle. The chalice from the palace has the brew that is true.

Court Jester (1955 film; words spoken—with difficulty—by Danny Kaye)

4 I'll take a lemonade! . . . In a dirty glass!

Road to Utopia (1946 film; words spoken by Bob Hope)

Dame Christabel Pankhurst
1880–1958

5 Never lose your temper with the Press or the public is a major rule of political life.

Unshackled (1959) ch. 5

6 We are here to claim our right as women, not only to be free, but to fight for freedom. That it is our right as well as our duty. It is our privilege, as well as our pride and our joy, to take some part in this militant movement which, as we believe, means the regeneration of all humanity.

Speech in London, 23 Mar. 1911, in *Votes for Women* 31 Mar. 1911

Emmeline Pankhurst 1858–1928

7 After all, is not a woman's life, is not her health, are not her limbs more valuable than panes of glass? There is no doubt of that, but most important of all, does not the breaking of glass produce more effect upon the Government?

Speech on 16 Feb. 1912, in *My Own Story* (1914) p. 213

8 There is something that Governments care far more for than human life, and that is the security of property, and so it is through property that we shall strike the enemy. . . . Be militant each in your own way. Those of you who can express your militancy by going to the House of Commons and refusing to leave without satisfaction, as we did in the early days—do so. . . . And my last word is to the Government: I incite this meeting to rebellion. I say to the Government: You have not dared to take the leaders of Ulster for their incitement to rebellion. Take me if you dare.

Speech at Albert Hall, 17 Oct. 1912, in *My Own Story* (1914) p. 265

Emmeline Pankhurst 1858–1928,
Dame Christabel Pankhurst
1880–1958, and Annie Kenney
1879–1953

9 We laid our plans to begin this work at a great meeting to be held in the Free Trade Hall, Manchester [on 13 Oct. 1905] with Sir Edward Grey as the principal speaker. We intended to get seats in the gallery, directly facing the platform and we made for the occasion a large banner with the words 'Will the Liberal Party Give Votes for Women?' . . . At the last moment, however, we had to alter the plan because it was impossible to get the gallery seats we wanted. There was no way in which we could use our large banner, so . . . we cut out and made a small banner with the three-word inscription 'Votes for Women'. Thus, quite accidentally, there came into existence the present slogan of the suffrage movement around the world.

Emmeline Pankhurst *My Own Story* (1914) ch. 3

Charlie Parker 1920–1955

1 Music is your own experience, your thoughts, your wisdom. If you don't live it, it won't come out of your horn.

> In Nat Shapiro and Nat Hentoff *Hear Me Talkin' to Ya* (1955) p. 358

Dorothy Parker 1893–1967

2 One more drink and I'd have been under the host.

> In Howard Teichmann *George S. Kaufman* (1972) p. 68

3 You can always tell that the crash is coming when I start getting tender about Our Dumb Friends. Three highballs and I think I'm St Francis of Assisi.

> *Here Lies* (1939) 'Just a Little One'

4 And I'll stay off Verlaine too; he was always chasing Rimbauds.

> *Here Lies* (1939) 'The Little Hours'

5 I'm never going to be famous. My name will never be writ large on the roster of Those Who Do Things. I don't do anything. Not one single thing. I used to bite my nails, but I don't even do that any more.

> *Here Lies* (1939) 'The Little Hours'

6 Sorrow is tranquillity remembered in emotion.

> *Here Lies* (1939) 'Sentiment'. Cf. *Oxford Dictionary of Quotations* (1979) 583:10

7 At intermission [in the 1933 premiere of *The Lake*], Dorothy Parker turned to a companion and made her famous quip: 'Katharine Hepburn runs the gamut from A to B.'

> In G. Carey *Katharine Hepburn* (1985) ch. 6

8 The affair between Margot Asquith and Margot Asquith will live as one of the prettiest love stories in all literature.

> Review of Margot Asquith's *Lay Sermons* in *New Yorker* 22 Oct. 1927, in *A Month of Saturdays* (1970) p. 10

9 And it is that word 'hummy', my darlings, that marks the first place in 'The House at Pooh Corner' at which Tonstant Weader fwowed up.

> *New Yorker* 20 Oct. 1928 (review by Dorothy Parker as 'Constant Reader')

10 Where's the man could ease a heart like a satin gown?

> *Not So Deep as a Well* (1937) 'The Satin Dress'

11 By the time you say you're his,
Shivering and sighing
And he vows his passion is
Infinite, undying—
Lady, make a note of this:
One of you is lying.

> *Not So Deep as a Well* (1937) 'Unfortunate Coincidence'

12 Four be the things I'd been better
    without:
Love, curiosity, freckles, and doubt.

> *Not So Deep as a Well* (1937) 'Inventory'

13 Oh, life is a glorious cycle of song,
A medley of extemporanea;
And love is a thing that can never go
    wrong;
And I am Marie of Roumania.

> *Not So Deep as a Well* (1937) 'Comment'

14 Razors pain you
Rivers are damp;
Acids stain you;
And drugs cause cramp.
Guns aren't lawful;
Nooses give;
Gas smells awful;
You might as well live.

> *Not So Deep as a Well* (1937) 'Résumé'

15 Why is it no one ever sent me yet
One perfect limousine, do you suppose?
Ah no, it's always just my luck to get
One perfect rose.

> *Not So Deep as a Well* (1937) 'One Perfect Rose'

16 Men seldom make passes
At girls who wear glasses.

> *Not So Deep as a Well* (1937) 'News Item'

17 Woman wants monogamy;
Man delights in novelty.
Love is woman's moon and sun;
Man has other forms of fun.
Woman lives but in her lord;
Count to ten, and man is bored.
With this the gist and sum of it,
What earthly good can come of it?

> *Not So Deep as a Well* (1937) 'General Review of the Sex Situation'

18 Whose love is given over-well
Shall look on Helen's face in hell

Whilst they whose love is thin and wise
Shall see John Knox in Paradise.
  Not So Deep as a Well (1937) 'Partial
  Comfort'

1 Accursed from birth they be
Who seek to find monogamy,
Pursuing it from bed to bed—
I think they would be better dead.
  Not So Deep as a Well (1937) 'Reuben's
  Children'

2 If, with the literate, I am
Impelled to try an epigram,
I never seek to take the credit;
We all assume that Oscar said it.
  Not So Deep as a Well (1937) 'A Pig's-Eye
  View of Literature'

3 Drink and dance and laugh and lie,
Love, the reeling midnight through,
For tomorrow we shall die!
(But, alas, we never do.)
  Not So Deep as a Well (1937) 'The Flaw in
  Paganism'

4 He lies below, correct in cypress wood,
And entertains the most exclusive
  worms.
  Not So Deep as a Well (1937) 'Tombstones in
  the Starlight'

5 Scratch a lover, and find a foe.
  Not So Deep as a Well (1937) 'Ballade of
  a Great Weariness'

6 There's a hell of a distance between
wise-cracking and wit. Wit has truth in
it; wise-cracking is simply callisthenics
with words.
  In *Paris Review* Summer 1956, p. 81

7 *House Beautiful* is play lousy.
  Review in *New Yorker* (1933), in Phyllis
  Hartnoll *Plays and Players* (1984) p. 89

8 Excuse My Dust.
  Suggested epitaph for herself (1925), in
  Alexander Woollcott *While Rome Burns*
  (1934) 'Our Mrs Parker'

9 That woman speaks eighteen languages,
and can't say No in any of them.
  In Alexander Woollcott *While Rome Burns*
  (1934) 'Our Mrs Parker'

10 And there was that wholesale libel on
a Yale prom. If all the girls attending it
were laid end to end, Mrs Parker said,
she wouldn't be at all surprised.
  Alexander Woollcott *While Rome Burns*
  (1934) 'Our Mrs Parker'

11 'Good work, Mary,' our Mrs Parker
wired collect [to Mrs Sherwood on the
arrival of her baby]. 'We all knew you
had it in you.'
  Alexander Woollcott *While Rome Burns*
  (1934) 'Our Mrs Parker'

12 How do they know?
  Reaction to the death of President Calvin
  Coolidge in 1933, in Malcolm Cowley
  Writers at Work 1st Series (1958) p. 65

13 As artists they're rot, but as providers
they're oil wells; they gush.
  Comment on lady novelists in Malcolm
  Cowley *Writers at Work* 1st Series (1958)
  p. 69

14 Hollywood money isn't money. It's
congealed snow, melts in your hand,
and there you are.
  In Malcolm Cowley *Writers at Work* 1st
  Series (1958) p. 81

15 Brevity is the soul of lingerie, as the
Petticoat said to the Chemise.
  Caption written for *Vogue* (1916) in John
  Keats *You Might as well Live* (1970) p. 32.
  Cf. Shakespeare's *Hamlet* act 2, sc. 2:
  'Brevity is the soul of wit'

16 You can lead a horticulture, but you
can't make her think.
  On being challenged to use 'horticulture' in
  a sentence, in John Keats *You Might as well
  Live* (1970) p. 46

17 It serves me right for putting all my eggs
in one bastard.
  On her abortion, in John Keats *You Might as
  well Live* (1970) pt. 2, ch. 3

Dorothy Parker 1893–1967, Alan Campbell 1905–1963, and Robert Carson 1910–1983

18 A star is born.
  Title of film (1937)

Ross Parker 1914–1974 and Hugh Charles 1907–

19 There'll always be an England
While there's a country lane,
Wherever there's a cottage small
Beside a field of grain.
  There'll always be an England (1939 song)

20 We'll meet again, don't know where,
Don't know when,
But I know we'll meet again some sunny
  day.
  We'll Meet Again (1939 song)

C. Northcote Parkinson 1909–

1 Expenditure rises to meet income.
  The Law and the Profits (1960) opening
  sentence

2 Work expands so as to fill the time
  available for its completion.
  Parkinson's Law (1958) p. 4

3 It might be termed the Law of Triviality.
  Briefly stated, it means that the time
  spent on any item of the agenda will be
  in inverse proportion to the sum
  involved.
  Parkinson's Law (1958) 'High Finance'

4 It is now known, however, that men
  enter local politics solely as a result of
  being unhappily married.
  Parkinson's Law (1958) 'Pension Point'

'Banjo' Paterson (Andrew Barton Paterson) 1864–1941

5 Once a jolly swagman camped by
    a billabong,
  Under the shade of a coolibah tree;
  And he sang as he watched and waited
    till his 'Billy' boiled:
  'You'll come a-waltzing, Matilda, with
    me.'
  Waltzing Matilda (1903 song)

Alan Paton 1903–

6 Cry, the beloved country.
  Title of novel (1948)

Norman Vincent Peale 1898–

7 The power of positive thinking.
  Title of book (1952)

Charles S. Pearce

8 Keep that schoolgirl complexion.
  Advertising slogan for Palmolive soap, from
  1917, in Nigel Rees *Slogans* (1982) p. 113

Hesketh Pearson 1887–1964

9 Misquotation is, in fact, the pride and
  privilege of the learned. A widely-read
  man never quotes accurately, for the
  rather obvious reason that he has read
  too widely.
  Common Misquotations (1934) Introduction

10 There is no stronger craving in the
   world than that of the rich for titles,

except perhaps that of the titled for
riches.
  The Pilgrim Daughters (1961) ch. 6

Lester Pearson 1897–1972

11 The grim fact is that we prepare for war
   like precocious giants and for peace like
   retarded pygmies.
   Speech in Toronto, 14 Mar. 1955

12 Not only did he [Dean Acheson] not
   suffer fools gladly, he did not suffer them
   at all.
   Time 25 Oct. 1971, p. 20

Charles Péguy 1873–1914

13 *Qui ne gueule pas la vérité, quand il sait la
   vérité, se fait le complice des menteurs et
   des faussaires.*

   He who does not bellow the truth when
   he knows the truth makes himself the
   accomplice of liars and forgers.
   Lettre du Provincial 21 Dec. 1899, in *Basic
   Verities* (1943) 'Honest People'

14 *La tyrannie est toujours mieux organisée
   que la liberté.*

   Tyranny is always better organised than
   freedom.
   In *Basic Verities* (1943) 'War and Peace'

Vladimir Peniakoff 1897–1951

15 That night a message came on the
   wireless for me. It said: 'SPREAD ALARM
   AND DESPONDENCY'. So the time had
   come, I thought, Eighth Army was
   taking the offensive. The date was,
   I think, May 18th, 1942.
   Private Army (1950) pt. 2, ch. 5

William H. Penn
See ALBERT H. FITZ

S. J. Perelman 1904–1979

16 Crazy like a fox.
   Title of book (1944)

17 I have Bright's disease and he has mine,
   sobbed the panting palooka.
   Judge 16 Nov. 1929

S. J. Perelman 1904–1979, Will B. Johnstone, and Arthur Sheekman

1 Do you suppose I could buy back my introduction to you?
   Monkey Business (1931 film), in *The Four Marx Brothers in Monkey Business and Duck Soup* (1972) p. 18

2 Look at me. Worked myself up from nothing to a state of extreme poverty.
   Monkey Business (1931 film), in *The Four Marx Brothers in Monkey Business and Duck Soup* (1972) p. 54

Carl Perkins 1932–

3 It's one for the money,
Two for the show,
Three to get ready,
Now go, cat, go!
But don't you step on my Blue Suede Shoes.
You can do anything but lay off my Blue Suede Shoes.
   Blue Suede Shoes (1956 song)

Frances Perkins 1882–1965

4 Why not 'Madam Secretary', if that form is to be used at all? One is accustomed to 'madam chairman' . . . so it comes more naturally, don't you think?
   When asked how she should be addressed as the first US woman cabinet member, in *New York Times* 6 Mar. 1933, p. 14. Cf. Howard Lindsay and Russel Crouse

Juan Perón 1895–1974

5 If I had not been born Perón, I would have liked to be Perón.
   In *Observer* 21 Feb. 1960

Ted Persons

6 Things ain't what they used to be.
   Title of song (1941; music by Mercer Ellington). Cf. Frank Norman and Lionel Bart

Henri Philippe Pétain 1856–1951

7 To write one's memoirs is to speak ill of everybody except oneself.
   In *Observer* 26 May 1946

Laurence Peter 1919– and Raymond Hull

8 My analysis . . . led me to formulate *The Peter Principle*: In a Hierarchy Every Employee Tends to Rise to His Level of Incompetence.
   The Peter Principle (1969) ch. 1

9 In time, every post tends to be occupied by an employee who is incompetent to carry out its duties. . . . Work is accomplished by those employees who have not yet reached their level of incompetence.
   The Peter Principle (1969) ch. 1

10 Competence, like truth, beauty and contact lenses, is in the eye of the beholder.
   The Peter Principle (1969) ch. 3

Kim Philby (Harold Adrian Russell Philby) 1912–1988

11 To betray, you must first belong. I never belonged.
   In *Sunday Times* 17 Dec. 1967, p. 2

Prince Philip, Duke of Edinburgh 1921–

12 I don't think doing it [killing animals] for money makes it any more moral. I don't think a prostitute is more moral than a wife, but they are doing the same thing.
   Speech in London, 6 Dec. 1988, comparing participation in blood sports to selling slaughtered meat, in *The Times* 7 Dec. 1988

13 I never see any home cooking. All I get is fancy stuff.
   In *Observer* 28 Oct. 1962

14 If you stay here much longer you'll all be slitty-eyed.
   Remark to Edinburgh University students in Peking, 16 Oct. 1986, in *The Times* 17 Oct. 1986

15 Just at this moment we are suffering a national defeat comparable to any lost military campaign, and, what is more, it is self-inflicted. I could use any one of the several stock phrases or platitudes about this. But I prefer one I picked up during the war. It is brief and to the point: Gentlemen, I think it is about time we 'pulled our fingers out'. . . . If

we want to be more prosperous we've
simply got to get down to it and work
for it. The rest of the world does not owe
us a living.

> Speech in London, 17 Oct. 1961, in *Daily
> Mail* 18 Oct. 1961

1 We now look upon it [the
English-Speaking Union] as including
those countries which use English as an
inter-Commonwealth language. I include
'pidgin-English' in this even though
I am referred to in that splendid
language as 'Fella belong Mrs Queen'.

> Speech to English-Speaking Union, Ottawa,
> 29 Oct. 1958, in *Prince Philip Speaks* (1960)
> pt. 2, ch. 3

Morgan Phillips 1902–1963

2 The Labour Party owes more to
Methodism than to Marxism.

> In James Callaghan *Time and Chance* (1987)
> ch. 1

Stephen Phillips 1864–1915

3 Behold me now
A man not old, but mellow, like good
   wine.
Not over-jealous, yet an eager husband.

> *Ulysses* (1902) act 3, sc. 2

Eden Phillpotts 1862–1960

4 Now old man's talk o' the days behind
   me;
My darter's youngest darter to mind me;
A little dreamin', a little dyin',
A little lew corner of airth to lie in.

> *Miniatures* (1942) 'Gaffer's Song'

Pablo Picasso 1881–1973

5 I paint objects as I think them, not as
I see them.

> In John Golding *Cubism* (1959) p. 60

6 God is really only another artist. He
invented the giraffe, the elephant, and
the cat. He has no real style. He just
goes on trying other things.

> Remark to Françoise Gilot in 1944, in
> Françoise Gilot and Carlton Lake *Life With
> Picasso* (1964) pt. 1

7 Every positive value has its price in
negative terms, and you never see
anything very great which is not, at the

same time, horrible in some respect. The
genius of Einstein leads to Hiroshima.

> Remark to Françoise Gilot in 1946, in
> Françoise Gilot and Carlton Lake *Life With
> Picasso* (1964) pt. 2

8 We all know that Art is not truth. Art is
a lie that makes us realize truth, at least
the truth that is given us to understand.

> In Dore Ashton *Picasso on Art* (1972) 'Two
> statements by Picasso'

9 Everyone wants to understand art. Why
not try to understand the song of a bird?
Why does one love the night, flowers,
everything around one, without trying
to understand them? But in the case of
a painting people have to *understand*. . . .
People who try to explain pictures are
usually barking up the wrong tree.

> In Dore Ashton *Picasso on Art* (1972) 'Two
> statements by Picasso'

Wilfred Pickles 1904–

10 Are yer courtin'?

> Catch-phrase in *Have a Go!* (BBC radio quiz
> programme, 1946–67)

11 Give him the money, Barney.

> Catch-phrase in *Have a Go!* (BBC radio quiz
> programme, 1946–67)

Harold Pinter 1930–

12 'But what would you say your plays
were *about*, Mr Pinter?' 'The weasel
under the cocktail cabinet.'

> In J. Russell Taylor *Anger and After* (1962)
> p. 231

13 I said to this monk, here, I said, look
here, mister, he opened the door, big
door, he opened it, look here mister,
I said, I showed him these, I said, you
haven't got a pair of shoes, have you,
a pair of shoes, I said, enough to help me
on my way. Look at these, they're
nearly out, I said, they're no good to me.
I heard you got a stock of shoes here.
Piss off, he said to me.

> *The Caretaker* (1960) act 1

14 I can't drink Guinness from a thick mug.
I only like it out of a thin glass.

> *The Caretaker* (1960) act 1

15 If only I could get down to Sidcup! I've
been waiting for the weather to break.
He's got my papers, this man I left them

with, it's got it all down there, I could
prove everything.
  The Caretaker (1960) act 1

Luigi Pirandello 1867–1936

1 *Sei personaggi in cerca d'autore.*

Six characters in search of an author.
  Title of play (1921)

2 *Quando i personaggi son vivi, vivi
veramente davanti al loro autore, questo
non fa altro che seguirli nelle parole, nei
gesti ch'essi appunto gli propongono.*

When the characters are alive, really
alive before their author, the latter
merely follows them in the words and
actions which they in fact suggest to
him.
  Sei personaggi in cerca d'autore (Six
  Characters in search of an Author, 1921) in
  Three Plays (1964) p. 64

Armand J. Piron

3 I wish I could shimmy like my sister
  Kate,
  She shivers like the jelly on a plate.
  Shimmy like Kate (1919 song)

Robert Pirosh, George Seaton, and George Oppenheimer

4 (*Feeling patient's pulse*): Either he's dead,
or my watch has stopped.
  A Day at the Races (1937 film; line spoken
  by Groucho Marx)

5 Emily, I've a little confession to make.
I really am a horse doctor. But marry
me, and I'll never look at any other
horse!
  A Day at the Races (1937 film; lines spoken
  by Groucho Marx)

Robert M. Pirsig 1928–

6 Zen and the art of motorcycle
maintenance.
  Title of book (1974)

Walter B. Pitkin 1878–1953

7 Life begins at forty.
  Title of book (1932)

Ruth Pitter 1897–

8 I dream

Already that I hear my lover's voice;
What music shall I have—what dying
  wails—
The seldom female in a world of males!
  On Cats (1947) 'Kitten's Eclogue'

Sylvia Plath 1932–1963

9 Love set you going like a fat gold watch.
The midwife slapped your footsoles, and
  your bald cry
Took its place among the elements.
  Ariel (1965) 'Morning Song'

10 Dying,
Is an art, like everything else.
I do it exceptionally well.
  Encounter Oct. 1963, 'Lady Lazarus'

11 Every woman adores a Fascist,
The boot in the face, the brute
Brute heart of a brute like you.
  Encounter Oct. 1963, 'Daddy'

William Plomer 1903–1973

12 They took the hill (Whose hill? What
  for?)
But what a climb they left to do!
Out of that bungled, unwise war
An alp of unforgiveness grew.
  Collected Poems (1960) 'The Boer War'

13 On a sofa upholstered in panther skin
Mona did researches in original sin.
  Collected Poems (1960) 'Mews Flat Mona'

14 A rose-red sissy half as old as time.
  The Dorking Thigh (1945) 'Playboy of the
  Demi-World'. Cf. *Oxford Dictionary of
  Quotations* (1979) 108:4

15 A family portrait not too stale to record
Of a pleasant old buffer, nephew to
  a lord,
Who believed that the bank was
  mightier than the sword,
And that an umbrella might pacify
  barbarians abroad:
Just like an old liberal
Between the wars.
  The Dorking Thigh (1945) 'Father and Son'

16 Fissures appeared in football fields
And houses in the night collapsed.
The Thames flowed backward to its
  source,
The last trickle seen to disappear
Swiftly, like an adder to its hole,
And here and there along the river-bed
The stranded fish gaped among empty
  tins,

Face downward lay the huddled suicides
Like litter that a riot leaves.
  Visiting the Caves (1936) 'The Silent Sunday'

Henri Poincaré 1854–1912

1 Science is built up of facts, as a house is
built of stones; but an accumulation of
facts is no more a science than a heap of
stones is a house.
  Science and Hypothesis (1905) ch. 9

Georges Pompidou 1911–1974

2 A statesman is a politician who places
himself at the service of the nation.
A politician is a statesman who places
the nation at his service.
  In *Observer* 30 Dec. 1973

Arthur Ponsonby (first Baron Ponsonby of Shulbrede) 1871–1946

3 When war is declared, Truth is the first
  casualty.
  Kommt der Krieg ins Land
  Gibt's Lügen wie Sand.

  [When war enters a country
  It produces lies like sand.]
  Epigraphs to *Falsehood in Wartime* (1928)
  p. 11

Sir Karl Popper 1902–

4 We may become the makers of our fate
when we have ceased to pose as its
prophets.
  The Open Society and its Enemies (1945)
  Introduction

5 We must plan for freedom, and not only
for security, if for no other reason than
that only freedom can make security
secure.
  The Open Society and its Enemies (1945)
  vol. 2, ch. 21

6 There is no history of mankind, there
are only many histories of all kinds of
aspects of human life. And one of these
is the history of political power. This is
elevated into the history of the world.
  The Open Society and its Enemies (1945)
  vol. 2, ch. 25

7 Piecemeal social engineering resembles
physical engineering in regarding the
ends as beyond the province of
technology.
  Poverty of Historicism (1957) pt. 3, sect. 21

8 For this, indeed, is the true source of our
ignorance—the fact that our knowledge
can only be finite, while our ignorance
must necessarily be infinite.
  Lecture to British Academy, 20 Jan. 1960,
  in *Proceedings of the British Academy* (1960)
  vol. 46, p. 69

Cole Porter 1891–1964

9 In olden days a glimpse of stocking
Was looked on as something shocking
Now, heaven knows,
Anything goes.
  Anything Goes (1934 song)

10 When they begin the Beguine
It brings back the sound of music so
  tender,
It brings back a night of tropical
  splendour,
It brings back a memory ever green.
  Begin the Beguine (1935 song)

11 Oh, give me land, lots of land
Under starry skies above
DON'T FENCE ME IN.
  Don't Fence Me In (1934 song; revived in
  1944 film *Hollywood Canteen*)

12 I get no kick from champagne,
Mere alcohol doesn't thrill me at all,
So tell me why should it be true
That I get a kick out of you?
  I Get a Kick Out of You (1934 song)

13 I've got you under my skin.
  Title of song (1936)

14 So goodbye dear, and Amen,
Here's hoping we meet now and then,
It was great fun,
But it was just one of those things.
  Just One of Those Things (1935 song)

15 Birds do it, bees do it,
Even educated fleas do it.
Let's do it, let's fall in love.
  Let's Do It (1954 song; these words are not
  in the original 1928 version)

16 Miss Otis regrets (she's unable to lunch
today).
  Title of song (1934)

17 My heart belongs to Daddy.
  Title of song (1938)

18 Night and day, you are the one,

Only you beneath the moon and under
the sun.
Night and Day (1932 song)

1 SHE: Have you heard it's in the stars,
Next July we collide with Mars?
HE: Well, did you evah! What a swell
party this is.
Well, Did You Evah? (1956 song)

2 Who wants to be a millionaire?
Title of song (1956)

3 You're the top.
Title of song (1934)

Beatrix Potter 1866–1943

4 In the time of swords and periwigs and
full-skirted coats with flowered
lappets—when gentlemen wore ruffles,
and gold-laced waistcoats of paduasoy
and taffeta—there lived a tailor in
Gloucester.
Tailor of Gloucester (1903) p. 9

5 The tailor replied—'Simpkin, we shall
make our fortune, but I am worn to
a ravelling. Take this groat (which is our
last fourpence) and . . . with the last
penny of our fourpence buy me one
penn'orth of cherry-coloured silk. But do
not lose the last penny of the fourpence,
Simpkin, or I am undone and worn to
a thread-paper, for I have NO MORE
TWIST.'
Tailor of Gloucester (1903) p. 22

6 It is said that the effect of eating too
much lettuce is 'soporific'.
Tale of the Flopsy Bunnies (1909) p. 9

7 Once upon a time there were four little
Rabbits, and their names were—Flopsy,
Mopsy, Cottontail, and Peter.
Tale of Peter Rabbit (1902) p. 9

8 You may go into the fields or down the
lane, but don't go into Mr McGregor's
garden: your Father had an accident
there; he was put in a pie by Mrs
McGregor.
Tale of Peter Rabbit (1902) p. 10

9 Peter sat down to rest; he was out of
breath and trembling with fright. . . .
After a time he began to wander about,
going lippity-lippity—not very fast, and
looking all round.
Tale of Peter Rabbit (1902) p. 58

Gillie Potter (Hugh William Peel) 1887–1975

10 Good evening, England. This is Gillie
Potter speaking to you in English.
Heard at Hogsnorton (opening words of
broadcasts, 6 June 1946 and 11 Nov. 1947)

Stephen Potter 1900–1969

11 A good general rule is to state that the
bouquet is better than the taste, and
vice versa.
One-Upmanship (1952) ch. 14

12 *How to be one up*—how to make the
other man feel that something has gone
wrong, however slightly.
Some Notes on Lifemanship (1950) p. 14

13 'Yes, but not in the South', with slight
adjustments, will do for any argument
about any place, if not about any
person.
Some Notes on Lifemanship (1950) p. 43

14 The theory and practice of
gamesmanship or The art of winning
games without actually cheating.
Title of book (1947)

Ezra Pound 1885–1972

15 The author's conviction on this day of
New Year is that music begins to
atrophy when it departs too far from the
dance; that poetry begins to atrophy
when it gets too far from music.
ABC of Reading (1934) 'Warning'

16 Any general statement is like a cheque
drawn on a bank. Its value depends on
what is there to meet it.
ABC of Reading (1934) ch. 1

17 One of the pleasures of middle age is to
find out that one WAS right, and that one
was much righter than one knew at say
17 or 23.
ABC of Reading (1934) ch. 1

18 Literature is news that STAYS news.
ABC of Reading (1934) ch. 2

19 Real education must ultimately be
limited to one who INSISTS on knowing,
the rest is mere sheep-herding.
ABC of Reading (1934) ch. 8

1 Tching prayed on the mountain and
wrote MAKE IT NEW
on his bath tub.
Day by day make it new
cut underbrush,
pile the logs
keep it growing.
    Cantos (1954) no. 53

2 Hang it all, Robert Browning,
There can be but the one 'Sordello'.
    Draft of XXX Cantos (1930) no. 2

3 And even I can remember
A day when the historians left blanks in
    their writings,
I mean for things they didn't know.
    Draft of XXX Cantos (1930) no. 13

4 Great literature is simply language
charged with meaning to the utmost
possible degree.
    How To Read (1931) pt. 2

5 For three years, out of key with his time,
He strove to resuscitate the dead art
Of poetry; to maintain 'the sublime'
In the old sense. Wrong from the start—

No, hardly, but seeing he had been born
In a half savage country, out of date.
    Hugh Selwyn Mauberley (1920) 'E. P. *Ode
    pour l'élection de son sépulchre*'

6 His true Penelope was Flaubert,
He fished by obstinate isles;
Observed the elegance of Circe's hair
Rather than the mottoes on sundials.
    Hugh Selwyn Mauberley (1920) 'E. P. *Ode
    pour l'élection de son sépulchre*'

7 The age demanded an image
Of its accelerated grimace,
Something for the modern stage,
Not, at any rate, an Attic grace;

Not, not certainly, the obscure reveries
Of the inward gaze;
Better mendacities
Than the classics in paraphrase!
    Hugh Selwyn Mauberley (1920) 'E. P. *Ode
    pour l'élection de son sépulchre*'

8 Christ follows Dionysus
Phallic and ambrosial
Made way for macerations;
Caliban casts out Ariel.
    Hugh Selwyn Mauberley (1920) 'E. P. *Ode
    pour l'élection de son sépulchre*'

9 There died a myriad,
And of the best, among them,

For an old bitch gone in the teeth,
For a botched civilization.
    Hugh Selwyn Mauberley (1920) 'E. P. *Ode
    pour l'élection de son sépulchre*'

10 The tip's a good one, as for literature
It gives no man a sinecure.

And no one knows, at sight,
    a masterpiece.
And give up verse, my boy,
There's nothing in it.
    Hugh Selwyn Mauberley (1920) 'E. P. *Ode
    pour l'élection de son sépulchre*'

11 Poetry must be *as well written as prose*.
    Letter to Harriet Monroe, Jan. 1915, in
    D. D. Paige (ed.) *Selected Letters of Ezra
    Pound* (1950) p. 48

12 Artists are the antennae of the race, but
the bullet-headed many will never learn
to trust their great artists.
    Literary Essays (1954) 'Henry James'

13 Winter is icummen in,
Lhude sing Goddamm,
Raineth drop and staineth slop,
And how the wind doth ramm!
Sing: Goddamm.
    Lustra (1916) 'Ancient Music'. Cf. *Oxford
    Dictionary of Quotations* (1979) 7:18

14 The apparition of these faces in the
    crowd;
Petals on a wet, black bough.
    Lustra (1916) 'In a Station of the Metro'

15 Bah! I have sung women in three cities,
But it is all the same;
And I will sing of the sun.
    Personae (1908) 'Cino'

16 The ant's a centaur in his dragon world.
Pull down thy vanity, it is not man
Made courage, or made order, or made
    grace,
Pull down thy vanity, I say pull down.
Learn of the green world what can be
    thy place
In scaled invention or true artistry,
Pull down thy vanity,
Paquin pull down!
The green casque has outdone your
    elegance.
    Pisan Cantos (1948) no. 81

17 Pull down thy vanity
Thou art a beaten dog beneath the hail,
A swollen magpie in a fitful sun,
Half black half white

Nor knowst'ou wing from tail
Pull down thy vanity.
Pisan Cantos (1948) no. 81

Anthony Powell 1905–

1 He fell in love with himself at first sight
and it is a passion to which he has
always remained faithful.
Acceptance World (1955) ch. 1

2 Self-love seems so often unrequited.
Acceptance World (1955) ch. 1

3 Dinner at the Huntercombes' possessed
'only two dramatic features—the wine
was a farce and the food a tragedy'.
Acceptance World (1955) ch. 4

4 Books do furnish a room.
Title of novel (1971)

5 Parents—especially step-parents—are
sometimes a bit of a disappointment to
their children. They don't fufil the
promise of their early years.
A Buyer's Market (1952) ch. 2

6 A dance to the music of time.
Title of a novel sequence (1951–75), after
title given by Giovanni Pietro Bellori to
a painting by Nicolas Poussin, *Le 4 stagioni
che ballano al suono del tempo*

7 Growing old is like being increasingly
penalized for a crime you haven't
committed.
Temporary Kings (1973) ch. 1

Enoch Powell 1912–

8 All political lives, unless they are cut off
in midstream at a happy juncture, end
in failure, because that is the nature of
politics and of human affairs.
Joseph Chamberlain (1977) epilogue

9 History is littered with the wars which
everybody knew would never happen.
Speech to Conservative Party Conference,
19 Oct. 1967, in *The Times* 20 Oct. 1967

10 As I look ahead, I am filled with
foreboding. Like the Roman, I seem to
see 'the River Tiber foaming with much
blood'.
Speech at Annual Meeting of West Midlands
Area Conservative Political Centre,
Birmingham, 20 Apr. 1968, in *Observer*
21 Apr. 1968

Sandy Powell 1900–1982

11 Can you hear me, mother?
Catch-phrase: see *Can You Hear Me,
Mother? Sandy Powell's Lifetime of Music-Hall*
(1975) p. 62

Vince Powell and Harry Driver

12 Never mind the quality, feel the width.
Title of ITV comedy series, 1967–9

Jacques Prévert 1900–1977

13 *C'est tellement simple, l'amour.*

Love is so simple.
Les Enfants du Paradis (1945 film)

14 *Notre Père qui êtes aux cieux
Restez-y
Et nous nous resterons sur la terre
Qui est quelquefois si jolie.*

Our Father which art in heaven
Stay there
And we will stay on earth
Which is sometimes so pretty.
Paroles (revised ed., 1949) 'Pater Noster'

J. B. Priestley 1894–1984

15 To say that these men paid their
shillings to watch twenty-two hirelings
kick a ball is merely to say that a violin
is wood and catgut, that *Hamlet* is so
much paper and ink. For a shilling the
Bruddersford United AFC offered you
Conflict and Art.
Good Companions (1929) bk. 1, ch. 1

16 An inspector calls.
Title of play (1947)

17 This little steamer, like all her brave and
battered sisters, is immortal. She'll go
sailing proudly down the years in the
epic of Dunkirk. And our
great-grand-children, when they learn
how we began this war by snatching
glory out of defeat, and then swept on to
victory, may also learn how the little
holiday steamers made an excursion to
hell and came back glorious.
Radio broadcast, 5 June 1940, in *Listener*
13 June 1940

1 God can stand being told by Professor
Ayer and Marghanita Laski that He
doesn't exist.
  In *Listener* 1 July 1965, p. 12

2 It is hard to tell where the MCC ends
and the Church of England begins.
  In *New Statesman* 20 July 1962, p. 78

V. S. Pritchett 1900–

3 The principle of procrastinated rape is
said to be the ruling one in all the great
best-sellers.
  The Living Novel (1946) 'Clarissa'

4 What Chekhov saw in our failure to
communicate was something positive
and precious: the private silence in
which we live, and which enables us to
endure our own solitude. We live, as his
characters do, beyond any tale we
happen to enact.
  Myth Makers (1979) 'Chekhov, a doctor'

5 The detective novel is the
art-for-art's-sake of our yawning
Philistinism, the classic example of
a specialized form of art removed from
contact with the life it pretends to build
on.
  New Statesman 16 June 1951, 'Books in
  General'

Marcel Proust 1871–1922

6 *A la recherche du temps perdu.*

In search of lost time.
  Title of novel (1913–27), translated by C. K.
  Scott-Moncrieff and S. Hudson, 1922–31, as
  'Remembrance of things past'

7 *Longtemps, je me suis couché de bonne
heure.*

For a long time I used to go to bed early.
  Du côté de chez Swann (Swann's Way, 1913,
  translated 1922 by C. K. Scott-Moncrieff,
  vol. 1, p. 1)

8 *Je portai à mes lèvres une cuillerée du thé
où j'avais laissé s'amollir un morceau de
madeleine. . . . Et tout d'un coup le
souvenir m'est apparu. Ce goût c'était celui
du petit morceau de madeleine que le
dimanche matin à Combray . . . ma tante
Léonie m'offrait après l'avoir trempé dans
son infusion de thé ou de tilleul.*

I raised to my lips a spoonful of the tea in
which I had soaked a morsel of cake. . . .
And suddenly the memory returns.

The taste was that of the little crumb of
madeleine which on Sunday mornings
at Combray . . . my aunt Léonie used to
give me, dipping it first in her own cup
of real or of lime-flower tea.
  Du côté de chez Swann (Swann's Way, 1913,
  translated 1922 by C. K. Scott-Moncrieff,
  vol. 1, pp. 46 and 61)

9 *Et il ne fut plus question de Swann chez les
Verdurin.*

After which there was no more talk of
Swann at the Verdurins'.
  Du côté de chez Swann (Swann's Way, 1913,
  translated 1922 by C. K. Scott-Moncrieff,
  vol. 2, p. 99)

10 *Dire que j'ai gâché des années de ma vie,
que j'ai voulu mourir, que j'ai eu mon plus
grand amour, pour une femme qui ne me
plaisait pas, qui n'était pas mon genre!*

To think that I have wasted years of my
life, that I have longed for death, that
the greatest love that I have ever known
has been for a woman who did not
please me, who was not my style!
  Du côté de chez Swann (Swann's Way, 1913,
  translated 1922 by C. K. Scott-Moncrieff,
  vol. 2, p. 228)

11 *On devient moral dès qu'on est malheureux.*

As soon as one is unhappy one becomes
moral.
  A l'ombre des jeunes filles en fleurs (Within
  a Budding Grove, 1918, translated 1924 by
  C. K. Scott-Moncrieff, vol. 1, p. 290)

12 *Tout ce que nous connaissons de grand nous
vient des nerveux. Ce sont eux et non pas
d'autres qui ont fondé les religions et
composé les chefs-d'œuvre. Jamais le monde
ne saura tout ce qu'il leur doit et surtout ce
qu'eux ont souffert pour le lui donner.*

All the greatest things we know have
come to us from neurotics. It is they and
they only who have founded religions
and created great works of art. Never
will the world be conscious of how
much it owes to them, nor above all of
what they have suffered in order to
bestow their gifts on it.
  Le côté de Guermantes (Guermantes Way,
  1921, translated 1925 by C. K.
  Scott-Moncrieff, vol. 1, p. 418)

13 *Il n'y a rien comme le désir pour empêcher
les choses qu'on dit d'avoir aucune
ressemblance avec ce qu'on a dans la pensée.*

There is nothing like desire for
preventing the thing one says from
bearing any resemblance to what one
has in mind.

> *Le côté de Guermantes* (Guermantes Way,
> 1921, translated 1925 by C. K.
> Scott-Moncrieff, vol. 2, p. 60)

1 *Un artiste n'a pas besoin d'exprimer
directement sa pensée dans son ouvrage
pour que celui-ci en reflète la qualité; on
a même pu dire que la louange la plus haute
de Dieu est dans la négation de l'athée qui
trouve la Création assez parfaite pour se
passer d'un créateur.*

An artist has no need to express his
mind directly in his work for it to
express the quality of that mind; it has
indeed been said that the highest praise
of God consists in the denial of Him by
the atheist, who finds creation so perfect
that it can dispense with a creator.

> *Le côté de Guermantes* (Guermantes Way,
> 1921, translated 1925 by C. K.
> Scott-Moncrieff, vol. 2, p. 147)

2 *Du reste, continua Mme de Cambremer, j'ai
horreur des couchers de soleil, c'est
romantique, c'est opéra.*

'Anyhow,' Mme de Cambremer went on,
'I have a horror of sunsets, they're so
romantic, so operatic.'

> *Sodome et Gomorrhe* (Cities of the Plain,
> 1922, translated by C. K. Scott-Moncrieff,
> vol. 1, p. 296)

3 *Une de ces dépêches dont M. de Guermantes
avait spirituellement fixé le modèle:
'Impossible venir, mensonge suit'.*

One of those telegrams of which the
model had been wittily invented by M.
de Guermantes: 'Impossible to come, lie
follows'.

> *Le temps retrouvé* (Time Regained, 1926,
> translated 1931 by S. Hudson, ch. 1, p. 7).
> Cf. Lord Charles Beresford

4 *Les vrais paradis sont les paradis qu'on
a perdus.*

The true paradises are paradises we
have lost.

> *Le temps retrouvé* (Time Regained, 1926,
> translated 1931 by S. Hudson, ch. 3,
> p. 215)

5 *Le bonheur seul est salutaire pour le corps,
mais c'est le chagrin qui développe les forces
de l'esprit.*

Happiness is salutary for the body but
sorrow develops the powers of the spirit.

> *Le temps retrouvé* (Time Regained, 1926,
> translated 1931 by S. Hudson, ch. 3,
> p. 259)

Olive Higgins Prouty 1882–1974

6 She [Charlotte] drew in her breath
sharply as if he had touched a nerve. 'O
Jerry,' she said when she could trust her
voice. 'Don't let's ask for the moon! We
have the stars!'

> THE END
>
> *Now, Voyager* (1941) ch. 29 (words spoken
> by Bette Davis in the 1942 film version)

John Pudney 1909–1977

7 Do not despair
For Johnny-head-in-air;
He sleeps as sound
As Johnny underground.

Fetch out no shroud
For Johnny-in-the-cloud;
And keep your tears
For him in after years.

Better by far
For Johnny-the-bright-star,
To keep your head,
And see his children fed.

> *Dispersal Point* (1942) 'For Johnny'

Mario Puzo 1920–

8 He's a businessman. . . . I'll make him
an offer he can't refuse.

> *The Godfather* (1969) ch. 1

9 A lawyer with his briefcase can steal
more than a hundred men with guns.

> *The Godfather* (1969) ch. 1

10 Mario had called George Mandel to say
he'd heard Joe [Heller] was paralysed.
'No, Mario. . . . He's got something
called Guillain-Barré.' 'My God,' Mario
blurted out. 'That's terrible!' A surprised
George murmured, 'Hey Mario, you
know about Guillain-Barré?' 'No,
I never heard nothing about it,' Mario
replied. 'But when they name any
disease after two guys, it's got to be
terrible!'

> Joseph Heller *No Laughing Matter* (1986)
> p. 44

Q

See Sir Arthur Quiller-Couch

Salvatore Quasimodo 1901–1968

1 Poetry ... is the revelation of a feeling that the poet believes to be interior and personal—which the reader recognizes as his own.
  Speech in New York, 13 May 1960, in *New York Times* 14 May 1960, p. 47

Peter Quennell 1905–

2 He [André Gide] was very bald ... with ... the general look of an elderly fallen angel travelling incognito.
  The Sign of the Fish (1960) ch. 2

Sir Arthur Quiller-Couch ('Q') 1863–1944

3 Literature is not an abstract science, to which exact definitions can be applied. It is an Art rather, the success of which depends on personal persuasiveness, on the author's skill to give as on ours to receive.
  Inaugural Lecture at Cambridge University, 1913, in *On the Art of Writing* (1916) p. 16

4 The best is the best, though a hundred judges have declared it so.
  Oxford Book of English Verse (1900) preface

5 Know you her secret none can utter? Hers of the Book, the tripled Crown?
  Poems (1929) 'Alma Mater'

6 He that loves but half of Earth Loves but half enough for me.
  Poems and Ballads (1896) 'The Comrade'

7 Not as we wanted it, But as God granted it.
  Poems and Ballads (1896) 'To Bearers'

James Rado 1939–
and Gerome Ragni 1942–

8 When the moon is in the seventh house, And Jupiter aligns with Mars, Then peace will guide the planets, And love will steer the stars; This is the dawning of the age of Aquarius, The age of Aquarius.
  Aquarius (1967 song; music by Galt MacDermot)

John Rae 1931–

9 War is, after all, the universal perversion. We are all tainted: if we cannot experience our perversion at first hand we spend our time reading war stories, the pornography of war; or seeing war films, the blue films of war; or titillating our senses with the imagination of great deeds, the masturbation of war.
  The Custard Boys (1960) ch. 13

Milton Rakove 1918–1983

10 The second law, Rakove's law of principle and politics, states that the citizen is influenced by principle in direct proportion to his distance from the political situation.
  In *Virginia Quarterly Review* (1965) vol. 41, p. 349

Sir Walter Raleigh 1861–1922

11 In Examinations those who do not wish to know ask questions of those who cannot tell.
  Laughter from a Cloud (1923) 'Some Thoughts on Examinations'

12 We could not lead a pleasant life, And 'twould be finished soon, If peas were eaten with the knife, And gravy with the spoon. Eat slowly: only men in rags And gluttons old in sin Mistake themselves for carpet bags And tumble victuals in.
  Laughter from a Cloud (1923) 'Stans Puer ad Mensam'

13 I wish I loved the Human Race; I wish I loved its silly face; I wish I liked the way it walks; I wish I liked the way it talks; And when I'm introduced to one I wish I thought *What Jolly Fun!*
  Laughter from a Cloud (1923) 'Wishes of an Elderly Man'

14 An anthology is like all the plums and orange peel picked out of a cake.
  Letter to Mrs Robert Bridges, 15 Jan. 1915, in *Letters of Sir Walter Raleigh* (1926) vol. 2, p. 411

Srinivasa Ramanujan 1887–1920

15 I remember once going to see him when he was lying ill at Putney. I had ridden in taxi-cab No. 1729, and remarked that the number (7.13.19) seemed to me rather a dull one. 'No,' he replied, 'it

—1975
cosmetics; in the
1976) ch. 8

900–1978
ide,
ky-tacky,
ide;
d a pink one
yellow one
ut of ticky-tacky
the same.
)

1902–1965
al adage which
'em, jine 'em.'
41) ch. 1

—1902
ationality he would
ety-nine out of
ou that they would
hen.
ecil Rhodes (1913)

me [in December
s friend Albert Grey
ight in Bulawayo to
had ever considered
as to be alive and in
have been born an
so many millions of
s had no such luck.
C. M. Woodhouse *Rhodes*

uch to do.
ell on the day he died, in
f Rhodes (1910) vol. 2,

Gwendolen Rees
0–1979
day is the same
y, melancholy,
e when they say 'As it
hing, is now, and ever
ithout end.'
k (1934) ch. 4, pt. 1

Grantland Rice 1880–1954

8 All wars are planned by old men
In council rooms apart.
  The Final Answer (1955) 'The Two Sides of War'

9 Outlined against a blue-gray October sky, the Four Horsemen rode again. In dramatic lore they were known as Famine, Pestilence, Destruction, and Death. These are only aliases. Their real names are Stuhldreher, Miller, Crowley, and Layden. They formed the crest of the South Bend cyclone before which another fighting Army football team was swept over the precipice at the Polo Grounds yesterday afternoon as 55,000 spectators peered down on the bewildering panorama spread on the green below.
  Report of football match on 18 Oct. 1924 between US Military Academy at West Point NY and University of Notre Dame, in *New York Tribune* 19 Oct. 1924

10 For when the One Great Scorer comes to mark against your name,
He writes—not that you won or lost—but how you played the Game.
  Only the Brave (1941) 'Alumnus Football'

Tim Rice 1944–

11 Don't cry for me Argentina.
  Title of song (1976; music by Andrew Lloyd Webber)

12 Prove to me that you're no fool
Walk across my swimming pool.
  Herod's Song (1970; music by Andrew Lloyd Webber)

Mandy Rice-Davies 1944–

13 MR BURGE: Do you know Lord Astor has made a statement to the police saying that these allegations of yours are absolutely untrue?
MANDY RICE-DAVIES: He would, wouldn't he? (*Laughter*).
  At the trial of Stephen Ward, 29 June 1963, in *Guardian* 1 July 1963

14 An American tourist, seeing me the centre of a crowd, came up to me. 'Hello, my dear, may I have your autograph. And would you mind telling me who you are?' I hated having to say my name. For years Mandy Rice-Davies was such an embarrassment to me. It is

is a very interesting number; it is the smallest number expressible as a sum of two cubes in two different ways.'
  G. H. Hardy in *Proceedings of the London Mathematical Society* 26 May 1921, p. 57. (The two ways are $1^3 + 12^3$ and $9^3 + 10^3$)

John Crowe Ransom 1888–1974

1 Here lies a lady of beauty and high degree.
Of chills and fever she died, of fever and chills,
The delight of her husband, her aunts, an infant of three,
And of medicos marvelling sweetly on her ills.
  Chills and Fever (1924) 'Here Lies a Lady'

Arthur Ransome 1884–1967

2 Mother smiled, and read the telegram aloud: BETTER DROWNED THAN DUFFERS IF NOT DUFFERS WONT DROWN. 'Does that mean Yes?' asked Roger. 'I think so.'
  Swallows and Amazons (1930) ch. 1

Frederic Raphael 1931–

3 He glanced with disdain at the big centre table where the famous faces of the Cambridge theatre were eating a loud meal. 'So this is the city of dreaming spires,' Sheila said. 'Theoretically speaking that's Oxford,' Adam said. 'This is the city of perspiring dreams.'
  Glittering Prizes: (1976) ch. 3. Cf. *Oxford Dictionary of Quotations* (1979) 15:4

Terence Rattigan 1911–1977

4 The headmaster said you ruled them with a rod of iron. He called you the Himmler of the lower fifth.
  The Browning Version (1948) (spoken by Peter Gilbert to Andrew Crocker-Harris)

5 Let us invent a character, a nice respectable, middle-class, middle-aged, maiden lady, with time on her hands and the money to help her pass it. She enjoys pictures, books, music, and the theatre and though to none of these arts (or rather, for consistency's sake, to none of these three arts and the one craft) does she bring much knowledge or discernment, at least, as she is apt to tell her cronies,

she 'does know what she likes'. Let us call her Aunt Edna. . . . Aunt Edna is universal, and to those who may feel that all the problems of the modern theatre might be solved by her liquidation, let me add that I have no doubt at all that she is also immortal.
  Collected Plays (1953) vol. 2, preface

6 KENNETH: If you're so hot, you'd better tell me how to say she has ideas above her station.
BRIAN: Oh, yes, I forgot. It's fairly easy, old boy. Elle a des idées au-dessus de sa gare.
KENNETH: You can't do it like that. You can't say *au-dessus de sa gare*. It isn't that sort of station.
  French without Tears (1937) act 1

7 Do you know what 'le vice Anglais'—the English vice—really is? Not flagellation, not pederasty—whatever the French believe it to be. It's our refusal to admit our emotions. We think they demean us, I suppose.
  In Praise of Love (1973) act 2

8 You can be in the Horseguards and still be common, dear.
  Separate Tables (1954) 'Table Number Seven' sc. 1

Gwen Raverat 1885–1957

9 I have defined Ladies as people who did not do things themselves. Aunt Etty was most emphatically such a person.
  Period Piece (1952) ch. 7

Irving Ravetch and Harriet Frank

10 The long hot summer.
  Title of film (1958), based on stories by William Faulkner

Ted Ray (Charles Olden) 1906–1977

11 Ee, it was agony, Ivy.
  Catch-phrase in *Ray's a Laugh* (BBC radio programme, 1949–61)

12 He's loo-vely, Mrs Hoskin . . . he's loo . . . ooo . . . vely!
  Catch-phrase in *Ray's a Laugh* (BBC radio programme, 1949–61) in *Raising the Laughs* (1952) p. 158

Sam Rayburn 1882–1961

1 If you want to get along, go along.
   In Neil MacNeil *Forge of Democracy* (1963)
   ch. 6

Sir Herbert Read 1893–1968

2 Do not judge this movement kindly. It is
not just another amusing stunt. It is
defiant—the desperate act of men too
profoundly convinced of the rottenness
of our civilization to want to save
a shred of its respectability.
   Introduction to International Surrealist
   Exhibition Catalogue, New Burlington
   Galleries, London, 11 June—4 July 1936

3 I saw him stab
And stab again
A well-killed Boche.

This is the happy warrior,
This is he. . . .
   Naked Warriors (1919) 'The Scene of War,
   4. The Happy Warrior'

Nancy Reagan 1923–

4 A woman is like a teabag—only in hot
water do you realise how strong she is.
   In *Observer* 29 Mar. 1981

Ronald Reagan 1911–

5 You can tell a lot about a fellow's
character by his way of eating
jellybeans.
   In *New York Times* 15 Jan. 1981

6 So in your discussions of the nuclear
freeze proposals, I urge you to beware
the temptation of pride—the temptation
blithely to declare yourselves above it all
and label both sides equally at fault, to
ignore the facts of history and the
aggressive impulses of an evil empire, to
simply call the arms race a giant
misunderstanding and thereby remove
yourself from the struggle between right
and wrong, good and evil.
   Speech to National Association of
   Evangelicals, 8 Mar. 1983, in *New York
   Times* 9 Mar. 1983

7 My fellow Americans, I am pleased to
tell you I just signed legislation which
outlaws Russia forever. The bombing
begins in five minutes.
   Said during radio microphone test, 11 Aug.
   1984, in *New York Times* 13 Aug. 1984

8 We are especially not going to tolerate
these attacks from outlaw states run by
the strangest collection of misfits,
Looney Tunes and squalid criminals
since the advent of the Third Reich.
   Speech following the hi-jack of a US plane,
   8 July 1985, in *New York Times* 9 July 1985

9 We know that this mad dog of the
Middle East has a goal of a world
revolution, Muslim fundamentalist
revolution, which is targeted on many of
his own Arab compatriots and where we
figure in that I don't know.
   Said of Col. Gadaffi of Libya at press
   conference, 9 Apr. 1986, in *New York Times*
   10 Apr. 1986, p. A 22

10 Politics is supposed to be the second
oldest profession. I have come to realize
that it bears a very close resemblance to
the first.
   At a conference in Los Angeles, 2 Mar.
   1977, in Bill Adler *Reagan Wit* (1981) ch. 5

Erell Reaves

11 Lady of Spain, I adore you.
Right from the night I first saw you,
My heart has been yearning for you,
What else could any heart do?
   Lady of Spain (1931 song; music by
   Tolchard Evans)

Henry Reed 1914–1986

12 Today we have naming of parts.
   Yesterday,
We had daily cleaning. And tomorrow
   morning,
We shall have what to do after firing.
   But today,
Today we have naming of parts.
   Japonica
Glistens like coral in all of the neighbour
   gardens,
And today we have naming of parts.
   A Map of Verona (1946) 'Lessons of the
   War: 1, Naming of Parts'

13 They call it easing the Spring: it is
   perfectly easy
If you have any strength in your
   thumb: like the bolt,
And the breech, and the cocking-piece,
   and the point of balance,

Which in our case we ha[...]
   the almond blossom
Silent in all of the gardens[...]
   going backwards and fo[...]
For today we have naming[...]
   A Map of Verona (1946) 'Less[...]
   War: 1, Naming of Parts'

1 And the various holds and [...]
   throws and breakfalls
Somehow or other I always [...]
   put
In the wrong place. And as [...]
   wars
Were global from the start.
   A Map of Verona (1946) 'Lesson[...]
   War: 3, Unarmed Combat'

2 As we get older we do not get[...]
   younger.
Seasons return, and today I an[...]
And this time last year I was fi[...]
And this time next year I shall [...]
   sixty-two.
   A Map of Verona (1946) 'Chard W[...]
   Eliot's Sunday Evening Postscript)'

3 It is, we believe,
Idle to hope that the simple
   stirrup-pump
Can extinguish hell.
   A Map of Verona (1946) 'Chard Whi[...]
   Eliot's Sunday Evening Postscript)'

4 And the sooner the tea's out of th[...]
   the sooner we can get out the gin,[...]
   Private Life of Hilda Tablet (1954 radio[...]
   in *Hilda Tablet and Others: four pieces f[...]
   radio* (1971) p. 60

5 DUCHESS: Of course we've all *dream*[...]
   reviving the *castrati*; but it's need[...]
   Hilda to take the first practical ste[...]
   towards making them a reality.
REEVES: P-practical steps?
DUCHESS: Yes, thank God. She's dra[...]
   up a list of well-known singers wh[...]
   she thinks would benefit from . . .
   treatment. Some of them have been[...]
   singing baritone, or even bass, for[...]
   years. It's only a question of getting[...]
   them to agree.
   Private Life of Hilda Tablet (1954 radio play[...]
   in *Hilda Tablet and Others: four pieces for
   radio* (1971) p. 72

John Reed 1887–1920

6 Ten days that shook the world.
   Title of book (1919)

Charles Revson 1906[...]

1 In the factory we make [...]
store we sell hope.
   In A. Tobias *Fire and Ice*[...]

Malvina Reynolds 1[...]

2 Little boxes on the hills[...]
Little boxes made of tic[...]
Little boxes on the hills[...]
Little boxes all the sam[...]
There's a green one an[...]
And a blue one and a [...]
And they're all made [...]
And they all look just [...]
   Little Boxes (1962 song[...]

Quentin Reynolds [...]

3 There is an old politic[...]
says 'If you can't lick[...]
   Wounded Don't Cry (1[...]

Cecil Rhodes 185[...]

4 Ask any man what [...]
prefer to be, and nin[...]
a hundred will tell y[...]
prefer to be English[...]
   In Gordon Le Sueur [...]
   p. 40

5 Rhodes chose this ti[...]
1896] to awaken h[...]
from his sleep one [...]
ask him whether h[...]
how fortunate he w[...]
good health and to[...]
Englishman, when [...]
other human being[...]
   J. G. Lockhart and [...]
   (1963) p. 29

6 So little done, so [...]
   Said to Lewis Mich[...]
   Lewis Michell *Life* [...]
   ch. 39

Jean Rhys (Ell[...] Williams) ?189[...]

7 The feeling of Su[...]
everywhere, hea[...]
standing still. Li[...]
was in the begin[...]
shall be, world [...]
   Voyage in the Da[...]

only in recent times I have been able to
say my name without a quiver of
discomfort. 'Call me Lady Hamilton,'
I said.

Mandy (1980) ch. 16

Dicky Richards

1 My Goodness, My Guinness.

Advertising slogan (1935) in B. Sibley *Book
of Guinness Advertising* (1985) p. 83

Frank Richards (Charles Hamilton) 1876–1961

2 My postal-order hasn't come yet.

Magnet (1908) vol. 1, no. 2 'The Taming of
Harry'

3 Hazeldene looked from one to the
other—from the well-set-up, athletic
Lancashire lad, to the fat greedy owl of
the Remove, and burst into a laugh.

Magnet (1909) vol. 3, no. 72 'The Greyfriars
Photographer'

4 'I—I say, you fellows—'
'Shut up, Bunter.'
'But—but I say—'
'Keep that cush over his chivvy.'
'I—I say—groo—groo—yarooh!'
And Bunter's remarks again tailed off
under the cushion.

Magnet (1909) vol. 3, no. 85 'The Greyfriars
Visitors'

I. A. Richards 1893–1979

5 It is very probable that the Hindenburg
Line to which the defence of our
traditions retired as a result of the
onslaughts of the last century will be
blown up in the near future. If this
should happen a mental chaos such as
man has never experienced may be
expected. We shall then be thrown back
. . . upon poetry. It is capable of saving
us; it is a perfectly possible means of
overcoming chaos.

Science and Poetry (1926) ch. 7

Sir Ralph Richardson 1902–1983

6 'Acting,' Ralph Richardson of the Old
Vic pronounced last week, 'is merely the
art of keeping a large group of people
from coughing.'

New York Herald Tribune 19 May 1946,
pt. 5, p. 1

Hans Richter 1843–1916

7 Your damned nonsense can I stand
twice or once, but sometimes always, by
God, Never.

In *Hansard* 13 Feb. 1958, col. 574

Rainer Maria Rilke 1875–1926

8 *Kunst-Werke sind von einer unendlichen
Einsamkeit und mit nichts so wenig
erreichbar als mit Kritik. Nur Liebe kann
sie erfassen und halten und kann gerecht
sein gegen sie.*

Works of art are of an infinite
solitariness, and nothing is less likely to
bring us near to them than criticism.
Only love can apprehend and hold them,
and can be just towards them.

Briefe an einem jungen Dichter (Letters to
a Young Poet, 1929, translated by Reginald
Snell, 1945) 23 Apr. 1903

9 *Und diese menschlichere Liebe (die
unendlich rücksichtsvoll und leise, und gut
und klar in Binden und Lösen sich
vollziehen wird) wird jener ähneln, die wir
ringend und mühsam vorbereiten, der Liebe,
die darin besteht, dass zwei Einsamkeiten
einander schützen, grenzen und grüssen.*

And this more human love (which will
consummate itself infinitely thoughtfully
and gently, and well and clearly in
binding and loosing) will be something
like that which we are preparing with
struggle and toil, the love which consists
in the mutual guarding, bordering and
saluting of two solitudes.

Briefe an einem jungen Dichter (Letters to
a Young Poet, 1929, translated by Reginald
Snell, 1945) 14 May 1904

10 *Wer hat uns also umgedreht, dass wir,
was wir auch tun, in jener Haltung sind
von einem, welcher fortgeht? Wie er auf
dem letzten Hügel, der ihm ganz sein Tal
noch einmal zeigt, sich wendet, anhält,
weilt—,
so leben wir und nehmen immer Abschied.*

Who's turned us around like this, so
that we always,
do what we may, retain the attitude
of someone who's departing? Just as he,
on the last hill, that shows him all his
valley

for the last time, will turn and stop and
  linger,
we live our lives, for ever taking leave.
  Duineser Elegien (Duino Elegies, translated by
  J. B. Leishman and Stephen Spender, 1948)
  no. 8

1 *Ich halte für die höchste Aufgabe einer
  Verbindung zweier Menschen diese: dass
  einer dem andern seine Einsamkeit
  bewache.*

  I hold this to be the highest task for
  a bond between two people: that each
  protects the solitude of the other.
  Letter to Paula Modersohn-Becker, 12 Feb.
  1902, in *Gesammelte Briefe* (Collected
  Letters, 1904) vol. 1, p. 204

Hal Riney 1932–

2 It's morning again in America.
  Slogan for Ronald Reagan's election
  campaign, 1984, in *Newsweek* 6 Aug. 1984

Robert L. Ripley 1893–1949

3 Believe it or not.
  Title of syndicated newspaper feature (from
  1918)

César Ritz 1850–1918

4 *Le client n'a jamais tort.*

  The customer is never wrong.
  In R. Nevill and C. E. Jerningham *Piccadilly
  to Pall Mall* (1908) p. 94

Joan Riviere 1883–

5 Civilization and its discontents.
  Title of translation of Sigmund Freud's *Das
  Unbehagen in der Kultur* (1930)

Lord Robbins (Lionel Charles Robbins, Baron Robbins) 1898–1984

6 Economics is the science which studies
  human behaviour as a relationship
  between ends and scarce means which
  have alternative uses.
  *Essay on the Nature and Significance of
  Economic Science* (1932) ch. 1, sect. 3

Leo Robin 1900–

7 Diamonds are a girl's best friend.
  Title of song (1949; music by Jule Styne)

Leo Robin 1900–   and Ralph Rainger

8 Thanks for the memory.
  Title of song (1937)

Edwin Arlington Robinson 1869–1935

9 So on we worked, and waited for the
  light,
  And went without meat, and cursed the
  bread;
  And Richard Cory, one calm summer
  night,
  Went home and put a bullet through his
  head.
  Children of the Night (1897) 'Richard Cory'

10 I shall have more to say when I am
  dead.
  The Three Taverns (1920) 'John Brown' (last
  line)

11 Miniver loved the Medici,
  Albeit he had never seen one;
  He would have sinned incessantly
  Could he have been one.
  The Town down the River (1910) 'Miniver
  Cheevy'

Rt. Revd John Robinson (Bishop of Woolwich) 1919–1983

12 What Lawrence is trying to do, I think,
  is to portray the sex relation as
  something sacred. . . . I think Lawrence
  tried to portray this relation as in a real
  sense an act of holy communion. For
  him flesh was sacramental of the spirit.
  Said as defence witness in case brought
  against Penguin Books for publishing *Lady
  Chatterley's Lover*, 27 Oct. 1960, in *The
  Times* 28 Oct. 1960

John D. Rockefeller 1839–1937

13 The growth of a large business is merely
  a survival of the fittest. . . . The
  American beauty rose can be
  produced in the splendour and fragrance
  which bring cheer to its beholder only
  by sacrificing the early buds which grow
  up around it.
  In W. J. Ghent *Our Benevolent Feudalism*
  (1902) p. 29

Knute Rockne 1888–1931

See JOSEPH P. KENNEDY

Cecil Rodd

1 Stop me and buy one.
   Advertising slogan for Wall's ice cream
   (from spring 1922) in *Wall's Magazine*
   Summer 1957, p. 33

Gene Roddenberry 1921–1991

2 Space—the final frontier. . . . These are
the voyages of the starship *Enterprise*. Its
five-year mission: to explore strange
new worlds, to seek out new life and
new civilizations, to boldly go where no
man has gone before.
   Introduction to *Star Trek* (television series)
   1966 onwards, in James A. Lely *Star Trek*
   (1979) p. 32

3 Beam us up, Mr Scott.
   Star Trek (television series 1966 onwards)
   'Gamesters of Triskelion' (often quoted as
   the catch-phrase 'Beam me up, Scotty',
   which was not actually used in the series)

Theodore Roethke 1908–1963

4 I wake to sleep, and take my waking
   slow.
   I feel my fate in what I cannot fear.
   I learn by going where I have to go.
   The Waking (1953) p. 120

Will Rogers 1879–1935

5 There is only one thing that can kill the
Movies, and that is education.
   Autobiography of Will Rogers (1949) ch. 6

6 The more you read and observe about
this Politics thing, you got to admit that
each party is worse than the other. The
one that's out always looks the best.
   Illiterate Digest (1924) 'Breaking into the
   Writing Game'

7 The Income Tax has made more Liars
out of the American people than Golf
has. Even when you make one out on
the level, you don't know when it's
through if you are a Crook or a Martyr.
   Illiterate Digest (1924) 'Helping the Girls
   with their Income Taxes'

8 Everything is funny as long as it is
happening to Somebody Else.
   Illiterate Digest (1924) 'Warning to Jokers:
   lay off the prince'

9 Well, all I know is what I read in the
papers.
   New York Times 30 Sept. 1923

10 You know everybody is ignorant, only
on different subjects.
   In *New York Times* 31 Aug. 1924

11 You can't say civilization don't advance,
however, for in every war they kill you
in a new way.
   New York Times 23 Dec. 1929

12 Half our life is spent trying to find
something to do with the time we have
rushed through life trying to save.
   Letter in *New York Times* 29 Apr. 1930

13 I bet you if I had met him [Trotsky] and
had a chat with him, I would have
found him a very interesting and human
fellow, for I never yet met a man that
I didn't like.
   In *Saturday Evening Post* 6 Nov. 1926

14 I don't make jokes—I just watch the
government and report the facts.
   In *Saturday Review* 25 Aug. 1962

15 Communism is like prohibition, it's a
good idea but it won't work.
   Weekly Articles (1981) vol. 3, p. 93 (first
   pubd. 1927)

16 Heroing is one of the shortest-lived
professions there is.
   Newspaper article, 15 Feb. 1925, in Paula
   McSpadden Grove *The Will Rogers Book*
   (1961) p. 193

Frederick William Rolfe ('Baron Corvo') 1860–1913

17 'There is no Holiness here,' George
interrupted, in that cold, white, candent
voice which was more caustic than
silver nitrate and more thrilling than
a scream.
   Hadrian VII (1904) ch. 21

18 Pray for the repose of His soul. He was
so tired.
   Hadrian VII (1904) ch. 24

Angelo Giuseppe Roncalli
See POPE JOHN XXIII

Eleanor Roosevelt 1884–1962

19 No one can make you feel inferior
without your consent.
   In *Catholic Digest* Aug. 1960, p. 102

Franklin D. Roosevelt 1882–1945

1 It is fun to be in the same decade with you.

Cable to Winston Churchill, replying to congratulations on Roosevelt's 60th birthday, in W. S. Churchill *Hinge of Fate* (1950) ch. 4

2 These unhappy times call for the building of plans that . . . build from the bottom up . . . that put their faith once more in the forgotten man at the bottom of the economic pyramid.

Radio address, 7 Apr. 1932, in *Public Papers* (1938) vol. 1, p. 625

3 I pledge you, I pledge myself, to a new deal for the American people. Let us all here assembled constitute ourselves prophets of a new order of competence and of courage. This is more than a political campaign; it is a call to arms. Give me your help, not to win votes alone, but to win in this crusade to restore America to its own people.

Speech to Democratic Convention in Chicago, 2 July 1932, accepting nomination for presidency, in *Public Papers* (1938) vol. 1, p. 647

4 First of all, let me assert my firm belief that the only thing we have to fear is fear itself—nameless, unreasoning, unjustified terror which paralyses needed efforts to convert retreat into advance.

Inaugural address, 4 Mar. 1933, in *Public Papers* (1938) vol. 2, p. 11

5 In the field of world policy I would dedicate this Nation to the policy of the good neighbour.

Inaugural address, 4 Mar. 1933, in *Public Papers* (1938) vol. 2, p. 14

6 I have seen war. I have seen war on land and sea. I have seen blood running from the wounded. I have seen men coughing out their gassed lungs. I have seen the dead in the mud. I have seen cities destroyed. I have seen 200 limping, exhausted men come out of line—the survivors of a regiment of 1,000 that went forward 48 hours before. I have seen children starving. I have seen the agony of mothers and wives. I hate war.

Speech at Chautauqua, NY, 14 Aug. 1936, in *Public Papers* (1936) vol. 5, p. 289

7 I see one-third of a nation ill-housed, ill-clad, ill-nourished.

Second inaugural address, 20 Jan. 1937, in *Public Papers* (1941) vol. 6, p. 5

8 When peace has been broken anywhere, the peace of all countries everywhere is in danger.

'Fireside Chat' radio broadcast, 3 Sept. 1939, in *Public Papers* (1941) vol. 8, p. 461

9 I am reminded of four definitions: A Radical is a man with both feet firmly planted—in the air. A Conservative is a man with two perfectly good legs who, however, has never learned to walk forward. A Reactionary is a somnambulist walking backwards. A Liberal is a man who uses his legs and his hands at the behest—at the command—of his head.

Radio address to *New York Herald Tribune* Forum, 26 Oct. 1939, in *Public Papers* (1941) vol. 8, p. 556

10 And while I am talking to you mothers and fathers, I give you one more assurance. I have said this before, but I shall say it again and again and again: Your boys are not going to be sent into any foreign wars.

Speech in Boston, 30 Oct. 1940, in *Public Papers* (1941) vol. 9, p. 517

11 We have the men—the skill—the wealth—and above all, the will. . . . We must be the great arsenal of democracy.

'Fireside Chat' radio broadcast, 29 Dec. 1940, in *Public Papers* (1941) vol. 9, p. 643

12 In the future days, which we seek to make secure, we look forward to a world founded upon four essential human freedoms. The first is freedom of speech and expression—everywhere in the world. The second is freedom of every person to worship God in his own way—everywhere in the world. The third is freedom from want—which, translated into world terms, means economic understanding which will secure to every nation a healthy peacetime life for its inhabitants— everywhere in the world. The fourth is freedom from fear—which, translated into world terms, means a world-wide reduction of armaments to such a point and in such a thorough fashion that no nation will be in a position to

commit an act of physical aggression against any neighbour—anywhere in the world.
Message to Congress, 6 Jan. 1941, in *Public Papers* (1941) vol. 9, p. 672

1 Yesterday, December 7, 1941—a date which will live in infamy—the United States of America was suddenly and deliberately attacked by naval and air forces of the Empire of Japan.
Address to Congress, 8 Dec. 1941, in *Public Papers* (1950) vol. 10, p. 514

2 The work, my friend, is peace. More than an end of this war—an end to the beginnings of all wars. Yes, an end forever to this impractical, unrealistic settlement of the differences between governments by the mass killings of peoples.
Undelivered address for Jefferson Day, 13 Apr. 1945
(the day after Roosevelt died) in *Public Papers* (1950) vol. 13, p. 615

3 The only limit to our realization of tomorrow will be our doubts of today. Let us move forward with strong and active faith.
Undelivered address for Jefferson Day, 13 Apr. 1945, final lines, in *Public Papers* (1950) vol. 13, p. 616

4 We all know that books burn—yet we have the greater knowledge that books can not be killed by fire. People die, but books never die. No man and no force can abolish memory. No man and no force can put thought in a concentration camp forever. No man and no force can take from the world the books that embody man's eternal fight against tyranny of every kind. In this war, we know, books are weapons. And it is a part of your dedication always to make them weapons for man's freedom.
'Message to the Booksellers of America' read at banquet, 6 May 1942, in *Publisher's Weekly* 9 May 1942

Theodore Roosevelt 1858–1919

5 The first requisite of a good citizen in this Republic of ours is that he shall be able and willing to pull his weight.
Speech in New York, 11 Nov. 1902, in *Addresses and Presidential Messages 1902–4* (1904) p. 85

6 A man who is good enough to shed his blood for the country is good enough to be given a square deal afterwards. More than that no man is entitled to, and less than that no man shall have.
Speech at the Lincoln Monument, Springfield, Illinois, 4 June 1903, in *Addresses and Presidential Messages 1902–4* (1904) p. 224

7 [William] McKinley has no more backbone than a chocolate éclair!
In H. T. Peck *Twenty Years of the Republic* (1906) p. 642

8 There is a homely old adage which runs: 'Speak softly and carry a big stick; you will go far.' If the American nation will speak softly, and yet build and keep at a pitch of the highest training a thoroughly efficient navy, the Monroe Doctrine will go far.
Speech at Chicago, 3 Apr. 1903, in *New York Times* 4 Apr. 1903

9 There can be no fifty-fifty Americanism in this country. There is room here for only 100 per cent. Americanism, only for those who are Americans and nothing else.
Speech in Saratoga, 19 July 1918, in *Roosevelt Policy* (1919) vol. 3, p. 1079

10 I wish to preach, not the doctrine of ignoble ease, but the doctrine of the strenuous life.
Speech to the Hamilton Club, Chicago, 10 Apr. 1899, in *Works*, Memorial edition (1925), vol. 15, p. 267

11 No man is justified in doing evil on the ground of expediency.
In *Works*, Memorial edition (1925) vol. 15, p. 388 'Latitude and Longitude among Reformers'

12 The men with the muck-rakes are often indispensable to the well-being of society; but only if they know when to stop raking the muck.
Speech in Washington, 14 Apr. 1906, in *Works*, Memorial edition (1925) vol. 18, p. 574

13 A hyphenated American is not an American at all. This is just as true of the man who puts 'native' before the hyphen as of the man who puts German or Irish or English or French before the hyphen. Americanism is a matter of the spirit and of the soul. Our allegiance must be purely to the United States. We

must unsparingly condemn any man who holds any other allegiance.
Speech in New York, 12 Oct. 1915, in *Works*, Memorial edition (1925) vol. 20, p. 457

1 There are the foolish fanatics always to be found in such a movement and always discrediting it—the men who form the lunatic fringe in all reform movements.
Autobiography (1913) ch. 7, in *Works*, Memorial edition (1925) vol. 22, p. 247

2 I wish in this campaign to do ... whatever is likely to produce the best results for the Republican ticket. I am as strong as a bull moose and you can use me to the limit.
Letter to Mark Hanna, 27 June 1900, in *Works*, Memorial edition (1926) vol. 23, p. 162 ('Bull Moose' became the popular name of the Progressive Party)

3 One of our defects as a nation is a tendency to use what have been called 'weasel words'. When a weasel sucks eggs the meat is sucked out of the egg. If you use a 'weasel word' after another, there is nothing left of the other.
Speech in St Louis, 31 May 1916, in *Works*, Memorial edition (1926) vol. 24, p. 483

4 Good to the last drop.
Said to Joel Cheek in 1907 about Maxwell House coffee, and subsequently used as an advertising slogan

Arthur Rose and Douglas Furber

5 Any time you're Lambeth way,
Any evening, any day,
You'll find us all
Doin' the Lambeth Walk.
Lambeth Walk (1937 song; music by Noel Gay)

Billy Rose 1899–1966

6 Me and my shadow.
Title of song (1927; music by Al Jolson and Dave Dreyer)

Billy Rose 1899–1966 and Marty Bloom

7 Does the spearmint lose its flavour on the bedpost overnight?
Title of song (1924; music by Ernest Breuer; revived in 1959 by Lonnie Donegan with the title 'Does your chewing-gum lose its flavour on the bedpost overnight?')

Billy Rose 1899–1966 and Willie Raskin 1896–1942

8 Fifty million Frenchmen can't be wrong.
Title of song (1927; music by Fred Fisher). Cf. Texas Guinan

William Rose 1918–1987

9 The Russians are coming, the Russians are coming.
Title of film (1966)

Lord Rosebery (Archibald Philip Primrose, 5th Earl of Rosebery) 1847–1929

10 There is no need for any nation, however great, leaving the Empire, because the Empire is a commonwealth of nations.
Speech in Adelaide, Australia, 18 Jan. 1884, in Marquess of Crewe *Lord Rosebery* (1931) vol. 1, ch. 7

11 And now we cannot but observe that it is beginning to be hinted that we are a nation of amateurs.
Rectorial Address at Glasgow University, 16 Nov. 1900, in *The Times* 17 Nov. 1900

12 I must plough my furrow alone. That is my fate, agreeable or the reverse; but before I get to the end of that furrow it is possible that I may find myself not alone.
Speech at City of London Liberal Club, 19 July 1901, on remaining outside Liberal Party leadership, in *The Times* 20 July 1901

Ethel Rosenberg 1916–1953 and Julius Rosenberg 1918–1953

13 We are innocent, as we have proclaimed and maintained from the time of our arrest. This is the whole truth. To forsake this truth is to pay too high a price even for the priceless gift of life—for life thus purchased we could not live out in dignity and self-respect.
Petition for executive clemency, filed 9 Jan. 1953, in Ethel Rosenberg *Death House Letters* (1953) p. 149

14 Ethel wants it made known that we are the first victims of American Fascism.
Letter from Julius to Emanuel Bloch before their execution for espionage, 19 June 1953, in Ethel Rosenberg *Testament of Ethel and Julius Rosenberg* (1954) p. 187

Alan S. C. Ross 1907–1980

1 U and Non-U. An essay in sociological
linguistics.
   Title of essay in Nancy Mitford *Noblesse
   Oblige* (1956), first published in
   Neuphilologische Mitteilungen (1954)

Harold Ross 1892–1951

2 Usually he [Ross] confined himself to
written comments. His later famed
'What mean?' 'Who he?' and the like
began to appear on manuscripts and
proofs.
   Dale Kramer *Ross and The New Yorker*
   (1952) ch. 13

3 The *New Yorker* will be the magazine
which is not edited for the old lady in
Dubuque.
   In James Thurber *The Years with Ross*
   (1959) ch. 4

4 'I don't want you to think I'm not
incoherent,' he [Ross] once rattled off to
somebody in '21'.
   James Thurber *The Years with Ross* (1959)
   ch. 5

5 I understand the hero [of Hemingway's
A Farewell to Arms] keeps getting in bed
with women, and the war wasn't fought
that way.
   In James Thurber *The Years with Ross*
   (1959) ch. 7

Sir Ronald Ross 1857–1932

6 This day relenting God
Hath placed within my hand
A wondrous thing; and God
Be praised. At his command,

Seeking His secret deeds
With tears and toiling breath,
I find thy cunning seeds,
O million-murdering Death.

I know this little thing
A myriad men will save,
O Death, where is thy sting?
Thy victory, O Grave?
   Philosophies (1910) 'In Exile' pt. 7
   (describing his part in discovering the
   life-cycle of the malaria parasite in 1897; cf.
   Oxford Dictionary of Quotations (1979) 77:1)

Jean Rostand 1894–1977

7 *Mon pessimisme va jusqu'à suspecter la
sincérité des pessimistes.*

My pessimism goes to the point of
suspecting the sincerity of the pessimists.
   Journal d'un caractère (Journal of a Character,
   1931)

8 *Être adulte, c'est être seul.*

To be adult is to be alone.
   Pensées d'un biologiste (Thoughts of
   a Biologist, 1954) p. 134

9 *On tue un homme, on est un assassin. On
tue des millions d'hommes, on est
conquérant. On les tue tous, on est un dieu.*

Kill a man, and you are an assassin. Kill
millions of men, and you are a
conqueror. Kill everyone, and you are
a god.
   Pensées d'un biologiste (Thoughts of
   a Biologist, 1939) p. 116

Leo Rosten 1908–

10 The only thing I can say about W. C.
Fields, whom I have admired since the
day he advanced upon Baby LeRoy with
an ice pick, is this: any man who hates
dogs and babies can't be all bad.
   Speech at Hollywood dinner in honour of
   W. C. Fields, 16 Feb. 1939, in *Saturday
   Review* 12 June 1976

Philip Roth 1933–

11 A Jewish man with parents alive is
a fifteen-year-old boy, and will remain
a fifteen-year-old boy until *they die!*
   Portnoy's Complaint (1967) p. 111

12 Doctor, my doctor, what do you say,
LET'S PUT THE ID BACK IN YID!
   Portnoy's Complaint (1967) p. 124

Dan Rowan 1922–1987 and
Dick Martin 1923–

13 Very interesting . . . but stupid.
   Catch-phrase in *Rowan and Martin's
   Laugh-In* (American television series,
   1967–73)

Helen Rowland 1875–1950

14 A husband is what is left of a lover, after
the nerve has been extracted.
   A Guide to Men (1922) p. 19

15 Somehow a bachelor never quite gets
over the idea that he is a thing of beauty
and a boy forever.
   A Guide to Men (1922) p. 25

1 The follies which a man regrets most, in his life, are those which he didn't commit when he had the opportunity.
  A Guide to Men (1922) p. 87

2 When you see what some girls marry, you realize how they must hate to work for a living.
  Reflections of a Bachelor Girl (1909) p. 45

Richard Rowland ?1881–1947

3 The lunatics have taken charge of the asylum.
  Comment on take-over of United Artists by Charles Chaplin, Mary Pickford, Douglas Fairbanks and D. W. Griffith, in Terry Ramsaye *A Million and One Nights* (1926) vol. 2, ch. 79

Maude Royden 1876–1956

4 The Church should go forward along the path of progress and be no longer satisfied only to represent the Conservative Party at prayer.
  Address at Queen's Hall, London, 16 July 1917, in *The Times* 17 July 1917

Naomi Royde-Smith ?1875–1964

5 I know two things about the horse
  And one of them is rather coarse.
  Weekend Book (1928) p. 231

Paul Alfred Rubens 1875–1917

6 Oh! we don't want to lose you but we
    think you ought to go
  For your King and your Country both
    need you so;
  We shall want you and miss you but
    with all our might and main
  We shall cheer you, thank you, kiss you
  When you come back again.
  Your King and Country Want You (1914 song)

Damon Runyon 1884–1946

7 I do see her in tough joints more than somewhat.
  Collier's 22 May 1930, 'Social Error'

8 'You are snatching a hard guy when you snatch Bookie Bob. A very hard guy, indeed. In fact,' I say, 'I hear the softest thing about him is his front teeth.'
  Collier's 26 Sept. 1931, 'Snatching of Bookie Bob'

9 I always claim the mission workers came out too early to catch any sinners on this part of Broadway. At such an hour the sinners are still in bed resting up from their sinning of the night before, so they will be in good shape for more sinning a little later on.
  Collier's 28 Jan. 1933, 'The Idyll of Miss Sarah Brown'

10 'In fact,' Sam the Gonoph says, 'I long ago come to the conclusion that all life is 6 to 5 against.'
  Collier's 8 Sept. 1934, 'A Nice Price'

11 'My boy,' he says, 'always try to rub up against money, for if you rub up against money long enough, some of it may rub off on you.'
  Cosmopolitan Aug. 1929, 'A Very Honourable Guy'

Dean Rusk 1909–

12 We're eyeball to eyeball, and I think the other fellow just blinked.
  Comment on Cuban missile crisis, 24 Oct. 1962, in *Saturday Evening Post* 8 Dec. 1962

Bertrand Russell (Bertrand Arthur William, third Earl Russell) 1872–1970

13 Three passions, simple but overwhelmingly strong, have governed my life: the longing for love, the search for knowledge, and unbearable pity for the suffering of mankind.
  Autobiography (1967) vol. 1, prologue

14 I was told that the Chinese said they would bury me by the Western Lake and build a shrine to my memory. I have some slight regret that this did not happen as I might have become a god, which would have been very *chic* for an atheist.
  Autobiography (1968) vol. 2, ch. 3

15 Men who are unhappy, like men who sleep badly, are always proud of the fact.
  Conquest of Happiness (1930) ch. 1

1 Boredom is therefore a vital problem for the moralist, since half the sins of mankind are caused by the fear of it.
Conquest of Happiness (1930) ch. 4

2 One of the symptoms of approaching nervous breakdown is the belief that one's work is terribly important, and that to take a holiday would bring all kinds of disaster. If I were a medical man, I should prescribe a holiday to any patient who considered his work important.
Conquest of Happiness (1930) ch. 5

3 Envy is the basis of democracy.
Conquest of Happiness (1930) ch. 6

4 One should as a rule respect public opinion in so far as is necessary to avoid starvation and to keep out of prison, but anything that goes beyond this is voluntary submission to an unnecessary tyranny, and is likely to interfere with happiness in all kinds of ways.
Conquest of Happiness (1930) ch. 9

5 A sense of duty is useful in work, but offensive in personal relations. People wish to be liked, not to be endured with patient resignation.
Conquest of Happiness (1930) ch. 10

6 Of all forms of caution, caution in love is perhaps the most fatal to true happiness.
Conquest of Happiness (1930) ch. 12

7 To be able to fill leisure intelligently is the last product of civilization, and at present very few people have reached this level.
Conquest of Happiness (1930) ch. 14

8 Aristotle maintained that women have fewer teeth than men; although he was twice married, it never occurred to him to verify this statement by examining his wives' mouths.
Impact of Science on Society (1952) ch. 1

9 The fact that an opinion has been widely held is no evidence whatever that it is not utterly absurd; indeed in view of the silliness of the majority of mankind, a widespread belief is more likely to be foolish than sensible.
Marriage and Morals (1929) ch. 5

10 To fear love is to fear life, and those who fear life are already three parts dead.
Marriage and Morals (1929) ch. 19

11 Mathematics may be defined as the subject in which we never know what we are talking about, nor whether what we are saying is true.
Mysticism and Logic (1917) ch. 4

12 Only on the firm foundation of unyielding despair, can the soul's habitation henceforth be safely built.
Philosophical Essays (1910) no. 2

13 Mathematics, rightly viewed, possesses not only truth, but supreme beauty— a beauty cold and austere, like that of sculpture.
Philosophical Essays (1910) no. 4

14 It is undesirable to believe a proposition when there is no ground whatever for supposing it is true.
Sceptical Essays (1928) 'On the Value of Scepticism'

15 The infliction of cruelty with a good conscience is a delight to moralists. That is why they invented Hell.
Sceptical Essays (1928) 'On the Value of Scepticism'

16 Every man, wherever he goes, is encompassed by a cloud of comforting convictions, which move with him like flies on a summer day.
Sceptical Essays (1928) 'Dreams and Facts'

17 Machines are worshipped because they are beautiful, and valued because they confer power; they are hated because they are hideous, and loathed because they impose slavery.
Sceptical Essays (1928) 'Machines and Emotions'

18 We have, in fact, two kinds of morality side by side: one which we preach but do not practise, and another which we practise but seldom preach.
Sceptical Essays (1928) 'Eastern and Western Ideals of Happiness'

19 It is obvious that 'obscenity' is not a term capable of exact legal definition; in the practice of the Courts, it means 'anything that shocks the magistrate'.
Sceptical Essays (1928) 'Recrudescence of Puritanism'

20 The fundamental defect of fathers, in our competitive society, is that they want their children to be a credit to them.
Sceptical Essays (1928) 'Freedom versus Authority in Education'

1 Man is a credulous animal, and must believe *something*; in the absence of good grounds for belief, he will be satisfied with bad ones.

> *Unpopular Essays* (1950) 'Outline of Intellectual Rubbish'

2 Fear is the main source of superstition, and one of the main sources of cruelty. To conquer fear is the beginning of wisdom, in the pursuit of truth as in the endeavour after a worthy manner of life.

> *Unpopular Essays* (1950) 'Outline of Intellectual Rubbish'

Dora Russell (Countess Russell)
1894–1986

3 We want better reasons for having children than not knowing how to prevent them.

> *Hypatia* (1925) ch. 4

George William Russell
See AE

John Russell 1919–

4 Certain phrases stick in the throat, even if they offer nothing that is analytically improbable. 'A dashing Swiss officer' is one such. Another is 'the beautiful Law Courts'.

> *Paris* (1960) ch. 11

Ernest Rutherford (Baron Rutherford of Nelson) 1871–1937

5 I do not ... want to give the impression that the use of large machines or of elaborate techniques is always justified; sometimes it contributes merely to the sense of self-importance of the investigator, and it is always salutary to remember Rutherford's 'We haven't got the money, so we've got to think!'

> R. V. Jones in *Bulletin of the Institute of Physics* (1962) vol. 13, p. 102

6 All science is either physics or stamp collecting.

> In J. B. Birks *Rutherford at Manchester* (1962) p. 108

Gilbert Ryle 1900–1976

7 A myth is, of course, not a fairy story. It is the presentation of facts belonging to one category in the idioms appropriate to another. To explode a myth is accordingly not to deny the facts but to re-allocate them. And this is what I am trying to do.

> *Concept of Mind* (1949) introduction

8 Philosophy is the replacement of category-habits by category-disciplines.

> *Concept of Mind* (1949) introduction

9 Such in outline is the official theory. I shall often speak of it, with deliberate abusiveness, as 'the dogma of the Ghost in the Machine'.

> *Concept of Mind* (1949) ch. 1 (referring to Descartes' mental-conduct concepts)

Rafael Sabatini 1875–1950

10 He was born with a gift of laughter and a sense that the world was mad. And that was all his patrimony.

> *Scaramouche* (1921) bk. 1, ch. 1

Oliver Sacks 1933–

11 The man who mistook his wife for a hat.

> Title of book (1985)

Victoria ('Vita') Sackville-West
1892–1962

12 The greater cats with golden eyes
Stare out between the bars.
Deserts are there, and different skies,
And night with different stars.

> *King's Daughter* (1929) pt. 2, no. 1 'The Greater Cats with Golden Eyes'

13 The country habit has me by the heart,
For he's bewitched for ever who has seen,
Not with his eyes but with his vision, Spring
Flow down the woods and stipple leaves with sun.

> *The Land* (1926) 'Winter'

Françoise Sagan 1935–

14 *Rien n'est plus affreux que le rire pour la jalousie.*

To jealousy, nothing is more frightful than laughter.

> *La Chamade* (1965) ch. 9

Antoine de Saint-Exupéry
1900–1944

1 *Les grandes personnes ne comprennent jamais rien toutes seules, et c'est fatigant, pour les enfants, de toujours et toujours leur donner des explications.*

Grown-ups never understand anything for themselves, and it is tiresome for children to be always and forever explaining things to them.
Le Petit Prince (The Little Prince, 1943) ch. 1

2 *On ne voit bien qu'avec le cœur. L'essentiel est invisible pour les yeux.*

It is only with the heart that one can see rightly; what is essential is invisible to the eye.
Le Petit Prince (The Little Prince, 1943) ch. 21

3 *L'expérience nous montre qu'aimer ce n'est point nous regarder l'un l'autre mais regarder ensemble dans la même direction.*

Experience shows us that love does not consist in gazing at each other but in looking together in the same direction.
Terre des Hommes (translated as 'Wind, Sand and Stars', 1939) ch. 8

George Saintsbury 1845–1933

4 I have never yet given a second-hand opinion of any thing, or book, or person.
Notes on a Cellar-Book (1920) 'Preliminary'

Saki (Hector Hugh Munro)
1870–1916

5 'But why should you want to shield him?' cried Egbert; 'the man is a common murderer.' 'A common murderer, possibly, but a very uncommon cook.'
Beasts and Super-Beasts (1914) 'The Blind Spot'

6 'Waldo is one of those people who would be enormously improved by death,' said Clovis.
Beasts and Super-Beasts (1914) 'The Feast of Nemesis'

7 He's simply got the instinct for being unhappy highly developed.
Chronicles of Clovis (1911) 'The Match-Maker'

8 'I think oysters are more beautiful than any religion,' he resumed presently. 'They not only forgive our unkindness to them; they justify it, they incite us to go on being perfectly horrid to them. Once they arrive at the supper-table they seem to enter thoroughly into the spirit of the thing. There's nothing in Christianity or Buddhism that quite matches the sympathetic unselfishness of an oyster.'
Chronicles of Clovis (1911) 'The Match-Maker'

9 All decent people live beyond their incomes nowadays, and those who aren't respectable live beyond other peoples'. A few gifted individuals manage to do both.
Chronicles of Clovis (1911) 'The Match-Maker'

10 The people of Crete unfortunately make more history than they can consume locally.
Chronicles of Clovis (1911) 'The Jesting of Arlington Stringham'

11 His socks compelled one's attention without losing one's respect.
Chronicles of Clovis (1911) '"Ministers of Grace"'

12 People may say what they like about the decay of Christianity; the religious system that produced green Chartreuse can never really die.
Reginald (1904) 'Reginald on Christmas Presents'

13 Every reformation must have its victims. You can't expect the fatted calf to share the enthusiasm of the angels over the prodigal's return.
Reginald (1904) 'Reginald on the Academy'

14 I always say beauty is only sin deep.
Reginald (1904) 'Reginald's Choir Treat'

15 Her frocks are built in Paris, but she wears them with a strong English accent.
Reginald (1904) 'Reginald on Worries'

16 The young have aspirations that never come to pass, the old have reminiscences of what never happened.
Reginald (1904) 'Reginald at the Carlton'

17 There may have been disillusionments in the lives of the medieval saints, but they would scarcely have been better pleased if they could have forseen that their

names would be associated nowadays chiefly with racehorses and the cheaper clarets.

Reginald (1904) 'Reginald at the Carlton'

1 The cook was a good cook, as cooks go; and as good cooks go, she went.

Reginald (1904) 'Reginald on Besetting Sins'

2 Women and elephants never forget an injury.

Reginald (1904) 'Reginald on Besetting Sins'

3 The Young Turkish candidate, who had conformed to the Western custom of one wife and hardly any mistresses, stood by helplessly while his adversary's poll swelled to a triumphant majority.

Reginald in Russia (1910) 'A Young Turkish Catastrophe'

4 The death of John Pennington had left his widow in circumstances which were more straitened than ever, and the Park had receded even from her notepaper, where it had long been retained as a courtesy title on the principle that addresses are given to us to conceal our whereabouts.

Reginald in Russia (1910) 'Cross Currents'

5 But, good gracious, you've got to educate him first. You can't expect a boy to be vicious till he's been to a good school.

Reginald in Russia (1910) 'The Baker's Dozen'

6 I should be the last person to say anything against temptation, naturally, but we have a proverb down here 'in baiting a mouse-trap with cheese, always leave room for the mouse'.

The Square Egg (1924) 'The Infernal Parliament'

7 A little inaccuracy sometimes saves tons of explanation.

The Square Egg (1924) 'Clovis on the Alleged Romance of Business'

8 Children with Hyacinth's temperament don't know better as they grow older; they merely know more.

Toys of Peace and Other Papers (1919) 'Hyacinth'

9 A buzz of recognition came from the front rows of the pit, together with a craning of necks on the part of those in less favoured seats. It heralded the arrival of Sherard Blaw, the dramatist who had discovered himself, and who

had given so ungrudgingly of his discovery to the world.

The Unbearable Bassington (1912) ch. 13

J. D. Salinger 1919–

10 If you really want to hear about it, the first thing you'll probably want to know is where I was born, and what my lousy childhood was like, and how my parents were occupied and all before they had me, and all that David Copperfield kind of crap, but I don't feel like going into it.

Catcher in the Rye (1951) ch. 1

11 What really knocks me out is a book that, when you're all done reading it, you wish the author that wrote it was a terrific friend of yours and you could call him up on the phone whenever you felt like it.

Catcher in the Rye (1951) ch. 3

12 Sex is something I really don't understand too hot. You never know *where* the hell you are. I keep making up these sex rules for myself, and then I break them right away.

Catcher in the Rye (1951) ch. 9

13 The only thing old Phoebe liked was when Hamlet patted this dog on the head. She thought that was funny and nice, and it was. What I'll have to do is, I'll have to read that play. The trouble with me is, I always have to read that stuff by myself. If an actor acts it out, I hardly listen. I keep worrying about whether he's going to do something phoney every minute.

Catcher in the Rye (1951) ch. 16

14 Take most people, they're crazy about cars. They worry if they get a little scratch on them, and they're always talking about how many miles they get to a gallon, and if they get a brand-new car already they start thinking about trading it in for one that's even newer. I don't even like *old* cars. I mean they don't even interest me. I'd rather have a goddam horse. A horse is at least *human*, for God's sake.

Catcher in the Rye (1951) ch. 17

15 'You know that song "If a body catch a body comin' through the rye"? I'd like—'

'It's "If a body *meet* a body coming through the rye"!' old Phoebe said. 'It's a poem. By Robert *Burns*.'

'I *know* it's a poem by Robert Burns.'

She was right, though. It *is* 'If a body meet a body coming through the rye'. I didn't know it then, though.

'I thought it was "If a body catch a body",' I said. 'Anyway, I keep picturing all these little kids playing some game in this big field of rye and all. Thousands of little kids, and nobody's around—nobody big, I mean—except me. And I'm standing on the edge of some crazy cliff. What I have to do, I have to catch everybody if they start to go over the cliff—I mean if they're running and they don't look where they're going I have to come out from somewhere and catch them. That's all I'd do all day. I'd just be the catcher in the rye and all. I know it's crazy, but that's the only thing I'd really like to be. I know it's crazy.'

Catcher in the Rye (1951) ch. 22

1 A confessional passage has probably never been written that didn't stink a little bit of the writer's pride in having given up his pride.

Seymour: an Introduction (1959) in *Raise High the Roof Beam, Carpenters and Seymour: an Introduction* (1963) p. 195

Lord Salisbury (*Robert Arthur James Gascoyne-Cecil, fifth Marquess of Salisbury*) 1893–1972

2 He is, as we all know, a man of most unusual intellectual brilliance; and he is, moreover, both brave and resolute. Those are valuable and not too common attributes in politics. But the fact remains that I believe he has adopted, especially in his relationship to the white communities of Africa, a most unhappy and an entirely wrong approach. He has been too clever by half.

Said of Iain Macleod, Colonial Secretary, in *Hansard* (House of Lords) 7 Mar. 1961, col. 307

Anthony Sampson 1926–

3 Members [of civil service orders] rise from CMG (known sometimes in Whitehall as 'Call Me God') to the KCMG ('Kindly Call Me God') to—for a select few governors and super-ambassadors—the GCMG ('God Calls Me God').

Anatomy of Britain (1962) ch. 18

Lord Samuel (*Herbert Louis, first Viscount Samuel*) 1870–1963

4 A library is thought in cold storage.

A Book of Quotations (1947) p. 10

5 It takes two to make a marriage a success and only one a failure.

A Book of Quotations (1947) p. 115

6 Without doubt the greatest injury of all was done by basing morals on myth. For, sooner or later, myth is recognized for what it is, and disappears. Then morality loses the foundation on which it has been built.

Romanes Lecture, 1947, p. 14

Carl Sandburg 1878–1967

7 Poetry is the opening and closing of a door, leaving those who look through to guess about what is seen during a moment.

Atlantic Monthly Mar. 1923 'Poetry Considered'

8 Poetry is the achievement of the synthesis of hyacinths and biscuits.

Atlantic Monthly Mar. 1923 'Poetry Considered'

9 Hog Butcher for the World,
Tool Maker, Stacker of Wheat,
Player with Railroads and the Nation's Freight Handler;
Stormy, husky, brawling,
City of the Big Shoulders.

Chicago Poems (1916) 'Chicago'

10 The fog comes
on little cat feet.

It sits looking
over harbor and city
on silent haunches
and then moves on.

Chicago Poems (1916) 'Fog'

11 I tell you the past is a bucket of ashes.

Cornhuskers (1918) 'Prairie'

12 When Abraham Lincoln was shovelled into the tombs,

he forgot the copperheads and the assassin . . .
in the dust, in the cool tombs.
Cornhuskers (1918) 'Cool Tombs'

1 Pile the bodies high at Austerlitz and Waterloo.
Shovel them under and let me work—
I am the grass; I cover all.
Cornhuskers (1918) 'Grass'

2 I am an idealist. I don't know where I'm going but I'm on the way.
Incidentals (1907) p. 8

3 Slang is a language that rolls up its sleeves, spits on its hands and goes to work.
In *New York Times* 13 Feb. 1959, p. 21

4 Little girl. . . . Sometime they'll give a war and nobody will come.
The People, Yes (1936) (cf. Charlotte Keyes in *McCall's* Oct. 1966 'Suppose They Gave a War and No One Came?'; a 1970 American film was entitled 'Suppose They Gave a War and Nobody Came?')

5 Why is there always a secret singing When a lawyer cashes in?
Why does a hearse horse snicker Hauling a lawyer away?
Smoke and Steel (1920) 'The Lawyers Know Too Much'

Henry 'Red' Sanders

6 Sure, winning isn't everything. It's the only thing.
In *Sports Illustrated* 26 Dec. 1955 (often attributed to Vince Lombardi)

William Sansom 1926–1976

7 A writer lives, at best, in a state of astonishment. Beneath any feeling he has of the good or the evil of the world lies a deeper one of wonder at it all. To transmit that feeling, he writes.
Blue Skies, Brown Studies (1961) 'From a Writer's Notebook'

George Santayana 1863–1952

8 The young man who has not wept is a savage, and the old man who will not laugh is a fool.
Dialogues in Limbo (1925) ch. 3

9 Fanaticism consists in redoubling your effort when you have forgotten your aim.
Life of Reason (1905) vol. 1, Introduction

10 Happiness is the only sanction of life; where happiness fails, existence remains a mad and lamentable experiment.
Life of Reason (1905) vol. 1, ch. 10

11 Progress, far from consisting in change, depends on retentiveness. . . . Those who cannot remember the past are condemned to repeat it.
Life of Reason (1905) vol. 1, ch. 12

12 It takes patience to appreciate domestic bliss; volatile spirits prefer unhappiness.
Life of Reason (1905) vol. 2, ch. 2

13 An artist is a dreamer consenting to dream of the actual world.
Life of Reason (1905) vol. 4, ch. 3

14 Music is essentially useless, as life is: but both have an ideal extension which lends utility to its conditions.
Life of Reason (1905) vol. 4, ch. 4

15 An artist may visit a museum, but only a pedant can live there.
Life of Reason (1905) vol. 4, ch. 7

16 Nothing is really so poor and melancholy as art that is interested in itself and not in its subject.
Life of Reason (1905) vol. 4, ch. 8

17 The truth is cruel, but it can be loved, and it makes free those who have loved it.
Little Essays (1920) 'Ideal Immortality'

18 England is the paradise of individuality, eccentricity, heresy, anomalies, hobbies, and humours.
Soliloquies in England (1922) 'The British Character'

19 There is no cure for birth and death save to enjoy the interval.
Soliloquies in England (1922) 'War Shrines'

20 It is a great advantage for a system of philosophy to be substantially true.
The Unknowable (1923) p. 4

21 For an idea ever to be fashionable is ominous, since it must afterwards be always old-fashioned.
Winds of Doctrine (1913) ch. 2

22 Intolerance itself is a form of egoism, and to condemn egoism intolerantly is to share it.
Winds of Doctrine (1913) ch. 4

'Sapper' (Herman Cyril MacNeile) 1888–1937

1 Hugh pulled out his cigarette-case. 'Turkish this side—Virginia that.'
   Bull-dog Drummond (1920) ch. 8

John Singer Sargent 1856–1925

2 Every time I paint a portrait I lose a friend.
   In N. Bentley and E. Esar *Treasury of Humorous Quotations* (1951)

Leslie Sarony 1897–1985

3 Ain't it grand to be blooming well dead?
   Title of song (1932)

4 I lift up my finger and I say 'tweet tweet'.
   Title of song (1929)

Nathalie Sarraute 1902–

5 Today, thanks to technical progress, the radio and television, to which we devote so many of the leisure hours once spent listening to parlour chatter and parlour music, have succeeded in lifting the manufacture of banality out of the sphere of handicraft and placed it in that of a major industry.
   Times Literary Supplement 10 June 1960

Jean-Paul Sartre 1905–1980

6 *Quand les riches se font la guerre ce sont les pauvres qui meurent.*

   When the rich wage war it's the poor who die.
   Le Diable et le bon Dieu (The Devil and the Good Lord, 1951) act 1, first tableau

7 *L'écrivain doit donc refuser de se laisser transformer en institution.*
   A writer must refuse, therefore, to allow himself to be transformed into an institution.
   Declaration read at Stockholm, 22 Oct. 1964, refusing the Nobel Prize, in Michel Contat and Michel Rybalka (eds.) *Les Écrits de Sartre* (1970) p. 403

8 *L'existence précède et commande l'essence.*

   Existence precedes and rules essence.
   L'Être et le néant (Being and Nothingness, 1943) pt. 4, ch. 1

9 *Je suis condamné à être libre.*

   I am condemned to be free.
   L'Être et le néant (Being and Nothingness, 1943) pt. 4, ch. 1

10 *L'homme est une passion inutile.*

   Man is a useless passion.
   L'Être et le néant (Being and Nothingness, 1943) pt. 4, ch. 2

11 *Alors, c'est ça l'Enfer. Je n'aurais jamais cru. ... Vous vous rappelez: le soufre, le bûcher, le gril. ... Ah! quelle plaisanterie. Pas besoin de gril, l'Enfer, c'est les Autres.*

   So that's what Hell is: I'd never have believed it. ... Do you remember, brimstone, the stake, the gridiron?. ... What a joke! No need of a gridiron, Hell is other people.
   Huis Clos (Closed Doors, 1944) sc. 5

12 *Il n'y a pas de bon père, c'est la règle; qu'on n'en tienne pas grief aux hommes mais au lien de paternité qui est pourri. Faire des enfants, rien de mieux; en avoir, quelle iniquité!*

   There is no good father, that's the rule. Don't lay the blame on men but on the bond of paternity, which is rotten. To beget children, nothing better; to *have* them, what iniquity!
   Les Mots (The Words, 1964) 'Lire'

13 *Les bons pauvres ne savent pas que leur office est d'exercer notre générosité.*

   The poor don't know that their function in life is to exercise our generosity.
   Les Mots (The Words, 1964) 'Lire'

14 *Elle [ma grand-mère] ne croyait à rien; seul, son scepticisme l'empêchait d'être athée.*

   She [my grandmother] believed in nothing; only her scepticism kept her from being an atheist.
   Les Mots (The Words, 1964) 'Lire'

15 *Comme tous les songe-creux, je confondis le désenchantement avec la vérité.*

   Like all dreamers, I mistook disenchantment for truth.
   Les Mots (The Words, 1964) 'Écrire'

16 *Je confondis les choses avec leurs noms: c'est croire.*

   I confused things with their names: that is belief.
   Les Mots (The Words, 1964) 'Écrire'

1 *Trois heures, c'est toujours trop tard ou trop tôt pour ce qu'on veut faire.*

Three o'clock is always too late or too early for anything you want to do.
   La Nausée (Nausea, 1938) 'Vendredi'

2 *Ma pensée, c'est moi: voilà pourquoi je ne peux pas m'arrêter. J'existe par ce que je pense . . . et je ne peux pas m'empêcher de penser.*

My thought is *me*: that's why I can't stop. I exist by what I think . . . and I can't prevent myself from thinking.
   La Nausée (Nausea, 1938) 'Lundi'

3 *Je déteste les victimes quand elles respectent leurs bourreaux.*

I hate victims who respect their executioners.
   Les Séquestrés d'Altona (The Condemned of Altona, 1960) act 1, sc. 1

4 *Je me méfie des incommunicables, c'est la source de toute violence.*

I distrust the incommunicable: it is the source of all violence.
   Les Temps Modernes July 1947, p. 106, 'Qu'est-ce que la littérature?' (What is Literature?)

Siegfried Sassoon 1886–1967

5 Soldiers are citizens of death's gray land, Drawing no dividend from time's tomorrows.
   Counter-Attack (1918) 'Dreamers'

6 In the great hour of destiny they stand, Each with his feuds, and jealousies, and sorrows.
Soldiers are sworn to action; they must win
Some flaming, fatal climax with their lives.
Soldiers are dreamers; when the guns begin
They think of firelit homes, clean beds, and wives.
   Counter-Attack (1918) 'Dreamers'

7 If I were fierce, and bald, and short of breath,
I'd live with scarlet Majors at the Base,
And speed glum heroes up the line to death.
You'd see me with my puffy petulant face,

Guzzling and gulping in the best hotel,
Reading the Roll of Honour. 'Poor young chap',
I'd say—'I used to know his father well;
Yes, we've lost heavily in this last scrap.'
And when the war is done and youth stone dead,
I'd toddle safely home and die—in bed.
   Counter-Attack (1918) 'Base Details'

8 'Good-morning; good morning!' the General said
When we met him last week on our way to the line.
Now the soldiers he smiled at are most of 'em dead,
And we're cursing his staff for incompetent swine.
'He's a cheery old card,' grunted Harry to Jack
As they slogged up to Arras with rifle and pack.

But he did for them both by his plan of attack.
   Counter-Attack (1918) 'The General'

9 Does it matter?—losing your legs? . . .
For people will always be kind,
And you need not show that you mind
When the others come in after hunting
To gobble their muffins and eggs.

Does it matter?—losing your sight? . . .
There's such splendid work for the blind;
And people will always be kind,
As you sit on the terrace remembering
And turning your face to the light.
   Counter-Attack (1918) 'Does it Matter?'

10 Who will remember, passing through this Gate,
The unheroic Dead who fed the guns?
Who shall absolve the foulness of their fate,—
Those doomed, conscripted, unvictorious ones?
   The Heart's Journey (1928) 'On Passing the New Menin Gate'

11 I am making this statement as an act of wilful defiance of military authority, because I believe that the War is being deliberately prolonged by those who have the power to end it.
   Memoirs of an Infantry Officer (1930) pt. 10, ch. 2

1 I'd like to see a Tank come down the
    stalls,
  Lurching to rag-time tunes, or 'Home,
    sweet Home',—
  And there'd be no more jokes in
    Music-halls
  To mock the riddled corpses round
    Bapaume.
  The Old Huntsman (1917) 'Blighters'

2 And he'd come home again to find it
    more
  Desirable than it ever was before.
  How right it seemed that he should
    reach the span
  Of comfortable years allowed to man!
  Splendid to eat and sleep and choose
    a wife,
  Safe with his wound, a citizen of life.
  He hobbled blithely through the garden
    gate,
  And thought: 'Thank God they had to
    amputate!'
  The Old Huntsman (1917) 'The One-Legged
  Man'

3 Why do you lie with your legs ungainly
    huddled,
  And one arm bent across your sullen
    cold
  Exhausted face? It hurts my heart to
    watch you,
  Deep-shadow'd from the candle's
    glittering gold;
  And you wonder why I shake you by the
    shoulder;
  Drowsy, you mumble and sigh and turn
    your head . . .
  *You are too young to fall asleep for ever;
  And when you sleep you remind me of the
  dead.*
  War Poems (1919) 'The Dug-Out'

4 But the past is just the same,—and
    War's a bloody game . . .
  Have you forgotten yet? . . .
  Look down, and swear by the slain of
    the War that you'll never forget.
  War Poems (1919) 'Aftermath'

5 Everyone suddenly burst out singing;
  And I was filled with such delight
  As prisoned birds must find in freedom
  Winging wildly across the white
  Orchards and dark green fields; on; on;
    and out of sight.

  Everyone's voice was suddenly lifted,
  And beauty came like the setting sun.

My heart was shaken with tears and
    horror
  Drifted away . . . O but every one
  Was a bird; and the song was wordless;
    the singing will never be done.
  War Poems (1919) 'Everyone Sang'

Erik Satie 1866–1925

6 *Ravel refuse la Légion d'Honneur, mais son
  œuvre l'accepte.*

  Ravel refuses the Legion of Honour, but
  all his music accepts it.
  In Jean Cocteau *Le Discours d'Oxford* (1956)
  p. 49

Telly Savalas 1926–

7 Who loves ya, baby?
  Catch-phrase in American TV series *Kojak*
  (1973–8)

Dorothy L. Sayers 1893–1957

8 I admit it is better fun to punt than to be
  punted, and that a desire to have all the
  fun is nine-tenths of the law of chivalry.
  Gaudy Night (1935) ch. 14

9 With a gesture of submission he bowed
  his head and stood gravely, the square
  cap dangling in his hand. 'Placetne,
  magistra?' 'Placet.'
  Gaudy Night (1935) ch. 23 (Lord Peter
  Wimsey's marriage proposal to Harriet
  Vane, and her acceptance)

10 Plain lies are dangerous: the only
  weapons left him [the advertiser] are the
  suggestio falsi and the *suppressio veri*, and
  his use even of these would be very
  much more circumscribed if one person
  in ten had ever been taught how to
  read. . . . Those who prefer their English
  sloppy have only themselves to thank if
  the advertisement writer uses his
  mastery of vocabulary and syntax to
  mislead their weak minds. . . . The moral
  of all this . . . is that we have the kind of
  advertising we deserve.
  Spectator 19 Nov. 1937 'The Psychology of
  Advertising'

11 As I grow older and older,
  And totter towards the tomb,
  I find that I care less and less
  Who goes to bed with whom.
  'That's Why I Never Read Modern Novels',
  in Janet Hitchman *Such a Strange Lady*
  (1975) ch. 12

Al Scalpone

1 The family that prays together stays together.

> Slogan devised for the Roman Catholic Family Rosary Crusade in 1947: see Patrick Peyton *All for Her* (1967) p. 144

Hugh Scanlon (Baron Scanlon) 1913–

2 Of course liberty is not licence. Liberty in my view is conforming to majority opinion.

> Television interview, 9 Aug. 1977, in *Listener* 11 Aug. 1977

Arthur Scargill 1938–

3 Parliament itself would not exist in its present form had people not defied the law.

> Said in evidence to House of Commons Select Committee on Employment, 2 Apr. 1980, in *House of Commons Paper no. 462 of Session 1979–80* p. 55

Age Scarpelli, Luciano Vincenzoni 1926– , and Sergio Leone 1921–

4 *Il buono, il bruto, il cattivo.*

The good, the bad, and the ugly.

> Title of film (1966)

Moritz Schlick

5 The meaning of a proposition is the method of its verification.

> *Philosophical Review* (1936) vol. 45, p. 341 'Meaning and Verification'

Artur Schnabel 1882–1951

6 The notes I handle no better than many pianists. But the pauses between the notes—ah, that is where the art resides!

> In *Chicago Daily News* 11 June 1958

7 Applause is a receipt, not a note of demand.

> In *Saturday Review of Literature* 29 Sept. 1951

8 I don't think there was ever a piece of music that changed a man's decision on how to vote.

> *My Life and Music* (1961) pt. 2, ch. 8

9 When I am asked, 'What do you think of our audience?' I answer, 'I know two kinds of audiences only—one coughing, and one not coughing.'

> *My Life and Music* (1961) pt. 2, ch. 10

Arnold Schoenberg 1874–1951

10 If it is art, it is not for the masses. 'If it is for the masses it is not art' is a topic which is rather similar to a word of yourself.

> Letter to W. S. Schlamm, 1 July 1945, in Erwin Stein *Arnold Schoenberg Letters* (1964) p. 235

Budd Schulberg 1914–

11 You don't understand. I could have had class. I could have been a contender. I could have been somebody—instead of a bum, which is what I am, let's face it.

> *On the Waterfront* (1954 film; words spoken by Marlon Brando)

12 What makes Sammy run?

> Title of novel (1941)

Diane B. Schulder 1937–

13 Law is a reflection and a source of prejudice. It both enforces and suggests forms of bias.

> In Robin Morgan *Sisterhood is Powerful* (1970) p. 139

E. F. Schumacher 1911–1977

14 Call a thing immoral or ugly, soul-destroying or a degradation of man, a peril to the peace of the world or to the well-being of future generations: as long as you have not shown it to be 'uneconomic' you have not really questioned its right to exist, grow, and prosper.

> *Small is Beautiful* (1973) pt. 1, ch. 3

15 Small is beautiful. A study of economics as if people mattered.

> Title of book (1973)

Albert Schweitzer 1875–1965

16 *Am Abend des dritten Tages, als wir bei Sonnenuntergang gerade durch eine Herde Nilpferde hindurchfuhren, stand urplötzlich, von mir nicht geahnt und nicht gesucht, das Wort "Ehrfurcht vor dem Leben" vor mir.*

Late on the third day, at the very moment when, at sunset, we were making our way through a herd of hippopotamuses, there flashed upon my mind, unforeseen and unsought, the phrase, 'Reverence for Life'.

Aus meinem Leben und Denken (My Life and Thought, 1933) ch. 13

1 *"Heda, kamerad," rufe ich, "willst du uns nicht ein wenig helfen?" "Ich bin ein Intellektueller und trage kein Holz," lautete die Antwort. "Hast du Glück," erwiderte ich; "auch ich wollte ein Intellektueller werden, aber es ist mir nicht gelungen."*

'Hullo! friend,' I call out, 'Won't you lend us a hand?' 'I am an intellectual and don't drag wood about,' came the answer. 'You're lucky,' I reply. 'I too wanted to become an intellectual, but I didn't succeed.'

Mitteilungen aus Lambarene (1928, tr. by C. T. Campion, 1931 as *More from the Primeval Forest*) ch. 5

2 *Die Wahrheit hat keine Stunde. Ihre Zeit ist immer und gerade dann wenn sie am unzeitgemässsesten scheint.*

Truth has no special time of its own. Its hour is now—always, and indeed then most truly when it seems most unsuitable to actual circumstances.

Zwischen Wasser und Urwald (On the Edge of the Primeval Forest, 1922) ch. 11

Kurt Schwitters 1887–1948

3 *Ich bin Maler, ich nagle meine Bilder.*

I am a painter and I nail my pictures together.

Remark to Raoul Hausmann, 1918, in Raoul Hausmann *Courrier Dada* (1958) p. 63

Martin Scorsese 1942– and Mardik Martin

4 You don't make up for your sins in church; you do it in the street, you do it at home. The rest is bullshit and you know it.

Mean Streets (1973 film) in Michael Bliss *Martin Scorsese and Michael Cimino* (1985) ch. 3

C. P. Scott 1846–1932

5 A newspaper is of necessity something of a monopoly, and its first duty is to shun the temptations of monopoly. Its primary office is the gathering of news. At the peril of its soul it must see that

the supply is not tainted. Neither in what it gives, nor in what it does not give, nor in the mode of presentation must the unclouded face of truth suffer wrong. Comment is free, but facts are sacred.

Manchester Guardian 5 May 1921

Paul Scott 1920–1978

6 The jewel in the crown.

Title of novel (1966)

Robert Falcon Scott 1868–1912

7 Great God! this [the South Pole] is an awful place and terrible enough for us to have laboured to it without the reward of priority.

Diary, 17 Jan. 1912, in *Scott's Last Expedition* (1913) vol. 1, ch. 18

8 For God's sake look after our people.

Diary, 29 Mar. 1912, in *Scott's Last Expedition* (1913) vol. 1, ch. 20

9 Make the boy interested in natural history if you can; it is better than games; they encourage it in some schools.

Final letter to his wife, in *Scott's Last Expedition* (1913) vol. 1, ch. 20

10 Had we lived, I should have had a tale to tell of the hardihood, endurance, and courage of my companions which would have stirred the heart of every Englishman. These rough notes and our dead bodies must tell the tale.

'Message to the Public' in *Scott's Last Expedition* (1913) vol. 1, ch. 20

Florida Scott-Maxwell

11 No matter how old a mother is she watches her middle-aged children for signs of improvement.

Measure of my Days (1968) p. 16

Alan Seeger 1888–1916

12 I have a rendezvous with Death
At some disputed barricade,
When Spring comes round with rustling shade
And apple blossoms fill the air.
I have a rendezvous with Death

When Spring brings back blue days and fair.

North American Review Oct. 1916 'I Have a Rendezvous with Death'

Pete Seeger 1919–

1 Where have all the flowers gone?
The girls have picked them every one.
Oh, when will you ever learn?
Where Have all the Flowers Gone? (1961 song)

See also ANONYMOUS 9:13

Erich Segal 1937–

2 Love means not ever having to say you're sorry.
Love Story (1970) ch. 13

W. C. Sellar 1898–1951 and R. J. Yeatman 1898–1968

3 For every person who wants to teach there are approximately thirty who don't want to learn—much.
And Now All This (1932) introduction

4 The Roman Conquest was, however, a *Good Thing*, since the Britons were only natives at the time.
1066 and All That (1930) ch. 1

5 The conversion of England was thus effected by the landing of St Augustine in Thanet and other places, which resulted in the country being overrun by a Wave of Saints. Among these were St Ive, St Pancra, the great St Bernard (originator of the clerical collar), St Bee, St Ebb, St Neot (who invented whisky), St Kit and St Kin, and the Venomous Bead (author of The Rosary).
1066 and All That (1930) ch. 3

6 Edward III had very good manners. One day at a royal dance he noticed some men-about-court mocking a lady whose garter had come off, whereupon to put her at her ease he stopped the dance and made the memorable epitaph: 'Honi soie qui mal y pense' ('Honey, your silk stocking's hanging down').
1066 and All That (1930) ch. 24

7 Shortly after this the cruel Queen died and a post-mortem examination revealed the word 'CALLOUS' engraved on her heart.
1066 and All That (1930) ch. 32

8 The utterly memorable Struggle between the Cavaliers (Wrong but Wromantic) and the Roundheads (Right but Repulsive).
1066 and All That (1930) ch. 35

9 Charles II was always very merry and was therefore not so much a king as a Monarch.
1066 and All That (1930) ch. 36

10 The National Debt is a very Good Thing and it would be dangerous to pay it off, for fear of Political Economy.
1066 and All That (1930) ch. 38

11 Napoleon's armies always used to march on their stomachs shouting: 'Vive l'Intérieur!' and so moved about very slowly (*ventre-à-terre*, as the French say) thus enabling Wellington to catch them up and defeat them.
1066 and All That (1930) ch. 48

12 Gladstone also invented the Education Rate by which it was possible to calculate how soon anybody could be educated, and he spent his declining years trying to guess the answer to the Irish Question; unfortunately whenever he was getting warm, the Irish secretly changed the Question.
1066 and All That (1930) ch. 57

13 AMERICA was thus clearly top nation, and History came to a .
1066 and All That (1930) ch. 62

14 Do not on any account attempt to write on both sides of the paper at once.
1066 and All That (1930) 'Test Paper 5'

Robert W. Service 1874–1958

15 Ah! the clock is always slow;
It is later than you think.
Ballads of a Bohemian (1921) 'It Is Later Than You Think'

16 When we, the Workers, all demand:
'What are WE fighting for?' . . .
Then, then we'll end that stupid crime,
that devil's madness—War.
Ballads of a Bohemian (1921) 'Michael'

17 This is the law of the Yukon, that only the Strong shall thrive;
That surely the Weak shall perish, and only the Fit survive.
Dissolute, damned and despairful, crippled and palsied and slain,

This is the Will of the Yukon,—Lo, how
she makes it plain!
Songs of a Sourdough (1907) 'The Law of the
Yukon'

1 A bunch of the boys were whooping it
up in the Malamute saloon;
The kid that handles the music-box was
hitting a jag-time tune;
Back of the bar, in a solo game, sat
Dangerous Dan McGrew,
And watching his luck was his
light-o'-love, the lady that's known as
Lou.
Songs of a Sourdough (1907) 'The Shooting of
Dan McGrew'

2 A promise made is a debt unpaid, and
the trail has its own stern code.
Songs of a Sourdough (1907) 'Cremation of
Sam McGee'

Anne Sexton 1928–1974

3 In a dream you are never eighty.
All My Pretty Ones (1962) 'Old'

James Seymour and Rian James
1899–

4 You're going out a youngster but you've
got to come back a star.
42nd Street (1933 film)

Peter Shaffer 1926–

5 All my wife has ever taken from the
Mediterranean—from that whole vast
intuitive culture—are four bottles of
Chianti to make into lamps, and two
china condiment donkeys labelled Sally
and Peppy.
Equus (1973) act 1, sc. 18

6 Passion, you see, can be destroyed by
a doctor. It cannot be created.
Equus (1973) act 2, sc. 35

Eileen Shanahan

7 The length of a meeting rises with the
square of the number of people present.
Attributed

Bill Shankly 1914–1981

8 Some people think football is a matter of
life and death. I don't like that attitude.

I can assure them it is much more
serious than that.
In *Sunday Times* 4 Oct. 1981

Tom Sharpe 1928–

9 The South African police would leave no
stone unturned to see that nothing
disturbed the even terror of their lives.
Indecent Exposure (1973) ch. 1

10 Skullion had little use for contraceptives
at the best of times. Unnatural, he called
them, and placed them in the lower
social category of things along with
elastic-sided boots and made-up bow
ties. Not the sort of attire for
a gentleman.
Porterhouse Blue (1974) ch. 9

George Bernard Shaw 1856–1950

11 All great truths begin as blasphemies.
Annajanska (1919) p. 262

12 One man that has a mind and knows it
can always beat ten men who havnt
and dont.
The Apple Cart (1930) act 1

13 What Englishman will give his mind to
politics as long as he can afford to keep
a motor car?
The Apple Cart (1930) act 1

14 Breakages, Limited, the biggest
industrial corporation in the country.
The Apple Cart (1930) act 1

15 I never resist temptation because I have
found that things that are bad for me do
not tempt me.
The Apple Cart (1930) interlude

16 Arms and the man.
Title of play (1898). Cf. Virgil in *Oxford
Dictionary of Quotations* (1979) 557:8

17 You can always tell an old soldier by the
inside of his holsters and cartridge
boxes. The young ones carry pistols and
cartridges; the old ones, grub.
Arms and the Man (1898) act 1

18 Oh, you are a very poor soldier—a
chocolate cream soldier!
Arms and the Man (1898) act 1

19 I never apologize!
Arms and the Man (1898) act 3

20 Youre not a man, youre a machine.
Arms and the Man (1898) act 3

1 You see things; and you say 'Why?' But I dream things that never were; and I say 'Why not?'
Back to Methuselah (1921) pt. 1, act 1

2 Make me a beautiful word for doing things tomorrow; for that surely is a great and blessed invention.
Back to Methuselah (1921) pt. 1, act 1

3 I enjoy convalescence. It is the part that makes illness worth while.
Back to Methuselah (1921) pt. 2

4 Silence is the most perfect expression of scorn.
Back to Methuselah (1921) pt. 5

5 Life is not meant to be easy, my child; but take courage: it can be delightful.
Back to Methuselah (1921) pt. 5

6 A strange lady giving an address in Zurich wrote him [Shaw] a proposal, thus: 'You have the greatest brain in the world, and I have the most beautiful body; so we ought to produce the most perfect child.' Shaw asked: 'What if the child inherits my body and your brains?'
In Hesketh Pearson *Bernard Shaw* (1942) p. 310

7 He is a barbarian, and thinks that the customs of his tribe and island are the laws of nature.
Caesar and Cleopatra (1901) act 2 (said by Caesar of his secretary, a Briton)

8 When a stupid man is doing something he is ashamed of, he always declares that it is his duty.
Caesar and Cleopatra (1901) act 3

9 He who has never hoped can never despair.
Caesar and Cleopatra (1901) act 4

10 A man of great common sense and good taste, meaning thereby a man without originality or moral courage.
Notes to Caesar and Cleopatra (1901) 'Julius Caesar'

11 We have no more right to consume happiness without producing it than to consume wealth without producing it.
Candida (1898) act 1

12 Do you think that the things people make fools of themselves about are any less real and true than the things they behave sensibly about? They are more

true: they are the only things that are true.
Candida (1898) act 1

13 It is easy—terribly easy—to shake a man's faith in himself. To take advantage of that to break a man's spirit is devil's work.
Candida (1898) act 1

14 I'm only a beer teetotaller, not a champagne teetotaller.
Candida (1898) act 3

15 The worst sin towards our fellow creatures is not to hate them, but to be indifferent to them: thats the essence of inhumanity.
The Devil's Disciple (1901) act 2

16 Martyrdom . . . is the only way in which a man can become famous without ability.
The Devil's Disciple (1901) act 3

17 I never expect a soldier to think.
The Devil's Disciple (1901) act 3

18 SWINDON: What will history say?
BURGOYNE: History, sir, will tell lies as usual.
The Devil's Disciple (1901) act 3

19 Your friend the British soldier can stand up to anything except the British War Office.
The Devil's Disciple (1901) act 3

20 There is at bottom only one genuinely scientific treatment for all diseases, and that is to stimulate the phagocytes.
The Doctor's Dilemma (1911) act 1

21 All professions are conspiracies against the laity.
The Doctor's Dilemma (1911) act 1

22 I don't believe in morality. I am a disciple of Bernard Shaw.
The Doctor's Dilemma (1911) act 3

23 I believe in Michael Angelo, Velasquez, and Rembrandt; in the might of design, the mystery of colour, the redemption of all things by Beauty everlasting, and the message of Art that has made these hands blessed. Amen. Amen.
The Doctor's Dilemma (1911) act 4

24 Parentage is a very important profession, but no test of fitness for it is ever imposed in the interest of the children.
Everybody's Political What's What? (1944) ch. 9

1 A government which robs Peter to pay Paul can always depend on the support of Paul.
   Everybody's Political What's What? (1944) ch. 30

2 It's all that the young can do for the old, to shock them and keep them up to date.
   Fanny's First Play (1914) 'Induction'

3 You don't expect me to know what to say about a play when I don't know who the author is, do you?
   Fanny's First Play (1914) epilogue

4 If it's by a good author, it's a good play, naturally. That stands to reason.
   Fanny's First Play (1914) epilogue

5 Home life as we understand it is no more natural to us than a cage is natural to a cockatoo.
   Getting Married (1911) preface 'Hearth and Home'

6 The one point on which all women are in furious secret rebellion against the existing law is the saddling of the right to a child with the obligation to become the servant of a man.
   Getting Married (1911) preface 'The Right to Motherhood'

7 Physically there is nothing to distinguish human society from the farm-yard except that children are more troublesome and costly than chickens and calves, and that men and women are not so completely enslaved as farm stock.
   Getting Married (1911) preface 'The Personal Sentimental Basis of Monogamy'

8 What God hath joined together no man ever shall put asunder: God will take care of that.
   Getting Married (1911) p. 216

9 Sam wanted to make a Goldwyn writer of George Bernard Shaw. They discussed it over tea one day in London. . . . A version of the conversation was cabled over to Howard Dietz, Goldwyn's publicity chief; he compressed Shaw's words into: 'The trouble, Mr Goldwyn, is that you are only interested in art and I am only interested in money.' This was cabled back to London and released there. It added considerably to Shaw's reputation as a wit.
   Alva Johnson *The Great Goldwyn* (1937) ch. 3

10 I am a woman of the world, Hector; and I can assure you that if you will only take the trouble always to do the perfectly correct thing, and to say the perfectly correct thing, you can do just what you like.
   Heartbreak House (1919) act 1

11 Go anywhere in England where there are natural, wholesome, contented, and really nice English people; and what do you always find? That the stables are the real centre of the household.
   Heartbreak House (1919) act 3

12 The captain is in his bunk, drinking bottled ditch-water; and the crew is gambling in the forecastle. She will strike and sink and split. Do you think the laws of God will be suspended in favour of England because you were born in it?
   Heartbreak House (1919) act 3

13 Money is indeed the most important thing in the world; and all sound and successful personal and national morality should have this fact for its basis.
   The Irrational Knot (1905) preface

14 Reminiscences make one feel so deliciously aged and sad.
   The Irrational Knot (1905) ch. 14

15 A man who has no office to go to—I don't care who he is—is a trial of which you can have no conception.
   The Irrational Knot (1905) ch. 18

16 An Irishman's heart is nothing but his imagination.
   John Bull's Other Island (1907) act 1

17 My way of joking is to tell the truth. Its the funniest joke in the world.
   John Bull's Other Island (1907) act 2

18 What really flatters a man is that you think him worth flattering.
   John Bull's Other Island (1907) act 4

19 There are only two qualities in the world: efficiency and inefficiency, and

only two sorts of people: the efficient and the inefficient.

John Bull's Other Island (1907) act 4

1 The greatest of evils and the worst of crimes is poverty . . . our first duty—a duty to which every other consideration should be sacrificed—is not to be poor.

Major Barbara (1907) preface

2 The universal regard for money is the one hopeful fact in our civilization, the one sound spot in our social conscience. Money is the most important thing in the world. It represents health, strength, honour, generosity and beauty as conspicuously and undeniably as the want of it represents illness, weakness, disgrace, meanness and ugliness. Not the least of its virtues is that it destroys base people as certainly as it fortifies and dignifies noble people.

Major Barbara (1907) preface

3 Cusins is a very nice fellow, certainly: nobody would ever guess that he was born in Australia.

Major Barbara (1907) act 1

4 Nobody can say a word against Greek: it stamps a man at once as an educated gentleman.

Major Barbara (1907) act 1

5 I am a Millionaire. That is my religion.

Major Barbara (1907) act 2

6 I can't talk religion to a man with bodily hunger in his eyes.

Major Barbara (1907) act 2

7 Wot prawce Selvytion nah?

Major Barbara (1907) act 2

8 Alcohol is a very necessary article. . . . It makes life bearable to millions of people who could not endure their existence if they were quite sober. It enables Parliament to do things at eleven at night that no sane person would do at eleven in the morning.

Major Barbara (1907) act 2

9 He knows nothing; and he thinks he knows everything. That points clearly to a political career.

Major Barbara (1907) act 3

10 The sixth Undershaft wrote up these words: NOTHING IS EVER DONE IN THIS WORLD UNTIL MEN ARE PREPARED TO KILL ONE ANOTHER IF IT IS NOT DONE.

Major Barbara (1907) act 3

11 Like all young men, you greatly exaggerate the difference between one young woman and another.

Major Barbara (1907) act 3

12 But a lifetime of happiness! No man alive could bear it: it would be hell on earth.

Man and Superman (1903) act 1

13 We are ashamed of everything that is real about us; ashamed of ourselves, of our relatives, of our incomes, of our accents, of our opinions, of our experience, just as we are ashamed of our naked skins.

Man and Superman (1903) act 1

14 The more things a man is ashamed of, the more respectable he is.

Man and Superman (1903) act 1

15 Vitality in a woman is a blind fury of creation. She sacrifices herself to it.

Man and Superman (1903) act 1

16 The true artist will let his wife starve, his children go barefoot, his mother drudge for his living at seventy, sooner than work at anything but his art.

Man and Superman (1903) act 1

17 Of all human struggles there is none so treacherous and remorseless as the struggle between the artist man and the mother woman.

Man and Superman (1903) act 1

18 There is no love sincerer than the love of food.

Man and Superman (1903) act 1

19 Very nice sort of place, Oxford, I should think, for people that like that sort of place. They teach you to be a gentleman there. In the Polytechnic they teach you to be an engineer or such like.

Man and Superman (1903) act 2

20 You think that you are Ann's suitor; that you are the pursuer and she the pursued; that it is your part to woo, to persuade, to prevail, to overcome. Fool: it is you who are the pursued, the marked down quarry, the destined prey.

Man and Superman (1903) act 2

1 It is a woman's business to get married as soon as possible, and a man's to keep unmarried as long as he can.
  Man and Superman (1903) act 2

2 MENDOZA: I am a brigand: I live by robbing the rich.
  TANNER: I am a gentleman: I live by robbing the poor.
  Man and Superman (1903) act 3

3 Hell is full of musical amateurs: music is the brandy of the damned.
  Man and Superman (1903) act 3

4 Englishmen never will be slaves: they are free to do whatever the Government and public opinion allow them to do.
  Man and Superman (1903) act 3

5 An Englishman thinks he is moral when he is only uncomfortable.
  Man and Superman (1903) act 3

6 In the arts of life man invents nothing; but in the arts of death he outdoes Nature herself, and produces by chemistry and machinery all the slaughter of plague, pestilence and famine.
  Man and Superman (1903) act 3

7 In the arts of peace Man is a bungler.
  Man and Superman (1903) act 3

8 As an old soldier I admit the cowardice: it's as universal as sea sickness, and matters just as little.
  Man and Superman (1903) act 3

9 When the military man approaches, the world locks up its spoons and packs off its womankind.
  Man and Superman (1903) act 3

10 What is virtue but the Trade Unionism of the married?
  Man and Superman (1903) act 3

11 Those who talk most about the blessings of marriage and the constancy of its vows are the very people who declare that if the chain were broken and the prisoners were left free to choose, the whole social fabric would fly asunder. You can't have the argument both ways. If the prisoner is happy, why lock him in? If he is not, why pretend that he is?
  Man and Superman (1903) act 3

12 Beauty is all very well at first sight; but who ever looks at it when it has been in the house three days?
  Man and Superman (1903) act 4

13 There are two tragedies in life. One is not to get your hearts desire. The other is to get it.
  Man and Superman (1903) act 4

14 Revolutions have never lightened the burden of tyranny: they have only shifted it to another shoulder.
  Man and Superman (1903) 'The Revolutionist's Handbook', foreword

15 Do not do unto others as you would that they should do unto you. Their tastes may not be the same.
  Man and Superman (1903) 'Maxims for Revolutionists: The Golden Rule'

16 The golden rule is that there are no golden rules.
  Man and Superman (1903) 'Maxims for Revolutionists: The Golden Rule'

17 The art of government is the organization of idolatry. The bureaucracy consists of functionaries; the aristocracy, of idols; the democracy, of idolators. The populace cannot understand the bureaucracy: it can only worship the national idols.
  Man and Superman (1903) 'Maxims for Revolutionists: Idolatry'

18 Democracy substitutes election by the incompetent many for appointment by the corrupt few.
  Man and Superman (1903) 'Maxims for Revolutionists: Democracy'

19 Liberty means responsibility. That is why most men dread it.
  Man and Superman (1903) 'Maxims for Revolutionists: Liberty and Equality'

20 The vilest abortionist is he who attempts to mould a child's character.
  Man and Superman (1903) 'Maxims for Revolutionists: Education'

21 He who can, does. He who cannot, teaches.
  Man and Superman (1903) 'Maxims for Revolutionists: Education'

22 Marriage is popular because it combines the maximum of temptation with the maximum of opportunity.
  Man and Superman (1903) 'Maxims for Revolutionists: Marriage'

1 Titles distinguish the mediocre, embarrass the superior, and are disgraced by the inferior.
   Man and Superman (1903) 'Maxims for Revolutionists: Titles'

2 When domestic servants are treated as human beings it is not worth while to keep them.
   Man and Superman (1903) 'Maxims for Revolutionists: Servants'

3 If you strike a child take care that you strike it in anger, even at the risk of maiming it for life. A blow in cold blood neither can nor should be forgiven.
   Man and Superman (1903) 'Maxims for Revolutionists: How to Beat Children'

4 Beware of the man whose god is in the skies.
   Man and Superman (1903) 'Maxims for Revolutionists: Religion'

5 Self-denial is not a virtue: it is only the effect of prudence on rascality.
   Man and Superman (1903) 'Maxims for Revolutionists: Virtues and Vice'

6 In heaven an angel is nobody in particular.
   Man and Superman (1903) 'Maxims for Revolutionists: Greatness'

7 A moderately honest man with a moderately faithful wife, moderate drinkers both, in a moderately healthy house: that is the true middle class unit.
   Man and Superman (1903) 'Maxims for Revolutionists: Moderation'

8 The reasonable man adapts himself to the world: the unreasonable one persists in trying to adapt the world to himself. Therefore all progress depends on the unreasonable man.
   Man and Superman (1903) 'Maxims for Revolutionists: Reason'

9 The man who listens to Reason is lost: Reason enslaves all whose minds are not strong enough to master her.
   Man and Superman (1903) 'Maxims for Revolutionists: Reason'

10 Decency is Indecency's conspiracy of silence.
   Man and Superman (1903) 'Maxims for Revolutionists: Decency'

11 Life levels all men: death reveals the eminent.
   Man and Superman (1903) 'Maxims for Revolutionists: Fame'

12 Home is the girl's prison and the woman's workhouse.
   Man and Superman (1903) 'Maxims for Revolutionists: Women in the Home'

13 Every man over forty is a scoundrel.
   Man and Superman (1903) 'Maxims for Revolutionists: Stray Sayings'

14 Youth, which is forgiven everything, forgives itself nothing: age, which forgives itself everything, is forgiven nothing.
   Man and Superman (1903) 'Maxims for Revolutionists: Stray Sayings'

15 Take care to get what you like or you will be forced to like what you get.
   Man and Superman (1903) 'Maxims for Revolutionists: Stray Sayings'

16 It is dangerous to be sincere unless you are also stupid.
   Man and Superman (1903) 'Maxims for Revolutionists: Stray Sayings'

17 Beware of the man who does not return your blow: he neither forgives you nor allows you to forgive yourself.
   Man and Superman (1903) 'Maxims for Revolutionists: Stray Sayings'

18 Self-sacrifice enables us to sacrifice other people without blushing.
   Man and Superman (1903) 'Maxims for Revolutionists: Self-Sacrifice'

19 There is nothing so bad or so good that you will not find Englishmen doing it; but you will never find an Englishman in the wrong. He does everything on principle. He fights you on patriotic principles; he robs you on business principles; he enslaves you on imperial principles; he bullies you on manly principles; he supports his king on loyal principles and cuts off his king's head on republican principles.
   Man of Destiny (1898) p. 201

20 Anybody on for a game of tennis?
   Misalliance (1914) p. 25 (perhaps the origin of the phrase 'Anyone for tennis?', said to be typical of drawing-room comedies; cf. Humphrey Bogart)

21 Anarchism is a game at which the police can beat you.
   Misalliance (1914) p. 85

22 The only way for a woman to provide for herself decently is for her to be good

to some man that can afford to be good to her.
Mrs Warren's Profession (1898) act 2

1 A great devotee of the Gospel of Getting On.
Mrs Warren's Profession (1898) act 4 (said of Miss Warren)

2 [Dancing is] a perpendicular expression of a horizontal desire.
In *New Statesman* 23 Mar. 1962

3 Youll never have a quiet world til you knock the patriotism out of the human race.
O'Flaherty V.C. (1919) p. 178

4 As long as I have a want, I have a reason for living. Satisfaction is death.
Overruled (1916) p. 72

5 There is, on the whole, nothing on earth intended for innocent people so horrible as a school. To begin with, it is a prison. But it is in some respects more cruel than a prison. In a prison, for instance, you are not forced to read books written by the warders and the governor . . . and beaten or otherwise tormented if you cannot remember their utterly unmemorable contents.
Parents and Children (1914) 'School'

6 The secret of being miserable is to have leisure to bother about whether you are happy or not. The cure for it is occupation.
Parents and Children (1914) 'Children's Happiness'

7 A perpetual holiday is a good working definition of hell.
Parents and Children (1914) 'Children's Happiness'

8 The fickleness of the women I love is only equalled by the infernal constancy of the women who love me.
The Philanderer (1898) act 2

9 There is only one religion, though there are a hundred versions of it.
Plays Pleasant and Unpleasant (1898) vol. 2, preface

10 The English have no respect for their language, and will not teach their children to speak it. They spell it so abominably that no man can teach himself what it sounds like. It is impossible for an Englishman to open his mouth without making some other Englishman hate or despise him.
Pygmalion (1916) preface

11 Hes a gentleman: look at his boots.
Pygmalion (1916) act 1

12 Remember that you are a human being with a soul and the divine gift of articulate speech: that your native language is the language of Shakespear and Milton and The Bible; and don't sit there crooning like a bilious pigeon.
Pygmalion (1916) act 1

13 I don't want to talk grammar, I want to talk like a lady.
Pygmalion (1916) act 2

14 PICKERING: Have you no morals, man?
DOOLITTLE: Can't afford them, Governor. Neither could you if you was as poor as me.
Pygmalion (1916) act 2

15 I'm one of the undeserving poor: that's what I am. Think of what that means to a man. It means that he's up agen middle-class morality all the time.
Pygmalion (1916) act 2

16 My aunt died of influenza: so they said. But it's my belief they done the old woman in.
Pygmalion (1916) act 3

17 Gin was mother's milk to her.
Pygmalion (1916) act 3

18 FREDDY: Are you walking across the Park, Miss Doolittle? If so—
LIZA: Walk! Not bloody likely. I am going in a taxi.
Pygmalion (1916) act 3

19 I have to live for others and not for myself: thats middle-class morality.
Pygmalion (1916) act 5

20 The Churches must learn humility as well as teach it.
Saint Joan (1924) preface

21 If ever I utter an oath again may my soul be blasted to eternal damnation!
Saint Joan (1924) sc. 2

22 A miracle, my friend, is an event which creates faith. That is the purpose and nature of miracles. . . . Frauds deceive. An event which creates faith does not deceive: therefore it is not a fraud, but a miracle.
Saint Joan (1924) sc. 2

1 We were not fairly beaten, my lord. No Englishman is ever fairly beaten.
Saint Joan (1924) sc. 4

2 How can what an Englishman believes be heresy? It is a contradiction in terms.
Saint Joan (1924) sc. 4

3 Must then a Christ perish in torment in every age to save those that have no imagination?
Saint Joan (1924) epilogue

4 With the single exception of Homer, there is no eminent writer, not even Sir Walter Scott, whom I can despise so entirely as I despise Shakespeare when I measure my mind against his. The intensity of my impatience with him occasionally reaches such a pitch, that it would positively be a relief to me to dig him up and throw stones at him, knowing as I do how incapable he and his worshippers are of understanding any less obvious form of indignity.
Saturday Review 26 Sept. 1896 (reviewing a production of *Cymbeline*)

5 Assassination is the extreme form of censorship.
Shewing-Up of Blanco Posnet (1911) 'Limits to Toleration'

6 'Do you know what a pessimist is?' 'A man who thinks everybody is as nasty as himself, and hates them for it.'
An Unsocial Socialist (1887) ch. 5

7 We dont bother much about dress and manners in England, because, as a nation, we dont dress well and weve no manners.
You Never Can Tell (1898) act 1

8 Well, sir, you never can tell. Thats a principle in life with me, sir, if youll excuse my having such a thing, sir.
You Never Can Tell (1898) act 2

9 The great advantage of a hotel is that it's a refuge from home life.
You Never Can Tell (1898) act 2

10 My speciality is being right when other people are wrong.
You Never Can Tell (1898) act 4

11 The younger generation is knocking at the door, and as I open it there steps spritely in the incomparable Max.
Saturday Review 21 May 1898 'Valedictory' (on handing over the theatre review column to Max Beerbohm)

Sir Hartley Shawcross (Baron Shawcross) 1902–

12 'But,' said Alice, 'the question is whether you can make a word mean different things.' 'Not so,' said Humpty-Dumpty, 'the question is which is to be the master. That's all.' We are the masters at the moment, and not only at the moment, but for a very long time to come.
Hansard 2 Apr. 1946, col. 1213. Cf. *Oxford Dictionary of Quotations* (1979) 135:22

Patrick Shaw-Stewart 1888–1917

13 I saw a man this morning
Who did not wish to die;
I ask and cannot answer
If otherwise wish I.
Poem (1916) in M. Baring *Have You Anything to Declare?* (1936) p. 39

14 He [Shaw-Stewart] once asked me if I knew a certain Duke's eldest son, and when I said no, and from what I heard I didn't think we should like him if we did, he answered: 'I've yet to meet the Duke I couldn't like.'
Edward Marsh *A Number of People* (1939) ch. 9

Gloria Shayne

15 Goodbye cruel world.
Title of song (1961)

E. A. Sheppard
See CHARLES COLLINS

Burt Shevelove 1915–1982 and Larry Gelbart ?1928–

16 A funny thing happened on the way to the Forum.
Title of musical (1962; music and lyrics by Stephen Sondheim)

Emanuel Shinwell (Baron Shinwell) 1884–1986

17 We know that the organised workers of the country are our friends. As for the rest, they don't matter a tinker's cuss.
Speech to Electrical Trades Union conference at Margate, 7 May 1947, in *Manchester Guardian* 8 May 1947

Jean Sibelius 1865–1957

1 'Never pay any attention to what critics say,' he [Sibelius] proceeded, and expatiated on this theme. When I ventured to put in the remark that their articles might sometimes be of great importance, he cut me short. 'Remember,' he said, 'a statue has never been set up in honour of a critic!'
> In Bengt de Törne *Sibelius: A Close-Up* (1937) ch. 2

Walter Sickert 1860–1942

2 Nothing knits man to man, the Manchester School wisely taught, like the frequent passage from hand to hand of cash.
> *New Age* 28 July 1910 'The Language of Art'

Maurice Sigler 1901–1961 and Al Hoffman 1902–1960

3 Little man, you've had a busy day.
> Title of song (1934)

Alan Sillitoe 1928–

4 The loneliness of the long-distance runner.
> Title of novel (1959)

Frank Silver 1892–1960 and Irving Cohn 1898–1961

5 Yes! we have no bananas, We have no bananas today.
> *Yes! We Have No Bananas* (1923 song)

Georges Simenon 1903–1989

6 *J'ai eu 10,000 femmes depuis l'âge de 13 ans et demi. Ce n'était pas du tout un vice. Je n'ai aucun vice sexuel, mais j'avais besoin de communiquer.*

I have made love to 10,000 women since I was 13½. It wasn't in any way a vice. I've no sexual vices. But I needed to communicate.
> Interview with Federico Fellini in *L'Express* 21 Feb. 1977

7 Writing is not a profession but a vocation of unhappiness.
> Interview in *Paris Review* Summer 1955

James Simmons 1933–

8 For every year of life we light A candle on your cake To mark the simple sort of progress Anyone can make, And then, to test your nerve or give A proper view of death, You're asked to blow each light, each year, Out with your own breath.
> *In the Wilderness and Other Poems* (1969) 'A Birthday Poem'

Paul Simon 1942–

9 And here's to you, Mrs Robinson Jesus loves you more than you will know. God bless you please, Mrs Robinson Heaven holds a place for those who pray.
> *Mrs Robinson* (1968 song; used in the film *The Graduate*)

Harold Simpson

10 Down in the forest something stirred: It was only the note of a bird.
> *Down in the Forest* (1906 song; music by Landon Ronald)

Kirke Simpson

11 [Warren] Harding of Ohio was chosen by a group of men in a smoke-filled room early today as Republican candidate for President.
> News report, 12 June 1920

N. F. Simpson 1919–

12 Knocked down a doctor? With an ambulance? How could she? It's a contradiction in terms.
> *One Way Pendulum* (1960) act 1

Noble Sissle 1889–1975 and Eubie Blake 1883–1983

13 I'm just wild about Harry.
> Title of song (1921)

C. H. Sisson 1914–

14 Here lies a civil servant. He was civil To everyone, and servant to the devil.
> In *The London Zoo* (1961) p. 29

Dame Edith Sitwell 1887–1964

1 Jane, Jane,
Tall as a crane,
The morning light creaks down again.
Bucolic Comedies (1923) 'Aubade'

2 The fire was furry as a bear.
Bucolic Comedies (1923) 'Façade: Dark Song'

3 I have often wished I had time to
cultivate modesty. . . . But I am too busy
thinking about myself.
In *Observer* 30 Apr. 1950

4 Virginia Woolf, I enjoyed talking to her,
but thought nothing of her writing.
I considered her 'a beautiful little
knitter'.
Letter to Geoffrey Singleton, 11 July 1955,
in John Lehmann and Derek Palmer (eds.)
Selected Letters (1970)

5 Daisy and Lily,
Lazy and silly,
Walk by the shore of the wan grassy
sea—
Talking once more 'neath
a swan-bosomed tree.
Song of the Cold (1948) 'Waltz'

6 Still falls the Rain—
Dark as the world of man, black as our
loss—
Blind as the nineteen hundred and forty
nails
Upon the Cross.
Street Songs (1942) 'The Raids, 1940. Night
and Dawn'

7 Mr [Percy Wyndham] Lewis's pictures
appeared, as a very great painter said to
me, to have been painted by a mailed fist
in a cotton glove.
Taken Care Of (1965) ch. 11

Sir Osbert Sitwell 1892–1969

8 The British Bourgeoise
Is not born,
And does not die,
But, if it is ill,
It has a frightened look in its eyes.
At the House of Mrs Kinfoot (1921) p. 8

9 In reality, killing time
Is only the name for another of the
multifarious ways
By which Time kills us.
Poems about People (1958) 'Milordo Inglese'

10 *Educ*: during the holidays from Eton.
Entry in *Who's Who* (1929)

'Red Skelton' (Richard Skelton) 1913–

11 Well, it only proves what they always
say—give the public something they
want to see, and they'll come out for it.
Comment on crowds attending the funeral
of Harry Cohn on 2 Mar. 1958, in Bob
Thomas *King Cohn* (1967) 'Foreground'

B. F. Skinner 1904–1990

12 Education is what survives when what
has been learned has been forgotten.
New Scientist 21 May 1964

Elizabeth Smart 1913–1986

13 By Grand Central Station I sat down and
wept.
Title of book (1945). Cf. Psalm 137:1

Alfred Emanuel Smith 1873–1944

14 No sane local official who has hung up
an empty stocking over the municipal
fireplace, is going to shoot Santa Claus
just before a hard Christmas.
Comment on the New Deal, in *New Outlook*
Dec. 1933

15 The crowning climax to the whole
situation is the undisputed fact that
William Randolph Hearst gave him
[Ogden Mills] the kiss of death.
Comment on Hearst's support for Smith's
unsuccessful opponent for governor of New
York State in *New York Times* 25 Oct. 1926

16 All the ills of democracy can be cured by
more democracy.
Speech in Albany, 27 June 1933, in *New
York Times* 28 June 1933

Sir Cyril Smith 1928–

17 This place is the longest running farce in
the West End.
Comment to journalists on the House of
Commons, July 1973, in *Big Cyril* (1977)
ch. 8

Dodie Smith 1896–1990

18 And so I give you our toast. From that
young man upstairs who has had the
impudence to make me a great-uncle, to
Mother and Father on their Golden
Wedding; through four generations of
us, and to those who have gone, and
those who are to come. To the

family—that dear octopus from whose
tentacles we never quite escape, nor, in
our inmost hearts, ever quite wish to.
Dear Octopus (1938) p. 120

1 Noble deeds and hot baths are the best
cures for depression.
I Capture the Castle (1949) pt. 1, ch. 3

Edgar Smith 1857–1938

2 You may tempt the upper classes
With your villainous demi-tasses,
But; Heaven will protect a working-girl!
Heaven Will Protect the Working-Girl (1909
song; music by A. Baldwin Sloane)

F. E. Smith (*Earl of Birkenhead*)
1872–1930

3 We have the highest authority for
believing that the meek shall inherit the
Earth; though I have never found any
particular corroboration of this aphorism
in the records of Somerset House.
Contemporary Personalities (1924) 'Marquess
Curzon'

4 Judge Willis ... after a long wrangle
with F. E. Smith, whom by this time he
must have come to loathe, upon a point
of procedure asked plaintively: 'What do
you suppose I am on the Bench for, Mr
Smith?' 'It is not for me, Your Honour,
to attempt to fathom the inscrutable
workings of Providence.'
In Second Earl of Birkenhead *F. E. The Life of
F. E. Smith First Earl of Birkenhead* (1959
ed.) ch. 9

5 JUDGE: I have read your case, Mr Smith,
and I am no wiser now than I was
when I started.
SMITH: Possibly not, My Lord, but far
better informed.
In Second Earl of Birkenhead *F. E. The Life of
F. E. Smith First Earl of Birkenhead* (1959
ed.) ch. 9

6 JUDGE WILLIS: You are extremely
offensive, young man.
F. E. SMITH: As a matter of fact, we
both are, and the only difference
between us is that I am trying to be,
and you can't help it.
In Second Earl of Birkenhead *Frederick Edwin
Earl of Birkenhead* (1933) vol. 1, ch. 9

7 MR JUSTICE DARLING: And who is
George Robey?

F. E. SMITH: Mr George Robey is the
Darling of the music halls, m'lud.
In A. E. Wilson *The Prime Minister of Mirth*
(1956) ch. 1

8 The world continues to offer glittering
prizes to those who have stout hearts
and sharp swords.
Rectorial Address, Glasgow University,
7 Nov. 1923, in *The Times* 8 Nov. 1923

Ian Smith 1919–

9 Let me say again, I don't believe in black
majority rule in Rhodesia—not in
a thousand years. I believe in blacks and
whites working together.
Broadcast speech, 20 Mar. 1976, in *Sunday
Times* 21 Mar. 1976

Logan Pearsall Smith 1865–1946

10 Happiness is a wine of the rarest vintage,
and seems insipid to a vulgar taste.
Afterthoughts (1931) 'Life and Human
Nature'

11 There are two things to aim at in life:
first, to get what you want; and, after
that, to enjoy it. Only the wisest of
mankind achieve the second.
Afterthoughts (1931) 'Life and Human
Nature'

12 How awful to reflect that what people
say of us is true!
Afterthoughts (1931) 'Life and Human
Nature'

13 How many of our daydreams would
darken into nightmares if there seemed
any danger of their coming true!
Afterthoughts (1931) 'Life and Human
Nature'

14 There are few sorrows, however
poignant, in which a good income is of
no avail.
Afterthoughts (1931) 'Life and Human
Nature'

15 An improper mind is a perpetual feast.
Afterthoughts (1931) 'Life and Human
Nature'

16 There is more felicity on the far side of
baldness than young men can possibly
imagine.
Afterthoughts (1931) 'Age and Death'

17 What music is more enchanting than
the voices of young people, when you
can't hear what they say?
Afterthoughts (1931) 'Age and Death'

1 The denunciation of the young is a necessary part of the hygiene of older people, and greatly assists the circulation of their blood.
   Afterthoughts (1931) 'Age and Death'

2 I cannot forgive my friends for dying; I do not find these vanishing acts of theirs at all amusing.
   Afterthoughts (1931) 'Age and Death'

3 Those who set out to serve both God and Mammon soon discover that there is no God.
   Afterthoughts (1931) 'Other People'

4 Most people sell their souls, and live with a good conscience on the proceeds.
   Afterthoughts (1931) 'Other People'

5 All Reformers, however strict their social conscience, live in houses just as big as they can pay for.
   Afterthoughts (1931) 'Other People'

6 When they come downstairs from their Ivory Towers, Idealists are very apt to walk straight into the gutter.
   Afterthoughts (1931) 'Other People'

7 Married women are kept women, and they are beginning to find it out.
   Afterthoughts (1931) 'Other People'

8 You cannot be both fashionable and first-rate.
   Afterthoughts (1931) 'In the World'

9 It is the wretchedness of being rich that you have to live with rich people.
   Afterthoughts (1931) 'In the World'

10 To suppose, as we all suppose, that we could be rich and not behave as the rich behave, is like supposing that we could drink all day and keep absolutely sober.
   Afterthoughts (1931) 'In the World'

11 The test of a vocation is the love of the drudgery it involves.
   Afterthoughts (1931) 'Art and Letters'

12 A best-seller is the gilded tomb of a mediocre talent.
   Afterthoughts (1931) 'Art and Letters'

13 People say that life is the thing, but I prefer reading.
   Afterthoughts (1931) 'Myself'

14 Thank heavens, the sun has gone in, and I don't have to go out and enjoy it.
   Afterthoughts (1931) 'Myself'

15 What I like in a good author is not what he says, but what he whispers.
   All Trivia (1933) 'Afterthoughts' pt. 5

16 Two weeks before his death, a friend asked him half-jokingly if he had discovered any meaning in life. 'Yes,' he replied, 'there is a meaning, at least for me, there is one thing that matters—to set a chime of words tinkling in the minds of a few fastidious people.'
   Cyril Connolly 'Logan Pearsall Smith', obituary notice in *New Statesman* 9 Mar. 1946

Stevie Smith (*Florence Margaret Smith*) 1902–1971

17 This Englishwoman is so refined She has no bosom and no behind.
   A Good Time was had by All (1937) 'This Englishwoman'

18 Nobody heard him, the dead man, But still he lay moaning: I was much further out than you thought And not waving but drowning.

   Poor chap, he always loved larking And now he's dead It must have been too cold for him his heart gave way, They said.

   Oh, no no no, it was too cold always (Still the dead one lay moaning) I was much too far out all my life And not waving but drowning.
   Not Waving but Drowning (1957) title poem

19 People who are always praising the past And especially the times of faith as best Ought to go and live in the Middle Ages And be burnt at the stake as witches and sages.
   Not Waving but Drowning (1957) 'The Past'

20 There you are you see, quite simple. If you cannot have your dear husband for a comfort and a delight, for a breadwinner and a crosspatch, for a sofa, chair or a hot-water bottle, one can use him as a Cross to be Borne.
   Novel on Yellow Paper (1936) p. 247

21 Oh I am a cat that likes to Gallop about doing good.
   Scorpion and Other Poems (1972) 'The Galloping Cat'

22 I long for the Person from Porlock

To bring my thoughts to an end,
I am growing impatient to see him
I think of him as a friend.
  Selected Poems (1962) 'Thoughts about the
  "Person from Porlock"'

1 Private Means is dead
God rest his soul, officers and
fellow-rankers said.
  Selected Poems (1962) 'Private Means is
  Dead'

2 Why does my Muse only speak when
  she is unhappy?
She does not, I only listen when I am
unhappy
When I am happy I live and despise
writing
For my Muse this cannot but be
dispiriting.
  Selected Poems (1964) 'My Muse'

John Snagge 1904–

3 His [Snagge's] famous gaffe [in
a commentary on the Boat Race] to the
effect that he couldn't see who was in
the lead but it was either Oxford or
Cambridge he had no recollection of
until he heard a recording afterwards.
  C. Dodd *Oxford and Cambridge Boat Race*
  (1983) ch. 14

C. P. Snow (*Baron Snow of Leicester*) 1905–1980

4 The official world, the corridors of
power, the dilemmas of conscience and
egotism—she disliked them all.
  Homecomings (1956) ch. 22

5 I believe the intellectual life of the whole
of western society is increasingly being
split into two polar groups. . . . Literary
intellectuals at one pole—at the other
scientists, and as the most
representative, the physical scientists.
Between the two a gulf of mutual
incomprehension.
  The Two Cultures and the Scientific Revolution
  (1959 Rede Lecture) p. 3

6 A good many times I have been present
at gatherings of people who, by the
standards of the traditional culture, are
thought highly educated and who have
with considerable gusto been expressing
their incredulity at the illiteracy of
scientists. Once or twice I have been

provoked and have asked the company
how many of them could describe the
Second Law of Thermodynamics. The
response was cold: it was also negative.
  The Two Cultures and the Scientific Revolution
  (1959 Rede Lecture) p. 14

Philip Snowden (*Viscount Snowden*) 1864–1937

7 It would be desirable if every
Government, when it comes to power,
should have its old speeches burnt.
  In C. E. Bechofer Roberts ('Ephesian') *Philip
  Snowden* (1929) ch. 12

8 I hope you have read the election
programme of the Labour Party: It is the
most fantastic and impracticable
programme ever put before the electors.
All the derelict industries are to be taken
over by the State, and the taxpayer is to
shoulder the losses. The banks and
financial houses are to be placed under
national ownership and control, which
means, I suppose, that they are to be
run by a joint committee of the Labour
Party and the Trades Union Council.
Your investments are to be ordered by
some board, and your foreign
investments are to be mobilized to
finance this madcap policy. This is not
Socialism. It is Bolshevism run mad.
  BBC radio election broadcast, 17 Oct. 1931,
  in *The Times* 19 Oct. 1931

Alexander Solzhenitsyn 1918–

9 А между тем ВНУТРЕННИХ ДЕЛ
вообще не осталось на нашей тесной
Земле! И спасение человечества
только в том, чтобы всем было дело
до всего: людям Востока было бы
сплошь небезразлично, что думают
на Западе; людям Запада — сплошь
небезразлично, что совершается на
Востоке.

Meanwhile no such thing as INTERNAL
AFFAIRS remains on our crowded
Earth. Mankind's salvation lies
exclusively in everyone's making
everything his business, in the people of
the East being anything but indifferent
to what is thought in the West, and in
the people of the West being anything

but indifferent to what happens in the East.

Nobel Prize Lecture, 1970, in John W. Dunlop, Richard Haugh and Alexis Klimoff (eds.) *Aleksandr Solzhenitsyn: Critical Essays and Documentary Materials* (1974) p. 574

1 Если десятки лет за десятками лет не разрешать рассказывать то, как оно есть, — непоправимо разблуживаются человеческие мозги, и уже соотечественника понять труднее, чем марсианина.

If decade after decade the truth cannot be told, each person's mind begins to roam irretrievably. One's fellow countrymen become harder to understand than Martians.

Раковый Корпус (Cancer Ward, 1968) pt. 2, ch. 32

2 Вы сильны лишь постольку, поскольку отбираете у людей *не всё*. Но человек, у которого вы отобрали *всё* — уже не подвластен вам, он снова свободен.

You only have power over people as long as you don't take *everything* away from them. But when you've robbed a man of *everything* he's no longer in your power—he's free again.

В Кругу Первом (The First Circle, 1968) ch. 17

3 Yes, we are still the prisoners of communism, and yet, for us in Russia, communism is a dead dog, while for many people in the West it is still a living lion.

Broadcast on BBC Russian Service, in *Listener* 15 Feb. 1979

4 У нас ложь стала не просто нравственной категорией, но и государственным столпом.

In our country the lie has become not just a moral category but a pillar of the State.

1974 interview, printed in appendix to Водался Теленок с дубом (The Oak and the Calf, 1975)

Anastasio Somoza 1925–1980

5 Indeed, you won the elections, but I won the count.

Reply to accusation of ballot-rigging, in *Guardian* 17 June 1977

Stephen Sondheim 1930–

6 Everything's coming up roses.

Title of song (1959; music by Jule Styne)

7 Send in the clowns.

Title of song (1973)

Susan Sontag 1933–

8 Interpretation is the revenge of the intellect upon art.

Evergreen Review Dec. 1964

9 Real art has the capacity to make us nervous. By reducing the work of art to its content, and then interpreting *that*, one tames the work of art. Interpretation makes art manageable, conformable.

Evergreen Review Dec. 1964

10 The camera makes everyone a tourist in other people's reality, and eventually in one's own.

New York Review of Books 18 Apr. 1974

11 A photograph is not only an image (as a painting is an image), an interpretation of the real; it is also a trace, something directly stencilled off the real, like a footprint or a death mask.

New York Review of Books 23 June 1977

12 Illness is the night-side of life, a more onerous citizenship. Everyone who is born holds dual citizenship, in the kingdom of the well and in the kingdom of the sick. Although we all prefer to use only the good passport, sooner or later each of us is obliged, at least for a spell, to identify ourselves as citizens of that other place.

New York Review of Books 26 Jan. 1978

13 The truth is that Mozart, Pascal, Boolean algebra, Shakespeare, parliamentary government, baroque churches, Newton, the emancipation of women, Kant, Marx, Balanchine ballet *et al.*, don't redeem what this particular civilization has wrought upon the world. The white race *is* the cancer of human history, it is the white race, and it alone—its ideologies and inventions—which eradicates autonomous civilizations wherever it spreads, which has upset the ecological balance of the planet, which now threatens the very existence of life itself.

Partisan Review Winter 1967, p. 57

Donald Soper (Baron Soper) 1903–

1 The quality of debate [in the House of Lords] is pretty high—and it is, I think, good evidence of life after death.
   Radio interview, in *Listener* 17 Aug. 1978

Charles Hamilton Sorley 1895–1915

2 When you see millions of the mouthless dead
   Across your dreams in pale battalions go,
   Say not soft things as other men have said,
   That you'll remember. For you need not so.
   Give them not praise. For, deaf, how should they know
   It is not curses heaped on each gashed head?
   Marlborough and Other Poems (1916) 'A Sonnet'

Henry D. Spalding d. 1990

3 I like Ike.
   US button badge first used in 1947 when General Eisenhower was seen as a potential presidential nominee, in *New Republic* 27 Oct. 1947

Muriel Spark 1918–

4 Parents learn a lot from their children about coping with life.
   The Comforters (1957) ch. 6

5 'I am putting old heads on your young shoulders,' Miss Brodie had told them at that time, 'and all my pupils are the crème de la crème.'
   Prime of Miss Jean Brodie (1961) ch. 1

6 Give me a girl at an impressionable age, and she is mine for life.
   Prime of Miss Jean Brodie (1961) ch. 1

7 One's prime is elusive. You little girls, when you grow up, must be on the alert to recognise your prime at whatever time of your life it may occur. You must live it to the full.
   Prime of Miss Jean Brodie (1961) ch. 1

John Sparrow 1906–1992

8 That indefatigable and unsavoury engine of pollution, the dog.
   Letter in *The Times* 30 Sept. 1975

Countess Spencer (Raine Spencer) 1929–

9 Alas, for our towns and cities. Monstrous carbuncles of concrete have erupted in gentle Georgian Squares.
   The Spencers on Spas (1983) p. 14. Cf. Prince Charles 50:2

Sir Stanley Spencer 1891–1959

10 Painting is saying "Ta" to God.
   In letter from Spencer's daughter Shirin, *Observer* 7 Feb. 1988

Stephen Spender 1909–

11 Never being, but always at the edge of Being.
   Poems (1933) no. 10

12 My parents kept me from children who were rough
   And who threw words like stones and who wore torn clothes.
   Poems (1933) no. 12

13 What I had not foreseen
   Was the gradual day
   Weakening the will
   Leaking the brightness away.
   Poems (1933) no. 13

14 Who live under the shadow of a war,
   What can I do that matters?
   Poems (1933) no. 17

15 The names of those who in their lives fought for life
   Who wore at their hearts the fire's centre.
   Born of the sun they travelled a short while towards the sun,
   And left the vivid air signed with their honour.
   Poems (1933) no. 23 'I think continually of those who were truly great'

16 After the first powerful plain manifesto
   The black statement of pistons, without more fuss
   But gliding like a queen, she leaves the station.
   Poems (1933) no. 26 'The Express'

17 Now over these small hills they have built the concrete
   That trails black wire:
   Pylons, those pillars
   Bare like nude, giant girls that have no secret.
   Poems (1933) no. 28 'The Pylons'

1 Consider: only one bullet in ten
   thousand kills a man.
   Ask: was so much expenditure justified
   On the death of one so young and so
   silly
   Stretched under the olive trees, Oh,
   world, Oh, death?
   Stephen Spender and John Lehmann (eds.)
   Poems for Spain (1939) 'Regum Ultimo
   Ratio'

2 ... their collected
   Hearts wound up with love, like little
   watch springs.
   Still Centre (1939) 'The Past Values'

3 People sometimes divide others into
   those you laugh at and those you laugh
   with. The young Auden was someone
   you could laugh-at-with.
   W. H. Auden (address delivered at Auden's
   memorial service at Christ Church
   Cathedral, Oxford, 27 Oct. 1973)

Oswald Spengler 1880–1936

4 *Der Sozialismus ist nichts als der
   Kapitalismus der Unterklasse.*

   Socialism is nothing but the capitalism
   of the lower classes.
   Jahre der Entscheidung (The Hour of Decision,
   1933) pt. 1

Steven Spielberg 1947–

5 Close encounters of the third kind.
   Title of film (1977)

Dr Benjamin Spock 1903–

6 You know more than you think you do.
   Common Sense Book of Baby and Child Care
   (1946) [later *Baby and Child Care*], opening
   words

7 To win in Vietnam, we will have to
   exterminate a nation.
   Dr Spock on Vietnam (1968) ch. 7

William Archibald Spooner
1844–1930

8 Mr Spooner has a habit of transferring
   his syllables, so that it is no unusual
   experience for the members of New
   College to hear their late Dean give out
   in chapel a well-known sentence in the

unintelligible guise of 'Kinkering Kongs
their tykles tate'.
Echo 4 May 1892

9 A famous New College personality ...
   was Warden Spooner. ... 'You have
   tasted your worm,' he is reputed to have
   said to an undergraduate, 'you have
   hissed my mystery lectures, and you
   must leave by the first town drain.' He
   was also responsible for proposing
   a toast to 'our queer old dean'.
   Oxford University What's What (1948) p. 8
   (William Hayter in *Spooner* (1977) ch. 6
   maintains these sayings are apocryphal)

10 Mr Huxley assures me that it's no
   farther from the north coast of
   Spitzbergen to the North Pole than it is
   from Land's End to John of Gaunt.
   Julian Huxley in *SEAC* (Calcutta) 27 Feb.
   1944

11 You will find as you grow older that the
   weight of rages will press harder and
   harder upon the employer.
   In William Hayter *Spooner* (1977) ch. 6

12 Poor soul, very sad; her late husband,
   you know, a very sad death—eaten by
   missionaries—poor soul!
   In William Hayter *Spooner* (1977) ch. 6

Sir Cecil Spring Rice 1859–1918

13 I vow to thee, my country—all earthly
   things above—
   Entire and whole and perfect, the service
   of my love,
   The love that asks no question: the love
   that stands the test,
   That lays upon the altar the dearest and
   the best:
   The love that never falters, the love that
   pays the price,
   The love that makes undaunted the final
   sacrifice.
   Poems (1920) 'I Vow to Thee, My Country'

14 And there's another country, I've heard
   of long ago—
   Most dear to them that love her, most
   great to them that know.
   Poems (1920) 'I Vow to Thee, My Country'

15 And her ways are ways of gentleness
   and all her paths are Peace.
   Poems (1920) 'I Vow to Thee, My Country'

16 I am the Dean of Christ Church, Sir:
   There's my wife; look well at her.

She's the Broad and I'm the High;
We are the University.
The Masque of Balliol in W. G. Hiscock (ed.)
The Balliol Rhymes (1939) p. 29

Bruce Springsteen 1949–

1 We gotta get out while we're young,
'Cause tramps like us, baby, we were
born to run.
Born to Run (1975 song)

Sir J. C. Squire 1884–1958

2 But I'm not so think as you drunk I am.
M. Baring et al. *One Hundred and One
Ballades* (1931 'Ballade of Soporific
Absorption')

3 It did not last: the Devil howling 'Ho!
Let Einstein be!' restored the status quo.
Poems (1926) 'In continuation of Pope on
Newton'. Cf. *Oxford Dictionary of Quotations*
(1979) 378:7

Joseph Stalin (Iosif Vissarionovich Dzhugashvili) 1879–1953

4 Государство есть машина в руках
господствующего класса для
подавления сопротивления своих
классовых противников.

The State is an instrument in the hands
of the ruling class, used to break the
resistance of the adversaries of that
class.
Foundations of Leninism (1924) section 4/6

5 Mr Churchill, Mr Prime Minister, how
many divisions did you say the Pope
had?
At the Potsdam Conference, reported by
Harry S. Truman in speech to American
Association for the Advancement of Science,
in *New York Times* 14 Sept. 1948, p. 24
(reporting Stalin's reaction to Churchill's
statement that the Pope would not like the
Communists to take over the Catholic part of
Poland)

6 Вопрос о *возможности* построения
социализма силами одной страны, на
что должен быть дан положительный
ответ.

First of all there is the question: Can
Socialism *possibly* be established in one
country alone by that country's unaided

strength? The question must be
answered in the affirmative.
Problems of Leninism (1926) ch. 6

Charles E. Stanton 1859–1933

7 *Lafayette, nous voila!*

Lafayette, we are here.
At the tomb of Lafayette in Paris, 4 July
1917, in *New York Tribune* 6 Sept. 1917

Frank L. Stanton 1857–1927

8 Sweetes' li'l' feller,
Everybody knows;
Dunno what to call him,
But he's mighty lak' a rose!
Mighty Lak' a Rose (1901 song; music by
Ethelbert Nevin)

Dame Freya Stark 1893–

9 The great and almost only comfort
about being a woman is that one can
always pretend to be more stupid than
one is and no one is surprised.
The Valleys of the Assassins (1934) ch. 2

Enid Starkie 1897–1970

10 Unhurt people are not much good in the
world.
Letter, 18 June 1943, in Joanna Richardson
Enid Starkie (1973) pt. 6, ch. 18

Christina Stead 1902–1983

11 If all the rich people in the world divided
up their money among themselves there
wouldn't be enough to go round.
House of All Nations (1938) 'Credo'

12 A self-made man is one who believes in
luck and sends his son to Oxford.
House of All Nations (1938) 'Credo'

Sir David Steel 1938–

13 I have the good fortune to be the first
Liberal leader for over half a century
who is able to say to you at the end of
our annual assembly: go back to your
constituencies and prepare for
government.
Speech at Liberal Party Assembly,
Llandudno, 18 Sept. 1981, in *The Times*
19 Sept. 1981

Lincoln Steffens 1866-1936

1 I have seen the future; and it works.
   Letter to Marie Howe, 3 Apr. 1919, in
   Letters (1938) vol. 1, p. 463 (describing
   a visit to the Soviet Union in 1919; cf.
   Steffens's *Autobiography* (1931) ch. 18: 'So
   you've been over into Russia?' said Bernard
   Baruch, and I answered very literally, 'I
   have been over into the future, and it
   works')

Gertrude Stein 1874-1946

2 Hemingway ... brought the manuscript
   he intended sending to America. He
   handed it to Gertrude Stein. He had
   added to his stories a little story of
   meditations and in these he said that
   The Enormous Room was the greatest
   book he had ever read. It was then that
   Gertrude Stein said, Hemingway,
   remarks are not literature.
   Autobiography of Alice B. Toklas (1933) ch. 7

3 Anyone who marries three girls from St
   Louis hasn't learned much.
   Said of Ernest Hemingway in James R.
   Mellow *Charmed Circle: Gertrude Stein and
   Company* (1974) ch. 16

4 Anything scares me, anything scares
   anyone but really after all considering
   how dangerous everything is nothing is
   really very frightening.
   Everybody's Autobiography (1937) ch. 2

5 It takes a lot of time to be a genius, you
   have to sit around so much doing
   nothing, really doing nothing.
   Everybody's Autobiography (1937) ch. 2

6 What was the use of my having come
   from Oakland it was not natural to have
   come from there yes write about it if
   I like or anything if I like but not there,
   there is no there there.
   Everybody's Autobiography (1937) ch. 4

7 Ezra Pound failed to impress her [Stein].
   ... She said he was a village explainer,
   excellent if you were a village, but if you
   were not, not.
   Janet Hobhouse *Everyone who was Anybody*
   (1975) ch. 6

8 You are so afraid of losing your moral
   sense that you are not willing to take it
   through anything more dangerous than
   a mud-puddle.
   Fernhurst, Q.E.D., and Other Early Writings
   (1971) 'Q.E.D.' (1903) bk. 1

9 Pigeons on the grass alas.
   Four Saints in Three Acts (1934) act 3, sc. 2

10 In the United States there is more space
   where nobody is than where anybody is.
   That is what makes America what it is.
   The Geographical History of America (1936)

11 Just before she [Stein] died she asked,
   'What *is* the answer?' No answer came.
   She laughed and said, 'In that case what
   is the question?' Then she died.
   Donald Sutherland *Gertrude Stein,
   A Biography of her Work* (1951) ch. 6

12 Disillusionment in living is the finding
   out nobody agrees with you not those
   that are and were fighting with you.
   Disillusionment in living is the finding
   out nobody agrees with you not those
   that are fighting for you. Complete
   disillusionment is when you realise that
   no one can for they can't change.
   Making of Americans (1934) ch. 5

13 Rose is a rose is a rose is a rose, is a rose.
   Sacred Emily (1913) p. 187

14 You are all a lost generation.
   In Ernest Hemingway *The Sun Also Rises*
   (1926) epigraph (Gertrude Stein heard the
   phrase 'a lost generation' (*une génération
   perdue*) from a French garage-owner: see
   James R. Mellow *Charmed Circle* (1974)
   ch. 10)

John Steinbeck 1902-1968

15 Man, unlike any other thing organic or
   inorganic in the universe, grows beyond
   his work, walks up the stairs of his
   concepts, emerges ahead of his
   accomplishments.
   Grapes of Wrath (1939) ch. 14

16 I know this—a man got to do what he
   got to do.
   Grapes of Wrath (1939) ch. 18

17 Okie use' ta mean you was from
   Oklahoma. Now it means you're a dirty
   son-of-a-bitch. Okie means you're scum.
   Don't mean nothing itself, it's the way
   they say it.
   Grapes of Wrath (1939) ch. 18

Gloria Steinem 1934-

18 Now, we are becoming the men we
   wanted to marry.
   Ms July/Aug. 1982

1 A woman without a man is like a fish
without a bicycle.
  Attributed

James Stephens 1882–1950

2 Women are stronger than men—they do
not die of wisdom.
They are better than men because they
do not seek wisdom.
They are wiser than men because they
know less and understand more.
  The Crock of Gold (1912) bk. 1, ch. 2

3 Finality is death. Perfection is finality.
Nothing is perfect. There are lumps in it.
  The Crock of Gold (1912) bk. 1, ch. 4

4 I hear a sudden cry of pain!
There is a rabbit in a snare:
Now I hear the cry again,
But I cannot tell from where. . . .
Little one! Oh, little one!
I am searching everywhere.
  Songs from the City (1915) 'The Snare'

Andrew B. Sterling 1874–1955

5 Wait till the sun shines, Nellie,
When the clouds go drifting by.
  Wait till the Sun Shines, Nellie (1905 song;
  music by Harry von Tilzer)

Wallace Stevens 1879–1955

6 Poetry is the supreme fiction, madame.
  Harmonium (1923) 'A High-Toned old
  Christian Woman'

7 Call the roller of big cigars,
The muscular one, and bid him whip
In kitchen cups concupiscent curds.
Let the wenches dawdle in such dress
As they are used to wear, and let the
  boys
Bring flowers in last month's
  newspapers.
Let be be finale of seem.
The only emperor is the emperor of
  ice-cream.
  Harmonium (1923) 'The Emperor of
  Ice-Cream'

8 Complacencies of the peignoir, and late
Coffee and oranges in a sunny chair,
And the green freedom of a cockatoo
Upon a rug mingle to dissipate
The holy hush of ancient sacrifice.
  Harmonium (1923) 'Sunday Morning, I'

9 Just as my fingers on these keys
Make music, so the self-same sounds

On my spirit make a music, too.

Music is feeling, then, not sound;
And thus it is that what I feel,
Here in this room, desiring you,

Thinking of your blue-shadowed silk,
Is music.
  Harmonium (1923) 'Peter Quince at the
  Clavier' pt. 1

10 Beauty is momentary in the mind—
The fitful tracing of a portal;
But in the flesh it is immortal.
The body dies; the body's beauty lives.
  Harmonium (1923) 'Peter Quince at the
  Clavier' pt. 4

11 I do not know which to prefer,
The beauty of inflections
Or the beauty of innuendoes,
The blackbird whistling
Or just after.
  Harmonium (1923) ' Thirteen Ways of
  Looking at a Blackbird'

12 The man bent over his guitar,
A shearsman of sorts. The day was
  green.

They said, 'You have a blue guitar,
You do not play things as they are.'

The man replied, 'Things as they are
Are changed upon the blue guitar.'
  The Man with the Blue Guitar (1937) title
  poem

13 They will get it straight one day at the
  Sorbonne.
We shall return at twilight from the
  lecture
Pleased that the irrational is rational.
  Notes Toward a Supreme Fiction (1942) 'It
  must give Pleasure'

14 The poet is the priest of the invisible.
  Opus Posthumous (1957) 'Adagia'

Adlai Stevenson 1900–1965

15 I suppose flattery hurts no one, that is, if
he doesn't inhale.
  TV broadcast, 30 Mar. 1952, in N. F. Busch
  Adlai E. Stevenson (1952) ch. 5

16 I have been thinking that I would make
a proposition to my Republican friends
. . . that if they will stop telling lies
about the Democrats, we will stop telling
the truth about them.
  Speech during 1952 Presidential Campaign,
  in J. B. Martin *Adlai Stevenson and Illinois*
  (1976) ch. 8

1 We must be patient—making peace is harder than making war.

> Speech to Chicago Council on Foreign Relations, 21 Mar. 1946, in *Chicago Daily News* 22 Mar. 1946

2 In America any boy may become President and I suppose it's just one of the risks he takes!

> Speech in Indianapolis, 26 Sept. 1952, in *Major Campaign Speeches of Adlai E. Stevenson; 1952* (1953) p. 174

3 My definition of a free society is a society where it is safe to be unpopular.

> Speech in Detroit, 7 Oct. 1952, in *Major Campaign Speeches of Adlai E. Stevenson; 1952* (1953) p. 218

4 We hear the Secretary of State [John Foster Dulles] boasting of his brinkmanship—the art of bringing us to the edge of the abyss.

> Speech in Hartford, Connecticut, 25 Feb. 1956, in *New York Times* 26 Feb. 1956, p. 64

5 She [Eleanor Roosevelt] would rather light a candle than curse the darkness, and her glow has warmed the world.

> Comment on learning of Mrs Roosevelt's death, in *New York Times* 8 Nov. 1962

6 A funny thing happened to me on the way to the White House.

> Speech in Washington, 13 Dec. 1952 (after his defeat in the Presidential election), in Alden Whitman *Portrait: Adlai E. Stevenson* (1965) ch. 1

7 Let's face it. Let's talk sense to the American people. Let's tell them the truth, that there are no gains without pains, that we are now on the eve of great decisions, not easy decisions, like resistance when you're attacked, but a long, patient, costly struggle which alone can assure triumph over the great enemies of man—war, poverty and tyranny—and the assaults upon human dignity which are the most grievous consequences of each.

> Speech of Acceptance at the Democratic National Convention, Chicago, Illinois, 26 July 1952, in *Speeches of Adlai Stevenson* (1952) p. 20

8 A hungry man is not a free man.

> Speech at Kasson, Minnesota, 6 Sept. 1952, in *Speeches of Adlai Stevenson* (1952) 'Farm Policy'

9 There is no evil in the atom; only in men's souls.

> Speech at Hartford, Connecticut, 18 Sept. 1952, in *Speeches of Adlai Stevenson* (1952) 'The Atomic Future'

10 It reminds me of the small boy who jumbled his biblical quotations and said: 'A lie is an abomination unto the Lord, and a very present help in trouble.'

> In Bill Adler *The Stevenson Wit* (1966) p. 84 (cf. Proverbs 12:22, Psalms 46:1)

Anne Stevenson 1933–

11 Blackbirds are the cellos of the deep farms.

> *Minute by Glass Minute* (1982) 'Green Mountain, Black Mountain'

Caskie Stinnett 1911–

12 A diplomat ... is a person who can tell you to go to hell in such a way that you actually look forward to the trip.

> *Out of the Red* (1960) ch. 4

Rt. Revd Mervyn Stockwood 1913–

13 A psychiatrist is a man who goes to the Folies-Bergère and looks at the audience.

> In *Observer* 15 Oct. 1961

Tom Stoppard 1937–

14 It's not the voting that's democracy, it's the counting.

> *Jumpers* (1972) act 1

15 My problem is that I am not frightfully interested in anything, except myself. And of all forms of fiction autobiography is the most gratuitous.

> *Lord Malquist and Mr Moon* (1966) pt. 2

16 The House of Lords, an illusion to which I have never been able to subscribe—responsibility without power, the prerogative of the eunuch throughout the ages.

> *Lord Malquist and Mr Moon* (1966) pt. 6. Cf. Rudyard Kipling

17 A foreign correspondent is someone who lives in foreign parts and corresponds, usually in the form of essays containing no new facts. Otherwise he's someone who flies around from hotel to hotel and thinks that the most interesting thing

about any story is the fact that he has arrived to cover it.
Night and Day (1978) act 1

1 WAGNER: You don't care much for the media, do you, Ruth?
RUTH: The media. It sounds like a convention of spiritualists.
CARSON: Ruth has mixed feelings about reporters.
Night and Day (1978) act 1

2 MILNE: No matter how imperfect things are, if you've got a free press everything is correctable, and without it everything is concealable.
RUTH: I'm with you on the free press. It's the newspapers I can't stand.
Night and Day (1978) act 1

3 We do on stage things that are supposed to happen off. Which is a kind of integrity, if you look on every exit as being an entrance somewhere else.
Rosencrantz and Guildenstern Are Dead (1967) act 1

4 GUILDENSTERN: Well then—one of the Greeks, perhaps? You're familiar with the tragedies of antiquity, are you? The great homicidal classics? Matri, patri, sorori, uxori and it goes without saying—suicidal—hm? Maidens aspiring to godheads—
ROSENCRANTZ: And vice versa.
Rosencrantz and Guildenstern Are Dead (1967) act 1

5 I can do you blood and love without the rhetoric, and I can do you blood and rhetoric without the love, and I can do you all three concurrent or consecutive, but I can't do you love and rhetoric without the blood. Blood is compulsory—they're all blood, you see.
Rosencrantz and Guildenstern Are Dead (1967) act 1

6 To sum up: your father, whom you love, dies, you are his heir, you come back to find that hardly was the corpse cold before his young brother popped onto his throne and into his sheets, thereby offending both legal and natural practice. Now why exactly are you behaving in this extraordinary manner?
Rosencrantz and Guildenstern Are Dead (1967) act 1

7 We're *actors*—we're the opposite of people! ... Think, in your head, *now*,

think of the most ... *private* ... *secret* ... *intimate* thing you have ever done secure in the knowledge of its privacy. ... Are you thinking of it? ... *Well, I saw you do it!*
Rosencrantz and Guildenstern Are Dead (1967) act 2

8 Eternity's a terrible thought. I mean, where's it all going to end?
Rosencrantz and Guildenstern Are Dead (1967) act 2

9 The bad end unhappily, the good unluckily. That is what tragedy means.
Rosencrantz and Guildenstern Are Dead (1967) act 2. Cf. *Oxford Dictionary of Quotations* (1979) 573:3

10 Life is a gamble at terrible odds—if it was a bet, you wouldn't take it.
Rosencrantz and Guildenstern Are Dead (1967) act 3

11 I doubt that art needed Ruskin any more than a moving train needs one of its passengers to shove it.
Times Literary Supplement 3 June 1977

12 War is capitalism with the gloves off and many who go to war know it but they go to war because they don't want to be a hero.
Travesties (1975) act 1

Lytton Strachey 1880–1932

13 [Samuel] Johnson's aesthetic judgements are almost invariably subtle, or solid, or bold; they have always some good quality to recommend them—except one: they are never right.
Books and Characters (1922) 'Lives of the Poets'

14 The history of the Victorian Age will never be written: we know too much about it. For ignorance is the first requisite of the historian—ignorance, which simplifies and clarifies, which selects and omits, with a placid perfection unattainable by the highest art.
Eminent Victorians (1918) preface

15 The time was out of joint, and he [Hurrell Froude] was only too delighted to have been born to set it right.
Eminent Victorians (1918) 'Cardinal Manning' pt. 2. Cf. *Oxford Dictionary of Quotations* (1979) 431:26

1 Miss Nightingale, however, with all her experience of public life, never stopped to consider the question whether God might not be a Limited Monarchy. Yet her conception of God was certainly not orthodox. She felt towards Him as she might have felt towards a glorified sanitary engineer; and in some of her speculations she seems hardly to distinguish between the Deity and the Drains.

    Eminent Victorians (1918) 'Florence Nightingale' pt. 4

2 His legs, perhaps, were shorter than they should have been.

    Eminent Victorians (1918) 'Dr Arnold'

3 Asked by the chairman [of a military tribunal] the usual question: 'I understand, Mr Strachey, that you have a conscientious objection to war?' he replied (in his curious falsetto voice), 'Oh no, not at all, only to *this* war.' Better than this was his reply to the chairman's other stock question, which had previously never failed to embarrass the claimant. 'Tell me, Mr Strachey, what would you do if you saw a German soldier trying to violate your sister?' With an air of noble virtue: 'I would try to get between them.'

    Robert Graves *Good-bye to All That* (1929) ch. 23

4 Discretion is not the better part of biography.

    In Michael Holroyd *Lytton Strachey* vol. 1 (1967) preface

5 He [Max Beerbohm] has the most remarkable and seductive genius—and I should say about the smallest in the world.

    Letter to Clive Bell, 4 Dec. 1917, in Michael Holroyd *Lytton Strachey* vol. 2 (1968) pt. 1, ch. 5

6 'If this is dying,' he remarked quietly, just before falling into unconsciousness, 'then I don't think much of it.'

    Michael Holroyd *Lytton Strachey* vol. 2, (1968) pt. 2, ch. 6

Igor Stravinsky 1882–1971

7 Music is, by its very nature, essentially powerless to *express* anything at all ... music expresses itself.

    In *Esquire* Dec. 1972

8 My music is best understood by children and animals.

    In *Observer* 8 Oct. 1961

Simeon Strunsky 1879–1948

9 People who want to understand democracy should spend less time in the library with Aristotle and more time on the buses and in the subway.

    No Mean City (1944) ch. 2

10 Famous remarks are very seldom quoted correctly.

    No Mean City (1944) ch. 38

G. A. Studdert Kennedy 1883–1929

11 Waste of Muscle, waste of Brain,
Waste of Patience, waste of Pain,
Waste of Manhood, waste of Health,
Waste of Beauty, waste of Wealth,
Waste of Blood, and waste of Tears,
Waste of youth's most precious years,
Waste of ways the saints have trod,
Waste of Glory, waste of God,
War!

    More Rough Rhymes of a Padre by 'Woodbine Willie' (1919) 'Waste'

12 When Jesus came to Golgotha they hanged Him on a tree,
They drave great nails through hands and feet, and made a Calvary.
They crowned Him with a crown of thorns, red were His wounds and deep,
For those were crude and cruel days, and human flesh was cheap.
When Jesus came to Birmingham they simply passed Him by,
They never hurt a hair of Him, they only let Him die.
For men had grown more tender and they would not give Him pain,
They only just passed down the street, and left Him in the rain.

    Peace Rhymes of a Padre (1921) 'Indifference'

Terry Sullivan

13 She sells sea-shells on the sea-shore,
The shells she sells are sea-shells, I'm sure,

For if she sells sea-shells on the
    sea-shore,
Then I'm sure she sells sea-shore shells.
She Sells Sea-Shells (1908 song; music by
Harry Gifford)

Arthur Hays Sulzberger
1891–1968

1 We [journalists] tell the public which
way the cat is jumping. The public will
take care of the cat.
Time 8 May 1950

Edith Summerskill 1901–1980

2 The housewife is the Cinderella of the
affluent state. . . . She is wholly
dependent on the whim of an individual
to give her money for the essentials of
life. If she complains she is a nagger—for
nagging is the repetition of unpalatable
truths.
Speech to Married Women's Association,
House of Commons, 14 July 1960, in *The
Times* 15 July 1960

Jacqueline Susann (Mrs Irving
Mansfield) 1921–1974

3 Valley of the dolls.
Title of novel (1966)

Hannen Swaffer 1879–1962

4 Perhaps it was about now [*c.*1902] that
he [Swaffer] began to formulate a dictum
which, though not always attributed to
him, has often been quoted (among
others, by witnesses before the first
Royal Commssion on the Press):
'Freedom of the press in Britain means
freedom to print such of the proprietor's
prejudices as the advertisers don't object
to.'
Tom Driberg *Swaff* (1974) ch. 2

Herbert Bayard Swope 1882–1958

5 The First Duty of a newspaper is to be
Accurate. If it is Accurate, it follows that
it is Fair.
Letter to *New York Herald Tribune* 16 Mar.
1958

6 He [Swope] enunciated no rules for
success, but offered a sure formula for
failure: *Just try to please everyone.*
In E. J. Kahn Jr. *World of Swope* (1965) p. 7
See also BERNARD BARUCH

Eric Sykes and Max Bygraves
1922–

7 Eric Sykes had this quick ear and could
tell by any inflection I put into a line
how to make it a catch phrase—at one
time I had more catch phrases than
I could handle. I had the whole country
saying things like 'I've arrived and to
prove it I'm here!' 'A good idea—son'
'Bighead!' 'Dollar lolly'.
Max Bygraves *I Wanna Tell You a Story!*
(1976) p. 96 (describing catch-phrases on
Educating Archie, 1950–3 BBC radio comedy
series)

John Millington Synge 1871–1909

8 'A man who is not afraid of the sea will
soon be drownded,' he said 'for he will
be going out on a day he shouldn't. But
we do be afraid of the sea, and we do
only be drownded now and again.'
Aran Islands (1907) pt. 2

9 'A translation is no translation,' he said,
'unless it will give you the music of
a poem along with the words of it.'
Aran Islands (1907) pt. 3

10 When I was writing 'The Shadow of the
Glen', some years ago, I got more aid
than any learning could have given me
from a chink in the floor of the old
Wicklow house where I was staying,
that let me hear what was being said by
the servant girls in the kitchen.
Playboy of the Western World (1907) preface

11 Oh my grief, I've lost him surely. I've
lost the only Playboy of the Western
World.
Playboy of the Western World (1907) act 3
(last lines)

Thomas Szasz 1920–

12 A child becomes an adult when he
realizes that he has a right not only to
be right but also to be wrong.
The Second Sin (1973) 'Childhood'

13 Masturbation: the primary sexual
activity of mankind. In the nineteenth

century, it was a disease; in the
twentieth, it's a cure.
The Second Sin (1973) 'Sex'

1 Traditionally, sex has been a very
private, secretive activity. Herein
perhaps lies its powerful force for uniting
people in a strong bond. As we make sex
less secretive, we may rob it of its power
to hold men and women together.
The Second Sin (1973) 'Sex'

2 Happiness is an imaginary condition,
formerly often attributed by the living to
the dead, now usually attributed by
adults to children, and by children to
adults.
The Second Sin (1973) 'Emotions'

3 The stupid neither forgive nor forget;
the naïve forgive and forget; the wise
forgive but do not forget.
The Second Sin (1973) 'Personal Conduct'

4 Two wrongs don't make a right, but
they make a good excuse.
The Second Sin (1973) 'Social Relations'

5 If you talk to God, you are praying; if
God talks to you, you have
schizophrenia. If the dead talk to you,
you are a spiritualist; if God talks to you,
you are a schizophrenic.
The Second Sin (1973) 'Schizophrenia'

6 Formerly, when religion was strong and
science weak, men mistook magic for
medicine; now, when science is strong
and religion weak, men mistake
medicine for magic.
The Second Sin (1973) 'Science and
Scientism'

George Szell 1897–1970

7 Conductors must give unmistakable and
suggestive signals to the orchestra—not
choreography to the audience.
Newsweek 28 Jan. 1963

Albert von Szent-Györgyi
1893–1986

8 Discovery consists of seeing what
everybody has seen and thinking what
nobody has thought.
In Irving Good (ed.) *The Scientist Speculates*
(1962) p. 15

Sir Rabindranath Tagore
1861–1941

9 Bigotry tries to keep truth safe in its
hand
With a grip that kills it.
Fireflies (1928) p. 29

Nellie Talbot

10 Jesus wants me for a sunbeam.
Title of hymn (1921), in *CSSM Choruses* No.
1

S. G. Tallentyre (E. Beatrice Hall)
1868–

11 'On the Mind' [*De l'Esprit*] became not
the success of the season, but one of the
most famous books of the century. The
men who had hated it, and had not
particularly loved Helvétius, flocked
round him now. Voltaire forgave him all
injuries, intentional or unintentional.
. . . 'I disapprove of what you say, but
I will defend to the death your right to
say it,' was his attitude now.
The Friends of Voltaire (1906) ch. 7 (often
attributed to Voltaire but not found in his
works)

Booth Tarkington 1869–1946

12 There are two things that will be
believed of any man whatsoever, and
one of them is that he has taken to
drink.
Penrod (1914) ch. 10

A. J. P. Taylor 1906–1990

13 He [Lord Northcliffe] aspired to power
instead of influence, and as a result
forfeited both.
English History, 1914–1945 (1965) ch. 1

14 Communism continued to haunt Europe
as a spectre—a name men gave to their
own fears and blunders. But the crusade
against Communism was even more
imaginary than the spectre of
Communism.
Origins of the Second World War (1962) ch. 2

15 A racing tipster who only reached
Hitler's level of accuracy would not do
well for his clients.
Origins of the Second World War (1962) ch. 7

Bert Leston Taylor 1866–1901

1 A bore is a man who, when you ask him how he is, tells you.
The So-Called Human Race (1922) p. 163

Norman Tebbit 1931–

2 We cannot ignore the price that unemployment today is exacting from the failures of the past. I have known about these things. I grew up in the Thirties with our unemployed father. He did not riot, he got on his bike and looked for work.
Speech at Conservative Party Conference, 15 Oct. 1981, in *Daily Telegraph* 16 Oct. 1981

Archbishop William Temple 1881–1944

3 In place of the conception of the power-state we are led to that of the welfare-state.
Citizen and Churchman (1941) ch. 2

4 It is a mistake to suppose that God is only, or even chiefly, concerned with religion.
In R. V. C. Bodley *In Search of Serenity* (1955) ch. 12

5 Christianity is the most materialistic of all great religions.
Readings in St John's Gospel vol. 1 (1939) introduction

A. S. J. Tessimond 1902–1962

6 Cats, no less liquid than their shadows,
Offer no angles to the wind.
They slip, diminished, neat, through loopholes
Less than themselves.
Cats (1934) p. 20

Margaret Thatcher 1925–

7 We have to get our production and our earnings into balance. There's no easy popularity in what we are proposing, but it is fundamentally sound. Yet I believe people accept there is no real alternative.
Speech at Conservative Women's Conference, 21 May 1980, in *Daily Telegraph* 22 May 1980

8 A triumphant Prime Minister declared 'Rejoice, rejoice' last night. . . . 'Let us congratulate our armed forces and the Marines,' she added.
On recapture of South Georgia, 25 Apr. 1982, *Daily Telegraph* 26 Apr. 1982

9 In church on Sunday morning—it was a lovely morning and we haven't had many lovely days—the sun was coming through a stained glass window and falling on some flowers, falling right across the church. It just occurred to me that this was the day I was meant not to see. Then all of a sudden I thought, 'there are some of my dearest friends who are not seeing this day.'
Television interview, 15 Oct. 1984, after the Brighton bombing, in *Daily Telegraph* 16 Oct. 1984

10 We're going to be rather lucky to be living at a time when you get the turn of the thousand years and we really ought to set Britain's course for the next century as well as this. . . . Yes, I hope to go on and on.
Television interview, 11 May 1987, in *Independent* 12 May 1987

11 I don't mind how much my Ministers talk, as long as they do what I say.
In *Observer* 27 Jan. 1980

12 I am extraordinarily patient, provided I get my own way in the end.
In *Observer* 4 Apr. 1989

13 Ladies and gentlemen, I stand before you tonight in my red chiffon evening gown, my face softly made up, my fair hair gently waved . . . the Iron Lady of the Western World! Me? A cold war warrior? Well, yes—if that is how they wish to interpret my defence of values and freedoms fundamental to our way of life.
Speech at Finchley, 31 Jan. 1976, in *Sunday Times* 1 Feb. 1976

14 I was asked whether I was trying to restore Victorian values. I said straight out I was. And I am.
Speech to British Jewish Community, 21 July 1983, in M. McFadyean & M. Renn *Thatcher's Reign* (1984) p. 114

15 We shall not be diverted from our course. To those waiting with bated breath for that favourite media catch-phrase, the U-turn, I have only

this to say. 'You turn if you want; the lady's not for turning.'

Speech at Conservative Party Conference in Brighton, 10 Oct. 1980, in *The Times* 11 Oct. 1980

1 Let me make one thing absolutely clear. The National Health Service is safe with us.

Speech at Conservative party Conference, 8 Oct. 1982, in *The Times* 9 Oct. 1982

2 The Prime Minister [Mrs Thatcher] said yesterday that she liked Mr Gorbachev— 'we can do business together'— and that she was cautiously optimistic for detente and world peace in the new year.

The Times 18 Dec. 1984

3 We must try to find ways to starve the terrorist and the hijacker of the oxygen of publicity on which they depend.

Speech to American Bar Association in London, 15 July 1985, in *The Times* 16 July 1985

4 No one would remember the Good Samaritan if he'd only had good intentions. He had money as well.

Television interview, 6 Jan. 1986, in *The Times* 12 Jan. 1986

5 Mrs Margaret Thatcher informed the world with regal panache yesterday that her daughter-in-law had given birth to a son. 'We have become a grandmother,' the Prime Minister said.

The Times 4 Mar. 1989

6 There is no such thing as Society. There are individual men and women, and there are families.

Woman's Own 31 Oct. 1987

Sam Theard and Fleecie Moore

7 Let the good times roll.

Title of song (1946)

Diane Thomas

8 Romancing the stone.

Title of film (1984)

Dylan Thomas 1914–1953

9 One Christmas was so much like another, in those years around the sea-town corner now and out of all sound except the distant speaking of the voices I sometimes hear a moment before sleep, that I can never remember whether it snowed for six days and six nights when I was twelve or whether it snowed for twelve days and twelve nights when I was six.

A Child's Christmas in Wales (1954) p. 5

10 Years and years and years ago, when I was a boy, when there were wolves in Wales, and birds the colour of red-flannel petticoats whisked past the harp-shaped hills, when we sang and wallowed all night and day in caves that smelt like Sunday afternoons in damp front farmhouse parlours, and we chased, with the jawbones of deacons, the English and the bears, before the motor car, before the wheel, before the duchess-faced horse, when we rode the daft and happy hills bareback, it snowed and it snowed.

A Child's Christmas in Wales (1954) p. 11

11 Do not go gentle into that good night, Old age should burn and rave at close of day;
Rage, rage against the dying of the light.

Collected poems (1952) 'Do Not Go Gentle into that Good Night'

12 After the first death, there is no other.

Deaths and Entrances (1946) 'A Refusal to Mourn the Death, by Fire, of a Child in London'

13 It was my thirtieth year to heaven Woke to my hearing from harbour and neighbour wood
And the mussel pooled and the heron Priested shore.
The morning beckon.

Deaths and Entrances (1946) 'Poem in October'

14 Pale rain over the dwindling harbour And over the sea wet church the size of a snail
With its horns through mist and the castle
Brown as owls
But all the gardens
Of spring and summer were blooming in the tall vales
Beyond the border and under the lark full cloud.
There could I marvel

My birthday
Away but the weather turned around.
Deaths and Entrances (1946) 'Poem in
October'

1 Now as I was young and easy under the
apple boughs
About the lilting house and happy as the
grass was green.
Deaths and Entrances (1946) 'Fern Hill'

2 Oh as I was young and easy in the
mercy of his means,
Time held me green and dying
Though I sang in my chains like the sea.
Deaths and Entrances (1946) 'Fern Hill'

3 The land of my fathers [Wales]. My
fathers can have it.
In *Adam* Dec. 1953

4 The force that through the green fuse
drives the flower
Drives my green age; that blasts the
roots of trees
Is my destroyer.
And I am dumb to tell the crooked rose
My youth is bent by the same wintry
fever.
18 Poems (1934) 'The Force that through
the Green Fuse drives the Flower'

5 Light breaks where no sun shines;
Where no sea runs, the waters of the
heart
Push in their tides.
18 Poems (1934) 'Light Breaks Where No
Sun Shines'

6 Dylan talked copiously, then stopped.
'Somebody's boring me,' he said, 'I
think it's me.'
Rayner Heppenstall *Four Absentees* (1960)
ch. 16

7 Dylan himself once defined an alcoholic
as a man you don't like who drinks as
much as you do.
Constantine Fitzgibbon *Life of Dylan Thomas*
(1965) ch. 6

8 Portrait of the artist as a young dog.
Title of book (1940); cf. James Joyce's
Portrait of the Artist as a Young Man (1916)

9 Too many of the artists of Wales spend
too much time talking about the position
of the artists of Wales. There is only one
position for an artist anywhere: and
that is, upright.
Quite Early One Morning (1954) pt. 2 'Wales
and the Artist'

10 The hand that signed the paper felled
a city;
Five sovereign fingers taxed the breath,
Doubled the globe of dead and halved
a country;
These five kings did a king to death.
25 Poems (1936) 'The Hand that Signed the
Paper Felled a City'

11 The hand that signed the treaty bred
a fever,
And famine grew, and locusts came;
Great is the hand that holds dominion
over
Man by a scribbled name.
25 Poems (1936) 'The Hand That Signed
the Paper Felled a City'

12 Though they go mad they shall be sane,
Though they sink through the sea they
shall rise again;
Though lovers be lost love shall not;
And death shall have no dominion.
25 Poems (1936) 'And Death Shall Have No
Dominion'. Cf. Romans 6:9

13 To begin at the beginning: It is spring,
moonless night in the small town,
starless and bible-black, the cobblestreets
silent and the hunched
courters'-and-rabbits' wood limping
invisible down to the sloeblack, slow,
black, crowblack, fishingboat-bobbing
sea.
Under Milk Wood (1954) p. 1

14 MR PRITCHARD: I must dust the blinds
and then I must raise them.
MRS OGMORE-PRITCHARD: And before
you let the sun in, mind it wipes its
shoes.
Under Milk Wood (1954) p. 16

15 Alone until she dies, Bessie Bighead,
hired help, born in the workhouse,
smelling of the cowshed, snores bass and
gruff on a couch of straw in a loft in Salt
Lake Farm and picks a posy of daisies in
Sunday Meadow to put on the grave of
Gomer Owen who kissed her once by the
pig-sty when she wasn't looking and
never kissed her again although she was
looking all the time.
Under Milk Wood (1954) p. 19

16 Me, Polly Garter, under the washing
line, giving the breast in the garden to
my bonny new baby. Nothing grows in
our garden, only washing. And babies.
And where's their fathers live, my love?

Over the hills and far away. You're
looking up at me now. I know what
you're thinking, you poor little milky
creature. You're thinking, you're no
better than you should be, Polly, and
that's good enough for me. Oh, isn't life
a terrible thing, thank God?
Under Milk Wood (1954) p. 30

1 MAE ROSE COTTAGE: I'm fast. I'm a bad
lot. God will strike me dead. I'm
seventeen. I'll go to hell.
SECOND VOICE: She tells the goats.
MAE ROSE COTTAGE: You just wait. I'll
sin till I blow up!
SECOND VOICE: She lies deep, waiting
for the worst to happen; the goats
champ and sneer.
Under Milk Wood (1954) p. 78

Edward Thomas 1878–1917

2 Out in the dark over the snow
The fallow fawns invisible go
With the fallow doe;
And the winds blow
Fast as the stars are slow.
Last Poems (1918) 'Out in the Dark'

3 If I should ever by chance grow rich
I'll buy Codham, Cockridden, and
Childerditch,
Roses, Pyrgo, and Lapwater,
And let them all to my elder daughter.
Poems (1917) 'If I Should Ever By Chance'

4 The past is the only dead thing that
smells sweet.
Poems (1917) 'Early One Morning'

5 Yes; I remember Adlestrop—
The name, because one afternoon
Of heat the express-train drew up there
Unwontedly. It was late June.
Poems (1917) 'Adlestrop'

6 As well as any bloom upon a flower
I like the dust on the nettles, never lost
Except to prove the sweetness of
a shower.
Poems (1917) 'Tall Nettles'

7 I have come to the borders of sleep,
The unfathomable deep
Forest where all must lose
Their way, however straight
Or winding, soon or late;
They can not choose.
Poems (1917) 'Lights Out'

Gwyn Thomas 1913–

8 There are still parts of Wales where the
only concession to gaiety is a striped
shroud.
Punch 18 June 1958

Francis Thompson 1859–1907

9 Wake! for the Ruddy Ball has taken
flight
That scatters the slow Wicket of the
Night;
And the swift Batsman of the Dawn has
driven
Against the Star-spiked Rails a fiery
smite.
'Wake! for the Ruddy Ball has Taken Flight'
(parody of Edward Fitzgerald) in J. C. Squire
Apes and Parrots (1929) p. 173

10 The fairest things have fleetest end,
Their scent survives their close:
But the rose's scent is bitterness
To him that loved the rose!
Poems (1913) vol. 1 'Daisy'

11 She went her unremembering way,
She went and left in me
The pang of all the partings gone,
And partings yet to be.

She left me marvelling why my soul
Was sad that she was glad;
At all the sadness in the sweet,
The sweetness in the sad.
Poems (1913) vol. 1 'Daisy'

12 Nothing begins, and nothing ends,
That is not paid with moan;
For we are born in other's pain,
And perish in our own.
Poems (1913) vol. 1 'Daisy'

13 Summer set lip to earth's bosom bare,
And left the flushed print in a poppy
there.
Poems (1913) vol. 1 'The Poppy'

14 The sleep-flower sways in the wheat its
head,
Heavy with dreams, as that with bread:
The goodly grain and the sun-flushed
sleeper
The reaper reaps, and Time the reaper.

I hang 'mid men my needless head,
And my fruit is dreams, as theirs is
bread:
The goodly men and the sun-hazed
sleeper
Time shall reap, but after the reaper

The world shall glean of me, me the
　sleeper.
　Poems (1913) vol. 1 'The Poppy'

1 Look for me in the nurseries of heaven.
　Poems (1913) vol. 1 'To My Godchild
　Francis M.W.M.'

2 I fled Him, down the nights and down
　　the days;
　I fled Him, down the arches of the
　　years;
　I fled Him, down the labyrinthine ways
　Of my own mind; and in the mist of
　　tears
　I hid from Him, and under running
　　laughter.
　Poems (1913) vol. 1 'Hound of Heaven' pt. 1

3 But with unhurrying chase,
　And unperturbèd pace,
　Deliberate speed, majestic instancy,
　They beat—and a Voice beat
　More instant than the Feet—
　All things betray thee, who betrayest
　　Me.
　Poems (1913) vol. 1 'Hound of Heaven' pt. 1

4 For, though I knew His love Who
　　followèd,
　Yet was I sore adread
　Lest, having Him, I must have naught
　　beside.
　Poems (1913) vol. 1 'Hound of Heaven' pt. 2

5 Fear wist not to evade, as Love wist to
　　pursue.
　Poems (1913) vol. 1 'Hound of Heaven' pt. 2

6 I said to Dawn: Be sudden—to Eve:
　Be soon.
　Poems (1913) vol. 1 'Hound of Heaven' pt. 2

7 To all swift things for swiftness did I sue;
　Clung to the whistling mane of every
　　wind.
　Poems (1913) vol. 1 'Hound of Heaven' pt. 2

8 Still with unhurrying chase,
　And unperturbèd pace,
　Deliberate speed, majestic instancy,
　Came on the following Feet,
　And a Voice above their beat—
　'Naught shelters thee, who wilt not
　　shelter Me.'
　Poems (1913) vol. 1 'Hound of Heaven' pt. 2

9 I was heavy with the even,
　When she lit her glimmering tapers
　Round the day's dead sanctities.
　Poems (1913) vol. 1 'Hound of Heaven' pt. 3

10 My harness piece by piece Thou hast
　　hewn from me,
　And smitten me to my knee.
　Poems (1913) vol. 1 'Hound of Heaven' pt. 4

11 Yea, faileth now even dream
　The dreamer, and the lute the lutanist;
　Even the linked fantasies, in whose
　　blossomy twist
　I swung the earth a trinket at my wrist.
　Poems (1913) vol. 1 'Hound of Heaven' pt. 4

12 Ah! must—
　Designer infinite!—
　Ah! must Thou char the wood ere Thou
　　canst limm with it?
　Poems (1913) vol. 1 'Hound of Heaven' pt. 4

13 Such is: what is to be?
　The pulp so bitter, how shall taste the
　　rind?
　Poems (1913) vol. 1 'Hound of Heaven' pt. 4

14 Yet ever and anon a trumpet sounds
　From the hid battlements of Eternity;
　Those shaken mists a space unsettle,
　　then
　Round the half-glimpsèd turrets slowly
　　wash again.
　Poems (1913) vol. 1 'Hound of Heaven' pt. 4

15 Now of that long pursuit
　Comes on at hand the bruit;
　That Voice is round me like a bursting
　　sea:
　'And is thy earth so marred,
　Shattered in shard on shard?
　Lo, all things fly thee, for thou fliest
　　Me!'
　Poems (1913) vol. 1 'Hound of Heaven' pt. 5

16 All which I took from thee I did but take,
　Not for thy harms,
　But just that thou might'st seek it in My
　　arms.
　Poems (1913) vol. 1 'Hound of Heaven' pt. 5

17 Halts by me that footfall:
　Is my gloom, after all,
　Shade of His hand, outstretched
　　caressingly?
　'Ah, fondest, blindest, weakest,
　I am He whom thou seekest!
　Thou dravest love from thee, who
　　dravest Me.'
　Poems (1913) vol. 1 'Hound of Heaven' pt. 5

18 And thou—what needest with thy
　　tribe's black tents
　Who hast the red pavilion of my heart?
　Poems (1913) vol. 1 'Arab Love-Song'

1 It is little I repair to the matches of the
   Southron folk,
Though my own red roses there may
   blow;
It is little I repair to the matches of the
   Southron folk,
Though the red roses crest the caps
   I know.
For the field is full of shades as I near the
   shadowy coast,
And a ghostly batsman plays to the
   bowling of a ghost,
And I look through my tears on
   a soundless-clapping host
As the run-stealers flicker to and fro,
To and fro:—
O my Hornby and my Barlow long ago!
   Poems (1913) vol. 1 'At Lord's'

2 There is no expeditious road
To pack and label men for God,
And save them by the barrel-load.
Some may perchance, with strange
   surprise,
Have blundered into Paradise.
   Poems (1913) vol. 1 'Epilogue to "A
   Judgement in Heaven"'

3 Go, songs, for ended is our brief, sweet
   play;
Go, children of swift joy and tardy
   sorrow:
And some are sung, and that was
   yesterday,
And some unsung, and that may be
   to-morrow.
   Poems (1913) vol. 1 'Envoy'

4 Ah, for a heart less native to high
   Heaven,
A hooded eye, for jesses and restraint,
Or for a will accipitrine to pursue!
   Poems (1913) vol. 2 'Dread of Height'

5 Spring is come home with her
   world-wandering feet,
And all things are made young with
   young desires.
   Poems (1913) vol. 2 'From the Night of
   Forebeing'

6 Let even the slug-abed snail upon the
   thorn
Put forth a conscious horn!
   Poems (1913) vol. 2 'From the Night of
   Forebeing'

7 And, while she feels the heavens lie
   bare,
She only talks about her hair.
   Poems (1913) vol. 2 'The Way of a Maid'

8 Pontifical Death, that doth the crevasse
   bridge
To the steep and trifid God.
   Poems (1913) vol. 2 'An Anthem of Earth'

9 And all man's Babylons strive but to
   impart
The grandeurs of his Babylonian heart.
   Poems (1913) vol. 2 'The Heart' no. 2

10 What heart could have thought you?—
   Past our devisal
   (O filigree petal!)
   Fashioned so purely,
   Fragilely, surely,
   From what Paradisal
   Imagineless metal,
   Too costly for cost?
   Poems (1913) vol. 2 'To a Snowflake'

11 Insculped and embossed,
   With His hammer of wind,
   And His graver of frost.
   Poems (1913) vol. 2 'To a Snowflake'

12 O world invisible, we view thee,
   O world intangible, we touch thee,
   O world unknowable, we know thee,
   Inapprehensible, we clutch thee!
   Poems (1913) vol. 2 'The Kingdom of God'

13 The angels keep their ancient places;—
   Turn but a stone, and start a wing!
   'Tis ye, 'tis your estrangèd faces,
   That miss the many-splendoured thing.

   But (when so sad thou canst not sadder)
   Cry;—and upon thy so sore loss
   Shall shine the traffic of Jacob's ladder
   Pitched betwixt Heaven and Charing
   Cross.

   Yea, in the night, my Soul, my
   daughter,
   Cry,—clinging Heaven by the hems;
   And lo, Christ walking on the water
   Not of Gennesareth, but Thames!
   Poems (1913) vol. 2 'The Kingdom of God'

Hunter S. Thompson 1939–

14 Fear and loathing in Las Vegas.
   Title of two articles in *Rolling Stone* 11 and
   25 Nov. 1971 (under the pseudonym 'Raoul
   Duke')

Lord Thomson (Roy Herbert Thomson, Baron Thomson of Fleet) 1894–1976

1/It is just like having a licence to print your own money.

> On the profitability of commercial television in Britain, in R. Braddon *Roy Thomson* (1965) ch. 32

Jeremy Thorpe 1929–

2 Greater love hath no man than this, that he lay down his friends for his life.

> Comment on Harold Macmillan sacking many of his Cabinet, 13 July 1962 , in D. E. Butler and Anthony King *General Election of 1964* (1965) ch. 1

James Thurber 1894–1961

3 I suppose that the high-water mark of my youth in Columbus, Ohio, was the night the bed fell on my father.

> *My Life and Hard Times* (1933) ch. 1

4 Her own mother lived the latter years of her life in the horrible suspicion that electricity was dripping invisibly all over the house.

> *My Life and Hard Times* (1933) ch. 2

5 All right, have it your own way—you heard a seal bark!

> Cartoon caption in *New Yorker* 30 Jan. 1932

6 That's my first wife up there and this is the *present* Mrs Harris.

> Cartoon caption in *New Yorker* 16 Mar. 1933

7 The war between men and women.

> Title of series of cartoons in *New Yorker* 20 Jan.–28 Apr. 1934

8 It's a naïve domestic Burgundy without any breeding, but I think you'll be amused by its presumption.

> Cartoon caption in *New Yorker* 27 Mar. 1937

9 Well, if I called the wrong number, why did you answer the phone?

> Cartoon caption in *New Yorker* 5 June 1937

10 There is no safety in numbers, or in anything else.

> *New Yorker* 4 Feb. 1939 'The Fairly Intelligent Fly'

11 Early to rise and early to bed makes a male healthy and wealthy and dead.

> *New Yorker* 18 Feb. 1939 'The Shrike and the Chipmunks'

12 It's our *own* story *exactly*! He bold as a hawk, she soft as the dawn.

> Cartoon caption in *New Yorker* 25 Feb. 1939

13 Then, with that faint fleeting smile playing about his lips, he faced the firing squad; erect and motionless, proud and disdainful, Walter Mitty, the undefeated, inscrutable to the last.

> *New Yorker* 18 Mar. 1939 'The Secret Life of Walter Mitty'

14 You might as well fall flat on your face as lean over too far backward.

> *New Yorker* 29 Apr. 1939 'The Bear Who Let It Alone'

15 You can fool too many of the people too much of the time.

> *New Yorker* 29 Apr. 1939 'The Owl who was God'

16 'Humour,' he said, 'is emotional chaos remembered in tranquillity.'

> In *New York Post* 29 Feb. 1960. Cf. *Oxford Dictionary of Quotations* (1979) 583:10

Paul Tillich 1886–1965

17 Neurosis is the way of avoiding non-being by avoiding being.

> *The Courage To Be* (1952) pt. 2, ch. 3

18 He who knows about depth knows about God.

> *The Shaking of the Foundations* (1948) ch. 7

Dion Titheradge

19 And her mother came too!

> Title of song (1921; music by Ivor Novello)

Alvin Toffler 1928–

20 Future shock.

> Title of book (1970)

J. R. R. Tolkien 1892–1973

21 In a hole in the ground there lived a hobbit. Not a nasty, dirty, wet hole, filled with the ends of worms and an oozy smell, nor yet a dry, bare, sandy hole with nothing in it to sit down on or to eat: it was a hobbit-hole, and that means comfort.

> *The Hobbit* (1937) ch. 1

1 One Ring to rule them all, One Ring to
find them
One Ring to bring them all and in the
darkness bind them.
Lord of the Rings, pt. 1 *The Fellowship of the
Ring* (1954) epigraph

Nicholas Tomalin

2 The only qualities for real success in
journalism are ratlike cunning,
a plausible manner and a little literary
ability. . . . The capacity to steal other
people's ideas and phrases—that one
about ratlike cunning was invented by
my colleague Murray Sayle—is also
invaluable.
Sunday Times Magazine 26 Oct. 1969

Barry Took and Marty Feldman

3 Hello, I'm Julian and this is my friend,
Sandy.
Catch-phrase in *Round the Horne* (BBC radio
series, 1965–8)

Sue Townsend

4 The secret diary of Adrian Mole aged
13¾.
Title of book (1982)

Pete Townshend 1945–

5 Hope I die before I get old.
My Generation (1965 song)

Polly Toynbee 1946–

6 Feminism is the most revolutionary idea
there has ever been. Equality for women
demands a change in the human psyche
more profound than anything Marx
dreamed of. It means valuing
parenthood as much as we value
banking.
Guardian 19 Jan. 1987

Sir Herbert Beerbohm Tree
1852–1917

7 To a man who was staggering in the
street under the weight of a grandfather
clock. 'My poor fellow, why not carry
a watch?'
Hesketh Pearson *Beerbohm Tree* (1956)
ch. 12

8 His own note books inform us that
a gramophone company asked him for
a testimonial, and he replied that he
never gave testimonials to objects of
merchandise. The company begged him
to favour their special case, since his
own voice had been reproduced by this
means. So he wrote the following: 'Sirs,
I have tested your machine. It adds
a new terror to life and makes death
a long-felt want.' He was asked to
amend this, as the public might
misconstrue it; but he answered that it
was not open to misconstruction. 'The
immortalism must stand,' said he; but it
was not used as an advertisement by the
company.
Hesketh Pearson *Beerbohm Tree* (1956)
ch. 19

9 He [Israel Zangwill] is an old bore. Even
the grave yawns for him.
In Max Beerbohm *Herbert Beerbohm Tree*
(1920) appendix 4

10 He [Beerbohm Tree] approved cheerfully
enough of everything until he came to
the collection of damsels that had been
dragged into the theatre as ladies in
waiting to the queen. He looked at them
in pained and prolonged dissatisfaction
and then said what we have all wanted
to say of the extra-women in nearly
every throne-room and ball-room and
school-room scene since the theatre
began. 'Ladies,' said Tree, peering at
them plaintively through his monacle,
'just a little more virginity, if you don't
mind.'
Alexander Woollcott *Shouts and Murmurs*
(1923) 'Capsule Criticism'

Herbert Trench 1865–1923

11 Come, let us make love deathless, thou
and I.
Deirdre Lived and Other Poems (1901) 'Come,
let us make love deathless'

G. M. Trevelyan 1876–1962

12 Disinterested intellectual curiosity is the
life-blood of real civilization.
English Social History (1942) introduction

13 It [education] has produced a vast
population able to read but unable to
distinguish what is worth reading, an

easy prey to sensations and cheap
appeals.
English Social History (1942) ch. 18

Tommy Trinder 1909–1989

1 Overpaid, overfed, oversexed, and over
here.
Describing American troops in Britain
during World War II, in *Sunday Times* 4 Jan.
1976

Leon Trotsky (*Lev Davidovich Bronstein*) 1879–1940

2 Old age is the most unexpected of all
things that happen to a man.
Diary in Exile (1959) 8 May 1935

3 Цивилизация сделала крестьянина
своим вьючным ослом. Буржуазия в
конце концов изменила лишь форму
вьюка.

Civilization has made the peasantry its
pack animal. The bourgeoisie in the long
run only changed the form of the pack.
History of the Russian Revolution (1933)
vol. 3, ch. 1

4 Вы — жалкие единицы, вы —
банкроты, ваша роль сыграна,
отправляйтесь туда, где вам отныне
надлежит быть: в сорную корзину
истории!

You [the Mensheviks] are pitiful isolated
individuals; you are bankrupts; your
role is played out. Go where you belong
from now on—into the dustbin of
history!
History of the Russian Revolution (1933)
vol. 3, ch. 10

5 Where force is necessary, it must be
applied boldly, decisively and completely.
But one must know the limitations of
force; one must know when to blend
force with a manœuvre, a blow with an
agreement.
What Next? (1932) ch. 14

Harry S. Truman 1884–1972

6 I never give them [the public] hell. I just
tell the truth, and they think it is hell.
In *Look* 3 Apr. 1956

7 I used to have a saying that applies here,
and I note that some people have picked

it up: 'If you can't stand the heat, get
out of the kitchen.'
Mr Citizen (1960) ch. 15 (see also Harry
Vaughan)

8 A politician is a man who understands
government, and it takes a politician to
run a government. A statesman is
a politician who's been dead 10 or 15
years.
In *New York World Telegram and Sun* 12 Apr.
1958

9 It's a recession when your neighbour
loses his job; it's a depression when you
lose yours.
In *Observer* 13 Apr. 1958

10 All the President is, is a glorified public
relations man who spends his time
flattering, kissing and kicking people to
get them to do what they are supposed
to do anyway.
Letter to his sister, 14 Nov. 1947, in *Off the
Record: the Private Papers of Harry S. Truman*
(1980) p. 119

11 I didn't fire him [General MacArthur]
because he was a dumb son of a bitch,
although he was, but that's not against
the law for generals. If it was, half to
three-quarters of them would be in jail.
In Merle Miller *Plain Speaking* (1974) ch. 24

12 When the decision is up before
you—and on my desk I have a motto
which says 'The buck stops here'—the
decision has to be made.
Speech at National War College, 19 Dec.
1952, in *Public Papers 1952–53* (1966)
p. 1094

13 Wherever you have an efficient
government you have a dictatorship.
Lecture at Columbia University, 28 Apr.
1959, in *Truman Speaks* (1960) p. 51

Barbara W. Tuchman 1912–1989

14 Dead battles, like dead generals, hold the
military mind in their dead grip and
Germans, no less than other peoples,
prepare for the last war.
August 1914 (1962) ch. 2

15 No more distressing moment can ever
face a British government than that
which requires it to come to a hard, fast
and specific decision.
August 1914 (1962) ch. 9

1 For one August in its history Paris was French—and silent.
   August 1914 (1962) ch. 20

Sophie Tucker 1884–1966

2 From birth to 18 a girl needs good parents. From 18 to 35, she needs good looks. From 35 to 55, good personality. From 55 on, she needs good cash. I'm saving my money.
   In Michael Freedland *Sophie* (1978) p. 214

Walter James Redfern Turner 1889–1946

3 When I was but thirteen or so
   I went into a golden land,
   Chimborazo, Cotopaxi
   Took me by the hand.
   The Hunter and Other Poems (1916) 'Romance'

Mark Twain (Samuel Langhorne Clemens) 1835–1910

4 'The Adventures of Tom Sawyer' ... was made by Mr Mark Twain, and he told the truth, mainly. There was things which he stretched, but mainly he told the truth.
   The Adventures of Huckleberry Finn (1884) ch. 1

5 There was some books. ... One was 'Pilgrim's Progress', about a man that left his family it didn't say why. I read considerable in it now and then. The statements was interesting, but tough. Another was 'Friendship's Offering', full of beautiful stuff and poetry; but I didn't read the poetry.
   The Adventures of Huckleberry Finn (1884) ch. 17

6 All kings is mostly rapscallions.
   The Adventures of Huckleberry Finn (1884) ch. 23

7 Hain't we got all the fools in town on our side? and ain't that a big enough majority in any town?
   The Adventures of Huckleberry Finn (1884) ch. 26

8 If there was two birds setting on a fence, he would bet you which one would fly first.
   The Celebrated Jumping Frog (1867) p. 10

9 I don't see no p'ints about that frog that's any better'n any other frog.
   The Celebrated Jumping Frog (1867) p. 16

10 An experienced, industrious, ambitious, and quite often picturesque liar.
   Century Magazine Dec. 1885 'Private History of a Campaign that Failed'

11 Be virtuous and you will be eccentric.
   A Curious Dream (1872) 'Mental Photographs'

12 Soap and education are not as sudden as a massacre, but they are more deadly in the long run.
   A Curious Dream (1872) 'Facts concerning the Recent Resignation'

13 Barring that natural expression of villainy which we all have, the man looked honest enough.
   A Curious Dream (1872) 'A Mysterious Visit'

14 Truth is the most valuable thing we have. Let us economize it.
   Following the Equator (1897) ch. 7

15 It is by the goodness of God that in our country we have those three unspeakably precious things: freedom of speech, freedom of conscience, and the prudence never to practise either of them.
   Following the Equator (1897) ch. 20

16 'Classic.' A book which people praise and don't read.
   Following the Equator (1897) ch. 25. Cf. Twain's speech to the 19th Century Club in New York, 20 Nov. 1900, in *Speeches* (1910) p. 194: 'It's a classic, just as Professor [Caleb] Winchester says, and it meets his definition of a classic—something that everybody wants to have read and nobody wants to read.'

17 Man is the Only Animal that Blushes. Or needs to.
   Following the Equator (1897) ch. 27

18 Let us be thankful for the fools. But for them the rest of us could not succeed.
   Following the Equator (1897) ch. 28

19 There are several good protections against temptations, but the surest is cowardice.
   Following the Equator (1897) ch. 36

20 By trying we can easily learn to endure adversity. Another man's, I mean.
   Following the Equator (1897) ch. 39

21 It takes your enemy and your friend, working together, to hurt you to the

heart: the one to slander you and the other to get the news to you.
Following the Equator (1897) ch. 45

1 I must have a prodigious quantity of mind; it takes me as much as a week, sometimes, to make it up.
The Innocents Abroad (1869) ch. 7

2 They spell it Vinci and pronounce it Vinchy; foreigners always spell better than they pronounce.
The Innocents Abroad (1869) ch. 19

3 I do not want Michael Angelo for breakfast—for luncheon—for dinner—for tea—for supper—for between meals.
The Innocents Abroad (1869) ch. 27

4 Lump the whole thing! say that the Creator made
Italy from designs by Michael Angelo!
The Innocents Abroad (1869) ch. 27

5 That joke was lost on the foreigner—guides cannot master the subtleties of the American joke.
The Innocents Abroad (1869) ch. 27

6 If you've got a nice *fresh* corpse, fetch him out!
The Innocents Abroad (1869) ch. 27

7 The report of my death was an exaggeration.
New York Journal 2 June 1897 (correcting newspaper reports which erroneously said that he was ill or dead, confusing him with his cousin, James Ross Clemens, who had been seriously ill in London)

8 He [Thomas Carlyle] said it in a moment of excitement, when chasing Americans out of his backyard with brickbats. They used to go there and worship. At bottom he was probably fond of them, but he was always able to conceal it.
New York World 10 Dec. 1899, 'Mark Twain's Christmas Book'

9 What a good thing Adam had. When he said a good thing he knew nobody had said it before.
Notebooks (1935) p. 67

10 Familiarity breeds contempt—and children.
Notebooks (1935) p. 237

11 Good breeding consists in concealing how much we think of ourselves and how little we think of the other person.
Notebooks (1935) p. 345

12 Adam was but human—this explains it all. He did not want the apple for the apple's sake; he wanted it only because it was forbidden.
Pudd'nhead Wilson (1894) ch. 2

13 Whoever has lived long enough to find out what life is, knows how deep a debt of gratitude we owe to Adam, the first great benefactor of our race. He brought death into the world.
Pudd'nhead Wilson (1894) ch. 3

14 Training is everything. The peach was once a bitter almond; cauliflower is nothing but cabbage with a college education.
Pudd'nhead Wilson (1894) ch. 5

15 One of the most striking differences between a cat and a lie is that a cat has only nine lives.
Pudd'nhead Wilson (1894) ch. 7

16 When angry, count four; when very angry, swear.
Pudd'nhead Wilson (1894) ch. 10

17 As to the Adjective: when in doubt, strike it out.
Pudd'nhead Wilson (1894) ch. 11

18 Put all your eggs in the one basket, and—WATCH THAT BASKET.
Pudd'nhead Wilson (1894) ch. 15

19 Few things are harder to put up with than the annoyance of a good example.
Pudd'nhead Wilson (1894) ch. 19

20 It were not best that we should all think alike; it is difference of opinion that makes horse-races.
Pudd'nhead Wilson (1894) ch. 19

21 There is a sumptuous variety about the New England weather that compels the stranger's admiration—and regret. The weather is always doing something there; always attending strictly to business; always getting up new designs and trying them on the people to see how they will go. But it gets through more business in spring than in any other season. In the spring I have counted one hundred and thirty-six different kinds of weather inside of four-and-twenty hours.
Speech to New England Society in New York, 22 Dec. 1876, in *Speeches* (1910) p. 59

1 There's plenty of boys that will come
hankering and grovelling around you
when you've got an apple, and beg the
core off of you; but when they've got
one, and you beg for the core and
remind them how you give them a core
one time, they say thank you 'most to
death, but there ain't-a-going to be no
core.
  Tom Sawyer Abroad (1894) ch. 1

2 There ain't no way to find out why
a snorer can't hear himself snore.
  Tom Sawyer Abroad (1894) ch. 10

3 The cross of the Legion of Honour has
been conferred upon me. However, few
escape that distinction.
  A Tramp Abroad (1880) ch. 8

4 All you need in this life is ignorance and
confidence; then success is sure.
  Letter to Mrs Foote, 2 Dec. 1887, in B.
  DeCasseres *When Huck Finn Went Highbrow*
  (1934) p. 7

Kenneth Tynan 1927–1980

5 Forty years ago he [Noel Coward] was
Slightly in *Peter Pan*, and you might say
that he has been wholly in *Peter Pan*
ever since.
  Curtains (1961) pt. 1, p. 59

6 What, when drunk, one sees in other
women, one sees in Garbo sober.
  Curtains (1961) pt. 2, p. 347

7 A critic is a man who knows the way
but can't drive the car.
  In *New York Times Magazine* 9 Jan. 1966,
  p. 27

8 A good drama critic is one who
perceives what is happening in the
theatre of his time. A great drama critic
also perceives what is *not* happening.
  Tynan Right and Left (1967) foreword

Miguel de Unamuno 1864–1937

9 *La vida es duda,*
  y la fe sin la duda es sólo muerte.

  Life is doubt,
  And faith without doubt is nothing but
    death.
  Poesías (1907) 'Salmo II'

10 *Cúrate de la afección de preocuparte cómo*
  apareces a los demás. Cuídate sólo de cómo
  apareces a Dios, cuídate de la idea que de ti
  Dios tenga.

Cure yourself of the condition of
bothering about how you look to other
people. Concern yourself only with how
you appear to God, with the idea that
God has of you.
  Vida de Don Quixote y Sancho (Life of Don
  Quixote and Sancho, 1905) pt. 1

John Updike 1932–

11 One out of three hundred and twelve
Americans is a bore, for instance, and
a healthy male adult bore consumes
each year one and a half times his own
weight in other people's patience.
  Assorted Prose (1965) 'Confessions of a Wild
  Bore'

12 The difficulty with humorists is that they
will mix what they believe with what
they don't; whichever seems likelier to
win an effect.
  Rabbit, Run (1960) p. 160

Sir Peter Ustinov 1921–

13 I was irrevocably betrothed to laughter,
the sound of which has always seemed
to me the most civilized music in the
world.
  Dear Me (1977) ch. 3

14 Contrary to general belief, I do not
believe that friends are necessarily the
people you like best, they are merely the
people who got there first.
  Dear Me (1977) ch. 5

15 Laughter would be bereaved if snobbery
died.
  In *Observer* 13 Mar. 1955

16 If Botticelli were alive today he'd be
working for *Vogue*.
  In *Observer* 21 Oct. 1962

17 As for being a General, well at the age of
four with paper hats and wooden swords
we're all Generals. Only some of us
never grow out of it.
  Romanoff and Juliet (1956) act 1

18 A diplomat these days is nothing but
a head-waiter who's allowed to sit down
occasionally.
  Romanoff and Juliet (1956) act 1

Paul Valéry 1871–1945

19 *Un poème n'est jamais achevé—c'est*
  toujours un accident qui le termine,
  c'est-à-dire qui le donne au public.

A poem is never finished; it's always an accident that puts a stop to it—i.e. gives it to the public.

> Littérature (1930) p. 46

1 *Il faut n'appeler Science: que l'ensemble des recettes qui réussissent toujours.—Tout le reste est littérature.*

'Science' means simply the aggregate of all the recipes that are always successful. All the rest is literature.

> Moralités (1932) p. 41

2 *Dieu créa l'homme, et ne le trouvant pas assez seul, il lui donne une compagne pour lui faire mieux sentir sa solitude.*

God created man and, finding him not sufficiently alone, gave him a companion to make him feel his solitude more keenly.

> Tel Quel 1 (1941) 'Moralités'

3 *La politique est l'art d'empêcher les gens de se mêler de ce qui les regarde.*

Politics is the art of preventing people from taking part in affairs which properly concern them.

> Tel Quel 2 (1943) 'Rhumbs'

Paul Vance *and* Lee Pockriss

4 Itsy bitsy teenie weenie, yellow polkadot bikini.

> Title of song (1960)

Vivian van Damm ?1889–1960

5 I did not coin the slogan 'We Never Closed' [for the Windmill Theatre in London]. It was merely a statement of fact.

> Tonight and Every Night (1952) ch. 18

Laurens van der Post 1906–

6 Human beings are perhaps never more frightening than when they are convinced beyond doubt that they are right.

> Lost World of the Kalahari (1958) ch. 3

Bartolomeo Vanzetti 1888–1927

7 If it had not been for these thing, I might have live out my life talking at street corners to scorning men. I might have die, unmarked, unknown, a failure. Now we are not a failure. This is our career and our triumph. Never in our

full life could we hope to do such work for tolerance, for joostice, for man's onderstanding of man as now we do by accident.

Our words—our lives—our pains—nothing! The taking of our lives—lives of a good shoemaker and a poor fish-peddler—all! That last moment belongs to us—that agony is our triumph.

> Statement after being sentenced, 9 Apr. 1927, in M. D. Frankfurter and G. Jackson *Letters of Sacco and Vanzetti* (1928) preface

8 Sacco's name will live in the hearts of the people and in their gratitude when Katzmann's and yours bones will be dispersed by time, when your name, his name, your laws, institutions, and your false god are but a deem rememoring of a cursed past in which man was wolf to the man.

> Note by Vanzetti of what he wanted to say at his trial, 9 Apr. 1927, in M. D. Frankfurter and G. Jackson *Letters of Sacco and Vanzetti* (1928) p. 380

Harry Vaughan

9 If you can't stand the heat, get out of the kitchen.

> In *Time* 28 Apr. 1952 (often used by Harry S. Truman, q.v.)

Ralph Vaughan Williams 1872–1958

10 I don't know whether I like it [the 4th symphony], but it's what I meant.

> In Christopher Headington *Bodley Head History of Western Music* (1974) p. 293

11 On arrival on a visit to the United States, Ralph Vaughan Williams was met by a crowd of reporters. One of them seized him by the arm and said, 'Tell me, Dr Vaughan Williams, what do you think about music?' The old man peered quizzically into his face and made the solemn pronouncement: 'It's a Rum Go!'

> Leslie Ayr *The Wit of Music* (1966) p. 43

Thorstein Veblen 1857–1929

12 Conspicuous consumption of valuable goods is a means of reputability to the gentleman of leisure.

> Theory of the Leisure Class (1899) ch. 4

1 So it is something of a homiletical
commonplace to say that the outcome of
any serious research can only be to
make two questions grow where one
question grew before.
   University of California Chronicle (1908)
   vol. 10, no. 4, 'Evolution of the Scientific
   Point of View'

Gore Vidal 1925–

2 It is not enough to succeed. Others must
fail.
   In G. Irvine *Antipanegyric for Tom Driberg*
   8 Dec. 1976, p. 2

3 It is the spirit of the age to believe that
any fact, no matter how suspect, is
superior to any imaginative exercise, no
matter how true.
   Encounter Dec. 1967, 'French Letters:
   Theories of the New Novel'

4 A triumph of the embalmer's art.
   In *Observer* 26 Apr. 1981 (describing Ronald
   Reagan)

5 I'm all for bringing back the birch, but
only between consenting adults.
   In *Sunday Times Magazine* 16 Sept. 1973

6 Whenever a friend succeeds, a little
something in me dies.
   In *Sunday Times Magazine* 16 Sept. 1973

7 American writers want to be not good
but great; and so are neither.
   Two Sisters (1970) p. 65

King Vidor 1895–1982

8 Take it from me, marriage isn't a word
... it's a *sentence*!
   The Crowd (1928 film)

José Antonio Viera Gallo 1943–

9 *El socialismo puede llegar solo en bicicleta.*

Socialism can only arrive on a bicycle.
   Said when Assistant Secretary of Justice in
   Chilean Government, in Ivan Illich *Energy
   and Equity* (1974) p. 11

John Wain 1925–

10 Poetry is to prose as dancing is to
walking.
   BBC radio broadcast, 13 Jan. 1976

Jerry Wald 1911–1962 and Richard Macaulay

11 Naughty but nice.
   Title of film (1939)

Prince of Wales
See PRINCE CHARLES

Arthur Waley 1889–1966

12 What is hard today is to censor one's
   own thoughts—
To sit by and see the blind man
On the sightless horse, riding into the
   bottomless abyss.
   Censorship

Edgar Wallace 1875–1932

13 What is a highbrow? He is a man who
has found something more interesting
than women.
   New York Times 24 Jan. 1932, sec. 8, p. 6

14 Dreamin' of thee! Dreamin' of thee!
   Writ in Barracks (1900) 'T. A. in Love'
   (popularised in 1930 broadcast by Cyril
   Fletcher)

George Wallace 1919–

15 Segregation now, segregation tomorrow
and segregation forever!
   Inaugural speech as Governor of Alabama,
   Jan. 1963, in *Birmingham World* 19 Jan.
   1963

Henry Wallace 1888–1965

16 The century on which we are
entering—the century which will come
out of this war—can be and must be the
century of the common man.
   Speech, 8 May 1942, in *Vital Speeches*
   (1942) vol. 8, p. 483

Graham Wallas 1858–1932

17 The little girl had the making of a poet
in her who, being told to be sure of her
meaning before she spoke, said, 'How
can I know what I think till I see what
I say?'
   Art of Thought (1926) ch. 4. Cf. E. M. Forster
   83:9

Sir Hugh Walpole 1884–1941

1 'Tisn't life that matters! 'Tis the courage
you bring to it.
  Fortitude (1913) bk.1, ch. 1

Andy Warhol 1927–1987

2 It's the place where my prediction from
the sixties finally came true: 'In the
future everyone will be famous
for fifteen minutes.' I'm bored with
that line. I never use it anymore. My
new line is, 'In fifteen minutes
everybody will be famous.'
  Andy Warhol's Exposures (1979) 'Studio 54'

3 Being good in business is the most
fascinating kind of art.
  In *Observer* 1 Mar. 1987

4 An artist is someone who produces
things that people don't need to have
but that he—for some reason—thinks it
would be a good idea to give them.
  *Philosophy of Andy Warhol (From A to B and
  Back Again)* (1975) ch. 10

Jack Warner (Horace Waters) 1895–1981

5 Mind my bike!
  Catch-phrase used in the BBC radio series
  Garrison Theatre, 1939 onwards, in D.
  Parker *Radio: the Great Years* (1977) p. 94

Ned Washington

6 Hi diddle dee dee (an actor's life for me).
  Title of song (1940; music by Leigh Harline)

7 When you wish upon a star.
  Title of song (1940; music by Leigh Harline)

Sir William Watson 1858–1935

8 April, April,
Laugh thy girlish laughter;
Then, the moment after,
Weep thy girlish tears!
  Poems (1905) vol. 1, 'Song'

9 These and a thousand tricks and ways
   and traits
I noted as of Demos at their root,
And foreign to the staid, conservative
Came-over-with-the Conqueror type of
   mind.
  Poems (1905) vol. 1, 'A Study in Contrasts'

Evelyn Waugh 1903–1966

10 Brideshead revisited.
  Title of novel (1945)

11 A shriller note could now be heard
rising from Sir Alastair's rooms; any
who have heard that sound will shrink
at the recollection of it; it is the sound of
English county families baying for
broken glass.
  Decline and Fall (1928) 'Prelude'. Cf. Hilaire
  Belloc 25:9

12 I expect you'll be becoming
a schoolmaster, sir. That's what most of
the gentlemen does, sir, that gets sent
down for indecent behaviour.
  Decline and Fall (1928) 'Prelude'

13 'We class schools, you see, into four
grades: Leading School, First-rate
School, Good School, and School.
Frankly,' said Mr Levy, 'School is pretty
bad.'
  Decline and Fall (1928) pt. 1, ch. 1

14 For generations the British bourgeoisie
have spoken of themselves as gentlemen,
and by that they have meant, among
other things, a self-respecting scorn of
irregular perquisites. It is the quality
that distinguishes the gentleman from
both the artist and the aristocrat.
  Decline and Fall (1928) pt. 1, ch. 6

15 'I often think,' he continued, 'that we
can trace almost all the disasters of
English history to the influence of
Wales!'
  Decline and Fall (1928) pt. 1, ch. 8

16 I haven't been to sleep for over a year.
That's why I go to bed early. One needs
more rest if one doesn't sleep.
  Decline and Fall (1928) pt. 2, ch. 3

17 Apparently he has been reading a series
of articles by a popular bishop and has
discovered that there is a species of
person called a 'Modern Churchman'
who draws the full salary of a beneficed
clergyman and need not commit himself
to any religious belief.
  Decline and Fall (1928) pt. 2, ch. 4

18 I came to the conclusion many years
ago that almost all crime is due to the
repressed desire for aesthetic expression.
  Decline and Fall (1928) pt. 3, ch. 1

1 Any one who has been to an English
public school will always feel
comparatively at home in prison. It is
the people brought up in the gay
intimacy of the slums, Paul learned,
who find prison so soul-destroying.
Decline and Fall (1928) pt. 3, ch. 4

2 Punctuality is the virtue of the bored.
Michael Davie (ed.) *Diaries of Evelyn Waugh*
(1976) 'Irregular Notes 1960–65', 26 Mar.
1962

3 Randolph Churchill went into hospital
. . . to have a lung removed. It was
announced that the trouble was not
'malignant'. Seeing Ed Stanley in
White's, on my way to Rome,
I remarked that it was a typical triumph
of modern science to find the only part
of Randolph that was not malignant and
remove it.
Michael Davie (ed.) *Diaries of Evelyn Waugh*
(1976) 'Irregular Notes 1960–65', Mar.
1964

4 You never find an Englishman among
the under-dogs—except in England, of
course.
The Loved One (1948) ch. 1

5 In the dying world I come from
quotation is a national vice. No one
would think of making an after-dinner
speech without the help of poetry. It
used to be the classics, now it's lyric
verse.
The Loved One (1948) ch. 9

6 Manners are especially the need of the
plain. The pretty can get away with
anything.
In *Observer* 15 Apr. 1962

7 'The Beast stands for strong mutually
antagonistic governments everywhere,'
he [Lord Copper] said. 'Self-sufficiency at
home, self-assertion abroad.'
Scoop (1938) bk. 1, ch. 1

8 Mr Salter's side of the conversation was
limited to expressions of assent. When
Lord Copper was right, he said,
'Definitely, Lord Copper'; when he was
wrong, 'Up to a point'.
Scoop (1938) bk. 1, ch. 1

9 'He [Boot]'s supposed to have
a particularly high-class style:
'Feather-footed through the plashy fen
passes the questing vole' . . . would that

be it?' 'Yes,' said the Managing Editor.
'That must be good style.'
Scoop (1938) bk. 1, ch. 1

10 News is what a chap who doesn't care
much about anything wants to read.
And it's only news until he's read it.
After that it's dead.
Scoop (1938) bk. 1, ch. 5

11 'I will not stand for being called
a woman in my own house,' she [Mrs
Earl Russell Jackson] said.
Scoop (1938) bk. 2, ch. 1

12 Other nations use 'force'; we Britons
alone use 'Might'.
Scoop (1938) bk. 2, ch. 5

13 All this fuss about sleeping together. For
physical pleasure I'd sooner go to my
dentist any day.
Vile Bodies (1930) ch. 6

14 Lady Peabury was in the morning room
reading a novel; early training gave
a guilty spice to this recreation, for she
had been brought up to believe that to
read a novel before luncheon was one of
the gravest sins it was possible for
a gentlewoman to commit.
Work Suspended (1942) 'An Englishman's
Home'

15 The trouble with the Conservative Party
is that it has not turned the clock back
a single second.
Attributed

Frederick Weatherly 1848–1929

16 Where are the boys of the old Brigade,
Who fought with us side by side?
The Old Brigade

17 Roses are flowering in Picardy,
But there's never a rose like you.
Roses of Picardy (1916 song)

Beatrice Webb 1858–1943

18 If I ever felt inclined to be timid as I was
going into a room full of people, I would
say to myself, 'You're the cleverest
member of one of the cleverest families
in the cleverest class of the cleverest
nation in the world, why should you be
frightened?'
In Bertrand Russell *Autobiography* (1967)
vol. 1, ch. 4

See also SIDNEY WEBB AND BEATRICE WEBB

Geoffrey Webb and Edward J. Mason

1 An everyday story of country folk.
   Introduction to *The Archers* (BBC radio serial, 1950 onwards)

Jim Webb 1946–

2 Up, up and away.
   Title of song (1967)

Sidney Webb (Baron Passfield) 1859–1947

3 First let me insist on what our opponents habitually ignore, and indeed, what they seem intellectually incapable of understanding, namely the inevitable gradualness of our scheme of change.
   Presidential address at Labour Party Conference in London, 26 June 1923, in *Report* (1923) p. 178

Sidney Webb (Baron Passfield) 1859–1947 and Beatrice Webb 1858–1943

4 Sidney would remark, 'I know just what Beatrice is saying at this moment. She is saying, "as Sidney always says, marriage is the waste-paper basket of the emotions."'
   Bertrand Russell *Autobiography* (1967) vol. 1, ch. 4

Simone Weil 1909–1943

5 What a country calls its vital economic interests are not the things which enable its citizens to live, but the things which enable it to make war. Gasoline is much more likely than wheat to be a cause of international conflict.
   In W. H. Auden *A Certain World* (1971) p. 384

6 *La culture est un instrument manié par des professeurs pour fabriquer des professeurs qui à leur tour fabriqueront des professeurs.*

   Culture is an instrument wielded by professors, to manufacture professors, who when their turn comes will manufacture professors.
   L'Enracinement (The Need for Roots, 1949) 'Déracinement ouvrier'

7 *Tous les Péchés sont des tentatives pour combler des vides.*

   All sins are attempts to fill voids.
   La Pesanteur et la grâce (Gravity and Grace, 1948) p. 27

Johnny Weissmuller 1904–1984

8 I didn't have to act in 'Tarzan, the Ape Man'—just said, 'Me Tarzan, you Jane.'
   Photoplay Magazine June 1932 (the words 'Me Tarzan, you Jane' do not occur in the 1932 film)

Thomas Earle Welby 1881–1933

9 'Turbot, Sir,' said the waiter, placing before me two fishbones, two eyeballs, and a bit of black mackintosh.
   The Dinner Knell (1932) 'Birmingham or Crewe?'

Fay Weldon 1931–

10 Natalie had left the wives and joined the women.
   Heart of the Country (1987) p. 51

11 The life and loves of a she-devil.
   Title of novel (1984)

Colin Welland 1934–

12 The British are coming.
   Speech accepting an Oscar for his *Chariots of Fire* screenplay, 30 Mar. 1982, in *Sight & Sound* Summer 1982

Orson Welles 1915–1985

13 To his associate, Richard Wilson ... Orson [Welles] then declared, 'This [the RKO studio] is the biggest electric train set any boy ever had!'
   Peter Noble *The Fabulous Orson Welles* (1956) ch. 7

14 In Italy for thirty years under the Borgias they had warfare, terror, murder, bloodshed—they produced Michelangelo, Leonardo da Vinci and the Renaissance. In Switzerland they had brotherly love, five hundred years of

democracy and peace and what did that produce . . . ? The cuckoo clock.
The Third Man (1949 film; words added by Welles to the script, in Graham Greene and Carol Reed *The Third Man* (1969) p. 114

H. G. Wells 1866–1946

1 If Max [Beaverbrook] gets to Heaven he won't last long. He will be chucked out for trying to pull off a merger between Heaven and Hell . . . after having secured a controlling interest in key subsidiary companies in both places, of course.
In A. J. P. Taylor *Beaverbrook* (1972) ch. 8

2 The thing his [Henry James's] novel is *about* is always there. It is like a church lit but without a congregation to distract you, with every light and line focussed on the high altar. And on the altar, very reverently placed, intensely there, is a dead kitten, an egg-shell, a bit of string.
Boon (1915) ch. 4

3 It is leviathan retrieving pebbles. It is a magnificent but painful hippopotamus resolved at any cost, even at the cost of its dignity, upon picking up a pea which has got into a corner of its den. Most things, it insists, are beyond it, but it can, at any rate modestly, and with an artistic singleness of mind, pick up that pea.
Boon (1915) ch. 4 (on Henry James)

4 He [James Holroyd] was a practical electrician but fond of whisky, a heavy, red-haired brute with irregular teeth. He doubted the existence of the Deity but accepted Carnot's cycle, and he had read Shakespeare and found him weak in chemistry.
Complete Short Stories (1927) 'Lord of the Dynamos'

5 But Nunez advanced with the confident steps of a youth who enters upon life. All the old stories of the lost valley and the Country of the Blind had come back to his mind, and through his thoughts ran this old proverb, as if it were a refrain—
In the Country of the Blind the One-Eyed Man is King.
The Country of the Blind (1904; revised 1939) p. 52

6 'Sesquippledan,' he would say. 'Sesquippledan verboojuice.'
History of Mr Polly (1909) ch. 1, pt. 5

7 'I'm a Norfan, both sides,' he would explain, with the air of one who had seen trouble.
Kipps (1905) bk. 1, ch. 6, pt. 1

8 'I expect,' he said, 'I was thinking jest what a Rum Go everything is. I expect it was something like that.'
Kipps (1905) bk. 3, ch. 3, pt. 8

9 The Social Contract is nothing more or less than a vast conspiracy of human beings to lie to and humbug themselves and one another for the general Good. Lies are the mortar that bind the savage individual man into the social masonry.
Love and Mr Lewisham (1900) ch. 23

10 Human history becomes more and more a race between education and catastrophe.
Outline of History (1920) vol. 2, ch. 41, pt. 4

11 The shape of things to come.
Title of book (1933)

12 The war that will end war.
Title of book (1914). Cf. David Lloyd-George 138:8

13 Moral indignation is jealousy with a halo.
The Wife of Sir Isaac Harman (1914) ch. 9, sect. 2

14 In England we have come to rely upon a comfortable time-lag of fifty years or a century intervening between the perception that something ought to be done and a serious attempt to do it.
The Work, Wealth and Happiness of Mankind (1931) ch. 2

Arnold Wesker 1932–

15 And then I saw the menu, stained with tea and beautifully written by a foreign hand, and on top it said—God I hated that old man—it said 'Chips with everything'. Chips with every damn thing. You breed babies and you eat chips with everything.
Chips with Everything (1962) act 1, sc. 2

Mae West 1892–1980

16 It's better to be looked over than overlooked.
Belle of the Nineties (1934 film)

1 A man in the house is worth two in the
street.
Belle of the Nineties (1934 film)

2 You ought to get out of those wet
clothes and into a dry Martini.
Every Day's a Holiday (1937 film). A similar
line is spoken by Robert Benchley in the
1942 film *The Major and the Minor*, written
by Charles Brackett and Billy Wilder. Cf.
7:12

3 I always say, keep a diary and some day
it'll keep you.
Every Day's a Holiday (1937 film)

4 Beulah, peel me a grape.
I'm No Angel (1933 film)

5 I've been things and seen places.
I'm No Angel (1933 film)

6 When I'm good, I'm very, very good,
but when I'm bad, I'm better.
I'm No Angel (1933 film)

7 It's not the men in my life that counts—
it's the life in my men.
I'm No Angel (1933 film)

8 Give a man a free hand and he'll try to
put it all over you.
Klondike Annie (1936 film)

9 Between two evils, I always pick the one
I never tried before.
Klondike Annie (1936 film)

10 I've been in *Who's Who*, and I know
what's what, but it'll be the first time
I ever made the dictionary.
Letter to the RAF, early 1940s, on having
an inflatable life jacket named after her, in
Fergus Cashin *Mae West* (1981) ch. 9

11 'Goodness, what beautiful diamonds!'
'Goodness had nothing to do with it,
dearie.'
Night After Night (1932 film)

12 Is that a gun in your pocket, or are you
just glad to see me?
In Joseph Weintraub *Peel Me a Grape* (1975)
p. 47

13 I used to be Snow White . . . but
I drifted.
In Joseph Weintraub *Peel Me a Grape* (1975)
p. 47

14 Why don't you come up sometime, and
see me? I'm home every evening.
She Done Him Wrong (1933 film; often
misquoted as 'Come up and see me
sometime', which became Mae West's
catch-phrase)

Dame Rebecca West (Cicily Isabel Fairfield) 1892–1983

15 Journalism—an ability to meet the
challenge of filling the space.
New York Herald Tribune 22 Apr. 1956, sec.
6, p. 2

16 He [Michael Arlen] is every other inch
a gentleman.
In Victoria Glendinning *Rebecca West* (1987)
pt. 3, ch. 5

17 God forbid that any book should be
banned. The practice is as indefensible
as infanticide.
The Strange Necessity (1928) 'The Tosh
Horse'

18 Just how difficult it is to write biography
can be reckoned by anybody who sits
down and considers just how many
people know the truth about his or her
love affairs.
Vogue 1 Nov. 1952

Edith Wharton 1862–1937

19 She sang, of course, 'M'ama!' and not
'he loves me'; since an unalterable and
unquestioned law of the musical world
required that the German text of French
operas sung by Swedish artists should be
translated into Italian for the clearer
understanding of English-speaking
audiences.
Age of Innocence (1920) bk. 1, ch. 1

20 She keeps on being Queenly in her own
room with the door shut.
The House of Mirth (1905) bk. 2, ch. 1

21 Another unsettling element in modern
art is that common symptom of
immaturity, the dread of doing what has
been done before.
The Writing of Fiction (1925) ch. 1

22 Mrs Ballinger is one of the ladies who
pursue Culture in bands, as though it
were dangerous to meet it alone.
Xingu and Other Stories (1916) 'Xingu'

E. B. White 1899–1985

23 MOTHER: It's broccoli, dear.
CHILD: I say it's spinach, and I say the
hell with it.
New Yorker 8 Dec. 1928 (cartoon caption)

1 Democracy is the recurrent suspicion
that more than half of the people are
right more than half of the time.
New Yorker 3 July 1944

2 Commuter—one who spends his life
In riding to and from his wife;
A man who shaves and takes a train,
And then rides back to shave again.
Poems and Sketches (1982) 'The Commuter'

T. H. White 1906–1964

3 The Victorians had not been anxious to
go away for the weekend. The
Edwardians, on the contrary, were
nomadic.
Farewell Victoria (1933) pt. 4

4 The once and future king.
Title of novel (1958)

Alfred North Whitehead
1861–1947

5 Life is an offensive, directed against the
repetitious mechanism of the Universe.
Adventures of Ideas (1933) pt. 1, ch. 5

6 It is more important that a proposition
be interesting than that it be true. This
statement is almost a tautology. For the
energy of operation of a proposition in
an occasion of experience is its interest,
and is its importance. But of course
a true proposition is more apt to be
interesting than a false one.
Adventures of Ideas (1933) pt. 4, ch. 16

7 There are no whole truths; all truths are
half-truths. It is trying to treat them as
whole truths that plays the devil.
Dialogues (1954) prologue

8 Intelligence is quickness to apprehend as
distinct from ability, which is capacity to
act wisely on the thing apprehended.
Dialogues (1954) 15 Dec. 1939

9 What is morality in any given time or
place? It is what the majority then and
there happen to like, and immorality is
what they dislike.
Dialogues (1954) 30 Aug. 1941

10 Art is the imposing of a pattern on
experience, and our aesthetic enjoyment
is recognition of the pattern.
Dialogues (1954) 10 June 1943

11 Civilization advances by extending the
number of important operations which
we can perform without thinking about
them.
Introduction to Mathematics (1911) ch. 5

12 The safest general characterization of
the European philosophical tradition is
that it consists of a series of footnotes to
Plato.
Process and Reality (1929) pt. 2, ch. 1

Bertrand Whitehead

13 Drinka Pinta Milka Day.
Slogan for the British Milk Marketing Board,
1958

Katharine Whitehorn 1926–

14 No nice men are good at getting taxis.
Observer 1977

15 Hats divide generally into three classes:
offensive hats, defensive hats, and
shrapnel.
Shouts and Murmurs (1963) 'Hats'

16 I wouldn't say when you've seen one
Western you've seen the lot; but when
you've seen the lot you get the feeling
you've seen one.
Sunday Best (1976) 'Decoding the West'

George Whiting

17 My blue heaven.
Title of song (1927; music by Walter
Donaldson)

18 When you're all dressed up and have no
place to go.
Title of song (1912; music by Newton
Harding)

Gough Whitlam 1916–

19 Well may he say 'God Save the Queen'.
But after this nothing will save the
Governor-General. . . . Maintain your
rage and your enthusiasm through the
campaign for the election now to be held
and until polling day.
Speech in Canberra, 11 Nov. 1975, in *The
Times* 12 Nov. 1975

Charlotte Whitton 1896–1975

20 Whatever women do they must do twice
as well as men to be thought half as
good. Luckily, this is not difficult.
In *Canada Month* June 1963

William H. Whyte 1917–

1 This book is about the organization man. . . . I can think of no other way to describe the people I am talking about. They are not the workers, nor are they the white-collar people in the usual, clerk sense of the word. These people only work for the Organization. The ones I am talking about *belong* to it as well.
The Organization Man (1956) ch. 1

Anna Wickham (Edith Alice Mary Harper) 1884–1947

2 It is well within the order of things
That man should listen when his mate sings;
But the true male never yet walked
Who liked to listen when his mate talked.
The Contemplative Quarry (1915) 'The Affinity'

Richard Wilbur 1921–

3 We milk the cow of the world, and as we do
We whisper in her ear, 'You are not true.'
Ceremony and Other Poems (1950) 'Epistemology'

Billy Wilder (Samuel Wilder) 1906–

4 Hindsight is always twenty-twenty.
In J. R. Columbo *Wit and Wisdom of the Moviemakers* (1979) ch. 7

Billy Wilder 1906–
and I. A. L. Diamond

5 GERRY: We can't get married at all. . . . I'm a man.
OSGOOD: Well, nobody's perfect.
Some Like It Hot (1959 film; closing words)

Thornton Wilder 1897–1975

6 Marriage is a bribe to make
a housekeeper think she's a householder.
Merchant of Yonkers (1939) act 1

7 The fights are the best part of married life. The rest is merely so-so.
Merchant of Yonkers (1939) act 2

8 Literature is the orchestration of platitudes.
In *Time* 12 Jan. 1953

Kaiser Wilhelm II 1859–1941

9 We have . . . fought for our place in the sun and have won it. It will be my business to see that we retain this place in the sun unchallenged, so that the rays of that sun may exert a fructifying influence upon our foreign trade and traffic.
Speech in Hamburg, 18 June 1901, in *The Times* 20 June 1901

Geoffrey Willans 1911–1958 and Ronald Searle 1920–

10 The only good things about skool are the BOYS wizz who are noble brave fearless etc. although you hav various swots, bulies, cissies, milksops, greedy guts and oiks with whom i am forced to mingle hem-hem.
Down With Skool! (1953) p. 7

11 This is wot it is like when we go back on the skool trane. There are lots of new bugs and all there maters blub they hav every reason if they knew what they were going to. For us old lags however it is just another stretch same as any other and no remision for good conduc. We kno what it will be like at the other end Headmaster beaming skool bus ratle off leaving trail of tuck boxes peason smugling in a box of flat 50 cigs fotherington-tomas left in the lugage rack and new bugs stand as if amazed.
How To Be Topp (1954) ch. 1

12 There is no better xsample of a goody-goody than fotherington-tomas in the world in space. You kno he is the one who sa Hullo Clouds Hullo Sky and skip about like a girly.
How To Be Topp (1954) ch. 4

13 Still xmas is a good time with all those presents and good food and i hope it will never die out or at any rate not until i am grown up and hav to pay for it all.
How To Be Topp (1954) ch. 11

Harry Williams 1874–1924

14 I'm afraid to come home in the dark.
Title of song (1907; music by Egbert van Alstyne)

Kenneth Williams 1926–1988

1 The nice thing about quotes is that they give us a nodding acquaintance with the originator which is often socially impressive.
Acid Drops (1980) preface

Tennessee Williams (Thomas Lanier Williams) 1911–1983

2 We have to distrust each other. It's our only defence against betrayal.
Camino Real (1953) block 10

3 We're all of us guinea pigs in the laboratory of God. Humanity is just a work in progress.
Camino Real (1953) block 12

4 What is the victory of a cat on a hot tin roof?—I wish I knew. . . . Just staying on it, I guess, as long as she can.
Cat on a Hot Tin Roof (1955) act 1

5 BRICK: Well, they say nature hates a vacuum, Big Daddy.
BIG DADDY: That's what they say, but sometimes I think that a vacuum is a hell of a lot better than some of the stuff that nature replaces it with.
Cat on a Hot Tin Roof (1955) act 2. Cf. *Oxford Dictionary of Quotations* (1979) 403:27

6 Mendacity is a system that we live in. Liquor is one way out an' death's the other.
Cat on a Hot Tin Roof (1955) act 2

7 I didn't go to the moon, I went much further—for time is the longest distance between two places.
The Glass Menagerie (1945) p. 123

8 We're all of us sentenced to solitary confinement inside our own skins, for life!
Orpheus Descending (1958) act 2, sc. 1

9 Turn that off! I won't be looked at in this merciless glare!
A Streetcar Named Desire (1947) sc. 1

10 I have always depended on the kindness of strangers.
A Streetcar Named Desire (1947) sc. 11 (Blanche's final words)

William Carlos Williams 1883–1963

11 I will teach you my townspeople

how to perform a funeral
for you have it over a troop
of artists—
unless one should scour the world—
you have the ground sense necessary.
Book of Poems Al Que Quiere! (1917) 'Tract'

12 Minds like beds always made up,
(more stony than a shore)
unwilling or unable.
Paterson (1946) bk. 1, preface

13 so much depends
upon

a red wheel
barrow

glazed with rain
water

beside the white
chickens.
Spring and All (1923) 'The Red Wheelbarrow'

14 Is it any better in Heaven, my friend Ford,
Than you found it in Provence?
The Wedge (1944) 'To Ford Madox Ford in Heaven'

Ted Willis (Edward Henry Willis, Baron Willis of Chislehurst) 1918–

15 Evening, all.
Opening words spoken by Jack Warner as Sergeant Dixon in *Dixon of Dock Green* (BBC television series, 1956–76)

Wendell Willkie 1892–1944

16 The constitution does not provide for first and second class citizens.
An American Programme (1944) ch. 2

17 Freedom is an indivisible word. If we want to enjoy it, and fight for it, we must be prepared to extend it to everyone, whether they are rich or poor, whether they agree with us or not, no matter what their race or the colour of their skin.
One World (1943) ch. 13

Sir Angus Wilson 1913–1991

18 'God knows how you Protestants can be expected to have any sense of direction,' she said. 'It's different with us, I haven't been to mass for years, I've got every mortal sin on my conscience, but I know when I'm doing wrong. I'm still

a Catholic, it's there, nothing can take it away from me.' 'Of course, duckie,' said Jeremy . . . 'once a Catholic always a Catholic.'

The Wrong Set (1949) p. 168. Cf. Mary O'Malley

Charles E. Wilson 1890–1961

1 For years I thought what was good for our country was good for General Motors and vice versa. The difference did not exist. Our company is too big. It goes with the welfare of the country. Our contribution to the nation is quite considerable.

Testimony to the Senate Armed Services Committee on his proposed nomination to be Secretary of Defence, 15 Jan. 1953, in *New York Times* 24 Feb. 1953, p. 8

Edmund Wilson 1895–1972

2 Of all the great Victorian writers, he [Dickens] was probably the most antagonistic to the Victorian age itself.
The Wound and the Bow (1941) 'Dickens: the Two Scrooges'

Harold Wilson (*Baron Wilson of Rievaulx*) 1916–

3 Traders and financiers all over the world had been listening to the Chancellor. For months he had said that if he could not stop the wage claims, the country was 'facing disaster'. . . . Rightly or wrongly these people believed him. For them, 5th September—the day that the Trades Union Congress unanimously rejected the policy of wage restraint—marked the end of an era. And all these financiers, all the little gnomes in Zurich and the other financial centres about whom we keep on hearing, started to make their dispositions in regard to sterling.
Hansard 12 Nov. 1956, col. 578

4 The Smethwick Conservatives can have the satisfaction of having topped the poll, and of having sent here as their Member one who, until a further General Election restores him to oblivion, will serve his term here as a Parliamentary leper.
Hansard 3 Nov. 1964, col. 71

5 My hon. Friends know that if one buys land on which there is a slag heap 120

ft. high and it costs £100,000 to remove that slag, that is not land speculation in the sense that we condemn it. It is land reclamation.
Hansard 4 Apr. 1974, col. 1441

6 If I had the choice between smoked salmon and tinned salmon, I'd have it tinned. With vinegar.
In *Observer* 11 Nov. 1962

7 The Monarchy is a labour-intensive industry.
In *Observer* 13 Feb. 1977

8 Harold Wilson . . . was unable to remember when he first uttered his dictum to the effect that: A week is a long time in politics. . . . Inquiries among political journalists led to the conclusion that in its present form the phrase was probably first uttered at a meeting between Wilson and the Parliamentary lobby in the wake of the Sterling crisis shortly after he first took office as Prime Minister in 1964. However, Robert Carvel . . . recalled Wilson at a Labour Party conference in 1960 saying 'Forty-eight hours is a long time in politics.'
Nigel Rees *Sayings of the Century* (1984) p. 149

9 This Party [the Labour Party] is a moral crusade or it is nothing.
Speech at Labour Party Conference, 1 Oct. 1962, in *The Times* 2 Oct. 1962

10 The Prime Ministers [at the Lagos Conference, 9–12 Jan. 1966] noted the statement by the British Prime Minister that on the expert advice available to him the cumulative effects of the economic and financial sanctions might well bring the rebellion to an end within a matter of weeks rather than months.
The Times 13 Jan. 1966

11 From now the pound abroad is worth 14 per cent or so less in terms of other currencies. It does not mean, of course, that the pound here in Britain, in your pocket or purse or in your bank, has been devalued.
Ministerial broadcast, 19 Nov. 1967, in *The Times* 20 Nov. 1967

12 Everyone wanted more wage increases, he [Mr Wilson] said, believing that prices would remain stable; but one

man's wage increase was another
man's price increase.
> Speech at Blackburn, 8 Jan. 1970, in *The
> Times* 9 Jan. 1970

McLandburgh Wilson 1892–

1 'Twixt the optimist and pessimist
The difference is droll:
The optimist sees the doughnut
But the pessimist sees the hole.
> *Optimist and Pessimist*

Sandy Wilson 1924–

2 It's never too late to have a fling,
For Autumn is just as nice as Spring,
And it's never too late to fall in love.
> *It's Never too Late to Fall in Love* (1953 song)

Woodrow Wilson 1856–1924

3 It must be a peace without victory. . . .
Only a peace between equals can last.
Only a peace the very principle of which
is equality and a common participation
in a common benefit.
> Speech to US Senate, 22 Jan. 1917, in
> *Messages and Papers* (1924) vol. 1, p. 352

4 Sometimes people call me an idealist.
Well, that is the way I know I am an
American. America, my fellow
citizens—I do not say it in
disaparagement of any other great
people—America is the only idealistic
Nation in the world.
> Speech at Sioux Falls, South Dakota, 8 Sept.
> 1919, in *Messages and Papers* (1924) vol. 2,
> p. 822

5 Once lead this people into war and they
will forget there ever was such a thing
as tolerance.
> In John Dos Passos *Mr Wilson's War* (1917)
> pt. 3, ch. 12

6 We have stood apart, studiously neutral.
> Speech to Congress, 7 Dec. 1915, in *New
> York Times* 8 Dec. 1915, p. 4

7 America can not be an ostrich with its
head in the sand.
> Speech at Des Moines, 1 Feb. 1916, in *New
> York Times* 2 Feb. 1916, p. 1

8 A little group of wilful men representing
no opinion but their own, have rendered

the Great Government of the United
States helpless and contemptible.
> Statement, 4 Mar. 1917, after a successful
> filibuster against Wilson's bill to arm
> American merchant ships, in *New York
> Times* 5 Mar. 1917, p. 1

9 Liberty has never come from the
government. Liberty has always come
from the subjects of government. The
history of liberty is the history of
resistance. The history of liberty is
a history of the limitation of
governmental power, not the increase of
it.
> Speech to New York Press Club in New
> York, 9 Sept. 1912, in *Papers of Woodrow
> Wilson* (1978) vol. 25, p. 124

10 No nation is fit to sit in judgement upon
any other nation.
> Speech in New York, 20 Apr. 1915, in
> *Selected Addresses* (1918) p. 79

11 There is such a thing as a man being too
proud to fight; there is such a thing as
a nation being so right that it does
not need to convince others by force
that it is right.
> Speech in Philadelphia, 10 May 1915, in
> *Selected Addresses* (1918) p. 88

12 Armed neutrality is ineffectual enough
at best.
> Speech to Congress, 2 Apr. 1917, in *Selected
> Addresses* (1918) p. 190

13 The world must be made safe for
democracy. Its peace must be planted
upon the tested foundations of political
liberty.
> Speech to Congress, 2 Apr. 1917, in *Selected
> Addresses* (1918) p. 195

14 The right is more precious than peace.
> Speech to Congress, 2 Apr. 1917, in *Selected
> Addresses* (1918) p. 197

15 The programme of the world's peace . . .
is this:
1. Open covenants of peace, openly
arrived at, after which there shall be no
private international understandings of
any kind but diplomacy shall proceed
always frankly and in the public view.
> Speech to Congress, 8 Jan. 1918, in *Selected
> Addresses* (1918) p. 247

Robb Wilton 1881–1957

16 The day war broke out.
> Catch-phrase, from *c.*1940

Arthur Wimperis 1874–1953

1 I've gotter motter
  Always merry and bright!
  Look around and you will find
  Every cloud is silver-lined;
  The sun will shine
  Altho' the sky's a grey one;
  I've often said to meself, I've said,
  'Cheer up, curly you'll soon be dead!
  A short life and a gay one!'
    My Motter (1909 song; music by Lionel
    Monckton and Howard Talbot)

Owen Wister 1860–1938

2 Therefore Trampas spoke. 'You bet, you
  son-of-a—' The Virginian's pistol came
  out, and ... he issued his orders to the
  man Trampas:—'When you call me
  that, *smile!*'
    The Virginian (1902) ch. 2

Ludwig Wittgenstein 1889–1951

3 If there were a verb meaning 'to believe
  mistakenly', it would not have a
  significant first person, present
  indicative.
    Philosophical Investigations (1953) pt. 2,
    sec. 10

4 *Was sich überhaupt sagen lässt, lässt sich
  klar sagen; und wovon man nicht reden
  kann, darüber muss man schweigen.*

  What can be said at all can be said
  clearly; and whereof one cannot speak
  thereof one must be silent.
    Tractatus Logico-Philosophicus (1922) preface

5 *Die Welt ist alles, was der Fall ist.*

  The world is everything that is the case.
    Tractatus Logico-Philosophicus (1922) p. 30

6 *Die Logik muss für sich selber sorgen.*

  Logic must take care of itself.
    Tractatus Logico-Philosophicus (1922) p. 126

7 *Die Grenzen meiner Sprache bedeuten die
  Grenzen meiner Welt.*

  The limits of my language mean the
  limits of my world.
    Tractatus Logico-Philosophicus (1922) p. 148

8 *Die Welt des Glücklichen ist eine andere als
  die des Unglücklichen.*

  The world of the happy is quite different
  from that of the unhappy.
    Tractatus Logico-Philosophicus (1922) p. 184

P. G. Wodehouse 1881–1975

9 Chumps always make the best
  husbands. When you marry, Sally, grab
  a chump. Tap his forehead first, and if it
  rings solid, don't hesitate. All the
  unhappy marriages come from the
  husbands having brains. What good are
  brains to a man? They only unsettle
  him.
    The Adventures of Sally (1920) ch. 10

10 It is never difficult to distinguish
  between a Scotsman with a grievance
  and a ray of sunshine.
    Blandings Castle and Elsewhere (1935) 'The
    Custody of the Pumpkin'

11 At this point in the proceedings there
  was another ring at the front door.
  Jeeves shimmered out and came back
  with a telegram.
    Carry On, Jeeves! (1925) 'Jeeves Takes
    Charge'

12 He spoke with a certain what-is-it in his
  voice, and I could see that, if not
  actually disgruntled, he was far from
  being gruntled, so I tactfully changed the
  subject.
    The Code of the Woosters (1938) ch. 1

13 Slice him where you like, a hellhound is
  always a hellhound.
    The Code of the Woosters (1938) ch. 1

14 It is no use telling me that there are bad
  aunts and good aunts. At the core, they
  are all alike. Sooner or later, out pops
  the cloven hoof.
    The Code of the Woosters (1938) ch. 2

15 Roderick Spode? Big chap with a small
  moustache and the sort of eye that can
  open an oyster at sixty paces?
    The Code of the Woosters (1938) ch. 2

16 To my daughter Leonora without whose
  never-failing sympathy and
  encouragement this book would have
  been finished in half the time.
    The Heart of a Goof (1926) dedication

17 The lunches of fifty-seven years had
  caused his chest to slip down into the
  mezzanine floor.
    The Heart of a Goof (1926) 'Chester Forgets
    Himself'

18 I turned to Aunt Agatha, whose
  demeanour was now rather like that of
  one who, picking daisies on the railway,

has just caught the down express in the small of the back.
The Inimitable Jeeves (1923) ch. 4

1 Sir Roderick Glossop, Honoria's father, is always called a nerve specialist, because it sounds better, but everybody knows that he's really a sort of janitor to the looney-bin.
The Inimitable Jeeves (1923) ch. 7

2 As a rule, you see, I'm not lugged into Family Rows. On the occasions when Aunt is calling to Aunt like mastodons bellowing across primeval swamps and Uncle James's letter about Cousin Mabel's peculiar behaviour is being shot round the family circle ('Please read this carefully and send it on to Jane'), the clan has a tendency to ignore me. It's one of the advantages I get from being a bachelor—and, according to my nearest and dearest, practically a half-witted bachelor at that.
The Inimitable Jeeves (1923) ch. 16

3 It was my Uncle George who discovered that alcohol was a food well in advance of medical thought.
The Inimitable Jeeves (1923) ch. 16

4 It is a good rule in life never to apologize. The right sort of people do not want apologies, and the wrong sort take a mean advantage of them.
The Man Upstairs (1914) title story

5 She fitted into my biggest armchair as if it had been built round her by someone who knew they were wearing armchairs tight about the hips that season.
My Man Jeeves (1919) 'Jeeves and the Unbidden Guest'

6 What with excellent browsing and sluicing and cheery conversation and what-not, the afternoon passed quite happily.
My Man Jeeves (1919) 'Jeeves and the Unbidden Guest'

7 'What ho!' I said.
'What ho!' said Motty.
'What ho! What ho!'
'What ho! What ho! What ho!'
After that it seemed rather difficult to go on with the conversation.
My Man Jeeves (1919) 'Jeeves and the Unbidden Guest'

8 I spent the afternoon musing on Life. If you come to think of it, what a queer thing Life is! So unlike anything else, don't you know, if you see what I mean.
My Man Jeeves (1919) 'Rallying Round Old George'

9 Ice formed on the butler's upper slopes.
Pigs Have Wings (1952) ch. 5

10 The Right Hon. was a tubby little chap who looked as if he had been poured into his clothes and had forgotten to say 'When!'.
Very Good, Jeeves (1930) 'Jeeves and the Impending Doom'

Humbert Wolfe 1886–1940

11 You cannot hope
to bribe or twist,
thank God! the
British journalist.

But, seeing what
the man will do
unbribed, there's
no occasion to.
The Uncelestial City (1930) 'Over the Fire'

Thomas Wolfe 1900–1938

12 Most of the time we think we're sick, it's all in the mind.
Look Homeward, Angel (1929) pt. 1, ch. 1

13 'Where they got you stationed now, Luke?' said Harry Tugman peering up snoutily from a mug of coffee. 'At the p-p-p-present time in Norfolk at the Navy base,' Luke answered, 'm-m-making the world safe for hypocrisy.'
Look Homeward, Angel (1929) pt. 3, ch. 36

14 You can't go home again.
Title of novel (1940)

Tom Wolfe 1931–

15 The bonfire of the vanities.
Title of novel (1987)

Woodbine Willie

See G. A. STUDDERT KENNEDY

Lt.-Commander Thomas Woodroofe 1899–1978

1 At the present moment, the whole Fleet's lit up. When I say 'lit up', I mean lit up by fairy lamps.
Radio broadcast, 20 May 1937

Harry Woods

2 Oh we ain't got a barrel of money,
Maybe we're ragged and funny,
But we'll travel along
Singin' a song,
Side by side.
Side by Side (1927 song)

3 When the red, red, robin comes bob, bob, bobbin' along.
Title of song (1926)

Virginia Woolf 1882–1941

4 Righteous indignation . . . is misplaced if we agree with the lady's maid that high birth is a form of congenital insanity, that the sufferer merely inherits diseases of his ancestors, and endures them, for the most part very stoically, in one of those comfortably padded lunatic asylums which are known, euphemistically, as the stately homes of England.
The Common Reader (1925) 'Lady Dorothy Nevill'. Cf. *Oxford Dictionary of Quotations* (1979) 244:21

5 We are nauseated by the sight of trivial personalities decomposing in the eternity of print.
The Common Reader (1925) 'The Modern Essay'

6 Each had his past shut in him like the leaves of a book known to him by heart; and his friends could only read the title.
Jacob's Room (1922) ch. 5

7 Never did I read such tosh [as James Joyce's *Ulysses*]. As for the first two chapters we will let them pass, but the 3rd 4th 5th 6th—merely the scratching of pimples on the body of the bootboy at Claridges.
Letter to Lytton Strachey, 24 Apr. 1922, in *Letters* (1976) vol. 2, p. 551

8 A woman must have money and a room of her own if she is to write fiction.
A Room of One's Own (1929) ch. 1

9 Women have served all these centuries as looking-glasses possessing the magic and delicious power of reflecting the figure of a man at twice its natural size.
A Room of One's Own (1929) ch. 2

10 Literature is strewn with the wreckage of men who have minded beyond reason the opinions of others.
A Room of One's Own (1929) ch. 3

11 So that is marriage, Lily thought, a man and a woman looking at a girl throwing a ball.
To the Lighthouse (1927) pt. 1, ch. 13

12 Things have dropped from me. I have outlived certain desires; I have lost friends, some by death—Percival—others through sheer inability to cross the street.
The Waves (1931) p. 202

Alexander Woollcott 1887–1943

13 A broker is a man who takes your fortune and runs it into a shoestring.
In Samuel Hopkins Adams *Alexander Woollcott* (1945) ch. 15

14 I have no need of your God-damned sympathy. I only wish to be entertained by some of your grosser reminiscences.
Letter to Rex O'Malley, 1942, in Samuel Hopkins Adams *Alexander Woollcott* (1945) ch. 34

15 She [Dorothy Parker] is so odd a blend of Little Nell and Lady Macbeth. It is not so much the familiar phenomenon of a hand of steel in a velvet glove as a lacy sleeve with a bottle of vitriol concealed in its folds.
While Rome Burns (1934) 'Our Mrs Parker'

16 All the things I really like to do are either illegal, immoral, or fattening.
In R. E. Drennan *Wit's End* (1973)

Frank Lloyd Wright 1867–1959

17 The necessities were going by default to save the luxuries until I hardly knew which were necessities and which luxuries.
Autobiography (1945) bk. 2, p. 108

18 The physician can bury his mistakes, but the architect can only advise his client to plant vines—so they should go

as far as possible from home to build their first buildings.

New York Times 4 Oct. 1953, sec. 6, p. 47

Woodrow Wyatt (*Baron Wyatt*) 1919–

1 A man falls in love through his eyes, a woman through her ears.

To the Point (1981) p. 107

Laurie Wyman

2 Left hand down a bit!

The Navy Lark (BBC radio series, 1959–77)

George Wyndham 1863–1913

3 Over the construction of Dreadnoughts. ... What the people said was, 'We want eight, and we won't wait.'

Speech in Wigan, 27 Mar. 1909, in *The Times* 29 Mar. 1909

Tammy Wynette (*Wynette Pugh*) 1942– and Billy Sherrill

4 Stand by your man.

Title of song (1968)

R. J. Yeatman 1898–1968

See W. C. SELLAR AND R. J. YEATMAN

W. B. Yeats 1865–1939

5 I think it better that at times like these
We poets keep our mouths shut, for in truth
We have no gift to set a statesman right;
He's had enough of meddling who can please
A young girl in the indolence of her youth
Or an old man upon a winter's night.

'A Reason for Keeping Silent' in Edith Wharton (ed.) *The Book of the Homeless* (1916) p. 45

6 We had fed the heart on fantasies,
The heart's grown brutal from the fare,
More substance in our enmities
Than in our love; Oh, honey-bees

Come build in the empty house of the stare.

The Cat and the Moon (1924) 'Meditations in Time of Civil War 6: The Stare's Nest by my Window'

7 Out-worn heart, in a time out-worn,
Come clear of the nets of wrong and right;
Laugh, heart, again in the gray twilight;
Sigh, heart, again in the dew of morn.

The Celtic Twilight (1893) 'Into the Twilight'

8 When you are old and grey and full of sleep,
And nodding by the fire, take down this book
And slowly read and dream of the soft look
Your eyes had once, and of their shadows deep.

How many loved your moments of glad grace,
And loved your beauty with love false or true,
But one man loved the pilgrim soul in you,
And loved the sorrows of your changing face.

And bending down beside the glowing bars
Murmur, a little sad, 'From us fled Love.
He paced upon the mountains far above,
And hid his face amid a crowd of stars.'

The Countess Kathleen (1892) 'When You Are Old'

9 A pity beyond all telling,
Is hid in the heart of love.

The Countess Kathleen (1892) 'The Pity of Love'

10 I will arise and go now, and go to Innisfree,
And a small cabin build there, of clay and wattles made;
Nine bean rows will I have there, a hive for the honey bee,
And live alone in the bee-loud glade.

And I shall have some peace there, for peace comes dropping slow,
Dropping from the veils of the morning to where the cricket sings;
There midnight's all a glimmer, and noon a purple glow,
And evening full of the linnet's wings.

I will arise and go now, for always night and day

I hear lake water lapping with low
  sounds by the shore;
While I stand on the roadway or on the
  pavements gray,
I hear it in the deep heart's core.
  The Countess Kathleen (1892) 'The Lake Isle
  of Innisfree'

1 We make out of the quarrel with others,
  rhetoric, but of the quarrel with
  ourselves, poetry.
  Essays (1924) 'Anima Hominis' sec. 5

2 Why, what could she have done being
  what she is?
  Was there another Troy for her to burn?
  The Green Helmet and Other Poems (1910)
  'No Second Troy'

3 The fascination of what's difficult
  Has dried the sap out of my veins, and
  rent
  Spontaneous joy and natural content
  Out of my heart.
  The Green Helmet and Other Poems (1910)
  'The Fascination of What's Difficult'

4 But where's the wild dog that has
  praised his fleas?
  The Green Helmet and Other Poems (1910)
  'To a Poet, Who would have Me Praise
  certain bad Poets, Imitators of His and of
  Mine'

5 When I was young,
  I had not given a penny for a song
  Did not the poet sing it with such airs,
  That one believed he had a sword
  upstairs.
  The Green Helmet and Other Poems (1910)
  'All Things can Tempt Me'

6 Where, where but here have Pride and
  Truth,
  That long to give themselves for wage,
  To shake their wicked sides at youth
  Restraining reckless middle age?
  The Green Helmet and Other Poems (1912)
  'On hearing that the Students of our New
  University have joined the Agitation against
  Immoral Literature'

7 I said 'a line will take us hours maybe,
  Yet if it does not seem a moment's
  thought
  Our stitching and unstitching has been
  naught.'
  In the Seven Woods (1903) 'Adam's Curse'

8 The land of faery,
  Where nobody gets old and godly and
  grave,

Where nobody gets old and crafty and
  wise,
Where nobody gets old and bitter of
  tongue.
  The Land of Heart's Desire (1894) p. 12

9 Land of Heart's Desire,
  Where beauty has no ebb, decay no
  flood,
  But joy is wisdom, Time an endless
  song.
  The Land of Heart's Desire (1894) p. 36

10 Measurement began our might:
  Forms a stark Egyptian thought,
  Forms that gentler Phidias wrought.
  Michaelangelo left a proof
  On the Sistine Chapel roof,
  Where but half-awakened Adam
  Can disturb globe-trotting Madam
  Till her bowels are in heat,
  Proof that there's a purpose set
  Before the secret working mind:
  Profane perfection of mankind.
  Last Poems (1939) 'Under Ben Bulben' pt. 4

11 Irish poets, learn your trade,
  Sing whatever is well made,
  Scorn the sort now growing up
  All out of shape from toe to top,
  Their unremembering hearts and heads
  Base-born products of base beds.
  Sing the peasantry, and then
  Hard-riding country gentlemen,
  The holiness of monks, and after
  Porter-drinkers' randy laughter.
  Last Poems (1939) 'Under Ben Bulben' pt. 5

12 Cast your mind on other days
  That we in coming days may be
  Still the indomitable Irishry.
  Last Poems (1939) 'Under Ben Bulben' pt. 5

13 Under bare Ben Bulben's head
  In Drumcliffe churchyard Yeats is laid.
  An ancestor was rector there
  Long years ago, a church stands near,
  By the road an ancient cross.
  No marble, no conventional phrase;
  On limestone quarried near the spot
  By his command these words are cut:
    Cast a cold eye
    On life, on death.
    Horseman pass by!
  Last Poems (1939) 'Under Ben Bulben' pt. 6

14 Pythagoras planned it. Why did the
  people stare?
  His numbers, though they moved or
  seemed to move

In marble or in bronze, lacked character.
But boys and girls, pale from the
    imagined love
Of solitary beds, knew what they were,
That passion could bring character
    enough,
And pressed at midnight in some public
    place
Live lips upon a plummet-measured face.

No! Greater than Pythagoras, for the
    men
That with a mallet or a chisel modelled
    these
Calculations that look but casual flesh,
    put down
All Asiatic vague immensities,
And not the banks of oars that swam
    upon
The many-headed foam at Salamis.
Europe put off that foam when Phidias
Gave women dreams and dreams their
    looking glass.
    Last Poems (1939) 'The Statues'

1 When Pearse summoned Cuchulain to
    his side
What stalked through the Post Office?
    What intellect,
What calculation, number,
    measurement, replied?
We Irish, born into that ancient sect
But thrown upon this filthy modern tide
And by its formless spawning, fury
    wrecked,
Climb to our proper dark, that we may
    trace
The lineaments of a plummet-measured
    face.
    Last Poems (1939) 'The Statues'

2 Our master Caesar is in the tent
Where the maps are spread,
His eyes fixed upon nothing,
A hand under his head.

Like a long-legged fly upon the stream
His mind moves upon silence.
    Last Poems (1939) 'Long-Legged Fly'

3 Now that my ladder's gone
I must lie down where all ladders start
In the foul rag and bone shop of the
    heart.
    Last Poems (1939) 'The Circus Animals'
    Desertion' pt. 3

4 I have met them at close of day
Coming with vivid faces
From counter or desk among grey

Eighteenth-century houses.
I have passed with a nod of the head
Or polite meaningless words,
Or have lingered awhile and said
Polite meaningless words,
And thought before I had done
Of a mocking tale or a gibe
To please a companion
Around the fire at the club,
Being certain that they and I
But lived where motley is worn:
All changed, changed utterly:
A terrible beauty is born.
    Michael Robartes and the Dancer (1920)
    'Easter, 1916'

5 Too long a sacrifice
Can make a stone of the heart.
O when may it suffice?
    Michael Robartes and the Dancer (1920)
    'Easter, 1916'

6 I write it out in a verse—
MacDonagh and MacBride
And Connolly and Pearse
Now and in time to be,
Wherever green is worn,
Are changed, changed utterly:
A terrible beauty is born.
    Michael Robartes and the Dancer (1920)
    'Easter, 1916'

7 Turning and turning in the widening
    gyre
The falcon cannot hear the falconer;
Things fall apart; the centre cannot
    hold;
Mere anarchy is loosed upon the world,
The blood-dimmed tide is loosed, and
    everywhere
The ceremony of innocence is drowned;
The best lack all conviction, while the
    worst
Are full of passionate intensity.
    Michael Robartes and the Dancer (1920) 'The
    Second Coming'

8 The darkness drops again but now
    I know
That twenty centuries of stony sleep
Were vexed to nightmare by a rocking
    cradle,
And what rough beast, its hour come
    round at last,
Slouches towards Bethlehem to be born?
    Michael Robartes and the Dancer (1920) 'The
    Second Coming'

9 An intellectual hatred is the worst,

So let her think opinions are accursed.
Have I not seen the loveliest woman
    born
Out of the mouth of Plenty's horn,
Because of her opinionated mind
Barter that horn and every good
By quiet natures understood
For an old bellows full of angry wind?
   Michael Robartes and the Dancer (1920) 'A
   Prayer for My Daughter'

1 The ghost of Roger Casement
  Is beating on the door.
   New Poems (1938) 'The Ghost of Roger
   Casement'

2 Think where man's glory most begins
    and ends
  And say my glory was I had such
    friends.
   New Poems (1938) 'The Municipal Gallery
   Re-visited'

3 You think it horrible that lust and rage
  Should dance attendance upon my old
    age;
  They were not such a plague when I was
    young;
  What else have I to spur me into song?
   New Poems (1938) 'The Spur'

4 I thought no more was needed
  Youth to prolong
  Than dumb-bell and foil
  To keep the body young.
  Oh, who could have foretold
  That the heart grows old?
   Nine Poems (1918) 'A Song'

5 That is no country for old men. The
    young
  In one another's arms, birds in the
    trees—
  Those dying generations—at their song,
  The salmon-falls, the mackerel-crowded
    seas,
  Fish flesh or fowl, commend all summer
    long
  Whatever is begotten born and dies.
  Caught in that sensual music all neglect
  Monuments of unageing intellect.
   October Blast (1927) 'Sailing to Byzantium'

6 An aged man is but a paltry thing,
  A tattered coat upon a stick, unless
  Soul clap its hands and sing, and louder
    sing
  For every tatter in its mortal dress.
   October Blast (1927) 'Sailing to Byzantium'

7 And therefore I have sailed the seas and
    come
  To the holy city of Byzantium.
   October Blast (1927) 'Sailing to Byzantium'

8 O body swayed to music, O brightening
    glance
  How can we know the dancer from the
    dance?
   October Blast (1927) 'Among School
   Children'

9 The Light of Lights
  Looks always on the motive, not the
    deed,
  The Shadow of Shadows on the deed
    alone.
   Poems (1895) 'The Countess Cathleen' act 3

10 The years like great black oxen tread the
     world,
   And God the herdsman goads them on
     behind,
   And I am broken by their passing feet.
   Poems (1895) 'The Countess Cathleen' act 4

11 Red Rose, proud Rose, sad Rose of all
     my days!
   Come near me, while I sing the ancient
     ways.
   Poems (1895) 'To the Rose upon the Rood of
   Time'

12 Rose of all Roses, Rose of all the World!
   Poems (1895) 'The Rose of Battle'

13 Down by the salley gardens my love and
     I did meet;
   She passed the salley gardens with little
     snow-white feet. She bid me take love
     easy, as the leaves grow on the tree;
     But I, being young and foolish, with
     her would not agree.
   In a field by the river my love and I did
     stand,
   And on my leaning shoulder she laid her
     snow-white hand.
   She bid me take life easy, as the grass
     grows on the weirs;
   But I was young and foolish, and now
     am full of tears.
   Poems (1895) 'Down by the Salley Gardens'

14 In dreams begins responsibility.
   Responsibilities (1914) epigraph

15 Was it for this the wild geese spread
   The grey wing upon every tide;
   For this that all that blood was shed,

For this Edward Fitzgerald died,
And Robert Emmet and Wolfe Tone,
All that delirium of the brave;
Romantic Ireland's dead and gone,
It's with O'Leary in the grave.
Responsibilities (1914) 'September, 1913'

1 I made my song a coat
Covered with embroideries
Out of old mythologies
From heel to throat;
But the fools caught it,
Wore it in the world's eye
As though they'd wrought it.
Song, let them take it
For there's more enterprise
In walking naked.
Responsibilities (1914) 'A Coat'

2 A woman of so shining loveliness
That men threshed corn at midnight by
a tress,
A little stolen tress.
The Secret Rose (1897) 'To the Secret Rose'

3 When shall the stars be blown about the
sky,
Like the sparks blown out of a smithy,
and die?
Surely thine hour has come, thy great
wind blows,
Far off, most secret, and inviolate Rose?
The Secret Rose (1897) 'To the Secret Rose'

4 Bald heads forgetful of their sins,
Old, learned, respectable bald heads
Edit and annotate the lines
That young men, tossing on their beds,
Rhymed out in love's despair
To flatter beauty's ignorant ear.

All shuffle there; all cough in ink;
All wear the carpet with their shoes;
All think what other people think;
All know the man their neighbour
knows.
Lord, what would they say
Did their Catullus walk that way?
Selected Poems (1929) 'The Scholars'

5 Does the imagination dwell the most
Upon a woman won or woman lost?
If on the lost, admit you turned aside
From a great labyrinth out of pride.
The Tower (1928) 'The Tower' pt. 2

6 A sudden blow: the great wings beating
still
Above the staggering girl, her thighs
caressed

By the dark webs, her nape caught in
his bill,
He holds her helpless breast upon his
breast.

How can those terrified vague fingers
push
The feathered glory from her loosening
thighs?
The Tower (1928) 'Leda and the Swan'

7 A shudder in the loins engenders there
The broken wall, the burning roof and
tower
And Agamemnon dead.
The Tower (1928) 'Leda and the Swan'

8 Never to have lived is best, ancient
writers say;
Never to have drawn the breath of life,
never to have looked into the eye of
day;
The second best's a gay goodnight and
quickly turn away.
The Tower (1928) 'From *Oedipus at Colonus*'

9 I mourn for that most lonely thing; and
yet God's will be done,
I knew a phoenix in my youth so let
them have their day.
The Wild Swans at Coole (1917) 'His
Phoenix'

10 I see a schoolboy when I think of him
With face and nose pressed to
a sweet-shop window,
For certainly he sank into his grave
His senses and his heart unsatisfied,
And made—being poor, ailing and
ignorant,
Shut out from all the luxury of the
world,
The ill-bred son of a livery
stable-keeper—
Luxuriant song.
The Wild Swans at Coole (1917) 'Ego
Dominus Tuus' [of Keats]

11 Nor law, nor duty bade me fight,
Nor public man, nor angry crowds,
A lonely impulse of delight
Drove to this tumult in the clouds;
I balanced all, brought all to mind,
The years to come seemed waste of
breath,
A waste of breath the years behind
In balance with this life, this death.
The Wild Swans at Coole (1919) 'An Irish
Airman Foresees his Death'

12 And pluck till time and times are done,

The silver apples of the moon,
The golden apples of the sun.
The Wind Among the Reeds (1899) 'Song of
Wandering Aengus'

1 Had I the heavens' embroidered cloths,
Enwrought with golden and silver light,
The blue and the dim and the dark
cloths
Of night and light and the half light,
I would spread the cloths under your
feet:
But I, being poor, have only my dreams;
I have spread my dreams under your
feet;
Tread softly because you tread on my
dreams.
The Wind Among the Reeds (1899) 'Aedh
Wishes for the Cloths of Heaven'

2 The light of evening, Lissadell,
Great windows open to the south,
Two girls in silk kimonos, both
Beautiful, one a gazelle.
The Winding Stair (1929) 'In Memory of Eva
Gore Booth and Con Markiewicz'

3 The innocent and the beautiful
Have no enemy but time.
The Winding Stair (1929) 'In Memory of Eva
Gore Booth and Con Markiewicz'

4 Nor dread nor hope attend
A dying animal;
A man awaits his end
Dreading and hoping all.
The Winding Stair (1929) 'Death'

5 He knows death to the bone—
Man has created death.
The Winding Stair (1929) 'Death'

6 What lively lad most pleasured me
Of all that with me lay?
I answer that I gave my soul
And loved in misery,
But had great pleasure with a lad
That I loved bodily.

Flinging from his arms I laughed
To think his passion such
He fancied that I gave a soul
Did but our bodies touch,
And laughed upon his breast to think
Beast gave beast as much.
The Winding Stair (1929) 'A Woman Young
and Old' pt. 9

7 We were the last romantics—chose for
theme
Traditional sanctity and loveliness;

Whatever's written in what poets name
The book of the people; whatever most
can bless
The mind of man or elevate a rhyme;
But all is changed, that high horse
riderless,
Though mounted in that saddle Homer
rode
Where the swan drifts upon a darkening
flood.
The Winding Stair and Other Poems (1933)
'Coole and Ballylee, 1931'

8 A woman can be proud and stiff
When on love intent;
But Love has pitched his mansion in
The place of excrement;
For nothing can be sole or whole
That has not been rent.
The Winding Stair and Other Poems (1933)
'Crazy Jane Talks with the Bishop'

9 A starlit or a moonlit dome distains
All that man is;
All mere complexities,
The fury and the mire of human veins.
Words for Music Perhaps and Other Poems
(1932) 'Byzantium'

10 Those images that yet
Fresh images beget,
That dolphin-torn, that gong-tormented
sea.
Words for Music Perhaps and Other Poems
(1932) 'Byzantium'

11 While on the shop and street I gazed
My body of a sudden blazed;
And twenty minutes more or less
It seemed, so great my happiness,
That I was blessèd and could bless.
Words for Music Perhaps and Other Poems
(1932) 'Vacillation'

12 The intellect of man is forced to choose
Perfection of the life, or of the work,
And if it take the second must refuse
A heavenly mansion, raging in the dark.
Words for Music Perhaps and Other Poems
(1932) 'Coole Park and Ballylee, 1932'

13 Only God, my dear,
Could love you for yourself alone
And not your yellow hair.
Words for Music Perhaps and Other Poems
(1932) 'Anne Gregory'

14 Swift has sailed into his rest;
Savage indignation there
Cannot lacerate his breast.
Imitate him if you dare,

World-besotted traveller; he
Served human liberty.
  Words for Music Perhaps and Other Poems
  (1932) 'Swift's Epitaph'

1 Out of Ireland have we come.
Great hatred, little room,
Maimed us at the start.
I carry from my mother's womb
A fanatic heart.
  Words for Music Perhaps and Other Poems
  (1932) 'Remorse for Intemperate Speech'

2 What were all the world's alarms
To mighty Paris when he found
Sleep upon a golden bed
That first night in Helen's arms?
  Words for Music Perhaps and Other Poems
  (1932) 'Lullaby'

Jack Yellen 1892–1991

3 Happy days are here again!
The skies above are clear again.
Let us sing a song of cheer again,
Happy days are here again!
  Happy Days Are Here Again (1929 song;
  music by Milton Ager)

4 I'm the last of the red-hot mamas.
  Title of song (1928; popularized by Sophie
  Tucker)

Michael Young 1915–

5 The rise of the meritocracy 1870–2033.
  Title of book (1958)

Waldemar Young et al.

6 We have ways of making men talk.
  Lives of a Bengal Lancer (1935 film; the
  words became a catch-phrase as 'We have
  ways of making you talk')

Darryl F. Zanuck 1902–1979

7 For God's sake don't say yes until I've
finished talking.
  In Philip French *The Movie Moguls* (1969)
  ch. 5

Emiliano Zapata 1879–1919

8 *Muchos de ellos, por complacer a tiranos,
por un puñado de monedas, o por cohecho o*

*soborno, están derramando la sangre de sus
hermanos.*

Many of them, so as to curry favour
with tyrants, for a fistful of coins, or
through bribery or corruption, are
shedding the blood of their brothers.
  Plan de Ayala 28 Nov. 1911, para. 10
  (referring to the maderistas who, in Zapata's
  view, had betrayed the revolutionary cause)

Frank Zappa 1940–

9 Rock journalism is people who can't
write interviewing people who can't talk
for people who can't read.
  In Linda Botts *Loose Talk* (1980) p. 177

Robert Zemeckis 1952–
and Bob Gale 1952–

10 Back to the future.
  Title of film (1985)

Ronald L. Ziegler 1939–

11 Reminded of the President's previous
statements that the White House was
not involved [in the Watergate affair],
Ziegler said that Mr Nixon's latest
statement 'is the Operative White House
Position . . . and all previous statements
are inoperative.'
  Boston Globe 18 Apr. 1973

Grigori Zinoviev 1883–1936

12 Armed warfare must be preceded by
a struggle against the inclinations to
compromise which are embedded among
the majority of British workmen, against
the ideas of evolution and peaceful
extermination of capitalism. Only then
will it be possible to count upon
complete success of an armed
insurrection.
  Letter to the British Communist Party,
  15 Sept. 1924, in *The Times* 25 Oct. 1924
  (the 'Zinoviev Letter', said by some to be
  a forgery: see *Listener* 17 Sept. 1987)

Index

acting: A. is a masochistic form   OLIV 223:4
  a. is therefore the lowest   MOORE 212:13
  A. is merely the art   RICH 247:6
  people in them, a.   LARK 178:11
action: A. is consolatory   CONR 81:17
  can only be grasped by a.   BRON 54:3
  Every public a.   CORN 84:2
actions: there are disinterested a.   GIDE 124:7
activated: A. SLUDGE   JENN 154:12
actor: about an a. or an actress   AGATE 3:5
  a. is a kind of a guy   GLASS 125:4
  a.'s life for me   WASH 305:6
  If an a. acts it out   SAL 258:13
actors: A. are cattle   HITC 141:5
  We're a.—we're the opposite   STOP 287:7
actress: about an actor or an a.   AGATE 3:5
  For an a. to be a success   BARR 26:17
acts: second a. in American   FITZ 110:17
  which a. the most slowly   DIMN 92:7
Adam: A. and Eve were dispossessed   BOUL 50:8
  A. sat under the Tree   KIPL 169:12
  A. was a gardener   KIPL 171:4
  A. was but human   TWAIN 301:12
  gratitude we owe to A.   TWAIN 301:13
  past Eve and A.'s   JOYCE 157:10
  What a good thing A. had   TWAIN 301:9
  Where but half-awakened A.   YEATS 319:10
  would have made A. and Bruce   BRY 57:2
adamant: a. for drift, solid   CHUR 74:1
adapt: a. the world to himself   SHAW 272:8
adaptation: successful a. to the universal
                                 JUNG 160:3
adder: like an a. to its hole   PLOM 235:16
addicted: Salteena was not very a.   ASHF 14:6
addiction: Every form of a. is bad   JUNG 159:16
  prisoners of a.   ILL 150:12
addictive: All sin tends to be a.   AUDEN 18:3
addresses: a. are given to us to conceal SAKI 258:4
adds: It a. a new terror   TREE 298:8
adherents: Socialism is its a.   ORW 225:15
adieu: A., mes amis. Je vais   DUNC 96:8
  A. tristesse   ÉLUA 106:6
adjective: As to the A.: when in doubt
                                 TWAIN 301:17
adjectives: slogan and a few vapid a.   OGIL 222:18
adjust: a. your dress before leaving   CHUR 75:8
Adler: [Irene A.]   DOYLE 94:1
Adlestrop: Yes; I remember A.   THOM 294:5
admiral: doorman but a rear a.   BENC 36:8
admiralty: If blood be the price of a.   KIPL 174:4
admiration: A., n. Our polite recognition
                                 BIER 46:5
admirations: are moulded by their a.
                                 BOWEN 50:12
admire: a. without desiring   BRAD 52:1
admired: poet is to be a.   COCT 78:4
adolescence: a. and obsolescence   LINK 188:12
  suffering from petrified a.   BEVAN 44:9

adolescence (cont.):
  Theory of Permanent A   CONN 80:13
adopted: Byroads not 'a'.   BETJ 43:11
adorable: a. pancreas   KERR 164:8
  strongly a. tennis-girl's hand BETJ 43:11
adore: Lady of Spain, I a. you   REAV 244:11
  Pam, I a. you, Pam   BETJ 44:4
adorns: a. my legs   HOUS 144:5
adread: Yet was I sore a.   THOM 295:4
adulation: subject of a. by the many
                                 BROWN 56:11
adult: A child becomes an a. when   SZASZ 289:12
  occupation of an a.   OLIV 223:4
  To be a. is to be alone   ROST 253:8
adulterous: less and it would be a.   BENC 36:9
adultery: a. being a most conventional
                                 NAB 216:12
  a. than in provincialism   HUXL 148:7
  I've committed a.   CART 64:6
adults: attributed by a. to children   SZASZ 290:2
  marriage is not that a.   DE VR 91:15
  only between consenting a.   VIDAL 304:5
advance: say civilization don't a.   ROG 249:11
advantage: a. for a system of philosophy
                                 SANT 260:20
  a. of doing one's praising   BUTL 60:11
  take a mean a. of them   WOD 316:4
advantages: I have not had your a.   BOTT 50:7
adventure: a. is only an inconvenience   CHES 68:4
  most beautiful a.   FROH 117:8
  out into a. and sunshine   FORS 114:11
  will be an awfully big a.   BARR 25:19
adventures: a. of his soul among masterpieces
                                 FRAN 116:7
adversaries: resistance of the a.   STAL 283:4
adversity: A., if a man is set down   BUTL 60:8
  easily learn to endure a.   TWAIN 300:20
advertisement: read a patent medicine a.
                                 JER 155:9
advertisements: ideals of a nation by its a.
                                 DOUG 93:12
advertisers: proprietor's prejudices as the a.
                                 SWAF 289:4
advertising: A. may be described   LEAC 182:10
  kind of a. we deserve   SAY 263:10
  money I spend on a.   LEV 186:14
advice: a. is in nine cases out   COLL 79:8
  a. I've been turning over   FITZ 110:13
  A., n. The smallest current   BIER 46:6
advise: A. the prince   ELIOT 103:11
  STREETS FLOODED. PLEASE A.   BENC 35:15
advised: If I demur, for, be a.   HEAN 136:13
advocates: potent a. of peace upon   GEOR 123:4
aeroplanes: it wasn't the a.   CREE 86:1
Aeschylean: A. phrase   HARDY 134:8
aesthetic: Between a. and religious   BELL 32:9
  degree of my a. emotion   BELL 32:9
  desire for a. expression   WAUGH 305:18
  our a. enjoyment   WHIT 310:10

affair: a. between Margot Asquith   PARK 230:8
   man's love a. with America   MAIL 199:9
affairs: about his or her love a.   WEST 309:18
   a. of the nation   JOHN 156:13
   from taking part in a.   VALÉ 303:3
   Let them mind their own a.   HOUS 145:3
affectionate: have a really a. mother
                      MAUG 205:17
affirmation: a. of all that constitutes   JUNG 160:3
affirmative: Latch on to the a.   MERC 207:6
affliction: some a. or defect either   BEER 30:9
affluence: face the economics of a.   GALB 121:3
afford: Can't a. them, Governor   SHAW 273:14
   people could a. to pay   LEWIS 187:11
   some man that can a.   SHAW 272:22
   which no democracy can a.   BEV 45:10
Afghanistan: wounded and left on A.'s   KIPL 169:5
afraid: And in short, I was a.   ELIOT 103:10
   I, a stranger and a.   HOUS 145:4
   I'm a. to come home in the dark   WILL 311:14
   it is that he is a.   FORS 114:2
   neither tarnished nor a.   CHAN 66:9
   not that I'm a. to die   ALLEN 4:6
   stop because you are a.   NANS 217:8
   things is to be a.   FAUL 107:11
   were a. to ask   REUB 245:14
   who is not a. of the sea   SYNGE 289:8
   Who's a. of the big bad wolf   CHUR 72:4
   Who's a. of Virginia Woolf   ALBEE 3:10
   you what you are a.   BENC 36:7
Africa: Out of A.   DIN 92:8
   sloggin' over A.   KIPL 170:12
   Till China and A. meet   AUDEN 16:12
   When a white man in A.   LESS 186:8
   white communities of A.   SAL 259:2
   with A. than my own body   ORTON 224:3
African: A. national consciousness   MACM 197:3
after: A. each war there is a little   ATK 15:14
   A. the first death   THOM 292:12
   A. you, Claude   KAV 162:3
   Or just a.   STEV 285:11
after-dinner: a. speech without the help
                      WAUGH 306:5
aftermath: triumphs that are the a. of war
                      HOOV 143:4
afternoon: At five in the a.   LORCA 190:21
   Christ were coming this a.   CART 64:4
   could lose the war in an a.   CHUR 76:14
   Lovely and willing every a.   AUDEN 19:12
   On a winter's a.   ELIOT 102:6
   Summer afternoon—summer a.   JAMES 152:11
aftersight: mind to a. and foresight   ELIOT 102:3
again: except play it over a.   LAMB 177:14
   Happy days are here a.   YELL 324:3
   I'll come in a.   CHAP 67:10
   I'll see you a.   COW 84:9
   Once a. we stop the mighty   ANON 10:9
   walk down a. with them off   HARG 135:2

again (cont.):
   You can't go home a.   WOLFE 316:14
against: a. everything all the time   KENN 164:5
   A. the beautiful   GREE 128:12
   anyone who wasn't a. war   LOW 191:6
   He was a. it   COOL 82:9
   I always vote *a.*   FIEL 109:8
   that all life is 6 to 5 a.   RUNY 254:10
Agamemnon: And A. dead   YEATS 322:7
   When A. cried aloud   ELIOT 102:13
Agatha: A.! Mary! come   ELIOT 101:18
   I turned to Aunt A.   WOD 315:18
age: a. has consisted of crises   ATK 15:15
   a. of miracles hadn't passed   GERS 123:6
   a. of pamphleteers   HOGB 142:10
   A. shall not weary them   BINY 47:5
   a. should burn and rave   THOM 292:11
   a. we are now entering   ELLIS 106:4
   a., which forgives itself   SHAW 272:14
   attendance upon my old a.   YEATS 321:3
   But perhaps a new a.   BERD 40:1
   dawning of the a. of Aquarius   RADO 242:8
   essentially a tragic a.   LAWR 181:7
   In every a.   ATK 15:15
   leaden a. o'ercargoed   FLEC 112:3
   past a. of the earth   JEANS 154:5
   Restraining reckless middle a.   YEATS 319:6
   scientific a.   HOLM 142:13
   That men call a.; and those   BROO 54:12
   The a. demanded an image   POUND 238:7
   then the only end of a.   LARK 179:15
   threshold of old a.   CORN 84:1
aged: a. man is but a paltry   YEATS 321:6
   An a. thrush, frail   HARDY 134:2
   deliciously a. and sad   SHAW 269:14
agèd: Of an a. face   CAMP 61:8
ageless-ancient: And mother-naked and a.
                      DAY-L 89:5
agenda: a. will be in inverse proportion
                      PARK 232:3
ages: a. of twenty and forty   AUDEN 18:7
   In the middle a.   JER 155:6
   live in the Middle A.   SMITH 278:19
   Somewhere a. and ages hence   FROST 118:8
aggravating: She was an a. child   BELL 33:9
aggression: against the menace of a.   ASQ 14:19
   a. against any neighbour   ROOS 250:12
   weapon of a.   ADLER 3:1
aggressive: They were not a. creatures
                      FORS 114:13
agin': Rapidly a.   DYLAN 97:13
agnostic: compliment to be called an a.   DARR 88:8
agog: a. at the plasterer   HEAN 136:9
agonizing: compel an a. reappraisal   DULL 96:6
agony: But only a., and that has   BROO 54:10
   Ee, it was a., Ivy   RAY 243:11
   Hard and bitter a. for us   ELIOT 100:10
   that a. is our triumph   VANZ 303:7
agree: Birds in their little nests a.   BELL 34:4

agree (*cont.*):

When you did a., he was	LLOY 190:4

agreeable: just as a. as optimism — BENN 38:13
agreement: a. signed last night — CHAM 66:5
agrees: a. with you not those — STEIN 284:12
ahead: If you want to get a. — ANON 8:15
a-hold: And always keep a. of Nurse — BELL 32:18
aid: entitled to claim the a. — CHUR 74:5
Aids: A. pandemic is a classic — ANNE 6:12
   misbehaving will not catch A. — CURR 87:11
aim: have forgotten your a. — SANT 260:9
   oneself an impossible a. — GREE 128:13
   things to a. at in life — SMITH 277:11
   You ask, what is our a. — CHUR 74:4
aimer: *qu'a. ce n'est point nous* — SAINT 257:3
aims: Had other a. than my delight — HARDY 134:9
ain't: a. a fit night out — FIEL 109:7
   a.-a-going — TWAIN 302:1
   A. it all a bleedin shame — ANON 10:15
   A. we got fun — KAHN 161:3
   It a. necessarily — HEYW 140:6
   There a. gonna be no war — MACM 196:17
   There a. no Sanity Claus — KAUF 161:9
   You a. heard nuttin' yet — JOLS 157:3
air: a. A Conservative — ROOS 250:9
   a. as inexperienced people — CONR 81:14
   a. a voice without a face — AUDEN 20:9
   burning fills the startled A. — BELL 35:7
   But merely vans to beat the a. — ELIOT 100:12
   Clear the a. — ELIOT 102:10
   conscience-stricken a. — HOUS 144:8
   Dust in the a. suspended — ELIOT 102:2
   His happy good-night a. — HARDY 134:2
   Into my heart an a. that kills — HOUS 146:11
   I take the a. there willingly — BECK 29:1
   since the day of the a. — BALD 23:5
   The a. is full of our cries — BECK 29:14
   This is the death of a. — ELIOT 102:2
   your room full of good a. — LEAC 182:14
airconditioning: with respectability and a. — BAR 24:14
airing: The toothbrush too is a. — BETJ 44:1
airline: a. ticket to romantic places — MARV 202:8
airmen: out to the British a. — CHUR 74:8
airports: a. almost deserted — AUDEN 17:3
airs: poet sing it with such a. — YEATS 319:5
aitches: nothing to lose but our a. — ORW 225:19
Alamein: A. we never had a victory — CHUR 76:7
à la mode: It began *à*. — DOBS 92:14
alarm: I viewed the morning with a. — GERS 123:6
   SPREAD A. AND DESPONDENCY — PEN 232:15
alarms: What were all the world's a. — YEATS 324:2
alas: A. but cannot help — AUDEN 20:11
   A., Time stays, *we* go — DOBS 93:1
   a.! we return — FORS 114:11
   And some, a., with Kate — AUDEN 18:17
   But, a., we never do — PARK 231:3
   Hugo—a. — GIDE 124:8
   Pigeons on the grass a. — STEIN 284:9

albatross: And I thought of the a. — LAWR 180:10
Albert: Frankie and A. were lovers — ANON 8:1
   takes to fill the A. Hall — LENN 185:8
   Went there with young A. — EDGAR 98:3
alcohol: a. doesn't thrill me — PORT 236:12
   A. is a very necessary article — SHAW 270:8
   a. produces a delightful — BENN 38:11
   a. was a food well in advance — WOD 316:3
   have taken more out of a. — CHUR 72:7
   narcotic be a. or morphine — JUNG 159:16
alcoholic: a. as a man you don't like — THOM 293:7
alcoholism: high smoking and a. — CURR 87:12
Aldershot: burnish'd by A. sun — BETJ 43:9
ale: a.'s the stuff to drink — HOUS 146:15
   drink your a. — HOUS 145:1
Alexander: A.'s ragtime band — BERL 40:4
alibi: He always has an a. — ELIOT 102:12
Alice: Robin went down with A. — MILNE 209:15
alien: a. people clutching — ELIOT 100:10
alike: a. are the groans of love — LOWRY 192:5
   think a. — TWAIN 301:20
alive: dead but a. and working — ANON 8:4
   hills are a. with the sound — HAMM 132:3
   how it feels to be a. — BARZ 27:11
   If Botticelli were a. today — UST 302:16
   Is that he is no longer a. — BENT 39:11
   Is that thing a. — BERR 41:10
   Not while I'm a. 'e aint — BEVIN 45:14
   that Lord Jones was a. — CHES 71:11
   What still a. at twenty-two — KING 167:11
   When I was man a. — HOUS 146:6
all: A. before my little room — BROO 55:7
   a. depends what you mean — JOAD 155:14
   A. God's children are not — LEB 183:7
   a. go together when we — LEHR 184:5
   A. human beings are born — ANON 11:16
   a. human life is there — JAMES 152:18
   A. I need to make a comedy — CHAP 67:4
   a. life is 6 to 5 against — RUNY 254:10
   A. men are creative — GOOD 126:13
   A. men are equal — FORS 115:1
   a. men are rapists — FREN 117:1
   A. my shows are great — GRADE 127:4
   A. quiet on the western front — REM 245:10
   A. the President's men — BERN 41:8
   A. the way with LBJ — ANON 6:14
   a. things fly thee — THOM 295:15
   And a. shall be well — ELIOT 102:7
   Evening, a. — WILL 312:15
   Fair Shares for A. — JAY 154:3
   fool a. of the people — ADAMS 2:5
   From a. that terror teaches — CHES 70:7
   slum you've seen them a. — AGNEW 3:6
allegiance: Any victim demands a. — GREE 128:15
   which you have pledged a. — BALD 22:12
alley: I think we are in rats' a. — ELIOT 105:1
alleys: a. in London do not present — DOYLE 94:8
alliance: A., *n*. In international — BIER 46:7

alliance (*cont.*):

rapture there is a family a.	BELL 32:8

Allies: A. had blundered — NEV 219:3
alligator: See you later, a. — GUID 130:5
allow: would a. such a conventional — BARR 27:1
all-powerful: a. to be impotent — CHUR 74:1
all-round: was a wonderful a. man — BEER 30:13
alone: a. against smiling enemies — BOWEN 51:4
  a. in the room there — KEYN 165:6
  a. you leave it to a torrent — CHES 70:3
  And I lie down a. — HOUS 145:10
  dangerous to meet it a. — WHAR 309:22
  fastest who travels a. — KIPL 175:4
  I want to be a. — GARBO 122:2
  must plough my furrow a. — ROS 252:12
  not good for man to be a. — BARR 26:18
  not sufficiently a. — VALÉ 303:2
  One is always a. — ELIOT 101:3
  To be adult is to be a. — ROST 253:8
  We live, as we dream — a. — CONR 81:10
  were a. with the quiet day — JAMES 153:9
  You'll never walk a. — HAMM 132:5
  You're never a. with a Strand — MAY 206:1
along: He keeps on rollin' a. — HAMM 132:1
  If you want to get along, go a. — RAYB 244:1
alp: An a. of unforgiveness grew — PLOM 235:12
Alps: beneath some snow-deep A. — ELIOT 100:5
also: The sun a. rises — HEM 138:12
altar: a. the dearest — SPR 282:13
  And on the a., very reverently — WELLS 308:2
  high a. on the move — BOWEN 50:14
alterations: carried on as usual during a. — CHUR 72:10
alternation: a. between two rhythms — JOAD 155:15
alternative: accept there is no real a. — THAT 291:7
  a. to war and destruction — KING 167:5
  Considering the a. — CHEV 71:12
alternatives: exhausted all other a. — EBAN 97:16
  have to decide between a. — BONH 49:4
always: a. another one walking — ELIOT 105:9
  a. at the edge — SPEN 281:11
  a. depended on the kindness — WILL 312:10
  a. had mornings like — MILNE 209:14
  A. merry and bright — WIMP 315:1
  a. night and day — YEATS 318:10
  out is a. through — FROST 119:3
  soul it is a. three o'clock — FITZ 110:12
  There is a. a forgotten thing — CHES 68:11
am: Where I a., I don't know — BECK 29:3
amateur: 'Eavy-sterned a. old men — KIPL 170:13
amateurs: disease that afflicts a. — CHES 69:10
  Hell is full of musical a. — SHAW 271:3
  that we are a nation of a. — ROS 252:11
amaze: these cogitations still a. — ELIOT 103:17
amazement: And to her a. she discovered — EWART 107:1
Amazon: She was an A. Her whole — BLAN 47:10
ambassador: A. in Berlin handed — CHAM 66:7

ambassador (*cont.*):

  choose a less provocative A. — HOUS 144:7
ambiguity: Seven types of a. — EMPS 106:8
ambition: A., *n.* An overmastering — BIER 46:8
  specimens, the lilies of a. — DOUG 93:6
ambitions: a. are lawful except those — CONR 81:20
  deceives with whispering a. — ELIOT 100:7
ambitious: on a much less a. project — ANON 8:4
ambrosial: Phallic and a. — POUND 238:8
ambulance: down a doctor? With an a. — SIMP 275:12
âme: *les aventures de son â.* — FRAN 116:7
amends: I must make a. — JOPL 157:6
America: A. can not be an ostrich — WILS 314:7
  A. is the only idealistic — WILS 314:4
  A. is the way parents obey — EDW 98:10
  A.'s present need is not — HARD 133:1
  A. there are two classes — BENC 36:10
  A. was thus clearly top — SELL 266:13
  A. will think tomorrow — KIPL 170:5
  arts in A. — BEEC 30:3
  God bless A. — BERL 40:6
  I, too, sing A. — HUGH 147:13
  It's morning again in A. — RINEY 248:2
  next to of course god a. i — CUMM 87:2
  restore A. to its own people — ROOS 250:3
  The greening of A. — REICH 245:8
  what A. will do for you — KENN 164:1
  what makes A. what it — STEIN 284:10
  which A. is the proof — MCC 193:14
American: about to send A. boys — JOHN 156:12
  acts in A. lives — FITZ 110:17
  A hyphenated A. is not — ROOS 251:13
  A. as cherry pie — BROWN 56:9
  A. Express — ANON 6:15
  A. gentlemen are the best — LOOS 190:16
  A. heiress wants to buy — MCC 193:13
  A. literature comes from — HEM 138:5
  A. people is business — COOL 82:13
  A. system of life — HOOV 143:7
  A. system of rugged individualism — HOOV 143:6
  A. white man to find — BALD 22:9
  A. who had spoken disparagingly — BURNS 58:5
  A. women shoot the hippopotamus — FORS 114:4
  A. writers want to be not — VIDAL 304:7
  I am a free man, an A. — JOHN 156:15
  I am A. bred — MILL 208:7
  idea I'm knocking the A. — CAP 63:8
  imported, elderly A. — JENK 154:10
  justice and the A. way — ANON 7:23
  process whereby A. girls — HAMP 132:7
  rooted in the A. dream — KING 166:10
  root of the A. Negro problem — BALD 22:9
  The A. beauty rose can — ROCK 248:13
Americanism: can be no fifty-fifty A. — ROOS 251:9
  McCarthyism is A. with its sleeves — MCC 193:11
Americans: A. have a perfect right — BEER 31:14
  new generation of A. — KENN 163:8
  twelve A. is a bore — UPD 302:11

Amis: [by Kingsley A.]   MAUG 205:15
ammunition: Lord and pass the a.   FORGY 113:15
amor: A. vincit insomnia   FRY 119:21
amour: C'est tellement simple, l'a.   PRÉV 239:13
  Il y a l'a. bien sûr   ANOU 12:12
  Vous savez bien que l'a.   ANOU 12:13
amours: Et nos a., faut-il qu'il   APOL 12:15
amputate: Thank God they had to a.   SASS 263:2
amuse: A talent to a.   COW 84:8
amusing: am generally rather a.   BEER 30:17
  besides being very a.   BUTL 59:10
analogies: A. decide nothing   FREUD 117:5
analysis: writings of Marx whose a.   BENN 37:2
anarchism: A. is a game   SHAW 272:21
  A., then, really   GOLD 126:3
anarchist: up a small a. community   BENN 37:12
anarchy: a. is loosed upon the world   YEATS 320:7
Anatomie: Die A. ist das Schicksal   FREUD 117:2
anatomy: A. is destiny   FREUD 117:2
  portions of the human a.   HELP 138:1
ANC: brought to you by the A.   MAND 200:1
ancestors: all classes, our a.   CHES 70:2
  a. lost no time in abandoning   LANC 178:2
anchor: a. in nonsense   GALB 121:3
ancient: burning for the a. heavenly   GINS 125:1
  In a. shadows and twilights   AE 3:3
  while I sing the a. ways   YEATS 321:11
and: including 'a.'   MCC 193:12
Andrea: A. del Sarto appears   BEER 30:20
Andromache: kissed his sad A. goodbye
                                           CORN 83:13
angel: a. travelling incognito   QUEN 242:2
  enough for an a. to pass   FIRB 109:12
  In heaven an a. is nobody   SHAW 272:6
angelheaded: a. hipsters burning   GINS 125:1
angels: A. can fly because they   CHES 70:4
  a. keep their ancient places   THOM 296:13
  a. over the prodigal's   SAKI 257:13
  a. play only Bach in praising   BARTH 27:3
  Hark! the herald a. sing   BEEC 30:4
  treefull of a. at Peckham Rye   BENÉT 37:1
anger: a. of men who have no opinions
                                           CHES 69:11
  life of telegrams and a.   FORS 115:2
  monstrous a. of the guns   OWEN 227:13
Anglais: know what 'le vice A.'   RATT 243:7
angles: Offer no a. to the wind   TESS 291:6
Anglo-Irish: A. slurred   BOWEN 51:5
Anglo-Irishman: He was an A.   BEHAN 31:22
Anglo-Saxons: public-school men or even of A.
                                           FORS 114:1
angry: a. if any one gives me   BUTL 60:7
  Knelt down with a. prayers   HODG 142:2
  known as the A. Young Man   FEAR 108:2
  looking for an a. fix   GINS 125:1
  were a. and poor and happy   CHES 70:12
  when very a., swear   TWAIN 301:16
anguish: A gay modulating a.   FRY 119:18

anguish (cont.):
  going to be howls of a.   HEAL 136:7
animal: A dying a.   YEATS 323:4
  a. ever invented anything   CHES 68:5
  a. on a planet which would   HALD 131:2
  Bang! Now the a.   DE L 91:7
  Be a good a., true   LAWR 182:3
  Only A. that Blushes   TWAIN 300:17
  The only a. in the world   LAWR 180:8
animals: All a., except man   BUTL 60:10
  a. are equal but some animals   ORW 224:12
  distinguishes man from a.   OSLER 227:3
  The a. will not look   AUDEN 20:11
ankle socks: about women who wear a.
                                           BENN 38:1
Ann: A., Ann   DE L 91:1
Anna: A. Livia! I want to hear all   JOYCE 158:2
annals: War's a. will cloud into night
                                           HARDY 133:15
annihilating: means for a. itself   BORN 50:2
anno: only a. domini, but that's   HILT 141:3
annotate: Edit and a. the lines   YEATS 322:4
annoyance: a. of a good example   TWAIN 301:19
another: a. nice mess you've gotten   LAUR 180:4
  tomorrow is a. day   MITC 211:9
answer: A. to the Great Question   ADAMS 1:14
  a. to the Irish Question   SELL 266:12
  a. yes without having asked   CAMUS 62:11
  asked, 'What is the a.?'   STEIN 284:11
  Please a. my question   BEER 31:19
  short a. is 'himself'   IBSEN 150:6
  Speak now, and I will a.   HOUS 146:10
  The a., my friend, is blowin'   DYLAN 97:3
  way to a pertinent a.   BRON 54:4
  why did you a. the phone   THUR 297:9
answered: They a., as they took   BELL 33:1
ant: a.'s a centaur in his dragon   POUND 238:16
antagonistic: a. governments everywhere
                                           WAUGH 306:7
  a. to the Victorian age   WILS 313:2
antennae: Artists are the a.   POUND 238:12
anthology: a. is like all the plums   RAL 242:14
anthropology: most familiar facts of a.   FRAZ 116:8
anti-christ: against the a. of Communism
                                           BUCH 57:7
anti-clerical: understand a. things so well
                                           BELL 33:13
anti-destin: L'art est un a.   MALR 199:14
antimilitarists: a. propose no substitute
                                           JAMES 153:14
anti-Semitic: have never been that [a.]
                                           MAUG 205:3
anvil: England's on the a.   KIPL 174:1
  The Church is an a.   MACL 196:2
any: a. man who hates dogs   ROST 253:10
  A. old iron, any old iron   COLL 79:7
anybody: A. can be pope   JOHN 156:1
  A. can Win, unless there   ADE 2:16
  a. could become President   DARR 88:7

anybody (*cont.*):

Has a. here seen Kelly	MURP 216:3
Is there a. there	DE L 90:11

anyone: never said 'Tennis, a.?'   BOG 48:9

anything: A. goes   PORT 236:9

a. never does run smooth	BUTL 59:7
I can do a. better than you	BERL 40:5
Remembering him like a.	CHES 70:10
Who could ask for a. more	GERS 123:7

anyway: Whose life is it a.   CLARK 76:16

anywhere: a. in the world   ROOS 250:12

apart: fall a.   YEATS 320:7

In council rooms a.	RICE 246:8
We have stood a., studiously	WILS 314:6
You mean a. from my own	GABOR 120:12

apartheid: are going to dismantle a.   MAND 200:1

apathy: a. of human beings   KELL 162:9

ape: naked a. self-named *Homo*   MORR 213:14

The gorgeous buttocks of the a.	HUXL 148:19
their manners from the A.	BELL 32:14

apes: And a. and peacocks   MAS 202:16

aphrodisiac: But a circumambulating a.
   FRY 119:17

Power 'is great a.'   KISS 175:13

Aphrodite: Blonde A. rose up excited
   AUDEN 20:12

Apollo: A young A., golden-haired   CORN 83:11

apologies: people do not want a.   WOD 316:4

apologize: I never a.   SHAW 267:19

Never a.	FISH 110:4
rule in life never to a.	WOD 316:4

apology: An a. for the Devil   BUTL 59:21

are God's a. for relations   KING 167:10

appeal: basic a. of movies   KAEL 160:5

appear: Blessed Cecilia, a. in visions   AUDEN 20:13

with how you a. to God   UNAM 302:10

appearance: a. leaves the world   BRAD 52:4

applause: A. is a receipt, not   SCHN 264:7

A., *n*. The echo of a platitude   BIER 46:9

apple: a. falling towards England   AUDEN 19:3

a. for the apple's sake	TWAIN 301:12
a. trees will never get	FROST 118:14
easy under the a. boughs	THOM 293:1
you when you've got an a.	TWAIN 302:1

apples: On moon-washed a. of wonder
   DRIN 95:17

The silver a. of the moon   YEATS 322:12

applications: And a. for situations   AUDEN 19:16

apply: The fundamental things a.   HUPF 148:5

You know my methods. A. them   DOYLE 95:6

appointment: a. by the corrupt few   SHAW 271:18

I had an a. with him	LOW 191:8
we have kept our a.	BECK 29:11

appreciated: *craving to be a.*   JAMES 153:11

appreciation: developing his faculty of a.
   CECIL 65:9

total dependence on the a.   CONN 80:10

apprehend: Intelligence is quickness to a.
   WHIT 310:8

apprehension: passionate a. of form   BELL 32:6

apprentice: become an a. once more   BEAV 28:5

apprenticeship: cannot be any a. for freedom
   BAR 24:13

approve: a. of your young sons   GRIF 129:8

But I do not a.   MILL 207:16

apricot: And the a. tree   CAUS 65:4

April: And A.'s in the west wind   MAS 204:2

April, A.	WATS 305:8
A. is the cruellest month	ELIOT 104:10
bright cold day in A.	ORW 225:2

aquarium: The a. is gone   LOW 191:12

Aquarius: dawning of the age of A.   RADO 242:8

Arab: A. compatriots and where   REAG 244:9

Arabia: with the spell of far A.   DE L 90:10

Arabs: ragged little street A.   DOYLE 95:7

Arbeit: *A. macht frei.*   ANON 6:16

archbishop: a. had come to see me   BURG 57:16

Archer: [Jeffrey A.'s book]   BANK 24:11

Mary A. in the witness box   CAUL 65:3

arches: down the a. of the years   THOM 295:2

Underneath the A.   FLAN 111:3

archetypes: are known as *a*.   JUNG 160:4

architect: An a. who saw this sight   MORG 213:9

a. can only advise	WRIG 317:18
Great A. of the Universe	JEANS 154:7

architecture: a. a certain inhumanity   CLARK 77:1

A. is the art of how	JOHN 157:1
A., of all the arts	DIMN 92:7
cuckoo clock style of a.	HEM 138:13
fall of English a.	BETJ 43:2
left leg, it's modern a.	BANK 24:10
New styles of a., a change	AUDEN 20:4

ardent: children a. for some desperate
   OWEN 227:14

are: sees things as they a.   BIER 46:16

so very indubitably *a*.   BEER 30:12

argent: *d'a. et de grosses armées*   ANOU 12:11

Argentina: Don't cry for me A.   RICE 246:11

argue: don't want to a. about it   AGATE 3:5

hero is a man who would a.   MAIL 199:10

argument: a. is that War makes rattling
   HARDY 133:4

once in the use of an a.   BENN 38:12

arias: Clear a. of light thrilling   DAY-L 89:7

arise: a. and make them miserable   HUXL 148:14

I will a. and go now   YEATS 318:10

aristocracy: a. in a republic is like   MITF 211:13

a. to what is decent	HOPE 143:10
while a. means government	CHES 69:16

aristocrat: both the artist and the a.
   WAUGH 305:14

Aristotle: A. maintained that women   RUSS 255:8

Arkangels: like he'd come from A.   JOYCE 158:7

arm: Give me your a., old toad   LARK 179:10

skin from the a.   ELIOT 102:10

armaments: a. that cause wars   MAD 198:9

a. to such a point   ROOS 250:12

armchair: a. which provides relaxation
MAT 204:8
armchairs: a. tight about the hips WOD 316:5
armed: A. neutrality is ineffectual WILS 314:12
  A. warfare must be preceded ZIN 324:12
  women. We should be a. O'BR 221:15
armées: *d'argent et de grosses a.* ANOU 12:11
Armenteers: Mademoiselle from A. ANON 9:19
armful: that's very nearly an a. GALT 121:8
armies: interested in a. and fleets AUDEN 17:1
  plenty of money and large a. ANOU 12:11
  stronger than all the a. ANON 11:7
armistice: conditions of the a. LLOY 189:9
  it is an a. for twenty FOCH 113:1
arms: A. and the man SHAW 267:16
  a. around him yes and drew JOYCE 159:10
  a. went round her waist MAS 203:8
  But in my a. till break of day AUDEN 17:10
  In one another's a. YEATS 321:5
  might'st seek it in My a. THOM 295:16
  simply call the a. REAG 244:6
  world in a. is not spending EIS 100:2
army: A. is the non-commissioned KIPL 174:12
  contemptible little a. ANON 7:24
  honour of the British A. KITC 175:15
aroma: a. of performing seals HART 135:10
around: Away but the weather turned a.
THOM 292:14
arranging: knack of so a. the world FRIS 117:7
arrest: a. of attention BELL 35:13
  But neither a. nor movement ELIOT 101:8
arrested: was a. one fine morning KAFKA 160:7
arrive: Will be to a. where we started ELIOT 102:4
arrived: a. and to prove it I'm SYKES 289:7
  that he has a. to cover it STOP 286:17
arrows: living a. are sent forth GIBR 124:3
ars: *A. gratia artis.* DIETZ 92:5
arse: a. for fifty years MACN 197:12
  politician is an a. upon CUMM 87:6
arsenal: great a. of democracy ROOS 250:11
arsenic: A. and old lace KESS 164:9
art: are only interested in a. SHAW 269:9
  A. and Religion BELL 32:8
  A. distils sensation BARZ 27:12
  A. does not reproduce KLEE 176:2
  a. for art's sake DIETZ 92:5
  a.-for-art's-sake PRIT 240:5
  a. has no importance whatever NAB 217:5
  a. has something to do BELL 35:13
  a. has the capacity SONT 280:9
  A. is a lie that makes PIC 234:8
  a. is an appeal to a reality MACC 193:9
  A. is a revolt against fate MALR 199:14
  A. is born of humiliation AUDEN 21:2
  A. is meant to disturb BRAQ 52:13
  A. is significant deformity FRY 120:3
  A. is something BARN 25:7
  a. is that common symptom WHAR 309:21

art (*cont.*):
  A. is the imposing WHIT 310:10
  A. is the objectification LANG 178:8
  a. is the only thing BOWEN 50:15
  A. is vice DEGAS 89:13
  a. must be parochial MOORE 212:11
  a. needed Ruskin any more STOP 287:11
  a. of balance MAT 204:8
  a. of being wise JAMES 153:16
  a. of keeping a large group RICH 247:6
  A. of the Possible BUTL 58:9
  a. should carry its justification CONR 81:16
  a. student wears coloured BRAT 52:15
  A. that has made these SHAW 268:23
  a. that is interested SANT 260:16
  at anything but his a. SHAW 270:16
  A triumph of the embalmer's a. VIDAL 304:4
  But hating, my boy, is an a. NASH 218:3
  compassion of the healer's a. ELIOT 101:15
  element of a. in their being CHES 69:10
  fascinating kind of a. WARH 305:3
  For a. establishes KENN 163:4
  gamesmanship or The a. of winning
POTT 237:14
  good a. than the pram CONN 80:9
  if it be an a. at all MOORE 212:13
  intellect upon a. SONT 280:8
  Interpretation makes a. SONT 280:9
  Irish a. JOYCE 158:16
  Is an a., like everything else PLATH 235:10
  It is an A. rather QUIL 242:3
  It's clever, but is it A. KIPL 170:1
  It's pretty, but is it A. KIPL 169:12
  know that A. is not truth PIC 234:8
  L'a. a pour objet de lui ANOU 12:14
  masses it is not a. SCH 264:10
  not the a. of the possible GALB 121:5
  not works of a. at all BLUNT 48:2
  offered you Conflict and A. PRIE 239:15
  people start on all this A. HERB 139:6
  Religion and a. spring CATH 64:13
  responsibility is to his a. FAUL 107:10
  sensitive one is to great a. BEER 30:19
  society a. is not a weapon KENN 163:5
  The A. of Being Ruled LEWIS 187:7
  The history of a. BUTL 59:19
  The object of a. is actually ANOU 12:14
  this so-called modern a. MUNN 215:15
  trade and half an a. INGE 151:9
  wants to understand a. PIC 234:9
  war is the necessary a. DULL 96:5
  where the a. resides SCHN 264:6
  Who talk about the Aims of A. KIPL 168:4
  Works of a. are of an infinite RILKE 247:8
article: being the correct a. ASHF 14:9
  first a. of my faith GAND 122:1
  Fortieth A. DENN 91:1
artifact: I have seen visible, Death's a. ABSE 1:3
artifice: it by every a. possible ANOU 12:14

artificer: old a., stand me now   JOYCE 158:12
artifices: *par tous les a. possibles*   ANOU 12:14
artificial: said it was a. respiration   BURG 58:1
artisan: To give employment to the a.   BELL 34:1
artist: An a. may visit a museum   SANT 260:15
   a. and the aristocrat   WAUGH 305:14
   a. has no need to express   PROU 241:1
   a. is a dreamer consenting   SANT 260:13
   a. is not a special kind   COOM 83:1
   a. is someone who produces   WARH 305:4
   a. will let his wife starve   SHAW 270:16
   a. writes his own autobiography   ELLIS 106:5
   given me by a very good a.   BELL 32:6
   grant the a. his subject   JAMES 153:6
   Never trust the a.   LAWR 182:2
   Portrait of the a.   THOM 293:8
   position for an a. anywhere   THOM 293:9
   really only another a.   PIC 234:6
   struggle between the a. man   SHAW 270:17
   The a., like the God   JOYCE 158:9
   West and from now on an a.   CONN 80:14
artistes: *passionnément par des a. inconnus*   BART 27:5
artistic: a. temperament is a disease   CHES 69:10
   intellectual and a.   BERL 40:13
artists: A. are not engineers   KENN 163:5
   A. are the antennae   POUND 238:12
   As a. they're rot   PARK 231:3
   creative a. very seldom   CHES 69:8
   creative but few are a.   GOOD 126:13
   most a. and all humbugs   CONN 80:11
   with passion by unknown a.   BART 27:5
arts: a. in America are a gigantic   BEEC 30:3
   a. of death   SHAW 271:6
   a. of life man invents   SHAW 271:6
   interested in the a.   AYCK 21:7
   therefore the lowest of the a.   MOORE 212:13
ascribe: a. to an opponent motives   BARR 26:5
ash: A. on an old man's sleeve   ELIOT 102:2
   Than Oak, and A., and Thorn   KIPL 172:12
ashamed: And be a.   HUGH 147:13
   a. of ourselves, of our   SHAW 270:13
   doing something he is a.   SHAW 268:8
   more things a man is a.   SHAW 270:14
ashes: Are a. under Uricon   HOUS 146:8
   Distinction between the A.   DOYLE 95:3
   fire and was burnt to a.   GRAH 127:8
   past is a bucket of a.   SAND 259:11
   will be sour grapes and a.   ASHF 14:11
Asian: A. boys ought to be doing   JOHN 156:12
aside: they have not stood a.   GREE 128:11
ask: A. any man what nationality   RHOD 246:4
   a. not what your country   KENN 164:1
   a. the hard question   AUDEN 20:6
   a. why   AUDEN 20:8
   Don't a. me, ask   FREUD 117:3
   Don't let's a. for the moon   PROU 241:6
   I a. and cannot answer   SHAW-274:13

ask (*cont.*):
   I intend to a. of them   KENN 163:7
   Never a. of money spent   FROST 118:5
   never does any harm to a.   KRUT 177:2
   still have to a.   ARMS 13:9
   that is all we a.   OWEN 227:11
   were afraid to a.   REUB 245:14
   when you a. him how   TAYL 291:1
   Who could a. for anything more   GERS 123:7
asking: refrain from a. it to dinner   HALS 131:8
asleep: Half a. as they stalk   HARDY 133:15
   Not to fall a. is distinguished   BELL 35:12
   ships sail like swans a.   FLEC 112:3
asphalt: Their only monument the a. road   ELIOT 104:2
aspidistra: Keep the a. flying   ORW 224:19
   The biggest a. in the world   HARP 135:5
aspirations: The young have a.   SAKI 257:16
aspires: Any work that a., however   CONR 81:16
Asquith: affair between Margot A.   PARK 230:8
   kept calling Margot A.   ASQ 15:4
   twenty years he [H. H. A.]   AMERY 5:11
ass: kiss my a. in Macy's window   JOHN 156:2
assassin: copperheads and the a.   SAND 259:12
   you are an a.   ROST 253:9
assassination: A. is the extreme form   SHAW 274:5
assent: being has ever given his a.   HUXL 149:10
asset: a. any country can have   CHUR 73:2
assistance: a. called Lend-Lease   CHUR 75:3
associate: a. with a lot of priests   BELL 33:13
assurance: a. of a sleepwalker   HITL 141:7
   One of the low on whom a. sits   ELIOT 105:6
asthmatic: a., I know nothing   DOYLE 94:19
astonish: A. me   DIAG 92:2
astonished: a. to see him in Baghdad   LOW 191:8
astonishment: state of a.   SANS 260:7
Astor: A. has made a statement   RIC 246:13
astride: give birth a. of a grave   BECK 29:13
astronomers: Confounding her a.   HODG 142:4
asylum: flourishes is the lunatic a.   ELLIS 106:3
   lunatic a. run by lunatics   LLOY 190:3
   taken charge of the a.   ROWL 254:3
Athanasian: have him reciting the A.   AUDEN 18:4
atheism: a., breast-feeding   ORTON 224:5
atheist: a. brooding and blaspheming   CHES 71:3
   a. is man who has no invisible   BUCH 57:6
   been very *chic* for an a.   RUSS 254:14
   denial of Him by the a.   PROU 241:1
   He was an embittered a.   ORW 224:16
   kept her from being an a.   SART 261:14
   Thanks to God, I am still an a.   BUÑ 57:14
atheists: There are no a. in the foxholes   CUMM 87:9
Athens: what Pericles felt of A.   KEYN 164:11
Atkins: Thank you, Mister A.   KIPL 168:10
atmosphere: delightful social a.   BENN 38:11
atom: A holy war with a. bombs   BENN 37:2
   a. bomb is a paper tiger   MAO 200:12
   a. possesses certain exceptional   JEANS 154:6

atom (cont.):
 defence against the a. bomb   ANON 7:3
 grasped the mystery of the a.   BRAD 52:6
 power of the a. has changed   EINS 99:8
 There is no evil in the a.   STEV 286:9
atomic: handling of a. technology   BORN 50:2
 win an a. war is to make   BRAD 52:5
atoms: a. of each of them   O'BR 222:6
 colourless movement of a.   BRAD 52:4
atrabilious: bowl with a. liquor   HUXL 149:1
atrophy: that music begins to a.   POUND 237:15
attack: a. the monkey when   BEVAN 45:5
 both by his plan of a.   SASS 262:8
 occasional heart a.   BENC 36:5
 That dared a. my Chesterton   BELL 35:5
attacking: a. the Foreign Secretary   BEVAN 45:5
 situation excellent, I am a.   FOCH 112:13
attempt: a. to cover the universe   FORS 114:9
attempted: A. to Believe Matilda   BELL 33:3
attempts: All sins are a. to fill voids WEIL 307:7
attendant: Am an a. lord, one that will do
                                      ELIOT 103:11
attention: a. in the midst of distraction BELL 35:13
 give their entire a. to it   BENN 38:17
 So a. must be paid   MILL 208:8
 socks compelled one's a.   SAKI 257:11
attentive: a. when she was in process FITZ 110:18
attire: sort of a. for a gentleman   SHAR 267:10
attitude: enchantingly wavering a.   FITZ 110:18
Attlee: A. is a charming and intelligent NIC 219:8
 A. reminds me of nothing   ORW 224:15
 [Clement A. is]   CHUR 72:8
 Mr A., whom Churchill once   CHUR 76:11
 opened [Clement] A. got out   CHUR 72:6
attracted: that they are a. by God   INGE 151:5
attracting: rhythm of a. people for fear
                                      JOAD 155:15
attraction: sexual a. through the potency
                                      HARD 132:16
attractive: they are in the least a. CAMP 62:4
attribute: moral a. of a Scotsman   BARR 26:14
auctioneer: A., n. The man who proclaims
                                      BIER 46:10
audace: Le tact dans l'a. c'est   COCT 78:3
audacity: a. is knowing how far   COCT 78:3
Auden: A., a sort of gutless   ORW 225:18
 A. was someone you could   SPEN 282:3
audience: Folies-Bergère and looks at the a.
                                      STOC 286:13
audiences: know two kinds of a. only SCHN 264:9
August: A. for the people   AUDEN 19:10
 A. in its history Paris   TUCH 300:1
 A. is a wicked month   O'BR 221:14
 In latter A. when the hay   LOW 192:1
aunt: A. like mastodons bellowing   WOD 316:2
 Her A. was off to the Theatre   BELL 33:4
 Her A., who, from her Earliest   BELL 33:3
 therefore when her A. returned   BELL 33:5
aunts: me that there are bad a.   WOD 315:14

aunts (cont.):
 Where his a., who are not   CHES 71:9
austere: beauty cold and a.   RUSS 255:13
Austerlitz: high at A. and Waterloo   SAND 260:1
Australia: So you're going to A.   MELBA 206:7
 that he was born in A.   SHAW 270:3
Australians: A. wouldn't give a XXXX ANON 6:17
Austria: A. is going to the war   CHES 70:6
authentic: a. mammon than a bogus   MACN 197:8
author: a. is not what he says   SMITH 278:15
 a. that wrote it was   SAL 258:11
 a. was executed for murdering   BARR 25:13
 characters in search of an a.   PIR 235:1
 don't know who the a.   SHAW 269:3
 If it's by a good a.   SHAW 269:4
 on the a.'s skill to give   QUIL 242:3
 really alive before their a.   PIR 235:2
 sincerely from the a.'s soul   HUXL 149:6
authoritarian: triumph of an a. state CLARK 77:1
authorities: a. whom we do not control
                                      CONN 81:6
 reported it to the proper a.   HELL 137:9
authority: And the lie of A.   AUDEN 17:12
 I don't like a., at least   BENS 39:3
 system can rest solely on a.   AYER 21:12
autobiography: a. is an obituary in serial
                                      CRISP 86:5
 a. is the most gratuitous   STOP 286:15
 Every artist writes his own a.   ELLIS 106:5
automatic: her hair with a. hand   ELIOT 105:7
automobile: And fix up his a.   CLAR 77:3
 l'a. est aujourd'hui l'équivalent   BART 27:5
autres: l'Enfer, c'est les A.   SART 261:11
autumn: a. always gets me badly   LAWR 181:3
 a. and the falling fruit   LAWR 181:10
 a. arrives in the early   BOWEN 50:11
 A. sunsets exquisitely   HUXL 148:19
avail: virtues are of no a.   HUXL 149:7
aventures: a. de son âme au milieu   FRAN 116:7
average: a. guy who could carry   CROS 86:9
avoid: subject and how to a. them   HEIS 137:3
avoiding: non-being by a. being   TILL 297:17
avoids: a. the sight of distress   MAUG 205:6
awaits: A man a. his end   YEATS 323:4
awakenings: bad dream between two a.
                                      O'NEI 223:11
aware: insignificant and is a.   BECK 28:12
 The infant child is not a.   HOUS 144:10
awareness: a. of the possibilities   LEAV 183:5
 positive signs of his a.   BLUNT 48:1
away: Up, up and a.   WEBB 307:2
awe: a. and dread   FRAZ 116:8
awful: a. place and terrible   SCOTT 265:7
 a. to reflect that what   SMITH 277:12
 nobody goes, it's a.   BECK 29:7
 The a. things that rabbits do   ANON 10:13
awfully: will be an a. big adventure BARR 25:19
awoke: a. one morning from uneasy   KAFKA 161:2
 Gently its touch a. him once   OWEN 228:1

axes: no a. are being ground — BROUN 56:5
Axis: under-belly of the A. — CHUR 75:2

B

Babbitt: B. He was forty-six years — LEWIS 187:11
babies: b. and you eat chips — WESK 308:15
  b. can't be all bad — ROST 253:10
  cut ribbons and kiss b. — KENT 207:12
  milk into b. — CHUR 73:2
  Other people's b. — HERB 139:4
baby: A B. in an ox's stall — BETJ 42:5
  b. laughed for the first — BARR 25:17
  bats with b. faces — ELIOT 105:10
  Burn, b., burn — ANON 7:8
  garden to my bonny new b. — THOM 293:16
  Make it one for my b. — MERC 207:7
  Who loves ya, b. — SAV 263:7
Babylonian: The grandeurs of his B. heart
  — THOM 296:9
Bach: angels play only B. — BARTH 27:3
  B. almost persuades me — FRY 120:4
bachelor: b. never quite gets over — ROWL 253:15
  facts that you are a b. — DOYLE 94:19
  half-witted b. — WOD 316:2
bachelors: All reformers are b. — MOORE 212:9
back: always give your b. a pat — LERN 185:21
  b. from time to time — ELIOT 105:4
  B. in the USSR — LENN 185:6
  B. to the future — ZEM 324:10
  B. to the garden — MITC 211:6
  b. upon the window-panes — ELIOT 103:7
  boys in the b. rooms — BEAV 28:9
  gets stabbed in the b. — GARD 122:4
  I counted them all b. — HANR 132:10
  I have a beast on my b. — DOUG 93:9
  safe to go b. in the water — ANON 9:6
  The Empire strikes b. — LUCAS 192:9
  what the boys in the b. — LOES 190:6
  when the eyes and b. — ELIOT 105:5
  Winston is b. — ANON 12:9
  you b. where you belong — HERM 139:20
backbone: b. of the Army is the non-commissioned
  — KIPL 174:12
  McKinley has no more b. — ROOS 251:7
backhand: your wonderful b. drive — BETJ 44:4
backing: I'm b. Britain — ANON 8:17
backs: On b. of tattered envelopes — HOPE 144:2
backward: B. ran sentences until reeled
  — GIBBS 124:1
  For life goes not b. — GIBR 124:3
  Leaned b. with a lipless grin — ELIOT 103:1
  lean over too far b. — THUR 297:14
  look b. to with pride — FROST 118:16
backwards: I'm walking b. for Christmas
  — MILL 209:5

backyards: all the clean American b. — MAIL 199:9
bacon: But b.'s not the only thing — KING 167:11
  When their lordships asked B. — BENT 39:6
bad: babies can't be all b. — ROST 253:10
  b. against the worse — DAY-L 89:8
  b. as we'd been saying — KENN 162:17
  b. aunts and good aunts — WOD 315:14
  b. book is as much — HUXL 149:6
  b. for me do not tempt — SHAW 267:15
  b. movies when they can — GOLD 126:12
  b. publicity except — BEHAN 32:5
  b. taste is better — BENN 38:8
  B. women never take — BROO 56:2
  believe a thing to be b. — MILN 211:2
  consistency is as b. for the mind — HUXL 148:12
  feeling is b. form — FORS 114:2
  Four legs good, two legs b. — ORW 224:11
  he is b. enough as it — CAMP 61:10
  her badness when she's b. — BARR 26:10
  I call you b., my little child — BELL 32:13
  I'm a b. lot — THOM 294:1
  it's not too b. at all — CHEV 71:12
  much b. in the best of us — ANON 11:8
  She was not really b. at heart — BELL 33:9
  Some of them are b. — GRADE 127:4
  The b. end unhappily — STOP 287:9
  The good, the b., and the ugly — SCAR 264:4
  they will come to a b. end — BEER 31:9
  told you b. things — CHUR 75:1
  when I'm b., I'm better — WEST 309:6
  world seemed none so b. — HOUS 146:16
badly: government by the b. educated — CHES 69:16
  it is worth doing b. — CHES 71:6
badness: b. of her badness when — BARR 26:10
Baghdad: astonished to see him in B. — LOW 191:6
bags: carry other people's b. — BRAC 51:14
Bailey: Won't you come home Bill B. — CANN 63:6
baiting: b. a mouse-trap with cheese — SAKI 258:6
baked: millionaires love a b. — FIRB 109:13
Baker: B. Street irregulars — DOYLE 95:7
balance: dream of is an art of b. — MAT 204:8
bald: [André Gide] was very b. — QUEN 242:2
  B. heads forgetful — YEATS 322:4
  Slightly b. — ANON 7:11
  two b. men over a comb — BORG 50:1
baldness: b. than young men can possibly
  — SMITH 277:16
Baldwin: Mr B. denouncing sanctions — BEAV 28:6
  never hears of B. nowadays — CHUR 73:4
Baldwins: two Mr B. on the stage — BEAV 28:6
ball: at a girl throwing a b. — WOOLF 317:11
  Ruddy B. has taken — THOM 294:9
  Take me out to the b. game — NORW 221:7
ballet: unearthly b. of bloodless — BRAD 52:4
ball-floor: Dance on this b. thin and wan
  — BLUN 47:12
Balliol: B. made me, Balliol fed me — BELL 35:3
  God be with you, B. men — BELL 35:3

balls: And a thousand lost golf b.   ELIOT 104:2
Ballymurphy: In B. Competence with pain
    HEAN 136:12
balmy: Ginger, you're b.   MURR 216:5
Baltimore: magazine and then you're in B.
    GORD 126:14
ban: B. the bomb   ANON 7:1
banality: b. out of the sphere   SARR 261:5
   word-and-thought-defying b. of evil AREN 13:4
banana: original b. man   PAGET 228:11
bananas: Yes! we have no b.   SILV 275:5
band: It's the best b. in the land   BERL 40:4
   rock 'n' roll b.   JAGG 152:5
   twilight! importunate b.   BETJ 43:11
   when the b. begins   KIPL 168:10
   when the wearied B.   HUXL 149:2
bands: people get into b. for three   GELD 122:10
   who pursue Culture in b.   WHAR 309:22
bang: A bigger b. for a buck   ANON 7:6
   b., goes the farmer's   GAY 122:8
   B.! Now the animal   DE L 91:7
   Bertha's got a b. on the boko   MARS 202:5
   If the big b. does come   OSB 226:14
   Not with a b. but a whimper   ELIOT 103:5
   The words 'Kiss Kiss B.B.'   KAEL 160:5
banished: B. from the herd he led   HODG 142:3
banishment: b. of its properly elected   CAIR 61:4
bank: all the way to the b.   LIB 188:3
   b. compared with founding   BREC 53:2
   b. is a place that will   HOPE 144:1
   b. was mightier   PLOM 235:15
   should tyrannize over his b.   KEYN 165:4
Bankhead: B. barged down the Nile   BROWN 56:12
banking: much as we value b.   TOYN 298:6
bankrupts: you are b.; your role   TROT 299:4
banks: b. and stones   KAV 161:12
   b. of the great grey-green   KIPL 171:15
   thanks, letters from b.   AUDEN 19:16
banned: that any book should be b.   WEST 309:17
Bapu: B. as we called him   NEHRU 218:17
bar: treat if met where any b.   HARDY 134:10
Barabbas: crowd will always save B.   COCT 78:5
barbarian: He is a b., and thinks   SHAW 268:7
barbarians: The B. are coming today   CAV 65:6
barbarism: methods of b. in South Africa
    CAMP 62:7
bard: this goat-footed b.   KEYN 165:3
bare: B. like nude, giant girls   SPEN 281:17
   Under b. Ben Bulben's head   YEATS 319:13
bareback: daft and happy hills b.   THOM 292:10
barged: Bankhead b. down the Nile   BROWN 56:12
baritone: have been singing b.   REED 245:5
bark: you heard a seal b.   THUR 297:5
barking: sound of Harold Hobson b.   GILL 124:10
Barlow: O my Hornby and my B. long ago
    THOM 296:1
barmaids: Are B. Chaste   MAS 203:8
barn: from the b. and the forge   HOUS 146:5

barn-cocks: Ere the b. say   HARDY 134:7
Barney: Give him the money, B.   PICK 234:11
barrel: decompose in a b. of porter   DONL 93:4
   Oh we ain't got a b. of money   WOODS 317:2
   out of the b. of a gun   MAO 201:2
barreltone: Ben Dollard had a base b.   JOYCE 159:6
barricade: At some disputed b.   SEEG 265:12
Barrie: [by J.M. B.]   LLEW 189:6
   clatter of Sir James B.'s   GUED 130:3
barring: B. that natural expression   TWAIN 300:13
Barrymore: B. would allow such a conventional
    BARR 27:1
bars: Between their silver b.   FLEC 111:15
barter: mental or physical b.   AUDEN 18:14
Barumph: King B. has a whim of iron
    HERF 139:19
base: b. people as certainly   SHAW 270:2
   had a b. barreltone voice   JOYCE 159:6
basement: faded female in a damp b.   HARD 132:16
basest: b. of all things   FAUL 107:11
basically: b. he's an underachiever   ALLEN 4:8
basin: Stare, stare in the b.   AUDEN 16:13
basis: have this fact for its b.   SHAW 269:13
basket: both come from the same b.   CONR 81:19
   WATCH THAT B.   TWAIN 301:18
bason: b. and a hose thing   ASHF 14:5
bastard: putting all my eggs in one b.
    PARK 231:17
   we knocked the b. off   HILL 140:13
bataille: La France a perdu une b.   DE G 90:3
bath: b. room said Bernard it   ASHF 14:5
   conifers, sound of the b.   BETJ 43:10
   I test my b. before I sit   NASH 217:18
   on his b. tub   POUND 238:1
   who watched the b. water   ABSE 1:4
bathroom: church as he goes to the b.   BLYT 48:4
   man in the b. cupboard   EWART 107:1
   revolutionary in a b.   LINK 188:11
bats: b. with baby faces   ELIOT 105:10
batsman: B. of the Dawn has driven   THOM 294:9
   I am the b. and the bat   LANG 178:6
battalions: your dreams in pale b. go   SORL 281:2
Battery: Bronx is up but the B.'s   COMD 79:10
battle: b. depends the survival   CHUR 74:7
   B., n. A method of untying   BIER 46:11
   b. of Waterloo was won   ORW 225:1
   France has lost a b.   DE G 90:3
   that out of b. I escaped   OWEN 228:5
battlements: came and perched on b.   BEER 31:17
   From the hid b. of Eternity   THOM 295:14
battles: b. are the only   MCAR 193:2
   Dead b., like dead generals   TUCH 299:14
   opening b.   ORW 225:1
battleship: Benchley, 'Get me a b.'   BENC 36:8
battu: mais de s'être bien b.   COUB 84:3
bawdy: While b. questions went about   MAS 203:8
bay: keeping feelings at b.   BROO 56:3
   steamer breaking from the b.   AUDEN 19:12

baying: county families b. for broken
    WAUGH 305:11
bayonet: b. is a weapon with a worker ANON 7:2
bayonets: himself a throne of b. INGE 151:8
bazaar: morning, Fate's great b. MACN 198:6
BBC: B. for interviewing HARD 132:16
  has demanded that the B. CRIT 86:7
be: But b. MACL 196:5
  Let b. be finale of seem STEV 285:7
  Such is: what is to b. THOM 295:13
beach: Along the hidden b. KIPL 170:9
  low voice: 'On the b.' CHES 69:12
  walk upon the b. ELIOT 103:12
beaches: enough for lazing upon b. BETJ 42:9
  We shall fight on the b. CHUR 74:6
Beachy Head: Birmingham by way of B.
    CHES 69:5
beam: B. us up, Mr Scott RODD 249:3
bean: Nine b. rows will I have YEATS 318:10
  The home of the b. and the cod BOSS 50:3
beanz: B. meanz Heinz DRAKE 95:16
bear: B. is looking so geometrical FRY 119:19
  B. of Very Little Brain MILNE 210:10
  B. them we can, and if HOUS 145:1
  Cannot b. very much reality ELIOT 101:7
  Grizzly B. is huge HOUS 144:10
  so b. ourselves CHUR 74:7
  The fire was furry as a b. SITW 276:2
  Their habits from the B. BELL 32:14
bearable: b. to millions of people SHAW 270:8
beard: has a fringe and a b. BRAT 52:15
bearer: b. of this letter ASHF 14:9
bearing: b. down on me now under JOYCE 158:7
bears: And dancing dogs and b. HODG 142:2
  b. might come with buns ISH 151:14
  Teddy B. have their Picnic KENN 162:12
beast: And what rough b. YEATS 320:8
  b. and the monk FORS 115:3
  B. gave beast as much YEATS 323:6
  B. stands for strong mutually WAUGH 306:7
  b. to the truly genteel HARDY 133:12
  I have a b. on my back DOUG 93:9
  night out for man or b. FIEL 109:7
  people call this b. to mind BELL 32:17
  was Beauty killed the B. CREE 86:1
beastly: b. incidents our memories O'NEI 223:13
  has been b. to the Bank CRIT 86:7
  How b. the bourgeois LAWR 181:15
  let's be b. to the Germans COW 84:7
Beat: had reading the B. novels CAP 63:10
  really a b. generation KER 164:6
  So we b. on, boats against FITZ 110:16
  The b. goes BONO 49:6
  They beat—and a Voice b. THOM 295:3
beaten: Englishman is ever fairly b. SHAW 274:1
  I was b. up by Quakers ALLEN 5:5
beating: b. of war drums KOES 176:8
  Is b. on the door YEATS 321:1

beatings: dread of b. BETJ 44:6
Beatles: And the B.' first LP LARK 179:3
  [the B. are] LENN 185:4
beats: B. like a fatalistic drum ELIOT 103:14
  Counting the slow heart b. GRAV 128:8
  It b. as it sweeps as it cleans PAG 229:1
Beattock: Pulling up B., a steady climb
    AUDEN 19:15
beaut: make a mistake, it's a b. LA G 177:6
beautiful: Against the b. and the clever
    GREE 128:12
  Another is 'the b. Law Courts' RUSS 256:4
  b. and simple as all truly HENRY 139:2
  B. comical things HARV 135:15
  b. I am HUGH 147:13
  B., one a gazelle YEATS 323:2
  b. stuff and poetry TWAIN 300:5
  b. things we have to keep O'NEI 223:13
  b. word for doing things SHAW 268:2
  Black is b. ANON 7:7
  find it a b. clean thought LAWR 182:4
  God's children are not b. LEB 183:7
  her 'a b. little knitter' SITW 276:4
  more b. than any religion SAKI 257:8
  most b. adventure FROH 117:8
  Of the forest b. HODG 142:3
  'Oh, how b.!' and sitting KIPL 171:3
  Oh, what a b. mornin' HAMM 131:13
  Small is b. SCH 264:15
  The b. and damned FITZ 110:8
  The b. and death-struck year HOUS 146:12
  The entirely b. AUDEN 17:10
  The innocent and the b. YEATS 323:3
  worshipped because they are b. RUSS 255:17
beauty: American b. rose can ROCK 248:13
  A terrible b. is born YEATS 320:4
  B. and the lust for learning BEER 31:12
  b. being only skin-deep KERR 164:8
  b. came like the setting SASS 263:5
  B. crieth in an attic BUTL 60:6
  B. for some provides escape HUXL 148:19
  B. is all very well at first SHAW 271:12
  B. is momentary in the mind STEV 285:10
  B. is the first test HARDY 133:2
  b. lives though lilies FLEC 111:7
  B.'s conquest of your face AUDEN 19:5
  B. she was statue cold FLEC 112:1
  B. took from those DE L 90:15
  b. what could be more beaut- CUMM 87:2
  body's b. lives STEV 285:10
  But b. vanishes; beauty passes DE L 90:13
  For such B., so descending BELL 34:14
  Has looked on B. bare MILL 208:2
  Her b. fed my common earth MAS 203:7
  It was B. killed the Beast CREE 86:1
  loveliest things of b. MAS 203:5
  say b. is only sin deep SAKI 257:14
  Say, is there B. yet to find BROO 56:1

beauty (*cont.*):

So is the b.	CAMP 61:8
The b. of inflections	STEV 285:11
thing of b. and a boy	ROWL 253:15
thought that where B. was	GALS 121:6
'Tisn't b., so to speak	KIPL 175:5
truth, but supreme b.	RUSS 255:13
Where b. has no ebb	YEATS 319:9
wildest b. in the world	OWEN 228:6

beaver: And cultivate a b. HUXL 148:6

Beaverbrook: [B.] gets to Heaven he won't

WELLS 308:1

B. is so pleased	BAXT 28:1
mind was that of Lord B.	ATTL 16:5

because: B. ANON 12:3

B. I do not hope to turn again	ELIOT 100:11
B. it's there	MALL 199:13
B. these wings are no longer	ELIOT 100:12
Done b. we are too menny	HARDY 133:6

beckon: The morning b. THOM 292:13

becoming: And b. the men we wanted STEI 284:18

bed: And bounced out of b. MILNE 210:4

'B.,' as the Italian proverb	HUXL 148:17
b. fell on my father	THUR 297:3
b. with me and she said	ALLEN 4:21
b. with my catamite when	BURG 57:16
Every b. is narrow	MILL 208:4
getting in b. with women	ROSS 253:5
[have stayed] in b.	JAC 152:3
I'd love to remain in b.	BERL 40:7
I toward thy b.	FLEC 111:12
it's nicer to lie in b.	LAUD 180:2
kneels at the foot of the b.	MILNE 210:6
Lying in b. would	CHES 71:2
mind is not a b. to be made	AGATE 3:5
Now can we go to b.	COPE 83:5
Out on the lawn I lie in b.	AUDEN 19:4
Pursuing it from b. to bed	PARK 231:1
stay in b. all day	BENC 36:1
That's why I go to b. early	WAUGH 305:16
Up to b.	DE L 91:2
used to go to b. early	PROU 240:7
Who goes to b. with whom	SAY 263:11

bedevilment: Of man's b. and God's HOUS 145:4

bedpost: lose its flavour on the b. ROSE 252:7

bedroom: b. as long as you don't CAMP 61:11

French widow in every b.	HOFF 142:9
Stranger, unless with b. eyes	AUDEN 16:10

The view from my b. of moss-dappled

BETJ 43:10

beds: Minds like b. always made up WILL 312:12

Of solitary b., knew what YEATS 319:14

bedside: I was at the b. making BENN 38:3

bee: butterfly, sting like a b. ALI 4:1

honeysuckle, I am the b. FITZ 110:6

Beecham's Pills: B. are just the thing BEEC 30:4

beef: Boiled b. and carrots COLL 79:6

Where's the b. FREE 116:13

beefsteak: b. and put some red blood CAMP 61:10

beefy: As b. ATS BETJ 43:7

bee-loud: And live alone in the b. glade

YEATS 318:10

been: I've b. things and seen places WEST 309:5

beer: I'm only a b. teetotaller SHAW 268:14

I'm only here for the b.	LEV 186:13
Pints and quarts of Ludlow b.	HOUS 146:16

Beerbohm: [Max B.] STR 288:5

beers: parts other b. cannot reach LOV 191:4

bees: Birds do it, b. do it PORT 236:15

Beethoven: B., and tell Tchaikovsky BERRY 41:9

greatest composers since B. BUCK 57:10

beetles: species of b. on this planet HALD 131:2

before: B. I built a wall I'd ask FROST 118:15

B. we were her people	FROST 119:9
B. you can call him a man	DYLAN 97:3
doing what has been done b.	WHAR 309:21

beg: b. in the streets FRAN 116:6

We cannot b. for pardon MACN 197:9

beget: passions, to get and b. OSLER 227:7

To b. children, nothing SART 261:12

beggar: You big black boundin' b. KIPL 169:1

begin: back to it and b. over FROST 118:9

So you have to b. there	HUXL 149:15
this planet. But let us b.	KENN 163:3
To b. at the beginning	THOM 293:13
When they b. the Beguine	PORT 236:10

beginning: begin at the b. THOM 293:13

classic formula of a b.	LARK 179:8
end is to make a b.	ELIOT 102:5
even the b. of the end	CHUR 73:5
In my b. is my end	ELIOT 101:11
In the b. was the Word	ELIOT 102:15
Is a new b., a raid	ELIOT 101:16
Movies should have a b.	GOD 125:7
that was the b. of fairies	BARR 25:17
What we call the b. is often	ELIOT 102:5

beginnings: start again at your b. KIPL 173:8

begins: b. in the heart of a man CATH 65:1

Church of England b.	PRIE 240:2
It b. in delight and ends	FROST 117:13
man's glory most b. and ends	YEATS 321:2

begotten: Whatever is b. born and dies

YEATS 321:5

beguile: songs b. your pilgrimage FLEC 111:7

Beguine: When they begin the B. PORT 236:10

begun: When the world was b. CART 64:7

behave: difficult to b. like gentlemen MACK 195:9

we must b. accordingly KISS 175:11

behaving: b. in this extraordinary STOP 287:6

behaviour: b. as a relationship between

ROBB 248:6

Christlike in my b. HUXL 148:6

behaviourism: Of course, B. 'works' AUDEN 18:4

behind: hair b. ELIOT 103:12

moment it will be b. me	REGER 245:7
Scratches its innocent b.	AUDEN 17:9
She has no bosom and no b.	SMITH 278:17

being: B. an old maid is like death	FERB 108:5
darkness of mere b.	JUNG 159:15
Never b., but always	SPEN 281:11
non-being by avoiding b.	TILL 297:17
not be worried into b.	FROST 118:2
particular living b.	JUNG 160:3
Belbroughton: B. Road is bonny, and pinkly	
	BETJ 44:1
Belgium: B. put the kibosh on the Kaiser	
	ELL 106:2
B. recovers in full measure	ASQ 14:19
yourself in France and B.	KITC 175:15
belief: b. in the occurrence	MENC 207:3
b. they done the old woman	SHAW 273:16
good grounds for b.	RUSS 256:1
their names: that is b.	SART 261:16
widespread b. is more	RUSS 255:9
believe: b. in life	DUB 96:2
b. in themselves are all	CHES 69:17
b. in the United States	PAGE 228:10
B. it or not	RIPL 248:3
b. that if I don't want	O'HARA 222:20
b. that the War is being	SASS 262:11
b. their wish has been	AUDEN 18:10
b. whether it call itself	JOYCE 158:13
b. with what they don't	UPD 302:12
Do you b. in fairies	BARR 26:1
Do you b. in the life to come	BECK 28:15
I b. in blacks and whites	SMITH 277:9
I b. in Michael Angelo	SHAW 268:23
I do not b. . . . . I know	JUNG 159:17
meaning 'to b. mistakenly'	WITT 315:3
must b. *something*	RUSS 256:1
Never b. in mirrors	OSB 226:9
Oh I b. in yesterday	LENN 185:18
Say quick that you b.	BARR 26:1
says 'I don't b. in fairies'	BARR 25:18
that what we b. is not	BELL 32:10
believed: things that will be b.	TARK 290:12
believer: Like every good b.	HUXL 148:6
bellows: old b. full of angry wind	YEATS 320:9
bells: B. are booming down	BETJ 44:2
b. of Hell go ting-a-ling-a-ling	ANON 10:8
Camberley, heavy with b.	BETJ 43:11
Oh, noisy b., be dumb	HOUS 146:4
silence beat the b.	FLEC 111:9
so floating many b. down	CUMM 86:15
The b. they sound so clear	HOUS 146:3
'Twould ring the b. of Heaven	HODG 142:2
would ring the b. of Ecstasy	GINS 124:12
belly-tension: b. between a man	GIBB 123:13
belong: about *b.* to it as well	WHYTE 311:1
B. TO ANY CLUB THAT WILL	MARX 202:11
have you back where you b.	HERM 139:20
I b. to Glasgow	FYFFE 120:10
so many of my readers b.	CHES 69:14
that is where we really b.	GREE 128:14
yet they b. not to you	GIBR 124:3

belong (*cont.*):	
you must first b.	PHIL 233:11
belongs: into the home—where it b.	HITC 141:4
Where it b.	ALD 3:13
beloved: Cry, the b. country	PATON 232:6
Love the B. Republic deserves	FORS 115:13
suspenders, Best B.	KIPL 171:8
belt: can't see a b. without	ASQ 15:8
belted: I've b. you and flayed you	KIPL 169:3
beneath: b. thy Chariot wheel	HOPE 144:3
I married b. me, all women do	ASTOR 15:11
benediction: movement of clouds in b.	DAY-L 89:7
benefactor: first great b. of our race	TWAIN 301:13
benefit: participation in a common b.	WILS 314:3
benison: The b. of hot water	BROO 54:9
Benn: B. flung himself	LEVIN 186:17
Bennett: essay on [Arnold] B.	LAWR 181:4
bent: b. by the same wintry	THOM 293:4
bereaved: would be b. if snobbery	UST 302:15
bereft: B. of life it rests	CHAP 67:9
Beresford: [Lord Charles B.]	CHUR 73:10
Berkeley: A nightingale sang in B. Square	
	MASC 202:15
Berle: by a man named Fulton B.	ACE 1:5
Berlin: British Ambassador in B.	CHAM 66:7
cross from East to West B.	KOES 176:9
Bernard: B. always had a few prayers	ASHF 14:6
B. muttered Ethel this	ASHF 14:12
Bernhardt: even to please Sarah [B.]	BEER 30:18
beset: b. by hardships	ATK 16:1
beside: I do like to be b. the seaside	GLOV 125:5
Bessie: B. Bighead, hired help	THOM 293:15
best: And so much bad in the b.	ANON 11:8
before you come to the b.	BUTL 59:17
b. defence against	ANON 7:3
b. lack all conviction	YEATS 320:7
b. minds of my generation	GINS 125:1
b. of all possible	BRAD 52:3
b. of all possible worlds	CAB 60:15
b.-seller	SMITH 278:12
b. way out is always through	FROST 119:3
dressed in his b.	EDGAR 98:3
loveliest and the b.	BELL 34:12
Mother knows b.	FERB 108:4
nightingale bills his b.	HARDY 133:8
Send forth the b. ye breed	KIPL 175:8
The b.	FRY 119:20
The best is the b.	QUIL 242:4
The b. things in life are free	DE SY 91:12
we will do our b.	CHUR 72:12
where the b. is like	KIPL 169:8
bestowed: you and not b. on me	EDW 98:11
bestseller: b. was a book which somehow	
	BOOR 49:8
best-sellers: one in all the great b.	PRIT 240:3
bet: he would b. you	TWAIN 300:8
if it was a b., you wouldn't	STOP 287:10
Once b. a pound	DE L 91:4

Bethlehem: Slouches towards B. to be born YEATS 320:8

betray: All things b. thee THOM 295:3
To b., you must first belong PHIL 233:11

betrayal: only defence against b. WILL 312:2
The b. of Ulster, the cynical CAIR 61:4

betrayed: Christ was b. AE 3:3

betraying: b. my country and betraying FORS 115:12

better: b. be changed in ourselves JUNG 160:2
B. by far PUDN 241:7
b. far write twaddle KATH 200:9
b. men than we go out KIPL 171:3
b. part of biography STR 288:4
B. red than dead ANON 7:4
b. than light and safer HASK 136:1
b. to be in chains KAFKA 161:1
b. to be looked over WEST 308:16
b. to die on your feet IBAR 149:17
confide in those who are b. CAMUS 62:13
far b. informed SMITH 277:5
heart may think it knows b. BOWEN 50:13
I am getting b. and better COUÉ 84:4
if they had been any b. CHAN 67:2
If way to the B. there HARDY 134:3
know b. as they grow older SAKI 258:8
music is b. than it sounds NYE 221:12
no b. than you should THOM 293:16
probably b. to have him JOHN 156:3
things I'd been b. without PARK 230:12
when I'm bad, I'm b. WEST 309:6
you can do, I can do b. BERL 40:5
You're a b. man than I am KIPL 169:3

betumble: showers b. the chestnut HARDY 133:8

between: B. my finger and my thumb HEAN 136:8
B. the idea ELIOT 103:4
I would try to get b. STR 288:3
within the sexes than b. COMP 80:3

Beulah: B., peel me a grape WEST 309:4

Bevan: [Aneurin B.] MACM 196:14
[Mr B.] changes his policy CHUR 75:4
on bad terms was Nye B. BEVIN 45:14

bevelled: b. edge of a sunlit mirror ABSE 1:3

Bevin: B. on a major occasion FOOT 113:3
capable hands of Ernest B. ATTL 16:7

bewache: *andern seine Einsamkeit b.* RILKE 248:1

beware: B. of rudely crossing it AUDEN 16:10
B. of the man who does not SHAW 272:17
B. of the man whose god SHAW 272:4
Sisters, I bid you b. KIPL 168:6

bewildered: Bewitched, bothered and b. HART 135:9
unprincipled to the utterly b. CAPP 63:13

bewitched: B., bothered and bewildered HART 135:9
b. for ever who has seen SACK 256:13

bewrapt: B. past knowing to what HARDY 133:14

beyond: b. the obvious facts DOYLE 94:19
But is there anything B. BROO 55:3

bias: suggests forms of b. SCH 264:13

biases: critic is a bundle of b. BALL 24:4
It b. the judgement DOYLE 95:9

Bible: So the B. said HOL 142:11

bible-black: town, starless and b. THOM 293:13

bicicleta: *puede llegar solo en b.* VIER 304:9

Bickleigh: murder his wife that Dr B. ILES 150:10

bicycle: can only arrive on a b. VIER 304:9
like a fish without a b. STEI 285:1
so is a b. repair kit CONN 80:5
Tomorrow the b. races AUDEN 20:10

bicycles: b. over the rocky roadsteads O'BR 222:6

bicyclists: illuminated trouser-clip for b. MORT 214:9

bid: She b. me take love easy YEATS 321:13

big: B. BROTHER IS WATCHING ORW 225:3
b. enough to take away FORD 113:10
B. ones, small ones HEAT 137:1
carry a b. stick ROOS 251:8
he was too b. for them BULM 57:12
I am b. It's the pictures BRAC 51:11
live in houses just as b. SMITH 278:5
victim to a b. lie HITL 141:11
Who's afraid of the b. bad wolf CHUR 72:4
Your feet's too b. BENS 39:2
You used to be b. BRAC 51:11

bigamy: And b., Sir, is a crime MONK 212:3
B. is having one husband ANON 7:5

bigger: A b. bang for a buck ANON 7:6
girls get b. every day LERN 186:5
The b. they FITZ 111:2

biggest: b. electric train WELL 307:13
b. industrial corporation SHAW 267:14
The b. aspidistra in the world HARP 135:5

bighead: 'B.!' 'Dollar lolly' SYKES 289:7

bigotry: B. may be roughly defined CHES 69:11
B. tries to keep truth TAG 290:9

bijoux: *jamais de b. artistiques* COL 79:3

bike: b. and looked for work TEBB 291:2
Mind my b. WARN 305:5

bikini: yellow polkadot b. VANCE 303:4

bill: her nape caught in his b. YEATS 322:6

billabong: swagman camped by a b. PAT 232:5

billboard: A b. lovely as a tree NASH 218:4

billion: And among that b. minus one HUXL 148:18

bills: By children and tradesmen's b. MACN 198:4
Just for paying a few b. LARK 179:6
nightingale b. his best HARDY 133:8
Receipted b. and invitations AUDEN 19:16

Billy: B., in one of his nice GRAH 127:8

bind: are the mortar that b. WELLS 308:9
darkness b. them TOLK 298:1
Go, b. your sons to exile KIPL 175:8

biographer: b. is an artist MACC 193:8

biography: b. can be reckoned by anybody WEST 309:18
b. is ultimately fiction MAL 199:12

biography (cont.):

B. should be written	BALF 24:2
But B. is about Chaps	BENT 39:7
not the better part of b.	STR 288:4
The Art of B.	BENT 39:7

birch: bringing back the b.   VIDAL 304:5
birches: than be a swinger of b.   FROST 118:9
bird: b. can fly   MILNE 210:12

b. that thinks two notes	DAV 88:14
I know why the caged b. sings	ANG 6:10
It's a b.! It's a plane	ANON 7:23
It was only the note of a b.	SIMP 275:10
like a b. on the wing	BOUL 50:9
Like the first b.	FARJ 107:6
She's a b. in a gilded cage	LAMB 177:13
Was a b.; and the song was	SASS 263:5

birds: And listen to the b.   GIBS 124:6

arms, b. in the trees	YEATS 321:5
b. came home to roost	MILL 208:10
B. do it, bees do it	PORT 236:15
B. in their little nests agree	BELL 34:4
b. must find in freedom	SASS 263:5
b., wild flowers	BALD 23:8
two b. setting on a fence	TWAIN 300:8

Birkenhead: B. is very clever but sometimes   ASQ 15:6
Birmingham: B. by way of Beachy Head   CHES 69:5

When Jesus came to B. they	KENN 288:12

birth: And with the trees to newer b.   GREN 129:5

at the b. of his child	ORTON 224:4
B., and copulation, and death	ELIOT 104:6
B. or Death	ELIOT 100:10
cure for b. and death	SANT 260:19
give b. astride of a grave	BECK 29:13
Rainbow gave thee b.	DAV 88:16
task in life is to give b.	FROMM 117:9
There was a B., certainly	ELIOT 100:10

birthday: afternoon of my eighty-first b.   BURG 57:16

Happy b. to you	HILL 140:12
it my b. or am I dying	ASTOR 15:13
My b.	THOM 292:14

birth-rate: Into a rising b.   FRY 119:17
biscuits: synthesis of hyacinths and b.   SAND 259:8
bisexuality: On b.: It immediately doubles   ALLEN 4:12
bishop: b. and has discovered   WAUGH 305:17

b. was feeling rather sea-sick	DOUG 93:11
blonde to make a b. kick	CHAN 66:11
hitting the niece of a b.	ORW 225:14
The sun like a B.'s bottom	ASQ 15:9

Bismarck: theory of politics was B.'s   KEYN 164:11
bit: b. in the corner you can't   BENN 37:10
bitch: old b. gone in the teeth   POUND 238:9

was a dumb son of a b.	TRUM 299:11

bitch-goddess: worship of the b. *success*   JAMES 153:12
bite: miseries, a b. and sup   HEAN 136:12

bites: But if a man b. a dog   BOG 48:10
biting: b. the hand that lays   GOLD 126:9
bits: have swallowed their b.   BETJ 42:10

Look at it, it's all in b.	AYCK 21:10

bitter: Failure makes people b.   MAUG 205:14
bitterness: But the rose's scent is b.   THOM 294:10

must have no hatred or b.	CAV 65:8

black: bit of b. mackintosh   WELBY 307:9

b. blood makes a man coloured	HUGH 147:12
b. face and a different	EDW 98:9
B. is beautiful	ANON 7:7
b. majority rule in Rhodesia	SMITH 277:9
b. people in this country	CARM 63:15
climb b. branches up	FROST 118:9
grace last night two b. owls	BEER 31:17
man, b. as our loss	SITW 276:6
rings b. Cyprus	FLEC 112:3
slow, b., crowblack	THOM 293:13
so long as it's b.	FORD 113:13
That old b. magic	MERC 207:8
The hump that is b. and blue	KIPL 171:12
vehicle the B. Panther Party	NEWT 219:5
Young, gifted and b.	IRV 151:13

blackbird: B. has spoken   FARJ 107:6

Bye bye b.	DIXON 92:10
The b. whistling	STEV 285:11

blackbirds: B. are the cellos   STEV 286:11
Blackburn: Four thousand holes in B.   LENN 185:8
black-eyed: The landlord's b. daughter   NOYES 221:10
blackguard: A b. whose faulty vision   BIER 46:16
Blackpool: seaside place called B.   EDGAR 98:3
Black Power: B. is one of the most legitimate   CARM 63:15
blacksmith: b. like our Norman King   KIPL 174:1
Black Widow: This is the B., death   LOW 192:2
blade: b. struck the water a full   COKE 78:14
Blake: B. saw a treefull of angels   BENÉT 37:1
blame: b. Marx for what was done   BENN 37:3

b. on men but on the bond	SART 261:12
It's the poor wot gets the b.	ANON 10:15
The police were to b.	GRANT 128:1
women never take the b.	BROO 56:2

blancmange: Of cold b. and rhubarb tart   KNOX 176:6
bland: b. lead the bland   GALB 121:2
blanket: right side of the b.   ASHF 14:9
blankets: Of b.; grainy wood   BROO 54:9
blasphemies: All great truths begin as b.   SHAW 267:11
blast-beruffled: In b. plume   HARDY 134:2
blasts: that b. the roots of trees   THOM 293:4
blazed: My body of a sudden b.   YEATS 323:11
blazing: At that Mother got proper b.   EDGAR 98:4
blazon: Their final b., and to prove   LARK 179:16
bleedin: Ain't it all a b. shame   ANON 10:15
bleeding: Beneath the b. hands we feel   ELIOT 101:15

bleeding (*cont.*):
b. to death of time | GRAV 128:8
instead of B, he sings | GARD 122:4
blend: b. of cold chalk soup | AMIS 5:13
blent: b. air all our compulsions | LARK 179:5
bless: B. 'em all! Bless 'em all | HUGH 147:11
was blessèd and could b. | YEATS 323:11
whatever most can b. | YEATS 323:7
blessed: B. Cecilia, appear in visions | AUDEN 20:13
Some b. Hope, whereof he knew | HARDY 134:2
blessing: b. or the greatest curse | BARR 26:3
boon and a b. to men | ANON 11:11
he has one matchless b. | EDW 98:11
simple b. of a rainbow | ABSE 1:3
Thou have paid thy utmost b. | DE L 90:15
blighted: Saying 'Farewell, b. love.' | ANON 10:15
blighty: Take me back to dear old B. | MILLS 209:9
blind: And old Maeonides the b. | FLEC 112:6
And wretched, b., pit ponies | HODG 142:2
b. side of the heart | CHES 68:11
Country of the B. the One-Eyed | WELLS 308:5
eyes were b. with stars | HODG 141:14
religion without science is b. | EINS 99:11
splendid work for the b. | SASS 262:9
though b., throbbing between | ELIOT 105:5
To sit by and see the b. man | WALEY 304:12
blindness: The 'eathen in 'is b. bows | KIPL 174:11
blinds: dusk a drawing-down of b. | OWEN 227:13
I must dust the b. | THOM 293:14
The b. let through the day | HOUS 145:5
blinked: other fellow just b. | RUSK 254:12
bliss: appreciate domestic b. | SANT 260:12
Gives promise of pneumatic b. | ELIOT 103:2
blitz: b. of a boy is Timothy | CAUS 65:5
blizzard: willingly to his death in a b. | ATK 16:1
blonde: b. and beautiful and had | MAIL 199:9
B. Aphrodite rose up excited | AUDEN 20:12
b. to make a bishop kick | CHAN 66:11
blondes: always seem to remember b. | LOOS 190:14
blood: at every jolt, the b. | OWEN 227:14
beefsteak and put some red b. | CAMP 61:10
b. and love without | STOP 287:5
b. be the price of admiralty | KIPL 174:4
b. of their brothers | ZAP 324:8
b. running from the wounded | ROOS 250:6
b.'s a rover | HOUS 145:14
For B., as all men know | HUXL 149:1
I would rather have b. | GREE 128:11
nothing to offer but b. | CHUR 74:3
poison the whole b. | EMPS 106:7
that all that b. was shed | YEATS 321:15
That one drop of Negro b. | HUGH 147:12
there's b. upon her gown | FLEC 112:1
Tiber foaming with much b. | POW 239:10
washed in the b. of the Lamb | LIND 188:8
We be one b., thou | KIPL 171:6
blood-dimmed: The b. tide is loosed | YEATS 320:7
bloodless: unearthly ballet of b. | BRAD 52:4

bloodshed: b. while war is politics | MAO 201:1
bloody: And sang within the b. wood | ELIOT 102:13
got was a b. good hiding | GRANT 128:1
Not b. likely | SHAW 273:18
Sunday, b. Sunday | GILL 124:11
bloom: As well as any b. upon a flower | THOM 294:6
B. ate with relish | JOYCE 159:4
Just now the lilac is in b. | BROO 55:7
look at things in b. | HOUS 145:13
risk of spoiling its b. | CONR 81:8
sort of b. on a woman | BARR 26:11
with b. along the bough | HOUS 145:13
bloomed: stallions, b. that spring | CRANE 85:10
blooming: grand to be b. well dead | SAR 261:3
stones and every b. | KAV 161:12
blossom: almond b. | REED 244:13
b. seethed and departed | BETJ 44:1
blossomed: B. Sarah | BERR 41:10
blots: senses know that absence b. | BOWEN 50:13
blow: A b. in cold blood neither | SHAW 272:3
A sudden b.: the great wings | YEATS 322:6
b. from which he never | MCL 196:10
B. out, you bugles | BROO 54:12
b. up the other half | LAING 177:10
could not b. his nose | CONN 80:17
does not return your b. | SHAW 272:17
For the hardest b. of all | BERL 40:7
I'll sin till I b. up | THOM 294:1
Spring is here, so b. your job | HART 135:12
blowin': b. in the wind | DYLAN 97:3
blowing: And thoughts go b. through | BROO 55:6
b. of a nose | FORS 115:7
by b. up the world | ADAMS 2:13
I'm forever b. bubbles | KENB 162:10
blows: From yon far country b. | HOUS 146:11
It b. so hard, 'twill soon | HOUS 146:8
blub: b. they hav every reason | WILL 311:11
blue: b. films of war | RAE 242:9
B. skies be your coverlet | HART 135:12
brings back b. days and fair | SEEG 265:12
deep b. air | LARK 178:10
Floating in the B. | MILNE 210:8
In his b. gardens | FITZ 110:14
lay off my B. Suede Shoes | PERK 233:3
My b. heaven | WHIT 310:17
those b. remembered hills | HOUS 146:11
University Statutes bound in b. | BETJ 44:7
Where the b. of the night | CROS 86:10
bluebirds: b. over the white cliffs | BURT 58:8
blunder: At so grotesque a b. | BENT 39:14
blundered: Have b. into Paradise | THOM 296:2
Blunt: Anthony B. | MUNN 215:15
blush: And b. at what they hear | KING 167:12
blushes: Animal that B. | TWAIN 300:17
blushing: other people without b. | SHAW 272:18
board: Everything goes by the b. | FAUL 107:10

board (*cont.*):

There wasn't any B., and now	HERB 139:12
boards: I sit upon her B.	DENN 91:11
boast: How many people can b.	BECK 29:11
boat: bonnie b., like a bird	BOUL 50:9
involuntary. They sank my b.	KENN 163:6
boats: b. against the current	FITZ 110:16
b. began to near the winning-post	COKE 78:14
simply messing about in b.	GRAH 127:13
bob: red, robin comes b.	WOODS 317:3
Boche: A well-killed B.	READ 244:3
bodies: b. high at Austerlitz	SAND 260:1
b. no sensible man directly	MACM 197:2
Did but our b. touch	YEATS 323:6
their b. but not their souls	GIBR 124:3
with well-developed b.	FORS 114:1
bodily: That I loved b.	YEATS 323:6
body: b. but sorrow develops	PROU 241:5
b. from the dominion	GOLD 126:3
b. I would throw it out	BECK 29:2
b.'s precious earth	MAS 203:9
inherits my b. and your brains	SHAW 268:6
mind as it is for the b.	HUXL 148:12
My b. of a sudden blazed	YEATS 323:11
O b. swayed to music	YEATS 321:8
Sick in soul and b. both	HODG 142:3
Still carry his b. around	FRY 119:13
The b. dies	STEV 285:10
truly have none in the b.	LAWR 181:17
who had one b. and one heart	DOUG 93:8
with Africa than my own b.	ORTON 224:3
Bog: upon the B. of Allen	JOYCE 157:9
Bognor: Bugger B.	GEOR 123:1
bogus: authentic mammon than a b.	MACN 197:8
bohreens: Bells are booming down the b.	
	BETJ 44:2
boiled: B. beef and carrots	COLL 79:6
parliamentarian is a bag of b. sweets	CRIT 86:6
boko: Bertha's got a bang on the b.	MARS 202:5
bold: He b. as a hawk, she soft	THUR 297:12
with one b. stare	ELIOT 105:6
boldly: b. go where no man has	RODD 249:2
Bolshevism: It is B. run mad	SNOW 279:8
bolt: your thumb: like the b.	REED 244:13
bomb: Ban the b.	ANON 7:1
b. them back into the Stone	LEMAY 184:10
defence against the atom b.	ANON 7:3
bombed: I'm glad we've been b.	THE Q 106:1
protect him from being b.	BALD 23:4
bomber: b. will always get through	BALD 23:4
bombing: b. begins in five minutes	REAG 244:7
bombs: Come, friendly b.	BETJ 42:2
bon: *b. critique est celui qui*	FRAN 116:7
Bonar Law: Unknown Prime Minister [B.]	
	ASQ 15:1
bond: b. between two people	RILKE 248:1
bonds: have slipped the surly b.	MAGEE 198:11
bone: b. to pick with graveyards	BECK 29:1
He knows death to the b.	YEATS 323:5

bone (*cont.*):

rag and a b. and a hank	KIPL 175:7
rag and b. shop	YEATS 320:3
take the muscle from b.	ELIOT 102:10
boneless: years to see the b. wonder	CHUR 73:13
bones: dead men lost their b.	ELIOT 105:1
bonfire: The b. of the vanities	WOLFE 316:15
bonheur: *b. seul est salutaire pour*	PROU 241:5
bonhomie: Overcame his natural *b.*	BENT 39:10
bonjour: *B. tristesse*	ÉLUA 106:6
bonkers: will be stark, raving b.	HAIL 130:14
bonnet: In her latest new b.	DOBS 92:14
bonnie: b. boat, like a bird	BOUL 50:9
bonny: Belbroughton Road is b.	BETJ 44:1
book: A b. which people praise	TWAIN 300:16
any b. should be banned	WEST 309:17
bad b. without showing	AUDEN 18:9
b. becomes a substitute	BURG 58:2
b. is as much of a labour	HUXL 149:6
b. known to him by heart	WOOLF 317:6
b. until I laid it down	MARX 202:10
b. was published I carried	BARR 26:7
b. which somehow sold	BOOR 49:8
b. you would have lying	GRIF 129:8
do not throw this b. about	BELL 32:12
encouragement this b.	WOD 315:16
Hers of the B., the tripled	QUIL 242:5
knocks me out is a b.	SAL 258:11
read one b. in my life	MITF 211:14
take down this b.	YEATS 318:8
when he can read the b.	BEVAN 45:4
write a b. about it	BRAB 51:10
book-keeping: inventor of double-entry b.	
	MULL 215:10
books: b. are alike in that they	HEM 138:2
B. are a load of crap	LARK 179:14
b. are either dreams	LOW 191:9
b. are undeservedly forgotten	AUDEN 18:8
B. are where things	BARN 25:8
b. at the British Museum	BUTL 60:7
b. can not be killed	ROOS 251:4
B. do furnish a room	POW 239:4
B. from Boots' and country	BETJ 44:5
B. make sense of life	BARN 25:8
B. say	BARN 25:8
b. written by the warders	SHAW 273:5
don't have to know about b.	LUML 192:12
Few b. today are forgivable	LAING 177:8
has written all the b.	BUTL 59:21
Have you read any good b.	MURD 216:1
his b. were read	BELL 34:10
I do not like b. I believe	BUTL 60:7
Long b., when read	FORS 114:10
my b. had been any worse	CHAN 67:2
only b. that influence	FORS 115:15
read b. of quotations	CHUR 75:13
study of mankind is b.	HUXL 148:11
The more b. we read	CONN 80:18
write it in the b. of law	JOHN 156:7

boom: groaning as the guns b.   CHES 70:6
booming: Bells are b. down the bohreens
                                  BETJ 44:2
boon: b. and a blessing to men   ANON 11:11
boot: imagine a b. stamping   ORW 225:9
  The b. in the face, the brute   PLATH 235:11
bootboy: b. at Claridges   WOOLF 317:7
Booth: B. died blind and still   LIND 188:9
  B. led boldly   LIND 188:8
Boots: Books from B.' and country BETJ 44:5
  b. and made-up bow ties   SHAR 267:10
  b.—movin' up and down again   KIPL 170:12
  He carries his heart in his b. HERB 139:11
  Hes a gentleman: look at his b. SHAW 273:11
  school without any b.   BULM 57:12
  Their b. are heavy on the floor AUDEN 19:8
  their heart is in their b.   CHES 68:18
  These b. are made for walkin'   HAZL 136:4
booze: with b. until he's fifty   FAUL 108:1
boozes: man who "b." by the company BURT 58:7
Border: Night Mail crossing the B. AUDEN 19:15
borders: I have come to the b. of sleep THOM 294:7
bore: A b. is a man   TAYL 291:1
  b. him in the right way   MAUG 205:2
  B., n. A person who talks   BIER 46:12
  b. one another seems   MENC 206:19
  [Israel Zangwill] is an old b. TREE 298:9
  twelve Americans is a b.   UPD 302:11
  was not only a b.   MUGG 215:8
bored: And said, 'I feel a little b.' CHES 70:15
  because I know that I am b.   JOAD 155:15
  begins there is that b.   MILL 208:13
  Ever to confess you're b.   BERR 41:13
  he b. for England   MUGG 215:8
  virtue of the b.   WAUGH 306:2
  world is quickly b.   MAUG 205:6
boredom: B. is therefore a vital RUSS 255:1
  b. on a large scale   INGE 151:3
  Life is first b., then fear   LARK 179:15
Borgias: B. they had warfare   WELL 307:14
  last night with the B.   BEER 30:11
boring: b. about somebody else's
  friends, is b. We must   BERR 41:12
  Somebody's b. me   THOM 293:6
born: already b. before my lips   MAND 200:2
  Art is b. of humiliation   AUDEN 21:2
  A star is b.   PARK 231:18
  A terrible beauty is b.   YEATS 320:4
  be b. is the best for man   AUDEN 19:2
  been b. to set it right   STR 287:15
  b. an Englishman and remained   BEHAN 31:21
  b. falls into a dream like   CONR 81:14
  b. in 1896 and my parents   ACK 1:10
  b. in a house seventy years   JEANS 154:5
  B. of the sun they travelled   SPEN 281:15
  B. on the fourth of July   COHAN 78:13
  b. with a gift of laughter   SAB 256:10
  b. with your legs apart   ORTON 224:9

born (cont.):
  England because you were b.   SHAW 269:12
  ever b. in a conference   FITZ 110:9
  For we are b. in other's pain   THOM 294:12
  human beings are b. free   ANON 11:16
  I am not yet b.; O fill me   MACN 198:8
  Is not b.   SITW 276:8
  I've been b., and once   ELIOT 104:6
  lad that's b. to be king   BOUL 50:9
  One is not b. a woman   BEAU 89:9
  seeing he had been b.   POUND 238:5
  that he was b. in Australia   SHAW 270:3
  Then surely I was b.   CHES 71:7
  They are b. three thousand   DEL 91:9
  towards Bethlehem to be b.   YEATS 320:8
  We all are b. mad   BECK 29:12
  we extol thee who are b.   BENS 39:4
  we were b. to run   SPR 283:1
borne: b. back ceaselessly   FITZ 110:16
  It is b. in upon me I am   HARE 134:14
borrow: well enough to b. from   BIER 46:4
boshaft: aber b. ist er nicht   EINS 99:5
bosom: She has no b. and no behind
                                  SMITH 278:17
  Thou hast not felt thy b. keep DAV 89:1
boss: b. there is always   MARQ 201:13
bossing: shorter hours and nobody b. ORW 225:17
Boston: And this is good old B.   BOSS 50:3
botanize: Hardy went down to b.   CHES 71:3
botch: I am a sundial, and I make a b. BELL 34:17
bother: I never b. with people I hate HART 135:11
  long words B. me   MILNE 210:10
bothered: Bewitched, b. and bewildered
                                  HART 135:9
Botticelli: B. were alive today he'd UST 302:16
bottle: chair or a hot-water b.   SMITH 278:20
bottles: English have hot-water b. MIKES 207:14
  put new wine into old b.   ATTL 16:4
bottom: at the b. of our garden   FYL 120:11
  forgotten man at the b.   ROOS 250:2
  The sun like a Bishop's b.   ASQ 15:9
  Which will reach the b. first   GRAH 127:9
bottoms: b. of my trousers rolled ELIOT 103:12
  office—with 'b. on seats'   HALL 131:6
bough: Petals on a wet, black b. POUND 238:14
  with bloom along the b.   HOUS 145:13
boughs: easy under the apple b.   THOM 293:1
  than ever on orchard b.   DRIN 95:17
bought: when I've just b. some   BREC 53:8
boum: 'B.' is the sound as far   FORS 115:7
bound: And b. for the same bourn HOUS 146:12
bounds: wider shall thy b. be set BENS 39:4
bouquet: b. is better than the taste POTT 237:11
bouquets: broken Anne of gathering b.
                                  FROST 119:4
bourgeois: b. always bounces up   CONN 80:16
  'B.,' I observed   HOPE 143:10
  b. origin goes through   ORW 225:13
  b. prefers comfort to pleasure HESSE 140:3

bourgeois (*cont.*):

How beastly the b.	LAWR 181:15
small-town b. at heart	NAB 216:12

bourgeoise: The British B. SITW 276:8

bourgeoisie: b. have spoken of themselves

	WAUGH 305:14
The b. in the long run	TROT 299:3
The discreet charm of the b.	BUÑ 57:13

bourn: And bound for the same b. HOUS 146:12

bourne: b. from which no hollingsworth

	MORT 214:8

bourreaux: *elles respectent leurs b.* SART 262:3

boutique: hour ago from this very b. CHAP 67:9

Bovril: B. HARR 135:8

made into B. when she dies ASQ 15:3

bow: elastic-sided boots and made-up b.

	SHAR 267:10
What of the b.	DOYLE 95:15

bowed: B. by the weight of centuries MARK 201:3

bowels: Have molten b.; your vision BOTT 50:5

Till her b. are in heat YEATS 319:10

bower: The b. we shrined to Tennyson

	HARDY 133:7

bowl: b. aloft and intoned JOYCE 158:14

b. with atrabilious	HUXL 149:1
Life is just a b. of cherries	BROWN 56:13

bowler: *I* am the b. and the ball LANG 178:6

bows: b. from which your children GIBR 124:3

box: documents I have to have a b. HOME 143:2

with cash at the b. office HALL 131:6

boxes: Little b. all the same REYN 246:2

boy: A b. brought the white sheet LORCA 190:21

And I were the only b.	GREY 129:6
Being read to by a b.	ELIOT 100:6
b. [Edward VIII] will	GEOR 122:12
b. is that the Chattanooga	GORD 126:14
b. may become President	STEV 286:2
B. Scout demonstrating	LEVIN 186:17
b. somebody ought to have	CAMP 61:9
But what can a poor b. do	JAGG 152:5
electric train set any b.	WELL 307:13
fifteen-year-old b.	ROTH 253:11
I am the Yankee Doodle B.	COHAN 78:13
Mad about the b.	COW 84:12
misfortunes can befall a b.	MAUG 205:17
O are you the b.	CAUS 65:4
parent who could see his b.	LEAC 182:9
seat sat the journeying b.	HARDY 133:14
thing of beauty and a b.	ROWL 253:15
you like your blueeyed b.	CUMM 87:3
You silly twisted b.	MILL 209:1

boyhood: In the lost b. of Judas AE 3:3

boys: b. are not going ROOS 250:10

b. are still there	BAR 27:9
b. in the back rooms	BEAV 28:9
b. in the back room will	LOES 190:6
b. of the old Brigade	WEAT 306:16
B. shout	DAV 88:15
b. were whooping	SERV 267:1

boys (*cont.*):

Not in the hands of b.	OWEN 227:13
send American b. 9 or 10	JOHN 156:12
The lightfoot b. are laid	HOUS 146:14
Till the b. come Home	FORD 113:14
were b. when I was a boy	BELL 35:1

brace: b. ourselves to our duty CHUR 74:7

braces: powerful liquid which rots b. MORT 214:7

Bradford: hat on a B. millionaire ELIOT 105:6

Bradshaw: The vocabulary of 'B.' DOYLE 95:13

brain: Bear of Very Little B. MILNE 210:10

b. attic stocked with all	DOYLE 94:7
B., *n.* An apparatus	BIER 46:13
dry b. in a dry season	ELIOT 100:8
My b.? It's my second favourite	ALLEN 5:4
through which the b. explores	DOUG 93:9
why did He give us a b.	LUCE 192:11

brains: b. of a Minerva BARR 26:17

gentleman said a girl with b.	LOOS 190:13
inherits my body and your b.	SHAW 268:6
rifle and blow out your b.	KIPL 169:5
sometimes his b. go to his head	ASQ 15:6
What good are b. to a man	WOD 315:9
with no b. at all	HERB 139:9

brain-washing: pre-empted it is called b.

	GREER 129:1

branches: black b. up a snow-white FROST 118:9

brandy: B. for the Parson KIPL 172:15

b. of the damned SHAW 271:3

brass: facts when you come to b. ELIOT 104:6

brassière: Art is not a *b.* BARN 25:7

b. is the French BARN 25:7

brave: All that delirium of the b. YEATS 321:15

b. causes left	OSB 226:14
heard her cry, 'you are b.'	GRAH 127:11
Then I was clean and b.	HOUS 146:2

braw: b. bricht moonlicht nicht MORR 214:1

bread: b. and butter that feels MACK 195:10

cursed the b.	ROB 248:9
don't bother about the b.	MILNE 210:9
In eating B. he made no Crumbs	BELL 33:10
The holy b., the food unpriced	MAS 203:10
To eat dusty b.	BOGAN 48:8
your b. and your butter	KIPL 171:1

break: b. a man's spirit is devil's SHAW 268:13

b. the bloody glass you	MACN 197:13
Crack and sometimes b.	ELIOT 101:9
Never give a sucker an even b.	FIEL 109:2
then I b. them right away	SAL 258:12
To b. earth's sleep at all	OWEN 228:2

Breakages: B., Limited, the biggest SHAW 267:14

breakdown: approaching nervous b. RUSS 255:2

Madness need not be all b. LAING 177:12

breakers: like b. cliffward leaping CRANE 85:10

breakfalls: rolls and throws and b. REED 245:1

breakfast: embarrassment and b. BARN 25:5

teatime, clears her b.	ELIOT 105:5
That B., Dinner, Lunch, and Tea	BELL 33:2
want Michael Angelo for b.	TWAIN 301:3

breakfast-time: period in matrimony is b.
HERB 139:16
breaking: You're b. my heart
BERN 41:5
breaks: be there when it b.
CAMP 61:12
Light b. where no sun shines
THOM 293:5
break-through: It may also be b.
LAING 177:12
breast: helpless b. upon his breast
YEATS 322:6
laughed upon his b. to think
YEATS 323:6
breastless: And b. creatures underground
ELIOT 103:1
breasts: b. all perfume yes
JOYCE 159:10
Twye was soaping her b.
EWART 107:1
with wrinkled female b.
ELIOT 105:5
breath: B.'s a ware that will not keep
HOUS 145:14
Out with your own b.
SIMM 275:8
breathless: B., we flung us
BROO 54:8
Bredon: In summertime on B.
HOUS 146:3
'Tis Summer Time on B.
KING 167:12
breed: it's a marvel they can b.
LAWR 180:11
breeding: b. consists in concealing
TWAIN 301:11
Burgundy without any b.
THUR 297:8
cruellest month, b.
ELIOT 104:10
breeds: Chaos often b. life
ADAMS 2:9
Or lesser b. without the Law
KIPL 173:5
breeze: And quivers in the sunny b.
GREN 129:5
comes forth in every b.
DAV 89:1
brevity: B. is the soul of lingerie
PARK 231:15
brew: from the palace has the b.
PAN 229:3
bribe: b. or twist
WOLFE 316:11
b. to make a housekeeper
WILD 311:6
bribes: How many b. he had taken
BENT 39:6
bricht: It's a braw b. moonlicht
MORR 214:1
brick: b. without hitting
ORW 225:14
paved with yellow b.
BAUM 27:13
They threw it a b. at a time
HARG 135:3
brickbats: his backyard with b.
TWAIN 301:8
bricks: That carries the b. to Lewley
BETJ 44:3
bride: all jealousy to the b.
BARR 26:2
b. to be he murmered several
ASHF 14:12
Can ser' him for a b.
MACD 194:11
Never the blushing b.
LEIGH 184:8
Brideshead: B. revisited
WAUGH 305:10
bridesmaid: Why am I always the b.
LEIGH 184:8
bridge: Champagne, and B.
BELL 34:13
Come shooting through the b.
BETJ 43:7
might be going a b. too far
BROW 56:15
See her on the b. at midnight
ANON 10:15
bridges: build b. and throw railroads
BROUN 56:7
poor to sleep under b.
FRAN 116:6
brief: To the end of a b. episode
MERC 207:7
briefest: b. statement imaginable
KAEL 160:5
brigade: boys of the old B.
WEAT 306:16
B. of Guards
MACM 197:2
fire b. and the fire
CHUR 73:12
brigand: I am a b.: I live by robbing
SHAW 271:2
brigands: b. demand your money or
BUTL 59:9
Briggs: Matilda B. . . . was a ship
DOYLE 94:9

bright: Always merry and b.
WIMP 315:1
B.'s disease and he has
PER 232:17
brightness: Leaking the b. away
SPEN 281:13
brilliance: b. is needed in the law
MORT 214:3
brilliant: far less b. pen than mine
BEER 31:5
sound like a b. drawing-room
DE VR 91:13
The dullard's envy of b.
BEER 31:9
brim: b. the bowl with atrabilious
HUXL 149:1
bring: difficult is it to b. it home
DOYLE 94:6
'Tis the courage you b.
WALP 305:1
bringing: B. the cheque and the postal
AUDEN 19:15
b. up a young and inexperienced
JER 155:8
brings: he b. down the whip
LESS 186:8
brink: We walked to the b.
DULL 96:5
brinkmanship: boasting of his b.
STEV 286:4
Britain: B. a fit country for heroes
LLOY 190:1
B. as an independent European
GAIT 121:1
B. has lost an empire
ACH 1:8
B. is about to begin
CHUR 74:7
B. needs is a new social
CALL 61:6
B. will be honoured
HARL 135:4
B. would fight on alone
CHUR 73:1
I'm backing B.
ANON 8:17
Britannia: you've shouted 'Rule B.'
KIPL 168:5
British: B. have the distinction
ATTL 16:4
B. Museum had lost
GERS 123:6
B. nation is unique
CHUR 75:1
B. people have taken
CHUR 72:10
I would rather be B. than just
PAIS 229:2
majority of B. workmen
ZIN 324:12
No sex please — we're B.
MARR 202:4
The B. are coming
WELL 307:12
[the B. Museum]
BEER 30:19
those who aren't B.
BARN 25:5
We are B., thank God
MONT 212:4
you B. soldier
KIPL 169:6
you broke a B. square
KIPL 169:1
Britishers: Which the B. won't wear
COW 84:13
British Museum: at the B. and at Mudie's
BUTL 60:7
Britons: B. were only natives
SELL 266:4
we B. alone use 'Might'
WAUGH 306:12
broad: B. of Church
BETJ 43:6
By brooks too b. for leaping
HOUS 146:14
She's the B. and I'm the High
SPR 282:16
broadcasters: important to be left to the b.
BENN 37:5
broadcasting: B. is really too important
BENN 37:5
broadened: has b. into a brotherhood
JOHN 156:8
Broadway: Give my regards to B.
COHAN 78:11
sinners on this part of B.
RUNY 254:9
broccoli: It's b., dear
WHITE 309:23
broke: If it ain't b., don't
LANCE 178:3
broken: baying for b. glass
WAUGH 305:11
b. Anne of gathering bouquets
FROST 119:4
b. by their passing feet
YEATS 321:10
b. the lock and splintered
AUDEN 19:8

broken (*cont.*):

Don't tell me peace has b.	BREC 53:8
He liked the Sound of B. Glass	BELL 34:3
mould. Can it be b.	JENK 154:11
peace has been b. anywhere	ROOS 250:8
whose tongues were all b.	DYLAN 97:5

broken-hearted: b. woman tends the grave

	HAYES 136:3
broker: b. is a man who takes	WOOL 317:13
Bronx: B. is up but the Battery's	COMD 79:10
bronze: B. cloud	FREE 116:14
Stone, b., stone	ELIOT 104:9
brook: b. was troubled for new	MAS 203:13
Fish say, in the Eternal B.	BROO 55:5
brooks: By b. too broad for leaping	HOUS 146:14
The b. were frozen	AUDEN 17:3
brothels: bars and b. of Westminster	LIV 189:4
brother: be the white man's b.	KING 166:9
BIG B. IS WATCHING YOU	ORW 225:3
B. can you spare a dime	HARB 132:12
B., thy tail hangs down behind	KIPL 171:7
I am the darker b.	HUGH 147:13
My B., good morning	BELL 35:9
stick more close than a b.	KIPL 173:10
Strong b. in God and last	BELL 34:7
brotherhood: b. of man is evoked	LAING 177:10
has broadened into a b.	JOHN 156:8
brother-in-law: man's brother, not his b.	
	KING 166:9
brotherly: Switzerland they had b.	WELL 307:14
brothers: together as b. or perish	KING 167:6
brought: government should be b.	MACM 196:16
great party is not to be b.	HAIL 130:13
He b. death into the world	TWAIN 301:13
brow: hope to meet my Maker b.	CORN 83:10
Slowly her white b. among	FREE 116:14
brown: b. fog of a winter dawn	ELIOT 104:14
old b. hills	MAS 204:2
quick b. fox jumps over	ANON 10:12
strong b. god	ELIOT 101:10
Browning: Hang it all, Robert B.	POUND 238:2
safety-catch of my B.	JOHST 157:2
brows: The pallor of girls' b.	OWEN 227:13
browsing: b. and sluicing and cheery	WOD 316:6
Bruce: would have made Adam and B.	BRY 57:2
Bruckner: [by B.]	BEEC 29:19
bruit: *Dont meurt le b. parmi le vent*	APOL 12:16
brush: And never b. their hair	BELL 32:14
brutal: grown b. from the fare	YEATS 318:6
brute: b. and blackguard made	HOUS 144:13
B. heart of a brute like you	PLATH 235:11
should be treated as a b.	EDW 98:9
brutes: Exterminate all the b.	CONR 81:11
bubbles: I'm forever blowing b.	KENB 162:10
buck: A bigger bang for a b.	ANON 7:6
day they pass the b.	AYRES 21:14
says 'The b. stops here'	TRUM 299:12
bucket: past is a b. of ashes	SAND 259:11

Buckingham: They're changing guard at B.

	MILNE 209:15
Buffalo Bill: B.'s	CUMM 87:3
bugger: B. Bognor	GEOR 123:1
buggers: b. can't be choosers	BOWRA 51:7
bugler: Is to hear the b. call	BERL 40:7
bugles: are the b. blowin'	KIPL 168:8
Blow out, you b., over	BROO 54:12
b. calling for them from	OWEN 227:13
bugs: lugage rack and new b.	WILL 311:11
build: And so easy to b.	IBSEN 149:19
b. from the bottom up	ROOS 250:2
b. their first buildings	WRIG 317:18
building: it's a very old b.	OSB 226:6
built: Before I b. a wall I'd	FROST 118:15
frocks are b. in Paris	SAKI 257:15
It is not what they b.	FENT 108:3
built-in: good writer is a b.	HEM 138:11
bull: b. by both horns he kissed	ASHF 14:12
b. moose and you can use	ROOS 252:2
See an old unhappy b.	HODG 142:3
bullet: b. in ten thousand kills	SPEN 282:1
b. may just as well have	COLL 79:9
Faster than a speeding b.	ANON 7:23
put a b. through his head	ROB 248:9
bullets: With b. made of platinum	BELL 32:16
bullshit: The rest is b. and you	SCOR 265:4
bum: Indicat Motorem B.	GODL 125:8
instead of a b.	SCH 264:11
bumpy: it's going to be a b.	MANK 200:4
bunch: b. of the boys were whooping	SERV 267:1
none better left on the b.	BUTL 59:17
bungler: arts of peace Man is a b.	SHAW 271:7
bunk: History is more or less b.	FORD 113:12
bunny: I am a b. rabbit	AYRES 21:14
buns: bears might come with b.	ISH 151:14
Bunter: Shut up, B.	RICH 247:4
burden: b. of responsibility	EDW 98:11
I lay down my b.	EDW 98:11
sometimes break, under the b.	ELIOT 101:9
Take up the White Man's b.	KIPL 175:8
bureaucrats: Guidelines for b.	BOREN 49:9
Burgundies: B. is that I hate them	AMIS 5:13
burgundy: B. without any breeding	THUR 297:8
burial: its b., except	MACM 196:14
buried: B. beneath some snow-deep Alps	
	ELIOT 100:5
Burlington: I'm B. Bertie	HARG 135:2
Burma: There's a B. girl a-settin'	KIPL 169:6
burn: age should b. and rave	THOM 292:11
another Troy for her to b.	YEATS 319:2
B., baby, burn	ANON 7:8
Hurry! We b.	DAY-L 89:5
burned: House, were B.	BELL 33:5
burning: A smell of b. fills	BELL 35:7
b. of the leaves	BINY 47:3
b. roof and tower	YEATS 322:7
hipsters b. for the ancient	GINS 125:1
Is Paris b.	HITL 141:10

burning (*cont.*):

Keep the Home-fires b.	FORD 113:14

burnish'd: Furnish'd and b. by Aldershot

	BETJ 43:9
burnished: sat in, like a b. throne	ELIOT 104:15
Burns: it's a poem by Robert B.	SAL 258:15
burnt: ash the B. roses leave	ELIOT 102:2
b. at the stake as witches	SMITH 278:19
got myself b. or hanged	JER 155:6

burnt-out: The b. ends of smoky days

	ELIOT 103:13
burst: suddenly b. out singing	SASS 263:5
bursting: round me like a b. sea	THOM 295:15
Burton: Or why was B. built on Trent	
	HOUS 146:15
bury: b. my body in Sussex grass	BENÉT 36:17
B. my heart at Wounded Knee	BENÉT 36:17
The physician can b.	WRIG 317:18
want one to b. my sister	MITF 211:10
We will b. you	KHR 166:2
bus: Can it be a Motor B.	GODL 125:8
he missed the b.	CHAM 66:8
I'm not even a b., I'm a tram	HARE 134:14
She tumbled off a b.	GRAH 127:7
stepping in front of a b.	OSB 226:14
buses: more time on the b.	STR 288:9
business: American people is b.	COOL 82:13
any other decent b. man	LEWIS 187:13
B. carried on as usual	CHUR 72:10
b. is the most fascinating	WARH 305:3
b. without really trying	MEAD 206:5
had attended b. college	ADE 2:15
It is the b. of the wealthy man	BELL 34:1
Liberty is always unfinished b.	ANON 9:14
making everything his b.	SOLZ 279:9
Murder is a serious b.	ILES 150:10
no b. like show business	BERL 40:10
That's no b. That's social	BRAC 51:14
The growth of a large b.	ROCK 248:13
we can do b. together	THAT 292:2
woman's b. to get married	SHAW 271:1
businessman: He's a b.	PUZO 241:8
businessmen: My message to the b.	CURR 87:11
bust: Uncorseted, her friendly b.	ELIOT 103:2
bustin': June is b. out all over	HAMM 131:10
busy: But I am too b. thinking	SITW 276:3
Little man, you've had a b. day	SIGL 275:3
But: And If and Perhaps and B.	ELIOT 101:4
butcher: b. but his mother was	ASHF 14:9
Hog B. for the World	SAND 259:9
butchers: become policemen or b.	CONN 80:7
butler: on the b.'s upper slopes	WOD 316:9
The b. did it	ANON 7:9
butlers: In my opinion, B. ought	BELL 33:6
butter: B., eh	MILNE 210:4
Can you tell Stork from b.	ANON 7:12
Could we have some b.	MILNE 210:3
like a little bit of b.	MILNE 210:5
rather have b. or guns	GOER 125:10

butter (*cont.*):

We can manage without b.	GOEB 125:9
butterfly: Float like a b.	ALI 4:1
The b. upon the road	KIPL 170:6
buttocks: The gorgeous b. of the ape	HUXL 148:19
button: By each b., hook, and lace	LOW 191:7
job of sewing on a b.	BROUN 56:7
buttons: b. off an' cut his stripes	KIPL 168:9
butty: He's an oul' b. o' mine	O'CAS 222:7
buy: b. a single vote more	KENN 162:16
b. back my introduction	PER 233:1
shall b. it like an honest	NORT 221:5
Stop me and b. one	RODD 249:1
won't you b. me a Mercedes	JOPL 157:6
buys: public b. its opinions	BUTL 60:4
buzz: B.! Buzz! Buzz	MILNE 210:7
by: B.	MCC 194:4
bye: B. bye blackbird	DIXON 92:10
Byron: B.!—he would be all forgotten	BEER 31:20
Byronic: think all poets were B.	COPE 83:4
Byzantium: And the Soldan of B.	CHES 70:5
To the holy city of B.	YEATS 321:7

C

cab: said, 'Get me a c.'	BENC 36:8
cabbage: c. with a college education	
	TWAIN 301:14
cabin: small c. build there	YEATS 318:10
Cabinet: another to mislead the C.	ASQ 14:18
C. ministers are educated	BENN 39:1
Cabots: Lowells talk to the C.	BOSS 50:3
cad: Flopshus C., an Outrageous	KIPL 175:2
cadence: reverent c. and subtle psalm	
	AUDEN 20:12
Cadogan: One-eighty-nine C. Square	BETJ 44:5
Caesar: Our master C. is in the tent	YEATS 320:2
Caesars: worship the C. and Napoleons	
	HUXL 148:14
café: heart in ev'ry street c.	HAMM 131:11
cage: He keeps a lady in a c.	CHES 68:17
natural to us than a c.	SHAW 269:5
We cannot c. the minute	MACN 197:9
caged: I know why the c. bird sings	ANG 6:10
cake: had soaked a morsel of c.	PROU 240:8
peel picked out of a c.	RAL 242:14
calamities: C. are of two kinds	BIER 46:14
calamity: Oh, c.	HARE 135:1
calculating: Party is a desiccated c.	BEVAN 44:11
calculations: C. that look but casual	YEATS 319:14
calf: c. to share the enthusiasm	SAKI 257:13
The lion and the c. shall	ALLEN 4:9
Caliban: C. casts out Ariel	POUND 238:8
California: C. is a fine place to live	ALLEN 4:3
From C. to the New York Island	GUTH 130:10
call: All, is Labour's C.	JAY 154:3
C. me Lady Hamilton	RIC 246:14

call (*cont.*):

C. me madam	LIND 188:7
C. no man foe, but never	BENS 39:5
c. of the running tide	MAS 203:15
do you c. that a rose	AYCK 21:10
Dunno what to c. him	STAN 283:8
Let's c. the whole thing off	GERS 123:9
May I c. you 338	COW 84:10
The c. of the wild	LOND 190:9
When you c. me	WIST 315:2
Whitehall as 'C. Me God'	SAMP 259:3
Work is the c.	MORR 213:15

called: if I c. the wrong number — THUR 297:9

calling: Followed their mercenary c. — HOUS 145:7

Germany c.! Germany calling — JOYCE 159:12

callisthenics: simply c. with words — PARK 231:6

callous: C. — SELL 266:7

calls: If anybody c. — BENT 39:8

calm: c. on the lap of the Line — KIPL 170:8

there we sit in peaceful c. — HUXL 149:2

calves: peculiarly susceptible to c. — HUXL 149:8

Camberley: Into nine-o'clock C. — BETJ 43:11

Cambridge: C. ladies who live in furnished — CUMM 87:4

C. theatre were eating	RAPH 243:3
dons from C. or junior	AMIS 5:13
For C. people rarely smile	BROO 55:10
gently back at Oxford or C.	BEER 30:16

Cambridgeshire: And C., of all England — BROO 55:10

came: I c. through and I shall — MAC 193:5

cameelious: C. hump — KIPL 171:12

camel: c. is a horse designed — ANON 7:10

Take my c., dear	MAC 193:6
The c. has a single hump	NASH 217:9
The C.'s hump is an ugly lump	KIPL 171:11

camera: c. makes everyone a tourist — SONT 280:10

I am a c. with its shutter — ISH 151:15

campaigning: years organizing and c. — BROD 54:2

can: C. I do you now, sir — KAV 162:4

C. you tell Stork from butter	ANON 7:12
Gizza job. . . . I c. do	BLEA 47:11
He who c., does. He	SHAW 271:21
Pass me the c., lad	HOUS 144:11
talent which does what it c.	BAR 25:1

Canadian: [Definition of a C.:] — BERT 41:15

canal: swimming along in the old c. — BETJ 44:3

Canalettos: Then the C. go — MACM 197:7

cancer: c. of human history — SONT 280:13

Obscene as c., bitter — OWEN 227:14

candidate: Republican c. for President — SIMP 275:11

candidates: when c. appeal — ADAMS 2:3

candle: A c. on your cake — SIMM 275:8

As a white c.	CAMP 61:8
c. in that great turnip	CHUR 73:4
c. than curse the darkness	STEV 286:5
My c. burns at both ends	MILL 207:17

candles: c. may be held to speed — OWEN 227:13

candles (*cont.*):

The c. burn their sockets — HOUS 145:5

candy: C. — NASH 218:8

canna: c. expect to be baith grand — BARR 25:15

cannibal: progress if a c. uses knife — LEC 183:12

cannon: then the c., and he comes — CHES 70:6

cannot: And c. come again — HOUS 146:11

He who c., teaches — SHAW 271:21

canoe: how to make love in a c. — BERT 41:15

cant: c. about the common interests — ATK 15:16

can't: When you c. find your way home — COLL 79:5

capable: am c. of higher things — FORS 114:5

c. of being humiliated — AUDEN 21:2

capacities: with it than his own c. — BEEC 29:23

capacity: c. for getting its possessors — BUTL 59:20

infinite c. for taking	HUXL 149:14
which is c. to act wisely	WHIT 310:8

capital: c. mistake to theorize — DOYLE 95:9

interests of c. and labour	ATK 15:16
lived long in a great c.	FORS 114:11

capitalism: c. of the lower classes — SPEN 282:4

definition of c. I would say	HAMP 132:7
I think that C., wisely	KEYN 165:2
peaceful extermination of c.	ZIN 324:12
talk about c. and communism	BAR 27:10
unacceptable face of c.	HEATH 136:14
War is c. with the gloves	STOP 287:12

capitalist: forces of a c. society — NEHRU 219:2

slave of c. society — CONN 81:7

captain: The c. is in his bunk — SHAW 269:12

captains: Star c. glow — FLEC 112:2

The c. and the kings depart	KIPL 173:3
The c. and the kings depart	KNOX 176:6

car: afford to keep a motor c. — SHAW 267:13

can't drive the c.	TYNAN 302:7
c. has become an article	MCL 196:11
c. has become the carapace	MCL 196:12
c. was poetry and tragedy	LEWIS 187:12
elegant c.	BELL 35:11

carapace: The car has become the c. — MCL 196:12

caravan: Put up your c. — HODG 141:12

carbon: only because the c. atom — JEANS 154:6

carborundum: Nil c. illegitimi. — ANON 10:2

carbuncle: like a monstrous c. — CHAR 68:3

carbuncles: c. of concrete have erupted — SPEN 281:9

carbuncular: He, the young man c., arrives — ELIOT 105:6

card: c. to play for Honours — BENN 39:1

card-indexes: Our memories are c. consulted — CONN 81:6

cards: Never play c. with a man — ALGR 3:14

With a wicked pack of c. — ELIOT 104:13

care: c. if you criticize us — OWEN 227:11

C. of his Mother	MILNE 210:1
c. what you say about me	COHAN 78:10
c. where the water goes	CHES 68:15
don't c. too much for money	LENN 185:7

care (*cont.*):
I didn't c. who knew	CHAN 66:10
I find that I c. less and less	SAY 263:11
Logic must take c. of itself	WITT 315:6
she don't c.	LENN 185:14
taken better c. of myself	BLAKE 47:9
Teach us to c. and not to care	ELIOT 100:12
The public will take c.	SULZ 289:1

cared: Suppose everybody c. enough — BUCH 57:8
career: nothing in his long c. — ANON 12:5
our c. and our triumph	VANZ 303:7
which might damage his c.	BARR 26:14

careless: C. talk costs lives — ANON 7:13
carelessness: With carefullest c. — BETJ 43:9
Carew: tends the grave of Mad C. — HAYES 136:3
cargo: c. boats that sail — KIPL 174:6
With a c. of ivory	MAS 202:16

cargoes: Deep c. of gigantic tomes — BELL 35:6
caricatures: c. are the most penetrating

HUXL 149:9
Carlyle: [Thomas C.] — TWAIN 301:8
very good of God to let C.	BUTL 59:10

carnation: nude with a c. up my nose — MCK 196:1
Carnegie: wisecrack that played C. — LEV 186:10
Carnot: Deity but accepted C.'s — WELLS 308:4
carol: chimes ring out with a c. — BOND 49:2
Carolina: have your ham'n eggs in C.

GORD 126:14
Caroline: [Queen C. of Brunswick] — BEER 31:3
carollings: So little cause for c. — HARDY 134:2
car park: c. till twenty to one — BETJ 43:12
car-park: c. the dance has begun — BETJ 43:11
carpenter: I said to the c. — CART 64:8
carpet: c. with their shoes — YEATS 322:4
figure in the c.	JAMES 152:15
Mistake themselves for c. bags	RAL 242:12

carried: And c. half-way home, or near

HOUS 146:16
carrots: Boiled beef and c. — COLL 79:6
carry: c. his body around — FRY 119:13
C. the lad that's born	BOUL 50:9
conviction and the will to c.	LIPP 189:1
Speak softly and c. a big	ROOS 251:8

cars: c. today are almost — BART 27:5
they're crazy about c.	SAL 258:14

casbah: Come with me to the C. — BOYER 51:9
case: A suitable c. for treatment — MERC 207:5
c. a certain little lady	GAY 122:7
everything that is the c.	WITT 315:5
heard one side of the c.	BUTL 59:21
over I would make a c.	BALD 23:6
working on a c. of Scotch	BENC 36:11

Casement: The ghost of Roger C. — YEATS 321:1
cash: And the C. that goes therewith — CHES 70:9
from hand to hand of c.	SICK 275:2
she needs good c.	TUCK 300:2
therefore pay you c. to go away	KIPL 170:16

cask: allowed to mature in the c. — O'FAO 222:17
Cassidy: C.'s hanging hill — KAV 161:13

Cassiopeia: C. was over — KAV 161:13
cast: C. *a cold eye* — YEATS 319:13
c. the first rock	LOOS 190:20
C. your mind on other days	YEATS 319:12

castles: C. in the air — IBSEN 149:19
castrati: *dreamed* of reviving the c. — REED 245:5
casualty: Truth is the first c. — PONS 236:3
cat: C. — NASH 217:10
c. and a lie	TWAIN 301:15
C. of such deceitfulness	ELIOT 102:12
c. with bright green eyes	MONRO 212:4
cosmic Cheshire c.	HUXL 149:16
My c. and i just smile	MCG 195:3
Oh I am a c. that likes	SMITH 278:21
The umpire, the pavilion c.	LANG 178:6
victory of a c. on a hot	WILL 312:4
which way the c. is jumping	SULZ 289:1
wild animals was the C.	KIPL 172:4

cataclysm: been unaltered in the c. — CHUR 73:11
their c. but one poor Noah	HUXL 148:18

catalogue: lamentable c. of human crime

CHUR 74:4
read a time-table or a c.	MAUG 205:13

catalyst: c. that sparks the revolution — DURY 97:1
catamite: I was in bed with my c. — BURG 57:16
catastrophe: between education and c.

WELLS 308:10
toward unparalleled c.	EINS 99:8

Catch: some catch, that C.-22 — HELL 137:4
catcher: c. in the rye and all — SAL 258:15
catching: The tune is c. and will — AUDEN 19:2
category-habits: replacement of c. — RYLE 256:8
caterpillar: world for a moss or a c. — BARB 24:15
caterpillars: Fat c. drift around — BROO 55:5
cathédrales: *des grandes c. gothiques* — BART 27:5
cathedrals: Gothic c. — BART 27:5
Catherine: child of Karl Marx and C. — ATTL 16:8
Catholic: C. always a Catholic — WILS 312:18
C. and the Communist	ORW 225:10
currently did not attend was C.	AMIS 6:3
Gentlemen, I am a C.	BELL 33:12
I was a fire-breathing C. C.O	LOW 191:13
now quite lawful for a C.	MENC 206:18
Once a C. always a Catholic	O'MAL 223:5
Roman C. Church	MACM 197:2
She had once been a C.	FITZ 110:18

catholics: C. and Communists have committed

GREE 128:11
Hitler attacked the C.	NIEM 219:12

cats: C. and monkeys — JAMES 152:18
C., no less liquid	TESS 291:6
C. seem to go on the principle	KRUT 177:2
How C. Spend their Time	BARB 24:16
melodious c. under the moon	HUXL 148:9
The greater c. with golden eyes	SACK 256:12
where c. are cats	MARQ 201:10

cattle: Actors are c. — HITC 141:5
The c. rise and listen	KING 167:12

cattle (*cont.*):

these who die as c. OWEN 227:13

Catullus: Did their C. walk that way YEATS 322:4

caught: And c. our youth, and wakened BROO 54:10

But the fools c. it YEATS 322:1

inferno had c. up with me BELL 35:11

cauliflower: c. is nothing but cabbage TWAIN 301:14

cause: c. as the world has ever BROUN 56:5

c. is he identified BENN 38:6

c. may be inconvenient BENN 38:15

c. of cheering us all up BENN 38:6

do some work for the c. BUCH 57:5

Rebel without a c. LIND 188:5

So little c. for carollings HARDY 134:2

statistics that some c. AUDEN 20:9

causes: brave c. left OSB 226:14

c. that they represent FORS 115:15

I hate the idea of c. FORS 115:12

caustic: voice which was more c. ROLFE 249:17

caution: c. in love is perhaps RUSS 255:6

Cavaliers: Struggle between the C. SELL 266:8

cave: burst stomach like a c. DOUG 93:8

The echo in a Marabar c. FORS 115:7

cease: War will c. when men refuse ANON 11:21

ceased: It has c. CHAP 67:9

Cecil: No, after you, C. KAV 162:3

Cecilia: Blessed C., appear in visions AUDEN 20:13

ceiling: enough to draw on the c. CHES 71:2

lines of the c. ÉLUA 106:6

celebrate: Unfortunately poetry cannot c. AUDEN 18:12

celebrity: c. is a person who is known BOOR 49:7

mathematical c. DOYLE 94:8

celestially: And mud, c. fair BROO 55:5

cell: c. whose walls are mirrors O'NEI 223:8

cello: [the c.] CAS 64:9

cellos: c. of the deep farms STEV 286:11

cells: These little grey c. CHR 72:2

Celtic: enchanted woods of C. antiquity KEYN 165:3

Cemetery: Help me down C. Road LARK 179:10

censor: c. one's own thoughts WALEY 304:12

censorship: extreme form of c. SHAW 274:5

cent: What he did with every c. FROST 118:5

centre: c. cannot hold YEATS 320:7

dead c. of middle age ADAMS 2:4

left and is now in the c. MOSL 214:11

Mon c. cède, ma droite FOCH 112:13

My c. is giving way FOCH 112:13

real c. of the household SHAW 269:11

cents: Today I feel like thirty c. ADE 2:19

centuries: Through what wild c. DE L 90:8

century: born in this c., tempered KENN 163:8

c. of the common man WALL 304:16

C. was the size of each MAIL 199:8

next c. as well as this THAT 291:10

cerebration: The deep well of unconscious c. JAMES 152:9

ceremony: The c. of innocence is drowned YEATS 320:7

certain: case a c. little lady GAY 122:7

my case of which I'm c. ANKA 6:11

one thing is c. too MAC 195:7

you can be c. of improving HUXL 149:15

certainty: And C.? and Quiet kind BROO 56:1

The c. of power DAY-L 89:6

We for a c. are not the first HOUS 144:13

cesspit: c. of their own making AND 6:8

cesspool: that great c. DOYLE 95:8

Cetacean: Noble and generous C. KIPL 171:9

Chablis: C. or Pouilly Fuissé AMIS 5:13

chaff: that the c. is printed HUBB 147:4

chagrin: *c. qui développe les forces* PROU 241:5

chain: tuppence for your old watch c. COLL 79:7

chains: be in c. than to be free KAFKA 161:1

chair: gain a c. of literature ALGR 3:16

The C. she sat in, like ELIOT 104:15

chaise-longue: hurly-burly of the c. CAMP 61:13

Chaliapin: C. is from my voice BENT 39:15

chalice: The c. from the palace PAN 229:3

chalk: c. cliffs of Dover BALD 23:5

challenge: times of c. and controversy KING 167:1

chamber: C. selected by the Whips FOOT 113:4

into the conference c. BEVAN 45:2

Chamberlain: C. NIC 219:7

Listening to a speech by C. BEVAN 44:10

[Neville C.] BEVAN 45:3

[Neville C.] CHUR 74:2

chambers: Steel c., late the pyres HARDY 134:4

champagne: C., and Bridge BELL 34:13

c. and the stars FITZ 110:14

I get no kick from c. PORT 236:12

It's like c. or high heels BENN 38:15

not a c. teetotaller SHAW 268:14

Champmédy: You may bury my tongue at C. BENÉT 36:17

chance: c. with one of the lords LAWR 180:10

Give peace a c. LENN 185:9

Chancellor: been listening to the C. WILS 313:3

talk with the German C. CHAM 66:5

chances: have to take c. for peace DULL 96:5

change: architecture, a c. of heart AUDEN 20:4

c. the possibilities LEAV 183:5

c. we think we see in life FROST 119:2

gradualness of our scheme of c. WEBB 307:3

leave it to a torrent of c. CHES 70:3

The wind of c. is blowing MACM 197:3

things will have to c. LAMP 178:1

Unionist when you want to c. BEVIN 45:16

wish to c. in the child JUNG 160:2

changed: Are changed, c. utterly YEATS 320:6

Are c. upon the blue guitar STEV 285:12

piece of music that c. SCHN 264:8

power of the atom has c. EINS 99:8

changes: c. in the deluge CHUR 73:11

changes (*cont.*):
Mr Norris c. trains ISH 151:16
changing: c. a typewriter ribbon BENC 36:4
c. guard at Buckingham MILNE 209:15
one fixed point in a c. DOYLE 94:13
stress on not c. one's mind MAUG 205:9
channel: C. in the mad March days MAS 203:1
channels: That through the c. of the ear
AUDEN 19:6
chaos: C. often breeds life ADAMS 2:9
c. remembered in tranquillity THUR 297:16
In c. of vacancy shone DE L 90:14
means of overcoming c. RICH 247:5
stillness in the midst of c. BELL 35:13
view there is mounting c. CALL 61:7
chap: second eleven sort of c. BARR 25:12
chapel: secluded c. ELIOT 102:6
Chapman: C. & Hall BENT 39:13
chaps: But Biography is about C. BENT 39:7
chapter: now to write the next c. JOHN 156:7
character: attempts to mould a child's c.
SHAW 271:20
c. but the determination JAMES 153:5
c. by his way of eating REAG 244:5
enormous lack of c. LEV 186:11
keep a c. of their own BOWEN 51:2
man's c. is the health CONN 81:3
Miss, I knows an undesirable c. FRY 120:2
Simplicity of c. is no MORL 213:11
suffering ennobles the c. MAUG 205:7
characteristic: c. sounds of the English
GILL 124:10
characters: Six c. in search of an author PIR 235:1
When the c. are alive PIR 235:2
charge: I'm in c. FORS 116:3
One thing alone I c. you DUB 96:2
When in c., ponder BOREN 49:9
charging: marching, c. feet, oh JAGG 152:5
Charing Cross: Pitched betwixt Heaven and C.
THOM 296:13
chariot: beneath thy C. wheel HOPE 144:3
Charles: C. II was always very merry SELL 266:9
It was used by C. the First COW 85:8
charm: But some have c. for none BARR 26:11
C. . . . it's a sort of bloom BARR 26:11
Completing the c. ELIOT 101:19
discreet c. of the bourgeoisie BUÑ 57:13
Museum had lost its c. GERS 123:6
You know what c. CAMUS 62:11
charme: *Vous savez ce qu'est le c.* CAMUS 62:11
charming: c. people have something CONN 80:10
C. spot BECK 29:6
Charrington: smudge the ledger, C. BETJ 43:8
chart: enigma of the fever c. ELIOT 101:15
Chartreuse: C. can never really die SAKI 257:12
chase: But with unhurrying c. THOM 295:3
Still with unhurrying c. THOM 295:8
chasing: c. Americans out TWAIN 301:8
he was always c. Rimbauds PARK 230:4

chasm: There exists a great c. BERL 40:13
chassis: worl's in a state o' c. O'CAS 222:8
chaste: like a c. whore MUGG 215:6
men ask, Are Barmaids C. MAS 203:8
chastity: C.—the most unnatural HUXL 148:15
chat: [Trotsky] and had a c. ROG 249:13
Chattanooga: Pardon me boy is that the C.
GORD 126:14
Chatterley: Between the end of the C. ban
LARK 179:3
book [*Lady C.'s Lover . . .*] GRIF 129:8
cheap: how potent c. music COW 85:3
cheaper: c. seats clap your hands LENN 185:3
c. to do this than to keep BUTL 60:4
cheat: so monosyllabic as to c. FRY 120:1
The sweet c. gone DE L 90:14
cheating: games without actually c. POTT 237:14
period of c. between BIER 46:24
Checkers: named it C. And you know
NIXON 220:10
cheeks: A girl whose c. are covered NASH 218:7
cheer: C. up, curly you'll soon WIMP 315:1
C. up! the worst is yet to come JOHN 156:16
cheerful: so c. as keeps me going KAV 162:8
cheeriness: Oh! Chintzy, Chintzy c. BETJ 43:3
cheering: had no need for c. dreams CHUR 76:5
with the great cause of c. BENN 38:6
cheerio: it s c. MARQ 201:11
cheers: 3 C. for Pooh MILNE 211:1
Two c. for Democracy FORS 115:13
cheese: eggs, apples, and c. KIPL 171:1
has 246 varieties of c. DE G 90:4
like some valley c. AUDEN 18:5
such thing as a *bad* c. FAD 107:4
cheesed: humanity soon had me c. BENN 38:2
chefs-d: *au milieu des c.'œuvre* FRAN 116:7
Chekhov: C. saw in our failure PRIT 240:4
chemistry: c. and machinery all SHAW 271:6
cheque: Bringing the c. and the postal
AUDEN 19:15
statement is like a c. POUND 237:16
cherished: My no longer c. MILL 208:5
cheroot: whackin' white c. KIPL 169:7
cherries: Life is just a bowl of c. BROWN 56:13
cherry: It is as American as c. BROWN 56:9
Loveliest of trees, the c. now HOUS 145:13
Cheshire: cosmic C. cat HUXL 149:16
chess-players: c. do CHES 69:18
chest: c. to slip down WOD 315:17
Chesterton: That dared attack my C. BELL 35:5
chestnut: showers betumble the c. HARDY 133:8
chew: fart and c. gum JOHN 156:4
chewing: Was c. little bits of String BELL 32:19
chewing gum: so much c. for the eyes ANON 11:2
Chianti: are four bottles of C. SHAF 267:5
chic: very c. for an atheist RUSS 254:14
chicken: republic is like a c. MITF 211:13
Some c. CHUR 73:1

chickens: c.   WILL 312:13
chicks: have been a crowd of c.   AYRES 21:16
chief: The C. Defect of Henry King   BELL 32:19
child: at the birth of his c.   ORTON 224:4
    Become a C. on earth for me   BETJ 42:5
    But God bless the c. that's   HOL 142:11
    c. becomes an adult when   SZASZ 289:12
    C.! do not throw this book   BELL 32:12
    c. if I were a young Macaulay   BARB 24:17
    c. inherits my body   SHAW 268:6
    c. of seven or eight years   BLUNT 48:2
    c. take care that you strike   SHAW 272:3
    Every time a c. says   BARR 25:18
    find I am to have his c.   BURG 58:1
    He has devoured the infant c.   HOUS 144:10
    I call you bad, my little c.   BELL 32:13
    I get when I see a c.'s   BELL 33:11
    illegitimate c. of Karl Marx   ATTL 16:8
    I speak like a c.   NAB 217:4
    It's not fair to the c.   FROST 119:4
    Proves the c. ephemeral   AUDEN 17:10
    She was an aggravating c.   BELL 33:9
    The nicest c. I ever knew   BELL 33:10
    what it is like to be a c.   JARR 154:2
    wish to change in the c.   JUNG 160:2
    Wretched C. expires   BELL 33:2
childbirth: Death and taxes and c.   MITC 211:7
childhood: c., adolescence and obsolescence   LINK 188:12
    C. is not from birth   MILL 208:6
    moment in c. when the door   GREE 128:18
    what my lousy c. was   SAL 258:10
    Where c. had strayed   AE 3:3
childish: puts away c. things   MILL 208:6
children: all our lives raising c.   EDGAR 98:4
    And c. listen   BERL 40:12
    best understood by c.   STR 288:8
    better reasons for having c.   RUSS 256:3
    breeds contempt — and c.   TWAIN 301:10
    By c. and tradesmen's bills   MACN 198:4
    by c. to adults   SZASZ 290:2
    c. ardent for some desperate   OWEN 227:14
    C. are dumb to say how   GRAV 128:7
    c. are no longer children   JACK 151:17
    C. aren't happy with nothing   NASH 218:5
    c. for signs of improvement   SCOT 265:11
    C. have never been very   BALD 22:13
    c. to be a credit to them   RUSS 255:20
    c. to be always and forever   SAINT 257:1
    c. will not know   LARK 178:13
    C. with Hyacinth's temperament   SAKI 258:8
    disappointment to their c.   POW 239:5
    farm-yard except that c.   SHAW 269:7
    first class, and with c.   BENC 36:10
    generally hate *people and c.*   CAMP 62:3
    God's c. are not beautiful   LEB 183:7
    Goodnight, c...everywhere   MCC 194:9
    hands of young c.   DYLAN 97:5

children (*cont.*):
    he cried the little c.   AUDEN 17:1
    he reappears in your c.   CONN 80:16
    I have seen c. starving   ROOS 250:6
    interest of the c.   SHAW 268:24
    learn a lot from their c.   SPARK 281:4
    not much about having c.   LODGE 190:5
    parents kept me from c.   SPEN 281:12
    rich and the poor get c.   KAHN 161:3
    sleepless c.'s hearts are glad   BETJ 42:5
    teach their c. to speak it   SHAW 273:10
    that c. produce adults   DE VR 91:15
    that their c. are naïve   NASH 217:11
    The labouring c. can look out   CLEG 77:7
    To beget c., nothing better   SART 261:12
    violations committed by c.   BOWEN 50:16
    way parents obey their c.   EDW 98:10
    Your c. are not your children   GIBR 124:3
Chile: earthquake in C.   COCK 78:2
chills: Of c. and fever she died   RANS 243:1
chilly: although the room grows c.   GRAH 127:8
Chimborazo: C., Cotopaxi   TURN 300:3
chime: c. of words tinkling   SMITH 278:16
chimes: c. ring out with a carol   BOND 49:2
China: C. is not the powerful   BRAD 52:7
    On a slow boat to C.   LOES 190:7
    Till C. and Africa meet   AUDEN 16:12
    up like thunder outer C.   KIPL 169:6
    your land armies in C.   MONT 212:7
Chinamen: With C., but not with me   BELL 34:4
Chinese: C. said they would bury   RUSS 254:14
    The C. wouldn't dare   COW 84:13
chintzy: Oh! Chintzy, C. cheeriness   BETJ 43:3
chips: said 'C. with everything'   WESK 308:15
chisel: That with a mallet or a c.   YEATS 319:14
chivalry: nine-tenths of the law of c.   SAY 263:8
chocolate: c. cream soldier   SHAW 267:18
choir: joined the c. invisible   CHAP 67:9
choirs: demented c. of wailing shells   OWEN 227:13
choose: As those who c.   BROW 56:14
    c. to be a plumber   EINS 99:10
    c. to run for President   COOL 82:14
    man is forced to c.   YEATS 323:12
    must c. whether to be rich   ILL 150:11
    They can not c.   THOM 294:7
choosers: buggers can't be c.   BOWRA 51:7
chooses: "boozes" by the company he c.   BURT 58:7
choosing: c. between the disastrous   GALB 121:5
chord: play the c. of C major   BEEC 29:22
chords: c. of summer sustained   DAY-L 89:7
choreography: not c. to the audience   SZELL 290:7
choristers: Of linen go the chanting c.   LAWR 181:11
choses: *les c. avec leurs noms*   SART 261:16
Christ: And lo, C. walking on the water   THOM 296:13
    C. follows Dionysus   POUND 238:8
    C. perish in torment   SHAW 274:3

Christ (cont.):

C. was betrayed AE 3:3
C. went deeper than I have HARR 135:6
C. were coming this afternoon CART 64:4
Christian: But the souls of C. peoples CHES 70:9
C. ideal has not been tried CHES 71:5
C. people who wouldn't CURR 87:11
C. religion doubted BUTL 60:9
C. teaching at the time BENN 37:3
persuades me to be a C. FRY 120:4
Christianity: A local thing called C. HARDY 133:3
C. is the most materialistic TEMP 291:5
C., of course . . . but why BALF 23:14
C. will go LENN 185:4
from C. and journalism BALF 23:14
Christlike: C. in my behaviour HUXL 148:6
Christmas: C.-morning BETJ 42:5
C. was so much like another THOM 292:9
Claus just before a hard C. SMITH 276:14
I'm dreaming of a white C. BERL 40:12
I'm walking backwards for C. MILL 209:5
Let them know it's C. time GELD 122:11
Christopher: C. Robin MORT 214:5
C. Robin is saying his prayers MILNE 210:6
C. Robin went down with Alice MILNE 209:15
chuck: C. it, Smith CHES 70:9
chumps: C. always make the best WOD 315:9
c., you may be quite sure BENN 38:16
church: Broad of C. BETJ 43:6
But get me to the c. on time LERN 185:20
C. can feed and sleep ELIOT 102:14
c. he currently did not AMIS 6:3
C. is an anvil which has MACL 196:2
c. lit but without a congregation WELLS 308:2
C. should go forward along ROYD 254:4
c. stands near YEATS 319:13
Come all to c., good people HOUS 146:4
he goes to c. as he goes BLYT 48:4
Stands the C. clock BROO 56:1
The C.'s Restoration BETJ 43:4
up for your sins in c. SCOR 265:4
Waiting at the c., waiting LEIGH 184:7
wet c. the size of a snail THOM 292:14
churches: C. must learn humility SHAW 273:20
Churchill: C. but the mind was ATTL 16:5
C. on top of the wave has BEAV 28:11
[C.] was a young man BALF 24:1
[C.] you see all his faults LYTT 193:1
compared to Winston [C.] NIC 219:8
Randolph C. went into hospital WAUGH 306:3
think Winston C. wants war BEVAN 45:1
[Winston C.] BEVAN 44:9
[Winston C.] MURR 216:9
churchman: As for the British c. BLYT 48:4
person called a 'Modern C.' WAUGH 305:17
Church of England: ends and the C. begins PRIE 240:2
churchyard: In Drumcliffe c. Yeats is laid YEATS 319:13

chute: Vivre est une c. horizontale. COCT 78:7
cigar: really good 5-cent c. MARS 202:6
cigarette: c. that bears a lipstick's MARV 202:8
cigars: Call the roller of big c. STEV 285:7
Cinderella: The housewife is the C. SUMM 289:2
cinema: The c. is truth 24 times GOD 125:6
circle: He drew a c. that shut me out MARK 201:4
Round and round the c. ELIOT 101:19
circulation: assists the c. of their blood SMITH 278:1
c. I could only entertain ASQ 15:2
circumambulating: But a c. aphrodisiac FRY 119:17
circumstance: escape from c. to ecstasy BELL 32:8
circus: celebrated Barnum's c. CHUR 73:13
have no right in the c. MAXT 205:19
citadels: Where from c. on high AUDEN 19:5
cities: streets of a hundred c. HOOV 143:7
citizen: c. in this Republic ROOS 251:5
his wound, a c. of life SASS 263:2
I am a c. of the world EINS 99:7
that the c. is influenced RAK 242:10
To the c. or the police AUDEN 17:12
citizens: c. dream of the south HARDY 133:8
c. of death's gray land SASS 262:5
c. of that other place SONT 280:12
first and second class c. WILL 312:16
citizenship: who is born holds dual c. SONT 280:12
city: A big hard-boiled c. CHAN 67:1
c. is not a concrete jungle MORR 213:13
C. is the centre CHAM 65:12
c. of dreaming spires RAPH 243:3
C. of the Big Shoulders SAND 259:9
this c., is Null an' O'CAS 222:11
Unreal C. ELIOT 104:14
civil: A c. servant doesn't make jokes ION 151:12
Always be c. to the girls MITF 211:11
Here lies a c. servant SISS 275:14
civilised: c. outrage HEAN 136:10
civilization: authenticating sign of c. BIER 46:22
can't say c. don't advance ROG 249:11
C. advances by extending WHIT 310:11
C. and its discontents RIV 248:5
C. and profits go hand in hand COOL 82:12
C. has made the peasantry TROT 299:3
C. is nothing more ORT 224:2
c. of one epoch becomes CONN 81:1
farmyard c. of the Fabians INGE 151:3
For a botched c. POUND 238:9
hopeful fact in our c. SHAW 270:2
last product of c. RUSS 255:7
life-blood of real c. TREV 298:12
rottenness of our c. READ 244:2
survival of Christian c. CHUR 74:7
you think of modern c. GAND 121:9
civilized: most c. music in the world UST 302:13
civil servants: wonderfully gifted c. CLARK 77:1

Civil Service: C. is profoundly deferential

CROS 86:11

claim: c. which I have to make   HITL 141:8
   entitled to c. the aid of all   CHUR 74:5
clairvoyante: Madame Sosostris, famous c.

ELIOT 104:13

clap: believe, c. your hands   BARR 26:1
   cheaper seats c.   LENN 185:3
   Don't c. too hard   OSB 226:6
   Soul c. its hands   YEATS 321:6
Clara: C. threw the twins she nursed   GRAH 127:9
clarets: racehorses and the cheaper c.   SAKI 257:17
Claridges: body of the bootboy at C.   WOOLF 317:7
class: got a better c. of enemy   MILL 209:8
   I could have had c.   SCH 264:11
   passes, c. distinction   BETJ 44:5
   This is a new c.   MAUG 205:15
   true middle c. unit   SHAW 272:7
   use of *force* by one c.   LENIN 184:15
   violence by which one c.   MAO 200:11
   while there is a lower c.   DEBS 89:11
classes: c. which need sanctuary   BALD 23:8
   divisible into two great c.   BEER 30:10
   there are two c. of travel   BENC 36:10
classic: 'C.' A book which people   TWAIN 300:16
   C. music is th'kind   HUBB 147:7
classics: c. is an enemy to the human   MILL 208:14
   Than the c. in paraphrase   POUND 238:7
clatter: c. of Sir James Barrie's   GUED 130:3
Claude: After you, C.   KAV 162:3
clause: what they call a sanity c.   KAUF 161:9
claws: been a pair of ragged c.   ELIOT 103:9
   right place to use his c.   CHUR 76:10
clay: c. and wattles made   YEATS 318:10
   C. is the word and clay   KAV 162:1
   C. lies still, but blood's   HOUS 145:14
   make pure c. of time's mud   MAL 199:12
   this the c. grew tall   OWEN 228:2
Clayhanger: C. trilogy *is* good   BENN 38:3
clean: c. the pasture spring   FROST 118:12
   c. the sky   ELIOT 102:10
   meadow for a c. place   KAV 162:2
   Not a c. & in-between-   MCG 195:2
   one more thing to keep c.   FRY 119:14
   Then I was c. and brave   HOUS 146:2
cleaning: We had daily c. And tomorrow

REED 244:12

cleanness: swimmers into c. leaping   BROO 54:10
cleans: It beats as it sweeps as it c.   PAG 229:1
clear: C. arias of light thrilling   DAY-L 89:7
   c. language is insincerity   ORW 226:2
   C. the air   ELIOT 102:10
   climbin' c. up to the sky   HAMM 131:12
   literature c. and cold   LEWIS 187:10
   On a c. day   LERN 186:3
   The bells they sound so c.   HOUS 146:3
clearing-house: c. of the world   CHAM 65:12
clearly: C. through a flint wall see   GRAV 128:5

Clemenceau: [C.] felt about France what

KEYN 164:11

   M. C.   LLOY 190:2
Cleopatra: Nile last night as C.   BROWN 56:12
clercs: *La trahison des c.*   BENDA 36:14
clergyman: c. and need not commit

WAUGH 305:17

clerk: 'Baccy for the C.   KIPL 172:15
   small house agent's c.   ELIOT 105:6
clever: c. and the successful   GREE 128:12
   c. enough to get all   CHES 71:10
   c. ones learn Latin   CHUR 75:10
   c. people round me here   CAMP 62:1
   has been too c. by half   SAL 259:2
   It's c., but is it Art   KIPL 170:1
   silliest woman can manage a c.   KIPL 172:10
   The c. men at Oxford   GRAH 127:16
cleverest: c. member of one   WEBB 306:18
cliché: c. and an indiscretion   MACM 197:1
   have used every c. except   CHUR 75:8
client: am mistaken, is our c.   DOYLE 94:10
   Le c. n'a jamais tort.   RITZ 248:4
cliff: edge of some crazy c.   SAL 258:15
cliffs: chalk c. of Dover   BALD 23:5
   white c. of Dover   BURT 58:8
climate: Now but a whole c. of opinion

AUDEN 17:2

   still spring in their c.   DOUG 93:6
climb: But what a c. they left to do   PLOM 235:12
   c. black branches up   FROST 118:9
   C. ev'ry mountain   HAMM 131:9
   C. to our proper dark   YEATS 320:1
climbin': c. clear up to the sky   HAMM 131:12
climbing: go by c. a birch tree   FROST 118:9
cling: c. to the old rugged cross   BENN 37:9
clinging: they c. to their crosses   CHES 70:8
Clive: What I like about C.   BENT 39:11
clock: Ah! the c. is always slow   SERV 266:15
   Church c. at ten to three   BROO 56:1
   c. back a single second   WAUGH 306:15
   I see the Time and Motion c.   AYRES 21:16
   rock around the c.   DE KN 90:7
   The c. has stopped in the dark   ELIOT 101:18
clocks: c. were striking   ORW 225:2
   The morning c. will ring   HOUS 145:15
clockwork: ever heard of a c. orange   BURG 57:15
clods: Only a man harrowing c.   HARDY 133:15
close: C. encounters of the third kind   SPIE 282:5
   c. my eyes, open my legs   HILL 141:2
   c. your eyes before you   AYCK 21:6
   Far away is c. at hand   GRAV 128:9
   fatter man trying to c.   AMIS 6:2
   peacefully towards its c.   DAWS 89:3
   Trod beside me, c. and dear   HOUS 146:12
closed: Philadelphia, but it was c.   FIEL 109:3
   slogan 'We Never C.'   VAN D 303:5
closer: 'Come c., boys,' Childers   CHIL 71:14
closes: it is about you that c.   CUMM 87:5

closes (cont.):
Satire is what c. Saturday KAUF 161:6
closest: c. friends won't tell you ANON 7:20
close-up: I'm ready for my c. now BRAC 51:12
closing: c. time in the gardens CONN 80:14
Poetry is the opening and c. SAND 259:7
cloth: c. coat is to look BALM 24:6
clothes: been poured into his c. WOD 316:10
Fold your c. up neat and trim DE L 91:8
On the state of her c. NASH 218:11
stones and who wore torn c. SPEN 281:12
The good smell of old c. BROO 54:9
wet c. and into a dry WEST 309:2
clothes-brush: mind and manner of a c. NIC 219:7
clothing: A sheep in sheep's c. GOSSE 127:2
sheep in sheep's c. CHUR 76:11
cloths: heavens' embroidered c. YEATS 323:1
cloud: Don't you know each c. contains BURKE 58:3
How sweet to be a C. MILNE 210:8
Turn the dark c. inside out FORD 113:14
War's annals will c. into night HARDY 133:15
clouds: blue-massing c.; the keen BROO 54:9
Hullo C. Hullo Sky WILL 311:12
movement of c. in benediction DAY-L 89:7
When the c. go drifting STER 285:5
cloud–waves: Bronze c. that ebbed FREE 116:14
clover: I'm looking over a four leaf c. DIXON 92:11
sort of pig in c. LAWR 181:4
cloverleaf: flower is the concrete c. MUMF 215:14
clowns: Send in the c. SOND 280:7
club: ANY C. THAT WILL ACCEPT MARX 202:11
Around the fire at the c. YEATS 320:4
I rose politely in the c. CHES 70:15
most exclusive c. there NASH 218:10
She drove to the c. BETJ 43:11
clue: almost invariably a c. DOYLE 94:6
Clun: Clungunford and C. HOUS 146:13
Clunbury: Clunton and C. HOUS 146:13
clung: C. to the whistling mane THOM 295:7
Clungunford: C. and Clun HOUS 146:13
Clunton: C. and Clunbury HOUS 146:13
clutch: Inapprehensible, we c. thee THOM 296:12
clutching: people c. their gods ELIOT 100:10
Clyde: On the bonnie banks o' C. LAUD 180:3
C major: chord of C. twenty times BEEC 29:22
CMG: [service orders] rise from C. SAMP 259:3
coal: c. and surrounded by fish BEVAN 44:13
coals: no more c. to Newcastle GEOR 122:13
coarse: And one of them is rather c. ROYD 254:5
coaster: c. with a salt-caked smoke MAS 203:1
coat: eternal Footman hold my c. ELIOT 103:10
Grab your c., and get your hat FIEL 108:11
I made my song a c. YEATS 322:1
tattered c. upon a stick YEATS 321:6
coats: In c. of red DE L 91:2
cobble-stones: On c. I lay FLAN 111:3
cobra: who thinks he's a c. BANK 24:11
cocaine: C. habit-forming BANK 24:9

cock: Nationalism is a silly c. crowing ALD 3:12
cockatoo: cage is natural to a c. SHAW 269:5
cockerel: calls with a c.'s tongue LEE 183:17
might have been a c. fine AYRES 21:16
Cocklecarrot: C. began the hearing MORT 214:6
cocktail: The weasel under the c. PINT 234:12
cocoa: C. is a cad and coward CHES 69:4
cocoanuts: I've got a loverly bunch of c. HEAT 137:1
cod: bean and the c. BOSS 50:3
c. passeth all understanding LUTY 192:13
Though we yawned like dying c. ASQ 15:9
code: trail has its own stern c. SERV 267:2
codes: their laws, and their c. FREN 117:1
co-exist: that we must peacefully c. KHR 166:2
coffee: C. and oranges in a sunny STEV 285:8
if this is c., I want ARM 13:6
life with c. spoons ELIOT 103:8
would put poison in your c. ASTOR 15:12
coffee bar: loafs in a c. BRAT 52:15
coffin: grave in a Y-shaped c. ORTON 224:9
cogitations: Sometimes these c. still amaze ELIOT 103:17
coherent: C. miseries, a bite and sup HEAN 136:12
coin: The smallest current c. BIER 46:6
coins: fistful of c. ZAP 324:8
Colbert: logical solutions that C. CLARK 77:1
cold: A blow in c. blood neither SHAW 272:3
A c. coming we had of it ELIOT 100:9
A c. war warrior THAT 291:13
Cast a c. eye YEATS 319:13
clear and c. and pure LEWIS 187:10
c. and are not clothed EIS 100:2
c. and unemotional manner DOYLE 95:2
c. as yesterday's mashed FIEL 108:9
c. doesn't crouch over LAWR 181:3
c. for him his heart gave SMITH 278:18
c. his blood with the thought MAS 203:12
Far away from the c. night air LERN 186:6
Had a bad c., nevertheless ELIOT 104:13
hands were loath and c. OWEN 228:8
How c. my toes MILNE 209:11
it was too c. always SMITH 278:18
midst of a c. war BAR 27:8
statue c. FLEC 112:1
straight past the common c. AYRES 22:1
The c., gray dawn ADE 2:19
The spy who came in from the c. LE C 183:13
We called a c. a cold BENN 38:5
colder: seas c. than the Hebrides FLEC 112:2
collapse: youth c. FORS 114:13
collarbone: And my silly old c.'s bust BETJ 42:11
collect: pass go. Do not c. £200 DARR 88:6
collective: call the c. unconscious JUNG 160:4
sense of c. responsibility ALD 3:2
collectors: great c. before me DOUG 93:6
college: Bearing from C. to their homes BELL 35:6
cabbage with a c. education TWAIN 301:14

cabbage (*cont.*):

had attended business c.	ADE 2:15
The c. arms upon the lid; Tokay	BETJ 44:7

colonel: C.'s Lady an' Judy O'Grady | KIPL 174:10

colony: status of a fuzzy wuzzy c. | CAIR 61:4

colors: c. dont quite match | ASHF 14:4

colour: c. of children's pee | AMIS 5:13

c. that of a tea-tray painter	BLUNT 48:2
have the Model T in any c.	FORD 113:13
Her c. comes and goes	DOBS 92:15
I know the c. rose	ABSE 1:2
Life is C. and Warmth	GREN 129:5
mystery of c.	SHAW 268:23
prison for the c. of his hair	HOUS 144:8
problem of the c. line	DUB 96:3
'twas hanging for the c.	HOUS 144:8

coloured: And see the c. counties | HOUS 146:3

black blood makes a man c.	HUGH 147:12

colourless: C. green ideas sleep furiously

	CHOM 71:16
some c. movement of atoms	BRAD 52:4

colours: With c. that never fade | BOND 49:2

Columbus: mark of my youth in C. | THUR 297:3

columnists: political c. say | ADAMS 2:3

columns: enormous fluted Ionic c. | MACN 198:2

comb: two bald men over a c. | BORG 50:1

combat: *le triomphe mais le c.* | COUB 84:3

come: believe in the life to c. | BECK 28:15

Christmas-morning bells say 'C.'	BETJ 42:5
C. all to church	HOUS 146:4
c. back till it's over	COHAN 78:12
C., friendly bombs	BETJ 42:2
C. mothers and fathers	DYLAN 97:13
C. on down	CROW 86:13
C. then, let us go forward	CHUR 74:5
c. to thee by moonlight	NOYES 221:11
c. to the end of a perfect	BOND 49:2
C. with me to the Casbah	BOYER 51:9
C. you back to Mandalay	KIPL 169:6
don't you c. up sometime	WEST 309:14
I go — I c. back	KAV 162:7
In the room the women c. and go	ELIOT 103:7
No! Let 'em all c.	KNIG 176:3
Out of Ireland have we c.	YEATS 324:1
sailed the seas and c.	YEATS 321:7
The shape of things to c.	WELLS 308:11
they'll c. out	RED 276:11
war and nobody will c.	SAND 260:4
When you c. back again	RUB 254:6
worst is yet to c.	JOHN 156:16

comedian: c. is whether you laugh | NATH 218:14

comedy: brilliant drawing-room c. | DE VR 91:13

make a c. is a park	CHAP 67:4

comes: c. as sincerely from | HUXL 149:6

it c. up here	HODG 142:5
nobody c., nobody goes	BECK 29:7
shirt or collar ever c.	LEAC 183:3
then just as it c.	BETJ 43:1

cometh: The iceman c. | O'NEI 223:7

comfort: bourgeois prefers c. to pleasure

	HESSE 140:3
c. about being a woman	STARK 283:9
I tell you naught for your c.	CHES 68:9
moments of c. and convenience	KING 167:1
That c. cruel men	CHES 70:7
that means c.	TOLK 297:21
your dear husband for a c.	SMITH 278:20

comfortable: be baith grand and c. | BARR 25:15

c. and the accepted	GALB 121:2
into something more c.	BEHN 106:15
not. Progress is a c. disease	CUMM 87:7

comfortably: Are you sitting c. | LANG 178:7

comforting: cloud of c. convictions | RUSS 255:16

c. thought	MARQ 201:13

comical: Beautiful c. things | HARV 135:15

comin': C. in on a wing and a pray'r | ADAM 2:14

coming: A cold c. we had of it | ELIOT 100:9

be c. for us that night	BALD 22:11
Everything's c. up roses	SOND 280:6
good both going and c.	FROST 118:9
I was c. to that	GRAV 128:2
The Barbarians are c. today	CAV 65:6
The British are c.	WELL 307:12
The Russians are c.	ROSE 252:9
We'll be over, we're c. over	COHAN 78:12

command: Are beyond your c. | DYLAN 97:13

Love shall come at your c.	GRAV 128:9

comment: C. is free, but facts | SCOTT 265:5

C. voulez-vous gouverner	DE G 90:4

commit: c. when he had the opportunity

	ROWL 254:1

committed: c. suicide 25 years after | BEAV 28:10

I've c. adultery	CART 64:6
You have c. every crime	CHUR 72:12

committee: C.—a group of men who individually

	ALLEN 4:5
horse designed by a c.	ANON 7:10

common: century of the c. man | WALL 304:16

c. interest	ATK 15:16
C. Law of England has been	HERB 139:14
find no c. denominator	AUDEN 18:16
happiness of the c.	BEV 45:11
Horseguards and still be c.	RATT 243:8
I'm only a c. old working chap	FYFFE 120:10
man is a c. murderer	SAKI 257:5
nor lose the c. touch	KIPL 173:9
Nothing but c. sense	MORT 214:3
The c. cormorant	ISH 151:14
The c. man, I think	BEVIN 45:15

commonplace: featureless and c. a crime

	DOYLE 94:6
great minds in the c.	HUBB 147:5
The most c. crime is often	DOYLE 95:11

commonwealth: because the Empire is a c.

	ROS 252:10
C. and its Empire lasts	CHUR 74:7

communicate: But I needed to c. | SIM 275:6

communicate (*cont.*):

   c. was something positive   PRIT 240:4

communication: being dead: the c.   ELIOT 102:1

communion: sense an act of holy c.   ROB 248:12

   weeks of perfect c.   AUDEN 20:10

communism: about capitalism and c.   BAR 27:10

   against the anti-Christ of C.   BUCH 57:7

   C. continued to haunt Europe   TAYL 290:14

   c. is a dead dog   SOLZ 280:3

   C. is like prohibition   ROG 249:15

   C. is Soviet power plus   LENIN 184:12

   [Russian C. is]   ATTL 16:8

Communist: The Catholic and the C.   ORW 225:10

communists: Catholics and C. have committed

       GREE 128:11

community: life, a c. of thought   ADAMS 2:10

   up a small anarchist c.   BENN 37:12

commuter: C.—one who spends his life

       WHITE 310:2

compact: C. of ancient tales, and port   BELL 35:6

companion: gave him a c. to make   VALÉ 303:2

company: "boozes" by the c. he chooses

       BURT 58:7

   When c. comes   HUGH 147:13

compassion: sharp c. of the healer   ELIOT 101:15

compel: c. an agonizing reappraisal   DULL 96:6

competence: C., like truth, beauty   PETER 233:10

   In Ballymurphy. C. with pain   HEAN 136:12

complacencies: C. of the peignoir, and late

       STEV 285:8

complaining: triple-towered sky, the dove c.

       DAY-L 89:4

complaint: that's the most fatal c.   HILT 141:3

completely: something c. different   CHAP 67:7

completing: C. the charm   ELIOT 101:19

completion: time available for its c.   PARK 232:2

complexes: chiefly the *feeling-toned* c.   JUNG 160:4

complexion: c. or slightly flatter   CONR 81:9

   Keep that schoolgirl c.   PEAR 232:8

complexities: All mere c.   YEATS 323:9

complicated: A c. gesture learned from

       BOLT 48:13

compliment: rather a c.   DARR 88:8

composer: c. on leaving the theatre   BEEC 29:22

   requirement for a c. is to be dead   HON 143:3

composers: greatest c. since Beethoven

       BUCK 57:10

composing: C. mortals with immortal fire

       AUDEN 20:13

compromise: c. which are embedded among

       ZIN 324:12

compulsions: whose blent air all our c.

       LARK 179:5

compulsory: Blood is c.—they're all   STOP 287:5

computer: things up requires a c.   ANON 11:14

comrade: surprise us with a lady C.   ERAC 51:13

conceal: c. our whereabouts   SAKI 258:4

   people have something to c.   CONN 80:10

   was always able to c. it   TWAIN 301:8

concealable: without it everything is c.

       STOP 287:2

concealing: c. how much we think   TWAIN 301:11

conceit: curst c. o' bein' richt   MACD 194:10

concentrate: I am unable to c.   GEOR 123:3

concentration: c. of talent and genius   KENN 163:2

conception: dad is present at the c.   ORTON 224:4

   some c. of how men   FORS 114:6

concepts: up the stairs of his c.   STEI 284:15

concern: Since our c. was speech   ELIOT 102:3

concerned: I am not c. with Poetry   OWEN 227:12

concert: c. I make them play   BEEC 30:5

   self-imposed torture, the c.   MILL 208:13

concession: where the only c. to gaiety

       THOM 294:8

conclusion: The c. of your syllogism   O'BR 222:3

conclusions: sufficient c. from insufficient

       BUTL 59:14

concrete: city is not a c. jungle   MORR 213:13

   flower is the c. cloverleaf   MUMF 215:14

   Hurries down the c. station   BETJ 42:8

   Monstrous carbuncles of c.   SPEN 281:9

   they have built the c.   SPEN 281:17

condemn: c. egoism intolerantly   SANT 260:22

   c. recourse to war   BRIA 53:11

   nor the years c.   BINY 47:5

condemned: I am c. to be free   SART 261:9

   past are c. to repeat   SANT 260:11

   They c. millions of first-class   BEVAN 45:8

condition: A c. of complete simplicity   ELIOT 102:7

conditions: c. of tyranny it is far   AREN 13:3

   get better living c.   BAR 27:10

   universal c. of existence   JUNG 160:3

conductor: greatest c. in this country   BEEC 29:21

conductors: C. must give unmistakable

       SZELL 290:7

   these third-rate foreign c.   BEEC 30:5

cones: eat the c. under his pines   FROST 118:14

conference: naked into the c. chamber

       BEVAN 45:2

   was ever born in a c.   FITZ 110:9

conferred: Legion of Honour has been c.

       TWAIN 302:3

confession: after the sweetness of c.   FIRB 109:14

confessional: c. passage has probably   SAL 259:1

confide: c. in those who are better   CAMUS 62:13

confidence: ignorance and c.   TWAIN 302:4

confier: *la c. à des militaires*   CLEM 77:8

confinement: c. inside our own skins   WILL 312:8

confions: *c. rarement à ceux qui*   CAMUS 62:13

conflict: cause of international c.   WEIL 307:5

   human c. was so much owed   CHUR 74:8

   offered you C. and Art   PRIE 239:15

   spreading c.   JOHN 156:11

   We are in an armed c.   EDEN 98:1

conflicts: solution of all disputes or c.   BRIA 53:11

conform: not always c. to our whim   REST 245:12

confound: c. strangeness with mystery
DOYLE 95:11
confounding: C. her astronomers HODG 142:4
confused: c. doesn't really understand
MURR 216:7
congeals: When love c. HART 135:10
Congo: Then I saw the C., creeping LIND 188:10
congratulate: c. our armed forces THAT 291:8
conifers: The scent of the c. BETJ 43:10
Conn: [Billy C.] LOUIS 191:3
connect: soul of every man. Only c. FORS 115:3
connected: country are necessarily c.
JOHN 155:17
connection: heavenly c. to the starry GINS 125:1
connive: Who would c. HEAN 136:10
conquer: How shall we c.? Like a wind FLEC 112:6
    possible to c. poverty JOHN 156:5
    To c. fear is the beginning RUSS 256:2
conqueror: you are a c. ROST 253:9
conquest: Beauty's c. of your face AUDEN 19:5
    The c. of the earth CONR 81:9
conscience: C. is thoroughly well-bred BUTL 59:8
    C.: the inner voice MENC 206:16
    cruelty with a good c. RUSS 255:15
    freedom of c. TWAIN 300:15
    good c. on the proceeds SMITH 278:4
    had sufficient c. to bother LLOY 189:11
    happiness or a quiet c. BERL 41:2
    sound spot in our social c. SHAW 270:2
    uncreated c. of my race JOYCE 158:12
    will not cut my c. HELL 137:9
consciences: c. of the citizens JOHN 155:16
conscience-stricken: wearing such a c. air
HOUS 144:8
consciousness: c. of possessing a deep MCL 196:8
    human c. control events BURR 58:6
consent: inferior without your c. ROOS 249:19
consenting: only between c. adults VIDAL 304:5
consequences: prevent it and to damn the c.
MILN 211:2
    renounce war for its c. FOSD 116:4
conservatism: c. is based upon the idea CHES 70:3
conservative: A C. is a man with two ROOS 250:9
    c. man in this world BEVIN 45:16
    C., n. A statesman BIER 46:15
    c. on the day after AREN 13:5
    C. Party at prayer ROYD 254:4
    C. Party is that it has WAUGH 306:15
    stomach is nothing if not c. BUTL 59:16
    which makes a man more c. KEYN 164:14
    would make me c. when old FROST 118:4
Conservatives: Life's better with the C. ANON 9:16
considering: C. the alternative CHEV 71:12
consistency: c. is as bad for the mind HUXL 148:12
consistent: c. people are the dead HUXL 148:12
conspicuous: C. consumption of valuable
VEBL 303:12
    Vega c. overhead AUDEN 19:4
conspiracies: are c. against the laity SHAW 268:21

conspiracy: c. of human beings to lie WELLS 308:9
    Indecency's c. of silence SHAW 272:10
constancy: c. of the women who love SHAW 273:8
constant: c. in human sufferings JOYCE 158:11
constellations: c. of feeling DOUG 93:9
constituencies: c. and prepare for government
STEEL 283:13
constitution: c. does not provide WILL 312:16
    nightmare is over. Our C. works FORD 113:8
constructed: defences of peace must be c.
ANON 8:7
consume: history than they can c. SAKI 257:10
consumer: c. society there are inevitably
ILL 150:12
    The c. isn't a moron OGIL 222:18
consumes: that c. without producing ORW 224:10
consuming: deathly inner c. fire HESSE 140:3
consumption: Conspicuous c. of valuable goods
VEBL 303:12
    c. things are very different GALB 121:4
contemplation: grasped by action, not by c.
BRON 54:3
    Has left for c. BETJ 43:4
    Of all the solemn talk of c. KAV 161:12
contempt: Familiarity breeds c. TWAIN 301:10
contemptible: French's c. little army ANON 7:24
contender: I could have been a c. SCH 264:11
content: C. in the tight hot cell BOGAN 48:8
    That is the land of lost c. HOUS 146:11
    their skin but by the c. KING 166:10
contentment: Preaches c. to that toad KIPL 170:6
contest: victory but the c. COUB 84:3
continent: C. people have good food MIKES 207:13
    Thou knowest of no strange c. DAV 89:1
continental: C. people have sex life MIKES 207:14
continentally: Learn to think c. CHAM 65:13
continents: nations and three separate c.
DOYLE 95:4
contingent: c. and the unforeseen FISH 109:15
contraception: fast word about oral c. ALLEN 4:21
contraceptives: c. at the best of times SHAR 267:10
contract: c. into which men enter CHUR 73:9
    c. now needs to be re-negotiated BENN 37:6
    needs is a new social c. CALL 61:6
    The Social C. is nothing WELLS 308:9
    verbal c. isn't worth GOLD 126:7
contracting: high c. powers solemnly BRIA 53:11
contraction: clever c. derived from ACE 1:5
contradict: Never c. FISH 110:4
contradiction: It is a c. in terms SHAW 274:2
    It's a c. in terms SIMP 275:12
contradictory: c. beliefs in one's mind ORW 225:7
contrary: Consistency is c. to nature HUXL 148:12
    c. to the way JENK 154:9
contrast: intense enjoyment from a c.
FREUD 117:4
control: authorities whom we do not c.
CONN 81:6

control (cont.):
   Ground c. to Major Tom   BOWIE 51:6
   kept under c.   MARQ 201:14
   some c. over their lives   CURR 87:12
controlling: c. interest in key subsidiary
     WELLS 308:1
controls: who c. the present controls ORW 225:5
controversy: times of challenge and c. KING 167:1
   when the man of c.   GALB 121:2
convalescence: enjoy c.   SHAW 268:3
convenience: c. to liberty, and a pleasant
     HESSE 140:3
   moments of comfort and c.   KING 167:1
convenient: There's never any c. time MITC 211:7
convent: The C. of the Sacred Heart ELIOT 102:13
conventional: adultery being a most c.
     NAB 216:12
   Barrymore would allow such a c.   BARR 27:1
   c. wisdom resists so stoutly   GALB 121:3
conversation: difficult to go on with the c.
     WOD 316:7
   ignorance cramps my c.   HOPE 143:11
   parlour c. to two sentences   ACE 1:5
conversion: c. of England was thus SELL 266:5
converted: You have not c. a man MORL 213:12
conveying: power of c. unlimited HARD 132:16
conviction: c. begins as a whim BROUN 56:6
   The best lack all c.   YEATS 320:7
convictions: cloud of comforting c. RUSS 255:16
convince: Only reason can c. us BELL 32:10
   reader wishes to c.   FORS 114:10
convinces: goes to the man who c. DARW 88:9
convincing: excuses are always less c. HUXL 149:5
cook: The cook was a good c. SAKI 258:1
   very uncommon c.   SAKI 257:5
cooking: home c. PHIL 233:13
cool: c. kindliness of sheets BROO 54:9
   c. waters where we used   HOPE 144:4
   c. white dress after   FIRB 109:14
   In the c. of the day   ELIOT 101:1
coolibah: Under the shade of a c. tree PAT 232:5
Coolidge: C. only snored MENC 206:8
   C.'s genius for inactivity   LIPP 188:13
   my admiration for Mr C.   ANON 11:13
cooling: like it for c. the blood FLAN 111:5
Cooper: C. killing off the Indians BALD 22:12
Copper: Definitely, Lord C. WAUGH 306:8
Copperfield: that David C. kind of crap SAL 258:10
copperheads: c. and the assassin SAND 259:12
coppers: like the old time 'c.' COLL 79:5
copse: c. was happy for old things MAS 203:13
copulating: skeletons c. on a corrugated
     BEEC 29:18
copulation: Birth, and c., and death ELIOT 104:6
core: ain't-a-going to be no c. TWAIN 302:1
   deep heart's c.   YEATS 318:10
   unerringly upon the human c.   JAMES 153:13
cork: I don't pop my c. FIEL 108:8
   took the c. out of my lunch   FIEL 109:1

corkscrews: heart are as crooked as c.
     AUDEN 19:2
cormorant: The common c. ISH 151:14
corn: about the Repeal of the C. BEER 31:20
   c. at midnight by a tress   YEATS 322:2
   c. is as high as an elephant's   HAMM 131:12
   c. that makes the holy   MAS 203:10
corner: Anyhow in a c., some untidy AUDEN 17:9
   at the c. of the street   GAY 122:7
   c. of the universe you   HUXL 149:15
   lew c. of airth to lie   PHIL 234:4
   little bit in the c.   BENN 37:10
   some c. of a foreign field   BROO 55:2
corners: into the c. of the evening ELIOT 103:7
corporation: biggest industrial c. SHAW 267:14
corps: c. of impudent snobs AGNEW 3:7
corpse: good wishes to the c. BARR 26:2
   got a nice *fresh* c.   TWAIN 301:6
corpses: To mock the riddled c. round SASS 263:1
correct: being the c. article ASHF 14:9
   c. in cypress wood   PARK 231:4
   perfectly c. thing   SHAW 269:10
correctable: press everything is c. STOP 287:2
correlative: finding an 'objective c.' ELIOT 104:4
corridors: admit princes to the c. DOUG 93:9
   c. of power, the dilemmas   SNOW 279:4
   c. under there is nothing   DRIN 95:17
   passages, contrived c.   ELIOT 100:7
corrugated: copulating on a c. tin BEEC 29:18
cors: *Les souvenirs sont c. de chasse* APOL 12:16
Cory: And Richard C., one calm ROB 248:9
cosmetics: factory we make c. REVS 246:1
cosmic: smile of a c. Cheshire HUXL 149:16
cosmopolitan: become c. in the end
     MOORE 212:11
cost: Bapu [Gandhi] knew the c. NAIDU 217:7
   But at what c.   BECK 28:14
   c. each other and the gods   AUDEN 20:7
   whatever the c. may   CHUR 74:6
costing: C. not less than everything ELIOT 102:7
costs: c. as much to keep up LLOY 189:12
costume: The same c. will LAVER 186:6
Cotopaxi: Chimborazo, C. TURN 300:3
cottage: Wherever there's a c. small PARK 231:19
Cottleston: C., Cottleston, Cottleston Pie
     MILNE 210:12
cotton-grass: Past c. and moorland border
     AUDEN 19:15
couché: *je me suis c. de bonne* PROU 240:7
coucher: *pauvre de c. sous les ponts* FRAN 116:6
couches: planned her, stilly c. she HARDY 134:4
couch-grass: From the heaps of c. HARDY 133:15
cough: all c. in ink YEATS 322:4
coughing: group of people from c. RICH 247:6
   one c., and one not coughing   SCHN 264:9
coughs: C. and sneezes spread diseases ANON 7:14
council: In c. rooms apart RICE 246:8
count: c. and calls her 'Miss' CHES 68:17

count (cont.):
c. four — TWAIN 301:16
C. to ten, and man is bored — PARK 230:17
I won the c. — SOM 280:5
counted: c. them all out and I counted — HANR 132:10
countenance: c. this person read — BRAM 52:11
countess: hear what the c. is saying — MAUG 204:12
counties: And see the coloured c. — HOUS 146:3
counting: C. the beats — GRAV 128:8
democracy, it's the c. — STOP 286:14
countries: come between these two c. — LAW 48:14
peace of all c. everywhere — ROOS 250:8
country: And there's another c. — SPR 282:14
An everyday story of c. folk — WEBB 307:1
Books from Boots' and c. lanes — BETJ 44:5
c. and betraying my friend — FORS 115:12
c. and they only saved — CHES 68:7
c. [Czechoslovakia] between — CHAM 66:4
c. gentleman — MACD 194:13
c. habit has me — SACK 256:13
c. has deliberately undertaken — HOOV 143:5
c. in which the office — HUXL 148:8
c. needs is a really good — MARS 202:6
C. of the Blind the One-Eyed — WELLS 308:5
c. 'tis of centuries come — CUMM 87:2
Cry, the beloved c. — PATON 232:6
fight for its King and C. — GRAH 127:5
fit c. for heroes to live — LLOY 190:1
foreign c. — HART 135:14
For your King and your C. — RUB 254:6
From yon far c. blows — HOUS 146:11
headed 'Your King and C.' — FIELD 108:7
How can you govern a c. — DE G 90:4
my c. — SPR 282:13
my c. and it may be yet — BLUN 47:14
My c., right or wrong — CHES 68:14
never let my c. die for me — KINN 168:2
Old C. must wake up if — GEOR 122:14
one day this c. of ours — COW 84:5
security and peace of each c. — JOHN 155:17
Switzerland is a small, steep c. — HEM 138:13
That is no c. for old men — YEATS 321:5
The trouble with this c. — ADAMS 2:5
This c. needs good farmers — NIXON 220:9
what was good for our c. — WILS 313:1
While there's a c. lane — PARK 231:19
you can do for your c. — KENN 164:1
countryman: c. must have praise — BLYT 48:5
countryside: smiling and beautiful c. — DOYLE 94:8
county: English c. families baying — WAUGH 305:11
cœur: voit bien qu'avec le c. — SAINT 257:2
courage: act of the greatest c. — JUNG 160:3
C. is the thing — BARR 26:6
c. to change what should — NIEB 219:10
C. was mine, and I had mystery — OWEN 228:7
c. you bring to it — WALP 305:1
originality or moral c. — SHAW 268:10
piety, c.—they exist — FORS 115:8

courage (cont.):
spirit of gallantry and c. — COW 84:5
Than C. of Heart or Holiness — BELL 35:2
course: c. of true anything never — BUTL 59:7
forgot his c. — FLEC 112:4
have them served to him c. — CHUR 74:2
court: C. him, elude him — BLUN 47:12
The C. is shaking — FARJ 107:7
courteous: Be invariably c., considerate — KITC 175:15
courtesy: c. title on the principle — SAKI 258:4
defence like elaborate c. — LUCAS 192:7
That the Grace of God is in C. — BELL 35:2
courtin': Are yer c. — PICK 234:10
courtmartialled: I was c. in my absence — BEHAN 31:24
courts: not enough c. to enforce — HUMP 148:2
covenants: Open c. of peace — WILS 314:15
coverlet: Blue skies be your c. — HART 135:12
cow: isn't grass to graze a c. — BETJ 42:2
Over the c. shed — O'HARA 222:19
The c. is of the bovine ilk — NASH 217:13
this than to keep a c. — BUTL 60:4
We milk the c. of the world — WILB 311:3
Coward: [Noel C.] — TYNAN 302:5
The sea hates a c. — O'NEI 223:12
cowardice: C., as distinguished from — HEM 138:6
soldier I admit the c. — SHAW 271:8
surest is c. — TWAIN 300:19
were guilty of Noel C. — DE VR 91:13
cows: Bulls and c. a thousand head — HODG 142:3
cowshed: smelling of the c. — THOM 293:15
cowslip: C. and shad-blow, flaked — CRANE 85:10
crack: And the c. in the tea-cup opens — AUDEN 16:13
C. and sometimes break — ELIOT 101:9
crackle: Snap! C.! Pop — ANON 10:17
cradle: c. rocks above an abyss — NAB 217:3
from the c. to the grave — CHUR 76:9
nightmare by a rocking c. — YEATS 320:8
craftsmen: was the work not of c. — CLARK 77:1
cramps: ignorance c. my conversation — HOPE 143:11
crane: Tall as a c. — SITW 276:1
crank: apprenticeship as a c. — BROUN 56:6
crap: Copperfield kind of c. — SAL 258:10
crash: c. is coming when I start — PARK 230:3
craving: c. in the world — PEAR 232:10
c. to be appreciated — JAMES 153:11
crawls: The sea-worm c.—grotesque — HARDY 134:4
crazed: c. with the spell of far — DE L 90:10
crazier: World is c. and more — MACN 198:7
crazy: C. like a fox — PER 232:16
Just two c. people together — HART 135:12
creaking: Came c. to the barn — LOW 192:1
creaks: The morning light c. down — SITW 276:1
creation: His divine system of c. — HELL 137:6
intrinsic evidence of his c. — JEANS 154:7

creation (*cont.*):
It took the whole of C.   HUGH 147:14
who finds c. so perfect   PROU 241:1
woman is a blind fury of c.   SHAW 270:15
world since the C.   NIXON 220:6
création: *une grande c. d'époque*   BART 27:5
creative: are c. but few are artists   GOOD 126:13
C. writers are always greater   FORS 115:16
creator: can dispense with a c.   PROU 241:1
concluded that the C.   HALD 131:2
say that the C. made   TWAIN 301:4
creature: Let the living c. lie   AUDEN 17:10
only c. that consumes   ORW 224:10
creatures: And breastless c. underground
    ELIOT 103:1
credit: I never seek to take the c.   PARK 231:2
In science the c. goes   DARW 88:9
people who get the c.   MORR 214:2
their children to be a c.   RUSS 255:20
credulities: upwards on the miseries or c.
    CONR 81:20
credulous: Man is a c. animal   RUSS 256:1
creed: last article of my c.   GAND 122:1
true meaning of its c.   KING 166:10
creep: c. again, leap again   DE L 91:7
creeper-nails: Sagged seats, the c. are rust
    HARDY 133:7
creeps: it c. like a rat   BOWEN 51:3
crème: all my pupils are the c.   SPARK 281:5
Crete: C. unfortunately make more   SAKI 257:10
crevasse: like a scream from a c.   GREE 128:16
crew: Set the c. laughing   FLEC 112:4
cricket: C. civilizes people   MUG 215:2
football and particularly c.   MANC 199:15
morning to where the c. sings   YEATS 318:10
Cricklewood: Midland, bound for C.   BETJ 43:8
cried: c. all the way   LIB 188:3
c. the little children   AUDEN 17:1
he c. out twice, a cry   CONR 81:12
cries: The air is full of our c.   BECK 29:14
crime: c. is due to the repressed   WAUGH 305:18
c. is often the most mysterious   DOYLE 95:11
c. you haven't committed   POW 239:7
featureless and commonplace a c.   DOYLE 94:6
have committed every c.   CHUR 72:12
lamentable catalogue of human c.   CHUR 74:4
Napoleon of c.   DOYLE 94:18
Napoleon of c.   ELIOT 102:12
we'll end that stupid c.   SERV 266:16
crimes: have committed great c.   GREE 128:11
worst of c. is poverty   SHAW 270:1
criminal: despise for ends I think c.   KEYN 164:10
while there is a c. element   DEBS 89:11
criminals: Looney Tunes and squalid c.
    REAG 244:8
crises: c. that seemed intolerable   ATK 15:15
crisis: cannot be a c. next week   KISS 175:12
critic: A great drama c. also   TYNAN 302:8
c. is a bundle of biases   BALL 24:4

critic (*cont.*):
c. is a man who knows   TYNAN 302:7
c. is to save the tale   LAWR 182:2
English c. is a don *manqué*   LAMB 177:15
function of the c.   BELL 32:9
set up in honour of a c.   SIB 275:1
The good c. is he who relates   FRAN 116:7
critical: at this c. moment   HAIG 130:12
c. period in matrimony   HERB 139:16
criticism: c. by the few than a subject
    BROWN 56:11
c. is applied only to what   JAMES 153:6
c. this past summer   ALGR 3:16
ignorance as regards c.   MACM 196:15
near to them than c.   RILKE 247:8
People ask you for c.   MAUG 205:10
two because it permits c.   FORS 115:13
criticisms: most penetrating of c.   HUXL 149:9
criticize: And don't c.   DYLAN 97:13
I don't care if you c.   OWEN 227:11
critics: C. are biased   BALL 24:4
c. is to be remembered   MOORE 212:12
that there are true c.   ALGR 3:16
critique: *Le bon c. est celui qui*   FRAN 116:7
crocodile: After 'while, c.   GUID 130:5
C. caught him   KIPL 172:1
croire: *avec leurs noms: c'est c.*   SART 261:16
Cromwell: bit of a ruin that C.   BEDF 29:15
C. said to the Long Parliament   AMERY 5:9
crook: their President is a c.   NIXON 220:8
you are a c. or a Martyr   ROG 249:7
crooked: are as c. as corkscrews   AUDEN 19:2
The c. be made straight   ELIOT 101:19
crooning: c. like a bilious pigeon   SHAW 273:12
cross: By the road an ancient c.   YEATS 319:13
cling to the old rugged c.   BENN 37:9
C. as the focus of longing   MUGG 215:7
c. of the Legion of Honour   TWAIN 302:3
C. to be Borne   SMITH 278:20
King's C.   FARJ 107:7
The c. be uncrossed   ELIOT 101:19
There's a little marble c.   HAYES 136:3
through sheer inability to c.   WOOLF 317:12
crosses: Between the c., row on row   MCCR 194:6
clinging to their c.   CHES 70:8
crossing: double c. of a pair of heels   HART 135:10
crossness: c. and dirt succeed where   FORS 114:9
crossroads: mankind faces a c.   ALLEN 4:13
crowblack: c., fishingboat-bobbing   THOM 293:13
crowd: c. flowed over London Bridge   ELIOT 104:14
c. will always save   COCT 78:5
have been a c. of chicks   AYRES 21:16
crowded: Across a c. room   HAMM 132:2
crowing: cock c. on its own dunghill   ALD 3:12
crown: c. of thorns *and* the thirty   BEVAN 44:12
exchange it some day for a c.   BENN 37:9
hairy gold c. on 'er 'ead   KIPL 169:4
Out of his C.   FARJ 107:7
The jewel in the c.   SCOTT 265:6

crowned: Into the c. knot of fire ELIOT 102:7
crowns: Give c. and pounds and guineas
　　　　　　　　　　　　　　　　HOUS 146:1
croyait: était un fou qui se c. COCT 78:8
cru: étonné quand il est c. DE G 90:5
crucified: choose who is to be c. COCT 78:5
　therefore the c. BONH 49:5
crucify: It's God they ought to c. CART 64:8
cruel: Goodbye c. world SHAY 274:15
　Not that he's c. LEAC 182:15
　That comfort c. men CHES 70:7
　The truth is c. SANT 260:17
cruellest: April is the c. month, breeding
　　　　　　　　　　　　　　　　ELIOT 104:10
　c. and most terrible War LLOY 189:9
cruelty: century inhumanity meant c.
　　　　　　　　　　　　　　　　FROMM 117:10
　c. with a good conscience RUSS 255:15
　main sources of c. RUSS 256:2
crumbling: C. between the fingers MACN 198:5
crumbs: bags to hold the c. ISH 151:14
　In eating Bread he made no C. BELL 33:10
crumpets: Over buttered scones and c.
　　　　　　　　　　　　　　　　ELIOT 100:5
crusade: c. against Communism was TAYL 290:14
　moral c. or it is nothing WILS 313:9
crushing: C. out life HOPE 144:4
cry: C., the beloved country PATON 232:6
　Don't c. for me Argentina RICE 246:11
　Forgot the c. of gulls ELIOT 105:8
　I hear a sudden c. of pain STEP 285:4
　your bald c. PLATH 235:9
crying: that wild high c. MAS 203:12
crystal: Why read the c. when BEVAN 45:4
cubes: c. in two different ways RAM 242:15
Cuchulain: When Pearse summoned C.
　　　　　　　　　　　　　　　　YEATS 320:1
cuckoo: And hear the pleasant c. DAV 88:14
　A rainbow and a c.'s song DAV 88:13
　hotels built on the c. HEM 138:13
　The c. clock WELL 307:14
　This is the weather the c. HARDY 133:8
cucumber: when c. is added to it MACK 195:10
cud: bitter as the c. OWEN 227:14
cult: After all, what's a c. ALTM 5:8
　c. of the individual decisively KHR 165:8
cultivate: And c. a beaver HUXL 148:6
　c. a few inhibitions LOOS 190:19
　which dictators may c. BEV 45:10
culturally: behind economically or c. DUBČ 95:18
culture: C. is an instrument wielded WEIL 307:6
　c. is no better AUDEN 20:7
　c. lives by sympathies JAMES 153:13
　C. may even be described ELIOT 102:11
　c. that a poet can earn AUDEN 18:6
　don't swallow the c. bait LAWR 181:14
　whole vast intuitive c. SHAF 267:5
　who pursue C. in bands WHAR 309:22

culture (cont.):
　word c. JOHST 157:2
cultured: intelligentsia and the c. BERD 40:1
cunning: exile, and c. JOYCE 158:13
　History has many c. passages ELIOT 100:7
cupboards: her c. opened HARDY 133:11
curate: c. at home as something FIRB 109:11
　c. who has strayed by mistake AUDEN 18:12
　The c. faced the laurels GRAH 127:11
　To sit upon the c.'s knee CHES 70:11
curates: C., long dust, will come and go
　　　　　　　　　　　　　　　　BROO 55:9
curb: snaffle and the c. CAMP 62:2
curds: kitchen cups concupiscent c. STEV 285:7
cure: But I wish that they could c. AYRES 22:1
　c. for birth and death SANT 260:19
　c. for it is occupation SHAW 273:6
　c. for this ill is not KIPL 171:13
　found a c. for most evils KELL 162:9
　no C. for this Disease BELL 33:1
　twentieth, it's a c. SZASZ 289:13
cured: be c. by more democracy SMITH 276:16
cures: best c. for depression SMITH 277:1
curiosity: intellectual c. is the life-blood
　　　　　　　　　　　　　　　　TREV 298:12
　Love, c., freckles, and doubt PARK 230:12
curious: c. incident of the dog DOYLE 94:16
　Yes; quaint and c. war HARDY 134:10
currency: than to debauch the c. KEYN 164:13
current: boats against the c. FITZ 110:16
currents: Cold c. thrid, and turn HARDY 134:4
curse: And the c. be ended ELIOT 101:19
　blessing or the greatest c. BARR 26:3
　c. to this country in time CHUR 75:4
curses: c. heaped on each gashed SORL 281:2
cursing: c. his staff for incompetent SASS 262:8
curtain: And so I face the final c. ANKA 6:11
　iron c. has descended CHUR 73:3
　sensuous c. BRAD 52:4
curtains: c. are drawn with care MONRO 212:4
　Nottingham lace of the c. BETJ 41:17
curtiosity: was full of 'satiable c. KIPL 171:14
curve: dear red c. of her lips MAS 203:5
custard: joke is ultimately a c. ORW 224:7
custom: c. of one wife and hardly SAKI 258:3
customer: The c. is never wrong RITZ 248:4
customs: thinks that the c. SHAW 268:7
cut: c. my conscience to fit HELL 137:9
　Was c. out of the grass CHES 68:8
　You can c., or you can drug LOW 191:9
cutting: c. edge of the mind BRON 54:3
　interest is that of c. ATK 15:16
cuttlefish: like a c. squirting out ORW 226:2
cycle: c. of deprivation JOS 157:8
cycle-clips: My c. in awkward reverence
　　　　　　　　　　　　　　　　LARK 179:4
cynic: C., n. A blackguard whose BIER 46:16
cynical: c. and entirely undemocratic CAIR 61:4
cynicism: C. is an unpleasant way HELL 137:8

cypress: little noise outside the c. LAWR 180:7
cypresses: Along the avenue of c. LAWR 181:11
Cyprus: black C. with a lake FLEC 112:3
Cyril: Nice one, C. ANON 10:4
Czechoslovakia: country [C.] between people
CHAM 66:4
C. and in the matters CHUR 74:2

D

dad: child can expect if the d. ORTON 224:4
that married dear old d. DILL 92:6
dada: encountered the mama of d. FAD 107:5
Daddy: D. sat up very late working BENC 36:11
My heart belongs to D. PORT 236:17
daffodils: d. were for Wordsworth LARK 179:9
daily: D. the steamers sidle up AUDEN 19:10
daintily: D. alights Elaine BETJ 42:8
dairymaid: The D. MILNE 210:3
daisies: d. in Sunday Meadow THOM 293:15
picking d. on the railway WOD 315:18
would be pushing up the d. CHAP 67:9
Daisy: D. and Lily SITW 276:5
dallied: But I dillied and d. COLL 79:5
Dalton: resignation of Hugh D. BIRCH 47:6
damage: which might d. his career BARR 26:14
dame: There is nothin' like a d. HAMM 132:4
damn: D. it all, you can't have BEVAN 44:12
d. the consequences MILN 211:2
d. you England OSB 226:15
It's 'D. you, Jack . . .' BONE 49:3
old man who said, 'D.' HARE 134:14
public doesn't give a d. BEEC 29:17
true that life is one d. MILL 208:3
damnation: be blasted to eternal d. SHAW 273:21
From sleep and from d. CHES 70:7
damned: better than any d. foreigner BEEC 29:21
brandy of the d. SHAW 271:3
D. from here to Eternity KIPL 169:9
If I were d. of body and soul KIPL 172:7
Life is just one d. thing HUBB 147:3
stink of the d. dead niggers ASQ 15:9
The beautiful and d. FITZ 110:8
damns: d. the vast majority o' MACD 194:10
damp: d. souls of housemaids ELIOT 103:15
female in a d. basement HARD 132:16
damps: d. there drip upon HARDY 133:7
dance: A d. to the music of time POW 239:6
And spectral d., before BROO 55:9
d. attendance upon my old YEATS 321:3
Dance, dance, d., little lady COW 84:6
Dance, d., dance till you drop AUDEN 19:2
d., for the figure AUDEN 19:2
d. in the old dame yet MARQ 201:7
D. on this ball-floor thin BLUN 47:12
dancer from the d. YEATS 321:8

dance (cont.):
d. round in a ring FROST 119:11
D. then wherever you may CART 64:7
D. till the stars come AUDEN 19:2
departs too far from the d. POUND 237:15
Each d. the others would DE L 91:4
from the car-park the d. BETJ 43:11
point, there the d. ELIOT 101:8
Shall we d. MILL 209:6
we d. at the Golf Club BETJ 43:10
danced: his didn't he d. his did CUMM 86:15
I d. in the morning CART 64:7
dancer: know the d. from the dance YEATS 321:8
dancers: d. are all gone under ELIOT 101:13
dances: Slightly bald. Also d. ANON 7:11
We shall have no time for d. MACN 197:10
dancing: And d. dogs and bears HODG 142:2
[D. is] SHAW 273:2
prose as d. is to walking WAIN 304:10
dandy: I'm a Yankee Doodle D. COHAN 78:13
Is d. NASH 218:8
Dane: You never get rid of the D. KIPL 170:16
Dane-geld: called paying the D. KIPL 170:16
danger: d. of their coming true SMITH 277:13
The d. of the future FROMM 117:10
The d. of the past was FROMM 117:10
dangereux: n'est plus d. qu'une idée ALAIN 3:9
dangerous: are d. for good or evil KEYN 165:5
d. everything is nothing STEIN 284:4
d. than sincere ignorance KING 167:2
d. to be sincere unless SHAW 272:16
more d. than a mud-puddle STEIN 284:8
more d. than an idea ALAIN 3:9
sat D. Dan McGrew SERV 267:1
were d. to meet it alone WHAR 309:22
dapper: d. from your napper COLL 79:7
dare: Do I d. to eat a peach ELIOT 103:12
Nobody'll d. HUGH 147:13
Take me if you d. PANK 229:8
Where eagles d. MACL 196:3
dares: Who d. wins ANON 12:7
dark: clock has stopped in the d. ELIOT 101:18
come home in the d. WILL 311:10
d. age made more sinister CHUR 74:7
d. and deep FROST 118:11
D. as the world of man SITW 276:6
d. night of the soul FITZ 110:2
day of his death was a d. AUDEN 17:3
I knew you in this d. OWEN 228:8
In the nightmare of the d. AUDEN 17:6
O d. dark dark ELIOT 101:14
Out in the d. over the snow THOM 294:2
raging in the d. YEATS 323:12
refuse a drink after d. MENC 206:17
The d. is light enough FRY 119:12
These are not d. days CHUR 72:13
They all go into the d. ELIOT 101:14
through the spaces of the d. ELIOT 103:14
want to go home in the d. HENRY 139:3

dark (cont.):

We work in the d.	JAMES 152:14
darken: Never d. my Dior again	LILL 188:4
darkening: swan drifts upon a d.	YEATS 323:7
darker: d. to the lighter	DUB 96:3
I am the d. brother	HUGH 147:13
speak of d. days	CHUR 72:13
darkness: between two eternities of d.	NAB 217:3
candle than curse the d.	STEV 286:5
d. among the gusty trees	NOYES 221:9
d. and put your hand	HASK 136:1
d. drops again but now	YEATS 320:8
d. of mere being	JUNG 159:15
Shares the d.—presently	MILL 208:4
there is d. everywhere	NEHRU 218:17
darlin': oh, he's a d. man	O'CAS 222:7
darling: Robey is the D. of the music	SMITH 277:7
Yes, my d. daughter	ANON 9:24
Yes, my d. daughter	DE L 91:8
dashing: A d. Swiss officer	RUSS 256:4
date: d. which will live in infamy	ROOS 251:1
keep them up to d.	SHAW 269:2
savage country, out of d.	POUND 238:5
daughter: all to my elder d.	THOM 294:3
And on her d.	ELIOT 105:4
D. am I in my mother's house	KIPL 170:7
Don't put your d. on the stage	COW 85:1
father would wish his d.	ANON 11:10
The landlord's black-eyed d.	NOYES 221:10
Translated D., come down	AUDEN 20:13
Yes, my darling d.	ANON 9:24
Yes, my darling d.	DE L 91:8
daughters: Your sons and your d.	DYLAN 97:13
David: King D. and King Solomon	NAYL 218:16
Davy: Sir Humphrey D.	BENT 39:9
dawn: brown fog of a winter d.	ELIOT 104:14
d. and sunset on moors	MAS 203:4
d. comes up like thunder	KIPL 169:6
D. is my brother	BELL 35:9
D. shall over Lethe break	BELL 34:14
gray d. of the morning	ADE 2:19
grey d. breaking	MAS 203:14
I said to D.: Be sudden—to Eve	THOM 295:6
see by the d.'s early	CUMM 87:2
she soft as the d.	THUR 297:12
through night hooting at d.	BEER 31:17
dawning: d. of the age of Aquarius	RADO 242:8
Dawson: Lord D. of Penn	MOYN 215:1
not been for that fool D.	ASQ 15:5
day: A long d.'s journey into night	O'NEI 223:10
And I work all d.	CHAP 67:6
bright cold d. in April	ORW 225:2
d. after the revolution	AREN 13:5
d. I was meant not to see	THAT 291:9
d. of his death was a dark	AUDEN 17:3
d. of small nations has	CHAM 66:1
d. when heaven was falling	HOUS 145:7
end of a perfect d.	BOND 49:2
Every d., in every way	COUÉ. 84:4

day (cont.):

every d. is a life	O'NEI 223:11
Go ahead, make my d.	FINK 109:9
I have met them at close of d.	YEATS 320:4
left alone with our d.	AUDEN 20:11
not a second on the d.	COOK 82:5
Oh, what a beautiful d.	HAMM 131:13
Round the d.'s dead sanctities	THOM 295:9
The blinds let through the d.	HOUS 145:5
The d. war broke out	WILT 314:16
daydreams: d. do not prevent her from	NAB 216:12
d. would darken into nightmares	SMITH 277:13
daylight: by d. and never to refuse	MENC 206:17
days: 1,000 d., nor in the life	KENN 163:11
And the d. grow short	AND 6:4
Cast your mind on other d.	YEATS 319:12
D. are where we live	LARK 179:12
d. of yore	GREN 129:4
good old d.' were a myth	ATK 15:15
Half to remember d.	FLEC 111:17
Happy d. are here again	YELL 324:3
In other d.	DE L 90:15
itself only three d.	JEANS 154:5
let us speak of darker d.	CHUR 72:13
Ten d. that shook the world	REED 245:6
The burnt-out ends of smoky d.	ELIOT 103:13
The d. go by, I remain	APOL 12:15
dazzled: Eyes still d. by the ways	LIND 188:9
dead: A d. sinner revised	BIER 47:1
After that it's d.	WAUGH 306:10
already three parts d.	RUSS 255:10
And he is d., who will not	GREN 129:5
be blooming well d.	SAR 261:3
Better red than d.	ANON 7:4
Chile. Not many d.	COCK 78:2
cold and pure and very d.	LEWIS 187:10
composer is to be d.	HON 143:3
consistent people are the d.	HUXL 148:12
curly you'll soon be d.	WIMP 315:1
d. fish swim with the stream	MUGG 215:5
d. had no speech	ELIOT 102:1
d. is tongued with fire	ELIOT 102:1
d. men lost their bones	ELIOT 105:1
D. religions do not produce	BREN 53:10
d. sound on the final stroke	ELIOT 104:14
d. that's what's wrong	CHAP 67:9
d. thing that smells sweet	THOM 294:4
d. to rapture and despair	MARK 201:3
democracy of the d.	CHES 70:2
does it make to the d.	GAND 121:10
Droops to sink among the D.	BELL 34:14
Either he's d.	PIR 235:4
Fame is a food that d. men	DOBS 92:13
For being d.	BENT 39:11
From the throat of a d. man	GRAV 128:5
gathered flowers are d.	FLEC 111:13
God is not d. but alive	ANON 8:4
healthy and wealthy and d.	THUR 297:11

dead (*cont.*):

her d. across the sea	BINY 47:4
If the d. talk to you	SZASZ 290:5
Is d. and dumb and done	DE L 91:7
kissed by the English d.	OWEN 228:3
like d. generals	TUCH 299:14
Lilacs out of the d. land	ELIOT 104:10
make sure he was d.	GOLD 126:11
millions of the mouthless d.	SORL 281:2
Mistah Kurtz — he d.	CONR 81:13
more to say when I am d.	ROB 248:10
move in a world of the d.	FORS 114:6
over the rich D.	BROO 54:12
Phoenician, a fortnight d.	ELIOT 105:8
Private Means is d.	SMITH 279:1
quick, and the d.	DEWAR 92:1
Remember me when I am d.	DOUG 93:7
rough notes and our d.'	SCOTT 265:10
saying 'Lord Jones D.'	CHES 71:11
servant's cut in half; he's d.	GRAH 127:10
shakes a d. geranium	ELIOT 103:14
somewhere that falls down d.	BARR 25:18
stars are d.	AUDEN 20:11
strove to resuscitate the d.	POUND 238:5
The d. don't die	LAWR 181:2
their wages and are d.	HOUS 145:7
There are no d.	MAET 198:10
The very d. of winter	ELIOT 100:9
they would be better d.	PARK 231:1
unheroic D. who fed the guns	SASS 262:10
When I am d., I hope it	BELL 34:10
Where d. men meet, on lips	BUTL 58:12
you remind me of the d.	SASS 263:3

deaded: I told you I'd be d.   MILL 209:4
deadener: But habit is a great d.   BECK 29:14
deadlock: Holy d.   HERB 139:7
deadly: more d. than the male   KIPL 173:11
   they are more d.   TWAIN 300:12
Deadwood: Tucson and D. and Lost Mule
           BENÉT 36:16
deaf: d., how should they know   SORL 281:2
deal: be given a square d.   ROOS 251:6

D. around me	ALGR 3:16
modest man who has a good d.	CHUR 72:8
new d. for the American	ROOS 250:3
There was a faith-healer of D.	ANON 11:9

dealing: used to d. with estate   DOUG 93:14
dean: D. of Christ Church   SPR 282:16
   The sly shade of a Rural D.   BROO 55:9
dear: D. 338171   COW 84:10
   D. One is mine as mirrors   AUDEN 19:1
death: After the first d.   THOM 292:12

And d. shall have no dominion	THOM 293:12
And d., who had the soldier	DOUG 93:8
A proper view of d.	SIMM 275:8
Birth, and copulation, and d.	ELIOT 104:6
Birth or D.	ELIOT 100:10
Black Widow, d.	LOW 192:2
bleeding to d. of time	GRAV 128:8

death (*cont.*):

brought d. into the world	TWAIN 301:13
d. and I will coquette	MARQ 201:7
D. and taxes and childbirth	MITC 211:7
d. could scarcely be bettered	BENN 38:3
D. destroys a man	FORS 115:4
D. devours all lovely things	MILL 208:4
d. in a blizzard to try	ATK 16:1
D. in Venice	MANN 200:5
[D. is]	ANON 7:15
d. is one of the few things	ALLEN 4:15
d. of one so young	SPEN 282:1
D. opens unknown doors	MAS 203:11
d. reveals the eminent	SHAW 272:11
'D.,' said Mark Staithes	HUXL 148:16
defend to the d. your right	TALL 290:11
doubt is nothing but d.	UNAM 302:9
enormously improved by d.	SAKI 257:6
fear d.	FROH 117:8
Finality is d. Perfection	STEP 285:3
friend and enemy is but D.	BROO 54:10
heroes up the line to d.	SASS 262:7
idea of D. saves him	FORS 115:4
I do not see why d. should	NAB 217:2
I have a rendezvous with D.	SEEG 265:12
I should be glad of another d.	ELIOT 100:10
Lead me from d. to life	KUMAR 177:4
maid is like a d. by drowning	FERB 108:5
Man has created d.	YEATS 323:5
morning I signed my d.	COLL 79:9
my d. was an exaggeration	TWAIN 301:7
no cure for birth and d.	SANT 260:19
O D., where is thy sting	ROSS 253:6

O D., where is thy sting-a-ling-a-ling
           ANON 10:8

[Ogden Mills] the kiss of d.	SMITH 276:15
O million-murdering D.	ROSS 253:6
one way out an' d.'s	WILL 312:6
On life, on d.	YEATS 319:13
only nervousness or d.	LEB 183:8
Peaceful out-of-breath d.	MCG 195:2
Pledges them that D. is ending	BELL 34:14
Pontifical D., that doth	THOM 296:8
prepare as though for d.	KATH 200:8
Satisfaction is d.	SHAW 273:4
seen visible, D.'s artifact	ABSE 1:3
suicide 25 years after his d.	BEAV 28:10
Swarm over, D.	BETJ 42:2
terror to life and makes d.	TREE 298:8
that I have longed for d.	PROU 240:10
The d. of hope and despair	ELIOT 102:2
The nearest thing to d. in life	ANON 10:1
The only possible d.	DUB 96:2
there a life before d.	HEAN 136:12
This is the d. of air	ELIOT 102:2
thought d. had undone so many	ELIOT 104:14
through the d. of some of her	MAS 203:7
until the arrival of d.	BERNE 41:6
was much possessed by d.	ELIOT 103:1

death (*cont.*):

you know, a very sad d.   SPOO 282:12

you're frightened of d.   DONL 93:3

deathless: let us make love d.   TREN 298:11

deathly: d. inner consuming   HESSE 140:3

death-sentence: d. without a whimper

LAWR 182:5

death-struck: The beautiful and d. year

HOUS 146:12

debate: d. forcefully and quote   HOGB 142:10

The quality of d.   SOPER 281:1

debt: A promise made is a d.   SERV 267:2

d. of gratitude we owe   TWAIN 301:13

midst of life we are in d.   MUMF 215:11

The National D. is a very   SELL 266:10

decade: d. after decade the truth   SOLZ 280:1

fun to be in the same d.   ROOS 250:1

decay: D. with imprecision   ELIOT 101:9

has no ebb, d. no flood   YEATS 319:9

deceitfulness: Cat of such d. and suavity

ELIOT 102:12

deceive: creates faith does not d.   SHAW 273:22

deceived: Let us not be d.   BAR 27:8

deceives: d. with whispering ambitions

ELIOT 100:7

December: From May to D.   AND 6:4

might have roses in D.   BARR 26:4

decency: D. is Indecency's conspiracy

SHAW 272:10

decent: aristocracy to what is d.   HOPE 143:10

d. people live beyond   SAKI 257:9

Here were d. godless people   ELIOT 104:2

decerated: d. dark red as I have somber ASHF 14:5

decide: d. between alternatives   BONH 49:4

You'll have to d.   DYLAN 97:14

decided: d. only to be undecided   CHUR 74:1

decision: d. has to be made   TRUM 299:12

fast and specific d.   TUCH 299:15

freedom of personal d.   JUNG 160:3

make a 'realistic d.'   MCC 194:2

monologue is not a d.   ATTL 16:6

questions of will or d.   CHOM 71:15

decisions: on the eve of great d.   STEV 286:7

deck: d. put on its leaves again   FLEC 112:5

declaration: There has been no d. of war

EDEN 98:1

declarations: And timid lovers' d.   AUDEN 19:16

declare: contracting powers solemnly d.

BRIA 53:11

d. before you all   ELIZ 105:12

declared: hundred judges have d.   QUIL 242:4

decline: d. utterly to be impartial   CHUR 73:12

went into a bit of a d.   ADAMS 2:1

decompose: d. in a barrel of porter   DONL 93:4

decomposing: d. in the eternity of print

WOOLF 317:5

decoration: some sort of d. for it   OSB 226:11

decorative: be d. and to do right   FIRB 109:10

decorum: The old Lie: Dulce et d. est

OWEN 227:14

deductions: features from which d.   DOYLE 95:11

dee: Hi diddle dee d.   WASH 305:6

deed: motive, not the d.   YEATS 321:9

right d. for the wrong   ELIOT 102:9

time the d. took place   ELIOT 102:12

deep: A gentle motion with the d.   DAV 89:1

are lovely, dark and d.   FROST 118:11

D. from human vanity   HARDY 134:4

D. in the heart of Texas   HERS 140:1

d. is the silence   DRIN 95:17

d. peace of the double-bed   CAMP 61:13

Oh, d. in my heart   ANON 12:6

say beauty is only sin d.   SAKI 257:14

deepens: It d. like a coastal shelf   LARK 179:2

deeper: Christ went d. than I have   HARR 135:6

This d. layer I call   JUNG 160:4

Deever: Danny D. in the mornin'   KIPL 168:9

defeat: Alamein we never had a d.   CHUR 76:7

d. comparable to any lost   PHIL 233:15

d. is an orphan   CIANO 76:15

In d.   CHUR 76:3

In d. unbeatable   CHUR 72:5

we know we should d. you   KIPL 170:16

defeated: be destroyed but not d.   HEM 138:10

History to the d.   AUDEN 20:11

we succeed in being d.   HELL 137:7

defect: The Chief D. of Henry King   BELL 32:19

defence: best d. against the atom   ANON 7:3

d. against the anti-Christ   BUCH 57:7

d. like elaborate courtesy   LUCAS 192:7

d. of England you no longer   BALD 23:5

d. of the indefensible   ORW 226:1

extremism in the d. of liberty   GOLD 126:4

only d. against betrayal   WILL 312:2

The only d. is in offence   BALD 23:4

defences: d. of peace must be constructed

ANON 8:7

defend: d. any one or anything   MENC 207:1

d. ourselves with guns   GOEB 125:9

D. the bad against the worse   DAY-L 89:8

I will d. to the death   TALL 290:11

we shall d. our island   CHUR 74:6

defiance: defeat: d. In victory   CHUR 76:3

d. of military authority   SASS 262:11

defiant: It is d.   READ 244:2

definition: capable of exact legal d.   RUSS 255:19

d. is the enclosing a wilderness   BUTL 60:2

d. of a free society   STEV 286:3

d. of a specialist as one   MAYO 206:3

d. of capitalism I would   HAMP 132:7

good working d. of hell   SHAW 273:7

deflowered: At last you are d.   COW 85:6

deformity: Art is significant d.   FRY 120:3

degree: d. of independence still   EINS 99:10

dei: *Introibo ad altare D*   JOYCE 158:14

deity: between the D. and the Drains   STR 288:1

D. but accepted Carnot's   WELLS 308:4

delegate: When in trouble, d.   BOREN 49:9
deleted: Expletive d.   ANON 7:22
Delia: D., if S-E-X ever rears   AYCK 21:6
deliberate: D. speed, majestic instancy
                                                   THOM 295:3
  Originality is d. and forced   HOFF 142:7
delicate-filmed: D. as new-spun silk   HARDY 134:1
delight: A lonely impulse of d.   YEATS 322:11
  And I was filled with such d.   SASS 263:5
  begins in d. and ends   FROST 117:13
  Had other aims than my d.   HARDY 134:9
  I most d. in Me   CAMP 62:1
  leaping light for your d.   AUDEN 19:6
  Moved to d. by the melody   AUDEN 20:12
  Teach us D. in simple things   KIPL 173:2
  The d. of her husband   RANS 243:1
  Till to d.   DE L 90:15
  visions for a simple human d.   BARB 24:15
delighted: literature is to be d.   CECIL 65:9
delightful: affording d. prospects   HOFF 142:9
  alcohol produces a d. social   BENN 38:11
  really d. sensation   FERB 108:5
  take courage: it can be d.   SHAW 268:5
delighting: But, O! d. me   HODG 142:4
delirium: All that d. of the brave   YEATS 321:15
deliver: D. us, good Lord   CHES 70:7
Del Monte: The man from D. says 'Yes'
                                                   ANON 9:22
deluge: d. subsides and the waters   CHUR 73:11
delusion: d. that one woman   MENC 206:12
delusions: gave us such insane d.   HELL 137:7
demand: not a note of d.   SCHN 264:7
demean: We think they d. us   RATT 243:7
demesne: Is private *pagus* or d.   AUDEN 16:10
demeure: *Les jours s'en vont, je d.*   APOL 12:15
democracies: d. it is the only sacred   FRAN 116:5
democracy: can be cured by more d.
                                                   SMITH 276:16
  capacity for justice makes d.   NIEB 219:9
  D. and proper drains   BETJ 44:5
  D. and socialism are means   NEHRU 219:1
  d. by universal suffrage   BENN 37:6
  d. can afford among   BEV 45:10
  D. is a *State* which recognizes   LENIN 184:15
  d. is that it has tolerated   BEVAN 45:3
  D. is the name we give   FLERS 112:11
  D. is the recurrent suspicion   WHITE 310:1
  D. is the theory   MENC 206:15
  d. is the worst form   CHUR 75:5
  D. means government   CHES 69:16
  D. means government by discussion   ATTL 16:9
  D. resumed her reign   BELL 34:13
  d. should spend less time   STR 288:9
  D. substitutes election   SHAW 271:18
  D. tells us not to neglect   CHES 70:2
  D. will not be salvaged   HOGB 142:10
  d. would have rallied   BALD 23:7
  Envy is the basis of d.   RUSS 255:3

democracy (*cont.*):
  great arsenal of d.   ROOS 250:11
  It is the d. of the dead   CHES 70:2
  little less d. to save   ATK 15:14
  must be made safe for d.   WILS 314:13
  political aspirant under d.   MENC 206:9
  puts in the place of d.   FOSD 116:4
  So Two cheers for D.   FORS 115:13
  voting that's d.   STOP 286:14
Democrat: D., in that order   JOHN 156:15
démocratie: *D. est le nom que nous*   FLERS 112:11
démocraties: *dans les d. elle est la*   FRAN 116:5
democrats: d. object to men being   CHES 70:2
  telling lies about the D.   STEV 285:16
demur: If I d., for, be advised   HEAN 136:13
denial: d. of Him by the atheist   PROU 241:5
denied: call that may not be d.   MAS 203:15
denizen: The spider is sole d.   HARDY 133:7
denominator: I can find no common d.
                                                   AUDEN 18:16
denouncing: d. some one or something
                                                   MENC 207:1
dentist: sooner go to my d. any day
                                                   WAUGH 306:13
denunciation: d. of the young is a necessary
                                                   SMITH 278:1
deoch-an-doris: Just a wee d.   MORR 214:1
depart: D., I say, and let us   AMERY 5:9
departing: someone who's d.   RILKE 247:10
department: fair sex is your d.   DOYLE 95:1
dépêches: *Une de ces d. dont M*   PROU 241:3
depended: always on the kindness   WILL 312:10
dependence: d. on the appreciation   CONN 80:10
depends: It all d. what you mean   JOAD 155:14
  so much d.   WILL 312:13
  That d. on the tip   BRAC 51:14
deposit: d. in my name at a Swiss   ALLEN 4:11
depression: are the best cures for d.   SMITH 277:1
  it's a d. when you lose   TRUM 299:9
deprivation: D. is for me what daffodils
                                                   LARK 179:9
  this as a 'cycle of d.'   JOS 157:8
depth: about d. knows about God   TILL 297:18
Derby: [the 17th Earl of D.]   HAIG 130:11
descended: iron curtain has d.   CHUR 73:3
désenchantement: *confondis le d. avec la vérité*
                                                   SART 261:15
desert: scare myself with my own d.   FROST 118:3
  The d. sighs in the bed   AUDEN 16:13
  Zuleika, on a d. island   BEER 31:8
deserts: D. are there, and different   SACK 256:12
  In the d. of the heart   AUDEN 17:7
  It's my d.; I'm a second   BARR 25:12
deserve: d. to get it good and hard   MENC 206:15
  war, but only d. it   CHUR 76:6
  you somehow haven't to d.   FROST 119:1
deserves: everyone has the face he d.   ORW 224:13
déshabille: *on dirait qu'elle se d.*   COL 79:2
desiccated: Party is a d. calculating   BEVAN 44:11

design: might of d.   SHAW 268:23
designed: horse d. by a committee   ANON 7:10
designer: D. infinite   THOM 295:12
designing: Say I am d. St Paul's   BENT 39:8
désir: d. pour empêcher les choses   PROU 240:13
desirable: D. than it ever was before   SASS 263:2
desire: d. for preventing the thing   PROU 240:13
   d. on the part   BUTL 59:15
   d. to be vilified by enemies   BIER 46:8
   d. to have all the fun   SAY 263:8
   d. to take medicine   OSLER 227:3
   From what I've tasted of d.   FROST 118:10
   Land of Heart's D.   YEATS 319:9
   Memory and d., stirring   ELIOT 104:10
   Yea, naught for your d.   CHES 68:9
desired: You who d. so much   CRANE 85:12
desires: d. of the heart   AUDEN 19:2
desireus: d. of being the correct   ASHF 14:9
desiring: admire without d.   BRAD 52:1
desk: From counter or d. among grey   YEATS 320:4
   Turn upward from the d.   ELIOT 105:5
desolation: witnesses to the d. of war   GEOR 123:4
despair: A minor form of d.   BIER 46:23
   d. and utter hopelessness   ALLEN 4:13
   D. is the price one pays   GREE 128:13
   Do not d.   PUDN 241:7
   foundation of unyielding d.   RUSS 255:12
   Lead me from d. to hope   KUMAR 177:4
   never hoped can never d.   SHAW 268:9
   or the quality of his d.   CONN 80:14
   Rhymed out in love's d.   YEATS 322:4
   The death of hope and d.   ELIOT 102:2
   without understanding d.   LAING 177:7
desperate: ardent for some d. glory   OWEN 227:14
   d. act of men too profoundly   READ 244:2
despise: d. Shakespeare when I measure
                                              SHAW 274:4
   Government I d. for ends   KEYN 164:10
despised: d. by the rest of society   BRAT 52:15
despondency: SPREAD ALARM AND D.   PEN 232:15
despondently: Sprouting d. at area gates
                                              ELIOT 103:15
destined: d. to live for three-score   JEANS 154:5
destinies: development of human d. the play
                                              FISH 109:15
   recognised, and robed as d.   LARK 179:5
destiny: Anatomy is d.   FREUD 117:2
   d. can determine how   BEAU 89:9
   D., n. A tyrant's authority   BIER 47:2
   I were walking with d.   CHUR 76:5
   We hug our little d. again   HEAN 136:12
destroy: D. him as you will   CONN 80:16
   necessary to d. the town   ANON 9:1
   When you d. a blade of grass   BOTT 50:4
   Whom the gods wish to d.   CONN 80:8
destroyed: be d. but not defeated   HEM 138:10
   can be d. by a doctor   SHAF 267:6

destroyed (cont.):
   generation d. by madness   GINS 125:1
destroyer: Is my d.   THOM 293:4
destroying: d. ourselves by violence   LAING 177:9
destroys: Death d. a man   FORS 115:4
destruction: by a brief fit of d.   BORN 50:2
   To say that for d. ice   FROST 118:10
   whether the mad d.   GAND 121:10
destructive: d. element submit yourself
                                              CONR 81:14
detachment: vigilance and a rare d.   MAUG 204:10
detected: d. only once in the use   BENN 38:12
detection: D. is, or ought   DOYLE 95:2
detective: d. novel is the art-for-art's-sake
                                              PRIT 240:5
detector: shock-proof shit d.   HEM 138:11
detente: d. and world peace   THAT 292:2
deteriorating: With shabby equipment always d.
                                              ELIOT 101:16
determination: character but the d. of incident
                                              JAMES 153:5
determine: that the means employed d.
                                              HUXL 148:13
dethrimental: temper till it would be d.
                                              O'CAS 222:14
de Valera: Negotiating with d.   LLOY 189:7
development: d. of human destinies   FISH 109:15
Devil: An apology for the D.   BUTL 59:21
   But the D. whoops   KIPL 170:1
   D. whispered behind   KIPL 169:12
   last: the D. howling   SQUI 283:3
   man's spirit is d.'s   SHAW 268:13
   that d.'s madness   SERV 266:16
   The D., having nothing else   BELL 34:11
   The d.'s walking parody   CHES 71:7
   up believing in the d.   KNOX 176:7
devils: And down on the d. we shot   ASQ 15:9
   d. to contest his vision   MAIL 199:10
devoid: entirely d. of interest   DOYLE 94:5
Devon: 'Twas Devon, glorious D.   BOUL 50:8
devoured: He has d. the infant child   HOUS 144:10
devours: Death d. all lovely things   MILL 208:4
dew: again in the d. of morn   YEATS 318:7
   drenched with d.   DE L 90:9
Dewey: D. threw his diaper   ICKES 150:9
   [Thomas D.]   DYKS 97:2
dews: Nor ask amid the d. of morning   HOUS 145:8
diagnostician: rectum makes a good d.
                                              OSLER 226:17
dial: D. 'M' for murder   KNOTT 176:4
dialect: picturesque use of d.   HARDY 133:12
   To purify the d. of the tribe   ELIOT 102:3
diametrically: d. opposed doctrines   HOOV 143:6
diamond: d. and safire bracelet   LOOS 190:16
diamonds: D. are a girl's best friend   ROBIN 248:7
   Goodness, what beautiful d.   WEST 309:11
   man enough to give him d.   GABOR 120:14
Diana: It's awf'lly bad luck on D.   BETJ 42:10
diaper: threw his d. into the ring   ICKES 150:9

diaries: keep d. to remember   O'NEI 223:13

diary: d. and some day it'll keep   WEST 309:3

    life of every man is a d.   BARR 25:14

    secret d. of Adrian Mole   TOWN 298:4

dice: [God] does not play d.   EINS 99:6

Dickens: D. as children but it never   BENN 38:2

    he [D.] was probably   WILS 313:2

dictated: We will not be d.   CHES 69:7

dictation: at d. speed what he knew   AMIS 6:1

dictator: been that the German d.   CHUR 74:2

dictators: D. ride to and fro upon   CHUR 76:8

    which d. may cultivate   BEV 45:10

dictatorship: government you have a d.   TRUM 299:13

    order to establish the d.   ORW 225:8

dictatorships: d. it puts   FOSD 116:4

dictionary: time I ever made the d.   WEST 309:10

did: d. for them both   SASS 262:8

didn't: D. she [or he or they] do well   FORS 116:1

die: better to d. on your feet   IBAR 149:17

    clean place to d.   KAV 162:2

    d. for my country   KINN 168:2

    D.? I should say not   BARR 27:1

    d. like a true-blue rebel   HILL 140:10

    d. will be an awfully big   BARR 25:19

    Don't d. of ignorance   ANON 7:18

    fifteen-year-old boy until *they* d.   ROTH 253:11

    fight and d.   HOOV 143:4

    he had to d. in my week   JOPL 157:7

    Hope I d. before I get old   TOWN 298:5

    I d. each time   HEM 138:4

    If I should d., think only   BROO 55:2

    If we must d., let it not   MCKAY 195:8

    It is most grand to d.   MAS 203:11

    Let me d. a youngman's death   MCG 195:2

    Live and let d.   FLEM 112:10

    not that I'm afraid to d.   ALLEN 4:6

    Old soldiers never d.   FOLEY 113:2

    People d., but books never   ROOS 251:4

    sky when you d.   HILL 140:11

    something he will d.   KING 166:8

    these who d. as cattle   OWEN 227:13

    they d. earlier   MENC 206:13

    they do not d. of wisdom   STEP 285:2

    they only let Him d.   KENN 288:12

    To d. and know it   LOW 192:2

    war it's the poor who d.   SART 261:6

    We must love one another or d.   AUDEN 17:12

    Who did not wish to d.   SHAW- 274:13

    Who went abroad to d.   LETTS 186:9

    work, work till we d.   LEWIS 187:5

    you asked this man to d.   AUDEN 20:8

died: d. if it had not been   ASQ 15:5

    d. to save their country   CHES 68:7

    foolish ideas have d.   FITZ 110:9

    He d. who loved to live   MCH 195:6

    If any question why we d.   KIPL 175:10

    Mithridates, he d. old   HOUS 147:1

died (*cont.*):

    Mother d. today. Or perhaps   CAMUS 62:15

    There d. a myriad   POUND 238:9

dies: begotten born and d.   YEATS 321:5

    d. fighting has increase   GREN 129:5

    into Bovril when she d.   ASQ 15:3

    kingdom where nobody d.   MILL 208:6

    little something in me d.   VIDAL 304:6

    When a lovely flame d.   HARB 132:11

    Who d. if England live   KIPL 170:15

diet: important part of a balanced d.   LEB 183:10

Dieu: D. est avec tout le monde   ANOU 12:11

    D. pour la rendre responsable   DUH 96:4

    le bon D. who drives it   CHR 72:3

    tue tous, on est un d.   ROST 253:9

difference: And that has made all the d.   FROST 118:8

    d. between accidental limitations   AUDEN 18:7

    d. between our talents   DE B 89:10

    d. does it make   GAND 121:10

    d. within the sexes   COMP 80:3

    greatly exaggerate the d.   SHAW 270:11

    it is d. of opinion   TWAIN 301:20

differences: unrealistic settlement of the d.   ROOS 251:2

different: had thought they were d.   ELIOT 100:10

    only on d. subjects   ROG 249:10

    something completely d.   CHAP 67:7

    They are d. from you   FITZ 110:7

    will not know it's a d.   LARK 178:13

    you'd have made them d.   O'BR 222:1

differently: one who thinks d.   LUX 192:14

    they do things d. there   HART 135:14

differs: delusion that one woman d.   MENC 206:12

difficult: at present, must be d.   ELIOT 104:8

    d. is what takes a little   NANS 217:8

    It has been found d.   CHES 71:5

    Luckily, this is not d.   WHIT 310:20

    The fascination of what's d.   YEATS 319:3

difficulties: up these little local d.   MACM 197:5

difficulty: quits the memory with d.   BEEC 30:2

dig: d. him up and throw stones   SHAW 274:4

    d. till you gently perspire   KIPL 171:13

    I'll d. with it   HEAN 136:8

    Let 'D. for Victory'   DORM 93:5

digestions: Few radicals have good d.   BUTL 59:16

digging: d. in the garden   ASHF 14:3

dignify: Dared d. the labor   CRANE 85:12

dignité: égaux en d. et en droits   ANON 11:16

dignity: d. and greatness and peace   COW 84:5

    equal in d. and rights   ANON 11:16

    Official d. tends to increase   HUXL 148:8

dillied: But I d. and dallied   COLL 79:5

dilly-dally: Don't d. on the way   COLL 79:5

dime: Brother can you spare a d.   HARB 132:12

    d. that we've got is honestly   NIXON 220:10

dine: going to d. with some men   BENT 39:8

dined: d. last night   BEER 30:11

    more d. against than dining   BOWRA 51:8

ding: D.! dong   LERN 185:20
dining: d. with the Borgias tonight   BEER 30:11
  more dined against than d.   BOWRA 51:8
dinky: Hinky, d., parley-voo   ANON 9:19
dinner: D. in the diner nothing   GORD 126:14
  I get too hungry for d.   HART 135:11
  refrain from asking it to d.   HALS 131:8
  The best number for a d.   GULB 130:7
  The man who came to d.   KAUF 161:7
dinner-knives: gravel paths with broken d.
   KIPL 171:3
diodes: terrible pain in all the d.   ADAMS 1:13
Dior: Never darken my D. again   LILL 188:4
diplomacy: D. is to do and say   GOLD 126:1
  d. shall proceed always   WILS 314:15
diplomat: A d.   STIN 286:12
  d. these days is nothing   UST 302:18
dipping: age o'ercargoed, d. deep   FLEC 112:3
direction: With no d. home   DYLAN 97:7
dirt: d. succeed where sweetness   FORS 114:9
  first four years the d.   CRISP 86:3
  insult sex, to do d. on it   LAWR 181:19
dirty: give pornography a d.   BARN 25:4
  In a d. glass   PAN 229:4
  'Jug Jug' to d. ears   ELIOT 104:16
  sex d.   ALLEN 4:7
  you d. rat   CAGN 60:18
Dirty Dick: At D.'s and Sloppy Joe's   AUDEN 18:17
dirty-mindedness: deliberate, journalistic d.
   LAWR 181:5
disadvantage: d. of being a hog   MORT 214:4
disagree: agree with us or d. with us   OWEN 227:11
disappeared: He d. in the dead of winter
   AUDEN 17:3
disappointed: Sir! you have d. us   BELL 33:7
disappointing: he'll be the least d.   BAR 27:7
disappointment: d. to their children   POW 239:5
disapprove: I d. of what you say   TALL 290:11
disaster: meet with Triumph and D.   KIPL 173:7
disasters: d. of English history   WAUGH 305:15
  d. of the world are due   CONN 81:1
disastrous: d. and the unpalatable   GALB 121:5
  war is as d. as to lose   CHR 72:1
discard: scientist to d. a pet hypothesis   LOR 191:2
discharge: There's no d. in the war   KIPL 170:12
disciple: am a d. of Bernard Shaw   SHAW 268:22
Discobolus: D. standeth and turneth   BUTL 60:6
discontents: Civilization and its d.   RIV 248:5
  source of all our d.   LEACH 182:8
discount: At a d.   FRY 119:15
discover: d. that I had no talent   BENC 36:13
  d. that there is no God   SMITH 278:3
discovered: dramatist who had d.   SAKI 258:9
discovering: process of d. who we   AUDEN 18:7
discovery: are the portals of d.   JOYCE 159:7
  D. consists of seeing what   SZEN 290:8
  his d. to the world   SAKI 258:9
  Medicinal d.   AYRES 22:1

discreet: The d. charm of the bourgeoisie
   BUÑ 57:13
discretion: D. is not the better part   STR 288:4
discriminate: do learn to d.   LAWR 181:14
discussion: means government by d.   ATTL 16:9
disease: But when they name any d.   PUZO 241:10
  d. that afflicts amateurs   CHES 69:10
  from the particular d.   JER 155:9
  I have Bright's d.   PER 232:17
  nineteenth century, it was a d.   SZASZ 289:13
  our national d.   JAMES 153:12
  sexually transmitted d.   ANON 9:15
  There is no Cure for this D.   BELL 33:1
diseases: d. is a sort of *Arabian*   OSLER 227:5
  scientific treatment for all d.   SHAW 268:20
  sneezes spread d.   ANON 7:14
disenchantment: I mistook d. for truth
   SART 261:15
disgrace: Intellectual d.   AUDEN 17:6
  It's no d. t'be poor   HUBB 147:8
  Its private life is a d.   ANON 10:13
disgruntled: if not actually d.   WOD 315:9
disgusting: murder of men is d.   EINS 99:4
dishonoured: To stain the stiff d. shroud
   ELIOT 102:13
disillusion: France; and one d.   KEYN 164:11
disillusionment: D. in living is the finding
   STEIN 284:12
disillusionments: d. in the lives   SAKI 257:17
disinterested: that there are d. actions   GIDE 124:7
dislike: d. it   MOORE 213:2
  I d. what I fancy I feel   ANON 11:9
  know whether I like or d.   FORS 115:5
disliked: day two things they d.   MAUG 205:4
disloyalty: not like subversion or d.   HELL 137:9
dismantle: d. apartheid ourselves   MAND 200:1
dismount: which they dare not d.   CHUR 76:8
disorder: d. by authorities whom   CONN 81:6
dispensation: ease here, in the old d.   ELIOT 100:10
dispiriting: Muse this cannot but be d.
   SMITH 279:2
disposed: way she d. of an empire   HARL 135:4
dispossessed: his little heart, d.   JAMES 153:9
disputes: d. or conflicts of whatever   BRIA 53:11
dissipated: still keep looking so d.   BENC 36:3
dissociation: d. of sensibility set   ELIOT 104:7
dissolution: at home? A lingering d.   BECK 28:13
distains: A starlit or a moonlit dome d.
   YEATS 323:9
distance: d. from the political situation
   RAK 242:10
  longest d. between two places   WILL 312:7
distempered: That questions the d. part
   ELIOT 101:15
distils: Art d. sensation and embodies   BARZ 27:12
distinction: British have the d.   ATTL 16:4
  d. at this dangerous moment   BELL 35:12
  D. between the Ashes   DOYLE 95:3

distinction (*cont.*):

few escape that d.	TWAIN 302:3
see you were a man of d.	FIEL 108:8

distinguish: d. human society from — SHAW 269:7
Give us the wisdom to d. — NIEB 219:10
distinguished: d. thing — JAMES 152:12
I write like a d. author — NAB 217:4
distortion: d. of the Marxist idea — BENN 37:3
distortions: d. of ingrown virginity — AUDEN 20:3
distraction: attention in the midst of d. — BELL 35:13
distress: avoids the sight of d. — MAUG 205:6
distressing: d. moment can ever face — TUCH 299:15
distrust: I d. the incommunicable — SART 262:4
We have to d. each other — WILL 312:2
disturb: Art is meant to d. — BRAQ 52:13
ourselves doesn't d. — HESSE 140:2
disturbing: upon as a d. influence — GALB 121:2
diver: Don't forget the d. — KAV 162:5
divided: D. by the morning tea — MACN 198:4
dividend: d. from time's tomorrows — SASS 262:5
divine: You look d. as you advance — NASH 217:12
divinely: D. subsidized to provoke — FRY 119:17
divisible: d. into two greed classes — BEER 30:10
divisions: d. did you say the Pope — STAL 283:5
divorced: Demand to be d. — CHES 71:9
my fault that we got d. — ALLEN 4:20
Dixon: D. . . . tried to flail his features — AMIS 5:14
do: Can I d. you now, sir — KAV 162:4
Diplomacy is to d. and say — GOLD 126:1
d. anything she hasn't — KAEL 160:6
D. evil in return — AUDEN 17:11
D. I dare to eat a peach — ELIOT 103:12
D. not do unto others — SHAW 271:15
D. not expect again a phoenix — DAY-L 89:4
D. not fold, spindle — ANON 7:16
d. something to *help* me — LAUR 180:5
d. the perfectly correct — SHAW 269:10
d. the right deed — ELIOT 102:9
d. those things — KEYN 165:1
d. well — FORS 116:1
D. what thou wilt shall — CROW 86:12
Goodness had nothing to d. — WEST 309:11
Let's d. it, let's fall — PORT 236:15
long as they d. what I say — THAT 291:11
not d. things themselves — RAV 243:9
So little done, so much to d. — RHOD 246:6
wild extremes I could d. — DURY 97:1
Doc: cards with a man called D. — ALGR 3:14
What's up, D. — AVERY 21:4
doctor: can be destroyed by a d. — SHAF 267:6
I really am a horse d. — PIR 235:5
Knocked a d. — SIMP 275:12
my d., what do you say — ROTH 253:12
doctors: We d. know — CUMM 87:8
doctrine: d. of ignoble ease — ROOS 251:10
how a d. so illogical — KEYN 164:15
doctrines: diametrically opposed d. — HOOV 143:6
documents: d. I have to have a box — HOME 143:2
dodo: The D. never had a chance — CUPPY 87:10

doe: With the fallow d. — THOM 294:2
dog: beaten d. beneath the hail — POUND 238:17
been working like a d. — LENN 185:10
But if a man bites a d. — BOG 48:10
But where's the wild d. — YEATS 319:4
d. and I just want to say — NIXON 220:10
d. is that you may make — BUTL 60:1
D. returns to his Vomit — KIPL 173:12
engine of pollution, the d. — SPAR 281:8
I'm a lean d., a keen dog — MCL 196:6
jumps over the lazy d. — ANON 10:12
mad d. of the Middle East — REAG 244:9
your heart to a d. to tear — KIPL 168:6
doggie: that d. in the window — MERR 207:9
dogma: d. of the Ghost — RYLE 256:9
will serve to beat a d. — GUED 130:1
dogmatism: ignorance the greater the d.
 — OSLER 227:6
dogs: All the d. of Europe bark — AUDEN 17:6
And dancing d. and bears — HODG 142:2
D. bark — DAV 88:15
d. go on with their doggy — AUDEN 17:9
hates d. and babies can't — ROST 253:10
keep parrots or puppy d. — CAMP 62:3
let's go to the d. tonight — HERB 139:10
Mad d. and Englishmen — COW 84:13
really kind to d. — BEER 31:11
doileys: Beg pardon, I'm soiling the d. — BETJ 43:1
doing: he's d. a grand job — FROST 117:12
dollar: D. lolly — SYKES 289:7
dolls: Valley of the d. — SUS 289:3
Dolly: Hello, D., well, hello Dolly — HERM 139:20
dolphin-torn: That d., that gong-tormented
 — YEATS 323:10
dome: moonlit d. distains — YEATS 323:9
domestic: naïve d. Burgundy without — THUR 297:8
respectable d. establishment — BENN 37:11
dominate: seeking to d. the world — BRAD 52:7
domination: d. of Prussia is wholly — ASQ 14:19
Soviet d. of Eastern Europe — FORD 113:9
domine: D., defende nos — GODL 125:8
dominion: And death shall have no d.
 — THOM 293:12
from the d. of religion — GOLD 126:3
hand that holds d. — THOM 293:11
domino: 'falling d.' principle — EIS 100:3
don: *c'est avant tout le d.* — ANOU 12:13
D. different from those — BELL 35:6
Remote and ineffectual D. — BELL 35:5
done: belief they d. the old woman — SHAW 273:16
D. because we are too — HARDY 133:6
d. very well out — BALD 23:2
have d. being what she — YEATS 319:2
he d. her wrong — ANON 8:1
Is dead and dumb and d. — DE L 91:7
Nothing to be d. — BECK 29:4
ought never to have d. — BEVIN 46:1
Something should be d. — EDW 99:1

donkeys: d. labelled Sally and Peppy   SHAF 267:5
Donne: another Newton, a new D.   HUXL 148:18
dons: D. admirable! Dons of Might   BELL 35:6
   technology d. from Cambridge   AMIS 5:13
don't: And d. criticize   DYLAN 97:13
   And d. go near the water   DE L 91:8
   But d. go near the water   ANON 9:24
   D. ask a man to drink and drive   ANON 7:17
   D. ask me, ask the horse   FREUD 117:3
   D. die of ignorance   ANON 7:18
   d. do it in the street   CAMP 61:11
   D. follow leaders   DYLAN 97:12
   D. forget the diver   KAV 162:5
   D. panic   ADAMS 1:11
   d. spare the horses   HILL 141:1
   D. tell my mother I'm living   HERB 139:8
   D. think twice, it's all right   DYLAN 97:4
   d. think you can't think   INGE 150:13
   George—d. do   GREN 129:3
doodle: A Yankee D., do or die   COHAN 78:13
Doolittle: across the Park, Miss D.   SHAW 273:18
door: childhood when the d.   GREE 128:18
   Converses at the d. apart   ELIOT 102:13
   generation is knocking at the d.   SHAW 274:11
   Is beating on the d.   YEATS 321:1
   lock and splintered the d.   AUDEN 19:8
   On the wrong side of the d.   CHES 68:11
   own room with the d. shut   WHAR 309:20
   that grows beside thy d.   HOPE 144:3
   Towards the d. we never opened   ELIOT 101:6
   We like to see them to the d.   MCG 195:3
doorbell: d. of a Mrs Renton   MORT 214:6
doors: Death opens unknown d.   MAS 203:11
   In Little Girls is slamming D.   BELL 33:8
   taxi-cab with both d.   HUGH 147:10
doorstep: Leave your worry on the d.   FIEL 108:11
Dorchester: Safe in the D. Hotel   BETJ 42:5
Dorset: vault for funeral Monday D.   BEER 31:18
dotage: Pedantry is the d. of knowledge
      JACK 151:18
double: about a joke with a d.   BARK 25:2
   it plies the saplings d.   HOUS 146:7
double-bed: d. after the hurly-burly   CAMP 61:13
doubled: D. the globe of dead   THOM 293:10
doubles: It immediately d.   ALLEN 4:12
doublethink: D. means the power   ORW 225:7
doubt: And troubled with religious d.   CHES 70:11
   d. is our passion and our   JAMES 152:14
   freckles, and d.   PARK 230:12
   Life is d.   UNAM 302:9
   Oh! let us never, never d.   BELL 33:18
   When in d., mumble   BOREN 49:9
   when in d., strike it   TWAIN 301:17
   yourself when all men d. you   KIPL 173:7
doubted: Christian religion d.   BUTL 60:9
doubts: will be our d. of today   ROOS 251:3
doughnut: The optimist sees the d.   WILS 314:1
Douglas-Home: [Alec D.]   CONN 80:12

dove: d. complaining   DAY-L 89:4
Dover: chalk cliffs of D.   BALD 23:5
   white cliffs of D.   BURT 58:8
down: Come on d.   CROW 86:13
   D. by the salley gardens   YEATS 321:13
   d., down into the darkness   MILL 207:16
   d. express in the small   WOD 315:18
   'd.' from Jimmy's university   OSB 226:12
   D. in the forest something   SIMP 275:10
   D. the passage which we   ELIOT 101:6
   D. these mean streets   CHAN 66:9
   D. to Gehenna or up   KIPL 175:4
   Had me low and had me d.   GERS 123:6
   meet 'em on your way d.   MIZN 212:1
   must d. to the seas again   MAS 203:14
downhearted: Are we d.   KNIG 176:3
   We are not d. The only   CHAM 66:2
Downing Street: Germany to D. peace   CHAM 66:6
   10 D.S. is an inconvenient   ASQ 15:2
dozed: d. off into a stupor when   BENC 36:2
dozen: d. dirty and ragged little   DOYLE 95:7
dozens: Mother to d.   HERB 139:4
dragging: d. themselves through   GINS 125:1
dragon: O to be a d.   MOORE 213:1
dragon-green: The d., the luminous   FLEC 111:14
drain: leave by the first town d.   SPOO 282:9
drained: Empire are irresistibly d.   DOYLE 95:8
drains: between the Deity and the D.   STR 288:1
   Democracy and proper d.   BETJ 44:5
drama: d. critic also perceives   TYNAN 302:8
dramatist: d. only wants more liberties
      JAMES 152:10
   d. who had discovered himself   SAKI 258:9
dramatize: ever-importunate murmur, 'D. it'
      JAMES 152:6
dravest: Thou d. love from thee   THOM 295:17
drawbacks: everything has its d.   JER 155:10
drawing: d. sufficient conclusions   BUTL 59:14
   The d. is on the level   BLUNT 48:2
drawing room: was flowing through my d.
      EDEN 98:2
drawing-room: brilliant d. comedy   DE VR 91:13
dread: d. of doing what has   WHAR 309:21
   d. with which the untutored   FRAZ 116:8
   Nor d. nor hope attend   YEATS 323:4
   That is why most men d. it   SHAW 271:19
   The d. of beatings   BETJ 44:6
dreadful: d. martyrdom must run   AUDEN 17:9
Dreadnoughts: construction of D.   WYND 318:3
   much to keep up as two D.   LLOY 189:12
dream: And slowly read and d.   YEATS 318:8
   A salesman is got to d.   MILL 208:9
   born falls into a d.   CONR 81:14
   But I d. things that never   SHAW 268:1
   citizens d. of the south   HARDY 133:8
   d. and dream that I am   FLEC 111:17
   d. between two awakenings   O'NEI 223:11
   d. of the days when work   CHES 70:12

dream (*cont.*):

I d. my dreams away	FLAN 111:3
If you can d.—and not make	KIPL 173:7
I have a d. that one day	KING 166:10
In a d. you are never eighty	SEXT 267:3
It was a d. I had last week	COPE 83:7
quiet sleep and a sweet d.	MAS 204:1
till you find your d.	HAMM 131:9
To follow the d.	CONR 81:14
True to the d. I am dreaming	COW 85:5
We live, as we d. — alone	CONR 81:10
Where we used to sit and d.	ARMS 13:7
Yea, faileth now even d.	THOM 295:11

dreamed: heaven and earth than are d.

	HALD 131:1

dreamer: An artist is a d. consenting SANT 260:13

dreamers: Like all d., I mistook SART 261:15

Soldiers are d.	SASS 262:6

dreamin': A little d., a little dyin' PHIL 234:4

D. of thee! Dreamin' of thee	WALL 304:14

dreaming: d. on the verge of strife CORN 83:11

I'm d. of a white Christmas	BERL 40:12
must be my excuse for d.	HALD 131:1

dreams: are either d. or swords LOW 191:9

city of perspiring d.	RAPH 243:3
d. and dreams their looking	YEATS 319:14
d. happy as her day	BROO 55:2
d. he found himself transformed	KAFKA 161:2
Facts are better than d.	CHUR 76:5
forgotten scream for help in d.	CAN 63:5
Heavy with d.	THOM 294:14
I have spread my d. under	YEATS 323:1
In d. begins responsibility	YEATS 321:14
Into the land of my d.	KING 167:8
Made holy by their d.	GIBS 124:6
Noon of my d., O noon	FLEC 112:1
That we who lived by honest d.	DAY-L 89:8

dreamt: I d. I went to Manderley DU M 96:7

dress: d. without which we feel MCL 196:11

Please adjust your d.	CHUR 75:8
we dont d. well and weve	SHAW 274:7
white d. after the sweetness	FIRB 109:14

dressed: All d. in his best EDGAR 98:3

D. in style, brand new tile	COLL 79:7
d. up and have no place	WHIT 310:18

dresser: Slept under the d. BENT 39:12

dressers: d. of this life BENN 37:10

dresses: d. so very soberly now JER 155:5

dried: A little life with d. tubers ELIOT 104:10

d. the sap out of my veins	YEATS 319:3

drift: adamant for d. CHUR 74:1

thus d. toward unparalleled	EINS 99:8

drifted: I d. WEST 309:13

drifting: When the clouds go d. STER 285:5

drink: Ale, man, ale's the stuff to d. HOUS 146:15

Couple them with d.	MCAR 193:2
Don't ask a man to d. and drive	ANON 7:17
d. all day and keep absolutely	SMITH 278:10
D. and dance and laugh and lie	PARK 231:3

drink (*cont.*):

d. and get beerier	LAWR 181:14
d. and I'd have been under	PARK 230:2
d. by daylight and never	MENC 206:17
d. he was drinking was	BENC 36:12
d. one another's healths	JER 155:4
d. to the spirit of gallantry	COW 84:5
d. your ale	HOUS 145:1
drunkenness—or so good as d.	CHES 68:5
intelligence to buy a d.	CUMM 87:1
One reason why I don't d.	ASTOR 15:10
or sleep or d. again	DE L 91:7
Shall sit and d. with me	BELL 35:1
She drove me to d.	FIEL 109:4
that he has taken to d.	TARK 290:12
your husband I would d.	ASTOR 15:12

drinka: D. Pinta Milka Day WHIT 310:13

drinks: couple of d. on a Saturday FYFFE 120:10

man you don't like who d.	THOM 293:7

drip: damps there d. upon HARDY 133:7

dripping: that electricity was d. THUR 297:4

drive: And d. the brute off LARK 179:6

Don't ask a man to drink and d.	ANON 7:17
That I was used to d.	HOUS 146:6
way but can't d. the car	TYNAN 302:7

driven: I'm as pure as the d. slush BANK 24:7

driver: he was in the d.'s seat BEAV 28:8

drives: D. my green age THOM 293:4

it is *le bon Dieu* who d.	CHR 72:3

droite: *ma d. recule, situation* FOCH 112:13

droits: *égaux en dignité et en d.* ANON 11:16

dromedary: The d., two NASH 217:9

droop: D. in a hundred A.B.C.'s ELIOT 100:5

droopingly: Lady Jane, a little d. LAWR 181:9

droops: D. on the little hands MILNE 210:6

D. to sink among the Dead	BELL 34:14

drop: dance till you d. AUDEN 19:2

Good to the last d.	ROOS 252:4
never said 'D. the gun . . .'	BOG 48:9
That one d. of Negro blood	HUGH 147:12
tune in and d. out	LEARY 183:4

dropped: Things have d. from me WOOLF 317:12

dropping: like d. a rose petal MARQ 202:2

peace comes d. slow	YEATS 318:10

drops: d. on gate-bars hang HARDY 133:9

drought: d. is destroying his roots HERB 139:11

drove: d. to the club in the late BETJ 43:11

She d. me to drink	FIEL 109:4

drown: Inns d. your empty selves BELL 34:18

drownded: no wrecks and nobody d. EDGAR 98:3

sea will soon be d.	SYNGE 289:8

drowned: ceremony of innocence is d.

	YEATS 320:7
D. THAN DUFFERS IF NOT	RANS 243:2
were d. in the deepest sea	KIPL 172:7

drowning: And not waving but d. SMITH 278:18

maid is like death by d.	FERB 108:5

drudgery: vocation is the love of the d.

	SMITH 278:11

drug: or you can d., with words — LOW 191:9
  powerful d. used by mankind — KIPL 175:1
drugs: And d. cause cramp — PARK 230:14
  Sex and d. and rock and roll — DURY 96:12
drum: Beats like a fatalistic d. — ELIOT 103:14
drummer: any kin to the snare d. — FREB 116:10
drumming: Down in the valley d. — AUDEN 19:7
drums: beating of war d. — KOES 176:8
  when the d. begin to roll — KIPL 168:11
drunk: d. if you can lie — MART 202:7
  d. with sight of power — KIPL 173:5
  not so think as you d. — SQUI 283:2
  when d., one sees in other — TYNAN 302:6
  Wordsworth d. and Porson sober — HOUS 144:6
drunkard: The rolling English d. made — CHES 69:5
drunkenness: d. would be the supremely — JAMES 153:18
  invented anything so bad as d. — CHES 68:5
  The d. of things being various — MACN 198:7
dry: clothes and into a d. Martini — WEST 309:2
  old man in a d. month — ELIOT 100:6
  Thoughts of a d. brain — ELIOT 100:8
Dublin: served in all the pubs in D. — DONL 93:4
  When I came back to D. — BEHAN 31:24
Dubuque: old lady in D. — ROSS 253:3
duchess: tomorrow every D. in London — MACD 194:12
duck: Honey, I just forgot to d. — DEMP 91:10
ducks: I turn to d. — HARV 135:15
duda: La vida es d. — UNAM 302:9
dude: Don't read too much now: the d. — LARK 179:14
duffers: Better drowned than d. — RANS 243:2
dugs: old man with wrinkled d. — ELIOT 105:6
duke: meet the D. I couldn't like — SHAW– 274:14
dukes: drawing room full of d. — AUDEN 18:12
  d. are just as great — LLOY 189:12
dulce: The old Lie: D. et decorum est — OWEN 227:14
dull: I am always deadly d. — BEER 30:17
dullard: d.'s envy of brilliant — BEER 31:9
dumb: Children are d. to say how — GRAV 128:7
  D. As old medallions — MACL 196:4
  d. to tell the crooked — THOM 293:4
  Ford is so d. he can't fart — JOHN 156:4
  Is dead and d. and done — DE L 91:7
  Oh, noisy bells, be d. — HOUS 146:4
  tender about Our D. Friends — PARK 230:3
  was a d. son of a bitch — TRUM 299:11
dumb-bell: Than d. and foil — YEATS 321:4
dump: What a d. — COFF 78:9
dungeon: life-sentence in the d. of self — CONN 81:4
dunghill: cock crowing on its own d. — ALD 3:12
Dunkirk: years in the epic of D. — PRIE 239:17
Dunn: Hunter D., Miss J. — BETJ 43:9
  Miss Joan Hunter D. — BETJ 43:12
Dupree: Weatherby George D. — MILNE 210:1
durch: Vorsprung d. Technik. — ANON 11:18

dure: ça d. ce que ça dure — DE G 90:1
dust: d. comes secretly day after — MEYN 207:11
  D. inbreathed was a house — ELIOT 102:2
  D. in the air suspended — ELIOT 102:2
  d., in the cool tombs — SAND 259:12
  d. the blinds and then — THOM 293:14
  d. upon the paper eye — DOUG 93:8
  Excuse My D. — PARK 231:8
  fear in a handful of d. — ELIOT 104:12
  In the city's d. you wait — HART 135:12
  Less than the d. — HOPE 144:3
  like the d. on the nettles — THOM 294:6
  our proud and angry d. — HOUS 145:1
  rich earth a richer d. — BROO 55:2
  voiced those rhymes is d. — HARDY 133:7
dustbin: into the d. of history — TROT 299:4
duty: body to do your d. — BAD 22:2
  declares that it is his d. — SHAW 268:8
  do his d. faithfully — BLUNT 48:1
  Do your d. bravely — KITC 175:15
  d. is useful in work — RUSS 255:5
  D. of a newspaper — SWOPE 289:5
  d. to have reported it — HELL 137:9
  d. to my country to love — PAGE 228:10
  it is our d. to try — MILN 211:2
  Nor law, nor d. bade me fight — YEATS 322:11
dwarfs: dozen red-bearded d. — MORT 214:6
dyin': A little dreamin', a little d. — PHIL 234:4
dying: achieve it through not d. — ALLEN 4:19
  A d. animal — YEATS 323:4
  against the d. of the light — THOM 292:11
  But I'm d. now and done — BETJ 42:9
  D. — PLATH 235:10
  'D.' he [Maugham] said — MAUG 205:1
  d. is more the survivors' — MANN 200:6
  forgive my friends for d. — SMITH 278:2
  'If this is d.,' he remarked — STR 288:6
  my birthday or am I d. — ASTOR 15:13
  shall I have—what d. wails — PITT 235:8
  sunsets exquisitely d. — HUXL 148:19
  Though we yawned like d. cod — ASQ 15:9
  time my father was d. — BENN 38:3
  with the thought of d. — MAS 203:12
dynamo: starry d. in the machinery — GINS 125:1
dynasties: Though D. pass — HARDY 133:15

E

each: mermaids singing, e. to each — ELIOT 103:12
eagle: e. or the snake — KIPL 170:4
  Fate is not an e. — BOWEN 51:3
  The e. has landed — HIGG 140:9
eagles: e. and the trumpets — ELIOT 100:5
  Where e. dare — MACL 196:3
ear: A stench in the e. — BIER 46:22
  e. with facility and quits — BEEC 30:2

ear (*cont.*):

have an e. for her music	DAY-L 89:7
penetrated into the e. of man	FORS 114:12
purse out of your wife's e.	MORT 214:4
We whisper in her e.	WILB 311:3

earl: e. and a knight — ATTL 16:2
fourteenth e. is concerned — HOME 143:1

early: E. to rise and early — THUR 297:11
I used to go to bed e. — PROU 240:7

earn: poet can e. much more money — AUDEN 18:6
set to e. their livings — GRAH 127:12

earned: e. everything I've got — NIXON 220:8

ears: And e. like errant wings — CHES 71:7
E. like bombs and teeth — CAUS 65:5
e. make him look like — HUGH 147:10
e. yielding like swinging — DOUG 93:9
'Jug Jug' to dirty e. — ELIOT 104:16
woman through her e. — WYATT 318:1

earth: advocates of peace upon e. — GEOR 123:4
And e. is but a star — FLEC 111:8
And I danced on the e. — CART 64:7
And is thy e. so marred — THOM 295:15
And we will stay on e. — PRÉV 239:14
are the scum of the e. — CHES 69:3
between the e. and skies — CAMP 62:5
But did thee feel the e. — HEM 138:4
E. and everything that's — KIPL 173:9
E. and Sky stand presently — KIPL 169:10
e. a richer dust concealed — BROO 55:2
e. a trinket at my wrist — THOM 295:11
E. in forgetful snow, feeding — ELIOT 104:10
e. is warm with Spring — GREN 129:5
E., receive an honoured guest — AUDEN 17:5
E.'s the right place — FROST 118:9
e. than are dreamed — HALD 131:1
He that loves but half of E. — QUIL 242:6
Let me enjoy the e. no less — HARDY 134:9
like to get away from e. — FROST 118:9
meek shall inherit the E. — SMITH 277:3
serious house on serious e. — LARK 179:5
Than anywhere else on e. — GURN 130:9
The conquest of the e. — CONR 81:9
The e. compels, upon it — MACN 197:10
vehicle E. zooming about — FULL 120:5
While e.'s foundations stand — HOUS 145:12

earthly: all e. things above — SPR 282:13

earthquake: Small e. in Chile — COCK 78:2

ease: doctrine of ignoble e. — ROOS 251:10
gold and heart's first e. — DAY-L 89:4
man could e. a heart like — PARK 230:10

easier: e. to fight for one's principles — ADLER 2:21
e. to love humanity — HOFF 142:6
e. to make war — CLEM 77:10
It will be e. for you — CHIL 71:14
tyranny it is far e. to act — AREN 13:3

easily: will more e. fall victim — HITL 141:11

easing: They call it e. the Spring — REED 244:13

east: e. all the way into Mississippi — KIPL 175:6
E. is East, and West — KIPL 169:10

east (*cont.*):

feel I can look the E.	THE Q 106:1
me somewheres e. of Suez	KIPL 169:8
tried to hustle the E.	KIPL 172:9

Eastern: Full of E. promise — ANON 8:2
Soviet domination of E. — FORD 113:9

Eastertide: Wearing white for E. — HOUS 145:13

easy: Life is not meant to be e. — SHAW 268:5
She bid me take love e. — YEATS 321:13
so e. to take refuge — IBSEN 149:19
terribly e.— to shake — SHAW 268:13
time an' the livin' is e. — HEYW 140:7
woman of e. virtue — HAIL 130:13
young and e. under the apple — THOM 293:1

eat: dare to e. a peach — ELIOT 103:12
E. or sleep or drink again — DE L 91:7
E. slowly: only men in rags — RAL 242:12
e. the cones under — FROST 118:14
e. wisely but not too well — MAUG 205:16
I'll try to e., but I cannot — ADE 2:19
me to e. in the kitchen — HUGH 147:13
You will e., bye and bye — HILL 140:11

eaten: e. by missionaries — SPOO 282:12
He has been e. by the bear — HOUS 144:10

'eathen: e. in 'is blindness bows — KIPL 174:11

eating: e. or opening a window — AUDEN 17:8
E. people is wrong — FLAN 111:6
Venice is like e. an entire — CAP 63:11

eccentric: Be virtuous and you will be e.
— TWAIN 300:11

ecclesiologist: A keen e. — BETJ 43:6

echo: e. in a Marabar cave — FORS 115:7
Footfalls e. in the memory — ELIOT 101:6
rose-garden. My words e. — ELIOT 101:6
The e. of a platitude — BIER 46:9
waiting for the e. — MARQ 202:2

éclair: backbone than a chocolate é. — ROOS 251:7

eclipses: e. and predominates — DOYLE 94:1

ecological: e. balance of the planet — SONT 280:13

economic: e. documents I have — HOME 143:2
e. ends than any alternative — KEYN 165:2
e. interests are not — WEIL 307:5
e. law on the side of destruction — KEYN 164:13
e. understanding — ROOS 250:12
social and e. experiment — HOOV 143:5

economical: being e. with the truth — ARMS 13:11

economically: behind e. or culturally — DUBČ 95:18

economics: E. and art are strangers — CATH 64:15
E. is the science — ROBB 248:6
face the e. of affluence — GALB 121:3
study of e. as if people — SCH 264:15

economists: e. and political philosophers
— KEYN 165:5

economize: Let us e. it — TWAIN 300:14

economy: E. is going without something
— HOPE 143:8
e. right in five years — BENN 37:8
fear of Political E. — SELL 266:10
Principles of Political E. — BENT 39:10

écrivain: *L'é. doit donc refuser*   SART 261:7

ecstasy: bells of E. and Forever   GINS 124:12
   circumstance to e.   BELL 32:8

ecstatic: Of such e. sound   HARDY 134:2

Eden: [Anthony E.]   BUTL 58:10
   E. submitted a long-winded   CHUR 75:8
   on E.'s green and gold   KIPL 169:12
   [Sir Anthony E.]   MUGG 215:8

edge: always at the e.   SPEN 281:11
   e. of the abyss   STEV 286:4

Edinburgh: travels north to E.   BEAV 28:6

edit: E. and annotate the lines   YEATS 322:4

editor: E.: a person employed   HUBB 147:4

Edna: Aunt E. is universal   RATT 243:5

educate: physician is to e.   OSLER 227:1

educated: Cabinet ministers are e.   BENN 39:1
   e. and who have with considerable   SNOW 279:6
   'e.' people tend to come   ORW 225:13
   once as an e. gentleman   SHAW 270:4

education: best kind of e.   BUCH 57:4
   between e. and catastrophe   WELLS 308:10
   cabbage with a college e.   TWAIN 301:14
   [e.] has produced a vast   TREV 298:13
   e. is the knowledge not   INGE 151:1
   E. is what survives when   SKIN 276:12
   e. must ultimately be limited   POUND 237:19
   E., *n.* That which discloses   BIER 46:17
   e. or of absence of self-control   BEVAN 44:11
   Gladstone also invented the E.   SELL 266:12
   just as in the case of e.   JAY 154:4
   Movies, and that is e.   ROG 249:5
   Soap and e. are not   TWAIN 300:12
   What poor e. I have received   BOTT 50:7

Edward: E. III had very good manners   SELL 266:6
   E. the Confessor   BENT 39:12
   [E. VIII]   GEOR 122:12

Edwardians: The E., on the contrary   WHITE 310:3

Eeyore: E., the old grey Donkey   MILNE 210:11

effect: e. upon the Government   PANK 229:7
   seems likelier to win an e.   UPD 302:12

effective: e. if you can stop people   ATTL 16:9

efficiency: e. and inefficiency   SHAW 269:19

efficient: e. government you have   TRUM 299:13

effort: e. is his own personality   FROMM 117:9
   e. nor the failure tires   EMPS 106:7
   e. when you have forgotten   SANT 260:9

effusive: The e. welcome of the pier   AUDEN 19:10

égalité: *majestueuse é. des lois*   FRAN 116:6

égaux: *libres et é. en dignité*   ANON 11:16

egg: And lay one more bloody e.   AYRES 21:16
   Go to work on an e.   ANON 8:6
   like eating an e. without   KIPL 175:3
   Wall St. lays an e.   ANON 11:20
   way of making another e.   BUTL 59:12

eggs: all my e. in one bastard   PARK 231:17
   Lays e. inside a paper bag   ISH 151:14
   your e. in the one basket   TWAIN 301:18

egoism: itself is a form of e.   SANT 260:22

egotist: E., *n.* A person of low   BIER 46:18

Ehrfurcht: *"E. vor dem Leben" vor mir*   SCHW 264:16

Eichmann: [E.] was summing up   AREN 13:4

eight: We want e., and we   WYND 318:3

eighth: I'm Henery the E., I am   MURR 216:6

eighty: In a dream you are never e.   SEXT 267:3

ein: *E. Reich, ein Volk, ein Führer*   ANON 7:19
   Nor can anyone understand E.   ANON 8:13

eine: I'll have e. kleine Pause   FERR 108:6

eingerichtet: *Wir sind so e., dass wir*   FREUD 117:4

Einsamkeit: *andern seine E. bewache*   RILKE 248:1

Einsamkeiten: *zwei E. einander schützen*   RILKE 247:9

Einstein: E. leads to Hiroshima   PIC 234:7
   Let E.   SQUI 283:3

einzurichten: *Kniff, die Welt so e.*   FRIS 117:7

either: E. war is obsolete or men   FULL 120:6

elderly: e. American [Ian MacGregor]   JENK 154:10
   Mr Salteena was an e. man   ASHF 14:2

elders: at listening to their e.   BALD 22:13

eldritch: e. light of sundown   DAY-L 89:4

election: Democracy substitutes e.   SHAW 271:18
   e. from my point of view   BALD 23:7
   e. now to be held and until   WHIT 310:19
   e. programme of the Labour   SNOW 279:8

elections: E. are won by men and women   ADAMS 2:6
   it's no go the e.   MACN 197:12
   you won the e.   SOM 280:5

electric: biggest e. train set   WELL 307:13
   tried to mend the E. Light   BELL 34:1

electrical: dark interludes in the e.   O'NEI 223:15

electrician: The E. is no longer there   BELL 35:7
   was a practical e.   WELLS 308:4

electricity: e. was dripping invisibly   THUR 297:4
   they must use less e.   JENK 154:8

electrification: Soviet power plus the e.   LENIN 184:12

electronic: e. interdependence recreates   MCL 196:7

elegance: casque has outdone your e.   POUND 238:16
   Has she e.? Has she fragrance   CAUL 65:3
   Observed the e. of Circe's hair   POUND 238:6

elegant: It's so e.   ELIOT 105:2
   Most intelligent, very e.   BUCK 57:9
   My e. car   BELL 35:11

elegies: e. are to this generation   OWEN 227:12

Elektra: [Strauss's E.]   BEEC 29:22

elementary: cried. 'E.,' said   DOYLE 94:17

elements: Took its place among the e.   PLATH 235:9

elephant: E.'s Child   KIPL 171:14
   high as an e.'s eye   HAMM 131:12
   shot an e. in my pajamas   KAUF 161:8

elephants: Women and e. never forget   SAKI 258:2

elevate: The mind of man or e. a rhyme
        YEATS 323:7
eleven: e. o'clock in the morning   CHAN 66:10
  e. o'clock that they were   CHAM 66:7
  second e. sort of chap   BARR 25:12
Elgar: Dear old E.—he is furious   BEEC 30:6
eliminated: you have e. the impossible
        DOYLE 95:5
Eliot: How unpleasant to meet Mr E. ELIOT 101:4
Elizabeth: grievous failing of E.'s HARDY 133:12
elm: tell me, e.! Night night   JOYCE 158:3
elopement: e. would be preferable ADE 2:18
  worked a love-story or an e. DOYLE 95:2
eloquence: e. is that which gets things LLOY 190:2
else: happening to Somebody E. ROG 249:8
  that I am not someone e. ALLEN 4:17
elsewhere: Altogether e., vast AUDEN 20:1
elude: Court him, e. him, reel BLUN 47:12
elusive: One's prime is e. SPARK 281:7
  That demmed, e. Pimpernel ORCZY 223:18
Elysium: Keep alive our lost E. BETJ 42:8
emancipation: preliminary to the e. of the mind
        KEYN 164:14
emancipator: whim so does every e. BROUN 56:6
embalmer: A triumph of the e.'s art VIDAL 304:4
embarrassment: land of e. and breakfast
        BARN 25:5
embittered: He was an e. atheist ORW 224:16
embroidered: Had I the heavens' e. cloths
        YEATS 323:1
embroideries: Covered with e. YEATS 322:1
emeralds: E. is paved with yellow BAUM 27:13
emergency: e. following upon another
        FISH 109:15
emeritus: called a *professor e.* LEAC 182:11
Emily: least sought for: E., hear CRANE 85:12
eminent: death reveals the e. SHAW 272:11
Emmet: And Robert E. and Wolfe Tone
        YEATS 321:15
emotion: degree of my aesthetic e. BELL 32:9
  dependable international e. ALSOP 5:7
  e. in the form of art ELIOT 104:4
  e. is immediately evoked ELIOT 104:4
  not a turning loose of e. ELIOT 104:3
  tranquillity remembered in e. PARK 230:6
emotional: Sentimentality is the e. promiscuity
        MAIL 199:5
emotions: have personality and e. ELIOT 104:3
  refusal to admit our e. RATT 243:7
  waste-paper basket of the e. WEBB 307:4
  world of the e. COL 79:1
emperor: E. and puts you in de Hall O'NEI 223:6
  E. himself can actually BREC 53:6
  e. of ice-cream STEV 285:7
  looking for the sacred E. BRAM 52:10
  That's presuming E. Long ICKES 150:8
emphasis: Is underlined for e. ELIOT 103:2
empire: Britain has lost an e. ACH 1:8

empire (*cont.*):
  E. are irresistibly DOYLE 95:8
  E. is a commonwealth ROS 252:10
  E. lasts for a thousand CHUR 74:7
  impulses of an evil e. REAG 244:6
  liquidation of the British E. CHUR 73:6
  our E. beyond the seas CHUR 74:6
  pledge our E. vast across HUXL 149:1
  remark to me, 'How's the E.?' GEOR 123:2
  The E. strikes back LUCAS 192:9
  way she disposed of an e. HARL 135:4
empires: e. of the future CHUR 76:1
  The day of E. has come CHAM 66:1
employee: Hierarchy Every E. Tends to Rise
        PETER 233:8
employer: harder upon the e. SPOO 282:11
employers: e. of past generations BALD 23:12
employment: happily known as gainful e. ACH 1:7
  To give e. to the artisan BELL 34:1
emptiness: And all the little e. of love BROO 54:10
  Panic and e. FORS 114:13
  The e. of ages in his face MARK 201:3
  Their hopeful plans to e. HOUS 144:13
empty: Bring on the e. horses CURT 88:1
  e. taxi arrived at 10 Downing CHUR 72:6
  me with their e. spaces FROST 118:3
enchanted: Some e. evening HAMM 132:2
enchantments: last e. of the Middle Age BEER 31:7
enclosing: definition is the e. a wilderness
        BUTL 60:2
encompassed: e. by a cloud of comforting
        RUSS 255:16
encounter: I go to e. for the millionth
        JOYCE 158:12
encounters: Close e. of the third kind SPIE 282:5
encourage: they e. it in some schools SCOTT 265:9
encouragement: e. this book would have
        WOD 315:16
encouraging: E. her to join the public AYCK 21:8
end: And now the e. is near ANKA 6:11
  beginning is often the e. ELIOT 102:5
  came to an e. all wars LLOY 189:9
  e. cannot justify the means HUXL 148:13
  e. forever to this ROOS 251:2
  e. is to make a beginning ELIOT 102:5
  e. of a thousand years GAIT 121:1
  e. of it's sittin' KIPL 174:8
  e. of the beginning CHUR 73:5
  great e. comes slowly DUB 96:2
  In my beginning is my e. ELIOT 101:11
  Keep right on to the e. LAUD 179:17
  middle and an e. GOD 125:7
  Our e. is Life. Put out to sea MACN 198:1
  patience is now at an e. HITL 141:9
  The bad e. unhappily STOP 287:9
  The e. is where we start from ELIOT 102:5
  there's an e. of May HOUS 144:11
  The war that will e. war WELLS 308:12
  Where it will all e., knows God GIBBS 124:2

end *(cont.)*:

where's it all going to e.	STOP 287:8
who have the power to e.	SASS 262:11
world will e. in fire	FROST 118:10

endeavours: e. are unlucky explorers DOUG 93:6

ended: And the curse be e. ELIOT 101:19

But he e. PM	ATTL 16:2
had e. his sport with Tess	HARDY 134:8
The song is e.	BERL 40:9

ending: e. a war is to lose it ORW 225:11

endless: I take my e. way HOUS 146:10

nowhere, and is e. LARK 178:10

ends: delight and e. in wisdom FROST 117:13

determine the nature of the e.	HUXL 148:13
e. and scarce means	ROBB 248:6
e. and the Church of England	PRIE 240:2
e. as beyond the province	POPP 236:7
e. I think criminal	KEYN 164:10
Out to the undiscovered e.	BELL 35:4
The burnt-out e. of smoky days	ELIOT 103:13

endure: easily learn to e. adversity TWAIN 300:20

man will not merely e. FAUL 107:12

endured: not to be e. with patient RUSS 255:5

enemies: against the common e. of man

KENN 163:12

alone against smiling e.	BOWEN 51:4
desire to be vilified by e.	BIER 46:8
e. of Freedom do not argue	INGE 151:2
e. will not believe you	HUBB 147:2

enemy: classics is an e. to the human MILL 208:14

e. if you want to save	BALD 23:4
e. of good art	CONN 80:9
e. of thought and the friend	CONR 81:17
friend and e. is but Death	BROO 54:10
got a better class of e.	MILL 209:8
Have no e. but time	YEATS 323:3
I am the e. you killed	OWEN 228:8
Sir, no man's e., forgiving all	AUDEN 20:3
sometimes his own worst e.	BEVIN 45:14
then there's life, its e.	ANOU 12:12
with the wrong e.	BRAD 52:7
written by an acute e.	BALF 24:2
your e. and your friend	TWAIN 300:21

enfants: *Faire des e., rien de* SART 261:12

pour les e., de toujours DE S 257:1

Enfer: *l'E., c'est les Autres* SART 261:11

enforce: courts to e. a law not HUMP 148:2

engaged: e. to Miss Joan Hunter BETJ 43:12

Engels: E. and Lenin he deceives KHR 165:9

engine: An e. that moves HARE 134:14

tremendous from her great e.	AUDEN 20:12
unsavoury e. of pollution	SPAR 281:8
when the human e. waits	ELIOT 105:5
you'll be a Really Useful E.	AWDRY 21:5

engineer: be an e. or such like SHAW 270:19

engineering: Piecemeal social e. resembles

POPP 236:7

engineers: Artists are not e. KENN 163:5

It is the age of the e. HOGB 142:10

England: And get me to E. once again BROO 55:10

apple falling towards E.	AUDEN 19:3
E. is a garden	KIPL 171:2
E. is finished and dead	MILL 208:7
E. is not the jewelled isle	ORW 224:20
E. is the paradise of individuality	SANT 260:18
E. mourns for her dead	BINY 47:4
E. shall bide till Judgement	KIPL 172:13
E.'s on the anvil	KIPL 174:1
E., their England	MACD 194:15
E. who only England know	KIPL 170:2
E. will have her neck wrung	CHUR 73:1
Establishment which we call E.	DENN 91:11
Florence, Elizabethan E.	INGE 151:7
For E.'s the one land, I know	BROO 55:10
God punish E.	FUNKE 120:9
Good evening, E. This	POTT 237:10
Gott strafe E.!	FUNKE 120:9
have lost the last of E.	BELL 34:18
History is now and E.	ELIOT 102:6
In E., justice is open	MATH 204:6
In E. people have good table manners	
	MIKES 207:13
lot that make up E. today	LAWR 180:11
my legs and think of E.	HILL 141:2
Noon strikes on E.	FLEC 112:1
Oh many a peer of E. brews	HOUS 146:15
Speak for E.	AMERY 5:10
stately homos of E.	CRISP 86:4
suspended in favour of E.	SHAW 269:12
That is for ever E.	BROO 55:2
The bow was made in E.	DOYLE 95:15
There'll always be an E.	PARK 231:19
think of the defence of E.	BALD 23:5
thoughts by E. given	BROO 55:2
Till then, damn you E.	OSB 226:15
Who dies if E. live	KIPL 170:15
With E.'s own coal	KIPL 171:1
You that love E., who have	DAY-L 89:7

English: An E. unofficial rose BROO 55:8

breathing E. air	BROO 55:2
But I was taught E.	CHUR 75:10
But marks our E. dead	KIPL 174:4
disagree the E. gentry	HALS 131:8
E. and the bears	THOM 292:10
E. have hot-water	MIKES 207:14
E. have no respect	SHAW 273:10
E. never smash in a face	HALS 131:8
E. sloppy have only themselves	SAY 263:10
E. up with which I will	CHUR 76:2
E. vice	RATT 243:7
E. without an accent now	BENC 35:14
game which the E.	MANC 199:15
if he went among the E.	BARR 26:12
mobilized the E. language	MURR 216:9
pause to consider the E.	NASH 218:10
Potter speaking to you in E.	POTT 237:10
really nice E. people	SHAW 269:11
stones kissed by the E. dead	OWEN 228:3

English (*cont.*):

Student of our sweet E. tongue	FLEC 112:7
The E. may not like music	BEEC 30:1
The wood of E. bows	DOYLE 95:15
words in the E. language	JAMES 152:11

Englishman: An E., even if he is alone

	MIKES 207:15
born an E. and remained	BEHAN 31:21
E. among the under-dogs	WAUGH 306:4
E. believes be heresy	SHAW 274:2
E. hate or despise him	SHAW 273:10
E. is ever fairly beaten	SHAW 274:1
E. is to belong	NASH 218:10
E. never enjoys himself	HERB 139:17
E. thinks he is moral when	SHAW 271:5
E. will give his mind	SHAW 267:13
find an E. in the wrong	SHAW 272:19
have been born an E.	RHOD 246:5
that the E. can't feel	FORS 114:2

Englishmen: But E. detest a siesta COW 84:13

E. act better than Frenchmen	BENN 38:7
E. don't think in the least	MCL 196:8
E. never will be slaves	SHAW 271:4
Mad dogs and E.	COW 84:13
they would prefer to be E.	RHOD 246:4

English-speaking: understanding of E. audiences

	WHAR 309:19

Englishwoman: This E. is so refined SMITH 278:17

Englishwomen: E.'s shoes look as if they

	HALS 131:7
Frenchwomen better than E.	BENN 38:7

enhanced: e. meaning in memorable BARZ 27:12

enigma: mystery inside an e. CHUR 75:6

Resolving the e. of the fever ELIOT 101:15

enjoy: business of life is to e. BUTL 60:10

e. it	SMITH 277:11
have to go out and e. it	SMITH 278:14
His duty is to e. himself	CECIL 65:9
I e. convalescence	SHAW 268:3
Let me e. the earth no less	HARDY 134:9

enjoyment: aesthetic e. is recognition

	WHIT 310:10
intense e. from a contrast	FREUD 117:4

enjoys: The Englishman never e. HERB 139:17

enmities: More substance in our e. YEATS 318:6

ennemie: *il y a la vie, son e.* ANOU 12:12

enormous: At the far end of the e. room

	AUDEN 19:13
With one e. chair	LERN 186:6

enough: e. in the world for everyone's BUCH 57:8

e. people to make a minority	ALTM 5:8
It is not e. to succeed	VIDAL 304:2
patriotism is not e.	CAV 65:8
The dark is light e.	FRY 119:12
wouldn't be e. to go round	STEAD 283:11

enslaved: completely e. as farm stock SHAW 269:7

ensured: Good-night. E. release HOUS 145:12

enterprise: For there's more e. YEATS 322:1

regeneration of industry and e. CHAR 68:2

enterprise (*cont.*):

starship E	RODD 249:2

entertain: could only e. my Liberal ASQ 15:2

entertained: e. by some of your grosser

	WOOL 317:14

entertaining: e. than half the novels

	MAUG 205:13

entertainment: Pictures are for e. GOLD 126:5

sort of *Arabian Nights* e. OSLER 227:5

entertains: e. the most exclusive worms

	PARK 231:4

enthusiasm: Above all no e. LAMB 177:15

little ordinary human e.	OSB 226:10
that e. moves the world	BALF 24:3

enthusiasts: e. can be trusted to speak BALF 24:3

entirely: The e. beautiful AUDEN 17:10

entitled: than that no man is e. ROOS 251:6

entrance: every exit as being an e. STOP 287:3

entrust: matter to e. to military CLEM 77:8

envelopes: On backs of tattered e. HOPE 144:2

envy: E. is the basis of democracy RUSS 255:3

into the mind, do not e. me	DOUG 93:9
prisoners of e.	ILL 150:12

enwrought: E. with golden and silver YEATS 323:1

Ep: E.'s statues are junk ANON 8:13

ephemeral: lacking which any story is e.

	FAUL 107:11
Proves the child e.	AUDEN 17:10

epic: e. poem, and the science MENC 206:19

epigram: E.: a wisecrack that played LEV 186:10

Impelled to try an e.	PARK 231:2
until it purrs like an e.	MARQ 202:3

episode: To the end of a brief e. MERC 207:7

epitaph: And were an e. to be my story

	FROST 119:10

epithet: e. which the riff-raff HOPE 143:10

epoch: e. when ladies apparently HUXL 149:8

Epstein: E.'s sculptures ANON 11:10

equal: All animals are e. ORW 224:12

All men are e.—all men	FORS 115:1
are e. is a proposition	HUXL 149:10
compel us to be e. upstairs	BARR 25:11
country about e. rights	JOHN 156:7
free and e. in dignity	ANON 11:16

equality: E. for women demands TOYN 298:6

e. in the servants' hall	BARR 25:11
'E.,' I spoke the word	DYLAN 97:11
majestic e. of the law	FRAN 116:6
not e. or fairness	BERL 41:2

equals: Only a peace between e. WILS 314:3

equipment: e. always deteriorating ELIOT 101:16

eradicate: e. from my heart a deep BEVAN 45:8

err: e. is human but to really ANON 11:14

To e.	ANON 12:10

errors: e. of those who think BID 46:3

His e. are volitional JOYCE 159:7

erstwhile: After all, my e. dear MILL 208:5

escape: Beauty for some provides e. HUXL 148:19

e. complex MCAR 193:2

escape (*cont.*):

e. from emotion	ELIOT 104:3
few e. that distinction	TWAIN 302:3
tentacles we never quite e.	SMITH 276:18
we women cannot e.	GIBB 123:11

escaped: that out of battle I e.   OWEN 228:5

Eskimo: Every Hottentot and every E.   LEHR 184:5

essay: e. on the life-history   BARB 24:16

essence: Existence precedes and rules e.
   SART 261:8

The e. of war is violence	FISH 110:1

essential: what is e. is invisible   DE S 257:2

established: like an e. society   GREE 128:11

establishment: E. which we call England
   DENN 91:11

estate: used to dealing with e.   DOUG 93:14

état: *un renforcement de l'É.*   CAMUS 63:2

eternal: e. Footman hold my coat   ELIOT 103:10

himself and her of an e. tie	AUDEN 19:3
I wish it could be e.	OSB 226:15
justice is e. publicity	BENN 38:14

eternities: between two e. of darkness   NAB 217:3

eternity: Are from e., and shall not   HOUS 145:1

Damned from here to E.	KIPL 169:9
decomposing in the e. of print	WOOLF 317:5
E.'s a terrible thought	STOP 287:8
From here to e.	JONES 157:4
themselves some conception of e.	MANC 199:15

Ethel: E. patted her hair and looked   ASHF 14:10

E. wants it made known	ROS 252:14
muttered E. this is so sudden	ASHF 14:12

etherized: Like a patient e. upon a table
   ELIOT 103:6

Ethiopia: E. and promptly stumbled   HELL 137:7

Eton: during the holidays from E.   SITW 276:10

feelings on leaving E.	CONN 80:13
playing-fields of E.	ORW 225:1
Spiritually I was at E.	BETJ 44:8

étonne: *É.-moi.*   DIAG 92:2

étonné: *é. quand il est cru sur*   DE G 90:5

Etruscans: secret of the long-nosed E.   LAWR 180:7

Ettie: E. [Lady Desborough]   ASQ 15:3

Etty: E. was most emphatically   RAV 243:9

Euclid: E. alone   MILL 208:2

fifth proposition of E.	DOYLE 95:2

eunuch: between a e. and a snigger   FIRB 109:11

prerogative of the e.	STOP 286:16

eunuchs: A seraglio of e.   FOOT 113:4

Europe: All the dogs of E. bark   AUDEN 17:6

alterations on the map of E.	CHUR 72:10
are going out all over E.	GREY 129:7
E. and many old and famous	CHUR 74:6
E. is the unfinished negative	MCC 193:14
E. may be free	CHUR 74:7
last gentleman in E.	LEV 186:15
smaller nationalities of E.	ASQ 14:19
The whole map of E. has	CHUR 73:11
wisest woman in E.	ELIOT 104:13

European: individualism and a E. philosophy
   HOOV 143:6

involved in a E. war this	BEAV 28:7

Euston: flushpots of E. and the hanging
   JOYCE 158:1

three in E. waiting-room	CORN 83:13

evah: Well, did you e.   PORT 237:1

eve: at e. our fancies blow   FLEC 112:6

Be sudden—to E.	THOM 295:6
From far, from e. and morning	HOUS 146:9
past E. and Adam's	JOYCE 157:10
The fallen sons of E.	CHES 69:1
When Adam and E. were dispossessed	
	BOUL 50:8

even: E. less am   HOPE 144:3

e. terror of their lives	SHAR 267:9
I was heavy with the e.	THOM 295:9

événements: *Tu ne prévois les é. que*   ION 151:11

evening: Any e., any day   ROSE 252:5

E., all	WILL 312:15
e. full of the linnet's	YEATS 318:10
e. is spread out against	ELIOT 103:6
e. that the first hour	BOWEN 50:11
Hello, good e., and welcome	FROST 117:11
into the corners of the e.	ELIOT 103:7
shadow at e. rising	ELIOT 104:12
Softly along the road of e.	DE L 90:9
Some enchanted e.	HAMM 132:2
The light of e., Lissadell	YEATS 323:2
The winter e. settles down	ELIOT 103:13

evensong: In a full-hearted e.   HARDY 134:2

events: e., mostly unimportant   BIER 46:20

Everest: down Mount E. in the nude   MCK 196:1

ever-importunate: The e. murmur   JAMES 152:6

everlasting: Thy e. mercy, Christ   MAS 203:10

every: candidates appeal to 'E.'   ADAMS 2:3

columnists say 'E. thinking'	ADAMS 2:3
e. day I have got up	MAUG 205:4
e. way, I am getting	COUÉ 84:4

everybody: E. wants to get inta the act   DUR 96:10

You know e. is ignorant	ROG 249:10

everyday: An e. story of country folk   WEBB 307:1

everyone: e. must know that a *short*   EDW 98:8

E. suddenly burst out singing	SASS 263:5
future e. will be famous	WARH 305:2
Kill e., and you	ROST 253:9

everything: Almost e. has been tried   BENN 37:4

E. exists, nothing has	FORS 115:8
E. goes by the board	FAUL 107:10
e. he's no longer	SOLZ 280:2
e. in its place and nothing	BEVAN 44:10
E. is funny as long as it	ROG 249:8
E. must be like something	FORS 114:3
E.'s coming up roses	SOND 280:6
E. you always wanted	REUB 245:14
I'm not young enough to know e.	BARR 25:10
it said 'Chips with e.'	WESK 308:15
Universe and E.	ADAMS 1:14
world is e. that is the case	WITT 315:5

everywhere: expression—e. in the world
ROOS 250:12
evidence: e. of life after death SOPER 281:1
e. of the lack of proper BEVAN 44:11
intrinsic e. of his creation JEANS 154:7
evil: Clear the land of e. KIPL 174:3
don't think that he's e. ALLEN 4:8
e. on the ground of expediency ROOS 251:11
He overcame e. with good KING 167:3
impulses of an e. empire REAG 244:6
it is a necessary e. BRAD 52:3
root of all e. BUTL 59:1
supernatural source of e. CONR 82:1
There is no e. in the atom STEV 286:9
Those to whom e. is done AUDEN 17:11
what people call e. GIDE 124:7
word-and-thought-defying *banality of e*
AREN 13:4
evils: Between two e., I always WEST 309:9
enamoured of existing e. BIER 46:15
e. and the worst of crimes SHAW 270:1
found a cure for most e. KELL 162:9
evolution: e. and peaceful extermination
ZIN 324:12
ev'rything: E.'s goin' my way HAMM 131:13
ev'rywhere: E. I hear the sound JAGG 152:5
exact: e. science, and should DOYLE 95:2
yet understand the e. HEAN 136:10
exaggerate: e. the difference between
SHAW 270:11
exaggerated: e. stress on not changing
MAUG 205:9
exaggeration: e. is a truth that has GIBR 124:5
report of my death was an e. TWAIN 301:7
examinations: E. those who do not wish
RAL 242:11
example: annoyance of a good e. TWAIN 301:19
exams: rigorous judging e. COOK 82:8
exception: I'll be glad to make an e. MARX 202:12
exceptional: possesses certain e. properties
JEANS 154:6
excesses: your guard against any e. KITC 175:15
exchange: And e. it some day for a crown
BENN 37:9
e. of one Nuisance ELLIS 106:4
excited: Blonde Aphrodite rose up e. AUDEN 20:12
exciting: films. They are too e. BERR 41:14
exclusively: e. in the right are generally
HUXL 149:11
excrement: The place of e. YEATS 323:8
excursion: e. to hell and came back PRIE 239:17
his perilous e. ashore LEWIS 187:12
excuse: E. me while I slip BEHN 106:15
E. My Dust PARK 231:8
e. not to play football LEB 183:11
must be my e. for dreaming HALD 131:1
they make a good e. SZASZ 290:4
Your e. is out of season JER 155:13

excuses: e. are always less convincing HUXL 149:5
execute: e. him, expropriate him CONN 80:16
execution: fascination of a public e. FOOT 113:3
executioners: victims who respect their e.
SART 262:3
executive: e. expression of human BRIT 54:1
executives: where e. would never AUDEN 17:4
exercise: e. for a research scientist LOR 191:2
exhaustion: The e. of weaning, the liar's
AUDEN 20:3
exhibitionism: masochistic form of e. OLIV 223:4
exile: silence, e., and cunning JOYCE 158:13
exist: have a perfect right to e. BEER 31:14
I e. by what I think SART 262:2
impression that we e. BECK 29:10
Laski that He doesn't e. PRIE 240:1
questioned its right to e. SCH 264:14
they e., but are identical FORS 115:8
war would e. between us CHAM 66:7
who does not e., you hate O'BR 222:1
existence: e. is but a brief crack NAB 217:3
E. precedes and rules essence SART 261:8
e. remains a mad and lamentable SANT 260:10
human e. is to kindle JUNG 159:15
may have the e. of mankind ADAMS 2:13
that He tolerates their e. BUTL 59:2
Their e. only adds MOUN 214:13
universal conditions of e. JUNG 160:3
very e. of life itself SONT 280:13
existential: enslavement and e. death
LAING 177:12
Existenz: *Sinn der menschlichen E.* JUNG 159:15
exists: And no one e. alone AUDEN 17:12
Everything e., nothing FORS 115:8
e. a great chasm between BERL 40:13
exit: e. as being an entrance STOP 287:3
ex-parrot: invisible! THIS IS AN E. CHAP 67:9
expect: Do not e. again a phoenix hour
DAY-L 89:4
e. a boy to be vicious SAKI 258:5
e. if the dad is present ORTON 224:4
That is what you may e. DOYLE 94:12
expectations: our talents and our e. DE B 89:10
revolution of rising e. CLEV 77:11
expected: I too awaited the e. guest ELIOT 105:6
expects: e. the Spanish Inquisition CHAP 67:10
expediency: always be sacrificed to e.
MAUG 204:13
evil on the ground of e. ROOS 251:11
expedition: come back, abandoning the e.
DOUG 93:6
expenditure: Ask: was so much e. justified
SPEN 282:1
E. rises to meet income PARK 231:9
expense: behalf, and at your e. COOK 82:7
repay the trouble and e. BELL 32:15
expensive: extremely e. it is to be poor BALD 22:14
experience: all my thirty years' e. CARR 64:2

experience (*cont.*):
benefit of much e.	BENN 37:4
E. is never limited	JAMES 153:4
E. is not what happens	HUXL 149:13
E. isn't interesting till	BOWEN 50:10
e. of life has been drawn	BEER 31:13
e. of women that extends	DOYLE 95:4
figure. A man of no e.	CURZ 88:2
had a wider range of e.	HARR 135:6
imposing of a pattern on e.	WHIT 310:10
much e.	MARQ 201:9
Music is your own e.	PARK 230:1
point of trying every e.	BAX 27:15
world that we need not e.	FRIS 117:7

experienced: An e., industrious — TWAIN 300:10
experiment: mad and lamentable e. — SANT 260:10
social and economic e. — HOOV 143:5
expert: e. is someone who knows — HEIS 137:3
expires: Wretched Child e. — BELL 33:2
explain: e. pictures are usually — PIC 234:9
e. why it didn't happen — CHUR 72:9
Never e. — FISH 110:4
Never e. — HUBB 147:2
one could never e. — BARZ 27:11
explained: Shut up he e. — LARD 178:9
explainer: said he was a village e. — STEIN 284:7
explaining: forever e. things to them — SAIN 257:1
explanation: fuss and with no e. — BLYT 48:4
sometimes saves tons of e. — SAKI 258:7
when he is the only e. — KNOX 176:7
explanations: loathe entering upon e. — BARR 25:16
expletive: E. deleted — ANON 7:22
exploding: like bombs poets e. — AUDEN 20:10
exploit: I'm sure you'd never e. one — COPE 83:5
exploitation: continue as forms of mutual e. — AUDEN 18:14
exploration: We shall not cease from e. — ELIOT 102:4
explore: e. strange new worlds — RODD 249:2
explorers: endeavours are unlucky e. — DOUG 93:6
exploring: And the end of all our e. — ELIOT 102:4
exposure: e. of the under-belly — CHUR 75:2
express: essentially powerless to *e.* — STR 288:7
E. declares that Great — BEAV 28:7
e. myself in some mode — JOYCE 158:13
He must not e. great joy — FORS 114:2
just caught the down e. — WOD 315:18
expressing: e. the inexpressible — HUXL 149:4
expression: desire for aesthetic e. — WAUGH 305:18
most perfect e. of scorn — SHAW 268:4
express-train: Of heat the e. drew up there — THOM 294:5
exquisitely: Or Autumn sunsets e. dying — HUXL 148:19
extend: prepared to e. it to everyone — WILL 312:17
extension: e. of the franchise — CHES 70:2
e. which lends utility — SANT 260:14
extérieure: *politique e., je fais* — CLEM 77:9
exterior: Underneath this flabby e. — LEV 186:11

exterminate: E. all the brutes — CONR 81:11
E.! Exterminate — NAT 218:15
will have to e. a nation — SPOCK 282:7
extinct: e. and that was all — CUPPY 87:10
extinction: The other, to total e. — ALLEN 4:13
extol: e. thee who are born — BENS 39:4
extra: And add some e., just for you — LARK 179:1
extraordinary: are interested in the e. — HUBB 147:5
can do the work of one e. — HUBB 147:6
extremes: E. meet—it's the only way I ken — MACD 194:10
wild e. I could do — DURY 97:1
extremism: e. and higher rates/taxes — HEW 140:5
e. in the defence of liberty — GOLD 126:4
E. in the pursuit — JOHN 156:13
eye: *Cast a cold e.* — YEATS 319:13
dust upon the paper e. — DOUG 93:8
e. of the beholder — PETER 233:10
e. of the storm — BELL 35:13
e. that can open an oyster — WOD 315:15
friend one must close one e. — DOUG 93:10
God caught his e. — MCC 194:4
high as an elephant's e. — HAMM 131:12
looked into the e. of day — YEATS 322:8
more important than the e. — BRON 54:3
There's no malice in me e. — AYRES 22:1
this than meets the e. — BANK 24:8
Wore it in the world's e. — YEATS 322:1
eyeball: We're e. to eyeball — RUSK 254:12
eyebrows: with e. made of platinum — FORS 114:4
eye-for-an-eye: e. philosophy would leave — KING 167:3
eyeing: Who gain a happiness in e. — HUXL 148:19
eyelids: When she raises her e. — COL 79:2
eyes: And each man fixed his e. — ELIOT 104:14
And their e. are burning — AUDEN 19:8
bodily hunger in his e. — SHAW 270:6
chewing gum for the e. — ANON 11:2
close your e. before you — AYCK 21:6
Crumbling behind the e. — MACN 198:5
e. are quickened — GRAV 128:5
e. as wide as a football-pool — CAUS 65:5
e. follow you about when — ORW 225:3
e. have seen what my hand — LOW 191:11
e. is deeper than all noses — CUMM 87:5
e. might be shining — LAWR 182:7
E. still dazzled — LIND 188:9
e. to ask again yes — JOYCE 159:10
e. were blind with stars — HODG 141:14
frightened look in its e. — SITW 276:8
Gasp and Stretch one's E. — BELL 33:3
good Lord made your e. — LEHR 184:4
If at times my e. are lenses — DOUG 93:9
love through his e. — WYATT 318:1
My e. are bleared, my coppers — ADE 2:19
on my bed, close my e. — HILL 141:2
Or was it his bees-winged e. — BETJ 41:17
Smoke gets in your e. — HARB 132:11

eyes (cont.):
They rape us with their e.	FREN 117:1
When Irish e. are smiling	OLC 223:2
when the e. and back	ELIOT 105:5
Your e. had once	YEATS 318:8

F

Fabians: civilization of the F. | INGE 151:3
| good man fallen among F. | LENIN 184:13 |
façade: f. of the National Gallery | CHAR 68:3
face: Accustomed to her f. | LERN 186:2
A f. peered. All the grey night	DE L 90:14
And hid his f. amid a crowd	YEATS 318:8
And so I f. the final curtain	ANKA 6:11
Beauty's conquest of your f.	AUDEN 19:5
dont quite match your f.	ASHF 14:4
Exhausted f.? It hurts	SASS 263:3
f. and a different religion	EDW 98:9
f. and promising himself	AMIS 5:14
f. looks like a wedding-cake	AUDEN 21:1
f. which gave a clearer	DOYLE 95:4
flat on your f. as lean	THUR 297:14
hand and touched the f.	MAGEE 198:11
has the f. he deserves	ORW 224:13
have the f. of a Venus	BARR 26:17
his listless form and f.	HARDY 133:14
I am the family f.	HARDY 133:13
I never forget a f.	MARX 202:12
I wish I loved its silly f.	RAL 242:13
only f. I like to see	CAMP 62:1
plummet-measured f.	YEATS 320:1
saved you only must save f.	HEAN 136:11
smash in a f.	HALS 131:8
smile on the f. of the tiger	ANON 10:11
stamping on a human f.	ORW 225:9
Stares from every human f.	AUDEN 17:6
strong men stand f. to face	KIPL 169:10
The rabbit has a charming f.	ANON 10:13
To get very red in the f.	BENT 39:6
unacceptable f. of capitalism	HEATH 136:14
we looked it in the f.	DULL 96:5
faced: he f. the firing squad	THUR 297:13
faces: baby f. in the violet	ELIOT 105:10
Coming with vivid f.	YEATS 320:4
Private f. in public places	AUDEN 20:2
public f. in private places	AUDEN 20:2
these f. in the crowd	POUND 238:14
facility: penetrates the ear with f.	BEEC 30:2
fact: believe that any f.	VIDAL 304:3
f. with respect	FISH 109:15
fatal futility of F.	JAMES 153:8
factory: f. we make cosmetics	REVS 246:1
facts: beyond the obvious f.	DOYLE 94:19
consists in ignoring f.	ADAMS 2:12
F. are better than dreams	CHUR 76:5
f. are lost forever	MAIL 199:7

facts (cont.):
f. are sacred	SCOTT 265:5
f. but to re-allocate them	RYLE 256:7
F. do not cease to exist	HUXL 149:12
f. when you come to brass	ELIOT 104:6
if the f. had been put	BEVIN 45:15
not of f. but of values	INGE 151:1
obvious f. about grown-ups	JARR 154:2
Science is built up of f.	POIN 236:1
will give you all the f.	AUDEN 19:9
fade: In fields where roses f.	HOUS 146:14
They simply f. away	FOLEY 113:2
faded: interviewing a f. female	HARD 132:16
fades: Until she f. away	CHES 68:17
fading: ruler but the last f. smile	HUXL 149:16
faery: The land of f.	YEATS 319:8
fail: succeed. Others must f.	VIDAL 304:2
was sure I should not f.	CHUR 76:5
We shall not f. or falter	CHUR 72:11
we shall not flag or f.	CHUR 74:6
failed: f. to inspire sympathy	BEER 31:11
remembered by what they f.	MOORE 212:12
they f. before	KING 167:9
failing: f. of Elizabeth's was her	HARDY 133:12
To you from f. hands we throw	MCCR 194:7
failure: end in f.	POW 239:8
F. makes people bitter	MAUG 205:14
formula for f.	SWOPE 289:6
His f. is ignominious	MENC 206:9
not the effort nor the f.	EMPS 106:7
Now we are not a f.	VANZ 303:7
success and only one a f.	SAM 259:5
there's no success like f.	DYLAN 97:8
faintly: F., faintlier afar	FREE 116:14
fair: f. and floral air	FLEC 112:1
f. sex is your department	DOYLE 95:1
F. Shares for All	JAY 154:3
flaying would be f.	HOUS 144:8
In a f. ground	KIPL 170:10
it follows that it is F.	SWOPE 289:5
It's not f. to the child	FROST 119:4
Ludlow come in for the f.	HOUS 146:5
noble, historically f.	LERN 185:21
remained at 'set f.'	BENN 38:4
fairest: f. things have fleetest	THOM 294:10
fairies: Do you believe in f.	BARR 26:1
f. at the bottom of our	FYL 120:11
I don't believe in f.	BARR 25:18
was the beginning of f.	BARR 25:17
fairly: Englishman is ever f. beaten	SHAW 274:1
f. with their men there	BALD 23:12
fairness: equality or f. or justice	BERL 41:2
fairy: course, not a f. story	RYLE 256:7
loves a f. when she's forty	HENL 138:14
there is a little f. somewhere	BARR 25:18
faith: creates f. does not deceive	SHAW 273:22
f. chiefly in the sense	AMIS 6:3
F. may be defined briefly	MENC 207:3
f. without doubt is nothing	UNAM 302:9

fast (cont.):

I'm f. I'm a bad lot — THOM 294:1

fasten: And if they think, they f. — HOUS 145:2

F. your seat-belts — MANK 200:4

faster: F. than a speeding bullet — ANON 7:23

fastest: f. who travels alone — KIPL 175:4

fastidious: minds of a few f. — SMITH 278:16

fat: ain't over 'til the f. — COOK 82:6

Butter merely makes us f. — GOER 125:10

f. greedy owl of the Remove — RICH 247:3

F. is a feminist issue — ORB 223:17

f. white woman whom nobody — CORN 83:12

Imprisoned in every f. man a thin — CONN 81:2

incredibly f. or incredibly thin — BARR 26:8

It is all f., without — LEWIS 187:8

Outside every f. man there — AMIS 6:2

thin man inside every f. — ORW 224:14

fatal: f. futility of Fact — JAMES 153:8

most f. complaint of all — HILT 141:3

most f. to true happiness — RUSS 255:6

fatalistic: Beats like a f. drum — ELIOT 103:14

fate: Art is a revolt against f. — MALR 199:14

f. in what I cannot fear — ROET 249:4

F. is not an eagle — BOWEN 51:3

F.'s great bazaar — MACN 198:6

f. when we have ceased — POPP 236:4

f. wilfully misunderstand — FROST 118:9

F. wrote her [Queen Caroline] — BEER 31:3

For all our children's f. — KIPL 170:14

foulness of their f. — SASS 262:10

I have a bone to pick with F. — NASH 217:17

fat-head: F. poet that nobody reads — CHES 69:15

father: As my poor f. used to say — HERB 139:6

even if he is our f. — CHES 70:2

f. gave me some advice — FITZ 110:13

f. of the nation — NEHRU 218:17

f. spent the first year — BREC 52:16

f. was the distinction — BOHR 48:11

f. would wish his daughter — ANON 11:10

Lloyd George knows my f. — ANON 9:17

night the bed fell on my f. — THUR 297:3

Our F. which art in heaven — PRÉV 239:14

There is no good f. — SART 261:12

time my f. was dying — BENN 38:3

your F. had an accident — POTT 237:8

your f., whom you love — STOP 287:6

fatherhood: Mirrors and f. are abominable — BORG 49:11

fathers: And where's their f. live — THOM 293:16

Come mothers and f. — DYLAN 97:13

f. and makes friends — MUMF 215:13

fundamental defect of f. — RUSS 255:20

My f. can have it — THOM 293:3

talking to you mothers and f. — ROOS 250:10

Tell them, because our f. lied — KIPL 175:10

Victory has a hundred f. — CIANO 76:15

fathom: f. the inscrutable workings — SMITH 277:4

fatigue: relaxation from physical f. — MAT 204:8

fattening: immoral, or f. — WOOL 317:16

Faulkner: F., and Steinbeck — ALGR 3:16

faults: f. of the age come from — BALF 23:14

They fill you with the f. — LARK 179:1

you see all his f. — LYTT 193:1

fauteuil: f. qui le délasse de ses — MAT 204:8

favour: being in and out of f. — FROST 119:2

I hold with those who f. fire — FROST 118:10

favourite: It's my second f. organ — ALLEN 5:4

people and their f. islands — AUDEN 19:10

fawns: The fallow f. invisible go — THOM 294:2

fear: direction of our f. — BERR 41:11

fate in what I cannot f. — ROET 249:4

F. and loathing in Las Vegas — THOM 296:14

F. God — KITC 175:15

F. is the main source — RUSS 256:2

f. it would make me conservative — FROST 118:4

f. love is to fear life — RUSS 255:10

f. of finding something — BELL 32:18

f. of life become publishers — CONN 80:7

F. wist not to evade — THOM 295:5

fourth is freedom from f. — ROOS 250:12

I f. those big words — JOYCE 159:1

Life is first boredom, then f. — LARK 179:15

never f. to negotiate — KENN 163:10

only thing we have to f. — ROOS 250:4

people for f. I may be lonely — JOAD 155:15

show you f. in a handful — ELIOT 104:12

state as required by its f. — MAD 198:9

The haunting f. that someone — MENC 206:14

till the f. of the Law — JOYCE 158:4

Why f. death — FROH 117:8

without f. the lawless roads — MUIR 215:9

feast: mind is a perpetual f. — SMITH 277:15

Paris is a movable f. — HEM 138:7

feather: To produce my foot, my each f. — HUGH 147:14

feathered: f. glory from her loosening — YEATS 322:6

feather-footed: F. through the plashy — WAUGH 306:9

featureless: more f. and commonplace — DOYLE 94:6

features: f. from which deductions — DOYLE 95:11

February: not Puritanism but F. — KRUT 177:1

fed: f. your hunger like — CRANE 85:12

feed: Church can f. and sleep — ELIOT 102:14

F. the world — GELD 122:11

will you still f. me — LENN 185:15

feel: Englishman can't f. — FORS 114:2

f. fierce and revolutionary — LINK 188:11

f. like a fugitive from — MAUL 205:18

f. the heart-break — GIBS 124:6

f. the machine slipping — LOW 191:14

f. with Norman that I have — AYCK 21:11

I dislike what I fancy I f. — ANON 11:9

I don't f. like going — SAL 258:10

I f. as I always have — BENC 36:5

It makes me f. good — LEV 186:12

make one f. more at home — FREUD 117:5

thee f. the earth move — HEM 138:4

feelin': I got a beautiful f. HAMM 131:13
feeling: constellations of f. DOUG 93:9
  f. of Sunday is the same RHYS 246:7
  f. that the poet believes QUAS 242:1
  If merely 'f. good' JAMES 153:18
  I get a funny f. inside of me GREGG 129:2
  mess of imprecision of f. ELIOT 101:16
  Music is f., then, not sound STEV 285:9
  Prevents that sinking f. HARR 135:8
  school that f. is bad FORS 114:2
feelings: keeping f. at bay BROO 56:3
feeling-toned: chiefly the *f. complexes* JUNG 160:4
fees: they took their F. BELL 33:1
feet: And palms before my f. CHES 71:8
  broken by their passing f. YEATS 321:10
  Came on the following F. THOM 295:8
  his eyes before his f. ELIOT 104:14
  Just direct your f. FIEL 108:11
  marching, charging f. JAGG 152:5
  on little cat f. SAND 259:10
  on your f. than to live IBAR 149:17
  Radical is a man with both f. ROOS 250:9
  stranger's f. may find the meadow HOUS 145:8
  wash their f. in soda ELIOT 105:4
  with little snow-white f. YEATS 321:13
  Your f.'s too big BENS 39:2
felicitous: F. phenomenon MOORE 213:1
felicity: f. on the far side of baldness SMITH 277:16
fell: bed f. on my father THUR 297:3
fella: F. belong Mrs Queen PHIL 234:1
felled: that signed the paper f. THOM 293:10
feller: Sweetes' li'l' f. STAN 283:8
fellow: other f. just blinked RUSK 254:12
fellows: For f. whom it hurts to think
                          HOUS 146:15
  I—I say, you f. RICH 247:4
felt: f. towards Him as she might STR 288:1
  rather f. you round my throat HOPE 144:4
  Thou hast not f. thy bosom keep DAV 89:1
female: faded f. in a damp basement HARD 132:16
  f. in a world of males PITT 235:8
  f. of the species is more KIPL 173:11
  f. will appear in society BEAU 89:9
  f. worker is the slave CONN 81:7
  vindictiveness of the f. CONN 80:20
feminism: F. is the most revolutionary TOYN 298:6
feminist: Fat is a f. issue ORB 223:17
femme: *f. qui ne me plaisait pas* PROU 240:10
  On ne naît pas f. BEAU 89:9
fen: plashy f. passes the questing WAUGH 306:9
fence: DON'T F. ME IN. PORT 236:11
  jonquils by sunny garden f. BETJ 44:1
  One time there was a picket f. MORG 213:9
  stately park and the f. MAUG 204:12
  two birds setting on a f. TWAIN 300:8
fences: f. make good neighbours FROST 118:14
Fermanagh: steeples of F. and Tyrone CHUR 73:11
fertile: In such a fix to be so f. NASH 218:9

fester: that f. are not springlike ABSE 1:2
fetch: *fresh* corpse, f. him out TWAIN 301:6
fetters: his f. fall GAND 121:11
fever: enigma of the f. chart ELIOT 101:15
  Of chills and f. she died RANS 243:1
  signed the treaty bred a f. THOM 293:11
fevers: Time and f. burn away AUDEN 17:10
fever-trees: all set about with f. KIPL 171:15
few: criticism by the f. BROWN 56:11
  death is one of the f. ALLEN 4:15
  F. thought he was even ATTL 16:2
  f. who would not rather HUXL 148:7
  owed by so many to so f. CHUR 74:8
fiancée: discerning young man his f. ANON 11:10
fickleness: f. of the women I love SHAW 273:8
fiction: biography is ultimately f. MAL 199:12
  f. autobiography STOP 286:15
  f. is a necessity CHES 68:12
  f. set to more or less MENC 207:2
  one form of continuous f. BEVAN 45:9
  Poetry is the supreme f. STEV 285:6
fiddle: important beyond all this f. MOORE 213:2
  tune played on an old f. BUTL 60:13
fiddler: village f. after Paganini NIC 219:8
fiddles: Oh some are fond of f. MAS 203:3
fiddlin': they were f. and small EDGAR 98:3
fidelity: Untruth. The stone f. LARK 179:16
field: Beside a f. of grain PARK 231:19
  corner of a foreign f. BROO 55:2
  f. by the river my love YEATS 321:13
  f. is full of shades THOM 296:1
  For Vaguery in the F. OSB 226:11
  Never in the f. of human CHUR 74:8
fields: f. and in the streets CHUR 74:6
  F. I would rather FIEL 109:6
  f. of millions of farms HOOV 143:7
  In f. where roses fade HOUS 146:14
  Strawberry f. forever LENN 185:13
  whispering of f. unsown OWEN 228:1
fiends: bloody and foreigners are f. MITF 211:16
fifteen: always f. years older BAR 27:6
  famous for f. minutes WARH 305:2
  f. minutes everybody will WARH 305:2
fifth: came f. and lost the job JOYCE 159:5
fifties: These are the tranquillized F. LOW 191:13
fifty: F. million Frenchmen can't ROSE 252:8
  It only leaves me f. more HOUS 145:13
  with booze until he's f. FAUL 108:1
fifty-fifty: f. Americanism in this ROOS 251:9
fight: bade me f. had told me EWER 107:2
  cease when men refuse to f. ANON 11:21
  dead, who will not f. GREN 129:5
  f. and fight and fight GAIT 120:16
  f. for freedom and truth IBSEN 150:2
  f. for its King and Country GRAH 127:5
  f. for one's principles ADLER 2:21
  man being too proud to f. WILS 314:11
  must f. on to the end HAIG 130:12

fight (*cont.*):

Nor law, nor duty bade me f.	YEATS 322:11
shall f. on the beaches	CHUR 74:6
that Britain would f.	CHUR 73:1
thought it wrong to f.	BELL 34:16
youth who must f. and die	HOOV 143:4

fighting: And who dies f. has increase — GREN 129:5

between two periods of f.	BIER 46:24
f. back	MCKAY 195:8
f. Blenheim all over again	BEVAN 45:1
f. for this woman's honour	KALM 161:4
right for f. in the street	JAGG 152:5
The f. man shall from the sun	GREN 129:5
those that are f. for you	STEIN 284:12
What are WE f.	SERV 266:16

fights: f. are the best part — WILD 311:7

figs: And f. grew upon thorn — CHES 71:7

figure: f. in the carpet — JAMES 152:15

f. of Juno	BARR 26:17
Not even a public f.	CURZ 88:2
The f. a poem makes	FROST 117:13
The f. is the same	FROST 117:13

figures: other f. in it — ELIOT 101:3

wit there is in those f. — FRY 120:3

Files-on-Parade: said F. — KIPL 168:8

fill: f. you with the faults — LARK 179:1

I am not yet born; O f. me	MACN 198:8
Sleep your f. — but when	BELL 34:14

filling: challenge of f. the space — WEST 309:15

films: I seldom go to f. They — BERR 41:14

filth: so is f. — FORS 115:8

final: And so I face the f. curtain — ANKA 6:11

dead sound on the f.	ELIOT 104:14
This is my f. word	BEAV 28:5

finality: Perfection is f. — STEP 285:3

financiers: And all these f. — WILS 313:3

Finchley: F. tried to mend the Electric — BELL 34:1

find: beginning to f. it out — SMITH 278:7

f. a friend one must close	DOUG 93:10
f. out what everyone	HERB 139:5
f. out why a snorer can't	TWAIN 302:2
f. the truth, to speak	NIXON 220:4
returns home to f. it	MOORE 212:10
Scratch a lover, and f. a foe	PARK 231:5
Someday I'll f. you	COW 85:5
till you f. your dream	HAMM 131:9
We always f. something	BECK 29:10
You will f. no new places	CAV 65:7

finds: War always f. a way — BREC 53:7

fine: A f. romance with no kisses — FIEL 108:9

California is a f. place	ALLEN 4:3
f. sense of the ridiculous	ALBEE 3:11
May will be f. next year	HOUS 144:12

finer: diner nothing could be f. — GORD 126:14

finest: This was their f. hour — CHUR 74:7

finger: Between my f. and my thumb — HEAN 136:8

chills the f. not a bit	NASH 217:18
f. do you want on the trigger	ANON 12:8
f. goes wabbling back	KIPL 173:12

FINGER (*cont.*):

f. in the throat and one	OSLER 226:17
It's f. lickin' good	ANON 9:7
lift up my f. and I say	SAR 261:4
like a rugged f. to Heaven	LLOY 189:13

fingernails: indifferent, paring his f. — JOYCE 158:9

fingers: Crumbling between the f. — MACN 198:5

Just as my f. on these keys	STEV 285:9
Let your f. do the walking	ANON 9:13
sovereign f. taxed the breath	THOM 293:10
those terrified vague f.	YEATS 322:6
time we 'pulled our f. out'	PHIL 233:15

fings: F. ain't wot they used t'be — NORM 221:4

finish: F. last — DUR 96:11

I've started so I'll f.	MAGN 199:1
start together and f.	BEEC 29:17
that you f. it	BENN 38:10
tools and we will f. the job	CHUR 72:11

finished: A poem is never f. — VALÉ. 302:19

f. in the first 100 days	KENN 163:11
married. Then he's f.	GABOR 120:13
world where England is f.	MILL 208:7
would have been f. in half	WOD 315:16

finishing: keep f. your sentences — LONS 190:12

finite: knowledge can only be f. — POPP 236:8

finned: f. cars nose forward like — LOW 191:12

fiords: probably pining for the f. — CHAP 67:9

fire: And nodding by the f. — YEATS 318:8

C'mon, baby, light my f	MORR 213:16
Cyprus with a lake of f.	FLEC 112:3
deathly inner consuming f.	HESSE 140:3
every time She shouted 'F.'	BELL 33:5
f. and the rose are one	ELIOT 102:7
f. and was burnt to ashes	GRAH 127:8
fire brigade and the f.	CHUR 73:12
f. next time	ANON 8:3
f. of my loins	NAB 217:1
F. your little gun	DE L 91:7
I didn't f. him [General]	TRUM 299:11
Into the crowned knot of f.	ELIOT 102:7
The f. next time	BALD 22:8
The f. was furry as a bear	SITW 276:2
wabbling back to the F.	KIPL 173:12
What of the faith and f.	HARDY 134:7
with f. beyond the language	ELIOT 102:1
with those who favour f.	FROST 118:10
world will end in f.	FROST 118:10

fired: ever got f. for buying IBM — ANON 10:3

fireplace: stocking over the municipal f. — SMITH 276:14

fires: Of her salamandrine f. — HARDY 134:4

firing: have what to do after f. — REED 244:12

he faced the f. squad — THUR 297:13

first: After the f. death — THOM 292:12

After the f. four years	CRISP 86:3
be done for the f. time	CORN 84:2
certainty are not the f.	HOUS 144:13
f. and second class citizens	WILL 312:16
f. message of India	FORS 115:9

first (*cont.*):

f. requirement for a composer	HON 143:3
f. requirement of a statesman	ACH 1:6
f. sign of old age	HICKS 140:8
f. team and who just miss	BRON 54:6
f. ten million years were	ADAMS 2:1
First things f., second	CONR 82:4
know the place for the f.	ELIOT 102:4
Like the f. bird	FARJ 107:6
Like the f. morning	FARJ 107:6
Non-violence is the f. article	GAND 122:1
people who got there f.	UST 302:14
significant f. person	WITT 315:3
team we have Who's on f.	ABB 1:1

first class: f., and with children   BENC 36:10
first-rate: A test of a f. work   BENN 38:10
fashionable and f.   SMITH 278:8
firwood: f. meditating on the nature   O'BR 222:2
fish: cars nose forward like f.   LOW 191:12
coal and surrounded by f.   BEVAN 44:13
f. gaped among empty tins   PLOM 235:16
F. say, they have   BROO 55:3
f. swim with the stream   MUGG 215:5
like a f. without a bicycle   STEI 285:1
much as a recently dead f.   ORW 224:15
pretty kettle of f.   MARY 202:13
There's a f. that *talks*   DE L 91:1
fishbones: placing before me two f.   WELBY 307:9
fished: f. down their throats   BETJ 42:10
fishes: invasion. So are the f.   CHUR 75:7
When f. flew and forests walked   CHES 71:7
fishingboat: crowblack, f.-bobbing sea
   THOM 293:13
fish-knives: Phone for the f., Norman   BETJ 42:12
fissures: F. appeared in football fields   PLOM 235:16
fist: mailed f. in a cotton glove   SITW 276:7
fistful: f. of coins   ZAP 324:8
fists: groan and shake their f.   HOUS 144:8
fit: ain't a f. night out   FIEL 109:7
Britain a f. country   LLOY 190:1
It isn't f. for humans now   BETJ 42:2
only the F. survive   SERV 266:17
fitness: no test of f.   SHAW 268:24
fits: And think by f. and starts   HOUS 145:2
frightened them all into f.   BETJ 42:10
fittest: survival of the f.   ROCK 248:13
fitting: f. that we should have   ASQ 15:1
Fitzgerald: For this Edward F. died   YEATS 321:15
five: At f. in the afternoon   LORCA 190:21
be only f. Kings left   FAR 107:8
economy right in f. years   BENN 37:8
F. go off in a caravan   BLYT 48:6
f. kings did a king   THOM 293:10
The bombing begins in f.   REAG 244:7
fivepence: We have saved f.   BECK 28:14
fix: ain't broke, don't f. it   LANCE 178:3
And f. up his automobile   CLAR 77:3
looking for an angry f.   GINS 125:1
fixed: f. point in a changing   DOYLE 94:13

fixed (*cont.*):

His eyes f. upon nothing   YEATS 320:2
flag: f. to which you have pledged   BALD 22:12
German f. will be hauled   BEAT 28:3
we shall not f. or fail   CHUR 74:6
flagellation: Not f., not pederasty   RATT 243:7
flag-flapper: Jelly-bellied F.   KIPL 175:2
flags: f. straining in the night-blasts   CHES 70:6
flame: And the roof-lamp's oily f.   HARDY 133:14
tongues of f. are in-folded   ELIOT 102:7
When a lovely f. dies   HARB 132:11
Flanders: In F. fields the poppies blow   MCCR 194:6
flannel: wear white f. trousers   ELIOT 103:12
flannelled: f. fools at the wicket   KIPL 170:11
flapped: filled the trees and f.   HODG 141:13
flare: The f. was up in the gymn   BETJ 44:3
flash: f. through the flowery   CHES 69:15
flatten: His hide is sure to f. 'em   BELL 32:16
flatter: To f. beauty's ignorant ear   YEATS 322:4
flattering: who spends his time f.   TRUM 299:10
you think him worth f.   SHAW 269:18
flattery: out of ten to tout for f.   COLL 79:8
suppose f. hurts no one   STEV 285:15
Flaubert: His true Penelope was F.   POUND 238:6
flaunt: when you got it, f. it   BROO 56:4
flavour: lose its f. on the bedpost   ROSE 252:7
flaying: enough and f. would be fair   HOUS 144:8
flea: literature's performing f.   O'CAS 222:15
fleas: Even educated f. do it   PORT 236:15
f. that tease in the High   BELL 34:9
that has praised his f.   YEATS 319:4
fled: I f. Him, down the nights   THOM 295:2
flee: Or watch the startled spirit f.   GRAV 128:5
fleece: forest f. the Wrekin heaves   HOUS 146:7
fleet: f. of stars is anchored   FLEC 112:2
whole F.'s lit up   WOOD 317:1
fleetest: The fairest things have f. end
   THOM 294:10
flesh: an' give us hearts o' f.   O'CAS 222:10
F. of her flesh they were   BINY 47:4
F. perishes, I live   HARDY 133:13
For him f. was sacramental   ROB 248:12
In that land of f. and bone   AUDEN 19:5
Neither f. nor fleshless   ELIOT 101:8
that look but casual f.   YEATS 319:14
word and clay is the f.   KAV 162:1
flew: f. between me and the sun   BLUN 47:14
flexible: Access—your f. friend   ANON 6:13
flick: f. of the wrist   HEAT 137:1
flicker: moment of my greatness f.   ELIOT 103:10
flies: like f. on a summer day   RUSS 255:16
Lord of the f.   GOLD 126:2
on his skin the swart f.   DOUG 93:8
fliest: fly thee, for thou f. Me   THOM 295:15
fling: Had chosen thus to f. his soul   HARDY 134:2
flinging: F. from his arms I laughed   YEATS 323:6
flints: soul would walk the f.   CARB 63:14
float: F. like a butterfly   ALI 4:1
floating: F. in the Blue   MILNE 210:8

flood: Empire vast across the f.	HUXL 149:1
flooded: STREETS F.	BENC 35:15
floor: f. without holding	MART 202:7
I sail across the f.	GREN 129:4
passing of the third f.	JER 155:7
floors: across the f. of silent	ELIOT 103:9
flop: f. than the organization	BAEZ 22:3
Flopsy: F., Mopsy, Cottontail	POTT 237:7
floraisons: *f. mois des métamorphoses*	ARAG 13:2
floral: f. air and the love	FLEC 112:1
florid: Let the f. music praise	AUDEN 19:5
flotilla: Where the old F. lay	KIPL 169:6
flow: F. down the woods and stipple	SACK 256:13
flower: f. is the concrete cloverleaf	MUMF 215:14
green fuse drives the f.	THOM 293:4
Pride is a f. that's free	COW 84:11
flowerings: O month of f., month	ARAG 13:2
flowers: f. the tenderness of patient	OWEN 227:13
gathered f. are dead	FLEC 111:13
her f. to love, her ways	BROO 55:2
Letting a hundred f. blossom	MAO 200:10
Say it with f.	O'KEE 223:1
Where have all the f. gone	SEEG 266:1
Who gave them f.	OWEN 228:4
flowery: you flash through the f.	CHES 69:15
flowing: if the Suez Canal was f.	EDEN 98:2
fluffy: But f., just fluffy	HERB 139:9
fluidity: *f. of self-revelation*	JAMES 152:7
solid for f., all-powerful	CHUR 74:1
flung: f. us on the windy hill	BROO 54:8
he f. himself from	LEAC 183:1
flush: f. to suffuse his face	AMIS 5:14
flushing: f. runneth from windows	BETJ 44:1
flushpots: f. of Euston and the hanging	
	JOYCE 158:1
flute: The f. and the trumpet	AUDEN 19:5
flutter: F. and bear him up	BETJ 42:4
fly: A f. can't bird, but a bird	MILNE 210:12
all things f. thee	THOM 295:15
And nestlings f.	HARDY 133:8
can f. because they take	CHES 70:4
God in His wisdom made the f.	NASH 218:2
He wouldn't hurt a f.	LEAC 182:15
long-legged f. upon the stream	YEATS 320:2
Oh! never f. conceals a hook	BROO 55:5
flyin'-fishes: Where the f. play	KIPL 169:6
flying: F. Scotsman is no less	BEAV 28:6
Keep the aspidistra f.	ORW 224:19
men in their f. machines	DAV 88:12
foam: off that f. when Phidias	YEATS 319:14
foe: Call no man f., but never	BENS 39:5
f. was folly and his weapon	ANON 8:12
Scratch a lover, and find a f.	PARK 231:5
foes: judge of a man by his f.	CONR 81:15
fog: brown f. of a winter dawn	ELIOT 104:14
The f. comes	SAND 259:10
yellow f. that rubs its back	ELIOT 103:7
foggy: A f. day in London Town	GERS 123:6

fold: Do not f., spindle	ANON 7:16
F. your clothes up neat	DE L 91:8
mill and the f.	HOUS 146:5
folded: To undo the f. lie	AUDEN 17:12
folds: spring has kept in its f.	ARAG 13:2
Folies-Bergère: F. and looks at the audience	
	STOC 286:13
folk: All music is f. music	ARMS 13:8
f. song is that once you	LAMB 177:14
f. that live in Liverpool	CHES 68:18
folk-dancing: excepting incest and f.	BAX 27:15
folklore: magicians of North European f.	
	KEYN 165:3
folks: Don't let the old f. know	HERB 139:8
follies: f. which a man regrets	ROWL 254:1
follow: contrived that the eyes f.	ORW 225:3
Don't f. leaders	DYLAN 97:12
expect to see when I f.	DOYLE 94:12
F. ev'ry rainbow, till	HAMM 131:9
My old man said, 'F. the van'	COLL 79:5
So, f. me, follow	FLAN 111:5
follows: Impossible to come, lie f.	PROU 241:3
folly: foe was f. and his weapon	ANON 8:12
f. like the back	AUDEN 17:1
lovely woman stoops to f.	ELIOT 105:7
fonctionnaire: *Un f. ne plaisante pas*	ION 151:12
fond: He was extremely f. of sums	BELL 33:10
was probably f. of them	TWAIN 301:8
food: And the sweet sticky f.	AYRES 21:15
Continent people have good f.	MIKES 207:13
discovered that alcohol was a f.	WOD 316:3
Fame is a f. that dead	DOBS 92:13
farce and the f. a tragedy	POW 239:3
F. comes first, then morals	BREC 53:1
F. enough for a week	MERR 207:10
F. is an important part	LEB 183:10
f. that raises	HANFF 132:9
lays out f. in tins	ELIOT 105:5
problem is f.	DONL 93:3
sincerer than the love of f.	SHAW 270:18
fool: clever woman to manage a f.	KIPL 172:10
f. all of the people all	ADAMS 2:5
f. lies here who tried	KIPL 172:9
f.'s excuse for failure	BIER 47:2
f. there was and he made	KIPL 175:7
f. too many of the people	THUR 297:15
f. us with how fast they	AUDEN 20:7
I'm not a bloody f.	LONS 190:12
make a f. of himself too	BUTL 60:1
Prove to me that you're no f.	RICE 246:12
shouldn't f. with booze	FAUL 108:1
that f. Dawson of Penn	ASQ 15:5
will not laugh is a f.	SANT 260:8
foolish: being young and f.	YEATS 321:13
f. ideas have died there	FITZ 110:9
f. their lack of understanding	BIER 46:17
more likely to be f.	RUSS 255:9
These f. things	MARV 202:8

fools: be thankful for the f. TWAIN 300:18
But the f. caught it YEATS 322:1
flannelled f. at the wicket KIPL 170:11
f. are in a terrible overwhelming IBSEN 150:1
F.! For I also had my hour CHES 71:8
f. in town on our side TWAIN 300:7
not suffer f. gladly PEAR 232:12
or perish together as f. KING 167:6
Poems are made by f. like me KILM 166:4
things people make f. SHAW 268:12
foot: f. less and it would BENC 36:9
Now I hold Creation in my f. HUGH 147:14
on an 'eathen idol's f. KIPL 169:7
We're f.—slog KIPL 170:12
football: f. is a matter of life SHAN 267:8
f. team was swept over RICE 246:9
good excuse not to play f. LEB 183:11
he's f. crazy, he's football MCGR 195:5
footfall: Halts by me that f. THOM 295:17
footfalls: F. echo in the memory ELIOT 101:6
footless: through f. halls of air MAGEE 198:11
footman: eternal F. hold my coat ELIOT 103:10
footnotes: series of f. to Plato WHIT 310:12
footprint: looking for a man's f. BEER 31:8
footprints: f. of a gigantic hound DOYLE 94:14
for: F. all we have KIPL 170:14
F. you but not for me ANON 10:8
F. your tomorrows these EDM 98:6
forbidden: only because it was f. TWAIN 301:12
forbids: which f. the rich as well FRAN 116:6
force: f. by one class against LENIN 184:15
'F.' is the food that raises HANFF 132:9
f. that through the green THOM 293:4
f. to the last resort ORT 224:2
know the limitations of f. TROT 299:5
may the f. LUCAS 192:10
nations use 'f.' WAUGH 306:12
United States by f. HARD 132:15
unofficial f. DOYLE 95:7
forced: Originality is deliberate and f. HOFF 142:7
forces: Certainly f. operating BURR 58:6
ford: F. is so dumb he can't JOHN 156:4
Heaven, my friend F. WILL 312:14
I am a F., not a Lincoln FORD 113:11
mountain, f. ev'ry stream HAMM 131:9
President F.'s campaign manager MORT 214:10
foreboding: I am filled with f. POW 239:10
forefathers: recover it from all his f. BUTL 59:5
Foreign: be sent into any f. wars ROOS 250:10
f. correspondent is someone STOP 286:17
jowled or hawk-like f. faces MACN 198:2
Life is a f. language MORL 213:10
past is a f. country HART 135:14
some corner of a f. field BROO 55:2
thing about f. affairs REST 245:12
third-rate f. conductors BEEC 30:8
wage war; my f. policy CLEM 77:9

foreigner: better than any damned f. BEEC 29:21
joke was lost on the f. TWAIN 301:5
foreigners: bloody and f. are fiends MITF 211:15
f. always spell better TWAIN 301:2
Foreign Secretary: F. naked into the conference BEVAN 45:2
He [a F.] is forever poised MACM 197:1
whatsoever in attacking the F. BEVAN 45:5
foreseen: What I had not f. SPEN 281:13
foresight: mind to aftersight and f. ELIOT 102:3
forest: f. fleece the Wrekin heaves HOUS 146:7
f. something stirred SIMP 275:10
F. where all must lose THOM 294:7
f. with a golden track LIND 188:10
Of the f. beautiful HODG 142:3
other answered: 'In the f.' CHES 69:12
forests: When fishes flew and f. walked CHES 71:7
foretell: f. what is going to happen CHUR 72:9
foretold: Oh, who could have f. YEATS 321:4
scene, and f. the rest ELIOT 105:6
forever: Ecstasy and F. be Itself GINS 124:12
I'm f. blowing bubbles KENB 162:10
safire bracelet lasts f. LOOS 190:16
Strawberry fields f. LENN 185:13
you can see f. LERN 186:3
forfeited: result f. both TAYL 290:13
forfeiting: has no intention of f. ORW 225:16
forge: f. and the mill HOUS 146:5
f. in the smithy JOYCE 158:12
forget: Deep meadows yet, for to f. BROO 56:1
do not quite f. CHES 70:13
Don't f. the diver KAV 162:5
elephants never f. SAKI 258:2
f. the lilac and the roses ARAG 13:2
Half to f. the wandering FLEC 111:17
I never f. a face MARX 202:12
I never forgive but I always f. BALF 23:15
into war and they will f. WILS 314:5
In violence, we f. who we MCC 194:1
Lest we f.—lest we forget KIPL 173:3
must *not* f. the suspenders KIPL 171:8
War that you'll never f. SASS 263:4
forgetful: Bald heads f. of their sins YEATS 322:4
Earth in f. snow, feeding ELIOT 104:10
forgivable: Few books today are f. LAING 177:8
forgive: allows you to f. yourself SHAW 272:17
can f. a man for the harm MAUG 205:8
f. my friends for dying SMITH 278:2
F., O Lord, my little jokes FROST 118:7
f. some sinner and wink MENC 207:4
hate here—much to f. MILL 208:7
I never f. but I always forget BALF 23:15
wise f. but do not SZASZ 290:3
forgiven: f. nothing SHAW 272:14
forgiveness: F. free of evil done KIPL 173:2
such knowledge, what f. ELIOT 100:7
forgives: God f. me for it CART 64:6
forgiving: Sir, no man's enemy, f. all AUDEN 20:3
forgot: And then f. to tell us why NASH 218:2

forgot (*cont.*):

f. his course	FLEC 112:4
f. the copperheads	SAND 259:12
Honey, I just f. to duck	DEMP 91:10
They never f.	AUDEN 17:9

forgotten: been learned has been f. SKIN 276:12

books are undeservedly f.	AUDEN 18:8
f. man at the bottom	ROOS 250:2
f. scream for help in dreams	CAN 63:5
f. the grandest moral attribute	BARR 26:14
f. what it is like	JARR 154:2
he would be all f. today	BEER 31:20
There is always a f. thing	CHES 68:11

fork: pick up mercury with a f. LLOY 189:7

form: bad f. FORS 114:2

his listless f. and face	HARDY 133:14
meaning in memorable f.	BARZ 27:12
passionate apprehension of f.	BELL 32:6
was f. behind which we	BELL 32:7

forme: *mais cela n'a pas de f.* ANOU 12:14

formed: perfectly f. one kept COOP 83:2

formerly: not what we were f. told BLUN 47:13

forms: F. a stark Egyptian thought YEATS 319:10

formula: classic f. of a beginning LARK 179:8

offered a sure f. for failure SWOPE 289:6

forsaken: have seen the righteous f. BLUN 47:13

Forster: F. never gets any further KATH 200:7

Fortescue: Was Charles Augustus F. BELL 33:10

fortieth: am become her F. Article DENN 91:11

fortissimo: exclaimed: 'F. at last!' MAHL 199:3

fortnight: looking beyond the next f. CHAM 65:11

Phoenician, a f. dead ELIOT 105:8

fortunate: f. he was to be alive RHOD 246:5

on Beauty bare. F. they MILL 208:2

fortune: f. and runs it into a shoestring

WOOL 317:13

good f. to others	BIER 46:14
You'll find your f. falling	BURKE 58:3

forty: Life begins at f. PITK 235:7

loves a fairy when she's f.	HENL 138:14
man over f. is a scoundrel	SHAW 272:13

forty-two: F. ADAMS 1:14

forum: happened on the way to the F.

SHEV 274:16

forward: look f. to with hope FROST 118:16

Foster: Mrs F., the hours I've AYCK 21:8

fotherington-tomas: f. left in the lugage rack

WILL 311:11

fou: *f. qui se croyait Victor* COCT 78:8

fought: f. because he had to fight MCH 195:6

war wasn't f.	ROSS 253:5
Who f. with us side by side	WEAT 306:16

foul: f. rag and bone shop YEATS 320:3

human but to really f. ANON 11:14

foule: *f. sauve toujours Barabbas* COCT 78:5

found: f. something more interesting WALL 304:13

has not yet f. a role	ACH 1:8
I f. it, I found it	ABSE 1:4
tragedy of a man who has f.	BARR 26:15

foundation: f. of unyielding despair RUSS 255:12

foundations: The hour when earth's f. fled

HOUS 145:7

While earth's f. stand HOUS 145:12

founding: bank compared with f. BREC 53:2

fountain: Let the healing f. start AUDEN 17:7

founts: f. falling in the Courts CHES 70:5

four: count f. TWAIN 301:16

first f. years the dirt	CRISP 86:3
f. essential human freedoms	ROOS 250:12
F. Horsemen rode again	RICE 246:9
F. legs good, two legs bad	ORW 224:11
f. with paper hats	UST 302:17
looking over a f. leaf clover	DIXON 92:11
that two plus two make f.	ORW 225:6

four-footed: On all f. things CHES 71:7

fourteenth: f. Mr Wilson HOME 143:1

fourth: f. time that infernal noise EDW 98:7

fourth-rate: f. country and I don't CHAR 68:2

fox: Better than that of the f. BLUNT 48:3

brown f. jumps over	ANON 10:12
Crazy like a f.	PER 232:16
f. came home and he went	MAS 203:13
They've shot our f.	BIRCH 47:6

foxes: second to the f. BERL 40:13

foxholes: There are no atheists in the f.

CUMM 87:9

frag: *f. das Pferd* FREUD 117:3

fragments: f. I have shored against ELIOT 105:11

Live in f. no longer FORS 115:3

fragrance: she elegance? Has she f.? CAUL 65:3

frame: Are all the Human F. requires BELL 33:2

France: Always it woke him, even in F.

OWEN 228:1

en F., est rétrospective	ARON 13:12
felt about F. what Pericles	KEYN 164:11
F. and Belgium in the true	KITC 175:15
F. and Germany remain apart	DULL 96:6
F. has lost a battle	DE G 90:3
F. is adequately secured	ASQ 14:19
F., is retrospective	ARON 13:12
F. will declare	EINS 99:7
F. wins wars	HELL 137:7
We shall fight in F.	CHUR 74:6

franchise: extension of the f. CHES 70:2

Francis: highballs and I think I'm St F.

PARK 230:3

frank: f. words in our respective COOK 82:7

Frankie: F. and Albert were lovers ANON 8:1

frankness: views with an appalling f. BALD 23:7

fraternize: I beckon you to f. AUDEN 16:10

fraud: therefore it is not a f. SHAW 273:22

frauds: then all great men are f. LAW 49:1

freckles: Love, curiosity, f., and doubt

PARK 230:12

free: A hungry man is not a f. man STEV 286:8

A man is either f.	BAR 24:13
born f. and equal in dignity	ANON 11:16

free (*cont.*):

chains than to be f.	KAFKA 161:1
Fallen in the cause of the f.	BINY 47:4
f. as they want	BALD 22:15
f. society is a society	STEV 286:3
f. society it	BEV 45:12
F. speech, free passes	BETJ 44:5
F. speech is about as good	BROUN 56:5
he's f. again	SOLZ 280:2
I am a f. man, an American	JOHN 156:15
I am condemned to be f.	SART 261:9
man a f. hand and he'll	WEST 309:8
Mother of the F.	BENS 39:4
prison, I am not f.	DEBS 89:15
soon write f. verse	FROST 118:6
such thing as a f. lunch	HEIN 137:2
The best things in life are f.	DE SY 91:12
they are f. to do whatever	SHAW 271:4
truth which makes men f.	AGAR 3:4
Was he f.	AUDEN 18:2
When people are f. to do	HOFF 142:7
worth nothin', but it's f.	KRIS 176:11

freedom: And the green f. of a cockatoo

	STEV 285:8
any apprenticeship for f.	BAR 24:13
better organised than f.	PÉGUY 232:14
can do for the f. of man	KENN 164:1
F. and slavery are mental	GAND 121:11
F. is always and exclusively	LUX 192:14
F. is an indivisible word	WILL 312:17
F. is not something	BALD 22:15
f. is reserved	COLL 79:4
F. is slavery	ORW 225:4
F. is the freedom to say	ORW 225:6
F. of mankind alike depend	HAIG 130:12
f. of personal decision	JUNG 160:3
f. of speech, freedom	TWAIN 300:15
F. of the press in Britain	SWAF 289:4
F.'s just another word	KRIS 176:11
go out to fight for f.	IBSEN 150:2
I gave my life for f.	EWER 107:2
O F., what liberties	GEOR 123:5
Our f. as free lances	MACN 197:10
The enemies of F. do not	INGE 151:2
there can be no f.	LENIN 185:1
things or in the f.	ILL 150:11
We must plan for f.	POPP 236:5
What stands if f. fall	KIPL 170:15

freedoms: four essential human f. — ROOS 250:12
freely: nature as f. as a lawyer — GIR 125:3
freemason: F., and an asthmatic — DOYLE 94:19
freemasonry: have a kind of bitter f. — BEER 31:10
freer: f., and more loving — BALD 22:10
  f. society — BERD 40:1
frees: He f. himself and shows — GAND 121:11
freeze: against those who would f. — MACN 198:8
freezes: Yours till Hell f. — FISH 110:2
frei: *Arbeit macht f.* — ANON 6:16
freiheit: *F. ist immer nur Freiheit* — LUX 192:14

French: F. for life-jacket — BARN 25:7

F. letters to the university	JOYCE 159:8
German text of F. operas	WHAR 309:19
how it's improved her F.	GRAH 127:6
No more Latin, no more F.	ANON 10:5
Paris was F.	TUCH 300:1
some are fond of F.	MAS 203:2
The only tribute a F. translator	BEER 30:18
There is a F. widow	HOFF 142:9
We are not F., and we	MONT 212:8

Frenchies: Those F. seek him everywhere

| | ORCZY 223:18 |

Frenchmen: Englishmen act better than F.

	BENN 38:7
Fifty million F. can't be wrong	GUIN 130:6
Fifty million F. can't be wrong	ROSE 252:8

Frenchwomen: F. better than Englishwomen

| | BENN 38:7 |

fresh: F. from the Lord — FARJ 107:6
  got a nice *f.* corpse — TWAIN 301:6
  noted for f. air and fun — EDGAR 98:3
Freud: trouble with [Sigmund] F. — DODD 93:2
friend: A f. in power is a friend lost — ADAMS 2:8

country and betraying my f.	FORS 115:12
Diamonds are a girl's best f.	ROBIN 248:7
down his wife for his f.	JOYCE 159:8
enemy of thought and the f.	CONR 81:17
f. and enemy is but Death	BROO 54:10
f. of yours and you could	SAL 258:11
I think of him as a f.	SMITH 278:22
much-loved and elegant f.	CHAR 68:3
my f., is blowin'	DYLAN 97:3
O f., unseen, unborn, unknown	FLEC 112:7
One f. in a lifetime	ADAMS 2:10
portrait I lose a f.	SARG 261:2
Strange f.	OWEN 228:6
The soul of a f. we've made	BOND 49:2
To find a f. one must close	DOUG 93:10
Whenever a f. succeeds	VIDAL 304:6
your enemy and your f.	TWAIN 300:21

friendly: nor yet is it f. — HOLM 142:13
friends: And the dear f. have to part — BOND 49:2

closest f. won't tell	ANON 7:20
country are our f.	SHIN 274:17
don't trust him, we are f.	BREC 53:5
down his f. for his life	THOR 297:2
foes as well as by his f.	CONR 81:15
forgive my f. for dying	SMITH 278:2
For golden f. I had	HOUS 146:14
F.	KING 167:10
f. are necessarily	UST 302:14
f. who are not seeing this	THAT 291:9
f. with its grandfathers	MUMF 215:13
glory was I had such f.	YEATS 321:2
God we can choose our f.	MUMF 215:12
have really no absent f.	BOWEN 50:13
his f. could only	WOOLF 317:6
I have lost f., some	WOOLF 317:12

friends (cont.):

laughter and the love of f.	BELL 35:4
little help from my f.	LENN 185:16
made ridiculous by f.	BIER 46:8
Money couldn't buy f.	MILL 209:8
My f. all drive Porsches	JOPL 157:6
some of my best f. both	MAUG 205:3
win f. and influence people	CARN 64:1
your f. do not need it	HUBB 147:2

friendship: f. called slight when BIER 46:4
F. needs a certain parallelism ADAMS 2:10
frighten: street and f. the horses CAMP 61:11
frightened: And f. them all into fits BETJ 42:10
It has a f. look in its eyes SITW 276:8
then you're f. of death DONL 93:3
why should you be f. WEBB 306:18
frightening: f. than when they are convinced VAN D 303:6
nothing is really very f. STEIN 284:4
fringe: lunatic f. in all reform ROOS 252:1
frivolity: precious is f. FORS 114:5
frocks: Her f. are built in Paris SAKI 257:15
frog: f. that's any better'n TWAIN 300:9
Frogs: 'F.,' he would say MITF 211:15
frog-spawn: They *can* nothing but f. LAWR 180:11
from: F. far, from eve and morning HOUS 146:9
F. here to eternity JONES 157:4
F. Russia with love FLEM 112:9
F. what I've tasted of desire FROST 118:10
Neither f. nor towards ELIOT 101:8
fromage: *quarante-six variétés de f.* DE G 90:4
front: All quiet on the western f. REM 245:10
which f. these were sent OWEN 228:4
frontier: on the edge of a new f. KENN 163:7
Space—the final f. RODD 249:2
That is where our f. lies BALD 23:5
The f. of my Person goes AUDEN 16:10
frontiers: old f. are gone BALD 23:5
Frost: F. has risen without trace MUGG 215:3
Froude: [Hurrell F.] STR 287:15
frowned: It is not true to say I f. CHES 70:15
this dark: for you so f. OWEN 228:8
frowning: f. at one another across COOP 83:2
frowst: Or f. with a book by the fire KIPL 171:13
Froyd: F. said that all I needed LOOS 190:19
frozen: f. in an out-of-date mould JENK 154:11
frozen-ground-swell: That sends the f. under it FROST 118:13
fruit: And my f. is dreams THOM 294:14
plucking the f. of memory CONR 81:8
veranda, and the f. AUDEN 19:12
with humid nightblue f. JOYCE 159:9
frying-pan: In the f. DE L 91:1
fuck: They f. you up, your mum LARK 179:1
zipless f. is the purest JONG 157:5
fudging: up with f. and mudging OWEN 227:9
fugitive: feel like a f. from th' law MAUL 205:18
fugues: been if he had written f. BUTL 59:18
fühlt: *man sich heimischer f.* FREUD 117:5

Führer: *Ein Reich, ein Volk, ein F.* ANON 7:19
fulfilment: longing and the image of f. MUGG 215:7
full: Are f. of passionate intensity YEATS 320:7
F. of Eastern promise ANON 8:2
Lord God, we ha' paid in f. KIPL 174:4
this life if, f. of care DAV 89:2
full-hearted: In a f. evensong HARDY 134:2
fun: Ain't we got f. KAHN 161:3
And certainly damps the f. COW 85:7
earth was all the f. BETJ 42:9
f. enough for far BETJ 42:9
f. I ever had without laughing ALLEN 5:1
F. is fun but no girl wants LOOS 190:18
f. to be in the same decade ROOS 250:1
f. to punt than to be punted SAY 263:8
f. where I've found it KIPL 174:8
Gladstone read Homer for f. CHUR 75:12
It was great f. PORT 236:14
I wish I thought *What Jolly F.!* RAL 242:13
must not do things for f. HERB 139:15
noted for fresh air and f. EDGAR 98:3
Oh, what f. DE L 91:7
function: everything must f. to perfection MUSS 216:10
f. in life is to exercise SART 261:13
fundament: is so frigid upon the f. NASH 217:18
fundamental: The f. things apply HUPF 148:5
funeral: f. expenses JER 155:10
f. was because they wanted GOLD 126:11
how to perform a f. WILL 312:11
should be jolly at my f. MOUN 214:12
vault for f. Monday Dorset BEER 31:18
funny: Everything is f. as long ROG 249:8
f. thing happened SHEV 274:16
f. thing happened to me STEV 286:6
Isn't it f. MILNE 210:7
What do you mean, f. HAY 136:2
Whatever is f. is subversive ORW 224:17
funny-peculiar: F. or funny ha-ha HAY 136:2
fur: On some other f. ANON 12:10
furiously: Colourless green ideas sleep f. CHOM 71:16
furnaces: Your worship is your f. BOTT 50:5
furnish: Books do f. a room POW 239:4
furnish'd: F. and burnish'd by Aldershot BETJ 43:9
furniture: f. that he is likely DOYLE 94:7
f. that used MACM 197:7
going to rearrange the f. MORT 214:10
furrow: plough my f. alone ROS 252:12
furry: The fire was f. as a bear SITW 276:2
furs: hot water; f. to touch BROO 54:9
further: f. out than you thought SMITH 278:18
f. they have to fall FITZ 111:2
fury: blind f. of creation SHAW 270:15
f. and the mire of human YEATS 323:9
f. like a non-combatant MONT 212:6

fury (cont.):
  f. like a woman looking   CONN 80:19
fuse: green f. drives the flower   THOM 293:4
fuss: f. about sleeping together   WAUGH 306:13
  f. and with no explanation   BLYT 48:4
fussy: A f. man   MILNE 210:5
  Now I'm not a f. woman   AYRES 22:1
futility: fatal f. of Fact   JAMES 153:8
future: Back to the f.   ZEM 324:10
  controls the f.   ORW 225:5
  door opens and lets the f.   GREE 128:18
  F. as a promised land   LEWIS 187:3
  f. everyone will be famous   WARH 305:2
  f. is not what it was   LEVIN 186:18
  F., *n.* That period   BIER 46:19
  f. of the human race   JEANS 154:5
  F. shock   TOFF 297:20
  orgastic f. that year   FITZ 110:16
  perhaps present in time f.   ELIOT 101:5
  seen the f.   STEF 284:1
  The danger of the f.   FROMM 117:10
  The empires of the f.   CHUR 76:1
  The once and f. king   WHITE 310:4
  want a picture of the f.   ORW 225:9
Fuzzy-Wuzzy: F., at your 'ome   KIPL 169:1
fwowed: which Tonstant Weader f. up
                         PARK 230:9
Fyfe: Is David Patrick Maxwell F.   ANON 10:1

G

gable: Skimming our g. and writing   HEAN 136:9
Gaels: For the great G. of Ireland   CHES 68:10
gag: tight g. of place   HEAN 136:11
gaiety: concession to g. is a striped   THOM 294:8
gaily: G. into Ruislip Gardens   BETJ 42:8
gainful: known as g. employment   ACH 1:7
gains: are no g. without pains   STEV 286:7
gale: The g., it plies the saplings   HOUS 146:8
gallant: died a very g. gentleman   ATK 16:1
gallantry: g. and courage that made   COW 84:5
galleon: Stately as a g., I sail   GREN 129:4
  The moon was a ghostly g.   NOYES 221:9
gallop: G. about doing good   SMITH 278:21
  withdrawn and watch them g.   DURY 97:1
galloping: No mad hooves g. in the sky   KAV 162:2
gallows: The g. in my garden   CHES 70:16
gamble: g. at terrible odds   STOP 287:10
game: g. at which the police   SHAW 272:21
  g. at which two can play   BEER 31:19
  g. of life seriously   LEARY 183:4
  g. within the view   LEAC 183:2
  how you played the G.   RICE 246:10
  I don't like this g.   MILL 209:7
  Take me out to the ball g.   NORW 221:7
games: all, the dread of g.   BETJ 44:6
  children's g. from the beginning   CHES 69:14

games (cont.):
  G. people play   BERNE 41:7
  it is better than g.   SCOTT 265:9
gamesmanship: g. or The art of winning
                      POTT 237:14
gamut: Katharine Hepburn runs the g.
                      PARK 230:7
Gandhi: [G.] knew the cost of setting   NAIDU 217:7
gang: g. at Forty-Second Street   COHAN 78:11
gangsters: have always acted like g.   KUBR 177:3
gaol: Woman's place was in the g.   BRAH 52:8
Garbo: one sees in G. sober   TYNAN 302:6
garden: And in that g., black   BROO 55:9
  at the bottom of our g.   FYL 120:11
  Back to the g.   MITC 211:6
  g. and I am parshial   ASHF 14:3
  G. *it shall never pass*   KIPL 171:4
  In a g. shady this holy lady   AUDEN 20:12
  I never promised you a rose g.   GREEN 128:10
  Lean on a g. urn   ELIOT 103:16
  nearer God's Heart in a g.   GURN 130:9
  Of the g. hard by Heaven   BOUL 50:8
  Our England is a g.   KIPL 171:2
  The gallows in my g.   CHES 70:16
  The sunlight on the g.   MACN 197:9
  who in his g. watching   AUDEN 19:3
Garden City: G. Café with its murals   BETJ 42:7
gardener: Oh, Adam was a g., and God   KIPL 171:4
  Will come the G. in white   FLEC 111:13
gardens: all of the neighbour g.   REED 244:12
  But all the g.   THOM 292:14
  g. with real toads in them   MOORE 213:3
  In his blue g., men   FITZ 110:14
  Leaving the g. tidy   LARK 179:13
  time in the g. of the West   CONN 80:14
gare: *idées au-dessus de sa g.*   RATT 243:6
gargling: g. from the froth-corrupted
                      OWEN 227:14
garments: g. were always in patchez   NASH 218:11
garter: An earl and a knight of the g.   ATTL 16:2
  Polly G., under   THOM 293:16
gas: G. smells awful   PARK 230:14
  The g. was on in the Institute   BETJ 44:3
gas-masks: trenches and trying on g.   CHAM 66:4
gasoline: G. is much more likely   WEIL 307:5
gasp: G. and Stretch one's Eyes   BELL 33:3
gate: g. where they're turning   AUDEN 19:8
  stood at the g. of the year   HASK 136:1
gate-bars: And drops on g. hang in a row
                      HARDY 133:9
gates: despondently at area g.   ELIOT 103:15
  g. to the glorious   FORS 114:11
gateway: Sex is the g. to life   HARR 135:7
gathering: broken Anne of g. bouquets
                      FROST 119:4
Gatsby: G. believed in the green   FITZ 110:16
gay: A g. modulating anguish   FRY 119:18
  g. goodnight and quickly   YEATS 322:8
  He has a g. appeal   COW 84:12

gay (*cont.*):
Her heart was warm and g.   HAMM 131:11
gays: g. and lesbians issue   HEW 140:5
gazed: shop and street I g.   YEATS 323:11
gazes: Yellow God forever g.   HAYES 136:3
gazing: does not consist in g.   DE S 257:3
Geduld: *meine G. jetzt zu Ende*   HITL 141:9
geese: Like g. about the sky   AUDEN 16:12
  this the wild g. spread   YEATS 321:15
gee-whiz: is the 'g.' emotion   MCEW 195:1
Gehenna: Down to G. or up to the Throne
           KIPL 175:4
gems: He's torn the g.   FARJ 107:7
General Motors: country was good for G.
           WILS 313:1
generals: against the law for g.   TRUM 299:11
  wooden swords we're all G.   UST 302:17
generation: elegies are to this g.   OWEN 227:12
  g. is knocking at the door   SHAW 274:11
  g. revolts against   MUMF 215:13
  minds of my g. destroyed   GINS 125:1
  reproduce themselves from g.   JOS 157:8
  this is really a beat g.   KER 164:6
  You are all a lost g.   STEIN 284:14
generations: Those dying g.—at their song
           YEATS 321:5
generosity: life is to exercise our g.   SART 261:13
genial: called in London 'g. Judas'   HAIG 130:11
geniessen: *den Kontrast intensiv g.*   FREUD 117:4
genitals: would only stare at his g.   ABSE 1:4
  you're breaking their g.   BERN 41:5
genius: G.   BUTL 59:20
  G. is one per cent inspiration   EDIS 98:5
  g. makes no mistakes   JOYCE 159:7
  g. of Einstein leads   PIC 234:7
  g. of its scientists   EIS 100:2
  g. which does what it must   BAR 25:1
  g. who had not to pay   BEER 30:9
  instantly recognizes g.   DOYLE 95:14
  I think like a g.   NAB 217:4
  lot of time to be a g.   STEIN 284:5
  Only an organizing g.   BEVAN 44:13
  remarkable and seductive g.   STR 288:5
geniuses: G. are the luckiest of mortals
           AUDEN 19:11
gent: gentleman is to a g.   BALD 23:10
genteel: beast to the truly g.   HARDY 133:12
Gentiles: Such boasting as the G. use   KIPL 173:5
gentle: A g. motion with the deep   DAV 89:1
  g. into that good night   THOM 292:11
gentleman: died a very gallant g.   ATK 16:1
  every other inch a g.   WEST 309:16
  g. from both the artist   WAUGH 305:14
  g. in Whitehall really   JAY 154:4
  g. with iron-grey whiskers   BEER 33:4
  Hes a g.: look at his boots   SHAW 273:11
  I am a g.: I live by robbing   SHAW 271:2
  I am not quite a g.   ASHF 14:3
  intelligentsia what a g. is to a gent   BALD 23:10

gentleman (*cont.*):
  last g. in Europe   LEV 186:15
  once as an educated g.   SHAW 270:4
  sort of attire for a g.   SHAR 267:10
  They teach you to be a g.   SHAW 270:19
gentlemen: difficult to behave like g.   MACK 195:9
  G. always seem to remember   LOOS 190:14
  G. do not take soup   CURZ 88:3
  people and creates good g.   MUG 215:2
  Three jolly g.   DE L 91:2
  what most of the g. does   WAUGH 305:12
  while the G. go   KIPL 172:15
gentlemen-rankers: G. out on the spree
           KIPL 169:9
gentleness: g. and all her paths   SPR 282:15
gentlewoman: possible for a g. to commit
           WAUGH 306:14
gently: G. they go, the beautiful   MILL 207:16
gentry: disagree the English g.   HALS 131:8
genuine: place for the g.   MOORE 213:2
geography: G. is about Maps   BENT 39:7
  Is different from G.   BENT 39:7
geometrical: The Great Bear is looking so g.
           FRY 119:19
George: And later by G. the Fourth   COW 85:8
  G.—don't do   GREN 129:3
  G. the Third   BENT 39:14
Georgia: G. the sons of former slaves   KING 166:10
  song keeps G. on my mind   GORR 127:1
Georgian: all the G. silver goes   MACM 197:7
  erupted in gentle G. Squares   SPEN 281:9
geranium: As a madman shakes a dead g.
           ELIOT 103:14
  leans through g. windows   LEE 183:17
German: been that the G. dictator   CHUR 74:2
  G. Emperor on August 19th   ANON 7:24
  G. flag will be hauled   BEAT 28:3
  G. soldier trying to violate   STR 288:3
  G. text of French operas   WHAR 309:19
  talk with the G. Chancellor   CHAM 66:5
Germans: let's be beastly to the G.   COW 84:7
  The G., if this Government   GEDD 122:9
  their dead grip and G.   TUCH 299:14
  They're G. Don't mention   CLEE 77:5
Germany: country is at war with G.   CHAM 66:7
  G. calling! Germany calling   JOYCE 159:12
  G. had become a menace   NEV 219:3
  G. loses and prospers   HELL 137:7
  G. to Downing Street peace   CHAM 66:6
  G. was rearming   BALD 23:7
  G. will claim me   EINS 99:7
  if France and G. remain   DULL 96:6
  I went first to G.   COOK 82:7
germs: g. in your handkerchief   ANON 7:14
Gershwin: George [G.] died on July 11
           O'HARA 222:20
Gert: G.'s writings are punk   ANON 8:13
Gestapo: G. and all the odious apparatus
           CHUR 74:6

gesture: Morality's a g.   BOLT 48:13
get: And you can g. it if you try   GERS 123:10
   g. and beget   OSLER 227:7
   g. by with a little help   LENN 185:16
   g. laid, to get fame   GELD 122:10
   g. me to the church   LERN 185:20
   G. out as early as you can   LARK 179:2
   g. out of these wet clothes   ANON 9:11
   g. out while we're young   SPR 283:1
   g. what you like or you   SHAW 272:15
   g. what you want   SMITH 277:11
   g. where I am today without   NOBBS 221:1
   got to g. up this morning   BERL 40:7
   governments had better g.   EIS 100:4
   He'd have to g. under   CLAR 77:3
   If you want to g. ahead   ANON 8:15
   If you want to g. along   RAYB 244:1
   It's nice to g. up   LAUD 180:2
   I want to g. off   NEWL 219:4
getting: devotee of the Gospel of G.   SHAW 273:1
ghastly: G. good taste, or a depressing
         BETJ 43:2
ghetto: wouldn't go into g. areas   AGNEW 3:6
ghost: G. in the Machine   RYLE 256:9
   g. of a crazy younger son   COW 85:9
   The g. of Roger Casement   YEATS 321:1
   thought to please my g.   MENC 207:4
ghostly: g. batsman plays   THOM 296:1
giant: one g. leap for mankind   ARMS 13:10
giants: g. and for peace like retarded
         PEAR 232:11
giblet: He liked thick g. soup   JOYCE 159:4
Gide: [André G.]   QUEN 242:2
gift: g. for a good writer   HEM 138:11
   g. of oneself   ANOU 12:13
   your g. survived it all   AUDEN 17:4
gifted: Young, g. and black   IRV 151:13
gigantic: footprints of a g. hound   DOYLE 94:14
   his bed into a g. insect   KAFKA 161:2
   shadows pass g. on the sand   FLEC 111:9
Gilbert: [W. S. G.'s]   ANON 8:12
gilded: She's a bird in a g. cage   LAMB 177:13
gin: g. joints in all the towns   EPST 106:9
   G. less than a' the world   MACD 194:11
   G. was mother's milk to her   SHAW 273:17
   sooner we can get out the g.   REED 245:4
Ginger: G., you're balmy   MURR 216:5
gingerbread: Off the g.   COW 85:7
Gipper: win just one for the G.   GIPP 125:2
gipsy: Time, you old g. man   HODG 141:12
giraffes: G.! — a People   CAMP 62:5
girders: Rumbling under blackened g.
         BETJ 43:8
girdle: g. when your hips stick   NASH 218:13
girl: Above the staggering g.   YEATS 322:6
   A pretty g. is like a melody   BERL 40:8
   at a g. throwing a ball   WOOLF 317:11
   big mountainous sports g.   BETJ 44:4

girl (cont.):
   Diamonds are a g.'s best friend   ROBIN 248:7
   first rock at a g.   LOOS 190:20
   g. at an impressionable   SPARK 281:6
   g. had the making   WALL 304:17
   g. in the indolence   YEATS 318:5
   g. needs good parents   TUCK 300:2
   g. next door   AUDEN 19:15
   g. wants to laugh all   LOOS 190:18
   g. whose cheeks are covered   NASH 218:7
   g. with brains ought   LOOS 190:13
   just like the g. that married   DILL 92:6
   only g. in the world   GREY 129:6
   policeman and a pretty g.   CHAP 67:4
   Poor little rich g.   COW 85:2
   Sex and the single g.   BROWN 56:10
   The naughtiest g. in the school   BLYT 48:7
   To the sweetest g. I know   JUDGE 159:13
   When I'm not near the g.   HARB 132:14
   your eye at some homely g.   MENC 207:4
girlish: Laugh thy g. laughter   WATS 305:8
girls: Always be civil to the g.   MITF 211:11
   And g. in slacks remember Dad   BETJ 42:5
   are like g. and roses   DE G 90:1
   At g. who wear glasses   PARK 230:16
   G. are simply the prettiest   MCG 195:3
   G. scream   DAV 88:15
   g. that have no secret   SPEN 281:17
   g. turn into American women   HAMP 132:7
   In Little G. is slamming Doors   BELL 33:8
   marries three g. from St Louis   STEIN 284:3
   men and g. came and went   FITZ 110:14
   see what some g. marry   ROWL 254:2
   The lads for the g.   HOUS 146:5
   The rose-lipt g. are sleeping   HOUS 146:14
girly: skip about like a g.   WILL 311:12
gist: With this the g. and sum of it   PARK 230:17
give: g. a war and nobody will   SAND 260:4
   G. crowns and pounds   HOUS 146:1
   G. him the money, Barney   PICK 234:11
   G. me a girl at an impressionable   SPARK 281:6
   G. me a light   HASK 136:1
   G. me a no-nonsense   AUDEN 18:4
   G. me the man who will surrender   BARB 24:15
   G. my regards to Broadway   COHAN 78:11
   g. the public something   SKEL 276:11
   G. us the tools and we   CHUR 72:11
   g. you anything but love   FIEL 108:10
   I couldn't g. it up   BENC 36:13
   would be a good idea to g.   WARH 305:4
given: that anybody can be g.   BALD 22:15
   who had g. so ungrudgingly   SAKI 258:9
gizza: G. job . . . . I can do   BLEA 47:11
G.K.C.: Poor G., his day is past   LUCAS 192:6
glacier: The g. knocks in the cupboard
         AUDEN 16:13
glad: g. green leaves like wings   HARDY 134:1
   gladness when she's g.   BARR 26:10
   I'm g. tomorrow's Thursday   AYRES 21:14

glad (*cont.*):

I'm in g. we've been bombed	THE Q 106:1
or are you just g. to see	WEST 309:12
Was sad that she was g.	THOM 294:11
you know you should be g.	LENN 185:12

glade: alone in the bee-loud g. YEATS 318:10

gladly: g. not to be standing here JOHN 156:6

gladness: g. of her gladness when BARR 26:10

Gladstone: G. also invented the Education SELL 266:12

G. laying upon Providence	LAB 177:5
Mr G. read Homer for fun	CHUR 75:12

glamour: The g. of childish days is upon me LAWR 181:13

glance: O brightening g. YEATS 321:8

glare: at in this merciless g. WILL 312:9

To protect you from the g. COW 84:13

Glasgow: G. belongs to me FYFFE 120:10

G. Empire Saturday night	DODD 93:2
G. to do some work	BUCH 57:5

glass: families baying for broken g. WAUGH 305:11

g. is falling hour by hour	MACN 197:13
g. produce more effect	PANK 229:7
hate you through the g.	BLUN 47:12
In a dirty g.	PAN 229:4
like it out of a thin g.	PINT 234:14
No g. of ours was ever raised	HEAN 136:13
sewer in a g.-bottomed	MIZN 212:2
Sound of Broken G.	BELL 34:3
The sun-comprehending g.	LARK 178:10
To g. the opulent	HARDY 134:4

glasses: At girls who wear g. PARK 230:16

with plenty of looking g. ASHF 14:7

gleam: They g. there for you and me DE SY 91:12

gleams: light g. an instant BECK 29:13

gliding: But g. like a queen SPEN 281:16

glimmers: holy g. of good-byes OWEN 227:13

glittering: g. prizes to those SMITH 277:8

gloamin': Roamin' in the g. LAUD 180:3

global: image of a g. village MCL 196:7

Were g. from the start REED 245:1

globe-trotting: Can disturb g. Madam YEATS 319:10

gloire: *mes amis. Je vais à la g.* DUNC 96:8

gloom: Upon the growing g. HARDY 134:2

glorious: g. and the unknown FORS 114:11

In that g. land above the sky HILL 140:11

leaves the world more g. BRAD 52:4

Mud! Mud! G. mud FLAN 111:5

glory: ardent for some desperate g. OWEN 227:14

g. of rulers and of races	BEV 45:11
G. of the Garden lies	KIPL 171:2
g. was I had such friends	YEATS 321:2
I am going to g.	DUNC 96:8
Land of Hope and G.	BENS 39:4
That the g. of this world	BRAD 52:4
What price g.	AND 6:5

Glossop: Sir Roderick G., Honoria's WOD 316:1

Gloucester: there lived a tailor in G. POTT 237:4

glove: mailed fist in a cotton g. SITW 276:7

velvet g. as a lacy sleeve WOOL 317:15

gloves: About people in g. and such CHES 69:15

capitalism with the g.	STOP 287:12
down the Strand with my g.	HARG 135:2
through the fields in g.	CORN 83:12

glow: g. in the heart CONR 82:2

her g. has warmed	STEV 286:5
Star captains g.	FLEC 112:2

glowing: life from the g. earth GREN 129:5

glow-worm: believe that I am a g. CHUR 76:13

Glücklichen: *G. ist eine andere als* WITT 315:8

glue: g. that holds Government FORD 113:7

gluttons: And g. old in sin RAL 242:12

Glyn: With Elinor G. ANON 12:10

gnomes: little g. in Zurich WILS 313:3

gnostics: For one of those g. BORG 49:11

gnu: I'm a g. FLAN 111:4

go: better 'ole, g. to it BAIR 22:5

boldly g. where no man	RODD 249:2
But I have a g., lady	OSB 226:8
Five g. off in a caravan	BLYT 48:6
G. ahead, make my day	FINK 109:9
g. along	RAYB 244:1
G. down like lumps of lead	HODG 142:1
g. home and sleep quietly	CHAM 66:6
Good-night—and g. to it	MORR 213:15
G. out into the darkness	HASK 136:1
g. the way that Providence	HITL 141:7
G. together like a horse	CAHN 60:19
go together when we g.	LEHR 184:5
G. to jail	DARR 88:6
G. to work on an egg	ANON 8:6
have no place to g.	WHIT 310:18
Here we g., here we go	ANON 8:11
hope to g. on	THAT 291:10
I can't g. on, I'll go	BECK 29:3
I g. — I come back	KAV 162:7
Inspiring prospects. Let's g.	BECK 29:6
In the name of God, g.	AMERY 5:9
let us g. forward together	CHUR 74:5
Let us g. then, you	ELIOT 103:6
mean streets a man must g.	CHAN 66:9
pass g.	DARR 88:6
pronouncement: 'It's a Rum G.!'	VAUG 303:11
They all g. into the dark	ELIOT 101:14
thinking jest what a Rum G.	WELLS 308:8
Victoria Station and g.	BEVIN 46:2
we think you ought to g.	RUB 254:6
will arise and g. now	YEATS 318:10

goal: moving freely without a g. KLEE 176:1

goals: And 'theories' and 'g.' KIPL 168:4

muddied oafs at the g. KIPL 170:11

goat: sort of fleecy hairy g. BELL 33:16

goats: g. champ and sneer THOM 294:1

goblins: The g. were right FORS 114:13

god: about depth knows about G. TILL 297:18

god (cont.):

A Jewish G.	BROW 56:14
And the Cabots talk only to G.	BOSS 50:3
A neck G. made for other use	HOUS 145:15
A thick skin is a gift from G.	ADEN 2:20
brown g.	ELIOT 101:10
But as G. granted it	QUIL 242:7
But O my G., what a relief	BARR 26:18
But only G. can make a tree	KILM 166:4
discover that there is no G.	SMITH 278:3
every cliché except "G. is love"	CHUR 75:8
G. be thanked Who has matched	BROO 54:10
G. be with you, Balliol men	BELL 35:3
G. bless America	BERL 40:6
G. bless the child that's	HOL 142:11
G. Calls Me God	SAMP 259:3
G. cannot alter the past	BUTL 59:2
G. can stand being told	PRIE 240:1
G. caught his eye	MCC 194:4
G. created man	VALÉ 303:2
[G.] does not play dice	EINS 99:6
G. gave Noah the rainbow sign	ANON 8:4
G. gave us memory	BARR 26:4
G. gives all men all earth	KIPL 170:10
G. gives us our relatives	MUMF 215:12
G. had wanted us to think	LUCE 192:11
G. has any validity	BALD 22:10
G. has been replaced	BAR 24:14
G. has more right	JOHN 155:16
G. has written all	BUTL 59:21
G. hath joined together	SHAW 269:8
G. in human form	BONH 49:5
God is a little tribal G.	BURR 58:6
G. is beginning to resemble	HUXL 149:16
G. is not dead but alive	ANON 8:4
G. is on everyone's side	ANOU 12:11
G. is really only another	PIC 234:6
G. is subtle but he is not	EINS 99:5
G. might not be a Limited	STR 288:1
G. punish England	FUNKE 120:9
G. rest his soul, officers	SMITH 279:1
G. si Love	FORS 115:9
G. that He has spared me	BELL 33:12
G. to arrange a virgin	JENK 154:9
G. to let Carlyle and Mrs	BUTL 59:10
G. to make it responsible	DUH 96:4
G., who does not exist	O'BR 222:1
G. who made thee mighty	BENS 39:4
G. will know the truth	LUCAS 192:6
G. works in a mysterious way	ELIOT 102:14
G. works in mysterious ways	AND 6:7
G. would give me some clear	ALLEN 4:11
G. would have made Adam	BRY 57:2
Had G. on his side	DYLAN 97:14
hand into the Hand of G.	HASK 136:1
Here is G.'s purpose	FULL 120:7
honest G.'s the noblest	BUTL 59:4
How do you know you're . . . G.	BARN 25:9
if G. talks to you	SZASZ 290:5

god (cont.):

In the name of G.	AMERY 5:9
It's G. they ought to crucify	CART 64:8
laboratory of G.	WILL 312:3
make gods, there is no G.	O'NEI 223:9
might have become a g.	RUSS 254:14
Not I: let G. and man decree	HOUS 145:3
Not only is there no G.	ALLEN 4:10
Of G.	EWER 107:3
only Bach in praising G.	BARTH 27:3
Only G., my dear	YEATS 323:13
out that there is a G.	ALLEN 4:8
Painting is saying "Ta" to G.	SPEN 281:10
problem was that G. is dead	FROMM 117:10
Strong brother in G.	BELL 34:7
suppose that G. is only	TEMP 291:4
Thank G. we're normal	OSB 226:7
Thanks to G., I am still	BUÑ 57:14
they are attracted by G.	INGE 151:5
This day relenting G.	ROSS 253:6
To justify G.'s ways to man	HOUS 146:15
To the steep and trifid G.	THOM 296:8
was a man who said, 'G. . . . .'	KNOX 176:5
What G. abandoned, these	HOUS 145:7
when you've sung 'G. save . . .'	KIPL 168:5
Where G. paints the scenery	HART 135:12
Where it will all end, knows G.	GIBBS 124:2
whose g. is in the skies	SHAW 272:4
with how you appear to G.	UNAM 302:10
you are a g.	ROST 253:9
godheads: Maidens aspiring to g.	STOP 287:4
godless: decent g. people	ELIOT 104:2
Godot: We're waiting for G.	BECK 29:6
gods: g. that made the gods	CHES 68:8
g. wish to destroy they	CONN 80:8
machine for making g.	BERG 40:3
not know much about g.	ELIOT 101:10
people clutching their g.	ELIOT 100:10
there are innumerable g.	BURR 58:6
what the g. had given him	BEER 30:9
When men make g.	O'NEI 223:9
Goebbels: inferno depicted by Dr G.	ORW 224:20
goes: All g. if courage goes	BARR 26:6
nobody g., it's awful	BECK 29:7
The beat g.	BONO 49:6
going: are g. out all over Europe	GREY 129:7
certain they are still g.	BIRK 47:8
cheerful as keeps me g.	KAV 162:8
Economy is g. without something	HOPE 143:8
g. down of the sun	BINY 47:5
g. out a youngster	SEYM 267:4
g. to be your next president	CART 64:5
good both g. and coming	FROST 118:9
I am g. to glory	DUNC 96:8
I learn by g. where I have	ROET 249:4
Safe shall be my g.	BROO 54:11
When the g. gets tough	KENN 164:4
gold: g. with plenty of looking	ASHF 14:7
Meets the g. of the day	CROS 86:10

gold (*cont.*):

rain of g. and heart's	DAY-L 89:4
rarer gifts than g.	BROO 54:12

golden: For g. friends I had HOUS 146:14

g. rule is that there	SHAW 271:16
hand that lays the g.	GOLD 126:9
I went into a g. land	TURN 300:3
Miles and miles of g. moss	AUDEN 20:1
Or west to the G. Gate	KIPL 175:6
Red hair she had and g. skin	BETJ 42:6
repeat that on the G.	HOUS 144:9
The g. apples of the sun	YEATS 322:12
through the forest with a g.	LIND 188:10
We are g.	MITC 211:6

Goldwyn: Mr G., is that you SHAW 269:9

golf: American people than G. has ROG 249:7

And a thousand lost g. balls	ELIOT 104:2
g. may be played on Sunday	LEAC 183:2
young to take up g. and too	ADAMS 2:4

golf-links: The g. lie so near the mill CLEG 77:7

Golgotha: G. they hanged Him KENN 288:12

gongs: g. groaning as the guns CHES 70:6

struck regularly, like g. COW 85:4

gong-tormented: That dolphin-torn, that g. sea

YEATS 323:10

good: And this is g. old Boston BOSS 50:3

another for the general G.	WELLS 308:9
be not g. but great	VIDAL 304:7
be thought half as g.	WHIT 310:20
bloody g. hiding	GRANT 128:1
every age 'the g. old days'	ATK 15:15
Gallop about doing g.	SMITH 278:21
God-willing, I will make g.	HITL 141:8
g. both going and coming	FROST 118:9
G., but not religious-good	HARDY 134:11
g. cooks go	SAKI 258:1
g. critic is he who relates	FRAN 116:7
G. evening, England	POTT 237:10
G. fences make good neighbours	FROST 118:14
g. for our country was	WILS 313:1
G. government could never	CAMP 62:8
G. taste and humour	MUGG 215:6
g. taste invariably have	ORTON 224:8
G. taste is better	BENN 38:8
G. Thing, since	SELL 266:4
g. to be out on the road	MAS 204:3
g. to say about anyone	LONG 190:11
g. to some man that can	SHAW 272:22
G. to the last drop	ROOS 252:4
g. unluckily	STOP 287:9
G. women always think it	BROO 56:2
have never had it so g.	MACM 197:4
Hello, g. evening, and welcome	FROST 117:11
If it's by a g. author	SHAW 269:4
Is g. enough for me	HERB 139:6
It's finger lickin' g.	ANON 9:7
know better what is g.	JAY 154:4
know when I am having a g.	ASTOR 15:10
Lady, be g.	GERS 123:8

good (*cont.*):

Let the g. times roll	THEA 292:7
like is not necessarily g.	BELL 32:10
makes rattling g. history	HARDY 133:4
Men have never been g.	BARTH 27:2
much g. in the worst of us	ANON 11:8
or so g. as drink	CHES 68:5
people are not much g.	STAR 283:10
policy of the g. neighbour	ROOS 250:5
simply say 'is g. for you'	GREE 128:19
stars and isles where g.	FLEC 111:7
that's g. enough for me	THOM 293:16
That would be a g. idea	GAND 121:9
The g., the bad, and the ugly	SCAR 264:4
those who go about doing g.	CREI 86:2
What earthly g. can come of it	PARK 230:17
what you fancy does you g.	LEIGH 184:9
When he said a g. thing	TWAIN 301:9
When I'm g., I'm very	WEST 309:6

goodbye: G. cruel world SHAY 274:15

G., moralitee	HERB 139:6
G., Piccadilly	JUDGE 159:13
G. to all	GRAV 128:3
he did not say g.	BARR 25:13
Just kiss yourself g.	JER 155:13
kissed his sad Andromache g.	CORN 83:13
So g. dear, and Amen	PORT 236:14
That's all. G.	AYRES 22:1

good-day: G. sadness ÉLUA 106:6

good-humoured: g. boy BEER 30:15

goodness: And g. only knowses CHES 69:2

G. had nothing to do	WEST 309:11
My G., My Guinness	RICH 247:1

good night: Has smiled and said 'G.' BELL 34:12

goodnight: gay g. and quickly turn YEATS 322:8

G., children . . . everywhere MCC 194:9

good-night: G. Ensured release HOUS 145:12

His happy g. air	HARDY 134:2
Thomas says g. to Lady Jane	LAWR 181:9

goods: both parties run out of g. AUDEN 18:14

consumption of valuable g.	VEBL 303:12
g. and services can	NOCK 221:3
private g. have full	GALB 121:4

goodwill: In peace: g. CHUR 76:3

goody-goody: g. than fotherington-tomas

WILL 311:12

Gorbachev: yesterday that she liked Mr G.

THAT 292:2

gorgeous: The g. buttocks of the ape HUXL 148:19

gospel: G. of Getting SHAW 273:1

gossip: For pines are g. pines FLEC 111:16

g. from all the nations AUDEN 19:16

got: man g. to do what STEI 284:16

when you g. it	BROO 56:4
youngster but you've g.	SEYM 267:4

Gotcha: G. ANON 8:5

Gothic: great G. cathedrals BART 27:5

gothiques: *grandes cathédrales g.* BART 27:5

Gott: G. *strafe England!* FUNKE 120:9

Gotto: its name is Ainsley G. ERWIN 106:14
Gourmont: out of Remy de G. HUXL 148:15
gouverner: *Comment voulez-vous g. un pays*
DE G 90:4
govern: Go out and g. New South Wales
BELL 33:7
How can you g. a country DE G 90:4
government: America as a g. of the people
PAGE 228:10
be desirable if every G. SNOW 279:7
constituencies and prepare for g. STEEL 283:13
Democracy means g. by discussion ATTL 16:9
forms of G. have been tried CHUR 75:5
glue that holds G. FORD 113:7
G. and public opinion allow SHAW 271:4
g. by the people themselves CAMP 62:8
G. feels in its inside BENN 38:16
G. I despise for ends KEYN 164:10
g. in peace and in war BEV 45:11
G. is big enough to give FORD 113:10
G. is not to do things KEYN 165:1
G. is the organization SHAW 271:17
g. should be brought down MACM 196:16
g. than that which requires TUCH 299:15
g. which robs Peter SHAW 269:1
g. you have a dictatorship TRUM 299:13
great Republic is a G. FORD 113:8
I just watch the g. ROG 249:14
It's no go the G. grants MACN 197:12
king and g. and nation KAV 161:12
means g. by the uneducated CHES 69:16
more effect upon the G. PANK 229:7
never come from the g. WILS 314:9
overthrow the G. of the United HARD 132:15
pleased to be in the G. BAXT 28:1
politician to run a g. TRUM 299:8
shackles and restraints of g. GOLD 126:3
too much in forms of g. BAR 27:10
worst form of G. CHUR 75:5
governments: g. had better get out EIS 100:4
Governor-General: nothing will save the G.
WHIT 310:19
gown: Or sail in amply billowing g. BELL 35:6
red chiffon evening g. THAT 291:13
there's blood upon her g. FLEC 112:1
grab: G. your coat, and get your hat FIEL 108:11
grace: g. last night two black BEER 31:17
G. of God is in Courtesy BELL 35:2
g. of Terpsichore BARR 26:17
g. under pressure HEM 138:8
He had at least the g. BENT 39:6
swallow, the g. of a boy BETJ 43:9
with what g. he throws FLEC 111:11
gracehoper: G. was always jigging ajog
JOYCE 158:6
grades: you see, into four g. WAUGH 305:13
gradient: The g.'s against her AUDEN 19:15
gradual: Was the g. day SPEN 281:13

gradualness: g. of our scheme of change
WEBB 307:3
Grafton: G. Gallery to look BLUNT 48:2
grain: rain is destroying his g. HERB 139:11
grammar: I don't want to talk g. SHAW 273:13
grammatical: 'g.' cannot be identified
CHOM 71:16
gramophone: And puts a record on the g.
ELIOT 105:7
g. company asked him TREE 298:8
grand: baith g. and comfortable BARR 25:15
doing a g. job FROST 117:12
G. Central Station I sat SMART 276:13
g. little lad was young EDGAR 98:2
g. to be blooming well SAR 261:3
It is most g. to die MAS 203:11
rose petal down the G. MARQ 202:2
grandeur: *g. en eux ne font pas de* CAMUS 62:10
grandeurs: The g. of his Babylonian heart
THOM 296:9
grandfather: weight of a g. clock TREE 298:7
grandfathers: makes friends with its g.
MUMF 215:13
grandmother: We have become a g. THAT 292:5
granites: g. which titanic wars had OWEN 228:5
grant: g. what I wish and snatch FROST 118:9
universities go on a Government g.
MAUG 205:15
Grantchester: The lovely hamlet G. BROO 55:10
granted: But as God g. it QUIL 242:7
taking things for g. HUXL 149:14
grape: Beulah, peel me a g. WEST 309:4
grapes: Always eat g. downwards BUTL 59:17
sour g. and ashes without ASHF 14:11
grasped: haven't g. the situation KERR 164:7
grass: g. grows on the weirs YEATS 321:13
g. is soft as the breast CORN 83:12
green g. and bursting trees GREN 129:5
happy as the g. was green THOM 293:1
He can watch a g. or leaf GRAV 128:5
I am the g.; I cover all SAND 260:1
just uninterrupted g. LAWR 182:4
kissed the lovely g. BROO 54:8
Pigeons on the g. alas STEIN 284:9
The g. will grow HOOV 143:7
Was cut out of the g. CHES 68:8
When you destroy a blade of g. BOTT 50:4
grassy: shore of the wan g. SITW 276:5
gratitude: G., like love, is never ALSOP 5:7
gratuitous: autobiography is the most g.
STOP 286:15
g. And that evil acts GIDE 124:7
grave: about life beyond the g. KHR 165:11
before us lies the open g. MCKAY 195:8
birth astride of a g. BECK 29:13
Even the g. yawns TREE 298:9
from the cradle to the g. CHUR 76:9
g. and constant in human JOYCE 158:11

grave (*cont.*):

g. in a Y-shaped coffin	ORTON 224:9
g. of Gomer Owen who kissed	THOM 293:15
his g. like an old dog	MILL 208:8
It's with O'Leary in the g.	YEATS 321:15
tends the g. of Mad Carew	HAYES 136:3
Thoughtful children, and the g.	AUDEN 17:10
Thy victory, O G.	ROSS 253:6

graver: And His g. of frost	THOM 296:11
graveyards: no bone to pick with g.	BECK 29:1
gravy: And g. with the spoon	RAL 242:12
It's the rich wot gets the g.	ANON 10:15
grease: slides by on g.	LOW 191:12
great: All my shows are g.	GRADE 127:4
distinguishing the few really g.	LEAV 183:5
forgive Thy g. big one on me	FROST 118:7
G. Architect	JEANS 154:7
G. Bear is looking so geometrical	FRY 119:19
g. end comes slowly	DUB 96:2
G. hatred, little room	YEATS 324:1
G. is the hand that holds	THOM 293:11
g. lies about his wooden	FLEC 112:4
g. life if you don't weaken	BUCH 57:5
g. minds in the commonplace	HUBB 147:5
g. party is not to be brought	HAIL 130:13
If I am a g. man, then	LAW 49:1
Is also a g.	FROST 118:10
streets where the g.	FLEC 112:1
The g. illusion	ANG 6:9
these are g. days	CHUR 72:13
time close to g. minds	BUCH 57:4
upward to the G. Society	JOHN 156:10
want to be not good but g.	VIDAL 304:7
Great Britain: G. was going to make war	BETH 41:16
G. will not be involved	BEAV 28:7
greater: always g. than the causes	FORS 115:16
G. love than this	JOYCE 159:8
g. the ignorance the greater	OSLER 227:6
greatest: Harrison are the g. composers	BUCK 57:10
I'm the g.	ALI 4:2
greatness: g. within them do not go	CAMUS 62:10
moment of my g. flicker	ELIOT 103:10
greed: enough for everyone's g.	BUCH 57:8
Greek: can say a word against G.	SHAW 270:4
G. as a treat	CHUR 75:10
G. divine-human form	BONH 49:5
G. one then is my hero	ABSE 1:4
Greeks: The G. had a word for it	AKINS 3:8
green: believed in the g. light	FITZ 110:16
Colourless g. ideas sleep	CHOM 71:16
evermore no g. life shoots	BOTT 50:4
G. how I love you green	LORCA 191:1
happy as the grass was g.	THOM 293:1
How g. was my valley	LLEW 189:5
sorts. The day was g.	STEV 285:12
that through the g. fuse	THOM 293:4
The g. plant groweth, menacing	CHES 68:11

green (*cont.*):

There's a g. one and a pink one	REYN 246:2
Wherever g. is worn	YEATS 320:6
greenery: In a mountain g.	HART 135:12
greenfly: sure there weren't any g.	AYCK 21:10
greening: The g. of America	REICH 245:8
greens: And healing g., leaves	ABSE 1:2
Grenzen: G. *meiner Sprache bedeuten*	WITT 315:7
grey: g. and full of sleep	YEATS 318:8
little g. cells	CHR 72:2
Night is growing g.	HARDY 134:7
The g. wing upon every tide	YEATS 321:15
Griddlebone: I might mention G.	ELIOT 102:12
grief: are quickened so with g.	GRAV 128:5
griefs: isolation and the busy g.	AUDEN 17:4
grievance: Scotsman with a g. and a ray	WOD 315:10
grieves: g. not and that never hopes	MARK 201:3
grimace: Of its accelerated g.	POUND 238:7
grin: backward with a lipless g.	ELIOT 103:1
g. on his face and a totem-symbol	KOES 176:9
grip: With a g. that kills it	TAG 290:9
Grishkin: G. is nice: her Russian eye	ELIOT 103:2
grisly: g. gang who work your wicked	CHUR 72:12
grizzly: The G. Bear is huge and wild	HOUS 144:10
groan: g. and shake their fists	HOUS 144:8
groans: alike are the g. of love	LOWRY 192:5
grocer: God made the wicked G.	CHES 68:16
groined: which titanic wars had g.	OWEN 228:5
Gromyko: G. of the Labour Party	HEAL 136:6
groom: even if he is our g.	CHES 70:2
grooves: In determinate g.	HARE 134:14
grope: Whose buildings g. the sky	AUDEN 17:12
grosser: your g. reminiscences	WOOL 317:14
Groucho: G. tendency	ANON 9:5
Je suis Marxiste—tendance G.	ANON 9:5
ground: G. control to Major Tom	BOWIE 51:6
Off the g.	DE L 91:4
proposition when there is no g.	RUSS 255:14
ride in a hole in the g.	COMD 79:10
group: g. of men who individually	ALLEN 4:5
grow: Every instant a g.; he can	GRAV 128:5
few people who g. up	CHES 69:14
g. where one question grew	VEBL 304:1
never g. out of it	UST 302:17
They shall g. not old	BINY 47:5
growing: keep it g.	POUND 238:1
grown: are g. and take our place	KIPL 173:1
I've g. accustomed to the trace	LERN 186:2
grown-ups: obvious facts about g.	JARR 154:2
g. never understand	SAIN 257:1
grows: Nothing g. in our garden	THOM 293:16
growth: g. of a large business	ROCK 248:13
grub: old ones, g.	SHAW 267:17
grubs: And Paradisal g. are found	BROO 55:5
grudge: politician will never g.	OLIV 223:3
gruntled: he was far from being g.	WOD 315:12
guarantee: one can g. success in war	CHUR 76:6

guard: changing g. at Buckingham MILNE 209:15
g. against the acquisition EIS 100:1
Must g. themselves LARK 178:12
guarding: consists in the mutual g. RILKE 247:9
guerre: *faire la g. que la paix* CLEM 77:10
g. *ce sont les pauvres* SART 261:6
La g., c'est une chose CLEM 77:8
guess: g. that he was born SHAW 270:3
guessing: G. so much and so much CHES 69:15
guest: Earth, receive an honoured g. AUDEN 17:5
I too awaited the expected g. ELIOT 105:6
tonight is my g. night HALL 131:5
guests: classes: hosts and g. BEER 30:10
guided: g. missiles and misguided KING 167:4
guides: g. cannot master the subtleties

TWAIN 301:5
G. us by vanities ELIOT 100:7
guile: packed with g. BROO 55:10
Guillain-Barré: got something called G.

PUZO 241:10
guilt: his sense of g. LESS 186:8
guilty: g. of several monographs DOYLE 95:3
g. until they are proved ORW 226:4
Mortal, g., but to me AUDEN 17:10
were g. of Noel Cowardice DE VR 91:13
guinea: g. pigs in the laboratory WILL 312:3
guineas: Give crowns and pounds and g.

HOUS 146:1
Guinness: drink G. from a thick mug PINT 234:14
'G.' the advertisements GREE 128:19
My Goodness, My G. RICH 247:1
guitar: Are changed upon the blue g. STEV 285:12
gulf: Between the two a g. SNOW 279:5
redwood forest to the G. GUTH 130:10
gulls: Forgot the cry of g. ELIOT 105:8
gum: chew g. at the same time JOHN 156:4
gun: barrel of a g. MAO 201:2
Every g. that is made EIS 100:2
Fire your little g. DE L 91:7
goes the farmer's g. GAY 122:8
I have no g., but I can spit AUDEN 16:10
never said 'Drop the g., Louie' BOG 48:9
that a g. in your pocket WEST 309:12
gun-boat: situation is send a g. BEVAN 45:1
gunfire: towards the sound of g. GRIM 129:10
Gunga: better man than I am, G. Din KIPL 169:3
guns: defend ourselves with g. GOEB 125:9
example, without g. GOEB 125:9
groaning as the g. boom CHES 70:6
G. aren't lawful PARK 230:14
rather have butter or g. GOER 125:10
saw g. and sharp swords DYLAN 97:5
Scarce heard amid the g. below MCCR 194:6
than a hundred men with g. PUZO 241:9
unheroic Dead who fed the g. SASS 262:10
when the g. begin SASS 262:6
when the g. begin to shoot KIPL 168:12
gush: they're oil wells; they g. PARK 231:13

gut: *Menschen aber waren nie g.* BARTH 27:2
gutless: sort of g. Kipling ORW 225:18
guts: g. to betray my country FORS 115:12
what do you mean by "g." HEM 138:8
gutter: so I lay down in the g. BURT 58:7
walk straight into the g. SMITH 278:6
guttural: The g. sorrow of the refugees

MACN 198:2
guy: actor is a kind of a g. GLASS 125:4
g. who could carry a tune CROS 86:9
guys: Nice g. DUR 96:11
gymn: The flare was up in the g. BETJ 44:3
gypsy: vagrant g. life MAS 204:1
gyre: turning in the widening g. YEATS 320:7

H

habit: But h. is a great deadener BECK 29:14
habitation: can the soul's h. henceforth

RUSS 255:12
habit-forming: Cocaine h.? Of course not

BANK 24:9
habitual: nothing is h. but indecision

JAMES 153:15
had: We all knew you h. it PARK 231:11
Haig: [Earl H.'s] BEAV 28:10
hail: beaten dog beneath the h. POUND 238:17
hair: And never brush their h. BELL 32:14
And not your yellow h. YEATS 323:13
colour of his h. HOUS 144:8
drew her long black h. ELIOT 105:10
grainy wood; live h. BROO 54:9
h. with automatic hand ELIOT 105:7
her voice, and her h. MAS 203:5
into her long black h. NOYES 221:10
never hurt a h. of Him KENN 288:12
part my h. behind ELIOT 103:12
patted her h. and looked ASHF 14:10
She only talks about her h. THOM 296:7
such a head of h. HOUS 144:8
sunlight in your h. ELIOT 103:16
half: H. dead and half alive BETJ 43:3
H. devil and half child KIPL 175:8
h. grant what I wish FROST 118:9
H. to forget the wandering FLEC 111:17
has been too clever by h. SAL 259:2
have been finished in h. WOD 315:16
He that loves but h. of Earth QUIL 242:6
I don't know which h. LEV 186:14
I knew h. of her O'BR 222:5
Send me the h. that's got GRAH 127:10
half-a-crown: Or help to h. HARDY 134:10
half-men: And h., and their dirty BROO 54:10
half-truths: all truths are h. WHIT 310:7
halitosis: from h. of the intellect ICKES 150:8
Hall: [H.] has always maintained HALL 131:6

Hall (*cont.*):

Meet her in the h.	COW 85:9
than the pram in the h.	CONN 80:9
The Absolute across the h.	BELL 35:6

hallelujah: thrilling voice cry out H. OSB 226:10

halo: indignation is jealousy with a h.

WELLS 308:13

Is a h.? It's only one more	FRY 119:14

halts: H. by me that footfall THOM 295:17

Hamilton: Call me Lady H. RIC 246:14

was Alexander H. . . . he left	CHAM 65:13

Hamlet: *H.* is so much paper PRIE 239:15

H. patted this dog	SAL 258:13
I am not Prince H.	ELIOT 103:11

hammer: who proclaims with a h. BIER 46:10

With His h. of wind	THOM 296:11

hammers: anvil—hear the h. ring KIPL 174:1

which has worn out many h.	MACL 196:2

ham'n eggs: have your h. in Carolina

GORD 126:14

Ha'nacker: Sally is gone from H. Hill BELL 34:8

hand: adorable tennis-girl's h. BETJ 43:11

A h. under his head	YEATS 320:2
biting the h. that lays	GOLD 126:9
darkness and put your h.	HASK 136:1
eyes have seen what my h.	LOW 191:11
from h. to hand of cash	SICK 275:2
Give a man a free h.	WEST 309:8
hair with automatic h.	ELIOT 105:7
h. and touched the face	MAGEE 198:11
h. in hand with love	NOYES 221:8
h. that holds dominion	THOM 293:11
h. that signed the paper	THOM 293:10
Hath placed within my h.	ROSS 253:6
If you can't lend your h.	DYLAN 97:13
laid her snow-white h.	YEATS 321:13
Left h. down a bit	WYMAN 318:2
My h.	CRANE 85:10
rare fine h.	KATH 200:7
The h. is the cutting	BRON 54:3
Took me by the h.	TURN 300:3
waltz, I take her h.	HUXL 149:2

handbag: hitting it with her h. CRIT 86:7

handclasp: Out where the h.'s a little CHAP 67:5

handcuffs: young sinner with the h. HOUS 144:8

handful: fear in a h. of dust ELIOT 104:12

handicraft: out of the sphere of h. SARR 261:5

handkerchief: damp h. and sometimes

MACK 195:10

h. binding her hair	CONN 81:5
on the state of the h.	CONN 80:17
tie and display h.	CHAN 66:10
Trap the germs in your h.	ANON 7:14

handles: There are no h. to a horse LEAC 182:12

hands: Beneath the bleeding h. we feel

ELIOT 101:15

h. could lay hold	BENÉT 37:1
h. I have built her up	AYCK 21:8
h. I loved beside the Shalimar	HOPE 144:4

hands (*cont.*):

h. of young children	DYLAN 97:5
h. that hold the aces	BETJ 42:3
has such small h.	CUMM 87:5
Holding h. at midnight	GERS 123:10
its h. and goes to work	SAND 260:3
my h. were loath	OWEN 228:8
prize-fighters shaking h.	MENC 206:11
Soul clap its h. and sing	YEATS 321:6
Their h. upon their hearts	HOUS 145:2
your h. from day to day	MACN 197:13

handsome: Hi! h. hunting man DE L 91:7

hang: H. it all, Robert Browning POUND 238:2

h. my hat is home sweet	JER 155:12
H. your clothes on a hickory	DE L 91:8
[Patrick Gray] h. there	EHRL 99:2
When they come to h. you, lad	KING 167:11
will not h. myself today	CHES 70:16

hanged: got myself burnt or h. JER 155:6

h. on the highest hill	KIPL 172:7

hangin': they're h. Danny Deever KIPL 168:9

hanging: Cassidy's h. hill KAV 161:13

h. for the colour	HOUS 144:8
h. garments of Marylebone	JOYCE 158:1
h. isn't bad enough	HOUS 144:8

hangman: And naked to the h.'s noose

HOUS 145:15

hank: rag and a bone and a h. KIPL 175:7

hansom: And was helped to a h. outside

BETJ 42:1

happen: are supposed to h. off STOP 287:3

don't know what will h. now	KING 166:11
everybody knew would never h.	POW 239:9
foretell what is going to h.	CHUR 72:9
It can't h. here	LEWIS 188:1
which started to h.	MARQ 202:1

happened: funny thing h. on the way

SHEV 274:16

h. to you and afterwards	HEM 138:2
things after they have h.	ION 151:11

happening: A way of h., a mouth AUDEN 17:4

perceives what is *not* h.	TYNAN 302:8

happens: be there when it h. ALLEN 4:6

Experience is not what h.	HUXL 149:13
judgement. It h. every day	CAMUS 62:14
Nothing h., nobody comes	BECK 29:7
something, h. anywhere	LARK 179:7

happiness: about somebody else's h. HUXL 149:3

away you take away his h.	IBSEN 150:7
But a lifetime of h.	SHAW 270:12
H. is an imaginary condition	SZASZ 290:2
H. is a wine of the rarest	SMITH 277:10
H. is salutary for the body	PROU 241:5
H. is the only sanction	SANT 260:10
h. is to admire without	BRAD 52:1
H. makes up in height	FROST 119:8
h. of the common man	BEV 45:11
h. or a quiet conscience	BERL 41:2
It seemed, so great my h.	YEATS 323:11

happiness (*cont.*):

more right to consume h.	SHAW 268:11
most fatal to true h.	RUSS 255:6
our h. is assured	BIER 46:19
politics of h.	HUMP 148:4
Who gain a h. in eyeing	HUXL 148:19

happy: A h. noise to hear

	HOUS 146:3
Farmer will never be h.	HERB 139:11
H. birthday to you	HILL 140:12
H. days are here again	YELL 324:3
h. home with his wife	EDW 98:11
H. the hare at morning	AUDEN 21:3
H. till I woke again	HOUS 146:16
His h. good-night air	HARDY 134:2
house and h. as the grass	THOM 293:1
I only wanted to make you h.	AYCK 21:9
peculiar ways of being h.	JAMES 153:17
remote from the h.	AUDEN 16:11
See the h. moron	ANON 10:14
somewhere, may be h.	MENC 206:14
The h. highways where I went	HOUS 146:11
The world of the h.	WITT 315:8
They are to be h.	LARK 179:12
This is the h. warrior	READ 244:3
Was he h.	AUDEN 18:2
were angry and poor and h.	CHES 70:12
whether you are h. or not	SHAW 273:6

harbour: Pale rain over the dwindling h.

	THOM 292:14

hard: ask the h. question

	AUDEN 20:6
A very h. guy, indeed	RUNY 254:8
h. rain's a gonna fall	DYLAN 97:5
it is awfully h. to get	HALD 131:3
It's been a h. day's night	LENN 185:10
soldier's life is terrible h.	MILNE 209:15

hard-boiled: h. city with no more personality

	CHAN 67:1

harder: We're number two. We try h.	ANON 12:2
hardest: President's h. task	JOHN 156:14
hard-faced: are a lot of h. men	BALD 23:2
Harding: H. of Ohio was chosen	SIMP 275:11
H. was not a bad man	LONG 190:10
hardships: his comrades, beset by h.	ATK 16:1
Hardy: H. went down to botanize	CHES 71:3

hare: Happy the h. at morning

	AUDEN 21:3
h. sitting up	LAWR 182:4
I like the hunting of the h.	BLUNT 48:3
that Caught the Pubic H.	BEHAN 31:23
hares: And little hunted h.	HODG 142:2

hark: H. the herald angels sing

	ANON 8:9
H.! the herald angels sing	BEEC 30:4
harlot: prerogative of the h.	KIPL 172:6
Harlow: H. kept calling Margot	ASQ 15:4
harm: forgive a man for the h.	MAUG 205:8
h. as those who go about	CREI 86:2
h. to ask for what you	KRUT 177:2
harms: Not for thy h.	THOM 295:16

harness: And hear the h. jingle

	HOUS 146:6
h. piece by piece Thou	THOM 295:10

harpsichord: [The h.]

	BEEC 29:18
Harris: Frank H. . . . said	BALF 23:14
this is the *present* Mrs H.	THUR 297:6
Harrison: George,H. are the greatest	BUCK 57:10
harrow: H. the house of the dead	AUDEN 20:4
worthy to pass into H.	CHUR 75:9
harrowing: Only a man h. clods	HARDY 133:15
Harry: I'm just wild about H.	SISS 275:13
Harvard: or the glass flowers at H.	MOORE 213:4

harvest: Oh, shine on, shine on, h. moon

	NORW 221:6
hassen: *Wenn wir einen Menschen h.*	HESSE 140:2

hat: get ahead, get a h.

	ANON 8:15
hang my h. is home sweet	JER 155:12
h. at a private view	EDW 98:8
He can't think without his h.	BECK 29:8
mistook his wife for a h.	SACKS 256:11
Queen to get away with a h.	LOOS 190:17
silk h. on a Bradford	ELIOT 105:6
The sun has got his h.	BUTL 58:11

hate: away this murdherin' h.

	O'CAS 222:10
bother with people I h.	HART 135:11
creatures is not to h. them	SHAW 268:15
Each sequestered in its h.	AUDEN 17:6
h. to get up in the morning	BERL 40:7
h. victims who respect	SART 262:3
h. what every poet hates	KAV 161:12
h. will outrun you yet	OSB 226:15
h. you through the glass	BLUN 47:12
have seen much to h. here	MILL 208:7
how I h. them	LAWR 180:11
If you h. a person	HESSE 140:2
I h. inaccuracy	BUTL 60:5
I think I know enough of h.	FROST 118:10
Lead me from h. to love	KUMAR 177:4
The man you love to h.	ANON 9:23
This is a letter of h.	OSB 226:15
you h. women, otherwise	O'BR 222:1
hated: never h. a man enough	GABOR 120:14
they are h. because they	RUSS 255:17

hates: any man who h. dogs

	ROST 253:10
h. them for it	SHAW 274:6
H. you 'cause your feet's	BENS 39:2
The sea h. a coward	O'NEI 223:12

Hathaway: reproductions of Anne H.'s cottage

	LANC 178:2

hating: But h., my boy, is an art

	NASH 218:3
special reason for h. school	BEER 30:15
hatless: H., I take off	LARK 179:4
hatred: h. for the Tory Party	BEVAN 45:8
have no h. or bitterness	CAV 65:8
intellectual h. is the worst	YEATS 320:9
undying h. it arouses	FOSD 116:4
hatreds: systematic organization of h.	ADAMS 2:7
hats: H. divide generally	WHIT 310:15
hauf-way: I'll ha'e nae h. hoose	MACD 194:10
hauled: German flag will be h.	BEAT 28:3
hauling: H. a lawyer away	SAND 260:5

haunches: on silent h.   SAND 259:10
haunted: A h. town it is to me   LANG 178:4
haunts: That h. you night and day   BERL 40:8
Havana: Our man in H.   GREE 128:17
have: But I h. a go, lady   OSB 226:8
   h. nothing whatever   MAUG 205:1
   h. to believe that if   O'HARA 222:20
   I h. to tell you now   CHAM 66:7
   long as you h. your life   JAMES 152:8
   Mama may h., papa may have   HOL 142:11
   something they must h.   BOWEN 51:1
   They h. to take you   FROST 119:1
   when you h. to go there   FROST 119:1
hawk: He bold as a h.   THUR 297:12
hay: So *that's* what h. looks like   MARY 202:14
   Work and pray, live on h.   HILL 140:11
hazards: h. whence no tears can   HARDY 134:7
hazy: ordinary human beings is so h.   OSB 226:11
he: H. would, wouldn't   RIC 246:13
   'Who h.?' and the like   ROSS 253:2
head: at the command—of his h.   ROOS 250:9
   ever rears its ugly h.   AYCK 21:6
   h. for that big star straight   MILL 208:11
   h. when all about you   KERR 164:7
   h. when there is anything   LEAC 182:12
   heaped on each gashed h.   SORL 281:2
   his brains go to his h.   ASQ 15:6
   If you can keep your h.   KIPL 173:7
   I hang 'mid men my needless h.   THOM 294:14
   Lady, when your lovely h.   BELL 34:14
   Lay your sleeping h., my love   AUDEN 17:10
   monstrous h. and sickening cry   CHES 71:7
   psychiatrist should have his h.   GOLD 126:10
   some as big as your h.   HEAT 137:1
   such a h. of hair   HOUS 144:8
   To keep your h.   PUDN 241:7
headmaster: H. beaming skool bus ratle   WILL 311:11
   h. said you ruled them   RATT 243:4
headmasters: H. have powers   CHUR 75:11
headpiece: H. filled with straw. Alas   ELIOT 103:3
head-waiter: h. who's allowed to sit   UST 302:18
healer: compassion of the h.'s art   ELIOT 101:15
healing: And h. greens, leaves   ABSE 1:2
   not h, but healing   HARD 133:1
heals: Time wounds all h.   BREC 52:17
health: case of nutrition and h.   JAY 154:4
   character is the h. of his wife   CONN 81:3
   His h., his honour   BLUN 47:13
   When you have both it's h.   DONL 93:3
healths: drink one another's h.   JER 155:4
healthy: all h. instinct for it   BUTL 60:3
   h. and wealthy and dead   THUR 297:11
   H. citizens are the greatest   CHUR 73:2
   h. stomach is nothing if   BUTL 59:16
heap: h. of all your winnings   KIPL 173:8
hear: And h. the harness jingle   HOUS 146:6
   And h. the larks so high   HOUS 146:3

hear (*cont.*):
   can't h. what they say   SMITH 277:17
   Can you h. me, mother   POW 239:11
   Come on and h.   BERL 40:4
   h. like ocean on a western   LANG 178:5
   h. the pleasant cuckoo   DAV 88:14
   h. what was being said   SYNGE 289:10
   If you could h.   OWEN 227:14
   I h. A gay modulating anguish   FRY 119:18
   I h. a sudden cry of pain   STEP 285:4
   I h. you, I will come   HOUS 146:4
   read music but can't h.   BEEC 29:16
   really want to h. about it   SAL 258:10
   Whenever I h. the word   JOHST 157:2
   which men prefer not to h.   AGAR 3:4
   who do not wish to h. it   BUTL 59:8
heard: ain't h. nuttin' yet   JOLS 157:3
   Have you h. it's in the stars   PORT 237:1
   h. one side of the case   BUTL 59:21
   h. shoes described   HALS 131:7
   should certainly have h.   AUDEN 18:2
   you h. a seal bark   THUR 297:5
hearing: assails our sense of h.   ELLIS 106:4
   Woke to my h. from harbour   THOM 292:13
Hearst: William Randolph H. gave him   SMITH 276:15

heart: A fanatic h.   YEATS 324:1
   An Irishman's h. is nothing   SHAW 269:16
   blind side of the h.   CHES 68:11
   bone shop of the h.   YEATS 320:3
   book known to him by h.   WOOLF 317:6
   Brute h. of a brute like you   PLATH 235:11
   Bury my h. at Wounded Knee   BENÉT 36:17
   But my h.'s right there   JUDGE 159:13
   But not your h. away   HOUS 146:1
   But since man's h. is small   KIPL 170:2
   Can make a stone of the h.   YEATS 320:5
   Can mean to a tired h.   BOND 49:2
   country begins in the h.   CATH 65:1
   Deep in the h. of Texas   HERS 140:1
   ease a h. like a satin   PARK 230:10
   engraved on her h.   SELL 266:7
   gold and h.'s first ease   DAY-L 89:4
   grandeurs of his Babylonian h.   THOM 296:9
   h. are as crooked   AUDEN 19:2
   h. attacks and he had   JOPL 157:7
   heart-break in the h.   GIBS 124:6
   h. could have thought you   THOM 296:10
   h. expands to tinker   MACN 198:6
   h. less native to high   THOM 296:4
   h. may think it knows better   BOWEN 50:13
   h. of man has long been   HOUS 145:6
   h. of the ridiculous   MAHON 199:4
   h. that one can see rightly   SAIN 257:2
   h. to poke poor Billy   GRAH 127:8
   h. wants to sing ev'ry   HAMM 132:3
   h. was shaken with tears   SASS 263:5
   He carries his h. in his boots   HERB 139:11
   Her h. was warm and gay   HAMM 131:11

heart (*cont.*):

his little h.	JAMES 153:9
In the deserts of the h.	AUDEN 17:7
Into my h. an air that kills	HOUS 146:11
I said to H.	BELL 35:8
It hurts my h. to watch	SASS 263:3
it in the deep h.'s core	YEATS 318:10
Land of H.'s Desire	YEATS 319:9
laughing h.'s long peace there	BROO 54:10
laughter of her h.	HAMM 131:11
let your h. be strong	LAUD 179:17
My h. belongs to Daddy	PORT 236:17
My h. was with the Oxford men	LETTS 186:9
occasional h. attack	BENC 36:5
Oh, deep in my h.	ANON 12:6
Out of my h.	YEATS 319:3
Out-worn h., in a time out-worn	YEATS 318:7
red pavilion of my h.	THOM 295:18
That the h. grows old	YEATS 321:4
The h. is a lonely hunter	MCC 194:8
The hills fill my h.	HAMM 132:3
verities and truths of the h.	FAUL 107:11
waters of the h.	THOM 293:5
We had fed the h. on fantasies	YEATS 318:6
What else could any h. do	REAV 244:11
who had one body and one h.	DOUG 93:8
With rue my h. is laden	HOUS 146:14
You're breaking my h.	BERN 41:5
You're my h.'s desire	ARMS 13:7

heart-break: feel the h. in the heart GIBS 124:6

hearth-fire: And the h. and the home-acre
  KIPL 172:14

heartless: For nature, h., witless nature
  HOUS 145:8

hearts:

H. wound up with love	SPEN 282:2
not to get your h. desire	SHAW 271:13
Their hands upon their h.	HOUS 145:2
tight hot cell of their h.	BOGAN 48:8
undeveloped h.	FORS 114:1
While your h. are yearning	FORD 113:14
Who sing to find your h.	FLEC 111:7

heat: you can't stand the h. TRUM 299:7
  you can't stand the h. VAUG 303:9

heathen: But Higgins is a H. CHES 71:9

heather: bonnie bloomin' h. LAUD 180:1

heaven: A lawyer's dream of h. BUTL 59:5

And h. endures	HOUS 145:12
And I came down from h.	CART 64:7
betwixt H. and Charing Cross	THOM 296:13
Cry,—clinging H. by the hems	THOM 296:13
day when h. was	HOUS 145:7
gets to H. he won't last	WELLS 308:1
h. an angel is nobody	SHAW 272:6
h. for a man like Adolf	BUCH 57:7
H. holds a place for those	SIMON 275:9
H. out of unbelievable	COW 84:5
H. will protect a working-girl	SMITH 277:2
Hell, and H. how high	BENÉT 37:1
Imagine there's no h.	LENN 185:2

heaven (*cont.*):

Is he in h.?—Is he in hell?	ORCZY 223:18
Is it any better in H.	WILL 312:14
It was my thirtieth year to h.	THOM 292:13
joy-bells ring in H.'s street	MAS 203:9
more things in h. and earth	HALD 131:1
My blue h.	WHIT 310:17
nurseries of h.	THOM 295:1
Of the garden hard by H.	BOUL 50:8
Pennies from h.	BURKE 58:3
that H. of all their wish	BROO 55:5
Toward h., till the tree	FROST 118:9
'Twould ring the bells of H.	HODG 142:2
under an English h.	BROO 55:2

heavenly: A h. mansion, raging YEATS 323:12
  ancient h. connection GINS 125:1

heavens: h.' embroidered cloths YEATS 323:1
  she feels the h. lie bare THOM 296:7

heaves: forest fleece the Wrekin h. HOUS 146:7

heavy: I was h. with the even THOM 295:9

Hebrides: seas colder than the H. FLEC 112:2

Hector: ago H. took off his plume CORN 83:13

hedgehogs: personality belongs to the h.
  BERL 40:13

  start throwing h. under me KHR 165:10

heels: crossing of a pair of h. HART 135:10
  nipping the h. of Hemingway ALGR 3:16

heigh-ho: H., heigh-ho MOREY 213:6

height: h. for what it lacks FROST 119:8
  not think up to the h. CHES 71:4

heimischer: *dass man sich h. fühlt*
  FREUD 117:5

Heineken: H. refreshes the parts other LOV 191:4

Heinz: Beanz meanz H. DRAKE 95:16

heiress: When an American h. wants MCC 193:13

Helen: Shall look on H.'s face in hell PARK 230:18
  That first night in H.'s arms YEATS 324:2

hell: Blake knew how deep is H. BENÉT 37:1

Can extinguish h.	REED 245:3
give them [the public] h.	TRUM 299:6
H. go ting-a-ling-a-ling	ANON 10:8
h. in such a way that you	STIN 286:12
H. is full of musical amateurs	SHAW 271:3
H. is oneself	ELIOT 101:3
H. is other people	SART 261:11
H., madam, is to love no more	BERN 41:4
interests of H.	FORS 114:9
I say the h.	WHITE 309:23
Is he in heaven?—Is he in h.?	ORCZY 223:18
it would be h. on earth	SHAW 270:12
made an excursion to h.	PRIE 239:17
merger between Heaven and H.	WELLS 308:1
out of unbelievable H.	COW 84:5
seventeen. I'll go to h.	THOM 294:1
They go to h. like lambs	CHES 68:18
though h. should bar the way	NOYES 221:11
What is h.	ELIOT 101:3
why they invented H.	RUSS 255:15
wicked as Lord George H.	BEER 31:6
wishful thinking in H.	LEWIS 187:2

hell (*cont.*):
  working definition of h.   SHAW 273:7
  Yours till H. freezes   FISH 110:2
hell-fires: An' dreamin' H. to see   KIPL 174:8
hellhound: h. is always a hellhound   WOD 315:13
Hellman: [Lillian H.]   MCC 193:12
hello: H., Dolly, well, hello Dolly   HERM 139:20
  H., good evening, and welcome   FROST 117:11
help: cannot h. nor pardon   AUDEN 20:11
  Give me your h., not   ROOS 250:3
  h. and support of the woman   EDW 98:11
  'h. me, heaven,' she prayed   FIRB 109:10
  How shall I h. you, say   HOUS 146:10
  Like whipping tops and h.   HODG 142:1
  little h. from my friends   LENN 185:16
  Or h. to half-a-crown   HARDY 134:10
  scream for h. in dreams   CAN 63:5
  very present h. in trouble   STEV 286:10
  you can't h. it   SMITH 277:6
  you do something to *h.*   LAUR 180:5
helpless: h. to hinder that or anything
   HARDY 133:11
helps: Mars a day h. you work   GAFF 120:15
hem-hem: am forced to mingle h.   WILL 311:10
Hemingway: nipping the heels of H.   ALGR 3:16
hen: better take a wet h.   KHR 166:1
  have been a farmyard h.   AYRES 21:16
  h. is only an egg's way   BUTL 59:12
Henery: I'm H. the Eighth, I am   MURR 216:6
Hepburn: H. runs the gamut from   PARK 230:7
herald: Hark! the h. angels sing   BEEC 30:4
herd: Banished from the h. he led   HODG 142:3
herds: H. of reindeer move across   AUDEN 20:1
herdsman: h. goads them on behind
   YEATS 321:10
here: And h.'s to you, Mrs Robinson   SIMON 275:9
  From h. to eternity   JONES 157:4
  H. comes the judge   MARK 201:5
  H. I am, an old man   ELIOT 100:6
  H.'s looking at you, kid   EPST 106:11
  H. we are   KNIG 176:3
  H. we go, here we go   ANON 8:11
  H. we go round the prickly pear   ELIOT 103:4
  H. were decent godless   ELIOT 104:2
  I'm only h. for the beer   LEV 186:13
  It can't happen h.   LEWIS 188:1
  Lafayette, we are h.   STAN 283:7
  stops h.   TRUM 299:12
  We're h. because   ANON 12:3
  We're h. because we're queer   BEHAN 32:4
heresies: Religions are kept alive by h.   BREN 53:10
heresy: Englishman believes be h.   SHAW 274:2
heretic: H., rebel, a thing to flout   MARK 201:4
  oppressor or a h.   CAMUS 63:3
heritage: And we have come into our h.
   BROO 55:1
hero: Greek one then is my h.   ABSE 1:4
  h. is a man who would argue   MAIL 199:10
  I understand the h.   ROSS 253:5

hero (*cont.*):
  Show me a h. and I will   FITZ 110:10
  they don't want to be a h.   STOP 287:12
Herod: hour of H.   HOPE 143:12
heroes: And its h. were made   AE 3:3
  Britain a fit country for h.   LLOY 190:1
  h. up the line to death   SASS 262:7
  land that has no h.   BREC 53:3
  land that needs h.   BREC 53:3
heroic: I'm not the h. type   ALLEN 5:5
heroics: present need is not h.   HARD 133:1
heroing: H. is one of the shortest-lived
   ROG 249:16
heroism: thing as splendour or h.   FORS 114:13
heron: mussel pooled and the h.   THOM 292:13
Herr: German Foreign Minister, H.   COOK 82:7
Herrgott: *Raffiniert ist der H.*   EINS 99:5
hers: H. of the Book, the tripled   QUIL 242:5
herself: playing h.   KAEL 160:6
Herzog: thought Moses H.   BELL 35:10
heure: *Vienne la nuit, sonne l'h.*   APOL 12:15
hey: H.! big spender   FIEL 108:8
  H.! Mr Tambourine Man   DYLAN 97:10
hi: H. diddle dee dee   WASH 305:6
hick: Sticks nix h. pix   ANON 11:3
hickory: your clothes on a h. limb   DE L 91:8
hid: h. his face amid a crowd   YEATS 318:8
  I h. from Him, and under   THOM 295:2
hidden: For Famagusta and the h. sun   FLEC 112:3
  The h. persuaders   PACK 228:9
hide: can run, but he can't h.   LOUIS 191:3
  h. of a rhinoceros   BARR 26:17
  His h. is sure to flatten 'em   BELL 32:16
hiding: got was a bloody good h.   GRANT 128:1
hier: *Ou peut-être h., je ne*   CAMUS 62:15
hierarchy: H. Every Employee Tends   PETER 233:8
high: And hear the larks so h.   HOUS 146:3
  By a h. star our course is set   MACN 198:1
  Every man who is h. up   BARR 26:16
  h. altar on the move   BOWEN 50:14
  h. as an elephant   HAMM 131:12
  h. contracting powers solemnly   BRIA 53:11
  H. o'er the fence leaps   HANFF 132:9
  hold my house in the h.   BELL 35:1
  lady's maid that h.   WOOLF 317:4
  She's the Broad and I'm the H.   SPR 282:16
  window at h. noon   JOHN 156:2
highballs: Three h. and I think I'm   PARK 230:3
highbrow: What is a h.? He is a man   WALL 304:13
higher: And find my own the h.   CORN 83:10
  implying 'I am capable of h. . . .'   FORS 114:5
highest: nation is the h. virtue   JOHN 156:13
high-mindedness: joss-sticks and honourable h.
   BRAM 52:12
high-tech: h. approach if you demolished
   CHAR 68:3
high-water: h. mark of my youth   THUR 297:3
  The h. mark, so to speak   ORW 225:18
highway: The h.'s under it   MILL 208:11

highway (*cont.*):

travelled each and ev'ry h.   ANKA 6:11
highwayman: The h. came riding   NOYES 221:9
highways: The happy h. where I went
    HOUS 146:11
hijacker: h. of the oxygen   THAT 292:3
hilarity: h. was like a scream from   GREE 128:16
Hilda: it's needed H.   REED 245:5
hill: are all gone under the h.   ELIOT 101:13
   Cassidy's hanging h.   KAV 161:13
   flung us on the windy h.   BROO 54:8
   h. as light fell short   HODG 141:13
   on the last h., that shows   RILKE 247:10
   They took the h.   PLOM 235:12
hills: h. are alive with the sound   HAMM 132:3
   h. fill my heart   HAMM 132:3
   h. of the South Country   BELL 34:19
   those blue remembered h.   HOUS 146:11
   we shall fight in the h.   CHUR 74:6
Himmler: He called you the H.   RATT 243:4
himself: His opinion of h.   BENN 38:4
   interested in h. than in me   BIER 46:18
   my short answer is 'h.'   IBSEN 150:6
Hindenburg: H. Line to which the defence
    RICH 247:5
hinder: she's helpless to h.   HARDY 133:11
hind-legs: standing a sheep on its h.   BEER 31:16
hindsight: H. is always twenty-twenty
    WILD 311:4
hinky: H., dinky, parley-voo   ANON 9:19
hinter: *Augenblick wird sie h. mir sein*   REGER 245:7
hip: H. is the sophistication   MAIL 199:6
Hippo: Lord H. suffered fearful loss   BELL 34:2
hippopotamus: h. resolved at any cost
    WELLS 308:3
   I shoot the H.   BELL 32:16
   shoot the h. with eyebrows   FORS 114:4
   The h.'s day   ELIOT 102:14
hips: armchairs tight about the h.   WOD 316:5
   your girdle when your h.   NASH 218:13
hipsters: angelheaded h. burning   GINS 125:1
hired: they h. the money   COOL 82:10
Hiroshima: Einstein leads to H.   PIC 234:7
historian: first requisite of the h.   STR 287:14
   h. must have a third quality   FORS 114:6
   one safe rule for the h.   FISH 109:15
   The h., essentially   JAMES 152:10
historians: h. can   BUTL 59:2
   h. left blanks   POUND 238:3
   H. repeat each other   GUED 130:2
   honoured by h. more for the way   HARL 135:4
   men who are not h. behave   FORS 114:6
history: A people without h.   ELIOT 102:6
   cancer of human h.   SONT 280:13
   disasters of English h.   WAUGH 305:15
   discerned in h. a plot   FISH 109:15
   from the lessons of h.   HUXL 148:10
   good h.   HARDY 133:4
   greatest week in the h.   NIXON 220:6

history (*cont.*):

h. becomes more and more   WELLS 308:10
H. came   SELL 266:13
H. has many cunning passages   ELIOT 100:7
H. is a combination of reality   COCT 78:6
h. is a pattern   ELIOT 102:6
H. is littered   POW 239:9
H. is more or less bunk   FORD 113:12
H. is now and England   ELIOT 102:6
h. is on our side   KHR 166:2
H., *n.* An account   BIER 46:20
h. of art is the history   BUTL 59:19
h. of every country begins   CATH 65:1
H. repeats itself   GUED 130:2
H., Stephen said   JOYCE 159:2
H. teaches us that men   EBAN 97:16
h. than they can consume   SAKI 257:10
h. to produce a little   JAMES 152:16
H. to the defeated   AUDEN 20:11
h. we make today   FORD 113:12
H. will absolve me   CAST 64:12
into the dustbin of h.   TROT 299:4
longest suicide note in h.   KAUF 161:10
memorable in the h. of our race   CHUR 72:13
natural h. if you can   SCOTT 265:9
Thames is liquid h.   BURNS 58:5
There is no h. of mankind   POPP 236:6
thousand years of h.   GAIT 121:1
What will h. say   SHAW 268:18
history-making: Man is a h. creature
    AUDEN 18:15
hit: H. the road, Jack   MAYF 206:2
Hitler: Even H. and Mussolini   LOW 191:6
   German Chancellor, Herr H.   CHAM 66:5
   H. attacked the Jews   NIEM 219:10
   H. knows that he will have   CHUR 74:7
   H.'s level of accuracy   TAYL 290:15
   H. swept out of his Berlin   ANON 9:3
   H. thought he might get   CHAM 66:8
   man like Adolf H.   BUCH 57:7
   one voice would say to H.   CHUR 72:12
hitting: was h. a jag-time tune   SERV 267:1
hive: h. for the honey bee   YEATS 318:10
ho: 'What h.!' I said   WOD 316:7
Hoares: no more H. to Paris   GEOR 122:13
hobbit: ground there lived a h.   TOLK 297:21
Hobson: sound of Harold H. barking   GILL 124:10
hock: at a weak h. and seltzer   BETJ 41:17
Hodgitts: 'O Mr H.!' I heard her   GRAH 127:11
hog: disadvantage of being a h.   MORT 214:4
   Not the whole h.   MILL 208:15
hogs: let it not be like h.   MCKAY 195:8
hoisted: h. again without permission   BEAT 28:3
hold: centre cannot h.   YEATS 320:7
   h. with those who favour   FROST 118:10
holds: h. and rolls and throws   REED 245:1
hole: h. with nothing in it   TOLK 297:21
   ride in a h. in the ground   COMD 79:10
holes: h. in Blackburn Lancashire   LENN 185:8

holiday: h. is a good working definition
SHAW 273:7
  h. to any patient who considered RUSS 255:2
holidays: *Educ*: during the h. from Eton
SITW 276:10
  Term, h., term LEWIS 187:5
holiness: Than Courage of Heart or H. BELL 35:2
  There is no H. here ROLFE 249:17
hollingsworth: bourne from which no h.
MORT 214:8
hollow: Down to the h. FLAN 111:5
  We are the h. men ELIOT 103:3
Hollywood: have been invited to H. CHAN 67:2
  H. is a place where people ALLEN 4:4
  H. money isn't money PARK 231:14
Holroyd: [James H.] WELLS 308:4
holy: H. deadlock HERB 139:7
  In a h. place CAMP 61:8
  totalitarianism or the h. name GAND 121:10
Holy Ghost: like to call on the H. LLOY 189:10
home: A house is not a h. ADLER 3:2
  can't find your way h. COLL 79:5
  dream that I am h. FLEC 111:17
  E.T. phone h. MATH 204:7
  h. again to find it more SASS 263:2
  h. discovers that he has DOUG 93:13
  H. is heaven and orgies NASH 218:12
  H. is the girl's prison SHAW 272:12
  H. is the place where FROST 119:1
  H. James, and don't spare HILL 141:1
  H. life as we understand SHAW 269:5
  I can hang my hat is h. JER 155:12
  I tank I go h. GARBO 122:3
  Look as much like h. as we can FRY 119:20
  [Lord H.] DOUG 93:14
  make one feel more at h. FREUD 117:5
  me so much nearer h. FROST 118:3
  murder into the h. HITC 141:4
  My h. policy CLEM 77:9
  My h. sweet home BERL 40:6
  never see any h. cooking PHIL 233:13
  street, you do it at h. SCOR 265:4
  that it's a refuge from h. SHAW 274:9
  The h. of the bean and the cod BOSS 50:3
  They dream of H. FORD 113:14
  Till the boys come H. FORD 113:14
  want to go h. in the dark HENRY 139:3
  what is it to be at h. BECK 28:13
  With no direction h. DYLAN 97:7
  You can't go h. again WOLFE 316:14
  you come h. Bill Bailey CANN 63:6
home-acre: And the hearth-fire and the h.
KIPL 172:14
home-fires: Keep the H. burning FORD 113:14
homeless: orphans and the h. GAND 121:10
Homer: Gladstone read H. for fun CHUR 75:12
  mounted in that saddle H. rode YEATS 323:7
homes: h. and first beginning BELL 35:4

homes (*cont.*):
  The Stately H. of England COW 85:7
  They think of firelit h. SASS 262:6
homeward: And rooks in families h. go
HARDY 133:9
  H., and brings the sailor ELIOT 105:5
homicidal: The great h. classics STOP 287:4
homme: *h. politique ne croit jamais* DE G 90:5
  L'h. est une passion inutile. SART 261:10
homo: naked ape self-named *H.* MORR 213:14
homos: stately h. of England CRISP 86:4
homosexuality: h. were the normal way BRY 57:2
honest: both h. and intelligent ORW 225:10
  h. God's the noblest work BUTL 59:4
  man looked h. enough TWAIN 300:13
  shall buy it like an h. NORT 221:5
  She was poor but she was h. ANON 10:15
  That we who lived by h. dreams DAY-L 89:8
honesty: h. is a good MARQ 201:14
honey: And is there h. still for tea BROO 56:1
  hive for the h. bee YEATS 318:10
  H. or condensed milk MILNE 210:9
  H., your silk stocking's SELL 266:6
  How a bear likes h. MILNE 210:7
  sun drips h. LEE 183:17
  Tiggers don't like h. MILNE 209:12
honey-bees: Than in our love; Oh, h.
YEATS 318:6
honeysuckle: h., I am the bee FITZ 110:6
honi: H. soie qui mal y pense SELL 266:6
honour: air signed with their h. SPEN 281:15
  Downing Street peace with h. CHAM 66:6
  Fear God. H. the King KITC 175:15
  fighting for this woman's h. KALM 161:4
  h. from me if Ye take away KIPL 174:5
  H. has come back BROO 55:1
  h. of the British Army KITC 175:15
  h. we had forgotten LLOY 189:13
  Let us h. if we can AUDEN 20:5
  Of h. and the sword CHES 70:7
  set up in h. of a critic SIB 275:1
  Though loss of h. was a wrench GRAH 127:6
honourably: h. ineligible for the struggle
CONN 80:12
honoured: will be h. by historians HARL 135:4
honours: good card to play for H. BENN 39:1
Honours List: H. and you can instantly
BENN 38:16
hoof: out pops the cloven h. WOD 315:14
hookah-mouth: sliding puffs from the h.
KIPL 169:11
hooray: Hip hip hip h. BUTL 58:11
hoot: literary mornings with its h. AUDEN 19:12
hooter: because the h. hoots CHES 68:18
hooting: h. at dawn flew away none BEER 31:17
Hoover: [J. Edgar H.] JOHN 156:3
hooves: No mad h. galloping in the sky KAV 162:2
hope: H., politeness, the blowing FORS 115:7
  h. that the simple stirrup-pump REED 245:3

hope (*cont.*):
- h. that the world will · JOHN 156:8
- I h. to go on · THAT 291:10
- Land of H. and Glory · BENS 39:4
- Lead me from despair to h. · KUMAR 177:4
- look forward to with h. · FROST 118:16
- Nor dread nor h. attend · YEATS 323:4
- Some blessed H., whereof · HARDY 134:2
- store we sell h. · REVS 246:1
- The death of h. and despair · ELIOT 102:2
- Whatever h. is yours · OWEN 228:6

hoped: never h. can never despair · SHAW 268:9

hopelessness: despair and utter h. · ALLEN 4:13
- The h. Whatever hope is yours · OWEN 228:6

hopes: h. of its children · EIS 100:2
- scribbled lines like fallen h. · HOPE 144:2

hoping: Here's h. we meet now and then
  · PORT 236:14

hop-yards: Say, for what were h. meant
  · HOUS 146:15

horizon: always somebody else's h. · GRAH 127:15
- The h. — the Three Wise Kings · KAV 161:13

horizontal: But the h. one · AUDEN 20:5
- Life is a h. fall · COCT 78:7
- perpendicular expression of a h. · SHAW 273:2

horn: mouth of Plenty's h. · YEATS 320:9
- Put forth a conscious h. · THOM 296:6
- won't come out of your h. · PARK 230:1

Hornby: O my H. and my Barlow long ago
  · THOM 296:1

horns: Memories are hunting h. · APOL 12:16
- sound of h. and motors · ELIOT 105:4

horrible: h. and the miserable · ALLEN 5:3
- h. in some respect · PIC 234:7

horror: h. of the Twentieth Century · MAIL 199:8
- I have a h. of sunsets · PROU 241:2
- imagination there is no h. · DOYLE 95:10
- The h.! The horror · CONR 81:12

horse: A h. is at least *human* · SAL 258:14
- are no handles to a h. · LEAC 182:12
- But where's the bloody h. · CAMP 62:2
- By putting money on a h. · BELL 34:2
- camel is a h. designed · ANON 7:10
- Don't ask me, ask the h. · FREUD 117:3
- Go together like a h. · CAHN 60:19
- heard no h. sing a song · ARMS 13:8
- h. is drawn by the cart · KIPL 170:1
- h. nosing around the meadow · KAV 162:2
- h. on the mountain · LORCA 191:1
- h. that stumbles and nods · HARDY 133:15
- I know two things about the h. · ROYD 254:5
- lies about his wooden h. · FLEC 112:4
- life and the torturer's h. · AUDEN 17:9
- never look at any other h. · PIR 235:5
- On the sightless h. · WALEY 304:12
- that high h. riderless · YEATS 323:7
- Why does a hearse h. snicker · SAND 260:5

Horseguards: H. and still be common · RATT 243:8

horseman: *H. pass by!* · YEATS 319:13

horsemen: Four H. rode again · RICE 246:9

horse-races: opinion that makes h. · TWAIN 301:20

horses: Bring on the empty h. · CURT 88:1
- don't spare the h. · HILL 141:1
- h. o' Kansas think to-day · KIPL 170:5
- oakleaves, h.' heels · ELIOT 104:9
- street and frighten the h. · CAMP 61:11
- They shoot h. don't they · MCCOY 194:5
- two h. you have no right · MAXT 205:19
- Women and H. and Power and War
  · KIPL 169:11

horticulture: You can lead a h. · PARK 231:16

hose: tip up bason and a h. · ASHF 14:5

Hoskin: He's loo-vely, Mrs H. · RAY 243:12

host: have been under the h. · PARK 230:2
- The h. with someone indistinct · ELIOT 102:13

hostile: This universe is not h. · HOLM 142:13

hostilities: others by their h. · BOWEN 50:12

hosts: h. and guests · BEER 30:10

hot: cat on a h. tin roof · WILL 312:4
- h. the scent · GRAV 128:7
- Noble deeds and h. baths · SMITH 277:1
- only in h. water do you · REAG 244:4
- Rosy and round and h. · ASQ 15:9
- The long h. summer · RAV 243:10

hotel: h. is that it's a refuge · SHAW 274:9
- h. offers stupendous · HOFF 142:9

hotels: h. built on the cuckoo · HEM 138:13

Hottentot: Every H. and every Eskimo
  · LEHR 184:5

hound: footprints of a gigantic h. · DOYLE 94:14
- H. that Caught the Pubic · BEHAN 31:23
- You ain't nothin' but a h. dog · LEIB 184:6

hour: At the violet h. · ELIOT 105:5
- expect again a phoenix h. · DAY-L 89:4
- Fools! For I also had my h. · CHES 71:8
- Have known the lightning's h. · DAY-L 89:6
- h. of destiny they stand · SASS 262:6
- h. of Herod · HOPE 143:12
- h. when earth's foundations · HOUS 145:7
- its h. come round at last · YEATS 320:8
- matched us with His h. · BROO 54:10
- night come, ring out the h. · APOL 12:15
- spring comes her h. · GIBB 123:11
- Surely thine h. has come · YEATS 322:3
- this h. and this trial · CHUR 76:5
- This was their finest h. · CHUR 74:7

hours: h. and nobody bossing you · ORW 225:17
- h. is a long time in politics · WILS 313:8
- h. I've put · AYCK 21:8
- Mary Woolnoth kept the h. · ELIOT 104:14
- than the speed, of h. · HOPE 144:3

house: A h. is a machine for living · LE C 183:14
- A h. is not a home · ADLER 3:2
- called a woman in my own h. · WAUGH 306:11
- Dust inbreathed was a h. · ELIOT 102:2
- dwell in the h. of tomorrow · GIBR 124:3
- Harrow the h. of the dead · AUDEN 20:4

house (*cont.*):

hold my h. in the high wood	BELL 35:1
H. Beautiful is play lousy	PARK 231:7
h. is built of stones	POIN 236:1
H. of Lords is the British	BENN 37:7
h. their bodies but not	GIBR 124:3
H. will in no circumstances	GRAH 127:5
h. with three poor staircases	ASQ 15:2
it has been born in a h.	JEANS 154:5
Make my h. your inn	MOORE 213:5
man in the h. is worth two	WEST 309:1
moon is in the seventh h.	RADO 242:8
serious h. on serious earth	LARK 179:5
small h. agent's clerk	ELIOT 105:6
The H. at Pooh Corner	PARK 230:9
The H. of Lords, an illusion	STOP 286:16
tragic the h. rose like magic	HARG 135:3
voice in her elected H.	DENN 91:11
young and inexperienced h.	JER 155:8

household: real centre of the h. SHAW 269:11

householder: housekeeper think she's a h.
WILD 311:6

housekeeper: bribe to make a h. WILD 311:6

housemaids: damp souls of h. ELIOT 103:15

houses: h. are all gone under ELIOT 101:13

It is not the h. It	FENT 108:3
live in h. just as big	SMITH 278:5

housewife: h. is the Cinderella SUMM 289:2

housework: need to do any h. at all CRISP 86:3

how: And H. and Where and Who KIPL 172:2

H. about you	FREED 116:12
H. can I tell what I think	FORS 114:8
H. can you govern a country	DE G 90:4
H. does it feel	DYLAN 97:7
H. do they know	PARK 231:12
H. many roads must a man	DYLAN 97:3
H. much is that doggie	MERR 207:9
H.'s the Empire	GEOR 123:2
H. shall we conquer	FLEC 112:6
H. to succeed in business	MEAD 206:5
H. to win friends and influence	CARN 64:1

Howe: [Sir Geoffrey H.'s] HEAL 136:5

howl: I hear a famisht h. BERR 41:10

howls: h. of anguish from HEAL 136:7

Howth: H. Castle and Environs JOYCE 157:10

Huckleberry: Mark Twain called *H. Finn*
HEM 138:5

hues: thee all her lovely h. DAV 88:16

huff: taxi you can leave in a h. KALM 161:5

huffy: Not h., or stuffy HERB 139:9

hug: We h. our little destiny again HEAN 136:12

huge: Bear is h. and wild HOUS 144:10

Hügel: *dem letzten H., der ihm* RILKE 247:10

Hugo: H.—alas GIDE 124:8

H. was a madman who thought COCT 78:8

hullo: H. Clouds Hullo Sky WILL 311:12

hum: Yes, the smell and hideous h. GODL 125:8

humains: *Tous les êtres h. naissent* ANON 11:16

human: All h. beings are born ANON 11:16

human (*cont.*):

all h. life is there	JAMES 152:18
Always h. beings will	DUB 96:2
apathy of h. beings	KELL 162:9
bombs could end the h.	BENN 37:2
But he's a h. being	MILL 208:8
classics is an enemy to the h.	MILL 208:14
expression of h. immaturity	BRIT 54:1
field of h. conflict was	CHUR 74:8
future of the h.	JEANS 154:5
horse is at least *h.*	SAL 258:14
H. beings are perhaps never	VAN D 303:6
h. beings have an almost	HUXL 149:14
H. beings have an inalienable	GREER 129:1
h. but to really foul	ANON 11:14
H. kind	ELIOT 101:7
H. Nature is the *craving*	JAMES 153:11
H. on my faithless arm	AUDEN 17:10
h. race commit suicide	ADAMS 2:13
h. race has today the means	BORN 50:2
importance of the h. factor	CHAR 67:11
it is a h. zoo	MORR 213:13
I wish I loved the H. Race	RAL 242:13
measles of the h.	EINS 99:3
on stars where no h. race	FROST 118:3
ordinary h. enthusiasm	OSB 226:10
own-goal scored by the h.	ANNE 6:12
people are only h.	COMP 80:1
robot may not injure a h.	ASIM 14:13
servants are treated as h.	SHAW 272:2
shame to h. nature	HOUS 144:8
simplification of the h.	FORS 114:9
socialism would not lose its h.	DUBČ 95:18
The h. race	CHES 69:14

humanity: deeper needs of h. BENN 37:2

'H.' and all such abstracts	CAMP 62:3
H. i love you	CUMM 87:1
H. is just a work in progress	WILL 312:3
It is easier to love h.	HOFF 142:6
regeneration of all h.	PANK 229:6
three-score years and ten, h.	JEANS 154:5
unremitting h. soon had me cheesed	BENN 38:2

humans: It isn't fit for h. now BETJ 42:2

humbled: maintains that I am h. CORN 83:10

humblest: h. hour is when he compares
BARR 25:14

humbugs: most artists and all h. CONN 80:11

humiliated: capable of being h. AUDEN 21:2

humiliation: Art is born of h. AUDEN 21:2

humility: learn h. as well as teach SHAW 273:20

hummy: And it is that word 'h.' PARK 230:9

humorists: h. is that they will mix UPD 302:12

humour: Good taste and h. MUGG 215:6

h. and irony is generally	BUTL 59:11
'H.,' he said	THUR 297:16
no sense of h.	ALBEE 3:11
possessing a deep sense of h.	MCL 196:8

hump: But uglier yet is the h. we get KIPL 171:11

The camel has a single h. NASH 217:9

hump (*cont.*):

We get the h.	KIPL 171:12
Hun: The H. is at the gate	KIPL 170:14
hundred: Droop in a h. A.B.C.'s	ELIOT 100:5
h. flowers blossom	MAO 200:10
hundred-horse-power: comes Winston with his h.	
	BALD 23:9
hundreds: lads in their h. to Ludlow	HOUS 146:5
hung: h. with bloom along	HOUS 145:13
hunger: H. allows no choice	AUDEN 17:12
theft from those who h.	EIS 100:2
with bodily h. in his eyes	SHAW 270:6
hungry: A h. man is not a free man	STEV 286:8
h. for dinner at eight	HART 135:11
tigers are getting h.	CHUR 76:8
Huns: better than H. or Wops	MITF 211:15
hunted: And little h. hares	HODG 142:2
H. and penned in an inglorious	MCKAY 195:8
others by their h.	LEWIS 187:4
hunter: The heart is a lonely h.	MCC 194:8
The H.'s waking thoughts	AUDEN 21:3
hunting: Hi! handsome h. man	DE L 91:7
I like the h. of the hare	BLUNT 48:3
life also; I went h. wild	OWEN 228:6
hurly-burly: h. of the chaise-longue	CAMP 61:13
hurrah: The last h.	O'CON 222:16
hurricane: crazy-eyed h. blowing	KIPL 170:8
hurry: H. up please it's time	ELIOT 105:3
H.! We burn	DAY-L 89:5
multitude of young men in a h.	CORN 84:1
So who's in a h.	BENC 36:12
hurt: has done the lover mortal h.	DOUG 93:8
h. you to the heart	TWAIN 300:21
The wish to h., the momentary	BRON 54:5
hurtig: Led go! You are h.	KIPL 172:1
hurting: once it has stopped h.	BOWEN 50:15
hurts: For fellows whom it h.	HOUS 146:15
husband: having one h. too many	ANON 7:5
h. for a comfort	SMITH 278:20
h. is a whole-time job	BENN 38:17
h. is what is left	ROWL 253:14
over-jealous, yet an eager h.	PHIL 234:3
words 'My h. and I'	ELIZ 105:13
your h. I would drink it	ASTOR 15:12
your own h. that took you	BEHAN 32:3
husbands: always make the best h.	WOD 315:9
hush: have said 'h.' just once	CAMP 61:9
H., hush	MORT 214:5
H.! Hush! Whisper who dares	MILNE 210:6
hushed-up: secretly, like wrongs h.	OWEN 228:4
hustle: who tried to h. the East	KIPL 172:9
hutch: Sitting in me h.	AYRES 21:14
hyacinths: synthesis of h. and biscuits	
	SAND 259:8
hygiene: h. of older people	SMITH 278:1
hymn: A lass was singing a h.	BETJ 44:3
hymns: And happy h. of farmers	KING 167:12
Sing on, with h. uproarious	BETJ 43:5
hyphen: before the h.	ROOS 251:13

hyphenated: h. American is not an American	
	ROOS 251:13
hypocrisy: H. is the most difficult	MAUG 204:10
m-m-making the world safe for h.	
	WOLFE 316:13
hypothesis: scientist to discard a pet h.	LOR 191:2
Hyssopps: H. of the Glen so you see	ASHF 14:9
hysterical: starving h. naked	GINS 125:1

I

I: I am a camera	ISH 151:15
I am a free man, an American	JOHN 156:15
I am a passenger on space	FULL 120:5
I am the family face	HARDY 133:13
I, a stranger and afraid	HOUS 145:4
I don't mind if I do	KAV 162:6
I go — I come back	KAV 162:7
I got rhythm	GERS 123:7
I grow old . . . I grow old	ELIOT 103:12
I only wanted to make you	AYCK 21:9
I should do	DOYLE 95:12
I tank I go home	GARBO 122:3
I, this incessant snow	DE L 91:6
It is I	DE L 91:6
I, too, am America	HUGH 147:13
I travel light; as light	FRY 119:13
I want to be alone	GARBO 122:2
I will show you fear	ELIOT 104:12
Thou a person becomes I	BUBER 57:3
words 'My husband and I'	ELIZ 105:13
IBM: got fired for buying I.	ANON 10:3
ice: always skating on thin i.	CAMP 61:12
I. formed on the butler's	WOD 316:9
i. on a hot stove the poem	FROST 118:2
lies to i. a wedding cake	ASQ 15:7
Some say in i.	FROST 118:10
To say that for destruction i.	FROST 118:10
ice-cream: emperor is the emperor of i.	
	STEV 285:7
iceman: The i. cometh	O'NEI 223:7
id: PUT THE I. BACK IN YID	ROTH 253:12
idea: A good i.—son	SYKES 289:7
An i., to be suggestive	JAMES 153:19
Between the i.	ELIOT 103:4
good i. but it won't work	ROG 249:15
good i. to give them	WARH 305:4
i. ever to be fashionable	SANT 260:21
i. is accepted it is time	JACK 152:1
i. of Death saves	FORS 115:4
i. was ever born in a conference	FITZ 110:9
i. whose time has come	ANON 11:7
i. within a wall of words	BUTL 60:2
I hate the i. of causes	FORS 115:12
more dangerous than an i.	ALAIN 3:9
respect for the i. of God	DUH 96:4

IDEAL

IMMATURITY

idea (cont.):
That would be a good i. GAND 121:9
whom the i. first occurs DARW 88:9
ideal: Christian i. has not been tried CHES 71:5
i. reader suffering from JOYCE 157:11
Youth would be an i. state ASQ 14:17
idealism: alcohol or morphine or i. JUNG 159:16
idealist: I am an i. I don't know SAND 260:2
Sometimes people call me an i. WILS 314:4
idealistic: America is the only i. WILS 314:4
idealists: I. are very apt to walk SMITH 278:6
ideals: i. of a nation by its advertisements
DOUG 93:12
ideas: has i. above her station RATT 243:6
I. can be too old OUSP 227:8
instead of genuine i. BENT 39:16
it is i., not vested interests KEYN 165:5
sound and original i. MACM 197:6
steal other people's i. TOM 298:2
idée: plus dangereux qu'une i. ALAIN 3:9
respecte trop l'i. de Dieu DUH 96:4
idées: i. au-dessus de sa gare RATT 243:6
identical: are i. FORS 115:8
identified: 'He's i.,' said the first BENN 38:6
idioms: i. appropriate to another RYLE 256:7
words and exhausted i. ORW 226:2
idle: I. to hope that the simple REED 245:3
idleness: i. and impotent stupidity BLUNT 48:2
idlers: loungers and i. of the Empire DOYLE 95:8
idling: impossible to enjoy i. JER 155:2
idol: i. to the north of Khatmandu HAYES 136:3
idolatry: organization of i. SHAW 271:17
If: And I. and Perhaps and But ELIOT 101:4
i. I had to choose FORS 115:12
I. it moves, salute it ANON 8:14
I. you've seen one city AGNEW 3:6
I. you want to get ahead ANON 8:15
I. you were the only girl GREY 129:6
ignoble: doctrine of i. ease ROOS 251:10
ignorance: dangerous than sincere i. KING 167:2
Don't die of i. ANON 7:18
i. and failing to realise CURR 87:12
I. is an evil weed BEV 45:10
i. is the first requisite STR 287:14
i. the greater the dogmatism OSLER 227:6
inhibition caused by i. MACM 196:15
life is i. and confidence TWAIN 302:4
slavery. I. is strength ORW 225:4
while our i. must necessarily POPP 236:8
Your i. cramps my conversation HOPE 143:11
ignorant: know everybody is i. ROG 249:10
where many i. men are sure DARR 88:8
ignore: happy with nothing to i. NASH 218:5
Most people i. most poetry MITC 211:3
ignored: exist because they are i. HUXL 149:12
Ike: I like I. SPAL 281:3
ill: But, if it is i. SITW 276:8
Government is dangerously i. BENN 38:16

ill-bred: i. son of a livery stable-keeper
YEATS 322:10
illegal: like to do are either i. WOOL 317:16
means that it is not i. NIXON 220:1
illegitimate: i. child of Karl Marx ATTL 16:8
illegitimi: Nil carborundum i. ANON 10:2
ill-housed: one-third of a nation i. ROOS 250:7
illimited: Of joy i. HARDY 134:2
illiteracy: at the i. of scientists SNOW 279:6
illness: I. is the night-side SONT 280:12
part that makes i. SHAW 268:3
ill-nourished: ill-clad, i. ROOS 250:7
ills: i. of democracy can SMITH 276:16
marvelling sweetly on her i. RANS 243:1
illuminated: i. trouser-clip for bicyclists
MORT 214:9
illusion: Bismarck's. He had one i. KEYN 164:11
The great i. ANG 6:9
visible universe was an i. BORG 49:11
illusions: It's life's i. I recall MITC 211:4
perils because of the i. MOUN 214:13
illustrate: simplify and i. the points HOME 143:2
illustration: i. of character JAMES 153:5
I'm: I. backing Britain ANON 8:17
I. in charge FORS 116:3
I. the greatest ALI 4:2
image: A photograph is not only an i.
SONT 280:11
c'est l'i. de la passion BART 27:4
consommée dans son i. BART 27:5
i. if not in usage BART 27:5
i. of myself which I try AUDEN 18:13
public wants is the i. BART 27:4
The age demanded an i. POUND 238:7
images: Fresh i. beget YEATS 323:10
imaginary: Happiness is an i. condition
SZASZ 290:2
imagination: Does the i. dwell the most
YEATS 322:5
functioning of the i. HEM 138:6
heart is nothing but his i. SHAW 269:16
'literalists of the i.' MOORE 213:3
lie in logic, not in i. CHES 69:18
no i. there is no horror DOYLE 95:10
save those that have no i. SHAW 274:3
schools for the i. GIR 125:3
imaginative: superior to any i. VIDAL 304:3
imagine: I. there's no heaven LENN 185:2
young men can possibly i. SMITH 277:16
imbecility: Moderation in war is i. FISH 110:1
imitate: I i. the Saviour HUXL 148:6
I. him if you dare YEATS 323:14
never failed to i. them BALD 22:13
poets i. ELIOT 104:5
they usually i. each other HOFF 142:7
imitation: i. of a semi-house-trained FOOT 113:5
immanent: I. Will that stirs HARDY 134:5
immature: I. poets imitate ELIOT 104:5
immaturity: expression of human i. BRIT 54:1

immaturity (*cont.*):

that common symptom of i.   WHAR 309:21
immense: Last night at twelve I felt i.   ADE 2:19
immensities: All Asiatic vague i.   YEATS 319:14
immoral: i., or fattening   WOOL 317:16
people looked on it as i.   GALS 121:6
immorality: i. is what they dislike   WHIT 310:9
immortal: No subject for i. verse   DAY-L 89:8
immortalism: The i. must stand   TREE 298:8
immortality: achieve i. through my work
                                   ALLEN 4:19
milk's leap toward i.   FAD 107:4
that millions long for i.   ERTZ 106:13
they gave, their i.   BROO 54:12
immortals: President of the I.   HARDY 134:8
impartial: decline utterly to be i.   CHUR 73:12
impatience: i. with him occasionally   SHAW 274:4
imperial: Her i. standards fly   AUDEN 19:5
imperially: Learn to think I.   CHAM 65:13
imperishable: I. peace   HOUS 145:12
impertinent: ask an i. question   BRON 54:4
importance: i. of the country   HUXL 148:8
important: Broadcasting is really too i.   BENN 37:5
i. thing in life is not   COUB 84:3
i. things a man has   BUTL 59:6
infinitely the most i.   DOYLE 94:4
Money is indeed the most i.   SHAW 269:13
Personal relations are the i.   FORS 115:2
The most i. product   FROMM 117:9
think that the most i.   BREN 53:9
imported: The withdrawal of an i.   JENK 154:10
imposing: Art is the i. of a pattern   WHIT 310:10
impossibility: i. of circulation I could   ASQ 15:2
im-possible: answer you in two words, "i."
                                   GOLD 126:8
impossible: have eliminated the i.   DOYLE 95:5
i. he is very probably   CLAR 77:2
i. is what takes   NANS 217:8
i. to carry the heavy burden   EDW 98:11
I. to come, lie follows   PROU 241:3
i. to enjoy idling thoroughly   JER 155:2
setting oneself an i. aim   GREE 128:13
imposters: those two i. just the same   KIPL 173:7
impotent: all-powerful to be i.   CHUR 74:1
idleness and i. stupidity   BLUNT 48:2
imprecision: Decay with i., will not   ELIOT 101:9
mess of i. of feeling   ELIOT 101:16
impresses: i. me most about America   EDW 98:10
impression: i. that we exist   BECK 29:10
impressionable: Give me a girl at an i.
                                   SPARK 281:6
impressive: i. sights in the world   BARR 26:13
imprisoned: I. in every fat man a thin   CONN 81:2
improbable: occurrence of the i.   MENC 207:3
whatever remains, *however* i.   DOYLE 95:5
improper: An i. mind is a perpetual feast
                                   SMITH 277:15
i. thoughts about   BRAD 51:15
proper or i.   FULL 120:7

impropriety: I. is the soul of wit   MAUG 205:5
improved: enormously i. by death   SAKI 257:6
improvement: children for signs of i.   SCOT 265:11
improving: you can be certain of i.   HUXL 149:15
impure: Puritan all things are i.   LAWR 181:6
in: being i. and out of favour   FROST 119:2
be i. *town tonight*   ANON 10:9
I. my beginning is my end   ELIOT 101:11
Meredith, we're i.   KITC 175:14
inability: i. to cross the street   WOOLF 317:12
inaccuracy: i. sometimes saves tons   SAKI 258:7
mind lying, but I hate i.   BUTL 60:5
inactivity: Coolidge's genius for i.   LIPP 188:13
inarticulate: raid on the i.   ELIOT 101:16
in-between: Don't mess with Mister I.
                                   MERC 207:6
inborn: acquisition but is i.   JUNG 160:4
inbreathed: Dust i. was a house   ELIOT 102:2
incest: excepting i. and folk-dancing   BAX 27:15
inch: other i. a gentleman   WEST 309:16
inches: Some thirty i. from my nose   AUDEN 16:10
incident: determination of i.   JAMES 153:5
To the curious i.   DOYLE 94:16
incite: i. this meeting to rebellion   PANK 229:8
inclined: I am i. to think   DOYLE 95:12
include: Gentlemen, i. me out   GOLD 126:6
incognito: fallen angel travelling i.   QUEN 242:2
incoherent: you to think I'm not i.   ROSS 253:4
income: Expenditure rises to meet i.   PARK 232:1
good i. is of no avail   SMITH 277:14
I. Tax has made more Liars   ROG 249:7
last slice of their i.   HEAL 136:7
organism to live beyond its i.   BUTL 59:15
incomes: beyond their i. nowadays   SAKI 257:9
incommunicable: I distrust the i.   SART 262:4
incomparable: steps spritely in the i. Max
                                   SHAW 274:11
incompetence: Rise to His Level of I.   PETER 233:8
incompetent: i. to carry out its duties   PETER 233:9
incomplete: A man in love is i. until
                                   GABOR 120:13
i. in the urban compound   MCL 196:11
inconsistency: human rights is a little i.
                                   OWEN 227:10
incontestable: Is i. It undercuts   FRY 119:15
inconvenience: i. is only an adventure   CHES 68:4
inconvenient: A cause may be i.   BENN 38:15
i. house with three   ASQ 15:2
increase: And who dies fighting has i.   GREN 129:5
dignity tends to i. in inverse   HUXL 148:8
i. was another man's price   WILS 313:12
indebted: thing I'm i. to her   FIEL 109:4
indecency: Decency is I.'s conspiracy
                                   SHAW 272:10
indecent: sent down for i. behaviour
                                   WAUGH 305:12
indecision: nothing is habitual but i.
                                   JAMES 153:15

indefensible: largely the defence of the i.
ORW 226:1

independence: that modest degree of i.
EINS 99:10

independent: end of Britain as an i.
GAIT 121:1

index: i. of a man's character
CONN 81:3

India: first message of I.
FORS 115:9

Indian: not sailed in I. Seas
DAV 89:1

treated like an I. widow
MITF 211:11

Indians: Cooper killing off the I.
BALD 22:12

that the I. are you
BALD 22:12

indicative: first person, present i.
WITT 315:3

indifference: i. of the majority
REST 245:13

indifferent: be i. to them
SHAW 268:15

established society, and been i.
GREE 128:11

friendly. It is simply i.
HOLM 142:13

i. to what is thought
SOLZ 279:9

well-meaning man of i.
BEAV 28:6

indignation: mists of righteous i.
MUGG 215:4

Moral i. is jealousy
WELLS 308:13

Righteous i.
WOOLF 317:4

Savage i. there
YEATS 323:14

indignity: He has spared me the i.
BELL 33:12

indiscretion: A lover without i. is no
HARDY 133:5

between a cliché and an i.
MACM 197:1

indistinct: The host with someone i.
ELIOT 102:13

individual: abolish the cult of the i.
KHR 165:8

I. beauty from
AUDEN 17:10

i. reader is important
NAB 217:5

that constitutes the i.
JUNG 160:3

There are i. men and women
THAT 292:6

individualism: rugged i. and a European
HOOV 143:6

individuality: England is the paradise of i.
SANT 260:18

realization of the innate i.
JUNG 160:3

without i. have no taste
BENN 38:8

indivisible: Freedom is an i. word
WILL 312:17

Peace is i.
LITV 189:3

indolence: A young girl in the i.
YEATS 318:5

indolent: i. expression and an undulating
BELL 33:16

indomitable: Still the i. Irishry
YEATS 319:12

indoors: 'Er i.
GRIF 129:9

indubitably: They so very i. *are*, you know
BEER 30:12

indulge: I. in loud unseemly jape
BELL 32:14

that I i. them privately
DENN 91:11

industrial: biggest i. corporation
SHAW 267:14

i. strategy for the period
BENN 37:4

industry: I. and all the virtues
HUXL 149:7

it in that of a major i.
SARR 261:5

labour-intensive i.
WILS 313:7

regeneration of i. and enterprise
CHAR 68:2

ineffectual: Remote and i. Don
BELL 35:5

inefficiency: efficiency and i.
SHAW 269:19

ineligible: honourably i. for the struggle
CONN 80:12

inevitable: i. gradualness of our scheme
WEBB 307:3

In Ireland the i. never
MAH 199:2

inexactitude: risk of terminological i.
CHUR 73:9

inexperienced: young and i. house
JER 155:8

inexpressible: expressing the i. is music
HUXL 149:4

inextinguishable: like it is i.
NIEL 219:11

infamy: date which will live in i.
ROOS 251:1

infancy: stages of man are i.
LINK 188:12

infant: i. mind even was bitter
BARB 24:17

What's a mixed i.
BEHAN 32:1

infanticide: indefensible as i.
WEST 309:17

inferior: are disgraced by the i.
SHAW 272:1

i. without your consent
ROOS 249:19

infernal: fourth time that i. noise
EDW 98:7

inferno: i. depicted by Dr Goebbels
ORW 224:20

i. of his passions has
JUNG 159:14

i. of insipidity and decay
LEWIS 187:7

moronic i. had caught
BELL 35:11

infinite: i. capacity for taking
HUXL 149:14

must necessarily be i.
POPP 236:8

infinite-resource-and-sagacity: because he was a man of i.
KIPL 171:10

infinitive: that when I split an i.
CHAN 66:12

inflections: The beauty of i.
STEV 285:11

infliction: i. of cruelty with a good
RUSS 255:15

influence: acquisition of unwarranted i.
EIS 100:1

How to win friends and i.
CARN 64:1

i. on human life than has
MULL 215:10

i. over the minds of men
KEYN 164:15

only books that i.
FORS 115:15

power instead of i.
TAYL 290:13

influenced: that the citizen is i.
RAK 242:10

influenza: can call it i. if ye like
BENN 38:5

My aunt died of i.
SHAW 273:16

in-folded: tongues of flame are i.
ELIOT 102:7

inform: i. the reader but to protect
ACH 1:9

informally: Quite i.
COW 85:8

information: knowledge we have lost in i.
ELIOT 104:1

informed: far better i.
SMITH 277:5

ingenious: i. machine for turning
DIN 92:9

inglorious: About as pointless and i.
OSB 226:14

inhale: if he doesn't i.
STEV 285:15

inherit: must i. the tribulation
HOOV 143:4

inhibition: i. caused by ignorance
MACM 196:15

inhibitions: was to cultivate a few i.
LOOS 190:19

inhumanity: century i. meant cruelty
FROMM 117:10

thats the essence of i.
SHAW 268:15

injury: least i. you can do him
JAMES 152:13

injustice: I. anywhere is a threat
KING 166:6

i. makes democracy necessary
NIEB 219:9

That's social i.
BRAC 51:14

ink: do you always drink i.
MILL 209:6

that the i. had not faded
BARR 26:7

there; all cough in i.
YEATS 322:4

inmate: i. in a long term institution
DURY 97:1

inn: Do you remember an I. BELL 34:9
Innisfree: go now, and go to I. YEATS 318:10
innocence: Everyone insists on his i. CAMUS 62:12
Never such i. LARK 179:13
The ceremony of i. is drowned YEATS 320:7
innocent: But to hurt i. people HELL 137:9
Chacun exige d'être i. CAMUS 62:12
The i. and the beautiful YEATS 323:3
until they are proved i. ORW 226:4
We are i., as we have proclaimed ROS 252:13
inns: And go to i. to dine CHES 68:16
From the towns all I. have BELL 34:18
I. are not residences MOORE 213:5
innuendoes: Or the beauty of i. STEV 285:11
inoperative: previous statements are i. ZIEG 324:11
Inquisition: Spanish I. CHAP 67:10
teaching at the time of the I. BENN 37:3
insanity: form of congenital i. WOOLF 317:4
inscrutable: undefeated, i. to the last THUR 297:13
insculped: I. and embossed THOM 296:11
insect: bed into a gigantic i. KAFKA 161:2
insects: i. and have abandoned BARB 24:16
inside: i. the tent pissing out JOHN 156:3
insignificance: And of the utmost i. CURZ 88:2
insignificant: i. and is aware of it BECK 28:12
insincere: Nor was he i. in saying MOORE 213:5
insincerity: clear language is i. ORW 226:2
i. of purpose to spend BRAM 52:10
i. possible between two BAUM 27:14
insipid: seems i. to a vulgar SMITH 277:10
insists: one who i. on knowing POUND 237:19
insomnia: Amor vincit i. FRY 119:21
suffering from an ideal i. JOYCE 157:11
inspect: i. new stock or to visit AUDEN 19:16
inspector: An i. calls PRIE 239:16
inspiration: Genius is one per cent i. EDIS 98:5
inspired: that I i. the nation CHUR 76:10
instability: taken to be a mark of i. GALB 121:2
instalment: serial form with the last i. CRISP 86:5
instant: light gleams an i. BECK 29:13
instinct: all healthy i. BUTL 60:3
his i. told him BUTL 60:12
i. for being unhappy highly SAKI 257:7
what we believe upon i. BRAD 52:2
instincts: animal, true to your i. LAWR 182:3
institute: I., Legion and Social BETJ 42:3
The gas was on in the I. BETJ 44:3
institution: inmate in a long term i. DURY 97:1
i. without hitting it CRIT 86:7
transformed into an i. SART 261:7
institutions: i. that has been unaltered CHUR 73:11
instruction: no i. book FULL 120:8
instrument: poet is a sensitive i. MACN 197:14
public and learning the i. BUTL 59:3
The State is an i. STAL 283:4

instruments: What i. we have agree AUDEN 17:3
insubordination: price of i. and insurrection MACG 195:4
insuccesso: *vuole riconoscere l'i.* CIANO 76:15
insufferable: Oxford that has made me i. BEER 30:15
insufficient: sufficient conclusions from i. BUTL 59:14
insult: do not consider it an i. DARR 88:8
insurance: i. for all classes CHUR 76:9
insurrection: A revolution is an i. MAO 200:11
insubordination and i. MACG 195:4
success of an armed i. ZIN 324:12
integrity: i. of their quarrel CHUR 73:11
Which is a kind of i. STOP 287:3
intellect: from halitosis of the i. ICKES 150:8
hindrance to subtlety of i. MORL 213:11
i. of man is forced YEATS 323:12
Monuments of unageing i. YEATS 321:5
revenge of the i. upon art SONT 280:8
intellectual: An i. hatred is the worst YEATS 320:9
i. and artistic personality BERL 40:13
i. curiosity is the life-blood TREV 298:12
I. disgrace AUDEN 17:6
i. is someone whose mind CAMUS 62:9
i. life of the whole SNOW 279:5
'I.' suggests straight AUDEN 19:14
wanted to become an i. SCHW 265:1
intellectuals: characterize themselves as i. AGNEW 3:7
intellectuel: *I. = celui qui se dédouble.* CAMUS 62:9
intelligence: I. is quickness to apprehend WHIT 310:8
i. is the ability to hold FITZ 110:11
science of arresting human i. LEAC 182:10
underestimating the i. MENC 206:10
intelligent: As i. Mr Toad GRAH 127:16
cannot be both honest and i. ORW 225:10
i. are to the intelligentsia BALD 23:10
i. readers soon discover BALL 24:4
Most i., very elegant BUCK 57:9
So i. ELIOT 105:2
intelligently: able to fill leisure i. RUSS 255:7
intelligentsia: i. and the cultured classes BERD 40:1
i. what a gentleman BALD 23:10
intend: Some day I i. reading MARX 202:10
intense: i. enjoyment from a contrast FREUD 117:4
intensity: Are full of passionate i. YEATS 320:7
intensiv: *Kontrast i. geniessen* FREUD 117:4
intention: i. to overthrow the Government HARD 132:15
intentions: if he'd only had good i. THAT 292:4
interdit: *qui i. au riche comme* FRAN 116:6
interest: common i. is that of cutting ATK 15:16
not entirely devoid of i. DOYLE 94:5
secured a controlling i. WELLS 308:1

interested: i. in art and I am only   SHAW 269:9
   wasn't particularly i.   BENC 36:2
   whatever he is most i.   BARR 26:9
   you're i. in the arts   AYCK 21:7
interesting: Experience isn't i. till   BOWEN 50:10
   have anything i. to say   CAP 63:10
   i. thing about any story   STOP 286:17
   something more i. than women   WALL 304:13
   that a proposition be i.   WHIT 310:6
   that it be i.   JAMES 153:3
   To see that I. Play   BELL 33:4
   Very i. . . . but stupid   ROWAN 253:13
interests: character in the i. of Hell   FORS 114:9
interfere: i. by violence with ours   JAMES 153:17
intérieure: *Politique i., je fais la*   CLEM 77:9
interior: poet believes to be i.   QUAS 242:1
interlude: present is an i.   O'NEI 223:14
interludes: dark i. in the electrical   O'NEI 223:15
internal: I. AFFAIRS remains   SOLZ 279:9
   i. combustion engine   BEVAN 44:11
international: dependable i. emotion   ALSOP 5:7
interpretation: also what is lost in i.   FROST 119:5
   I. is the revenge   SONT 280:8
   I. makes art manageable   SONT 280:9
interpreter: i. can do no more   BEEC 29:23
interprets: lawyer i. the truth   GIR 125:3
interrogate: can i. as well as observe   OSLER 226:16
interstellar: The vacant i. spaces   ELIOT 101:14
interval: death save to enjoy the i.   SANT 260:19
interviewing: BBC for i. a faded female   HARD 132:16
   i. people who can't talk   ZAPPA 324:9
intimacy: gay i. of the slums   WAUGH 306:1
   you should avoid any i.   KITC 175:15
intimate: i. when he is rich or famous   BIER 46:4
   tribal, i. revenge   HEAN 136:10
intolerable: crises that seemed i.   ATK 15:15
   Curing the i. neutral itch   AUDEN 20:3
   still with the i. wrestle   ELIOT 101:12
intolerance: I. itself is a form of egoism   SANT 260:22
intractable: sullen, untamed and i.   ELIOT 101:10
introduced: And when I'm i. to one   RAL 242:13
introduction: I could buy back my i.   PER 233:1
introibo: *I. ad altare Dei*   JOYCE 158:14
invasion: *l'i. promise de longue*   CHUR 75:7
   long-promised i.   CHUR 75:7
invent: inalienable right to i.   GREER 129:1
   To remember or i.   FROST 118:5
invented: i. for the sole purpose   CUPPY 87:10
   No animal ever i. anything   CHES 68:5
   Truth exists; only lies are i.   BRAQ 52:14
invention: great and blessed i.   SHAW 268:2
   Marriage is a wonderful i.   CONN 80:5
invents: arts of life man i.   SHAW 271:6
inverse: agenda will be in i.   PARK 232:3
   increase in i. ratio   HUXL 148:8

inversion: But will his negative i.   AUDEN 20:3
inverted: i. Victorianism   FORS 114:9
investigator: self-importance of the i.   RUTH 256:5
investment: i. for any community   CHUR 73:2
invisible: man who has no i. means   BUCH 57:6
   O world i., we view thee   THOM 296:12
   priest of the i.   STEV 285:14
   what is essential is i.   SAINT 257:2
invitations: i. and don't invite us   KHR 166:2
   Receipted bills and i.   AUDEN 19:16
involuntary: It was i. They sank my boat   KENN 163:6
involved: not be i. in a European   BEAV 28:7
inwardness: full i. of the situation   JAMES 153:14
Iowa: I. mistake each other   ALLEN 4:4
Ireland: For the great Gaels of I.   CHES 68:10
   I. has her madness   AUDEN 17:4
   I. hurt you into poetry   AUDEN 17:4
   I. is the old sow that eats   JOYCE 158:10
   I. the inevitable never   MAH 199:2
   Out of I. have we come   YEATS 324:1
   Romantic I.'s dead and gone   YEATS 321:15
   was general all over I.   JOYCE 157:9
   what I have got for I.   COLL 79:9
   words 'I.' and 'island'   BOWEN 51:5
Irish: Across the I. Sea   MILL 209:5
   guess the answer to the I. Question   SELL 266:12
   I. poets, learn your trade   YEATS 319:11
   Let the I. vessel lie   AUDEN 17:5
   symbol of I. art   JOYCE 158:16
   We I., born into that ancient   YEATS 320:1
   When I. eyes are smiling   OLC 223:2
Irishman: I.'s heart is nothing   SHAW 269:16
Irishry: Still the indomitable I.   YEATS 319:12
iron: Adriatic an i. curtain   CHUR 73:3
   Any old i., any old iron   COLL 79:7
   Barumph has a whim of i.   HERF 139:19
   I. Lady of the Western   THAT 291:13
   ruled them with a rod of i.   RATT 243:4
   The i. lady   ANON 8:19
ironies: Life's little i.   HARDY 133:10
irony: most perfect humour and i.   BUTL 59:11
irrational: that the i. is rational   STEV 285:13
irregulars: Baker Street i.   DOYLE 95:7
irresistibly: Empire are i. drained   DOYLE 95:8
irresolute: resolved to be i.   CHUR 74:1
is: I. Paris burning   HITL 141:10
   I. your journey *really* necessary   ANON 8:20
island: i. is made mainly of coal   BEVAN 44:13
   i. or a large part of it   CHUR 74:6
   'i.' to be synonymous   BOWEN 51:5
   Look, stranger, at this i. now   AUDEN 19:6
   The i., the veranda   AUDEN 19:12
   this i. or lose the war   CHUR 74:7
islands: their favourite i.   AUDEN 19:10
isles: stars and i. where good   FLEC 111:7
isolation: i. and the busy griefs   AUDEN 17:4
   robbed of the i.   FORS 115:3

issue: Fat is a feminist i.   ORB 223:17
  It *is* a moral i.   HALEY 131:4
  make an i. of my womanhood   BRAC 51:13
it: I. *is* a moral issue   HALEY 131:4
  It's just I. Some women'll   KIPL 175:5
Italian: I. for the clearer understanding
                 WHAR 309:19
Italy: I. for thirty years under   WELL 307:14
  I. from designs by Michael   TWAIN 301:4
  I. has been losing wars   HELL 137:7
  traveller who has gone to I.   FORS 115:11
itch: intolerable neutral i.   AUDEN 20:3
it's: I. for you-hoo   ANON 9:2
  I. that man again   ANON 9:3
itself: Ecstasy and Forever be I.   GINS 124:12
  i. and not in its subject   SANT 260:16
itsy: I. bitsy teenie weenie   VANCE 303:4
ivory: downstairs from their I. Towers
                 SMITH 278:6
Ivy: Ee, it was agony, I.   RAY 243:11

J

jabbed: me as you j. and killed   OWEN 228:8
Jack: It's 'Damn you, J. . . .'   BONE 49:3
jacket: j. is always worn   EDW 98:8
jack-knife: Just a j. has Macheath, dear
                 BREC 52:18
Jacob: traffic of J.'s ladder   THOM 296:13
jail: Go to j. Go directly   DARR 88:6
  stealin' dey gits you in j.   O'NEI 223:6
jails: There are not enough j.   HUMP 148:2
jake: j. then you're frightened   DONL 93:3
jalousie: *que le rire pour la j.*   SAGAN 256:14
jamais: j. triste archy jamais triste   MARQ 201:12
James: [Henry J.'s]   WELLS 308:2
  Home J., and don't spare   HILL 141:1
  J. I, James II   GUED 130:4
  J. James   MILNE 210:1
  Poor Henry [J.], he's spending   MAUG 204:12
Jane: Aunt J. observed, the second   GRAH 127:7
  good-night to Lady J.   LAWR 181:9
  J., Jane   SITW 276:1
  Me Tarzan, you J.   WEIS 307:8
janitor: j. to the looney-bin   WOD 316:1
Japan: forces of the Empire of J.   ROOS 251:1
Japanese: J. action with prudence   CHUR 72:14
  The J. don't care   COW 84:13
jape: Indulge in loud unseemly j.   BELL 32:14
japonica: have naming of parts. J.   REED 244:12
jargon: language, we have j.   BENT 39:16
j'attaque: *situation excellente, j.*   FOCH 112:13
jaw-jaw: j. is always better   CHUR 75:14
jealous: over-j.   PHIL 234:3
jealousy: indignation is j. with a halo
                 WELLS 308:13

jealousy (*cont.*):
  J. is no more than feeling   BOWEN 51:4
  j. to the bride and good   BARR 26:2
  To j., nothing is more   SAGAN 256:14
jeans: wears dirty j.   BRAT 52:15
Jeeves: J. shimmered out and came   WOD 315:11
Jefferies: J. to Swedenborg and Oscar   BARB 24:15
Jefferson: when Thomas J. ate alone   KENN 163:2
Jellicoe: J. was the only man on either   CHUR 76:14
jelly: She shivers like the j.   PIRON 235:3
jellybeans: by his way of eating j.   REAG 244:5
Jesus: J. came to Birmingham they   KENN 288:12
  J. for what was done   BENN 37:3
  J. is there only for others   BONH 49:5
  J. loves you more   SIMON 275:9
  J. wants me for a sunbeam   TALB 290:10
  Jolson is greater than J.   FITZ 111:1
  more popular than J. now   LENN 185:4
  teachings of J.   BENN 37:2
jeunes filles: *les j. et comme les roses*   DE G 90:1
Jew: declare that I am a J.   EINS 99:7
  I'm not really a J.   MILL 208:15
jewel: me in 'J. in the Crown'   ASHC 14:1
  The j. in the crown   SCOTT 265:6
jewellery: Don't ever wear artistic j.   COL 79:3
  you'll just rattle your j.   LENN 185:3
jewels: j. make women either incredibly
                 BARR 26:8
Jewish: A J. God   BROW 56:14
  J. man with parents alive   ROTH 253:11
  national home for the J.   BALF 23:13
Jew-*ish*: really a *Jew*. Just J.   MILL 208:15
Jews: But spurn the J.   BROW 56:14
  England and America are J.   MAUG 205:3
  Hitler attacked the J.   NIEM 219:12
  J. except they don't know   MAL 199:11
  J. in any other country   BALF 23:13
  The J.   EWER 107:3
jigsaw: just a piece in a j.   MANK 200:3
Jim: fence leaps Sunny J.   HANFF 132:9
  I'm worried about J.   ANON 8:18
jine: can't lick 'em, j. 'em   REYN 246:3
jingle: and hear the harness j.   HOUS 146:6
job: came fifth and lost the j.   JOYCE 159:5
  Gizza j. . . . . I can do   BLEA 47:11
  here, so blow your j.   HART 135:12
  he's doing a grand j.   FROST 117:12
  husband a whole-time j.   BENN 38:17
  it is a whole-time j.   MAUG 204:10
  neighbour loses his j.   TRUM 299:9
  we will finish the j.   CHUR 72:11
John: from Land's End to J.   SPOO 282:10
  J. had   MILNE 209:16
  Spiritually I was at Eton, J.   BETJ 44:8
Johnny: And now . . . heeeeere's J.   MCM 196:13
Johnny-head-in-air: For J.   PUDN 241:7
Johnson: J.'s aesthetic judgements   STR 287:13
joie: *j. venait toujours après*   APOL 12:15
joined: Close j. is far away   GRAV 128:9

joint: minute you walked in the j.	FIEL 108:8
joints: gin j. in all the towns	EPST 106:9
tough j. more than somewhat	RUNY 254:7
joke: every j. is ultimately	ORW 224:17
It's our only j.	BARR 26:16
Its the funniest j.	SHAW 269:17
j. with a double meaning	BARK 25:2
subtleties of the American j.	TWAIN 301:5
jokes: A civil servant doesn't make j.	ION 151:12
I don't make j.—I just	ROG 249:14
my little j. on Thee	FROST 118:7
no more j. in Music-halls	SASS 263:1
joking: j. is to tell the truth	SHAW 269:17
jolly: should be j. at my funeral	MOUN 214:12
Three j. Farmers	DE L 91:4
Three j. gentlemen	DE L 91:2
Jolson: J. is greater than Jesus	FITZ 111:1
Jolyon: [J.] was afflicted	GALS 121:6
Jones: saying 'Lord J. Dead'	CHES 71:11
jonquils: land-locked pools of j.	BETJ 44:1
Joseph: Someone must have traduced J.	
	KAFKA 160:7
Josephine: Not tonight, J.	DAVID 88:11
joss-sticks: j. and honourable high-mindedness	
	BRAM 52:12
journalism: course . . . but why j.	BALF 23:14
from Christianity and j.	BALF 23:14
J.—an ability to meet	WEST 309:15
j. are ratlike cunning	TOM 298:2
j. is people who can't	ZAPPA 324:9
j. largely consists in saying	CHES 71:11
j. what will be read once	CONN 80:6
journalist: British j.	WOLFE 316:11
journalists: J. say a thing that they	BENN 38:18
journey: A long day's j. into night	O'NEI 223:10
For a j., and such a long	ELIOT 100:9
Is your j. *really* necessary	ANON 8:20
j. I prepare	MANS 200:8
j. seem like to those	BARN 25:5
long j. towards oblivion	LAWR 181:10
On a j. North	COW 85:8
Up, lad: when the j.'s over	HOUS 145:14
journeying: third-class seat sat the j. boy	
	HARDY 133:14
jours: Les j. s'en vont, je demeure.	APOL 12:15
joy: But j. is wisdom, Time	YEATS 319:9
I know of no j.	FIRB 109:14
J. always came after pain	APOL 12:15
j. from girl and boy	AUDEN 19:16
j. of the working	KIPL 174:13
j. that the day has brought	BOND 49:2
must not express great j.	FORS 114:2
Of j. illimited	HARDY 134:2
politics of j.	HUMP 148:4
Strength through j.	LEY 188:2
Joyce: clumsy *olla putrida* James J.	LAWR 181:5
go for a Proust or a J.	COBB 78:1
joyicity: hoppy on akkant of his j.	JOYCE 158:6

Judas: called in London 'genial J.'	HAIG 130:11
In the lost boyhood of J.	AE 3:3
Whether J. Iscariot	DYLAN 97:14
judge: Here comes the j.	MARK 201:5
I could have been a j.	COOK 82:8
j. of a man by his foes	CONR 81:15
j. this movement kindly	READ 244:2
j. you don't have to know	LUML 192:12
judgement: at God's great J. Seat	KIPL 169:10
England shall bide till J. Tide	KIPL 172:13
It biases the j.	DOYLE 95:9
j. of our scientific age	HOLM 142:13
nation is fit to sit in j.	WILS 314:10
judgements: Johnson's aesthetic j.	STR 287:13
judges: j. have declared it	QUIL 242:4
She threw me in front of the J.	BETJ 42:11
judging: had the Latin for the j.	COOK 82:8
Judy: actually did say was 'J.'	CAGN 60:18
jug: 'J. Jug' to dirty ears	ELIOT 104:16
jugement: *N'attendez pas le j. dernier*	CAMUS 62:14
Juin: *sans nuage et J. poignardé*	ARAG 13:2
Julia: missed point completely, J.	ELIOT 101:2
Julian: J. and this is my friend	TOOK 298:3
Julias: Now the J., Maeves and Maureens	
	BETJ 44:2
July: Born on the fourth of J.	COHAN 78:13
January, June, or J.	NORW 221:6
Next J. we collide with Mars	PORT 237:1
jump: what Trojan 'orses will j.	BEVIN 45:13
jumps: fox j. over the lazy dog	ANON 10:12
June: I like *New York* in J.	FREED 116:12
J. is bustin' out all over	HAMM 131:10
May without cloud and J.	ARAG 13:2
Unwontedly. It was late J.	THOM 294:5
jungle: not a concrete j.	MORR 213:13
primitive in a giant j.	MAIL 199:6
this is the Law of the J.	KIPL 174:2
junior: Cambridge or j. television	AMIS 5:13
juniper-tree: leopards sat under a j.	ELIOT 101:1
junk: Ep's statues are j.	ANON 8:13
just: J. a wee deoch-an-doris	MORR 214:1
j. going outside and may	MAHON 199:4
j. going outside and may	OATES 221:13
J. like that!	COOP 83:3
j. one of those things	PORT 236:14
J. when you thought it was	ANON 9:6
J. you wait	HART 135:12
rather be British than j.	PAIS 229:2
The scrupulous and the j.	CONR 81:21
justice: j. and the American way	ANON 7:23
j. is open to all	MATH 204:6
j. makes democracy possible	NIEB 219:9
j. should not only be done	HEW 140:4
'J.' was done	HARDY 134:8
or j. or human happiness	BERL 41:2
price of j. is eternal	BENN 38:14
pursuit of j. is no virtue	GOLD 126:4
threat to j. everywhere	KING 166:6

justification: art should carry its j.   CONR 81:16
justify: The end cannot j. the means   HUXL 148:13
   To j. God's ways to man   HOUS 146:15
justifying: j. his position at whatever   AMERY 5:11

K

Kaiser: put the kibosh on the K.   ELL 106:2
Kansas: What the horses o' K. think   KIPL 170:5
Karajan: [Herbert von K. is]   BEEC 29:20
Kate: And some, alas, with K.   AUDEN 18:17
Kathaleen: K. Ní Houlihan, your road's
                                 CARB 63:14
Katy: K-K-K-Katy, beautiful K.   O'HARA 222:19
keats: *Prancing Nigger*, Blunden, K.   BETJ 44:7
keep: But k. your fancy free   HOUS 146:1
   diary and some day it'll k.   WEST 309:3
   He may k. that will and can   HOUS 145:3
   k. 'em down on the farm   LEWIS 187:9
   k. fat souls from sleep   MCL 196:6
   K. on truckin'   CRUMB 86:14
   K. right on to the end   LAUD 179:17
   K. that schoolgirl complexion   PEAR 232:8
   K. the aspidistra flying   ORW 224:19
   K. the Home-fires burning   FORD 113:14
   K. violence in the mind   ALD 3:13
   K. ye the law   KIPL 174:3
   k. your head when all about   KIPL 173:7
   To k. your head   PUDN 241:7
   ware that will not k.   HOUS 145:14
   worth while to k. them   SHAW 272:2
keeping: art of k.   MARQ 201:8
   I am so sorry for k. you   GEOR 123:3
   merely the art of k.   RICH 247:6
   usefully in k. feelings at bay   BROO 56:3
keeps: And gave it us for k.   AYRES 22:1
   cheerful as k. me going   KAV 162:8
   He just k. rollin'   HAMM 132:1
Kelly: K. from the Isle of Man   MURP 216:3
Kempis: Oscar Wilde to Thomas à K.   BARB 24:15
Kensal Green: Paradise by way of K.   CHES 69:6
kept: must be k. in their place   AWDRY 21:5
   'That I k. my word,' he said   DE L 90:12
Kerouac: can write, not even Mr K.   CAP 63:10
kettle: pretty k. of fish   MARY 202:13
Kew: down to K. in lilac-time   NOYES 221:8
key: k. is Russian national   CHUR 75:6
   looking for the k.   BENN 37:10
   out of k. with his time   POUND 238:5
keys: And all her shining k.   HARDY 133:11
   half that's got my k.   GRAH 127:10
kharki: gentleman in K. ordered South   KIPL 168:5
Khatmandu: idol to the north of K.   HAYES 136:3
kibosh: put the k. on the Kaiser   ELL 106:2
kick: k. a hole in a stained   CHAN 66:11
   k. around any more   NIXON 220:3

kick (*cont.*):
   Kiss 'em one day and k.   KIPL 172:6
   That I get a k. out of you   PORT 236:12
kicking: k. his something something   CHUR 73:7
   kissing and k. people   TRUM 299:10
kid: Here's looking at you, k.   EPST 106:11
kiddies: k. have crumpled the serviettes
                                   BETJ 42:12
kidnapped: k. and they snap into action
                                 ALLEN 4:18
kidneys: k. which gave to his palate   JOYCE 159:4
kids: And don't have any k. yourself   LARK 179:2
   k. playing some game   SAL 258:15
   many k. have you killed   ANON 9:10
kill: get out and k. something   LEAC 182:15
   K. a man, and you   ROST 253:9
   K. millions of men   ROST 253:9
   k. more women and children   BALD 23:4
   k. shall be thy kill if   KIPL 171:6
   MEN ARE PREPARED TO K.   SHAW 270:10
   Otherwise k. me   MACN 198:8
   sin to k. a mockingbird   LEE 183:15
   that can k. the Movies   ROG 249:5
   they k. you in a new way   ROG 249:11
   To k. a human being   JAMES 152:13
killed: Beauty k. the Beast   CREE 86:1
   Has k. lots of men   MOYN 215:1
   how many kids have you k.   ANON 9:10
   I am the enemy you k.   OWEN 228:8
   me as you jabbed and k.   OWEN 228:8
   The effort very nearly k. her   BELL 33:3
   who k. him   BELL 34:16
killer: For here the lover and k.   DOUG 93:8
killing: In reality, k. time   SITW 276:9
killings: mass k. of peoples   ROOS 251:2
kills: Into my heart an air that k.   HOUS 146:11
   With a grip that k. it   TAG 290:9
kilometres: Peeling off the k.   CONN 81:5
kimonos: Two girls in silk k., both   YEATS 323:2
kin: k. to the snare drummer   FREB 116:10
kind: been very k. to me here   CAV 65:8
   encounters of the third k.   SPIE 282:5
   For people will always be k.   SASS 262:9
   Human k.   ELIOT 101:7
   k. of a people do they   CHUR 72:14
   Too kind, too k.   NIGH 219:13
kindle: existence is to k. a light   JUNG 159:15
kindliness: cool k. of sheets   BROO 54:9
kindly: K. Call Me God   SAMP 259:3
   Sally is gone that was so k.   BELL 34:8
kindness: depended on the k. of strangers
                                   WILL 312:10
   with the milk of human k.   GUED 130:3
king: down unless you're a k.   HULL 148:1
   duty as K. and Emperor   EDW 98:11
   fight for its K. and Country   GRAH 127:5
   K. and Country need you   FIELD 108:7
   k. and government and nation   KAV 161:12
   K. and your Country both   RUB 254:6

king (*cont.*):

K. [George V] told me	ASQ 15:5
K. John was not a good man	MILNE 209:13
K.'s Cross	FARJ 107:7
K.'s life is moving peacefully	DAWS 89:3
K.'s Moll Reno'd in Wolsey's	ANON 9:8
lad that's born to be k.	BOUL 50:9
Like a k. in exile	LAWR 180:10
mile of kingdom, I am k.	KAV 161:12
Mrs Simpson's pinched our k.	ANON 8:9
much a k. as a Monarch	SELL 266:9
Northcliffe has sent for the K.	ANON 8:10
One-Eyed Man is K.	WELLS 308:5
self-dedication of the K. himself	BLUNT 48:1
The Chief Defect of Henry K.	BELL 32:19
The K. asked	MILNE 210:3
The man who would be k.	KIPL 172:8
The once and future k.	WHITE 310:4

kingdom: A road, a mile of k., I am king

	KAV 161:12
k. of the well	SONT 280:12
k. where nobody dies	MILL 208:6

kingdoms: our places, these K. | ELIOT 100:10

kings: All k. is mostly rapscallions | TWAIN 300:6

godly k. had built her	FLEC 112:1
The captains and the k. depart	KIPL 173:3
there will be only five K.	FAR 107:8
These five k. did a king	THOM 293:10
walk with K.	KIPL 173:9

kinkering: K. Kongs their tykles | SPOO 282:8

Kinnock: K. in a thousand generations

	KINN 168:3

Kipling: sort of gutless K. | ORW 225:18

kiss: I want him to k. my ass | JOHN 156:2

Just k. yourself goodbye	JER 155:13
K. 'em one day and kick	KIPL 172:6
k. is still a kiss	HUPF 148:5
k. of death	SMITH 276:15
Leans to the sun's k. glorying	GREN 129:5
ribbons and k. babies	MICH 207:12
rough male k.	BROO 54:9
thank you, k. you	RUB 254:6
The k. of the sun for pardon	GURN 130:9
When women k. it always	MENC 206:11
will be wanting to k. me	MACD 194:12
words 'K. Kiss Bang Bang'	KAEL 160:5

kissed: Hasn't been k. for forty years | ANON 9:19

k. by a man who *didn't*	KIPL 175:3
k. his sad Andromache goodbye	CORN 83:13
k. the lovely grass	BROO 54:8
wasn't looking and never k.	THOM 293:15

kisses: A fine romance with no k. | FIEL 108:9

k. on an 'eathen idol's	KIPL 169:7

kissing: I wasn't k. her, I was | MARX 202:9

I wonder who's k. her now	ADAMS 2:2
k. and kicking people	TRUM 299:10

Kissinger: he [K.] has observed | KISS 175:13

kit-bag: troubles in your old k. | ASAF 13:13

kitchen: get out of the k. | TRUM 299:7

kitchen (*cont.*):

get out of the k.	VAUG 303:9
servant girls in the k.	SYNGE 289:10
They send me to eat in the k.	HUGH 147:13

Kitchener: K. is a great poster | ASQ 14:14

kith: If one's own kin and k. | NASH 218:6

kitten: dead k., an egg-shell | WELLS 308:2

The trouble with a k.	NASH 217:10

kleinsten: k. *Zimmer in meinem Hause* | REGER 245:7

knack: k. of so arranging | FRIS 117:7

knee: And smitten me to my k. | THOM 295:10

Picture you upon my k.	CAES 60:16

knees: than to live on your k. | IBAR 149:17

work is done upon his k.	KIPL 171:4

knew: all k. you had it in you | PARK 231:11

blessed Hope, whereof he k.	HARDY 134:2
k. practically everything	BENC 36:2
k. that the lower classes	CURZ 88:4

knife: If peas were eaten with the k. | RAL 242:12

progress if a cannibal uses k.	LEC 183:12
wind's like a whetted k.	MAS 204:1

Kniff: *als* K., *die Welt so einzurichten* | FRIS 117:7

knight: An earl and a k. of the garter | ATTL 16:2

knit: The stuff of life to k. me | HOUS 146:9

knits: Nothing k. man to man | SICK 275:2

knitter: beautiful little k. | SITW 276:4

knives: The Night of the Long K. | HITL 141:6

knock: Don't k. masturbation | ALLEN 5:2

knocked: It is what they k. down | FENT 108:3

K. down a doctor	SIMP 275:12
we k. the bastard off	HILL 140:13

knocking: K. on the moonlit door | DE L 90:11

k. the American system	CAP 63:8

knot: Into the crowned k. of fire | ELIOT 102:7

So the k. be unknotted	ELIOT 101:19
teeth a political k.	BIER 46:11

know: because I wish to k. | ASTOR 15:10

Eh? K. what I mean	CHAP 67:8
enough to k. everything	BARR 25:10
He must k. sumpin'	HAMM 132:1
How do they k.	PARK 231:12
How do you k. you're . . . God	BARN 25:9
I do not believe. . . . I k.	JUNG 159:17
I Don't K. is on third	ABB 1:1
I don't k. where I'm going	SAND 260:2
I k. nothing whatever	DOYLE 94:19
I k. two things about the horse	ROYD 254:5
I k. what I like	BEER 31:15
I k. what I like	JAMES 153:7
I k. why the caged bird sings	ANG 6:10
I think I k. enough of hate	FROST 118:10
K. all that there	GRAH 127:16
k. anything about music	BEER 31:15
k. ask questions of those	RAL 242:11
k. a woman until you have	LEV 186:16
k. better than anybody	AGATE 3:15
k. I know you know I know	GUNN 130:8
k. is what I read	ROG 249:9
k. less and understand	STEP 285:2

know (*cont.*):

k. more than you think	SPOCK 282:6
k. such a frightful lot	CHES 69:15
k. that summer sang	MILL 208:1
k. the man their neighbour	YEATS 322:4
k. the place for the first	ELIOT 102:4
k. what is right	JOHN 156:14
k. what I think till	WALL 304:17
k. what they have said	CHUR 73:10
k. what we are talking	RUSS 255:11
not k. much about gods	ELIOT 101:10
Not many people k.	CAINE 61:3
She knows, you k.	BAKER 22:6
The kind old sun will k.	OWEN 228:1
they k. enough who know	ADAMS 2:11
they merely k. more	SAKI 258:8
things they didn't k.	POUND 238:3
wanted to k. about sex	REUB 245:14
We Americans k., although	JOHN 156:11
Where I am, I don't k.	BECK 29:3
Whitehall really does k.	JAY 154:4
You k. my methods. Apply them	DOYLE 95:6
you k. you should be glad	LENN 185:12

knowing: Bewrapt past k. to what HARDY 133:14

For lust of k. what should	FLEC 111:10
one who INSISTS on k.	POUND 237:19

knowingly: He asked him k. . . . nudge CHAP 67:8

never k. undersold	LEWIS 187:6

knowledge: After such k., what forgiveness

ELIOT 100:7

k. we have lost in information	ELIOT 104:1
our k. can only be finite	POPP 236:8
Pedantry is the dotage of k.	JACK 151:18
search for k.	RUSS 254:13
wisdom we have lost in k.	ELIOT 104:1

known: k. for his well-knownness BOOR 49:7

light and safer than a k.	HASK 136:1
more than they have k.	BROO 55:6

knows: He k. death to the bone YEATS 323:5

He k. nothing	SHAW 270:9
k. an undesirable character	FRY 120:2
k. not whither nor why	MAS 204:3
man who k. the way	TYNAN 302:7
She k., you know	BAKER 22:6
sits in the middle and k.	FROST 119:11
specialist as one who 'k. . . .'	MAYO 206:3
that has a mind and k.	SHAW 267:12
What one k. is, in youth	ADAMS 2:11
you k. of a better 'ole	BAIR 22:5

Knox: Shall see John K. in Paradise PARK 230:18

kongs: guise of 'Kinkering K.'	SPOO 282:8
Kontrast: *wir nur den K. intensiv*	FREUD 117:4
Krieg: *Kommt der K. ins Land*	PONS 236:3
kritik: *Ich habe Ihre K. vor mir*	REGER 245:7
wenig erreichbar als mit K.	RILKE 247:8
Kruger: killing K. with your mouth	KIPL 168:5
Ku: K. Klux Klanner	KING 166:7
kultur: *Wenn ich K. höre*	JOHST 157:2
Kurtz: Mistah K. — he dead	CONR 81:13

L

laboratory: guinea pigs in the l. of God WILL 312:3

labour: be the Gromyko of the L. HEAL 136:6

Don't let L. ruin it	ANON 9:16
election programme of the L.	SNOW 279:8
interests of capital and l.	ATK 15:16
L. isn't working	ANON 9:9
L. Party is a desiccated	BEVAN 44:11
L. Party owes more to Methodism	PHIL 234:2
much of a l. to write	HUXL 149:6
programme of the L. party	HAIL 130:14
Shares for All, is L.'s Call	JAY 154:3
[the L. Party] is a moral	WILS 313:9
The 'loony L. left'	HEW 140:5
[the poor] have to l.	FRAN 116:6

labour-intensive: The Monarchy is a l. industry

WILS 313:7

labyrinth: From a great l. out of pride YEATS 322:5

labyrinthine: I fled Him, down the l. ways

THOM 295:2

lace: Arsenic and old l.	KESS 164:9
lacerate: Cannot l. his breast	YEATS 323:14
lack: best l. all conviction	YEATS 320:7
l. of ability to suspend	HEM 138:3
lacks: what it l. in length	FROST 119:8
lacy: glove as a l. sleeve	WOOL 317:15

lad: A grand little l. was young EDGAR 98:3

And I myself a sterling l.	HOUS 146:16
And many a lightfoot l.	HOUS 146:14
Carry the l. that's born	BOUL 50:9
great pleasure with a l.	YEATS 323:6
lively l. most pleasured me	YEATS 323:6

ladder: Now that my l.'s gone YEATS 320:3

plasterer on his l.	HEAN 136:9

laden: With rue my heart is l. HOUS 146:14

ladies: began. I am parshial to l. ASHF 14:3

L. as people who did not	RAV 243:9
l. in waiting to the queen	TREE 298:10
'L.,' said Tree	TREE 298:10
The l. of St James's	DOBS 92:15
when l. apparently rolled	HUXL 149:8
worth any number of old l.	FAUL 107:10

lads: l. for the girls HOUS 146:5

l. in their hundreds	HOUS 146:5
l. that will never be old	HOUS 146:5
Though your l. are far away	FORD 113:14

lady: called her his l. fair KIPL 175:7

case a certain little l.	GAY 122:7
Dance, dance, dance, little l.	COW 84:6
Iron L. of the Western	THAT 291:13
L., be good	GERS 123:8
L., make a note of this	PARK 230:11
l. of beauty and high degree	RANS 243:1
L. of Spain, I adore you	REAV 244:11
l. passing by was heard	BURT 58:7
l.'s not for turning	THAT 291:15

lady (cont.):

l. that's known as Lou	SERV 267:1
L., three white leopards	ELIOT 101:1
L., when your lovely head	BELL 34:14
old l. in Dubuque	ROSS 253:3
That's why the l. is a tramp	HART 135:11
The iron l.	ANON 8:19
The Liner she's a l.	KIPL 174:6
This l. of the West Country	DE L 90:13
want to talk like a l.	SHAW 273:13
whore like a lady and a l.	MIZN 212:1
young l. named Bright	BULL 57:11

Lafayette: L., we are here — STAN 283:7

lag: not l. behind economically — DUBČ 95:18

laid: attending it were l. end to end — PARK 231:10

get l., to get fame	GELD 122:10
The lightfoot boys are l.	HOUS 146:14
These l. the world away	BROO 54:12

lain: lovely muck I've l. — HOUS 146:16

laity: conspiracies against the l. — SHAW 268:21

lake: Cyprus with a l. of fire — FLEC 112:3

l. water lapping with low — YEATS 318:10

Lalun: L. is a member of the most — KIPL 171:5

lamb: blood of the L. — LIND 188:8

Lambeth: Doin' the L. Walk — ROSE 252:5

lambs: l. who've lost our way — KIPL 169:9

They go to hell like l. — CHES 68:18

lame: without religion is l. — EINS 99:11

lamp: Every street l. that I pass — ELIOT 103:14

lamp-post: leaning on a l. at the corner — GAY 122:7

lamps: l. are going out all over — GREY 129:7

land: A lane to the l. of the dead — AUDEN 16:13

citizens of death's gray l.	SASS 262:5
In that l. of flesh and bone	AUDEN 19:5
l. did not lag behind economically	DUBČ 95:18
l. of embarrassment	BARN 25:5
L. of Heart's Desire	YEATS 319:9
L. of Hope and Glory	BENS 39:4
L. of our birth, we pledge	KIPL 173:1
L.'s End to John of Gaunt	SPOO 282:10
L. that I love	BERL 40:6
l. was made for you	GUTH 130:10
l. was ours before we were	FROST 119:9
Oh, give me l., lots of land	PORT 236:11
That is the l. of lost content	HOUS 146:11
The l. of faery	YEATS 319:8
The l. of my fathers	THOM 293:3
There's a l. that I heard	HARB 132:13
There shall be no more l.	BROO 55:5
Throughout the l.	DYLAN 97:13
you l. of the pilgrims	CUMM 87:2

landed: The eagle has l. — HIGG 140:9

landing: fight on the l. grounds — CHUR 74:6

land-locked: l. pools of jonquils — BETJ 44:1

landlord: Bess, the l.'s daughter — NOYES 221:10

landslide: I'm going to pay for a l. — KENN 162:16

lane: A l. to the land of the dead — AUDEN 16:13

language: beyond the l. of the living — ELIOT 102:1

bottom the l. of the unheard — KING 167:7

language (cont.):

clear l. is insincerity	ORW 226:2
foreign l.	MORL 213:10
instead of l., we have	BENT 39:16
In such lovely l.	LAWR 181:18
l. an opera is sung	APPL 13:1
l. convey more than they	CONN 80:11
L. is a form of human reason	LÉ.V 187:1
l. of priorities	BEVAN 45:7
l. of Shakespear and Milton	SHAW 273:12
literature is simply l.	POUND 238:4
no respect for their l.	SHAW 273:10
Political l.	ORW 226:3
The limits of my l. mean	WITT 315:7

languages: woman speaks eighteen l. — PARK 231:9

words in our respective l. — COOK 82:7

lap: her l., legs, feet — O'BR 222:5

lapping: lake water l. with low — YEATS 318:10

large: So l. a trunk before — BELL 32:17

larger: can only be to make us l. — BALD 22:10

lark: Where never l., nor even — MAGEE 198:11

larks: And hear the l. so high — HOUS 146:3

The l., still bravely singing — MCCR 194:6

lash: sodomy and the l. — CHUR 73:8

lass: A l. was singing a hymn — BETJ 44:3

lassie: I love a l., a bonnie — LAUD 180:1

Wae my l. by my side — LAUD 180:3

last: bears the marks of the l. — HAIG 130:11

Don't wait for the l.	CAMUS 62:14
Good to the l. drop	ROOS 252:4
I'm the l. of the red-hot mamas	YELL 324:4
It did not l.: the Devil	SQUI 283:3
It will not l. the night	MILL 207:17
l. article of my creed	GAND 122:1
L. night at twelve I felt	ADE 2:19
L. night I dreamt I went	DU M 96:7
l. temptation is the greatest	ELIOT 102:9
laughs longest who laughs l.	MAS 204:4
look of the l. gentleman	LEV 186:15
lost the l. of England	BELL 34:18
my l. press conference	NIXON 220:3
Nice guys. Finish l.	DUR 96:11
prepare for the l. war	TUCH 299:14
that I could l. for ever	CONR 82:2
The l. hurrah	O'CON 222:16
The l. time I saw Paris	HAMM 131:11
they l. while they last	DE G 90:1
were the l. romantics	YEATS 323:7

Las Vegas: Fear and loathing in L. — THOM 296:14

late: be a little l. this year — LOES 190:8

damned fella will be l.	MITF 211:12
Dread of being l.	BETJ 44:6
l. to do anything but *accept*	CAMP 61:9
never come l.	HART 135:11
Steel chambers, l. the pyres	HARDY 134:4
that the people who are l.	LUCAS 192:8
This is a l. parrot	CHAP 67:9
too l. to have a fling	WILS 314:2

later: It is l. than you think — SERV 266:15

later (*cont.*):
See you l., alligator	GUID 130:5

Latin: clever ones learn L. — CHUR 75:10
L. for the judging — COOK 82:8
No more L., no more French — ANON 10:5
there no L. word for Tea — BELL 34:6
lattenzaun: *Es war einmal ein L.* — MORG 213:9
laugh: all of them make me l. — AUDEN 18:16
behind her a meaning l. — EWART 107:1
But I l. — HUGH 147:13
comedian is whether you l. — NATH 218:14
Fact, nothing to l. at at all — EDGAR 98:3
l. and he will think you — MAUG 205:2
l.-at-with — SPEN 282:3
l. broke into a thousand — BARR 25:17
L. thy girlish laughter — WATS 305:8
no girl wants to l. — LOOS 190:18
They l. uproariously in youth — BROO 55:11
we'll l. at the weather — HART 135:12
who will not l. is a fool — SANT 260:8
laughed: Flinging from his arms I l. — YEATS 323:6
L. in the sun, and kissed — BROO 54:8
l. when I sat down — CAPL 63:7
When he l., respectable — AUDEN 17:1
When the first baby l. — BARR 25:17
laughing: fun I ever had without l. — ALLEN 5:1
l. at anyone I am generally — BEER 30:17
Set the crew l., and forgot — FLEC 112:4
laughs: l. longest who laughs last — MAS 204:4
laughter: And l., learnt of friends — BROO 55:2
born with a gift of l. — SAB 256:10
But l. and the love of friends — BELL 35:4
irrevocably betrothed to l. — UST 302:13
I was convulsed with l. — MARX 202:10
l. of her heart in ev'ry — HAMM 131:11
L. would be bereaved if — UST 302:15
more frightful than l. — SAGAN 256:14
Porter-drinkers' randy l. — YEATS 319:11
under running l. — THOM 295:2
laundries: sunset where that Land of L. — BETJ 43:8
laundry: An' it all goes into the l. — KIPL 170:13
any first-class l. — LEAC 183:3
laurels: The curate faced the l. — GRAH 127:11
lavatory: l. door shut by extending — BANK 24:10
l. makes you fear the worst — COW 85:8
lavished: luxury was l. on you — ORTON 224:5
law: be the whole of the L. — CROW 86:12
brilliance is needed in the l. — MORT 214:3
enforce a l. not supported — HUMP 148:2
fugitive from th' l. — MAUL 205:18
Keep ye the l.—be swift — KIPL 174:3
L. is a reflection — SCH 264:13
l. is the most powerful — GIR 125:3
L. of the Jungle — KIPL 174:2
l. of the Yukon — SERV 266:17
lesser breeds without the L. — KIPL 173:5
majestic equality of the l. — FRAN 116:6
Nor l., nor duty bade me fight — YEATS 322:11
people not defied the l. — SCAR 264:3

law (*cont.*):
The Common L. of England — HERB 139:14
till the fear of the L. — JOYCE 158:4
write it in the books of l. — JOHN 156:7
Law Courts: Another is 'the beautiful L.' — RUSS 256:4
lawful: l. for a Catholic woman — MENC 206:18
lawn: Out on the l. I lie in bed — AUDEN 19:4
Lawrence: L. tried to portray this — ROB 248:12
L. was right when he had — GIBB 123:13
laws: island are the l. of nature — SHAW 268:7
L. for themselves and not — HOUS 145:3
l. made or the authorizations — JOHN 155:16
l. of God will be suspended — SHAW 269:12
their l., and their codes — FREN 117:1
The l. of God, the laws of man — HOUS 145:3
lawyer: A l.'s dream of heaven — BUTL 59:5
freely as a l. interprets — GIR 125:3
l. with his briefcase can — PUZO 241:9
When a l. cashes — SAND 260:5
lay: And l. one more bloody egg — AYRES 21:16
I l. down my burden — EDW 98:11
l. down his friends — THOR 297:2
L. your sleeping head, my love — AUDEN 17:10
layer: l. I call the *collective* — JUNG 160:4
or less superficial l. — JUNG 160:4
lays: constructing tribal l. — KIPL 168:7
hand that l. the golden — GOLD 126:9
l. out food in tins — ELIOT 105:5
Lazarus: Come forth, L. — JOYCE 159:5
lazy: jumps over the l. dog — ANON 10:12
L. and silly — SITW 276:5
LBJ: All the way with L. — ANON 6:14
L., how many kids have — ANON 9:10
lead: couldn't see who was in the l. — SNAG 279:3
Go down like lumps of l. — HODG 142:1
L. me from death to life — KUMAR 177:4
l. you all in the dance — CART 64:7
You can l. a horticulture — PARK 231:16
leaden: Because if I use l. ones — BELL 32:16
With l. age o'ercargoed — FLEC 112:3
leader: A fanatic is a great l. — BROUN 56:6
A political l. must keep — BAR 27:9
I'll be l., you can march — CAST 64:11
l. for the Labour Party — BEVAN 44:11
One realm, one people, one l. — ANON 7:19
Our beloved l., Bapu — NEHRU 218:17
Take me to your l. — ANON 11:5
The final test of a l. — LIPP 189:1
leaders: Don't follow l. — DYLAN 97:12
l. of a revolution — CONR 81:21
leaf: does a wise man hide a l. — CHES 69:12
He can watch a grass or l. — GRAV 128:5
lean: L. on a garden urn — ELIOT 103:16
l. over too far backward — THUR 297:14
l. to wild extremes I could — DURY 97:1
leaning: l. on a lamp-post — GAY 122:7
L. together — ELIOT 103:3
leap: creep again, l. again — DE L 91:7

leap (*cont.*):

milk's l. toward immortality	FAD 107:4
one giant l. for mankind	ARMS 13:10

leaping: And l. from place to place HARDY 133:13

By brooks too broad for l.	HOUS 146:14
l. light for your delight	AUDEN 19:6
swimmers into cleanness l.	BROO 54:10

leaps: It moves in mighty l. AYRES 22:1

o'er the fence l. Sunny Jim	HANFF 132:9

leapt: l. straight past the common AYRES 22:1

learn: Churches must l. humility	SHAW 273:20
Irish poets, l. your trade	YEATS 319:11
l. a lot from their children	SPARK 281:4
l. by going where I have	ROET 249:4
L. to think Imperially	CHAM 65:13
Oh, when will you ever l.	SEEG 266:1
thirty who don't want to l.	SELL 266:3

learned: An' I l. about women from 'er KIPL 174:9

been l. has been forgotten	SKIN 276:12
from St Louis hasn't l.	STEIN 284:3
privilege of the l.	PEAR 232:9

learning: And sleep—and l. of a sort BELL 35:6

Beauty and the lust for l.	BEER 31:12
public and l. the instrument	BUTL 59:3

leave: always l. room for the mouse SAKI 258:6

By all ye l. or do	KIPL 175:9
ever taking l.	RILKE 247:10
L. him alone	FARJ 107:7
l. in a taxi you can leave	KALM 161:5
L. them while you're looking	LOOS 190:15
L. your worry on the doorstep	FIEL 108:11
repeat his past nor l.	AUDEN 18:15
you l. them as they	CHES 70:3
you must l.	SPOO 282:9

leaves: burning of the l. BINY 47:3

glad green l. like wings	HARDY 134:1
only stop to rake the l.	FROST 118:12
thick on Severn snow the l.	HOUS 146:7
whole deck put on its l.	FLEC 112:5
woods and stipple l.	SACK 256:13

Leben: *Wort "Ehrfurcht vor dem L."* SCHW 264:16

lecture: And to l. rooms is forced CHES 71:9

at twilight from the l.	STEV 285:13

lectures: have hissed my mystery l. SPOO 282:9

led: L. go	KIPL 172:1
ledger: floor and smudge the l.	BETJ 43:8

left: be l. to the politicians DE G 90:6

L. hand down a bit	WYMAN 318:2
l. Him in the rain	KENN 288:12
l. thee all her lovely	DAV 88:16
l. the wives and joined	WELD 307:10
nobody l. to be concerned	NIEM 219:12
position was on the l.	MOSL 214:11
The 'loony Labour l.'	HEW 140:5
we that are l. grow	BINY 47:5

leg: extending your left l. BANK 24:10

legal: exact l. definition RUSS 255:19

legend: The past exudes l. MAL 199:12

legion: L. and Social Club BETJ 42:3

legion (*cont.*):

Ravel refuses the L.	SATIE 263:6
The cross of the L.	TWAIN 302:3

legs: Four l. good, two legs bad ORW 224:11

haricot vein in one of my l.	BUTL 60:13
His l., perhaps, were shorter	STR 288:2
losing your l.	SASS 262:9
not himself, adorns my l.	HOUS 144:5
The strongest l. in Pontefract	BETJ 42:6
two perfectly good l.	ROOS 250:9
were born with your l.	ORTON 224:9

Leicester: Farewell, L. Square JUDGE 159:13

Leidenschaften: *seiner L. gegangen ist* JUNG 159:14

leisure: gentleman of l. VEBL 303:12

l. intelligently	RUSS 255:7
miserable is to have l.	SHAW 273:6

lemon: squeezed as a l. is squeezed GEDD 122:9

lemonade: I'll take a l. PAN 229:4

Len: L. says one steady pull FROST 119:3

lend: If you can't l. your hand DYLAN 97:13

not well enough to l.	BIER 46:4
words would hardly l.	DOYLE 95:13

lend-lease: assistance called L. CHUR 75:3

length: l. of a meeting rises SHAN 267:7

what it lacks in l.	FROST 119:8

Lenin: Engels and L. he deceives KHR 165:9

L. was right	KEYN 164:13

Lennon: [John L.] MCC 194:3

John L., Paul McCartney	BUCK 57:10

lenses: beauty and contact l. PETER 233:10

If at times my eyes are l.	DOUG 93:9

Léonie: aunt L. used to give me PROU 240:8

Weep not for little L.	GRAH 127:6

leopards: l. sat under a juniper-tree ELIOT 101:1

leper: here as a Parliamentary l. WILS 313:4

Lesbia: L. with her sparrow MILL 208:4

lesbians: gays and l. issue HEW 140:5

less: l. in this than meets BANK 24:8

l. than that no man	ROOS 251:6
L. than the dust, beneath	HOPE 144:3
more and more about l.	MAYO 206:3

lesson: l. of the fearsome AREN 13:4

lessons: l. of history is the most HUXL 148:10

lest: l. they should be set GRAH 127:12

let: get out of the way and l. EIS 100:4

L. him twist slowly	EHRL 99:2
L. me enjoy the earth no less	HARDY 134:9
L. the florid music praise	AUDEN 19:5
l. their liquid siftings	ELIOT 102:13
L. them know it's Christmas	GELD 122:11
L. the train take the strain	ANON 9:12
L. us go then, you	ELIOT 103:6
L. your fingers do the walking	ANON 9:13
Not I: l. God and man decree	HOUS 145:3

Lethe: Dawn shall over L. break BELL 34:14

let's: L. all go down the Strand CAST 64:11

Let's do it, l.'s fall in love	PORT 236:5

letter: l. by strange letter HEAN 136:9

until you have had a l.	LEV 186:16

letters: L. for the rich, letters   AUDEN 19:15
   l. get   MILNE 210:14
   L. of thanks, letters from   AUDEN 19:16
   l. to *The Times* about   BEER 31:20
lettuce: much l. is 'soporific'   POTT 237:6
level: their l. of incompetence   PETER 233:9
leviathan: l. retrieving pebbles   WELLS 308:3
liar: exceptionally good l.   JER 155:1
   l. is he who makes   BUTL 60:12
   quite often picturesque l.   TWAIN 300:10
   still a l.   CORN 83:10
   They only answered 'Little L.!'   BELL 33:5
   virtue and a proved l.   HAIL 130:13
liars: himself the accomplice of l.   PÉGUY 232:13
   Income Tax has made more L.   ROG 249:7
liberal: a L. is a man who uses   ROOS 250:9
   could only entertain my L.   ASQ 15:2
   distinguished from the L.   BIER 46:15
   Just like an old l.   PLOM 235:15
   l. is a man who tells other   BAR 24:12
liberals: l. can understand everything BRUCE 57:1
   L. offer a mixture of sound   MACM 197:6
liberate: we shall l. this country   MAND 200:1
liberates: Work l.   ANON 6:16
liberation: l. of the human mind from   GOLD 126:3
   rescue and the l.   CHUR 74:6
liberties: dramatist only wants more l.
                               JAMES 152:10
   what l. are taken in thy   GEOR 123:5
liberty: can be no effective l.   BELL 32:10
   convenience to l.   HESSE 140:3
   course l. is not licence   SCAN 264:2
   defence of l. is no vice   GOLD 126:4
   foundations of political l.   WILS 314:13
   L. has never come from   WILS 314:9
   L. is always unfinished   ANON 9:14
   L. is liberty, not equality   BERL 41:2
   L. means responsibility   SHAW 271:19
   or the holy name of l.   GAND 121:10
   Served human l.   YEATS 323:14
   survival and the success of l.   KENN 163:8
   true that l. is precious   LENIN 184:14
   voices of l. be mute   CUMM 87:2
library: A l. is thought in cold storage SAM 259:4
   join the l.   AYCK 21:8
   l. of any literary man   BUTL 60:7
   Like one of his l. books   AYCK 21:11
   lumber room of his l.   DOYLE 94:7
   spend less time in the l.   STR 288:9
libre: *Je suis condemné à être l.*   SART 261:9
libres: *naissent l. et égaux en*   ANON 11:16
licence: course liberty is not l.   SCAN 264:2
   your own l. to print money   THOM 297:1
Licht: *ein L. anzünden in der*   JUNG 159:15
lick: says If you can't l. 'em   REYN 246:3
licorice: In the l. fields at Pontefract BETJ 42:6
lid: l. of the sardine tin   BENN 37:10

lie: And I l. down alone   HOUS 145:10
   And the l. of Authority   AUDEN 17:12
   Art is a l. that makes   PIC 234:8
   between a cat and a l.   TWAIN 301:15
   fall victim to a big l.   HITL 141:11
   Impossible to come, l. follows   PROU 241:3
   It is possible to l.   ADLER 3:1
   l. down where all ladders   YEATS 320:3
   L. follows by post   BER 40:2
   l. has become not just   SOLZ 280:4
   l. is an abomination unto   STEV 286:10
   l. than a truth misunderstood   JAMES 154:1
   l. with your legs ungainly   SASS 263:3
   My love and I would l.   HOUS 146:3
   not l. easy at Winchelsea   BENÉT 36:17
   old L.   OWEN 227:14
   writes is a l., including   MCC 193:12
Liebe: *Nur L. kann sie erfassen*   RILKE 247:8
   Und diese menschlichere L.   RILKE 247:9
   Wo die L. herrscht   JUNG 160:1
lied: because our fathers l.   KIPL 175:10
   But it l.   BELL 35:8
lies: combination of reality and l.   COCT 78:6
   From l. of tongue and pen   CHES 70:7
   great l. about his wooden   FLEC 112:4
   He l. below, correct   PARK 231:4
   Here l. a most beautiful lady   DE L 90:13
   It produces l. like sand   PONS 236:3
   l. about the Democrats   STEV 285:16
   L. are the mortar   WELLS 308:9
   l. it lives   FOSD 116:4
   L. on my ledge and dulls   MEYN 207:11
   l. sound truthful and murder   ORW 226:3
   Matilda told such Dreadful L.   BELL 33:3
   only l. are invented   BRAQ 52:14
   Plain l. are dangerous   SAY 263:10
   white l. to ice a wedding   ASQ 15:7
   Who l. beneath your spell   HOPE 144:4
   will tell l. as usual   SHAW 268:18
life: about l. beyond the grave   KHR 165:11
   actor's l. for me   WASH 305:6
   A little l. with dried tubers   ELIOT 104:10
   all human l. is there   JAMES 152:18
   all l. is 6 to 5 against   RUNY 254:10
   And then there's l.   ANOU 12:12
   And the Pride of L.   HARDY 134:4
   A short l. and a gay one   WIMP 315:1
   attempt to represent l.   JAMES 153:2
   believe in l.   DUB 96:2
   believe in the l. to come   BECK 28:15
   believe that since my l. began   COW 84:8
   broader and fuller l.   DUB 96:2
   business of l. is to enjoy it   BUTL 60:10
   change we think we see in l.   FROST 119:2
   children about coping with l.   SPARK 281:4
   Crushing out l.   HOPE 144:4
   doctrine of the strenuous l.   ROOS 251:10
   don't talk to me about L.   ADAMS 1:12

life (cont.):

drawn the breath of l.	YEATS 322:8
fear love is to fear l.	RUSS 255:10
football is a matter of l.	SHAN 267:8
For each one l. to give	KIPL 170:15
For l. is joy, and mind	MAS 203:9
gave my l. for freedom	EWER 107:2
good evidence of l. after	SOPER 281:1
great l. if you don't weaken	BUCH 57:5
his friends for his l.	THOR 297:2
I feel that l.	ALLEN 5:3
In balance with this l.	YEATS 322:11
I really don't know l. at all	MITC 211:4
isn't l. a terrible thing	THOM 293:16
It's not the men in my l.	WEST 309:7
it's the l. in my men	WEST 309:7
Lead me from death to l.	KUMAR 177:4
L. begins at forty	PITK 235:7
L. exists in the universe	JEANS 154:6
L., friends, is boring	BERR 41:12
l. goes not backward	GIBR 124:3
l. had been but a preparation	CHUR 76:5
L. has taught us that love	SAIN 257:3
l. in the village began	LEE 183:16
L. is a foreign language	MORL 213:10
L. is a gamble at terrible	STOP 287:10
L. is a glorious cycle	PARK 230:13
L. is a great surprise	NAB 217:2
L. is a horizontal fall	COCT 78:7
L. is a maze in which we	CONN 80:21
L. is an offensive	WHIT 310:5
L. is a sexually transmitted	ANON 9:15
L. is Colour and Warmth	GREN 129:5
L. is doubt	UNAM 302:9
L. is first boredom, then fear	LARK 179:15
L. is for each man a solitary	O'NEI 223:8
l. is in the past and future	O'NEI 223:14
L. is just a bowl of cherries	BROWN 56:13
L. is just one damned thing	HUBB 147:3
L. is like a sewer	LEHR 184:3
L. is like playing a violin	BUTL 59:3
L. is made up of sobs	HENRY 138:15
l. is mainly a process	BERNE 41:6
L. is not having been told	NASH 217:15
L. is not meant to be easy	SHAW 268:5
L. is one long process	BUTL 59:13
L. is perhaps most wisely	O'NEI 223:11
L. is something to do when	LEB 183:9
l. is spent in a perpetual	JOAD 155:15
L. is the art of drawing	BUTL 59:14
L. is the other way round	LODGE 190:5
L. is too short to stuff	CONR 82:3
L. is very nice, but it	ANOU 12:14
l. is washed	BARZ 27:11
l. is where things aren't	BARN 25:8
L. levels all men	SHAW 272:11
l. of every man is a diary	BARR 25:14
L. says	BARN 25:8
L.'s better with the Conservatives	ANON 9:16

life (cont.):

l. seems to have no plots	COMP 80:4
L.'s little ironies	HARDY 133:10
l. talking at street corners	VANZ 303:7
L., the Universe and Everything	ADAMS 1:14
L., to be sure, is nothing	HOUS 145:11
l. was coming to consist	AMIS 6:1
L. we have lost in living	ELIOT 104:1
l. will be sour grapes	ASHF 14:11
L. would ring the bells	GINS 124:12
L., you know, is rather	BENN 37:10
long as you have your l.	JAMES 152:8
measured out my l. with coffee	ELIOT 103:8
midst of l. we are in debt	MUMF 215:11
more a way of l.	ANON 10:7
much too far out all my l.	SMITH 278:18
Music is l., and like it	NIEL 219:11
my experience of l. has	BEER 31:13
nature, contrary to l.	HUXL 148:12
nearest thing to death in l.	ANON 10:1
not lead a pleasant l.	RAL 242:12
On l., on death.	YEATS 319:13
only sanction of l.	SANT 260:10
Our end is L. Put out to sea	MACN 198:1
outer l. of telegrams	FORS 115:2
part of l.'s rich pageant	MARS 202:5
People say that l.	SMITH 278:13
Perfection of the l.	YEATS 323:12
priceless gift of l.	ROS 252:13
problematical world and sells us l.	FRY 119:15
queer thing L.	WOD 316:8
Reverence for L.	SCHW 264:16
Sex is the gateway to l.	HARR 135:7
sons and daughters of L.'s	GIBR 124:3
struggle of l.	CONN 80:12
taking l. by the throat	FROST 119:6
terror to l. and makes death	TREE 298:8
That was how his l. happened	KAV 162:2
The l. and loves of a she-devil	WELD 307:11
there a l. before death	HEAN 136:12
'Tisn't l. that matters	WALP 305:1
University of L.	BOTT 50:7
Was my l. also	OWEN 228:6
What is this l. if	DAV 89:2
which makes l. worth living	ELIOT 102:11
which would support l.	HALD 131:2
Whose l. is it anyway	CLARK 76:16
you all that my whole l.	ELIZ 105:12
your money or your l.	BUTL 59:9
life-blood: l. of real civilization	TREV 298:12
life-insurance: I detest l. agents	LEAC 182:13
life-jacket: brassière is the French for l.	BARN 25:7
life-lie: l. away from the average	IBSEN 150:7
life-sentence: l. in the dungeon of self	CONN 81:4
l. which fate carries	LAWR 182:5
lifetime: But a l. of happiness	SHAW 270:12
lit again in our l.	GREY 129:7
light: against the dying of the l.	THOM 292:11
C'mon, baby, l. my fire	MORR 213:16

light (*cont.*):

Colour and Warmth and L.	GREN 129:5
eldritch l. of sundown	DAY-L 89:4
faces in the violet l.	ELIOT 105:10
I l. my lamp in the evening	BELL 34:19
I travel l.; as light	FRY 119:13
kindle a l. in the darkness	JUNG 159:15
l. and the half light	YEATS 323:1
l. at the end of the tunnel	DICK 92:3
l. at the end of the tunnel	LOW 191:10
l. between two eternities	NAB 217:3
L. breaks where no sun shines	THOM 293:5
l. gleams an instant	BECK 29:13
l. has gone out of our	NEHRU 218:17
l. of my life, fire	NAB 217:1
me a l. that I may tread	HASK 136:1
mend the Electric L.	BELL 34:1
Of L. and Mrs Humphry Ward	CHES 70:15
sweetness and l. failed	FORS 114:9
The dark is l. enough	FRY 119:12
The l. of evening, Lissadell	YEATS 323:2
The L. of Lights	YEATS 321:9
turning your face to the l.	SASS 262:9
waited for the l.	ROB 248:9
was far faster than l.	BULL 57:11
while the l. fails	ELIOT 102:6
lighter: darker to the l. races	DUB 96:3
lightfoot: And many a l. lad	HOUS 146:14
The l. boys are laid	HOUS 146:14
light-house: Keeping a l. with his eyes	CAMP 62:5
lightly: they take themselves l.	CHES 70:4
lightning: Have known the l.'s hour	DAY-L 89:6
It's to keep the l. out	ISH 151:14
lights: Turn up the l.; I don't	HENRY 139:3
lignes: *dans les l. du plafond*	ÉLUA 106:6
like: can do just what you l.	SHAW 269:10
Duke I couldn't l.	SHAW- 274:14
forced to l. what you get	SHAW 272:15
How shall we conquer? L. a wind	FLEC 112:6
I know what I l.	BEER 31:15
I know what I l.	JAMES 153:7
I l. Ike	SPAL 281:3
I l. the hunting of the hare	BLUNT 48:3
Just l. that!	COOP 83:3
L. a complete unknown	DYLAN 97:7
l. a little bit of butter	MILNE 210:5
L. a rolling stone	DYLAN 97:7
l. it [the 4th symphony]	VAUG 303:10
l. potato and I like po-tah-	GERS 123:9
l. the girl that married	DILL 92:6
l. to be beside the seaside	GLOV 125:5
l. to do are either illegal	WOOL 317:16
l. to get away from earth	FROST 118:9
l. who drinks as much	THOM 293:7
man that I didn't l.	ROG 249:13
people you l. best	UST 302:14
that what we l. is not	BELL 32:10
those whom I l. or admire	AUDEN 18:16
was l. to give offence	FROST 118:15

like (*cont.*):

what it is l. to be a child	JARR 154:2
whether I l. or dislike them	FORS 115:5
You're going to l. this	DAN 88:5
liked: I wish I l. the way it walks	RAL 242:13
I would have l.	PERÓN 233:5
People wish to be l.	RUSS 255:5
likely: Walk! Not bloody l.	SHAW 273:18
likes: does know what she l.	RATT 243:5
Somebody up there l. me	LEHM 184:1
lilac: forget the l. and the roses	ARAG 13:2
Just now the l. is in bloom	BROO 55:7
lilacs: L. out of the dead land, mixing	
	ELIOT 104:10
lilac-time: Go down to Kew in l.	NOYES 221:8
lilas: *jamais les l. ni les roses*	ARAG 13:2
lilies: beauty lives though l.	FLEC 111:7
l. of ambition	DOUG 93:6
lilting: l. house and happy	THOM 293:1
lily: It trembles to a l.	DOBS 92:15
morning glows the l.	FLEC 111:11
limb: clothes on a hickory l.	DE L 91:8
limbs: And if these poor l. die	BROO 54:11
l. that fester are not	ABSE 1:2
Yours are the l., my sweeting	NASH 217:12
limelight: politicians take in their l.	BELL 33:11
They do not sit in the l.	BEAV 28:9
limestone: On l. quarried near the spot	
	YEATS 319:13
limit: l. to our realization	ROOS 251:3
limitation: l. of governmental power	WILS 314:9
limitations: difference between accidental l.	
	AUDEN 18:7
must know the l. of force	TROT 299:5
limited: nervous and terse, but l.	DOYLE 95:13
limits: l. of my language mean	WITT 315:7
limm: wood ere Thou canst l.	THOM 295:12
limousine: l. and a ticket	MACN 197:11
One perfect l., do you suppose	PARK 230:15
Limpopo: greasy L. River, all set	KIPL 171:15
Lincoln: I am a Ford, not a L.	FORD 113:11
L. was shovelled	SAND 259:12
line: An active l. on a walk	KLEE 176:1
hammered into l.	KIPL 174:1
l. will take us hours maybe	YEATS 319:7
season-ticket on the l.	AMERY 5:11
lineage: We Poets of the proud old l.	FLEC 111:7
lineaments: l. of a plummet-measured	
	YEATS 320:1
liner: The L. she's a lady	KIPL 174:6
lines: Edit and annotate the l.	YEATS 322:4
l. of the ceiling	ÉLUA 106:6
scribbled l. like fallen	HOPE 144:2
lingerie: Brevity is the soul of l.	PARK 231:15
lingering: A l. dissolution	BECK 28:13
lingers: melody l.	BERL 40:9
linnet: behind with my old cock l.	COLL 79:5
lion: l. and the calf shall lie	ALLEN 4:9
l. the right place to use	CHUR 76:10

lion (*cont.*):
  that had the l.'s heart   CHUR 76:10
lions: l. to the roaring slaughter   CUMM 87:2
  To feed ruddy L.? Not me   EDGAR 98:4
lipless: Leaned backward with a l. grin
                   ELIOT 103:1
lippity-lippity: wander about, going l. POTT 237:9
lips: already born before my l.   MAND 200:2
  l. are not yet unsealed   BALD 23:6
  l. upon a plummet-measured YEATS 319:14
  on l. of living men   BUTL 58:12
  Red l. are not so red   OWEN 228:3
lipstick: cigarette that bears a l.'s MARV 202:8
  you've got on too much l.   NASH 218:13
liqueurs: chocolate l. in one go CAP 63:11
liquid: And let their l. siftings fall ELIOT 102:13
  less l. than their shadows TESS 291:6
  l. which rots braces   MORT 214:7
  Thames is l. history   BURNS 58:5
liquidation: preside over the l. CHUR 73:6
liquor: bowl with atrabilious l. HUXL 149:1
  But l.   NASH 218:8
  I don't drink l. I don't   LEV 186:12
  lads for the l.   HOUS 146:5
  L. is one way out an'   WILL 312:6
  Livelier l. than the Muse HOUS 146:15
  We drank our l. straight AUDEN 18:17
listen: acts it out, I hardly l. SAL 258:13
  l. to the birds and winds GIBS 124:6
  l. when his mate sings WICK 311:2
  only l. when I am unhappy SMITH 279:2
  Stop-look-and-l.   ANON 11:4
  when you wish him to l. BIER 46:12
listener: same applies to the l. BEEC 29:23
listening: good at l. to their elders BALD 22:13
  L. to a speech by Chamberlain BEVAN 44:10
  talking about him ain't l. GLASS 125:4
listless: on his l. form and face HARDY 133:14
lit: l. again in our lifetime GREY 129:7
  stared; the sky was l. HODG 141:14
  whole Fleet's l. up   WOOD 317:1
literalists: l. of the imagination MOORE 213:3
literary: beloved by l. pundits CONN 80:11
  Like an unsuccessful l. man BELL 33:16
  L. intellectuals at one SNOW 279:5
  smallest library of any l. BUTL 60:7
  The l. mornings with its hoot AUDEN 19:12
literate: If, with the l., I am PARK 231:2
literature: All modern American l. HEM 138:5
  All the rest is l.   VALÉ 303:1
  L. flourishes best when INGE 151:9
  L. is a luxury   CHES 68:12
  L. is mostly about having LODGE 190:5
  L. is news that STAYS news POUND 237:18
  L. is not an abstract science QUIL 242:3
  l. is simply language charged POUND 238:4
  L. is strewn with the wreckage WOOLF 317:10
  L. is the art of writing CONN 80:6
  L. is the orchestration WILD 311:8

literature (*cont.*):
  l. is to be delighted   CECIL 65:9
  L.'s always a good card BENN 39:1
  possible to gain a chair of l. ALGR 3:16
  produce a little l. JAMES 152:16
  professors like their l. clear LEWIS 187:10
  remarks are not l.   STEIN 284:2
  The tip's a good one, as for l. POUND 238:10
littérature: *Tout le reste est l.* VALÉ 303:1
little: For politics and l. else CAMP 62:6
  From having too l. to do KIPL 171:11
  Great hatred, l. room YEATS 324:1
  Life's l. ironies HARDY 133:10
  L. boxes on the hillside REYN 246:2
  L. Boy kneels at the foot MILNE 210:6
  L. man, you've had a busy day SIGL 275:3
  L. minds are interested HUBB 147:5
  l. of what you fancy does LEIGH 184:9
  L. one! Oh, little one STEP 285:4
  l. things are infinitely DOYLE 94:4
  Pooh always liked a l. MILNE 210:9
  shall we turn to l. things GIBS 124:6
  So l. done, so much to do RHOD 246:6
  Thank heaven for l. girls LERN 186:5
  These l. grey cells CHR 72:2
  these l. local difficulties MACM 197:5
littleness: always ruined by the l. BREC 53:6
  For the long l. of life CORN 83:11
live: As you l., believe   DUB 96:2
  enable its citizens to l. WEIL 307:5
  Flesh perishes, I l. HARDY 133:13
  he isn't fit to l.   KING 166:8
  I do not wish to l. MILL 208:7
  If you don't l. it PARK 230:1
  L. all you can JAMES 152:8
  L. and let die FLEM 112:10
  l. for a time close BUCH 57:4
  l. for others and not SHAW 273:19
  l. in a yellow submarine LENN 185:17
  L. in fragments no longer FORS 115:3
  l. in houses just as big SMITH 278:5
  l. our lives CART 64:4
  l. this long [100 years] BLAKE 47:9
  l. together as brothers KING 167:6
  l. under the shadow SPEN 281:14
  l. with a good conscience SMITH 278:4
  Long L. Free Quebec DE G 90:2
  must l. it to the full SPARK 281:7
  one's principles than to l. ADLER 2:21
  rich that you have to l. SMITH 278:9
  Sacco's name will l. VANZ 303:8
  than to l. on your knees IBAR 149:17
  To l. is like to love BUTL 60:3
  We l., as we dream — alone CONR 81:10
  which will l. in infamy ROOS 251:1
  You might as well l. PARK 230:14
lived: Had we l., I should have SCOTT 265:10
  I've l. a life that's full ANKA 6:11
  Never to have l. is best YEATS 322:8

livelier: L. liquor than the Muse **HOUS 146:15**
Liverpool: The folk that live in L. **CHES 68:18**
livery: The ill-bred son of a l. **YEATS 322:10**
lives: Careless talk costs l. **ANON 7:13**
  cat has only nine l. **TWAIN 301:15**
  Led merry, merry l. **NAYL 218:16**
  second acts in American l. **FITZ 110:17**
  The taking of our l. **VANZ 303:7**
  we live our l., for ever **RILKE 247:10**
livin': Summer time an' the l. is easy **HEYW 140:7**
living: language of the l. **ELIOT 102:1**
  Life we have lost in l. **ELIOT 104:1**
  L. and partly living **ELIOT 102:8**
  L. for today **LENN 185:2**
  l. in central London **GOWR 127:3**
  L. is abnormal **ION 151:10**
  man to find a way of l. **BALD 22:9**
  must hate to work for a l. **ROWL 254:2**
  reason for l. **SHAW 273:4**
  West it is still a l. lion **SOLZ 280:3**
  world does not owe us a l. **PHIL 233:15**
llama: L. is a woolly sort **BELL 33:16**
Lloyd George: L. arrived at his proper **BENN 38:12**
  [L.] did not seem to care **BEAV 28:8**
  L. knows my father **ANON 9:17**
  Minister [L.] has resigned **ANON 8:10**
load: 'l.' with manly pride **BURT 58:7**
loan: Norman that I have him on l. **AYCK 21:11**
loath: hands were l. and cold **OWEN 228:8**
loathe: l. entering upon explanations **BARR 25:16**
loathing: Fear and l. in Las Vegas **THOM 296:14**
lobby: into the l. against us **BALD 23:6**
local: A l. thing called Christianity **HARDY 133:3**
  little l. difficulties **MACM 197:5**
  l., but prized elsewhere **AUDEN 18:5**
lock: broken the l. and splintered **AUDEN 19:8**
  happy, why l. him **SHAW 271:11**
locked: L. and frozen in each eye **AUDEN 17:6**
locks: until his l. grew grey **CARB 63:14**
locusts: And famine grew, and l. came
    THOM 293:11
logic: any sense attacking l. **CHES 69:18**
  It is the l. of our times **DAY-L 89:8**
  L. must take care of itself **WITT 315:6**
loin: jusqu'où on peut aller trop l. **COCT 78:3**
loins: fire of my l. **NAB 217:1**
lois: majestueuse égalité des l. **FRAN 116:6**
Lolita: L., light of my life **NAB 217:1**
Loman: L. never made a lot **MILL 208:8**
London: A crowd flowed over L. Bridge
    ELIOT 104:14
  A foggy day in L. Town **GERS 123:6**
  As he gazed at the L. skies **BETJ 41:17**
  'Cause in sleepy L. town **JAGG 152:5**
  City of L. remains **CHAM 65:12**
  it isn't far from L. **NOYES 221:8**
  it travels south to L. **BEAV 28:6**
  living in central L. **GOWR 127:3**

London (cont.):
  L. and realize **HICKS 140:8**
  L. Pride has been handed **COW 84:11**
  L. spread out in the sun **LARK 179:11**
  L., that great cesspool **DOYLE 95:8**
  L. to Paris in 25 hours **DAV 88:12**
  L. with one voice would **CHUR 72:12**
  many MPs never see the L. **LIV 189:4**
  me on the train for L. **MILLS 209:9**
  One road leads to L. **MAS 203:6**
  roar of L.'s traffic **ANON 10:9**
  That I love L. **GREGG 129:2**
  that the 'L. Effect' **HEW 140:5**
  This—is L. **MURR 216:8**
  vilest alleys in L. **DOYLE 94:8**
  Yankee Doodle came to L. **COHAN 78:13**
Londoner: Maybe it's because I'm a L.
    GREGG 129:2
lone: walking by his wild l. **KIPL 172:5**
loneliness: l. of the long-distance **SILL 275:4**
lonely: A l. impulse of delight **YEATS 322:11**
  l. sea **MAS 203:14**
  mine as mirrors are l. **AUDEN 19:1**
  people for fear I may be l. **JOAD 155:15**
  The heart is a l. hunter **MCC 194:8**
lonesomeness: And starlight lit my l.
    HARDY 134:6
long: And l. 'tis like **HOUS 145:6**
  because time is l. **DUB 96:2**
  But it's a l., long while **AND 6:4**
  For the l. littleness of life **CORN 83:11**
  How l., I wondered **GERS 123:6**
  It's a l. way to Tipperary **JUDGE 159:13**
  Life is one l. process **BUTL 59:13**
  l. and the short **HUGH 147:11**
  L. books, when read **FORS 114:10**
  l. for the Person from **SMITH 278:22**
  l. run we are all dead **KEYN 165:7**
  l. time I used to go **PROU 240:7**
  Night of the L. Knives **HITL 141:6**
  The l. hot summer **RAV 243:10**
  The l. summer **FAUL 107:9**
  they keep on saying it l. **BENN 38:18**
  Too l. a sacrifice **YEATS 320:5**
  too l. without a war here **BREC 53:4**
  trouble with Senator L. **ICKES 150:8**
  was gonna live this l. **BLAKE 47:9**
  week is a l. time in politics **WILS 313:8**
longed: that I have l. for death **PROU 240:10**
longer: what takes a little l. **NANS 217:8**
longest: laughs l. who laughs last **MAS 204:4**
  l. running farce **SMITH 276:17**
  l. suicide note in history **KAUF 161:10**
longevity: L. has its place **KING 166:11**
Longfellow: have to be shown L.'s grave
    MOORE 213:4
long-haired: But I consort with l. things
    KIPL 168:4
longing: Cross as the focus of l. **MUGG 215:7**

longing (*cont.*):
l. for love, the search RUSS 254:13
longitude: A l. with no platitude FRY 119:16
long-legged: Like a l. fly upon the stream
YEATS 320:2
long-nosed: The l., sensitive-footed LAWR 180:7
longtemps: L., *je me suis couché* PROU 240:7
look: And they all l. just the same REYN 246:2
full l. at the worst HARDY 134:3
I can sit and l. at it JER 155:11
l. after our people SCOTT 265:8
L. at it, it's all AYCK 21:10
l. at things in bloom HOUS 145:13
L. for me by moonlight NOYES 221:1
L. for me in the nurseries THOM 295:1
l. forward to the trip STIN 286:12
l. of the last gentleman LEV 186:15
L., stranger, at this island AUDEN 19:6
l. the East End THE Q 106:1
L. thy last on all things DE L 90:15
L.! Up in the sky ANON 7:23
Stop-l.-and-listen ANON 11:4
They l. on and help LAWR 181:2
you l. to other people UNAM 302:10
looked: hair and l. very sneery ASHF 14:10
l. and three whin bushes KAV 161:13
l. at in this merciless WILL 312:9
l. at life from both sides MITC 211:4
l. over than overlooked WEST 308:16
looking: at dawn l. for an angry GINS 125:1
at each other but in l. SAINT 257:3
Here's l. at you, kid EPST 106:11
I'm l. over a four leaf clover DIXON 92:11
Leave them while you're l. LOOS 190:15
l. and never kissed her THOM 293:15
l. beyond the next fortnight CHAM 65:11
l. for the sacred Emperor BRAM 52:10
l. forward to the past OSB 226:13
that someone may be l. MENC 206:16
with plenty of l. glasses ASHF 14:7
lookingglass: The cracked l. of a servant
JOYCE 158:16
looking-glasses: l. possessing the magic
WOOLF 317:9
looks: l. at it when it has been SHAW 271:12
she needs good l. TUCK 300:2
looney: L. Tunes and squalid criminals
REAG 244:8
looney-bin: sort of janitor to the l. WOD 316:1
loony: The 'l. Labour left' HEW 140:5
loophole: l. through BRON 54:5
loopholes: neat, through l. TESS 291:6
loose: For the man who should l. LOW 191:7
loosed: anarchy is l. upon the world YEATS 320:7
loo-vely: He's l., Mrs Hoskin RAY 243:12
lord: Am an attendant l. ELIOT 103:11
am the L. of the Dance CART 64:7
Deliver us, good L. CHES 70:7
Fresh from the L. FARJ 107:6

lord (*cont.*):
L. of the flies GOLD 126:2
L., put beneath Thy special BETJ 44:5
L. survives the rainbow LOW 192:3
L., won't you buy me JOPL 157:6
talk it over with Our L. JOHN 155:18
[the L. Privy Seal] BAIL 22:4
The sapient sutlers of the L. ELIOT 102:15
lords: chance with one of the l. LAWR 180:10
L. is the British Outer BENN 37:7
[The House of L.] LLOY 189:8
lordship: l. may compel us BARR 25:11
lordships: When their l. asked Bacon BENT 39:6
lose: disastrous as to l. CHR 72:1
ending a war is to l. ORW 225:11
l. me temper till it would O'CAS 222:14
l. the war in an afternoon CHUR 76:14
l. you but we think you RUB 254:6
l. your temper PANK 229:5
nothing to l. but our aitches ORW 225:19
losers: winners, but all are l. CHAM 66:3
losing: l. theirs and blaming it KIPL 173:7
l. your legs SASS 262:9
l. your moral sense STEIN 284:8
trick lies in *l.* wars HELL 137:7
loss: And the profit and l. ELIOT 105:8
breathe a word about your l. KIPL 173:8
lost: And a thousand l. golf balls ELIOT 104:2
are paradises we have l. PROU 241:4
better to have loved and l. BUTL 60:14
Britain has l. an empire ACH 1:8
But France has not l. DE G 90:3
He never l. his cap, or tore BELL 33:10
In search of l. time PROU 240:6
In the l. boyhood of Judas AE 3:3
listens to Reason is l. SHAW 272:9
l. daddy I arsked tenderly LARD 178:9
L. Generation and the subsequent KER 164:6
lost than never to have l. BUTL 60:14
l. the last of England BELL 34:18
l. the only Playboy SYNGE 289:11
L. the van and don't know COLL 79:5
l. upon the roundabouts CHAL 65:10
make wherever we're l. FRY 119:20
Museum had l. its charm GERS 123:6
That is the land of l. content HOUS 146:11
what is l. in translation FROST 119:5
won or l. RICE 246:10
You are all a l. generation STEIN 284:14
lot: going to like this . . . not a l. DAN 88:5
I'm *fast*. I'm a bad l. THOM 294:1
Lou: lady that's known as L. SERV 267:1
loud: It's too l., man FREB 116:9
louder: again and play it rather l. LAMB 177:14
Louie: 'Drop the gun, L.' BOGA 48:9
loungers: l. and idlers of the Empire DOYLE 95:8
lousy: *House Beautiful* is play l. PARK 231:7
L. but loyal ANON 9:18
my l. childhood was like SAL 258:10

love: absolutely l. the noise it makes   BEEC 30:1
accept you and l.   CAMP 61:9
alike are the groans of l.   LOWRY 192:5
All you need is l.   LENN 185:5
A man falls in l. through   WYATT 318:1
among those whom I l.   AUDEN 18:16
And l. is not secure   CHES 68:11
And l. will steer the stars   RADO 242:8
And this more human l.   RILKE 247:9
caution in l. is perhaps   RUSS 255:6
Could l. you for yourself alone   YEATS 323:13
fear l. is to fear life   RUSS 255:10
field by the river my l.   YEATS 321:13
figure is the same as for l.   FROST 117:13
floral air and the l.   FLEC 112:1
From us fled L.   YEATS 318:8
give you anything but l.   FIEL 108:10
Green how I l. you green   LORCA 191:1
Hearts wound up with l.   SPEN 282:2
Heigho, if l. were all   COW 84:8
Hell, madam, is to l. no more   BERN 41:4
how to make l. in a canoe   BERT 41:15
I'd l. to get you   LOES 190:7
I'd l. to remain in bed   BERL 40:7
I'd l. to turn you   LENN 185:8
I have made l. to 10,000   SIM 275:6
I'll l. you, dear, I'll   AUDEN 16:12
I l. a lassie, a bonnie   LAUD 180:1
I l. *people.* Lovers   CAMP 62:3
I l. the girl I'm near   HARB 132:14
I l. you, Nellie Dean   ARMS 13:7
I'm tired of L.: I'm still   BELL 34:15
Is hid in the heart of l.   YEATS 318:9
It's sex with someone I l.   ALLEN 5:2
I wish I were in l. again   HART 135:10
knew His l. Who followèd   THOM 295:4
know very well that l.   ANOU 12:13
Land that I l.   BERL 40:6
laughter and the l. of friends   BELL 35:4
Lead me from hate to l.   KUMAR 177:4
Let's do it, let's fall in l.   PORT 236:15
let us make l. deathless   TREN 298:11
Life has taught us that l.   SAIN 257:3
little emptiness of l.   BROO 54:10
live is like to l.   BUTL 60:3
longing for l.   RUSS 254:13
L. and I had the wit   MARK 201:4
L. and marriage, love   CAHN 60:19
l. and toil in the years   KIPL 173:1
l. but not your thoughts   GIBR 124:3
L., curiosity, freckles   PARK 230:12
L. has pitched his mansion   YEATS 323:8
l. hath no man than this   THOR 297:2
l. is a thing that can   PARK 230:13
L. is like the measles   JER 155:3
L. is so simple   PRÉV 239:1
L. is the delusion   MENC 206:12
L. is woman's moon and sun   PARK 230:17

love (*cont.*):
L. like youth is wasted   CAHN 61:1
L. means not ever having   SEGAL 266:2
l. myself is very different   AUDEN 18:13
l. of the drudgery   SMITH 278:11
l. only means one thing   BENN 38:9
L. set you going like   PLATH 235:9
L. shall come at your command   GRAV 128:9
l. sincerer than the love   SHAW 270:18
l. that asks no question   SPR 282:13
L. to all men 'neath   KIPL 173:2
l. to sit and bay   MCL 196:6
l. will be seen   FORS 115:3
L. wist to pursue   THOM 295:5
l. with himself at first   POW 239:1
l. without the rhetoric   STOP 287:5
l. would follow me still   KIPL 172:7
Make l. not war   ANON 9:21
My l. and I would lie   HOUS 146:3
never l. a stranger   BENS 39:5
Now that l. is perished   MILL 208:5
Oh, when I was in l. with you   HOUS 146:2
Only l. can apprehend   RILKE 247:8
Only L. the Beloved Republic   FORS 115:13
pale from the imagined l.   YEATS 319:14
predominates, l. is lacking   JUNG 160:1
right place for l.   FROST 118:9
salley gardens my l.   YEATS 321:13
save the Party we l.   GAIT 120:16
school can l. like a fool   NASH 218:3
She bid me take l. easy   YEATS 321:13
Such a morning it is when l.   LEE 183:17
support of the woman I l.   EDW 98:11
than to l. one's neighbour   HOFF 142:6
that doesn't l. a wall   FROST 118:13
that the greatest l.   PROU 240:10
The man you l. to hate   ANON 9:23
There is l. of course   ANOU 12:12
They l. the Good   BROO 55:11
Thine own eternal l.   O'CAS 222:10
thing in the world is l.   BREN 53:9
time you hear your l. song   CAHN 61:1
too late to fall in l.   WILS 314:2
Try thinking of l.   FRY 119:21
Use him as though you l. him   BLUN 47:12
violence masquerading as l.   LAING 177:9
We must l. one another or die   AUDEN 17:12
What will survive of us is l.   LARK 179:16
When l. congeals   HART 135:10
Where l. rules, there   JUNG 160:1
While you l. your lover, let   HART 135:12
Whose l. is given over-well   PARK 230:18
wilder shores of l.   BLAN 47:10
words, 'God si L.'   FORS 115:9
Work is l. made visible   GIBR 124:4
You made me l. you   MCC 193:10
loved: And l. in misery   YEATS 323:6
better to have l. and lost   BUTL 60:14
I l. you, so I drew these   LAWR 182:7

loved (*cont.*):
  it can be l.   SANT 260:17
  I wish I l. the Human Race   RAL 242:13
  l. your moments of glad   YEATS 318:8
love-knot: l. into her long black   NOYES 221:10
loveliest: L. of trees, the cherry now   HOUS 145:13
  l. things of beauty God   MAS 203:5
  world the l. and the best   BELL 34:12
loveliness: A woman of so shining l.   YEATS 322:2
  I am weak from your l.   BETJ 43:9
  That fashioned forth its l.   HARDY 134:9
lovely: And down in l. muck I've lain

    HOUS 146:16
  And left thee all her l. hues   DAV 88:16
  As you are woman, so be l.   GRAV 128:6
  It gives a l. light   MILL 207:17
  It was the l. moon—she lifted   FREE 116:14
  Look thy last on all things l.   DE L 90:15
  L. and willing every afternoon   AUDEN 19:12
  l. day I thought it was   MAUG 205:12
  l. woman stoops to folly   ELIOT 105:7
  Oh what a l. war   LITT 189:2
  The woods are l.   FROST 118:11
lover: has done the l. mortal hurt   DOUG 93:8
  l. and killer are mingled   DOUG 93:8
  l.'s quarrel with the world   FROST 119:10
  l. without indiscretion   HARDY 133:5
  Scratch a l., and find a foe   PARK 231:5
  what is left of a l.   ROWL 253:14
  woman looking for a new l.   CONN 80:19
loverly: Oh, wouldn't it be l.   LERN 186:6
lovers: Almighty l. in the Spring   CHES 68:11
  And timid l.' declarations   AUDEN 19:16
  Frankie and Albert were l.   ANON 8:1
  l. be lost love shall not   THOM 293:12
  l. find their peace   FLEC 111:8
  people. L. of 'Humanity'   CAMP 62:3
loves: And our l., must I remember   APOL 12:15
  He that l. but half of Earth   QUIL 242:6
  She l. you, yeh, yeh, yeh   LENN 185:12
  The life and l. of a she-devil   WELD 307:11
  white woman whom nobody l.   CORN 83:12
  Who l. ya, baby   SAV 263:7
love-story: l. or an elopement   DOYLE 95:2
lovin': I ain't had no l.   NORW 221:6
loving: freer, and more l.   BALD 22:10
low: Had me l. and had me down   GERS 123:6
  Seem to murmur sweet and l.   ARMS 13:7
  with l. sounds by the shore   YEATS 318:10
lowbrow: was the first militant l.   BERL 41:1
Lowells: Where the L. talk to the Cabots

    BOSS 50:3
lower: capitalism of the l. classes   SPEN 282:4
  never knew that the l. classes   CURZ 88:4
  they are l. than vermin   BEVAN 45:8
loyal: Lousy but l.   ANON 9:18
loyalty: I want l. I want him   JOHN 156:2
  L. is the Tory's secret weapon   KILM 166:5
  l. we all feel to unhappiness   GREE 128:14

luck: always just my l. to get   PARK 230:15
  'Cause with a bit of l.   AYRES 21:14
  I had the l. to be called   CHUR 76:10
  It's awf'lly bad l. on Diana   BETJ 42:10
  l. and sends his son   STEAD 283:12
  l. was his light-o'-love   SERV 267:1
luckiest: Geniuses are the l. of mortals

    AUDEN 19:11
Ludlow: L. come in for the fair   HOUS 146:5
  Oh I have been to L. fair   HOUS 146:16
Lüge: *L. leichter zum Opfer als*   HITL 141:11
Lügen: *Gibt's L. wie Sand*   PONS 236:3
lullaby: Once in a l.   HARB 132:13
lumber: l. room of his library   DOYLE 94:7
lumberjack: I'm a l.   CHAP 67:6
lump: L. the whole thing   TWAIN 301:4
lumps: Go down like l. of lead   HODG 142:1
  There are l. in it   STEP 285:3
lunacy: fit of complete l.   BORN 50:2
lunatic: l. asylums which are known

    WOOLF 317:4
  l. fringe in all reform   ROOS 252:1
  themselves are all in l. asylums   CHES 69:17
lunatics: lunatic asylum run by l.   LLOY 190:3
  l. have taken charge   ROWL 254:3
lunch: she's unable to l. today   PORT 236:16
  such thing as a free l.   HEIN 137:2
  took the cork out of my l.   FIEL 109:1
luncheon: do not take soup at l.   CURZ 88:3
  read a novel before l.   WAUGH 306:14
lunches: l. of fifty-seven years   WOD 315:17
lungs: froth-corrupted l.   OWEN 227:14
  gold and l. of bronze   BELL 35:6
  using your l. all the time   LEAC 182:14
lurch: Tho' rather in the l.   COW 85:9
lurching: L. to rag-time tunes   SASS 263:1
lust: horrible that l. and rage   YEATS 321:3
  lot of women with l.   CART 64:6
  l. for learning   BEER 31:12
  l. of knowing what should   FLEC 111:10
lutanist: lute the l.   THOM 295:11
lutte: *l. elle-même vers les sommets*   CAMUS 63:4
luxuriant: L. song   YEATS 322:10
luxuries: necessities and which l.   WRIG 317:17
luxury: all the l. of the world   YEATS 322:10
  Literature is a l.   CHES 68:12
  l. was lavished on you   ORTON 224:5
lying: done as easily l. down   ALLEN 4:15
  I do not mind l.   BUTL 60:5
  L. in bed would be an altogether   CHES 71:2
  One of you is l.   PARK 230:11
  smallest amount of l.   BUTL 60:12
Lyme: There once was an old man of L.

    MONK 212:3
Lyonnesse: When I set out for L.   HARDY 134:6
lyre: 'Omer smote 'is bloomin' l.   KIPL 174:7
lyres: turn to rhythmic tidal l.   HARDY 134:4
lyric: now it's l. verse   WAUGH 306:5

M

Ma: Anyway, M., I made it GOFF 125:11
MacArthur: didn't fire him [General M.]
　　　　　　　　　　　　　　　TRUM 299:11
Macaulay: M. or Ruskin and secretly BARB 24:17
Macavity: M., Macavity, there's no ELIOT 102:12
Macbeth: Little Nell and Lady M. WOOL 317:15
Macdonald: boneless wonder [Ramsay M.]
　　　　　　　　　　　　　　　CHUR 73:13
　[Ramsay M.] LLOY 189:11
macerations: Made way for m. POUND 238:8
Macheath: Just a jack-knife has M., dear
　　　　　　　　　　　　　　　BREC 52:18
machine: A house is a m. for living LE C 183:14
Ghost in the M. RYLE 256:9
I have tested your m. TREE 298:8
ingenious m. for turning DIN 92:9
m. can do the work of fifty HUBB 147:6
m. for making gods BERG 40:3
Unpassioned beauty of a great m. BROO 54:9
We feel the m. slipping LOW 191:10
Youre not a man, youre a m. SHAW 267:20
machinery: dynamo in the m. of the night
　　　　　　　　　　　　　　　GINS 125:1
machines: M. are worshipped RUSS 255:17
M. for making more machines BOTT 50:5
m. or of elaborate techniques RUTH 256:5
men in their flying m. DAV 88:12
macht: Arbeit m. frei. ANON 6:16
die M. den Vorrang hat JUNG 160:1
mackintosh: bit of black m. WELBY 307:9
Macy: ass in M.'s window JOHN 156:2
mad: Are the men that God made m. CHES 68:10
born m. BECK 29:12
go m. they shall be sane THOM 293:12
How m. I am, sad I am BETJ 43:9
M. about the boy COW 84:12
M. at you 'cause your feet's BENS 39:2
m. dog of the Middle East REAG 244:9
M. dogs and Englishmen COW 84:13
or less m. on one point KIPL 172:11
Poets do not go m. CHES 69:18
sense that the world was m. SAB 256:10
madam: Call me m. LIND 188:7
Why not 'M. Secretary' PERK 233:4
made: has m. all the difference FROST 118:8
m. by someone who had often HALS 131:7
mind is not a bed to be m. AGATE 3:5
We are so m., that we can FREUD 117:4
You m. me love you MCC 193:10
madeleine: m. which on Sunday mornings
　　　　　　　　　　　　　　　PROU 240:8
mademoiselle: M. from Armenteers ANON 9:19
madman: As a m. shakes a dead geranium
　　　　　　　　　　　　　　　ELIOT 103:14
Hugo was a m. who thought COCT 78:8

madmen: M. in authority, who hear KEYN 165:5
madness: generation destroyed by m. GINS 125:1
has her m. and her weather AUDEN 17:4
M. need not be all breakdown LAING 177:12
The rest is the m. of art JAMES 152:14
Maeonides: And old M. the blind FLEC 112:6
Maggie: work on M.'s Farm no more DYLAN 97:9
magic: has succeeded where m. BRON 54:7
house rose like m. HARG 135:3
mistake medicine for m. SZASZ 290:6
That old black m. MERC 207:8
magical: M. mystery tour LENN 185:11
purely m. object BART 27:5
magique: un objet parfaitement m. BART 27:5
magistrate: anything that shocks the m.
　　　　　　　　　　　　　　　RUSS 255:19
The M. gave his opinion EDGAR 98:4
magnanimity: victory: m. In peace CHUR 76:3
magnificent: inconvenient, but it's m. BENN 38:15
m. men in their flying DAV 88:12
magpie: A swollen m. in a fitful sun
　　　　　　　　　　　　　　　POUND 238:17
Maguire: M. and his men KAV 162:1
Mahler: M. exclaimed MAHL 199:3
Mai: M. qui fut sans nuage et ARAG 13:2
maid: m. that high birth WOOLF 317:4
Yonder a m. and her wight HARDY 133:15
maiden: For many a rose-lipt m. HOUS 146:14
maidens: M. aspiring to godheads STOP 287:4
maids: m. come forth sprig-muslin HARDY 133:8
mail: Night M. crossing the Border AUDEN 19:15
maimed: M. us at the start YEATS 324:1
maiming: risk of m. it for life SHAW 272:3
maintenance: art of motorcycle m. PIRS 235:6
maison: m. est une machine-à-habiter LE C 183:14
majestic: face of the m. equality FRAN 116:6
majestueuse: travailler devant la m. égalité
　　　　　　　　　　　　　　　FRAN 116:6
Major: Ground control to M. Tom BOWIE 51:6
majority: big enough m. in any town
　　　　　　　　　　　　　　　TWAIN 300:7
conforming to m. opinion SCAN 264:2
indifference of the m. REST 245:13
m. never has right IBSEN 150:1
m. then and there happen WHIT 310:9
minority to the m. LENIN 184:15
rule the m. are wrong DEBS 89:12
make: Go ahead, m. my day FINK 109:9
M. do and mend ANON 9:20
M. love not war ANON 9:21
m. two questions grow where VEBL 304:1
m. way for an older man MAUD 204:9
m. wherever we're lost FRY 119:20
sometimes, to m. it up TWAIN 301:1
than a Scotsman on the m. BARR 26:13
wrote M. IT NEW POUND 238:1
You cannot m. him out at all BELL 33:17
maker: meet my M. brow to brow CORN 83:10

maker (*cont.*):

prepared to meet my M.	CHUR 75:15
The M. of the stars and sea	BETJ 42:5

makes: Happiness m. up in height   FROST 119:8

making: cesspit of their own m.   AND 6:8

egg's way of m. another egg	BUTL 59:12
m-m-m. the world safe	WOLFE 316:13
We have ways of m. men talk	YOUNG 324:6

Malamute: whooping it up in the M.   SERV 267:1

male: Especially the m. of the species

                                LAWR 181:15

more deadly than the m.	KIPL 173:11
rough m. kiss	BROO 54:9
true m. never yet walked	WICK 311:2
weapon of the m.	CONN 80:20

malenky: Then I read a m. bit out   BURG 57:15

malentendu: *c'est d'être admiré par m.*   COCT 78:4

malheureux: *moral dès qu'on est m.*   PROU 240:11

malice: There's no m. in me eye   AYRES 22:1

malicious: God is subtle but he is not m.   EINS 99:5

malignant: was not m. and remove it

                                WAUGH 306:3

mallet: m. or a chisel modelled   YEATS 319:14

malt: m. does more than Milton   HOUS 146:15

mama: encountered the m. of dada   FAD 107:5

M. may have, papa may have   HOL 142:11

maman: *m. est morte*   CAMUS 62:15

mamas: I'm the last of the red-hot m.   YELL 324:4

mammals: 8,000 species of m.   HALD 131:2

mammon: authentic m. than a bogus

                                MACN 197:8

man: All animals, except m.   BUTL 60:10

A m. not old, but mellow	PHIL 234:3
A m. who's untrue to his wife	AUDEN 19:14
A moderately honest m.	SHAW 272:7
A pint of plain is your only m.	O'BR 222:4
Arms and the m.	SHAW 267:16
artist m. and the mother	SHAW 270:17
Beware of the m. whose god	SHAW 272:4
blood makes a m. coloured	HUGH 147:12
boldly go where no m.	RODD 249:2
But if a m. bites a dog	BOG 48:10
century of the common m.	WALL 304:16
everyone has sat except a m.	CUMM 87:6
get to a m. in the case	KIPL 174:10
God created m.	VALÉ 303:2
God, the laws of m.	HOUS 145:3
good for m. to be alone	BARR 26:18
have you ever tasted M.	KIPL 171:9
He's no a m. ava'	MACD 194:11
He was her m., but he done	ANON 8:1
How many roads must a m.	DYLAN 97:3
I am a free m., an American	JOHN 156:15
I got my m.	GERS 123:7
I'm a m.	WILD 311:5
I met a m. who wasn't there	MEAR 206:6
I never hated a m. enough	GABOR 120:14
I saw a m. this morning	SHAW- 274:13
It's that m. again	ANON 9:3

man (*cont.*):

less than that no m.	ROOS 251:6
m. a free hand and he'll	WEST 309:8
m. and a woman looking	WOOLF 317:11
M., biologically considered	JAMES 153:10
m. by standing a sheep	BEER 31:16
m. can interrogate as well	OSLER 226:16
M. can leave the earth	KOES 176:9
m. could ease a heart like	PARK 230:10
M. delights in novelty	PARK 230:17
m. does with what happens	HUXL 149:13
m. ever shall put asunder	SHAW 269:8
m. falls in love through	WYATT 318:1
m. fixed his eyes before	ELIOT 104:14
m. from Del Monte says	ANON 9:22
m. got to do what he got	STEI 284:16
M. hands on misery to man	LARK 179:2
M. has created death	YEATS 323:5
m. in love is incomplete	GABOR 120:13
m. in the house is worth	WEST 309:1
M. is a credulous animal	RUSS 256:1
M. is a history-making creature	AUDEN 18:15
M. is a useless passion	SART 261:10
m. is either free	BAR 24:13
m. is that you think him	SHAW 269:18
M. is the Only Animal	TWAIN 300:17
m. is the only creature	ORW 224:10
m. more dined against	BOWRA 51:8
M. must choose whether	ILL 150:11
m. of genius who had not	BEER 30:9
m. over forty is a scoundrel	SHAW 272:13
m. shouldn't fool	FAUL 108:1
m. suffering from	BEVAN 44:9
M., unlike any other thing	STEI 284:15
m. who "boozes"	BURT 58:7
m. who goes to a psychiatrist	GOLD 126:10
m. who has no office	SHAW 269:15
m. who has not passed through	JUNG 159:14
m. who is high up loves	BARR 26:16
m. who is not afraid	SYNGE 289:8
m. who listens to Reason	SHAW 272:9
m. who mistook his wife	SACKS 256:11
m. who should loose me	LOW 191:7
m. who used to notice such	HARDY 134:1
m. will not merely endure	FAUL 107:12
m. without originality	SHAW 268:10
nastiest little m.	DYKS 97:2
night out for m. or beast	FIEL 109:7
noblest work of m.	BUTL 59:4
Of m.'s bedevilment and God's	HOUS 145:4
Ol' m. river, dat ol' man	HAMM 132:1
One m. in a thousand	KIPL 173:10
one small step for a m.	ARMS 13:10
Or an old m. upon a winter's	YEATS 318:5
Our m. in Havana	GREE 128:17
problem is that *m. is dead*	FROMM 117:10
reflecting the figure of a m.	WOOLF 317:9
right to be obeyed than m.	JOHN 155:16
Stand by your m.	WYN 318:4

man (cont.):

street fighting m.	JAGG 152:5
streets a m. must go	CHAN 66:9
the m. for others	BONH 49:5
The m. who came to dinner	KAUF 161:7
The m. who would be king	KIPL 172:8
The m. you love to hate	ANON 9:23
Then m. your ships	LUCAS 192:10
The Reasonable M.	HERB 139:14
The significance of m.	BECK 28:12
things that happen to a m.	TROT 299:2
This very remarkable m.	INGE 150:13
thy vanity, it is not m.	POUND 238:16
To justify God's ways to m.	HOUS 146:15
tragedy of a m. who has found	BARR 26:15
Ulcer M. on 4 Ulcer Pay	EARLY 97:15
were a m. of distinction	FIEL 108:8
what is m.? Wherefore	LENO 185:19
What ought a m.	IBSEN 150:6
When I was m. alive	HOUS 146:6
when the m. of controversy	GALB 121:2
without a m. is like a fish	STEI 285:1
woman be more like a m.	LERN 185:21
Women who love the same m.	BEER 31:10
you'll be a M., my son	KIPL 173:9
Youre not a m., youre a machine	SHAW 267:20
manage: m. without butter but not	GOEB 125:9
management: m. doesn't seem to understand	
	CHAR 67:11
manager: No m. ever got fired	ANON 10:3
Mandalay: Come you back to M.	KIPL 169:6
mandarin: called this style the M.	CONN 80:11
manderley: night I dreamt I went to M.	DU M 96:7
mane: whistling m. of every wind	THOM 295:7
manhood: upon me, my m. is cast	LAWR 181:13
manifestly: m. and undoubtedly be seen	
	HEW 140:4
manifesto: first powerful plain m.	SPEN 281:16
man-in-the-street: Of the sensual m.	
	AUDEN 17:12
To the m., who, I'm sorry	AUDEN 19:14
mankind: have put m. and posterity	INGE 151:7
have the existence of m.	ADAMS 2:13
Homes and the Freedom of m.	HAIG 130:12
m. faces a crossroads	ALLEN 4:13
m. is divisible into two	BEER 30:10
M. must put an end to war	KENN 163:1
silliness of the majority of m.	RUSS 255:9
suffering of m.	RUSS 254:13
The proper study of m. is books	HUXL 148:11
There is no history of m.	POPP 236:6
up the other half of m.	LAING 177:10
manner: All m. of thing shall be well	ELIOT 102:7
this extraordinary m.	STOP 287:6
manners: dress well and weve no m.	SHAW 274:7
Edward III had very good m.	SELL 266:6
M. are especially the need	WAUGH 306:6
people have good table m.	MIKES 207:13
Who take their m. from the Ape	BELL 32:14

manœuvring: could be a m. swine	MCC 194:3
man-o'-war: The M.'s 'er 'usband	KIPL 174:6
mansion: A heavenly m., raging	YEATS 323:12
But Love has pitched his m.	YEATS 323:8
mantled: M. in mist, remote from	AUDEN 16:11
manufacture: m. professors	WEIL 307:6
manufactures: m. therefore is a secondary	
	CHAM 65:12
manure: becomes the m. of the next	CONN 81:1
many: adulation by the m.	BROWN 56:11
m. a good tune played	BUTL 60:13
Not m. people know	CAINE 61:3
owed by so m. to so few	CHUR 74:8
many-splendoured: That miss the m. thing	
	THOM 296:13
map: m. of Europe has been changed	CHUR 73:11
maps: Geography is about M.	BENT 39:7
Where the m. are spread	YEATS 320:2
Marabar: echo in a M. cave is not	FORS 115:7
marble: Glowed on the m.	ELIOT 104:15
m. cross below the town	HAYES 136:3
march: Do not m. on Moscow	MONT 212:7
m. my troops towards	GRIM 129:10
m. of this retreating world	OWEN 228:7
m. on their stomachs shouting	SELL 266:11
Men who m. away	HARDY 134:7
you can m. behind	CAST 64:11
marched: Ten thousand women m. through	
	CHES 69:7
marching: hear the sound of m.	JAGG 152:5
Margery: Some went upstairs with M.	
	AUDEN 18:17
margin: m. this innocent virgin	AUDEN 20:12
Maria: M. flung herself on him	GRAH 127:11
Marie: And I am M. of Roumania	PARK 230:13
marijuana: m. in his hair	LOW 191:13
Marilyn: M. who was every man's	MAIL 199:9
Marines: armed forces and the M.	THAT 291:8
marionettes: though the m. are men	BENT 39:15
mark: Great Scorer comes to m.	RICE 246:5
Market Harborough: Am in M. Where ought	
	CHES 68:6
markets: m. by the sea shut fast	FLEC 111:8
marks: bears the m. of the last	HAIG 130:11
m. of the beast	HARDY 133:11
marmalade-downwards: m. incidence was	
statistically	JENN 154:13
Marquis: Abducted by a French M.	GRAH 127:6
marriage: long monotony of m.	GIBB 123:13
Love and m., love and marriage	CAHN 60:19
M. always demands the finest	BAUM 27:14
m. and the constancy	SHAW 271:11
m. a success and only one	SAM 259:5
M. is a bribe to make	WILD 311:6
M. is a wonderful invention	CONN 80:5
m. is not that adults produce	DE VR 91:15
m. isn't a word	VIDOR 304:8
M. is popular because it	SHAW 271:22

marriage (cont.):
  m. is the waste-paper basket   WEBB 307:4
  M., n. The state or condition   BIER 46:21
  So that is m., Lily thought   WOOLF 317:11
marriages: m. come from the husbands
     WOD 315:9
  The thousands of m.   LARK 179:13
married: although he was twice m.   RUSS 255:8
  are the best part of m.   WILD 311:7
  aunts, who are not m.   CHES 71:9
  I m. beneath me, all women do   ASTOR 15:11
  I'm getting m. in the morning   LERN 185:20
  incomplete until he has m.   GABOR 120:13
  M. women are kept women   SMITH 278:7
  my parents were m.   ACK 1:10
  So they were m.   MACN 198:4
  Trade Unionism of the m.   SHAW 271:10
  We can't get m. at all   WILD 311:5
  woman's business to get m.   SHAW 271:1
marries: m. three girls from St   STEIN 284:3
marry: alone, they'd never m.   HENRY 139:1
  But m. me, and I'll never   PIR 235:5
  Carlyle and Mrs Carlyle m.   BUTL 59:10
  get away to m. you today   LEIGH 184:7
  'm.' is an aphorism   MITF 211:11
  men we wanted to m.   STEI 284:18
  one thing, they m. later   MENC 206:13
  see what some girls m.   ROWL 254:2
  You don't m. it legitimately   DEGAS 89:13
Mars: M. a day helps you work   GAFF 120:15
  Next July we collide with M.   PORT 237:1
Martini: clothes and into a dry M.   ANON 9:11
  clothes and into a dry M.   WEST 309:2
  like a medium Vodka dry M.   FLEM 112:8
Martinis: M. did the work for me   ADE 2:19
martyr: you are a Crook or a M.   ROG 249:7
martyrdom: M. . . . . is the only   SHAW 268:16
  That even the dreadful m.   AUDEN 17:9
marvel: There could I m.   THOM 292:14
  They m. more and more   BELL 32:17
marvelling: She left me m. why my soul
     THOM 294:11
Marx: abandonment of the teaching of M.
     KHR 165:9
  anything M. dreamed   TOYN 298:6
  Karl M. and Catherine   ATTL 16:8
  M. whose analysis seems   BENN 37:2
  wholly wrong to blame M.   BENN 37:3
Marxism: Methodism than to M.   PHIL 234:2
Marxist: I am a M.—of the Groucho   ANON 9:5
  The distortion of the M.   BENN 37:3
Marxiste: Je suis M.—tendance Groucho.   ANON 9:5
Mary Jane: What is the matter with M.
     MILNE 210:2
Marylebone: hanging garments of M.
     JOYCE 158:1
Masefield: To M. something more   BEER 30:14
masochism: A spirit of national m.   AGNEW 3:7
masochistic: m. form of exhibitionism   OLIV 223:4

masonry: man into the social m.   WELLS 308:9
mass: After two thousand years of m.
     HARDY 134:13
  I go to M. every day   BELL 33:12
  Move between the fields to M.   BETJ 44:2
  The broad m. of a nation   HITL 141:11
massacre: are not as sudden as a m.
     TWAIN 300:12
masses: m. it is not art   SCH 264:10
mass-production: m. are being utilized
     LANC 178:2
mast: m. burst open with a rose   FLEC 112:5
master: community consisting of a m.   BIER 46:21
  M. shall praise us   KIPL 174:13
  not make dreams your m.   KIPL 173:7
  or can be m. of money   BEV 45:12
masterpiece: one knows, at sight, a m.
     POUND 238:10
  writer is to produce a m.   CONN 80:18
masterpieces: adventures of his soul among m.
     FRAN 116:7
masters: are the m. at the moment   SHAW 274:12
  Old M.   AUDEN 17:8
mastery: Wisdom was mine, and I had m.
     OWEN 228:7
mastiff: m. which is to watch over   LLOY 189:8
mastodons: calling to Aunt like m.   WOD 316:2
masturbation: knock m.   ALLEN 5:2
  M. is the thinking man's   HAMP 132:6
  m. of war   RAE 242:9
  M.: the primary sexual   SZASZ 289:13
match: dont quite m. your face   ASHF 14:4
matched: has m. us with His hour   BROO 54:10
matches: with that stick of m.   MAND 200:1
matchless: he has one m. blessing   EDW 98:11
mate: should listen when his m.   WICK 311:2
materialistic: Christianity is the most m.
     TEMP 291:5
  m. people I have ever met   MCC 193:13
materials: I use simple m.   LOWRY 192:4
mathematical: Moriarty of m. celebrity
     DOYLE 94:18
mathematician: appear as a pure m.   JEANS 154:7
mathematicians: M. go mad, and cashiers
     CHES 69:18
mathematics: M. may be defined   RUSS 255:11
  M., rightly viewed   RUSS 255:13
  pregnancy by a resort to m.   MENC 206:18
  world for ugly m.   HARDY 133:2
Matilda: M., and the House, were Burned
     BELL 33:5
  M. told such Dreadful Lies   BELL 33:3
  You'll come a-waltzing, M.   PAT 232:5
mating: Only in the m. season   MILL 209:6
matrimony: m. is breakfast-time   HERB 139:16
matter: But what's the m. wi' Glasgow
     FYFFE 120:10
  Does it m.   SASS 262:9

matter (*cont.*):
  don't m. a tinker's cuss   SHIN 274:17
  What is the m. with Mary Jane   MILNE 210:2
mattered: m. more than they should   BOLD 48:12
mattering: m. once it has stopped   BOWEN 50:15
matters: m. just as little   SHAW 271:8
  What can I do that m.   SPEN 281:14
mature: allowed to m. in the cask   O'FAO 222:17
  imitate; m. poets steal   ELIOT 104:5
  m. enough for offspring   DE VR 91:15
Maugham: he [M.] said to me   MAUG 205:1
Max: incomparable M.   SHAW 274:11
Maxim: The M. Gun, and they have not
                      BELL 33:14
maximum: m. of temptation   SHAW 271:22
May: From M. to December   AND 6:4
  M. month flaps its glad   HARDY 134:1
  M. will be fine next year   HOUS 144:12
  M. without cloud and June   ARAG 13:2
  On the first of M.   HART 135:12
  outside and m. be some time   MAHON 199:4
  outside and m. be some time   OATES 221:13
  there's an end of M.   HOUS 144:11
maybe: M. it's because I'm a Londoner
                     GREGG 129:2
Mayer: [Louis B. M.'s]   GOLD 126:11
mayor: finally married the M.   BAXT 28:1
  What did the m. do   GRAV 128:2
maze: Life is a m. in which we   CONN 80:21
mazy: A merry road, a m. road   CHES 69:5
MCC: M. ends and the Church   PRIE 240:2
McCarthyism: M. is Americanism   MCC 193:11
McCartney: Paul M. and George Harrison
                     BUCK 57:10
McGregor: go into Mr M.'s garden   POTT 237:8
McGrew: sat Dangerous Dan M.   SERV 267:1
McKinley: M. has no more backbone   ROOS 251:7
me: For you but not for m.   ANON 10:8
  I most delight in M.   CAMP 62:1
  interested in himself than in m.   BIER 46:18
  M. and my shadow   ROSE 252:6
  M. Tarzan, you Jane   WEIS 307:8
  rest of m.   BELL 32:11
meadow: And m. rivulets overflow   HARDY 133:9
  m. for a clean place   KAV 162:2
  stranger's feet may find the m.   HOUS 145:8
meadows: Deep m. yet, for to forget   BROO 56:1
meals: supper—for between m.   TWAIN 301:3
mean: A poem should not m.   MACL 196:5
  Down these m. streets   CHAN 66:9
  It all depends what you m.   JOAD 155:14
  It don't m. a thing   MILLS 209:10
  What m.?   ROSS 253:2
meaner: opponent motives m.   BARR 26:5
meaning: enhanced m. in memorable   BARZ 27:12
  Is there a m. to music   COPL 83:8
  language charged with m.   POUND 238:4
meaningful: with 'm.' or 'significant'
                     CHOM 71:16

meaningless: cryptic as to be almost m.
                     ANON 11:12
  Polite m. words   YEATS 320:4
meanings: words and m.   ELIOT 101:12
means: invisible m. of support   BUCH 57:6
  m. employed determine   HUXL 148:13
  m. think that the most   BREN 53:9
  mercy of his m.   THOM 293:2
  Private M. is dead   SMITH 279:1
meant: it's what I m.   VAUG 303:10
measles: It is the m. of the human   EINS 99:3
  Love is like the m.   JER 155:3
measure: m. of a man is not where   KING 167:1
measured: m. out my life with coffee   ELIOT 103:8
measurement: M. began our might   YEATS 319:10
meat: And went without m.   ROB 248:9
  I have no stomach for such m.   DOBS 92:13
  m. no woman in London will   CAMP 61:10
  opinions as it buys its m.   BUTL 60:4
Meccah: some to M. turn to pray   FLEC 111:12
mechanized: potato-gatherers like m. scarecrows
                     KAV 162:1
medal: it—a m. inscribed   OSB 226:11
medals: do with m. and ribbons   BELL 35:12
media: don't care much for the m.   STOP 287:1
medical: food well in advance of m.   WOD 316:3
Medici: Miniver loved the M.   ROB 248:11
medicinal: M. discovery   AYRES 22:1
medicine: masses not to take m.   OSLER 227:1
  m. advertisement without   JER 155:9
  men mistake m. for magic   SZASZ 290:6
  The desire to take m.   OSLER 227:3
Medicine Hat: The plumed war-bonnet of M.
                     BENÉT 36:16
medicos: m. marvelling sweetly   RANS 243:1
mediocre: Some men are born m.   HELL 137:5
  Titles distinguish the m.   SHAW 272:1
  Women want m. men   MEAD 206:4
mediocrity: M. knows nothing higher
                     DOYLE 95:14
meditating: middle of a firwood m.   O'BR 222:2
Mediterranean: encircling movement in the M.
                     CHUR 75:2
  ever taken from the M.   SHAF 267:5
medium: m. because nothing's well   ACE 1:5
  The m. is the message   MCL 196:9
medley: A m. of extemporanea   PARK 230:13
meek: m. shall inherit the Earth   SMITH 277:3
meet: m. my Maker brow to brow   CORN 83:10
  m. the Duke I couldn't   SHAW- 274:14
  We'll m. again, don't know   PARK 231:20
  Yet m. we shall, and part   BUTL 58:12
meetings: M. that do not come off   BOWEN 51:2
meets: this than m. the eye   BANK 24:8
meilleurs: *ceux qui sont m. que nous*   CAMUS 62:13
mellow: m., like good wine   PHIL 234:3
Mellstock: lie in M. churchyard now   BETJ 42:3
melodious: wailed like m. cats under   HUXL 148:9

mess (*cont.*):
who has made an awful m.   BURR 58:6
message: first m. of India   FORS 115:9
The medium is the m.   MCL 196:9
messages: m. should be delivered GOLD 126:5
sending of general m.   DOYLE 95:13
you get m. of sympathy   AYCK 21:7
Messer: *die Nacht der langen M.* HITL 141:6
messing: simply m. about in boats GRAH 127:13
met: m. a man that I didn't   ROG 249:13
metamorphoses: flowerings, month of m.
                                   ARAG 13:2
métamorphoses: *floraisons mois des m.* ARAG 13:2
metaphor: all m. is poetry   CHES 68:13
metaphysics: M. is the finding of bad BRAD 52:2
science of m.   MENC 206:19
meters: Watch the parkin' m.   DYLAN 97:12
Methodism: more to M. than to Marxism
                                   PHIL 234:2
methods: You know my m. Apply them
                                   DOYLE 95:6
Mexico: South of the Border—down M. way
                                   KENN 162:13
mezzanine: down into the m. floor WOD 315:17
Michael Angelo: Enter M. Andrea del Sarto
                                   BEER 30:20
Italy from designs by M.   TWAIN 301:4
not want M. for breakfast   TWAIN 301:3
Michelangelo: Talking of M.   ELIOT 103:7
they produced M.   WELL 307:14
Michelin: she with the M. beside me CONN 81:5
microbe: The M. is so very small BELL 33:17
middle: beginning, a m. and an end GOD 125:7
dead centre of m.   ADAMS 2:4
pleasures of m.   POUND 237:17
sinking m. class   ORW 225:19
sits in the m. and knows   FROST 119:11
stay in the m. of the road   BEVAN 45:6
Middle Age: enchantments of the M. BEER 31:7
middle-aged: watches her m. children
                                   SCOT 265:11
middle class: The M. was quite prepared BELL 33:7
middle-class: m. morality all the time
                                   SHAW 273:15
thats m. morality   SHAW 273:19
Middle East: this mad dog of the M. REAG 244:9
Middlesex: Elysium — rural M. again BETJ 42:8
midge: And lightly skims the m.   BETJ 43:7
Midlands: When I am living in the M. BELL 34:19
midnight: Holding hands at m.   GERS 123:10
Love, the reeling m. through   PARK 231:3
m. in some public place   YEATS 319:14
M. shakes the memory   ELIOT 103:14
See her on the bridge at m.   ANON 10:15
There m.'s all a glimmer   YEATS 318:10
troubled m. and the noon   ELIOT 103:17
midst: m. of life we are in debt MUMF 215:11
midwife: m. slapped your footsoles PLATH 235:9
mieux: *je vais de m. en mieux*   COUÉ 84:4

might: Because the all-enacting M. HARDY 134:9
Britons alone use 'M.'   WAUGH 306:12
mightier: believed that the bank was m.
                                   PLOM 235:15
make thee m. yet   BENS 39:4
spark-gap is m. than the pen   HOGB 142:10
mighty: And m. ships ten thousand ton
                                   HODG 142:1
But he's m. lak' a rose   STAN 283:8
God who made thee m.   BENS 39:4
stop the m. roar of London's   ANON 10:9
miles: 10,000 m. away from home   JOHN 156:12
60,000 m. per hour somewhere   FULL 120:5
And m. around the wonder grew   HOUS 146:2
And m. to go before I sleep   FROST 118:11
militaires: *pour la confier à des m.* CLEM 77:8
militant: m. each in your own way PANK 229:8
this m. movement   PANK 229:6
was the first m. lowbrow   BERL 41:1
military: Doing the M. Two-step   GREN 129:4
hold the m. mind   TUCH 299:14
matter to entrust to m.   CLEM 77:8
race has no m. purpose   MOUN 214:13
When the m. man approaches   SHAW 271:9
military-industrial: by the m. complex EIS 100:1
milk: Gin was mother's m. to her SHAW 273:17
M. and then just as it   BETJ 43:1
m. is more likely   BUTL 60:4
m. of human kindness   GUED 130:3
m. the cow of the world   WILB 311:3
One end is moo, the other, m.   NASH 217:13
putting m. into babies   CHUR 73:2
mill: golf-links lie so near the m. CLEG 77:7
John Stuart M.   BENT 39:10
m. and the fold   HOUS 146:5
old m. by the stream   ARMS 13:7
Under the m., under the mill   BROO 56:1
million: A m. million spermatozoa HUXL 148:18
Fifty m. Frenchmen can't   ROSE 252:8
m. Frenchmen can't be wrong   GUIN 130:6
really want to make a m.   HUBB 147:9
The first ten m. years   ADAMS 2:1
millionaire: And an old-fashioned m. FISH 110:5
As a silk hat on a Bradford m.   ELIOT 105:6
I am a M. That is my religion   SHAW 270:5
Who wants to be a m.   PORT 237:2
millionaires: All m. love a baked apple
                                   FIRB 109:13
full of rascals, m.   BENN 38:16
millions: Kill m. of men, and you ROST 253:9
m. long for immortality   ERTZ 106:13
m. of the mouthless dead   SORL 281:2
Milton: And malt does more than M. can
                                   HOUS 146:15
mind: are the empires of the m.   CHUR 76:1
Before the secret working m.   YEATS 319:10
Came-over-with-the Conqueror type of m.
                                   WATS 305:9

mind (*cont.*):

Cast your m. on other days   YEATS 319:12
Come back into my m.   BELL 34:19
consistency is as bad for the m.   HUXL 148:12
contradictory beliefs in one's m.   ORW 225:7
cutting edge of the m.   BRON 54:3
give his m. to politics   SHAW 267:13
His m. moves upon silence   YEATS 320:2
I do not m. lying   BUTL 60:5
I don't m. if I do   KAV 162:6
If I am out of my m.   BELL 35:10
improper m. is a perpetual   SMITH 277:15
it's all in the m.   WOLFE 316:12
joy, and m. is fruit   MAS 203:9
keeps Georgia on my m.   GORR 127:1
Keep violence in the m.   ALD 3:13
Let them m. their own affairs   HOUS 145:3
m. and body to do   BAD 22:2
m. and knows it can always   SHAW 267:12
m. begins to roam irretrievably   SOLZ 280:1
m. from the dominion   GOLD 126:3
m. is not a bed to be made   AGATE 3:5
M. my bike   WARN 305:5
m. of man or elevate   YEATS 323:7
Mr Churchill but the m.   ATTL 16:5
my m. is maturing late   NASH 217:17
Of my own m.   THOM 295:2
on not changing one's m.   MAUG 205:9
prodigious quantity of m.   TWAIN 301:1
resemblance to what one has in m.

                                     PROU 240:13
sentences until reeled the m.   GIBBS 124:1
someone whose m. watches   CAMUS 62:9
urge the m. to aftersight   ELIOT 102:3
while we have sex in the m.   LAWR 181:17
youngest darter to m. me   PHIL 234:4

minded: wreckage of men who have m.

                                     WOOLF 317:10
minds: best m. of my generation   GINS 125:1
fairly developed m.   FORS 114:1
great m. in the commonplace   HUBB 147:5
have comfortable m.   CUMM 87:4
Little m. are interested   HUBB 147:5
m. is the best kind   BUCH 57:4
M. like beds always made up   WILL 312:12
m. of a few fastidious   SMITH 278:16
mislead their weak m.   SAY 263:10
pervert climbs into the m.   BRON 54:5
since wars begin in the m.   ANON 8:7
Women never have young m.   DEL 91:9
mine: If they are m. or no   HOUS 145:8
M. is the only voice   CAMP 62:1
she is m. for life   SPARK 281:6
So be m., as I yours for ever   GRAV 128:6
miner: so I became a m. instead   COOK 82:8
miners: m. sweat their guts out   ORW 225:12
Mineworkers: National Union of M.   MACM 197:2
Ming Bing: what is known as the M.   MONT 212:7
miniature: every day is a life in m. O'NEI 223:11

minimum: with the m. of fuss   BLYT 48:4
mining: snakeskin-titles of m.-claims

                                     BENÉT 36:16
minister: been said that this M.   BAIL 22:4
deferential — 'Yes, M. . . .'   CROS 86:11
M. in order to preside   CHUR 73:6
ministers: mind how much my M. talk

                                     THAT 291:11
Miniver: M. loved the Medici   ROB 248:11
mink: doesn't have a m. coat   NIXON 220:10
The trick of wearing m.   BALM 24:6
minority: enough people to make a m. ALTM 5:8
m. to the majority   LENIN 184:15
The m. are right   DEBS 89:12
mint: pockets the mark of the m.   CHES 70:12
minute: leave in a m. and a huff   KALM 161:5
The m. you walked in the joint   FIEL 108:8
minutes: And twenty m. more or less

                                     YEATS 323:11
be famous for fifteen m.   WARH 305:2
going to say in twenty m.   BRAB 51:10
hundred and seventeen m.   BENN 38:12
m. the damned fella will   MITF 211:12
Mirabeau: M. Bridge flows the Seine APOL 12:15
Sous le pont M. coule la Seine   APOL 12:15
miracle: not a fraud, but a m.   SHAW 273:22
miracles: But the age of m. hadn't   GERS 123:6
Miranda: M.   BELL 34:9
mire: Sow returns to her M.   KIPL 173:12
mirror: bevelled edge of a sunlit m. ABSE 1:3
mirror'd: Lie m. on her sea   HODG 142:4
mirrors: believe in m. or newspapers OSB 226:9
cell whose walls are m.   O'NEI 223:8
mine as m. are lonely   AUDEN 19:1
M. and fatherhood   BORG 49:11
Over the m. meant   HARDY 134:4
The m. of the sea are strewn   FLEC 111:15
mirth: M. that has no bitter springs KIPL 173:2
The song of the birds for m.   GURN 130:9
miscarriages: pregnancies and at least four m.

                                     BEEC 29:19
miserable: arise and make them m.   HUXL 148:14
certain too, I'm m.   MAC 195:7
horrible and the m.   ALLEN 5:3
make only two people m.   BUTL 59:10
m. human being than one   JAMES 153:15
m. is to have leisure   SHAW 273:6
miseries: Coherent m., a bite and sup

                                     HEAN 136:12
m. or credulities of mankind   CONR 81:20
misery: Man hands on m. to man   LARK 179:2
misfits: strangest collection of m. REAG 244:8
misfortune: bored by the recital of m. MAUG 205:6
m. to ourselves, and good   BIER 46:14
misfortunes: m. can befall a boy   MAUG 205:17
misguided: guided missiles and m.   KING 167:4
mishtake: Shome m., surely   ANON 10:16
mislead: one to m. the public   ASQ 14:18

misplaced: rise of m. power exists EIS 100:1

mispronounce: language: all men m. it

 MORL 213:10

misquotation: M. is, in fact, the pride PEAR 232:9

missed: he m. the bus CHAM 66:8

 m. the point completely ELIOT 101:2

missing: M. so much and so much CORN 83:12

mission: Its five-year m. RODD 249:2

 m. workers came out too RUNY 254:9

missionaries: sad death—eaten by m.

 SPOO 282:12

Mississippi: day even the state of M. KING 166:10

 east all the way into M. KIPL 175:6

 What have you in the M. BURNS 58:5

Miss T: That whatever M. eats DE L 91:3

mist: White the m. along the grass BETJ 44:2

mistake: always made a new m. instead

 COPE 83:6

 capital m. to theorize DOYLE 95:9

 When I make a m., it's a beaut LA G 177:6

mistaken: unless I am m., is our DOYLE 94:10

mistakenly: meaning 'to believe m.' WITT 315:3

mistakes: genius makes no m. JOYCE 159:7

 m. that can be made HEIS 137:3

 nothing that make no m. CONR 81:18

mistook: man who m. his wife SACKS 256:11

mistress: But m. in my own KIPL 170:7

 m. and two slaves BIER 46:21

mistresses: wife and hardly any m. SAKI 258:3

mists: And low the m. of evening lie BETJ 43:7

 But when the m. in autumn KING 167:12

 m. of righteous indignation MUGG 215:4

 shaken m. a space unsettle THOM 295:14

misunderstand: May no fate wilfully m. me

 FROST 118:9

misunderstood: admired through being m.

 COCT 78:4

 I do not want to be m. JOS 157:8

 worse lie than a truth m. JAMES 154:1

Mithridates: M., he died old HOUS 147:1

Mitty: Walter M., the undefeated THUR 297:13

mixed: What's a m. infant BEHAN 32:1

moan: That is not paid with m. THOM 294:12

moanday: All m., tearsday, wailsday JOYCE 158:4

mock: m. the riddled corpses SASS 263:1

 yet m. what women meant OWEN 228:4

mockeries: No m. now for them OWEN 227:13

mocking: Of a m. tale or a gibe YEATS 320:4

mockingbird: it's a sin to kill a m. LEE 183:15

models: they have no other m. BALD 22:13

Model T: have the M. in any colour FORD 113:13

moderately: m. honest man with a moderately

 SHAW 272:7

moderation: M. in the affairs JOHN 156:13

 m. in the pursuit of justice GOLD 126:4

 M. in war is imbecility FISH 110:1

modern: called a 'M. Churchman' WAUGH 305:17

 it's m. architecture BANK 24:10

modern (cont.):

 this so-called m. art MUNN 215:15

modest: I was a m., good-humoured BEER 30:15

 m. man who has a good CHUR 72:8

modesty: had time to cultivate m. SITW 276:3

modulating: A gay m. anguish, rather FRY 119:18

moi: Pretentious? M. CLEE 77:6

mois: m. des floraisons mois ARAG 13:2

Mole: secret diary of Adrian M. TOWN 298:4

moll: King's M. Reno'd in Wolsey's ANON 9:8

Mom: at a place called M.'s ALGR 3:14

moment: m. in childhood when GREE 128:18

 m. of my greatness flicker ELIOT 103:10

 m. the slave resolves GAND 121:11

 phoenix DAY-L 89:5

 That last m. belongs to us VANZ 303:7

momentary: Beauty is m. in the mind STEV 285:10

moments: timeless m. ELIOT 102:6

Mona: M. did researches in original PLOM 235:13

monarch: so much a king as a M. SELL 266:9

monarchy: might not be a Limited M. STR 288:1

 M. is a labour-intensive WILS 313:7

Monday: On M., when the sun is hot

 MILNE 210:15

monde: m. des émotions qu'on nomme COL 79:1

 responsable d'un m. aussi absurde DUH 96:4

monedas: por un puñado de m. ZAP 324:8

money: am only interested in m. SHAW 269:9

 arms is not spending m. EIS 100:2

 demand your m. or your life BUTL 59:9

 earn much more m. writing AUDEN 18:6

 enough to get all that m. CHES 71:10

 For lack of m., and it LARK 178:12

 For m. can't buy me love LENN 185:7

 Give him the m., Barney PICK 234:11

 He had m. as well THAT 292:4

 Her voice is full of m. FITZ 110:15

 his m., and his religious BUTL 59:6

 Hollywood m. isn't money PARK 231:14

 I'm saving my m. TUCK 300:2

 It's one for the m. PERK 233:3

 leave them now is m. LARK 178:13

 m. among themselves there STEAD 283:11

 m. and large armies ANOU 12:11

 m. by underestimating MENC 206:10

 M. couldn't buy friends MILL 209:8

 M. doesn't talk, it swears DYLAN 97:6

 M. gives me pleasure all BELL 34:15

 m. if you can prove HOPE 144:1

 M. is better than poverty ALLEN 4:16

 M. is indeed the most important SHAW 269:13

 M. is like a sixth sense MAUG 205:11

 m. I spend on advertising LEV 186:14

 M. is the most important SHAW 270:2

 M., it turned out BALD 22:7

 must have m. and a room WOOLF 317:8

 Never ask of m. spent FROST 118:5

 no one shall work for m. KIPL 174:13

 Oh we ain't got a barrel of m. WOODS 317:2

money (cont.):
or can be master of m.	BEV 45:12
own licence to print m.	THOM 297:1
poor know that it is m.	BREN 53:9
Take the m. and run	ALLEN 4:14
there's no m. in poetry	GRAV 128:4
The want of m. is so quite	BUTL 59:1
they hired the m.	COOL 82:10
try to rub up against m.	RUNY 254:11
We haven't got the m.	RUTH 256:5
what to do with their m.	BAR 24:12
when you don't have any m.	DONL 93:3

monk: beast and the m. FORS 115:3
I said to this m. PINT 234:13
monkey: m. when the organ grinder BEVAN 45:5
surest way to make a m. BENC 36:6
monkeys: Cats and m.—monkeys JAMES 152:18
M., who very sensibly refrain GRAH 127:12
monks: The holiness of m., and after
YEATS 319:11
monogamy: too many. M. is the same ANON 7:5
Who seek to find m. PARK 231:1
monographs: been guilty of several m.
DOYLE 95:3
monologue: m. is not a decision ATTL 16:6
monopoly: shun the temptations of m.
SCOTT 265:5
monosyllabic: nothing so m. as to cheat FRY 120:1
monotony: long m. of marriage GIBB 123:13
Monroe: M. Doctrine will go ROOS 251:8
monster: pity this busy m., manunkind
CUMM 87:7
monsters: then even the m. we defy MCKAY 195:8
monstrous: m. carbuncle on the face CHAR 68:3
month: [£1,500 a m.] GOWR 127:3
April is the cruellest m. ELIOT 104:10
old man in a dry m. ELIOT 100:6
O m. of flowerings ARAG 13:2
months: weeks rather than m. WILS 313:10
Montparnasse: I shall not rest quiet in M.
BENÉT 36:17
Montreal: Stowed away in a M. lumber room
BUTL 60:6
monument: Their only m. the asphalt road
ELIOT 104:2
monuments: M. of unageing intellect YEATS 321:5
moo: And m. and coo with women-folk
KIPL 168:4
One end is m., the other, milk NASH 217:13
moocow: m. coming down along JOYCE 158:8
moon: And a white m. beams KING 167:8
And I danced in the m. CART 64:7
A ship, an isle, a sickle m. FLEC 111:15
Don't let's ask for the m. PROU 241:6
I didn't go to the m. WILL 312:7
It was the lovely m.—she lifted FREE 116:14
melodious cats under the m. HUXL 148:9
moment when the m. was blood CHES 71:7
M. and returning him safely KENN 164:2

moon (cont.):
m. and under the sun PORT 236:18
m. is in the seventh house RADO 242:8
m. shone bright on Mrs ELIOT 105:4
m. was a ghostly galleon NOYES 221:9
shine on, harvest m. NORW 221:6
Slowly, silently, now the m. DE L 91:5
The m. belongs to everyone DE SY 91:12
The m. is nothing FRY 119:17
The M. on the one hand BELL 35:9
The silver apples of the m. YEATS 322:12
Tryst with the m. DRIN 95:17
moonlight: Look for me by m. NOYES 221:11
M. behind you COW 85:5
road was a ribbon of m. NOYES 221:9
moonlit: A starlit or a m. dome distains
YEATS 323:9
Knocking on the m. door DE L 90:11
moons: Reason has m., but moons HODG 142:4
moon-washed: On m. apples of wonder
DRIN 95:17
Moorish: M. wall and I thought well
JOYCE 159:10
moorland: Past cotton-grass and m. AUDEN 19:15
moors: seen dawn and sunset on m. MAS 203:4
moose: strong as a bull m. ROOS 252:2
moral: afraid of losing your m. STEIN 284:8
being a form of m. effort LEAC 183:2
Englishman thinks he is m. SHAW 271:5
It is a m. issue HALEY 131:4
m. category but a pillar SOLZ 280:4
m. crusade or it WILS 313:9
m. flabbiness born JAMES 153:12
M. indignation is jealousy WELLS 308:13
m. system can rest solely AYER 21:12
prostitute is more m. than a wife PHIL 233:12
unhappy one becomes m. PROU 240:11
moralising: blow his nose without m. CONN 80:17
moralist: vital problem for the m. RUSS 255:1
moralists: conscience is a delight to m.
RUSS 255:15
moralitee: Goodbye, m. HERB 139:6
morality: I don't believe in m. SHAW 268:22
kinds of m. side by side RUSS 255:18
m. in any given time WHIT 310:9
m. loses the foundation SAM 259:6
m. should have this fact SHAW 269:13
M.'s not practical BOLT 48:13
thats middle-class m. SHAW 273:19
up agen middle-class m. SHAW 273:15
morals: done by basing m. on myth SAM 259:6
Food comes first, then m. BREC 53:1
Have you no m., man SHAW 273:14
more: joints m. than somewhat RUNY 254:7
m. people should see me ASHC 14:1
m. things a man is ashamed SHAW 270:14
m. things in heaven HALD 131:1
M. will mean worse AMIS 5:12
some animals are m. ORW 224:12

more (*cont.*):
The m. it snows	MILNE 209:11
To Masefield something m.	BEER 30:14
which is probably m.	KALM 161:4
wink wink, say no m.	CHAP 67:8

Moriarty: M. of mathematical celebrity
DOYLE 94:18

mornin': Oh, what a beautiful m. HAMM 131:13
morning: arrives in the early m. BOWEN 50:11
Good m., sir—was there	MURD 216:2
gray dawn of the m. after	ADE 2:19
hate to get up in the m.	BERL 40:7
I danced in the m.	CART 64:7
It's m. again in America	RINEY 248:2
I viewed the m. with alarm	GERS 123:6
Like the first m.	FARJ 107:6
m. glows the lily	FLEC 111:11
M. has broken	FARJ 107:6
m. I had another talk	CHAM 66:5
Praise for the m.	FARJ 107:6
shadow at m. striding	ELIOT 104:12
Such a m. it is when love	LEE 183:17
sun and in the m.	BINY 47:5
The m. light creaks down again	SITW 276:1
they take you in the m.	BALD 22:11
was arrested one fine m.	KAFKA 160:7
You've got to get up this m.	BERL 40:7

mornings: The literary m. with its hoot
AUDEN 19:12
we *always* had m. like MILNE 209:14
Mornington: made me a present of M.
HARG 135:3
Morocco: Dictionary, we're M. bound BURKE 58:4
moron: I wish I were a m. ANON 10:14
| See the happy m. | ANON 10:14 |
| The consumer isn't a m. | OGIL 222:18 |

moronic: m. inferno had caught up BELL 35:11
morphine: alcohol or m. or idealism JUNG 159:16
Morris: [William M.] BEER 30:13
mort: *compositeur, c'est d'être m.* HON 143:3
mortal: every tatter in its m. YEATS 321:6
M., guilty, but to me AUDEN 17:10
mortals: Composing m. with immortal
AUDEN 20:13
luckiest of m. because what AUDEN 19:11
mortar: Lies are the m. that bind WELLS 308:9
mortgaged: And frequently m. to the hilt
COW 85:7
morts: *Il n'y a pas de m.* MAET 198:10
Moscow: Do not march on M. MONT 212:7
M. to surprise us BRAC 51:13
moss: Miles and miles of golden m. AUDEN 20:1
m. or a caterpillar BARB 24:15
most: m. people vote against ADAMS 2:6
That [sex] was the m. fun ALLEN 5:1
mother: And her m. came too TITH 297:19
At that M. got proper blazing	EDGAR 98:4
Can you hear me, m.	POW 239:11
Care of his M.	MILNE 210:1

mother (*cont.*):
Don't tell my m. I'm living	HERB 139:8
For m. will be there	HERB 139:10
Gin was m.'s milk to her	SHAW 273:17
Glory, M. of the Free	BENS 39:4
man and the m. woman	SHAW 270:17
M. died today	CAMUS 62:15
M., give me the sun	IBSEN 150:4
m. is she watches her middle-aged	SCOT 265:11
M. knows best	FERB 108:4
m. lived the latter years	THUR 297:4
M. may I go and bathe	ANON 9:24
M. may I go out to swim	DE L 91:8
m. never realizes	JACK 151:17
M. to dozens	HERB 139:4
My m., drunk or sober	CHES 68:14
My m.'s life made me a man	MAS 203:7
my m. taught me as a boy	BERR 41:13
My m. used to say	AYCK 21:6
rate butcher but his m.	ASHF 14:9
really affectionate m.	MAUG 205:17
that I half knew my m.	O'BR 222:5
universal m.	CHES 71:6

mother-in-law: man said when his m. died
JER 155:10
savage contemplates his m. FRAZ 116:8
mother-naked: And m. and ageless-ancient
DAY-L 89:5
mothers: Come m. and fathers DYLAN 97:13
| M. of large families | BELL 32:15 |
| talking to you m. and fathers | ROOS 250:10 |

moths: m. among the whisperings FITZ 110:14
motion: A gentle m. with the deep DAV 89:1
Between the m.	ELIOT 103:4
Poetry in m.	KAUF 161:11
poetry of m.	GRAH 127:15

motive: Looks always on the m. YEATS 321:9
motives: opponent m. meaner BARR 26:5
motorcycle: art of m. maintenance PIRS 235:6
motoribus: Cincti Bis M. GODL 125:8
motors: The sound of horns and m. ELIOT 105:4
motto: speak is criticism's m. FORS 115:14
| that is my m. | MARQ 201:12 |
| The scouts' m. is founded | BAD 22:2 |

mottoes: Rather than the m. on sundials
POUND 238:6
mould: frozen in an out-of-date m. JENK 154:11
m. a child's character SHAW 271:20
moulded: m. by their admirations BOWEN 50:12
Moulmein: By the old M. Pagoda KIPL 169:6
mount: rejected the Sermon on the M. BRAD 52:6
mountain: And the river jumps over the m.
AUDEN 16:12
Climb ev'ry m., ford ev'ry	HAMM 131:9
In a m. greenery	HART 135:12
O'er the rugged m.'s brow	GRAH 127:9
We've been to the m. top	KING 166:11

mountainous: great big m. sports girl BETJ 44:4

mountains: He paced upon the m. far above
YEATS 318:8
mounting: view there is m. chaos   CALL 61:7
mourn: here is no cause to m.   OWEN 228:6
mourning: voice of m. save the choirs
OWEN 227:13
   waste any time in m.   HILL 140:10
mourns: England m. for her dead   BINY 47:4
mouse: leave room for the m.   SAKI 258:6
   wainscot and the m.   ELIOT 102:2
moustache: m. and the sort of eye   WOD 315:15
   who didn't wax his m. was   KIPL 175:3
mouth: A way of happening, a m.   AUDEN 17:4
   before he opens his m.   NATH 218:14
   just whispering in her m.   MARX 202:9
   keeping your m. shut   EINS 99:9
   m. too wide when he talks   FORS 114:2
   m. without making some   SHAW 273:10
mouths: examining his wives' m.   RUSS 255:8
   m. were made for tankards   MAS 203:3
   We poets keep our m. shut   YEATS 318:5
move: high altar on the m.   BOWEN 50:14
   Let us m. forward   ROOS 251:3
   M. him into the sun   OWEN 228:1
   m. in a world of the dead   FORS 114:6
moved: We shall not be m.   ANON 12:4
movement: But neither arrest nor m.   ELIOT 101:8
   intelligent may begin a m.   CONR 81:21
   m. of clouds in benediction   DAY-L 89:7
moves: His mind m. upon silence   YEATS 320:2
   If it m., salute it   ANON 8:14
   It m. in mighty leaps   AYRES 22:1
movies: basic appeal of m.   KAEL 160:5
   M. should have a beginning   GOD 125:7
   out and pay to see bad m.   GOLD 126:12
   that can kill the M.   ROG 249:5
moving: It is m. day   HART 135:12
   King's life is m. peacefully   DAWS 89:3
   Somebody stopped the m. stairs   MACN 198:3
Mozart: en famille they play M.   BARTH 27:3
   M. and Salieri we see   BAR 25:1
   The truth is that M.   SONT 280:13
MPs: M. never see the London   LIV 189:4
much: conflict was so m. owed   CHUR 74:8
   Guessing so much and so m.   CHES 69:15
   Missing so m. and so much   CORN 83:12
   M. as you said you were   HARDY 134:12
   seem m. for them   COMP 80:1
   So little done, so m. to do   RHOD 246:6
muck: can say is — sing 'em m.   MELBA 206:7
   lovely m. I've lain   HOUS 146:16
muck-rakes: m. are often indispensable
ROOS 251:12
mud: m. against a wall may   BLUNT 48:2
   M.! Mud! Glorious mud   FLAN 111:5
   M.'s sister, not himself   HOUS 144:5
   pure clay of time's m.   MAL 199:12
   universe with m.   FORS 114:9
muddied: wicket or the m. oafs   KIPL 170:11

mudging: up with fudging and m.   OWEN 227:9
Mudie's: British Museum and at M.   BUTL 60:7
mug: Guinness from a thick m.   PINT 234:14
Mulligan: plump Buck M. came from
JOYCE 158:14
multitude: m. of silent witnesses   GEOR 123:4
multitudes: Weeping, weeping m.   ELIOT 100:5
mum: you up, your m. and dad   LARK 179:1
mumble: When in doubt, m.   BOREN 49:9
Mungojerrie: I might mention M.   ELIOT 102:12
municipal: vast m. fire station   CHAR 68:3
murals: Garden City Café with its m.   BETJ 42:7
murder: brought back m. into the home
HITC 141:4
   Dial 'M' for m.   KNOTT 176:4
   even to m.   ADLER 3:1
   lies sound truthful and m.   ORW 226:3
   m. his wife that Dr Bickleigh   ILES 150:10
   M. is a serious business   ILES 150:10
   m. of men is disgusting   EINS 99:4
   We hear war called m.   MACD 194:14
murderer: man is a common m.   SAKI 257:5
murdering: executed for m. his publisher
BARR 25:13
murmur: Seem to m. sweet and low   ARMS 13:7
   The ever-importunate m.   JAMES 152:6
Murphy: M.'s Law to the statement   MURP 216:4
muscle: take the m. from bone   ELIOT 102:10
muse: Livelier liquor than the M.   HOUS 146:15
   M. only speak when she   SMITH 279:2
museum: An artist may visit a m.   SANT 260:15
mush: with m. and slush   OWEN 227:9
mushroom: *too short to stuff a m.*   CONR 82:3
music: A dance to the m. of time   POW 239:6
   alive with the sound of m.   HAMM 132:3
   all his m. accepts it   SATIE 263:6
   All m. is folk music   ARMS 13:8
   anguish, rather like m.   FRY 119:18
   anything about m. really   BEER 31:15
   Caught in that sensual m.   YEATS 321:5
   Classic m. is th'kind   HUBB 147:7
   Darling of the m.   SMITH 277:7
   English may not like m.   BEEC 30:1
   Extraordinary how potent cheap m.   COW 85:3
   have an ear for her m.   DAY-L 89:7
   I got m.   GERS 123:7
   inexpressible is m.   HUXL 149:4
   Is there a meaning to m.   COPL 83:8
   keep swinging after the m.   HELP 138:1
   me the most civilized m.   UST 302:13
   more or less lascivious m.   MENC 207:2
   m. begins there   MILL 208:13
   m. begins to atrophy when   POUND 237:15
   m. expresses itself   STR 288:7
   m. for a lilt upon   MAS 203:3
   m. goes 'round and around   HODG 142:5
   m. is best understood   STR 288:8
   M. is essentially useless   SANT 260:14

music (cont.):

M. is feeling, then, not sound	STEV 285:9
M. *is* life, and like it	NIEL 219:11
m. is more enchanting	SMITH 277:17
m. is that which penetrates	BEEC 30:2
m. is the brandy	SHAW 271:3
M. is your own experience	PARK 230:1
m. of a poem along	SYNGE 289:9
m. *per se* means nothing	BEEC 29:23
m. that changed a man's	SCHN 264:8
O body swayed to m.	YEATS 321:8
read m. but can't hear	BEEC 29:16
sound of m. so tender	PORT 236:10
The m. [the scherzo of Beethoven's 5th Symphony]	FORS 114:13
what do you think about m.	VAUG 303:11
What m. shall I have	PITT 235:8
whisper m. on those strings	ELIOT 105:10

musical: kind of m. Malcolm Sargent

BEEC 29:20

musicals: m. one day about the glamour-studded

MAC 195:7

musician: poet and not a m.   BUTL 59:18

musicians: M. did not like the piece   BEEC 29:22

To all m., appear and inspire   AUDEN 20:13

musicologist: m. is a man who can read

BEEC 29:16

musket: Sam, Sam, pick up tha' m.

HOLL 142:12

musky: close to the Crocodile's m.	KIPL 172:1
müssen: *wir sie nicht erleben m.*	FRIS 117:7
Mussolini: Even Hitler and M. were	LOW 191:6
must: I m. have no hatred	CAV 65:8
m. and the talent	BAR 25:1
mute: except that of m.	MACM 196:14
mutilate: spindle or m. in any way	ANON 7:16

mutilated: My elegant car . . . was m.

BELL 35:11

mutual: consists in the m. guarding

RILKE 247:9

forms of m. exploitation	AUDEN 18:14
my: My Goodness, M. Guinness	RICH 247:1
myriad: A m. men will save	ROSS 253:6
There died a m.	POUND 238:9
myself: Am quite m. again	HOUS 146:2
find I'm talking to m.	BARN 25:9

mysterious: crime is often the most m.

DOYLE 95:11

God works in a m. way   ELIOT 102:14

mystery: Courage was mine, and I had m.

OWEN 228:7

Magical m. tour	LENN 185:11
m. inside an enigma	CHUR 75:6
m. of the atom and rejected	BRAD 52:6
strangeness with m.	DOYLE 95:11

myth: A m. is, of course   RYLE 256:7

by basing morals on m.	SAM 259:6
curveship lend a m. to God	CRANE 85:11
were a m. No one ever	ATK 15:15

N

Nacht: *die N. der langen Messer*	HITL 141:6
nagging: n. is the repetition	SUMM 289:2
nail: painter and I n. my pictures	SCHW 265:3
nails: I used to bite my n.	PARK 230:5
nineteen hundred and forty n.	SITW 276:6
relatively clean finger n.	MORT 214:3
naissent: *humains n. libres et égaux*	ANON 11:16
naît: *On ne n. pas femme*	BEAU 89:9
naïve: n. domestic Burgundy without	THUR 297:8
the n. forgive and forget	SZASZ 290:3

naked: And n. to the hangman's noose

HOUS 145:15

ashamed of our n. skins	SHAW 270:13
In walking n.	YEATS 322:1
n. ape self-named *Homo*	MORR 213:14
orchid she rode quite n.	AUDEN 20:12
Secretary n. into the conference	BEVAN 45:2
starving hysterical n.	GINS 125:1

name: gable and writing our n.   HEAN 136:9

holy n. of liberty	GAND 121:10
its n. is Ainsley Gotto	ERWIN 106:14
liberties are taken in thy n.	GEOR 123:5
long as you spell my n.	COHAN 78:10
mark against your n.	RICE 246:10
may prefer a self-made n.	HAND 132:8
n. any disease after two	PUZO 241:10
n. at the top of the page	CHUR 75:9
n. of a man is a numbing	MCL 196:10
n. of totalitarianism	GAND 121:10
n. we give the people	MARQ 112:11
paper which bears his n.	CHAM 66:5
yet can't quite n.	LARK 178:11

nameless: n. and abominable colour HOUS 144:8

names: love with American n.	BENÉT 36:16
n. of those	SPEN 281:15
n. would be associated	SAKI 257:17
things with their n.	SART 261:16

naming: Today we have n. of parts REED 244:12

nape: her n. caught in his bill   YEATS 322:6

Napoleon: N. of crime	DOYLE 94:18
N. of Crime	ELIOT 102:12
N.'s armies always used	SELL 266:11

Napoleons: worship the Caesars and N.

HUXL 148:14

narcotic: n. be alcohol or morphine	JUNG 159:16
narrow: Every bed is n.	MILL 208:4
n. into a neighbourhood	JOHN 156:8
nastiest: n. little man I've ever	DYKS 97:2
The n. thing in the nicest way	GOLD 126:1
nasty: everybody is as n. as himself	SHAW 274:4
something n. in the woodshed	GIBB 123:12

Natchez: young belle of old N.   NASH 218:11

nation: A N. spoke to a Nation	KIPL 170:7
at the service of the n.	POMP 236:2
British n. is unique	CHUR 75:1

nation (cont.):

dream that one day this n.	KING 166:10
have to exterminate a n.	SPOCK 282:7
I want ours to be a n.	MUG 215:2
king and government and n.	KAV 161:12
Let every n. know, whether	KENN 163:8
mass of a n.	HITL 141:11
n. by its advertisements	DOUG 93:12
n. is fit to sit in judgement	WILS 314:10
n. is quite considerable	WILS 313:1
n. is the highest	JOHN 156:13
N. of many sovereign States	PAGE 228:10
N. shall speak peace unto	REND 245:11
n. talking to itself	MILL 208:12
n., we dont dress	SHAW 274:7
one-third of a n. ill-housed	ROOS 250:7
temptation to a rich and lazy n.	KIPL 170:16
that I inspired the n.	CHUR 76:10
was thus clearly top n.	SELL 266:13
we are a n. of amateurs	ROS 252:11
what our N. stands	BETJ 44:5

national: N. Debt is a very Good | SELL 266:10

n. home for the Jewish	BALF 23:13
N. Theatre when it was	HALL 131:6
our n. disease	JAMES 153:12
That key is Russian n.	CHUR 75:6

National Gallery: elegant façade of the N.

CHAR 68:3

National Health: N. Service is safe | THAT 292:1

nationalism: N. is an infantile sickness | EINS 99:3

N. is a silly cock crowing	ALD 3:12

nationalities: smaller n. of Europe | ASQ 14:19

nationality: Ask any man what n. | RHOD 246:4

nationals: we are not other n. | MONT 212:8

nations: And the living n. wait | AUDEN 17:6

gossip from all the n.	AUDEN 19:16
men and n. behave wisely	EBAN 97:16
n. have always acted like	KUBR 177:3
n. which have put mankind	INGE 151:7
Other n. use 'force'	WAUGH 306:12
The day of small n. has	CHAM 66:1

native: n. and sees the human being | LESS 186:8

'n.' before the hyphen	ROOS 251:13

natives: Britons were only n. | SELL 266:4

natural: n. man has only two primal | OSLER 227:7

n. to have come from there	STEIN 284:6
n. to us than a cage	SHAW 269:5

nature: Consistency is contrary to n. | HUXL 148:12

[Death is] n.'s way	ANON 7:15
For n., heartless, witless	HOUS 145:8
interpreted n. as freely	GIR 125:3
interrogate as well as observe n.	OSLER 226:16
N. and we women cannot	GIBB 123:11
n. not by force	BRON 54:7
n. of a protest	HOFF 142:7
necessary limitations of our n.	AUDEN 18:7
no spell to cast on n.	BRON 54:7
refined and sensitive n.	DOYLE 95:4
that n. replaces it	WILL 312:5

naught: I must have n. beside | THOM 295:4

I tell you n. for your comfort	CHES 68:9
N. broken save this body	BROO 54:10

naughtiest: The n. girl in the school | BLYT 48:7

naughty: N. but nice | WALD 304:11

Oh wasn't it n. of Smudges	BETJ 42:11

naval: me about n. tradition | CHUR 73:8

navel: water rise above his n. | ABSE 1:4

navies: Far-called our n. melt away | KIPL 173:4

navy: N. is that I am very much | CARS 64:3

They expect the n.	CHUR 72:10
thoroughly efficient n.	ROOS 251:8

nay: And Mr Hall's n. was nay | BENT 39:13

Nazi: odious apparatus of N. rule | CHUR 74:6

near: When I'm not n. the girl | HARB 132:14

nearer: n. God's Heart in a garden | GURN 130:9

nearest: n. to expressing the inexpressible

HUXL 149:4

The n. thing to death in life	ANON 10:1

neat: I was n., clean, shaved | CHAN 66:10

n. and adequately tall	CHES 70:16
You look n.	COLL 79:7

necessarily: It ain't n. | HEYW 140:6

necessary: everything in it is a n. evil | BRAD 52:3

into the war is the n. art	DULL 96:5
Is your journey *really* n.	ANON 8:20
n. limitations of our nature	AUDEN 18:7
n. to destroy the town	ANON 9:1

necessities: were n. and which luxuries

WRIG 317:17

necessity: luxury; fiction is a n. | CHES 68:12

neck: A n. God made for other use | HOUS 145:15

Some chicken! Some n.	CHUR 73:1

necklace: with our n., we shall | MAND 200:1

necks: comes and wrings our n. | AYRES 21:16

necktie: And left my n. God knows where

HOUS 146:16

need: All you n. is love | LENN 185:5

n. for living in central	GOWR 127:3
n. in this life is ignorance	TWAIN 302:4
n. thou hast in life	HOPE 144:3
n. to have	WARH 305:4
N. we say it was not love	MILL 208:5
present n. is nof heroics	HARD 133:1
Will you still n. me	LENN 185:15
world for everyone's n.	BUCH 57:8

needs: that Blushes. Or n. | TWAIN 300:17

negative: But will his n. inversion | AUDEN 20:3

Elim-my-nate the n.	MERC 207:6
n. of which America	MCC 193:14
n. peace which is the absence	KING 166:7

negotiate: never n. out of fear | KENN 163:10

negotiating: N. with de Valera | LLOY 189:7

Negro: drop of N. blood | HUGH 147:12

N.'s great stumbling block	KING 166:7
root of the American N.	BALD 22:9

neighbour: policy of the good n. | ROOS 250:5

whole than to love one's n.	HOFF 142:6

neighbourhood: will not narrow into a n.
    JOHN 156:8
neighbours: But just as all the n.   CHES 70:16
  Good fences make good n.   FROST 118:14
  happening to our n.   CHAM 66:2
  silk, will the n. say   HARDY 134:1
  thoughts about their n.   BRAD 51:15
neither: Will n. care nor know   HOUS 145:8
Nell: Little N. and Lady Macbeth   WOOL 317:15
Nellie: by the stream, N. Dean   ARMS 13:7
  Wait till the sun shines, N.   STER 285:5
neo-gothic: Pancras Station—n., you know
    BEEC 30:6
Nero: N. fiddled, but Coolidge   MENC 206:8
nerve: after the n. has been   ROWL 253:14
  all fat, without n.   LEWIS 187:8
  called a n. specialist   WOD 316:1
  test your n. or give   SIMM 275:8
nerveux: *grand nous vient des n.*   PROU 240:12
nervous: capacity to make us n.   SONT 280:9
  n. breakdown is the belief   RUSS 255:2
nervousness: There is only n. or death LEB 183:8
nest: warm n. of renaissance   DAY-L 89:5
nestlings: And n. fly   HARDY 133:8
nests: Birds in their little n. agree   BELL 34:4
net: old to rush up to the n.   ADAMS 2:4
  play tennis with the n.   FROST 118:6
  Whizzing them over the n.   BETJ 44:4
nets: n. of wrong and right   YEATS 318:7
nettles: like the dust on the n.   THOM 294:6
neurosis: N. is the way of avoiding   TILL 297:17
neurotics: have come to us from n.   PROU 240:12
neutral: stood apart, studiously n.   WILS 314:6
neutrality: Armed n. is ineffectual   WILS 314:12
  just for a word 'n.'   BETH 41:16
never: described but had n. seen   HALS 131:7
  have n. had it so good   MACM 197:4
  I n. promised you a rose garden   GREEN 128:10
  N. ask of money spent   FROST 118:5
  N. believe in mirrors   OSB 226:9
  N. explain   FISH 110:4
  N. explain   HUBB 147:2
  N. give a sucker an even break   FIEL 109:2
  n. go down to the end   MILNE 210:1
  n. hated a man enough   GABOR 120:14
  n. in the field of human   CHUR 74:8
  n. knowingly undersold   LEWIS 187:6
  N. mind the quality   POW 239:12
  N. on Sunday   DASS 88:10
  N. play cards with a man   ALGR 3:14
  second things n.   CONR 82:4
  slogan 'We N. Closed'   VAN D 303:5
  sometimes always, by God, N.   RICH 247:7
  they n. will be good   BARTH 27:2
  You'll n. walk alone   HAMM 132:5
  you n. can tell   SHAW 274:8
  You're n. alone with a Strand   MAY 206:1
nevermore: N. to peep again, creep   DE L 91:7

new: Day by day make it n.   POUND 238:1
  govern N. South Wales   BELL 33:7
  Is a n. beginning, a raid   ELIOT 101:16
  n. and neat and adequately   CHES 70:16
  n. deal for the American   ROOS 250:3
  N. England is not Puritanism   KRUT 177:1
  n. wine into old bottles   ATTL 16:4
  The shock of the n.   DUNL 96:9
  Youth is something very n.   CHAN 67:3
Newcastle: no more coals to N.   GEOR 122:13
New England: N. weather that compels
    TWAIN 301:21
news: And it still is n.   HOL 142:11
  bites a dog, that is n.   BOG 48:10
  Literature is n. that STAYS   POUND 237:18
  N. is what a chap who doesn't   WAUGH 306:10
  n. yet to hear and fine   CHES 69:6
  report all the n.   NIXON 220:3
  tell Tchaikovsky the n.   BERRY 41:9
newspaper: A good n., I suppose   MILL 208:12
  n. is of necessity something   SCOTT 265:5
  n. is to be Accurate   SWOPE 289:5
  Once a n. touches a story   MAIL 199:7
  person employed by a n.   HUBB 147:4
newspapers: I read the n. avidly   BEVAN 45:9
  It's the n. I can't stand   STOP 287:2
  Never believe in mirrors or n.   OSB 226:9
  n. are ceaselessly querulous   MENC 207:1
Newton: And make us as N. was   AUDEN 19:3
  another N., a new Donne   HUXL 148:18
New York: California to the N.   GUTH 130:10
  I like N. in June   FREED 116:12
  New York, N., — a helluva town   COMD 79:10
New Yorker: N. will be the magazine   ROSS 253:3
nexus: n. with the work of Ricardo   GALB 121:3
Niagara: On seeing N. Falls   MAHL 199:3
nice: Naughty but n.   WALD 304:11
  N. but nubbly   KIPL 171:9
  N. guys   DUR 96:11
  n. men are good at getting   WHIT 310:14
  N. one, Cyril   ANON 10:4
  n. to get up in the mornin'   LAUD 180:2
  n. to have you back where   HERM 139:20
  n. to people on your way   MIZN 212:1
  N. to see you—to see you, nice   FORS 116:2
  N. work if you can get it   GERS 123:10
nicely: That'll do n., sir   ANON 6:15
nicens: n. little boy named baby   JOYCE 158:8
nicest: nastiest thing in the n.   GOLD 126:1
nichts: *Vergleiche entscheiden n.*   FREUD 117:5
niece: hitting the n. of a bishop   ORW 225:14
niggers: stink of the damned dead n.   ASQ 15:9
night: acquainted with the n.   FROST 119:7
  A long day's journey into n.   O'NEI 223:10
  be coming for us that n.   BALD 22:11
  dark n. of the soul it   FITZ 110:12
  Every hour. Let no n.   DE L 90:15
  fit n. out for man   FIEL 109:7

night (cont.):

For one n. or the other night	FLEC 111:13
gentle into that good n.	THOM 292:11
Illness is the n.-side	SONT 280:12
It's been a hard day's n.	LENN 185:10
Last n. I dreamt I went	DU M 96:7
Let n. come, ring out the hour	APOL 12:15
machinery of the n.	GINS 125:1
moonless n. in the small	THOM 293:13
N. and day, you are the one	PORT 236:18
n. in her silver shoon	DE L 91:5
N. is growing grey	HARDY 134:7
N. Mail crossing the Border	AUDEN 19:15
n. of tropical splendour	PORT 236:10
n. of tyranny had descended	MURR 216:9
n. we went to Birmingham	CHES 69:5
returned on the previous n.	BULL 57:11
sleep; at n. he hunts	ELIOT 102:14
slow Wicket of the N.	THOM 294:9
That haunts you n. and day	BERL 40:8
The N. of the Long Knives	HITL 141:6
then it's n. once more	BECK 29:13
what closes Saturday n.	KAUF 161:6
Where the blue of the n.	CROS 86:10

night-blasts: flags straining in the n. CHES 70:6

nightingale: A n. sang in Berkeley Square

	MASC 202:15
brown n. bills his best	HARDY 133:8

nightingales: The n. are singing near

	ELIOT 102:13
Where the n. are singing	KING 167:8

nightmare: In the n. of the dark AUDEN 17:6

long national n. is over	FORD 113:8
n. from which I am	JOYCE 159:2

nightmares: daydreams would darken into n.

	SMITH 277:13

nights: down the n. and down THOM 295:2

nil: N. carborundum illegitimi. ANON 10:2

Nile: Bankhead barged down the N.

	BROWN 56:12

nimble: n. in the calling of selling LEWIS 187:11

nine: N. bean rows will I have YEATS 318:10

nineteen: it doesn't mean n. BENN 38:9

Nineveh: Is one with N., and Tyre KIPL 173:4

Is Solomon's temple, poets, N.	MEYN 207:11
N. from distant Ophir	MAS 202:16

nipping: n. the heels of Hemingway ALGR 3:16

nix: Sticks n. hick pix ANON 11:3

no: A man who says n. CAMUS 63:1

can't say N.	PARK 231:9
confirmed turophile n.	FAD 107:4
he's got n. business	GALS 121:7
land of the omnipotent N.	BOLD 48:12
n. go the merrygoround	MACN 197:11
N.! I am not Prince Hamlet	ELIOT 103:11
n. instruction book came	FULL 120:8
N. manager ever got fired	ANON 10:3
N. more coals to Newcastle	GEOR 122:13
N. more Latin, no more French	ANON 10:5

no (cont.):

n. plain women on television	FORD 113:6
n. real alternative	THAT 291:7
N. sex please — we're British	MARR 202:4
n. such thing as a free	HEIN 137:2
n. such thing as Society	THAT 292:6
n. such thing as splendour	FORS 114:13
N. tears in the writer	FROST 118:1
Oh, n. man knows	DE L 90:8
There is n. such thing	FAUL 108:1
Ulster says n.	ANON 11:17

Noah: cataclysm but one poor N. HUXL 148:18

God gave N. the rainbow sign	ANON 8:3
N. he often said	CHES 68:15

noble: dignifies n. people SHAW 270:2

Eternally n., historically	LERN 185:21
except for a n. purpose	HERB 139:17
N. deeds and hot baths	SMITH 277:1

nobleness: And N. walks in our ways again

	BROO 55:1

noblest: God's the n. work of man BUTL 59:4

nobody: And n. knows MILNE 209:11

And n.'s wife	HERB 139:4
n. comes, nobody goes	BECK 29:7
n. gets old and godly	YEATS 319:8
N. speaks the truth when	BOWEN 51:1
n. tells me anything	GALS 121:7
N. was ever meant	FROST 118:5
someone gave a war & N.	GINS 124:12
war and n. will come	SAND 260:4
Well, n.'s perfect	WILD 311:5
What n. is sure about	BELL 33:18
wrecks and n. drownded	EDGAR 98:3

Nod: Old N., the shepherd, goes DE L 90:9

passed with a n. of the head	YEATS 320:4

no-encouragement: read an expression of n.

	BRAM 52:11

noise: absolutely love the n. BEEC 30:1

A happy n. to hear	HOUS 146:3
fourth time that infernal n.	EDW 98:7
most sublime n.	FORS 114:12
N., n. A stench	BIER 46:22
n. outside the cypress	LAWR 180:7

noisy: Oh, n. bells, be dumb HOUS 146:4

nom: Démocratie est le n. que MARQ 112:11

nomadic: on the contrary, were n. WHITE 310:3

noms: choses avec leurs n. SART 261:16

non: Un homme qui dit n. CAMUS 63:1

non-being: avoiding n. by avoiding being

	TILL 297:17

non-combatant: War hath no fury like a n.

	MONT 212:6

non-commissioned: backbone of the Army is the n.

	KIPL 174:12

nonconformity: history of N. behind him

	ORW 225:16

none: n. of them know one half GRAH 127:13

some have charm for n.	BARR 26:11

nonexistence: either nonviolence or n. KING 167:5

non-fiction: make use of her n.   AYCK 21:8
non-interference: n. with their own peculiar
                                        JAMES 153:17
nonsense: anchor in n. than to put   GALB 121:3
  had discovered what n.   MAUG 204:11
  n. can I stand twice   RICH 247:7
  n. which was knocked out   BEER 30:16
nonsensical: are equally n.   CHOM 71:16
non-u: U and N. An essay in sociological
                                        ROSS 253:1
nonviolence: either n. or nonexistence KING 167:5
non-violence: N. is the first article   GAND 122:1
  organization of n.   BAEZ 22:3
noon: Is sayin' nearly n.   AYRES 21:16
  midnight and the n.'s repose   ELIOT 103:17
  n. and tell me it smells   JOHN 156:2
  n. a purple glow   YEATS 318:10
  N. strikes on England   FLEC 112:1
noose: And naked to the hangman's n.
                                        HOUS 145:15
  I tie the n. on in a knowing   CHES 70:16
nooses: N. give   PARK 230:14
norfan: I'm a N., both sides   WELLS 308:7
Norfolk: bear him up the N.   BETJ 42:4
normal: homosexuality were the n. way   BRY 57:2
  n. child and not as a prodigy   BARB 24:17
  Thank God we're n.   OSB 226:7
normalcy: nostrums but n.   HARD 133:1
Norman: blacksmith like our N.   KIPL 174:1
  I always feel with N.   AYCK 21:11
  Phone for the fish-knives, N.   BETJ 42:12
Norris: Mr N. changes trains   ISH 151:16
north: heart of the N. is dead   LAWR 181:3
  N.-East   KIPL 170:4
  n. you may run to the rime-ringed   KIPL 175:6
Northcliffe: has resigned and N. has   ANON 8:10
  [Lord N.]   TAYL 290:13
northern: N. reticence, the tight   HEAN 136:11
Norwegian: N. Blue   CHAP 67:9
nose: caught him by his little n.   KIPL 172:1
  Do not run up your n. dead   BALD 23:1
  Had a very shiny n.   MARKS 201:6
  his n. without moralising   CONN 80:17
  n. had gone to that bourne   MORT 214:8
  n. needs a constant struggle   ORW 226:5
  Some thirty inches from my n.   AUDEN 16:10
  what lies under one's n.   AUDEN 18:11
  with a carnation up my n.   MCK 196:1
noselessness: The N. of Man   CHES 69:2
noses: They haven't got no n.   CHES 69:1
  Where do the n. go   HEM 138:3
nostalgia: N. isn't what it used   ANON 10:6
nostrums: not n. but normalcy   HARD 133:1
not: gladly n. to be standing   JOHN 156:6
  if you were not, n.   STEIN 284:7
  I say 'Why n.?'   SHAW 268:1
  n. entirely devoid of interest   DOYLE 94:5
  N. huffy, or stuffy   HERB 139:9

not (cont.):
  n. I, but the wind   LAWR 181:12
  N. many people know   CAINE 61:3
  n. necessarily   GOD 125:7
  N. so much a programme   ANON 10:7
  N. tonight, Josephine   DAVID 88:11
  n. what we were formerly   BLUN 47:13
  N. while I'm alive 'e   BEVIN 45:14
  N. with a bang but a whimper   ELIOT 103:5
  they have n.   BELL 33:14
note: It was only the n. of a bird   SIMP 275:10
  once he sent me round a n.   LEIGH 184:7
  suicide n. in history   KAUF 161:10
noted: I n. as of Demos at their root   WATS 305:9
  n. for fresh air and fun   EDGAR 98:3
notes: bedside making copious n.   BENN 38:3
  n. and our dead bodies   SCOTT 265:10
  n. I handle no better   SCHN 264:6
  n. like little fishes vanish   MACN 198:6
  n. tremendous from her   AUDEN 20:12
nothin': just another word for n.   KRIS 176:11
  N. ain't worth nothin'   KRIS 176:11
  There is n. like a dame   HAMM 132:4
  You ain't n. but a hound dog   LEIB 184:6
nothing: absolutely n.—half so much
                                        GRAH 127:13
  Analogies decide n.   FREUD 117:5
  And n. will remain   HOUS 146:2
  diner n. could be finer   GORD 126:14
  Fact, n. to laugh at at all   EDGAR 98:3
  For n. can be sole or whole   YEATS 323:8
  Goodness had n. to do   WEST 309:11
  I have n. to say   CAGE 60:17
  It follows that n. should   CORN 84:2
  moral crusade or it is n.   WILS 313:9
  n. but as a group decide   ALLEN 4:5
  n. ever ran quite straight   GALS 121:6
  N. happens, nobody comes   BECK 29:7
  n. has value   FORS 115:8
  n. in his long career   ANON 12:5
  N. IS EVER DONE IN THIS   SHAW 270:10
  N. is more dangerous   ALAIN 3:9
  N. is wasted, nothing   HERB 139:13
  N., like something   LARK 179:7
  n. on in the [calendar]   MONR 212:5
  nothing, really doing n.   STEIN 284:5
  n. that make no mistakes   CONR 81:18
  N. to be done   BECK 29:4
  n. to look backward   FROST 118:16
  n. to lose but our aitches   ORW 225:19
  people of whom we know n.   CHAM 66:4
  remembering n. but the blue sky   FORS 115:11
  The moon is n.   FRY 119:17
  There's n. surer   KAHN 161:3
  under there is n. but sleep   DRIN 95:17
  ways will all be as n.   HARDY 133:11
  Worked myself up from n.   PER 233:2
  you know, she was n.   AYCK 21:8
notice: used to n. such things   HARDY 134:1

Nottingham: N. lace of the curtains BETJ 41:17
nought: N. but vast Sorrow was there DE L 90:14
noun: not a n. FULL 120:7
novel: advance we may hold a n. JAMES 153:3
  either a picture or a n. JAMES 153:5
  n. before luncheon was WAUGH 306:14
  n. is *about* is always WELLS 308:2
  n. is that it does attempt JAMES 153:2
  n. tells a story FORS 114:7
novelist: No poet or n. wishes AUDEN 18:10
novelists: major n. who count LEAV 183:5
novels: entertaining than half the n.
  MAUG 205:13
  had reading the Beat n. CAP 63:10
now: History is n. and England ELIOT 102:6
  n. for something completely CHAP 67:7
  N. is the time for the burning BINY 47:3
nubbly: 'Stute Fish. 'Nice but n.' KIPL 171:9
nuclear: n. arms race has no military
  MOUN 214:13
  n. freeze proposals REAG 244:6
nude: n. with a carnation MCK 196:1
nudge: nudge n., snap snap CHAP 67:8
nuggets: Nuts and n. in the window BETJ 43:8
nuisance: exchange of one N. ELLIS 106:4
  squalid n. in time of war CHUR 75:4
nuit: *Vienne la n., sonne l'heure* APOL 12:15
null: this city, is N. an' Void O'CAS 222:11
NUM: against the Pope or the N. BALD 23:1
number: if I called the wrong n. THUR 297:9
  n. for a dinner party GULB 130:7
  n. of the question '1' CHUR 75:9
  very interesting n. RAM 242:15
  We're n. two. We try harder ANON 12:2
  with the square of the n. SHAN 267:7
numbers: His n., though they moved
  YEATS 319:14
  There is no safety in n. THUR 297:10
numerals: on the nature of the n. O'BR 222:2
nun: An extremely rowdy N. COW 85:9
  I'd the upbringing a n. ORTON 224:3
nurse: And always keep a-hold of N. BELL 32:18
nurseries: Look for me in the n. of heaven
  THOM 295:1
nurses: let's play doctor and n. MILL 209:7
nutrition: case of n. and health JAY 154:4
nuts: N. MCAU 193:7
  N. and nuggets in the window BETJ 43:8
nuttin': heard n. yet JOLS 157:3

O

O: else's horizon! O bliss GRAH 127:15
  O dark dark dark ELIOT 101:14
  O Death, where is thy ANON 10:8
  O O O O that Shakespeherian ELIOT 105:2

oafish: And o. louts remember Mum BETJ 42:5
oafs: muddied o. at the goals KIPL 170:11
oak: stream of old o. beams LANC 178:2
  Than O., and Ash, and Thorn KIPL 172:12
oakleaves: o., horses' heels ELIOT 104:9
oar: o. was dipping COKE 78:14
oars: banks of o. that swam upon YEATS 319:14
Oates: O. of the Inniskilling ATK 16:1
oath: artist who is on o. MACC 193:8
  o. again may my soul SHAW 273:21
obedience: be swift in all o. KIPL 174:3
obey: o. the orders given it ASIM 14:13
  parents o. their children EDW 98:10
obeyed: right to be o. than man JOHN 155:16
obituary: autobiography is an o. in serial
  CRISP 86:5
  publicity except your own o. BEHAN 32:5
object: o. that it is not a trial KAFKA 160:8
  o. to people looking BIRK 47:8
  The o. of art is actually ANOU 12:14
objectification: Art is the o. of feeling LANG 178:8
objectionable: it is doubtless o. ANON 11:12
  many ways extremely o. KEYN 165:2
objective: finding an 'o. correlative' ELIOT 104:4
objet: *L'art a pour o. de lui* ANOU 12:14
obligation: o. to become the servant SHAW 269:6
oblivion: long journey towards o. LAWR 181:10
  Over o. HARDY 133:13
obscene: O. as cancer, bitter as the cud
  OWEN 227:14
obscenity: 'o.' is not a term capable RUSS 255:19
observe: interrogate as well as o. nature
  OSLER 226:16
  You see, but you do not o. DOYLE 94:2
observer: Is a keen o. of life AUDEN 19:14
obsolescence: adolescence and o. LINK 188:12
obsolete: Either war is o. or men FULL 120:6
obstacle: o. to professional writing BENC 36:4
obvious: o. facts about grown-ups JARR 154:2
occasional: o. heart attack BENC 36:5
occupation: The cure for it is o. SHAW 273:6
occupied: o. her time most usefully BROO 56:3
occurred: Ought never to have o. BENT 39:14
occurrence: o. of the improbable MENC 207:3
ocean: didn't think much to the O. EDGAR 98:3
  I'll love you till the o. AUDEN 16:12
  o.'s margin this innocent AUDEN 20:12
  They hear like o. on a western LANG 178:5
oceans: To the o. white with foam BERL 40:6
o'clock: soul it is always three o. FITZ 110:12
octopus: that dear o. from whose SMITH 276:18
odd: But not so o. BROW 56:14
  How o. EWER 107:3
  It's a very o. thing DE L 91:3
  Must think it exceedingly o. KNOX 176:5
  o. about women who wear BENN 38:1
odds: And how am I to face the o. HOUS 145:4
  gamble at terrible o. STOP 287:10

53

ODE

ONE

odds (cont.):
  o. are five to six — DICK 92:3
ode: I intended an O. — DOBS 92:14
  O. on a Grecian Urn — FAUL 107:10
odium: He lived in the o. — BENT 39:9
Odysseus: Like O., the President — KEYN 164:12
Odyssey: surge and thunder of the O. — LANG 178:5
o'ercargoed: With leaden age o. — FLEC 112:3
offence: whom I was like to give o. — FROST 118:15
offending: o. both legal and natural — STOP 287:6
offensive: Life is an o., directed — WHIT 310:5
  someone else is being o. — BROO 56:2
  You are extremely o. — SMITH 277:6
offer: nothing to o. but blood — CHUR 74:3
  o. he can't refuse — PUZO 241:8
office: A man who has no o. — SHAW 269:15
  country in which the o. — HUXL 148:8
  o. that Benchley and Dorothy — BENC 36:9
  o. was his pirate ship — LEWIS 187:12
officers: o. and fellow-rankers — SMITH 279:1
official: O. dignity tends to increase — HUXL 148:8
  o. who has hung up an empty — SMITH 276:14
  The o. world, the corridors — SNOW 279:4
  This high o., all allow — HERB 139:12
  What is o. — FRY 119:15
offspring: mature enough for o. — DE VR 91:15
O'Grady: Colonel's Lady an' Judy O. — KIPL 174:10
oiks: o. with whom i am forced — WILL 311:10
oil: providers they're o. wells — PARK 231:13
Okie: O. means you're scum — STEI 284:17
old: All wars are planned by o. men — RICE 246:8
  Any o. iron, any old iron — COLL 79:7
  Ash on an o. man's sleeve — ELIOT 102:2
  attendance upon my o. age — YEATS 321:3
  boys of the o. Brigade — WEAT 306:16
  country for o. men — YEATS 321:5
  don't even like o. cars — SAL 258:14
  Don't let the o. folks know — HERB 139:8
  first sign of o. age — HICKS 140:8
  grow o. simultaneously — CONN 81:1
  Hope I die before I get o. — TOWN 298:5
  Ideas can be too o. — OUSP 227:8
  I grow o. . . . I grow old — ELIOT 103:12
  lads that will never be o. — HOUS 146:5
  me conservative when o. — FROST 118:4
  Mithridates, he died o. — HOUS 147:1
  now am not too o. — BLUN 47:13
  o. age crept over them — NAYL 218:16
  o. age is always fifteen — BAR 27:6
  O. age is the most unexpected — TROT 299:2
  o. and grey and full — YEATS 318:8
  o. bold mate of Henry Morgan — MAS 203:3
  O. Country must wake up — GEOR 122:14
  o. have reminiscences — SAKI 257:16
  o. have rubbed it — MAUG 204:11
  o. heads on your young — SPARK 281:5
  o. is having lighted rooms — LARK 178:11
  o. is like being increasingly — POW 239:7
  o. maid is like death — FERB 108:5

old (cont.):
  o. man in a dry month — ELIOT 100:6
  o. man's talk o' the days — PHIL 234:4
  o. man upon a winter's — YEATS 318:5
  O. man with wrinkled female — ELIOT 105:5
  O. soldiers never die — FOLEY 113:2
  o. sweet song keeps Georgia — GORR 127:1
  o. to rush up to the net — ADAMS 2:4
  Or if ever I grow to be o. — BELL 35:1
  See an o. unhappy bull — HODG 142:3
  That o. black magic — MERC 207:8
  That the heart grows o. — YEATS 321:4
  The o. Lie — OWEN 227:14
  The O. Masters — AUDEN 17:8
  they get to feeling o. — BROO 55:11
  They shall grow not o. — BINY 47:5
  threshold of o. age — CORN 84:1
  tune played on an o. fiddle — BUTL 60:13
  was an o. man who said — HARE 134:14
  Where nobody gets o. — YEATS 319:8
  wine into o. bottles without — ATTL 16:4
  world must be getting o. — JER 155:5
  young can do for the o. — SHAW 269:2
older: Ah, but I was so much o. then — DYLAN 97:11
  always fifteen years o. — BAR 27:6
  As I grow o. and older — SAY 263:11
  must make way for an o. — MAUD 204:9
  O. men declare war — HOOV 143:4
  o. we do not get any younger — REED 245:2
old-fashioned: afterwards be always o.
 — SANT 260:21
  I want an o. house — FISH 110:5
  'ole: knows of a better 'o. — BAIR 22:5
O'Leary: It's with O. in the grave — YEATS 321:15
oligarchy: o. of those who merely — CHES 70:2
olive: Stretched under the o. trees — SPEN 282:1
olla putrida: clumsy o. James Joyce — LAWR 181:5
'Omer: 'O. smote 'is bloomin' lyre — KIPL 174:7
ominous: be fashionable is o. — SANT 260:21
omnipotence: final proof of God's o. — DE VR 91:14
omnipotent: In Scotland, land of the o. No
 — BOLD 48:12
omniscience: his specialism is o. — DOYLE 94:11
on: I hope to go o. — THAT 291:10
once: been tried at least o. — BENN 37:4
  can I stand twice or o. — RICH 247:7
  O. a Catholic always a Catholic — O'MAL 223:5
  O. again we stop the mighty — ANON 10:9
  O. I built a railroad — HARB 132:12
  O. in the racket you're — CAP 63:9
  o. is enough — ELIOT 104:6
  O. lead this people — WILS 314:5
  O. upon a time and a very — JOYCE 158:8
  The o. and future king — WHITE 310:4
oncoming: headlight of an o. train — DICK 92:3
  It's the light of the o. train — LOW 191:10
one: But the O. was Me — HUXL 148:18
  Dear O. is mine as mirrors — AUDEN 19:1
  fire and the rose are o. — ELIOT 102:7

one (*cont.*):

have o. without the other	CAHN 60:19
How to be o. up	POTT 237:12
It's o. for the money	PERK 233:3
It's only o. more thing	FRY 119:14
Make it o. for my baby	MERC 207:7
Night and day, you are the o.	PORT 236:18
o. acquainted	FROST 119:7
o. damn thing after another	MILL 208:3
O. friend in a lifetime	ADAMS 2:10
O. is always alone	ELIOT 101:3
o. is the shadow	JUNG 160:1
O. of you is lying	PARK 230:11
O. realm, one people	ANON 7:19
o. regret in life	ALLEN 4:17
O. thing alone I charge	DUB 96:2
park till twenty to o.	BETJ 43:12
win just o. for the Gipper	GIPP 125:2

one-and-twenty: When I was o. HOUS 146:1
one-eyed: Blind the O. Man is King WELLS 308:5

o. yellow idol to the north	HAYES 136:3
ones: like the o. I used to know	BERL 40:12
only: A pint of plain is your o. man	O'BR 222:4
be o. five Kings left	FAR 107:8
I o. wanted to make you happy	AYCK 21:9
It's the o. thing	SAND 260:6
O. a man harrowing clods	HARDY 133:15
o. a trial if I recognize	KAFKA 160:8
o. books that influence	FORS 115:15
O. connect	FORS 115:3
o. possible death	DUB 96:2
o. thing we haven't succeeded	HUXL 148:16
o. thing we have to fear	ROOS 250:4
O. thin smoke without flame	HARDY 133:15
o. those who have personality	ELIOT 104:3
onward: 'O.,' the sailors cry	BOUL 50:9
Yet this will go o. the same	HARDY 133:15
open: great o. spaces	MARQ 201:10
justice is o. to all	MATH 204:6
O. covenants of peace	WILS 314:15
that all questions are o.	BELL 32:10
you o. that Pandora's Box	BEVIN 45:13
opened: o. a tavern for his friends	DOUG 93:13
Towards the door we never o.	ELIOT 101:6
opening: o. a window or just walking	AUDEN 17:8
Poetry is the o. and closing	SAND 259:7
opera: mind what language an o.	APPL 13:1
o. ain't over 'til	COOK 82:6
O. is when a guy gets stabbed	GARD 122:4
o. plot can be sensible	AUDEN 20:14
poor man's o.	HUXL 148:17
operas: German text of French o.	WHAR 309:19
operatic: they're so romantic, so o.	PROU 241:2
operationally: O., God is beginning	HUXL 149:16
operations: o. which we can perform	WHIT 310:11
operative: O. White House Position	ZIEG 324:11
: Nineveh from distant O.	MAS 202:16
: A vagrant o. without visible	BIER 46:25
clear o. about them	BONH 49:4

opinion (*cont.*):

given a second-hand o.	SAIN 257:4
His o. of himself	BENN 38:4
historians of O.	KEYN 164:15
men representing no o.	WILS 314:8
neglect a good man's o.	CHES 70:2
Now but a whole climate of o.	AUDEN 17:2
o. has been widely held	RUSS 255:9
o. that makes horse-races	TWAIN 301:20
researchers into Public O.	AUDEN 18:1
rule respect public o.	RUSS 255:4
The Magistrate gave his o.	EDGAR 98:4

opinionated: Because of her o. mind YEATS 320:9
opinions: anger of men who have no o.

	CHES 69:11
his religious o.	BUTL 59:6
its o. as it buys its meat	BUTL 60:4
minded beyond reason the o.	WOOLF 317:10
o. for the time of year	AUDEN 18:1

opponent: ascribe to an o. motives BARR 26:5

o. cannot be both honest	ORW 225:10

opportunity: commit when he had the o.

	ROWL 254:1
o. to move not only toward	JOHN 156:10
with the maximum of o.	SHAW 271:22

opposed: ability to hold two o. FITZ 110:11
opposite: o. is also a profound truth BOHR 48:11

we're the o. of people	STOP 287:7

opposites: trivialities where o. BOHR 48:11
oppressor: day o' the O. is ended KIPL 170:5

ends as an o. or a heretic	CAMUS 63:3

optimism: just as agreeable as o. BENN 38:13

Of O. I have said	BRAD 52:3
when the place where o.	ELLIS 106:3

optimist: o. is a guy MARQ 201:9

o. proclaims that we live	CAB 60:15
The o. sees the doughnut	WILS 314:1

opulence: private o. and public GALB 121:4
opulent: To glass the o. HARDY 134:4
oral: word about o. contraception ALLEN 4:21
orange: clockwork o. BURG 57:15

you happen to be an o.	ALLEN 4:3

orators: one of those o. of whom CHUR 73:10
orchard: stiller than ever on o. boughs DRIN 95:17
orchestra: An o. is playing to the rich

	AUDEN 19:13
rehearsal I let the o. play	BEEC 30:5
rules for an o.	BEEC 29:17

orchestration: o. of platitudes WILD 311:8
orchid: White as an o. she rode AUDEN 20:12
ordeal: o. of meeting me is another CHUR 75:15
order: Democrat, in that o. JOHN 156:15

devoted to o. than to justice	KING 166:7
necessarily in that o.	GOD 125:7
never return, all is in o.	KATH 200:8
only war creates o.	BREC 53:4
o. of competence	ROOS 250:3
o., security and peace	JOHN 155:17
when o. breeds habit	ADAMS 2:9

orderly: keep themselves o.   LARK 178:12

ordinary: calmly before the o. folk   BEVIN 45:15

   I warn you not to be o.   KINN 167:13

organ: direction to point that o.   AUDEN 18:11

   my second favourite o.   ALLEN 5:4

   o. to enlarge her prayer   AUDEN 20:12

organ grinder: monkey when the o.   BEVAN 45:5

organism: o. to live beyond its income   BUTL 59:15

organization: book is about the o. man

   WHYTE 311:1

   government is the o. of idolatry   SHAW 271:17

   systematic o. of hatreds   ADAMS 2:7

   than the o. of non-violence   BAEZ 22:3

organize: any time in mourning—o.   HILL 140:10

organizing: o. and campaigning   BROD 54:2

organs: o. of beasts and fowls   JOYCE 159:4

orgasm: o. has replaced the Cross   MUGG 215:7

orgastic: o. future that year   FITZ 110:16

orgies: Home is heaven and o. are vile

   NASH 218:12

orgy: But you *need* an o.   NASH 218:12

   o. looks particularly alluring   MUGG 215:4

original: o. ideas is sound   MACM 197:6

   o. is unfaithful   BORG 49:10

originality: O. is deliberate and forced   HOFF 142:7

   when o. is taken   GALB 121:2

   without o. or moral courage   SHAW 268:10

Orion: O. plunges prone   HOUS 145:10

orisons: Can patter out their hasty o.

   OWEN 227:13

orphan: defeat is an o.   CIANO 76:15

orphans: o. and the homeless   GAND 121:10

orthodoxy: 'o.' not only no longer   CHES 69:8

Orwell: [George O.]   CONN 80:17

Oscar: We all assume that O. said it   PARK 231:2

ostrich: America can not be an o.   WILS 314:7

other: death, there is no o.   THOM 292:12

   did lots of o. things too   JOYCE 159:11

   every o. inch a gentleman   WEST 309:16

   have one without the o.   CAHN 60:19

   Hell is o. people   SART 261:11

   like o. people's authority   BENS 39:3

   not on o. people   HUXL 149:15

   o. people in the world   CALL 61:7

   O. voices, other rooms   CAP 63:12

others: Jesus is there only for o.   BONH 49:5

   o. by their hunted expression   LEWIS 187:4

   O. must fail   VIDAL 304:2

otherwise: admire him would wish o.   ANON 12:5

Otis: Miss O. regrets   PORT 236:16

oublierai: n'o. jamais les lilas ni   ARAG 13:2

ought: do what Asian boys o.   JOHN 156:12

   meritus, 'so he o. to be'   LEAC 182:11

   o. never to have done it   BEVIN 46:1

   Where o.   CHES 68:6

our: O. man in Havana   GREE 128:17

ours: The land was o. before we   FROST 119:9

ourselves: better be changed in o.   JUNG 160:2

out: best way o. is always   FROST 119:3

   can say he is o. of touch   DOUG 93:14

   Gentlemen, include me o.   GOLD 126:6

   get o. of the kitchen   TRUM 299:7

   I counted them all o.   HANR 132:10

   o. always looks the best   ROG 249:6

   O. of Africa   DIN 92:8

   O. where the handclasp's   CHAP 67:5

outcast: universal in sympathy and an o.

   BARN 25:6

outcome: o. of a war is decided   MAO 200:12

outdistanced: o. the ends for which we   KING 167:4

outer: o. life of telegrams   FORS 115:2

Outer Mongolia: British O. for retired   BENN 37:7

outlast: last for ever, o. the sea   CONR 82:2

outlaw: o. states run by the strangest   REAG 244:8

outlaws: legislation which o. Russia   REAG 244:7

outlived: I have o. certain desires   WOOLF 317:10

outrage: civilised o.   HEAN 136:10

outside: just going o. and may   MAHON 199:4

   just going o. and may   OATES 221:13

   O. every fat man there was   AMIS 6:2

   than o. pissing in   JOHN 156:3

out-worn: O. heart, in a time out-worn

   YEATS 318:7

Ovaltineys: We are the O.   ANON 11:22

oven: stove instead of the o.   JENK 154:8

over: Cassiopeia was o.   KAV 161:13

   come back till it's o.   COHAN 78:12

   oversexed, and o. here   TRIN 299:1

   O. there, over there   COHAN 78:12

   try to put it all o. you   WEST 309:8

overcame: O. his natural bonhomie   BENT 39:10

overcome: his passions has never o.   JUNG 159:14

   We shall o.   ANON 12:6

overflow: And meadow rivulets o.   HARDY 133:9

overlook: art of knowing what to o.

   JAMES 153:16

overlooked: be looked over than o.   WEST 308:16

   That I o. before   DIXON 92:11

overpaid: Is grossly o.   HERB 139:12

   O., overfed, oversexed   TRIN 299:1

overpraised: are usually o.   FORS 114:10

oversexed: o., and over here   TRIN 299:1

overthrow: intention to o. the Government

   HARD 132:15

owed: much o. by so many   CHUR 74:8

owl: greedy o. of the Remove   RICH 247:3

   O., and the Waverley   ANON 11:11

   said O.   MILNE 210:10

owls: o. came and perched   BEER 31:17

own: child that's got his o.   HOL 142:11

   money and a room of her o.   WOOLF 317:8

   provided I get my o. way   THAT 291:12

own-goal: o. scored by the human   ANNE 6:12

ox: brother to the o.   MARK 201:3

   [Lady Desborough] is an o.   ASQ 15:3

oxen: years like great black o.   YEATS 321:10

P

paragraphing: p. is to stroke a platitude
MARQ 202:3
parallelism: needs a certain p. of life ADAMS 2:10
pardon: cannot help nor p. AUDEN 20:11
P. me boy is that the Chattanooga GORD 126:14
The kiss of the sun for p. GURN 130:9
parent: p. who could see his boy LEAC 182:9
parentage: P. is a very important profession
SHAW 268:24
parenthood: p. as much as we value TOYN 298:6
parents: 1896 and my p. were married ACK 1:10
18 a girl needs good p. TUCK 300:2
A Jewish man with p. alive ROTH 253:11
America is the way p. obey EDW 98:10
how my p. were occupied SAL 258:10
P. — especially step-parents POW 239:5
p. finally realize ALLEN 4:18
p. kept me from children SPEN 281:12
P. learn a lot from SPARK 281:4
what a tangled web do p. NASH 217:11
what p. were created NASH 218:5
Paris: call it the school of P. MUNN 215:15
flew from London to P. DAV 88:12
frocks are built in P. SAKI 257:15
Is P. burning HITL 141:10
its history P. was French TUCH 300:1
no more Hoares to P. GEOR 122:13
P. is a movable feast HEM 138:7
pictures sent over from P. BLUNT 48:2
The last time I saw P. HAMM 131:11
To mighty P. when he found YEATS 324:2
parish: The p. of rich women AUDEN 17:4
park: make a comedy is a p. CHAP 67:4
Parker: [Dorothy P.] WOOL 317:15
P. shared in the Metropolitan BENC 36:9
parkin': Watch the p. meters DYLAN 97:12
parking: And put up a p. lot MITC 211:5
parley-voo: Hinky, dinky, p. ANON 9:19
parliament: [p.] are a lot of hard-faced BALD 23:2
P. itself would not exist SCAR 264:3
P. to do things at eleven SHAW 270:8
parliamentarian: p. is a bag of boiled sweets
CRIT 86:6
parliamentary: term here as a P. leper WILS 313:4
parochial: than provincial—he was p.
JAMES 152:17
that art must be p. MOORE 212:11
parodies: P. and caricatures HUXL 149:9
parody: The devil's walking p. CHES 71:7
parried: I p.; but my hands were OWEN 228:8
parrot: p. what I purchased not CHAP 67:9
parrots: keep p. or puppy dogs CAMP 62:3
parshial: garden and I am p. to ladies ASHF 14:3
parsley: P. NASH 218:5
parson: And after him the p. ran CHES 69:5
If P. lost his senses HODG 142:2
part: p. in affairs which properly VALÉ 303:3
p. of life's rich pageant MARS 202:5
p. of ourselves doesn't HESSE 140:2

part (cont.):
p. of the solution or you're CLEA 77:4
p. of the universe BECK 28:12
p. that makes illness worth SHAW 268:3
prepared to play a p. MACM 196:14
Shall I p. my hair behind ELIOT 103:12
that it is your p. to woo SHAW 270:20
Yet meet we shall, and p. BUTL 58:12
parties: both p. run out of goods AUDEN 18:14
partings: The pang of all the p. gone THOM 294:11
partly: Living and p. living ELIOT 102:8
parts: naming of p. REED 244:12
refreshes the p. other beers LOV 191:4
party: dinner p. of more than two MENC 206:19
p. is not to be brought HAIL 130:13
p. is worse than the other ROG 249:6
P. line is that there DJIL 92:12
save the P. we love GAIT 120:16
The p.'s over COMD 79:11
pasarán: *No p.* IBAR 149:18
pass: Do not p. go DARR 88:6
Horseman p. by! YEATS 319:13
Lord and p. the ammunition FORGY 113:15
P. me the can, lad HOUS 144:11
p. out into adventure FORS 114:11
pay us, p. us; but do CHES 70:13
They shall not p. ANON 8:16
They shall not p. IBAR 149:18
passage: Down the p. which we did ELIOT 101:6
p. from hand to hand SICK 275:2
passages: History has many cunning p.
ELIOT 100:7
passageways: With smell of steaks in p.
ELIOT 103:13
passed: just p. down the street KENN 288:12
That p. the time BECK 29:9
passenger: I am a p. on space vehicle FULL 120:5
passengers: train needs one of its p. STOP 287:11
passeront: *Ils ne p. pas.* ANON 8:16
passes: Men seldom make p. PARK 230:16
passing: The p. of the third floor back JER 155:7
passing-bells: p. for these who die OWEN 227:13
passion: *c'est l'image de la p.* BART 27:4
connect the prose and the p. FORS 115:3
Man is a useless p. SART 261:10
our p. is our task JAMES 152:14
p. could bring character YEATS 319:14
passion, not p. itself BART 27:4
p. to which he has always POW 239:1
P., you see, can be destroyed SHAF 267:6
To think his p. such YEATS 323:6
passionate: Are full of p. intensity YEATS 320:7
p. apprehension of form BELL 32:6
passions: his p. has never overcome JUNG 159:14
Three p., simple but overwhelmingly
RUSS 254:13
passport: My p.'s green HEAN 136:13
past: always praising the p. SMITH 278:19
And talk about the p. MCG 195:3

past (cont.):

As changed itself to p.	LARK 179:13
ceaselessly into the p.	FITZ 110:16
looking forward to the p.	OSB 226:13
or nothing but the p.	KEYN 164:14
p. is a bucket of ashes	SAND 259:11
p. is a foreign country	HART 135:14
p. is just the same	SASS 263:4
p. is not getting any better	LEVIN 186:18
p. is the only dead thing	THOM 294:4
p. shut in him like	WOOLF 317:6
present controls the p.	ORW 225:5
rather absurd about the p.	BEER 31:4
remember the p. are condemned	SANT 260:11
repeat his p. nor leave	AUDEN 18:15
The danger of the p. was	FROMM 117:10
The p. exudes legend	MAL 199:12
Time present and time p.	ELIOT 101:5

pasture: clean the p. spring FROST 118:12
paternalism: p. and state socialism HOOV 143:6
paternity: men but on the bond of p. SART 261:12
path: bedroom of moss-dappled p. BETJ 43:10

down our particular p.	FORS 115:15
it by any p. whatsoever	KRIS 176:10
One p. leads to despair	ALLEN 4:13

pathetic: That's what it is. P. MILNE 210:11
pathos: managed to murmur, P., piety
FORS 115:8
paths: all her p. are Peace SPR 282:15
patience: my p. is now at an end HITL 141:9

P., n. A minor form	BIER 46:23
p. to appreciate domestic	SANT 260:12
weight in other people's p.	UPD 302:11

patient: I am extraordinarily p. THAT 291:12
p. etherized upon a table ELIOT 103:6
patois: p. which is something like CHAN 66:12
patria: Pro p. mori OWEN 227:14
patrimony: And that was all his p. SAB 256:10
patriot: thing that no p. CHES 68:14
patriotism: P. is a lively sense ALD 3:12

realize that p. is not enough	CAV 65:8
world til you knock the p.	SHAW 273:3

patted: Ethel p. her hair ASHF 14:10
pattern: history is a p. ELIOT 102:6

imposing of a p. on experience	WHIT 310:10
In a p. called a war	LOW 191:7
predetermined p.	FISH 109:15
The dance's p., dance while	AUDEN 19:2

paucity: p. of its reverberation MAIL 199:8
paupières: Quand elle lève ses p. COL 79:2
pause: I'll have eine kleine P. FERR 108:6
There was a p. — just long FIRB 109:12
pauses: But the p. between SCHN 264:6
pauvres: la guerre ce sont les p. SART 261:6

[les p.]	FRAN 116:6
p. ne savent pas que leur	SART 261:13

pavement: Stand on the highest p. ELIOT 103:16
pavements: roadway or on the p. YEATS 318:10
pavilion: red p. of my heart THOM 295:18

paving: Over the p. ELIOT 104:9
pawn: when you're hard up you p. CUMM 87:1
pay: And wonders what's to p. HOUS 145:5

genius who had not to p.	BEER 30:9
hav to p. for it all	WILL 311:13
must p. for one by one	KIPL 170:3
Not a penny off the p.	COOK 82:5
p. a million priests	HARDY 134:13
Smile at us, p. us, pass us	CHES 70:13
sum of things for p.	HOUS 145:7
that we shall p. any price	KENN 163:8
Ulcer Man on 4 Ulcer P.	EARLY 97:15
We won't p., we won't pay	FO 112:12

paying: called p. the Dane-geld KIPL 170:16
pays: p. us poor beggars in red KIPL 169:4
voulez-vous gouverner un p. DE G 90:4
pea: p. which has got WELLS 308:3
peace: advocates of p. upon earth GEOR 123:4

all her paths are P.	SPR 282:15
believe it is p. for our time	CHAM 66:6
deep p. of the double-bed	CAMP 61:13
Downing Street p. with honour	CHAM 66:6
even lovers find their p.	FLEC 111:8
Georgia, Georgia, no p. I find	GORR 127:1
Give p. a chance	LENN 185:9
Imperishable p.	HOUS 145:12
In p.	CHUR 76:3
I were the Prince of P.	HOUS 144:7
Let p. fill our heart	KUMAR 177:4
make war than to make p.	CLEM 77:10
more precious than p.	WILS 314:14
my friend, is p.	ROOS 251:2
Nation shall speak p. unto	REND 245:11
not a p. treaty	FOCH 113:1
Only a p. between equals	WILS 314:13
Open covenants of p.	WILS 314:15
p. among our peoples let	KIPL 174:3
p. and what did that produce	WELL 307:14
p. at the price of ultimate	NIC 219:7
p. comes dropping slow	YEATS 318:10
p. is harder than making	STEV 286:1
P. is indivisible	LITV 189:3
P. is nothing but slovenliness	BREC 53:4
P. is poor reading	HARDY 133:4
p. Man is a bungler	SHAW 271:7
p. must be constructed	ANON 8:7
P., n. In international	BIER 46:24
p. of all countries everywhere	ROOS 250:8
P. on earth and mercy mild	BEEC 30:4
peace. P. is the way	MUSTE 216:11
P. upon earth	HARDY 134:13
precocious giants and for p.	PEAR 232:11
security and p. of each country	JOHN 155:17
such thing as inner p.	LEB 183:8
take chances for p.	DULL 96:5
tell me p. has broken out	BREC 53:8
Then p. will guide the planets	RADO 242:8
think that people want p.	EIS 100:4

peace (cont.):
  this country in time of p.   CHUR 75:4
  War is p.   ORW 225:4
  When there was p., he was   AUDEN 18:1
peaceful: ideas of evolution and p.   ZIN 324:12
peacefully: moving p. towards its close DAWS 89:3
  summer sustained p.   DAY-L 89:7
peace-time: p. choice between the American
      HOOV 143:6
peach: Do I dare to eat a p.   ELIOT 103:12
  The p. was once a bitter   TWAIN 301:14
peacock: P. that was ever sent   LAWR 182:1
peacocks: on the terraces and p.   KIPL 171:2
peal: The wildest p. for years   HODG 142:2
pear: Here we go round the prickly p. ELIOT 103:4
pearls: Give p. away and rubies   HOUS 146:1
  string the p. were strung   JAMES 152:15
pearly: And he shows them p. white BREC 52:18
Pearse: P. summoned Cuchulain   YEATS 320:1
peas: p. were eaten   RAL 242:12
peasantry: Sing the p., and then   YEATS 319:11
pebble: does a wise man hide a p.   CHES 69:12
pebbles: leviathan retrieving p.   WELLS 308:3
péchés: P. sont des tentatives   WEIL 307:7
pecker: want his p. in my pocket   JOHN 156:2
Peckham: treefull of angels at P.   BENÉT 37:1
pedant: only a p. can live   SANT 260:15
pedantry: P. is the dotage of knowledge
      JACK 151:18
peddler: be a plumber or a p.   EINS 99:10
pederasty: Not flagellation, not p.   RATT 243:7
pedestal: place my wife under a p. ALLEN 4:20
pedestrians: only two classes of p. DEWAR 92:1
pee: colour of children's p.   AMIS 5:13
peel: Beulah, p. me a grape   WEST 309:4
  plums and orange p.   RAL 242:14
peeling: P. off the kilometres   CONN 81:5
peep: Nevermore to p. again   DE L 91:7
peeps: p. at it to make sure   BARR 26:7
peepshow: ticket for the p.   MACN 197:11
peer: Oh many a p. of England brews
      HOUS 146:15
peerage: When I want a p.   NORT 221:5
peignoir: Complacencies of the p. STEV 285:8
peine: venait toujours après la p. APOL 12:15
pelican: Oh, a wondrous bird is the p.
      MERR 207:10
pellet: p. with the poison's   PAN 229:3
pellets: And then me spray of p. AYRES 21:16
pen: far less brilliant p.   BEER 31:5
  From lies of tongue and p.   CHES 70:7
  mightier than the p.   HOGB 142:10
  The squat p. rests   HEAN 136:8
  Waverley p.   ANON 11:11
pencil: p. long enough to draw   CHES 71:2
Penelope: His true P. was Flaubert POUND 238:6
penetrating: most p. of criticisms HUXL 149:9
penitence: p. condemns to silence BRAD 51:16
pennies: P. from heaven   BURKE 58:3

Pennsylvania: P. station 'bout a quarter
      GORD 126:14
penny: I had not given a p. for a song YEATS 319:5
  Not a p. off the pay   COOK 82:5
pensée: Ma p., c'est moi: voilà   SART 262:2
pension: hang your hat on a p.   MACN 197:12
people: alien p. clutching   ELIOT 100:10
  And p. came to theirs   HODG 142:2
  A p. without history   ELIOT 102:6
  Before we were her p.   FROST 119:9
  between p. of whom we know   CHAM 66:4
  can fool all of the p.   ADAMS 2:5
  For p. will always be kind   SASS 262:9
  government by the p.   CAMP 62:8
  government of the p.   PAGE 228:10
  half p. and half bicycles   O'BR 222:6
  Hell is other p.   SART 261:11
  Here the p. rule   FORD 113:8
  I never bother with p. I hate   HART 135:11
  kind of a p. do they think   CHUR 72:14
  love p.   CAMP 62:3
  Most p. ignore most poetry   MITC 211:3
  Most p. sell their souls   SMITH 278:4
  name we give the p.   MARQ 112:11
  new p. takes the land   CHES 70:14
  Not many p. know   CAINE 61:3
  One realm, one p., one leader   ANON 7:19
  outside, not on other p.   HUXL 149:15
  p. and their favourite   AUDEN 19:10
  p. are free to do as they   HOFF 142:7
  p. are only human   COMP 80:1
  p. are right more   WHITE 310:1
  P. can clean their teeth   JENK 154:8
  p. don't do such things   IBSEN 150:5
  p. get into bands for three   GELD 122:10
  p. know what they want   MENC 206:15
  P. must not do things   HERB 139:15
  P. say that life   SMITH 278:13
  people than the p.   JAY 154:4
  p. too much of the time   THUR 297:15
  p. want peace so much   EIS 100:4
  p. we followed a policy   DUBČ 95:18
  P. who are always praising   SMITH 278:19
  p. who are late are often   LUCAS 192:8
  p. who are really powerful   MAO 200:13
  p. who do things and people   MORR 214:2
  p. who get the credit   MORR 214:2
  p. who got there first   UST 302:14
  p. will get to the promised   KING 166:11
  P. you know, yet can't   LARK 178:11
  Power to the p.   ANON 10:10
  sake look after our p.   SCOTT 265:8
  study of economics as if p.   SCH 264:15
  Top p. take The Times   ANON 11:15
  we are the p. of England   CHES 70:13
  were decent godless p.   ELIOT 104:2
  we're the opposite of p.   STOP 287:7
  what p. say of us is true   SMITH 277:12

Peoria: It will play in P.   ANON 9:4
perceived: P. the scene, and foretold   ELIOT 105:6
percentage: It's a reasonable p.   BECK 29:5
perception: p. that something ought
                            WELLS 308:14
perdu: A la recherche du temps p.   PROU 240:6
   France n'a pas p. la guerre   DE G 90:3
père: Il n'y a pas de bon p.   SART 261:12
   Notre P. qui êtes aux cieux   PRÉV 239:14
perfect: come to the end of a p. day   BOND 49:2
   Nothing is p. There   STEP 285:3
   Well, nobody's p.   WILD 311:5
perfection: everything must function to p.
                            MUSS 216:10
   P., of a kind, was what   AUDEN 17:1
   P. of the life, or of the work   YEATS 323:12
   p. unattainable   STR 287:14
perfectly: p. formed one kept   COOP 83:2
perform: operations which we can p.   WHIT 310:11
performing: English literature's p. flea
                           O'CAS 222:15
   The faint aroma of p. seals   HART 135:10
Perhaps: And If and P. and But   ELIOT 101:4
Pericles: France what P. felt of Athens
                           KEYN 164:11
perils: And spotted the p. beneath   AYRES 21:15
   p. because of the illusions   MOUN 214:13
period: critical p. in matrimony   HERB 139:16
   p. of cheating between   BIER 46:24
   p. of silence on your part   ATTL 16:7
   p. would need a far less   BEER 31:5
periphrastic: p. study in a worn-out   ELIOT 101:12
perish: But if it had to p. twice   FROST 118:10
   Must then a Christ p.   SHAW 274:3
   or p. together as fools   KING 167:6
   slide, p.   ELIOT 101:9
   They too shall p. unconsoled   LANG 178:6
permanent: Theory of P. Adolescence   CONN 80:13
   there is no p. place   HARDY 133:2
permeated: p. with the odour of joss-sticks
                           BRAM 52:12
Perón: I had not been born P.   PERÓN 233:5
perpendicular: [Dancing is] a p. expression
                           SHAW 273:2
perpetual: An improper mind is a p. feast
                           SMITH 277:15
perquisites: self-respecting scorn of irregular p.
                         WAUGH 305:14
persist: p. to the threshold   CORN 84:1
person: I long for the P. from Porlock
                         SMITH 278:22
   The frontier of my P. goes   AUDEN 16:10
   To us he is no more a p.   AUDEN 17:2
personaggi: Sei p. in cerca d'autore.   PIR 235:1
personal: it the p. unconscious   JUNG 160:4
   P. relations are the important   FORS 115:2
personality: From 35 to 55, good p.   TUCK 300:2
   his effort is his own p.   FROMM 117:9

personality (cont.):
   P. is the supreme realization   JUNG 160:3
   who have p. and emotions   ELIOT 104:3
perspiration: ninety-nine per cent p.   EDIS 98:5
perspire: And dig till you gently p.   KIPL 171:13
perspiring: city of p. dreams   RAPH 243:3
persuade: that is to p. oneself   LESS 186:7
persuaders: The hidden p.   PACK 228:9
persuades: p. me to be a Christian   FRY 120:4
persuasiveness: depends on personal p.
                           QUIL 242:3
pertinent: way to a p. answer   BRON 54:4
perversion: universal p.   RAE 242:9
perversions: unnatural of all the sexual p.
                           HUXL 148:15
pervert: p. climbs into the minds   BRON 54:5
pessimism: p. goes to the point   ROST 253:7
   P., when you get used   BENN 38:13
pessimist: But the p. sees the hole   WILS 314:1
   Do you know what a p.   SHAW 274:6
   p. fears this   CAB 60:15
pessimists: p. abandon themselves   BENN 38:13
   sincerity of the p.   ROST 253:7
pestle: vessel with the p.   PAN 229:3
pet: And kept it for a p.   BELL 33:15
petal: rose p. down the Grand   MARQ 202:2
petals: P. on a wet, black bough   POUND 238:14
   she'd peel all the p.   AYCK 21:10
Peter: Cottontail, and P.   POTT 237:7
   formulate The P. Principle   PETER 233:8
   government which robs P.   SHAW 269:1
Peter Pan: has been wholly in P.   TYNAN 302:5
petrified: suffering from p. adolescence
                           BEVAN 44:9
pettiness: A p.   LAWR 180:10
petty: makes men p. and vindictive   MAUG 205:7
peuple: que nous donnons au p.   FLERS 112:11
pews: Talk about the p. and steeples   CHES 70:9
Pferd: Weiss ich, frag das P.   FREUD 117:3
phagocytes: stimulate the p.   SHAW 268:20
phallic: P. and ambrosial   POUND 238:8
Ph.D.: P. I saw how it was possible   ALGR 3:16
phenomenon: Felicitous p.   MOORE 213:1
Phidias: Forms that gentler P. wrought
                           YEATS 319:10
Philadelphia: I went to P., but it was   FIEL 109:3
   rather be living in P.   FIEL 109:6
Philippines: In the P., there are lovely   COW 84:13
   this is relief of the P.   MAC 193:5
philistinism: art-for-art's-sake of our yawning P.
                         PRIT 240:5
philosophers: economists and political p.
                         KEYN 165:5
philosophical: p. tradition is that it   WHIT 310:12
philosophy: advantage for a system of p.
                         SANT 260:20
   European p. of diametrically   HOOV 143:6
   p. and a party program   LIPP 188:13
   P. is the replacement   RYLE 256:8

philosophy (*cont.*):

superstition to enslave a p.	INGE 151:4
why I have no p. myself	HALD 131:1

Phlebas: P. the Phoenician — ELIOT 105:8

phlegm: p. and tooth-decay — HELL 137:6

phobias: Tell us your p. and we — BENC 36:7

Phoenician: Phlebas the P., a fortnight — ELIOT 105:8

phoenix: Do not expect again a p. hour — DAY-L 89:4

p. in my youth so let them	YEATS 322:9
p. moment	DAY-L 89:5

phone: E.T. p. home — MATH 204:7

P. for the fish-knives, Norman	BETJ 42:12
p. whenever you felt like	SAL 258:11
why did you answer the p.	THUR 297:9

phoney: something p. every minute — SAL 258:13

photograph: A p. is not only an image — SONT 280:11

photographs: interested in . . . p.? Eh — CHAP 67:8

photography: P. is truth — GOD 125:6

Phyllida: But P., my Phyllida — DOBS 92:15

physical: are so lightly called p. — COL 79:1

For p. pleasure I'd sooner — WAUGH 306:13

physician: p. can bury his mistakes — WRIG 317:18

p. is to educate the masses — OSLER 227:1

physicians: P. of the Utmost Fame — BELL 33:1

physicists: p. have known sin — OPP 223:16

physics: resort to p. and chemistry — MENC 206:18

science is either p. or stamp — RUTH 256:6

physiques: *nomme, à la légère, p.* — COL 79:1

pianists: no better than many p. — SCHN 264:6

piano: great black p. appassionato — LAWR 181:13

when I sat down at the p. — CAPL 63:7

Picardy: Roses are flowering in P. — WEAT 306:17

Picasso: isn't as great as a P. — MUNN 215:15

P. coming down the street — CHUR 73:7

Piccadilly: Goodbye, P. — JUDGE 159:13

pick: I always p. the one — WEST 309:9

Sam, Sam, p. up tha' musket — HOLL 142:12

picked: have p. them every one — SEEG 266:1

pickle: had been weaned on a p. — ANON 11:13

Pickwick: The P., the Owl — ANON 11:11

picnic: Teddy Bears have their P. — KENN 162:12

picture: Every p. tells a story — ANON 7:21

express in a p. — BELL 32:6

It's no go the p. palace — MACN 197:12

p. is worth ten thousand — BARN 25:3

p. or a novel that is *not* — JAMES 153:5

P. you upon my knee — CAES 60:16

picture-painter: successful writer or p. — LEWIS 187:13

pictures: It's the p. that got small — BRAC 51:11

Of cutting all the p. out — BELL 32:12

painter and I nail my p. — SCHW 265:3

People who try to explain p. — PIC 234:9

P. are for entertainment — GOLD 126:5

You used to be in p. — BRAC 51:11

picturesque: quite often p. liar — TWAIN 300:10

pie: p. by Mrs McGregor — POTT 237:8

p. in the sky when you — HILL 140:11

pier: The effusive welcome of the p. — AUDEN 19:10

piercing: man, it's too p. — FREB 116:9

piety: Pathos, p., courage — FORS 115:8

piffle: are as p. before the wind — ASHF 14:8

pig: p. came up an' lay down — BURT 58:7

p. got up and slowly walked — BURT 58:7

sort of p. in clover — LAWR 181:4

pigeon: crooning like a bilious p. — SHAW 273:12

pigeons: P. on the grass alas — STEIN 284:9

pig-sty: p. when she wasn't looking — THOM 293:15

Pilate: hands than water like P. — GREE 128:11

pile: P. the bodies high at Austerlitz — SAND 260:1

p. the logs — POUND 238:1

pilgrim: loved the p. soul in you — YEATS 318:8

pilgrimage: with songs beguile your p. — FLEC 111:7

pilgrims: love you land of the p. — CUMM 87:2

Pilgrim's Progress: One was 'P.', about a man — TWAIN 300:5

pillar: category but a p. of the State — SOLZ 280:4

pillars: Pylons, those p. — SPEN 281:17

The seven p. of wisdom — LAWR 182:6

pillow: like the feather p. — HAIG 130:11

Pimpernel: That demmed, elusive P. — ORCZY 223:18

pimples: merely the scratching of p. — WOOLF 317:7

pin: If I sit on a p. — ANON 11:9

pinafore: His stockings or his p. — BELL 33:10

pinched: Mrs Simpson's p. our king — ANON 8:9

pines: cones under his p. — FROST 118:14

p. are gossip pines — FLEC 111:16

pining: probably p. for the fiords — CHAP 67:9

pink: With a p. hotel — MITC 211:5

pinkly: p. bursts the spray — BETJ 44:1

pinko-grey: white races are really p. — FORS 115:6

pins: They're like as a row of p. — KIPL 174:10

pint: amount [of blood], but a p. — GALT 121:8

A p. of plain is your only man — O'BR 222:4

pinta: Drinka P. Milka Day — WHIT 310:13

pints: P. and quarts of Ludlow beer — HOUS 146:16

pious: p. but Mr Salteena was — ASHF 14:6

pipe: p. might fall out if — FORS 114:2

Pippa: at a window. P. passes — BEER 30:20

pips: until the p. squeak — GEDD 122:9

piss: P. off, he said to me — PINT 234:13

worth a pitcher of warm p. — GARN 122:5

pissing: inside the tent p. out — JOHN 156:3

pistols: The young ones carry p. — SHAW 267:17

pit: And wretched, blind, p. ponies — HODG 142:2

p. of the stomach — HOUS 145:9

pitch-and-toss: And risk it on one turn of p. — KIPL 173:8

pitched: But Love has p. his mansion — YEATS 323:8

pitcher: isn't worth a p. of warm — GARN 122:5

pitchfork: Can't I use my wit as a p. — LARK 179:6

pits: This must be the p. — MCEN 194:17

pittance: p. from the BBC for interviewing
HARD 132:16
pity: And the seas of p. lie   AUDEN 17:6
A p. beyond all telling   YEATS 318:9
p. for the suffering   RUSS 254:13
P. is the feeling   JOYCE 158:11
The Poetry is in the p.   OWEN 227:12
thought it was a p. to get up   MAUG 205:12
pix: Sticks nix hick p.   ANON 11:3
place: And leaping from p. to place   HARDY 133:13
clean p. to die   KAV 162:2
everything in its p.   BEVAN 44:10
Home is the p. where   FROST 119:1
In p. of strife   CAST 64:10
know the p. for the first   ELIOT 102:4
must be kept in their p.   AWDRY 21:5
p. for street fighting   JAGG 152:5
p. in any political group   HELL 137:9
p. in the sun and have   WILH 311:9
p. in the world for ugly   HARDY 133:2
p. where a story ended   ELIOT 102:2
p. where optimism most   ELLIS 106:3
right p. for love   FROST 118:9
sleepy and there is no p.   DYLAN 97:10
tight gag of p.   HEAN 136:11
To know their p., and not   BELL 33:6
up and have no p. to go   WHIT 310:18
places: all p. were alike   KIPL 172:4
Are the quietest p.   HOUS 146:13
distance between two p.   WILL 312:7
I've been things and seen p.   WEST 309:5
P. they guarded, or kept   LARK 178:12
We returned to our p.   ELIOT 100:10
You will find no new p.   CAV 65:7
placetne: P., magistra   SAY 263:9
plafond: *inscrite dans les lignes du p.*   ÉLUA 106:6
plagiarism: from one author, it's p.   MIZN 212:1
plagiarize: P.! Let no one else's work   LEHR 184:4
plague: such a p. when I was young   YEATS 321:3
plain: A pint of p. is your only man   O'BR 222:4
especially the need of the p.   WAUGH 306:6
how she makes it p.   SERV 266:17
I see it shining p.   HOUS 146:11
no p. women on television   FORD 113:6
stays mainly in the p.   LERN 186:4
plan: both by his p. of attack   SASS 262:8
Commends a most practical p.   INGE 150:13
plane: It's a p.   ANON 7:23
p. trees going sha-sha-sha   CONN 81:5
planet: species of beetles on this p.   HALD 131:2
plans: hopeful p. to emptiness   HOUS 144:13
p. are always ruined   BREC 53:6
planted: p. another one down   BOUL 50:8
plants: come and talk to the p.   CHAR 68:1
plashy: Feather-footed through the p. fen
WAUGH 306:6
plasterer: at the p. on his ladder   HEAN 136:9
plates: they have hats like p.   COW 84:13
platform: p. on which they could   KINN 168:3

platinum: With bullets made of p.   BELL 32:16
with eyebrows made of p.   FORS 114:4
platitude: A longitude with no p.   FRY 119:16
Applause, *n.* The echo of a p.   BIER 46:9
p. is simply a truth repeated   BALD 23:3
stroke a p. until it purrs   MARQ 202:3
platitudes: orchestration of p.   WILD 311:8
Plato: series of footnotes to P.   WHIT 310:12
play: And watch the men at p.   CLEG 77:7
author, it's a good p.   SHAW 269:4
But when I started to p.   CAPL 63:7
concert I make them p.   BEEC 30:5
Games people p.   BERNE 41:7
House Beautiful is p. lousy   PARK 231:7
I can. P. it   EPST 106:10
I let the orchestra p.   BEEC 30:5
I'll have to read that p.   SAL 258:13
It will p. in Peoria   ANON 9:4
not p. things as they   STEV 285:12
our brief, sweet p.   THOM 296:3
p. a song for me   DYLAN 97:10
p. fair to win the trick   LAB 177:5
p. it over again and play   LAMB 177:14
p. of the contingent   FISH 109:15
p. the chord of C major   BEEC 29:22
p. when I don't know   SHAW 269:3
The structure of a p.   MILL 208:10
To see that Interesting P.   BELL 33:4
two can p.   BEER 31:19
verse as p. tennis   FROST 118:6
Work is x; y is p.   EINS 99:9
you work, rest and p.   GAFF 120:15
playboy: only P. of the Western   SYNGE 289:11
played: how you p. the Game   RICE 246:10
your role is p. out   TROT 299:4
playing: She's p. herself   KAEL 160:6
pleasant: And hear the p. cuckoo   DAV 88:14
please: *Just try to p. everyone*   SWOPE 289:6
P. get out of the new one   DYLAN 97:13
woman who did not p.   PROU 240:10
pleased: p. to be in the Government   BAXT 28:11
pleasure: gives me p. all the time   BELL 34:15
p. I get when I see a child's   BELL 33:11
p. of a poem itself   FROST 117:13
p. politicians take   BELL 33:11
prefers comfort to p.   HESSE 140:3
pleasured: What lively lad most p. me
YEATS 323:6
pleasures: not with their p.   HUXL 149:3
p. of middle age   POUND 237:17
pledge: p. our Empire vast across   HUXL 149:1
Pleiads: The rainy P. wester   HOUS 145:10
plies: wind it p. the saplings   HOUS 146:7
plight: Alexander Selkirk knew the p.   KAV 161:12
plis: *le printemps dans ses p.*   ARAG 13:2
plot: discerned in history a p.   FISH 109:15
opera p. can be sensible   AUDEN 20:14
plots: life seems to have no p.   COMP 80:4

plough: must p. my furrow alone ROS 252:12
  this morning held the p. BETJ 42:3
ploughing: Is my team p. HOUS 146:6
pluck: p. till time and times YEATS 322:12
plucking: p. the fruit of memory CONR 81:8
plumber: be a p. or a peddler EINS 99:10
  getting a p. on weekends ALLEN 4:10
plumbers: good p., good carpenters NIXON 220:9
plume: In blast-beruffled p. HARDY 134:2
plums: p. and orange peel picked RAL 242:14
plunder: cannot separately p. a third BIER 46:7
plunge: O p. your hands in water AUDEN 16:13
plunges: Orion p. prone HOUS 145:10
plural: Incorrigibly p. I peel MACN 198:7
plus: On the p. side, death ALLEN 4:15
PM: But he ended P. ATTL 16:2
pneumatic: Gives promise of p. bliss ELIOT 103:2
pocket: carried it about in my p. BARR 26:7
  Is that a gun in your p. WEST 309:12
  picked a p. with his tongue BIER 46:10
  p. or purse WILS 313:11
  p. that they cannot separately BIER 46:7
  want his pecker in my p. JOHN 156:2
pockets: The young man feels his p. HOUS 145:5
poem: A p. is never finished VALÉ 302:19
  A p. lovely as a tree KILM 166:3
  A p. should not mean MACL 196:5
  figure a p. makes FROST 117:13
  give you the music of a p. SYNGE 289:9
  ice on a hot stove the p. FROST 118:2
  pleasure of a p. itself to tell FROST 117:13
  P. should be palpable MACL 196:4
  wouldn't be much of a p. COPE 83:7
poems: P. are made by fools like me KILM 166:4
poet: A p.'s hope AUDEN 18:5
  better p. than Porson HOUS 144:6
  culture that a p. can earn AUDEN 18:6
  Fat-head p. that nobody reads CHES 69:15
  feeling that the p. QUAS 242:1
  had the making of a p. WALL 304:17
  I hate what every p. hates KAV 161:12
  I was a p., I was young FLEC 112:7
  Lawn Tennyson, gentleman p. JOYCE 159:3
  No p. ever interpreted GIR 125:3
  p. and not a musician BUTL 59:18
  p. can do today is warn OWEN 227:12
  p. is a sensitive instrument MACN 197:14
  p. is the priest STEV 285:14
  p. is to be admired COCT 78:4
  p. or novelist wishes AUDEN 18:10
  p. sing it with such airs YEATS 319:5
  The p.'s inward pride DAY-L 89:6
poète: Le pire drame pour un p. COCT 78:4
poetical: worn-out p. fashion ELIOT 101:12
poetry: all metaphor is p. CHES 68:13
  and that is p. CAGE 60:17
  book of p. is like dropping MARQ 202:2
  common-sense view of p. MACN 197:14

poetry (cont.):
  Emptied of its p. AUDEN 17:5
  has never written any p. CHES 70:1
  his motor car was p. LEWIS 187:12
  I didn't read the p. TWAIN 300:5
  Ireland hurt you into p. AUDEN 17:4
  most p. ignores most people MITC 211:3
  neither is there p. in money GRAV 128:4
  Of p.; to maintain POUND 238:5
  p. cannot celebrate them AUDEN 18:12
  p. he invented was easy AUDEN 17:1
  P. in motion KAUF 161:11
  P. is a comforting piece MENC 207:2
  P. is a way of taking life FROST 119:6
  P. is not a turning loose ELIOT 104:3
  P. is the achievement SAND 259:8
  P. is the opening and closing SAND 259:7
  P. . . . is the revelation QUAS 242:1
  P. is the supreme fiction STEV 285:6
  P. is to prose as dancing WAIN 304:10
  P. is what is lost in translation FROST 119:5
  p. makes nothing happen AUDEN 17:4
  P. must be as well written POUND 238:11
  p. strays into my memory HOUS 145:9
  power corrupts, p. cleanses KENN 163:4
  publicity rather than of p. LEAV 183:6
  quarrel with ourselves, p. YEATS 319:1
  read a little p. sometimes HOPE 143:11
  that p. begins to atrophy POUND 237:15
  The p. does not matter ELIOT 101:12
  The P. is in the pity OWEN 227:12
  The p. of motion GRAH 127:15
  upon p. It is capable RICH 247:5
  without the help of p. WAUGH 306:5
poets: Immature p. imitate ELIOT 104:5
  Irish p., learn your trade YEATS 319:11
  mature p. steal ELIOT 104:5
  Nor till the p. among us can MOORE 213:3
  P. do not go mad CHES 69:18
  p. in our civilization ELIOT 104:8
  p. keep our mouths shut YEATS 318:5
  powerful p. of the century ELIOT 104:7
  think all p. were Byronic COPE 83:4
  We P. of the proud old lineage FLEC 111:7
  written in what p. name YEATS 323:7
  young the p. exploding AUDEN 20:10
point: missed the p. completely ELIOT 101:2
  still p. of the turning ELIOT 101:8
  was wrong, 'Up to a p.' WAUGH 306:8
pointless: p. and inglorious as stepping
     OSB 226:14
points: simplify and illustrate the p. HOME 143:2
Poirot: [Hercule P.] CHR 72:2
poised: p. between a cliché MACM 197:1
poison: p. the whole blood stream EMPS 106:7
  was drinking was slow p. BENC 36:12
  With its sickening p. LARK 179:6
  with the p.'s in the vessel PAN 229:3
  would put p. in your coffee ASTOR 15:12

poison (cont.):
You p. England at her roots   BOTT 50:4
poison-gas: We've got as far as p.   HARDY 134:13
poisoning: p. and of deterioration   BORN 50:2
poissons: Les p. aussi   CHUR 75:7
poke: haven't the heart to p.   GRAH 127:8
Poland: withdraw their troops from P. CHAM 66:7
pole: returning from the P.   ATK 16:1
polecat: semi-house-trained p.   FOOT 113:5
police: encourage among p. officers ORTON 224:7
  game at which the p.   SHAW 272:21
  p. were to blame for what   GRANT 128:1
  To the citizen or the p.   AUDEN 17:12
policeman: p. and a pretty girl   CHAP 67:4
  The terrorist and the p.   CONR 81:19
policemen: become p. or butchers   CONN 80:7
  first time how young the p.   HICKS 140:8
  not enough p., not enough   HUMP 148:2
  P., like red squirrels   ORTON 224:6
policy: basic United States p.   DULL 96:6
  best p. to speak the truth   JER 155:1
  home p.   CLEM 77:9
  national p. towards each other   BRIA 53:11
  p. is to be able to take   BEVIN 46:2
  p. of the good neighbour   ROOS 250:5
  p. so that socialism would   DUBČ 95:18
polis: The P. as Polis, in this   O'CAS 222:11
polite: Our p. recognition   BIER 46:5
politeness: p., the blowing of a nose FORS 115:7
political: All p. lives, unless they POW 239:8
  clearly to a p. career   SHAW 270:9
  comfortable place in any p.   HELL 137:9
  fear of P. Economy   SELL 266:10
  history of p. power   POPP 236:6
  old p. adage which says   REYN 246:3
  p. aspirant under democracy   MENC 206:9
  p. columnists say   ADAMS 2:3
  P. language   ORW 226:3
  p. leader must keep looking   BAR 27:9
  p. person and could have   HELL 137:9
  P. power grows out   MAO 201:2
  p. speech and writing   ORW 226:1
  P. thought, in France   ARON 13:12
politician: A p. is a statesman   POMP 236:2
  p. does get an idea   MARQ 201:15
  p. is a man who understands   TRUM 299:8
  p. is an arse upon   CUMM 87:6
  p. never believes what   DE G 90:5
  p. was a person with whose   LLOY 190:4
  p. will never grudge   OLIV 223:3
  who wishes to become a p.   CHUR 72:9
politicians: matter to be left to the p. DE G 90:6
  not the p. and statesmen   AUDEN 18:12
  p. take in their limelight   BELL 33:11
  too many p. who believe   ADAMS 2:5
politics: All p., however, are based REST 245:13
  For p. and little else beside   CAMP 62:6
  In international p.   BIER 46:7
  In p., there is no use   CHAM 65:11

politics (cont.):
  law of principle and p.   RAK 242:10
  observe about this P. thing   ROG 249:6
  P. and the fate of mankind   CAMUS 62:10
  p. are too serious a matter   DE G 90:6
  P. are usually the executive   BRIT 54:1
  P., as a practice   ADAMS 2:7
  p. consists in ignoring   ADAMS 2:12
  P. is not the art   GALB 121:5
  P. is supposed   REAG 244:10
  P. is the art of preventing   VALÉ 303:3
  P. is the Art of the Possible   BUTL 58:9
  P. is war without bloodshed   MAO 201:1
  p. of happiness   HUMP 148:4
  p. of purpose   HUMP 148:4
  p. of the left and centre   JENK 154:11
  p. ought to be in America   HUMP 148:4
  p. solely as a result   PARK 232:4
  presented as 'realist p.'   BERD 40:1
  purpose and the p. of joy   HUMP 148:4
  week is a long time in p.   WILS 313:8
  will give his mind to p.   SHAW 267:13
politique: Comme un homme p. ne croit DE G 90:5
  La pensée p., en France   ARON 13:12
  p. est l'art d'empêcher   VALÉ 303:3
  p. et le sort des hommes   CAMUS 62:10
  P. intérieure, je fais   CLEM 77:9
pollution: unsavoury engine of p.   SPAR 281:8
Polly: P. Garter, under the washing THOM 293:16
Poltagrue: Went off to tempt My Lady P.
                                     BELL 34:11
polyphiloprogenitive: P.   ELIOT 102:15
polytechnic: In the P. they teach you
                                     SHAW 270:19
pomp: Lo, all our p. of yesterday   KIPL 173:4
pond: have their Stream and P.   BROO 55:3
ponder: When in charge, p.   BOREN 49:9
ponies: And wretched, blind, pit p. HODG 142:2
  Five and twenty p.   KIPL 172:15
  p. have swallowed   BETJ 42:10
Pontefract: In the licorice fields at P. BETJ 42:6
ponts: de coucher sous les p.   FRAN 116:6
poodle: Gentleman's [Mr Balfour's] p. LLOY 189:8
Pooh: 3 Cheers for P.   MILNE 211:1
  P. always liked a little   MILNE 210:9
Pooka: The P. MacPhellimey   O'BR 222:2
pool: Gentle and brown, above the p. BROO 56:1
  Walk across my swimming p.   RICE 246:12
poor: being p., have only   YEATS 323:1
  But what can a p. boy do   JAGG 152:5
  expensive it is to be p.   BALD 22:14
  help the many who are p.   KENN 163:9
  if you was as p. as me   SHAW 273:14
  It's no disgrace t'be p.   HUBB 147:8
  It's the p. wot gets the blame   ANON 10:15
  live by robbing the p.   SHAW 271:2
  object is p. or obscure   BIER 46:4
  one of the undeserving p.   SHAW 273:15
  Peace is p. reading   HARDY 133:4

poor (*cont.*):

p. don't know	SART 261:13
p. get children	KAHN 161:3
P. little rich girl	COW 85:2
p. man's opera	HUXL 148:17
rich richer and the p.	NEHRU 219:2
sacrificed—is not to be p.	SHAW 270:1
She was p. but she was honest	ANON 10:15
[the p.] have to labour	FRAN 116:6
The p. know that it	BREN 53:9
war it's the p. who die	SART 261:6

pop: p. my cork for every guy — FIEL 108:8
Snap! Crackle! P.! — ANON 10:17
popcorn: Everything else is mere p. — BELL 35:12
pope: against the P. or the NUM — BALD 23:1
Anybody can be p. — JOHN 156:1
But I'm the P. — JOHN 155:18
divisions did you say the P. — STAL 283:5
poppies: In Flanders fields the p. blow — MCCR 194:6
poppy: flushed print in a p. there — THOM 294:13
population: p. able to read but unable — TREV 298:13
porcupines: couple of p. under you — KHR 165:10
Porlock: I long for the Person from P. — SMITH 278:22
pornographic: impotent stupidity, a p. show — BLUNT 48:2
pornography: P. is the attempt to insult — LAWR 181:19

p. of war	RAE 242:9
show to give p. a dirty	BARN 25:4

Porsches: My friends all drive P. — JOPL 157:6
Porson: better poet than P. — HOUS 144:6
port: ancient tales, and p. — BELL 35:6
portal: The fitful tracing of a p. — STEV 286:1
porter: decompose in a barrel of p. — DONL 93:4
Mrs P. in the spring — ELIOT 105:4
portions: p. of the human anatomy — HELP 138:1
portrait: paint a p. I lose a friend — SARG 261:2
p. not too stale to record — PLOM 235:15
P. of the artist as a young dog — THOM 293:8
position: Its human p.; how it takes — AUDEN 17:8
My p. was on the left — MOSL 214:11
p. must be held — HAIG 130:12
p. of pre-eminence in her — GEOR 122:14
positive: ac-cent-tchu-ate the p. — MERC 207:6
p. peace which is the presence — KING 166:7
p. value has its price — PIC 234:7
that he gave more p. signs — BLUNT 48:1
The power of p. thinking — PEALE 232:7
possessed: I p., as you suggest — HARD 132:16
Webster was much p. by death — ELIOT 103:1
possession: p. of a book becomes — BURG 58:2
possibilities: awareness of the p. — LEAV 183:5
possible: It is p. to lie, and even — ADLER 3:1
not the art of the p. — GALB 121:5
Politics is the Art of the P. — BUTL 58:9
p. he is almost certainly — CLAR 77:2
p. to conquer poverty — JOHN 156:5

possible (*cont.*):

p. to gain a chair of literature	ALGR 3:16
world is the best of all p.	BRAD 52:3

Possum: said the Honourable P. — BERR 41:14
post: Lie follows by p. — BER 40:2
p. tends to be occupied — PETER 233:9
postal: Bringing the cheque and the p. — AUDEN 19:15
p. districts packed like — LARK 179:11
postal-order: My p. hasn't come yet — RICH 247:2
poster: Kitchener is a great p. — ASQ 14:14
posterity: decided to write for p. — ADE 2:17
have put mankind and p. — INGE 151:7
P. is as likely to be wrong — BROUN 56:8
p. on what he would have — OSLER 227:2
postern: p. behind my tremulous — HARDY 134:1
Post-Impressionist: P. pictures sent over from — BLUNT 48:2
postman: The p. always rings twice — CAIN 61:2
post office: stalked through the P. — YEATS 320:1
pot: *make them in the one p.* — JOYCE 158:17
potato: You like p. and I like po-tah- — GERS 123:9
potatoes: yesterday's mashed p. — FIEL 108:9
potato-gatherers: p. like mechanized scarecrows — KAV 162:1
potency: through the p. of my voice — HARD 132:16
potent: Extraordinary how p. cheap music — COW 85:3
p. advocates of peace upon — GEOR 123:4
potential: The p. for the disastrous — EIS 100:1
potentially: become what he p. — FROMM 117:9
Potter: This is Gillie P. speaking — POTT 237:10
Pouilly Fuissé: glasses of Chablis or P. — AMIS 5:13
pounces: p. unerringly upon — JAMES 153:13
pound: P. failed to impress her — STEIN 284:7
p. here in Britain — WILS 313:11
pounds: Fifty p.! An' tha's niver — LAWR 182:1
Give crowns and p. and guineas — HOUS 146:1
poured: P. forth her song in perfect — AUDEN 20:12
p. into his clothes — WOD 316:10
poverty: anything to do with p. — CURR 87:12
Money is better than p. — ALLEN 4:16
possible to conquer p. — JOHN 156:5
p. knows how extremely — BALD 22:14
setting him up in p. — NAIDU 217:7
state of extreme p. — PER 233:2
unconditional war on p. — JOHN 156:9
worst of crimes is p. — SHAW 270:1
power: A friend in p. is a friend lost — ADAMS 2:8
because they confer p. — RUSS 255:17
because we had p. — BENÉT 36:15
corridors of p. — SNOW 279:4
disastrous rise of misplaced p. — EIS 100:1
Horses and P. and War — KIPL 169:11
limitation of governmental p. — WILS 314:9
p. grows out of the barrel — MAO 201:2
P., he [Kissinger] has — KISS 175:13
p. instead of influence — TAYL 290:13
P. is not a means — ORW 225:8

power (*cont.*):

p. of conveying unlimited	HARD 132:16
p. of vested interests	KEYN 165:5
p. on earth that can protect	BALD 23:4
p. over people as long	SOLZ 280:2
p.-state	TEMP 291:3
p. to hold men and women	SZASZ 290:1
P. to the people	ANON 10:10
p. which stands on Privilege	BELL 34:13
P. without responsibility	KIPL 172:6
responsibility without p.	STOP 286:16
Send to us p. and light	AUDEN 20:3
shares p. much more widely	BENN 37:6
symbol of the p. of Heaven	MOORE 213:1
The certainty of p.	DAY-L 89:6
The p. of positive thinking	PEALE 232:7
unleashed p. of the atom	EINS 99:8
War knows no p.	BROO 54:11
when it comes to p.	SNOW 279:7
When p. corrupts	KENN 163:4
where p. predominates	JUNG 160:1
who have the p. to end it	SASS 262:11
powerful: be a p. person yourself	CORN 84:1
most p. of schools	GIR 125:3
rich society and the p.	JOHN 156:10
Sisterhood is p.	MORG 213:8
powerless: p. to *express* anything	STR 288:7
powers: contracting p. solemnly declare	
	BRIA 53:11
Headmasters have p.	CHUR 75:11
prostitute all their p.	FORS 114:5
practical: Commends a most p. plan	INGE 150:13
Morality's *not* p.	BOLT 48:13
practise: prudence never to p.	TWAIN 300:15
we preach but do not p.	RUSS 255:18
practised: at seeing it p.	BUTL 60:9
practising: art than he can by p. it	AUDEN 18:6
prairies: From the mountains to the p.	BERL 40:6
praise: countryman must have p.	BLYT 48:5
Let the florid music p.	AUDEN 19:5
people p. and don't read	TWAIN 300:16
P. for the singing	FARJ 107:6
p. of God consists	PROU 241:1
P. the Lord and pass	FORGY 113:15
Teach the free man how to p.	AUDEN 17:7
they only want p.	MAUG 205:10
things thou wouldst p.	DE L 90:15
whom must the p. be given	BEAV 28:9
praising: advantage of doing one's p.	BUTL 60:11
when I am p. anyone	BEER 30:17
who are always p. the past	SMITH 278:19
pram: Mr Shultz went off his p.	KINN 168:1
than the p. in the hall	CONN 80:9
prawce: Wot p. Selvytion nah	SHAW 270:7
pray: place for those who p.	SIMON 275:9
P. for the repose	ROLFE 249:18
p. to Him I find I'm talking	BARN 25:9
some to Meccah turn to p.	FLEC 111:12
Work and p., live on hay	HILL 140:11

prayer: Conservative Party at p.	ROYD 254:4
The wish for p. is a prayer	BERN 41:3
which characterizes p.	BELL 35:13
prayers: Bernard always had a few p.	ASHF 14:6
Knelt down with angry p.	HODG 142:2
p. would make me whole	KIPL 172:7
Robin is saying his p.	MILNE 210:6
pray'r: Comin' in on a wing and a p.	ADAM 2:14
prays: family that p. together stays	SCAL 264:1
preach: p. but do not practise	RUSS 255:18
preaching: p. and got myself burnt	JER 155:6
precedent: dangerous p.	CORN 84:2
precedes: Existence p. and rules essence	
	SART 261:8
precious: how p. is frivolity	FORS 114:5
so p. that it must be rationed	LENIN 184:14
The right is more p. than peace	WILS 314:14
predict: p. things after they have	ION 151:11
predominates: eyes she eclipses and p.	DOYLE 94:1
predominating: with sniffles p.	HENRY 138:15
pre-eminence: p. in her Colonial trade	
	GEOR 122:14
pre-empted: p. it is called brain-washing	
	GREER 129:1
prefer: I do not know which to p.	STEV 285:11
I p. reading	SMITH 278:13
may p. a self-made name	HAND 132:8
Or would you p.	ANON 12:10
which men p. not to hear	AGAR 3:4
preference: special p. for beetles	HALD 131:2
pregnancies: p. and at least four miscarriages	
	BEEC 29:19
pregnancy: p. by a resort to mathematics	
	MENC 206:18
pregnant: If men could get p.	KENN 162:11
prejudice: P., *n.* A vagrant opinion	BIER 46:25
p. the civil and religious	BALF 23:13
reflection and a source of p.	SCH 264:13
prejudices: p. as the advertisers don't	SWAF 289:4
their own and a critic's p.	BALL 24:4
premises: based upon licensed p.	O'BR 222:3
preparation: p. for this hour and this	CHUR 76:5
prepare: constituencies and p. for government	
	STEEL 283:13
p. for war like precocious	PEAR 232:11
prepared: am p. to meet my Maker	CHUR 75:15
BE p., which means	BAD 22:2
P. TO KILL ONE ANOTHER	SHAW 270:10
world is not yet p.	DOYLE 94:9
prerogative: p. of the eunuch throughout	
	STOP 286:16
p. of the harlot throughout	KIPL 172:6
present: know nothing but the p.	KEYN 164:14
p. controls the past	ORW 225:9
P. has latched its postern	HARDY 134:1
p. is an interlude	O'NEI 223:14
p. of Mornington Crescent	HARG 135:3
Time p. and time past	ELIOT 101:5

presents: it were not for the p.	ADE 2:18
p. and good food and i	WILL 311:13
preserve: P. it as your chiefest	BELL 32:12
p.'s full of stones	BETJ 43:1
Whom God P.	MORT 214:9
preside: p. over the liquidation	CHUR 73:6
presidency: P. is an unpardonable	JOHN 156:13
p. so much that he'll spend	BROD 54:2
President: All the P. is, is a glorified	TRUM 299:10
All the P.'s men	BERN 41:8
America any boy may become P.	STEV 286:2
anybody could become P.	DARR 88:7
going to be your next p.	CART 64:5
more than any other P.	MENC 206:8
not choose to run for P.	COOL 82:14
not their P. is a crook	NIXON 220:8
P. of the Immortals	HARDY 134:8
P.'s hardest task is not	JOHN 156:14
We are the P.'s men	KISS 175:11
When the P. does it	NIXON 220:1
press: Freedom of the p.	SWAF 289:4
racket is back in its p.	BETJ 43:9
with you on the free p.	STOP 287:2
pressed: P. into service means pressed	FROST 119:4
pressure: Hemingway said, 'grace under p.'	HEM 138:8
presumption: you'll be amused by its p.	THUR 297:8
pretend: I do not p. to know where	DARR 88:8
p. to be more stupid	STARK 283:9
We shall not p. that there	ANON 12:5
why p.	SHAW 271:11
Pretender: James II, and the Old P.	GUED 130:4
pretentious: And Harry says, 'P.'	CLEE 77:6
pretty: A p. girl is like a melody	BERL 40:8
It's p., but is it Art	KIPL 169:12
policeman and a p. girl	CHAP 67:4
The p. can get away	WAUGH 306:6
Which is sometimes so p.	PRÉV 239:14
prevail: merely endure, he will p.	FAUL 107:12
prevent: knowing how to p. them	RUSS 256:3
we have a right to p. it	MILN 211:2
prevented: could not have been p.	BEVIN 45:15
preventing: nothing like desire for p.	PROU 240:13
Politics is the art of p.	VALÉ 303:3
prévois: p. les événements que lorsqu'ils	ION 151:11
prey: p. to sensations and cheap	TREV 298:13
preys: p. systematically	JAMES 153:10
price: Despair is the p. one pays	GREE 128:13
increase was another man's p.	WILS 313:12
love that pays the p.	SPR 282:13
p. of championing human	OWEN 227:10
p. of insubordination	MACG 195:4
p. of justice is eternal	BENN 38:14
What p. glory	AND 6:5
prices: acting directly to reduce p.	HEATH 136:15
prickly: Here we go round the p. pear	ELIOT 103:4

pride: beware the temptation of p.	REAG 244:6
great labyrinth out of p.	YEATS 322:5
having given up his p.	SAL 259:1
here have P. and Truth	YEATS 319:6
London P. has been handed	COW 84:11
look backward to with p.	FROST 118:16
P. of Life that planned	HARDY 134:4
The poet's inward p.	DAY-L 89:6
priest: p. of the invisible	STEV 285:14
priests: And pay a million p.	HARDY 134:13
associate with a lot of p.	BELL 33:13
p. were infinitely more	FITZ 110:18
The p. in gold and black	LAWR 181:11
primal: has only two p. passions	OSLER 227:7
primary: p. object of a student	CECIL 65:9
prime: One's p. is elusive	SPARK 281:7
Prime Minister: best P. we have	BUTL 58:10
camouflage about the P.	PAGET 228:11
country gentleman than a p.	MACD 194:13
P. [Lloyd George] has	ANON 8:10
The next P. but three	BELL 33:7
triumphant P. declared	THAT 291:8
Unknown P.	ASQ 15:1
would have become P. before	CONN 80:12
Prime Ministers: P. have never yet been	CHUR 75:11
wild flowers, and P.	BALD 23:8
primeval: mastodons bellowing across p.	WOD 316:2
primitive: wise p. in a giant jungle	MAIL 199:6
prince: Advise the p.	ELIOT 103:11
I were the P. of Peace	HOUS 144:7
princes: admit p. to the corridors	DOUG 93:9
principle: He does everything on p.	SHAW 272:19
law of p. and politics	RAK 242:10
p. of Human Nature	JAMES 153:11
the 'falling domino' p.	EIS 100:3
useful thing about a p.	MAUG 204:13
principles: instead of p., slogans	BENT 39:16
one's p. than to live	ADLER 2:21
upon those p. of freedom	PAGE 228:10
print: decomposing in the eternity of p.	WOOLF 317:5
licence to p. money	THOM 297:1
p. such of the proprietor's	SWAF 289:4
seeing our names in p.	CHES 70:12
printemps: p. dans ses plis a gardé	ARAG 13:2
printing: p. press is either	BARR 26:3
printless: On lissom, clerical, p. toe	BROO 55:9
priorities: language of p. is the religion	BEVAN 45:7
priority: without the reward of p.	SCOTT 265:7
prison: begin with, it is a p.	SHAW 273:5
comparatively at home in p.	WAUGH 306:1
Home is the girl's p.	SHAW 272:12
In the p. of his days	AUDEN 17:7
p. for the colour	HOUS 144:8
there is a soul in p.	DEBS 89:11

prisoner: If the p. is happy SHAW 271:11
prisoners: p. of addiction ILL 150:12
still the p. of communism SOLZ 280:3
privacy: narrow p. and tawdry secrets
LEACH 182:8
private: his p. parts, his money BUTL 59:6
Its p. life is a disgrace ANON 10:13
P. faces in public places AUDEN 20:2
P. Means is dead SMITH 279:1
p. opulence and public GALB 121:4
with a silk hat at a p. EDW 98:8
privilege: power which stands on P. BELL 34:13
privy: nor a p., nor a seal BAIL 22:4
prized: local, but p. elsewhere AUDEN 18:5
prize-fighters: one of p. shaking hands
MENC 206:11
prizes: offer glittering p. SMITH 277:8
p. at the flower show BRON 54:6
problem: or you're part of the p. CLEA 77:4
p. is food DONL 93:3
p. of the colour line DUB 96:3
p. of the twentieth century DUB 96:3
quite a three-pipe p. DOYLE 94:3
that they can't see the p. CHES 71:1
problematical: The p. world and sells us life
FRY 119:15
problems: p. reproduce themselves JOS 157:8
proceeds: good conscience on the p. SMITH 278:4
process: attentive when she was in p. FITZ 110:18
p. whereby American girls HAMP 132:7
proclaims: p. with a hammer BIER 46:10
procrastination: p. is the art MARQ 201:8
prodigal: angels over the p.'s SAKI 257:13
prodigious: have a p. quantity of mind
TWAIN 301:1
prodigy: normal child and not as a p. BARB 24:17
producers: or junior television p. AMIS 5:13
produces: artist is someone who p. WARH 305:4
producing: that consumes without p. ORW 224:10
product: p. of the untalented CAPP 63:13
production: p. and reduce unemployment
HEATH 136:15
profanation: From sale and p. CHES 70:7
profane: P. perfection of mankind YEATS 319:10
profession: ancient p. in the world KIPL 171:5
be the second oldest p. REAG 244:10
not a p. but a vocation SIM 275:7
very important p. SHAW 268:24
professions: p. are conspiracies against
SHAW 268:21
shortest-lived p. there ROG 249:16
professor: called a p. emeritus LEAC 182:11
professors: instrument wielded by p. WEIL 307:6
p. like their literature LEWIS 187:10
profit: And the p. and loss ELIOT 105:8
p. is not always what motivates GIDE 124:7
profitable: it is not p. MARQ 201:14
profited: p. from public service NIXON 220:8

profits: Civilization and p. go COOL 82:12
profound: Down some p. dull tunnel OWEN 228:5
p. truths recognized BOHR 48:11
programme: Not so much a p. ANON 10:7
progress: beings will live and p. DUB 96:2
certain since Social P. began KIPL 173:12
p. depends on the unreasonable SHAW 272:8
P., far from consisting SANT 260:11
p. if a cannibal uses knife LEC 183:12
p. in the arts MAO 200:10
P. is a comfortable disease CUMM 87:7
p. is based upon a universal BUTL 59:15
'P.' is the exchange ELLIS 106:4
P. through technology ANON 11:18
The social p., order JOHN 155:17
They spoke of P. spiring round CHES 70:15
To mark the simple sort of p. SIMM 275:8
To swell a p., start ELIOT 103:11
prohibition: Communism is like p. ROG 249:15
project: much less ambitious p. ANON 8:4
projected: They stay as they were p. BOWEN 51:2
projections: Merely p. There is nothing
ELIOT 101:3
proletarian: p. socialist state in Russia
LENIN 184:11
prolong: Youth to p. YEATS 321:4
prolonged: p. by those who have SASS 262:11
Prometheus: P. reaches for the stars KOES 176:9
promiscuity: Sentimentality is the emotional p.
MAIL 199:5
promise: Full of Eastern p. ANON 8:2
Gives p. of pneumatic bliss ELIOT 103:2
p. made is a debt unpaid SERV 267:2
p. of a refined and sensitive DOYLE 95:4
p. of their early years POW 239:5
was a young man of p. BALF 24:1
promised: I never p. you a rose garden
GREEN 128:10
I've seen the p. land KING 166:11
think of the Future as a p. LEWIS 187:3
promises: But I have p. to keep FROST 118:11
he is a young man of p. BALF 24:1
Vote for the man who p. BAR 27:7
promising: destroy they first call p. CONN 80:8
prone: Orion plunges p. HOUS 145:10
pronounce: p. a judgment BECK 28:12
spell better than they p. TWAIN 301:2
proof: p. of God's omnipotence DE VR 91:14
which America is the p. MCC 193:14
proofs: p. and tell him or her CHAN 66:12
propaganda: purely for p. BEAV 28:4
proper: And lacks a p. pride MACD 194:11
p. or improper FULL 120:7
p. study of mankind HUXL 148:11
properties: certain exceptional p. JEANS 154:6
property: from the dominion of p. GOLD 126:3
own p. at the resurrection BUTL 59:5
p. that we shall strike PANK 229:8

property (*cont.*):
Thieves respect p.   CHES 69:13
prophets: ceased to pose as its p.   POPP 236:4
proportion: That's out of p.   LARK 179:6
proposition: all men are equal is a p.   HUXL 149:10
into the fifth p. of Euclid   DOYLE 95:2
p. be interesting   WHIT 310:6
p. is the method   SCHL 264:5
undesirable to believe a p.   RUSS 255:14
propriety: p. of some persons seems   BRAD 51:15
prose: *as well written as p*   POUND 238:11
Poetry is to p. as dancing   WAIN 304:10
p. and the passion   FORS 115:3
prose-song: Stein's p. is a cold   LEWIS 187:8
prospects: affording delightful p.   HOFF 142:9
prosper: which our affairs p.   BIER 46:19
prosperity: p. arrived at in a single   BUTL 60:8
prostitute: can p. all their powers   FORS 114:5
p. is more moral   PHIL 233:12
prostitutes: small nations like p.   KUBR 177:3
protect: Heaven will p. a working   SMITH 277:2
inform the reader but to p.   ACH 1:9
p. its own existence   ASIM 14:13
protected: squirrels, must be p.   ORTON 224:6
protection: millions of farms if that p. HOOV 143:7
protections: p. against temptations   TWAIN 300:19
protects: p. the solitude   RILKE 248:1
protest: partakes of the nature of a p.   HOFF 142:7
Protestant: A P. with a horse   BEHAN 31:22
attacked me and the P. church   NIEM 219:12
Protestants: P. can be expected to have
                                                         WILS 312:18
proud: are always p. of the fact   RUSS 254:15
A woman can be p. and stiff   YEATS 323:8
It makes him very p.   MILNE 210:8
man being too p. to fight   WILS 314:11
p. of seeing our names   CHES 70:12
Proust: go for a P. or a Joyce   COBB 78:1
prove: I could p. everything   PINT 234:15
I've arrived and to p.   SYKES 289:7
you money if you can p.   HOPE 144:1
proved: something or other could be p.
                                                         FRY 119:19
virtue and a p. liar   HAIL 130:13
whole you have p.   HARDY 134:12
Provence: Than you found it in P.   WILL 312:14
Proverbs: King Solomon wrote the P.
                                                         NAYL 218:16
providence: I go the way that P. dictates
                                                         HITL 141:7
inscrutable workings of P.   SMITH 277:4
p. to kill you before you   BUTL 59:17
provident: They are p. instead   BOGAN 48:8
providers: p. they're oil   PARK 231:13
provincial: he was worse than p.   JAMES 152:17
provincialism: adultery than in p.   HUXL 148:7
provocative: choose a less p. Ambassador
                                                         HOUS 144:7
provoke: subsidized to p. the world   FRY 119:17

prudence: effect of p. on rascality   SHAW 272:5
p. never to practise   TWAIN 300:15
prudent: stage, a p. Mr Baldwin   BEAV 28:6
prunus: p. and forsythia across   BETJ 44:1
Prussia: military domination of P.   ASQ 14:19
psalm: reverent cadence and subtle p.
                                                         AUDEN 20:12
Psalms: And King David wrote the P.
                                                         NAYL 218:16
psychiatrist: Any man who goes to a p.
                                                         GOLD 126:10
p. is a man who goes   STOC 286:13
psychical: For P. Research   COW 85:9
psychology: p. of human relationships
                                                         BERNE 41:7
pub: any p. on Saturday night   ORW 225:17
wasn't a p. open in the city   BEHAN 32:3
Will someone take me to a p.   CHES 70:15
pubic: that Caught the P. Hare   BEHAN 31:23
public: British p. falls for this   HAIL 130:14
Ce que le p. réclame   BART 27:4
describe holding p. office   ACH 1:7
gives it to the p.   VALÉ 302:19
glorified p. relations   TRUM 299:10
I and the p. know   AUDEN 17:11
now quit altogether p.   EDW 98:11
one to mislead the p.   ASQ 14:18
opulence and p. squalor   GALB 121:4
Private faces in p. places   AUDEN 20:2
p. buys its opinions   BUTL 60:4
p. school will always feel   WAUGH 306:1
p. something they want   SKEL 276:11
p. wants is the image   BART 27:4
p. will take care   SULZ 289:1
researchers into P. Opinion   AUDEN 18:1
solo in p. and learning   BUTL 59:3
The p. doesn't give   BEEC 29:17
whatever the Government and p.   SHAW 271:4
yourself and have no p.   CONN 80:15
publicity: hijacker of the oxygen of p. THAT 292:3
justice is eternal p.   BENN 38:14
p. except your own obituary   BEHAN 32:5
p. rather than of poetry   LEAV 183:6
qualities which create p.   ATTL 16:3
publics: can impose on their p.   BENN 38:8
public-school: p. men or even of Anglo-Saxons
                                                         FORS 114:1
published: after my first book was p.   BARR 26:7
publisher: executed for murdering his p.
                                                         BARR 25:13
publishers: fear of life become p.   CONN 80:7
Turned Down by numerous P.   ADE 2:17
pubs: all the p. in Dublin   DONL 93:4
pudding: Take away that p.   CHUR 76:12
puddle: dangerous than a mud-p.   STEIN 284:8
puffed: P. its sulphur to the sunset   BETJ 43:8
pull: Len says one steady p. more   FROST 119:3
P. down thy vanity   POUND 238:16

pull (*cont.*):

willing to p. his weight	ROOS 251:5
pulls: p. a lady through	MARQ 201:11
pulp: The p. so bitter, how shall	THOM 295:13
pulse: And two people with the one p.	
	MACN 198:3
p. in the eternal mind	BROO 55:2
puñado: *por un p. de monedas*	ZAP 324:8
punctuality: P. is the virtue of the bored	
	WAUGH 306:2
punctures: And it p. my skin	ANON 11:9
punk: Gert's writings are p.	ANON 8:13
punt: it is better fun to p.	SAY 263:8
pupils: p. are the crème de la	SPARK 281:5
purchased: life thus p. we could	ROS 252:13
pure: appear as a p. mathematician	JEANS 154:7
cold and p. and very dead	LEWIS 187:10
I'm as p. as the driven slush	BANK 24:7
p. as the lily in the dell	LAUD 180:1
purest: fuck is the p. thing there	JONG 157:5
purify: To p. the dialect of the tribe	ELIOT 102:3
puritan: P. all things are impure	LAWR 181:6
puritanism: England is not P. but February	
	KRUT 177:1
P. The haunting fear	MENC 206:14
purple: His P. Robe	FARJ 107:7
noon a p. glow	YEATS 318:10
purpose: Here is God's p.	FULL 120:7
himself except for a noble p.	HERB 139:17
politics of p. and the politics	HUMP 148:4
Proof that there's a p. set	YEATS 319:10
p. of human existence	JUNG 159:15
Sole p. of visit	HARD 132:15
purring: Is suddenly p. there	MONRO 212:4
purrs: until it p. like an epigram	MARQ 202:3
pursue: those who p. many ends	BERL 40:13
who p. Culture in bands	WHAR 309:22
pursued: it is you who are the p.	SHAW 270:20
The villain still p. her	NOBL 221:2
pursuit: moderation in the p. of justice	
	GOLD 126:4
Now of that long p.	THOM 295:15
p. of the Presidency	JOHN 156:13
push: without trying to p. it	O'CAS 222:12
put: Our end is Life. P. out to sea	MACN 198:1
p. out on the troubled	GALB 121:3
what p. me up to it	BEVIN 46:1
with which I will not p.	CHUR 76:2
putting: way of p. it	ELIOT 101:12
pygmies: peace like retarded p.	PEAR 232:11
pyjamas: I in p. for the heat	LAWR 180:9
pylons: P., those pillars	SPEN 281:17
pyramid: bottom of the economic p.	ROOS 250:2
Pyrenees: that tease in the High P.	BELL 34:9
pyres: Steel chambers, late the p.	HARDY 134:4
Pythagoras: P. planned it	YEATS 319:14
python: sheep in the stare of a p.	BANK 24:11
Who bought a P. from a man	BELL 33:15

Q

quad: no one about in the Q.	KNOX 176:5
quaint: Yes; q. and curious war	HARDY 134:10
Quakers: I was beaten up by Q.	ALLEN 5:5
qualification: q. for being put	CARS 64:3
qualities: only two q. in the world	SHAW 269:19
q. which create publicity	ATTL 16:3
quality: have a third q. as well	FORS 114:6
Never mind the q.	POW 239:12
quantity: prodigious q. of mind	TWAIN 301:1
quarks: Three q. for Muster Mark	JOYCE 158:5
quarrel: lover's q. with the world	FROST 119:10
out of the q. with others	YEATS 319:1
q. in a far away country	CHAM 66:4
reality only one to make a q.	INGE 151:6
quarters: Ere to the wind's twelve q.	HOUS 146:10
quay: Who would wait on the q.	CAUS 65:4
Quebec: Long Live Free Q.	DE G 90:2
Queen: Fella belong Mrs Q.	PHIL 234:1
Q. to get away with a hat	LOOS 190:17
To toast *The Q.*	HEAN 136:13
queenly: Q. in her own room	WHAR 309:20
queer: toast to 'our q. old dean'	SPOO 282:9
We're here because we're q.	BEHAN 32:4
what a q. thing Life	WOD 316:8
queerer: universe is not only q.	HALD 131:1
questing: fen passes the q. vole	WAUGH 306:9
question: ask an impertinent q.	BRON 54:4
down the number of the q.	CHUR 75:9
having asked any clear q.	CAMUS 62:11
If any q. why we died	KIPL 175:10
questions grow where one q.	VEBL 304:1
q. that has never been	FREUD 117:6
secretly changed the Q.	SELL 266:12
that case what is the q.	STEIN 284:11
The q. is absurd	AUDEN 18:2
To ask the hard q. is simple	AUDEN 20:6
questions: no q. isn't told a lie	KIPL 172:15
not wish to know ask q.	RAL 242:11
q. and form a clear opinion	BONH 49:4
q. of will or decision	CHOM 71:15
that all q. are open	BELL 32:10
That q. the distempered part	ELIOT 101:15
queue: forms an orderly q. of one	MIKES 207:15
quick: Come! q. as you can	DE L 91:1
q., and the dead	DEWAR 92:1
q. brown fox jumps over	ANON 10:12
quickened: His eyes are q. so with grief	
	GRAV 128:5
quicker: Is q.	NASH 218:8
quickest: q. way to start	HUBB 147:9
quiet: All q. on the western front	REM 245:10
q. world til you knock	SHAW 273:3
were alone with the q.	JAMES 153:9
quietest: Are the q. places	HOUS 146:13
quietly: Q. sweating palm to palm	HUXL 149:2

quietly (cont.):
Q. they go, the intelligent   MILL 207:16
quinquireme: Q. of Nineveh from distant
   MAS 202:16
quinsy: weaning, the liar's q.   AUDEN 20:3
quit: q. altogether public affairs   EDW 98:11
quite: q. a gentleman but you   ASHF 14:3
quivers: And q. in the sunny breeze   GREN 129:5
quotation: from q. is a national vice
   WAUGH 306:5
quotations: man to read books of q.   CHUR 75:13
q. from the Bible   LAWR 181:5
quote: debate forcefully and q.   HOGB 142:10
monkey of a man is to q.   BENC 36:6
quoted: remarks are very seldom q.   STR 288:10
quotes: man never q. accurately   PEAR 232:9
q. is that they give us   WILL 312:1

R

rabbit: I am a bunny r.   AYRES 21:14
Run, r., run   GAY 122:8
The r. has a charming face   ANON 10:13
There is a r. in a snare   STEP 285:4
rabbits: there were four little R.   POTT 237:5
race: As men and women with our r.   KIPL 173:1
flag as the r. wore   COKE 78:14
r. between education   WELLS 308:10
r. or the colour   WILL 312:17
r. relations in our time   CARM 63:15
racehorses: r. and the cheaper clarets   SAKI 257:17
races: darker to the lighter r.   DUB 96:3
r. are really pinko-grey   FORS 115:6
racing: r. tipster who only reached   TAYL 290:15
racist: r. institutions and values   CARM 63:15
rack: r. and new bugs stand   WILL 311:11
racket: Once in the r. you're always   CAP 63:9
r. is back in its press   BETJ 43:9
r. run by unscrupulous   BEEC 30:3
radar: r. and all great writers   HEM 138:11
radiance: strain of this trial — a r.   CAUL 65:3
radical: I never dared be r. when young
   FROST 118:4
R. is a man with both feet   ROOS 250:9
r. revolutionary will become   AREN 13:5
radicals: one of these goddam r.   CAP 63:8
r. have good digestions   BUTL 59:16
radio: I had the r.   MONR 212:5
r. and television   SARR 261:5
raffiniert: R. ist der Herrgott   EINS 99:5
rafters: stars come down with the r.   AUDEN 19:2
rag: foul r. and bone shop   YEATS 320:3
r. and a bone and a hank   KIPL 175:7
That Shakespearian r.   BUCK 57:9
that Shakespeherian R.   ELIOT 105:2
rage: horrible that lust and r.   YEATS 321:3
Maintain your r.   WHIT 310:19

rage (cont.):
r. against the dying   THOM 292:11
rages: older that the weight of r.   SPOO 282:11
ragged: been a pair of r. claws   ELIOT 103:9
rushed a dozen dirty and r.   DOYLE 95:7
raging: r. in the dark   YEATS 323:12
ragtime: Alexander's r. band   BERL 40:4
R . . . but when the wearied Band   HUXL 149:2
raid: r. on the inarticulate   ELIOT 101:16
railroad: Once I built a r. Now   HARB 132:12
railroads: build bridges and throw r.   BROUN 56:7
railway: picking daisies on the r.   WOD 315:18
various r. termini   FORS 114:11
rain: boy, waiting for r.   ELIOT 100:6
Dull roots with spring r.   ELIOT 104:10
hard r.'s a gonna fall   DYLAN 97:5
left Him in the r.   KENN 288:12
not even the r., has such   CUMM 87:5
r. in Spain stays mainly   LERN 186:4
r. is destroying his grain   HERB 139:11
r. over the dwindling harbour   THOM 292:14
Singin' in the r.   FREED 116:11
Still falls the R.   SITW 276:6
Sudden the r. of gold   DAY-L 89:4
wedding-cake left out in the r.   AUDEN 21:1
rainbow: A r. and a cuckoo's song   DAV 88:13
Follow ev'ry r., till   HAMM 131:9
God gave Noah the r. sign   ANON 8:3
It was the R. gave thee birth   DAV 88:16
simple blessing of a r.   ABSE 1:3
Somewhere over the r.   HARB 132:13
The Lord survives the r.   LOW 192:3
rain-green: over the r. grass   LEE 183:17
raining: It isn't r. rain to me   LOV 191:5
rains: Every time it rains, it r.   BURKE 58:3
rainy: The r. Pleiads wester   HOUS 145:10
raised: No glass of ours was ever r.   HEAN 136:13
raises: food that r. him   HANFF 132:9
rake: stop to r. the leaves   FROST 118:12
raking: when to stop r. the muck   ROOS 251:12
Ramsay: come to me and say 'R.'   MACD 194:13
Ramsbottom: And Mr and Mrs R.   EDGAR 98:3
ran: I r. the paper [Daily Express]   BEAV 28:4
nothing ever r. quite straight   GALS 121:6
ranches: r. of isolation   AUDEN 17:4
randy: Porter-drinkers' r. laughter   YEATS 319:11
R.—where   BELL 32:11
range: wider r. of experience   HARR 135:6
Rangoon: chunkin' from R. to Mandalay
   KIPL 169:6
rape: legitimately, you r. it   DEGAS 89:13
r. is said to be the ruling   PRIT 240:3
They r. us with their eyes   FREN 117:1
rapidly: R. agin'   DYLAN 97:13
Yes, but not so r.   BECK 29:9
rapists: with women, all men are r.   FREN 117:1
rapscallions: All kings is mostly r.   TWAIN 300:6
rapture: r. there is a family alliance   BELL 32:8
rare: how r., how precious   FORS 114:5

rare (*cont.*):

r. in our pockets the mark | CHES 70:12
rarer: r. than the unicorn | JONG 157:5
rascality: effect of prudence on r. | SHAW 272:5
rascals: Honours List is full of r. | BENN 38:16
rash: He was not r. | GRAH 127:11
r. my dear your colors | ASHF 14:4
rat: giant r. of Sumatra | DOYLE 94:9
it creeps like a r. | BOWEN 51:3
Mmm, you dirty r. | CAGN 60:18
rather: I would r. have blood | GREE 128:11
would you r. be a country | MACD 194:13
ratio: inverse r. to the importance | HUXL 148:8
rational: r. and that it was all | AYER 21:13
that the irrational is r. | STEV 285:13
ratlike: success in journalism are r. | TOM 298:2
rattle: Shake, r. and roll | CALH 61:5
stuttering rifles' rapid r. | OWEN 227:13
rave: age should burn and r. | THOM 292:11
Ravel: R. refuses the Legion | SATIE 263:6
ravish: can't r. a tin of sardines | LAWR 181:8
raw: R. towns that never believe | AUDEN 17:4
ray: grievance and a r. of sunshine | WOD 315:10
razor: mirror and a r. lay crossed | JOYCE 158:14
that the r. ceases to act | HOUS 145:9
razors: R. pain you | PARK 230:14
reach: parts other beers cannot r. | LOV 191:4
reaction: third r. of man upon | HOLM 142:13
reactionaries: All r. are paper tigers | MAO 200:13
reactionary: R. is a somnambulist walking
| ROOS 250:9
read: bothered to r. another | MITF 211:14
countenance this person r. | BRAM 52:11
Don't r. too much now: the dude | LARK 179:14
ever been taught how to r. | SAY 263:10
his books were r. | BELL 34:10
I r., much of the night | ELIOT 104:11
journalism what will be r. | CONN 80:6
man who can r. music | BEEC 29:16
never having r. either | COBB 78:1
only news until he's r. it | WAUGH 306:10
people praise and don't r. | TWAIN 300:16
people who can't r. | ZAPPA 324:9
r. and dream of the soft | YEATS 318:8
r. any good books lately | MURD 216:1
R. out my words at night | FLEC 112:7
r. that stuff by myself | SAL 258:13
r. the crystal when | BEVAN 45:4
she cannot r. | AUDEN 21:3
that he has r. too widely | PEAR 232:9
vast population able to r. | TREV 298:13
what I r. in the papers | ROG 249:9
reader: no tears in the r. | FROST 118:1
only the individual r. | NAB 217:5
r. recognizes as his own | QUAS 242:1
r. wishes to convince others | FORS 114:10
That ideal r. suffering | JOYCE 157:11
readers: are biased, and so are r. | BALL 24:4
so many of my r. belong | CHES 69:14

reading: becomes a substitute for r. | BURG 58:2
Peace is poor r. | HARDY 133:4
R. isn't an occupation we | ORTON 224:7
thing, but I prefer r. | SMITH 278:13
reads: Fat-head poet that nobody r. | CHES 69:15
ready: r. for my close-up now | BRAC 51:12
those for which we are r. | FORS 115:15
real: directly stencilled off the r. | SONT 280:11
everything that is r. about us | SHAW 270:13
r. and true than the things | SHAW 268:12
R. life seems to have no | COMP 80:4
The r. way to travel | GRAH 127:15
washed in the speechless r. | BARZ 27:11
realist: presented as 'r. politics' | BERD 40:1
realistic: make a 'r. decision' | MCC 194:2
reality: And the r. | ELIOT 103:4
art is an appeal to a r. | MACC 193:9
Cannot bear very much r. | ELIOT 101:7
combination of r. and lies | COCT 78:6
sense of ultimate r. | BELL 32:7
tourist in other people's r. | SONT 280:10
realization: limit to our r. of tomorrow
| ROOS 251:3
r. of the innate individuality | JUNG 160:3
re-allocate: deny the facts but to r. | RYLE 256:7
really: you'll be a R. Useful Engine | AWDRY 21:5
realm: One r., one people, one leader | ANON 7:19
reap: Time shall r., but after | THOM 294:14
reaping: without looking up, 'r. | BOTT 50:6
reappears: he r. in your children | CONN 80:16
reappraisal: compel an agonizing r. | DULL 96:6
rearming: said that Germany was r. | BALD 23:7
rearrange: r. the furniture | MORT 214:10
rears: S-E-X ever r. its ugly head | AYCK 21:6
reason: all r. is against it | BUTL 60:3
I have a r. for living | SHAW 273:4
Language is a form of human r. | LÉV 187:1
r. can convince us of those | BELL 32:10
R. enslaves all whose | SHAW 272:9
r. for the existence | JAMES 153:2
R. has moons, but moons | HODG 142:4
r. so many people showed | GOLD 126:11
r. why he should be treated | EDW 98:9
r. why I don't drink | ASTOR 15:10
r. why we should be anything | ASQ 14:16
right deed for the wrong r. | ELIOT 102:9
You needn't try to r. | JER 155:13
reasonable: figure of 'The R. Man' | HERB 139:14
It's a r. percentage | BECK 29:5
rather be right than be r. | NASH 217:19
r. man adapts himself | SHAW 272:8
r. man could have expected | HERB 139:18
reasons: care anything about r. | JAMES 153:7
r. for having children | RUSS 256:3
r. for what we believe | BRAD 52:2
simple rock and roll r. | GELD 122:10
reassures: disturb, science r. | BRAQ 52:13
rebel: R. without a cause | LIND 188:5

rebel (cont.):

true-blue r.	HILL 140:10
What is a r.? A man who says no	CAMUS 63:1
rebellion: incite this meeting to r.	PANK 229:8
might well bring the r.	WILS 313:10
r. against the existing	SHAW 269:6
recall: r. he would be willing	BRAD 51:16
receipt: Applause is a r.	SCHN 264:7
received: undertaking has been r.	CHAM 66:7
recession: r. when your neighbour	TRUM 299:9
recherche: A la r. du temps perdu.	PROU 240:6
recipes: r. that are always successful	VALÉ 303:1
reciting: r. the Athanasian Creed	AUDEN 18:4
reckless: r. Mr Baldwin	BEAV 28:6
reclaimed: man r. his own property	BUTL 59:5
reclamation: condemn it. It is land r.	WILS 313:5
recognition: aesthetic enjoyment is r.	WHIT 310:10
r. of another's resemblance	BIER 46:5
recognize: only a trial if I r.	KAFKA 160:8
record: kind of r. seemed vital	COPE 83:7
r. of sin than does	DOYLE 94:8
r. on the gramophone	ELIOT 105:7
recover: r. it from all his forefathers	BUTL 59:5
recovers: from which he never r.	MCL 196:10
rector: An ancestor was r. there	YEATS 319:13
rectum: r. makes a good diagnostician	OSLER 226:17
red: Better r. than dead	ANON 7:4
it's not even r. brick	OSB 226:12
R. hair she had and golden	BETJ 42:6
r. house in a red mahogany	BETJ 42:4
R. lips are not so red	OWEN 228:3
r. wheel	WILL 312:13
Their r. it never dies	DOBS 92:15
When the r., red, robin	WOODS 317:3
redeemed: Is not r. from time	ELIOT 102:6
redemption: r. of all things	SHAW 268:23
red-haired: r. girls scamper like roses	LEE 183:17
red-hot: I'm the last of the r. mamas	YELL 324:4
reduced: I would not be r. to accepting	HARD 132:16
redwood: r. forest to the Gulf Stream	GUTH 130:10
reeled: sentences until r. the mind	GIBBS 124:1
reference: r. to fun in any Act	HERB 139:15
refined: Good looking, so r.	FIEL 108:8
r. and sensitive nature	DOYLE 95:4
r. out of existence	JOYCE 158:9
This Englishwoman is so r.	SMITH 278:17
reflecting: r. the figure of a man	WOOLF 317:9
reform: lunatic fringe in all r.	ROOS 252:1
reformation: r. must have its victims	SAKI 257:13
reformer: r. is a guy who rides through	MIZN 212:2
reformers: All r. are bachelors	MOORE 212:9
All R., however strict	SMITH 278:5
refrain: R. from the unholy pleasure	BELL 32:12
sensibly r. from speech	GRAH 127:12
They merely r. from asking	HALS 131:8

refreshes: Heineken r. the parts	LOV 191:4
refuge: are so easy to take r.	IBSEN 149:19
that it's a r. from home	SHAW 274:9
refugees: The guttural sorrow of the r.	MACN 198:2
refusal: r. to admit our emotions	RATT 243:7
refuse: daylight and never to r.	MENC 206:17
men r. to fight	ANON 11:21
offer he can't r.	PUZO 241:8
regard: r. for religion as we can	O'CAS 222:13
regarder: r. ensemble dans la même	SAIN 257:3
regards: Give my r. to Broadway	COHAN 78:11
regeneration: r. of all humanity	PANK 229:6
Regent: who revelled with the R.	BEER 31:6
regiment: R. an' pokes the 'eathen	KIPL 174:11
regret: My one r. in life	ALLEN 4:17
r. in the theatre	BARR 26:19
regrets: follies which a man r.	ROWL 254:1
Miss Otis r.	PORT 236:16
rehearsal: r. I let the orchestra	BEEC 30:5
rehearse: obvious reluctance to r.	BEEC 30:7
Reich: Ein R., ein Volk, ein Führer.	ANON 7:19
reindeer: Herds of r. move across	AUDEN 20:1
Rudolph, the Red-Nosed R.	MARKS 201:6
reject: accepted it is time to r. it	JACK 152:1
r. me on account	BELL 33:12
rejoice: Prime Minister declared 'R.'	THAT 291:8
relate: r. everything to a single	BERL 40:13
relation: r. of the darker	DUB 96:3
relations: are God's apology for r.	KING 167:10
offensive in personal r.	RUSS 255:5
Personal r. are the important	FORS 115:2
relationships: psychology of human r.	BERNE 41:7
r. begin and most of them	AUDEN 18:14
relative: In a r. way	BULL 57:11
Success is r.	ELIOT 101:17
relatives: God gives us our r.	MUMF 215:12
relativity: If my theory of r. is proven	EINS 99:7
relaxation: r. from physical fatigue	MAT 204:8
release: Good-night. Ensured r.	HOUS 145:12
I r. the safety-catch	JOHST 157:2
we have found r. there	BROO 54:10
relegation: r. to the status of a fuzzy	CAIR 61:4
relenting: This day r. God	ROSS 253:6
reliable: r. walls of youth collapse	FORS 114:13
relief: But O my God, what a r.	BARR 26:18
religion: Art and R. are, then	BELL 32:8
Christian r. doubted	BUTL 60:9
concerned with r.	TEMP 291:4
face and a different r.	EDW 98:9
from the dominion of r.	GOLD 126:3
me on account of my r.	BELL 33:12
Millionaire. That is my r.	SHAW 270:5
more beautiful than any r.	SAKI 257:8
priorities is the r. of Socialism	BEVAN 45:7
reason to bring r. into it	O'CAS 222:13
R. and art spring from	CATH 64:13
r. is whatever he is most	BARR 26:9

religion (cont.):
  r. to a man with bodily   SHAW 270:6
  r. without science   EINS 99:11
  science is strong and r.   SZASZ 290:6
  Science without r. is lame   EINS 99:11
  start your own r.   HUBB 147:9
  There is only one r.   SHAW 273:9
  To become a popular r.   INGE 151:4
religions: materialistic of all great r.   TEMP 291:5
  r. and created great works   PROU 240:12
  R. are kept alive by heresies   BREN 53:10
religious: aesthetic and r. rapture   BELL 32:8
  himself to any r. belief   WAUGH 305:17
  his r. opinions   BUTL 59:6
  r. system that produced   SAKI 257:12
religious-good: Good, but not r.   HARDY 134:11
reluctance: r. to rehearse on a morning   BEEC 30:7
remain: roll over but the rocks r.   HERB 139:13
  The days go by, I r.   APOL 12:15
  We all are born mad. Some r.   BECK 29:12
remained: born an Englishman and r.   BEHAN 31:21
remains: whatever r., *however improbable*   DOYLE 95:5
remarkable: This very r. man   INGE 150:13
remarks: r. are not literature   STEIN 284:2
  r. are very seldom quoted   STR 288:10
remedy: r. for the worst of them   KELL 162:9
remember: Ah yes! I r. it well   LERN 186:1
  always seem to r. blondes   LOOS 190:14
  And even I can r.   POUND 238:3
  Do you r. an Inn   BELL 34:9
  r. days that have gone   FLEC 111:17
  R. me when I am dead   DOUG 93:7
  R. no man's foot can pass   BOTT 50:4
  r. the Good Samaritan if   THAT 292:4
  r. the past are condemned   SANT 260:11
  To r. or invent   FROST 118:5
  We will r. them   BINY 47:5
  Who will r., passing through   SASS 262:10
  Yes; I r. Adlestrop   THOM 294:5
  You must r. this, a kiss   HUPF 148:5
remembered: critics is to be r.   MOORE 212:12
  none are undeservedly r.   AUDEN 18:8
  tranquillity r. in emotion   PARK 230:6
  What are those blue r. hills   HOUS 146:11
remembering: R. him like anything   CHES 70:10
  r. nothing but the blue   FORS 115:11
remembrance: Down in the flood of r.   LAWR 181:13
remind: R. me of you   MARV 202:8
reminiscences: old have r. of what   SAKI 257:16
  R. make one feel so deliciously   SHAW 269:14
  some of your grosser r.   WOOL 317:14
r-e-m-o-r-s-e : R.!   ADE 2:19
remote: R. and ineffectual Don   BELL 35:5
Remove: fat greedy owl of the R.   RICH 247:3
renaissance: Wake in her warm nest of r.   DAY-L 89:5

rendezvous: I have a r. with Death   SEEG 265:12
Reno'd: Moll R. in Wolsey's Home   ANON 9:8
renounce: recourse to war and r.   BRIA 53:11
  r. war for its consequences   FOSD 116:4
renowned: r. both far and wide   CAMP 62:6
rent: That has not been r.   YEATS 323:8
  They r. out my room   ALLEN 4:18
repair: r. to the matches   THOM 296:1
repeal: about the R. of the Corn   BEER 31:20
repeat: interesting till it begins to r.   BOWEN 50:10
  past are condemned to r.   SANT 260:11
  r. his past nor leave it   AUDEN 18:15
  r. that on the Golden Floor   HOUS 144:9
  would be willing to r.   BRAD 51:16
repelled: they are only r. by man   INGE 151:5
repetition: nagging is the r.   SUMM 289:2
repetitious: r. mechanism of the Universe   WHIT 310:5
replacement: r. of category-habits   RYLE 256:8
report: r. of my death was an exaggeration   TWAIN 301:7
  r. what the candidate says   NIXON 220:3
reporters: mixed feelings about r.   STOP 287:1
repose: midnight and the noon's r.   ELIOT 103:17
represent: causes that they r.   FORS 115:16
  does attempt to r. life   JAMES 153:2
representative: indignity of being your r.   BELL 33:12
repressed: r. desire for aesthetic   WAUGH 305:18
  r. sadists are supposed   CONN 80:7
reproduce: r. themselves from generation   JOS 157:8
republic: Only Love the Beloved R.   FORS 115:13
  R. is a Government of laws   FORD 113:8
  r. is like a chicken   MITF 211:13
republican: king's head on r. principles   SHAW 272:19
  proposition to my R. friends   STEV 285:16
  results for the R. ticket   ROOS 252:2
reputation: it wrecks a woman's r.   COL 79:3
  your r. is assured   MAUG 205:2
require: he thought 'e might r.   KIPL 174:7
requirement: first r. for a composer   HON 143:3
  first r. of a statesman   ACH 1:6
requisite: first r. of the historian   STR 287:14
rescue: r. and the liberation   CHUR 74:6
research: steal from many, it's r.   MIZN 212:1
researchers: r. into Public Opinion   AUDEN 18:1
researches: Mona did r. in original sin   PLOM 235:13
resemblance: recognition of another's r.   BIER 46:5
  r. to what one has in mind   PROU 240:13
resemble: r. not a ruler   HUXL 149:16
resented: Who r. it   COW 85:9
residence: And built of them a r.   MORG 213:9
residences: Inns are not r.   MOORE 213:5
resigned: approve. And I am not r.   MILL 207:16
  has r. and Northcliffe   ANON 8:10

resigned (*cont.*):
  r. to the way they have   CATH 65:2
resistance: liberty is the history of r.   WILS 314:9
  r. of the adversaries   STAL 283:4
resolution: In war: r. In defeat   CHUR 76:3
resolved: r. to be irresolute   CHUR 74:1
resolving: R. the enigma of the fever   ELIOT 101:1
resonance: r. of his solitude   CONN 80:14
resources: inner r., because I am heavy
                        BERR 41:13
respect: may more perfectly r. it   CHES 69:13
  r. for the idea of God   DUH 96:4
  r. public opinion   RUSS 255:4
  who r. their executioners   SART 262:3
  without losing one's r.   SAKI 257:11
respectability: r. and airconditioning   BAR 24:14
  save a shred of its r.   READ 244:2
respectable: more r.   SHAW 270:14
  r. live beyond other peoples'   SAKI 257:9
  riff-raff apply to what is r.   HOPE 143:10
respecte: r. *trop l'idée de Dieu*   DUH 96:4
respective: words in our r. languages   COOK 82:7
respects: To pay us his r.   AYRES 21:16
respiration: said it was artificial r.   BURG 58:1
respond: they r. I find   CHAR 68:1
responsable: *la rendre r. d'un monde*   DUH 96:4
responsibility: collective r.   ALD 3:12
  heavy burden of r.   EDW 98:11
  In dreams begins r.   YEATS 321:14
  Liberty means r.   SHAW 271:19
  Power without r.   KIPL 172:6
  r. without power, the prerogative   STOP 286:16
  writer's only r. is to his art   FAUL 107:10
responsible: idea of God to make it r.   DUH 96:4
  r. for this work of development   BEAV 28:9
rest: eyes before you see the r.   AYCK 21:6
  r. and play   GAFF 120:15
  r. if one doesn't sleep   WAUGH 305:16
  r. is mere sheep-herding   POUND 237:19
  r. quiet in Montparnasse   BENÉT 36:17
  To talk about the r. of us   ANON 11:8
  where's the r. of me   BELL 32:11
resting: r. up from their sinning   RUNY 254:9
restoration: not revolution, but r.   HARD 133:1
  The Church's R.   BETJ 43:4
restraint: r. with which they write   CAMP 62:2
restricted: R. to What Precisely   ELIOT 101:4
rests: Bereft of life it r.   CHAP 67:9
resurrection: own property at the r.   BUTL 59:5
resuscitate: He strove to r. the dead art
                      POUND 238:5
retain: r. the ability to function   FITZ 110:11
retainer: The Old R. night and day   BELL 33:6
reticence: Northern r., the tight   HEAN 136:11
retired: British Outer Mongolia for r.   BENN 37:7
retirement: there must be no r.   HAIG 130:12
retreat: convert r. into advance   ROOS 250:4
  Never keep a line of r.   NANS 217:8
retreating: Have you seen yourself r.   NASH 217:12

retrospective: r. or utopian   ARON 13:12
return: alas! we r.   FORS 114:11
  r. at twilight from   STEV 285:13
  Should I never r.   KATH 200:8
  through and I shall r.   MAC 193:5
  who does not r. your blow   SHAW 272:17
returned: And r. on the previous night
                      BULL 57:11
reveal: they r. the sardines   BENN 37:10
revelation: with the force of a r.   JAMES 153:19
revelations: stupendous r.   HOFF 142:9
revelled: who r. with the Regent   BEER 31:6
revenge: r. of the intellect   SONT 280:8
  tribal, intimate r.   HEAN 136:10
revenue: tariff for r.   HOOV 143:7
reverberation: paucity of its r.   MAIL 199:8
reverence: My cycle-clips in awkward r.
                      LARK 179:4
  phrase, 'R. for Life'   SCHW 264:16
  r. can you have for a Supreme   HELL 137:6
reverting: explains why r. to old ideas
                      OUSP 227:8
review: have your r. before me   REGER 245:7
  r. a bad book without showing   AUDEN 18:9
revisited: Brideshead r.   WAUGH 305:10
revivals: art is the history of r.   BUTL 59:19
reviving: *dreamed* of r. the *castrati*   REED 245:5
revolt: Art is a r. against fate   MALR 199:14
révolté: *Qu'est-ce qu'un homme r.*   CAMUS 63:1
revolution: A r. is an insurrection   MAO 200:11
  catalyst that sparks the r.   DURY 97:1
  leaders of a r.   CONR 81:21
  not r., but restoration   HARD 133:1
  on the day after the r.   AREN 13:5
  order to safeguard a r.   ORW 225:8
  r. impossible will make   KENN 164:3
  r. of rising expectations   CLEV 77:11
revolutionaries: r. are potential Tories
                      ORW 224:18
revolutionary: Feminism is the most r.
                      TOYN 298:6
  fierce and r. in a bathroom   LINK 188:11
  r. ends as an oppressor   CAMUS 63:3
  r. phrases is mistaken   KHR 165:11
  r. will become a conservative   AREN 13:5
revolutionized: it has already r.   ACE 1:5
révolutionnaire: *r. finit en oppresseur*   CAMUS 63:3
revolutions: It is a main cause of r.   INGE 151:3
  r. have ended in a reinforcement   CAMUS 63:2
  R. have never lightened   SHAW 271:14
reward: without the r. of priority   SCOTT 265:7
Reynolds: R. isn't as great   MUNN 215:15
rhetoric: love without the r.   STOP 287:5
  quarrel with others, r.   YEATS 319:1
Rhine: you think of the R.   BALD 23:5
rhinoceros: hide of a r.   BARR 26:17
Rhodes: R. had not enabled them   BEER 31:14

rhubarb: Of cold blancmange and r. tart
    KNOX 176:6
rhyme: man or elevate a r. YEATS 323:7
  still more tired of R. BELL 34:15
rhymes: voiced those r. is dust HARDY 133:7
rhyming: r. North Battersea slogan JAY 154:3
rhythm: I got r. GERS 123:7
  r., a predetermined FISH 109:15
  r. of attracting people JOAD 155:15
rhythmic: turn to r. tidal lyres HARDY 134:4
ribbon: changing a typewriter r. BENC 36:4
  road was a r. of moonlight NOYES 221:9
  soldier's r. on a tunic ABSE 1:3
ribbons: cut r. and kiss babies KENT 207:12
  medals and r. BELL 35:12
Ribstone: Right as a R. Pippin BELL 35:8
Ricardo: R. and face the economics GALB 121:3
rice: r. pudding for dinner again MILNE 210:2
rich: behave as the r. behave SMITH 278:10
  Do you sincerely want to be r. CORN 83:9
  ever by chance grow r. THOM 294:3
  If I ever become a r. man BELL 35:1
  intimate when he is r. BIER 46:4
  It's the r. wot gets the gravy ANON 10:15
  live by robbing the r. SHAW 271:2
  orchestra is playing to the r. AUDEN 19:13
  Poor little r. girl COW 85:2
  r. are the scum CHES 69:3
  r. enough to pay over 75% HEAL 136:7
  r. get rich and the poor KAHN 161:3
  r. people in the world STEAD 283:11
  r. richer and the poor NEHRU 219:2
  r. society and the powerful JOHN 156:10
  r. that you have to live SMITH 278:9
  r. wage war it's the poor SART 261:6
  save the few who are r. KENN 163:9
  tell you about the very r. FITZ 110:7
  that of the r. for titles PEAR 232:10
  whether to be r. in things ILL 150:11
  which forbids the r. FRAN 116:6
riche: qui interdit au r. comme FRAN 116:6
riches: material and spiritual r. KHR 165:11
  that of the titled for r. PEAR 232:10
richesse: la r. est chose sacrée FRAN 116:5
rid: r. of them because I know JOAD 155:15
  time we got r. of Him BALD 22:10
riddle: Ask me a r. and I reply MILNE 210:12
  It is a r. wrapped CHUR 75:6
  The r. of the sands CHIL 71:13
ride: Just to r. the ponies COHAN 78:13
  r. two horses you have MAXT 205:19
  She's got a ticket to r. LENN 185:14
  Sweet to r. forth at evening FLEC 111:9
  Who went for a r. on a tiger ANON 10:11
rides: r. back to shave again WHITE 310:2
ridiculous: At the heart of the r. MAHON 199:4
  fine sense of the r. ALBEE 3:11
  r. by friends when dead BIER 46:8
  To the R. GRAH 127:7

riding: r. at breakneck speed towards BLAN 47:10
  The highwayman came r. NOYES 221:9
rien: R. n'est plus dangereux ALAIN 3:9
riff-raff: epithet which the r. HOPE 143:10
rifle: r. and blow out your brains KIPL 169:5
Riga: There was a young lady of R. ANON 10:11
right: are exclusively in the r. HUXL 149:11
  be r. than be reasonable NASH 217:19
  claim our r. as women PANK 229:6
  decorative and to do r. FIRB 109:10
  defend to the death your r. TALL 290:11
  Don't think twice, it's all r. DYLAN 97:4
  do the r. deed ELIOT 102:9
  doubt that they are r. VAN D 303:6
  Earth's the r. place FROST 118:9
  every single one of them is r. KIPL 168:7
  find out that one was r. POUND 237:17
  half of the people are r. WHITE 310:1
  has more r. to be obeyed JOHN 155:16
  have been, a man of the r. MOSL 214:11
  have no r. in the circus MAXT 205:19
  it's all r. with me BELL 35:10
  Jack — I'm all r. BONE 49:3
  My country, r. or wrong CHES 68:14
  my r. is retreating FOCH 112:13
  no longer means being r. CHES 69:8
  not to do what is r. JOHN 156:14
  Only if it's done r. ALLEN 4:7
  questioned its r. to exist SCH 264:14
  R. as a Ribstone Pippin BELL 35:8
  r. but also to be wrong SZASZ 289:12
  R. but Repulsive SELL 266:8
  r. for fighting JAGG 152:5
  r. is more precious WILS 314:14
  r. side of the blanket ASHF 14:9
  r. that it does not need WILS 314:11
  r. to a child SHAW 269:6
  r. to be heard does not HUMP 148:3
  r. to be taken seriously HUMP 148:3
  r. to consume happiness SHAW 268:11
  r. to invent themselves GREER 129:1
  speciality is being r. SHAW 274:10
  The majority never has r. IBSEN 150:1
  they are never r. STR 287:13
  wrongs don't make a r. SZASZ 290:4
righteous: have seen the r. forsaken BLUN 47:13
  R. indignation WOOLF 317:4
righter: r. than one knew at say POUND 237:17
rights: country about equal r. JOHN 156:7
  equal in dignity and r. ANON 11:16
  r. is a little inconsistency OWEN 227:10
  r. to which this nation KENN 163:8
  until the r. of the smaller ASQ 14:19
right-side-up: The toast fell r. JENN 154:13
rigorous: My God, what a r. exam COOK 82:8
rigour: They're noted for their r. COOK 82:8
Rimbauds: he was always chasing R. PARK 230:4
rime: The r. was on the spray HARDY 134:6

Rime Intrinsica: R., Fontmell Magna   BETJ 42:3
rind: how shall taste the r.   THOM 295:13
ring: his diaper into the r.   ICKES 150:9
  night come, r. out the hour   APOL 12:15
  One R. to rule them all   TOLK 298:1
  r. with Mr Tolstoy unless   HEM 138:9
  round in a r. and suppose   FROST 119:11
  'Twould r. the bells of Heaven   HODG 142:2
rings: r. black Cyprus   FLEC 112:3
  The postman always r. twice   CAIN 61:2
rinky-dink: r. of a voice and all   MAIL 199:9
Rio: Go rolling down to R.   KIPL 172:3
riot: He did not r., he got   TEBB 291:2
  r. is at bottom the language   KING 167:7
ripens: But not when it r. in a tumour   ABSE 1:2
rire: le r. pour la jalousie   SAGAN 256:14
rise: Every Employee Tends to R.   PETER 233:8
  r. at ten thirty and saunter   HARG 135:2
  r. of misplaced power exists   EIS 100:1
  r. of the meritocracy 1870   YOUNG 324:5
risen: Frost has r. without trace   MUGG 215:3
rises: The sun also r.   HEM 138:12
rising: Into a r. birth-rate   FRY 119:17
  revolution of r. expectations   CLEV 77:11
  your shadow at evening r.   ELIOT 104:12
risks: one of the r. he takes   STEV 286:2
  r. of spreading conflict   JOHN 156:11
Ritz: like the R. Hotel   MATH 204:6
rivalry: thought, a r. of aim   ADAMS 2:10
river: field by the r. my love   YEATS 321:13
  I think that the r.   ELIOT 101:10
  laughs the immortal r. still   BROO 56:1
  Ol' man r., dat ol' man river   HAMM 132:1
  O Sleepless as the r. under   CRANE 85:11
  r. jumps over the mountain   AUDEN 16:12
riverrun: r., past Eve and Adam's   JOYCE 157:10
rivers: R. are damp   PARK 230:14
rivulets: And meadow r. overflow   HARDY 133:9
road: And not the r.   NASH 217:16
  And one more for the r.   MERC 207:7
  A r., a mile of kingdom   KAV 161:12
  Golden R. to Samarkand   FLEC 111:9
  good to be out on the r.   MAS 204:3
  hard the r. may   CHUR 74:4
  Hit the r., Jack   MAYF 206:2
  look ahead up the white r.   ELIOT 105:9
  middle of the r.   BEVAN 45:6
  monument the asphalt r.   ELIOT 104:2
  One r. leads to London   MAS 203:6
  On every r. I wandered   HOUS 146:12
  r. in dangerous circumstances   BALD 23:11
  r. through the woods   KIPL 173:6
  r. to the City of Emeralds   BAUM 27:13
  r. was a ribbon of moonlight   NOYES 221:9
  rolling English r.   CHES 69:5
  Softly along the r. of evening   DE L 90:9
  There is no expeditious r.   THOM 296:2
  Your old r.   DYLAN 97:13

road (cont.):
  your r.'s a thorny way   CARB 63:14
roads: And without fear the lawless r.   MUIR 215:9
  By r. 'not adopted'   BETJ 43:11
  How many r. must a man   DYLAN 97:3
  two r. by which men escape   BELL 32:8
  Two r. diverged in a wood   FROST 118:8
roadway: r. or on the pavements   YEATS 318:10
roam: love, her ways to r.   BROO 55:2
  person's mind begins to r.   SOLZ 280:1
roamin': R. in the gloamin'   LAUD 180:3
roar: called upon to give the r.   CHUR 76:10
  mighty r. of London's   ANON 10:9
roareth: What is this that r. thus   GODL 125:8
roaring: But R. Bill   BELL 34:16
rob: If a writer has to r.   FAUL 107:10
robbed: We was r.   JAC 152:2
robbing: r. a bank compared   BREC 53:2
robe: His Purple R.   FARJ 107:7
Robey: R. is the Darling   SMITH 277:7
robin: r. comes bob, bob   WOODS 317:3
Robinson: And here's to you, Mrs R.   SIMON 275:9
robot: r. may not injure   ASIM 14:13
Robotics: Rules of R.   ASIM 14:13
robots: that men may become r.   FROMM 117:10
robs: government which r. Peter   SHAW 269:1
rock: cast the first r. at a girl   LOOS 190:20
  r. around the clock   DE KN 90:7
  R. journalism is people   ZAPPA 324:9
  Sex and drugs and r. and roll   DURY 96:12
rocket: every r. fired signifies   EIS 100:2
rock 'n' roll: It's only r.   JAGG 152:4
  r. or Christianity   LENN 185:4
rocks: roll over but the r. remain   HERB 139:13
  throwing r. at the stork   BREC 52:16
rocky: iron bicycles over the r.   O'BR 222:6
rode: r. madly off in all directions   LEAC 183:1
  R. their horses   DE L 91:2
role: has not yet found a r.   ACH 1:8
roll: Let the good times r.   THEA 292:7
  R. over, Beethoven   BERRY 41:9
  seas r. over but the rocks   HERB 139:13
  Sex and drugs and rock and r.   DURY 96:12
  Shake, rattle and r.   CALH 61:5
rolled: apparently r. along on wheels   HUXL 149:8
  bottoms of my trousers r.   ELIOT 103:12
roller: The r., pitch, and stumps   LANG 178:6
rollin': He keeps on r. along   HAMM 132:1
rolling: Go r. down to Rio   KIPL 172:3
  Like a r. stone   DYLAN 97:7
  r. English drunkard made   CHES 69:5
Roman: R. came to Rye or out   CHES 69:5
  R. ever was able to say   BEER 30:11
  The R. Conquest was   SELL 266:4
  Thundered out on the R. air   AUDEN 20:12
  To-day the R. and his trouble   HOUS 146:8
romance: A fine r. with no kisses   FIEL 108:9
romancing: R. the stone   THOM 292:8

romantic: An airline ticket to r. places MARV 202:8
  R. Ireland's dead and gone YEATS 321:15
  The r. lie in the brain AUDEN 17:12
  they're so r., so operatic PROU 241:2
romanticism: attempted to tinge it with r. DOYLE 95:2
romantics: We were the last r. YEATS 323:7
Rome: For R. so near us DAY-L 89:5
Ronald: Lord R. said nothing LEAC 183:1
roof: cat on a hot tin r. WILL 312:4
  He has restored the r. BETJ 43:5
  on a corrugated tin r. BEEC 29:18
roof-lamp: And the r.'s oily flame HARDY 133:14
roof-wrecked: Is r.; damps there drip upon HARDY 133:7
rooks: And r. in families homeward go HARDY 133:9
  r. came home in scramble HODG 141:13
room: Across a crowded r. HAMM 132:2
  All before my little r. BROO 55:7
  All I want is a r. somewhere LERN 186:6
  although the r. grows chilly GRAH 127:8
  A r. with a view FORS 115:10
  Books do furnish a r. POW 239:4
  end of the enormous r. AUDEN 19:13
  Fifty springs are little r. HOUS 145:13
  Here in this r., desiring you STEV 285:9
  In the r. the women come and go ELIOT 103:7
  just entering the r. BROUN 56:6
  men in a smoke-filled r. SIMP 275:11
  money and a r. of her own WOOLF 317:8
  R. at the top BRAI 52:9
  sitting in the smallest r. REGER 245:7
rooms: boys in the back r. BEAV 28:9
  old is having lighted r. LARK 178:11
  Other voices, other r. CAP 63:12
Roosevelt: [Eleanor R.] STEV 286:5
  [President R.] CHUR 75:3
  R.'s New Deal promised KENN 163:7
  R. told me that he was CHUR 76:4
  will give to President R. CHUR 72:11
roost: birds came home to r. MILL 208:10
root: money is the r. of all evil BUTL 59:1
  r. of the American Negro BALD 22:9
rooting: are r. for Gary Cooper BALD 22:12
roots: drought is destroying his r. HERB 139:11
  Dull r. with spring rain ELIOT 104:10
  You poison England at her r. BOTT 50:4
rosary: every day. This is a r. BELL 33:12
rose: An English unofficial r. BROO 55:8
  But he's mighty lak' a r. STAN 283:8
  But R. crossed the road DOBS 92:14
  fire and the r. are one ELIOT 102:7
  His supplication to the r. FLEC 111:11
  If you gave Ruth a r. AYCK 21:10
  I know the colour r. ABSE 1:2
  inviolate R. YEATS 322:3
  I r. politely in the club CHES 70:15

rose (cont.):
  It wavers to a r. DOBS 92:15
  mast burst open with a r. FLEC 112:5
  One perfect r. PARK 230:15
  promised you a r. garden GREEN 128:10
  R. is a rose is a rose STEIN 284:13
  R. of all Roses, Rose YEATS 321:12
  r.'s scent is bitterness THOM 294:10
  Roves back the r. DE L 90:8
  sad R. of all my days YEATS 321:11
  scent is of the summer r. GRAV 128:7
  tell the crooked r. THOM 293:4
  The American beauty r. ROCK 248:13
Rosebud: R. is just a piece MANK 200:3
rose-garden: Into the r. My words echo ELIOT 101:6
rose-lipt: For many a r. maiden HOUS 146:14
rose-red: A r. sissy half as old as time PLOM 235:14
roses: all the ash the burnt r. ELIOT 102:2
  Everything's coming up r. SOND 280:6
  forget the lilac and the r. ARAG 13:2
  girls and r. DE G 90:1
  In fields where r. fade HOUS 146:14
  jamais les lilas ni les r. ARAG 13:2
  might have r. in December BARR 26:4
  own red r. there may blow THOM 296:1
  R. are flowering in Picardy WEAT 306:17
  smells like r. JOHN 156:2
rosy: R. and round and hot ASQ 15:9
rot: As artists they're r. PARK 231:13
rots: liquid which r. braces MORT 214:7
rotted: Or simply r. early NASH 217:17
rotten: You r. swines MILL 209:4
rottenness: r. of our civilization READ 244:2
rough: And what r. beast, its hour YEATS 320:8
  r. male kiss BROO 54:9
round: For it's going r. and round FYFFE 120:10
  music goes 'r. and around HODG 142:5
  Rosy and r. and hot ASQ 15:9
  R. and round the circle ELIOT 101:19
  R. both the shires they HOUS 146:3
  R. up the usual suspects EPST 106:12
roundabouts: What's lost upon the r. CHAL 65:10
Roundheads: R. (Right but Repulsive) SELL 266:8
rouse: If anything might r. him now OWEN 228:1
Rousseau: R. was the first militant BERL 41:1
rover: blood's a r. HOUS 145:14
row: are a-standing in a r. HEAT 137:1
Rowe: R.'s Rule DICK 92:3
rows: not lugged into Family R. WOD 316:2
royal: The R. slice of bread MILNE 210:3
rub: if you r. up against RUNY 254:11
rubies: Give pearls away and r. HOUS 146:1
ruddy: R. Ball has taken THOM 294:9
rude: Because a manner r. and wild BELL 32:13
  But only rather r. and wild BELL 33:9
Rudolph: R., the Red-Nosed Reindeer MARKS 201:6

rue: With r. my heart is laden	HOUS 146:14
rugged: cling to the old r. cross	BENN 37:9
system of r. individualism	HOOV 143:6
ruin: r. himself in twelve months	GEOR 122:12
r. that Cromwell knock'd	BEDF 29:15
ruined: always r. by the littleness	BREC 53:6
ruins: have shored against my r.	ELIOT 105:11
Ruislip: Gaily into R. Gardens	BETJ 42:8
rule: major r. of political life	PANK 229:5
One Ring to r. them all	TOLK 298:1
Rowe's R.	DICK 92:3
r. in life never to apologize	WOD 316:4
safe r. for the historian	FISH 109:15
ruled: 'The Art of Being R.' might	LEWIS 187:7
ruler: r. but the last fading	HUXL 149:16
rulers: are brought about by r.	BIER 46:20
Rules: fundamental R. of Robotics	ASIM 14:13
golden r. for an orchestra	BEEC 29:17
people wouldn't obey the r.	BENN 37:12
simple little r. and few	BELL 33:15
there are no golden r.	SHAW 271:16
ruling: hands of the r. class	STAL 283:4
rum: It's a R. Go	VAUG 303:11
It's nothing but r.	CHUR 73:8
thinking jest what a R. Go	WELLS 308:8
run: choose to r. for President	COOL 82:14
He [Billy Conn] can r.	LOUIS 191:3
R., rabbit, run	GAY 122:8
r. up your nose dead against	BALD 23:1
Take the money and r.	ALLEN 4:14
They get r. down	BEVAN 45:6
we were born to r.	SPR 283:1
What makes Sammy r.	SCH 264:12
runic: r. tales to sigh or sing	FLEC 111:16
runner: long-distance r.	SILL 275:4
runs: r. away at the first snarl	LLOY 189:8
run-stealers: As the r. flicker to and fro	THOM 296:1
rupture: getting r. or something	DONL 93:3
rush: r. through the fields	CHES 69:15
rushed: with the time we have r.	ROG 249:12
Ruskin: doubt that art needed R.	STOP 287:11
young Macaulay or R.	BARB 24:17
Russia: developed in R. was as great	BENN 37:3
From R. with love	FLEM 112:9
outlaws R. forever	REAG 244:7
proletarian socialist state in R.	LENIN 184:11
you the action of R.	CHUR 75:6
Russian: Grishkin is nice: her R. eye	ELIOT 103:2
Russians: The R. are coming	ROSE 252:9
rust: creeper-nails are r.	HARDY 133:7
Less than the r., that never	HOPE 144:3
rustic: A swear-word in a r. slum	BEER 30:14
Ruth: If you gave R. a rose	AYCK 21:10
ruthless: r. if he is a good one	FAUL 107:10
You must be r., relentless	FISH 110:3
Rye: Before the Roman came to R.	CHES 69:5
be the catcher in the r.	SAL 258:15

S

Sacco: S.'s name will live	VANZ 303:8
sack: S. the lot	FISH 110:3
sacrament: abortion would be a s.	KENN 162:11
sacramental: flesh was s. of the spirit	ROB 248:12
sacred: facts are s.	SCOTT 265:5
The Convent of the S. Heart	ELIOT 102:13
wealth is a s. thing	FRAN 116:5
sacrée: richesse est chose s.	FRAN 116:5
sacrifice: A woman will always s.	MAUG 204:14
great pinnacle of S.	LLOY 189:13
Self-sacrifice enables us to s.	SHAW 272:18
Still stands Thine ancient S.	KIPL 173:3
The holy hush of ancient s.	STEV 285:8
Too long a s.	YEATS 320:5
undaunted the final s.	SPR 282:13
sacrificed: always be s. to expediency	MAUG 204:13
sacrifices: s. he makes on her account	MAUG 205:8
sad: And all their songs are s.	CHES 68:10
deliciously aged and s.	SHAW 269:14
her sadness when she's s.	BARR 26:10
s. subject for any publicity	ATTL 16:3
something s. about the boy	COW 84:12
The sweetness in the s.	THOM 294:11
saddest: s. life is that of a political	MENC 206:9
sadists: As repressed s. are supposed	CONN 80:7
sadness: At all the s. in the sweet	THOM 294:11
Farewell s.	ÉLUA 106:6
Good-day s.	ÉLUA 106:6
s. of her sadness when	BARR 26:10
safe: be made s. for democracy	WILS 314:13
it is s. to be unpopular	STEV 286:3
National Health Service is s.	THAT 292:1
S. shall be my going	BROO 54:11
S. though all safety's	BROO 54:11
s. to go back in the water	ANON 9:6
S. upon solid rock	MILL 207:18
S. with his wound	SASS 263:2
woman in London will be s.	CAMP 61:10
world s. for hypocrisy	WOLFE 316:13
safer: s. than a known way	HASK 136:1
safety: 'S. first' does not mean	BALD 23:11
strike against the public s.	COOL 82:11
There is no s. in numbers	THUR 297:10
The s. of our Homes	HAIG 130:12
safety-catch: release the s. of my Browning	JOHST 157:2
sagged: S. seats, the creeper-nails	HARDY 133:7
said: at all can be s. clearly	WITT 315:4
I hope it may be s.	BELL 34:10
nobody had s. it before	TWAIN 301:9
s. by the servant girls	SYNGE 289:10
s. to the man who stood	HASK 136:1
There is a great deal to be s.	BENT 39:11

sail: I s. across the floor — GREN 129:4
Or s. in amply billowing gown — BELL 35:6
sailed: hast not s. in Indian Seas — DAV 89:1
have s. the seas and come — YEATS 321:7
sailing: s. proudly down the years — PRIE 239:17
sailor: brings the s. home from sea — ELIOT 105:5
sailors: 'Onward,' the s. cry — BOUL 50:9
sails: Red s. in the sunset — KENN 162:15
To the white dipping s. — MAS 203:6
saint: S., n. A dead sinner — BIER 47:1
Saint Mary Woolnoth: To where S. kept the hours — ELIOT 104:14
saints: lives of the medieval s. — SAKI 257:17
overrun by a Wave of S. — SELL 266:5
S. should always be judged — ORW 226:4
We are not s., but we have — BECK 29:11
sake: my s. do not be rash — GRAH 127:11
salamandrine: Of her s. fires — HARDY 134:4
Salamis: The many-headed foam at S. — YEATS 319:14
sale: From s. and profanation — CHES 70:7
salesman: A s. is got to dream — MILL 208:9
Salieri: In Mozart and S. we see — BAR 25:1
salley: by the s. gardens my love — YEATS 321:13
s. gardens with little — YEATS 321:13
Sally: S. is gone that was so kindly — BELL 34:8
salmon: And the s. sing in the street — AUDEN 16:12
smoked s. and tinned salmon — WILS 313:6
Salteena: S. was an elderly man — ASHF 14:2
S. was not very addicted — ASHF 14:6
salute: If it moves, s. it — ANON 8:14
salvaged: Democracy will not be s. by men — HOGB 142:10
salvation: s. lies exclusively — SOLZ 279:9
Sam: nephew of my Uncle S.'s — COHAN 78:13
Sam, S., pick up tha' musket — HOLL 142:12
wouldn't have a Willie or a S. — MURR 216:6
Samaritan: would remember the Good S. — THAT 292:4
Samarkand: Along the Golden Road to S. — FLEC 111:9
Samarra: with him tonight in S. — LOW 191:8
same: are doing the s. thing — PHIL 233:12
I'm having the s. — LOES 190:6
s. the whole world over — ANON 10:15
Sighted sub, sank s. — MASON 204:5
Yet this will go onward the s. — HARDY 133:15
Sammy: What makes S. run — SCH 264:12
sanction: Happiness is the only s. of life — SANT 260:10
sanctions: s. might well bring — WILS 313:10
sanctities: Round the day's dead s. — THOM 295:9
sanctity: untrespassed s. of space — MAGEE 198:11
sanctuary: three classes which need s. — BALD 23:8
sand: It produces lies like s. — PONS 236:3
palace built upon the s. — MILL 207:18
pass gigantic on the s. — FLEC 111:9
with its head in the s. — WILS 314:7

sandal: massive s. set on stone — MILL 208:2
sandalwood: S., cedarwood, and sweet — MAS 202:16
sands: are as various as the s. — FORS 114:1
The riddle of the s. — CHIL 71:13
Sandy: this is my friend, S. — TOOK 298:3
sane: go mad they shall be s. — THOM 293:12
no s. human being has ever — HUXL 149:10
s. person would do at eleven — SHAW 270:8
sang: And s. themselves to sleep — HODG 141:13
s. as he watched and waited — PAT 232:5
s. in my chains like — THOM 293:2
sanitary: glorified s. engineer — STR 288:1
sanity: what they call a s. clause — KAUF 161:9
sank: certainly he s. into his grave — YEATS 322:10
Sighted sub, s. same — MASON 204:5
Santa: going to shoot S. Claus — SMITH 276:14
Santa Claus: arrival of death, or S. — BERNE 41:6
sap: Has dried the s. out — YEATS 319:3
sapient: The s. sutlers of the Lord — ELIOT 102:15
saplings: it plies the s. double — HOUS 146:7
sapristi: S. Nuckoes — MILL 209:6
Sarah: Blossomed S. — BERR 41:10
sardines: can't ravish a tin of s. — LAWR 181:8
like opening a tin of s. — BENN 37:10
Sargent: kind of musical Malcolm S. — BEEC 29:20
sashes: one of his nice new s. — GRAH 127:8
sat: everyone has s. except a man — CUMM 87:6
last person who has s. — HAIG 130:11
s. too long here — AMERY 5:9
Station I s. down and wept — SMART 276:13
when I s. down at the piano — CAPL 63:7
'satiable: was full of 's. curtiosity — KIPL 171:14
satin: ease a heart like a s. — PARK 230:10
satire: S. is what closes Saturday — KAUF 161:6
satiric: have the s. temperament — BEER 30:17
satisfaction: S. is death — SHAW 273:4
satisfactory: putting it—not very s. — ELIOT 101:12
Saturday: date on S. night — ALLEN 4:12
played the Glasgow Empire S. — DODD 93:2
Satire is what closes S. night — KAUF 161:6
sausage: s., by-the-yard — LEWIS 187:8
savage: s. contemplates his mother-in-law — FRAZ 116:8
Standing among s. scenery — HOFF 142:9
who has not wept is a s. — SANT 260:8
savaged: being s. by a dead sheep — HEAL 136:5
save: And s. them by the barrel-load — THOM 296:2
destroy the town to s. — ANON 9:1
exist in order to s. us — DE VR 91:14
little less democracy to s. — ATK 15:14
saved you only must s. face — HEAN 136:11
s. the Governor-General — WHIT 310:19
s. the Party we love — GAIT 120:16
s. those that have no imagination — SHAW 274:3
s. your world you asked — AUDEN 20:8
through life trying to s. — ROG 249:12
will always s. Barabbas — COCT 78:5

saved: could have s. sixpence BECK 28:14
  One of the thieves was s. BECK 29:5
  s. his friend from a wetting MILNE 211:1
  s. you only must save face HEAN 136:11
  they only s. the world CHES 68:7
saves: idea of Death s. him FORS 115:4
  sometimes s. tons of explanation SAKI 258:7
saving: It is capable of s. us RICH 247:5
savings: oven, all sorts of s. JENK 154:8
saviour: I imitate the S. HUXL 148:6
  it's 'S. of 'is country' KIPL 168:12
saw: I s. you do it STOP 287:7
  s. guns and sharp swords DYLAN 97:5
  s. ten thousand talkers DYLAN 97:5
  s. the skull beneath ELIOT 103:1
Sawyer: The Adventures of Tom S. TWAIN 300:4
Saxon: from our S. good and evil KEYN 165:3
say: disapprove of what you s. TALL 290:11
  don't care what you s. COHAN 78:10
  don't s. nothin' HAMM 132:1
  having to s. you're sorry SEGAL 266:2
  I have nothing to s. CAGE 60:17
  I—I s., you fellows RICH 247:4
  I s. the hell with it WHITE 309:23
  Journalists s. a thing BENN 38:18
  long as they do what I s. THAT 291:11
  more to s. when I am dead ROB 248:10
  S. it with flowers O'KEE 223:1
  s. no more CHAP 67:8
  s. the perfectly SHAW 269:10
  s. what you are going BRAB 51:10
  Some s. the world will FROST 118:10
  think till I see what I s. WALL 304:17
  We must not s. BERR 41:12
  what they are going to s. CHUR 73:10
  you s. nothing HEAN 136:11
saying: I am s. it CAGE 60:17
  s. it long enough it will BENN 38:18
Sayle: my colleague Murray S. TOM 298:2
says: author is not what he s. SMITH 278:15
scaffold: s. he said goodbye BARR 25:13
scales: someone is practising s. MACN 198:6
scandal: s. by a woman of easy virtue HAIL 130:13
scare: s. me with their empty FROST 118:3
  s. myself with my own desert FROST 118:3
scarecrows: potato-gatherers like mechanized s.
                    KAV 162:1
scares: Anything s. me, anything STEIN 284:4
scarlet: His sins were s. BELL 34:10
  Only the s. soldiers, dear AUDEN 19:7
scene: start a s. or two ELIOT 103:11
scenery: Standing among savage s. HOFF 142:9
  Where God paints the s. HART 135:12
scent: How hot the s. GRAV 128:7
  s. comes forth DAV 89:1
  Their s. survives their close THOM 294:10
  The s. of the conifers BETJ 43:10
scepticism: s. kept her from being SART 261:14

sceptre: He's thrown his S. FARJ 107:7
schedule: My s. is already full KISS 175:12
Schicksal: Die Anatomie ist das S. FREUD 117:2
schizoid: means s. self-alienation FROMM 117:10
schizophrenia: S. cannot be understood
                    LAING 177:7
schizophrenic: s. is a special strategy
                    LAING 177:11
  talks to you, you are a s. SZASZ 290:5
scholar: better s. than Wordsworth HOUS 144:6
  scientist or s. or teacher EINS 99:10
scholarship: slender indications of s. CHUR 75:9
school: he's been to a good s. SAKI 258:5
  people so horrible as a s. SHAW 273:5
  s. is all put gently back BEER 30:16
  S. is pretty bad WAUGH 305:13
  S.'s out DAV 88:15
  s. that feeling is bad FORS 114:2
  s. without any boots it BULM 57:12
  special reason for hating s. BEER 30:15
  The naughtiest girl in the s. BLYT 48:7
  till we leave s. LEWIS 187:5
schoolboy: I see a s. when I think of him
                    YEATS 322:10
  s. who wipes his fingers BLUNT 48:2
schoolchildren: What all s. learn AUDEN 17:11
schoolgirl: Keep that s. complexion PEAR 232:8
schoolmaster: you'll be becoming a s.
                    WAUGH 305:12
schools: encourage it in some s. SCOTT 265:9
  s. for the imagination GIR 125:3
  s. of thought contend MAO 200:10
  We class s., you see WAUGH 305:13
schreit: s. im Traum um Hilfe CAN 63:5
science: human s. is at a loss CHOM 71:15
  ought to be, an exact s. DOYLE 95:2
  religion without s. is blind EINS 99:11
  S. is built up of facts POIN 236:1
  s. is either physics RUTH 256:6
  s. is strong and religion SZASZ 290:6
  S. may have found a cure KELL 162:9
  s. may have the existence ADAMS 2:13
  'S.' means simply the aggregate VALÉ 303:1
  s. of arresting human intelligence LEAC 182:10
  s. reassures BRAQ 52:13
  s. the credit goes DARW 88:9
  S. without religion is lame EINS 99:11
  That is the essence of s. BRON 54:4
  This is why s. has succeeded BRON 54:7
  typical triumph of modern s. WAUGH 306:3
scientific: judgement of our s. age HOLM 142:13
  s. power has outrun our KING 167:4
scientist: research s. to discard LOR 191:2
  s. says that something CLAR 77:2
scientists: at the illiteracy of s. SNOW 279:6
  myself in the company of s. AUDEN 18:12
  representative, the physical s. SNOW 279:5
scold: only will he not s. you BUTL 60:1

scones: afternoon tea-cakes and s. BETJ 43:1
Over buttered s. and crumpets ELIOT 100:5
score: from seventy springs a s. HOUS 145:13
scorer: S. comes to mark against RICE 246:10
scorn: perfect expression of s. SHAW 268:4
S. the sort now growing up YEATS 319:11
Scot: S. summed it all up very BAX 27:15
Scotch: Mary, ma S. Bluebell LAUD 180:1
working on a case of S. BENC 36:11
Scotland: In S., land of the omnipotent
BOLD 48:12
Scotsman: moral attribute of a S. BARR 26:14
S. of your ability let BARR 26:12
S. with a grievance WOD 315:10
The Flying S. is no less BEAV 28:6
world than a S. on the make BARR 26:13
Scott: Beam us up, Mr S. RODD 249:3
scoundrel: Every man over forty is a s.
SHAW 272:13
scouts: s.' motto is founded BAD 22:2
scramble: And rooks came home in s. sort
HODG 141:13
scrap: just for a s. of paper BETH 41:16
scratch: S. a lover, and find a foe PARK 231:5
scratches: S. its innocent behind AUDEN 17:9
scratchin': S. in the sun AYRES 21:16
scratching: s. of pimples on the body
WOOLF 317:7
scream: like a s. from a crevasse GREE 128:16
scribbled: And s. lines like fallen hopes
HOPE 144:2
Man by a s. name THOM 293:11
scrotumtightening: The snotgreen sea. The s. sea
JOYCE 158:15
scrupulous: The s. and the just CONR 81:21
sculpture: austere, like that of s. RUSS 255:13
scum: are the s. of the earth CHES 69:3
Okie means you're s. STEI 284:17
They are s. MAUG 205:15
scuttling: S. across the floors ELIOT 103:9
sea: And the s. rises higher CHES 68:9
are all gone under the s. ELIOT 101:13
deep s. keep you up CONR 81:14
her dead across the s. BINY 47:4
if Ye take away the s. KIPL 174:5
In a solitude of the s. HARDY 134:4
Lie mirror'd on her s. HODG 142:4
my chains like the s. THOM 293:2
Over the s. to Skye BOUL 50:9
ride slowly towards the s. CHES 70:14
round me like a bursting s. THOM 295:15
sailor home from s. ELIOT 105:5
s. for a thousand years KIPL 174:4
s. will soon be drownded SYNGE 289:8
serpent-haunted s. FLEC 111:14
snotgreen s. JOYCE 158:15
that gong-tormented s. YEATS 323:10
that I am very much at s. CARS 64:3

sea (cont.):
The mirrors of the s. FLEC 111:15
The s. hates a coward O'NEI 223:12
The swaying sound of the s. AUDEN 19:6
Where no s. runs, the waters THOM 293:5
Who hath desired the S. KIPL 170:8
Within a walk of the s. BELL 35:1
sea-fogs: And here the s. lap and cling KIPL 170:9
seal: heard a s. bark THUR 297:5
Minister [the Lord Privy S.] BAIL 22:4
S. thy sense in deathly slumber DE L 90:15
search: characters in s. of an author PIR 235:1
In s. of lost time PROU 240:6
s. for knowledge RUSS 254:13
travels the world in s. MOORE 212:10
searching: I am s. everywhere STEP 285:4
seas: floors of silent s. ELIOT 103:9
I must down to the s. again MAS 203:14
mackerel-crowded s. YEATS 321:5
new places, no other s. CAV 65:7
not sailed in Indian S. DAV 89:1
sailed the s. and come YEATS 321:7
s. roll over but the rocks HERB 139:13
these out to s. colder FLEC 112:2
troubled s. of thought GALB 121:3
sea-shells: She sells s. on the sea-shore
SULL 288:13
sea-sick: bishop was feeling rather s. DOUG 93:11
seaside: I do like to be beside the s. GLOV 125:5
s. place called Blackpool EDGAR 98:3
season: dry brain in a dry s. ELIOT 100:8
Your excuse is out of s. JER 155:13
seasons: S. return, and today REED 245:2
season-ticket: has held a s. on the line
AMERY 5:11
seat: s. of this sensation HOUS 145:9
third-class s. sat the journeying HARDY 133:14
seat-belts: Fasten your s., it's going MANK 200:4
seated: looked wiser when he was s. KEYN 164:12
seats: Sagged s., the creeper-nails HARDY 133:7
with 'bottoms on s.' HALL 131:6
seawards: My road leads me s. MAS 203:9
sea-worm: The s. crawls HARDY 134:4
secluded: afternoon, in a s. chapel ELIOT 102:6
second: first and s. class citizens WILL 312:16
happens to be a S. Entry ADE 2:16
I'm a s. eleven sort BARR 25:12
not a s. on the day COOK 82:5
s. acts in American lives FITZ 110:17
s. oldest profession REAG 244:10
s. things never CONR 82:4
s. time in our history CHAM 66:6
s. time you hear your love CAHN 61:1
struck the water a full s. COKE 78:14
The s. best is a formal order AUDEN 19:2
truth 24 times per s. GOD 125:6
second-best: anything but the s. LESS 186:2
second-hand: s. opinion of any thing SAIN 257:4
second-rate: many s. ones of our own BEEC 30:8

secret: giant girls that have no s.   SPEN 281:17
Know you her s. none can utter   QUIL 242:5
s. diary of Adrian Mole   TOWN 298:4
s. of the long-nosed Etruscans   LAWR 180:7
S. sits in the middle   FROST 119:11
Vereker's s., my dear man   JAMES 152:15
secretary: Why not 'Madam S.'   PERK 233:4
secretive: As we make sex less s.   SZASZ 290:1
secretly: S. armed against all death's   BROO 54:11
So s., like wrongs hushed-up   OWEN 228:4
secrets: narrow privacy and tawdry s.
   LEACH 182:8
secure: And love is not s.   CHES 68:11
security: freedom can make s. secure   POPP 236:5
otherwise styled s.   MAD 198:9
s. and peace of each country   JOHN 155:17
see: And s. the coloured counties   HOUS 146:3
are you just glad to s.   WEST 309:12
Besides, they'll s. how   HUGH 147:13
heart that one can s.   SAIN 257:2
I'll s. you again   COW 84:9
I'll s. you later   BARR 25:13
I think that I shall never s.   KILM 166:3
I think that I shall never s.   NASH 218:4
Nice to s. you—to see you, nice   FORS 116:2
not as I s. them   PIC 234:5
Oh shall I s. the Thames again   BETJ 43:7
s. a belt without hitting   ASQ 15:8
S. an old unhappy bull   HODG 142:3
s. it often since you've   AUDEN 19:12
S. the happy moron   ANON 10:14
s. what is in front   ORW 226:5
s. who was in the lead   SNAG 279:3
S. you later, alligator   GUID 130:5
takes little talent to s.   AUDEN 18:11
then can he s. clearly   BARN 25:6
think till I s. what I say   WALL 304:17
through a flint wall s.   GRAV 128:5
what I think till I s.   FORS 114:8
You s., but you do not observe   DOYLE 94:2
You s. things   SHAW 268:1
seeds: I find thy cunning s.   ROSS 253:6
seed-time: Ought I to regret my s.   LOW 191:13
seeing: at s. it practised   BUTL 60:9
Discovery consists of s.   SZEN 290:8
friends who are not s.   THAT 291:9
seek: s. not to make them like   GIBR 124:3
s. what is happily known   ACH 1:7
We s. him here, we seek   ORCZY 223:18
We still s. no wider war   JOHN 156:11
seekest: I am He whom thou s.   THOM 295:17
seems: s. that I have spent   AYER 21:13
seen: fine things to be s.   CHES 69:6
I have s. the future   STEF 284:1
manifestly and undoubtedly be s.   HEW 140:4
s. one Western you've seen   WHIT 310:16
s. the righteous forsaken   BLUN 47:13
s. war on land and sea   ROOS 250:6

seen (cont.):
you've s. one city slum   AGNEW 3:6
sees: one s. in other women   TYNAN 302:6
segregation: S. now, segregation tomorrow
   WALL 304:15
Seine: Mirabeau Bridge flows the S.   APOL 12:15
pont Mirabeau coule la S.   APOL 12:15
self: life-sentence in the dungeon of s.   CONN 81:4
public and have no s.   CONN 80:15
that's your own s.   HUXL 149:15
self-alienation: schizoid s.   FROMM 117:10
self-assertion: Self-sufficiency at home, s. abroad
   WAUGH 306:7
self-control: education or of absence of s.
   BEVAN 44:11
self-denial: S. is not a virtue   SHAW 272:5
self-importance: s. of the investigator   RUTH 256:5
self-indulgence: her favourite form of s.
   MAUG 204:14
self-love: S. seems so often unrequited   POW 239:2
self-made: s. man is one who believes
   STEAD 283:12
s. man may prefer a self-made   HAND 132:8
self-revelation: The terrible *fluidity of s*
   JAMES 152:7
self-sacrifice: S. enables us to sacrifice
   SHAW 272:18
self-sufficiency: S. at home, self-assertion
   WAUGH 306:7
Selkirk: Alexander S. knew the plight   KAV 161:12
sell: I'll s. him   LEAC 182:9
selling: because it was s. well   BOOR 49:8
nimble in the calling of s.   LEWIS 187:11
writers are always s.   DID 92:4
sells: problematical world and s. us life   FRY 119:15
seltzer: He sipped at a weak hock and s.
   BETJ 41:17
selvytion: Wot prawce S. nah   SHAW 270:7
semi-house-trained: imitation of a s. polecat
   FOOT 113:5
senator: United States S.   JOHN 156:15
senators: respectable s. burst   AUDEN 17:1
send: S. in the clowns   SOND 280:7
S. me the half that's got   GRAH 127:10
s. me to eat in the kitchen   HUGH 147:13
situation is s. a gun-boat   BEVAN 45:1
sending: s. of general messages   DOYLE 95:13
sends: s. his son to Oxford   STEAD 283:12
s. the frozen-ground-swell   FROST 118:13
sensation: Art distils s. and embodies   BARZ 27:12
really delightful s.   FERB 108:5
seat of this s. is the pit   HOUS 145:9
sense: common s. and good taste   SHAW 268:10
fine s. of the ridiculous   ALBEE 3:11
ground s. necessary   WILL 312:11
Money is like a sixth s.   MAUG 205:11
s. that that is where   GREE 128:14
s. to the American people   STEV 286:7
senses: If Parson lost his s.   HODG 142:2

senses (*cont.*):
s. and his heart unsatisfied   YEATS 322:10
s. know that absence   BOWEN 50:13
sensibility: century a dissociation of s.   ELIOT 104:7
it is an immense s.   JAMES 153:4
sensible: No opera plot can be s.   AUDEN 20:14
sensitive: more s. one is   BEER 30:19
sensual: Of the s. man-in-the-street   AUDEN 17:12
that s. music all neglect   YEATS 321:5
sentence: it's a s.   VIDOR 304:8
ordinary British s.   CHUR 75:10
sentenced: courtmartialled in my absence and s.
    BEHAN 31:24
s. to solitary confinement   WILL 312:8
sentences: Backward ran s. until reeled
    GIBBS 124:1
keep finishing your s.   LONS 190:12
sentiment: those who have no s.   MAIL 199:5
sentimental: Of its s. value   FRY 119:13
sentimentality: S. is the emotional promiscuity
    MAIL 199:5
separate: s. the wheat from the chaff   HUBB 147:4
September: When you reach S.   AND 6:4
sequestered: Each s. in its hate   AUDEN 17:6
seraglio: A s. of eunuchs   FOOT 113:4
serene: that unhoped s.   BROO 54:12
serenity: s. to accept what cannot   NIEB 219:10
serial: autobiography is an obituary in s.
    CRISP 86:5
serious: It's nice to meet s. people   COPE 83:5
much more s.   SHAN 267:8
Murder is a s. business   ILES 150:10
s. house on serious earth   LARK 179:5
that politics are too s.   DE G 90:6
too s. a matter to entrust   CLEM 77:8
You cannot be s.   MCEN 194:16
seriously: right to be taken s.   HUMP 148:3
S., though, he's doing   FROST 117:12
take the game of life s.   LEARY 183:4
sermon: rejected the S. on the Mount   BRAD 52:6
serpent-haunted: s. sea   FLEC 111:14
servant: obligation to become the s.   SHAW 269:6
Our ugly comic s.; and then   AUDEN 19:12
s. girls in the kitchen   SYNGE 289:10
s. to the devil   SISS 275:14
Your s.'s cut in half   GRAH 127:10
servants: equality in the s.'hall   BARR 25:11
s. are treated as human   SHAW 272:2
wish your wife or your s.   GRIF 129:8
serve: s. both God and Mammon   SMITH 278:3
s. that in which I no longer   JOYCE 158:13
To s. your captives' need   KIPL 175:8
served: have things daintily s.   BETJ 42:12
s. to him course by course   CHUR 74:2
which I thought s. him   CHUR 75:12
service: places the nation at his s.   POMP 236:2
Pressed into s. means pressed   FROST 119:4
service of our imperial   ELIZ 105:12
services: s. can be paid for   NOCK 221:3

serviettes: kiddies have crumpled the s.
    BETJ 42:12
servility: savage s.   LOW 191:12
serving-men: I keep six honest s.   KIPL 172:2
sesquippledan: S. verboojuice   WELLS 308:6
set: s. down from the carrier's   LEE 183:16
She s. out one day   BULL 57:11
settlement: s. of the differences between
    ROOS 251:2
settles: war s. *nothing*   CHR 72:1
seul: *Être adulte, c'est être s.*   ROST 253:8
seven: s. pillared worthy house   LAWR 182:7
S. types of ambiguity   EMPS 106:8
The s. pillars of wisdom   LAWR 182:6
seventy: S. minutes had passed before   BENN 38:12
take from s. springs   HOUS 145:13
several: s. excuses are always less   HUXL 149:5
Severn: from the S. to the Tyne   KIPL 174:1
thick on S. snow the leaves   HOUS 146:7
sewer: Life is like a s.   LEHR 184:3
through a s. in a glass   MIZN 212:2
sewing: remarked brightly, 's.?'   BOTT 50:6
s. on a button is beyond   BROUN 56:7
sex: attempt to insult s.   LAWR 181:19
Battles and s.   MCAR 193:2
Continental people have s. life   MIKES 207:14
fair s. is your department   DOYLE 95:1
Is s. dirty   ALLEN 4:7
It's s. with someone   ALLEN 5:2
No s. please — we're British   MARR 202:4
practically conceal its s.   NASH 218:9
predominates the whole of her s.   DOYLE 94:1
S. and drugs and rock and roll   DURY 96:12
S. and not much about having   LODGE 190:5
S. and the single girl   BROWN 56:10
s. has been a very private   SZASZ 290:1
S. is the gateway to life   HARR 135:7
s. rears its ugly 'ead   ALL 5:6
s. relation as something   ROB 248:12
[s.] was the most fun   ALLEN 5:1
these s. rules for myself   SAL 258:12
wanted to know about s.   REUB 245:14
was exactly like s.   BALD 22:7
we have s. in the mind   LAWR 181:17
women are a s. by themselves   BEER 31:2
you have money, it's s.   DONL 93:3
S-E-X: if S. ever rears its ugly   AYCK 21:6
sexes: within the s. than between   COMP 80:3
saxophones: s. wailed like melodious   HUXL 148:9
sexual: all the s. perversions   HUXL 148:15
I've no s. vices   SIM 275:6
primary s. activity   SZASZ 289:13
S. intercourse began   LARK 179:3
unlimited s. attraction   HARD 132:16
sexually: s. transmitted disease   ANON 9:15
sex-war: s. thoughtlessness   CONN 80:2
shabby: For tamed and s. tigers   HODG 142:2
s. equipment always deteriorating   ELIOT 101:16

shackles: s. and restraints of government GOLD 126:3
shad-blow: Cowslip and s., flaked like CRANE 85:10
shade: A whiter s. of pale REID 245:9
s. of a coolibah tree PAT 232:5
s. your eyes but plagiarize LEHR 184:4
The sly s. of a Rural Dean BROO 55:9
shadow: Falls the S. ELIOT 103:4
Me and my s. ROSE 252:6
s. at evening rising ELIOT 104:12
s. at morning striding ELIOT 104:12
S. of Shadows on the deed YEATS 321:9
The one is the s. JUNG 160:1
Who live under the s. of a war SPEN 281:14
shadows: In ancient s. and twilights AE 3:3
less liquid than their s. TESS 291:6
s. pass gigantic FLEC 111:9
shag: (or s.) ISH 151:14
shake: S., rattle and roll CALH 61:5
s. their wicked sides YEATS 319:6
shaken: S. and not stirred FLEM 112:8
shakes: As a madman s. a dead geranium ELIOT 103:14
Midnight s. the memory ELIOT 103:14
Shakespeare: entirely as I despise S. SHAW 274:4
S. and found him weak WELLS 308:4
S., another Newton HUXL 148:18
S. I am struck with wonder LAWR 181:18
S. is not to translate BEER 30:18
S. remained more a theme BROWN 56:11
'S.,' she recalls HULL 148:1
souls most fed with S.'s CHES 70:10
Shakespearian: That S. rag BUCK 57:9
Shakespeherian: O O O O that S. Rag ELIOT 105:2
shaking: s. them to make certain BIRK 47:8
The Court is s. FARJ 107:7
Shalimar: hands I loved beside the S. HOPE 144:4
shame: Ain't it all a bleedin s. ANON 10:15
s. on you ARMS 13:9
'Tis a s. to human nature HOUS 144:8
who have known s. BROO 54:10
Shannon: dark mutinous S. waves JOYCE 157:9
shape: All out of s. from toe to top YEATS 319:11
it has no s. ANOU 12:14
means pressed out of s. FROST 119:4
The s. of things to come WELLS 308:11
shapely: it's s. and its name ERWIN 106:14
shard: Shattered in s. on shard THOM 295:15
shares: Fair S. for All JAY 154:3
shark: s. has pretty teeth BREC 52:18
sharp: s. compassion of the healer's ELIOT 101:15
shaved: s. and sober, and I didn't CHAN 66:10
shaves: A man who s. and takes a train WHITE 310:2
Shaw: disciple of Bernard S. SHAW 268:22
[George Bernard S.] LENIN 184:13
Mr S. CHES 70:1

Shaw (cont.):
S. a beefsteak and put CAMP 61:10
she: S. sells sea-shells SULL 288:13
s. who voiced those rhymes HARDY 133:7
shearsman: A s. of sorts STEV 285:12
sheath: s. the sword which we have ASQ 14:19
shed: s. his blood for the country ROOS 251:6
she-devil: The life and loves of a s. WELD 307:11
sheep: being savaged by a dead s. HEAL 136:5
black s. who've gone astray KIPL 169:9
s. in sheep's clothing CHUR 76:11
s. in sheep's clothing GOSSE 127:2
s. in the stare of a python BANK 24:11
s. to pass resolutions INGE 151:6
standing a s. on its hind-legs BEER 31:16
sheep-bells: The s. and the ship-bells ring KIPL 170:9
sheep-herding: rest is mere s. POUND 237:19
sheet: A boy brought the white s. LORCA 190:21
sheets: cool kindliness of s. BROO 54:9
shell: protective and aggressive s. MCL 196:12
underneath that gloomy s. ANON 10:1
shells: demented choirs of wailing s. OWEN 227:13
shelter: To s. me from the cold BELL 35:1
shelters: Naught is thee, who wilt THOM 295:8
shepherd: Old Nod, the s., goes DE L 90:9
sherry: And s. in the cupboard BETJ 44:7
shifted: s. it to another shoulder SHAW 271:14
shilling: s. the Bruddersford United PRIE 239:15
shilling life: s. will give you all AUDEN 19:9
shimmered: Jeeves s. out and came WOD 315:11
shimmy: s. like my sister Kate PIRON 235:3
shine: Boy you can gimme a s. GORD 126:14
s. on, harvest moon NORW 221:6
S. on, shine AUDEN 19:5
that's where I s. BENC 35:16
shines: Light breaks where no sun s. THOM 293:5
When the m-m-m-moon s. O'HARA 222:19
shining: A woman of so s. loveliness YEATS 322:2
dead; look s. AUDEN 20:4
dulls my s. things MEYN 207:11
I see it s. plain HOUS 146:11
London town the sun was s. GERS 123:6
s. keys will be took from HARDY 133:11
street in all his s. ABSE 1:4
Through the dark cloud s. FORD 113:14
ship: built your s. of death LAWR 181:10
It was so old a s. FLEC 112:5
S. me somewheres east KIPL 169:8
tall s. and a star MAS 203:14
The s. on the sea LORCA 191:1
ship-bells: The sheep-bells and the s. ring KIPL 170:9
ships: And mighty s. ten thousand ton HODG 142:1
s. and stars and isles FLEC 111:7
s. sail like swans asleep FLEC 112:3
stately s. are twirled HODG 142:1
Then man your s. LUCAS 192:10

ships (cont.):
wrong with our bloody s.   BEAT 28:2
Shiraz: wine of S. into urine   DIN 92:9
shires: calling for them from sad s.   OWEN 227:13
Round both the s. they ring   HOUS 146:3
shirt: s. or collar ever comes   LEAC 183:3
shit: shock-proof s. detector   HEM 138:11
shivers: s. like the jelly   PIRON 235:3
shock: Future s.   TOFF 297:20
Neither the sudden s.   CHUR 72:11
s. around the age of 5   BALD 22:12
s. them and keep them   SHAW 269:2
The s. of the new   DUNL 96:9
shocking: Was looked on as something s.
                                            PORT 236:9
shock-proof: s. shit detector   HEM 138:11
shocks: that s. the magistrate   RUSS 255:19
shoe: In its s.   FARJ 107:7
shoemaker: lives of a good s.   VANZ 303:7
shoes: Englishwomen's s. look   HALS 131:7
got a stock of s. here   PINT 234:13
mind it wipes its s.   THOM 293:14
step on my Blue Suede S.   PERK 233:3
shoestring: fortune and runs it into a s.
                                            WOOL 317:13
shome: S. mishtake, shurely   ANON 10:16
shone: that once had s.   FLEC 111:8
shook: Ten days that s. the world   REED 245:6
shoot: could s. me in my absence   BEHAN 31:24
I s. the Hippopotamus   BELL 32:16
They s. horses don't they   MCCOY 194:5
they shout and they s.   INGE 151:2
They up and s. themselves   BROO 55:11
women s. the hippopotamus   FORS 114:4
You s. a fellow down   HARDY 134:10
shop: bone s. of the heart   YEATS 320:3
s. and street I gazed   YEATS 323:11
The s. at the corner   AUDEN 19:15
shops: might shun the awful s.   CHES 68:16
shore: s. of the wan grassy sea   SITW 276:5
with low sounds by the s.   YEATS 318:10
shored: have s. against my ruins   ELIOT 105:11
shores: wilder s. of love   BLAN 47:10
short: And the days grow s.   AND 6:4
A s. life and a gay one   WIMP 315:1
be but a s. time tonight   BALD 23:6
Life is too s. to stuff   CONR 82:3
s. and the tall   HUGH 147:11
s. one ready for my own   FROST 119:10
step is s. from the Sublime   GRAH 127:7
who was s. and stout   CHES 70:11
shorter: were s. than they should   STR 288:2
shorts: zephyr and khaki s. girl   BETJ 44:4
shot: A long s., Watson   DOYLE 94:15
s. an elephant in my pajamas   KAUF 161:8
They've s. our fox   BIRCH 47:6
shoulder: shifted it to another s.   SHAW 271:14
s. all the time to see   BAR 27:9
s. she laid her snow-white   YEATS 321:13

shoulder (cont.):
S. the sky, my lad   HOUS 145:1
shoulders: City of the Big S.   SAND 259:9
s. held the sky suspended   HOUS 145:7
shout: s. and bang and roar   BELL 35:6
There was a s. about my ears   CHES 71:8
they s. and they shoot   INGE 151:2
shouting: chased the s. wind along   MAGEE 198:11
The tumult and the s. dies   KIPL 173:3
shoved: s. aside in favour of things   BROUN 56:5
shovel: S. them under and let me work
                                            SAND 260:1
shovelling: S. white steam over her   AUDEN 19:15
show: I will s. you fear   ELIOT 104:12
S. me a hero and I will   FITZ 110:10
s. to give pornography   BARN 25:4
There's no business like s.   BERL 40:10
shower: Yes, this is our finest s.   OSB 226:7
showers: s. betumble the chestnut   HARDY 133:8
showing: review a bad book without s.
                                            AUDEN 18:9
showman: That's what the s. said   HEAT 137:1
shows: All my s. are great   GRADE 127:4
And he s. them pearly white   BREC 52:18
shrapnel: picking s. out of your head   LUML 192:12
shrill: It's too s., man   FREB 116:9
shrimp: until a s. learns to whistle   KHR 165:9
shrine: build a s. to my memory   RUSS 254:14
shrined: The bower we s. to Tennyson
                                            HARDY 133:7
shroud: Fetch out no s.   PUDN 241:7
gaiety is a striped s.   THOM 294:8
stiff dishonoured s.   ELIOT 102:13
shtick: does her own s.   KAEL 160:6
shudder: s. in the loins engenders   YEATS 322:7
shuffle: All s. there; all cough in ink   YEATS 322:4
Shultz: Mr S. went off his pram   KINN 168:1
shurely: Shome mishtake, s.   ANON 10:16
shut: Each had his past s.   WOOLF 317:6
great markets by the sea s.   FLEC 111:8
S. up he explained   LARD 178:9
sick: I'll be s. tonight   LLEW 189:6
kingdom of the s.   SONT 280:12
Oh, Mummy, I'm s. with disgust   BETJ 42:11
s. hearts that honour could   BROO 54:10
s. horse nosing around   KAV 162:2
S. in soul and body both   HODG 142:3
The cattle then are s.   KING 167:12
time we think we're s.   WOLFE 316:12
sickle: A ship, an isle, a s. moon   FLEC 111:15
sickness: Nationalism is an infantile s.   EINS 99:3
universal as sea s.   SHAW 271:8
Sid: Tell S.   ANON 11:6
Sidcup: I could get down to S.   PINT 234:15
side: S. by side   WOODS 317:2
s. with plenty of money   ANOU 12:11
This s. the tomb   DAV 88:13
side-fall: Along the s. of the hill   KAV 162:1
sides: I'm a Norfan, both s.   WELLS 308:7

sides (*cont.*):
looked at life from both s.   MITC 211:4
on both s. of the paper   SELL 266:14
sideways: more up and down than s.   HEM 138:13
Siegfried: out the washing on the S.   KENN 162:14
siesta: But Englishmen detest a s.   COW 84:13
siftings: And let their liquid s. fall   ELIOT 102:13
sigh: A s. is just a sigh   HUPF 148:5
full of runic tales to s.   FLEC 111:16
telling this with a s.   FROST 118:8
sighs: S., short and infrequent   ELIOT 104:14
sight: And he keeps it out of s.   BREC 52:18
losing your s.   SASS 262:9
sighted: S. sub, sank same   MASON 204:5
sightless: On the s. horse, riding   WALEY 304:12
sights: Her s. and sounds   BROO 55:2
s. in the world   BARR 26:13
sign: would give me some clear s.   ALLEN 4:11
signalling: thin one is wildly s.   CONN 81:2
signals: suggestive s. to the orchestra   SZELL 290:7
signed: hand that s. the paper   THOM 293:10
morning I s. my death warrant   COLL 79:9
s. legislation which outlaws   REAG 244:7
significance: s. of man   BECK 28:12
significant: Art is s. deformity   FRY 120:3
would follow that 's. form'   BELL 32:7
signs: positive s. of his awareness   BLUNT 48:1
silence: activities and a period of s.   ATTL 16:7
After s., that which comes   HUXL 149:4
deep is the s.   DRIN 95:17
His mind moves upon s.   YEATS 320:2
Indecency's conspiracy of s.   SHAW 272:10
myself to use, s., exile   JOYCE 158:13
penitence condemns to s.   BRAD 51:16
private s. in which we live   PRIT 240:4
S. is the most perfect expression   SHAW 268:4
through the s. beat the bells   FLEC 111:9
silenced: because you have s. him   MORL 213:12
silent: And s. be   AUDEN 19:6
floors of s. seas   ELIOT 103:9
In a slow s. walk   HARDY 133:15
I stood upon that s. hill   HODG 141:14
multitude of s. witnesses   GEOR 123:4
Paris was French—and s.   TUCH 300:1
S. as the sleeve-worn stone   MACL 196:4
thereof one must be s.   WITT 315:4
The s. sullen peoples   KIPL 175:9
The *t* is s., as in *Harlow*   ASQ 15:4
silently: S. and very fast   AUDEN 20:1
Slowly, s., now the moon   DE L 91:5
silk: Delicate-filmed as new-spun s.   HARDY 134:1
s. hat on a Bradford millionaire   ELIOT 105:6
s. purse out of your wife's   MORT 214:4
your blue-shadowed s.   STEV 285:9
silkworm: power of Heaven—of s.   MOORE 213:1
silliest: s. woman can manage a clever   KIPL 172:10
silliness: s. of the majority of mankind   RUSS 255:9
silly: They are s. things   AWDRY 21:5

silly (*cont.*):
You s. twisted boy   MILL 209:1
You were s. like us   AUDEN 17:4
silver: all the Georgian s.   MACM 197:7
Between their s. bars   FLEC 111:15
There's a s. lining   FORD 113:14
The s. apples of the moon   YEATS 322:12
thirty pieces of s.   BEVAN 44:12
Walks the night in her s.   DE L 91:5
With the s. penny   CAUS 65:4
simple: I'm a s. man, and I use   LOWRY 192:4
It was beautiful and s.   HENRY 139:2
Love is so s.   PRÉ.V 239:13
To ask the hard question is s.   AUDEN 20:6
simplicity: A condition of complete s.   ELIOT 102:7
S. of character is no hindrance   MORL 213:11
simplification: s. of the human character
    FORS 114:9
simplify: And s. me when I'm dead   DOUG 93:7
s. and illustrate the points   HOME 143:2
Simpson: Mrs S.'s pinched our king   ANON 8:9
sin: beauty is only s. deep   SAKI 257:14
I'll s. till I blow up   THOM 294:1
lips were shaped for s.   BETJ 42:6
loins. My s., my soul   NAB 217:1
more dreadful record of s.   DOYLE 94:8
mother I'm living in s.   HERB 139:8
physicists have known s.   OPP 223:16
researches in original s.   PLOM 235:13
s. tends to be addictive   AUDEN 18:3
s. towards our fellow creatures   SHAW 268:15
s. ye do by two and two   KIPL 170:3
There's only one real s.   LESS 186:7
what did he say about s.   COOL 82:9
Would you like to s.   ANON 12:10
sincere: It is dangerous to be s.   SHAW 272:16
sincerely: comes as s. from the author   HUXL 149:6
Do you s. want to be rich   CORN 83:9
sincerity: s. of the pessimists   ROST 253:7
test of your s.   BENN 38:10
sinecure: It gives no man a s.   POUND 238:10
sing: And I will s. of the sun   POUND 238:15
heart wants to s. ev'ry song   HAMM 132:3
I, too, s. America   HUGH 147:13
Lhude s. Goddamm   POUND 238:13
never heard no horse s.   ARMS 13:8
second best to s. them   BELL 34:5
s. 'em muck   MELBA 206:7
s. for a rock 'n' roll   JAGG 152:5
s. to find your hearts   FLEC 111:7
S. whatever is well made   YEATS 319:11
Soul clap its hands and s.   YEATS 321:6
think that they will s.   ELIOT 103:12
was said. We s. it   HARDY 134:13
while I s. the ancient ways   YEATS 321:11
singer: The s. not the song   LIND 188:6
singers: s. who she thinks would   REED 245:5
singin': S. in the rain   FREED 116:11

slaughter: machinery all the s. of plague
    SHAW 271:6
slave: s. of capitalist   CONN 81:7
  The moment the s. resolves   GAND 121:11
slavery: because they impose s.   RUSS 255:17
  Freedom and s. are mental   GAND 121:11
  s. in the extreme acceptance   CHUR 73:9
  state is a state of S.   GILL 124:9
slaves: Englishmen never will be s.   SHAW 271:4
  inevitably two kinds of s.   ILL 150:12
  mistress and two s.   BIER 46:21
  was that men became s.   FROMM 117:10
sleep: And miles to go before I s.   FROST 118:11
  And sang themselves to s.   HODG 141:13
  And s.—and learning of a sort   BELL 35:6
  been to s. for over a year   WAUGH 305:16
  calf won't get much s.   ALLEN 4:9
  Church can feed and s.   ELIOT 102:14
  come to the borders of s.   THOM 294:7
  Eat or s. or drink again   DE L 91:7
  From s. and from damnation   CHES 70:7
  green ideas s. furiously   CHOM 71:16
  grey and full of s.   YEATS 318:8
  hear a moment before s.   THOM 292:9
  I s. all night   CHAP 67:6
  Is passed in s.; at night   ELIOT 102:14
  I wake to s., and take   ROET 249:4
  Let us s. now   OWEN 228:8
  like men who s. badly   RUSS 254:15
  Never s. with a woman   ALGR 3:14
  poor to s. under bridges   FRAN 116:6
  recommend you to go home and s.   CHAM 66:6
  s. and a sweet dream when   MAS 204:1
  S. upon a golden bed   YEATS 324:2
  s. you remind me   SASS 263:3
  S. your fill   BELL 34:14
  there is nothing but s.   DRIN 95:17
  There'll be time enough to s.   HOUS 145:14
  To break earth's s. at all   OWEN 228:2
  twenty centuries of stony s.   YEATS 320:8
  We shall not s.   MCCR 194:7
  when you can't get to s.   LEB 183:9
sleeper: sun-flushed s.   THOM 294:14
sleep-flower: s. sways in the wheat   THOM 294:14
sleeping: fuss about s. together   WAUGH 306:13
  Lay your s. head, my love   AUDEN 17:10
  The rose-lipt girls are s.   HOUS 146:14
  wakened us from s.   BROO 54:10
sleepless: O S. as the river under thee
    CRANE 85:11
sleeps: He s. as sound   PUDN 241:7
sleepwalker: with the assurance of a s. HITL 141:7
sleepy: 'Cause in s. London town   JAGG 152:5
  s. and there is no place   DYLAN 97:10
sleeve: Ash on an old man's s.   ELIOT 102:2
  bringing an ace down his s.   LAB 177:5
  s. with a bottle of vitriol   WOOL 317:15
sleeves: Americanism with its s.   MCC 193:11
  language that rolls up its s.   SAND 260:3

sleigh: To hear s. bells in the snow   BERL 40:12
slender: s. indications of scholarship   CHUR 75:9
slept: He s. in the hall   BENT 39:12
  He s. more than any other   MENC 206:8
  s. soundly and had no need   CHUR 76:5
slice: S. him where you like   WOD 315:13
slide: slip, s., perish   ELIOT 101:9
slight: friendship called s.   BIER 46:4
Slightly: he [Noel Coward] was S.   TYNAN 302:5
slime: Is wetter water, slimier s.   BROO 55:4
slip: Excuse me while I s.   EST 106:15
  tension, s., slide   ELIOT 101:9
  They s., diminished   TESS 291:6
slipped: s. the surly bonds of earth MAGEE 198:11
slippered: A s. Hesper; and there   BROO 55:8
slitty-eyed: longer you'll all be s.   PHIL 233:14
slob: He was just a s.   LONG 190:10
slogan: rhyming North Battersea s.   JAY 154:3
  s. and a few vapid adjectives   OGIL 222:18
slogans: instead of principles, s.   BENT 39:16
slogged: s. up to Arras with rifle   SASS 262:8
slopes: on the butler's upper s.   WOD 316:9
Sloppy Joe: At Dirty Dick's and S.'s AUDEN 18:17
slouches: S. towards Bethlehem   YEATS 320:8
slouching: S. in the undergrowth   HODG 142:3
Slough: bombs, and fall on S.   BETJ 42:2
slovenliness: Peace is nothing but s.   BREC 53:4
slow: Ah! the clock is always s.   SERV 266:15
  In a s. silent walk   HARDY 133:15
  On a s. boat to China   LOES 190:7
  sloeblack, s., black   THOM 293:13
  was drinking was s. poison   BENC 36:12
  way of telling you to s. down   ANON 7:15
slowly: angel to pass, flying s.   FIRB 109:12
  great end comes s.   DUB 96:2
  pig got up and s. walked   BURT 58:7
  s. in the wind   EHRL 99:2
  S., silently, now the moon   DE L 91:5
sludge: simply says: ACTIVATED S.   JENN 154:12
sluicing: excellent browsing and s.   WOD 316:6
slum: A swear-word in a rustic s.   BEER 30:14
  free diversions in s. life   MCAR 193:2
  you've seen one city s.   AGNEW 3:6
slumber: Seal thy sense in deathly s. DE L 90:15
slums: gay intimacy of the s.   WAUGH 306:1
slush: I'm as pure as the driven s.   BANK 24:7
  with mush and s.   OWEN 227:9
sly: The s. shade of a Rural Dean   BROO 55:9
small: day of s. nations has   CHAM 66:1
  pictures that got s.   BRAC 51:11
  S. is beautiful   SCH 264:15
  That's one s. step for a man   ARMS 13:10
  The Microbe is so very s.   BELL 33:17
  while your s., but perfectly   COOP 83:2
smallest: about the s. in the world   STR 288:5
  Advice, n. The s. current coin   BIER 46:6
  s. amount of lying go   BUTL 60:12
  s. room of my house   REGER 245:7

small-talking: this s. world can I find FRY 119:16
smarter: who thought themselves s. ATTL 16:2
smash: English never s. in a face HALS 131:8
  This great society is going s. AUDEN 20:7
smell: s. by the ferocity ELLIS 106:4
  s. of burning fills BELL 35:7
  s. of steaks in passageways ELIOT 103:13
  The good s. of old clothes BROO 54:9
  Yes, the s. and hideous hum GODL 125:8
smells: dead thing that s. sweet THOM 294:4
  pine-woody, evergreen s. BETJ 43:11
  tell me it s. like roses JOHN 156:2
Smethwick: S. Conservatives can have
                           WILS 313:4
smile: And s., smile, smile ASAF 13:13
  fading s. of a cosmic HUXL 149:16
  For Cambridge people rarely s. BROO 55:10
  S. at us, pay us, pass CHES 70:13
  s. dwells a little longer CHAP 67:5
  s. on the face of the tiger ANON 10:11
  s. playing about his lips THUR 297:13
  When you call me that, s. WIST 315:2
smiled: Has s. and said BELL 34:12
smiles: s., with sniffles HENRY 138:15
smiling: alone against s. enemies BOWEN 51:4
  they start not s. back MILL 208:9
smite: Star-spiked Rails a fiery s. THOM 294:9
Smith: Chuck it, S.! CHES 70:9
  F. E. S. CHES 70:8
smithy: forge in the s. JOYCE 158:12
smoke: coaster with a salt-caked s. MAS 203:1
  Only thin s. without flame HARDY 133:15
  S. gets in your eyes HARB 132:11
smoke-filled: s. room early today SIMP 275:11
smoking: high s. and alcoholism CURR 87:12
smoky: The burnt-out ends of s. days
                          ELIOT 103:13
smooth: anything never does run s. BUTL 59:7
smug: s. self-satisfaction BALD 23:11
snaffle: s. and the curb all right CAMP 62:2
snail: slug-abed s. upon the thorn THOM 296:6
snake: A s. came to my water-trough LAWR 180:9
  handy in case I see a s. FIEL 109:5
  The S. is living yet BELL 33:15
snakeskin: The s.-titles of mining-claims
                        BENÉT 36:16
snap: I'm kidnapped and they s. ALLEN 4:18
  S.! Crackle! Pop ANON 10:17
snare: kin to the s. drummer FREB 116:10
snatch: grant what I wish and s. FROST 118:9
  when you s. Bookie Bob RUNY 254:8
snatching: instead of s. his victuals CHUR 74:2
sneery: hair and looked very s. ASHF 14:10
sneeze: it's like having a good s. LAWR 181:1
sneezes: Coughs and s. spread diseases ANON 7:14
snicker: Footman hold my coat, and s.
                        ELIOT 103:10
sniffles: sobs, s., and smiles HENRY 138:15

snigger: between a eunuch and a s. FIRB 109:11
snobbery: would be bereaved if s. UST 302:15
snobs: effete corps of impudent s. AGNEW 3:7
snore: snorer can't hear himself s. TWAIN 302:2
snored: Coolidge only s. MENC 206:8
  have simply sat and s. CHES 70:15
snorer: way to find out why a s. TWAIN 302:2
snores: s. bass and gruff THOM 293:15
snotgreen: The s. sea JOYCE 158:15
snow: Earth in foretful s., feeding ELIOT 104:10
  I, this incessant s. DE L 91:6
  It's congealed s. PARK 231:14
  Out in the dark over the s. THOM 294:2
  Severn s. the leaves HOUS 146:7
  s. disfigured the public AUDEN 17:3
  s. was general all over JOYCE 157:9
  To hear sleigh bells in the s. BERL 40:12
  To see the cherry hung with s. HOUS 145:13
snow-deep: Buried beneath some s. Alps
                        ELIOT 100:5
snowed: it s. and it snowed THOM 292:10
  s. for six days and six THOM 292:9
snows: Said our Lady of the S. KIPL 170:7
  The more it s. MILNE 209:11
Snow White: I used to be S ... but I drifted
                        WEST 309:13
snow-white: branches up a s. trunk FROST 118:9
  shoulder she laid her s. hand YEATS 321:13
so: And s. do I HARDY 133:8
  S. farewell then ANON 11:1
soap: S. and education are not TWAIN 300:12
sob: S., heavy world AUDEN 16:15
sober: But men at whiles are s. HOUS 145:2
  keep absolutely s. SMITH 278:10
  one sees in Garbo s. TYNAN 302:6
  shaved and s. CHAN 66:10
  when I was one-third s. BURT 58:7
  Wordsworth drunk and Porson s. HOUS 144:6
soberly: it dresses so very s. JER 155:5
Sobranies: Balkan S. in a wooden box BETJ 44:7
sobs: Life is made up of s. HENRY 138:15
so-called: s. white races are really FORS 115:6
sociable: I am a s. worker BEHAN 32:2
social: breakdown in the s. contract BENN 37:6
  delightful s. atmosphere BENN 38:11
  Legion and S. Club BETJ 42:3
  needs is a new s. contract CALL 61:6
  s. and economic experiment HOOV 143:5
  S. Contract is nothing WELLS 308:9
  s. engineering resembles POPP 236:7
  s. fabric would fly asunder SHAW 271:11
  The s. progress, order JOHN 155:17
socialism: Democracy and s. are means
                        NEHRU 219:1
  followed a policy so that s. DUBČ 95:18
  paternalism and state s. HOOV 143:6
  priorities is the religion of S. BEVAN 45:7
  S. can only arrive on a bicycle VIER 304:9

socialism (*cont.*):

S. does not mean much	ORW 225:17
S. is its adherents	ORW 225:15
S. is nothing but the capitalism	SPEN 282:4
S. must always remain	KEYN 164:15
S. *possibly* be established	STAL 283:6
This is not S. It	SNOW 279:8

socialist: proletarian s. state in Russia

	LENIN 184:11
s. culture in our land	MAO 200:10
S. literature is W. H. Auden	ORW 225:18
s. whose political commitment	BENN 37:2
The typical S.	ORW 225:16

socially: often s. impressive WILL 312:1

société: *la s. la femelle humaine* BEAU 89:9

society: altering the *shape* of s. ORW 224:18

importance whatever to s.	NAB 217:5
In a consumer s. there	ILL 150:12
no such thing as S.	THAT 292:6
return to a non-utopian s.	BERD 40:1
rich s. and the powerful	JOHN 156:10
slave of capitalist s.	CONN 81:7
s. cannot help the many	KENN 163:9
s. where it is safe	STEV 286:3
This great s. is going smash	AUDEN 20:7
upward to the Great S.	JOHN 156:10

sockets: The candles burn their s. HOUS 145:5

socks: s. compelled one's attention SAKI 257:11

student wears coloured s. BRAT 52:15

Socratic: S. manner is not a game BEER 31:19

soda: They wash their feet in s. ELIOT 105:4

sodden: That are s. and unkind BELL 34:19

sodium: Of having discovered S. BENT 39:9

sodomy: s. and the lash CHUR 73:8

sofa: s. upholstered in panther PLOM 235:13

soft: she s. as the dawn THUR 297:12

softest: s. thing about him RUNY 254:8

softly: S. along the road of evening DE L 90:9

s. because you tread	YEATS 323:1
s. through the silence	FLEC 111:9

softness: s. of my body will be guarded LOW 191:7

soiling: Beg pardon, I'm s. the doileys BETJ 43:1

soils: Six days of the week it s. LARK 179:6

solar: somewhere in the s. system FULL 120:5

sold: book which somehow s. BOOR 49:8

Soldan: S. of Byzantium is smiling CHES 70:5

soldier: An' go to your Gawd like a s. KIPL 169:5

A s.'s life is terrible hard	MILNE 209:15
can always tell an old s.	SHAW 267:17
chocolate cream s.	SHAW 267:18
I never expect a s. to think	SHAW 268:17
side of the Unknown S.	ASQ 15:1
s. can stand up to anything	SHAW 268:19
s. of the King to help	KITC 175:15
s.'s ribbon on a tunic	ABSE 1:3
who had the s. singled	DOUG 93:8

soldiers: are to bring the s. home LARK 178:12

mostly knaves, and s.	BIER 46:20
Old s. never die	FOLEY 113:2

soldiers (*cont.*):

S. are citizens of death's	SASS 262:5
S. are dreamers	SASS 262:6
s. he smiled at are most	SASS 262:8
S., this solitude	DE L 91:6
The s. coming	AUDEN 19:7
What is the world, O s.	DE L 91:6

sole: For nothing can be s. or whole YEATS 323:8

S. purpose of visit	HARD 132:15
The spider is s. denizen	HARDY 133:7

soleil: *horreur des couchers de s.* PROU 241:2

solemn: more s. of our number said BETJ 44:8

s. beauty like slow old MAS 203:4

solicitor: s., a Freemason DOYLE 94:19

solid: Safe upon s. rock the ugly MILL 207:18

s. for fluidity, all-powerful CHUR 74:1

solidity: appearance of s. to pure wind ORW 226:3

solitary: sentenced to s. confinement WILL 312:8

solitude: endure our own s. PRIT 240:4

In a s. of the sea	HARDY 134:4
make him feel his s.	VALÉ 303:2
resonance of his s.	CONN 80:14
Soldiers, this s.	DE L 91:6
that each protects the s.	RILKE 248:1

solitudes: saluting of two s. RILKE 247:9

Solomon: Is S.'s temple, poets, Nineveh

	MEYN 207:11
King David and King S.	NAYL 218:16
One man in a thousand, S. says	KIPL 173:10

solution: s. for the problem of habitual BENC 36:1

that they can't see the s.	CHES 71:1
you're either part of the s.	CLEA 77:4

somber: decorated dark red as I have s. ASHF 14:5

sombre: s. picture presented BERNE 41:6

some: S. chicken CHUR 73:1

S. enchanted evening	HAMM 132:2
S. men are born mediocre	HELL 137:5
S. say the world will end	FROST 118:10

somebody: I could have been s. SCH 264:11

S. up there likes me LEHM 184:1

someday: S. I'll find you COW 85:5

somehow: you s. haven't to deserve FROST 119:1

someone: S. must have traduced Joseph

KAFKA 160:7

something: Everything must be like s. FORS 114:3

Good morning, sir—was there s.	MURD 216:2
s. nasty in the woodshed	GIBB 123:12
s. or other could be proved	FRY 119:19
S. should be done to get	EDW 99:1
S. there is that doesn't	FROST 118:13
S. you somehow haven't	FROST 119:1
Time for a little s.	MILNE 210:13
When there's s. doing	KNIG 176:3
you say s. about me	COHAN 78:10

sometime: Why don't you come up s.

WEST 309:14

somewhat: tough joints more than s. RUNY 254:7

somewhere: S. over the rainbow HARB 132:13

somnambulist: A Reactionary is a s. ROOS 250:9

son: good idea—s.' 'Bighead!'   SYKES 289:7
    his little s. should cry   CORN 83:13
    s. of a bitch stole   MAC 193:3
    you'll be a Man, my s.   KIPL 173:9
song: A rainbow and a cuckoo's s.   DAV 88:13
    given a penny for a s.   YEATS 319:5
    have I to spur me into s.   YEATS 321:3
    I made my s. a coat   YEATS 322:1
    Luxuriant s.   YEATS 322:10
    old sweet s. keeps Georgia   GORR 127:1
    play a s. for me   DYLAN 97:10
    Poured forth her s. in perfect   AUDEN 20:12
    s. was wordless   SASS 263:5
    s. well sung   MAS 203:3
    that thinks two notes a s.   DAV 88:14
    The singer not the s.   LIND 188:6
    The s. is ended   BERL 40:9
    The s. of the birds for mirth   GURN 130:9
    Time an endless s.   YEATS 319:9
    time you hear your love s.   CAHN 61:1
    wants to sing ev'ry s.   HAMM 132:3
songe-creux: Comme tous les s.   SART 261:15
songs: all trades, to make s.   BELL 34:5
    And all their s. are sad   CHES 68:10
    s. beguile your pilgrimage   FLEC 111:7
    s., for ended is our brief   THOM 296:3
    s. they have sung   HAMM 132:3
    their dirty s.   BROO 54:10
sonne: Vienne la nuit, s. l'heure   APOL 12:15
sonnet: And it turned to a S.   DOBS 92:14
sonnets: S. and birds descend   MACN 197:10
sons: approve of your young s.   GRIF 129:8
    further s. to their name   EDGAR 98:4
    s. acclaim your glorious   CUMM 87:2
    s. and daughters of Life's   GIBR 124:3
    The fallen s. of Eve   CHES 69:1
    Your s. and your daughters   DYLAN 97:13
soon: Be s.   THOM 295:6
    curly you'll s. be dead   WIMP 315:1
    it's awfully s.   KAEL 160:6
    s. as one is unhappy one   PROU 240:11
    s. write free verse   FROST 118:6
sophism: more precisely, a s.   BORG 49:11
sophistication: s. of the wise primitive   MAIL 199:6
soporific: too much lettuce is 's.'   POTT 237:6
Sordello: There can be but the one 'S.'
    POUND 238:2
sordid: s. thing sound like a brilliant   DE VR 91:13
sore: man has long been s.   HOUS 145:6
sores: s. on innocent tongues   OWEN 227:14
sorrow: Nought but vast S. was there   DE L 90:14
    salutary for the body but s.   PROU 241:5
    s., and the triumphs   HOOV 143:4
    s. enough in the natural   KIPL 168:6
    S. is tranquillity remembered   PARK 230:6
sorrows: s. of your changing face   YEATS 318:8
    There are few s., however   SMITH 277:14
    The world's great s. were born   AE 3:3

sorry: having to say you're s.   SEGAL 266:2
    S. for itself   LAWR 181:16
    s. for keeping you waiting   GEOR 123:3
    Very s. can't come   BER 40:2
    who, I'm s. to say   AUDEN 19:14
sort: And sleep—and learning of a s.   BELL 35:6
sorts: only two s. of people   SHAW 269:19
so-so: The rest is merely s.   WILD 311:7
Sosostris: Madame S., famous clairvoyante
    ELIOT 104:13
Soudan: at your 'ome in the S.   KIPL 169:1
soul: By which the s. of man is fed   MAS 203:10
    He fancied that I gave a s.   YEATS 323:6
    his s. among masterpieces   FRAN 116:7
    most surely, on the s.   DIMN 92:7
    night of the s. it is always   FITZ 110:12
    oath again may my s.   SHAW 273:21
    repose of His s.   ROLFE 249:18
    Sick in s. and body both   HODG 142:3
    sincerely from the author's s.   HUXL 149:6
    S. clap its hands and sing   YEATS 321:6
    there is a s. in prison   DEBS 89:11
    The s. of a friend we've made   BOND 49:2
souls: bodies but not their s.   GIBR 124:3
    damp s. of housemaids   ELIOT 103:15
    only in men's s.   STEV 286:9
    people sell their s.   SMITH 278:4
    s. most fed with Shakespeare's   CHES 70:10
    s. of Christian peoples   CHES 70:9
sound: alive with the s. of music   HAMM 132:3
    hear the s. of marching   JAGG 152:5
    it is sheer s.   BEEC 29:23
    Music is feeling, then, not s.   STEV 285:9
    s. ideas is original   MACM 197:6
    S. of Broken Glass   BELL 34:3
    s. of English county families   WAUGH 305:11
    s. of Harold Hobson   GILL 124:10
    s. which reverberates through   KOES 176:8
    s. which so thrills   AUDEN 19:7
    The s. of surprise   BALL 24:5
    Whose s. dies on the wind   APOL 12:16
sounds: music is better than it s.   NYE 221:12
soup: not take s. at luncheon   CURZ 88:3
sour: life will be s. grapes   ASHF 14:11
sous: S. le pont Mirabeau coule   APOL 12:15
south: citizens dream of the s.   HARDY 133:8
    go s. in the winter   ELIOT 104:11
    great hills of the S.   BELL 34:19
    I want to go s., where   LAWR 181:3
    more seriously down S.   CURR 87:12
    not in the S.   POTT 237:13
    Or s. to the blind Horn's hate   KIPL 175:6
    S. of England where you   ORW 225:14
    S. of the Border   KENN 162:13
South Africa: methods of barbarism in S.
    CAMP 62:7
    S., renowned both far and wide   CAMP 62:6

South African: S. police would leave no
SHAR 267:9
Southampton: Yes, weekly from S. KIPL 172:3
South Pole: [the S.] SCOTT 265:7
Southron: matches of the S. folk THOM 296:1
souvenirs: Les s. sont cors de chasse APOL 12:16
sovereign: power and light, a s. touch
AUDEN 20:3
soviet: S. domination of Eastern FORD 113:9
S. power plus the electrification LENIN 184:12
sow: his Vomit and the S. KIPL 173:12
Ireland is the old s. JOYCE 158:10
space: art of how to waste s. JOHN 157:1
beyond S. and Time BROO 55:4
challenge of filling the s. WEST 309:15
passenger on s. vehicle FULL 120:5
S.—the final frontier RODD 249:2
s. where nobody STEIN 284:10
spaces: And through the s. of the dark
ELIOT 103:14
It is the s. between FENT 108:3
me with their empty s. FROST 118:3
Removed the s. from the fence MORG 213:9
vacant interstellar s. ELIOT 101:14
spaceship: fact regarding S. Earth FULL 120:8
spade: s. is never so merely FRY 120:1
Spain: Lady of S., I adore you REAV 244:11
The rain in S. stays mainly LERN 186:4
Spanish: expects the S. Inquisition CHAP 67:10
some are fond of S. wine MAS 203:2
spanner: their throats with a s. BETJ 42:10
spare: Brother can you s. a dime HARB 132:12
don't s. the horses HILL 141:1
s. time and in his working GILL 124:9
spared: has s. me the indignity BELL 33:12
spark-gap: The s. is mightier HOGB 142:10
sparks: s. blown out of a smithy YEATS 322:3
speak: He must s. in calm BEVAN 44:11
I s. like a child NAB 217:4
let us s. of darker days CHUR 72:13
Nation shall s. peace REND 245:11
one's memoirs is to s. ill PÉT 233:7
S. for England AMERY 5:10
S. now, and I will answer HOUS 146:10
S. softly and carry ROOS 251:8
s. thereof one must WITT 315:4
Think before you s. FORS 115:14
speaker: public s. NIC 219:8
speaking: their watches when I am s. BIRK 47:8
This is Henry Hall s. HALL 131:5
when they are s. CHUR 73:10
spearmint: s. lose its flavour ROSE 252:7
special: s. kind of artist COOM 83:1
We are all s. cases CAMUS 62:12
specialism: his s. is omniscience DOYLE 94:11
specialist: definition of a s. as one MAYO 206:3
specialists: All other men are s. DOYLE 94:11
speciality: s. is being right when SHAW 274:10
species: s. is more deadly KIPL 173:11

species (cont.):
s. of beetles on this planet HALD 131:2
systematically on its own s. JAMES 153:10
specimens: s., the lilies of ambition DOUG 93:6
spectators: be anything more than s. ASQ 14:16
spectre: haunt Europe as a s. TAYL 290:14
speculation: s. in the sense that we WILS 313:5
speech: divine gift of articulate s. SHAW 273:12
freedom of s. and expression ROOS 250:12
freedom of s., freedom TWAIN 300:15
sensibly refrain from s. GRAH 127:12
Since our concern was s. ELIOT 102:3
s. in the slack moments BROUN 56:5
s. without the help WAUGH 306:5
what the dead had no s. ELIOT 102:1
speeches: From all the easy s. CHES 70:7
should have its old s. SNOW 279:7
speechless: washed in the s. real BARZ 27:11
speed: candles may be held to s. OWEN 227:13
Less than the s., of hours HOPE 144:3
S., bonnie boat, like BOUL 50:9
s. glum heroes up the line SASS 262:7
s. towards the wilder shores BLAN 47:10
S. with the light-foot GREN 129:5
Unsafe at any s. NADER 217:6
war s. MORR 213:15
speeding: Faster than a s. bullet ANON 7:23
spell: foreigners always s. better TWAIN 301:2
no s. to cast on nature BRON 54:7
Who lies beneath your s. HOPE 144:4
with the s. of far Arabia DE L 90:10
you s. my name right COHAN 78:10
spelling: My s. is Wobbly MILNE 210:14
spend: I want to s., and spend NICH 219:6
s. a little time FIEL 108:8
spender: A real big s. FIEL 108:8
Where the s. thinks it went FROST 118:5
spending: arms is not s. money alone EIS 100:2
spent: Never ask of money s. FROST 118:5
spermatozoa: A million million s. HUXL 148:18
spider: The s. is sole denizen HARDY 133:7
spiders: s. marching through LOW 192:1
spider-web: kind of huge s. JAMES 153:4
spill: stone and let them not s. MACN 198:8
spin: Sob as you s. AUDEN 16:11
spinach: I say it's s., and I say WHITE 309:23
spindle: s. or mutilate ANON 7:16
spinster: s. from being treated like MITF 211:11
spires: city of dreaming s. RAPH 243:3
I saw the s. of Oxford LETTS 186:9
What s., what farms are those HOUS 146:11
spirit: break a man's s. is devil's SHAW 268:13
develops the powers of the s. PROU 241:5
Or watch the startled s. flee GRAV 128:5
s. of her spirit BINY 47:4
s. of national masochism AGNEW 3:7
was sacramental of the s. ROB 248:12
spirits: S. of well-shot woodcock BETJ 42:4
spiritual: has outrun our s. power KING 167:4

spiritual (*cont.*):
  not being a s. people   MANC 199:15
spiritualist: talk to you, you are a s.   SZASZ 290:5
spiritualists: like a convention of s.   STOP 287:1
spiritually: S. I was at Eton, John   BETJ 44:8
spit: I have no gun, but I can s.   AUDEN 16:10
spiteful: write when I feel s.   LAWR 181:1
splendid: men with S. Hearts may go   BROO 55:10
  s. in the morning glows   FLEC 111:11
  S. to eat and sleep   SASS 263:2
  With few but with how s. stars   FLEC 111:15
splendour: show of some fuller s.   BRAD 52:4
  such thing as s. or heroism   FORS 114:13
splintered: lock and s. the door   AUDEN 19:8
splinters: bombs and teeth like s.   CAUS 65:5
split: when I s. an infinitive   CHAN 66:12
spoil: healths, and s. our own   JER 155:4
spoke: And sometimes no one s. to him
                                                 MILNE 209:13
spoken: possible to the s. one   CONN 80:11
  s. to like this before   CARR 64:2
  s. with greater regret   BALD 23:6
  that never have s. yet   CHES 70:13
spontaneous: S. joy and natural content
                                                 YEATS 319:3
spoons: my life with coffee s.   ELIOT 103:8
  world locks up its s.   SHAW 271:9
sport: had ended his s. with Tess   HARDY 134:8
sportsman: A s. is a man   LEAC 182:15
spot: corner, some untidy s.   AUDEN 17:9
  each one s. shall prove   KIPL 170:10
  penned in an inglorious s.   MCKAY 195:8
  sumpshous s. all done up in gold   ASHF 14:7
Sprache: *Die Grenzen meiner S. bedeuten*
                                                 WITT 315:7
spray: And then me s. of pellets   AYRES 21:16
  pinkly bursts the s.   BETJ 44:1
  The rime was on the s.   HARDY 134:6
spread: S. ALARM AND DESPONDENCY   PEN 232:15
  s. my dreams under   YEATS 323:1
spreading: risks of s. conflict   JOHN 156:11
sprig-muslin: And maids come forth s. drest
                                                 HARDY 133:8
spring: clean the pasture s.   FROST 118:12
  first hour of s. strikes   BOWEN 50:11
  It is s., moonless night   THOM 293:13
  Mrs Porter in the s.   ELIOT 105:4
  naked earth is warm with S.   GREN 129:5
  S. breaks through again   COW 84:9
  s. comes her hour is upon   GIBB 123:11
  S. comes round with rustling   SEEG 265:12
  s. has kept in its folds   ARAG 13:2
  S. is come home with her   THOM 296:5
  S. is here, so blow your job   HART 135:12
  s. summer autumn winter   CUMM 86:15
  s. than in any other season   TWAIN 301:21
  S. will be a little late   LOES 190:8
  They call it easing the S.   REED 244:13

spring (*cont.*):
  with his vision, S.   SACK 256:13
springing: Praise for them, s.   FARJ 107:6
springlike: that fester are not s.   ABSE 1:2
springs: from seventy s. a score   HOUS 145:13
sprouting: S. despondently at area gates
                                                 ELIOT 103:15
spun: ships are twirled and s.   HODG 142:1
spunk: their s. is that watery   LAWR 180:11
spur: have I to s. me into song   YEATS 321:3
spurn: But s. the Jews   BROW 56:14
spy: s. who came in from   LE C 183:13
squad: s. took up their positions   CHIL 71:14
squalid: he was a s. nuisance   CHUR 75:4
squalor: opulence and public s.   GALB 121:4
square: given a s. deal afterwards   ROOS 251:6
  like this on the public s.   CAV 65:6
  so thoroughly s.   LERN 185:21
  s. of the number of people   SHAN 267:7
squares: districts packed like s.   LARK 179:11
  Tree-muffled s., and look   LARK 178:13
squat: s., and packed with guile   BROO 55:10
squawking: And the seven stars go s.
                                                 AUDEN 16:12
squeak: s. of a boot   FORS 115:7
  until the pips s.   GEDD 122:9
squeezed: s. as a lemon is squeezed   GEDD 122:9
squires: s. ride slowly towards   CHES 70:14
squirrels: like red s., must be protected
                                                 ORTON 224:6
squirt: I 'spec me s. of water   AYRES 21:16
St: S. Andrews by the Northern sea   LANG 178:4
stab: I saw him s.   READ 244:3
stabbed: guy gets s. in the back   GARD 122:4
stable: Stand s. here   AUDEN 19:6
stables: s. are the real centre   SHAW 269:11
stage: Something for the modern s.   POUND 238:7
  s. things that are supposed   STOP 287:3
  your daughter on the s.   COW 85:1
stages: four s. of man are infancy   LINK 188:12
staggered: He s. — and, terrible-eyed   BETJ 42:1
staid: And foreign to the s.   WATS 305:9
stain: s. the stiff dishonoured   ELIOT 102:13
stained: that never s. thy Sword   HOPE 144:3
stained glass: kick a hole in a s. window
                                                 CHAN 66:11
stair: As I was walking up the s.   MEAR 206:6
staircases: house with three poor s.   ASQ 15:2
stalk: Half asleep as they s.   HARDY 133:15
stalks: starvation that s.   FOSD 116:4
stall: A Baby in an ox's s.   BETJ 42:5
stalls: Tank come down the s.   SASS 263:1
stamp: either physics or s.   RUTH 256:6
  s. collection waits   BETJ 42:4
stamping: boot s. on a human face   ORW 225:9
stamps: it s. a man at once   SHAW 270:4
stand: British soldier can s.   SHAW 268:15
  God can s. being told   PRIE 240:1
  If she can s. it, I can   EPST 106:10

stand (*cont.*):

If you can't s. the heat	TRUM 299:7
If you can't s. the heat	VAUG 303:9
s. apart imaginatively	BECK 28:12
S. beside her and guide her	BERL 40:6
S. by your man	WYN 318:4
s. for being called a woman	WAUGH 306:11
S. me now and ever	JOYCE 158:12
S. on the highest pavement	ELIOT 103:16
S. up and take the war	KIPL 170:14
time to s. and stare	DAV 89:2
standards: Her imperial s. fly	AUDEN 19:5
standing: given gladly not to be s.	JOHN 156:6
S. among savage scenery	HOFF 142:9
stands: And s. about the woodland ride	
	HOUS 145:13
man who s. most alone	IBSEN 150:3
S. the Church clock	BROO 56:1
star: And earth is but a s.	FLEC 111:8
A s. is born	PARK 231:18
his separate s.	KIPL 174:13
Just head for that big s.	MILL 208:11
S. captains glow	FLEC 112:2
tall ship and a s.	MAS 203:14
When you wish upon a s.	WASH 305:7
you've *got* to come back a s.	SEYM 267:4
starboard: But we stuck to our s. triggers	
	ASQ 15:9
stardust: We are s.	MITC 211:6
stare: empty house of the s.	YEATS 318:6
no time to stand and s.	DAV 89:2
S., stare in the basin	AUDEN 16:13
Why did the people s.	YEATS 319:14
stared: stood and s.	HODG 141:14
stares: S. from every human face	AUDEN 17:6
stark: I think it will be s.	HAIL 130:14
starless: s. and bible-black	THOM 293:13
starlight: And s. lit my lonesomeness	
	HARDY 134:6
starlit: A s. or a moonlit dome distains	
	YEATS 323:9
starry: connection to the s. dynamo	GINS 125:1
'Neath is s. sky	GERS 123:10
stars: And night with different s.	SACK 256:12
And the seven s. go squawking	AUDEN 16:12
champagne and the s.	FITZ 110:14
eyes were blind with s.	HODG 141:14
Fast as the s. are slow	THOM 294:2
Have you heard it's in the s.	PORT 237:1
mistake each other for s.	ALLEN 4:4
moon! We have the s.	PROU 241:6
s. be blown about the sky	YEATS 322:3
s. grew bright in the winter	MAS 203:13
s. hung with humid nightblue	JOYCE 159:9
stars, what is the s.	O'CAS 222:9
s. where no human race	FROST 118:3
The sky was s. all over it	HODG 141:14
The s. are dead	AUDEN 20:11
The s. belong to everyone	DE SY 91:12

stars (*cont.*):

Where the fleet of s.	FLEC 112:2
with how splendid s.	FLEC 111:15
starship: voyages of the s. *Enterprise*	RODD 249:2
start: s. a scene or two	ELIOT 103:11
s. together and finish	BEEC 29:17
s. your own religion	HUBB 147:9
The end is where we s. from	ELIOT 102:5
started: I've s. so I'll finish	MAGN 199:1
Will be to arrive where we s.	ELIOT 102:4
starter: Few thought he was even a s.	ATTL 16:2
Your s. for ten	GASC 122:6
startle: come down and s.	AUDEN 20:13
starts: make certain it never s.	BRAD 52:5
starvation: s. that stalks	FOSD 116:4
starving: s. hysterical naked	GINS 125:1
state: Democracy is a S.	LENIN 184:15
little from a s. of things	FREUD 117:4
no such thing as the S.	AUDEN 17:12
pillar of the S.	SOLZ 280:4
reinforcement of the S.	CAMUS 63:2
S. is an instrument	STAL 283:4
s. is a state of Slavery	GILL 124:9
s. is or can be master	BEV 45:12
s. my case of which I'm	ANKA 6:11
While the S. exists	LENIN 185:1
Youth would be an ideal s.	ASQ 14:17
stately: S. as a galleon, I sail	GREN 129:4
s. homes of England	WOOLF 317:4
s. homos of England	CRISP 86:4
s. park and the fence	MAUG 204:12
S., plump Buck Mulligan	JOYCE 158:14
s. ships are twirled	HODG 142:1
The S. Homes of England	COW 85:7
statement: made my manic s.	LOW 191:13
perhaps the briefest s.	KAEL 160:5
s. is like a cheque drawn	POUND 237:16
The black s. of pistons	SPEN 281:16
statements: previous s. are inoperative	
	ZIEG 324:11
states: Nation of many sovereign S.	PAGE 228:10
slavery are mental s.	GAND 121:11
statesman: A s. is a politician who's	TRUM 299:8
A s. who is enamoured	BIER 46:15
did agree, he was a s.	LLOY 190:4
first requirement of a s.	ACH 1:6
gift to set a s. right	YEATS 318:5
s. is a politician	POMP 236:2
station: has ideas above her s.	RATT 243:6
Hurries down the concrete s.	BETJ 42:8
she leaves the s.	SPEN 281:16
walls of that antique s.	BEER 31:7
statistics: s. that some cause was	AUDEN 20:9
statuary: s. which no careful father	ANON 11:10
statue: Beauty she was s. cold	FLEC 112:1
s. has never been set up	SIB 275:1
s. inside every block	ORW 224:14
statues: disfigured the public s.	AUDEN 17:3
Ep's s. are junk	ANON 8:13

statutes (*cont.*):

s. on the terraces	KIPL 171:2
s. will be standing	LARK 178:13
towers and tombs and s.	FLEC 112:1

status: relegation to the s.   CAIR 61:4

    restored the s. quo   SQUI 283:3

stay: behind my tremulous s.   HARDY 134:1

If we want things to s.	LAMP 178:1
it so it will s. split	CHAN 66:12
s. as they were projected	BOWEN 51:2
S. there	PRÉV 239:14
will not s. in place	ELIOT 101:9
Yet will not s.	GRAV 128:9

stay-at-home: Sweet S., sweet Well-content
     DAV 89:1

stayed: [i.e. have s.]   JAC 152:3

stays: Literature is news that S. news
     POUND 237:18

    that prays together s.   SCAL 264:1

steaks: smell of s. in passageways   ELIOT 103:13

steal: if you s. from many   MIZN 212:1

imitate; mature poets s.	ELIOT 104:5
s. bread	FRAN 116:6
s. more than a hundred	PUZO 241:9
s. other people's ideas	TOM 298:2

stealin': s. dey gits you in jail   O'NEI 223:6

steam: Shovelling white s. over   AUDEN 19:15

steamer: s. breaking from the bay   AUDEN 19:12

    This little s., like all   PRIE 239:17

steamers: Daily the s. sidle up to meet
     AUDEN 19:10

going to, all you Big S.	KIPL 171:1
Great s., white and gold	KIPL 172:3

steel: S. chambers, late the pyres   HARDY 134:4

s. in a velvet glove	WOOL 317:15
stone, s., stone	ELIOT 104:9
wounded surgeon plies the s.	ELIOT 101:15

steeple: Each in his lone religious s.   CAMP 62:5

steeples: In s. far and near   HOUS 146:3

s. of Fermanagh and Tyrone	CHUR 73:11
Talk about the pews and s.	CHES 70:9

steer: ugly 'ead it's time to s.   ALL 5:6

Stein: I don't like the family S.   ANON 8:13

    S.'s prose-song is a cold   LEWIS 187:8

Steinbeck: Faulkner, and S.   ALGR 3:16

Stellenbosh: For fear o' S.   KIPL 170:13

stench: A s. in the ear   BIER 46:22

stenographers: then went off to become a s.
     CHES 69:7

step: Light of s. and heart was she   DE L 90:13

one small s. for a man	ARMS 13:10
s. is short from the Sublime	GRAH 127:7
s. on my Blue Suede Shoes	PERK 233:3

step-parents: Parents — especially s.   POW 239:5

steps: s. spritely in the incomparable
     SHAW 274:11

sterling: And I myself a s. lad   HOUS 146:16

sterner: rather speak of s. days   CHUR 72:13

Stettin: S. in the Baltic to Trieste   CHUR 73:3

stewed: Seem far too familiar. Get s.   LARK 179:14

stick: big s.   ROOS 251:8

phrases s. in the throat	RUSS 256:4
s. more close than a brother	KIPL 173:10
s. with an 'orse's 'ead	EDGAR 98:3
tattered coat upon a s.	YEATS 321:6
we going to make it s.	MACG 195:4

sticks: S. nix hick pix   ANON 11:3

sticky: himself in a rather s. voice   MILNE 210:9

stiff: A woman can be proud and s.   YEATS 323:8

    stain the s. dishonoured   ELIOT 102:13

stiffen: before it has had time to s.   ORW 224:15

stigma: Any s., as the old saying   GUED 130:1

still: Clay lies s., but blood's   HOUS 145:14

If you s. have to ask	ARMS 13:9
S. falls the Rain	SITW 276:6
s. it is not we	CHES 70:14
s. point of the turning	ELIOT 101:8

stiller: s. than ever on orchard   DRIN 95:17

stillness: A s. which characterizes   BELL 35:13

s. in the midst of chaos	BELL 35:13
that s. ultimately best	CRANE 85:12

stilly: planned her, s. couches she   HARDY 134:4

stimulant: s. handy in case I see   FIEL 109:5

stimulate: s. the phagocytes   SHAW 268:20

sting: O Death, where is thy s.   ROSS 253:6

    s. like a bee   ALI 4:1

sting-a-ling-a-ling: O Death, where is thy s.
     ANON 10:8

stink: s. of the damned dead niggers   ASQ 15:9

stinker: Outrageous S.   KIPL 175:2

stirred: forest something s.   SIMP 275:10

    Shaken and not s.   FLEM 112:8

stirrup-pump: Idle to hope that the simple s.
     REED 245:3

stirs: Will that s. and urges   HARDY 134:5

stitching: s. and unstitching has   YEATS 319:7

St James: The ladies of S.'s   DOBS 92:15

St Louis: girls from S. hasn't learned   STEIN 284:3

    S. team we have Who's   ABB 1:1

stocking: In olden days a glimpse of s.   PORT 236:9

s. over the municipal fireplace	SMITH 276:14
your silk s.'s hanging	SELL 266:6

stolen: They have s. his wits away   DE L 90:10

stolid: S. and stunned, a brother   MARK 201:3

stomach: burst s. like a cave   DOUG 93:8

I have no s. for such meat	DOBS 92:13
sensation is the pit of the s.	HOUS 145:9
s. is nothing if not conservative	BUTL 59:16

stomachs: used to march on their s.   SELL 266:11

stone: bomb them back into the S.   LEMAY 184:10

Can make a s. of the heart	YEATS 320:5
Like a rolling s.	DYLAN 97:7
massive sandal set on s.	MILL 208:2
Romancing the s.	THOM 292:8
s. and let them not spill	MACN 198:8
S., bronze, stone	ELIOT 104:9
s. unturned to see	SHAR 267:9

stone (*cont.*):

take our hearts o' s.	O'CAS 222:10
take the s. from stone	ELIOT 102:10
Turn but a s., and start	THOM 296:13
written of me on my s.	FROST 119:10

stones: house is built of s. POIN 236:1

s. and every blooming	KAV 161:12
s. kissed by the English	OWEN 228:3

stony: more s. than a shore WILL 312:12

stood: I s. and stared HODG 141:14

s. [i.e. have stayed] JAC 152:3

stop: again we s. the mighty ANON 10:9

effective if you can s.	ATTL 16:9
s. because you are afraid	NANS 217:8
s. everyone from doing	HERB 139:5
S.-look-and-listen	ANON 11:4
S. me and buy one	RODD 249:1
S. the world, I want to get off	NEWL 219:4
s. to rake the leaves away	FROST 118:12

stopper: Pull out the s. LERN 185:20

stops: says 'The buck s. here' TRUM 299:12

storage: A library is thought in cold s. SAM 259:4

store: s. we sell hope REVS 246:1

stories: love s. in all literature PARK 230:8

S., like whiskey, must O'FAO 222:17

stork: Can you tell S. from butter ANON 7:12

throwing rocks at the s. BREC 52:16

storm: sleek-barrelled swell before s. KIPL 170:8

story: And were an epitaph to be my s.

FROST 119:10

Ere their s. die	HARDY 133:15
Every picture tells a s.	ANON 7:21
he means to write one s.	BARR 25:14
It's our *own* s. *exactly*	THUR 297:12
Marks the place where a s.	ELIOT 102:2
newspaper touches a s.	MAIL 199:7
novel tells a s.	FORS 114:7
s. for which the world	DOYLE 94:9
s. is ephemeral and doomed	FAUL 107:11

stout: who was short and s. CHES 70:11

stove: Her s., and lays out food ELIOT 105:5

ice on a hot s. the poem	FROST 118:2
s. instead of the oven	JENK 154:8

stowed: S. away in a Montreal lumber BUTL 60:6

St Pancras: Towers of S. Station BEEC 30:6

St Paul's: Say I am designing S. BENT 39:8

Strabismus: Dr S. MORT 214:9

strafe: *Gott s. England!* FUNKE 120:9

straight: nothing ever ran quite s. GALS 121:6

s. one day at the Sorbonne	STEV 285:13
The crooked be made s.	ELIOT 101:19

strain: Let the train take the s. ANON 9:12

Words s. ELIOT 101:9

Strand: Let's all go down the S. CAST 64:11

S. with my gloves	HARG 135:2
You're never alone with a S.	MAY 206:1

strange: knowest of no s. continent DAV 89:1

s. dark interludes	O'NEI 223:15
'S. friend,' I said	OWEN 228:6

strange (*cont.*):

s. interlude in which we O'NEI 223:14

strangeness: confound s. with mystery

DOYLE 95:11

stranger: From the wiles of the s. NASH 218:6

I, a s. and afraid	HOUS 145:4
Look, s., at this island now	AUDEN 19:6
never love a s.	BENS 39:5
S., unless with bedroom eyes	AUDEN 16:10
You may see a s.	HAMM 132:2

strangers: depended on the kindness of s.

WILL 312:10

Economics and art are s. CATH 64:13

strangling: Than s. in a string HOUS 145:15

Strasser: Major S. has been shot EPST 106:12

straw: Headpiece filled with s. Alas ELIOT 103:3

Of the s. for a bedding BELL 34:9

strawberry: S. fields forever LENN 185:13

strayed: shabby curate who has s. AUDEN 18:12

stream: dead fish swim with the s. MUGG 215:5

have their S. and Pond	BROO 55:3
long-legged fly upon the s.	YEATS 320:2
mountain, ford ev'ry s.	HAMM 131:9
old mill by the s.	ARMS 13:7

street: at the corner of the s. GAY 122:7

fighting in the s.	JAGG 152:5
it in the s. and frighten	CAMP 61:11
out my life talking at s.	VANZ 303:7
Picasso coming down the s.	CHUR 73:7
place for s. fighting man	JAGG 152:5
shop and s. I gazed	YEATS 323:11
To the sunny side of the s.	FIEL 108:11
worth two in the s.	WEST 309:1
you do it in the s.	SCOR 265:4

street-bred: s. people that vapour KIPL 170:2

streets: children died in the s. AUDEN 17:1

fields and in the s.	CHUR 74:6
mean s. a man must go	CHAN 66:9
s. at dawn looking	GINS 125:1
S. FLOODED	BENC 35:15
s. of a hundred cities	HOOV 143:7
s. on a Sunday morning	BEHAN 32:3
s. that no longer exist	FENT 108:3
s. where the great men	FLEC 112:1

strength: S. through joy LEY 188:2

that country's unaided s.	STAL 283:6
together with our united s.	CHUR 74:5
triumphant conviction of s.	CONR 82:2

strenuous: doctrine of the s. life ROOS 251:10

stretched: was things which he s. TWAIN 300:4

striding: Your shadow at morning s. ELIOT 104:12

strife: In place of s. CAST 64:10

strike: child take care that you s. SHAW 272:3

s. against the public safety	COOL 82:11
when in doubt, s. it out	TWAIN 301:17

strikes: The Empire's back LUCAS 192:9

string: egg-shell, a bit of s. WELLS 308:2

Than strangling in a s.	HOUS 145:15
Was chewing little bits of S.	BELL 32:19

strings: whisper music on those s.   ELIOT 105:10
striped: gaiety is a s. shroud   THOM 294:8
striving: And a s. evermore for these   GREN 129:5
stroke: paragraphing is to s. a platitude

          MARQ 202:3
  The s. of midnight ceases   HOUS 145:10
strong: Is a s. brown god   ELIOT 101:10
  only the S. shall thrive   SERV 266:17
  S. brother in God and last   BELL 34:7
  S. gongs groaning   CHES 70:6
  s. people that they can   BONH 49:4
  those who think they are s.   BID 46:3
  you realise how s. she   REAG 244:4
stronger: thing s. than all the armies   ANON 11:7
  Women are s. than men   STEP 285:2
strongest: s. man in the world   IBSEN 150:3
struck: Certain women should be s.   COW 85:4
structure: s. of a play is always   MILL 208:10
  s. of the ordinary British   CHUR 75:10
struggle: burden of a long twilight s.   KENN 163:12
  But today the s.   AUDEN 20:10
  ineligible for the s. of life   CONN 80:12
  nose needs a constant s.   ORW 226:5
  s. against the inclinations   ZIN 324:12
  s. between the artist man   SHAW 270:17
  s. everybody is engaged   BAR 27:10
  s. itself towards the heights   CAMUS 63:4
  would carry on the s.   CHUR 74:6
struts: He s. sitting down   DYKS 97:2
stuck: all s. over   HEM 138:13
  And they s. it   NIXON 220:2
student: S. of our sweet English tongue

          FLEC 112:7
  s. wears coloured socks   BRAT 52:15
studio: [the RKO s.]   WELL 307:13
studiously: We have stood apart, s. neutral

          WILS 314:6
study: periphrastic s. in a worn-out   ELIOT 101:12
  proper s. of mankind   HUXL 148:11
stuff: Ale, man, ale's the s. to drink   HOUS 146:15
  short to s. a mushroom   CONR 82:3
  s. of which tyrants   BEAV 28:11
  The s. of life to knit me   HOUS 146:9
stuffed: We are the s. men   ELIOT 103:3
stuffy: Not huffy, or s., not tiny   HERB 139:9
stumbles: With an old horse that s.   HARDY 133:15
stunt: just another amusing s.   READ 244:2
stupendous: hotel offers s. revelations   HOFF 142:9
stupid: always pretend to be more s.   STARK 283:9
  be s. enough to want it   CHES 71:10
  s. man is doing something   SHAW 268:8
  s. neither forgive   SZASZ 290:3
  unless you are also s.   SHAW 272:16
  Very interesting . . . but s.   ROWAN 253:13
stupidity: idleness and impotent s.   BLUNT 48:2
  ignorance and conscientious s.   KING 167:2
stupor: just dozed off into a s.   BENC 36:2
style: He has no real s.   PIC 234:6

style (cont.):
  particularly high-class s.   WAUGH 306:9
  this s. the Mandarin style   CONN 80:11
  who was not my s.   PROU 240:10
suavity: such deceitfulness and s.   ELIOT 102:12
sub: Sighted s., sank same   MASON 204:5
subject: grant the artist his s.   JAMES 153:6
  I should be a sad s.   ATTL 16:3
  itself and not in its s.   SANT 260:16
  My s. is War, and the pity   OWEN 227:12
  No s. for immortal verse   DAY-L 89:8
subjectification: s. of nature   LANG 178:8
subjects: from the s. of government   WILS 314:9
sublime: audience yelled 'You're s.   HARG 135:3
  Of poetry; to maintain 'the s.'   POUND 238:5
  ridiculous, the s.   MAHON 199:4
  Symphony is the most s. noise   FORS 114:12
  The step is short from the S.   GRAH 127:7
submit: destructive element s.   CONR 81:14
subsidized: Divinely s. to provoke   FRY 119:17
substitute: becomes a s. for reading   BURG 58:2
  can be no s. for victory   MAC 193:4
  There is no s. for talent   HUXL 149:7
substitutes: Ours is the age of s.   BENT 39:16
subtle: s. but he is not malicious   EINS 99:5
subtleties: s. of the American joke   TWAIN 301:5
  subtlety: hindrance to s. of intellect   MORL 213:11
suburban: urban and s. man   MCL 196:12
suburbs: s. on summer evenings   AUDEN 20:10
subversion: s. or disloyalty   HELL 137:9
subversive: Whatever is funny is s.   ORW 224:17
succeed: enough to s.   VIDAL 304:2
  How to s. in business   MEAD 206:5
  rest of us could not s.   TWAIN 300:18
  we s. in being defeated   HELL 137:7
succeeds: Whenever a friend s.   VIDAL 304:6
success: bitch-goddess s   JAMES 153:12
  can guarantee s. in war   CHUR 76:6
  confidence; then s. is sure   TWAIN 302:4
  For an actress to be a s.   BARR 26:17
  his s. is disgraceful   MENC 206:9
  If A is a s. in life   EINS 99:9
  interested in, and yours is S.   BARR 26:9
  s. and only one a failure   SAM 259:5
  S. is relative   ELIOT 101:17
  s. spoils people by making   MAUG 205:14
  Sweet smell of s.   LEHM 184:2
  there's no s. like failure   DYLAN 97:8
successful: clever and the s.   GREE 128:12
  most s. adaptation   JUNG 160:3
  s. writer or picture-painter   LEWIS 187:13
Süchtigkeit: Form von S. ist von übel   JUNG 159:16
sucker: Never give a s. an even break   FIEL 109:2
sucking: s. at the bung   MAS 203:3
sudden: I said to Dawn: Be s.—to Eve   THOM 295:6
  muttered Ethel this is so s.   ASHF 14:12
  S. the rain of gold   DAY-L 89:4
suddenly: For, s., I saw you there   GERS 123:6
Sudeten: problem of the S. Germans   HITL 141:9

Sudetenland: [the S.] HITL 141:8
suet-pudding: prose-song is a cold, black s.
LEWIS 187:8
Suez: somewheres east of S. KIPL 169:8
S. Canal was flowing through EDEN 98:2
suffer: be prepared to s. for it BENN 38:15
he did not s. them PEAR 232:12
sufferer: unites it with the human s.
JOYCE 158:11
suffering: About s. they were never wrong
AUDEN 17:8
If he sees s., privation BEVAN 44:11
pity for the s. of mankind RUSS 254:13
s. ennobles the character MAUG 205:7
s. from halitosis ICKES 150:8
s. from the particular JER 155:9
sufferings: constant in human s. JOYCE 158:11
suffice: And would s. FROST 118:10
O when may it s. YEATS 320:5
sufficient: s. to keep him straight LLOY 189:11
suffragettes: The s. were triumphant BRAH 52:8
sugared: s. about by the old men KIPL 170:13
suggestive: An idea, to be s. JAMES 153:19
suicide: human race commit s. ADAMS 2:13
It is not: it is s. MACD 194:14
It is s. to be abroad BECK 28:13
longest s. note in history KAUF 161:10
s. 25 years after his death BEAV 28:10
suicides: downward lay the huddled s.
PLOM 235:16
suitable: A s. case for treatment MERC 207:5
suitor: think that you are Ann's s. SHAW 270:20
sukebind: when the s. hangs heavy GIBB 123:11
sullen: s., untamed and intractable ELIOT 101:10
The silent s. peoples KIPL 175:9
sulphur: Puffed its s. to the sunset BETJ 43:8
sum: s. of things for pay HOUS 145:7
To s. up STOP 287:6
Sumatra: with the giant rat of S. DOYLE 94:9
summer: fulness o' s. GIBB 123:11
I only know that s. sang in me MILL 208:1
s. afternoon JAMES 152:11
S. set lip to earth's bosom THOM 294:13
s.'s here and the time JAGG 152:5
s. sustained peacefully DAY-L 89:7
S. time an' the livin' is easy HEYW 140:7
The long hot s. RAV 243:10
The long s. FAUL 107:9
'Tis S. Time on Bredon KING 167:12
summertime: In s. on Bredon HOUS 146:3
sumpshous: s. spot all done up ASHF 14:7
sums: He was extremely fond of s. BELL 33:10
sun: And I will sing of the s. POUND 238:15
before you let the s. THOM 293:14
Born of the s. they travelled SPEN 281:15
breaks where no s. shines THOM 293:5
burnish'd by Aldershot s. BETJ 43:9
climbed towards the s. CHES 71:3

sun (cont.):
Courts of the s. CHES 70:5
flew between me and the s. BLUN 47:14
For Famagusta and the hidden s. FLEC 112:3
Go out in the midday s. COW 84:13
Laughed in the s. BROO 54:8
Let the hot s. AUDEN 19:5
Mother, give me the s. IBSEN 150:4
Move him into the s. OWEN 228:1
our place in the s. WILH 311:9
Scratchin' in the s. AYRES 21:16
s. and in the morning BINY 47:5
s. enough for lazing upon BETJ 42:9
s. goes down with a flaming BOND 49:2
s. has gone SMITH 278:14
s. not shining and a look CHAN 66:10
s. was shining everywhere GERS 123:6
swollen magpie in a fitful s. POUND 238:17
The golden apples of the s. YEATS 322:12
The kind old s. will know OWEN 228:1
The s. also rises HEM 138:12
The s. has got his hat BUTL 58:11
The s. like a Bishop's bottom ASQ 15:9
Under the s. HOUS 146:13
Wait till the s. shines STER 285:5
zooming about the S. at 60,000 FULL 120:5
sunbeam: Jesus wants me for a s. TALB 290:10
sunbeams: O what made fatuous s. toil
OWEN 228:2
Sunday: For this is S. morning MACN 198:6
Here of a S. morning HOUS 146:3
Never on S. DASS 88:10
off the streets on a S. BEHAN 32:3
on a rainy S. afternoon ERTZ 106:13
S., bloody Sunday GILL 124:11
S. is the sound of Harold GILL 124:10
S. that goes FLEC 111:8
The feeling of S. RHYS 246:7
sundial: I am a s., and I make a botch BELL 34:17
sundown: eldritch light of s. DAY-L 89:4
sung: And some are s. THOM 296:3
sunlight: keep that s. out of sight BETJ 42:9
The s. on the garden MACN 197:9
weave the s. in your hair ELIOT 103:16
sunlit: s. uplands CHUR 74:7
sunny: meet again some s. day PARK 231:20
To the s. side of the street FIEL 108:11
sunrise: Had seen their s. pass CHES 68:8
sunset: Puffed its sulphur to the s. BETJ 43:8
Red sails in the s. KENN 162:15
sunsets: I have a horror of s. PROU 241:2
Or Autumn s. exquisitely dying HUXL 148:19
sunshine: grievance and a ray of s. WOD 315:10
into adventure and s. FORS 114:11
sup: miseries, a bite and s. HEAN 136:12
superficial: s. layer of the unconscious
JUNG 160:4
superior: embarrass the s. SHAW 272:1
S. people never make long MOORE 213:4

superior (*cont.*):
s. persons can remain superior ORW 225:12
Superman: It's a plane! It's S. ANON 7:23
supermarionettes: are men, the men are s.
BENT 39:15
supernatural: s. source of evil is not CONR 82:1
superstition: main source of s. RUSS 256:2
s. to enslave a philosophy INGE 151:4
supplication: His s. to the rose FLEC 111:11
supply: that the s. is not tainted SCOTT 265:5
support: depend on the s. of Paul SHAW 269:1
help and s. of the woman EDW 98:11
no invisible means of s. BUCH 57:6
without visible means of s. BIER 46:25
supportable: s. with equanimity by most
BUTL 60:8
supported: enforce a law not s. HUMP 148:2
suppose: round in a ring and s. FROST 119:11
S. everybody cared enough BUCH 57:8
supposed: they are s. to do anyway TRUM 299:10
supreme: I mean the s. creation BART 27:5
Personality is the s. realization JUNG 160:3
Poetry is the s. fiction STEV 285:6
reverence can you have for a S. HELL 137:6
sure: Make ye s. to each his own KIPL 174:3
many ignorant men are s. DARR 88:8
wanted to make s. he was dead GOLD 126:11
What nobody is s. about BELL 33:18
surer: There's nothing s. KAHN 161:3
surest: s. way to make a monkey BENC 36:6
surge: s. and thunder of the Odyssey LANG 178:5
surgeon: The wounded s. plies the steel
ELIOT 101:15
surprise: Life is a great s. NAB 217:2
Our chief weapon is s. CHAP 67:10
The sound of s. BALL 24:5
surprised: Don't be s. HEAN 136:13
one is and no one is s. STARK 283:9
she wouldn't be at all s. PARK 231:10
s. to be taken at his word DE G 90:5
surrealist: theatre of the s. BENT 39:15
surrender: me the man who will s. BARB 24:15
we shall never s. CHUR 74:6
surroundings: s. and if I do not preserve
ORT 224:1
survival: merely a s. of the fittest ROCK 248:13
victory, there is no s. CHUR 74:4
survive: Dare hope to s. HUXL 148:18
s. for two thousand million JEANS 154:5
survives: Education is what s. when SKIN 276:12
makes nothing happen: it s. AUDEN 17:4
survivors: man's dying is more the s.'
MANN 200:6
susceptible: peculiarly s. to calves HUXL 149:8
suspect: no matter how s. VIDAL 304:3
suspects: Round up the usual s. EPST 106:12
suspend: lack of ability to s. HEM 138:6
suspended: shoulders held the sky s. HOUS 145:7
s. in favour of England SHAW 269:12

suspenders: must *not* forget the s. KIPL 171:8
suspicion: Democracy is the recurrent s.
WHITE 310:1
Sussex: And the story of S. told BELL 35:1
may bury my body in S. BENÉT 36:17
shall the S. songs be sung BELL 35:1
Yea, S. by the sea KIPL 170:10
su-superior: Don't be sucked in by the s.
LAWR 181:14
sutlers: The sapient s. of the Lord ELIOT 102:15
swagman: s. camped by a billabong PAT 232:5
swallow: The speed of a s., the grace BETJ 43:9
swan: black s. as death came AUDEN 20:12
s.-bosomed SITW 276:5
s. drifts upon a darkening YEATS 323:7
Swann: was no more talk of S. PROU 240:9
swans: ships sail like s. asleep FLEC 112:3
swarm: S. over, Death BETJ 42:2
swaying: The s. sound of the sea AUDEN 19:6
swear: And now the farmers s. KING 167:12
s. by the slain SASS 263:4
when very angry, s. TWAIN 301:16
swears: Money doesn't talk, it s. DYLAN 97:6
swear-word: A s. in a rustic slum BEER 30:14
sweat: s. of its laborers EIS 100:2
toil, tears and s. CHUR 74:3
sweating: Quietly s. palm to palm HUXL 149:2
Swedenborg: Jefferies to S. and Oscar Wilde
BARB 24:15
Sweeney: S. to Mrs Porter in the spring
ELIOT 105:4
sweeps: It beats as it s. as it cleans PAG 229:1
sweet: At all the sadness in the s. THOM 294:11
dead thing that smells s. THOM 294:4
Seem to murmur s. and low ARMS 13:7
S. smell of success LEHM 184:2
S. Stay-at-Home, sweet DAV 89:1
S. to ride forth at evening FLEC 111:9
sweetest: s. way to me is a ship's KIPL 170:4
To the s. girl I know JUDGE 159:13
sweetness: after the s. of confession FIRB 109:14
succeed where s. and light FORS 114:9
The s. in the sad THOM 294:11
sweets: parliamentarian is a bag of boiled s.
CRIT 86:6
sweet-shop: pressed to a s. window YEATS 322:10
swell: deep sea s. ELIOT 105:8
his best; quite a s. EDGAR 98:3
To s. a progress, start ELIOT 103:11
What a s. party this PORT 237:1
Swift: S. has sailed into his rest YEATS 323:14
s. things for swiftness THOM 295:7
swim: Mother may I go out to s. DE L 91:8
swimmers: s. into cleanness leaping BROO 54:10
swimming: S. from tree to tree LOW 192:1
swindles: simple as all truly great s. HENRY 139:2
swine: could be a manoeuvring s. MCC 194:3
swines: rotten s. MILL 209:4

swing: If it ain't got that s.   MILLS 209:10
  s. for it   KING 167:11
swinger: than be a s. of birches   FROST 118:9
swinging: A boutique, and a s. hot spot
                                        MITC 211:5
  my ears yielding like s. doors   DOUG 93:9
  s. after the music had   HELP 138:1
swings: roundabouts we pulls up on the s.
                                        CHAL 65:10
swirling: s. about in a human cesspit   AND 6:8
Swiss: A dashing S. officer   RUSS 256:4
  deposit in my name at a S.   ALLEN 4:11
  way a S. waiter talks   CHAN 66:12
Switzerland: S. is a small, steep country
                                        HEM 138:13
  S. they had brotherly love   WELL 307:14
swoons: S. to a waltz, I take her hand HUXL 149:2
sword: believed he had a s. upstairs   YEATS 319:5
  I gave them a s.   NIXON 220:2
  Of honour and the s.   CHES 70:7
  shall never sheath the s.   ASQ 14:19
  that never stained thy S.   HOPE 144:3
sword-pen: against this I raise my s.   BURG 57:15
swords: are either dreams or s.   LOW 190:4
  saw guns and sharp s.   DYLAN 97:5
swore: S. not at all   BENT 39:13
swots: although you hav various s.   WILL 311:10
syllogism: The conclusion of your s.   O'BR 222:3
symbol: It is a s. of Irish art   JOYCE 158:16
sympathize: s. with people's pains   HUXL 149:3
sympathy: boys a little tea and s.   AND 6:6
  need of your God-damned s.   WOOL 317:14
  you get messages of s.   AYCK 21:7
symphony: drastically cutting his A flat s.
                                        BEEC 30:6
  Fancy a s. by Wordsworth   BUTL 59:18
  S. is the most sublime   FORS 114:12
synthesis: s. of hyacinths and biscuits SAND 259:8
system: His divine s. of creation   HELL 137:6
  Mendacity is a s.   WILL 312:6
  somewhere in the solar s.   FULL 120:5
  wholly alter our American s.   HOOV 143:7
systematic: s. organization of hatreds ADAMS 2:7

T

t: The t is silent   ASQ 15:4
ta: Painting is saying "T." to God   SPEN 281:10
table: his victuals from the t.   CHUR 74:2
  I'll sit at the t.   HUGH 147:13
  patient etherized upon a t.   ELIOT 103:6
tact: t. dans l'audace c'est   COCT 78:3
tactful: t. in audacity is knowing   COCT 78:3
tail: At such a little t. behind   BELL 32:17
  t. must wag the dog   KIPL 170:1
  thy t. hangs down behind   KIPL 171:7

tailor: lived a t. in Gloucester   POTT 237:4
tails: Brushin' off my t.   BERL 40:11
take: God will t. care   SHAW 269:8
  T. away that pudding   CHUR 76:12
  t. everything away from   SOLZ 280:2
  t. from seventy springs   HOUS 145:13
  T. me back to dear old Blighty   MILLS 209:9
  T. me out to the ball game   NORW 221:7
  T. me to your leader   ANON 11:5
  T. the money and run   ALLEN 4:14
  they t. themselves lightly   CHES 70:4
  they t. you in the morning   BALD 22:11
  Will someone t. me to a pub   CHES 70:15
  You can't t. it with you   HART 135:13
taken: quite surprised to be t.   DE G 90:5
  right to be t. seriously   HUMP 148:3
  t. charge of the asylum   ROWL 254:3
  t. more out of alcohol   CHUR 72:7
takes: T. two to tango   HOFF 142:8
taking: t. things for granted   HUXL 149:14
  way of t. life   FROST 119:6
talcum: A bit of t.   NASH 217:14
tale: any t. we happen to enact   PRIT 240:4
  artist. Trust the t.   LAWR 182:2
  I should have had a t.   SCOTT 265:10
  t. that I heard told   HOUS 147:1
  This most tremendous t. of all   BETJ 42:5
talent: A t. to amuse   COW 84:8
  gilded tomb of a mediocre t.   SMITH 278:12
  greatest concentration of t.   KENN 163:2
  his one really notable t.   MENC 206:8
  I had no t. for writing   BENC 36:13
  substitute for t.   HUXL 149:7
  t. instantly recognizes   DOYLE 95:14
  t. to see clearly what   AUDEN 18:11
  what it must and the t.   BAR 25:1
talents: t. and our expectations   DE B 89:10
tales: runic t. to sigh or sing   FLEC 111:16
  T., marvellous tales   FLEC 111:7
talk: And the Cabots t. only to God   BOSS 50:3
  And the land t. slid north   KIPL 169:11
  by men who t. fluently   HOGB 142:10
  Careless t. costs lives   ANON 7:13
  come and t. to the plants   CHAR 68:1
  If you t. to God, you   SZASZ 290:5
  interviewing people who can't t.   ZAPPA 324:9
  I want to t. like a lady   SHAW 273:13
  Money doesn't t., it swears   DYLAN 97:6
  much my Ministers t.   THAT 291:11
  nor good t. necessarily   KIPL 175:5
  possible to t. to the unborn   BARZ 27:11
  solemn t. of contemplation   KAV 161:12
  t. about capitalism   BAR 27:10
  T. about the pews and steeples   CHES 70:9
  t. it over with Our Lord   JOHN 155:18
  t. of Swann at the Verdurins'   PROU 240:9
  t. on 'Sex and Civics'   BETJ 42:7
  t. well but not too wisely   MAUG 205:16

talk (*cont.*):
t. with crowds and keep	KIPL 173:9
t. with the German Chancellor	CHAM 66:5
To t. about the rest of us	ANON 11:8
We have ways of making men t.	YOUNG 324:6

talked: listen when his mate t. WICK 311:2

talkers: thousand t. whose tongues DYLAN 97:5

talking: I find I'm t. to myself BARN 25:9
more money writing or t.	AUDEN 18:6
nation t. to itself	MILL 208:12
never know what we are t.	RUSS 255:11
soon leaves off t.	BUTL 59:8
T. of Michelangelo	ELIOT 103:7
t. to you by telephone	NIXON 220:5
until I've finished t.	ZAN 324:7
was myself t. to myself	BENC 36:2

talks: A person who t. when you BIER 46:12
She only t. about her hair THOM 296:7

tall: neat and adequately t. CHES 70:16
short and the t.	HUGH 147:11
T. as a crane	SITW 276:1
t. ship and a star to steer	MAS 203:14
this the clay grew t.	OWEN 228:2

Tallulah: T. [Bankhead] is always skating
CAMP 61:12

tambourine: Mr T. Man, play a song DYLAN 97:10

tamed: For t. and shabby tigers HODG 142:2

tames: one t. the work of art SONT 280:9

tamper: Would never want to t. AUDEN 17:4

tangled: t. web do parents weave NASH 217:11

tango: Takes two to t. HOFF 142:8

tank: T. come down the stalls SASS 263:1

Tanqueray: The Second Mrs T. BELL 33:4

tanstaafl: Oh, "t.". Means HEIN 137:2

tapers: When she lit her glimmering t.
THOM 295:9

tar: wine that tasted of the t. BELL 34:9

tariff: competitive t. for revenue HOOV 143:7

tarnished: neither t. nor afraid CHAN 66:9

tart: t. who has finally married BAXT 28:1

tarts: by the action of two t. MACM 196:16

Tarzan: Me T., you Jane WEIS 307:8

task: President's hardest t. JOHN 156:14
t. in life is to give birth	FROMM 117:9
There is but one t. for all	KIPL 170:15

taste: A person of low t. BIER 46:18
bouquet is better than the t.	POTT 237:11
common sense and good t.	SHAW 268:10
Ghastly good t., or a depressing	BETJ 43:2
Good t. and humour	MUGG 215:6
individuality have no t.	BENN 38:8
invariably have very bad t.	ORTON 224:8
taste is better than bad t.	BENN 38:8
together by a sense of t.	BALL 24:4

tasted: From what I've t. of desire FROST 118:10

tastes: t. may not be the same SHAW 271:15

tatter: t. in its mortal dress YEATS 321:6

tattered: A t. coat upon a stick, unless
YEATS 321:6

tavern: has merely opened a t. DOUG 93:13

taverns: t. while the tempest hurled HOUS 144:13

tax: [t.] on the last slice HEAL 136:7

taxes: Death and t. and childbirth MITC 211:7

taxi: An empty t. arrived CHUR 72:6
Like a t. throbbing waiting	ELIOT 105:5
you can't leave in a t.	KALM 161:5

taxi-cab: t. with both doors open HUGH 147:10

taxis: are good at getting t. WHIT 310:14

taxpayer: t. is to shoulder the losses SNOW 279:8

tay: t. and stuff fit only MAS 203:2

Tchaikovsky: tell T. the news BERRY 41:9

tea: ain't going to be no t. KATH 200:7
I makes t. I makes tea	JOYCE 158:17
little t. and sympathy	AND 6:6
Lunch, and T.	BELL 33:2
T., although an Oriental	CHES 69:4
t. for two and two	CAES 60:16
t. in which I had soaked	PROU 240:8
t. is brought at five o'clock	MONRO 212:4
t.'s out of the way	REED 245:4
there honey still for t.	BROO 56:1
there no Latin word for T.	BELL 34:6
this is coffee, I want t.	ARM 13:6

teabag: woman is like a t. REAG 244:4

tea-cakes: With afternoon t. and scones
BETJ 43:1

teach: humility as well as t. SHAW 273:20
T. the free man how to praise	AUDEN 17:7
t. there are approximately	SELL 266:3
T. us to care and not to care	ELIOT 100:12
t. you to be a gentleman	SHAW 270:19

teaches: From all that terror t. CHES 70:7
He who cannot, t. SHAW 271:21

tea-cup: And the crack in the t. opens
AUDEN 16:13

team: Is my t. ploughing HOUS 146:6

tears: And keep your t. PUDN 241:7
mist of t.	THOM 295:2
No t. in the writer	FROST 118:1
now am full of t.	YEATS 321:13
t. and sweat	CHUR 74:3
t. on a soundless-clapping	THOM 296:1
t. would come down to me	KIPL 172:7
To hazards whence no t.	HARDY 134:7
wind but t. are in my eyes	MAS 204:2

tease: t. in the High Pyrenees BELL 34:9

tea-shops: Emperor in the low-class t.
BRAM 52:10

teatime: The typist home at t. ELIOT 105:5

tea-tray: colour that of a t. painter BLUNT 48:2

Tebbit: [Norman T.] FOOT 113:5

Technik: *Diskussion mit Hanna!—über T.*
FRIS 117:7

Vorsprung durch T. ANON 11:18

techniques: machines or of elaborate t.
RUTH 256:5

technology: beyond the province of t. POPP 236:7

technology (*cont.*):

Discussion with Hanna—about t.	FRIS 117:7
Progress through t.	ANON 11:18
t. dons from Cambridge	AMIS 5:13
t. with the enthusiasm	LEVIN 186:17
tedding: And the t. and the spreading	BELL 34:9
teenie: Itsy bitsy t. weenie	VANCE 303:4
teeth: about him is his front t.	RUNY 254:8
I'd looked after me t.	AYRES 21:15
old bitch gone in the t.	POUND 238:9
People can clean their t.	JENK 154:8
shark has pretty t.	BREC 52:18
that women have fewer t.	RUSS 255:8
untying with the t.	BIER 46:11
teetotaller: I'm only a beer t.	SHAW 268:14
t. and often with vegetarian	ORW 225:16
telegram: t. to my wife in London	CHES 68:6
telegrams: life of t. and anger	FORS 115:2
telephone: historic t. call ever made	NIXON 220:5
television: are no plain women on t.	FORD 113:6
junior t. producers	AMIS 5:13
radio and t.	SARR 261:5
see bad t. for nothing	GOLD 126:12
sentences: 'What's on t.?'	ACE 1:5
T. has brought back murder	HITC 141:4
t. programmes are so much	ANON 11:2
thinking man's t.	HAMP 132:6
tell: closest friends won't t.	ANON 7:20
How can I t. what I think	FORS 114:8
I t. you	FRY 120:2
not t. with such high zest	OWEN 227:14
poem itself to t.	FROST 117:13
t. a lot about a fellow's	REAG 244:5
t. an old soldier	SHAW 267:17
T. me all	JOYCE 158:2
Tell me, t. me, tell me	JOYCE 158:3
T. Sid	ANON 11:6
t. Tchaikovsky	BERRY 41:9
T. them, because our fathers	KIPL 175:10
T. them I came, and no	DE L 90:12
t. them of us and say	EDM 98:6
T. us your phobias and we	BENC 36:7
t. you naught	CHES 68:9
those who cannot t.	RAL 242:11
you never can t.	SHAW 274:8
telling: A pity beyond all t.	YEATS 318:9
I shall be t. this with a sigh	FROST 118:8
tells: ask him how he is, t. you	TAYL 291:1
temper: Never lose your t.	PANK 229:5
t. till it would be dethrimental	O'CAS 222:14
truth that has lost its t.	GIBR 124:5
temperature: t. to the deathly inner	HESSE 140:3
tempered: this century, t. by war	KENN 163:8
tempest: taverns while the t.	HOUS 144:13
temps: *A la recherche du t. perdu.*	PROU 240:6
tempt: are bad for me do not t.	SHAW 267:15
T. me no more	DAY-L 89:6
t. My Lady Poltagrue	BELL 34:11

temptation: combines the maximum of t.	SHAW 271:22
oughtn't to yield to t.	HOPE 143:9
t. because I have found	SHAW 267:15
t. is the greatest treason	ELIOT 102:9
t. to a rich and lazy nation	KIPL 170:16
temptations: protections against t.	TWAIN 300:19
t. both in wine and women	KITC 175:15
ten: Church clock at t.	BROO 56:1
It will probably take t.	BENN 37:8
T. Commandments an' a man	KIPL 169:8
T. days that shook the world	REED 245:6
Your starter for t.	GASC 122:6
tenants: T. of the house	ELIOT 100:8
tendance: *Je suis Marxiste—t. Groucho.*	ANON 9:5
tendency: Groucho t.	ANON 9:5
tennis: Anybody on for a game of t.	SHAW 272:20
juvenile I never said 'T., anyone?'	BOGA 48:9
play t. with the net down	FROST 118:6
Tennyson: Lawn T., gentleman poet	JOYCE 159:3
[T.] could not think up	CHES 71:4
T. was not Tennysonian	JAMES 153:1
The bower we shrined to T.	HARDY 133:7
tension: Under the t., slip	ELIOT 101:9
tent: inside the t. pissing	JOHN 156:3
Our master Caesar is in the t.	YEATS 320:2
tentacles: dear octopus from whose t.	SMITH 276:18
term: formula, 'T., holidays, ...'	LEWIS 187:5
terminated: be t. when one or both	AUDEN 18:14
terminological: risk of t. inexactitude	CHUR 73:9
terrestrial: Was written on t. things	HARDY 134:2
terrible: A t. beauty is born	YEATS 320:4
isn't life a t. thing	THOM 293:16
it's got to be t.	PUZO 241:10
made them so t. to Helen	FORS 114:13
t. pain in all the diodes	ADAMS 1:13
that t. football club	MCGR 195:5
words T. Vaudeville	ACE 1:5
terrified: those t. vague fingers push	YEATS 322:6
territory: It comes with the t.	MILL 208:9
terror: adds a new t. to life	TREE 298:8
From all that t. teaches	CHES 70:7
nothing disturbed the even t.	SHAR 267:9
T. is the feeling	JOYCE 158:11
t. which paralyses needed	ROOS 250:4
victory in spite of all t.	CHUR 74:4
terrorist: t. and the hijacker	THAT 292:3
t. and the policeman both	CONR 81:19
Tess: had ended his sport with T.	HARDY 134:8
test: Beauty is the first t.	HARDY 133:2
t. of a first-rate intelligence	FITZ 110:13
t. of a leader	LIPP 189:1
t. of a vocation	SMITH 278:11
testament: Have you your t.	BEHAN 32:2
Texas: Deep in the heart of T.	HERS 140:1
Thames: Into the T.	FARJ 107:7
Not of Gennesareth, but T.	THOM 296:13
Oh shall I see the T. again	BETJ 43:7

Thames (*cont.*):

T. flowed backward	PLOM 235:16
T. is liquid history	BURNS 58:5

thank: terrible thing, t. God — THOM 293:16
T. heaven for little girls — LERN 186:5
thanked: God be t. Who has matched — BROO 54:10
thankful: be t. for the fools — TWAIN 300:18
thanks: T. for the memory — ROBIN 248:8
thanksgiving: With proud t., a mother — BINY 47:4
that: And t. — MILNE 209:16
T. was the week that was — BIRD 47:7
thatch: build a house with deep t. — BELL 35:1
Thatcher: [Margaret T.] — CRIT 86:7
Margaret T. wins on Thursday — KINN 167:13
thcream: t. and thcream and thcream — CROM 86:8
theatre: happening in the t. of his time — TYNAN 302:8
Her Aunt was off to the T. — BELL 33:4
I like the t., but never — HART 135:11
My only regret in the t. — BARR 26:19
t. might be solved by her — RATT 243:5
t. of farce is the theatre — BENT 39:15
t. of the surrealist — BENT 39:15
thee: Dreamin' of t.! Dreamin' — WALL 304:14
theft: t. from those who hunger — EIS 100:2
them: T. that's got shall get — HOL 142:11
theme: pudding — it has no t. — CHUR 76:12
themselves: women are a sex by t. — BEER 31:2
theories: And 't.' and 'goals' — KIPL 168:4
theorize: capital mistake to t. — DOYLE 95:9
theory: t. of relativity is proven — EINS 99:7
there: Because it's t. — MALL 199:13
be t. when it happens — ALLEN 4:6
Over there, over t. — COHAN 78:12
T. is always something rather — BEER 31:4
t. is no there there — STEIN 284:6
T. was a young lady of Riga — ANON 10:11
thermodynamics: describe the Second Law of T. — SNOW 279:6
they: t. know enough who know — ADAMS 2:11
T. shall not pass — IBAR 149:18
thick: A t. skin is a gift from God — ADEN 2:20
thcream till I'm t. — CROM 86:8
t. and exactly in the right — BUTL 60:11
t. on Severn snow the leaves — HOUS 146:7
thicker: men know, than Water's t. — HUXL 149:1
thieves: One of the t. was saved — BECK 29:5
T. respect property — CHES 69:13
union of two t. — BIER 46:7
thighs: glory from her loosening t. — YEATS 322:6
staggering girl, her t. caressed — YEATS 322:6
thin: incredibly fat or incredibly t. — BARR 26:8
t. man inside every fat — ORW 224:14
t. one is wildly signalling — CONN 81:2
T. red line of 'eroes — KIPL 168:11
whose love is t. and wise — PARK 230:18
thing: Courage is the t. — BARR 26:6
Good T., since — SELL 266:4
Let's call the whole t. off — GERS 123:9

thing (*cont.*):

love only means one t. — BENN 38:9
machine, a t. — MACN 198:8
only t. we have to fear — ROOS 250:4
purest t. there is — JONG 157:5
that if a t. is worth doing — CHES 71:6
T. as he sees It — KIPL 174:13
t. of beauty and a boy — ROWL 253:15
t. stronger than all — ANON 11:7
t. you have ever done secure — STOP 287:7
things: confused t. with their names — SART 261:16
deeds are concerned with t. — AUDEN 18:12
I mean for t. they didn't know — POUND 238:3
It means twenty t. — BENN 38:9
I've been t. and seen places — WEST 309:5
people don't do such t. — IBSEN 150:5
real and true than the t. — SHAW 268:12
The fundamental t. apply — HUPF 148:5
The shape of t. to come — WELLS 308:11
t. a' didn't wish — HARDY 133:11
T. ain't what they used — PERS 233:6
t. are as piffle before — ASHF 14:8
T. fall apart — YEATS 320:7
t. or in the freedom — ILL 150:11
t. people make fools — SHAW 268:12
t. to stay as they — LAMP 178:1
used to notice such t. — HARDY 134:1
was just one of those t. — PORT 236:14
think: All t. what other people think — YEATS 322:4
And t. by fits and starts — HOUS 145:2
But I can't t. for you — DYLAN 97:14
concealing how much we t. — TWAIN 301:11
Don't t. twice, it's all right — DYLAN 97:4
He can't t. without his hat — BECK 29:8
If you can t.—and not make — KIPL 173:7
I never expect a soldier to t. — SHAW 268:17
I paint objects as I t. — PIC 234:5
I t. like a genius — NAB 217:4
know what I t. till I see — WALL 304:17
legs and t. of England — HILL 141:2
people do they t. — CHUR 72:14
something with them besides t. — LOOS 190:13
so t. you drunk I am — SQUI 283:2
so we've got to t. — RUTH 256:5
then I don't t. much of it — STR 288:6
T. before you speak is criticism's — FORS 115:14
t. how it's improved her — GRAH 127:6
t. I'm not incoherent — ROSS 253:4
t. just with our wombs — LUCE 192:11
t. only this of me — BROO 55:2
t. that they will sing — ELIOT 103:12
t. the laws of God will — SHAW 269:12
t. up to the height — CHES 71:4
time we t. we're sick — WOLFE 316:12
To t. that two and two are four — HOUS 145:6
we should all t. alike — TWAIN 301:20
which we t. that we think — BIER 46:13
who t. they are strong — BID 46:3
you can't make her t. — PARK 231:16

think (cont.):

You know more than you t.	SPOCK 282:6

thinking: But I am too busy t. about   SITW 276:3

columnists say 'Every t. man.'	ADAMS 2:3
prevent myself from t.	SART 262:2
The power of positive t.	PEALE 232:7
t. and we thus drift toward	EINS 99:8
t. jest what a Rum Go everything	WELLS 308:8
t. man's television	HAMP 132:6
t. what nobody has thought	SZEN 290:8
Try t. of love, or something	FRY 119:21

thinks: he t. he knows everything   SHAW 270:9

third: Close encounters of the t. kind	SPIE 282:5
t. who walks always beside	ELIOT 105:9

third-class: t. seat sat the journeying
                      HARDY 133:14

third-rate: t. foreign conductors around
                      BEEC 30:8

thirst: an' a man can raise a t.	KIPL 169:8
thirteen: clocks were striking t.	ORW 225:2
When I was but t.	TURN 300:3

thirtieth: It was my t. year to heaven
                      THOM 292:13

thirty: my t. years' experience	CARR 64:2
t. pieces of silver	BEVAN 44:12
this: T.—is London	MURR 216:8
T. is the way the world ends	ELIOT 103:5
Thomas: little T.	AWDRY 21:5
T. says good-night to Lady	LAWR 181:9
Wilde to T. à Kempis	BARB 24:15

Thoreau: be of his [T.'s] talent   JAMES 152:17

thorn: Than Oak, and Ash, and T.	KIPL 172:12
thorns: crown of t. and the thirty	BEVAN 44:12
thorny: your road's a t. way	CARB 63:14
thou: T. a person becomes I	BUBER 57:3

thought: A library is t. in cold storage   SAM 259:4

Eternity's a terrible t.	STOP 287:8
Hugo was a madman who t.	COCT 78:8
I wish I t. What Jolly Fun!	RAL 242:13
My t. is me	SART 262:2
not seem a moment's t.	YEATS 319:7
t. in a concentration camp	ROOS 251:4
t. that is big and strong	BOND 49:2
t. we were done with these	BENÉ.T 36:15
troubled seas of t.	GALB 121:3
you t. of nothing else	BALD 22:7

thoughtful: T. children, and the grave
                      AUDEN 17:10

thoughtlessness: In the sex-war t.   CONN 80:20

thoughts: censor one's own t.   WALEY 304:12

The Hunter's waking t.	AUDEN 31:3
t. go blowing through them	BROO 55:6
T. of a dry brain	ELIOT 100:8
To bring my t. to an end	SMITH 278:22
your love but not your t.	GIBR 124:3

thousand: After two t. years of mass
                      HARDY 134:13

And a t. lost golf balls	ELIOT 104:2
Bulls and cows a t. head	HODG 142:3

thousand (cont.):

end of a t. years of history	GAIT 121:1
its Empire lasts for a t.	CHUR 74:7
not in a t. years	SMITH 277:9
picture is worth ten t. words	BARN 25:3
Said it three t. years ago	FLEC 112:6
saw ten t. talkers whose	DYLAN 97:5
they have sung for a t.	HAMM 132:3
t. blows deal one deathblow	MCKAY 195:8
t. tricks and ways	WATS 305:9

three: always t. o'clock   FITZ 110:12

itself only t. days old	JEANS 154:5
no occasion to give t.	FORS 115:13
people get into bands for t.	GELD 122:10
Refused about the age of t.	CHES 70:11
Though he was only t.	MILNE 210:1
t. classes which need sanctuary	BALD 23:8
T. jolly Farmers	DE L 91:4
T. jolly gentlemen	DE L 91:2
T. o'clock is always too	SART 262:1
t. white leopards sat	ELIOT 101:1
T. Wise Kings	KAV 161:13

three-pipe: It is quite a t. problem   DOYLE 94:3

threescore: Now, of my t. years and ten
                      HOUS 145:13

threshold: persist to the t. of old	CORN 84:1
threw: t. me in front of the Judges	BETJ 42:11
thrid: Cold currents t.	HARDY 134:4
thrilling: more t. than a scream	ROLFE 249:17
thrills: that sound which so t.	AUDEN 19:7
throat: cutting each other's t.	ATK 15:16
From the t. of a dead man	GRAV 128:5
One finger in the t.	OSLER 226:17
phrases stick in the t.	RUSS 256:4
rather felt you round my t.	HOPE 144:4
taking life by the t.	FROST 119:6
your t. 'tis hard to slit	KING 167:11

throbbing: Like a taxi t. waiting   ELIOT 105:5

t. between two lives   ELIOT 105:5

throne: A T. sent word to a Throne   KIPL 170:7

Gehenna or up to the T.	KIPL 175:4
himself a t. of bayonets	INGE 151:8
like a burnished t.	ELIOT 104:15

through: best way out is always t.   FROST 119:3

Progress t. technology	ANON 11:18
t. you but not from you	GIBR 124:3

throw: do not t. this book about   BELL 32:12

thrush: An aged t., frail	HARDY 134:2
thrust: mediocrity t. upon them	HELL 137:5
thunder: comes up like t. outer China	KIPL 169:6
thundered: T. out on the Roman air	AUDEN 20:12
Tiber: T. foaming with much blood	POW 239:10
ticket: She's got a t. to ride	LENN 185:14
t. at Victoria Station	BEVIN 46:2
t. for the peepshow	MACN 197:11

ticky-tacky: And they're all made out of t.
                      REYN 246:2

tidal: rhythmic t. lyres	HARDY 134:4
tide: are turning the t.	CHUR 74:8

tide (*cont.*):
  call of the running t.   MAS 203:15
tides: Push in their t.   THOM 293:5
  so I drew these t.   LAWR 182:7
tie: father's old green t.   COLL 79:7
  t. the noose on in a knowing   CHES 70:16
  with double-end evening t.   BETJ 43:10
tiger: On a t.skin   ANON 12:10
  smile on the face of the t.   ANON 10:11
  t.'s terrible heart   BENÉT 37:1
  T. well repay the trouble   BELL 32:15
  Who went for a ride on a t.   ANON 10:11
tigers: And the t. are getting   CHUR 76:8
  For tamed and shabby t.   HODG 142:2
  There *were* no t. *That* was   ELIOT 101:2
tiggers: T. don't like honey   MILNE 209:12
tight: t. gag of place   HEAN 136:11
tights: she played it in t.   BEER 31:3
tile: Dressed in style, brand new t.   COLL 79:7
  red brick, but white t.   OSB 226:12
time: against her, but she's on t.   AUDEN 19:15
  Alas, T. stays, *we* go   DOBS 93:1
  And pluck till t. and times   YEATS 322:12
  As t. goes by   HUPF 148:5
  because t. is long   DUB 96:2
  be done for the first t.   CORN 84:2
  beyond Space and T.   BROO 55:4
  bleeding to death of t.   GRAV 128:8
  By the t. you say you're   PARK 230:11
  By which T. kills us   SITW 276:9
  chew gum at the same t.   JOHN 156:4
  Have no enemy but t.   YEATS 323:3
  Hurry up please it's t.   ELIOT 105:3
  In search of lost t.   PROU 240:6
  I see the T. and Motion clock   AYRES 21:16
  it is peace for our t.   CHAM 66:6
  Just the worst t. of the year   ELIOT 100:9
  knew how women pass the t.   HENRY 139:1
  long t. in politics   WILS 313:8
  lot of t. to be a genius   STEIN 284:5
  me pleasure all the t.   BELL 34:15
  never *is* in such cases 't.'   JAMES 153:8
  new direction of T.   LAWR 181:12
  no t. to stand and stare   DAV 89:2
  not redeemed from t.   ELIOT 102:6
  Now's the t. to trust   HART 135:12
  outside and may be some t.   MAHON 199:4
  outside and may be some t.   OATES 221:13
  people too much of the t.   THUR 297:15
  perhaps present in t. future   ELIOT 101:5
  sissy half as old as t.   PLOM 235:14
  summer's here and the t. is oh   JAGG 152:5
  that is an idea whose t.   ANON 11:7
  That passed the t.   BECK 29:9
  The fire next t.   BALD 22:8
  There'll be t. enough to sleep   HOUS 145:14
  The t. was out of joint   STR 287:15
  Through t. to times anon   HARDY 133:13
  T. and fevers burn away   AUDEN 17:10

time (*cont.*):
  T. an endless song   YEATS 319:9
  t. available for its completion   PARK 232:2
  T. for a little something   MILNE 210:13
  t. for mirth and laughter   ADE 2:19
  T. has transfigured them   LARK 179:16
  T. held me green and dying   THOM 293:2
  t. in every man's life   MAUD 204:9
  t. in the library   STR 288:9
  t. is the longest distance   WILL 312:7
  t. of swords and periwigs   POTT 237:4
  t. on the buses   STR 288:9
  T. present and time past   ELIOT 101:5
  t. spent on any item   PARK 232:3
  time, t. is all I lacked   DOUG 93:6
  t. to cultivate modesty   SITW 276:3
  t. trying to make life   AYER 21:13
  t. until the arrival   BERNE 41:6
  T. was away and somewhere else   MACN 198:3
  t. we have rushed through   ROG 249:12
  T. wounds all heals   BREC 52:17
  T., you old gipsy man   HODG 141:12
  Truth has no special t.   SCHW 265:2
  we have not the t.   KIPL 170:16
  what takes a little t.   NANS 217:8
time-lag: t. of fifty years   WELLS 308:14
timeless: Of t. moments   ELIOT 102:6
times: For the t. they are a-changin'   DYLAN 97:13
  It is the logic of our t.   DAY-L 89:8
  Let the good t. roll   THEA 292:7
  The T. about the Repeal   BEER 31:20
  Top people take *The T*   ANON 11:15
  truth 24 t. per second   GOD 125:6
  year's experience 30 t.   CARR 64:2
time-table: t. or a catalogue   MAUG 205:13
timid: t. as I was going   WEBB 306:18
tin: corrugated t. roof   BEEC 29:18
  opening a t. of sardines   BENN 37:10
ting-a-ling-a-ling: The bells of Hell go t.
     ANON 10:8
tinge: t. it with romanticism   DOYLE 95:2
tinker: Man's heart expands to t.   MACN 198:6
  they don't matter a t.'s   SHIN 274:17
tinkling: words t. in the minds   SMITH 278:16
tinned: between smoked salmon and t.
     WILS 313:6
tins: lays out food in t.   ELIOT 105:5
tip: That depends on the t.   BRAC 51:14
Tipperary: It's a long way to T.   JUDGE 159:13
tipster: t. who only reached Hitler's   TAYL 290:15
tiptoe: T. through the tulips   DUBIN 96:1
tire: shall not weaken or t.   CHUR 72:11
tired: His soul. He was so t.   ROLFE 249:18
  I'm t. of Love   BELL 34:15
  long process of getting t.   BUTL 59:13
  round him has always t.   BEER 30:13
  Tho' you're t. and weary   LAUD 179:17
Tiresias: T., though blind   ELIOT 105:5
tiring: she recalls, 'is so t.'   HULL 148:1

'tis: 't. better to have loved   BUTL 60:14
Titanic: furniture on the deck of the T.
                    MORT 214:10
titivating: We watch them t.   MCG 195:3
title: But I love the t.   COPE 83:7
  could only read the t.   WOOLF 317:6
titled: that of the t. for riches   PEAR 232:10
titles: T. distinguish the mediocre   SHAW 272:1
Toad: As intelligent Mr T.   GRAH 127:16
  Give me your arm, old t.   LARK 179:10
  The t. beneath the harrow knows   KIPL 170:6
toads: imaginary gardens with real t.
                    MOORE 213:3
toast: t. fell right-side-up   JENN 154:13
  To t. *The Queen*   HEAN 136:13
tobaccos: Ashes of the Various T.   DOYLE 95:3
today: But t. the struggle   AUDEN 20:10
  doubts of t.   ROOS 251:3
  get where I am t. without   NOBBS 221:1
  Here t.—in next week tomorrow   GRAH 127:15
  T. I feel like thirty cents   ADE 2:19
  T. we have naming of parts   REED 244:12
  tomorrows these gave their t.   EDM 98:6
  will not hang myself t.   CHES 70:16
to–day: T. the Roman and his trouble   HOUS 146:8
toddle: t. safely home and die   SASS 262:7
toe: clerical, printless t.   BROO 55:9
toes: How cold my t.   MILNE 209:11
  t. you will have trodden   CORN 84:1
toff: saunter along like a t.   HARG 135:2
toffees: All the t. I chewed   AYRES 21:15
together: May never come t. again   DAV 88:13
  never again so much t.   MACN 198:4
toil: t., tears and sweat   CHUR 74:3
Tokay: college arms upon the lid; T.   BETJ 44:7
told: like to be t. the worst   CHUR 75:1
  what we were formerly t.   BLUN 47:13
tolerance: was such a thing as t.   WILS 314:5
tolerated: democracy is that it has t.   BEVAN 45:3
tolerates: that He t. their existence   BUTL 59:2
Tolstoy: any ring with Mr T.   HEM 138:9
Tom: Ground control to Major T.   BOWIE 51:6
tomato: t. and I like to-mah-to   GERS 123:9
tomatoes: like a couple of hot t.   FIEL 108:9
tomb: This side the t.   DAV 88:13
  t. of a mediocre talent   SMITH 278:12
tombs: dust, in the cool t.   SAND 259:12
  towers and t. and statues   FLEC 112:1
tombstone: fight is a t. white   KIPL 172:9
tomes: Deep cargoes of gigantic t.   BELL 35:6
Tommy: O it's T. this, an' Tommy   KIPL 168:10
tomorrow: cleaning. And t. morning   REED 244:12
  dwell in the house of t.   GIBR 124:3
  For t. we shall die   PARK 231:3
  Leave t. behind   COW 84:6
  today—in next week t.   GRAH 127:15
  T. I'll sit at the table   HUGH 147:13
  t. every Duchess in London   MACD 194:12

tomorrow (*cont.*):
  T. for the young the poets   AUDEN 20:10
  t. is another day   MITC 211:9
  t. will be our doubts   ROOS 251:3
  word for doing things t.   SHAW 268:2
to-morrow: t. we will run faster   FITZ 110:16
tomorrows: dividend from time's t.   SASS 262:5
  For your t. these gave   EDM 98:6
ton: mighty ships ten thousand t.   HODG 142:1
Tone: And Robert Emmet and Wolfe T.
                    YEATS 321:15
tones: t. as dry and level   AUDEN 20:9
tongue: From lies of t. and pen   CHES 70:7
  our sweet English t.   FLEC 112:7
  picked a pocket with his t.   BIER 46:10
  t. into the corners   ELIOT 103:7
  t. taking a trip of three   NAB 217:1
  would not yield to the t.   BIER 46:11
tongued: dead is t. with fire beyond   ELIOT 102:1
tongues: t. of flame are in-folded   ELIOT 102:7
  t. that have not Thee   KIPL 173:5
  whose t. were all broken   DYLAN 97:5
tonic: wicked as a ginless t.   COPE 83:4
tonight: air to be *in town t*   ANON 10:9
  Not t., Josephine   DAVID 88:11
  t. is my guest night   HALL 131:5
too: Done because we are t.   HARDY 133:6
  golf and t. old to rush   ADAMS 2:4
  Three o'clock is always t.   SART 262:1
  T. kind, too kind   NIGH 219:13
  t. young to take up golf   ADAMS 2:4
took: 'E went an' t.—the same as me   KIPL 174:7
  t. from thee I did   THOM 295:16
tools: t. and we will finish   CHUR 72:1
toothbrush: t. too is airing in this   BETJ 44:1
tooth-decay: t. in His divine system   HELL 137:6
toothpaste: t. is out of the tube   HALD 131:3
tooth-point: Exactly where each t. goes
                    KIPL 170:6
top: Room at the t.   BRAI 52:9
  T. of the world   GOFF 125:11
  T. people take *The Times*   ANON 11:15
  You're the t.   PORT 237:3
top hat: I'm puttin' on my t.   BERL 40:11
tops: whipping t. and help   HODG 142:1
torch: The t.; be yours to hold   MCCR 194:7
  t. has been passed   KENN 163:8
torchlight: T. crimson on the copper   CHES 70:6
tories: revolutionaries are potential T.
                    ORW 224:18
torrent: leave it to a t. of change   CHES 70:3
torture: form of self-imposed t.   MILL 208:13
  So does t.   AUDEN 18:4
torturer: life and the t.'s horse   AUDEN 17:9
Tory: burning hatred for the T.   BEVAN 45:8
  T.'s secret weapon   KILM 166:5
tosh: Never did I read such t.   WOOLF 317:7
totalitarianism: name of t. or the holy
                    GAND 121:10

totem: And under the t. poles   MACN 198:2
totem-symbol: grin on his face and a t.
   KOES 176:9
totter: And t. towards the tomb   SAY 263:11
touch: t. with us from time   BEEC 30:7
tough: t. get going   KENN 164:4
toujours: t. gai toujours gai   MARQ 201:7
tour: Magical mystery t.   LENN 185:11
tourist: camera makes everyone a t.   SONT 280:10
   t. the last enchantments   BEER 31:7
tournament: We in the t. — you against me
   BETJ 43:9
tous: T. les êtres humains naissent   ANON 11:16
   T. les jours, à tous points   COUÉ. 84:4
tout: ten to t. for flattery   COLL 79:8
toward: T. heaven, till the tree   FROST 118:9
towards: Neither from nor t.   ELIOT 101:8
towering: height of his own t.   CHES 71:4
towers: t. and tombs and statues   FLEC 112:1
town: A haunted. it is to me   LANG 178:4
   air to be in t. tonight   ANON 10:9
   All over t.   BURKE 58:3
   anyone lived in a pretty how t.   CUMM 86:15
   destroy the t. to save   ANON 9:1
   down to the end of the t.   MILNE 210:1
   Enormous through the Sacred T.   BELL 35:6
   enough majority in any t.   TWAIN 300:7
   helluva t.   COMD 79:10
   means our own dear t. to us   COW 84:11
   night in the small t.   THOM 293:13
   The t. will follow you   CAV 65:7
towns: t. all Inns have been driven   BELL 34:18
   t. in all the world   EPST 106:9
townspeople: I will teach you my t.   WILL 312:11
toy: eyes gleam over a new t.   BELL 33:11
trace: Frost has risen without t.   MUGG 215:3
   it is also a t., something   SONT 280:11
   Projecting trait and t.   HARDY 133:13
   t. almost all the disasters   WAUGH 305:15
track: T. twenty nine   GORD 126:14
trade: half a t. and half an art   INGE 151:9
   Irish poets, learn your t.   YEATS 319:11
   pre-eminence in her Colonial t.   GEOR 122:14
   There isn't any T.   HERB 139:12
   What is virtue but the T.   SHAW 271:10
trades: It is the best of all t.   BELL 34:5
trade unionist: T. when you want to change
   BEVIN 45:16
trade unions: first snarl of the t.   LLOY 189:8
tradition: T. may be defined   CHES 70:2
   We don't want t.   FORD 113:12
traduced: Someone must have t. Joseph
   KAFKA 160:7
Trafalgar Square: T. and started again   CHAR 68:3
traffic: mighty roar of London's t.   ANON 10:9
tragedies: There are two t. in life   SHAW 271:13
   with the t. of antiquity   STOP 287:4
tragedy: farce and the food a t.   POW 239:3

tragedy (cont.):
   I will write you a t.   FITZ 110:10
   most tremendous t.   BEER 31:3
   That is what t. means   STOP 287:9
   t. for a poet   COCT 78:4
   t. of a man who has found   BARR 26:15
   washy way of true t.   KAV 162:2
tragic: acted so t. the house   HARG 135:3
   essentially a t. age   LAWR 181:7
trahison: La t. des clercs.   BENDA 36:14
trail: long, long t. awinding   KING 167:8
   t. has its own   SERV 267:2
train: electric t. set any boy   WELL 307:13
   headlight of an oncoming t.   DICK 92:3
   Let the t. take the strain   ANON 9:12
   Runs the red electric t.   BETJ 42:8
   t. and tram alternate go   BETJ 43:8
   t. for London town   MILLS 209:9
   t. needs one of its passengers   STOP 287:11
   t. of events has carried   AMERY 5:11
   Trust the t., Mademoiselle   CHR 72:3
   who shaves and takes a t.   WHITE 310:2
   will pack, and take a t.   BROO 55:10
training: T. is everything   TWAIN 301:14
trains: through the fields in t.   CHES 69:15
trait: Projecting t. and trace   HARDY 133:13
traité: n'est pas un t. de paix   FOCH 113:1
traités: Les t., voyez-vous   DE G 90:1
tram: I'm not even a bus, I'm a t.   HARE 134:14
   train and t. alternate   BETJ 43:8
tramp: That's why the lady is a t.   HART 135:11
trance: off this traveller's t.   DAY-L 89:5
tranquillity: chaos remembered in t.   THUR 297:16
   Sorrow is t. remembered   PARK 230:6
tranquillized: These are the t. Fifties   LOW 191:13
transform: those who t. the world   AUDEN 18:12
transformed: dreams he found himself t.
   KAFKA 161:2
   t. into an institution   SART 261:7
translate: Shakespeare is not to t.   BEER 30:18
translated: T. Daughter, come down
   AUDEN 20:13
translation: A t. is no translation   SYNGE 289:9
   Poetry is what is lost in t.   FROST 119:5
   unfaithful to the t.   BORG 49:10
translations: T.   CAMP 62:4
transmit: To t. that feeling   SANS 260:7
transsexuals: only to aspiring male t.   LEB 183:11
Tranter Reuben: While T., T. S   BETJ 42:3
trap: baiting a mouse-t.   SAKI 258:6
traum: schreit im T. um Hilfe   CAN 63:5
travailler: t. devant la majestueuse   FRAN 116:6
travel: classes of t.   BENC 36:10
   I t. light; as light   FRY 119:13
   man can t. who will   FRY 119:13
   The real way to t.   GRAH 127:15
   t. in the direction   BERR 41:11
travelled: care which way he t.   BEAV 28:8
   I took the one less t.   FROST 118:8

travelled (*cont.*):
t. each and ev'ry highway | ANKA 6:11
traveller: t. who has gone to Italy | FORS 115:11
World-besotted t. | YEATS 323:14
Travellers: sit outside at 'The T.' | HARDY 133:8
travelling: been t. round the world | COOK 82:7
travels: t. the fastest who travels | KIPL 175:4
t. the world in search | MOORE 212:10
trays: cheap tin t. | MAS 203:1
tread: me a light that I may t. | HASK 136:1
Tread softly because you t. | YEATS 323:1
treason: temptation is the greatest t. | ELIOT 102:9
treasure: it as your chiefest t. | BELL 32:12
treat: And he who gives a child a t. | MAS 203:9
Talk about a t. | COLL 79:7
t. if met where any bar | HARDY 134:10
treaties: T., you see, are like girls | DE G 90:1
treatment: A suitable case for t. | MERC 207:5
scientific t. for all diseases | SHAW 268:20
t. Some of them have been | REED 245:5
treaty: not a peace t. | FOCH 113:1
signed the t. bred a fever | THOM 293:11
tree: A billboard lovely as a t. | NASH 218:4
A-hanging on the t. | CART 64:8
A poem lovely as a t. | KILM 166:3
by climbing a birch t. | FROST 118:9
If he finds that this t. | KNOX 176:5
trees: And with the t. to newer birth | GREN 129:5
darkness among the gusty t. | NOYES 221:9
green grass and bursting t. | GREN 129:5
Loveliest of t., the cherry now | HOUS 145:13
My apple t. will never get | FROST 118:14
t. and flapped and fought | HODG 141:13
t. because they seem more | CATH 65:2
t. that grow so fair | KIPL 172:12
tree-tops: Where the t. glisten | BERL 40:12
trembled: could think there t. through | HARDY 134:2
trembles: It t. to a lily | DOBS 92:15
tremulous: postern behind my t. stay | HARDY 134:1
trenches: t. and trying on gas-masks | CHAM 66:4
Trent: Or why was Burton built on T. | HOUS 146:15
trespass: And t. there and go | HOUS 145:8
cannot t. with impunity | AUDEN 18:7
tress: A little stolen t. | YEATS 322:2
trial: object that it is not a t. | KAFKA 160:8
this hour and this t. | CHUR 76:5
t. of which you can have | SHAW 269:15
trials: t. of vigilance and exertion | CHUR 72:11
tribal: constructing t. lays | KIPL 168:7
t. God who has made | BURR 58:6
t., intimate revenge | HEAN 136:10
tribe: To purify the dialect of the t. | ELIOT 102:3
with thy t.'s black tents | THOM 295:18
tribulation: who must inherit the t. | HOOV 143:4
tribute: t. a French translator | BEER 30:18
trick: A T. that everyone abhors | BELL 33:8

trick (*cont.*):
dream when the long t.'s | MAS 204:1
play fair to win the t. | LAB 177:5
t. lies in *losing* wars | HELL 137:7
t. of wearing mink | BALM 24:6
tricks: These and a thousand t. | WATS 305:9
tried: been t. and found wanting | CHES 71:5
has been t. at least once | BENN 37:4
pick the one I never t. | WEST 309:9
Trieste: Stettin in the Baltic to T. | CHUR 73:3
trifling: most t. of his works | OSLER 227:2
trigger: finger do you want on the t. | ANON 12:8
triggers: stuck to our starboard t. | ASQ 15:9
trilogy: Clayhanger t. *is* good | BENN 38:3
trinket: I swung the earth a t. | THOM 295:11
trinkets: ye returned to your t. | KIPL 170:11
triomphe: *point le t. mais le combat* | COUB 84:3
trip: look forward to the t. | STIN 286:12
t. through a sewer | MIZN 212:2
triple: There be t. ways to take | KIPL 170:4
tripled: Hers of the Book, the t. Crown | QUIL 242:5
triple-towered: The t. sky, the dove complaining | DAY-L 89:4
tristesse: *Adieu t.* | ÉLUA 106:6
Bonjour t. | ÉLUA 106:6
triumph: A t. of the embalmer's art | VIDAL 304:4
meet with T. and Disaster | KIPL 173:7
our career and our t. | VANZ 303:7
t. of modern science | WAUGH 306:3
triumphs: t. | HOOV 143:4
trivial: t. people should muse | LAWR 181:18
t. personalities decomposing | WOOLF 317:5
trivialities: t. where opposites | BOHR 48:11
trod: T. beside me, close and dear | HOUS 146:12
trois: *T. heures, c'est toujours* | SART 262:1
Trojan: T. 'orses will jump out | BEVIN 45:13
troops: I intend to march my t. | GRIM 129:10
tropical: brings back a night of t. | PORT 236:10
Trotsky: [T.] and had a chat | ROG 249:13
trotting: T. through the dark | KIPL 172:15
trouble: The t. with Senator Long | ICKES 150:8
time of t. when | MARQ 201:13
To-day the Roman and his t. | HOUS 146:8
t. of all kinds and keeping | BUTL 59:20
t. with [Sigmund] Freud | DODD 93:2
t. with this country | ADAMS 2:5
very present help in t. | STEV 286:10
Wenlock Edge the wood's in t. | HOUS 146:7
When in t., delegate | BOREN 49:9
When there's t. brewing | KNIG 176:3
You have to take t. | BENN 38:3
troubled: And t. with religious doubt | CHES 70:11
put out on the t. seas | GALB 121:3
t. midnight and the noon's | ELIOT 103:17
troubles: all my t. seemed so far | LENN 185:18
From t. of the world | HARV 135:15
has got over all its t. | JER 155:8
sleep with a woman whose t. | ALGR 3:14
t. of our proud and angry | HOUS 145:1

troubles (*cont.*):

your t. in your old kit-bag ASAF 13:13

trouser-clip: illuminated t. for bicyclists

MORT 214:9

trousers: bottoms of my t. rolled ELIOT 103:12

t. on when you go out IBSEN 150:2

wear white flannel t. ELIOT 103:12

trowel: With his t. point, letter HEAN 136:9

Troy: another T. for her to burn YEATS 319:2

truce: no t. or parley with you CHUR 72:12

truckin: Keep on t.' CRUMB 86:14

trucks: lot to learn about t. AWDRY 21:5

t. along the lines below BETJ 43:8

true: And is it t.? And is it true BETJ 42:5

believe is not necessarily t. BELL 32:10

be substantially t. SANT 260:20

course of t. anything BUTL 59:7

danger of their coming t. SMITH 277:13

her ear, 'You are not t. WILB 311:3

long enough it *will* be t. BENN 38:18

no matter how t. VIDAL 304:3

Of t. wood, of yew wood DOYLE 95:15

only things that are t. SHAW 268:12

people say of us is t. SMITH 277:12

pessimist fears this is t. CAB 60:15

supposing it is t. RUSS 255:14

t. men of action in our AUDEN 18:12

t. proposition is more WHIT 310:6

what we are saying is t. RUSS 255:11

true-blue: die like a t. rebel HILL 140:10

truer: t. than if they had really HEM 138:2

trumpet: The flute and the t. AUDEN 19:5

Yet ever and anon a t. sounds THOM 295:14

trumpets: are the eagles and the t. ELIOT 100:5

trunk: branches up a snow-white t. FROST 118:9

So large a t. before BELL 32:17

trust: Because I don't t. him BREC 53:5

can't t. the 'specials' COLL 79:5

Never t. the artist LAWR 182:2

T. the train, Mademoiselle CHR 72:3

t. thou hast in me HOPE 144:3

t. yourself when all men KIPL 173:7

trusted: it is not to be t. BROD 54:2

truth: An exaggeration is a t. GIBR 124:5

Art is not t. PIC 234:8

Bigotry tries to keep t. TAG 290:9

decade after decade the t. SOLZ 280:1

economical with the t. ARMS 13:11

fable becomes the t. COCT 78:6

here have Pride and T. YEATS 319:6

I just tell the t. TRUM 299:6

improbable, must be the t. DOYLE 95:5

joking is to tell the t. SHAW 269:17

lawyer interprets the t. GIR 125:3

Let's tell them the t. STEV 286:7

mainly hid the t. TWAIN 300:4

mistook disenchantment for t. SART 261:15

murder, for the t. ADLER 3:1

never ending battle for t. ANON 7:23

truth (*cont.*):

Nobody speaks the t. when BOWEN 51:1

Now God will know the t. LUCAS 192:6

opposite is also a profound t. BOHR 48:11

Photography is t. GOD 125:6

platitude is simply a t. BALD 23:3

policy to speak the t. JER 155:1

possesses not only t. RUSS 255:13

Strict Regard for T. BELL 33:3

telling the t. about them STEV 285:16

than a t. misunderstood JAMES 154:1

that T. is a pathless land KRIS 176:10

The t. is cruel, but it SANT 260:17

truer than the t. ANOU 12:14

trusted to speak the t. BALF 24:3

t. about his or her love WEST 309:18

truth and to live the t. NIXON 220:4

T. exists BRAQ 52:14

T. has no special time SCHW 265:2

t. is often a terrible ADLER 3:1

t. is something that everyone MCC 193:15

T. is the first casualty PONS 236:3

t. is the glue that holds FORD 113:7

T. is the most valuable TWAIN 300:14

t. is to pay too high ROS 252:13

t. when he knows the truth PÉGUY 232:13

t. which makes men free AGAR 3:4

unpleasant way of saying the t. HELL 137:8

truthful: true Poets must be t. OWEN 227:12

truths: between the two sorts of t. BOHR 48:11

repetition of unpalatable t. SUMM 289:2

There are no new t. MCC 193:15

There are no whole t. WHIT 310:7

t. begin as blasphemies SHAW 267:11

t. being in and out FROST 119:2

T. that become old become OUSP 227:8

t. which must serve KENN 163:4

t. without a recogniton BELL 32:10

verities and t. of the heart FAUL 107:11

try: *Just t. to please everyone* SWOPE 289:6

T. thinking of love FRY 119:21

t. to get between them STR 288:3

We're number two. We t. harder ANON 12:2

trying: business without really t. MEAD 206:5

He just goes on t. other PIC 234:6

that I am t. SMITH 277:6

t. every experience once BAX 27:15

t. we can easily learn TWAIN 300:20

tryst: T. with the moon, and deep DRIN 95:17

tube: toothpaste is out of the t. HALD 131:3

tubers: A little life with dried t. ELIOT 104:10

tuckets: Then the t., then the trumpets CHES 70:6

tuckoo: little boy named baby t. JOYCE 158:8

Tucson: T. and Deadwood and Lost BENÉT 36:16

tue: *On t. un homme, on est* ROST 253:9

tulips: Here t. bloom as they are told BROO 55:8

Tiptoe through the t. DUBIN 96:1

tumble: And t. victuals RAL 242:12

tumour: But not when it ripens in a t. ABSE 1:2

tumult: Drove to this t. in the clouds
       YEATS 322:11
 The t. and the shouting dies KIPL 173:3
 The t. and the shouting dies KNOX 176:6
tune: good t. played on an old BUTL 60:13
 guy who could carry a t. CROS 86:9
 thinkin'll turn into a t. HUBB 147:7
 t. in and drop out LEARY 183:4
 t. is catching and will AUDEN 19:2
 we complain about the t. BEVAN 45:5
tunes: beauty like slow old t. MAS 203:4
tunic: soldier's ribbon on a t. ABSE 1:3
tunnel: Down some profound dull t. OWEN 228:5
 light at the end of the t. DICK 92:3
 light at the end of the t. LOW 191:10
tuppence: t. for your old watch chain COLL 79:7
turbot: 'T., Sir,' said the waiter WELBY 307:9
Turkish: T. this side SAP 261:1
turn: Because I do not hope to t. ELIOT 100:11
 goodnight and quickly t. YEATS 322:8
 I t. to ducks HARV 135:15
 To t. you out, to turn KIPL 168:8
 T. that off WILL 312:9
 T. up the lights HENRY 139:3
 you must t. on, tune LEARY 183:4
turned: t. us around like this RILKE 247:10
turning: And t. your face to the light SASS 262:9
 gate where they're t. AUDEN 19:8
 lady's not for t. THAT 291:15
 point of the t. world ELIOT 101:8
 some advice I've been t. FITZ 110:13
 t. before we have learnt CONN 80:21
 t. in the widening gyre YEATS 320:7
 t. the tide of world war CHUR 74:8
turnip: candle in that great t. CHUR 73:4
turophile: t. no such thing as a *bad* FAD 107:4
turtle: t. lives 'twixt plated NASH 218:9
tusky: t. mouth, and the Crocodile KIPL 172:1
TV: T. — a clever contraction ACE 1:5
twaddle: But better far write t. MANS 200:9
twain: never the t. shall meet KIPL 169:10
twangs: t. and breaks at the end MACN 198:5
tweet: my finger and I say 't.' SAR 261:4
twelve: At t. noon, the natives swoon COW 84:13
 will ruin himself in t. GEOR 122:12
twelve-winded: And yon t. sky HOUS 146:9
twentieth: The problem of the t. century DUB 96:3
 t. century BEVAN 45:1
twenty: armistice for t. years FOCH 113:1
 chord of C major t. BEEC 29:22
 It means t. things BENN 38:9
 t. minutes you ought BRAB 51:10
 T. will not come again HOUS 145:13
twenty-four: then we shall be t. HOUS 144:12
twenty-twenty: Hindsight is always t. WILD 311:4
twice: But if it had to perish t. FROST 118:10
 Don't think t., it's all right DYLAN 97:4
 nonsense can I stand t. or once RICH 247:7
 something that will be read t. CONN 80:6

twice (*cont.*):
 The postman always rings t. CAIN 61:2
 t. as often as any other COKE 78:14
 t. as well as men WHIT 310:20
twigs: The bleak t. overhead HARDY 134:2
twilight: again in the gray t. YEATS 318:7
 full Surrey t.! importunate BETJ 43:11
 In a t. dim with rose DE L 90:9
twilights: In ancient shadows and t. AE 3:3
twins: Clara threw the t. she nursed GRAH 127:9
twirled: ships are t. and spun HODG 142:1
twist: Give 'em a t., a flick HEAT 137:1
 I have NO MORE T. POTT 237:5
 Let him t. slowly EHRL 99:2
twisted: And they t. it with relish NIXON 220:2
two: Between t. evils, I always WEST 309:9
 game at which t. can play BEER 31:19
 Just tea for t. and two CAES 60:16
 making in all, t. BIER 46:21
 Takes t. to tango HOFF 142:8
 To think that t. and two HOUS 145:6
 T. cheers for Democracy FORS 115:13
 t. classes of pedestrians DEWAR 92:1
 T. for a woman, one BEEC 30:4
 t. glasses and two chairs MACN 198:3
 t. people miserable instead BUTL 59:10
 t. things about the horse ROYD 254:5
 t. things that will TARK 290:12
 t. things they disliked MAUG 205:4
 worth t. in the street WEST 309:1
Twye: T. was soaping her breasts EWART 107:1
Tyne: from the Severn to the T. KIPL 174:1
types: Seven t. of ambiguity EMPS 106:8
typewriter: changing a t. ribbon BENC 36:4
typing: writing at all — it's t. CAP 63:10
typist: The t. home at teatime ELIOT 105:5
tyrannize: t. over his bank balance KEYN 165:4
tyranny: against a monstrous t. CHUR 74:4
 conditions of t. it is far easier AREN 13:3
 lightened the burden of t. SHAW 271:14
 long dark night of t. MURR 216:9
 submission to an unnecessary t. RUSS 255:4
 T. is always better organised PÉGUY 232:14
tyrant: A t.'s authority for crime BIER 47:2
tyrants: curry favour with t. ZAP 324:8
 stuff of which t. BEAV 28:11
Tyre: Is one with Nineveh, and T. KIPL 173:4
 which men still call T. FLEC 112:3
Tyrone: steeples of Fermanagh and T.
        CHUR 73:11

U

U: U and Non-U ROSS 253:1
ugly: Once sex rears its u. 'ead ALL 5:6
 The good, the bad, and the u. SCAR 264:4
 upon solid rock the u. MILL 207:18

ugly (*cont.*):

world for u. mathematics   HARDY 133:2

ulcer: I am an 8 U. Man on 4 Ulcer   EARLY 97:15

Ulster: The betrayal of U.   CAIR 61:4

   U. says no   ANON 11:17

Ulysses: hand that wrote U.   JOYCE 159:11

   touching on one aspect of U.   FORS 114:9

umbrella: Be sure that your u.   BURKE 58:3

   u. might pacify barbarians   PLOM 235:15

umbrellas: say, who possess u.   FORS 115:1

umpire: The u., the pavilion cat   LANG 178:6

unable: I am u. to concentrate   GEOR 123:3

unacceptable: u. face of capitalism   HEATH 136:14

unaltered: u. in the cataclysm   CHUR 73:11

unattractive: not against the u.   GREE 128:12

Unaufrichtigkeit: *U. zwischen Mensch*   BAUM 27:14

unaware: And I was u.   HARDY 134:2

unbearable: unbeatable: in victory u.   CHUR 72:5

unbeatable: defeat u.   CHUR 72:5

unbeautiful: u. and have comfortable   CUMM 87:4

unborn: possible to talk to the u.   BARZ 27:11

unbribed: u.   WOLFE 316:11

uncomfortable: moral when he is only u.

         SHAW 271:5

uncommon: very u. cook   SAKI 257:5

unconditional: u. war on poverty in America

         JOHN 156:9

unconscious: call it the *personal u*   JUNG 160:4

   call the *collective u*   JUNG 160:4

   irony is generally quite u.   BUTL 59:11

   The deep well of u. cerebration   JAMES 152:9

uncorseted: U., her friendly bust   ELIOT 103:2

uncrossed: The cross be u.   ELIOT 101:19

undaunted: u. by odds, unwearied   CHUR 74:8

undecided: decided only to be u.   CHUR 74:1

under: get out and get u.   CLAR 77:3

   I'd have been u. the host   PARK 230:2

   I've got you u. my skin   PORT 236:13

   U. Mirabeau Bridge flows   APOL 12:15

underachiever: that basically he's an u.

         ALLEN 4:8

under-belly: exposure of the u. of the Axis

         CHUR 75:2

undercuts: Is incontestable. It u.   FRY 119:15

under-dogs: Englishman among the u.

         WAUGH 306:4

underestimating: money by u. the intelligence

         MENC 206:10

undergraduates: U. owe their happiness chiefly

         BEER 30:16

underground: And breastless creatures u.

         ELIOT 103:1

undergrowth: Slouching in the u.   HODG 142:3

underlined: Is u. for emphasis   ELIOT 103:2

underneath: Though u. that gloomy shell

         ANON 10:1

   U. the Arches   FLAN 111:3

   U. this flabby exterior   LEV 186:11

undersold: never knowingly u.   LEWIS 187:6

understand: confused doesn't really u.

         MURR 216:7

   Everyone wants to u. art   PIC 234:9

   Grown-ups never u. anything   DE S 257:1

   It's all they can u.   MELBA 206:7

   Nor can anyone u. Ein   ANON 8:13

   people who don't u. them   BRUCE 57:1

   really don't u. too hot   SAL 258:12

   The shire for Men who U.   BROO 55:10

   think I u. people very well   FORS 115:5

   u. what is happening   CHAM 66:2

   What you can't u.   DYLAN 97:13

   yet u. the exact   HEAN 136:10

understanding: cod passeth all u.   LUTY 192:13

   foolish their lack of u.   BIER 46:17

   not by force but by u.   BRON 54:7

understood: how well they u.   AUDEN 17:8

   music is best u. by children   STR 288:8

   u. this liking for war   BENN 37:11

undertakers: nothing against u. personally

         MITF 211:10

undertaking: such u. has been received

         CHAM 66:7

undeserving: I'm one of the u. poor   SHAW 273:15

undesirable: Miss, I knows an u. character

         FRY 120:2

   u. to believe a proposition   RUSS 255:14

undeveloped: u. hearts   FORS 114:1

undo: To u. the folded lie   AUDEN 17:12

undone: not thought death had u.   ELIOT 104:14

undressing: it is as if she is u.   COL 79:2

undulating: indolent expression and an u.

         BELL 33:16

uneasy: one morning from u. dreams

         KAFKA 161:2

uneconomic: 'u.' you have not really   SCH 264:14

uneducated: government by the u.   CHES 69:16

   u. man to read books   CHUR 75:13

unemotional: same cold and u.   DOYLE 95:2

unemployment: production and reduce u.

         HEATH 136:15

   u. today is exacting from   TEBB 291:2

unexpected: Old age is the most u.   TROT 299:2

   u. constantly occurs   MAH 199:2

unfaithful: u. to the translation   BORG 49:10

unfathomable: The u. deep   THOM 294:7

unfinished: Liberty is always u. business

         ANON 9:14

unforeseen: contingent and the u.   FISH 109:15

unforgiveness: An alp of u. grew   PLOM 235:12

unforgiving: If you can fill the u. minute

         KIPL 173:9

unhappily: result of being u. married   PARK 232:4

   The bad end u., the good   STOP 287:9

unhappiness: loyalty we all feel to u.   GREE 128:14

   profession but a vocation of u.   SIM 275:7

   U. is best defined   DE B 89:10

unhappiness (*cont.*):

volatile spirits prefer u.	SANT 260:12

unhappy: As soon as one is u. one   PROU 240:11

different from that of the u.	WITT 315:8
instinct for being u.	SAKI 257:7
Men who are u., like men	RUSS 254:15
only speak when she is u.	SMITH 279:2
See an old u. bull	HODG 142:3
U. the land that has no	BREC 53:3
U. the land that needs	BREC 53:3
which make us so u.	JOYCE 159:1

unhealthy: unscrupulous men for u.   BEEC 30:3

unheard: language of the u.   KING 167:7

unholy: Refrain from the u. pleasure   BELL 32:12

unhurt: U. people are not much good

	STAR 283:10

unicorn: it is rarer than the u.   JONG 157:5

uniform: The u. 'e wore   KIPL 169:2

uninterested: can exist is an u. person   CHES 69:9

uninteresting: earth as an u. subject   CHES 69:9

unions: there would have been no u.   BALD 23:12

u. and the industrialists	NIEM 219:12

unique: The British nation is u.   CHUR 75:1

unite: people in this country to u.   CARM 63:15

United: U. States by force   HARD 132:15

United States: including the U.   CHUR 74:7

must be purely to the U.	ROOS 251:13
U. helpless and contemptible	WILS 314:8

universal: adaptation to the u. conditions

	JUNG 160:3
it's as u. as sea sickness	SHAW 271:8
The writer must be u.	BARN 25:6

universe: cover the u. with mud   FORS 114:9

essential function of the u.	BERG 40:3
good u. next door	CUMM 87:8
Great Architect of the U.	JEANS 154:7
Life exists in the u. only	JEANS 154:6
our world, our u.	KUMAR 177:4
repetitious mechanism of the U.	WHIT 310:5
that part of the u.	BECK 28:12
This u. is not hostile	HOLM 142:13
U. and Everything	ADAMS 1:14
u. from one tiny part	BENÉT 37:1
u. is not only queerer	HALD 131:1
u. you can be certain	HUXL 149:15
visible u. was an illusion	BORG 49:11

universities: u. go on a Government grant

	MAUG 205:15

university: be able to get to a u.   KINN 168:3

benefiting from u. training	AMIS 5:12
French letters to the u.	JOYCE 159:8
from Jimmy's u. According	OSB 226:12
gained in the U. of Life	BOTT 50:7
We are the U.	SPR 282:16

unkempt: U. about those hedges blows   BROO 55:8

unkind: That are sodden and u.   BELL 34:19

unknotted: So the knot be u.   ELIOT 101:19

unknown: buried the U. Prime Minister   ASQ 15:1

glorious and the u.	FORS 114:11

unknown (*cont.*):

Like a complete u.	DYLAN 97:7
O friend unseen, unborn, u.	FLEC 112:7
side of the U. Soldier	ASQ 15:1
tread safely into the u.	HASK 136:1

unleashed: u. power of the atom has   EINS 99:8

unlike: So u. anything else   WOD 316:3

unlimited: conveying u. sexual attraction

	HARD 132:16

unlivable: live in an u. situation   LAING 177:11

unluckily: good u.   STOP 287:9

unlucky: It was his u. night   MCH 195:6

who is so u.	MARQ 202:1

unmarried: keep u. as long as he can   SHAW 271:1

unmemorable: their utterly u. contents

	SHAW 273:5

unnatural: most u. of all the sexual   HUXL 148:15

U., he called them	SHAR 267:10

unnecessary: said at once 'The U. War'

	CHUR 76:4

unnerved: As Cook is a little u.   BETJ 42:12

unofficial: An English u. rose   BROO 55:8

It is the u. force	DOYLE 95:7

unpalatable: disastrous and the u.   GALB 121:5

unparalleled: drift toward u. catastrophe

	EINS 99:8

unpardonable: Presidency is an u. vice

	JOHN 156:13

unpicked: their climate, still u.   DOUG 93:6

unpleasant: Cynicism is an u. way   HELL 137:8

How u. to meet Mr Eliot	ELIOT 101:4

unpopular: I was not u. there   BEER 30:15

where it is safe to be u.	STEV 286:3

unprepared: Magnificently u.   CORN 83:11

unprincipled: sold by the u.   CAPP 63:13

unravelled: must all be u. from within   CHR 72:2

unreal: U. City   ELIOT 104:14

unreality: u. of the fable becomes   COCT 78:6

unreasonable: progress depends on the u.

	SHAW 272:8

unregulated: And there the u. sun   BROO 55:8

unremembering: She went her u. way

	THOM 294:11
Their u. hearts and heads	YEATS 319:11

unremitting: u. humanity soon had me

	BENN 38:2

unrequited: Self-love seems so often u.   POW 239:2

unsafe: U. at any speed   NADER 217:6

unscrupulous: by u. men for unhealthy   BEEC 30:3

unseen: O friend u., unborn, unknown

	FLEC 112:7

unselfish: u. and unsordid financial   CHUR 75:3

unselfishly: U. so we might have today   MCH 195:6

unselfishness: sympathetic u. of an oyster

	SAKI 257:8

unsettle: They only u. him   WOD 315:9

unsuccessful: Like an u. literary man   BELL 33:16

unsung: And some u., and that may   THOM 296:3

untalented: product of the u.   CAPP 63:13

untamed: u. and intractable — ELIOT 101:10
untidy: corner, some u. spot — AUDEN 17:9
until: u. the pips squeak — GEDD 122:9
untilled: And all the u. air between — AUDEN 16:10
untried: difficult; and left u. — CHES 71:5
untrue: A man who's u. to his wife — AUDEN 19:14
untruth: U. The stone fidelity — LARK 179:16
untutored: with which the u. savage — FRAZ 116:8
untying: u. with the teeth a political — BIER 46:11
unvictorious: u. ones — SASS 262:10
unwarranted: acquisition of u. influence — EIS 100:1
unwearied: u. in their constant challenge — CHUR 74:8
unyielding: foundation of u. despair — RUSS 255:12
up: sort of English u. — CHUR 76:2
  U., lad: when the journey's — HOUS 145:14
  U., up and away — WEBB 307:2
  was wrong, 'U. to a point' — WAUGH 306:8
upbringing: u. a nun would envy — ORTON 224:3
uplands: forward into broad, sunlit u. — CHUR 74:7
  light thrilling over her u. — DAY-L 89:7
uplift: u. and self-confidence — BARN 25:7
upper: Like many of the U. Class — BELL 34:3
  To prove the u. classes — COW 85:7
upside: Is u. down — BURKE 58:3
upstairs: compel us to be equal u. — BARR 25:11
  Some went u. with Margery — AUDEN 18:17
upstanding: A clean u. chap like you — KING 167:11
upward: u. to the Great Society — JOHN 156:10
urban: Being u., squat, and packed — BROO 55:10
  incomplete in the u. — MCL 196:11
urge: u. the mind to aftersight — ELIOT 102:3
urgency: u. in our outlook — CHAR 68:2
urges: Will that stirs and u. — HARDY 134:5
Uricon: Are ashes under U. — HOUS 146:8
urine: tang of faintly scented u. — JOYCE 159:4
  wine of Shiraz into u. — DIN 92:9
urn: Lean on a garden u. — ELIOT 103:16
usage: consumed in image if not in u. — BART 27:5
  sinon dans son u. — BART 27:5
use: must u. less electricity — JENK 154:8
  No u. to talk to me — HOUS 146:1
  picturesque u. of dialect words — HARDY 133:12
  U. him as though you love him — BLUN 47:12
  What's the u. of worrying — ASAF 13:13
used: accept that I may well be u. — AND 6:7
  Fings ain't wot they u. t'be — NORM 221:4
  man who u. to notice such — HARDY 134:1
  Things ain't what they u. — PERS 233:6
  You u. to be in pictures — BRAC 51:11
useful: Really U. Engine — AWDRY 21:5
  u. thing about a principle — MAUG 204:13
  u. to Him in this respect — BUTL 59:2
useless: Man is a u. passion — SART 261:10
  Music is essentially u. — SANT 260:14
uselessness: u. of men above sixty years — OSLER 227:4
using: I've been u. it for years — BANK 24:9

USSR: Back in the U. — LENN 185:6
usual: u. during alterations — CHUR 72:10
utility: extension which lends u. — SANT 260:14
Utopia: view as an infernal U. — LEWIS 187:7
utopian: retrospective or u. — ARON 13:12
utopias: Life is moving towards u. — BERD 40:1
  U. and the farmyard civilization — INGE 151:3
  U. are realizable — BERD 40:1
utopique: *est rétrospective ou u.* — ARON 13:12
utter: her secret none can u. — QUIL 242:5
  u. and get rid of the element — CHES 69:10
U-turn: U., I have only this — THAT 291:15

V

vacancy: In chaos of v. shone — DE L 90:14
vacant: v. interstellar spaces — ELIOT 101:14
vacuum: v. is a hell of a lot better — WILL 312:5
vagrant: A v. opinion without visible — BIER 46:25
vaguery: inscribed 'For V. in the Field' — OSB 226:11
vain: nothing is in v. — HERB 139:13
  v. citadels that are not — OWEN 228:7
vaincu: *v. mais de s'être bien* — COUB 84:3
vais: *Je v. à la gloire* — DUNC 96:8
vales: blooming in the tall v. — THOM 292:14
valid: supremely v. human experience — JAMES 153:18
valley: Down in the v. drumming — AUDEN 19:7
  How green was my v. — LLEW 189:5
  v. of its saying where — AUDEN 17:4
  V. of the dolls — SUS 289:3
valuable: Truth is the most v. thing — TWAIN 300:14
  v. than panes of glass — PANK 229:7
value: exists, nothing has v. — FORS 115:8
  Its v. depends on what — POUND 237:16
  Of its sentimental v. — FRY 119:13
  Though we v. none — AUDEN 20:5
values: not of facts but of v. — INGE 151:1
  restore Victorian v. — THAT 291:14
van: man said, 'Follow the v. — COLL 79:5
vanishing: I do not find these v. — SMITH 278:2
  Guides us by v. — ELIOT 100:7
vanities: The bonfire of the v. — WOLFE 316:15
vanity: Deep from human v. — HARDY 134:4
  Pull down thy v. — POUND 238:16
vans: But merely v. to beat the air — ELIOT 100:12
vapour: street-bred people that v. — KIPL 170:2
variety: v. and two because it permits — FORS 115:13
various: As you are lovely, so be v. — GRAV 128:6
  constant, constant as v. — GRAV 128:6
  drunkenness of things being v. — MACN 198:7
  v. as the sands — FORS 114:1
vast: Empire v. across the flood — HUXL 149:1
vaudeville: from the words Terrible V. — ACE 1:5

vault: v. for funeral Monday Dorset   BEER 31:18
Vega: V. conspicuous overhead   AUDEN 19:4
vegetarian: teetotaller and often with v.
  ORW 225:16
vegetarianism: resolutions in favour of v.
  INGE 151:6
vehicle: space v. Earth zooming   FULL 120:5
veils: v. of the morning to where   YEATS 318:10
vein: haricot v. in one of my legs   BUTL 60:13
veins: mire of human v.   YEATS 323:9
  white of egg in their v.   LAWR 180:11
velvet: In v. collar-rolls   KIPL 168:4
  steel in a v. glove   WOOL 317:15
Venice: Death in V.   MANN 200:5
  V. and immediately wired   BENC 35:15
  V. is like eating an entire   CAP 63:11
venomous: V. Bead   SELL 266:5
vent: *meurt le bruit parmi le v.*   APOL 12:16
venture: Each v.   ELIOT 101:16
Venus: have the face of a V.   BARR 26:17
veranda: v., and the fruit   AUDEN 19:12
verb: v.   FULL 120:7
verbal: v. contract isn't worth   GOLD 126:7
verboojuice: Sesquippledan v.   WELLS 308:6
verboten: Where *das Betreten*'s not v   BROO 55:8
verde: *Verde que te quiero v.*   LORCA 191:1
Vereker: V.'s secret, my dear man   JAMES 152:15
Verfahren: *ja überhaupt kein V. ist*   KAFKA 160:8
verge: brought to the v. of war   DULL 96:5
  Stands dreaming on the v.   CORN 83:11
vergessen: *Alles was man v. hat*   CAN 63:5
Vergleiche: *V. entscheiden nichts*   FREUD 117:5
verheiratet: *V. sein verlangt immer*   BAUM 27:14
verification: method of its v.   SCHL 264:5
vérité: *désenchantement avec la v.*   SART 261:15
  Qui ne gueule pas la v.   PÉGUY 232:13
verities: v. and truths of the heart   FAUL 107:11
Verlaine: And I'll stay off V. too   PARK 230:4
vermin: lower than v.   BEVAN 45:8
verse: And give up v., my boy   POUND 238:10
  free v. as play tennis   FROST 118:6
  I write it out in a v.   YEATS 320:6
versions: are a hundred v. of it   SHAW 273:9
vertical: The v. man   AUDEN 20:5
very: V. interesting . . . but stupid   ROWAN 253:13
vessel: Let the Irish v. lie   AUDEN 17:5
  v. with the pestle   PAN 229:3
vexed: v. to nightmare by a rocking   YEATS 320:8
vicars: A hundred V. down the lawn   BROO 55:9
vice: Art is v.   DEGAS 89:13
  defence of liberty is no v.   GOLD 126:4
  English v.   RATT 243:7
  quotation is a national v.   WAUGH 306:5
  unpardonable v.   JOHN 156:13
  v. that any man can pursue   MAUG 204:10
  wasn't in any way a v.   SIM 275:6
vice-presidency: v. isn't worth a pitcher
  GARN 122:5

vicious: can't expect a boy to be v.   SAKI 258:5
victim: Any v. demands allegiance   GREE 128:15
  fall v. to a big lie   HITL 141:11
victims: hate v. who respect   SART 262:3
  reformation must have its v.   SAKI 257:13
  revolution. They are its v.   CONR 81:21
  v. of American Fascism   ROS 252:14
victor: But my shock-headed v.   BETJ 43:9
  may call itself the v.   CHAM 66:3
Victoria: ticket at V. Station and go   BEVIN 46:2
Victorian: antagonistic to the V.   WILS 313:2
  rather stuffy V. family   ORW 224:20
  trying to restore V. values   THAT 291:14
  V. Age will never be written   STR 287:14
Victorianism: inverted V.   FORS 114:9
Victorians: V. had not been anxious   WHITE 310:3
victory: Alamein we never had a v.   CHUR 76:7
  be no substitute for v.   MAC 193:4
  In v. magnanimity   CHUR 76:3
  Let 'Dig for V.'   DORM 93:5
  must be a peace without v.   WILS 314:3
  Thy v., O Grave   ROSS 253:6
  v. at all costs, victory   CHUR 74:4
  v. but the contest   COUB 84:3
  V. gave us such insane   HELL 137:7
  V. has a hundred fathers   CIANO 76:15
  v. of a cat on a hot tin   WILL 312:4
  v. unbearable   CHUR 72:5
  without v., there   CHUR 74:4
victuals: snatching his v. from the table
  CHUR 74:2
vida: *La v. es duda*   UNAM 302:9
vie: *C'est très jolie la v.*   ANOU 12:14
  Et puis il y a la v.   ANOU 12:12
Vietnam: Murrow once said about V.   MURR 216:7
  To win in V., we will   SPOCK 282:7
Vietnamese: [the North V.]   LEMAY 184:10
view: A room with a v.   FORS 115:10
  O world invisible, we v. thee   THOM 296:12
  v. from my bedroom of moss-dappled
  BETJ 43:10
vigilance: v. and a rare detachment   MAUG 204:10
vilified: desire to be v. by enemies   BIER 46:8
village: blaspheming over the v. idiot   CHES 71:3
  excellent if you were a v.   STEIN 284:7
  terror my life in the v.   LEE 183:16
  v. which men still call   FLEC 112:3
villagers: gold and black, the v.   LAWR 181:11
villages: from the v. most   BELL 34:18
villain: The v. still pursued her   NOBL 221:2
villainy: v. which we all have   TWAIN 300:13
Vinci: V. and pronounce it Vinchy   TWAIN 301:2
vincit: *Amor v.* insomnia   FRY 119:21
vindicated: were now so terribly v.   CHUR 76:5
vindictive: makes men petty and v.   MAUG 205:7
vindictiveness: v. of the female   CONN 80:20
vinegar: have it tinned. With v.   WILS 313:6
vines: his client to plant v.   WRIG 317:18

vingt: *un armistice de v. ans*   FOCH 113:1
vintage: wine of the rarest v.   SMITH 277:10
violations: v. committed by children
    BOWEN 50:16
viole: *légitimement, on le v.*   DEGAS 89:13
violence: act of v.   MAO 200:11
  destroying ourselves by v.   LAING 177:9
  In v., we forget who we   MCC 194:1
  I say v. is necessary   BROWN 56:9
  I wanted to avoid v.   GAND 122:1
  Keep v. in the mind   ALD 3:13
  organization of v.   BAEZ 22:3
  source of all v.   SART 262:4
  war is v.   FISH 110:1
violent: impossible will make v.   KENN 164:3
violet: At the v. hour, the evening   ELIOT 105:5
  At the v. hour, when   ELIOT 105:5
  faces in the v. light   ELIOT 105:10
  V. Elizabeth complacently   CROM 86:8
violets: It's raining v.   LOV 191:5
violin: v. is wood and catgut   PRIE 239:15
  v. solo in public and learning   BUTL 59:3
virgin: margin this innocent v.   AUDEN 20:12
  past God to arrange a v.   JENK 154:9
Virginia: Turkish this side—V.   SAP 261:1
virginity: distortions of ingrown v.   AUDEN 20:3
  just a little more v.   TREE 298:10
virtue: crowds and keep your v.   KIPL 173:9
  disguised as a v.   BIER 46:23
  easy v. and a proved liar   HAIL 130:13
  nation is the highest v.   JOHN 156:13
  Punctuality is the v. of the bored   WAUGH 306:2
  pursuit of justice is no v.   GOLD 126:4
  Self-denial is not a v.   SHAW 272:5
  v. but the Trade Unionism   SHAW 271:10
virtues: spend in discovering his v.   LYTT 193:1
  v. are of no avail   HUXL 149:7
virtuous: Be v. and you will be eccentric
    TWAIN 300:11
visible: does not reproduce the v.   KLEE 176:2
  Work is love made v.   GIBR 124:4
vision: blackguard whose faulty v.   BIER 46:16
  devils to contest his v.   MAIL 199:10
  Have molten bowels; your v.   BOTT 50:5
  single central v.   BERL 40:13
  v. of her will probably   CAUL 65:3
visions: Blessed Cecilia, appear in v.   AUDEN 20:13
visit: inspect new stock or to v.   AUDEN 19:16
  Sole purpose of v.   HARD 132:15
  which you cannot v.   GIBR 124:3
visits: people never make long v.   MOORE 213:4
vitality: The lower one's v.   BEER 30:19
  V. in a woman is a blind   SHAW 270:15
vitriol: sleeve with a bottle of v.   WOOL 317:15
vittoria: *La v. trova cento padri*   CIANO 76:15
vive: *V. Le Québec Libre.*   DE G 90:2
vivid: v. air signed   SPEN 281:15
vivre: *C'est une chose anormale de v.*   ION 151:10
  V. est une chute horizontale.   COCT 78:7

vivre *(cont.):*
vocabulary: The v. of 'Bradshaw'   DOYLE 95:13
vocation: test of a v. is the love   SMITH 278:11
  v. of unhappiness   SIM 275:7
Vodka: medium V. dry Martini   FLEM 112:8
Vogue: he'd be working for *V*   UST 302:16
voice: All I have is a v.   AUDEN 17:12
  Are her v., and her hair   MAS 203:5
  At once a v. outburst among   HARDY 134:2
  Her v. is full of money   FITZ 110:15
  His v. rose to a sharp   BELL 32:11
  inner v. which warns   MENC 206:16
  Mine is the only v. I care   CAMP 62:1
  Out of the air a v. without   AUDEN 20:9
  that I hear my lover's v.   PITT 235:8
  through the potency of my v.   HARD 132:16
  v. but because he has   FAUL 107:12
  v. was suddenly lifted   SASS 263:5
  v. we heard was   ATTL 16:5
  v. which was more caustic   ROLFE 249:17
voiced: she who v. those rhymes   HARDY 133:7
voices: Other v., other rooms   CAP 63:12
  v. of young people   SMITH 277:17
voids: are attempts to fill v.   WEIL 307:7
volatile: v. spirits prefer unhappiness   SANT 260:12
vole: passes the questing v.   WAUGH 306:9
voler: *dans les rues et de v.*   FRAN 116:6
volitional: His errors are v.   JOYCE 159:7
Volk: *Ein Reich, ein V., ein Führer.*   ANON 7:19
volume: v. as it is with what   BARR 25:14
vomit: V. and the Sow returns   KIPL 173:12
Vorsprung: *V. durch Technik.*   ANON 11:18
vote: because most people v.   ADAMS 2:6
  Don't buy a single v.   KENN 162:16
  I never v. *for* anybody   FIEL 109:8
  man's decision on how to v.   SCHN 264:8
  The v., I thought   O'BR 221:15
  V. early. Vote often   ANON 11:19
  V. for the man who promises   BAR 27:7
voter: Every intelligent v.   ADAMS 2:3
votes: inscription 'V. for Women'   PANK 229:9
  v. to the most obscure   CHES 70:2
voting: v. that's democracy   STOP 286:14
vow: As if a wedding v.   DYLAN 97:11
  I v. to thee, my country   SPR 282:13
vowel: nice ear for v. sounds   BOWEN 51:5
voyages: v. of the starship *Enterprise*   RODD 249:2
vrai: *plus vrai que le v.*   ANOU 12:14
vulgar: let the v. stuff alone   BELL 34:6
  seems insipid to a v.   SMITH 277:10
vulgarizing: succeeded in completely v.   HUXL 148:16

W

wage: It is to w. war, by sea   CHUR 74:4
  I w. war   CLEM 77:9
  policy of w. restraint   WILS 313:3
  w. increase was another   WILS 313:12

wage/price: w. spiral by acting directly
HEATH 136:15
wages: And took their w. and are dead
HOUS 145:7
w. and shorter hours ORW 225:17
Wagner: W.'s music is better NYE 221:12
Wahrheit: *Die W. hat keine Stunde* SCHW 265:2
wail: voice rose to a sharp w. BELL 32:11
wailed: sexophones w. like melodious HUXL 148:9
wains: hangs heavy from the w. GIBB 123:11
wainscot: The wall, the w. and the mouse
ELIOT 102:2
wait: eight, and we won't w. WYND 318:3
Must you w. HART 135:12
Tomorrow, just you w. and see BURT 58:8
w. and not be tired KIPL 173:7
w. for the last judgement CAMUS 62:14
W. till the sun shines, Nellie STER 285:5
w. to watch the water clear FROST 118:12
w. until a shrimp learns KHR 165:9
We had better w. and see ASQ 14:15
who have to w. for them LUCAS 192:8
waiter: dam' good head w. GULB 130:7
waiting: There was I, w. at the church
LEIGH 184:7
though they keep us w. MCG 195:3
w. at the k-k-k-kitchen O'HARA 222:19
w. for rain ELIOT 100:6
w. for the long-promised CHUR 75:7
We're w. for Godot BECK 29:6
What are we all w. CAV 65:6
waits: Someone w. for me CROS 86:10
wake: Old Country must w. GEOR 122:14
They come, they w. us LARK 179:12
W.! for the Ruddy Ball THOM 294:9
W. in her warm nest DAY-L 89:5
wakeful: W. they lie GRAV 128:8
wakened: w. us from sleeping BROO 54:10
wakes: And w. a vague unpunctual star
BROO 55:8
waking: take my w. slow ROET 249:4
Wales: Go out and govern New South W.
BELL 33:7
influence of W. WAUGH 305:15
land of my fathers [W.] THOM 293:3
One road runs to W. MAS 203:6
position of the artists of W. THOM 293:9
there were wolves in W. THOM 292:10
W. where the only concession THOM 294:8
walk: An active line on a w. KLEE 176:1
A w. for walk's sake KLEE 176:1
A w. on the wild side ALGR 3:15
before we have learnt to w. CONN 80:21
Idealists are very apt to w. SMITH 278:6
In a slow silent w. HARDY 133:15
Or w. with Kings KIPL 173:9
W. across my swimming pool RICE 246:12
w. through the fields CORN 83:12

walk (*cont.*):
w. upon the beach ELIOT 103:12
Within a w. of the sea BELL 35:1
You'll never w. alone HAMM 132:5
walked: He w. by himself KIPL 172:4
pig got up and slowly w. BURT 58:7
w. to the brink and we DULL 96:5
walkin': These boots are made for w. HAZL 136:4
walking: act of w. round BEER 30:13
I'm w. backwards for Christmas MILL 209:5
I were w. with destiny CHUR 76:5
Let your fingers do the w. ANON 9:13
opening a window or just w. AUDEN 17:8
prose as dancing is to w. WAIN 304:10
walks: The w. by the lake AUDEN 20:10
Who is the third who w. ELIOT 105:9
Yet in my W. it seems to me BELL 35:2
wall: Before I built a w. I'd FROST 118:15
that doesn't love a w. FROST 118:13
The broken w., the burning YEATS 322:7
The w., the wainscot ELIOT 102:2
turneth his face to the w. BUTL 60:6
Watch the w., my darling KIPL 172:15
walled: citadels that are not w. OWEN 228:7
walling: was w. in or walling out FROST 118:15
wallow: And there let us w. FLAN 111:5
walls: reliable w. of youth collapse FORS 114:13
w. of that antique station BEER 31:7
Wall St.: W. lays an egg ANON 11:20
waltz: Swoons to a w., I take HUXL 149:2
waltzing: You'll come a-w., Matilda PAT 232:5
wander: May w. like a river AUDEN 19:6
wandering: Half to forget the w. and pain
FLEC 111:17
wanderlust: To your w. HART 135:12
want: All I w. is a room somewhere LERN 186:6
As long as I have a w. SHAW 273:4
believe that if I don't w. O'HARA 222:20
be stupid enough to w. CHES 71:10
I didn't w. to do it MCC 193:10
I w. to be alone GARBO 122:2
public something they w. SKEL 276:11
something you probably won't w. HOPE 143:8
The w. of money BUTL 59:1
third is freedom from w. ROOS 250:12
We w. eight, and we won't WYND 318:3
What does a woman w. FREUD 117:6
You can do what you w. INGE 150:13
wanted: I only w. to make you happy AYCK 21:9
Not as we w. it QUIL 242:7
w. to make sure he was GOLD 126:11
wanting: been tried and found w. CHES 71:5
wants: Everybody w. to get inta the act DUR 96:10
war: After each w. there ATK 15:14
against w. LOW 191:6
are the aftermath of w. HOOV 143:4
at all, only to *this* w. STR 288:3
because I believe that the W. SASS 262:11

war (cont.):

been no declaration of w.	EDEN 98:1
big w., by a brief	BORN 50:2
Britain was going to make w.	BETH 41:16
brought to the verge of w.	DULL 96:5
can wage a pitiless w.	GREE 128:12
cruellest and most terrible W.	LLOY 189:9
desolation of w.	GEOR 123:4
Don't mention the w.	CLEE 77:5
Either w. is obsolete	FULL 120:6
ending a w. is to lose	ORW 225:11
essence of w. is violence	FISH 110:1
except the British W. Office	SHAW 268:19
give a w. and nobody will	SAND 260:4
gone too long without a w.	BREC 53:4
great protection against w.	BEVIN 45:15
guarantee success in w.	CHUR 76:6
harder than making w.	STEV 286:1
has been a w. yet	BEVIN 45:15
Horses and Power and W.	KIPL 169:11
involved in a European w.	BEAV 28:7
involve us in the wrong w.	BRAD 52:7
In w.: resolution	CHUR 76:3
In w., whichever side may	CHAM 66:3
It is easier to make w.	CLEM 77:10
lose the w. in an afternoon	CHUR 76:14
Make love not w.	ANON 9:21
men declare w.	HOOV 143:4
midst of a cold w.	BAR 27:8
moral equivalent of w.	JAMES 153:14
mothers and wives. I hate w.	ROOS 250:6
must take chances in w.	DULL 96:5
My argument is that W.	HARDY 133:4
My subject is W.	OWEN 227:12
nuisance in time of w.	CHUR 75:4
Oh what a lovely w.	LITT 189:2
once 'The Unnecessary W.'	CHUR 76:4
only w. creates order	BREC 53:4
Out of that bungled, unwise w.	PLOM 235:12
recourse to w. and renounce	BRIA 53:11
rich wage w. it's the poor	SART 261:6
someone gave a w. & Nobody	GINS 124:12
state of w. would exist	CHAM 66:7
still seek no wider w.	JOHN 156:11
than an end of this w.	ROOS 251:2
that devil's madness—W.	SERV 266:16
that 'w. is war'	CAMP 62:7
that w. settles *nothing*	CHR 72:1
The day w. broke out	WILT 314:16
There ain't gonna be no w.	MACM 196:17
The w. between men and women	THUR 297:7
The w. that will end war	WELLS 308:12
unconditional w. on poverty	JOHN 156:9
understood this liking for w.	BENN 37:11
under the shadow of a w.	SPEN 281:14
very well out of the w.	BALD 23:2
W. always finds a way	BREC 53:7
w. and they will forget	WILS 314:5

war (cont.):

w. for its consequences	FOSD 116:4
W. hath no fury like a non-combatant	MONT 212:6
W. is, after all, the universal	RAE 242:9
W. is capitalism	STOP 287:12
W. is peace	ORW 225:4
W. is too serious a matter	CLEM 77:8
W. knows no power	BROO 54:11
w. like precocious giants	PEAR 232:11
W.'s a bloody game	SASS 263:4
W.'s annals will cloud	HARDY 133:15
w. should ever come between	BON 48:14
w. they kill you in a new	ROG 249:11
w. wasn't fought	ROSS 253:5
w. we hadn't a chance	HELL 137:7
W. will cease when men refuse	ANON 11:21
w. will put an end to mankind	KENN 163:1
w. with atom bombs could	BENN 37:2
w. with one another again	CHAM 66:5
waste of God, W.	STUD 288:11
way to win an atomic w.	BRAD 52:5
We hear w. called murder	MACD 194:14
When is a w. not a war	CAMP 62:7
when there was w.	AUDEN 18:1
When w. enters a country	PONS 236:3
When w. is declared	PONS 236:3
which enable it to make w.	WEIL 307:5
Winston Churchill wants w.	BEVAN 45:1
without bloodshed while w.	MAO 201:1
Work at w. speed	MORR 213:15
Yes; quaint and curious w.	HARDY 134:10
Ward: Of Light and Mrs Humphry W.	CHES 70:15
ware: w. that will not keep	HOUS 145:14
warfare: Armed w. must be preceded	ZIN 324:12
Borgias they had w.	WELL 307:14
warm: earth is w. with Spring	GREN 129:5
Her heart was w. and gay	HAMM 131:11
pitcher of w. piss	GARN 122:5
Wake in her w. nest	DAY-L 89:5
Winter kept us w., covering	ELIOT 104:10
warmed: her glow has w.	STEV 286:5
warming: further than w. the teapot	MANS 200:7
warmth: Colour and W. and Light	GREN 129:5
warn: poet can do today is w.	OWEN 227:12
w. you not to be ordinary	KINN 167:13
warning: w. to all persons	BALD 23:11
warnings: w. over the last six years	CHUR 76:5
warrior: Me? A cold war w.	THAT 291:13
This is the happy w.	READ 244:3
wars: All w. are planned by old men	RICE 246:8
And as for war, my w.	REED 245:1
armaments that cause w.	MAD 198:9
beginnings of all w.	ROOS 251:2
Between the w.	PLOM 235:15
For all their w. are merry	CHES 68:10
littered with the w.	POW 239:9
sent into any foreign w.	ROOS 250:10
trick lies in *losing* w.	HELL 137:7

wars (*cont.*):

w. begin in the minds	ANON 8:7
W. cannot be fought	MOUN 214:13
which titanic w. had groined	OWEN 228:5
warship: every w. launched	EIS 100:2
war-war: always better than to w.	CHUR 75:14
was: That was the week that w.	BIRD 47:7
W. he free	AUDEN 18:2
wash: can w. your hands and pray	KIPL 171:4
never comes out in the w.	KIPL 170:13
w. their feet in soda water	ELIOT 105:4
w. the wind	ELIOT 102:10
washed: W. by the rivers, blest	BROO 55:2
w. in the blood	LIND 188:8
w. in the speechless	BARZ 27:11
washing: under the w. line	THOM 293:16
w. on the Siegfried Line	KENN 162:14
washy: w. way of true tragedy	KAV 162:2
waste: come seemed w. of breath	YEATS 322:11
w. all our lives raising	EDGAR 98:4
w. any time in mourning	HILL 140:10
W. of Muscle, waste of Brain	STUD 288:11
w. remains and kills	EMPS 106:7
What a w., what a waste	DURY 97:1
wasted: he has not w. his time	FORS 114:10
Nothing is w., nothing	HERB 139:13
that it was all w.	AYER 21:13
youth is w. on the young	CAHN 61:1
waste-paper: marriage is the w. basket	
	WEBB 307:4
watch: done much better by a w.	BELL 34:17
going like a fat gold w.	PLATH 235:9
He can w. a grass or leaf	GRAV 128:5
like little w. springs	SPEN 282:2
never sit out front and w.	BARR 26:19
or my w. has stopped	PIR 235:4
The son of a bitch stole my w.	MAC 193:3
wait to w. the water clear	FROST 118:12
W. for me by moonlight	NOYES 221:11
W. THAT BASKET	TWAIN 301:18
W. the parkin' meters	DYLAN 97:12
why not carry a w.	TREE 298:7
withdrawn and w. them gallop	DURY 97:1
watched: beautiful, I w. in vain	FLEC 112:5
He w. the ads	NASH 217:16
watches: someone whose mind w.	CAMUS 62:9
their w. when I am speaking	BIRK 47:8
watching: BIG BROTHER IS W. YOU	ORW 225:3
water: And don't go near the w.	DE L 91:8
And wait to watch the w.	FROST 118:12
benison of hot w.	BROO 54:9
But don't go near the w.	ANON 9:24
Christ walking on the w.	THOM 296:13
don't care where the w.	CHES 68:15
drank rapidly a glass of w.	CUMM 87:2
hands than w. like Pilate	GREE 128:11
He's fallen in the w.	MILL 209:3
Is wetter w., slimier slime	BROO 55:4
makes w. I makes water	JOYCE 158:17

water (*cont.*):

No more w., the fire next time	ANON 8:3
Oh, is the w. sweet and cool	BROO 56:1
replied that there was w.	BURNS 58:5
safe to go back in the w.	ANON 9:6
struck the w. a full second	COKE 78:14
surrounded by w. took	BOWEN 51:5
than W.'s thicker	HUXL 149:1
Waterloo: high at Austerlitz and W.	SAND 260:1
Probably the battle of W.	ORW 225:1
waterproof: W. Boots on	MILNE 209:16
waters: Across the waste of w. die	BETJ 43:7
And the w. as they flow	ARMS 13:7
hitherandthithering w.	JOYCE 158:3
On those cool w. where we	HOPE 144:4
w. of the heart	THOM 293:5
Watson: A long shot, W.; a very	DOYLE 94:15
Good old W.! You	DOYLE 94:13
wattles: clay and w. made	YEATS 318:10
wave: Churchill on top of the w.	BEAV 28:11
overrun by a W. of Saints	SELL 266:5
w. follows upon wave	FISH 109:15
wavering: enchantingly w. attitude	FITZ 110:18
Waverley: W. pen	ANON 11:11
wavers: It w. to a rose	DOBS 92:15
waves: The w., they were fiddlin'	EDGAR 98:3
waving: And not w. but drowning	SMITH 278:18
than w. me farewell	HOPE 144:4
waxed: man has just w. the floor	NASH 217:15
way: All the w. with LBJ	ANON 6:14
every w., I am getting	COUÉ 84:4
Ev'rything's goin' my w.	HAMM 131:13
get you out of the w.	CORN 84:1
going but I'm on the w.	SAND 260:2
happened on the w. to the Forum	SHEV 274:16
have it your own w.	THUR 297:5
I had to make my own w.	ORTON 224:5
I take my endless w.	HOUS 146:10
It's a long w. to Tipperary	JUDGE 159:13
it's the w. they say it	STEI 284:17
knows the w. but can't drive	TYNAN 302:7
more a w. of life	ANON 10:7
nice to people on your w.	MIZN 212:1
Or the w. of a man with a maid	KIPL 170:4
Poetry is a w. of taking	FROST 119:6
provided I get my own w.	THAT 291:12
shows the w. to others	GAND 121:11
than this. I did it my w.	ANKA 6:11
Their w., however straight	THOM 294:7
There is no w. to peace	MUSTE 216:11
they kill you in a new w.	ROG 249:11
This is the w. the world ends	ELIOT 103:5
unpleasant w. of saying the truth	HELL 137:8
War always finds a w.	BREC 53:7
was a w. of putting it	ELIOT 101:12
washy w. of true tragedy	KAV 162:2
w. he travelled providing	BEAV 28:8
w. of telling you to slow	ANON 7:15
w. she disposed	HARL 135:4

water (*cont*.):

w. to the Better there	HARDY 134:3
w. to the White House	STEV 286:6
W. up high	HARB 132:13

ways: And if my w. are not as theirs HOUS 145:3

To justify God's w. to man	HOUS 146:15
w. deep and the weather	ELIOT 100:9
w. will all be as nothing	HARDY 133:11
We have w. of making men talk	YOUNG 324:6

we: slogan 'W. Never Closed' VAN D 303:5

still it is not w.	CHES 70:14
W. are the hollow men	ELIOT 103:3
W. are the Ovaltineys	ANON 11:22
W. are the stuffed men	ELIOT 103:3
W. have become a grandmother	THAT 292:5
W. shall not be moved	ANON 12:4
W. shall not pretend	ANON 12:5
W. shall overcome	ANON 12:6
W. was robbed	JAC 152:2

weak: But the w., washy way KAV 162:2

surely the W. shall perish	SERV 266:17
The w. have one weapon	BID 46:3
w. always have to decide	BONH 49:4
w. from your loveliness	BETJ 43:9
w. men he laid an exaggerated	MAUG 205:9

weaken: great life if you don't w. BUCH 57:5

we shall not w. or tire CHUR 72:11

weak-minded: very w. fellow I am HAIG 130:11

weakness: oh! w. of joy BETJ 43:9

wealth: w. is a sacred thing FRAN 116:5

w. without producing it SHAW 268:11

wealthy: business of the w. BELL 34:1

weaned: had been w. on a pickle ANON 11:13

weapon: art is not a w. KENN 163:5

bayonet is a w. with a worker	ANON 7:2
folly and his w. wit	ANON 8:12
Loyalty is the Tory's secret w.	KILM 166:5
Our chief w. is surprise	CHAP 67:10
terrible w. of aggression	ADLER 3:1
weak have one w.	BID 46:3

weapons: fought with nuclear w. MOUN 214:13

we know, books are w. ROOS 251:4

wearied: Ragtime . . . but when the w. Band

HUXL 149:2

wearing: w. armchairs tight about WOD 316:5

w. such a conscience-stricken	HOUS 144:8
W. white for Eastertide	HOUS 145:13

wears: she w. them SAKI 257:15

weary: Age shall not w. them BINY 47:5

weasel: If you use a 'w. word' ROOS 252:3

w. took the cork out	FIEL 109:1
w. under the cocktail cabinet	PINT 234:12

weather: Away but the w. turned around

THOM 292:14

her madness and her w.	AUDEN 17:4
places and how the w. was	HEM 138:2
rains we'll laugh at the w.	HART 135:12
The ways deep and the w. sharp	ELIOT 100:9
waiting for the w. to break	PINT 234:15

weather (*cont*.):

W. and rain have undone	KIPL 173:6
w. inside of four-and-twenty	TWAIN 301:21
w. the cuckoo likes	HARDY 133:8
w. when good fellows get	BURT 58:7
you won't hold up the w.	MACN 197:13

weave: w. the sunlight ELIOT 103:16

Webb: When Captain W. the Dawley man

BETJ 44:3

webs: By the dark w., her nape YEATS 322:6

Webster: Like W.'s Dictionary BURKE 58:4

W. was much possessed by death ELIOT 103:1

wedding: As if a w. vow DYLAN 97:11

white lies to lie a w. ASQ 15:7

wedding-cake: my face looks like a w.

AUDEN 21:1

wee: Just a w. deoch-an-doris MORR 214:1

Of the 'w. six' I sing HEAN 136:11

weed: Ignorance is an evil w. BEV 45:10

Less than the w., that grows HOPE 144:3

weeds: than mundane w. are there BROO 55:5

w. from gravel paths	KIPL 171:3
w. will overrun the fields	HOOV 143:7

week: he had to die in MY w. JOPL 157:7

takes me as much as a w.	TWAIN 301:1
That was the w. that was	BIRD 47:7
w. in the history	NIXON 220:6
w. is a long time in politics	WILS 313:8

weekend: anxious to go away for the w.

WHITE 310:3

The w. starts here ANON 12:1

weekends: getting a plumber on w. ALLEN 4:10

weeks: w. rather than months WILS 313:10

weep: But she would w. to see today DOUG 93:8

I w. like a child	LAWR 181:13
W. not for little Léonie	GRAH 127:6
W. thy girlish tears	WATS 305:8

weeping: W., weeping multitudes ELIOT 100:5

weigh: Shall w. your God and you KIPL 175:9

weight: w. of rages will press SPOO 282:11

willing to pull his w. ROOS 251:5

welcome: Hello, good evening, and w.

FROST 117:11

on your part would be w.	ATTL 16:7
The effusive w. of the pier	AUDEN 19:10
W., O life! I go to encounter	JOYCE 158:12

welfare: w.-state TEMP 291:3

with the w. of the country WILS 313:1

well: And all shall be w. ELIOT 102:7

Didn't she [or he or they] do w.	FORS 116:1
He does himself extremely w.	ANON 10:1
How w. I did behave	HOUS 146:2
I do it exceptionally w.	PLATH 235:10
talk w. but not too	MAUG 205:16
w. of unconscious cerebration	JAMES 152:9

well-bred: Conscience is thoroughly w. BUTL 59:8

well-content: Sweet Stay-at-Home, sweet W.

DAV 89:1

well-developed: into it with w. bodies FORS 114:1

well-knownness: who is known for his w.
BOOR 49:7
well-meaning: w. man of indifferent judgement
BEAV 28:6
wells: at evening from the w.   FLEC 111:9
Welsh: about in the W. jungle   BANK 24:11
Welt: *Die W. ist alles, was der*   WITT 315:5
die W. so einzurichten   FRIS 117:7
wench: stuff fit only for a w.   MAS 203:2
Wenlock: W. Edge the wood's in trouble
HOUS 146:7
wept: has not w. is a savage   SANT 260:8
Station I sat down and w.   SMART 276:13
were: w. we led all that way   ELIOT 100:10
we're: W. here   ANON 12:3
W. number two. We try harder   ANON 12:2
west: another one down in the w.   BOUL 50:8
gardens of the W.   CONN 80:14
Or w. to the Golden Gate   KIPL 175:6
running farce in the W.   SMITH 276:17
That's where the W. begins   CHAP 67:5
This lady of the W. Country   DE L 90:13
warm wind, the w. wind   MAS 204:2
W. of these out to seas   FLEC 112:2
wester: The rainy Pleiads w.   HOUS 145:10
western: All quiet on the w. front   REM 245:10
be delivered by W. Union   GOLD 126:5
only Playboy of the W.   SYNGE 289:11
when you've seen one W.   WHIT 310:16
Westminster: bars and brothels of W.   LIV 189:4
wet: Let's get out of these w.   ANON 9:11
w. clothes and into a dry   WEST 309:2
wetting: He saved his friend from a w.
MILNE 211:1
Weygand: General W. called   CHUR 74:7
what: are W. and Why and When   KIPL 172:2
But w. can a poor boy do   JAGG 152:5
His later famed 'W. mean   ROSS 253:2
I know what's w.   WEST 309:10
luckiest of mortals because w.   AUDEN 19:11
Oh, w. a beautiful mornin'   HAMM 131:13
Restricted to W. Precisely   ELIOT 101:4
w. is which   MILNE 210:15
W. a dump   COFF 78:9
W. a waste, what a waste   DURY 97:1
W. does a woman want   FREUD 117:6
'W. ho!' I said   WOD 316:7
W. if someone gave a war   GINS 124:12
W. is hell   ELIOT 101:3
W. is man, when you come   DIN 92:9
W. is she a-doin'   ANON 10:15
W. of the bow   DOYLE 95:15
W. of the faith and fire   HARDY 134:7
W. one knows is, in youth   ADAMS 2:11
W.'s up, Doc   AVERY 21:4
W. we call the beginning   ELIOT 102:5
w. we can make of the mess   ELIOT 101:17
w. you may expect to see   DOYLE 94:12

what's: W. on second, I Don't   ABB 1:1
W. on television   ACE 1:5
wheat: it is to separate the w.   HUBB 147:4
sleep-flower sways in the w.   THOM 294:14
w. to be a cause of international   WEIL 307:5
wheel: beneath thy Chariot w.   HOPE 144:3
w.'s kick and the wind's   MAS 203:14
wheels: apparently rolled along on w.   HUXL 149:8
when: had forgotten to say 'W.!'   WOD 316:10
Oh, w. will you ever learn   SEEG 266:1
w. a guy gets stabbed   GARD 122:4
W. a lovely flame dies   HARB 132:11
W. I am dead, I hope it   BELL 34:10
W. I'm not near the girl   HARB 132:11
W. in doubt, strike it   TWAIN 301:17
W. there was peace   AUDEN 18:1
W. you call me   WIST 315:2
W. you go home, tell them   EDM 98:6
w. you got it, flaunt   BROO 56:4
W. you have eliminated   DOYLE 95:5
whence: Or w. he came   HARDY 133:14
W. did he whence   LENO 185:19
whenever: W. I hear the word culture
JOHST 157:2
where: But w.'s the bloody horse   CAMP 62:2
W. are the eagles   ELIOT 100:5
W. have all the flowers gone   SEEG 266:1
W. it will all end, knows God   GIBBS 124:2
W. there is no imagination   DOYLE 95:10
whereabouts: conceal our w.   SAKI 258:4
wherefore: W. does he why   LENO 185:19
where's: w. the rest of me   BELL 32:11
wherever: Dance then w. you may   CART 64:7
make w. we're lost   FRY 119:20
which: W. will reach the bottom   GRAH 127:9
while: But it's a long, long w.   AND 6:4
w. there is a lower class   DEBS 89:11
whim: Barumph has a w. of iron   HERF 139:19
conviction begins as a w.   BROUN 56:6
strangest w. has seized me   CHES 70:16
tempted by a private w.   BELL 34:11
whimper: Not with a bang but a w.   ELIOT 103:5
whin: I looked and three w. bushes   KAV 161:13
whip: he brings down the w.   LESS 186:8
whipping: w. tops and help   HODG 142:1
Whips: Chamber selected by the W.   FOOT 113:4
whiskers: gentleman with iron-grey w.
BEER 31:20
whiskey: bad w. Some whiskeys   FAUL 108:1
Stories, like w.   O'FAO 222:17
whisper: Hush! Hush! W. who dares   MILNE 210:6
We w. in her ear   WILB 311:3
w. music on those strings   ELIOT 105:10
w. to the tourist the last   BEER 31:7
w. was already born before   MAND 200:2
whispering: Come w.   HARDY 133:15
deceives with w. ambitions   ELIOT 100:7
was just w. in her mouth   MARX 202:9

wilder: speed towards the w. shores BLAN 47:10
wilderness: enclosing a w. of idea BUTL 60:2
Women have no w. in them BOGAN 48:8
wildest: The w. peal for years HODG 142:2
w. of all the wild animals KIPL 172:4
wilful: w. men representing no WILS 314:8
will: above all, the w. ROOS 250:11
By all ye w. or whisper KIPL 175:9
Immanent W. that stirs HARDY 134:5
questions of w. or decision CHOM 71:15
there is no w. to power JUNG 160:1
Weakening the w. SPEN 281:13
w. accipitrine to pursue THOM 296:4
w. across the sky in stars LAWR 182:7
W. of the Yukon SERV 266:17
Without a wish, without a w. HODG 141:14
Willie: wouldn't have a W. or a Sam MURR 216:6
willing: Lovely and w. every afternoon
                                AUDEN 19:12
Wilson: [Harold W.] BULM 57:12
I suppose Mr [Harold] W. HOME 143:1
W.'s New Freedom promised KENN 163:7
[Woodrow W.] KEYN 164:12
wilt: Do what thou w. shall CROW 86:12
win: action; they must w. SASS 262:6
Anybody can W., unless ADE 2:16
How to w. friends CARN 64:1
To w. in Vietnam, we will SPOCK 282:7
w. an atomic war BRAD 52:5
w. and lose and still somehow MITC 211:4
w. a war is as disastrous CHR 72:1
w. just one for the Gipper GIPP 125:2
Winchelsea: I shall not lie easy at W.
                                BENÉT 36:17
wind: And how the w. doth ramm POUND 238:13
And the w. shall say ELIOT 104:2
bellows full of angry w. YEATS 320:9
blowin' in the w. DYLAN 97:3
Ere to the w.'s twelve quarters HOUS 146:10
How shall we conquer? Like a w. FLEC 112:6
It's a warm w., the west MAS 204:2
Offer no angles to the w. TESS 291:6
piffle before the w. ASHF 14:8
slowly in the w. EHRL 99:2
solidity to pure w. ORW 226:3
wash the w. ELIOT 102:10
whistling mane of every w. THOM 295:7
Whose sound dies on the w. APOL 12:16
w. came keen with a tang MAS 203:13
w. it plies the saplings HOUS 146:7
w. of change is blowing MACM 197:3
w. that blows LAWR 181:12
w. was a torrent of darkness NOYES 221:9
windage: w. of their own and a critic's BALL 24:4
window: appears for a moment at a w.
                                BEER 30:20
hole in a stained glass w. CHAN 66:11
Macy's w. at high noon JOHN 156:2

stained-glass w.'s hue BETJ 42:5
that doggie in the w. MERR 207:9
throw it out of the w. BECK 29:2
whistled a tune to the w. NOYES 221:10
window-panes: Drift across w. ELIOT 102:15
rubs its back upon the w. ELIOT 103:7
windows: flushing runneth from w. BETJ 44:1
Great w. open to the south YEATS 323:2
then shut up the w. LEAC 182:14
thought of high w. LARK 178:10
winds: And the w. blow THOM 294:2
W. of the World, give answer KIPL 170:2
w. will blow the profit MACN 197:13
with the light-foot w. GREN 129:5
windscreen: w. yellowing with crushed
                                CONN 81:5
Windsor: 'eard o' the Widow at W. KIPL 169:4
wine: are fond of Spanish w. MAS 203:2
doesn't get into the w. CHES 68:15
last companion, W. BELL 34:7
mellow, like good w. PHIL 234:3
new w. into old bottles ATTL 16:4
sweet white w. MAS 202:16
Sweet w. of youth BROO 54:12
temptations both in w. and women KITC 175:15
w. bars and brothels LIV 189:4
w. of Shiraz into urine DIN 92:9
w. of the rarest vintage SMITH 277:10
w. that tasted of the tar BELL 34:9
w. was a farce POW 239:3
wing: Comin' in on a w. and a pray'r ADAM 2:14
like a bird on the w. BOUL 50:9
Nor knowst'ou w. from tail POUND 238:17
wings: Because these w. are no ELIOT 100:12
glad green leaves like w. HARDY 134:1
great w. beating still YEATS 322:6
w. like he'd come from JOYCE 158:7
wink: forgive some sinner and w. MENC 207:4
wink w., say no more CHAP 67:8
winners: there are no w., but all CHAM 66:3
winning: gamesmanship or The art of w.
                                POTT 237:14
w. isn't everything SAND 260:6
winnings: one heap of all your w. KIPL 173:8
wins: Who dares w. ANON 12:7
Winston: W. is back ANON 12:9
W. with his hundred-horse-power BALD 23:9
W. would go up to his Creator LLOY 189:10
winter: brown fog of a w. dawn ELIOT 104:14
go south in the w. ELIOT 104:11
On a w.'s afternoon ELIOT 102:6
The very dead of w. ELIOT 100:9
The w. evening settles down ELIOT 103:13
W. is icummen POUND 238:13
W. kept us warm, covering ELIOT 104:10
Winters: Timothy W. comes to school CAUS 65:5
wintry: bent by the same w. THOM 293:4
wipes: mind it w. its shoes THOM 293:14

wire: And I'll bite the w. nettin' AYRES 21:16
wisdom: beginning of w. RUSS 256:2
  But joy is w., Time YEATS 319:9
  But there's w. in women BROO 55:6
  ends in w. FROST 117:13
  The seven pillars of w. LAWR 182:6
  want of human w. BON 48:14
  we had power, we had w. BENÉT 36:15
  why the conventional w. GALB 121:3
  w. to choose correctly ALLEN 4:13
  w. to distinguish one from NIEB 219:10
  W. was mine, and I had mastery OWEN 228:7
  w. we have lost in knowledge ELIOT 104:1
wise: I heard a w. man say HOUS 146:1
  The art of being w. JAMES 153:16
  w. and disguises from BIER 46:17
  w. forgive but do not forget SZASZ 290:3
  w. man hide a pebble CHES 69:12
wisecrack: w. that played Carnegie LEV 186:10
wise-cracking: distance between w. and wit
                                     PARK 231:6
wisely: men and nations behave w. EBAN 97:16
  party one should eat w. MAUG 205:16
wiser: Are w. and nicer AUDEN 20:2
  are w. than their own BROO 55:6
  looked w. when he was seated KEYN 164:12
  that they are w. than they MAUG 204:11
  w. now than I was when SMITH 277:5
  w. than men because they STEP 285:2
wisest: w. woman in Europe ELIOT 104:13
wish: because I w. to know ASTOR 15:10
  I do w. he did not look ANON 11:13
  If otherwise w. SHAW- 274:13
  I w. I loved the Human Race RAL 242:13
  I w. I were in love again HART 135:10
  I wish, I w. he'd stay away MEAR 206:6
  They merely w. the property CHES 69:13
  When you w. upon a star WASH 305:7
  w. for prayer is a prayer BERN 41:3
  w. I'd looked after me AYRES 21:15
  w. that he gave more positive BLUNT 48:1
  w. that is kind and true BOND 49:2
  w. they were the only one AUDEN 18:10
  Without a w., without a will HODG 141:14
wishes: w. and ways will all HARDY 133:11
wishful: w. thinking in Hell LEWIS 187:2
wit: folly and his weapon w. ANON 8:12
  Impropriety is the soul of w. MAUG 205:5
  use my w. as a pitchfork LARK 179:6
  W. has truth in it PARK 231:6
  w. there is in those figures FRY 120:3
withdraw: w. their troops from Poland
                                     CHAM 66:7
withdrawn: yawn and be w. and watch
                                     DURY 97:1
within: difference w. the sexes COMP 80:3
without: get where I am today w. NOBBS 221:1
witless: heartless, w. nature HOUS 145:8

witnesses: silent w. to the desolation GEOR 123:4
wits: They have stolen his w. away DE L 90:10
wives: And many, many w. NAYL 218:16
  like w. CAMP 62:4
  w. and joined the women WELD 307:10
wizz: about skool are the BOYS w. WILL 311:10
wobbles: good spelling but it W. MILNE 210:14
woe: this world of sin and w. CHUR 75:5
woke: Happy till I w. again HOUS 146:16
  W. to my hearing from harbour THOM 292:13
Woking: Although he's playing for W. BETJ 44:4
wolf: while the w. remains INGE 151:6
  Who's afraid of the big bad w. CHUR 72:4
  W. that shall keep it may KIPL 174:2
Wolsey: King's Moll Reno'd in W.'s ANON 9:8
wolves: there were w. in Wales THOM 292:10
woman: [Irene Adler] is always the w. DOYLE 94:1
  artist man and the mother w. SHAW 270:17
  As you are w., so be lovely GRAV 128:6
  A w. can be proud and stiff YEATS 323:8
  A w. is like a teabag REAG 244:4
  A w. of so shining loveliness YEATS 322:2
  belief they done the old w. SHAW 273:16
  broken-hearted w. tends the grave HAYES 136:3
  called a w. in my own house WAUGH 306:11
  comfort about being a w. STARK 283:9
  delusion that one w. differs MENC 206:12
  difference between one young w. SHAW 270:11
  Every w. adores a Fascist PLATH 235:11
  Every w. knows BARR 26:16
  fighting for this w.'s honour KALM 161:4
  hours I've put into that w. AYCK 21:8
  I am a w. of the world SHAW 269:10
  like a beautiful w. CAS 64:9
  lovely w. stoops to folly ELIOT 105:7
  maintaining the prime truth of w. CHES 71:6
  man to strike a w. COW 85:4
  Now I'm not a fussy w. AYRES 22:1
  One is not born a w. BEAU 89:9
  scandal by a w. of easy HAIL 130:13
  seen the loveliest w. born YEATS 320:9
  sort of bloom on a w. BARR 26:11
  support of the w. I love EDW 98:11
  There is no fury like a w. CONN 80:19
  Upon a w. won or woman lost YEATS 322:5
  What does a w. want FREUD 117:6
  white w. whom nobody loves CORN 83:12
  w. be more like a man LERN 185:21
  w. can forgive a man MAUG 205:8
  w. drew her long black ELIOT 105:10
  w. is a blind fury SHAW 270:15
  w. is of special interest LEB 183:11
  w. looking at a girl WOOLF 317:11
  w. must have money WOOLF 317:8
  w.'s business to get married SHAW 271:1
  W.'s place was in the gaol BRAH 52:8
  w. that you forsake her KIPL 172:14
  w. through her ears WYATT 318:1

woman (*cont.*):
w. to provide for herself SHAW 272:22
W. wants monogamy PARK 230:17
w. who did not care KIPL 175:7
w. who did not please me PROU 240:10
w. who is really kind BEER 31:11
w. who lives for others LEWIS 187:4
w. will always sacrifice MAUG 204:14
w. without a man is like STEI 285:1
wrecks a w.'s reputation COL 79:3
You don't know a w. until LEV 186:16
you give him meat no w. CAMP 61:10
womanhood: Don't make an issue of my w.
BRAC 51:13
womankind: spoons and packs off its w.
SHAW 271:9
womb: In the dark w. where I began MAS 203:7
wombs: think just with our w. LUCE 192:11
women: American w. shoot FORS 114:4
And goes with W., and Champagne BELL 34:13
An' I learned about w. from KIPL 174:9
An' learn about w. from me KIPL 174:8
better time of it than w. MENC 206:13
But there's wisdom in w. BROO 55:6
claim our right as w. PANK 229:6
concern for the rights of w. COPE 83:5
Equality for w. demands TOYN 298:6
getting in bed with w. ROSS 253:5
girls turn into American w. HAMP 132:7
Good w. always think it BROO 56:2
if they yet mock what w. OWEN 228:4
I married beneath me, all w. do ASTOR 15:11
In an experience of w. DOYLE 95:4
infernal constancy of the w. SHAW 273:8
inscription 'Votes for W.' PANK 229:9
In the room the w. come and go ELIOT 103:7
knew how w. pass the time HENRY 139:1
Married women are kept w. SMITH 278:7
means nothing to w. O'BR 221:15
more interesting than w. WALL 304:13
not exist, you hate w. O'BR 222:1
one sees in other w. TYNAN 302:6
plain w. on television FORD 113:6
Some w.'ll stay in a man's KIPL 175:5
Some w., the few BARR 26:11
sung w. in three cities POUND 238:15
temptations both in wine and w. KITC 175:15
that many jewels make w. BARR 26:8
The parish of rich w. AUDEN 17:4
The war between men and w. THUR 297:7
we w. cannot escape GIBB 123:11
whereas w. require both BUTL 59:9
wives and joined the w. WELD 307:10
W. and elephants never forget SAKI 258:2
W. and Horses and Power KIPL 169:11
w. are a sex by themselves BEER 31:2
w. are in furious secret SHAW 269:6
w. are not so young BEER 31:1
W. are stronger than men STEP 285:2

women (*cont.*):
w. come out to cut up what KIPL 169:5
W. do not find it difficult MACK 195:9
w. do they must do twice WHIT 310:20
w. have fewer teeth RUSS 255:8
W. have no wilderness in them BOGAN 48:8
W. have served all these WOOLF 317:9
w. kiss it always reminds MENC 206:11
w. marched through CHES 69:7
W. never have young minds DEL 91:9
w. should be struck regularly COW 85:4
W. want mediocre men MEAD 206:4
W. who love the same man BEER 31:10
w. who wear ankle socks BENN 38:1
W. would rather be right NASH 217:19
you have to kill more w. BALD 23:4
won: I w. the count SOM 280:5
not that you w. or lost RICE 246:10
w. but to have run COUB 84:3
wonder: And miles around the w. grew
HOUS 146:2
And w. what you've missed AUDEN 16:13
boneless w. [Ramsay Macdonald] CHUR 73:13
I w. who's kissing her now ADAMS 2:2
I w. why he does MILNE 210:7
One can only w. BENT 39:14
On moon-washed apples of w. DRIN 95:17
wonderland: with love in summer's w.
NOYES 221:8
wonders: And w. what's to pay HOUS 145:5
w. out of natural personal JENK 154:9
wondrous: Oh, a w. bird is the pelican
MERR 207:10
wood: And sang within the bloody w.
ELIOT 102:13
don't drag w. about SCHW 265:1
Edge the w.'s in trouble HOUS 146:7
grainy w. BROO 54:9
roads diverged in a w. FROST 118:8
The w. of English bows DOYLE 95:15
w. ere Thou canst limm THOM 295:12
w. limping invisible down THOM 293:13
woodcock: Spirits of well-shot w. BETJ 42:4
wooden: lies about his w. horse FLEC 112:4
woodland: And stands about the w. ride
HOUS 145:13
woodlanded: by w. ways BETJ 43:11
woodlands: About the w. I will go HOUS 145:13
woods: Flow down the w. and stipple SACK 256:13
If you go down in the w. today KENN 162:12
no better than its w. AUDEN 20:7
once a road through the w. KIPL 173:6
The w. are lovely, dark FROST 118:11
through the Wet Wild W. KIPL 172:5
w. against the world BLUN 47:15
woodshed: something nasty in the w.
GIBB 123:12
Woolf: Virginia W., I enjoyed SITW 276:4
Who's afraid of Virginia W. ALBEE 3:10

woolly: The Llama is a w. sort   BELL 33:16
Woolworth's: paying a visit to W.   BEVAN 44:10
  The finest that W. could sell   EDGAR 98:3
Wops: better than Huns or W.   MITF 211:15
word: Clay is the w. and clay is the flesh
    KAV 162:1
  fast w. about oral contraception   ALLEN 4:21
  hear the w. culture   JOHST 157:2
  If you use a 'weasel w.'   ROOS 252:3
  interview that every w. she   MCC 193:12
  In the beginning was the W.   ELIOT 102:15
  just another w. for nothin'   KRIS 176:11
  merely a spade as the w.   FRY 120:1
  Send the w., send the word   COHAN 78:12
  send the w. to beware   COHAN 78:12
  The Greeks had a w. for it   AKINS 3:8
  w. for doing things tomorrow   SHAW 268:2
  w. go forth from this time   KENN 163:8
  w. mean different things   SHAW 274:12
wordless: A poem should be w.   MACL 196:4
words: idea within a wall of w.   BUTL 60:2
  I fear those big w.   JOYCE 159:1
  long w. Bother me   MILNE 210:10
  Read out my w. at night, alone   FLEC 112:7
  rose-garden. My w. echo   ELIOT 101:6
  simply callisthenics with w.   PARK 231:6
  take the w. 'Ireland'   BOWEN 51:5
  With w. and meanings   ELIOT 101:12
  w. and exhausted idioms   ORW 226:2
  W. are, of course   KIPL 175:1
  w. comes the thought   LARK 178:10
  'W. fail me,' he replied   BEEC 29:22
  w. like stones   SPEN 281:12
  W. strain   ELIOT 101:9
  w. would hardly lend itself   DOYLE 95:13
  worth ten thousand w.   BARN 25:3
  you can drug, with w.   LOW 191:9
Wordsworth: better scholar than W.   HOUS 144:6
  symphony by W.   BUTL 59:18
  what daffodils were for W.   LARK 179:9
wore: W. it in the world's eye   YEATS 322:1
work: And no further w. is done   COW 84:13
  Any w. that aspires   CONR 81:16
  bike and looked for w.   TEBB 291:2
  day's hard w. in thy life   LAWR 182:1
  day's w. in his life   BENN 38:6
  dream of the days when w.   CHES 70:12
  good idea but it won't w.   ROG 249:15
  grows beyond his w.   STEI 284:15
  has plenty of w. to do   JER 155:2
  hate to w. for a living   ROWL 254:2
  I like w.: it fascinates   JER 155:11
  its hands and goes to w.   SAND 260:3
  It's off to w. we go   MOREY 213:6
  leave school, and then w.   LEWIS 187:5
  Let no one else's w. evade   LEHR 184:4
  life, or of the w.   YEATS 323:12
  Mars a day helps you w.   GAFF 120:15

work (*cont.*):
  most of my w. sitting down   BENC 35:16
  My w. is left behind   BELL 34:19
  Nice w. if you can get it   GERS 123:10
  stopped w. at this age   OSLER 227:4
  test of a first-rate w.   BENN 38:10
  The w., my friend   ROOS 251:2
  We w. in the dark   JAMES 152:14
  Whistle while you w.   MOREY 213:7
  Why should I let the toad w.   LARK 179:6
  w. and in that work does   COLL 79:4
  W. and pray, live on hay   HILL 140:11
  w. at anything   SHAW 270:16
  w. done and still keep   BENC 36:3
  W. expands so as to fill   PARK 232:2
  W. is accomplished by those   PETER 233:9
  W. is love made visible   GIBR 124:4
  w. is terribly important   RUSS 255:2
  W. is the call   MORR 213:15
  W. is x EINS 99:9
  W. liberates   ANON 6:16
  w. of one extraordinary   HUBB 147:6
  w. on Maggie's Farm no   DYLAN 97:9
worked: So on we w., and waited   ROB 248:9
  W. myself up from nothing   PER 233:2
worker: bayonet is a weapon with a w.   ANON 7:2
  sociable w.   BEHAN 32:2
  w. is the slave of capitalist   CONN 81:7
  w. would sooner have   BLYT 48:5
workers: They are not the w.   WHYTE 311:1
  W., all demand   SERV 266:16
  w. of the country are our   SHIN 274:17
workhouse: prison and the woman's w.
    SHAW 272:12
working: And I've been w. like a dog   LENN 185:10
  Labour isn't w.   ANON 9:9
  To the ordinary w. man   ORW 225:17
  will protect a w.-girl   SMITH 277:2
  w. class where we belong   ORW 225:19
  w. on a case of Scotch   BENC 36:11
  w. on a much less ambitious   ANON 8:4
workings: inscrutable w. of Providence
    SMITH 277:4
workmen: majority of British w.   ZIN 324:12
works: future; and it w.   STEF 284:1
  W. of art are of an infinite   RILKE 247:8
workshop: other nation may be its w.
    CHAM 65:12
  w. for anything   FAUL 107:11
world: am a citizen of the w.   EINS 99:7
  anarchy is loosed upon the w.   YEATS 320:7
  blackguard made the w.   HOUS 144:13
  brought death into the w.   TWAIN 301:13
  by blowing up the w.   ADAMS 2:13
  dream of the actual w.   SANT 260:13
  Feed the w.   GELD 122:11
  In a w. I never made   HOUS 145:4
  into a w. of whose richness   FORS 114:1
  into the history of the w.   POPP 236:6

world (*cont.*):

lover's quarrel with the w.	FROST 119:10
making the w. safe	WOLFE 316:13
march of this retreating w.	OWEN 228:7
mean the limits of my w.	WITT 315:7
move in a w. of the dead	FORS 114:6
new w., with all	CHUR 74:6
Oh, w., Oh	SPEN 282:1
only girl in the w.	GREY 129:6
O w. invisible, we view thee	THOM 296:12
problematical w. and sells	FRY 119:15
responsible for such an absurd w.	DUH 96:4
say the w. will end	FROST 118:10
so arranging the w.	FRIS 117:7
Sob, heavy w.	AUDEN 16:11
Stop the w., I want to get off	NEWL 219:4
subsidized to provoke the w.	FRY 119:17
Ten days that shook the w.	REED 245:6
that the w. will not narrow	JOHN 156:8
Their w. gives way and dies	MACN 198:5
Then the w. seemed none so bad	HOUS 146:16
The seldom female in a w.	PITT 235:8
they only saved the w.	CHES 68:7
This is the way the w. ends	ELIOT 103:5
this small-talking w.	FRY 119:16
Top of the w.	GOFF 125:11
towns in all the w.	EPST 106:9
turning w.	ELIOT 101:8
What is the w., O soldiers	DE L 91:6
When the w. was begun	CART 64:7
woods against the w.	BLUN 47:15
w. can only be grasped	BRON 54:3
w. empty of people	LAWR 182:4
w. grown old and cold	BROO 54:10
w. in arms is not spending	EIS 100:2
w. is becoming like a lunatic	LLOY 190:3
W. is crazier and more	MACN 198:7
w. is everything	WITT 315:5
w. is made of people	BRON 54:6
w. is not yet prepared	DOYLE 94:9
w. is quickly bored	MAUG 205:6
w. is the best of all possible	BRAD 52:3
w. locks up its spoons	SHAW 271:9
w. must be getting old	JER 155:5
w. must be made safe	WILS 314:13
w. of the emotions	COL 79:1
w. of the happy is quite	WITT 315:8
w.'s great sorrows were	AE 3:3
w. the loveliest	BELL 34:12
w. til you knock the patriotism	SHAW 273:3
W., you have kept faith	HARDY 134:12
worlds: best of all possible w.	CAB 60:15
worm: And the w. that never dies	BROO 55:5
You have tasted your w.	SPOO 282:9
worms: entertains the most exclusive w.	
	PARK 231:4
We are all w. But I do	CHUR 76:13
worn-out: study in a w. poetical	ELIOT 101:12
worried: I'm w. about Jim	ANON 8:18

worried (*cont.*):

may not be w. into being	FROST 118:2
worry: Don't W. Me	EARLY 97:15
Leave your w. on the doorstep	FIEL 108:11
worrying: What's the use of w.	ASAF 13:13
worse: Defend the bad against the w.	DAY-L 89:8
dirt doesn't get any w.	CRISP 86:3
finding something w.	BELL 32:18
More will mean w.	AMIS 5:12
my books had been any w.	CHAN 67:2
w. than be a swinger	FROST 118:9
worship: Good; they w. Truth	BROO 55:11
men w. the Caesars	HUXL 148:14
w. God in his own way	ROOS 250:12
w. of the bitch-goddess	JAMES 153:12
Your w. is your furnaces	BOTT 50:5
worst: But the w. that you can	ALLEN 4:8
Cheer up! the w. is yet to come	JOHN 156:16
conviction, while the w.	YEATS 320:7
exacts a full look at the w.	HARDY 134:3
found no remedy for the w.	KELL 162:9
intellectual hatred is the w.	YEATS 320:9
like to be told the w.	CHUR 75:1
so much good in the w.	ANON 11:8
wicked will. You do your w.	CHUR 72:12
w. advertisement for Socialism	ORW 225:15
w. is that which delays	LLOY 190:2
w. thing I can say about	BEVAN 45:3
worth: contract isn't w. the paper	GOLD 126:7
that if a thing is w.	CHES 71:6
w. any number of old ladies	FAUL 107:10
Worthington: daughter on the stage, Mrs W.	
	COW 85:1
worthy: after a w. manner of life	RUSS 256:2
wotthehell: w. wotthehell	MARQ 201:7
would: He w., wouldn't	RIC 246:13
W. this man, could he see	AUDEN 20:8
W. you like to sin	ANON 12:10
wound: Hearts w. up with love	SPEN 282:2
wounded: The w. surgeon plies the steel	
	ELIOT 101:15
w. and left on Afghanistan's	KIPL 169:5
Wounded Knee: Bury my heart at W.	
	BENÉT 36:17
wounds: Time w. all heals	BREC 52:17
wreckage: w. of men who have minded	
	WOOLF 317:10
wrecks: w. and nobody drownded	EDGAR 98:3
Wrekin: fleece the W. heaves	HOUS 146:7
Wren: Sir Christopher W.	BENT 39:8
wrench: Though loss of honour was a w.	
	GRAH 127:6
wrestle: with the intolerable w.	ELIOT 101:12
wretched: And w., blind, pit ponies	HODG 142:2
wretches: How shall w. live like us	GODL 125:8
wrings: comes and w. our necks	AYRES 21:16
wrinkled: man with w. female breasts	ELIOT 105:5
W. with age, and drenched	DE L 90:9
write: decided to w. for posterity	ADE 2:17

years (*cont.*):

The wildest peal for y.	HODG 142:2
thousand y. of history	GAIT 121:1
three-score y. and ten	JEANS 154:5
y. he [H. H. Asquith]	AMERY 5:11
y. like great black oxen	YEATS 321:10

Yeats: Drumcliffe churchyard Y. — YEATS 319:13

William Y. is laid to rest	AUDEN 17:5

yellow: And not your y. hair — YEATS 323:13

Emeralds is paved with y. brick	BAUM 27:13
he put down *The Y. Book*	BETJ 42:1
one-eyed y. idol	HAYES 136:3
We all live in a y. submarine	LENN 185:17
Who's y. and keeps the store	LARK 179:14
y. fog that rubs its back	ELIOT 103:7
Y. God forever gazes down	HAYES 136:3
y. outside and a softer	PAGET 228:11
y. polkadot bikini	VANCE 303:4

yes: from Del Monte says 'Y.' — ANON 9:22

getting the answer y.	CAMUS 62:11
Y., but not in the South	POTT 237:13
y. I said yes I will Yes	JOYCE 159:10
Y., Minister! No	CROS 86:11
Y., my darling daughter	ANON 9:24
Y., my darling daughter	DE L 91:8
Y.—oh dear yes	FORS 114:7
y. until I've finished	ZAN 324:7

yesterday: backward nor tarries with y.

	GIBR 124:3
have naming of parts. Y.	REED 244:12
Or perhaps it was y.	CAMUS 62:15
up with y.	MARQ 201:8
Y., all my troubles seemed	LENN 185:18
Y., December 7, 1941	ROOS 251:1
Y.'s men	KING 167:9

yet: ain't heard nuttin' y. — JOLS 157:3

yew: Of true wood, of y. wood — DOYLE 95:15

yid: LET'S PUT THE ID BACK IN Y. — ROTH 253:12

ying: Y. tong iddle I po — MILL 209:2

you: anything better than y. — BERL 40:5

For y. but not for me	ANON 10:8
How about y.	FREED 116:12
Y. ain't heard nuttin'	JOLS 157:3
Y. can't take it with you	HART 135:13
Y. come too	FROST 118:12

you-hoo: It's for y. — ANON 9:2

young: being y. and foolish — YEATS 321:13

country for old men. The y.	YEATS 321:5
dared be radical when y.	FROST 118:4
denunciation of the y.	SMITH 278:1
enchanting than the voices of y.	SMITH 277:17
get out while we're y.	SPR 283:1
how y. the policemen look	HICKS 140:8
I have been y., and now	BLUN 47:13
I'm as y. as ever I was	BUTL 60:13
I was a poet, I was y.	FLEC 112:7
made y. with young desires	THOM 296:5
Most women are not so y.	BEER 31:1
multitude of y. men in a hurry	CORN 84:1

young (*cont.*):

Portrait of the artist as a y.	THOM 293:8
putting old heads on your y.	SPARK 281:5
side of baldness than y.	SMITH 277:16
That y. men, tossing	YEATS 322:4
think it is, and we were y.	HOUS 145:11
To keep the body y.	YEATS 321:4
Tomorrow for the y. the poets	AUDEN 20:10
too y. to take up golf	ADAMS 2:4
up a y. and inexperienced	JER 155:8
When I was y.	YEATS 319:5
y. and easy under the apple	THOM 293:1
Y. as he was, his instinct	BUTL 60:12
y. can do for the old	SHAW 269:2
y. enough to know everything	BARR 25:10
Y., gifted and black	IRV 151:13
y. had discovered what	MAUG 204:11
y. have aspirations	SAKI 257:16
y. ones carry pistols	SHAW 267:17
y. to fall asleep for ever	SASS 263:3
youth is wasted on the y.	CAHN 61:1

younger: I'm y. than that now — DYLAN 97:11

older we do not get any y.	REED 245:2
y. with time	CAS 64:9

youngman: Let me die a y.'s death — MCG 195:2

youngster: out a y. but you've *got* — SEYM 267:4

yours: So be mine, as I y. for ever — GRAV 128:6

Y. till Hell freezes	FISH 110:2

yourself: Could love you for y. alone — YEATS 323:13

youth: And caught our y. — BROO 54:10

done and y. stone dead	SASS 262:7
from her Earliest Y.	BELL 33:3
it is y. who must fight	HOOV 143:4
it is y. who must inherit	HOOV 143:4
knew a phoenix in my y.	YEATS 322:9
Love like y. is wasted	CAHN 61:1
Sweet wine of y.; gave up	BROO 54:12
their wicked sides at y.	YEATS 319:6
The situation of our y.	BALD 22:13
walls of y. collapse	FORS 114:13
What one knows is, in y.	ADAMS 2:11
y. and the feeling	CONR 82:2
y. is bent by the same	THOM 293:4
Y. is something very new	CHAN 67:3
Y. to prolong	YEATS 321:4
Y., which is forgiven everything	SHAW 272:14
Y. would be an ideal state	ASQ 14:17

Yucatan: I had an Aunt in Y. — BELL 33:15

Yukon: This is the Will of the Y. — SERV 266:17

Z

Zarathustra: saith Z., sometime regius

	JOYCE 159:8

Zen: Z. and the art of motorcycle — PIRS 235:6

Zimbabwe: everyone to play cricket in Z.

	MUG 215:2

zipless: z. fuck is the purest thing   JONG 157:5
zoo: it is a human z.   MORR 213:13
    well you may see at the Z.   KIPL 171:11

zooming: Earth z. about the Sun   FULL 120:5
Zuleika: Z., on a desert island   BEER 31:8
Zurich: little gnomes in Z.   WILS 313:3